THE SHIRE HORSE

KEITH CHIVERS

THE SHIRE HORSE

A History of the Breed, the Society and the Men

J. A. ALLEN

LONDON

ISBN 0 85131 245 4

Published in 1976 by
J. A. ALLEN & COMPANY LIMITED
1, Lower Grosvenor Place,
Buckingham Palace Road,
London, SW1W 0EL.

Book production Bill Ireson

Set in 11/12 point Monotype Bembo,
printed and bound by The Garden City Press Limited,
Letchworth,
Hertfordshire SG6 1JS

Foreword

by
His Royal Highness, The Prince Philip
Duke of Edinburgh, K.G., K.T.

In this high speed mechanical age it is difficult to imagine that barely fifty years ago the heavy horse was still the prime mover in agriculture. Before the coming of the railways, barely 150 years ago, the horse was the only power available for transport on land. After the railways and before the coming of the motor lorry there was even more work for them as they had to move every load both to and from the railway yard. These great horses were therefore of the very greatest importance and breeders were constantly trying to provide the most suitable types of horses for all the many different uses to which they were put. Of the heavy horses the Shire was one of the most popular and it certainly had a particular hold on the public imagination. Giants of strength yet with the gentlest of characters they served men's needs patiently and willingly.

Since I took to driving carriage horses I have come to understand something of the remarkable relationship which develops between a driver and his team. There is no denying the skill of the heavy lorry drivers but with a team of horses every job is a co-operative undertaking between a group of intelligent and independent beings. It is this extraordinary relationship between man and animal which this book is all about. It is the story of the men who bred the Shire horses and their understanding of the characters and abilities of their animals.

Sandringham
Norfolk
1976

Contents

PART B: THE SEVEN LINES OF BLOOD

APPENDICES

REFERENCES AND NOTES

INDICES

List of Illustrations

Dedication

To all true Shire men, past and present, this book is dedicated – men of genius such as Robert Bakewell, and simple men of whom we have no memorial; men of every social position, from King George V to those whose lives were humble and their death obscure; countrymen and townsmen; breeders, owners, veterinary surgeons, grooms, drivers, carters, ploughmen, and all who went to work with Shires.

In particular, it is dedicated to the 3rd Earl of Ellesmere, Fred Street, Edward Coke, and the others who founded the Society for improving the English sort of cart-horse; and to those who have devoted themselves to promoting their object.

In honouring the Shire, I have no mind to dishonour other breeds of Great Horse and the men who favoured them. In particular among those, I call to mind Lawrence Drew, who preached and practised that the Clydesdale and the Shire were one breed; and Herman Biddell, Suffolk horseman and historian, who has been my exemplar.

The Shire Horse did more than any other animal, and than most men, to break down the barriers of class in this country, especially in the nineteenth century and the early years of this one. In him, men of all ranks found their common interest and were helped to realise their true brotherhood.

Sponsors

THE whole cost of the research and writing of this book (and, as is explained in the Acknowledgements, this was very considerable) has been borne by the following bodies and companies, whose generosity enables royalties to be payable to the Shire Horse Society. They will be devoted to the furtherance of the work it has pursued ever since its foundation – the promotion of the "Old English breed of Cart Horses".

The Nuffield Foundation

Courage Limited

Hull Brewery Company Limited

J. R. Parkington and Company Limited

Watney Mann Limited

Whitbread and Company Limited

Young and Company's Brewery Limited

Shire Horse Society

Acknowledgements

THIS attempt to study the history of the Shire Horse was handicapped by a dire poverty of documentary evidence about many important matters (made infinitely worse by the loss of most of the breed society's own records in 1941), by an overwhelming plethora of ephemeral writings that were mostly trivial but which required panning for their occasional traces of pure gold, and by the fact that much of what I needed to know about the recent past (the last one or two hundred years) was in private hands.

When I tracked this personal material down, it was only rarely that I could afford not to spend long hours accumulating notes about individual breeders or owners – masses of paper superfluous to my immediate requirements. The reason is simple. Books in libraries and papers in achives can be left there until they are needed. Privately-owned documents must be attended to at once. Often, their present owner is likely to be their last owner before they are confined to the fire. Even when his successors are more appreciative of the raw material of history, he himself is often the only man capable of adding flesh to their dry bones by his own reminiscence or from knowledge handed down by his forefathers, because the next generation has lost the horse tradition. Indeed, he may be the last man able even to assemble their skeleton at all. I have therefore been forced (admittedly by love as much as by sense of duty) to collect the material for twenty books simultaneously with the writing of one. Someone, one day, may need it.

All this would have been impossible without considerable financial help. I gratefully record that all expenses, not to mention my "wages" for those three years when my hobby became my whole-time occupation (lucky man!), have been met by those generous sponsors listed on page xix. I hope only that my efforts will not have fallen too far short of what this deserves.

I wish also to acknowledge the generosity of spirit of successive Presidents and the entire Council of the Shire Horse Society. If I had not gained a deep understanding of the special, somewhat old-fashioned, attributes of typical "Shire men", I would stand amazed at my complete freedom to review the history of their breed entirely in my own way, both as to detail and in general perspective, without any restriction whatever. They have never even considered the proposition that "he who pays the piper calls the tune". The tune I have played is entirely mine, and no other members of the Society must be blamed either for its wrong notes or for any errors of interpretation in it.

As to names, I owe a special debt to John A. Young and to J. David Kay, who have been particularly involved with this project, for their unfailing encouragement and support. But it is no exaggeration that if the Secretary of the Society, Roy W. Bird, had not taken up the idea in the first place with enthusiasm and carried me along in the strength of his tremendous energy, the work would neither have properly started nor failed to founder in any number of difficult and rocky waters. No plea for help has been too troublesome for him to tackle with gusto, even at times when his work as Secretary of the East of England Agricultural Society pressed hard upon him. Mrs. Pat Wakefield, the Assistant Secretary of the Shire Horse Society, has comforted me with more moral support and practical help than I can even remember, because it has been accorded so unsparingly that I have come to take it for granted. Roy Bird's predecessor, the late Albert Holland, gave unstintingly of his vast knowledge, and his death was a bitter blow, not least for personal reasons.

I would not care to estimate how much of this book is inspired by John Porter, whose friendship sprang from its writing, for we had never met until I began it. His knowledge of Shire history in the past hundred years is compendious and accurate, and my debt to him is enormous. For example, the chapters on the descendants of Harold and William the Conqueror (that is, the bloodlines of the modern Shire) stem from his investigations and are grounded on his research. Joan Chivers and Kathleen Porter both have enormous tolerance for husbands who must have often bored them to tears when they were not neglecting, through their preoccupation, even the common courtesies of meal-time conversation.

To Harold Burrow, Emeritus Professor of Veterinary Medicine, Royal Veterinary College, University of London, I am uniquely indebted. No living practitioner has had more personal experience with Shire horses than he—any deficiency in the pages that deal with their breeding, or their care, is due solely to my inadequacy—for his patience in helping me has been inexhaustible. In addition, both he and John Porter read the draft of my text, but it is not their fault if I have persisted in any errors. I wish also to record my deep obligation to C. R. Hannis, whose advice, whenever asked (and that was frequently), never failed to rescue me.

I am particularly grateful to Lesley Thomas for cheerfully deciphering my extraordinary handwriting and my quaint tapes. I estimate that, counting notes that were never intended for this general history, she has typed nearly two million words about the Shire.

The number of others to whom I am indebted for information that only they could give, or for ideas that I was incapable of conceiving for myself, is so phenomenal that I immediately apologise to any that I have inadvertently omitted here, though not really forgotten. I have unfortunately found it impossible to name all the archivists and librarians, both professional and amateur, who have gone often far out of their way to help, as is their nature. Similar omissions are necessary of the secretaries of societies who have done likewise and of all those clergymen who, as custodians of parish registers, have willingly responded to my cries for help.

ACKNOWLEDGEMENTS xxiii

For obvious reasons, the following names are given in alphabetical order, which causes a former Sovereign to appear at the foot of it. On no other topic could the names of those who have taken a contributory interest in the compiling of a book, range so completely across the social spectrum. A few of these names are, alas, already not longer with us:

Robert Adams, Arthur Addicott, T. H. Balderston, Richard Beard, John M. Belcher, Denys F. Benson, Cynthia Bettaney, George Brooks, Hubert Brown, R. A. Brown, Sam Bower, F. H. Bowser, B. H. Bury, Charlie Butler, Mrs. Clark (snr.) and B. J. M. Clark, Hugh Close, J. B. Cooke, W. C. Cotterill, P. K. Cottrell, Fred Croft, Lt. Col. R. J. C. Crowden, W. J. Cumber, John Cumber, Col. T. W. Daniel, R. F. Daplyn, D. R. T. Davies, Ivy Day, Lady Denham, The Dinam Estates Company and W. H. Williams, The Duchess of Devonshire and many members, past and present, of the Chatsworth staff, Mrs. R. G. N. Edwards, John Evans, J. Downes Evans, Richard Forshaw, Jack Freer, B. H. Gadsby, W. A. Gilbey, Tom Golledge, F. D. Goodson, Members of the Great Eccleston S.H.S., Ronald Greaves and Mrs. Lilian Bailey, Arthur Gutteridge, J. W. Hiles, Henry Hobbs, E. J. Holland, H. C. Horrell, John Hothersall, Sidney Hubbard, Robert Hull, Ernest and John Hutton, Mrs. Muriel Hutton, George and Arthur Ivatt, Stephen James, Tom Kirk, E. A. Lane, Mary Lawton, The Earl of Leicester and Dr. W. O. Hassall, The Marquess of Londonderry, The Misses R. L. and M. Lynn, John Malliband, T. Baker Marsh, Frank R. Marshall, John Martinson, J. C. Matthews, David Morbey, R. H. Morgan, W. A. Mudell, Reg. Nunn, S. T. Parker, H. T. Parsons, Bill Pearce, Mrs. M. Rackham, Harry Ranson, Bill Rastall, H. Eady Robinson, Tom Robinson, Charlie Roffe, Mrs. M. M. Roger, Coriolanus Rowles, Philip Ryder-Davies, Mrs. Shepherd, W. B. Shipman, William Simpson, Mrs. Gwen Smith, Mrs. M. Thompson, Margaret Thompson, Nancy and Betty Todd, William Townley, G. S. Turner, Mr. and Mrs. T. G. Twell, A. E. Vyse (Secretary) and members of the British Percheron Horse Society, Mrs. T. W. Warren, Dick Watson, Mrs. Wyn Wheatcroft, John Whitehurst, Dorian Williams, Mrs. E. J. Williams, The Duke of Windsor, R. F. Wyatt.

Illustrations Acknowledgement

I WISH to record my thanks to the following for supplying illustrations, or for allowing pictures in their ownership to be used:

COLOUR PLATES
1 and 2. Young and Company's Brewery Limited; 3. Daniel Thwaites and Company Limited; 4. Watney Mann and Truman Brewers Limited; 5. Major R. W. Gleadow; 6. Courage Shire Horse Centre; 7. Wadworth and Company Limited; 8. Whitbread and Company Limited.

BLACK AND WHITE PLATES
The relevant plate number is shown in brackets, after each contributor. Richard Beard (26); John M. Belcher (51); British Rail (Western Region) (45, 46, 60); Professor Harold Burrow (56); Esso Petroleum Company Limited (27); Richard Forshaw (32); W. A. Gilbey (17, 18, 42); C. R. Hannis (54, 55 and others); The Marquess of Londonderry (19, 20); John Malliband (22); *Radio Times* Hulton Picture Library (6, 36, 37, 38, 39); Rothamsted Experimental Station Library (3, 4 and 7 to 14 inclusive); *The Times* (53); Whitbread and Company Limited (5); and Denis Wood (28).

Preface

The Shire Horse, like every other heavy-horse, is a descendant of the Great Horse. The Great Horse was bred up from the so-called cold-blood horses of Central Europe. The latter, like all other horses, were derived ultimately from Eohippus, or whatever primitive ancestor the paleontologists have yet to discover or devise. But Shire history, if by this we mean the history of pedigree (and in this book we do), begins only about the year A.D. 1760.

The history of a breed is a family history. Your family history, and mine, extends only as far as our knowledge of who was whose father and mother. If your name happens to be Baldwin or Godwin, you can assume a Saxon origin in the male line, but a pre-Norman earl or sheriff will not serve as part of your genealogy if you cannot find the connecting links between him and your ancestor John in 1595 or your grandfather George in 1895. Even a complete genealogy does not make a proper history unless we know what the members of the family listed in it were like and what they did.

If we could only discover the pedigrees, and could find out more precisely the conformation and points of the animals, a history of the two English heavy breeds, the Suffolk and the Shire, could begin in the year 1066, when Great Horses or destriers first came to this country in sufficient numbers to make them anything but imported rarities. If we wanted to begin earlier, we would have to go overseas and trace the breeding back through the dark ages, perhaps to the time described theatrically by Professor David Low. "In an evil hour", he wrote, "the Barbarians poured their swarms into Southern Europe, (and) the Great Black Horse of the North became an instrument of destruction, and an object of terror, living long in many a legend and tale of blood, and becoming associated in the minds of the distracted people with ideas of the anger of the gods and the power of the demons!"[1] But we cannot do any of these things. We shall have to skate over almost exactly seven centuries of pre-history and devote all the rest of our space to a couple of hundred years. Most of that must be allotted to the brief six glorious decades when Shire-horse breeding was not only of high importance to industry, commerce, transport and agriculture as well as to the ordinary daily lives of tens of thousands of people, but was highly organised. That last period ended about 1939, which is where this narrative virtually ends. But since, happily, Shire-breeding has continued still to be properly organised, by young new men as well as by old ones, something has been added to bring the story down to the present time, though it must be the task of someone else, in time to come, to view these latter years objectively and to pass a judgement upon them.

It would be most exciting to be able to pierce the mists that envelop even the 1750s, and to discover the sire of *The Packington Blind Horse* or the dam of Oldacre's *Old Kirby*, or who bred, *Bumper* and how. But 1760 is really not bad. Suffolk horse pedigrees go back to the same date, and only the Thorough-bred can go farther. There are cart-horses foaled in 1976 whose genealogy extends through almost as many generations in two hundred years as you can boast in nine, if you can prove unbroken descent from a Norman baron.

PART A

THE CHRONICLES OF THE CART-HORSE

CHAPTER I

1066–1660

The Great Horse

I. WILLIAM I TO KING JOHN: 1066–1216

"THE Battle of Hastings", wrote J. A. Frost in 1915,[1] with more truth than originality, "was waged between Harold's English army of infantrymen and William the Conqueror's army of horsemen, ending in a victory for the latter." Doubtless, few of his readers were startled by the statement. But he was absolutely right to begin his historical sketch of the Shire horse with that event, and to refuse idle speculation about pre-Norman animals. The horses that pulled Boudicca's chariots have little to do with the case: nor need we concern ourselves with any others which were to be found in the land during the 1,005 years that passed between the death of the savage queen and the arrival of the invaders with their Spanish and Norman destriers, or heavy war-horses, on that autumn day in 1066.

By a strange coincidence of names, the story that we shall follow here culminates in a contest between another Harold and another William the Conqueror. But before we reach even the birth of those two great horses, in 1881 and 1862 respectively, there is a long road to travel, and it will be longer still before we see how the battle of bloodlines ended in a victory, this time, for Harold.

In so far as one can generalise about the types of people who engage themselves in certain occupations, it cannot be disputed that the men who throughout these last nine centuries bred and owned heavy horses, and the men who still do so, are on the whole a gentle, honest, likeable, unpretentious, strong and silent sort of people. It is therefore quite uncharacteristic that the earliest name that we can associate with the importation into Britain of great heavy Continental stallions for breeding purposes was also one of the nastiest characters in our history. This was Robert de Bellême, the eldest son of Roger, Lord of Montgomery in Normandy, Lord of Arundel and Chichester, Earl of Shrewsbury and founder and Lord of Montgomery in Wales. When his father died in 1094, Robert succeeded to the Norman possessions and his younger brother Hugh to the English earldom and estates. Unfortunately, Hugh died four years later and Robert became master of all. He settled at Bridgnorth and rapidly became the most powerful lord of any who owed homage to William II. Tall and strong in physique and daring in spirit, he fostered to a remarkable degree his exceptional traits of savagery, greed, irreligion and cruelty, especially the last. Almost the only good thing he did was to introduce Continental destriers to his Welsh lands. When, in response to forty-five charges brought against him, Henry I brought an army and turned him out of the country in 1102, there was great applause and rejoicing throughout England and Montgomery. The date of his death no one knows now and no one cared then, though all piously hoped that he died as loathsomely as he lived. But his horse enterprise flourished, and in 1188 Giraldus Cambrensis mentioned "many excellent studs set apart for breeding" in Powys, all originating from the repulsive Robert's Percheron stallions.[2]

How many Great Horses were brought from Europe during the hundred years that followed the invasion, it would be folly to try to guess. It is certain that they were numerous, and that Henry II, in importing more, was continuing a regular policy. His four Norman predecessors had found it no small task to provide the country with the horses it required for modern warfare, but the success which they had achieved is made pretty clear by the fact that, half way through the reign of the first of the Plantagenets, this type of horse was readily available on the London market.

William FitzStephen's description, in 1171, of the horse sale held every Friday at Smithfield has been quoted by every writer on horse history – almost always so incompletely as to distort it. In fact, only one horse-book[3] has taken the trouble to give the full Latin text and an English translation. Since the latter can scarcely be improved, here is that part which is relevant: "There is a fair where the sight of well-bred horses for sale is well-known. Either to look on or to buy, everyone who is in town comes – earls, barons, knights, and many burgesses." Here follow sentences describing the palfreys or amblers, the cobs, various sorts of colts, and the pack-horses, and next the heavy-horses: "Here are expensive chargers of handsome conformation and impressive height, switching their ears and arching their necks: they have massive quarters. When these are run up, the prospective buyers first watch the slower paces and then the faster ones, in which the fore-feet are alternately raised and set down and then the hind-feet likewise . . . a shout goes up to take the common horses aside. Here are mares for ploughing or draught in sled or double harness cart. Some of them are heavy in foal. Yet others have brought forth foals which frisk about, their progeny not yet weanable." As Mr. Dent and Miss Goodall have pointed out, these heavy-horses, these destriers, trotted because they were trotters by nature. Their "original home was in marsh land", just like the historical trotting Shire's true home was, centuries later.

Times have changed less than we often assume. Any modern Shire man would have felt perfectly at home at Smithfield, where the horses were first walked and then trotted for inspection. The use of brood-mares for farm-work, too, would have fitted in with his scheme of things, though the amount of cultivation done by horses was of course small compared with the work done by oxen. The chief difference he would have noticed is that the surplus colts were not castrated in those days. The breeder hoped to make his money from stallions for war, not geldings for the peaceful drudgery of the towns.

(If horse writers, with rare exceptions such as the authors already quoted, have been generally pretty vague about history in general, it is also true that historians have rarely or never paused to think about horses. For example, when Charles Oman wrote *The Art of War in the Middle Ages*, which inevitably was largely about cavalry fighting, it did not occur to him to wonder about the horses on which the cavalry sat – not even to the extent of contemplating the difference between the ponderous trot of the medieval charger, culminating in a sickening thud on impact, and the high mobility of the galloping ancient Scythian or modern light horse. The cavalry horse of the middle ages was scarcely a charger in the modern sense of the word. He was himself charged or loaded, as the French verb still signifies: that is, he was a weight-carrier.[4])

King John's importation, about 1200, of 100 stallions from the Low Countries specifically for breeding purposes, and his careful distribution of them in the most promising districts, was obviously a renewed attempt to improve the weight and size and numerical strength of the English Great Horse. This was a very large number. Even in the years 1900 to 1914, when our heavy-horse population was at its height, 100 foreign stallions put to the task of covering, between them, something approaching 10,000 mares every year would soon have changed the breed out of all recognition, especially if their best half-bred sons were set to the same task. Perhaps it was just that which John's horses achieved. If it is legitimate to see the modern Suffolk as a descendant of William the Conqueror's horses, the black Flemish hairy-legged stallions that John brought over can be regarded as the foundation of the Shire. In any event, his pride in them qualifies him to rank, one suspects, with George V himself as a heavy-horse man, though not perhaps as a constitutional and well-loved sovereign.

2. HENRY III TO RICHARD II: 1216–1399

As no doubt had been the case for a century and a half, there was money in breeding heavy-horses and perhaps John had spread the industry wider through the country than ever before. Long after his death, too, their cost was enormous. An inventory of horses killed at the battle of Falkirk in 1298 valued the cheapest charger at sixty marks, and the dearest hack at ten.

During the twenty years allowed to the wretched Edward II before he was deposed and murdered in 1327, and the fifty years of his son's rule, the importation of breeding stock from the Low Countries continued. Edward III spent enormous sums on Great Horses, one consignment from the Count of Hainault costing 25,000 florins. Breeding at home was a specialised and expensive undertaking, something of which is revealed by the account rolls of the Fitzalan manors in west Shropshire. These relate to the years 1313 to 1394.

Edmund Fitzalan (1285–1326) had succeeded his father as Earl of Arundel in 1302, and his Shropshire estates included those of Oswestry, which had been in the family for about 200 years, and of Clun, which they had held for nearly 150. In the nonconformist tradition of his ancestor John Fitzalan, who had been prominent in the confederation of barons against King John, he was one of the five earls who in 1312 formed a league against Piers Gaveston and removed his

head. The following year, the rolls refer to Richard Cocus or Coccus who led
Edmund's destrier, a horse called Morel Lestrange, round the various manors
where the brood mares were kept, and William de Wyrcester was in charge of
two grooms and twelve colts on the same business. They visited Rednal,
Ruyton, Shrawardine, Wroxeter, Withyford and Lydley Heys.

Whether the stallion had any blood in him from the horses imported by
Robert de Bellême two centuries before, would be anyone's guess. But it is
fairly safe to assume, from his name, that he had been bred by John Lestrange,
sixth baron of Knokyn. The Lestrange family held extensive estates in Shropshire and Norfolk. John's grandfather had been a loyal servant of the crown,
serving under King John in 1214 at Poitou, and had been appointed in 1233
constable of the castles of Montgomery, Shrewsbury, Bridgnorth and Chester.
In 1310, John Lestrange himself gave his manor of Hunstanton to his younger
brother, from whom the famous Norfolk Lestranges were descended. The
following year, John died, and it is not unreasonable to guess that the horses we
are interested in then passed to Fitzalan.

In 1314, Morel Lestrange and nine of the other entire horses got mange, and
the farrier from Ness was called in to treat them. He knew Morel well, because
he had bred him – his official position being stud groom to the Lord of Great
Ness, who was none other than the new John Lestrange. The horse's feet were
duly bled, and the fee, together with the bill for pig's fat, olive oil, honey and
other necessary things, amounted to 4s. 2¾d. What a modern veterinary surgeon
may think of the treatment is immaterial, because the cure was successful and
the stallion-round was done as usual. This may seem an unlikely story in view
of the fact that the battle of Bannockburn took place on 24th June, when all
destriers should not be serving mares at all but fighting far away. Nevertheless,
it is true that the stallion stayed at home, simply because his owner was one of
those who refused to accompany Edward II to the relief of Stirling, and so contributed to the disaster two miles to the south of that castle. Fitzalan completely
changed his attitude later and supported the royal cause. But this brought him
only temporary benefit (he became justice of Wales and Warden of the Welsh
marshes, and acquired much extra land), since he was executed on 17th November 1326 and his estates were forfeited, less than a year before the miserable
King himself was murdered.

However, the stud continued as usual. In 1381, Rednal and Ruyton were
still stallion headquarters, as they had been all along – the numbers rising sometimes to four senior stock-horses and fifteen younger ones. Other places where
mares were kept, in addition to those mentioned in the round of 1313, were
Bromhurst or Bromwich Park at Maesbury and the Upper and Lower Parks at
Oswestry, where there were twenty-three mares and fifty-two colts and fillies.
In 1394 eighty-six loads of hay were made at West Felton for the horses and
deer in the parks, and forty quarters of oats were bought for the mares in Bromhurst. In addition, twenty-seven bushels of peas were required to make bread
for the stallion "at the time of the leaping of the mares" (carefully recorded as

being from April to the first day of August), during which time, to judge from his feeding, he was expected to be busy. The expenses of the stallion and groom during the season amounted to £2. 2s. 8½d. This seems an enormous sum, but the various items – groom's wages, shoeing, veterinary expenses, oats and bran, halter reins, surcingles, oil and tallow to dress the horses – were all accounted for. The entire horses were stabled throughout the year, except for a few weeks after the season. In 1314, the cost of mowing grass for the horses at Ruyton was 21s. 6d.: in 1349, nineteen women were employed for ten weeks to mow grass for the colts, and were paid £4. 17s. 10½d.

The accounts refer also to palfreys, coursers, and mountain ponies, but it is the King's horses and carts kept on the manor of Adderley – in the north-east of the county, twenty-four miles as the crow flies from Oswestry and twenty from Ruyton – which are of most present interest. They were stabled at night and, except for two or three weeks at grass, were given hay and oats throughout the year. These draught animals, presumably second-grade destriers, were kept in steady work, as the regular expense of repairs to the carts and harness show, and had occasional special jobs. In 1321, for example, they took wool from Newport to London and, in July 1323, a team left Adderley to join the King for the Scottish war, returning at Michaelmas in the following year. These were additional to the affri, or farm-horses, to whose feeding, shoeing and duties there are frequent references.[5]

Edward II, in his disastrous and overwhelming defeat at Bannockburn, had lost an enormous number of Great Horses, captured or killed. It is therefore not surprising that his son, engaged in continual campaigns north of the border, prohibited their exportation, especially to Scotland. A German dealer who brought some to England on speculation was allowed to take them out again when he could not sell them – but they had to go overseas. From this time onward for many years, it was a felony to sell horses to the Scots, whose less successful efforts to import direct from Holland and Flanders left them in desperate need of good stock. There were never enough Great Horses in England either (the German dealer's horses cannot have been much good) and at the age of nineteen Richard II found it necessary in 1386 to control their price by proclamation in the counties of Lincoln, Cambridge and the East and North Ridings. By the time he was removed from the throne, the situation had considerably improved, not only in those areas but elsewhere, including no doubt those Shropshire manors which the travelling stallions still visited so methodically and at such great expense.

3. HENRY IV TO HENRY VII: 1399–1509

Richard's Lancastrian successor found not only more Great Horses, but bigger and better ones, than had been available before. At last, supply was beginning to match the demand. But, half a century later, the Wars of the Roses caused a serious set-back. Civil strife was a different matter from international warfare. Ordinary men saw no point in breeding strong horses for

Yorkists or Lancastrians to seize. If they had a chance of doing it without being caught, many sent their best animals abroad, some as far as Italy. But those who lived in the north sneaked them over the border to Scotland, where James II in the middle decades of the century was glad to have every one he could get. From his time onwards for 100 years, Great Horses from Poland, Denmark, Sweden, Hungary and elsewhere came to sow their seed in Scotland, with remarkably unimpressive results.

When, on Bosworth Field in the afternoon of 22nd August 1485, the crown that had fallen off Richard III's head was placed upon that of Henry Tudor, the new King therefore acquired a pretty sorry stock. Since foreign wars had no place in his policy, there was time to repair the damage. However, it is folly to fill a leaking cistern and, as the Continental demand for good Great Horses was insatiable, he was determined to stop the exodus. In 1496 exportation was prohibited anew by an Act, "Who only may carry a horse out of this land without the King's licence: the custom and price of a mare to be transported."[6] Mares could not be exported, except under licence, unless they were at least three years old and worth no more than 6s. 8d. Even then, duty was payable and this rose to 6s. 8d. for those for which a licence was required. Anyone caught attempting to evade these restrictions forfeited his mare. However, the owner received compensation and the head officers of the town where she was seized were required to sell her openly at the best price obtainable, the balance, after compensation had been paid, being divided between the King and the officer who had apprehended her. If, on the other hand, any private person could spot an unlicensed mare about to be carried over the water before the King's officer could do so, he could offer the owner 7s., and take the mare. This incentive to the enforcement of the law led to some pretty strange dealings. A stallion could not be exported at all, even under licence. But the owner could take one with him, provided that he swore on oath before the Customer or Searcher of the port that it was for his own use and that he had no intention of selling him. The concession was of course abused. Some men travelled much, and their horse ran away or was stolen every time. The Act was largely a failure.

A more sensible development in this reign was the new practice of gelding, an operation apparently invented by the ancient Scythians but hitherto ignored in England. It was, of course, still considered necessary to use only stallions for the cavalry, but at last breeders were beginning to recognise the impossibility of making much headway towards improvement when all males, big and small, good and bad, were left entire, and all stock (except that of the privileged classes) had to be pastured together in large fields late in the season after the harvest, when a valuable mare which had failed to conceive to a Great Horse was likely to be got in foal in the autumn by the persistent efforts of a collection of weeds and misfits. Castration grew only very slowly in popularity and three centuries were to pass before it became a standard operation upon colts which were not specifically selected as possible coming sires. But at least a start was made.

4. HENRY VIII, EDWARD VI AND MARY I: 1509–1558

Most of Henry VIII's considerable legislation about horses was enacted in the later years of his reign. In 1532, exportation of stallions, or (except under licence) of any mares worth more than 6s. 8d., already prohibited under his father's law, became a felony, with a staggering fine of £40.[7] Scotland, being the only foreign country not separated by water from England, was specially dealt with. No horse, mare or gelding was to be sold, exchanged, given, conveyed or delivered into the realm of Scotland: nor, in England, might one be sold, exchanged or delivered to any Scottish man for him to convey north of the border. These regulations were pretty successful, and in 1540 an Act of Parliament in Scotland limited the right to appear mounted on the battlefield to generals only. In this deplorable condition, the Scots could do little in the line of real warfare. But they could annoy the English, for light horses suitable for the interminable unofficial border skirmishes were plentiful.

Not satisfied with forbidding export, the King attempted in a series of later laws to control and promote horse-breeding within the realm. The very notion that this could be done by legislation was absurd – especially at that time. If the farm-land of Tudor England had been all enclosed, and if there had been a twentieth-century Ministry of Agriculture and constabulary, the thing might have been just possible, though any government which tried to do it as Henry did would provide plenty of amusement for the opposition. The laws themselves became progressively ridiculous. For their utter futility, they could be ignored here, were it not for certain points of interest in them.

The preamble to the first of these Acts[8] said that the King, "calling to his most gracious memory the great decay of the generation and breeding of good, and swift, and strong horses, which heretofore have been bred in this realm, to the great defence, profit and common commodity of the same", was convinced that degeneration would continue "if speedy remedy be not sooner provided in that behalf." Accordingly, any owner of an enclosed deer park with a circumference of one mile was required, from 1st May 1537, to keep two brood mares of 13-hands at least: in a park with a circumference of four miles or more, four such mares had to be kept. The penalty for non-compliance was 40s. for each month, with three months' grace for the purpose of replacing any mare that died. The owners must not "willingly suffer any of the said mares to be covered or leapt with any stoned horse under the stature of fourteen handful[9] ... upon pain of forfeiture of 40s." Half of the fines went to the King, and half to the informant. It is difficult to imagine any legislation more productive, even at best, of doubt and confusion. At the worst, evil persons could arrange quite a profitable shemozzle by slyly introducing a little entire horse through a gap in the hedge, ditch, wall or pale and then informing all the appropriate authorities. It is debatable what action the owner was then required to take in order to be seen not to "willingly suffer" the situation. The counties of Westmorland, Cumberland and Northumberland and the Bishopric of Durham were exemped from the Act's demands, not so much because they could not fulfil them as because they were too close to the border. Also exempt were parks and other enclosed grounds in which tenants or other neighbours had the right or privilege of grazing stock – that is, where the fencing was simply for the purpose of keeping in the deer of the lord of the manor. James V of Scotland in 1535 also tried to increase the size of horses by law, but with equally little result.

A further Act,[10] five years later, was far more stringent and positive. It made two distinct requirements. The first had to do with the size of stallions. No one was allowed to put an entire horse above the age of two years and below the height of 15-hands into any "forest, chase, moor, marish, heath, common or waste ground" where mares and fillies were normally kept, in twenty-five specified counties. (In all other shires, similar regulations applied, but the minimum height was 14-hands.) The modern breeder cannot fail to be aghast at the omission from the 15-hand list of Derbyshire, Nottinghamshire, the Soke of Peterborough, Rutland and Hertfordshire: nor can the pony lover be other than appalled at the inclusion of the whole of Wales, and also of Hampshire (the only southern county, except for Kent, to come under the Act). Enforcement depended on the usual incentive to informers, who were to go to the keeper of the forest or chase or, in other cases, the appropriate constable, bailiff, headborough, bursholder or tithingman, and require him to come and bring the suspect stallion to the pound so as to be measured in the presence of three honest men. If the informer was correct, the horse was his to keep, "as his own proper goods and chattels for ever, without let, interruption, vexation, suit, or trouble of the owner." In the event of the officer or any of the three honest men refusing to carry out their duty or not measuring truly, they could be fined 40s. each time, half going to the King and half to anyone who cared to sue for it. However, every undersized stallion was allowed one free break-out each year from his own pasture or ground into a place where mares were kept, provided he did so against the will and mind of his owner. When that happened, open notice and knowledge had to be given at the owner's dwelling-house or published on a Sunday or other festival day at the parish church. The owner then had four days to get him back again before the law could be put in operation.

The second requirement of this law was an autumn round-up of all mares, fillies, foals and geldings in forests and chases and on commons, moors, marishes, heaths and waste grounds. This had to be done on Michaelmas Day or within fifteen days thereafter. Any female that "shall be thought not to be able, nor like to grow to be able, to bear foals of reasonable stature" or any horse at all, including a gelding, unlikely to be able to do "profitable labours" was to be killed "and the bodies of them to be buried in the ground, or otherwise bestowed, as no noyance thereby shall come or grow to the people there near inhabiting or thither resorting." In the event of a difference of opinion – and, in view of the fact that no minimum height was specified, this could only arise out of personal enmity or spite among the various owners concerned – decision was by majority vote. Disputes were to be dealt with in Quarter Sessions. The penalty for failure to carry out the drive was 40s., forfeited to the King: on the other hand, additional drives could be made at any time of the year. (An extra clause made it an offence, incurring a 10s. fine, to put a horse of any sex or description into the places mentioned above if it was affected by scab or mange.)

These laws were not an attempt, either laudable or lunatic, to preserve and increase the number of Great Horses so much as an effort to convert all ponies into horses and to kill off all those that were not being bred bigger. The whole thing was a fiasco. As the authors of *The Foals of Epona* have pointed out, there was no resulting scarcity which caused the value of ponies to rise, nor was the price of leather brought down by the glut which the law might be expected to bring about.

However, Henry's last horse Act,[11] the following year, did try to be more positive by requiring wealthier persons to keep stoned trotting horses for the saddle at least three years old and 14-hands in height. Archbishops and Dukes had to provide and maintain seven, and lesser personages five, three, two or one, according to their status and financial position. The one-stallion men were clergy with between £100 and 500 marks (£333.33) and any layman whose wife wore a gown of silk, a French hood or bonnet of velvet, and so on. The penalty for non-compliance was £10 for each three months. Two years were allowed for the replacement of stallions which were requisitioned for the wars and lost – sufficient time to bring on a home-bred colt.

Henry VIII's only real success with horses was in preventing good ones getting into Scotland. His enthusiasm for the Great Horse cannot be doubted. But the truth is that the heaviest and slowest variety of this animal was now becoming gradually out-dated as a war-horse, except to carry heavy fat men such as the King himself. Its breeding, like all horse-breeding, was now entering a phase when objectives were not clear, and it is certain that no improvement in any stock ever takes place unless men can see an ideal to aim at. Loss of purpose seems to have sent even the King's own stud adrift. Thirty years after his death, William Harrison remarked that "King Henrie the eight erected a noble stud-derie" (i.e. for breeding horses, especially of the Great sort) "and for a time had verie good successe with them, till the officers waxing wearie, produced a mixed breed of bastard races, whereby his good purpose came to little effect."[12]

In the first year of Edward VI, a new Act[13] confirmed much of his father's law of 1532 with reference to selling horses both overseas and to Scottish men. However, its whole purpose was destroyed by various relaxations. For example, the King could grant licences to export, and authorise others by warrant to issue such licences, each document specifying the number of animals permitted. In respect of Scotland, "to the intent that the King's Majesty shall not hereafter be deceived in the number of such horses, mares or geldings", the number of horses licensed to cross the border had to be calendered in a book and also endorsed "on the backside of the said licence" by one of the three Wardens of the Marches. A second relaxation allowed people going overseas once again to take horses for their own use – and not just one horse only, as in the time of

Henry VII. Cheap mares could also be exported again, and the maximum value
of these was now raised to 10s. Further, the Warden of the Five Ports could
give six horses or geldings at his pleasure in any one year to persons beyond the
seas who were "in amity with the King's Highness".

This law, naturally, was immediately abused and the rest of the horse legislation in Edward's reign was no smarter. Another law in his first year[14] had
made the stealing of horses, mares or geldings a felony without benefit of
clergy. But there was doubt whether it was felonious to steal just one horse, so
another Act[15] was required to resolve the matter.

In the reign of Edward's elder half-sister, their father's Act compelling wealthy
people to keep heavy trotting stallions was partially repealed. In her reign also
was passed the famous Act[16] which required that, at fairs and markets, toll-
takers or book-keepers should enter the names of buyers and sellers of horses in
a register. Before the sale could become effective, the animal must stand in the
open fair one hour in the presence of all parties to the contract, so that they
could be challenged. Laws directed against horse-stealing now became a regular
feature of most reigns, and the problem proved a more lasting one than that of
preventing the Scottish men obtaining English horses.

5. ELIZABETH I: 1558–1603

English achievements on the high seas obscure the undoubted degeneration of
our horses during Elizabeth's reign. Had we depended upon these and not upon
ships, we would have been in a sorry plight, no matter how thrustful and bold
our adventuring men. But of course we knew we did not depend on them, and
this knowledge, together with the decreasing importance of sheer strength and
weight in the war-horse, was responsible for the lack of incentive to match the
power and size that continued to characterise the Low Countries horses.
Nevertheless, it is in this reign that a new need for size and power, for quite
different purposes, first really began to make itself plain. Let us consider the
deterioration of the war-horse first, and the beginnings of specialist draught-
horse development afterwards.

Elizabeth began briskly, in the first year of her reign, by adding a year's
imprisonment[17] to Henry's £40 fine for exporting horses to Scotland. Four
years later, she repealed that part of Edward's Act which allowed men to take
horses abroad "for their only occupation in their journeys". As the new Act[18]
explained, "many evil-disposed persons of a covetous and greedy desire do
daily transport out of this realm very great numbers of horses and geldings,
and do exchange and sell the same in the parts beyond the seas, for their own
private lucre and gain". It was practically impossible to stop them, because they
had only to perjure themselves – such offences were "no otherwise to be tried
or judged but only by the oath of the offender himself; therefore the offenders
therein do escape unpunished, and thereby many persons are greatly encouraged
daily to commit the like offences".

Also in 1562, on 7th May, she issued a Proclamation about "the decay of horses within the realm, which partly riseth by stealing and carrying numbers of horses, geldings, mares, and colts out of the realm, and by neglecting the breeding and keeping of horses within the realm, according to the laws provided". Regarding the former offence, she warned her people "not to trust in any remission of penalties therefor provided". As for the latter, she thought the laws had been "by divers persons so long forgotten that it will seem hard to have the same speedily put in execution". There would be a muster-roll taken in September, and also the following January, and thereafter every half-year.[19] Another Proclamation of the same date detailed the existing regulations about horse-breeding and keeping, and reminded everyone that it was also a felony to deliver a horse to any place in the "Debateable Land" between England and Scotland.[20]

A third Act about horses followed in 1565, but this was to do with their breeding and, so far from being an attempt to increase the number of big and powerful animals, was an admission of defeat. It is also the clearest and most startling reminder we could possibly have that the whole pattern and plan of heavy horse breeding, as we have become familiar with it in the last two centuries, not only did not exist, but could not exist, in sixteenth-century England.

Let us look ahead to about 1765, when the so-called "English" draught horse was on its way to becoming the biggest and heaviest in the world. For this, one part of England alone, the Fens, was responsible. It was only there that the greatest weight and power were developed. Most of the Fen horses were of Flemish descent and so the soil merely had to add to already existing immensity. All draught horses bred in other places, if they were of the greatest size, could be traced back, within a generation or two, to the Fens. Once Fen blood was cut off, a skilful breeder could produce more quality perhaps, but he began to lose sheer massiveness. This was so in Bakewell's time and it remained so.

But in 1565, 200 years before Bakewell, and for many years to come as well, these Fens really were Fens. They could support very little. They were quite unable to maintain the 15-hands stallion that Henry VIII had demanded in forests, chases, marishes and commons. They could not even support the 14-hands stallions that he had required in Derbyshire, Nottinghamshire and other lesser parts. (And here is another reminder that, in the heavy-horse sense, these times were still pre-historic. It was in these counties that Fens massiveness was converted in classical times to a perfect combination of powerful muscle and fine hard bone.)

This 1565 Act[21] explained that "divers and sundry great and manifold hurts, hindrances, and losses have happened and chanced as well to the inhabitants of the moors, marishes, and fen grounds within the Isle of Ely, situate, lying and being in the said County of Cambridge, as also to the inhabitants of other moors, marishes, and fen grounds within the said Shire, together with the Counties of Huntingdon, Northampton, Lincoln, Norfolk, and Suffolk next adjoining and bordering upon the same Isle: for that the said moors, marishes, and fen grounds, because of the rottenness, unfirmness, moisture, and waterishness,

were never able ne yet are to breed, bear, or bring forth such great breed
of stoned horses of such bignesss and high stature as within the aforesaid statute
are expressed, without danger and peril of the miring, drowning, and perishing
of the same". The result had been that unscrupulous persons had enforced the
law by removing poor men's little horses, and so no one dare put a stallion in
the Fens, "to the utter subversion and decay of all the tilliage and carriage within
the said Isle and others the countries round about the same, in time to come".
The Act therefore reduced the minimum height of stallions allowed to depasture
in marishes and seggy fen grounds in that area to only 13-hands.

The Queen was fighting a losing battle, as her father had done, in the attempt
to maintain the Great Horse population. In March 1580, a muster of horse and
armour showed an appalling state of affairs and so on 14th April she issued her
fourth Proclamation on the subject. "The Queen's most excellent Majesty,
finding by the view of the last certificate of musters the number of horsemen,
especially in certain countries, to be much less than she looked for, considering
the great charge that from time to time hath been given", pointed out that
"great numbers of her Majesty's subjects be in danger of great penalties, if her
Majesty should seek the due execution of her laws". She had appointed a commission of noblemen and gentlemen to go into the matter. "The punishment
with all severity of such as be found offenders therein is very necessary."
Justices of peace and others who received instructions from the commissioners
would ignore them "at their uttermost peril".[22]

Eight years later, the Armada was on its way. A mere 3,000 cavalry could be
mustered throughout the length and breadth of England, and it was fortunate
that they were not required. The year after the Spanish horses were all drowned,
Sir John Smythe contemptuously called them "deformed light-bellied beasts".
Compared with Henry VIII's idea of a cavalry horse, perhaps they were. But in
England there were few even of these. The vast majority of horses, now and for
years to come, were not what we should call horses at all. They were ponies,
and if the Queen's most dear father could have seen them, still about in such
numbers, he would have played old Harry.

To turn now to the new development in this reign, it is an odd coincidence
that 1564, the year preceding the Act which admitted that the Fens could
support only ponies of a height that a eleven-year-old might ride, may be
regarded as the most significant early date in the history of the horse as a modern
draught animal. That year, Her Majesty acquired a coach and appointed a
Dutchman, Guylliam Boonen, to drive it. She was not the first person in England to own one. Two years before she became Queen, Sir Thomas Hoby had
offered to let Lady Cecil have a ride in his. But a royal example was important.
In 1572, she made a journey to Warwick behind six of the biggest and strongest
horses available, and as a result was unable to sit down for days. Within another
eight years, so many people had put caste before comfort that there was an
outcry against the evil effects these machines would have upon the art of riding.

(For some reason, the legend survived that it was Henry, 18th Earl of Arundel and the last of the Fitzalans to bear that title, who presented the Queen with her first coach. He brought it back from Padua and rode in it through Canterbury, Blackheath and London before offering it to her, together with her "first pair of silk stockings". He then returned by water to his house in the Strand. Alas for romance, this was in 1567 and she already had not only a coach but silk stockings as well. Her silk-woman, Mrs. Montague, had given her a pair of black ones in 1561, since when she had never worn cloth hose again.)

With perhaps even greater significance, it was in 1564 or thereabouts that the first public stage wagon also made its appearance. People who were unable to ride had the opportunity now of travelling far more slowly and agonisingly than those who could. And goods could now be tugged along less efficiently behind eight massive draught-horses, if they could be found, than they could be carried by a greater number of less expensive pack animals. But it was the beginning of progress, and we are fortunate in having a contemporary description of this new form of cartage and transport.

William Harrison (1534–1593), rector of Radwinter in Essex and Canon of Windsor, contributed the *Historicall Description of the Iland of Britaine* to Raphael Holinshed's *Chronicles* (1577), and we have already noted his comment on the dismal failure of Henry VIII's stud. In the chapter entitled "Of cattell kept for profit", he described cart and pack-horses (which were not gelded) and riding horses (commonly gelded) and bewailed the deceits practised by horse-keepers, dealers and hostelers – "an honest meaning man shall have verye good lucke among them, if he be not deceyved by some false tricke or other".

His first paragraph on horses is worth reading in full. After praising our oxen, he says "Our horses, moreover, are highe, and although not commonly of such huge greatnesse as in other places of the maine, yet yf you respect the easinesse of theyr pace, it is harde to saye where their lyke are to be had. Our lande doth yielde no Asses, and therefore the most parte of our caryage is made by these, which remaining stoned, are either reserved for the cart, or appointed to bear such burthens, as are convenient for them: Our Carte horses therfore are commonly so strong, that five of them will drawe three thousande weyght of the greatest tale wyth ease for a long journey. Such as are kept also for burden, will cary foure hundreth waight commonly without any hurt, or hinderance. Thys furthermore is to be noted, that our Princesse and the Nobilitye, have their cariage commonly made by cartes, whereby it commeth to passe, that when the Queenes maiestie doth remoove from any one place to another, there are usually 400 cartwares" (teams, OED: the 1587 text adds "which amount to the summe of 2400 horses") "appointed out of the Countryes adioyning, whereby hir caryage is conveighed safely unto the appointed place, whereby also the auncient use of sommers and sumpter horses, is in maner utterly relinquished."[23]

6. BLUNDEVILLE ON BREEDS AND BREEDING

Canon Harrison's observation that English horses were not usually so big as those in parts of the Continent is mild: his task was to describe, not to criticise or advise. And he described only the native sorts. "Of such outlandish horses as are dailie brought over unto us I speake not, as the genet of Spaine, the courser of Naples, the hobbie of Ireland, the Flemish roile,[24] and the Scottish nag, bicause that further speech of them commeth not within the compasse of this treatise."

Thomas Blundeville, however, who lived at Newton Flotman, seven miles south of Norwich, was a horseman, not a churchman, and he therefore wrote quite differently. In 1565 he had issued *The Art of Ryding and Breaking Greate Horses*, but this was only a translation of three Continental works on equitation, management and feeding. In 1580 a second and enlarged edition appeared under the title *The Foure Chiefest Offices belonging to Horsemanship*. The new first office, that of breeding, was entirely his own. He remedied Harrison's failure to describe the foreign horses which were regularly imported, and in addition explained the various breeding methods that were used in his time. Both are of the utmost interest. (In his Epistle Dedicatory, addressed to the Earl of Leicester, Master of the Queen's Horse, he had, incidentally, put in a plea that Her Majesty should not only enforce the law about horses more rigorously, but also make a contribution herself by finding room for some horse-breeding in her parks, which were wholly devoted to the keeping of deer, "a pleasure without profit".)

Three of the foreign horses that Blundeville described, during that transitional period in which he lived, when the virtues of the heavy horse were being gradually adapted from weight-carrying to weight-hauling, are of concern to cart-horse history. These are the German, the Flemish, and the Frisian. A fourth is, literally, of only passing interest, even though it was the choicest and most expensive. Few people could afford to import a Napolitan stallion – "both comelie and stronglie made and of so much goodness, of so gentle a nature and so high a courage as anie horse is". He was marked out from other breeds by his "no lesse cleane than stronge makinge".[25] But his part in English cart-horse history is, from now on, negligible. His future lay as a great riding horse and he was admirably adaptable to the coming requirements of the newer type of cavalry. To see the path that he was to tread, we look to the mounts on which our kings of the next century are depicted.

There was cart-horse potential in the North German horse, the "High Almaine", which was bred over a wide area west of the Elbe. Indeed, even in Blundeville's description we pass almost unawares from Great Horse to Cart Horse. He is "commonlie a great horse, and though not finelie yet verie stronglie made, and therefore more meete for the shocke [of battle] than to passe a cariere, or to make a swift manege, because they be verie grosse and heavie, yet by industrie they are made lighter behind than before: for their riders do use in their maneging to make them to turne alwaies with their hinder parts, and not with their fore parts: like Jacke anapes, when he is made to come over the chaine, whereby they keepe their Horses heade alwaies upon the enimie. The disposition of this Horse (his heavie mould considered) is not evill, for he is verie tractable, and will labour indifferentlie well by the way, for his pace for the most part is a verie hard trot."

Now we turn to the heaviest horse of the sixteenth century, the true ancestor many times over of the modern Shire. "The Flanders Horse in his shape, disposition and pace, differeth in a maner nothing from the Almaine Horse: saving that for the most part he is of a greater stature, and more puissant. The Mares also of Flanders be of a great stature, strong, long, large, faire and fruitfull, and besides that, will endure great labour, as is well seene, for that the Flemings do use none other draught, but with those Mares in their wagons, in the which I have seene two or three Mares to go lightlie awaie with such a burthen, as is almost incredible." If Anne of Cleves fitted the description Henry VIII had given her, he might have done better not to have divorced her so quickly.

Finally, the Frisian horse, which was to play a smaller but more subtle role in the formation of the English cart-horse of the future. "The Frizeland Horse is no verie great Horse, but rather of a meane stature" (Blundeville was using the word which signifies "middling", not the other "mean", synonymous with "contemptible") "being therewith strong and well compact together, and hath verie good legs." But he did not like its temperament. "The disposition of this Horse is so devilish, so stubborne, and so froward, as unlesse the rider which first breaketh him be verie bold, and therewith circumspect to correct him in time, he shall never bring him to any good: for he will do nothing without stripes, which also being given out of time, will make him so restiefe, that neither faire meanes nor fowle meanes, will ever win him from that vice againe. The pace of this Horse is a good comelie trot."

Blundeville deplored the degeneration of the great horses of his day, and offered advice to those who should want to breed them. There were other men who would desire ambling horses or swift runners. "But now to content the countrieman his desire, which seeketh to breede Horses for draught, or burthen, where should I wish him to provide himselfe of Mares and Stallions better than here in England, wheras he maie easilie find a number of strong Jades, more meete for that purpose, than for the saddle?" The reason for the plenty of these common sorts was a "lacke of good order of breeding". If this could only be put right, "I beleeve there would be so good and so faire Horses bred here, as in anie place in Christendome." If this was a pregnant thought, so also was his acute observation of the way in which the Flanders horse became modified on introduction to this country. It was huge and heavy and gross because it came out of "wet grounds": in England it became "finer limmed, cleaner made, and therewith lighter and more nimble, than they be at home". When the Fens, in years to come, became able to support heavy horses, it produced a type possessing Flemish weight and coarseness, and the modification could be observed within our own realm and in the short distance that separated, say, Deeping from Derby.

What were the points of a cart-horse? "So that he be great of stature, deepe ribbed, side bellied,[26] and have strong legs, and good hoofes: and therewith will stoope to his worke, and laie sure hold on the ground with his feete, and stoutlie pull at a pinch, it maketh no matter how fowle or evill favoured he be." Maybe so, but his next remark reassures us that English ideas were not all disorderly. "Notwithstanding, I have knowne some carriers that go with cartes, to be so exquisite in their choice of Horses, as unlesse they had beene as comelie to the eie as good in their worke, they would not buie them, in so much as I have seene sometime drawing in their cartes better proportioned Horses, than I have knowne to be finelie kept in stables."

As for breeding, Blundeville listed three methods of mating, which, in view of the specialised system that was later to be developed, are most important to notice. "The first and best waie, and speciallie for him that hath manie Mares and Stallions, is to put everie one of his Stallions by himselfe (being before well rested and well fed for the purpose) into a severall pasture." Then, from the beginning of May until the middle of June, "you may turne into everie one of these Stallions so manie Mares as he is well able to cover, which abilitie is to be measured by his youth, strength, and lustinesse. For if he be young and lustie, he maie cover ix or x Mares verie well, and if he be old and feeble, he had need to cover the fewer; for to cover manie is a great feeblishing to the Horse."

The second method was only a small step from the first and almost "natural" way. Those who had only one stallion and a few mares could put in one mare after another. "By this meanes the Stallion shall not beate himselfe so much, nor spend more seede upon one Mare than upon an other."

The third way, though recommended only for those who did not happen to have a paddock big enough to let the stallion run with his mares, was a some-what surprising introduction of the modern method of bringing the horse to the mare. The modern breeder will recognise points of similarity with his own method: but, having done so, will be even more surprised that the obvious advantages of the system were not realised. The mare should be watched for her season and then should be put in "some pretie close yard or court made of purpose. Well, the Mare then being thus brought in, ye may cause your horse-keeper to bring forth your Stallion, who if he hath bene well fed, and modera-telie exercised, as I said before, so soone as he seeth and smelleth the Mare, he will immediatelie fetch three or foure saults, and bound aloft with all foure for joie, even in your horsekeepers hand, who must not be afraid, but rather readie to helpe the Horse in his businesse, so soone as he shall leape the Mare, by putting his yard with his hand into the right place, whereby the Mare shall be the more speedilie, the more easilie, and also the more substantially served, by meanes that the Horse shall spend no labour in vaine, nor waste anie part of his seede. And after that the Mare hath been covered once, let your horsekeeper lead the Stallion a little aside, and walke him a while faire and softlie behind some house or wall cleane out of hir sight, to breathe him. And when he is well breathed, bring him in againe, and let him cover the mare the second time, and then lead him out againe, and so the third time if ye will, continuing to do this everie evening and morning the space of two or three daies, untill you thinke that she be sped." And at the end of every last covering, "bestowe one pale of water on the reines of hir backe, and cast another into her taile, and that shall make hir to hold." One would have thought that, in spite of the notorious difficulties in achieving conception, twelve or more leaps in two or three days would have made it unnecessary to seal the mare with pails of water.

No one at that time had thought of the idea of putting the stallion to a dozen or so *different* mares in so short a period. Like Harrison, and for that matter any writer with pretensions to education, Blundeville referred to Strabo's statement[27] that in ancient Syria the King's stud of 30,000 mares was served by only 300 stallions. But it did not occur to anyone that the proportion of one to 100 might only have been achieved by a slightly more economical system than this. Perhaps Blundeville had visions of one horse performing over 1,200 leaps a season in that golden age, for he commented that "it seemeth that Horses in times past have bene of a farre stronger nature than they be now in these our daies."

Blundeville coined the phrase "such sire and damme, such colt", re-worded later as the maxim "like begets like". But one cannot expect too much of him, expert as he no doubt was. He was a product of his times. On the subject of the best age for stud stallions, he only mildly criticised the fact that "in most places of this Realme, they appoint no Horses to that use, but such as be verie old, and therewith perhaps both lame and blind. Yet the men in the old time made a great matter thereof, and allowed no Stallion to be verie good, but from v. yeares to xiiij." Mares, he said, should be covered at the age of three onwards. This was considerably more sensible, but he quoted, without condemning, the "pretie meanes and sleights men of old time used" – for example, of tying up the left stone of a stallion with a "thredden lace" in order to beget a horse foal, and the right one to ensure a mare foal. Those who did not have a strong preference could prognosticate the sex of a foal by observing whether the horse covered the mare on the third day before the full moon, or when the wind was blowing in the north, or whether he dismounted her on the right side, all of which would be indications of a colt foal, whereas the opposites would foretell a filly foal. It is difficult to have much sympathy with these old horsemen's tales, or with his own belief that if the stallion were not restricted in his drinking it would make his seed 'thin and waterie.' But one can understand his puzzlement over the infertility of stallions. He had a sort of rule of thumb test to see whether "the seede be good or not. Take of it betwixt your thumbe and finger, or in a locke of wooll, and if in your feeling and towsing of the wooll it seemeth to be firme, fast and slimie, it is good, but if it be liquid or waterish, it is naught." But now, as his contemporary, Canon Harrison would have concluded, to leave this, let us see what may be said of James VI and I.

7. JAMES VI AND I, CHARLES I AND THE COMMONWEALTH:
1603–1660

When the Scottish King took the English crown as well, the way was opened at last for the free sale and transit of horses across the border, though over three years passed before a new Act officially made such traffic no longer a felony.[28] Of the true position of horse-breeding in Scotland at that time, no one has ever claimed to know even half as much as is known of the situation in England, and that is little. There are two Scottish authorities with whom no one, in either country, would lightly dispute – Archibald M'Neilage (Secretary of the Clydesdale Horse Society 1881–1931 and editor of *The Scottish Farmer*) and Lawrence Drew (1826–1884), the nineteenth-century Bakewell of British cart-horse breeding. Neither of these gentlemen could find anything to say of heavy horses in their land prior to 1603. M'Neilage commented that, as Scotland often had greater intercourse with France and Flanders than with England, Norman and Flemish horses could have come in: Drew believed that more Great Horses came illegally from England than from across the water, but that in general his countrymen did little or nothing in the way of improving what poor creatures they had.

James VI and I did little or nothing about anything, particularly in the last five years of his life. But when, at the end of 1620, he appeared to be about to send an expedition to help his son-in-law, Frederick V the Prince Palatine (who had been elected King of Bohemia, but was now in the process of being driven from both his domains by the Emperor and by Spain), he appointed a council of war to estimate the cost. It was staggering. 1,150 baggage carts, each carrying one ton, would require eight cart-horses each, and 380 hospital wagons would need three each. A large proportion of these could probably be hired in the Low Countries at 2s. per day, including driver and keep, or could be bought there outright for £9 each. 200 superior horses – that is, horses of a size and strength more nearly approaching what we should now recognise as a cart-horse – for the ordnance and munition would have to be supplied from England at £15 each. This, of course, was only part of it. There were cavalry horses to be found as well. The estimate for the whole expedition was a quarter of a million pounds as initial cost, and £900,000 per annum for maintenance. The King deceptively told the Commons it would be much less. They voted him far less still and the plan petered out.

However, it was in James's reign that the draining of the Fens at last began to be transformed from a dream to a practical enterprise. It had taken long enough. Over a century earlier, John Morton, Bishop of Ely (and afterwards Archbishop of Canterbury), who had been a political refugee in Flanders in 1483–5, had cut a drain from Peterborough to Wisbech, forty feet wide and four deep, which still goes under the name of Morton's Leam. What might be achieved, with energy and enterprise, in the vast Fens had been indicated by the drainage of marshes in the London area in the time of Henry VIII, such as Wapping Marsh by Cornelius Vanderdelf in 1544, and Plumstead and Greenwich Marshes. Near the end of Elizabeth's reign, in 1601, an Act had been passed for the drainage of the Great Fens or Great Level, and Commissioners and Courts of Sewers were appointed.

Part of the Isle of Ely was reclaimed under a local Act of 1606, but James scarcely used his divine right to demand that the waters should be speedily gathered into one place and that the dry land should appear without delay. In 1621, Cornelius Vermuyden, a young man of about twenty-six from St. Maartensdijk on the island of Tholen in the province of Zeeland, who had been employed to repair damage and complete the drainage of the Havering and Dagenham area, undertook to reclaim 360,000 acres of fen land in the counties of Northampton, Lincoln and Cambridge. (There was a row as to whether he had really succeeded in the former project but four months after James's death, Charles in July 1625 gave him much of the reclaimed land.) In 1626, Vermuyden also agreed to drain Hatfield Chase, between Doncaster and Scunthorpe. Here, difficulties showed themselves in the pattern that was to become so familiar – the unpopularity of the foreign workmen, the opposition of those who lived by fishing and fowling, and criticism of Vermuyden's methods. In September 1628, he was knighted by Charles and in 1630 contracted to drain the Great Fens.

Among those who had shares in the company which the 4th Earl of Bedford had formed to back this project was Sir Edmund Verney of Claydon House in Buckinghamshire. He had to live in London to dance attendance as Knight Marshal on Charles I and in 1634 rented a large new house on the Bedford estate in Covent Garden. From there, he used to send detailed instructions and advice to his beloved eldest son Ralph about the management of things at home. For example, "I think it will do the colts no hurt to play abroade in the heate of the day, but I heare the pied coult got his mischance by a stroake of one of the cart horses, and that must be by carelessness of servants." In 1635, before Vermuyden had even officially "completed" his operations, Sir Edmund wrote home suggesting "I would send as many cart horses as I could to the fenns, there they would gather flesh at an easy charge."[29]

This sentence is so significant that one is almost tempted to suggest that the date 1635 should be regarded as the 1066 of Shire horse history. Only on the drained Fens, where previously a pony of Charles I's height, 13.2-hands, was almost too big to be supported, could the massive size and weight of the imported Flanders horse be not only maintained but even increased. Unfortunately, however, the work was largely a failure and the Earl of Bedford stood to lose the £100,000 he had invested. Charles took the matter into his own hands and re-appointed Vermuyden, and a new Company of Adventurers stolidly pursued the task.

If things had gone more peacefully in the next few years, and that part of the Fens had been made something more than mere "summer ground", perhaps Verney might have started actually breeding cart-horses there. If so, his voluminuous correspondence, so largely preserved, would have been sure to record it. As it is, we have but the dimmest and mistiest picture of the contractors' Flemish horses, which were brought over to help make the new rich lands and stayed to beget progeny which would help to farm it. As soon as dry land appeared, these horses trod it and waxed exceedingly great upon it.

In 1642, Sir Edmund was killed at the battle of Edgehill. The Civil War brought drainage work almost to a standstill for seven years, and saboteurs had the chance to do what they could to restore the new lands to their former seggy and marishy condition. The emergence of the Fens as the breeding ground of the heaviest of all horses, the central depot from which breeders all over England drew their basic requirements, cannot after all be marked by any convenient and simple ten-sixty-six. It was not a sharp and straightforward Norman Conquest, but prolonged and confused like the Saxon invasions.

To return to the diminutive King Charles, he had been warned by Sir Edward Harwood that, horse for horse, England could not field 2,000 to match the best 2,000 of the French. As it turned out, that did not matter, at least in the early stages of his only war, since it was domestic. Inferior or not by European standards, the cavalry in that struggle was the "Queen of the Battlefield". At first, both sides tried to adapt old methods to modern conditions. Cavalry was drawn up in six ranks on each wing of the battle order, and the charge consisted of an advance at the trot, halt, discharge of pistols when within firing range, and then close in to fight it out with sword and sheer weight and power. But Prince Rupert suddenly transformed the whole method of cavalry fighting. Following the innovations of King Gustavus Adolphus of Sweden, he drew up his cavalry only three deep and made them rush at a full gallop straight into the enemy without stopping. If that was to be the order of things from now on, the Great Horse was obsolete almost overnight.

The paradox lay, of course, in the fact that the war (as the Shire historian we first quoted would have put it) "ended in a victory for the Roundheads", even though it was the Royalists who began with most of the best horses. There were two reasons why the Parliament party had the better ones in the end. They were strongest in the eastern counties and, indeed, almost all those areas where the biggest and best horses were to be found, Oliver Cromwell himself being a Huntingdonshire man. And secondly, though there were more European countries inclined to give moral support to the King than to his enemies, none of them gave much practical help to either side. When it was a matter of selling strong Great Horses for cash (and Europeans were interested in that) it was the Parliament men who got by far the most, because they controlled the most convenient ports. When the war ended, there were many more Great Horses in the country than before it started. But the old-fashioned sort would never be of use again, even in England, to sit on and to fight from.

Oliver Cromwell's brilliance as a cavalry commander is irrelevant here, but it is worth remembering that it partly stemmed from his personal skill as a horseman and his knowledge of horses. For example, he dared to oppose the Earl of Manchester's orders to prepare for battle at Winceby in October 1643, "our horse being extremely wearied with hard duty two or three days together". And in November 1644, after the second battle of Newbury, he was again insubordinate. The Earl ordered him and his cavalry to check the King's march. Three days earlier, Cromwell had been eager to advance, but he was now equally certain that they must not move, on the grounds that the horses were spent and harassed.[30]

It is fitting that Cromwell may be given the credit of inventing a new name for the successor to the old Great Horse, or at least of being the first user of it that can be traced. Like all good names, it was a simple one. On 31st January 1644, he wrote from Stilton to Samuel Squire, "Dear Sir, Buy those horses, but do not give more than 18 or 20 pieces each" (i.e. "broad pieces" or gold sovereigns) "for them. That is enough for Dragooners" (as it would be: being mere mounted infantry, they rode any old horses). But he continued, "I will give you 60 pieces for that Black you won at Horncastle (if you hold to a mind to sell him) for my son, who has a mind to him. Sir, I am Your Friend, Oliver Cromwell."[31] Another letter, six months later, shows that he employed the word "Black" regularly.

The Black that young Richard Cromwell coveted was almost certainly a Frisian horse, the creature of middling size which Blundeville had commented on in 1580. Cromwell himself certainly had Frisians of his own which he drove in the more leisured times of the Commonwealth. It is a safe guess, though nothing more, that plenty of Frisians had turned up, as well as Flemish horses, in the drainage operations in the Fens, and they were absolutely ideal for the new sort of cavalry warfare. Black, indeed, they were, and black they have all remained, to this day. Cromwell was therefore scarcely thinking of a cart-horse when he used the word "Black", but the English cart-horses acquired plenty of Frisian blood and it was to the cart-horse that the name Black became attached. The Fens and the midland counties heavy-horses of the next century were to become the "Black Horse" breed – and (since memories were conveniently short) were soon called the "Old English Black Horses". Really, they would have been better described as English Flemish-Frisian Horses. When the supporters of the Cleveland Bay wished to explain that their breed was free both of cart-horse and of thoroughbred influence, they used to say it was "neither blood nor black".[32]

The importance of the Frisian horse in the history of the Shire and perhaps the Clydesdale is greater than used to be supposed, largely because, far too often, he has not been given his correct name, being classed vaguely with "Dutch", "Flemish" or "Belgian" horses in varying degrees of inaccuracy. But it is the true Flanders horse, as Blundeville knew it and as it was to remain for many a year, that was the main fount and origin of all British heavy-horses, other than the Suffolks. In this connexion, we must turn again to Scotland during the Civil War, because there used to be an old legend that "one of the Dukes of Hamilton" had six fine black stallions from Flanders at Strathaven castle in the middle of the seventeenth century. If he did, it is the first fact that anyone can point to about a heavy-horse in Scotland. Drew and M'Neilage both referred to it, but were too cautious to comment.

This mysterious Duke can only have been the 1st Duke, James Hamilton, who was born in 1606 and was beheaded on the 9th March 1649. The 2nd Duke was his brother, who only briefly survived him, being killed at the battle of Worcester in 1651. Their sister Anne succeeded them and she surrendered her honours in favour of her son James Douglas, the 4th Duke, who was born too late (1658) to fit the legend. The 1st Duke had succeeded his father as 3rd Marquess of Hamilton and 2nd Earl of Cambridge in 1625, and was the next heir to the throne of Scotland after the descendants of James VI. He failed in an expedition to Germany (1631–1634). He failed as Charles' commissioner in Scotland to pacify the country after the prayer-book disturbances. In 1648 he led an army of 20,000, which grew to 24,000, against the Parliament, but was so badly beaten by 9,000 English that Cromwell was able to smash his army up, regiment by regiment, in the so-called battle of Preston. He had, of course, been abroad, and he owned property both in England and Scotland, so he could have obtained Flemish stallions direct or second-hand. He has been described as a man who was easily brought to imagine that "all future tasks were easy and all present obstacles insuperable". It may be that he thought that Great Black Horses could be easily grown in seventeenth-century Scotland. But it is also possible that Scottish memories have confused him with his great-great-nephew the 6th Duke, also called James, who about 1750 actually did have a Black Flemish stallion. Would the first Duke really be remembered as "one of the Dukes"? Perhaps his only connexion with the Scottish cart-horse was nominal: when, in 1643, he was created Duke of Hamilton, he also became the first Marquess of Clydesdale.

When the Commonwealth was established, the 5th Earl of Bedford resumed his father's undertaking in the Fens and re-appointed Vermuyden as engineer. A prompt start was made in 1649, and the work was completed in 1652, though the Southern level remained to be drained. However, 150 years were to pass before all those rich Fen grounds were to be properly reclaimed where great Shires were produced in the nineteenth century. In 1653, Sir Cornelius went to Holland with what Gardiner called "the most astounding proposal ever made by an Englishman to the minister of a foreign state"[33] – that of a perpetual alliance with England, to include the partition of the world between the two powers, the admission to civil rights in each country of the citizens of both, and a declaration of war upon any state maintaining the Inquisition. Vermuyden seems to have thought of the idea and Cromwell's party in the Council of State approved, but the Dutch were not impressed. The last we hear of Vermuyden is in 1655–6, when he was attempting to drain Sedgemoor. He died in poverty and in an obscurity as dense as that which hides the names of the horses, and their pioneer breeders, in those part-drained Fens with which his name will always be associated.

CHAPTER II

1660–1760

Horses for the wagon, coach or cart

I. HEAVY WHEELED TRANSPORT

IT is a fairly reasonable generalisation to say that, when the monarchy was restored in 1660, four-wheeled vehicles in the form of public stage wagons and private coaches had been travelling the so-called roads of England for about 100 years. The one innovation in that time had been the public stage coach, which made its first appearance just before the Civil War. For long it was a cumbrous vehicle with six to eight passengers inside, a few stuffed into the boot, and none on top (where they could only have remained if they had been lashed down with ropes), grinding on its way by the might and main of the horses.

During the next 100 years – precisely a century elapsed between the coronation of Charles II and the accesssion of George III in 1760 – there was virtually no new development, and little improvement, in the transport either of goods or of people. Progress began to be rapid only just after the period with which we are now concerned. Indeed, 1760 will serve as well as any other date to mark the beginning of the canal age. And it was in 1762 that any coach was first hung on steel springs, and 1784 when the first mail coach, London to Bristol, was introduced. From 1660 to 1760, therefore, the whole weight of responsibility continued to rest either on the back of some kind of horse or else upon a cart, wagon or coach which could be dragged only very slowly, by the tremendous exertions of the most powerful horses obtainable.

It is somewhat illusory during this period to draw a distinction between coach horses, wagon horses, dray horses and cart-horses, because a good specimen of any of them would have been ideal for all types of draught, particularly in winter. When in 1729 Lady Irwin expected that her journey from Bath to Althorp, less than 100 miles, would take four days, her only hope of improving on the time would have been to be provided with relays of the best brewers' dray horses from London. In Sussex, there were virtually no good coach or wagon horses, and the mud would have been too much for any but the finest and biggest in the country. Daniel Defoe in 1722, in a village near Lewes, saw "an ancient lady, and a lady of very good quality, I assure you, drawn to church in her coach with six oxen; nor was it done in frolic or humour ,but meer necessity, the way being so stiff and deep that no horse could go in it."[1]

This state of affairs explains why Dr. John Burton, travelling in Sussex in 1751 on horseback, and gaining the impression that the women, the oxen and the swine all had long legs, accounted for it by a theory that the constant pulling of the feet out of the mud stretched the muscles and lengthened the bones. Further west, the year before his journey, the very first wheeled vehicle for passengers, public or private, in the whole county of Devon had made its appearance.

Such progress as was made during this 100-year period lay not in the roads, but in the horses. In former days, ridiculously under-sized animals had struggled, ten or more in a team, with loads no greater than 3 or 3½ tons. Now, stage-wagons were pulled by eight, or sometimes even six, big heavy-horses. The first regular connection Shrewsbury had with London was the opening of the stage service in 1737. Drawn by eight horses, the wagon was scheduled to complete the journey in seven to nine days. Somewhat ironically, it was named Gee-hoo.

It is not difficult to understand why, in spite of the increase of wagons and coaches, pack-horse transport was far from being ousted. When, about 1730, Matthew Pickford took over the old business that ever afterwards was to go by his name, it was by pack-horses that he extended his enterprise into other parts of Lancashire and to Staffordshire and Yorkshire. By 1760, pack-horses were more numerous in this country than they had ever been.

2. SIR RICHARD HUTTON'S MIXED BREEDING, 1670–1686

In the second half of the seventeenth century, the 1st Duke of Newcastle[2] was the great authority on horsemanship but, among the plethora of livestock and farming books dating from the later years of Elizabeth onwards, the works of Gervase Markham (1568–1637) were still very popular. Mr. Markham had once been a soldier but became a prolific writer of plays, poems and treatises on country pursuits, the art of war and horses. His first volume on this last subject was the *Discourse on Horsemanshippe* (1593), but he wrote so much and borrowed so recklessly, both from his own writings and from other people's, that his several publishers became just as confused about his works as every librarian has been ever since. In 1617, he was forced to sign a promise never to write any more books on animal diseases, but in 1623 there appeared his *Maister-peece, Containing all knowledge belonging to a smith, farrier or horse-leech . . . etc*. This went through any number of editions during the next 100 years.

The Perfect horse-man, or, the experienced secrets of Mr. Markham's fifty years' practice, a resumé or hotch-potch of his equine writings, first appeared thirty years or so after his death. His advice about the best method of covering mares, like the language in which it is couched, is typical of his time. For example, "to know when your Mares are ready (if it be in a wild State) observe their chasing and galloping up and down morning and evening, and their inconstancy of abiding in any one place, especially throwing their noses to the North and South, the lifting up of their tails, riding one anothers backs, wooding[3] one another, oft pissing, and opening of their shares and closing them again, all are signs of Lust: if you will make a more particular trial, then prove them with some stoned Tit or Jade". The teaser having done his work, the breeder should then take the proved mare and the stallion and "put them together into some close-walled Paddock, where there is store of sweet grass and sweet water, just upon the going down of the sun, as near as you can observe, either three days after the change, or three days before the full of the Moon, and let them remain close together two whole nights and one day, and take the Horse from her at sunrise".

A copy of the 1668 edition of this book was bought by Sir Richard Hutton of Poppleton, near York. He appears to have followed Markham's suggestions pretty closely and on the blank pages at the end he recorded the dates when his mares were served. The earliest entry is for 1670 and the last was made in 1687, the year of his death. His notes typify the confusion of the age. As a later writer sarcastically remarked of the breeders of this time, "the weight of their knowledge of what they were about did not much oppress their brains."[4]

These are the sorts of things Hutton wrote in his register:

1672: "Aprill ye 29 my dun mare tooke my great coachhorse and the next morning. She since did run to horse and was covered by my chesnut horse the nineteen day of May."

1683: "Mr. Chas Hares stoned Nag covered my Grey filly April 24 and 25". Under the heading "Mares covered by Mr. Hamonds chesnut colt Anno 1683" appear the entries "The Ball mare put to him about May Day, next the three year old Turke and ran with him till May 27 when ye Spanish filly was put to him. The old cart mare put to him June 6."

Unfortunately, there is no telling whether Hamond's colt got a better foal out of the Turk or the Spanish than he did out of the cart mare. The next year, Hutton was also using the blood horse Diamond, belonging to Charles II (with whom he had gone into exile in the old days). For example, "My grey mare was covered by Diamond June 2 1684: the Browne mare was covered by Diamond June 1684." Before the next season began, the King had died – according to family tradition, owing the Hutton family £10,000, as a token of which they received only two pictures. This may be not quite true, for one branch of the family seems to have inherited from his Majesty a library in Chancery Lane and, when the royal racing stud was broken up, many of the horses passed to the D'Arcy family, into which Sir Richard's cousin, Matthew Hutton of Marske, had married. In any event, Diamond went on serving Hutton mares. For example:

"Mares covered by Diamond in the year 1685. Turk Filly covered May 15 1685. Spanish Filly May 17 1685. Browne filly June 2. Spanish again June 6. Turke again June 12, the Dun mare the night and morning June 24".

This appears to show more system in the breeding, but in 1686 a number of mares covered by Diamond were later put to the great coach-horse, which was of course a heavy-horse, possibly a Great Horse. Incidentally, the methods advocated by Markham were no more successful than any others tried before or since, if we may judge by the frequency of entries usually expressed as "She took horse again" (date) "and ran with him" (so many) "days". Sir Richard died the next year, at the age of seventy-five and there are no more entries.[5]

In the horse-breeding disorder of the late seventeenth century, the "racer" was the only "pure-bred" horse and was therefore the only candidate for the term "Thoroughbred". Nevertheless, though no one knows their names, there were men who tried to maintain, and not to mix, the blood of the Great Horse and to produce heavy draught horses by mating a Black stallion, whether fresh from Flanders or with a generation or two of English breeding behind him, with Black mares of similar type. When James II had been got rid of in 1688, William III imported not only Barbs, Turks and Arabs but also (not surprisingly) more big black Dutch stallions. He was the last monarch for a couple of centuries for whom we can claim any intimate association with heavy-horses unless we count Farmer George. Their breeding now became the task of humble men, who made it their living to produce a special strong sort of horse for the wagons, carts, drays and coaches. While breeders in general were muddling about, they were as dedicated to their ideal as were those, in more exalted circles, who strove by finding a Marske to breed an Eclipse.

3. THE HORSES THAT DANIEL DEFOE SAW: 1722

In the sixty years that separated the beginning of Charles I's war against his Parliament and the accession of his younger grand-daughter Anne in 1702, the revolution in the fortunes and work of the Great Horse had been completed. The great long-tailed mares which pulled the heavy Queen about in her massive coach were symbolic of the change. They were creatures of peace. They were pulling weights, not carrying them. And, if they had trotted, they would have shaken everything and everyone behind them to pieces on those roads.

The work for which these draught animals were required was rapidly increasing. The only town in England which was neither on the sea-coast nor on a navigable river, and which yet had any transport links with the rest of the country other than by road, was Exeter. In 1564–1566, the Corporation of that city had built a canal, one-and-three-quarter miles long, to the Exe below Countess Wear. Other than this, there was to be another period of nearly sixty years from the beginning of Anne's reign before men began seriously constructing canals. But as population and trade increased, there was more and more work for heavy draught. Many were the occupiers of land whose main income was derived from supplying horses and men to take farm-produce, or timber, or iron, or bricks, or stone, from where it was produced to where it was needed, or to take foreign goods from port to inland town. Each journey made every road even worse than it was before, and more demanding of powerful horses.

If Celia Fiennes, writing in the first year of Queen Anne about her journeys in the two previous reigns, had been as interested in kinds of horses as she was in enclosures, or cloth manufacture or houses and gardens, we would indeed have a wonderful description of them. But she is almost entirely silent on the subject. Even Daniel Defoe's *Tour through the Whole Island of Great Britain*, made in 1722 and published in 1724–1726, is a disappointment. He went into raptures about the great numbers of top quality saddle horses he saw at Penkridge Fair in Staffordshire,[6] but says nothing of the heavy ones there. He was impressed by the importance, as a horse-mart, of Northampton,[6] where they had no less than four horse-fairs a year, but does not appear to have seen one of them. In London, he tells us that Smithfield was still a great horse-market on Friday afternoons, but mainly for riding animals "of the highest price".[7] He remarks that Montgomeryshire "is noted for an excellent breed of Welch horses, which, though not very large, are exceedingly valuable, and much esteem'd all over England",[8] but says nothing else about them. He writes at great length on the Fens,[9] which he entered first from the east and, on a later journey, from the north: but he offers not a word about their horses, his most serious omission of all. Many hundreds of thousands of Fen acres were still "drowned" in his day. But where drainage had been more or less satisfactory, he notes occasionally the size of the livestock which were produced. For example, in a reference to Boston, he says that the land was very rich and "feeds prodigious numbers of large sheep, and also oxen of the largest size, the overplus and best of which all goes to London market". In the Lincolnshire fens, as in the Isle of Ely and elsewhere, "we see innumerable number of cattle, which are fed up to an extraordinary size by the richness of the soil".[10]

The other and older side of the picture is shown by his remark that from King's Lynn "they pass over here in boats into the fenn-country, and over the famous washes into Lincolnshire, but the passage is very dangerous and uneasy, and where passengers often miscarry and are lost; but then it is usually on their venturing at improper times, and without the guides, which if they would be persuaded not to do, they would very rarely fail of going or coming safe". And, having had his view of Cambridge from Gogmagog Hills, "As we descended westward, we saw the fenn country on our right, almost all cover'd with water like a sea, the Michaelmas rains having been very great that year, they had sent down great floods of water from the upland countries, and those fenns being, as may be very properly said, the sink of no less than thirteen counties: that is to say, that all the water, or most part of the water of thirteen counties, falls into them, they are often thus overflow'd". He added, "As these fenns appear cover'd with water, so I observ'd too, that they generally at this latter part of the year appear also cover'd with foggs, so that when the Downs and higher grounds of the adjacent country were gilded by the beams of the sun, the Isle of Ely look'd as if wrapp'd up in blankets, and nothing to be seen, but now and then, the lanthorn or cupola of Ely Minster. One could hardly see this from the hills and not pity the many thousands of families that were bound to or confin'd in those foggs, and had no other breath to draw than what must be mix'd with those vapours, and that steam which so universally overspread the country: But notwithstanding this, the people, especially those that are used to it, live unconcern'd, and as healthy as other folks, except now and then an ague, which they make light of, and there are great numbers of very antient people among them."[11]

Duck were still to be taken in vast quantities on those very lands where, later, some of the finest heavy-horses were to be bred. "There is a duckoy not far from Ely, which pays to the landlord, Sir Tho. Hare 500 l a year rent, besides the charge of maintaining a great number of servants for the management; and from which duckoy alone they assured me at St. Ives (a town on the Ouse, where the fowl they took was always brought to be sent to London;) that they generally sent up three thousand couple a week. There are more of these about Peterbro' who send the fowl up twice a week in waggon loads at a time, whose waggons before the late Act of Parliament to regulate carriers, I have seen drawn by ten, and twelve horses a piece, they were loaden so heavy."[12]

Defoe tells us about the heavy-horses of only two counties – Leicestershire and, astonishingly, Somerset. The former county, obviously, he can hardly ignore. "The horses produced here, or rather fed here, are the largest in England, being generally the great black coach horses and dray horses, of which so great a number are continually brought up to London, that one would think so little a spot as this of Leicestershire could not be able to supply them."[7] Having got this far, somewhat unconvincingly, he seems to be deserted both by facts and even by the powerful Defoe imagination and, realising that he does not know what he is talking about, somewhat feebly adds that "the adjoining counties of Northampton and Bedford" have "of late come into the same business". Why he mentions Bedford, which sixty years later was certainly not much of a county for breeding Blacks, and omits Lincolnshire, which in his own day definitely was, it is difficult to explain, except on the assumption that he is out of his depth, a situation he was so fearful of getting into in the undrained parts of the Fens. Daniel was a true middle class Londoner and, though he knew ten times more about horses than the average Londoner of today, he was more interested in rushing from town to town than in lingering on a farm, and much keener on trade and commerce than stock-breeding or industry.

Though silent on the horses of the eastern counties' Fens, drained or still undrained, he is specific about the horses in the Somerset Levels, that miniature fen-land of between 200 and 300 square miles between Mendip and the Quantock Hills, wherein were once the prehistoric lake villages of Glastonbury and Meare, and where Alfred also had his island fortress of Athelney and made his treaty with the Danes at Wedmore. When Monmouth, one Sunday night in July 1685, had ridden out from Bridgwater into the mist-laden marshes of Sedgemoor to his inevitable defeat amongst the rhines, Daniel Defoe, then a young man of 25, had been with him.[13] As, thirty-seven years later, he now revisits that area, he once more approaches from Bridgwater, though this time in daylight. "There is", he says, "a road to Bristol, which they call the Lower Way; the Upper Way, and which is the more frequented road, being over

Mendip Hills. This Lower Way also is not always passable, being subject to floods and dangerous inundations." All this part of the country "lies low and is wholly imployed in breeding and feeding of cattle, as are also the moors or marsh grounds, which extend themselves up to the rivers Perrot and Ivill". From here, he says, they export, "fat oxen, as large, and good, as any in England; large Cheddar cheese, the greatest, and best, of the kind in England; and colts bred in great numbers in the moors, and sold into the northern counties, where the horse copers, as they are called, in Staffordshire and Leicestershire buy them again, and sell them to London for cart-horses, and coach horses, the breed being very large".[14]

All of this is extremely puzzling. Defoe was surely right. No place in England, save only the real Fens, was better fitted to grow cart-horses of enormous size. But what happened to them between 1722 (or the survivors of the 1685 battle of the yokels against the King, if Defoe was relying in 1722 more on his memory than his eyes) and the end of the century? When Billingsley drafted his report on the agriculture of Somerset in 1794, he noted that the horse-breeders were "very inattentive to the selection of males and females for breeding". If stallions had not entered the county from farther north each spring, "the breed would be contemptible indeed". Why did the men of the Somerset Levels become as careless and thoughtless as the Fenmen were cunning and skilful? We are left to wonder at the incongruity, as we tour with Defoe, of being introduced to the then weighty horses of Somerset and of not even meeting the Lincolnshire Black.

One thing seems certain. These "very large" horses of Defoe's time, so suitable for heavy draught, must have been the purest descendants of the last Great Horses in England, the least modified by importation with a view to sheer draughting qualities. And he does not even tell us what they were like! Did they have very hairy legs, or clean ones? Were they black – or grey – or brown – or even chestnut? We are left in a Sedgemoor fog. The first Somerset heavy-horse breeder that it is possible to name was a Mr. Kirby of Hutton, three miles inland from Weston-super-Mare and just on the edge of this flat district. He bred a brown horse. But that was in 1846 and the sire came from Lancashire, and that is modern history, nothing at all to do with the early eighteenth century – as far as we know. The dam is unrecorded. Perhaps she was descended from one of those that Defoe had seen, and that is about as illuminating a speculation as to assert that you and I are descended from our ancestors.

4. A FOREIGN IMPRESSION IN 1748

The difficulty of obtaining a clear idea of the conformation of horses in any particular area at any particular time in the past is due to their being so commonplace. No one bothered to describe them. And, unlike tables or cooking pots or clothes, they do not survive to be placed in museums. Furthermore, the artist is not so much uninformative as positively misleading. With one or two notable exceptions, of whom Leonardo da Vinci is of course the foremost, artists before the time of George Stubbs (who was born in the year that the first part of Defoe's *Tour* was published and whose *Anatomy of the Horse* appeared in 1766) were careless of the type of horses that they depicted because they were only a background to their human subjects. To study horse-breeds by looking at the works of the great masters is about as sensible as to learn history by reading Shakespeare. Even after Stubbs, it is not safe to assume that a painted horse in any way resembled an actual breed unless the artist, like him, is specifically delineating the animal and not merely providing atmosphere for a human portrait.

Defoe was a Londoner touring England as a sightseer and so, disappointing as he is for our purposes, what he said is of interest. The foreigner is likely to be more useful, because so many sights were remarkable to him which to Defoe were no different from what he saw daily in London. Pehr Kalm, who visited England in 1748, had the extra qualification, as a young member of the Swedish Academy of Sciences, of being a skilled and exact observer.[15]

Unfortunately his travels were confined to the Home Counties but, even so, it is significant that he never referred to seeing oxen at work, either on farms or in haulage. At Little Gaddesdon, he saw pease being harrowed by six harrows bound side by side and pulled by six horses, one to each harrow. He was amazed to notice they were all controlled by two young boys. At "Carrington" (wherever that was) he saw three harrows and three horses likewise, all controlled by "one single little boy". He was intrigued by horse-troughs, by water-carts and mounting-blocks, and the prettiness of Gravesend. He was enchanted by the sight of farmers, day-labourers and "clodhoppers" all going about their daily work with peruques on their heads. He was dubious about men doing the milking – "England is a paradise for ladies and women". He was struck by the enormous number of lush meadows ringing London, fertilised with massive quantities of town manure in the autumn and supporting milch cows, beasts awaiting the butcher and the huge horses that were the pride of brewers and other enthusiastic owners of Blacks. He was amazed to find nearly all the church yards in Kent and Essex occupied by grazing horses. He saw very big horses even in Kent, which surprises us now. He was told that the Cumberland horses were not so large as those in the Home Counties, which is not at all surprising.

"For ordinary coaches, a pair of horses is harnessed abreast, as with us in Sweden; or, when they are heavier, two, three, or more pairs, one after another. But for wagons on which all sorts of things are carried, and for carts, where they are large, the horses are harnessed or spanned in quite a peculiar manner . . . all in a single row, the one after the other. I have seen as many as eight such horses spanned all in a row one after another. Nevertheless, it is rare to see so many. Commonly five or six horses are used for one of the large baggage-wagons, so harnessed tandem." He said that the chains were so heavy that "any other than English horses" would hardly be able to support them. English horses were as tall as the largest cavalry-horses in Sweden, but "fat and of an uncommon strength". He was astounded that no reins were used, but the horses were "steered wherever he wished, or to stop or go faster, only by the various and particular calls of the driver. Also, one never sees more than a single *carl* accompany and drive a wagon and six horses all spanned in a row."

He was particularly curious about docking. "All English horses, at least as many as I saw, have had the tail cut off about six inches from the root, so that the whole stump of the tail was only four or six inches long. On my asking the reason for this, some Englishmen have answered that it is the custom of the country to have the horses so bob-tailed." (If he had had time to visit Suffolk, he would have been even more surprised at the sight of the bung-tails there.) He had to work out his own answer – that "When they are all harnessed in a row, and close behind each other, the horse going before may not strike the next in the eyes with his dirty and muddy tail". Docking may have accounted for the large number of ladies he saw in London with horse-hair hats, which "look incomparably well". Be that as it may, we must finish with Pehr Kalm, though the subject of docking is far from done with.

5. OVER THE BORDER: 1689–1758

It would be presumptuous, if not impudent, on the part of an Englishman, and a Shire historian at that, to advance his own theories about how the sister breed of Clydesdale was developed. On the other hand, error of the opposite sort will not be avoided if he unquestioningly accepts the views of Scottish patriots. Those who speak of the Shire as the "Old English Cart-horse" are wrong, because it is Flemish/Dutch in origin. If courtesy let the Clydesdale be dubbed the "native breed of Scotland", the error would be doubled, because its origin is mainly Anglo-Flemish/Dutch.

But who said that? Archibald M'Neilage and Lawrence Drew said it, and they have already been mentioned (Chapter I.7). To them we add Thomas Dykes, agricultural correspondent of *The Glasgow News* prior to acting briefly as first secretary of the Clydesdale Horse Society until succeeded by M'Neilage in 1880. The pioneer of descriptive reporting on horse shows, Dykes continued thereafter for many years to devote himself to the study of the Clydesdale horse. Upon the views of these three Scotsmen all that is written in these pages about the Clydesdale up to the year 1880 is entirely based, and it is hoped that Scotsmen will pardon the omission of any further expression of indebtedness in later chapters to these gentlemen, other than acknowledgement when their writings are actually quoted.

The Scottish men may not have been very happy at the notion of having Mary II and her Dutch William to rule over them, but it was only then that, in the opinion of M'Neilage, heavy-horses had a chance to establish themselves. "The art of the breeder is definitely an art of peace, and until the Revolution Settlement in 1689 gave the land rest from war, there was no opportunity to pursue it. And it was precisely the Clydesdale and Avondale districts to which the settlement brought peace."[16] The Act of Union in 1707 confirmed it.

The true story of the Clydesdale may begin in a small way with one John Paterson of Lochlyoch in Carmichael parish in the Upper Ward of Lanarkshire. He appears to have had a black Flemish stallion about the years 1715–1720. M'Neilage says that he brought him from England, but unfortunately does not give any authority for the statement. The Lochlyoch mares were famous fifty years later and remained so for another fifty, and they may have had in them the blood of this horse. Dykes spoke in 1878 to an ancient lady more than ninety years of age who could remember two things clearly – dancing on Tinto at the news of Waterloo, and the Lochlyoch mares. They were black, with streaks of grey hairs on the under parts of their bodies. The streaks were held to be signs of Scotch hardiness remaining in the otherwise typical Flemish Black. Mr. Dykes also pointed out, however, that the Low Countries horses were not all of one "breed". "There were several standards of size and weight amongst the Flemish or Flamand Border breeds introduced into this country, and those brought into Lanarkshire most likely were about 14 cwt, which was about a couple of cwt over the weight of the Scottish native stock."[17]

The fame of the Lochlyoch Stud cast a special legendary glory on John Paterson's Flemish stallion. But by his time there were probably many other Blacks in Scotland. Dykes discovered a notice in *The Caledonian Mercury* of 16th October 1721 about the displenishing sale of a gentleman who was "very curious in breeding". It began: "There are to be exposed for sale by public roup upon Wednesday, 1st of November at the Miln of Alva in Stirlingshire" (here followed the precise location) "in the house of Robert Murray, inn-keeper, five fine bay-coloured stone horses, young and well-marked, proper for coach or saddle; one fine large black stallion, four well-sized black English mares, all of them with foals at their foot, with several other colts and fillies . . ." etc.

Drew maintained that James, 6th Duke of Hamilton, who succeeded to the title in 1742 and died in 1758, imported a dark brown Flemish stallion for the use of his tenants free of charge. He ought to know something about it, as he worked for the 11th Duke. And he had in fact spoken to a man (this would be about 1850) who well remembered the groom that had travelled the horse on his round. (It is possible that this stallion gave rise to the legend about the *first* Duke having brought in a Flemish stallion in Cromwell's time: see Chapter I.7.) We see but dimly into this period of the Scottish horse, and perhaps we do not miss much. Dykes went so far as to say that "till at least twenty years after the rebellion of 1745 there was small demand for agricultural horses of the modern lorry or dray type".[18]

6. THEIR LORDSHIPS' FRISIANS

Of all the great personages that strutted across the eighteenth-century scene, the man whom one would be least likely to associate with any new development in cart-horse breeding is Philip Dormer Stanhope. Born in 1694, he ended his official education with one year at Oxford University. He left it, he said, a pedant. After a tour of Flanders, which made him a man of the world, he became a Member of Parliament in 1715 and had not reached his twenty-first birthday when he made his maiden speech. If anyone knew he was under age, no one stopped him. He became the choicest ornament of urbane society, and the complete urban man. Bretby, the family seat in Derbyshire not far from Burton-on-Trent, was rural and therefore to him inevitably barbarous and disgusting. However, in 1725 his father fell ill and a visit was necessary. There, it has been written, "the rustic seclusion excited his spleen" and he hastened back to civilisation as soon as was decent. In January of the following year, his father's death made him the 4th Earl of Chesterfield and so he duly took his seat in what he termed the "hospital for incurables". On 23rd April, 1728 he set out for The Hague as ambassador, a post he held until ill-health forced his resignation in 1732.

William Marshall, writing nearly sixty years later, accounted for the improvement in the black cart-horses of Derbyshire at that time in these words: "This variety is generally and well understood to have taken its rise in six Zealand" (sic, i.e. Zeeland) "mares, sent over from The Hague by the late Lord Chesterfield, during his embassy at that court. These mares finally resting at his Lordship's seat at Bretby in the Derbyshire quarter of this district" (i.e. of the Midlands) "the breed of that quarter became improved, and Derbyshire for some time took the lead in this species of stock."[19] What sort of mares these were, is not absolutely clear, but it is more than likely that they were Frisians. If they were the usual "Flanders" mares, they would neither have improved or changed the breed, nor have been worthy of comment. They were presumably a diplomatic gift. It is doubtful if his Lordship could have picked them out for himself and he possibly did not appreciate their value or the special privilege of being allowed to export them. Lord Chesterfield paid one more visit to The Hague, in 1745, but this was only a brief mission to persuade the Dutch to join in the war of the Austrian succession, certainly not to buy horses. Since he studiously avoided visiting the uncouth yokels of Derbyshire, he presumably never even saw his contribution to cart-horse breeding. His celebrated wit was directed only at the civilities of London life. Of sexual pleasures, he said that "the posture is ridiculous, the pleasure transient, and the price damnable".[20] What he would have said, had he known he would appear in a book about breeding cart-horses, it would be interesting to know.

Castle Donington is only ten miles east of Bretby, but is in Leicestershire. Thither, according to George Culley, one of the Earls of Huntingdon "brought home with him a set of coach-horses of the black breed from the Continent. Most of these being stallions, he with some difficulty prevailed upon his tenants by the Trent-side to put their mares to them: which cross answered so well, that the breed in that neighbourhood has been in the greatest repute ever since."[21] Culley certainly obtained the information from Robert Bakewell (see next chapter), but he seems to have muddled his facts slightly. He says that Lord Huntingdon imported these horses when "returning from an embassy to the States-General". This was the Earl of Chesterfield, but no Earl of Huntingdon.

He adds that Bakewell followed suit "many years afterwards". Bakewell in 1760, or not much later, could be said to be "many years" after the Earl of Chesterfield's mares of 1728–1732, but he was only a few years, if at all, after Lord Huntingdon. The 15th and present Earl is of the opinion that his predecessor in question was the 10th Earl, who succeeded his father in 1746 and died in 1789. Nearly all writers on the subject in the nineteenth century blindly copied out the errors originally stemming from Culley's faulty memory of what Bakewell had told him, and there grew up the legend that the Earl of *Chesterfield*'s mares were sent when he was "ambassador at The Hague about 1755–1760", which is absurd. If we switch this date to the Huntingdon importation of stallions, it fits the belief that it was the 10th Earl who was responsible.

Francis Hastings, the 10th Earl, travelled extensively in Europe. (A bust of him is still to be seen in the British Embassy in Paris.) In 1788, the year before his death, he was one of the founder members, like Bakewell, of the Leicestershire Agricultural Society. There is absolutely no doubt that his stallions were Frisian, and the initial reluctance of his Leicestershire tenants to use them on their Black mares is understandable: it was a very different matter from the Bretby estate introducing a different type of mare, which, if they proved unsuitable, could be a source of loss only to the proprietor.

(The 10th Earl was the son of Selina, the celebrated Countess of Huntingdon who, to the dismay of all her friends, turned Methodist. Some few years after the death of her husband, she sold her jewels to build her first regular chapel at Brighton in 1761 and became the main agent by which Methodism penetrated into aristocratic circles. She rebuked the Archbishop of Canterbury, Dr. Cornwallis, for holding "routs" and, since he took no notice, she requested George III and Queen Charlotte to do something about it. She was cordially received by both, but the King would have been much happier discussing Frisian stallions with her son, as, later, he did with Bakewell. She died in 1791, but "The Countess of Huntingdon's connexion" lived on as a sect of Methodism until eventually in recent times the respectability of the parent body made it superfluous.)

It is perhaps appropriate here to say something more of the Frisian horse, at the cost of abandoning the chronological limits of this chapter. Mr. Dent and Miss Goodall have drawn attention to the significance, for English horse and pony breeds, of the part that Friesland has played in English history, at least from the later years of the Roman occupation, when there was a Frisian cavalry squadron at the very central fort of Hadrian's wall. They have convincingly shown that the Dales and Fells ponies, which appear so remarkably like miniature versions of the modern Frisian horse, could in fact have originated in its cross with small native ponies.[22]

In a later article,[23] Mr. Dent points also to the close resemblance of the Frisian to the "Old English Black". This, too, is unarguable, but only in so far as that version of the Black is concerned which is represented by Bakewell's horses. And Bakewell's horses were produced by an "English"/Frisian cross, as indeed were the produce of the Bretby mares and, in the reverse direction, of the Castle Donington stallions. So the resemblance is scarcely surprising. It would seem therefore, unnecessary to take into account the Anglo-Saxon invasions, in which Frisian elements played their part, as the village names of Friston, Firsby, Monk Fryston, Ferry Fryston and a dozen or so others bear witness even today. (S. G. Wildman has suggested[24] that the "Black Horse" pubs of England commemorate the victories of King Arthur *against* the Saxon invaders.) Mr. Dent recalls that Hereward the Wake is traditionally supposed to have bought his horse Swallow in Friesland. But what horses the heroic "last of the English" had around him as he sacked the monastery of Peterborough, or stood on the island of Ely to make a vain stand against the Conqueror, can be of no real significance in Shire history. One stallion in 1750, or even half a dozen mares in 1730 is of more importance than 10,000 in 1069. Nevertheless, the reminder of the long connexion of British horse and pony breeding with Friesland horses is timely and valuable.

Nineteenth-century writers ignorantly and indiscriminately used the term "Flemish", or, later "Belgian" for a whole variety of breeds of horse, including the Frisian. Perhaps they were muddled by the fact that the latter had long since ceased to be confined to Friesland itself. The breed's stud-book authorities say that "in all probability horses of the Frisian breed, after several exchanges of blood, occurred between 1500 and 1600 in North and South Holland, Friesland, Groningen, Drente, Overijsel and Northern Germany. In those years grey, brown and black horses were still found."[25] W. J. Miles in his *Modern Practical Farriery* in 1868 referred to the "long-tailed blacks used in the funeral cortege" as "Dutch or Flemish": to be precise, they were Frisians. W. J. Gordon in *The Horse-world of London* (1893) called them "Flemings". Even John Tilling, whose grandfather once at the end of the last century disastrously tried to enter the specialist world of the undertaker, referred to the "long-tailed black-'uns" as "Flemish".[26] Many alive today will remember hearing them called, even more confusingly, "Belgian Blacks".

Billy Smart's circus, who have had magnificent Frisian stallions for many years, at last labelled them correctly. But they had John de Witt, a Dutchman, in charge. The only thing he had no experience of with these is that, if they are gelded, they turn from black to a shabby brown – which is how Tillings, thinking it preposterous to have a funeral carriage drawn by stallions, came to fail in the burial business. But a circus man does not work with geldings, anyway. One thing Mr. de Witt did to them, which would confuse any Englishman who was anxious to see the qualities they had transmitted to the Shire, was to cut all the plentiful hair off their legs as a time saving economy in grooming.

It is unfortunate that this wonderful breed from Friesland should have been known to Victorians only as a mourning horse, and even that by the wrong name. He was an important element in the Shire. And he is not as devilish, stubborn and forward as Blundeville found him, but gay, intelligent and beautiful: nasty tempered only when his particularly sensitive nature is not respected.

CHAPTER III

1760–1820

The Black Horse and the Sorrel

I. 1760: THE BEGINNING OF HISTORY

Now at last, with the accession of George III, we find the proper materials available for the study of cart-horses – accurate descriptions, names of breeders and of horses, and even pedigrees. The writings of Arthur Young, from about 1767 to 1809, and of William Marshall from 1787, together with the Agricultural Surveys of all the counties in England, Wales and Scotland commissioned by the new Board of Agriculture in 1783 (six of them written by Young himself) all combine, with the mass of other writings that they generated, to give us our first clear and coherent impression of what had become of the Great Horse.

By reading between Young's lines, we can actually get a glimpse of the cart-horse before 1760, for it can be safely assumed that, if the heavy-horses he mentioned had been modified much in his lifetime (he was born in 1741) or even in the time of his father at Bradfield in Suffolk, he would have said so. Furthermore, it is perfectly clear that, for him and his contemporaries, only two types of true heavy-horse were worth serious consideration – the Sorrel and the Black, or the Suffolk and the Lincolnshire or Leicestershire, or the Punch and the Dray-horse, or whatever one cared to call them. There were some other types, but they were either very localised or else their individuality was more apparent than real, as they were at the extremity of the many gradations of the Black that were to be found as one travelled farther from the Fens or the rich pastures of Leicester.

The year of Farmer George's accession, 1760, is also the very year when a certain W. Garthside, somewhere in Lincolnshire, bred a chestnut trotting colt which at the age of four was in the possession of Andrew Blake in the parish of St. Margaret's, Ipswich. Blake advertised him as "got by Mr. Walles's famous Golden Farmer, son of Rigby's Fearnought, his dam by Eyven's Stud, remarkable for strength and moving. He goes as well as any horse in the county, there are few able to perform with him . . . He will be at Woodbridge on Wednesdays, Saxmundham on Thursdays, and the other part of the week at home."[1] His fee was 12s. per mare. Herman Biddell, Suffolk breeder and historian and editor of the first Suffolk Stud-book (1880), was able to trace 131 stallions directly descended from Blake's horse in the male line, and so he is the earliest identifiable horse in the Suffolk genealogical tree. (Ironically, he was not in fact a Suffolk Punch at all: of this we must say more later.)

Shire history begins at the same time, though slightly more hazily, with the appearance of the Packington Blind Horse, who might have been foaled as early as 1755 and who might have been owned by a man called Hood, but who certainly stood in the village of Packington near Ashby-de-la-Zouch. From this horse, too, descendants and families can be traced, but this is not the place to discuss him or his relations.

If the Shire man wants something more positive than the shadowy Packington horse, he can console himself with the thought that it was in 1760 that Robert Bakewell took over full control of the farm from his father – and in 1766 bred his celebrated "K". And if the Suffolk supporter wants a real Suffolk and not an outsider, he must begin with 1768, the foaling date of Crisp's Horse of Ufford.

It is not coincidence that the earliest traceable ancestors of both breeds were almost exactly contemporaneous. Shire history and Suffolk history both have a largely oral basis. Cart-horse breeding was almost entirely in the hands of practical farmers who kept pedigrees in their heads, not on paper. The most that they needed to note down was a service date to enable them to remember when a foal would be due, and that could be scratched on a stable wall or door: or, if in a book, and if the book survives, it would illuminate a pedigree for us about as clearly as old Hutton's memorandum of the Great Coach Horse covering his old cart-mare in 1672. Few big landlords had had much personal interest in cart-horses since they had ceased to be Great Horses. If they did any breeding, it was left to the manager or to the stud-groom to organise. Indeed, a list survives of cart-horses at Holkham Hall in 1719, but this is a mere inventory and, though it reveals Thomas Coke's personal touch in their naming, tells us nothing of genealogy: nor even does a later list of 1817, of horses belonging to Thomas William Coke, Earl of Leicester. If Coke of Norfolk himself did not make and preserve pedigrees of his cart-horses no one else would be likely to do so.

In the 1870s, when men were turning their thoughts towards the value of putting these details in a permanent book of record, the limit of accurate memory stretched back just over 100 years. Old men remembered what their grandfathers had said, but the tales of a fourth generation back were only hearsay, vague and misty, entrancing but imprecise. Here is one example. In 1875 there was a very aged retired stud-groom who could remember being told about the days when his grandfather was head man for a family called Gallemore, owners of a famous stud of Black horses on the Croxden Abbey estate, where Derbyshire and Staffordshire meet. In 1745, when Bonny Prince Charlie marched on Derby, this grandfather had to hide his stallions in a place of safety. He managed it successfully, but if we want to know what the horses were called and how they were bred and what stock they left, it is too late to find out. Either the grandson had not been old enough to understand the details in the first place, or no one had enough sense to ask him when he was ancient. All we have to prove that the story was not a dream is that six genuinely historical stallions called "Gallemore", foaled between the years 1780 and 1839, appear in the first volume of the Shire Stud-book. (The earliest of them was bred by a man called Moore, near Burton-on-Trent.) No human Gallemores appear in Shire-breeding history until much later, but their importance in this business in the mid-eighteenth century is vouched for by the naming of these slightly later horses – just as Morel Lestrange in 1313 had been named after his breeder. According to one tradition, Hood's Packington Blind Horse himself had been bred by one of the Gallemore family.

Handbills and stud-cards, those fascinating founts of information, take us back no earlier than the late eighteenth century. Perhaps they were rarely printed before that. But one day someone may come across a card that will tell us who the Packington Blind Horse really was. One thing is certain: the great county record offices do not contain such a thing, for cart-horse breeding was in those days the work of humble men. Dutch William was the last King to import them: George III was interested in them: but Edward VII was the first to breed them.

2. A REVOLUTION IN BREEDING METHODS

Some revolutions are so sudden that a date can be assigned to them. Others take years to accomplish. Others again are so slow and imperceptible in their movement that it is difficult to mark their beginning, accurately trace their progress, or decide when they have been completed. But they are all revolutions if they end in a radical and general alteration of circumstances or of system. The change in the method of mating cart-horses, and of course others too, is of the last type.

Since the Creator had a certain amount of success with his evolutionary plans for horses, it is wise first to consider His method, obvious as that may be. The mare normally has only one foal at a time. (Let us discount twins, because they do not appear to be intended.)[2] She may have her first one when she is three. (Let us forget the precocious ones which, born early one spring and covered late the following year, have foals at the age of two. In the truly wild state, not exceptionally favourable to early growth and maturity, this does not seem to be part of the divine intention, either.) She may have her last foal when she is fifteen, or twenty, or older still. Who can tell, with so variable a creature? But one thing we can tell. A very fecund mare may have ten foals but if you subtract all the males, and all the females which for some reason do not have any foals themselves, and all the accidents and disasters, it is clear that, although in nature horses are preyed on rather than preying, they are intended to have a high survival rate. The Almighty saw no need to litter the earth with foals like kittens, rabbits or millions of baby eels, just to keep the population steady.

Man, after domesticating the horse, could attempt to improve upon nature in two ways. He could try to increase the horse population; and he could try to breed special sorts for his various purposes – faster ones, stronger ones, bigger ones, and so on.

Greater numbers could be achieved only by two means. He could try to obviate violent deaths and other wastage. And he could make an effort to rear those young animals which, in primitive conditions, would fail to survive to maturity because they were not robust enough to do so. The first would be a good thing, but the second was obviously of more questionable benefit. What he could certainly not do was to improve the birth-rate. In breeding pigs, he can take advantage of the fact that multiple births are normal, and concentrate on those individuals or types which are most fruitful in this respect, until he has produced a race whose litters are nearly always gratifyingly numerous. But anyone foolish enough to try to make a regular thing, by selection, of horse twins would soon have found the venture a disastrous failure. And if he thought that a mare might have progeny more regularly under his protection than when independent, he would have been disappointed. Most advanced animals which produce their young sparingly are fairly well catered for in this respect. It has been observed that, in the wild, a female chimpanzee in oestrus is likely to copulate in turn with all the males in the group, than which no better insurance for the continuation of the species could be devised. Though stallions do their best to keep their particular mares for themselves, nevertheless it is obvious that, with both sexes running free, the chances of a mare which is able to conceive failing actually to do so are pretty remote.

The second of man's aims under conditions of domestication, the improvement in quality, and the selection of special types, was easier to achieve. It was for long held up, as far as the ordinary farmer was concerned, by the fact that, until fields were enclosed, breeding had to be, in Lord Ernle's famous phrase, "the haphazard union of nobody's son with everybody's daughter", or what another writer had called "chance medley matings".[3] Great men had the facilities to breed Great Horses: ordinary men might be directed by their king to remove the worst stallions from circulation: but selective breeding in the true and full sense was impossible until those who owned horses were all able, like Sir Richard Hutton, to put a mare for a day or two in a little paddock with the chosen stallion.

After his time, the revolution really started. It was based simply on the fact that, whereas nothing at all could be done to make a mare have extra foals, a stallion could successfully cover an enormous number of mares – provided that he was always separate from them except for the few moments required for the actual mating. Blundeville in 1580 had held the key to this method when he recommended that those who had no suitable paddock where the horse and mare could run together should bring the stallion to her, supervise his mounting and then remove him at once. But he did not then follow this up by pointing out that the stallion, after the briefest "breathe", would be both able and willing to cover a second mare. Instead, he proposed that the horse should be taken back to the same one, and serve her thus a dozen times or so in two or three days. This seems preposterous in itself. In addition, a stallion with the appetite to cover the same mare three times in one evening would have no reluctance to mount half a dozen different females once each, for variety titillates desire. There may

be any one of three reasons why Blundeville did not proceed to this logical conclusion, or perhaps it may be a combination of all three. Firstly, logical "next
steps" are not necessarily taken quickly, even by the most intelligent people,
when new ideas are in the wind. (One may as well ask why early railway
trains and even early motor cars had doors like horse-drawn carriages instead of
proper train and car doors.) Secondly, in Elizabethan times economical use of
entire horses, and selective breeding only from the very best, did not enter into
man's calculations. And thirdly, he might have known a thing or two about the
difficulty of getting a mare in foal. If time and resources are of no particular
account, having her covered a dozen times in a few days is certainly the surest
way one can think of to achieve one's end.

John Lawrence, in a book published when he was an old man in 1809, drew
attention to the revolutionary nature of the new method of breeding. Referring
to Blundeville's comment about a "young and lusty Horse covering nine or ten
mares in a season", he asked "What would he have thought of the soundness of
their headpieces, which would suffer their mares to assist in making up the
round dozen covered by the same Horse *in one day*, could he have foretold that
such would be the case in the nineteenth century?"[4]

Both quality and selection for type were now the targets: therefore, the more
mares that could be served by one top quality stallion the better. A further
advantage accrued from the new system, though its full benefit did not show until later in the century, when the vast number of draught animals required for
haulage in towns and country made breeding a great industry. By that time,
everyone who was not a breeder wanted geldings, always dependable, least
liable to infirmities, and certainly never subject to the stirrings and passions that
troubled a stallion or mare and made them, particularly the former, a nuisance.
Under this revolutionary system, there was no waste. 100 mares were breeding
and working. One stallion was kept for stud. Ninety-nine geldings began quite
young on country work, spent their mature years in the town and then, if they
survived, found a call for their labour in the country again. The Creator had
never said "Let there be geldings" but, under the new artificial method, there
were geldings. And the perfection of the system was in its economy, which kept
the bills for haulage lower than they ever were after the invention of the motor
lorry and the tractor, and yet gave the breeder and dealer a good livelihood.

A side advantage of the spread of castration was a comparable decrease in the
practice of spaying, both of town mares and any others from which the
owners did not wish, for some reason, to breed. Though geldings did not begin
entirely to replace stallions even for town haulage until after the end of the
period under review, spaying did eventually become a completely obsolete
practice, except in the case of "wingey mares" suffering from cystic ovaries.
These are temperamentally unstable and difficult or dangerous to handle and
work: no one wants a draught mare that behaves permanently as if in full
season, or a brood mare that is at once nymphomaniac and infertile.

This novel system was beautifully simple. The stallion could stand always at one convenient centre or could walk an advertised route, starting from his headquarters on Monday morning and staying each night at a different place, until on Saturday he had traversed a circle of up to sixty miles: or, of course, he could operate a mean between the two extremes, perhaps visiting the town on market days and standing at home on others. It was, to begin with and for many years to come, almost entirely a matter of private enterprise on the part of the stallion owner, except where a group of mare owners negotiated some arrangement whereby a good horse might be brought into their district. The value of an outstanding stallion was enhanced. And yet, if he served 100 mares, the fee for each could be very reasonable and his owner would still make a profit handsome enough to provide against the manifold risks and disasters which in more sophisticated times he might wish to pass to an insurance company. Where the new system was adopted, it ran in much the same way as it was always to do ever after, except that privately travelled horses passed more of their nights at inns and pubs than their successors, which were hired by "clubs" and therefore were often accommodated by members. Most early travelling Suffolk stallions certainly stayed overnight at five or six different inns and were baited at midday at six other intermediate ones. This was a severe strain on their leaders' sobriety.

However, the new method had its drawbacks. Few species are less adapted physically and psychologically to mating during the briefest possible encounter than the horse, unless one were foolish enough to attempt to breed in this way from elephants or rhinoceroses or the few others, including humans, whose sexual organs are of the same general type. All their bodily arrangements presuppose a period of courtship without which the female cannot be either safely or successfully covered. But now the stallion, living most of the time in unnatural seclusion, was aware precisely of what was intended as soon as he was led into the presence of the mare and, as often as not, was ready to tolerate little delay. She, on the other hand, was there only because in the opinion of her owner or groom she would be ready. No one had told her of the intention. Her own views might be quite different. She might have shown every sympton in condition and behaviour, of desire for the horse – and yet when suddenly confronted by him react with a sudden and violent refusal: she might, on the other hand, have given little hint except to the intuition of an experienced man that she was in or near season at all, and nevertheless accept the horse gracefully and charmingly. The gradations of response between these two extremes, not only from one mare as compared with another but from the same mare at different times, made the whole affair both unpredictable and dangerous.

A mare's refusal was shown in no negative fashion by walking away, but positively with her shod feet. Stallions, being constructed in the way they are, offered a large and undefended target. Well-timed kicks killed them outright: less synchronised ones sent them rearing right over to break their backs: even if all physical injury was avoided by the skill of the men who held them, such a reception was not conducive to their good temper. A few frustrations and frights of this sort either made them savage in their treatment of mares or else disgusted them and discouraged their interest. If the human supervisors of this pantomime took special thought for the horse, the mare might suffer. Especially if she was hobbled and so rendered completely unable to deny the proceedings, physical injury at the time or psychological damage in respect of future occasions were equal possibilities. In brief, this new system, though perfectly workable by three patient and understanding men, was fraught with all sorts of absurd and perilous chances if operated by the brainless or brutish.

So far as actual results were concerned, these controlled matings reduced the chances of conception. In the mare, the interval between the end of one period of oestrus and the beginning of the next, though it averages about sixteen or seventeen days, is variable. The actual duration of her heat is quite unpredictable, but is likely to be shorter as the season wears on than at the beginning. Worst of all, ovulation occurs about twenty-four hours before the end of it. So who can tell when that may be? The stallion's spermatozoa, according to their condition and hers, could live for a week but might not survive more than a day. Therefore the best chance of conception is when copulation takes place a few hours, or up to a day, before ovulation. In natural conditions, or the pretence of them that formerly obtained, there was every chance that this would happen at least once, and perhaps twice, during this ideal twenty-four hour period. But, under this system, she would be covered only once during the whole of any one heat, because stallion-owners from the outset always laid it down as a strict rule that no mare would be served twice in seven days. If one takes into account that the stallion was sometimes close at hand and at other times less accessible, luck played too large a part altogether. The stallion man's rule was dictated by the fact that no charge was ever made for a mare returning to service, no matter how many times. The result was that the stallion was possibly called upon to serve the same mare four times during a season for one fee, whereas if he served her twice in the same heat that might well have proved sufficient. But then, of course, every mare owner would demand two services per oestrus, and those mares which really were barren after all would receive too much for their money. The stallion-owner realised, with the writer of Proverbs, that "There are three things that are never satisfied, yea, four that say not 'Enough': the grave; and the barren womb; the earth, that is not satisfied with water; and the fire . . ."

It would have been more economical and efficient, therefore, if two services within a week were allowed for one fee, lower than normally charged, a second fee being payable if a new heat showed that the mare was still not "stopped". For the same total number of services in the season, the stallion would generally have earned more and, probably, got more foals: at the same time, mare-owners would have had to take greater care to time affairs as cunningly as they could. However, the system was based on the idea that, if either party was at fault, it was the stallion, when in fact it was probably the mare, or, rather, her owner. This philosophy, that the customer is always right, was manifest also in the custom whereby mares which were barren one year were charged only half-fee to the same horse or his successor the next year, which was absurd. Either the horse was infertile, in which case any fee, however small, for his continued efforts was too much, or he was not.

The ideal way of working this new method of leaving only one stallion entire in every hundred was, of course, to send the mares to live at his premises until such time as they were got in foal. The onus was then on the stallion-owner, who had the whole of every day to keep the mare under surveillance. This version of the new system, as it was gradually developed for the breeding of valuable horses, meant that the mare could be brought every two days, or every day, or at critical times even twice a day, to the trying board, where the unfortunate teaser accepted all the frustrations, though none of the dangers nor any of the rewards, that in the travelling method had to be borne by the actual stallion proposed for service. When the teaser had proved the situation, his more valuable colleague could cover the mare, perhaps twice at carefully planned intervals at the discretion of his owner, though two services in these conditions were far less necessary than in the hit-and-miss affair at home. Everything that could be done to reduce the risk of accident and to enhance and expedite the chances of conception was available. Furthermore, causes of barrenness, either physical or medical, were more readily detectable than at home, where the pre-occupations of farming routine or (until comparatively modern times) too scanty veterinary knowledge were unlikely even to reveal the commonest troubles, such as the contraction of the entrance to the womb, which so frequently occurred in cart-mares bred from only irregularly or rather late in life. On the farm, the end of the season might come before much serious thought was given to why a particular mare had not been "stopped" or to why, perhaps, she had not even been served at all. Finally, much more was known about the fertility of the resident stallion at a stud than the ordinary farmer knew about the travelling horse in his district. In later times, when breeding was more organised, the situation naturally could be improved. But in 1760 or 1820, there was little hope of checking whether the unknown but impressively virile stallion who arrived in your district for the first time was only there because he had proved useless at the other end of the county. Furthermore, the expensive stallion standing at home always had less mares to cope with. The travelling stallion had to serve many more, because his comparatively low fee, when expenses were deducted, meant that his owner did not begin to make a profit until after the point at which his more aristocratic counterpart ceased operations. In addition, unless the stallion-leader were entirely honest, the horse's owner was left to wonder how many extra mares he covered "on the side", with a few shillings going into the man's pocket instead of a half-guinea or guinea finding its way home at the end.

However, the ideal way was, in cart-horse circles, an idle dream. The ordinary farmer could afford neither his money nor his mare's time to send her away. In the distant future of the years to come, there would be wealthy men who could breed from cart-mares in much the same way as they would breed from top-quality thoroughbreds. But they were to be the exception. Now, and for the most part always, the same pattern would have to hold good: all the mares would have to work as well as breed and all the colts would have to be cut, except the outstanding one that the stallion-owner would come along and pay good money for, in the chance that he would grow into a useful sire.

Now we have a surprise. No figures about foaling rates among cart-mares were ever compiled until the reign of George V had begun. But it is quite certain that, illogical as it may appear, the percentage of success among travelling stallions was not far behind, if it was behind at all, that attained under the most ideal conditions of the resident stud. In the French government studs of the mid-nineteenth century the results were infinitely worse. In the decade 1830–1840 each horse covered an average of only thirty-two mares a season – and left nine foals: in 1840–1845, an average of forty-two mares each and sixteen foals. It was not until 1851 that the percentage of successes rose above fifty. In any age, figures much below sixty-six would have spelt ruin for an owner of an English cart-stallion. Later still, among the most valuable and pampered creatures in the world, the percentage of mares in the General Stud-book officially returned as barren in 1884 was 27.6: twenty years afterwards, it was 28.3: another twenty years, 31.1: in 1964, 29.5 – that is, 2,571 barren mares out of 8,610 whose owners started the season with high hopes and ended it with lighter pockets. In comparison with this, the ordinary cart-mare who perhaps had a single day or just a few minutes off work for the purpose of conceiving a foal, did not do too badly, and her success was attributable to the skill and knowledge of the unlearned men who operated the travelling system. The method certainly stood the test of time, for it was never superseded, at the ordinary level, by any other. Even artificial insemination, when it became feasible, was rejected by cart-horse men.

Perhaps the greatest drawback of the travelling-stallion system was that, from the beginning to the end, it resulted in a high percentage of mares that appeared capable of breeding a foal only in alternate years. Mares suckling a foal come in heat as others do, but their oestrous periods are brief in duration – hours, rather than days. Unless running with the stallion or tried every day, they may miss service altogether for that year. Even if the owner of such a mare is aware that she is in heat, she may be past it before the travelling horse is able to meet her. But in many cases, owners failed to see any symptoms at all and became convinced that their mare was unable to breed every year. Many potential foals, and much valuable income, were probably lost in this way by "small men", the very men who could least afford to waste an opportunity.

3. THE SUFFOLK HORSE

Herman Biddell, writing in Volume 1 of the Suffolk Stud-book, called the years before the mid-eighteenth centruy "semi-prehistorical times". His worthy modern successor as a writer about the breed (albeit born and bred in Wales) is George Ewart Evans, and he makes two points about those days which are of great relevance to the student of Shire history. They explain why the Sorrel had such a flying start over the Black as a distinct and more or less pure breed, and they account for the fact that its usefulness was largely restricted to the farm, just as its breeding for a long time remained more or less confined to its county of origin.

Firstly, from Robert Reyce's *The Breviary of Suffolk*, written in 1618, he quotes a passage which suggests that the men of that county were pretty neglectful of the need to produce Great Horses for war. "Such is our slothfulness in this respect that for the most part we rather desire to be furnished from our dear fairs with the refuse of other countries, though after our long labour and great cost we commonly meet with pampered counterfeit or deceit." In contrast, the breeding of cart-horses was for Suffolk men a matter of care and concern. "Now for our horses of burden or draught, experience of long time . . . causeth us to esteem our own home bred the more, which every way proveth so well for our own use and profit that our husbandmen may justly compare in this respect with any other country whatsoever."[5] This was naughty of those individualists, the Suffolk men: concentrating on cart-horses, they had an unfair advantage over everyone else and did nothing to ease the military weakness of James and Charles.

Secondly, even by Reyce's time, much of Suffolk – and particularly the coastal area of the "Sandlings" where the true home of the breed seems to have been – had already been enclosed. Enclosures were the essential preliminary to any large scale selective breeding by ordinary men. In Suffolk therefore, the enthusiasm, and the opportunity also, had long been there to breed working horses. And, where there were enclosures, each man found it easier to work his own team – and it was quicker, and therefore cheaper, if that were a horse-team. Gone early were the days when the Suffolk plough-team was composed of A's ox, B's ox, C's ox, D's horse, E's ox and so on. The parish of Hawstead had transferred completely to horses so early that in 1784, the Reverend Sir John Cullum[6] was quite unable to say when oxen had last been used. For two centuries no lease had mentioned them, and horses only had been used even for hauling timber. Before the time of Young, the Sorrel had become an agricultural horse *par excellence*, and a carefully bred one.

The Suffolks of 1760 were as near as one could possibly get, without the aid of pedigree records printed in the form of a stud-book, to a true pure breed – as was proved by their uniformity of conformation and colour. (What we call chestnut and the Suffolk men, to show their difference from ordinary men, like to spell as "chesnut", was then called sorrel. Arthur Young called it a "bay sorrell". They were not bred for beauty. Young called them "one of the greatest curiosities of the county". Their form was "that of a true round barrel, remarkably short, and the legs the same: and lower over the forehand than in any part of the back, which they reckon here a point of consequence".[7] Later, he wrote of their "short legs, great carcases, large ill-made heads, slouching ugly ears, and low fore-hands. Worse points for a coach or saddle-horse could hardly be named. But for the true cart breed these are essential."[8] One sees here what the Suffolk men had been at, while the inhabitants of the Shires were quite unable to be so single-minded. A few years later still, when these true-bred Suffolks had become, alas, already the "old breed", Young repeated almost the same words, adding that "these horses could only walk and draw, they could trot no better than a cow".[9] Marshall referred to the old Suffolk as, "to speak from appearances, this half-horse, half-hog race of animals".[10] George Culley called them "a very plain made horse . . . the head large, ears wide, muzzle coarse, fore-end low, back long but very straight, sides flat, shoulders too far forward, hind quarters middling, but rather high about the hips, legs round and short in the pastern, deep-bellied, and full in the flanks".[11]

The Suffolk men certainly achieved what they bred for, particularly in the main centre of their breeding – "the coast, extending to Woodbridge, Debenham, Eye and Loestoff. The best of all were found some years ago upon the Sandlings south of Woodbridge and Orford."[12] Their power and courage were tremendous. "They are all taught with very great care to draw in concert; and many farmers are so attentive to this point, that they have teams, every horse of which will fall on his knees at the word of command twenty times running, in the full drawing attitude, and all at the same moment, but without exerting any strength till a variation in the word orders them to give all their strength – and then they will carry out amazing weights . . . I was assured by many people here, that four good horses in a narrow-wheeled waggon would, without any hurt or mischief from over working, carry 30 sacks of wheat, each of 4 bushels (near 9 gallon measure) 30 miles, if proper fair time was given them. A waggon weighs about 25 cwt" [and] "this weight therefore is very near 5 tons. And let me add that they have not a turnpike near them. One might venture to assert that there are not four Great Black horses in England that would do this."[13] (What the Great Blacks could do was never officially tested until the year 1924.) Young was a Suffolk man and had already claimed the local breed was stronger and hardier than any of the Great Black breeds either of Flanders or of the English Shires. Their drawing matches, with a wagon loaded with sand and the wheels sunk and obstructed, became famous and were held either for wagers or a silver cup. Culley, no Suffolk man at all, also drew attention to another virtue that the Suffolk has never lost. "We know from observation and experience, that all deep-bellied horses carry their food long, and consequently are enabled to stand longer and harder day's works . . . it is well known that the Norfolk and Suffolk farmers plough more land in a day than any other people in the island."[14]

My purpose in emphasising the odd appearance and the exceptional merit of the mid-eighteenth-century Suffolk is simply to contrast his uniformity with the variety to be found in the Blacks. Nevertheless, a change gradually came over this obviously well-established breed in the 1770s and after, and Young, and many others, regretted it. In 1784, he complained that the breeders now "aim a great deal too much at breeding for a handsome forehand, head, and ears: and a lighter carcase, for using in coaches and chaises as well as carts". He regretted, too, the old spirit of rivalry for the strongest and gamest drawers – "the best of twenty pulls" – and men like Mr. Mays of Ramsholt Dock, who was said to have drawn fifteen horses for 1,500 guineas. He suggested it would be better to give "royal rewards to the victors in such matches as these, which encourage a race of horses useful in a superior degree, rather than for running races with a breed that is good for nothing else . . ."[15]

It is typical of the crazy nature of our earliest pedigree knowledge that Andrew Blake's Farmer, bred by Garthside in 1760, is, as we have seen, both the first "pedigree" Suffolk and perhaps also the first to contaminate the only "pure" breed in the country. But, to the student of Shire history, there is a much more intriguing possibility that presents itself. As already mentioned, this horse was a Lincolnshire trotting stallion – some sort of "Black", even though actually chestnut in colour. His dam's sire was "Eyven's Stud", a stallion that was foaled, at the very latest, in 1754 and probably about 1735–40. Now Eyven or Eyvens is an odd name and it is difficult to resist the temptation of thinking that he must be the same as the "Ivens" whose several grey horses appear repeatedly in the pedigree of some of the highest-bred Blacks in Shire history – or, more probably, "Eyvens" was Ivens' father or grandfather, for Ivens who lived at Eydon in the south-west corner of Northamptonshire, has won his niche in cart-horse history for horses foaled about 1815–1825. Spelling, even of proper names, was of no importance to most cart-horse breeders until at least mid-Victorian times. Since a horse called Pledger's "Heart of Oak" in the mid-nineteenth century also figures in leading pedigrees of both the Suffolk and Shire breeds, the suggestion is not so unlikely as may at first appear. The sire of Blake's Farmer, "Mr. Wallet's famous Golden Farmer, son of Rigby's Fearnought" sounds like a true Suffolk and no doubt bequeathed his colour: if his dam was a Black, then "Eyven's Stud" is the earliest Shire name to figure in a continuous pedigree. It is somewhat damaging to both Suffolk and Shire pride that the pedigree concerned is a Suffolk one.

4. ROBERT BAKEWELL

At whatever aspect of modern Shire-breeding we gaze, we find Robert Bakewell's tall, broad-shouldered and corpulent figure there at the back of the picture, either as the actual originator and inventor of the method or as the inspiration of those who devised it. But our knowledge of pedigrees of Blacks in Bakewell's time and for many years afterwards is so deficient (and in the case of mares, amounts to almost total ignorance) that we have no way of telling the degree of permanent effect which his activities had on the breed. One suspects that it was in fact very considerable indeed – and more lasting than his influence on cattle breeds. So, we must try to consider him, ignoring his Leicesters and his Longhorns. (He was so identified in most people's minds with these that the Countess of Oxford once asked his much younger namesake Robert Bakewell the geologist if he was related to "the Mr. Bakewell who invented sheep". He had to reply that he was not. But Humphry Davy, in a lecture, muddled them up. The Dictionary of National Biography itself gets some dates in the breeder Bakewell's life wrong. Rarely can a celebrated genius of such recent times have been so poorly documented.)

Born on 23rd May 1725, his known pedigree stretched back nineteen generations to Henry II's chancellor, who was presented to the rectory of Bakewell in 1158. But it was his grandfather (1643–1716), the third of five successive Roberts, who first took the tenancy of Dishley Grange, which was owned then, as it still is, by the de Lisle family of Gracedieu Park. Only a little way out of Loughborough, lying low between the road to Derby and the Soar, and therefore on the Nottinghamshire boundary, the farm comprised 440 acres. The fourth Robert (1685–1773) was a model father, for he allowed the fifth to travel extensively as a very young man, learning the methods of others, and then gave him first a big share in the management of the farm and finally, at the age of thirty-five, complete control. This in itself is almost sufficient reason for calling the year 1760 the beginning of Shire history.

This fifth Robert Bakewell possessed a rare understanding of animals. Arthur Young was amazed at the gentleness with which he reared his cattle. "All his bulls stand still in the field to be examined: the way of driving them from one field to another, or home, is by a little swish; he or his men walk by their side, and guide them with the stick wherever they please; and they are accustomed to this method from being calves. A lad, with a stick three feet long and as big as his finger, will conduct a bull away from other bulls, and his cows, from one end of the farm to the other."[16] A bull so savage that it arrived at Dishley under the escort of six cows and a man on horseback holding a nine foot spike calmed down at once in his presence. A stallion was once sent to him as being utterly impossible to manage, but soon followed him up and down the Loughborough corn market like a dog. With men, whether prince or poor, friend or stranger, though the jealous called him secretive and egotistic, he was honest, polite and lavishly hospitable. His employees served him long, like William Peet, who was the Dishley stud-groom for nearly forty years.

Pondering how best to improve the breed of Black horses, Bakewell was greatly impressed by the possibilities of the type of animal that the Earl of Huntingdon had imported. He saw in it qualities – not so much excellent in themselves as likely to "nick" well with his own stock – that could not be obtained at home. So he determined to obtain some Frisians. William Pitt, writing some forty years later, shrewdly assessed Bakewell's burning determination to have better animals than anyone else. The Leicestershire Blacks were already outstandingly good horses in comparison with any to be found elsewhere, and there appeared to be less scope for improvement in them than in sheep or longhorns. "Where so many very good ones were bred, and amongst so many experienced competitors, he found it difficult to take the lead, and nothing less would satisfy his restless and aspiring genius."[17] It is typical of him that, in taking a hint from another, he did not blindly imitate. He decided to

get mares, not stallions. That way, he could create his own Dishley breed at
home before launching it on the market.

Pitt, who got his information from a neighbour, Mr. Ferryman, states that
"in company with Mr. Salisbury, (Bakewell) went through Holland and part
of Flanders, and there purchased some West Friezland mares, which excelled
in those points wherein he thought his own horses defective". But it is
Bakewell's friend and former pupil, that great Northumbrian farmer George
Culley, who has told us how on their visit across the German Ocean Bakewell
and Salisbury nearly met their match. The Frisian men were happy enough to
sell stallions, but not mares. They are still of the same mind today, as anyone
may discover for himself who tries to buy any. But the difficulties the two men
encountered only strengthened Bakewell's determination. "Mr. Bakewell says
that he never met with a man but he could have prevailed upon him to part
with his stock for money, except in Holland, where he met with a Dutch boor,
who would not sell one of his mares for any price he could offer; and anybody
who knows the above great breeder will be sensible that he would not pinch
for price who gave above seventy guineas, when beginning business, for a
cart-mare to breed from."[18] In the end, after much labour and expense, he
managed to buy six and returned home with them in triumph.

He put his precious mares to his own Leicestershire Black stallion and then
bred "in-and-in" to fix the type he aimed at – or, rather, the types, for his
"restless and aspiring genius" could never be content with one thing at a time.

It is only in his bigger sort that we are interested. His other kind, both
shorter and somewhat lighter, he intended for carriage and cavalry work. But,
as Culley pointed out, there was no future in it because, just about this time,
the nobility and gentry began to give up the use of heavy black horses to draw
them along (the roads were now allowing more speed and requiring less sheer
power) and the army were starting to use lighter horses also.

Other than the fact that he intensively inbred his horses, as he did all his
other stock, we are remarkably ignorant about Bakewell's activities. He never
wrote a book or even a single word for public print, in spite of Culley's efforts
to persuade him. If he left his business or breeding records behind him, they
have all perished. Though ever willing to help and advise the practical man who
genuinely wanted to learn, he had a horror of the agricultural journalist. Until
recently, the only known surviving Bakewell documents were a collection in
the British Museum of six short letters written by him to Arthur Young
between the years 1783 and 1791, and of two letters about him in 1811, sixteen
years after the great man's death, from George Culley to Young (who had been
first Secretary to the Board of Agriculture since its establishment in 1793).
This was all, apart from a copy in the Rothamsted Library of Bakewell's appeal
"to the nobility, gentry and others" to save him from bankruptcy in 1776.
However, Professor H. Cecil Pawson of the University of Durham was
fortunate in being invited by Mrs. Leather-Culley to look through some old
papers in her possession. Among them he found thirty-two long letters in

Bakewell's own hand dated between 11th April 1786 and 28th August 1792, all but eight of them addressed to George Culley. Professor Pawson has published them in their entirety.[19] With the formality typical of the times, they all begin "Dear Sir". They end either with such expressions as "Your most obliged Humble Servt. Rt. Bakewell" or, at their most familiar, "Yrs most sincerely, R.B." or "Best Compts. where due, R.B.", though the more formal subscriptions are not confined to the earlier letters. Perhaps the only hint in them of the friendship between master and former pupil is Bakewell's little joke protesting, more than once, at Culley adding the county after "Loughborough" on the address of his letters. Surely the fame of the place required no further information? "After Loughborough you add Leicestershire; pray when you write next to London say Middlesex."

The thirty-two "new" letters are invaluable, but we are still far too ignorant of the man. Of the writings of his contemporaries, only Arthur Young, who was quick to recognise and respect his greatness (somewhat grudgingly, when it came to horses, for Young was a Suffolk man) and perhaps William Marshall, can be trusted, apart from Culley himself. Our poverty of detailed knowledge is largely due to Bakewell's own strict secrecy about his breeding methods. Probably no one but himself and Will Peet ever knew what stallion was the sire of any Dishley foal. Our unquenched thirst for more knowledge resembles (if we may say so without blasphemy) the Christians' longing to know more than they do about their Master's life. A chronicle according to Peet would be, in a manner, as great a treasure as a Gospel according to St. Peter.

Bakewell was particularly secretive about his methods of breeding "in-and-in". A remark made by Culley suggests the reason. He said that popular prejudice against inbreeding was based on religious scruples. And Bakewell was strictly religious. He was a trustee of two Unitarian chapels, and would never show stock on a Sunday, no matter how important the visitor. And so it is not surprising if he did not care to discuss the mating of mother and son, father and daughter or brother and sister. He had enough small-minded enemies without seeking more. (Marshall, however, seems to think that inbreeding was not uncommon in the midland counties and had been learned from "the gentlemen of the turf at Newmarket").[20] But it was obvious to him, even if it was beyond the comprehension of his less intelligent neighbours, that inbreeding was doubly necessary with his horses. The foundation mares being of a different breed or type from the stallions, this alone could fix the characteristics obtained in the first cross. And time was not on his side, because three or four generations of horses took so long to produce.

Bakewell rarely sold good stallions of his special Dishley blend. He let them for the season only. Marshall believed him to be not in fact the originator, but "certainly the principal promoter, of this branch of rural business". The hiring of stallions later became such a commonplace method of overcoming the peculiar problems of cart-horse breeding, that it is difficult to accept the fact that, prior to Bakewell, it had been practised only "on a small scale", and that

Bakewell was at first ridiculed for letting out sires. Nevertheless, this was so. Even in Leicestershire, these were still the early experimental days of the new system of breeding. What letting had been done was mostly to individuals, who wished to travel the horses themselves as a business venture. A group of progressive farmers who clubbed together to hire a horse between them, or an enlightened landlord wishing to help his tenants, were preferable customers in Bakewell's eyes because he could then send his own employee in charge of the horse.

Marshall's explanation of the hiring system, therefore, appears naïve simply because he was writing about something fairly new. "A domestic industrious man", he wrote, "has a good horse; but is too attentive to the ordinary business of his farm, to follow him every week to three or four markets, and too diffident to set him off to advantage, and to enter into contests and unavoidable squabbles with stallion men: while, to a man of more leisure and less modesty, a loose calling is most agreeable. Thus both parties are served: the letter by receiving a sum certain and his horse again; the hirer by getting a greater number of mares than the owner could have got. This mode of disposal would of course give a loose to the breeding of stallions: for the breeder not only got rid of the disagreeable part of the business; but if his own neighbourhood were overstocked, he could by this means send them to other districts." The result of this letting of stallions "has probably been greater than was foreseen. The great improvement which has been made in the stock of this district is striking; but may be accounted for in this practice. A superior male, the best for instance, instead of being kept confined within the pale of his proprietor, or of being beneficial to a few neighbours only, became, through this practice, a treasure to the whole district; this year in one part of it, the next in another. Hence, *even one superior male may change considerably the breed of a country. But, in a year or two, his offspring are employed in forwarding the improvement. Such of his sons as prove of a superior quality are let out in a similar way; consequently the blood, in a short time, circulates through every part, and every man of spirit partakes of the advantage.*"[21]

The liberty of italicising the last four sentences has been taken because they could well have been adopted in 1880 as the motto of the Shire Society. It is a wonder that their truth did not seem obvious before the end of the eighteenth century, and even more surprising that the main point of them was not put fully into practice in a systematic way for another ninety years. But Bakewell certainly made full use of letting, and Professor Pawson has pointed out that this was not just a means of making money, but was his method of studying the influence of his stallions (as of his rams and bulls) on females of various types – that is, long before anyone else, he developed the system of progeny testing. And progeny testing in horses is an infinitely slower and more inexact business than in other stock. (Count François de la Rochefoucauld suggested in 1784 that it was the enormous number of males that Bakewell let, and the prodigious number of non-payers among his customers, that brought him in 1776 to the bankruptcy from which he was rescued by the subscriptions of his friends and admirers. Others have thought the disaster might have been largely due to the turning of Dishley into a sort of free hotel and showplace. But this is another matter.)

Of the many stallion-lettings that Bakewell arranged, we know even the barest details of only four districts – that is, apart from one or two of those sent to Scotland to help found the modern Clydesdale, and they will be mentioned later. The letters to Culley have occasional references to a stallion let to him and his neighbours. In a letter dated 11th April 1786, he said "The Horse was set forward about the time that was thought most proper with directions to call on Mr. Collings" (the famous Colling brothers near Darlington, pupils of Bakewell and Shorthorn improvers) "and I hope by this time is arrived safe and meets with the approbation of the majority of the Subscribers; all I do not expect he will please." On 8th December, he wrote, "Edward Porter and the Horse came home very well and I am pleased to hear they both gave satisfaction where they have been. I have not any doubt but the Horse both from his Form and Family will please wherever he goes." Stallion-leader Porter had told him that Mr. Culley would be likely to be using one or two of his own colts the following season and so Bakewell wanted to know whether a Dishley stallion would be required. "Far be it from me to send a Horse to injure you or your Friends. If you think you and your Friends would like to have him on the same Terms as last Year (Viz) Eighty Guineas, you bearing all Expences except me paying the Man's Wages, I will send him but not on any other Terms at present." The horse *was* wanted, and, after dispatching him, Bakewell commented in a letter dated 2nd May 1787, that "One of his Brothers had on Saturday the 14th Instant covered 38 mares at 2 Gs and half a Crown each" (i.e. the groom's fee) "what he has done since I know not. Another was at Dishley at 2Gs and like to (have) a good Season." Bakewell's idea of a good season seems to involve a pretty brisk start. On 30th June, he wrote "By yesterdays post I had a Letter from Mr. Robt. Mitchelson of Colwell near Hexham desiring to know the Price of the Horse E. Porter leads (he supposed for you). I have heard but once from E.P. since he left home. I have by this post returned answer to Mr. Mitchelson that if he will pay you One Hundred Guineas free of any deduction he may have the Horse but not at any less price." He added at the top of the letter "P.S. please to acquaint E. Porter with the contents of this relating to the Horse." On 31st August, he thanked Culley for the trouble he took about Mitchelson and E. Porter, but does not reveal whether a sale was concluded. In 1788, Ted Porter was in Northumberland again and there was an accident. On 19th July, Bakewell wrote "I am much obliged to you on E. Porter's Acct. and desire you will act as you think proper and inform him that I do not in the least blame him for the accident that has happened so that he may be perfectly easy on that account." The next year, Porter went north again and Bakewell thanked Culley for his "favourable account of Ed. Porter and his Horse".

This last letter, dated 8th May 1789, was written from the Swan Inn, Lad

Lane, London and mentions another letting. "I have let a Horse which came up Yesterday to stand at Mile End about a Mile from White Chappel Church." A stallion brought up the previous year had received a signal honour. He had written to Arthur Young on 10th March 1788 from the Black Bean, Piccadilly, "I left Dishley about a fortnight past, have brought a Black stallion to London which has been seen by the King, Prince of Wales and many other great personages to whom he gives more general satisfaction than others I have yet shown . . . I had near an hours conversation with the King on the subject of breeding which he seemed much pleased with and listened to what I said with great attention". It was in the courtyard of St. James's Palace that the horse was paraded, and no doubt George III put some of the master's ideas into practice on his Windsor farm. (This horse was "G", for which see Part B.III.2.)

The only other reference in the correspondence to stallion-letting occurs in a letter dated 13th April 1792. "Last year I had a Horse in South Wales hired by a Gentleman for the use of his Tenants and this Season I have one in North Wales to which they have entered into a Subscription for 100 Mares at 2 Gs and half a Crown each Mare." Young said that Bakewell's fees normally ranged from 25 to 150 guineas the season. £157. 10s. 0d. for the hire of one horse makes one wonder how Bakewell could ever have become bankrupt. Its value is best understood by seeing what a farmer in the Loughborough district could get for it, based on the local figures Young gives:[22]

		£.	s.
1 Year's wages for			
5 day labourers @ £18		90.	0.
3 lads @ £4		12.	0.
2 maids @ £3. 10s. to £4		7.	10.
Two new waggons (£16. to £20.)		36.	0.
One new cart		9.	0.
Complete set of harness (30s. to 40s.)		2.	0.
A pair of harrows		1.	0.
		£157.	10.

Young commented that one of Bakewell's horses covered at 5 guineas a mare. Two mares to this horse would more than pay a head-man's wages (£7 to £10) in that part of the county, or would buy a new cart and inexpensive set of harness. But Bakewell once said that the only way to improve the breed of anything was to keep up the price of the male: that would induce farmers to send only their best females. However, his fees for stallions pale before those for some of his other stock. He let his first ram in 1760 for 16s. and drove it to Leicester Fair himself: in 1786 he let twenty for over £1,000. His famous "Two-Pounder" once brought in 800 guineas for only two-thirds of a season, and another earned 1,200 guineas altogether. But we must turn from these details to his general ideas of the conformation of a cart horse.

(One or two of his stallions, entered a century later in the first Cart-horse Stud-book, and one or two others mentioned in pedigrees in the stud-book, are discussed in Part B.III.)

5. THE FIRST BREED ARGUMENT

Arguments about the rival merits of different breeds have long been the spice of life to many men, particularly in slack times when they have had leisure to promote or join a harmless slanging match in the Press. Robert Bakewell was at the centre of the first recorded battle of Sorrel versus Black and the outline of the argument is worth tracing, not just for light relief, but because it best conveys his idea of the true conformation of a draught horse. The dramatis personae, apart from Bakewell himself and some anonymous Ipswich men, are Arthur Young and William Marshall.

After his first visit to Dishley in 1770, Young wrote that Bakewell considered cart horses, like oxen, should have "thick and short bodies and very short legs".[23] Thirteen years later, Bakewell invited him to pay a second visit to see the horses before they left on their travels "and compare them with the Suffolk kind. Opinion of the true form of a horse puzzles me very much and my desire is to be open to invitation and to listen to information that may be rec'd, from any part of this or any other Kingdom."[24] When Young did come (16–18th March 1785), he thought the horses, "compactly formed", were the best Blacks he had seen.[25]

Writing to Culley on 8th December 1786, Bakewell referred to the horse that had been in Northumberland that year, and asked "What other kind of Horse either from Form or Action is likely to bear more Hardship of Labor, Food or Climate? If you know tell me what and where they may be found. Mr. Young says in Suffolk but if Mr. Barton who at his coming to that large Farm near Nottingham brought with him a Set of those kind of Horses and yet notwithstanding his Knowledge of their Use and his general Acquaintance with that part of the Kingdom has not yet had a second Sett but has used the Black Horses, what must we conclude but that he thinks the latter most suitable for his Purpose,

> We are best of all led to
> Men's Principles, by what they do.

And a Gentleman near Norwich had two Teams for the Purposes of hard Labor, one out of Suffolk, the other out of Lincolnshire, a county where in your Opinion and Mine the Horses are not of the most useful Form, yet these were able to do much more at hard Labor than the former."[26]

The criticism of the "Lincolnshire", presumably meaning "Fen", variety of the Blacks is not surprising. Marshall called them elephants, or alternatively, slugs.[27] At this time an ancestor of a great Shire breeder of the late nineteenth century, Anthony Hamond, in the fen-corner of Norfolk possessed a celebrated

Fen stallion which he actually named Dodman, which is the dialect word for snail.[28]

In 1788, Bakewell issued another invitation to Young to come and see a smaller variety of Black horses he had produced "which am fully persuaded are able to perform as much work in the farming way as any others of greater weight and with as little food".[29] No other remark could as fully reveal Bakewell's whole attitude to stock-breeding and his restless search for greater efficiency.

The crux of the matter is contained in a letter to Culley the following spring. This has been quoted, in *The Horse in the Furrow*, by G. E. Evans from the Suffolk point of view, but no apology is needed for repeating it. What Bakewell says is so important that, for ease of reading, the liberty has been taken of adding even more than we have in former quotations of the punctuation that he never bothered about. "On Monday last I was at Ipswich Fair where was a large Shew of Stallions, many of them of the true Suffolk kind which the Bigotry and Prejudice of the Farmers in that County lead them to believe and *roundly to assert* are the *best in the World*. And a few days past I saw one advertisement in a Welch Paper offering a Premium of 20 Gs. for He that should shew the best stallion. The preference would be given to a Suffolk Punch, but a Certificate must be produced that he was of that kind. This advertisement surely was drawn up on the other side of the Water, or why prefer Blood to form or action?

"From hearing what they said at Ipswich I proposed a Mode of examining their Stallions, venturing to give it as my Opinion that *a Horse either for figure or use, particularly the former, should have his fore end so formed that his Ears when he is shewn to advantage be as nearly as may be over his fore feet; that measuring a Horse from the fore part of his shoulder points to a little below the Tail, and divide that measure in to three parts, that from the Shoulders to the Hip should not be the longest, and when a Horse is shewn as Stallions commonly are he should be wider over the ribs than from Shoulder to Hip.*

"This Doctrine was new to them but I rather think will have some effect. I forgot your description of a Horse or probably might have availed myself of it."[30]

Marshall, commenting in 1790 that in Leicestershire the old "long fore-end, long back and long thick hairy legs" had all been shortened and improved, unreservedly praised Bakewells "K" as the "handsomest" Black he had ever seen: "He was, in reality, the fancied war horse of the German painters: who, in the luxuriance of imagination, never perhaps excelled the natural grandeur of this horse. A man of moderate size seemed to shrink behind his fore-end, which rose so perfectly upright that his ears stood (as Mr. Bakewell says every horse's ought to stand) perpendicularly over his fore feet. It may be said, with little latitude, that in grandeur and symmetry of form, viewed as a picturable object he exceeded as far the horse which this superior breeder had the honour of showing to his Majesty (i.e. "G") and which was afterwards shown publicly, some months ago in London, as that horse does the meanest of the breed. Nor was his form deficient in utility. He died, I think, in 1785, at the age of nineteen years." But he thought that a much younger horse, whose letter, maddeningly, he had forgotten, was more useful – "His carcase thick, his back short and straight and his legs short and clean; as strong as an ox; yet active as a pony; equally suitable for a cart or a lighter carriage."[31] (He could not forbear to add that, if it were fashionable to eat horse-flesh, he would have been as valuable to a farmer as an ox.)

Arthur Young, who had admitted that, as Blacks went, Bakewell's were good, allowed his native pride to re-assert itself when he reported on his native county in 1794. The Sorrel – the new lighter and handsomer Sorrel – was "an excellent breed; and if the comparison with others, and especially the great black horse of the midland counties, be fairly made, I have no doubt of their beating them in useful draft, that of the cart and the plough. But the fair comparison is this: let a given sum be invested in the purchase of each breed: and then, by means of which, will a thousand tons of earth be moved to a given distance by the smallest quantity of hay and oats? It is the oats and hay that are to be compared, not the number or size of the cattle."[32]

But Robert Bakewell could not respond to the idea of moving a thousand tons of earth, though the logic of the test no doubt appealed to him. He was now a sick man. The unfortunate John Monk, whose task it was to report on Leicestershire at this same time, found the old fellow too unwell to talk much and, furthermore, failed to see the horses. It was not a horse-showing day, and that was that. But even so, the politeness and attentive hospitality caused him to write "I shall always think of my visit to Dishley with pleasure".[33] It was left to William Pitt, author of the revised *General View*, already quoted, to speak more fully of Dishley.

The great man died on 1st October 1795. Young had already written, after his challenge to move a thousand tons of earth, that "a spirited and attentive breeder, upon a farm of 1000 or 1500 acres of various soils, that would admit two or three stallions, and 30 or 40 capital mares, might, by breeding "in-and-in" (that is, by copying Bakewell) advance the Suffolk "to a very high perfection". Bakewell had advanced the Leicester/Dutch black on 440 acres. But Arthur Young, like William Marshall, could not resist temptation, whenever he spoke of the draught horse. "It would be better," he observed, "to use the money and effort to improve the draught oxen."[34]

As a postscript to Bakewell's life, we have William Pitt's description of the horse-system at Dishley under his nephew and successor, Robert Honeyborn, who ran the farm for just over twenty years until his own death in 1816 at the age of fifty-four. Three or four "capital black stallions" were kept, and sometimes more – they had been much more numerous before the specialisation in sheep. They served at 1 or 2 guineas a mare. Eight to ten brood mares (no geldings) did all the farm work, with occasional help from the still-docile stallions, and bullocks and heifers. All mares were put to the horse, and it was reckoned to rear two foals a year from every three mares.[35]

6. THE FENS TYPE AND THE MIDLANDS SORTS

Though he wrote from north of the border, and half-way through the nineteenth century at that, Professor David Low's summary of Black horse territory can scarcely be bettered: "from the Humber to the Cam, occupying the rich fen lands of Lincoln and Cambridge, and extending westwards through the counties of Huntingdon, Northamptonshire, Leicestershire, Nottingham-shire, Derbyshire, Warwickshire and Stafford to the Severn".[36] He could have added "part of Shropshire". He could also have mentioned as newer "colonies", Cheshire and parts of Lancashire, particularly the wonderful district of the Fylde. The breed was indeed spreading south and west also, though many of those animals to be found in the counties nearer to London were geldings, on their way to the city streets. Elsewhere in England, to use Low's words again, "on the commons and poorer grounds it presents the coarse pack-horse form, distinctive of the greater part of the older horses of England".

At about the end of the eighteenth century, the distinction between the Fens type and the Midlands type was at its clearest, and the reasons lay partly in the difference of soil on which they were bred and partly in the fact that Flemish blood, immigrating pretty steadily into the country, had always remained for a generation or so where it landed – in the east. Unfortunately, Fen Blacks are remarkably poorly documented. We can almost watch the Midlands horse develop from the old Great Horse. But the dray-horse of the Fens, huge and ponderous, seems suddenly to emerge into full view, as it were in a rising and clearing of the mists and fogs, from the place where a couple of centuries earlier we had seen only little black ponies.

The varieties of Black can be described under three headings – their conformation; their colour; and their hair.

a. *Conformation*

Fen soil has the property of encouraging enormous weight and size in the animal it nourishes; the limestone of Derbyshire is particularly conducive to the formation of hard fine bone. The best of both were combined to make the modern Shire Horse, but if one could go back to, say, 1800 and examine a Fen bred Black and compare him with a Derbyshire bred, one would see animals almost as different from each other as the modern Suffolk and the modern Shire, and certainly less alike than the Shire and the Clydesdale were in, say, 1900.

The Lincoln was heavier, and coarser; with beefy legs, and bone that was too round and soft; feet frequently shallow and weak at the heels; a flowing mane and tail; a profusion of thick and wiry hair, which was often curly, on the legs; and a very dull temperament. The Derbyshire had a finer head, flintier bone and less hair; was hardier and a better "doer": but was not so weighty.

The chief faults that a later judge would have found in either type were the upright pasterns of the fore-leg: the want of muscle on the inside of the thighs and the roundness and lack of angle of the hocks – in fact the whole of the hind leg was so bent that the hocks were too far back and the feet too far forward; and the length and narrowness of the back and its "dip" behind the withers, the apparent length being accentuated by the last rib being too far forward and too short. Furthermore, the eyes and ears were both too small. The Lincoln's head was too large and the Derbyshire's too lean and narrow. And it is certain that when either horse was asked to walk and trot, his action both before and behind was as clumsy and slow as everything about him, from shoulder to hock, suggested.

b. *Colour*

The heavy-horses of the Fens and the rest of Lincolnshire were almost invariably of a sooty sort of colour: some of them could be described better as being of a slatey hue. In so far as "black" can be called a colour or can be said to vary, we must not think in terms of the glossy black that many so much admire today. Blackness became so synonymous with the area that "Lincolnshire Black" was already on its way to becoming a breed name and, if it had more or less stayed at home, like the Suffolk Sorrel or Punch, instead of colonising all the rest of England, we should now perhaps have had a distinct breed under that title. The Fens horse frequently had white markings on the legs and a small white star on the forehead.

In Derbyshire and Leicestershire, black was also universal, though there were many horses with more white in the face. "Blaze" was a common name during this period, and one can safely assume that any such horse hailed from one of these two counties. In Staffordshire, on the other hand, the regular colour was almost always brown, and any man who wanted to boast about the ancient local pedigree of his horses would say that they were descended from "the old brown Staffordshire breed". A black one, there, almost certainly had recent blood in him from further east.

The "slatiness" of many Blacks often gave way to grey. Some horses of this time were in fact described sometimes as black and sometimes as grey. Some of the "black-greys" may really have been blue roans. Bay was quite unknown. Any man who had a big bay, however heavy, which he claimed was really one of this breed was a patent liar. Such a horse contained light blood.

c. *Hair*

To a late eighteenth-century observer, the hair on a horse's face or legs would pretty clearly indicate where the animal came from, quite irrespective of the mere quantity of it on the cannons, fetlocks and coronets (coarser, longer and more profuse in Lincolnshire than in the more western areas). Peculiarities of hair distribution were of three distinct kinds.

Firstly, a certain strain of horses had a long thick moustache, and this was a Lincolnshire characteristic. In a black skinned animal, this hair was always black. The trait persisted in certain examples far into the nineteenth century, by which time an increasing number of cart-horses had patches of pink skin in certain parts of the body. The moustache was then composed either of white hairs or a mixture of black and white, according to the hue of the skin from which they sprang, but never of any other colour.

Secondly, there was a variety of horse whose lips, muzzle and eyelids were entirely devoid of hair, or at most covered with a very fine down. The skin in these parts was almost always flesh coloured, sometimes with small dark blotches or spots. There was a number of horses called "Bald", presumably for this reason. One of the most famous was Bulstrode's Bald Horse (93)[37] foaled in 1778 at Isley Walton, near Loughborough. Two celebrated "Blazes", Radford's (185) of Little Eaton in Derbyshire, foaled in 1786, and Knowles' (188) of Nailstone in Leicestershire (c. 1800), were also often known as "Bald".[38]

Finally, there were horses which had a long tuft of hair growing from the front of each knee – like Mr. Hamond's *Dodman* in 1780, *Old Ruff Knees* (probably belonging to a Mr. Storey of Kedleston, Derbyshire, though no doubt Fen bred, about 1800) and Brown's *Rough Knees*, which appears to have been a Fen horse travelling in Durham in 1831. Some even had a similar tuft growing out just below the point of the hock – quite separate from the hair lower down. The tufts were not a stallion characteristic, but appeared also on mares of this strain and sprouted as strongly on gelded animals also. These hairy-kneed and hairy-hocked types had become exceedingly rare by the 1870s, but it was in Wales, oddly enough, that the last examples could have been seen, no doubt owing to the influence of some now unknown but extremely pre-potent stallion from the Fens who long ago travelled those western regions. Similarly, the moustache and bald-face scattered and dissipated itself throughout the country.

7. THE OX AND HORSE ECONOMY

Oxen were advocated, and horses deplored, as farm workers by nearly all the late eighteenth-century writers. Young and Marshall were the protagonists, but most of the compilers of the County Reports from 1793 onwards appear to share their view, if not explicitly. Even John Monk, the first reporter on Leicestershire itself, commends Mr. Norton, a Catholic priest, who in France in 1777 had won a very handsome gold medal for "an essay upon the great utility of oxen in preference to horses for the farmers' use". [39] The essence of Marshall's argument is to be found embedded in a piece about the various breeds of cattle. If, he argued, there were 30,000 square miles of cultivated land in the Kingdom, and if five-sixths of the husbandry were done by horses at twenty to the square mile (or about three to 100 acres), then it was costing the country at least a million pounds a year in depreciation at £2 per annum. But if all the work were done by oxen, the extra beef available would supply 100,000 people with an extra pound of meat a day each.[40]

However, it was not on generalised appeals to the national interest that the ox versus horse arguments were generally based, but on the practical advantage to the farmer. A calculation made by Arthur Young at Rye is one of the clearest expositions of the case. An ox-man there used twelve draught beasts. Each year he bought six yearlings. These he kept until they were four years old, when they spent two years at work. He then sold them at six for fatting on the nearby marshes. His actual expenses, compared with the estimated cost of using horses, worked out as follows (the items in Young's calculation being slightly rearranged for the sake of clarity):[41]

COMPARATIVE ANNUAL COST OF DRAUGHT

By 12 oxen (actual cost)			By 6 horses (estimate)	
	£. s. d.			£. s. d.
Purchase of 6 yearlings	3. 0. 0.		Depreciation (£2 p.a. per horse)	12. 0. 0.
Grass @ 20s. per acre:			Grass @ 20s. per acre:	
12 yrlgs. & 2 yr. old	9 acres			
6 3 yr. old	12 ,,			
12 4 & 5 yr. old	36 ,,			
	——			
	57	57. 0. 0.	3 acres each	18. 0. 0.
Making hay, suppose	10. 0. 0.		Making hay, suppose	3. 0. 0.
			Oats (1 bushel per horse p.w. – 30 weeks @ 2s. 3d.)	20. 5. 0.
			Chaff @ 5s. per horse	1.10. 0.
			Vet attention, suppose	3. 0. 0.
Shoeing	3. 0. 0.		Shoeing	1.10. 0.
Tithe, rates etc.	16. 0. 0.		Tithe, rates etc.	5. 8. 0.
	————			
	89. 0. 0.			
Less: sale of 6 lean oxen				
6 yr. old, for fatting	60. 0. 0.			
	————			————
	29. 0. 0.			64.13. 0.
Cost per two oxen p.a.	4.16. 8.		Cost per one horse p.a.	10.15. 6.

The calculation is no doubt accurate. And certainly the four and five-year-old ox appreciated in value as he worked, while the five and six-year-old horse was on the point of depreciating until sooner or later – sooner, if anything untoward happened to him – he fetched only the knacker's price. So the argument was valid in a non-horse area, which Sussex surely was. However, Young's table of costs proves only that a man was a fool if he bought mature heavy geldings for his farm-work. This is the one thing that those who could play a part in the true horse economy would never do. There was a place for the ox and a place for the horse in late eighteenth-century farming, and the so-called controversy was rather a book argument than a real one. Marshall and Young were such partisans that their judgement was too often warped by the heat of their views. But Marshall is quite informative about the various stages of the horse economy: and, since the pattern remained more or less the same from his time until the year 1939, it is worth while to see what he says.

We begin with the stallion. In many cases a farmer merely retained a home-bred colt for his own use and for any neighbour who cared to send for it at a price of a few shillings. We do not need Marshall's hint to know how common a practice that was, for a century and a half later such casual easy-way-out breeding was still practised by the brainless or the idle. But he does also refer to the increasing number of stallion men whose business it was to have a stud of entire horses, some of which were for sale, others for hire, and others again to be travelled by the owner's employees at a fixed fee per mare. Some of these stallion men were also breeders: other only bought likely colts, retaining the best and castrating and selling those which did not fulfil their promise. Normal prices for good quality entires were from 50 to 200 guineas: 40 guineas to 80 or even 100, for a season's hire: and from half a guinea to 2 guineas for service. (Bakewell could charge 5 guineas for K and also for G, which he showed to George III.) The custom had already grown up of holding private stallion shows in March, where potential customers could select for purchase or hire or merely for service. There were also public shows at which the big man and the one-stallion man alike could show off the points of their stallions. But the only one Marshall mentions is Ashby-de-la-Zouch, where stallions came in on Maundy Thursday and Good Friday and were led out of the inn yard occasionally "into a back street to be shown to those who desire to see them out". But business was officially done on the Saturday and on Easter Monday. On 29th March 1785, when he was there, it was a poor show – only about thirty on view, though "all of the black cart horse breed (I saw but one coloured horse)". He claims that only two were sold (including the best horse in the show, for 100 guineas) and none let on the first two days, but cannot explain why, unless it was because other counties, benefiting from Leicestershire blood in the past, now had good horses of their own. He picked a bad year, obviously. But his description of the horses is more generally applicable. "Some of the two year old colts were of extraordinary size for their age. Mr. —— had one not less than 15-hands and a half or 16-hands high, and as well furnished as most aged horses. Short-backed, square made, full carcased horses, with four or five inches of fat on their ribs, were the favourites. A good deal of bone is still liked, and their manner of going much attended to: not so much as to activity, as to their trotting true."[42]

Mares were worked by the farmers until near their time of foaling and, after about a month off, moderately afterwards, the foals being shut up during working hours. Foaling in March or April was preferred, and weaning in October or November, so the covering season began towards the end of April. Some foals were taken with their dams to the autumn fairs, the most famous of which at that time were Ashby, Loughborough and Market Harborough. More were kept until they were eighteen months old, when the best places for disposal were the fairs at Burton-on-Trent, Rugby and Ashbourne. The Leicestershire and other Midlands graziers who bought them ran them for a year with their other stock and then disposed of them, preferably at the Stafford or Rugby sales, to arable farmers who broke them to harness and worked them until they were five years old or, more commonly, six. Then the dealers took them to town – chiefly, of course, London, "where they are finally purchased for drays, carts, wagons, coaches, the Army, or any other purpose they turn out to be fit for". In this sequence, the prices obtained (and here Marshall purports to offer a ten-year average) were 5–10 guineas for foals; 10–20 guineas for yearlings; 15–30 guineas for two-year-olds; and 25–40 guineas for six-year-olds, the profit in these four years of course deriving also from the work they did on the farm.

(William Pitt[43] gave the prices obtaining at Harborough Fair in October 1807. Two-year colts averaged 35 guineas. Prime weaning foals were 10–15 guineas; eighteen months, 20–30 guineas; 2½ years, 30–40 guineas. These figures reflect the general rise in farm produce of all kinds at this time of boom and enthusiasm. For ordinary country horses, he suggested 10 guineas for a yearling; 20 at two years old; 30 at three to six years; and then depreciation at 2 guineas per annum. John Lawrence[44] mentioned Lambourn Fair as a popular place for the farmers of Berkshire and Hampshire to buy dray-horses which would eventually end up in London.)

Marshall grudgingly admitted that the four or five men involved in the early stages (or the two or three, according to when the young animal was first sold) all did well out of it, and there was no other way by which the carman, the carrier, coachman or contractor, or the brewer or the miller, could obtain a mature animal. But he predictably pointed out that, if a horse went blind, or lame, or died, it was not marketable, because no one would eat it. And he thought even brood mares began to be unprofitable after the age of about six – an absurd argument, because in his day men were reluctant to breed from them until they were about five! He drew a dismal picture of "the majority of farmers, throughout the Kingdom, working even barren mares and geldings down the stage of decline: though they know it will terminate in a ditch or a dog kennel. But, with the same unconcern, some men go to the gallows".

Influences were already at work, of course, which were to make this bias eventually untenable. In the first place must be put the changes in farming practice itself. The light iron Rotherham plough had made its appearance in 1730 and was slowly, very slowly, becoming more common. With this, the ox could not match the horse's speed and efficiency. And of course it is a truism that all the new machinery that revolutionised farming in the nineteenth century was not only designed for horse husbandry but would have been useless behind the plodding ox. In the second place, the rapid growth of industry and commerce demanded an ever-increasing supply of the most powerful horses, aged at least five, and these neither grew on trees nor could be allowed to eat the corn of idleness while growing to maturity. (This demand, likewise, was of course to be accelerated beyond all expectation by the railways.) Thirdly, there was to come a time when people were almost as reluctant to eat a steer that had been developing its muscles for a couple of years before being rested and loaded with fat at the age of six, as they were to eat a lamed or worn-out cart-horse.

The worn-out cart-horse was himself to become a marketable commodity, as the numbers grew. And so, when the farmer of Rye had in the end to give up his oxen, he could buy cast-offs from the towns very cheaply, if he did not wish to take part in any of the original stages of the horse economy (which of course he could do more easily in the nineteenth century than in Young's time). A gelding that was past the drudgery of the hard stones often had several years' useful farm-life left in him, though this would naturally depend on the treatment he had received (which was often ignorant and brutal), his town owner's interpretation of the term "worn-out" and his final possessor's notion of what he was fit for. Although, in this case, it would be a farmer who in the end would have to send for the knacker, it was the town-user who, as usual, suffered the real depreciation, for if he had given £50 for his gelding, he sold it for £5 or, if £100, for perhaps £9. The number of small farmers round Bristol, for example, who staffed their holdings in this way was very considerable.

But this is to move beyond the limits of our period. In the last years of the eighteenth century, this horse economy was in too many cases insufficiently appreciated by those who criticised the seeming extravagance of many men's management – the use of four or more horses in ploughing, when, as Bakewell showed, it could be done with two (Bakewell had used cattle but, typically, he experimented with heifers instead of steers. When he turned to horses, he ploughed with two abreast, and was said to be the first man to do so.) Young on his way to Dishley to pay his second visit, stopped at Naseby, where Mr. Cowdell, a tenant farmer, obligingly showed him his Blacks. There were seventeen, "though ten or eleven would do his work". But this man bred Blacks and, though Young realised that the work of mares would be lost at busy times of the year, he did not really enquire whether the profit from the sales would make the seventeen considerably cheaper than a non-productive ten.[45]

George Culley criticised the extraordinary vanity of the Berkshire farmers. He had several times seen "a narrow-wheel'd waggon, with six stallions, one before another; the first horse, besides having on a huge bridle, covered with fringe and tassels, enough to half-load a common Yorkshire cart-horse, has six bells hung to it, the next five, and so to the last, which has only one. And it is really diverting to see with what a conceited air the driver struts and brandishes his long whip."[46] But he did not stop to ask whether the owner was using stallions because he was too old-fashioned or vainglorious to have geldings, or whether perhaps he was a stallion-owner, keeping his horses fit for a very lucrative spring season. Nor do those who criticised over-large teams of geldings tell us their age, and whether all or some were young horses being trained and hardened for haulage in the towns and docks.

We must leave the critics with Marshall's condemnation of show teams in the Midlands. Five horses were reckoned to make a team and a fashionable team would be worth £150. ("A shameful height of extravagance.") He says that it was considered a disgrace "unless the horses have three or four inches of fat upon their ribs. To bring them to this exquisite state, they are of course limited in work, and unstinted in provender. A strike a meal for six horses is counted fairish feeding. Two meals a day, fourteen strike a week; near two-and-a-half bushels a horse a week! The harness, too, especially the housing, is truly ridiculous; at once expensive and unornamental; standing up aukwardly high above the back of the horse; like the sail-fin of the nautilus; as if it were intended to catch the wind, and accelerate or retard the motion of the animal."[47]

Only one thing does Marshall commend. A man alone, on horseback, took care of each team, and a waggoner and a boy usually managed two teams between them, whereas in the south a man and a boy were usually allowed to four horses. Poor Marshall! Did he not realise that some men take a boyish glee – an enthusiasm it is difficult to imagine him possessed by – in their beautiful teams? If they were fools, there have been similar fools ever since. They may not approve, nowadays, of the three or four inches of fat on the ribs. *Autres temps, autres moeurs.* But men in the eighteenth century did not differ from their successors of the twentieth in seeing something more attractive than money when they looked at their horses.

William Pitt shared the view that Leicestershire men went too far in their passion for Black horses. But he was one of the few writers who really understood the horse economy of the Midlands. His summing-up was not only true at the time, but remarkably prophetic. In quoting him, one is tempted again to take the liberty of using italics. Having discussed the breeders' absorption with producing vast numbers of foals, he continued, "If the practice of rearing such colts were discontinued, or prohibited, from whence must the demand for strong black dray or road horses be supplied, as well as some of a secondary weight for coaching and the army, except from where they now are, Leicestershire and Derbyshire principally? If this subject be properly considered, it will appear that *agricultural horses are here principally a nursery for raising a supply for commercial purposes* . . . Horses are necessary in great numbers in a rich, commercial and luxurious country, for other purposes than those of agriculture. They can only be produced from the land, and therefore must be bred by farmers, to support and maintain that luxury which I believe, in a moderate degree, tends to encrease the comfort and happiness of a civilised society."[48]

8. THE LEICESTERSHIRE IN SCOTLAND

Glasgow, described by Trevelyan as a "pretty little country town" in the reign of Queen Anne, with a population of 12,500, a university, a market, and fifteen ships (which totalled 1,182 tons altogether and had to load twelve miles down the unnavigable river) had become by 1800 a booming commercial and industrial city of 80,000 people. The coalfields were producing over 1.6 million tons a year, more than half the output of Durham and Northumberland, and twice as much as Wales. The provisions of the Act of Union had made all this feasible: the industrial revolution (helped by the local boy, James Watt) had speeded the process. Urban industry, which found work for the English Black, called the Clydesdale into existence.

Individual names in what Thomas Dykes called the "Black horse wave" that spread over Scotland are not really traceable earlier than two newspaper notices in 1774. In *The Edinburgh Courant* of 4th May was advertised "To cover at Dalkeith, at one guinea a mare and a shilling the groom, A REMARKABLE STRONG BLACK HORSE, proper for getting either draught or carriage horses. His sire covered three years in Leicestershire at five guineas. This horse was bred by Mr. Bakewell, at Dishley in Leicestershire, and is thought to be the best of his sort that ever was in this country. N.B. Mr. John Dickson, Dalkeith House, will show the horse." He was the property of the Duke of Buccleugh. *The Edinburgh Advertiser*, the same month, carried this: "To cover this season at 15s. a mare. A BEAUTIFUL BLACK HORSE, known by the name of YOUNG SAMPSON. He is a four-year-old, 16.1 inch high, the property of MR. ROBERT BAKEWELL in Leicestershire, and is allowed to be the best black horse ever shown in Scotland."[49] He, and a Westmorland bay horse of 15.2, were to be met with in the Grassmarket on the first three days of the week and at the Crown, Linlithgow, on the last three. It is worthy of note that, whereas Bakewell had sold the one (possibly a son of K), the other had either been let to someone unnamed or was travelling for him privately, in accordance with the system he preferred.

The next Black invader that can be quoted by name is *Blaze*, brought into Scotland about 1780 by one of the Patersons of Lochlyoch already mentioned. M'Neilage reported that this horse was later spoken of as "having founded the famous Clydesdale breed of horses". He commented, very reasonably, that "this is a somewhat liberal tribute to the success of one horse, but doubtless careful selection and better treatment of the stock descended from him and the native Lanarkshire mares would effect wonders . . . *Blaze* undoubtedly left his mark on the Upper Ward of Lanarkshire, but he could have left no mark had there not been a breed there of such stock as a mark could be left upon."[50] Possibly a *Blaze* owned by Mr. Scott of Brownhill, and winner of a premium at Edinburgh Grassmarket stallion show in 1783, (or 1785, or both) was the same horse. The last that can be mentioned here is a *Farmer's Glory*, whose chief claim to immortality is as the sire of the dam of the famous Knockdon stud-horse Old Times.[51]

As to what the Clydesdale looked like by the end of the century, George

Culley is a knowledgeable guide. They "are probably as good and useful a draught horse as any we are possessed of. They are larger than the Suffolk Punches, being from 15- to 16½-hands high, strong, hardy, and remarkably true pullers, a restive horse being rarely found amongst them. In point of shape, they are in general plain-made about the head, sides and hind-legs; they are mostly of a grey or brown colour".[52] One wonders how short some of the Suffolks were in those days.

John Naismith, whose draft report for the Board of Agriculture was made in the same year as Culley's book, makes the most infuriating of all remarks – "The draught horses of Clydesdale have long been in high estimation, and are so well known that a description of them would be unnecessary."[53] He said that those of the Upper Ward were considered the best, and there had been much recent improvement carried out. "Dealers from different parts of England come to the Glasgow and Rutherglen market to purchase them, and prefer them to the Derbyshire blacks." This indication that the two-way movement of the following century had already begun is illuminating, but it is more likely that – at least in 1794 – the "different parts of England" were almost entirely the northern parts. Some people, Naismith reported, thought the Ayrshire horses were better than those of Clydesdale at this time.

It was Col. W. Fullarton, of Fullarton, twice an M.P., who reported on Ayrshire. 1793 was a busy year for him – he raised the 25th Light Dragoons, or Fullarton's Light Horse: he wrote his *General View*: and he imported a Flemish horse. Because the sort of horse he chose will interpret his views about other people's horses, we will start with that. The Netherlands government would not let him buy mares, so he had what he describes himself as "the strongest Flanders stallion, of a bay colour, and of that sort which brings their legs well under them, and are speedy in their movements. He weighs about 1200 weight, walks fast, and trots at the rate of 13 miles in the hour, being able to draw two tons".[54] Dykes adds that the horse was six years old, 15.3-hands, and called Vandernoot. He certainly proves to us that it is necessary not to jump to conclusions at the mention of the term Flanders. A Flemish horse could be one of many sorts, like an English one.

"The Ayrshire horses", boomed the worthy colonel, "are neither flat-footed, gummy-legged, clumsy animals, like the unwieldy breed which supplies the drays of London: nor are they by any means so slight and flimsy as the working stock of Yorkshire. On the contrary, they are short and active on their legs, hard in the hoofs, large in the arms, very deep and powerful in the counter, streight in the back, square in the body, and broad across the fillets. Their predominant defects are, a shortness and coarseness of the forehand, and a deficiency of that elegance of form and action, which only belong to particular descriptions of high-bred or foreign horses." (This last criticism seems a little unfair.)

Few stallions covered for more than 10s. or 15s. The colour was changing. The old black and grey were being challenged by bays and browns, no doubt

PLATES 1 and 2   Hairy horse and smooth horse. Dodman (*above*), foaled in 1780, belonged to an ancestor of Anthony Hamond (Shire Society President in 1888) at Westacre, Swaffham. Note the tuft of hair in front of the knee; (*below*) this unknown Leicestershire stallion is longer in the body, finer in the head and less hirsute. George Morland, who painted him, lived in Bakewell country between 1780 and 1795.

PLATE 3   A Bakewell Black, with Dishley Grange in the background. He is six-years-old and the picture is dated 1791, which means he could be G (890). Whoever he is, was he *really* like this? The Frisian look seems somewhat overdone.

PLATE 4   This is Elephant, foaled in 1788, at four years of age. Owned by Thomas Alsop of Marylebone, he was 16.1 hands high, eight feet in girth and "one of the most boney horses and of the greatest bulk for his length in the kingdom".

because the breed had been "improved by strong chapman stallions, covering from different parts of England". (He added a footnote that chapman stallions "are those which cover at the different fairs and markets, for coach and saddle stock; being neither thorough bred, like racers, nor so coarse as the dray and waggon breed". He said that they were "commonly half or three-quarter bred".) The colonel's idea of a horse no doubt coloured his "general view" of the county and his particular view of its horses. Eleven years later, with the turn of the century, *The Edinburgh Courant* carried a notice announcing "Roup of Mr. James Innis, Durris. To be sold on August 22, 1804, twelve work horses and mares, all of them good sizes, peaceable and in great order. They are chiefly bred from a valuable Lanarkshire Black Horse."

This brief discussion of Scottish Blacks in the 1760–1820 period must end with Glancer (335), which was usually referred to as Thompson's Black Horse, of whom M'Neilage wrote in 1891 "most of the best known modern Clydesdales trace their descent in at least one line, and some in more than one line, from this celebrated horse." His dam was "The Lampits mare" which was sold in 1808 by the Clarkson family at one of their sales at Shott's Hill Mill. They and the Patersons of Lochlyoch were inter-related and Dykes believed, on the strength of this, that this mare was descended from the chief Lochlyoch strain, in which case, M'Neilage said, "It is an easy matter thus to connect most of the leading families of Clydesdales in the present day with the old Lochlyoch breed, descended from the black stallion brought from England by John Paterson".[55] (Unfortunately, M'Neilage seems to have been thinking of the 1715–1720 Paterson, since he adds "about the time of the first Jacobite rising". One would have thought that the Blaze of 1780 was more likely to have been concerned.)

Glancer is recorded by Dykes in the Clydesdale Stud-book as having been foaled about 1810. But M'Neilage, his successor as secretary, advanced reasons, irrelevant to Shire history, for believing he was up to ten years younger. Elsewhere, he appears to be sceptical even that the Lampits mare was in fact the dam of Glancer. "The test of dates was not too rigorously applied by those who searched out the material",[56] for the first and retrospective volume of the Clydesdale Stud-book. This remark is true enough and applies, unfortunately, with equal force to those who produced the material for the first English book.

A travelling card of this great Glancer was extant many years later, and was reproduced in the first Stud-book. It informs us that his owner was James Thompson, tenant of Germiston in the vicinity of Tollcross, to the east of Glasgow. The fee was a modest guinea, with 1s. to the groom. But the card is undated, which is typical of the frustrations involved in a study of Black horse breeding in either Scotland or England. It could have been about 1820.

9. 1820: A FORGOTTEN BLACK

At last, on 29th January 1820, the old King's life, if the last ten years or so could be called that, flickered out. Biddell called the year of his accession the beginning of "historical times" for the Sorrel horse. It was so, too, for the Mid-lands Black. But of individual Black horses of the Fens, or of their breeders and owners, we know almost nothing until the year 1800, when the long reign was precisely two-thirds through. In that year was foaled the great foundation sire of the modern Shire horse, Wiseman's Honest Tom. The astounding success of the Honest Tom blood – a quite overwhelming success, because by 1939 there were few Shire horses which did not trace directly in the male line to him[57] – presupposes years of crafty thought and cunning breeding, particularly in that area of Lincolnshire called, so significantly for horsemen, Parts of Holland. But we can only guess at it, because, with the possible exception of Caswell's Honest Tom whose foaling date was either 1796 or 1806 (and he, by coincidence, was the foundation sire of the second greatest Shire line),[58] he is also the very first Fen horse about whose breeding anything whatever is known.

To discuss the great men and horses of those days, from there across to the Severn, and north and south, would only cause confusion here. They must receive the honour due to them in a separate review of the counties.[59] Yet "some there be, which have no memorial; who are perished as though they had not been, and are become as though they had not been born", as the son of Sirach in his wisdom reminds us. Or it would be wiser to say that there be many, rather than some. Fittingly therefore, we might conclude the survey of these formative years by rescuing just one Black horse, and his owner, from their oblivion – not an outstanding example (though of course his owner naturally claimed at the time that he was), but typical and representative of all.

John Savidge, who was born in 1782, came from a big family at Bassingham, about half-way between Newark and Lincoln, but about two miles to the east of the Fosse Way. In due course he took a farm at Carlton Scroop, six miles or more north of Grantham on the Lincoln road, as tenant of Sir John Thorold, Bt. When he was thirty-eight, he had a card printed as follows:

1820
To Cover this Season,
At One Guinea each Mare
That well-bred Black Horse

USEFUL:
The property of
Mr. John Savidge, of Carleton Scroop.

"Useful was bred out of one of the best black mares in Lincolnshire, and was got by Mr. Trimland's black horse, in Bicker Fen, son of that noted old horse of Mr. Bycroft's of Donnington, which was allowed, by judges, to be the best black Stallion in England. He has proved himself a most excellent Stock-getter" (Here follows the route) "The Money to be paid the last time round, or at Midsummer."

Neither Useful, nor his sire, nor his dam's sire, was ever put in the Shire Stud-book when it was started sixty years later. Nor did Messrs. Savidge, Trimland or Bycroft figure in the records that were then compiled. All had been forgotten, and their contribution to Shire history – like that of many thousands more, of horses and men – cannot now be truly assessed.

Between 1820 and 1828 John Savidge moved to Barrowby Vale, where his daughter was born in 1828. And this single stud card, in the possession of her grandson Arthur Gleeson over a century and a half later, forms the total record of one man's – three men's – noted old horses. But in 1820 things had already begun to happen which were to lower the standard of the Great Black horse, and a period of retrogression was starting which was to last pretty well another sixty years. During the Napoleonic wars, breeding had boomed, and the tremendous number of Enclosure Acts helped supply to keep up with the increasing demand for heavy industrial horses. But the coming of peace in 1815 brought about the beginning of a great confusion in their breeding, a confusion from which the Sorrel was almost wholly exempt and of which the canny Scottish men took the fullest advantage.

CHAPTER IV

1820–1874

The Degeneration of the Dray-horse

1. CONFUSION DURING THE DEPRESSION: 1820–1837

THREE times since he ceased to be a battle-stallion and became a gelding of peace, three times indeed since the death of Bakewell, wars have had an infinitely more calamitous effect upon the breeding of the Great Horse than anything else in his long history. A boom has been followed on each occasion by an exaggerated reaction. The first of these disasters followed the end of the Napoleonic wars.

As soon as the Congress of Vienna in 1815 had re-arranged European frontiers for peace, there was a tremendous demand for British horses, including the Blacks. Vast numbers went abroad to many countries of the Continent; not just any old horses or even good geldings, but many of the finest stallions. We could have sold every one there was, and very nearly did. It had taken us 750 years to import and blend the Black blood but now the shoe was on the other hoof. Everyone wanted our best breeding stock all at once. Wonderful prices were offered and, the longer the post-war farming depression went on at home, the more eagerly were they accepted. There was no man, and no organisation or department, to observe what was happening and to call a halt. The days had gone when it was the King's business to roar with rage and make export a felony: in any case, George IV and William IV were no Henry. Even the Board of Agriculture was dissolved in 1822.

Before anyone grasped the situation, good stallions had become so rare that half-ruined farmers could not afford to use them. Good mares began to be sold to pull heavy loads in London, like geldings. Small, misshapen and feeble ones were bred from. But what did that matter? You could not get a fair price for any horse in the home market, except perhaps for a few of the best in the big towns. Even as early as 1822, William Cobbett found that at Chertsey Fair "cart colts, two and three years old, were selling for less than a third of what they were sold for in 1813."[1] Thousands of four-year-olds, which had cost £25 to rear, were sold for £15.

Bakewell never wrote a book but, had he still been alive in 1831, he might have been provoked to do so by William Youatt, who did. Youatt's advice, in his volume on "The Horse" in *The Library of Useful Knowledge*, about heavy-horses would have appeared as idiotic to the great Leicestershire breeder as it does to us. To start with, Youatt's comments on the three main British breeds are somewhat odd. The passing of the old type of Suffolk was to be regretted, and the modern version was "a cross with the Yorkshire half or three-quarters bred". The Clydesdale he praised briefly as "a good kind of draught-horse, and particularly for farming business and in a hilly country"; it was being taken into England by many people "for the coach and the saddle". The Heavy Black Horse was too slow. He extolled "the farmer's horse", which a man could produce "if he has a few useful cart-mares, and crosses them with a well-knit half-bred horse". His special recommendation was to "let a dray-mare be selected, as perfect as can be obtained. Let her be put to the strongest, largest, most compact, thoroughbred horse. If the produce be a filly, let her be covered by a superior dray-horse, and the result of this cross, if a colt, will be precisely the animal required to breed from."[2] As if to destroy the memory of Bakewell for ever, he provided a wood-cut of "The Dray Horse" which was "the Suffolk crossed, although not as deeply as some, with the Flanders". The owners of this "favourite" must remain unnamed, for the picture offers as miserable a specimen of heavy horse-flesh as one could expect to see, a sort of nightmare of a horse. (He also supplied a cut showing a Cleveland, a Suffolk, a Clydesdale, and a "Northamptonshire", without explanation.)

The very need to quote Mr. Youatt, or even to mention him at all, is a criticism of the period under review, for in the matter of heavy-horses he led the ignorant and followed the blundering. But perhaps the most extraordinary thing about his book was its immense and continuing popularity. It was read by thousands, and was reprinted over and over again for many years. The fourth "edition" in 1898, twenty years after the heavy-breed societies had come into existence, still spoke of the Clydesdale being bred for the coach and saddle and for hilly country, and the value of covering cart-mares with a thoroughbred stallion, not to mention the choice of the jugular vein for general blood-letting or for specific bleeding to cure inflammation of the head. The pictures had been changed, and now depicted a shapeless Suffolk and a dray-horse which was one-quarter Flanders bred.

(It must not be assumed that Youatt was a fool or that the popularity of his book was luck. He was a veterinary surgeon who lived in Wells Street, off Oxford Street, and in the early 1830s was appointed at a salary of £199 to look after the animals, and staff, of the London Zoo. He was very able and conscientious, examining his charges in the former category twice weekly, and conducting post-mortems from his dispensary in the grounds until his death in 1847. After that, incredibly, the Zoological Society did not regularly hold post-mortems for another twenty years.)

Fifty of Youatt's 450 pages were taken up by an essay "On Draught", illustrated by forty-two figures and diagrams. The author, whose name was not mentioned at the time, was a young man called Isambard Kingdom Brunel. In 1831, he was twenty-six, and the Thames Tunnel was still an uncompleted failure. The Great Western Railway, his great steamships, his bridges and other triumphs were as yet only dreams of the future. This treatise, as may be expected, was exhaustively technical: it was also lively. For example, after considering the conical wheel, which had enjoyed some popularity for heavy vehicles, he observed that "If such a machine had been constructed for the express purpose of grinding the materials of the road to powder, or of serving as a check or drag to the waggon, it might indeed have been judicious, but as a *wheel* it was monstrous." It is a pity Mr. Brunel did not write about horses, as he would have been interesting. (The 1856 edition of Youatt acknowledged Brunel's authorship of the treatise. But it was still appearing almost unaltered, and once again anonymously, in the 1898 edition, almost forty years after his death.)

The effect of crossing and confusion during this period is seen in the changing colour of what had always been the Black or, sometimes, the Brown. When the first Stud-book, containing stallions, was compiled in 1879–1880, great care was taken to include only those whose blood was, as far as could be ascertained, 'pure'. Of the forty-eight which were foaled in the eighteenth century, the colour of only twenty-four was known, and they were all black or brown. The fifty-eight of known colour between 1801 and 1810 contained two greys and a chestnut. The ninety-six dated 1811–1820 included one roan – and the first bay. And bay is the one colour that is completely foreign to the "old breed". It can only have been introduced by light blood somewhere along the line. This first one was bred in 1819 by Samuel Heathcote at Earl Sterndale, south of Buxton and near the Dove. Its name, Hurricane (1129), is singularly inappropriate to a cart-horse, but all that is known of his pedigree gives no clue to the origin of his colour. His sire's line led straight back through the best-known breeders of Blacks to Bakewell himself, and his dam was by Hambleton's *Brown Horse*, a typical Staffordshire type. But somewhere in the secret recesses of his ancestry, and probably pretty recent, was a light or even a blood horse. In 1821–1830, there were six bays out of 131; and in 1831–1840, nineteen out of 144. Within another thirty years, bay was the commonest colour of all.

2. HIGH FARMING AND MORE CONFUSION: 1837–1874

It is a paradox that the neglect and degeneration of good cart-horse breeding, which was caused in the first place by post-war agricultural distress in the two decades up to 1837, owed its continuance to the increasing prosperity of the years that followed. In the better times which began to come shortly after the little Victoria became Queen and which reached their apogee, after a short recession in the late 'forties, in the golden years of the 'fifties and 'sixties, all kinds of crops became exceedingly profitable. And so were cattle and sheep, in the breeding of which immense pains were taken and great advances made. Calves and lambs, bred in large numbers, were a proper and rewarding object of study for the progressive scientific man. Foals, in ones and twos, or three here, and perhaps even six over there on a very large farm, could not be bred to a plan. In comparison with other livestock, their production was, as it always is, a chancy and expensive affair. When everything else on the farm was booming, why bother with them?

An expert, an instinctive horseman who thought and dreamed horses, could do well by producing the great dray-horses for the heaviest and showiest work of the towns. But most men made little out of it. In the 'forties, a four-year-old in the "useful heavy gelding" category was rarely worth more than £40. Assuming that he had fully earned his keep in the past year, he had still probably cost £26 to produce – stallion fee, keep of mare for a month at foaling, and all the expenses which followed. Some of the latter were ridiculous by later standards. The young animal was left to go wild, and then he was handed to a professional breaker. If he was sold at four or five, he was stuffed with food and left idle for weeks so that he could go off to the fair in true Billy Bunter condition. If anything went wrong to make him unsaleable, he was a very expensive proposition indeed.

But the horse was not a luxury. He was, as never before, a farming necessity. Especially in the 'fifties and after, mechanisation in the form of mowers, tedders, reapers and the like called upon more and more horses. Modern farming had made the labours of oxen, and many of the labours of men also, obsolete. High prosperity resulted in, or in some respects was caused by, great improvements in draining, cultivations and weed control. The agricultural horse population rose ever faster. Steam did indeed come in almost before the ox was out and, particularly for threshing, was a wonderful thing. When a method was eventually devised whereby two engines moving along the opposite ends of a field could plough efficiently, some people predicted that the value of the horse would be depressed for ever. But they were wrong, and steam never became the farmer's friend or the horse's rival in any universal or really significant sense. What hopes there were for it began to be dissipated when bad times and wet seasons came back in the late 'seventies.

So horses were enjoying a hey-day. But they were mostly mongrels. Few men even thought of the cart-horse as anything else. They had to have plenty of what Youatt had labelled the "useful farmer's horse" and that is what they bred or bought, without the slightest plan or thought as to what they were doing. The town horse, too, was fast approaching his hey-day and he too, inevitably, had to be largely a mongrel.

Mixing of common bloods was bad enough. But, in addition, there were many distinctive types of draught-horse which, earlier in the century, could have been easily developed into valuable breeds but which, in these years, were utterly lost and destroyed, most notably the Vardy horse of Northumberland and Durham. Some of them are not only lost but forgotten. A proliferation of draught breeds would not, perhaps, have been a good thing; better that they should have all been converted into Shires or Clydesdales or Suffolks. But to turn them into mongrels first was hardly the best and most promising foundation on which to build.

The railways were a contributory factor in this inglorious confusion, just as they were in the increased crossing that went on between Sorrel and Black – a one-way crossing, the putting of Suffolk stallions on over-sluggish and over-weight mares in an attempt to produce something handier. Of course, horses travelled miles before the railways were ever invented. But a transport system which enabled a Fens stallion or a Suffolk to be at home one morning and covering a Cornish mare the next evening undoubtedly accelerated the muddle.

The flow of Flemish blood, for breeding purposes, slowed and was coming to a point of coagulation by the 'sixties. But no one can tell how many thousands of English mares had been served by Low Countries stallions in the first half of the century. When the breed societies started up, this was a thing to be deliberately put out of mind, yet even in the Stud-book there is a faint trace of them, like a small plaque on a wall commemorating a thousand dead. In 1846 the Duke of Portland bred a stallion at Welbeck Abbey called *Prince Albert*, whose pedigree as far as it can be seen, looks distinctly Dutch. The Duke also had at this time a couple of immense geldings, which he had bred out of English mares by a Dutch stallion, and they lived to a great age. In 1848, the Duke of Rutland bred a horse called *Samson*, got by Berridge's *Samson*, a real old Black, out of a Flemish mare. Another *Samson*, bred in Yorkshire in 1861 out of a Flemish dam, covered a lot of mares in the Grimsby area. These three horses were not, of course, put in the Stud-book, but they were recorded, for some reason which must have appeared more sensible in 1879 than it does now, in an appendix to it.

To condemn these Flemish or Dutch horses would be to act the unfilial part of the successful young man who disowns his humble parents. Nevertheless, it would have been better if Bakewell's mares (and they, of course, were Frisians) had been the last of them. R.B. had done what was wanted, and other English breeders could have accomplished the rest without further help from overseas. The Bakewell Blacks required no further mothering or fathering. But the beautiful mares that Leicestershire was producing at the end of the eighteenth century were defiled for many years. And so, in the interests of truth rather than out of ingratitude, we may note what John Burke wrote in 1845 of these "cumbersome, ill-proportioned, and slow Flemish stallions" annually up for sale in considerable numbers in England. Many of the best proved attractive to some of the brewers, for they were traditionalists and thought stallions were better publicity than geldings. Others found their way to the country to supply the deficiency of good English sires.

"I have many times noticed these horses, and can safely aver, not only that I never yet saw a really well formed one, but that they are decidedly the very worst breed of draught horses I ever beheld. I never yet saw one whose feet were not flat, and whose fore legs, below the knee, were not of the worst description; the tendons at the back of the joint tied in, and the whole shank utterly disproportioned to the bulk of the horse. Indeed there is scarcely one in twenty whose legs can do much more than support his unwieldy carcase; and were it not for the large crests and heavy necks of these horses – points which some people imagine confer a stately appearance on them – there would be very few imported into this country.

"However, as many farmers are induced to make use of the first showy-looking stallion that is brought to them, I would warn them against putting any of their mares to these brutes. Few people can mistake the breed when they have once noticed it: and lest they should never have met with it, a Flemish stallion may be recognised by being mare-headed – heavy to excess in the neck and crest – flat-sided, and weak in the joints, quarters, and legs. With all these defects, or most of them, his long mane, his bulk (for he is prone to fatten) and his *tout ensemble*, coupled with a few flaunting ribbons about the head, and a gay bridle, do not fail to entrap the man who is unable to form a correct opinion of his principal points – the only true method of judging a horse."[3] (His own views lose some credibility, however, in so far as he was one of the misguided men who said one should never breed from a mare under the age of five or use a stallion less than seven or eight years old. Instead of the Flemish stallions, he suggested using "light Norman cart-stallions" – having never heard, presumably, of Bakewell.)

George Coates had published his *Shorthorn Herd Book* in 1822. The *Hereford Herd Book* first appeared in 1846, Davy's *Devon Herd Book* in 1851, the *Aberdeen-Angus Polled Herd Book* in 1862 and, in 1874, herd books for the newly-created Red Poll Cattle and for South Wales Black Cattle. Societies for these and other breeds were on the point of formation. All – in spite of the visitations of rinderpest, pleuro-pneumonia and foot and mouth disease – were in a state of development which made them ripe for this urgent step. In contrast, the heavy-horse was the only English farm product which was, in general, worse than it had been at any time in the sixty years of George III.

3. THE STAUNCH MINORITY

Those who kept the old breed going, and tried amid the confusion to improve it, were a minority. George MacQueen paid them a deserved tribute many years later when he wrote that "planned breeding was confined to the few men of genius, born horse men and enthusiasts, who on meeting began to talk of horses before the seat was warm – men who knew every horse of note in the county and a good many outside it, every horse of their lifetime, and the history of many that lived before their time – men who knew where to find a good mare, and the best horse to send her to."[4] These men were to be found where their like had ever been – in the Fens and in the Midland counties from Leicestershire to the Severn.

The Fenmen were the most conservative. David Low claimed in mid-century that their old type – the type that Bakewell deliberately refrained from using – still existed in small numbers in the possession of old farmers. Typical of the stock produced by low-lying marshy lands with rank pastures, they had coarse heads, large ears, thick lips with hair on them, cumbersome shoulders, shaggy limbs, broad hoofs and short upright pasterns. "They are strong, of a soft temperament, and eminently deficient in action, spirit and bottom." Even the more modern type retained many of these faults, only slightly modified. "The main defects of his conformation and temperament are his too great bulk of body, and want of action and mettle. For a pull with a heavy weight he is admirable: but he steps out short, and is slow in all his motions."[5]

In the 'seventies, Fenmen boasted that light blood had never adulterated their horses. This cannot have been absolutely true, because six of the first eleven bay stallions later registered in the Stud-book as true English cart-horses were Fenbred. But their claim was in general justifiable. So scrupulous were most of them that they never ceased to look upon even a Leicestershire horse as something foreign, to be treated with suspicion and certainly not to be invited to cover a Fen mare. This was of course absurd but, in view of the chaos that generally reigned, they were doing good for the breed's future by fixing a type, even if they could have benefited at the time from Bakewell blood. The result of their jealous insularity was remarkable. In the short term, nothing new that was good came into the Fens, and far too much went out, because anyone who wanted weight went there to purchase it.

A diagrammatic representation of the spread of the Black blood throughout the nineteenth century would be simple to produce – a map of England, with arrows pointing from the Fens west, south and north. In the long term, it has resulted in the fact that almost every good specimen of a modern pedigree Shire in the twentieth century is traceable in the direct male line to one or two horses bred in the Fens.

Among those in Leicestershire and Derbyshire and adjacent districts who were among the "born horse men and enthusiasts", the case was a little different. They were not ashamed to import Fen blood, but from their stocks too there was a steady exodus, chiefly in the form of mares being taken north to build up the Clydesdale breed. The temptation to sell was little resisted, the Scotsmen knew exactly what they wanted, and it was the best too often that made the journey.

At the end of the 'seventies, the most articulate of the Fen breeders summed up the whole history of more than half a century in one pithy remark. "That the Clydesdale has been improved by an intermixture with the Shire-horse, whilst the latter has been deteriorated by an introduction of Suffolk blood, is too notorious to be disputed."[6] It would be difficult to compose a more provocative sentence. But here let us notice only his use of the novel word "Shire-horse", which was itself to be a subject of sharp debate. The writer was Frederic Street, of Somersham. Of him we must treat in the next chapter. (Some of the other enthusiasts, from the Fens and the Shires, many by this time long dead, but all contributing to the Shire horse of the future, will be discussed in Part B.II).

4. THE DEVELOPMENT OF THE CLYDESDALE

The Scottish kind of Black horses, when the Highland and Agricultural Society started to have classes for them in the 1820s, "possessed little hair on their legs, and their fetlock joints and pasterns were well developed and easily apparent; while in the modern horse", (the writer, Thomas Dykes, was referring to the 'seventies) "the fetlock and pastern are not readily definable, owing to the superfluity of hair. They had also in those days better action; and it was not unusual for farmers to ride their best mares to market, as the late Mr. Frame of

Broomfield did with the dam of his noted horse, Glancer II (337), from which so many of our most noted Clydesdale stallions of the present day trace their descent."[7]

In these words, Dykes vividly sketches sixty years of change. One cannot imagine the 1820 Clydesdale as a successful Glasgow heavy gelding, nor picture his successor of 1880 being ridden to market. Elsewhere he quoted a celebrated Clydesdale breeder, Peter Crawford, who used to say of his earliest days, "We did not want such very big horses then, nor for a long time after; breeding was all for farm-work, and clever clean-legged horses with good action sold best."[8]

In 1845, David Low, from his Edinburgh chair, viewed the typical Clydesdale as a horse about 16-hands, predominantly still black, but with brown and bay both common and continually gaining. (Grey frequently appeared, but many men of that period always asserted they were never used to breed from.) He said it was longer in the body, less compact and muscular, and "inferior in weight and physical strength to the Black Horse, and in figure and showy action to the better class of the draught-horses of Northumberland and Durham".

At this point it is necessary to interrupt Professor Low. Why should the horses of that no-man's-land between Scotland, where action was so splendid, and England, where it was largely sluggish and clumsy, be best of all, and not of a middling standard? It is difficult to say, but there is ample reason why it should be good. In Northumberland, the old Vardy horse was a blend of the small, hardy and quick native type and the Bakewell Black. Though finally extinguished by the floods of the pedigree movement and now long since beyond recall, he was in Low's day distinctive enough to have his own name and, if only he had been kept separate, he might have had much to offer both Scotland and England at the end of the century.

We ought here to prolong our digression by moving westward to consider Cumberland. Much must be said soon about the vast numbers of Midlands mares that went north, from about 1850 onwards, to help make the "new" Clydesdale. But in the years before that, from perhaps the turn of the century, there had been considerable movement in the contrary direction. W. R. Trotter, a Northumbrian, was quite clear on this point. He wrote, in 1890, "There is no doubt that the heavy horses of England and Scotland are of one and the same family, and that an interchanging of breeding stock has been going on over the Border for the whole of this century, at any rate . . . According to several old horse books that have come under the notice of the writer, English dealers early this century travelled north to Rutherglen fair, and bought large lots of cart fillies, which were taken into Lancashire and several other counties. How long this trade continued it is not easy to define, but certain it is that in the neighbourhood of Carlisle, Longtown, and several other Border towns, tribes of horse dealers now exist, and have existed in the same families for generations, whose operations in their trade have been pursued from Preston in the South to Glasgow, Falkirk, and Edinburgh in the North. When they found they could dispose of good fillies in the North they often drew their supplies from the

South, and *vice versa*. The direction of the current undoubtedly varied, but according to available history it was certainly from North to South during the early half of this century."[9]

In spite of his modest apparent reliance on "old horse books", Trotter was a very knowledgeable person and, as befitted his geographical position, impartial. He continued by saying that the south to north migration of mares, from the Midlands to Scotland and by-passing the border regions, began only later, about mid-century. Unfortunately, more partisan writers tended to exaggerate movements in one direction and forgot those in the other. Only in one respect do Trotter's remarks require qualification, or perhaps explanation. The most southerly point he mentions is Preston. If we move it north as far as Carnforth, or perhaps even Kendal, we fix a frontier which is to hold good for future years. The Fylde was to become one of the greatest adopted homes of the English variety: but not far north of it one is, horse-wise, virtually in Scotland, and it was the southward movement of the Clydesdale in the first half of the nineteenth century that determined this boundary.

To return to the Clydesdales and to David Low, he remarked that their greatest virtues were their steady drawing powers, freedom from vice, great activity, and beautiful free action. Their long stride, he thought, came partly as a result of conformation and partly from training and habit. Archibald M'Neilage, later, wrote that, whereas a Hackney man meant by "action" a high-stepping movement, "a Clydesdale judge means clean lifting of the feet, not sciffling along, but the foot at every step must be lifted clean off the ground and the inside of every shoe must be made plain to the man standing behind."[10] He stressed that action also meant close movement – "the fore legs must be planted well under the shoulders, not on the outside like the legs of a bull-dog". As one continues to read his description however, one begins to wonder whether he is describing a Scottish or an English horse, for the ideal type of both was in most points remarkably the same. Even on the matter of action, it is perhaps as unfair to over-emphasise this point of the Clydesdale's superiority as it would be to harp on his inferiority in strength. No breeder, either Scottish or English, would have been anything but pleased if he happened to produce a crop of foals which had the size and weight associated with the one type combined with the movement of the other.

The truth is that both varieties or breeds all through this period were steadily growing more alike, or that the best specimens of them were. The Clydesdale gelding for example, had become, by the 'seventies, an extraordinarily useful town horse. His method of working in Glasgow was different from that of his London counterpart because he specialised in the four-wheeled single-horse lorry, weighing about 30 cwt. He usually pulled 3 or 3½ tons, up to four-and-a-half times his own weight, which was between 1,700 and 2,000 lb. He could do this on most gradients (though he needed a trace horse on such steep ascents as Buchanan Street or West Nile Street) because he was adept at zig-zagging to get the better of such a task. Perhaps the difference between the English and the

Scottish outlook lay in the fact that, whereas the former's motto was that "to move weight, you must have weight" the latter tended to cry "brains and spirit".

During the middle fifty years of the century, the Clydesdale type had spread from Lanark and Ayr to all other areas which were suitable for draught-horse breeding and to four in particular – Galloway, perhaps first and foremost; Argyllshire, and particularly the Kintyre peninsula; Cumberland; and Aberdeenshire, or the north-eastern part of it, and the adjacent lower lands of the eastern coast. The last-named area was the odd one out, perhaps because of its geographical separation from the others. Whereas generally the Clydesdale was now being steadily modified by the introduction of English mares, here there was at first a succession of English stallions. And a strange lot they were. In the 'twenties, a Mr. Ferguson of Pitfour kept what he called Suffolk stallions. Since they had hair up to their knees and the point of their hocks, it is possible that he was mistaken. But he was so enthusiastic about the good they could do, that he charged only 2s. 6d. a mare to his tenants, and 13s. to others. (Much later, there were real Suffolk entire horses in Buchan.) Mr. Boswell of Kingcausie brought in a Lincolnshire-bred stallion in the late 'thirties which he called "a very complete horse". It was whole white, had a curly mane reaching past its knees and a tail that almost touched the ground, and stood about 16-hands on rather straight hind legs. He left a great number of foals, but it was said that "none was quite equal to himself". A more orthodox specimen was the grey horse bred in 1838 by Jacob St. John Ackers in Gloucestershire on land now occupied by Prinknash Abbey. Known as *Black's Horse of Carnleith*, he had a long life and a multiplicity of progeny.

However, it is with the main heavy-horse breeding areas to the south that we are primarily concerned. Here, the steady progress towards approximation of the Scottish and English breeds was due almost entirely to the enormous number of mares imported every year from the Midlands. Naturally, this constant migration was not emphasised by early Clydesdale commentators, who either argued that most of them were the daughters of Scotch mares that had been bought up at Rutherglen, Lanark and Biggar Fairs and taken to England, or else claimed that they had been sired by Scotch stallions travelling in England.

Lawrence Drew, on the other hand, was in no doubt about the Englishness of the mares. His eminence, and the fact that he was a Scot, compels us to treat with some respect his statement of the matter. He (or one of his co-operators) wrote that "The facts which we allege – and we do so without the least hesitation – are these, that the number of brood mares alone of the best Clydesdale type which have been brought direct from England to Scotland within the last 40 years are more than sufficient to account for the present number and excellent breed of horses called Clydesdales. It is a well-known fact that draught horses of the very best quality could be purchased in England, less than 40 years ago, at prices ranging from £25 to £35, which were brought to Scotland and sold at prices ranging from £70 to £90. Some of our most extensive as well as most enterprising horse dealers soon became alive to this; and it is not too much to say, that much of the colossal fortunes which some of them have amassed is due to the enormous profits they made on these English horses; and notwithstanding the great prices paid by their customers here, particularly for the brood mares, the customers were almost invariably well pleased with their bargains. In fact, it is no uncommon thing yet for these customers, as well as their descendants, to enquire anxiously of the dealer for the pedigree of such and such a mare, in order to get others of the same strain of blood, her breeding powers and the stock she produced were so remarkable in excellence."[11]

Some of these dealers were listed. Michael Teenan of Dumfries, for upwards of twenty years of a successful horse dealing career, attended the Midland fairs and drafted in "a large number of mares and fillies for breeding purposes every year", in Dumfries and Galloway. James Clark of Glasgow, "than whom a better judge of Clydesdale horses did not exist", did the same for many years, and the mares found their way to Lanarkshire, Renfrew and Dunbarton. James M'Kinlay had premises in St. Mungo Street and his customers were scattered over the same three counties. Unlike most dealers, who walked them all the way, he collected mares in shiploads at Liverpool for the journey to Glasgow. John Brown of Biggar brought in at least fifty English brood mares annually for many years. "He found that greater profit could be made for himself on English mares, and his customers were better pleased, than with Scotch animals." As their farms extended from Biggar to the remotest parts of Lanarkshire, the mares "must have been distributed over the very localities where the best Clydesdales are now to be found". Robert M'William of Stranraer for many years had bought up fifty or more breeding mares and fillies from Derbyshire to take to the Rhins, "where they were readily disposed of in that district". Hugh Crawford of Kilbarchan, "than whom there is no more highly respected horse dealer in the county", was another large buyer of English mares, which went to his native Renfrew and to Ayr.[11] He once met a friend at Carlisle station and was asked where he had been. He replied that he had been to England for "a wheen horse". But on further enquiry, the "few horses" turned out to be a complete special train-load.[12]

In the north, English mares – all of a type – had superceded the more individualistic stallions of the early part of the period. Alexander M'Bey of Aberdeen had for nearly thirty years conveyed large numbers. And so had another Aberdeen dealer, Peter Elder, "who, during the time of the Crimean war, when wheat was dear, imported direct from England to Morayshire many hundreds of English mares for breeding purposes, all of which were readily bought by the Morayshire farmers. Hence the large number of prize horses of the Clydesdale type which year after year appear from the counties of Aberdeen, Moray, and Banff."[13]

David Riddell of Blackhall, Paisley, Drew's closest associate, in one single year, had imported from England "upwards of two hundred choice mares and fillies of the Clydesdale type for breeding purposes". By this, it is merely meant that Mr. Riddell would not go near the Fens, but confined his attention to the

Midlands. Drew himself bought many English mares of the highest class, but these must be considered in a later chapter.

Having followed Drew for so long, we do not apologise for quoting him again to summarise the change that had come over the Scottish draught-horse between about 1840, and about 1874. "Those who survive of the above named dealers are unanimous in stating that within their experience – that is within the last 30 or 40 years – the only horses for agricultural purposes which could be had for money at such places as Stranraer and the Rhins of Galloway, Dumfries, Ayr, Lanarkshire, Aberdeen and Morayshire, were hardy enough animals, with good feet and pasterns and excellent action, but clean legged. They possessed, however, neither the bone nor the size, the weight nor the symmetry of the horses which in these localities are now to be had in abundance. Whence then this marked and visible improvement in the breed of Scotch horses? Can it be by carefully selecting and mating the old, clean legged stock of Scotch horses? No. To look for such a result by any such process of selection and mating would be took for a physical impossibility. If it is impossible to bring about such a result – that is, to improve the breed – by keeping the purity of the old blood intact, what in nature or art could produce so desirable a change as has admittedly been effected in the breed of horses for agricultural purposes? Are we not forced to answer that it is only by the infusion of new blood?"[14]

The logical conclusion to which Drew proceeded from this argument must be left for another page. More immediately, we need to consider why, if English cart-horse breeding had been degenerating for fifty years or more, the Scots were so successful in achieving this improvement – apart, that is, from the simple subtraction and addition caused by the migration of thousands of the best mares to the north. (This was so extensive that Trotter was not exaggerating when he wrote that it "may account in a measure for the great difficulty there is in England to find mares with correct ankles, good feet, and clean coronets, because for years the Scotchmen took away only those animals which excelled in those cardinal points, thus leaving a residuum of short pasterned animals, with defective feet, and having of side-bones above an average crop".[15])

There were perhaps five reasons:

1. The Scotsman has a flair for this particular occupation, as for so many others. One has only to consider how many were employed on English estates as managers, particularly as managers of stock, to recognise the truth of this generalisation. It is instanced, in particular, by the fact that, all through the years when too many Englishmen who wanted weight looked only at impressive tops, the Scots developed as axiomatic the principle that, in cart-horse breeding, one looked first at feet and legs. Without quality and hardness there, they believed that anything else was useless. The English, for the most part, had still to learn that elementary lesson.

2. Given flair, it is simpler to make something out of very little (provided

that the very little is all of a type) by blending in new blood (provided that this, too, is carefully selected to be as uniform as possible), than it is to make improvements – or even to maintain the existing standards – when there is a multiplicity of breeds and types jostling each other closely. The English breeder, having lost his sense of direction, either through his own folly or through economic or other pressures, could not fail to fall into confusion. He proved unable either to keep his splendid variety of breeds, from light horses to the portly Suffolk, entirely separate, or to cross-breed in a planned and systematic fashion.

3. The compactness and comparative isolation of the suitable heavy-horse-breeding areas in Scotland was favourable to the development of a uniform and fixed type. For example the three counties of Lincoln, Nottingham and Leicester, of which every inch is suitable for heavy-horses, are nearly as extensive as Lanark, Ayr, Dumfries, Kirkcudbright and Wigtown, and considerably more extensive than those parts of these chief Clydesdale counties in which it was practicable to breed these horses. The Scotsman had something of the advantage of the Suffolk men in this respect – an advantage which, of course, only applies in the conditions then obtaining, a total lack of organisation or official pedigree recording.

4. The Clydesdale breeders had long learned the value of co-operation in obtaining the use of stallions, and their hiring system made all the difference to the general standard, which was remarkably uniform, of the annual crops of foals. The English breeders were unable to make any headway until they had copied their cousins in this. (The development of the hiring societies is discussed in the next chapter.)

5. The Scotsmen called their horses Clydesdales – even if they were bred in Aberdeen or Wigtown – and had done so universally since at least the 'twenties. The English had no recognised name for theirs. A large number of Clydesdale stallions and some mares were exported, from about 1850 onwards, to Australia and New Zealand. Mostly, the colonials were after comparatively clean legs and activity rather than ponderous weight; but they learned the name "Clydesdale" and that was what they asked for, not for some unpredictable form of English cart-horse. A York ham appears superior to a nameless ham, and a Chelsea or Bath bun is surely better than any old bun. At Highland Shows, it did not matter that the prize-lists were simply for "agricultural horses": only Scottish animals entered. In England, it did matter, and so classifications were adopted for the only two which had a name – the Suffolk and the Clydesdale: the old Black or the ex-Black was nameless and presumably breedless. The distinctive name of the Clydesdale had much to do with the Prince Consort's interest in it. And in the late 'seventies, the Earl of Beaconsfield, attending a meeting at Aylesbury, spoke to Frederic Street and asked him how it was that a

good Clydesdale had not been introduced into that district, it being the only pure breed of cart-horse. Mr. Street's reply was mild. "Because", he said, "we have better horses in England." He then proceeded to give the Prime Minister a short history lesson, explaining how the Scottish horses were a variety of the English breed. It was fortunate that Dizzy had not made his ignorant remarks in public. It would have been enough to drive all the English breeders into the arms of Mr. Gladstone.

5. SUFFOLK PROGRESS

George Mumford Sexton, auctioneer, knew something about the Suffolk breed of horses because he not only sold them but, like other members of his family, had bred them. And this was not surprising, because he lived at Wherstead Hall, near Ipswich, almost at the very heart of the best breeding area. He also knew much about the hairy-legged "English". His somewhat paradoxical association with the latter will be discussed later, but there was no man better qualified to write about either breed, or more likely to be fair to both.

"The English or Shire Horse", he wrote, "varies much in size, style, and character in the different counties of England, occasioned no doubt by the soil and the requirements of the different districts; light land naturally not wanting such heavy horses as some of the strongest clays, which require three or four powerful horses to plough up the land. Vast is the difference between horses of adjoining counties. Take Norfolk, Cambridge, and Lincolnshire, for instance: there is as much difference in the horses in some parts of these counties as between their native sheep; all are, no doubt, to a certain extent, indigenous to the soil."

This is a fair comment. In contrast, "the Suffolk is purely an agricultural, or plough horse, suited admirably to the light land district, where he is bred to perfection, and has no superior for the work he is able to perform. He is endowed with a marvellous constitution, which enables him to do an eight hours' journey at plough, and return to his stable looking little the worse for it. He is remarkable, too, for carrying his years well, frequently living and working for upwards of twenty years on the same farm, and at fifteen or sixteen years he looks in the prime of life. He is rather over-topped for his legs and feet, which is no doubt caused from the quality of the soil he is bred upon (being light and sandy) not containing the limestone, carbonates, and phosphates that other counties are favoured with to produce bone and the firm feet necessary to carry the heavy amount of iron that is put upon horses, to withstand the straining wear and tear of work imposed upon town horses now-a-days."[15]

The circumstances in which Sexton wrote compelled him to be circumspect, which is why he is worth quoting. Had he been free to adopt a more partisan attitude, one way or the other, he could have emphasised that neither the English nor any other horse could do his day's work, like the Suffolk, in one stretch, without returning home to bait. The small stomach of the species *equus* requires food little and often, but the Suffolk's deep-ribbed body showed why he, of all breeds, was least subject to this handicap. He could have said that any hundred Suffolks, on average, would outlive any hundred English – so much so, that it was a wry joke among breeders and dealers (and auctioneers) that the chief drawback of the breed was that customers required replacements too infrequently. On the other hand, he could have put the point about legs and feet more strongly, and said that the Suffolk's feet were useless except on light land, that he was sadly deficient in bone below the knee, and was often bent back, or "calf-kneed", at the cannon-bones.

However, whether biased or impartial, no one could dispute that the Suffolk, so far from being involved in the difficulties and confusions that had resulted in the deterioration of cart-horses in the rest of England, had remained comparatively pure and was therefore more uniform in type, and indeed had actually improved since 1820. The advantages which the breed enjoyed in former times, such as the early enclosures in the county, have already been discussed.

Those which enabled it to continue its progress during this late period can be clearly listed, and are seven in number.

1. Its name was distinctive. Even if anyone used the old-fashioned word "Sorrel" or talked of the "Punch", his listener would immediately recognise the Suffolk. It was a better name even than "Clydesdale" for it identified with only one county and appealed to local pride. If sent into Norfolk or Essex, or Surrey or Wales, it was still a Suffolk horse.

2. Its colour and conformation were equally distinctive. If you saw its silhouette in the dark, you would recognise the Suffolk. You would recognise the Fen bred horse in similar circumstances, but the vast majority of heavy-horses was not readily thus identifiable. In daylight, a Suffolk must appear as a chestnut: otherwise he was not a true Suffolk at all. Admittedly, other horses, too, might be chestnut, but they might be black, or brown, or grey, or bay or particoloured, or even dun.

3. The district where he was bred is compact and cohesive. The sea forms more than a quarter of the county boundary, and even on its other sides its division from the rest of England is in some manner more marked than that between most other counties. Its inhabitants have always had – again relatively to those of other counties, perhaps of all other counties except Cornwall – a certain distinctiveness. The district is, comparatively, quite small. Lincolnshire is not only vaster, but less homogeneous. Spalding, in the Fens, is almost as far from Scunthorpe as it is from Stafford. A Spalding horse sent to Shrewsbury became transformed into a Shropshire horse, of whose antecedents few men, if any, knew anything at all.

4. As Sexton pointed out, breeders were aiming almost exclusively at an

agricultural horse, primarily for home use. Their plans were not pulled this way and that by the uncertainty of town demand or of fashion, nor were they handicapped by the fact that an unsold gelding would be too big for the farm. Modifications during the nineteenth century were confined solely to the nice points raised by the continued new inventions in agricultural machinery.

5. Bakewell's lesson about in-breeding had been well learned. Modified versions of it, in the form of line-breeding, were easy to practise. There had been virtually no cross-breeding in Suffolk, and the exceptions were readily detectable. One silly man long ago, admiring Bakewell but not understanding him, had hired a stallion from him and called it Dishley. But even in the third and fourth generation, men knew where that Black blood still ran and, if they did not want it, could avoid it, and so easily saved themselves from the sudden appearance of non-Suffolk characteristics in the next generation. There had been an attempt to produce carriage horses by the use of Hunter blood, but it had been a failure. And any Suffolk man was in a position to know what horses, if any, bore in their veins the result of this experiment, too. Hundreds of Suffolk stallions were indeed put upon non-Suffolk mares of all types, from Black downwards. But this was in areas far away, leaving the confusion to be perpetuated in other men's fields. And one suspects that it was only the stallions of doubtful breeding or uncertain value that sought pastures new. Great efforts were made for patriotic reasons to keep the best at home. Manfred Biddell went to Mr. Barthropp's sale in 1862, and bought Canterbury Pilgrim (62) for 215 guineas. He did not want him at all, but saw a risk of his leaving the county. (This well-bred colt turned out a poor stallion. But that is by the way.) Seven years later, Richard Garrett bought Crisp's Cup-Bearer (416) for £493, solely to prevent his departure from home territory. (This horse sent him right to the top as a breeder. But that, too, is by the way.) Breeding heavy-horses in Suffolk was like blending coffees. Elsewhere, it was more like making minestrone soup.

6. The Suffolk Agricultural Association had been able to do for many years many of the tasks which elsewhere were the responsibility of no one. Founded in 1831 as the East Suffolk Agricultural Association (and all good Suffolk horses had originated in the east of the county), it had held its first show in 1832. In 1856 it took over the West Suffolk Society, and became a full county body. Its shows were virtually family affairs for the Suffolk horse, and no other type had anything like it, except perhaps the Clydesdale at the Highland shows. But it did more than provide a venue for all to compete at in the summer. In the early 'sixties it inaugurated strict veterinary inspections and would allow no prize to go to a horse with bad hereditary defects. Ringbone, sidebone and brittle feet, that had bid to become the scourge of the Suffolk horse, were being bred out of him at a time when, elsewhere in the country, it was only intelligent individuals that troubled at all about such matters. The bent hind legs and weak hocks of certain families in the breed were similarly disappearing, and so were respiratory

defects. (Many a roarer had won a prize in the early days.) The veterinary inspector in 1871, when the show was held at Beccles, reported that of thirty entries submitted to him, he "had not laid his hands on a sidebone during the day". And that, in those times, was a remarkable achievement. For nearly twenty years, the Suffolk Show was the only one with a veterinary inspection that was anything better than a farce. The Royal Agricultural Society made no requirement that a surgeon should examine the animals at all and the unsoundness of many Royal Show winners was laughable. A Suffolk could win there which the owner dare not exhibit at home. And what there was no veterinary man to detect the judges did not bother to see.

7. The Spring Fair at Woodbridge was another institution which did good to the breed in a way that no other such event (and of course there were very many of them up and down the country) was able to do, except, again, in Scotland at the Glasgow show. Its origin lost in the mists of time, it had long been the showground par excellence for the display of Suffolk stallions. 6th April was its date, and that was the day the stallions always set out for their rounds. The visitor would see all the best that were available for public use in the county. It was in fact a breed show for stallions. In the 'sixties, the number of horses on parade began seriously to decline, largely because the practice had grown up of starting the season a fortnight earlier. But the county horse was so important that in 1871 a town meeting was held which blithely transferred Fair Day to the third Friday in March. A special committee to organise prizes and draw up rules and regulations for cart stallions was appointed. The Fair became less of a general stock mart, but a better stallion parade than it had ever been. There were prizes for Thoroughbreds and Hackneys, but the only class of heavy-horse catered for was the pure-bred Suffolk. You could go to Woodbridge and see them all. If you asked questions, you could find out about their back-breeding, and if anyone told you a tale there would be somebody to correct it. At any other stallion parade in England, except perhaps in the Fens, you would see all miscellaneous kinds, and what blood they had in them you were very lucky if you discovered.

6. THE ROYAL SHOW: A MISGUIDING LIGHT

William Gun of Hope Park is the first man on record to have won a prize for a work-horse. This was in December 1756, when the Edinburgh Society for Encouraging Arts, Sciences, Manufactures and Agriculture, in the second year of its existence, offered £10 to the farmer who should keep the best stud stallion. This society collapsed in 1765, but the Highland and Agricultural Society of Scotland, founded in 1783, has proved to be a more durable successor. Horse-breeding was far from being the first thing it encouraged. For example, John Robertson won a gold medal in 1790 for a system of fire and smoke signals to vessels, indicating where shoals of herring had appeared on the coast. In 1809, Corporal Angus Mackay was awarded a similar medal for capturing a French general and not letting him go. George Clark, who played a pibroch in spite of being so severely wounded in battle that he could not sit down, was voted a handsome stand of bagpipes. Money was allocated for Gaelic dictionaries and translations. In 1816, premiums were given for the breed of work-horses. The first actual show was held in 1822, but it was not until 1826, when it was held at Glasgow, that there were prizes for Clydesdale horses.

Twelve years later, when the show was again at Glasgow and was attracting 121 horses, the English Agricultural Society was founded. Its first show was held at Oxford the following year, 1839. For Shorthorns a first prize was offered of 30 sovereigns, and four others brought the total to £80 altogether: there were similar awards for Herefords and for Devons. With nine prizes in other classes, the premiums for cattle totalled £385. Thomas Bates brought four of his Shorthorns from Kirklevington on Tees-side. He walked them to Hull: thence, they went by sea and by barge to Aylesbury, from where they were walked again the last twenty-three miles. But it was worth it, for they won the first four prizes.

Horses were not so well catered for. There was just one premium of £20 for the best cart-stallion, and one of £10 for cart-mare and foal. A premium of £30 was also offered to the best stallion for breeding hunters, carriage-horses or roadsters serving mares in 1839 at not more than £3, but it was not awarded, because none of the eight entries, aged two to seventeen, merited a prize. The ten cart-stallions on parade were a pretty unlikely lot, also. All except one came from not far afield, but it was that one which received the prize. William Bennett, forty years of age, had walked Mr. Thomas Freeman's eight-year-old Suffolk horse Briton all the way from Henham Hall (east of Halesworth). He had no pony, so when he got to a good high bank, he got on for a ride. By road today, the journey is over 150 miles and, even if Bennett had flown like the crow, he could not have reduced it much below 130.

The glory of winning the first national championship, and the more practical appreciation shown by his guv'nor, lightened the long journey home and the horse was ever afterwards known as Oxford Briton (540). Forty years later, honest William was still "a cheery man to speak with, a capital companion round a show yard, and withal always on his guard not to say an unkind thing about any man's cattle". He had provided Herman Biddell, who thus described him, with much useful information for the first Suffolk Stud-book.

The prize for mare with foal went to what we should now call a "Shire" – of sorts. She was shown by Joseph Osborne of Chilton, who had only a dozen miles to travel. Her name is now indiscoverable but she was bred by J. Darvell of Brill and was probably by his grey Champion (379), a horse that was entered in the stallion class. Osborne himself bred some good foals by this horse.

One might criticise the new society for offering such stingy prizes for horses, resulting in such a poor entry. But errors are to be expected in a new venture, and this one was perhaps not so serious as the mistake of letting the public examine the selected examples of wheat that it was proposed should be sown in order to decide who was to win the prize for that. Confusion and jostling among eager visitors resulted in much of the grain being knocked to the ground. Even worse, the contents of the various parcels were mixed and muddled together. The competition had to be abandoned. The next year, the new society became the Royal Agricultural Society of England, but the encouragement it gave to cart-horse breeding at the Cambridge show and, in 1841, at Liverpool remained faint and feeble. At the fourth Show at Bristol in 1842, the number of heavy horse prizes was increased to six.

For the first nine years the schedule usually referred to "cart" stallions and mares, though occasionally they were described as horses "for agricultural purposes". This led to many grievances on the part of those showing the heaviest types because, whatever the classification, judges usually had farm work in mind. At the 1847 show, at Northampton, one stallion was ruled out simply because he was "too big every way for farm-work, but just the type to draw a brewer's dray and to beget horses for that work". The judges recommended a separate class for dray-stallions. This was done the following year at York, though it was a derisory offer in comparison with the "agricultural" classes that headed the list.

The Royal Show was not merely a mirror of the times, but a guiding light. As a result of its policy, many began to believe that the future lay in smaller and lighter draught horses with cleaner legs. The pundits said so and the Royal seemed to prove it. From 1848 to 1853 inclusive, thirty-nine prizes went to Suffolks and nine to other breeds. In 1852 at Lewes, the Sorrels made a clean sweep. James Howard of Bedford later complained that, as a direct result of the prestige of the Royal Show, landed proprietors all over England (who otherwise took no part or interest in draught-horse breeding) introduced Suffolk stallions into their district with a view to "improving" the local horses.

In 1855, perhaps because the show was at Carlisle, the Suffolks did not win a single one of the prizes, which went to an astonishing assortment of other types – some of them Scottish, even though, in recognition of the locale of the meeting, Clydesdales had their own special classes as well. There was disorder. No one really knew what he had to do to win the glory of a Royal award – except the Suffolk breeders who, bar the freak occasions like this, knew they were all right. Dray-horses were tending to become an inferior form of life not worth the attention of a gentleman: and the offer of prizes for these was erratic, depending on the locality of the show each year.

Herman Biddell drew up a table to show that Suffolk horses, in the period to 1861, won far more Royal prizes than all other "agricultural" breeds combined. This was regarded by Midlands and Fen breeders as proof of the depths to which unabashed bias could make the judges sink. It is not, and cannot be, a particularly reliable table. For example the grey Young Inkerman, bred in Cambridgeshire, twice won prizes, in 1856 and 1857. He was described on the second occasion as a "Suffolk-and-Lincoln", by *Heart of Oak*. Later he appeared posthumously in the English Stud-book as Inkerman 1134, "Shire-Horse", by

Farmer's Glory (832). In 1858 at Chester the winners included (apart from Suffolks) a "Black Dishley Agricultural stallion" amid various unidentifiable types. In 1859, winners were listed as "Agricultural Warwickshire Stallion", "Agricultural Oxfordshire Stallion", "Agricultural Northamptonshire Stallion", and five Suffolks.

In 1862 at Battersea an attempt was made to end the confusion. Special classes were introduced for Suffolks, with twelve prizes: there were also twelve prizes for "agricultural horses not qualified to compete as Suffolks"; and four for "dray" stallions and mares. These classifications lasted three years until, at Devonport and Plymouth in 1865, the dray-horse classes were completely and finally dropped. In 1869 at Manchester, the final insult was offered. Clydesdales, as well as the Suffolks, were now given classes of their own. Robert Bakewell's bones must have turned when the news reached the Elysian pastures that the old Blacks had to appear as "Agricultural horses not qualified to compete as Suffolks or Clydesdales". Such was the social stigma under which the budding Shire horse laboured until the early 'eighties.

Veterinary inspection at Royal Shows had been, from the beginning, so perfunctory as to be farcical, at least in so far as hereditary defects were concerned. Nor were the judges themselves, for some inscrutable reason, encouraged to take these into particular consideration. It was notorious that sound stallions had to compete on unequal terms with showy over-topped animals which could have best served their respective breeds by being rendered unable to serve at all. In 1861, Professor W. C. Spooner of the Royal Veterinary College determined to do something about this deplorable situation. He reported all the very worst cases of roaring and sidebone to the judges, in case the burden of their duties on a hot day deprived them of the faculties of hearing and touch. It then became a rule that horses were not only inspected on arrival to make certain they had no infection which would spread to other exhibits, but were actually examined for soundness by a second officer. This lasted a brave eight years. Reporting on the 1871 show at Wolverhampton, the senior steward, Jacob Wilson of Morpeth, wrote that "prior to the Manchester show horse entries had dwindled down to a minimum, and were a disgrace to our national society. The *double* veterinary inspection, and the risk of losing a previous good reputation thereby, prevented the exhibition of even the *best* horses in the country. This difficulty has now been removed and horses are only subjected to veterinary examination at the discretion of the judges."[16] Back came the sidebones and the roaring, studiously unfelt and unheard by the judges. This did not prevent Welcher's Honest Tom winning six successive first prizes (1867–1872) at the Royal, which is a record: but he had to do so on most occasions in competition with stallions which under a more enlightened system would have never been left entire at all. This dismal lack of veterinary scruple went on until the early 'nineties.

As at the Royal, so also at even the smallest one-day shows. Hereditary diseases and unsoundnesses were ignored and stallions which, if not "added to the list" as they should have been, ought at least to have been left in obscurity, were given local fame and popularity. Outside the Fens and other staunch heavy-horse areas, classifications for "agricultural horses", aping the Royal, resulted in prizes being generally given for light-legged animals, and ensured that, below show level, there were too many weeds in the country. Another folly was the attempt to aggrandise the status of local shows by promoting a disproportionate number of open classes and giving them too much of the prize-money. By this means valuable stallions were enticed to the district, but there was a naïve failure to do anything to ensure that, having taken a big prize, they stayed to cover the mares. Meanwhile the humbler local men, with a good mare or two or even with a sound stallion, were frightened off from competing for the main honours at their very own show. But perhaps the ultimate absurdity was that yearlings and two-year-olds were largely judged on how big and forward they were. To win, they had to appear like fat-stock, which was fatuous. They were brought like lambs to the slaughter, and expected to live and work like Blacks.

7. WEIGHT FOR THE SHORT HAUL

The old long-distance road wagons, that had still rumbled on their cumbrous way wherever there were no canals, were superseded during this period as fast as the railways were built, and by the 1860s had become an old man's memory. W. C. Spooner, thinking of his "boyish days", wrote about the old-type wagon that had operated long before the fast passenger road-coaches had ever been thought of and still went on working even when six-mile-an-hour luggage vans, taking advantage of the better roads, had come in as a novelty. His memory of them is worthy of notice, if only because of the contrast it draws between the old England of 1820 and modern England in 1874. He could remember "the slow but sure approach of one of these ponderous vehicles with its eight or ten ton load, heralded perhaps by a cloud of dust ever stirred up by the heavy feet of the ten or twelve massive animals that moved it onward at the rate of some two miles an hour . . . It was a sight to behold these leviathans settle into their work after a short respite in the midst of a steep hill. The burly waggoner, too heavy to walk, and scorning to ride in his waggon, was mounted on one of those strong sure-footed ponies, usually white or pie-bald, which have long since disappeared. A crack from his long whip would send in to the collar with a twenty-horse power the ten hairy-legged but powerful brutes whose broad backs were rendered still broader in appearance by the absence of tails, for each horse was docked close to the stump, under the absurd idea that their strength would thereby be increased."[17]

Joseph Byford of Glemsford was one who refused to make peace with the railways and long continued to advertise his service to the Old Catherine Wheel at Bishopsgate via Braintree, Chelmsford and Romford – proudly "all the way by road". The family bred their own Suffolks and their district was suited only to the biggest sort, and so they made a brave show. (His son William had

Shires, and was a member of the breed society for the first fourteen years of its existence.) But it was ridiculous to fight the railways. In any case these required heavy-horses at almost every station, and were in fact doing much to increase the demand for the heavy-horse at the very job for which he is best suited, the short haul, to which we must now turn.

David Low, speaking of the brewers' carts and the wagons of the coal-merchants, wrote that "the stranger sees with admiration the vast numbers of enormous carriages in endless motion through the crowded streets, drawn by teams of the largest horses in the world". He was critical of mere size, which the users told him was necessary to cope with the jolting and sudden obstructions on the rough pavement. He argued that "it is muscular force, and not the *vis inertiae* of great weight of body, which best enables a horse to overcome continued obstacles". He also objected to the practice of harnessing several horses tandem – "usually attached in lines, which causes them to pull by sudden jerks, and with unequal force; and in turning the corners of narrow streets and lanes, it is often seen that the entire weight of the enormous carriage is thrown, for a time, on the shaft horse".[18]

In 1849, three years later, the Reverend John M. Wilson quoted an observer who was astonished at the docility and good temper of these gigantic horses. "I have often watched the facility with which one of them will back a waggon into a narrow street or archway, but a few inches wider than the vehicle itself, and guided only by the voice of the carman, aided perhaps by a few slight movements of his hand."[19] As a parson, Mr. Wilson was particularly concerned with moral feelings and intellectual habits. For example, in contrasting the litters of the carnivores with the one or two young produced by herbivorous creatures, he observed that "in animals, as well as in man, fruitfulness is the common attendant of monogamy and chastity". Debatable as that may be, he was an excellent commentator on the horse, which is why he is selected here from so many. But it is odd that this attitude did not lead him to comment on the fact that there were still some town horse-owners who did not conform to the increasing practice of not using stallions. As early as 1809, John Lawrence had commented that "the number of dray and cart stallions in the metropolis, formerly so considerable, is now reduced to few, and it is desirable that geldings may be entirely substituted" – they are "void of the trouble and of some of the diseases of the stoned-horse. Even in the view of humanity, it is a point gained to deprive the male by a temporary suffering of that powerful appetite, which must be perpetually recurring with no chance of gratification."[20]

His namesake, Richard Lawrence, did not agree with him. He thought, strangely, that the gelding was more delicate and less able to bear heat and cold. "Even the stallions which work on the brewers' drays in London, and which are never cloathed in the stable, and are often obliged to stand many hours in the streets, are always fuller of flesh and finer in their coats than the geldings of the same description."[21] This was as late as the 'thirties, but on the whole it was mainly some of the brewers who still preferred stallions, and continued to do so until, in an age of increasing refinement and delicacy, pressure of public opinion forced them to agree that a stallion in the shafts was as bad as a bull in a china-shop. (Since draught entire horses by mid-Victorian times excited criticism rather than admiration, the practice became confined, before dying out alto-gether, to small cartage men, the owners of perhaps only one animal, living in or near a town and working to and from it, who reckoned to supplement their income by a few casual shillings for obliging a mare-owner.)

William Miles, in the 'sixties, praised the brewers for their liberality towards worn-out horses, in having them destroyed instead of selling them for a small sum to be put to work they could no longer do in conditions that were less good than those to which they had been accustomed. The exceptions to this enlight-ened practice showed how much superior was the management of brewery horses to that of most others. "One was sold from being supposed to be lame: he turned out sound. Three tons and a half, including his cart, became his ordinary load, and with this he went all over London and the neighbourhood and never had, or required, any assistance, not even over the bridges, or up hills." He maintained his condition for several years after becoming a brewer's reject.

It is Miles who gives us perhaps the finest picture of a dray-horse team at its best.[22] A Scotsman told him, "I have been over most of the globe; I have seen many of its wonders; but the greatest I ever saw was in London. I saw a brewer's team lowering some butts of beer. The horse that performed this office, without any signal, raised the butts, and returned and lowered the rope: not a word or sign escaped the man at the top of the hole, who only waited to perform his part as methodically as his four footed mate did his. Two others were sometimes playing at intervals in apparent converse. The cellaring finished, the horse took his place by the team: the other loose horse, that had been going wherever he pleased, also came, and was hooked on. The man adjusted his dress, then walked away; the team followed. Not one word had passed, not even a motion of the whip, or any other intimation of what was to be done next." He added that he had never seen the same number of men work in such unison: it was wonderful, and if it was not reason, he thought the greater portion of mankind had better give up some part of their reason to learn sagacity from a dray-horse. "I fol-lowed some distance to see how it was that a man who seemed as if he could be crushed at any moment by these monsters, had such control over them. I ob-served he never touched them: between carriages where there hardly seemed room enough to squeeze through, he went without touching, and this, too by merely waving a bit of whipcord at the end of a long black rod . . . I was quite astounded . . . and can hardly prevail upon myself that it was not some necro-mancer waving an enchanted rod."

It is disappointing that one of the most acute of all observers of the English scene, the great but controversial French philosopher Hippolyte Taine, alluded only briefly to our draught-horses. He thought they were marvellous, like our policemen, who did not shout and gesticulate but, on point duty, never spoke.

"If there is any mix-up in the traffic, they simply raise an arm to stop the coach-man."[23] The horses resembled elephants. He met a farmer who had twelve, which he was presumably maturing for town work. "Glossy skins, muscular loins, colossal quarters. One of the horses, smaller, was French, and the farmer said it was not so strong, and less able to stand bad weather." That was no doubt meant to be one in the eye for Hippolyte, who nevertheless continued to study the man as dispassionately as he examined the horses, for he had a theory that there was a marked affinity between the horses and the inhabitants of every country. He classified Englishmen in three main types, of which one corres-ponded to the English dray-horse – "the robust man, big and solidly built . . . sometimes as much as six feet tall and broad in proportion . . . the face and flesh highly coloured . . . they might be taken for prime specimens selected for an exhibition of human beings, like vegetable show beetroots or cauliflowers. Basically good-humoured, often also good-natured, commonly rather awk-ward . . ."[24] Taine would have been surprised to hear it, but the robust English-man was breeding far too few elephantine horses.

8. STALLION AND MARE: FALLACIES AND FOLLIES

In 1874, improvement in the general standard of cart-horses was still being hampered among even the experts by fallacious ideas about heredity and, on a lower plane, by a variety of foolish practices. In between, good veterinary ad-vice was not plentiful.

a. *Some fallacies*

In general, perhaps these were not often particularly detrimental to breeding in a practical sense, but if wise men believed such tales as the following four, one should not be surprised at the ignorance of the foolish. (It must be remembered that, then, there was a wider gulf than there is now in knowledge, and fre-quently in intelligence, between the top ranks of farming and stock-raising and the lower reaches.)

1. It was still generally believed that the first stallion to cover a mare in-fluenced all her subsequent offspring by other stallions. And there were plenty of people willing to "prove" it. For example, a well-known veterinary expert quoted the case of an Arabian mare of nearly pure blood which was crossed with a quagga. The foal was the sort of hybrid that one would expect. She was subsequently served in two successive years by an Arab and in following years by other horses. She obliged with a foal each time, but each of her progeny had strong quagga markings and characteristics! (Even in 1976, this theory, or rather, superstition of telegony is not entirely dead, though fortunately the cranks who believe it are not to be found among practical breeders – or veterinary surgeons.) There was another belief based on the same ignorant absurdity – that if the same stallion covered the same mare year after year, the principle of "satura-tion" would result in each foal resembling its sire more completely than the last.

2. The sire determined the foal's conformation and outward characteristics, including its action: the dam contributed the internal structure and vital organs, constitution and temper. This principle was held to apply to diseases also – shivering would be inherited from the dam, sidebone only from the sire. The lady who suggested to George Bernard Shaw that they ought to marry, because a child with her beauty and his brains would be a great gift to humanity, was no doubt deluded by a contrary version of the theory. The great man countered with a more orthodox form of it when he replied that their offspring might suffer the disaster of inheriting his beauty and her brains.

3. Another absurdity (conflicting with the idea just referred to, but more commonly held lower down the scale of expertise) was that, to correct a fault in the dam, it was necessary to choose a stallion with the opposite fault. On this principle, a good way of producing a beautifully straight-limbed child would be, presumably, to marry a bandy man to a knock-kneed woman.

4. The stallion controlled the size of the foal at the time of parturition. There-fore, it was dangerous to put a big stallion on a small mare, because the foal, even if delivered without harm to its dam, would never get enough milk. This last point is rather a distortion of the truth than a simple error. Troubles of this sort arising from the use of mares whose conformation was far from ideal no doubt were responsible for it.

b. *Practical follies*
It is a dreary pastime to contemplate the faults, arising either from ignorance or from brutality, that were prevalent as late as the 1870s. However, since a wonderful transformation was effected in thirty years or so, it is impossible that anyone alive today should fully realise how stupidly his predecessors often acted a century ago, and therefore something must be said about it. This depressing subject can best be considered as six separate topics:

1. The people involved, whether farmers or grooms, were of an infinitely lower general status and education than their successors even one generation later. This is part of social history and is too complex a matter to enter into detail about here. But if one takes the stallion-leaders as just one example, it is true to say that, although some were "respectable", humane and sober, many or most were brutish, drunken and filthy. An owner of stallions who wanted to employ the better sort had a hard job of it to find them. The employment was not regarded as one to attract decent men.
This generalisation of course casts an unfair aspersion on the memory of Robert Bakewell's excellent Ed. Porter and on those fine fellows who now were his worthy successors – men who were in sole charge of a large, powerful and potentially dangerous animal for twenty-four hours of the day; who had to walk ten or twelve miles a day themselves and find their own comforts at the

end of it; who, often far from home, and not too comfortable on wet mornings after bad weather the day before, put their horse's well-being first at all times and never thought of cheating their employer, which would have been so easy; who were as sober as a judge and moral as the judge's maiden aunt; who knew their job thoroughly and carried it out with respect for the mare and her owner. But the general reputation of the profession was, regrettably, well earned by the rest of them who, however disreputable at home, regarded their thirteen weeks' travelling as an opportunity to cast off all restraint, particularly with regard to their own sexual activity. The sailor's proverbial interests at different ports were infantile compared with the stallion-man's alleged and concentrated excesses on his round. It has been suggested that the very nature of the business conducted at all his stopping-places was conducive to a sympathetic outlook among the local girls. There is the story of a man leading his stallion past the vicarage gate one spring morning and, in response to the parson's kind enquiry whether he was having a successful season, replying, "Not 'arf! We've only been on t'road a week, and I'm six ahead of him already." If the leaders fathered even half as many illegitimate children as popular opinion credited them with, the ease of their conquests must have some special reason in addition to whatever personal attractions they may have had. But we must not give them all the credit. The activity in the yard behind the pub or in the farm yard – an exciting highlight in an otherwise uneventful country week – made the more impulsive and less modest young ladies temporarily lose their heads to local lads as well. It might be an interesting study to correlate the bastardy figures and dates of some sample parishes with the stallion round.

2. The mating of stallion and mare was too often at this time connected with much absurd and even disgusting nonsense and mumbo-jumbo, not to say cruelty. All sorts of crude devices were adopted to make the mare stand to the horse or the horse mount the mare, none of them conducive to anything but savagery or terror in either. By 1874, of course, things were already improving. Richard Reynolds, the Liverpool Corporation veterinary superintendent, commented that "the barbarous customs much practised in former years by ignorant persons" were becoming less frequent. There remain now among us, a hundred years later, only the mysterious vestiges of the more charming folk-lore relics of that whole corpus of mystique and ritual which grew up around horse-breeding. The reality was for the most part ludicrous, and repulsively ludicrous at that. The frequent absence of all thought for any standard of hygiene would horrify a modern groom. Just as one wonders not so much at the infant mortality rate in Victorian times as at the fact that so many babies actually survived, so it is amazing that infection – in the form of contagious cellulitis or pink-eye, and of other diseases causing sterility or worse – was not passed on more frequently from mare, via the stallion, to mare. Perhaps, of all the common failings of the time, this was as reprehensible as any, for the horse in its shape and its nature is the cleanest and most fastidious of animals. It says much for the admirable way

in which the he and she were constructed that they survived these times, just as the fact that so many were well-mannered and tractable is a tribute to their character rather than to the way they were too often treated.[25]

3. With stallions, the most frequent error was their gross over-use. Two-year-old colts, which might be ready perhaps to try their powers on a dozen or so mares, frequently served forty, fifty or even sixty on the principle that "what a colt can do should be the measure of what he should do",[26] as Professor Axe had cause to complain even many years later in writing about these "baby sires". Those whose own growth, virility and fertility somehow managed to survive this precocious sexual excess and the over-stimulating food that they were given to keep them going, inevitably suffered from disastrous effects upon their young hind legs.

Mature stallions were also absurdly over-worked. Some covered 150 mares in a season, and some even 200. However, it must be admitted that they were not apparently the worse for it; nor did the mares necessarily suffer either. The famous Suffolk, Catlin's Duke (296), bred in 1846 was reckoned to have left more mares in foal than any other horse of the times – and not only because he covered so many, for it was claimed that his success percentage was phenomenal, though that cannot be checked. The most mares that his leader, Charlie Row, ever booked in to him in one season was 220. This may safely be accepted as the true figure, for Charlie was a good leader of undoubted integrity, most unlikely to ask the horse to do anything else "on the side". Duke was well known also for his exceptionally good temper. When he was sold at the age of nine in the autumn of 1855, he went somewhat feebly round the ring, but this was because his feet had become a little tender which perhaps is not surprising. Nevertheless, for three more seasons he continued his efforts on the mixed and undistinguished mares of Essex as readily and genially as he had served the purer ones of his native county.[27]

The Shire, King Dick, who was so irrepressible that, when not otherwise occupied, he engaged his energies in trying to break out of his quarters in order to wreak havoc on the main road a mile away from home, easily topped Duke's record. He covered 317 mares in the year 1870.[28] The palm, however, must be awarded to the Suffolks after all. Three of them, Moses, David and Catlin, in 1849 served 1,135 mares between them.[29] Another horse was reported as serving nine mares in two-and-a-half hours.[29] Stallions serving eight mares in a couple of hours, or not much longer, were by no means exceptional, and one hunter stallion has been recorded as having covered twenty-one mares in twenty-four hours and left nineteen of them in foal.[30] And Professor Axe, who was not a vendor of traveller's tales, stated that a well-known Shire stallion, "after completing a heavy season in Lancashire, was let for further work in the south. On reaching his destination, at three o'clock in the day, twenty-three mares were waiting for service. Of these, nineteen were found to be in season, and were served the same day, and thirteen proved to be in foal."[31]

All this is not say, of course, that there were no sensible owners or men – nor that there were none who still maintained the contrary lunacy, that a stallion should not be used as a stock-horse until the age of eight. If he were any good, that would be his best years wasted. If he were not very fertile (and the difference between one horse and another in sexual capacity and desire is enormous), he would by then have become enough of an old bachelor to be ill-disposed towards the business: he might refuse service altogether or even be prematurely impotent.

The stallions that regularly served these vast crowds of mares every year were, inevitably, the worst in quality and conformation. They were busy because they were cheap. These 15s. or 1 guinea horses often caused the owner of a good horse serving at, say, 3 guineas (which was worth every penny of the difference a hundred times over) to withdraw him, defeated, from a district where, with only thirty or forty mares coming to him, he could not even pay his way. Some landlords tried to improve the situation by providing their tenants with a good stallion cheaply, or even gratis. In some cases, the only mares sent to such a free horse were so bad that, if the owner had to pay for the service, he would not even have troubled to put them to a half-guinea scrub stallion. Some of these latter, not travelling but staying at home as uncastrated geldings, essentially labourers, were relics of the old system that had really been obsolete 100 years. They were handy to oblige a neighbour, but did more harm to the cart-horse breed than their limited opportunities would suggest.

Finally, the condition in which stallions, even quite good ones, too often began their season would cause derision among any men born in the twentieth century. After being boxed up and fed like pigs for weeks, they were too adipose even to walk much, let alone serve a mare either with enthusiasm or the seed of fertility. Within days or a week, many of them were suffering from laminitis, that agonising inflammation of the feet accompanied by fever. If they were able to resume their duties and continue without breaking down from some other cause, they ended them exhausted. The walking of a regular round, and the serving of mares en route, was an arduous test, but a horse in fit and hard condition was capable of finishing the season in as good a condition as he began.[32] But at this time, too few did. Unfortunately, emphasis on the wrong things at shows helped to make even the best stallions so obese as to be temporarily, or even permanently, sterile.

4. Mares generally suffered from the opposite follies to those which stallions were subjected to, certainly as far as the age of breeding was concerned. Even the best authorities held that it was wrong to put a two-year-old filly to the horse. Frederic Street, who advocated it, was one of the very few voices in the wilderness. Admittedly, it was better to miss the chance of breeding perhaps late in the season from a well-grown filly than to try to do so from any which were not sufficiently mature at that age and were therefore likely to suffer in

their own development. But the common view, that mares should not be covered until the age of five, was absurd. Not only were two, or three, valuable years wasted, but a mare whose first mating was delayed until then would be a far less ready and easy breeder than if she had started earlier.

The general result was that good healthy mares in excellent condition on farms where their work was regular but not excessive, contributed far too little to the next generation of cart-horses. Unsuitable mares, on the other hand, contributed far too much, or at least were expected to do so. It was commonly said of one which could not, for some reason, do satisfactory work, that "she will do to breed from", as if the sire could contribute all the virtues and the dam would reproduce none of her faults. Sometimes, the sole qualification upon which a mare was selected for breeding was that she was hot-tempered, or a kicker, or the possessor of some other vice. Motherhood would "sober her down". Even when it did, it was not the surest way to improve the image of the cart-horse as a willing and docile worker. Worst of all, many men bought worn-out old mares, perhaps some which had led a gelding's life in the town, and expected to get out of them both work and foals. Such unfortunate creatures were either shocked by the efforts directed towards motherhood, or else were at the same time nymphomaniac and barren, and therefore a dangerous nuisance, owing to the development of cysts in their ovaries.

5. Conformation was, therefore, sacrificed in the stallion's case to a showy top and sheer weight and, in the mare, to God knows what. The commonest defects which this ignorance produced were deficiency of bone below the knee; roundness, which inevitably meant softness, of bone; uprightness and shortness of the pasterns; fleshiness of the legs accompanied by coarse and curly hair, conducive to that offensive and troublesome condition known as grease; and narrow feet. These things inevitably created thoroughly bad action which led, through the sheer inefficiency of their possessor as a motive force, to a whole series of maladies.

6. These unsoundnesses developed into positive disablements, particularly in the unnatural conditions of town streets. Worse still, some of them, by a distorted sort of man-created evolution, were hereditary. Of the limbs that have been mentioned, the most serious and common hereditary unsoundnesses were sidebone, ringbone and bone spavin. But there were others, some of them more quickly developing in town conditions and, equally, more incapacitating. The heavy-horse was especially prone to hereditary diseases of the wind – in the form of roaring and whistling; of the nervous system – shivering and stringhalt; and of the eye – cataract. Where all these faults were not carefully bred out, they stayed in. (It is not accurate, strictly speaking, to speak of some of these unsoundnesses as hereditary. Horses were not born with sidebones or ringbones. But poor conformation, which *was* hereditary, inevitably called them into existence.)

PLATES 5 and 6   George Garrard in 1792 painted one of Messrs. Whitbread's geldings. This is a picture of supreme importance, showing that dray-horses of that time were real animals after all! It absolves us from having to believe what we see in most portraits of the period, which were "idealised" (if that can possibly be the right word). The coal-horses below are also credible. Having laboured uphill on a terrible "road", they now descend without any drag to ease the strain.

PLATE 7 Where is the hair? And why does he look like a seal? This claims to be the great England's Glory (705), foaled in 1814, son of Wiseman's Honest Tom. Artists who represented sheep as rectangles are, sadly, not to be trusted with horses.

PLATE 8 A puzzle. This "Old English Black Horse", bred by "Mr. Broome of Ormiston, Derby", was by Old Blacklegs (which one?) from "a mare of the Dishley breed". Dishley appears in the background—but the painting dates from between 1832 and 1841.

7. Foaling, which among wild equine creatures is apparently so simple, is of course fraught in the domesticated animal with all sorts of dangers, both during and after parturition. Most men could list a dozen possible accidents or diseases likely to occur at this time. That all these were magnified where the simplest standards of hygiene were neglected requires no elaboration.

We might therefore conclude an otherwise depressing discussion with a narrative told by Gilbert Murray who, in a little pamphlet full of excellent advice on cart-horse breeding, unaccountably became poetic about foaling night. "A trusty servant is left in charge, all have long since retired to rest, and even the weary watch-dog is fast asleep in his kennel. The mare stands quietly munching the last rip of hay. A certain uneasy feeling, unnoticed by the attendant, seems to steal over her, she rests now one leg then the other, the act of mastication is suspended, and again slowly proceeds. Meanwhile, the weary watcher, apprehending no immediate danger to his charge, stealthily retires to more comfortable quarters to enjoy the proverbial forty winks. Imbued with the most honest intentions, he throws himself down on the hay loft, or on a batten of straw in an empty stall, and is soon wrapped in balmy slumber. An hour passes, a second, nay, a third. When he wakes, trembling with nervous agitation, he rushes in haste to inspect his charge, but all too late to save the foal, which, from lack of careful assistance, was strangled at birth."[33] One hopes that Mr. Murray did not tell bed-time stories to children.

9. THE MISMANAGEMENT OF GELDINGS

As in the country, so also in town. The general standard of management was appalling. This does not mean that every owner and every carman was a fool or a brute. Many were. Many also were wise and gentle. There will always be both sorts, though the first in later years have been restrained by the law and by public opinion in a manner that then they were not. But it was the average level that was so low.

The whole economy of the country, all its manufacture and trade, its very life, depended upon the work of the heavy town or "commercial" gelding, just as vitally as it had grown to depend upon the railways. This is in itself a vast subject, with the details of which a breed history cannot be very deeply concerned. But some general remarks must be made, if only because the breeders, in improving their own methods, were to find themselves equally involved quite soon in the welfare of town horses. The chief evils of the commercial gelding's life can be listed under seven heads:

a. *Preparation*

As concerning the early life of horses destined ultimately for the town, comment should perhaps be confined to two subjects – their breaking and their ultimate move from the country:

1. Something has already been said about the absurd philosophy which often

governed the training of the young horse to work – the idea that, having let him begin by being unruled and unruly, the next step was to break him, as quickly as possible and as ruthlessly as necessary, to captive labour. Richard Reynolds remarked that "the education of horses is too often entrusted to men devoid of sufficient acumen to estimate the character, and who are deficient in that patient resolution so essential for the proper management of a colt. Intelligence is not by any means equally distributed amongst horses; some are very slow learners, whilst others appear to grasp at once what is required of them; yet ignorant men usually adopt the same means for the governance of the high-couraged percipient colt as for the dull lethargic dunce."[34] In this connexion, a very ancient horse breaker of the old school had once said to him, "There are no bad horses; bad men make 'em." In this Bakewell himself would have heartily agreed. But in the 'seventies, there were plenty of bad men, even if many were bad only in the sense that they were ignorant louts.

2. The final preparation of the gelding for town work, at the age of five, was usually quite as absurd, though its cruel effects were less quickly apparent. Horses sold via the fairs were usually made more attractive by being isolated for a time, without any exercise at all, in a darkened loose-box and fed with as much fattening food as they would take – including linseed cake, treacle and new milk. By this means, a horse was successfully rendered quite unfit for work of any description and, on his arrival in town, ripe for disease and sickness at the earliest possible moment. Like other lunacies, this was perhaps not so common in 1874 as it had been even in 1864, but thousands of men would not dream of selling a five-year-old in any other way, as long as there were those who would pay an extra pound or two for an animal which was less useful than he had been a couple of months earlier.

b. *Town life itself*

No owner, of course could avoid the basic unsuitability of urban conditions. But because town horses were so common, this fact must not for that reason be ignored. The new arrival found everything especially alarming, because the countryside was then quiet to a degree that is almost unimaginable now. And the hard stones and pavements were bad for feet, legs and general equine welfare. To take one apparently trivial example of the hardships, there was a civil suit in 1874 (*Benjamin* v. *Storr*) where it was held that the staling of horses left standing in a street outside business premises for an unreasonable time was a nuisance under the law, capable of being restrained by injunction. So, Mr. Storr was in the wrong, but it might be a nice point whether he would have been committing an offence if his horse had staled without first waiting an unreasonable time. What appears not to have concerned either the law or Mr. Benjamin is the unfortunate animal. Note that he did wait a long time, not in the vain hope of saving Storr from court proceedings or Benjamin from offence, but simply because, belonging to the cleanest of species, he hated splashing himself in this way on the hard pavement. One is left to wonder how Storr and his horse coped with the injunction.

c. *Gears and shoeing*

Apart from overworking him, which was common, there were two particular methods of making it difficult or impossible for a horse to do his work efficiently and without suffering. Both were practised on a large scale. Firstly, there were collars too large or too small or ill-fitting; collar and saddle linings that caused sores through being filthy or in bad repair; defective gearing of all kinds; an incorrect angle of draught. Examples of all these could be seen in a few minutes' walk in the heart of London. In the second place, there was bad shoeing, perhaps the most crass of all stupidities. If attempts to make the foot fit the shoe were cruel, the attempt to give a fine superficial appearance by rasping the whole outside of the hoof was crazy – the action of a man who, as one breeder of the day sarcastically remarked, would shave the bark off a tree to make it look handsome. Perhaps the most insidious evil was the contract-shoeing system, which was then interpreted by most farriers, or so-called farriers, as a challenge to keep every shoe on as long as possible. Parents who joined such a scheme for their children would soon appreciate the drawbacks of the arrangement. All in all, it was marvellous that some horses were able to walk at all. The standard was low in the countryside also, and it was only when such organisations as the Bath and West Society instituted competitions and arranged a travelling school, conducted by a master-smith, in the 'nineties that much improvement was made. The lay spectator who is fascinated by expert shoeing demonstrations at its shows today is unaware that they originated in an attempt, less than a hundred years ago, to provide education in a craft so ancient that there was no excuse at all for the ignorance that was prevalent.

d. *Management*

It would be pointless to enlarge upon the general subjects of bad stabling, either fetid and stuffy, or draughty and damp; inadequate grooming; general filth; bad feeding; or any of the other horrors which, if the imagination cannot picture them, there are no statistics to show. Since it will be necessary to return to this subject when we consider the 1880s, let it suffice here to mention two horse-owning companies that clearly ought to have set an example and yet who were only just beginning to practise the bare minimum of reasonable management.

The London and North Western Railway Company had, until very recently, lodged all their London horses in underground vaults at Camden Town. These were dark, damp and draughty. Admittedly, the animals had now (in 1874) been moved, and had been put there in the first place only because it was difficult to discover proper stabling close at hand. But this was many years in the finding. In other words, a sickness and death rate that was quite staggering was of no real consequence: it was just a minor waste of money that irritated the business instincts of the directors. Horses were rather like men. Better conditions would make them fitter and therefore cheaper in the long run. Neither mattered much in comparison with an expensive locomotive. (The L.N.W.R. is quoted here simply because it was overall not the worst, but the *best* manager of horses amongst the railway companies. An example of the lead it took occurs in the next section.)

Our second example is of over-indulgence, of horses almost killed by kindness. At a certain Durham colliery in the early 'seventies, 149 horses were employed at hauling coal from the pit head. Strong animals averaging about 16.2-hands, they were liberally fed at a cost of £1. 2s. 3d. per week each. But the management was worried, because their work was badly falling off. The eminent veterinary surgeon, Charles Hunting, was called in and found them in miserably poor condition. He promptly altered, and reduced, their diet, which had consisted of 168 lb of uncrushed oats and 154 lb of long hay per week. He substituted 109 lb of mixed crushed grains and 98 lb of chopped hay. Within three months, the horses were all in excellent health and their work had increased amazingly, at a saving of 9s. 5½d. per horse per week, or £3,664 a year for them all.

e. *Sickness*

The town horse often began by contracting a fever in his first week and, if he possessed any tendencies towards those hereditary unsoundnesses which have already been commented on (Section 8(b)6), they would soon find marked expression on city pavements. Obviously, the lower the standard of care and management, the more susceptible the animal would be to all those other troubles that affected horses in general and heavy ones in particular.

Hot or badly ventilated stables aggravated, if they did not cause, catarrh, inflammation of the lungs, pleurisy and, among infectious diseases, they certainly spread influenza rapidly. Overwork, or exposure to cold and wet followed by neglect, was a frequent contributory cause of congested lungs, bronchitis and rheumatism. Incorrect feeding or watering caused colic, spasmodic or flatulent, and inflammation of the bowels. The painful swelling of the hind leg known as weed or lymphangitis was the "Monday morning complaint" caused by Sunday's lack of all exercise combined with a failure to reduce rations accordingly; even this temporary trouble easily became chronic, by which time the leg was permanently much swollen. Bad shoeing, together with heavy work in hot weather, caused the agonising inflammation of the foot known as laminitis; neglect or excessive paring was responsible for thrush, and canker; sheer bad workmanship, such as wrongly driven nails, provided frequent and much simpler sources of foot trouble. When poor feet or poor action was not corrected by particular attention to shoeing, any one of a dozen other troubles could result, from seedy toe and shelly foot to "clicking" and the other permutations of one limb constantly knocking another during walking, some of them exaggerated by debility or tiredness.

Inadequate cleaning and grooming were responsible for cracked heels and mud fever and that particular scourge of the hairy-legged cart-horse, grease. This ailment, so irritating to the horse, and so offensive to man in its extreme condition (by which time it was incurable), could often be guarded against only by exceptional care, it is true: but it was caused simply by cold and wet and a dirty skin. Injuries were responsible for quittor in the foot, capped elbow and capped hock; and sprains developed into such troubles as thoroughpin and bog spavin. Parasites, whether internal in the form either of bots or of worms in their several and unpleasing varieties, or external, such as bloodsucking flies or lice or ringworm, also flourished more happily in bad conditions than good. The one ailment from which the town horse was generally free (as Jerome K. Jerome found himself free only of one malady, housemaid's knee[35]), simply because it normally affected only young animals and immunised them against its recurrence, was strangles, which was contagious.

f. *Contagious diseases*

When in 1865 the "cattle plague" or rinderpest invaded this country and spread with alarming rapidity, the first ineffective measures were soon followed by the Cattle Diseases Prevention Act which became law on 20th February the following year. Compulsory slaughter was accompanied by the entirely novel principle of compensation, paid for out of the county rates. Following this precedent, the Contagious Diseases (Animals) Act 1869 included among those which were notifiable a horse ailment – glanders. The primitive organisation at hand for dealing with rinderpest had proved surprisingly effective. But an endemic disease, spread over a scattered horse population, is a more cunning opponent (especially when horse-owners for the most part were determined to conceal cases if they possibly could) than a sudden epidemic. The authorities in whom power was vested were the Privy Council (the branch concerned being called from 1870 the Veterinary Department), the magistrates and local inspectors.

Under the 1869 Act, no one was to expose in a market or fair or any other public place, or lead or drive along a public way, or cause to be carried in any way, a horse with glanders. If they did, an inspector could seize and slaughter it. But if they kept a glandered horse at home, no action could be taken. Professor G. T. Brown, Chief Inspector of the Privy Council's Veterinary Department, reported that "it is known that in some large horse establishments a special stable is set apart for those animals which have been condemned as glandered by the veterinary surgeon in attendance. These horses, instead of being sent to the slaughter-house in accordance with the recommendation of the professional attendant, have been kept in the 'condemned cell' and employed exclusively for night work."[36]

Slaughter was often difficult to enforce, for it could not be carried out, if the owner objected, without reference to the Privy Council. Unfortunately, except that it was peculiar to the horse family, and highly contagious, not much was known about the disease or how to diagnose it in the early stages. It was not clear precisely how it was spread, but it was abundantly obvious that improper housing and feeding, and dirt, gave it a special invitation. It was rare among animals that were regularly fed, properly attended to, and not overworked: it was commonest among omnibus and cab horses and those employed in the rougher kinds of heavy draught. The period of incubation seemed variable, and the symptoms were sometimes dangerously disguised. But sooner or later they became painfully clear – fever, which subsided for a short while before re-appearing, accompanied by a yellow discharge from the nostrils, sores and ulcers, and enlargement of the glands of the lower jaw. In its acute form, it caused eventual death. In its chronic form it was especially dangerous, for the infected horse could even perform hard work. But this always gave way in the end to acute glanders. (Farcy, or "skin glanders", was added to the regulations in 1873.)

The official figures for 1874 showed that 401 stables were returned as affected by glanders and 121 by farcy. The number of horses infected during the year was 532 (and 132 by farcy). 477 (ninety-seven)were slaughtered; twenty-four (eleven) died, nineteen (twenty-one) were reported as "recovered", and twelve (three) were still under treatment at the end of the year. But the statistics are nonsensical. They represent only those cases where the inspectors could not be deceived. General ignorance about the danger was responsible for an attitude that was anti-social.

g. *Cruelty*

Sins of omission and of commission are supposed to be distinct, but the dividing line between neglect and positive cruelty is difficult sometimes to draw. The first Act in Britain for the protection of animals from human beings was passed in 1822, and Richard Martin became the object of general derision as a result of it. Nevertheless, the Royal Society for the Prevention of Cruelty to Animals was founded in 1824. It faced an uphill task and, as far as town horses were concerned, the problem in some senses grew worse during its first fifty years to 1874, because the direct connexion of the average carter with the civilising influence of the countryside from where his family had originated was becoming steadily weaker. The barbarising effect of urban life (so far as the poor were concerned) was more powerful than could be counteracted by the influx of young lads from the farms, anxious to try their luck in the town, who had a deeper understanding of the needs we all have, animals included, at our birth, life and death. There were fewer of these young fellows prior to 1874 than there were to be soon afterwards, when agricultural depression drove them out from their homes.

Our friend John Wilson the parson in 1849 wrote about cruelty. He stated the position somewhat strongly. "The driving of horses in wagon-draught, and especially in cart-draught, requires much attention, great care, and considerable kindness, and is, in a deplorable proportion of instances, very ill or even very cruelly performed. The driving of cart-horses on the streets and in the neigh-bourhood of large towns, in particular, is often performed in a manner alto-gether heartless or savage. Constant urging, frequent whipping, occasional kicking or striking, and general inattention to the several methods of averting pain, or of alleviating labour, are so often the characteristics of horse-driving in cities as to have been a main cause of procuring for Britons, among our con-tinental neighbours, the atrocious reputation of being the most cruel nation in Europe."

Perhaps we can argue with his last sentence, for brutality was not really such an English monopoly as he wished to shock us into thinking. It was, in 1849, a pretty general characteristic, at least of the civilised world. However that may be, it is a rather refreshing pleasure to see Mr. Wilson observing how things ought to be done. "A good driver sees that both the yoke and the load are properly adjusted: he avoids ruts and inequalities upon the road; he makes gradual deflexions in order to pass vehicles and obstructions, and uses general precaution against any jerk or sudden change of motion; he pursues an oblique line in winding upon an acclivity or upon a rough or adhesive level; he keeps constantly beside his horse and never rides on his cart or waggon when it is laden; he makes any occasional alterations in the centre of gravity which are requisite to equalise either the draught or the pressure; he does not permit his horse to stand with a strain upon him on a declivity; he forbears, except in extreme cases, all use of a whip; and in general, he acts with kindness, with consideration, and with a steady regard to both the comfort of the animal and the economising of his labour. Such a man takes more work out of an inferior horse than a bad driver can get out of a superior one; and he, at the same time, prevents all the outrage upon good moral order, and all the enormous indirect injury to society, which arise from the practice of cruelty."

It was only very slowly indeed that any progress at all was made towards a more considerate attitude to working horses in towns. The Metropolitan Free Drinking Fountain Association is a commendably early, and rare, example of a kind thought. Its first fountains, in 1859, were for people, but in 1864–1866 it put the first public animal troughs in London – at Highgate Hill, Roehampton, Maida Hill, Finsbury and Kilburn. Their siting was decided by the needs of cattle in transit rather than of resident horses, but the latter were welcome to use them. Shortly afterwards, the organisation was re-named the Metropolitan Drinking Fountain and Cattle Trough Association, and did much good work. But this sort of thing was a shining light in a dark age, and it was not really until Anna Sewell's only book was published – in 1877, three years after the end of this period, and the year before she died – that the public seriously began to think about the plight of many of the horses working in towns. It required *Black Beauty* to open their eyes, in the same way as they had not thought much about slavery until they read *Uncle Tom's Cabin*. If one makes an allowance for the sentimentality and accepts that she and her intended readers were genteel persons, we find she gives a picture of London horse life and management in the 'seventies that does not leave as much to the imagination as one might expect. Thinly disguised as a narrative, the book is really a series of little sermons. In the story of Ginger, the well-bred chestnut mare, she declaims against harsh methods of breaking, bearing-reins, docking and the use of blinkers. Cart-horses rarely appear in her book, but she does introduce one pair that was badly knocked about by their carter, who had clearly been drinking and poured forth some abusive language. The good Mr. Wright was introduced into the story especially to write down the name and address on the cart and to say, "I never see a wicked thing like this without doing what I can, and many a master has thanked me for letting him know how his horses have been used."

It is somewhat surprising that this semi-invalid spinster lady of Brighton (she was fifty-seven when the book was published) not only knew so much of her subject but trained her horse-characters to explain matters so clearly to those who knew less. Indeed, the continuance of cruelty was largely due to the thoughtless indifference of the general public. "It was a very rare thing for any one to notice the horse that had been working for him," said Black Beauty. "I have known ladies do it now and then, and this gentleman and one or two others have given me a pat and a kind word; but ninety-nine out of a hundred would as soon think of patting the steam-engine that drew the train."[37]

In the last year of the period under review, the tax on horses was abolished. Young William Pitt had started it all in 1784, when he proposed the idea as a "tax on luxury" to which only carriage and saddle horses would be subject. Amid the uproar that this provoked, there were many who warmly supported him and urged that it should be extended to farm horses – in order, of course, to encourage the greater use of oxen. At the end of the century, duty became payable on all horses.[38] Mares kept solely for breeding were exempted in 1819 and in 1822,[39] after six years' suspension, the tax on agricultural horses was abolished. But Governments had never resisted the attractions of obtaining revenue from the horse and so, when at last all such duty was finally abolished in 1874, there was great joy and relief. It gave a mild fillip to town-horse ownership, which was in any case beginning a period of rapid growth. But, if it affected gelding management at all, it was perhaps adversely. If we have to pay tax on something, we tend to take special care of it. But let us hope there were those who devoted to their horse the few extra shillings that the abolition of the tax left in their pocket.

10. LIVERPOOL POINTS THE WAY

In 1825, an American journalist dispatched to his New York paper a news-letter about Liverpool. "There is a striking peculiarity", he wrote, "in the carts and dray-horses of this town. Both are heavy beyond anything which has met my observation. One of the cars I should say outweighs four of ours, forming a load for an ordinary team. They are apparently more unwieldy than a Pennsylvania wagon. The horses, however, are proportionately large, being of the real Brobdignag breed. Their legs are like mill-posts. They are well fed, strong, but clumsy. They lumber along the streets with a jar like the carriages of heavy artillery, carrying sometimes three or four tons at a load. It is said that these horses degenerate when exported to other countries." So impressed was he by the sight of them that he recorded a story he had been told about a pair hauling timber from the quay side. The ship's captain, irritated by the slowness of the work, ordered the driver to whip them up: the load had somehow got hitched to the vessel and the horses responded by pulling away its stern as well. The editor printed the story but added a footnote, "This is a bouncer."

Bouncer or not, the size and strength of the dock and dray-horses of Liverpool had been remarkable from the early days of that city's rapid growth as a great port. Its demand for such great animals had already turned the Fylde into a considerable breeding-ground, the foundation stock always coming, and being continually replenished, from the eastern counties. And it is in Liverpool that in mid-century we see the growth of a custom into a movement which was in due course to improve the condition and management of town-horses and the status and self-respect of the men who had to work with them. And this was something which was more desperately needed, in view of the widening gap between town and country life among the poorest parts of the population, than it ever had been before.

The Liverpool May-Day Parade was inaugurated, according to the belief of those who managed it in more sophisticated Edwardian and Georgian times, in the year 1863. But in reality it began before that – how long before, it is impossible to say, because, to start with, it was not an organised affair at all. Thoroughly urban as it was (and no place except the most dismal slums of Manchester, Leeds or London was more divorced from rural life than Liverpool was then), it seems to have had its roots in country customs, or at least in some dim memory of them. That is, it was no creation of the social "do-gooders" or even of the horse-improvers, as the later London parade was to be, but was, in origin at least, spontaneous.

Since 1863 has been claimed as the foundation year, let us see what the *Liverpool Mercury* had to say about it then. "Yesterday being May-day, the usual custom of decorating the horses and carts and the omnibuses was observed, perhaps to a greater extent than on any previous occasion, ribbons, flowers, and favours of various kinds being profusely employed. The effect was, of course, heightened by the fineness of the weather, which, for once within the last few days, presented the appearance of warm and genial spring. With their accustomed activity, the London and North Western Railway Company were prominently represented in the display, the arrangements having been under the efficient direction of Mr. Charles Cooper, the superintendent of the northern division."

Mr. Cooper deserves full marks for his enthusiasm, because a history of the town-horse, when it is written, will not show the railways in the best of lights during the 'sixties. Thirty horses from Lime-street Station were there, and so were the parcels horses. "Another pleasing feature was that presented by the company's draught horses, whose fine appearance attracted considerable notice. They were all more or less gaily decorated, considerable pains having been taken by Mr. Livock, general superintendent of the horse department, to maintain the recognised superiority of the stud."

There seems to have been no general parade at all. "In various parts of the town might also have been seen throughout the day the carts of private firms whose employers seemed to vie with each other in making the most attractive display." In a long list of honourable mentions, there were brewers – W. J. Hammond, and Allsopps, for example; coal merchants – the Atherton, Haydock, and other companies; the Leigh Colliery; Thomas Leicester, of the Scotland-road Mills; and many others, as well as cab horse proprietors, and 'bus owners such as Messrs. Busby and the Omnibus Conveyance Company. But, to return to heavy horses, "As usual, the teams belonging to Messrs. Rose and Ellison, the contractors under the Corporation, were brought out, and made a very effective display."[40]

In 1866, in order to cope with the compulsory slaughter provisions of the Cattle Diseases Prevention Act, the Corporation resolved to employ its own veterinary surgeon. Up to that time, a private practitioner had occasionally been called in, at a fee of 1 guinea a time, to advise the inspectors of cattle when they needed him, but otherwise there was no local authority veterinary man. . Among those who applied for the post was Richard Sam Reynolds, then just twenty-five years of age. The son of a well-known veterinary surgeon at Mansfield, he had qualified at the Royal College of Veterinary Surgeons a month or two before his 21st birthday (there was not so much to learn in his day) and had since been assisting his father. A Council minute of 2nd January 1867 records laconically that it was resolved, "That Mr. Richard Reynolds, junior, of Mansfield, be appointed Veterinary Surgeon, at the salary of £200 per annum, he to devote his whole time to the duties of his office."

In fact, he was to devote thirty-five years to those duties, and it is doubtful whether any veterinary surgeon did more for the well-being of the town horse than he did. This is a somewhat large claim, in view of the number of outstanding contributors to that task, including his own successor. But it must be remembered that this young man was a missionary in very murky and unsanitary territory at a time when the town horse had travelled as far from the healthy life of the open plain and pastures as he ever was to do in all his history. He soon persuaded the Council that it would be more efficient and economical (that was the decisive point) to own its own draught-horses instead of relying upon contractors. He was, in addition, a great pioneer of the movement towards a pedigree system of breeding. From his very appointment he busily collected information about the ancestry of notable cart-stallions, as he had done from his youngest days in his father's Nottinghamshire practice. By 1874, he knew more about English Cart-horse or Black Horse pedigrees than any man in England. He was responsible for the 1,000 or so horses, heavy and others, that the Corporation now owned (a number that was later to rise to 3,700 tram horses and 300 draught horses), and was on the way to being regarded as the greatest authority in England on town-horse management and one of the best judges at shows.

Since 1874 is the terminus of this chapter, *The Mercury* account of the May-Day Parade of this year may be appropriate. The writer somewhat self-consciously drew attention to the fact that "fondness for the few festal days that still remain in the English calendar is as strong as of yore, although the manner of showing it may be different . . . In no particular, perhaps, is the distinction between 'town and country' more marked than in the way of keeping the first day of the merrie month . . . In the town celebration, it has lost nearly all its poetry. The display takes more a practical than a poetic shape. It tends to bring before the public eye the vast resources of a great commercial community: and this display, with its somewhat rude attempt at pageantry, has unquestionably many attractions . . .

"On no occasion was the celebration more successful than yesterday. The weather was all that could be desired, and in every way suitable for an out-door display. The streets were crowded by thousands of spectators, dressed in holiday attire, who turned out to see the grand May-Day spectacle. And a noble sight it was, and one which perhaps no other town in the world could equal. There were hundreds of gaily caparisoned horses which, for quality of breed, strength, and beauty, have never been excelled, and which called forth the admiration of all who had the pleasure of witnessing the gallant display. These fine animals, and the brightly-painted vehicles to which they were attached, with their drivers bright with ribbons and favours, made a right gay cavalcade.

"There were nearly all kinds of horses represented – the noble, strong-limbed, stately dapple grey, most used in Liverpool for dray purposes: the light, well-bred, fast-trotting butcher's galloway; and the miserable spavined screw, which began its career in aristocratic 'carriage work', but whose declining years are spent in dragging some broken-down coster's cart in Marybone. But all the drivers seemed proud of their vehicles and animals – whether it was the dignified-looking drayman, happy in his new hat and smock frock, or the poor rag collector in tattered garments, who, although somewhat untidy himself, had devoted his energies to the grooming and decoration of his donkey and the painting of his breakdown-looking cart . . .

"The corporation teams were exceptionally fine, and bespoke the skill which Mr. Reynolds had shown in their selection, and the care which had been disposed in their grooming and keep . . . This annual display seems to have its good effect not only in the horses being better looked after and attended to, and the waggons and carts kept in good order by having at least one good coat of paint annually, but it also stimulates the men in endeavouring themselves to present a respectable and tidy appearance."

The fire department led with two steam fire-engines, followed by a salvage cart, nightsoil carts, water-carts and so on to the number of eighty, one of them bearing the legend "Long life and success to our Queen, the Mayor, Aldermen,

Councillors and Burgesses of Liverpool". Two of the 120 Corporation horses, all decorated with artificial flowers over their harness and with gaudy loin cloths, had cost 200 guineas the pair – an enormous sum for cart horses at that time. Twenty-two different brewers and wine merchants were represented. One miller sent thirty two-horse flour wagons, with a band of music on the leading one. Carver & Co, the carriers, had twenty-four two-horse and fifty-two one-horse lorries there. The L.N.W.R. led the railways as usual, but the Lancashire & Yorkshire were represented, for the first time, with twelve lorries and a string of twenty unharnessed horses following them, thanks to the enthusiasm of the new manager, Mr. John O. Windle who took an interest "in all portions of the staff". The contractor to the Great Northern, the North British, and the Manchester, Sheffield & Lincolnshire railways had 100 horses and eighty lorries on view, some constructed to carry 20 tons when laden. The Mersey Steel & Iron Company had seven teams in the procession, "the waggons containing gigantic castings executed at the works". Innumerable coal merchants, corn merchants and timber merchants, potato dealers, general dealers, builders and other traders contributed to the heavy horse part of the affair.

The reporter, who wrote exhaustively, made no attempt to compute the number of heavy or other horses taking part. Sam Hague's minstrels were on a band carriage drawn by five pairs of greys, with postillions in pink and white striped jackets, buckskin breeches, and boots. Messrs. Bass, Ratcliff and Gretton stole a march on all the local brewers by giving a huge luncheon party with a liberal supply of best bitter and choice old ale. By the end of the day, however, their rivals had sold, not given away, vast quantities of their own brews in the crowded pubs. More important, many humble horses were clean and well-harnessed, and had been well looked after in preparation for the great day: what is more, many humble carters had had such a day, a day of glory. And similar junketings had been going on in Birkenhead, too.

CHAPTER V

1874-1878

The Stud-book Movement

(N.B. IN this and subsequent chapters, names of horses which are in the Stud-book are in Roman type, and of unregistered animals in *italic*. In the former case, the registration number has been generally omitted – but not always. For example it has been included where there might be confusion between two or more well-known animals of the same name. The same practice has been followed in the Index.)

I. AN END TO AGRICULTURAL PROSPERITY

If one of the principal causes of the neglect of good cart-horse breeding in the two middle quarters of the nineteenth century was the profitable nature of every other form of farm produce, animal and vegetable, it is equally true that the agricultural depression of the last quarter had the contrary effect, simply because heavy horses now became the only produce that was both easily saleable and steadily rising in price. 1874 is generally selected by historians (except those who are caught by the fashion of arguing the depression almost out of existence) as the date which marks the end of "high farming" and the beginning of the bad times. By a coincidence (it was no more than that), it was also the year when the first moves towards the formation of the national heavy-horse breeding societies were made.

In 1874, of course no one expected the agricultural community to face ruin. Two years later, 108 pages of *The Journal of the Royal Agricultural Society* were devoted to a symposium "On the relative profits to the farmer from Horses, Cattle, and Sheep Breeding, Rearing and Feeding in the United Kingdom".[1] The conclusion, drawn by W. Macdonald, editor of *The North British Agriculturist*, was what everyone had known for years – that horses were the least profitable. Hunter and carriage-horses could not be reared by ordinary rent-paying farmers with profit: draught-horses breeding could be done more extensively with benefit to the farmer, but was made difficult by the lack of good sound stallions. No one needed a panel of experts to tell him this. These gentlemen would have been more useful if they had been clairvoyant enough to see that, within fifteen years or so, many hundreds of tenant farmers would be quite unable to pay their rent and would face bankruptcy (if they had not been already overcome by it) and that hundreds more were to keep going simply by breeding and selling good cart foals. Many landlords also kept their heads above water both indirectly through this activity and directly by taking up the business themselves.

There are several reasons why the stud-book movement actually preceded this state of affairs, if only by a year or two. In the first place, the heavy-horse breeding industry was over-due for inclusion in the general pattern of scientific improvement and planning which marks Victorian husbandry: that is, the real question is not why the movement began before 1885 or 1895, but why it had not started in 1865 or 1855, and the answer is simply that no one had then "got round to it". Secondly, there was a combination of circumstances, more or less trivial in themselves, which simultaneously gave the breeders the push they needed. In the towns, there was a great deficiency of good sound heavy geldings in face of a growing demand, which caused prices to rise at least 25% between 1860 and 1875. This shortage began to be met, between 1874 and 1876, by a sudden increase in importations from Belgium (12,033 in 1874; 25,757 in 1875; 40,763 in 1876), to which great publicity was given and which was regarded as an affront and an insult to British farming, and therefore as a challenge. In Scotland, the activities of Lawrence Drew, though of incalculable benefit to heavy-horse breeding in general, precipitated a crisis which demanded quick and decisive action. In all non-Suffolk England, the Earl of Ellesmere emerged as the first enthusiast whose social position and wealth and personal abilities fitted him to be a leader of a hitherto unorganised industry. In Suffolk, they had been on the point of forming a society for some years. It was no coincidence, of course, that all three stud-books were ultimately organised within the same eleven months. It was merely a matter of rivalry.

Where it seems difficult to serve both logic and clarity in relating the events of these four or five busy years, the claims of clarity have been preferred. For this reason, the foundation of the Clydesdale Society is described before the work of Lawrence Drew. It is necessary also in some instances to reach back to events of fifty or more years earlier, but no apology is offered for this, either. An annalistic account of affairs, too rigidly adhered to, is sometimes meaningless.

2. THE EARL OF ELLESMERE

In 1757, the twenty-one year old Francis Egerton, 3rd (and last) Duke of Bridgewater, first came from London to his Worsley Hall estate near Manchester, and immediately began to plot with his agent, John Gilbert, how to carry coal faster and in greatly increased quantities from the mines to Manchester, and perhaps to the Mersey estuary, by means of a canal. Nineteen years later, James Brindley had completed the waterway that ran from Worsley over the Irwell at Barton to Stretford and, from there, right into Manchester at Castlefield basin in one direction and to Runcorn in the other.

The energetic young duke became eventually, in Charles Hadfield's words, the awesome "Grand Panjandrum"[2] of the British inland navigation system. When he died in 1803, the Bridgewater Trustees took over the control of the canal and his great-nephew, Lord Francis Leveson-Gower, succeeding to the estates, assumed the name of Egerton. He was created Earl of Ellesmere in 1846 and died in 1857. His son died five years later when thirty-nine and so, at the age of fifteen and still at Eton, Francis Charles Granville Egerton became the third Earl. He went up to Trinity College, Cambridge, took his degree at the age of twenty and then cast around for something additional to cricket, racing, shooting, the writing of novels, the ownership of about 13,300 superficial acres and of a vast mineral wealth below many of them, for the satisfaction of his enthusiasms. Almost his first action on coming of age was to appoint Captain Henry Heaton, a Fenman from Chatteris, as manager of the Worsley Hall farms. Even as they walked the estate, beneath their feet there still moved the coal-boats along the forty-two branching miles of fantastic underground canal driven far into the mines on four different levels, which his predecessor, also at the age of twenty-one, had planned 111 years before. The main surface canal wound its way through the park, from parts of which the chimneys of Manchester were visible, and to which vast multitudes of industrial workers looked as their favourite resort, with its pleasant lanes and trees and grass.

Next year (1869), the Earl and his manager went to the Royal Show, which happened to be at Manchester, and bought a two-year-old colt called Columbus which had won second prize for Thomas Shaw of Winmarleigh, in the Fylde. Bred by R. Burnett at Holbeach, he was by The Admiral, than whom no Fens horse could have had a better pedigree, since his sire was the celebrated Dack's Matchless and his dam by Seward's Major. (These horses are discussed in Part B. VIII.1 and V.4.) Columbus' dam was by England's Glory (731), a grandson of Seward's Major. His lordship liked the look of the horse and the captain knew what its breeding signified. They had made a good start. The following spring, Henry Heaton went to see Mr. Thacker at Benwick, only a few miles from his old home, and bought the famous stock-horse Heart of Oak, foaled in 1859 and now eleven. He was a massive black, with 13¼ inches of bone below the knee, the truest product of the Fens, bred at Bury near Ramsey by John Rowell, one of the best-known and most respected of breeders, as his son was to be after him. History was to make this horse one of the eight "foundation sires" of the modern breed. (See B. VIII.2.) The Earl of Ellesmere was now on the way to becoming the first great landowner, the first man with influence outside the circle either of his own neighbours or of the farming business, to have a stud of English cart-horses for the express purpose of breeding them on scientific principles of pedigree and conformation.

The stud farm was scarcely small – about 1,000 acres. All the buildings were specially planned and constructed, and included over 100 horse boxes. The animals were kept in a natural breeding state – the mares and foals and other young stock out at grass and the stallions in open sheds with large straw-yards for exercise. Shorthorns and Large White pigs were becoming the other Worsley specialities, but it was the cart-horses which their proprietor cherished. The shrewd and genial Heaton blessed the day when this opportunity had been offered him of showing what he knew about the breeding of these. He also picked a winner in appointing Edward McKenna as the stud-groom. In five years, a large number of mares and fillies was purchased, and eighteen stallions. Sixteen of the latter had been bred in the Fens, five of them at Chatteris itself by four different breeders: the other two were bred in the Fylde, but even they were by the most famous horse of his time, the Fen-bred Honest Tom (1105), of whom more will be said later.

In 1876 and the following year, the stud had a phenomenal success with the first horses entered for shows. At the Royal in Birmingham three firsts, one third and three reserve: at the Liverpool Royal the champion cup, five firsts, three seconds and four thirds. By the time the 1877 foals had arrived, the accommodation was strained to its limits. In spite of private sales constantly being made, there were over 100 horses. These included twenty stallions, many of them let to agricultural societies and noble landowners whom Lord Ellesmere was trying to fire with enthusiasm for the improving of their tenants' horses. So his lordship determined to have the first of what he always called his "weeding-out" sales. This took place on Wednesday, 13th February the following year and was conducted by G. M. Sexton of Ipswich. Cart-horse men from all parts, Scotland and Suffolk included, travelled to Manchester and made the fifteen minute railway journey from Victoria Station. Judged by the standards of even ten years later, either at Worsley or at other places where his example of having a "home-sale" was followed, the prices were far from spectacular. This was partly because it really was a weeding-out sale: only a few of the best animals were offered and these were surplus stallions. Among them was old Columbus, now eleven. One of his sons, *Young Admiral*, had been sold to a United States buyer for £800 and now he himself went for 290 guineas to James Howard, M.P., the farm-implement manufacturer of Bedford who, with his brother Charles, was an ardent cart-horse breeder on their Britannia farms. Some of the Ellesmere animals were Clydesdales or had Clydesdale blood. But it was not necessarily the Scotch ones that went to Scotland. For 310 guineas Mr. Wilson took back to Dumfries Honest Tom III whose pedigree, as far as can be traced over several generations, does not take us more than a dozen miles round the Isle of Ely. Another Mr. Wilson, of Kendal, bought for 165 guineas "the grand old Mrs. Muir", an eleven-year-old Clydesdale in foal to the Chatteris-bred Young Samson (i.e. 1980), but Mrs. Muir's yearling filly by Honest Tom III went only to the other side of Manchester for 70 guineas. Col. Williamson from Perthshire bought the three-year-old Roving Boy for 240 guineas, whose dam was reported as by a Clydesdale horse out of an English mare, whereas his sire was said to be by an English horse out of a Clydesdale mare. (He and his sire were both registered later in the English book when it was started.) The two-year-old Cambridge Tom (290 guineas) is an example of the vagueness of pedigree at that time. He was bred by one H. Edwards of Waterbeach out of "a prize mare by Bailey's horse" – presumably James Bailey of Wilburton, Ely and possibly his Honest Tom (1113). His sire is better authenticated. It was King Tom, bred and owned by Henry Bultitaft of Bedwell Hay, Ely, who like his father before him was a stallion owner in a big way of business.

The forty-five animals made £6,184. 10s. od., twenty-nine females averaging £101. 3s. 2¾d. and sixteen males £203. 3s. 6d. It was, incidentally, not the practice then to use 1st January in determining the age of cart-horses, and the animals appear in the catalogue as a year younger than they were by the later system of reckoning, introduced by the stud-book societies. Only one animal, the nine-year-old *Dainty*, had a reserved price on her, and she was unsold at 400 guineas. *Countess*, also nine, had gone temporarily lame, but Lord Ellesmere would not withdraw her, and at 45 guineas she was the best bargain of the sale. One very ordinary yearling colt was unfit, so he sportingly substituted Peeping Tom, which he had not really wanted to sell, and he made the highest price of the day at 370 guineas.

The Earl had played very fair with his customers and now he paraded before them his brood mares and his stock horses, to give them an idea of what they could expect in the future. The latter numbered five. The chief one was the Young Samson that had covered the grand old Mrs. Muir. He was a seven-year-old bay bred almost on the very banks of the Old Bedford River and bought from Frederic Street of Somersham Park, St. Ives. He had won a special £60 prize at the Birmingham Royal Show in 1876 and a £100 cup presented by the Mayor of Liverpool at the Royal Show there in 1877 for the best draught-horse of any breed. Standing 17.1-hands on very short legs, with massive bone and abundant hair, there was no doubt where he hailed from. Somewhat unexpectedly, he was a wonderful mover. His lordship announced he would never be shown again but would be available for fifty mares at 8 guineas. His three-year-old bright chestnut son Samson II, bred on the same farm, equally heavy-built, was also open to fifty nominations, at 5 guineas. Pride of the Shires, bay, Chatteris-bred through and through, five years old, would take 100 mares at 3 guineas. The three-year-old dark chestnut British Wonder was another that Captain Heaton had obtained from Frederic Street the year before, for 278 guineas. He was by none other than Charles Marsters' celebrated England's Wonder, the Old Strawberry, and would stand at 4 guineas. Last but not least was the old black horse himself, Heart of Oak, now nineteen. The odd thing about him, retrospectively, is that his service fee was only 3 guineas.

However, of far wider significance than the sale itself was the conversation that took place the evening before, when a large party of breeders of all kinds of cart-horses dined at the Queen's Hotel in Manchester as guests of Lord Ellesmere. His lordship wanted a particular word with Frederic Street who, he had learned from Henry Heaton, was due in less than three weeks' time to read a paper to the Farmers' Club in London on the breeding and management of cart-horses. (Arrangements for this had only just been concluded. Mr. Street had suggested, as late as November, that it was about time the subject was considered, and it had taken Mr. Druce, the secretary, several letters to persuade him to write the paper himself.) Lord Ellesmere button-holed the older man, and asked him whether he would be prepared to turn the occasion into a proposal to form a stud-book association for their type of horse. The Clydesdale men and the Suffolk men had both, within the past year, organised themselves in this way, and it was essential not to be left behind. James Howard, pleased with his purchase of Columbus, agreed to support Mr. Street if he raised the matter. And so, of course, did Henry Heaton. The Hon. Edward Coke was also a guest and told Mr. Street that he could put him down for any job of work he liked, to help the movement forward. This was a valuable capture.

With this dinner, the Earl of Ellesmere pushed English cart-horse breeding from its somewhat murky obscurity into the light of day. There was of course much banter between the supporters of rival breeds, and a difference of opinion between James Howard and Herman Biddell from Suffolk could have developed into something of a row, if they had not been his lordship's guests. Mr. Howard advanced the theory that, when they had been in open competition up to 1861, the Suffolks had won most of the Royal Show prizes simply because Suffolk men wholly ruled the Council and always managed to get Suffolk judges appointed for the cart-horses. Biddell regarded this as utterly preposterous. The discussion was eventually diverted to other topics, but both were left with somewhat ruffled feathers. (Biddell later claimed that he regarded Howard's argument "too feeble to live long". But when a few months later he found "this mouldy story dished up again . . . in an otherwise excellent article on Shire-breds, by Mr. Street",[3] he was enraged, particularly at the latter's appeal to R.A.S.E. records as evidence. He said that Street did not get any support at all from these records: he had merely "rescued the idea from the smoke and ashes of after-dinner cigars at Manchester".[4]

3. THE FYLDE: T. H. MILLER AND PARSON WOOD

Leonard Charles Wood, born on 12th May 1819, at Ash Hall, Glamorganshire, became a scholar of Jesus College, Oxford and then took holy orders. In 1843, after having served less than a year as deacon at Fleetwood, he was appointed by the lord of the manor, Joseph Hornby, to the vicarage of Singleton (five miles as the crow flies from the sands of Blackpool). In 1852, Alderman Thomas Miller, a very distinguished personage in the town of Preston, where he owned several cotton mills, bought the Singleton Park Estate from the Hornby family, pulled down the church (which had been built only fifty-three years earlier, to replace a tiny dilapidated building) and erected a handsome new edifice big enough to seat 300 people. He died in 1865, and was succeeded by his son Thomas Horrocks Miller, who was twenty-one years of age.

The new squire was a young man after Parson Wood's heart. Like his father, he was a staunch supporter of the Church. But he also had great ideas about improving the live-stock and horses in that part of the Fylde, which was Mr. Wood's great enthusiasm also. First, in 1869, they organised a small company of local landowners with a view to the encouragement of light-horse breeding. But Wood knew that the ordinary tenant farmers would gain most if a real impetus could be given to the breeding of heavy dray-horses. There was a wonderful market for these in the Lancashire towns, and the Fylde was as ideal a place to produce them as anywhere in England. So, in 1871, they gave up the first venture and founded the Fylde Cart-Horse Breeding Improvement Company. Parson Wood was the secretary and treasurer, and the third most prominent member was Thomas Townley Townley-Parker of Cuerden Hall, Preston. They bought a stallion called *Carbinier*. This was a useful sort of horse, but Miller was determined they should obtain the best. The most famous stallion in England was William Welcher's Honest Tom (1105). Welcher had bred him, and in 1867–1871 had won first prize with him at the Royal Show for five successive years. He was now six years old. Miller and Wood knew all about his soundness and his stock-getting qualities, and about his pedigree as well, and it was Miller himself who travelled to Watton in Norfolk to try to get him. According to legend, he was armed with gold sovereigns which he produced in instalments until Mr. Welcher's reluctance was overcome. But, since the final price was 500 guineas, this seems doubtful, unless he had extra pockets and a strong physique, or pushed them to the door of Griston Hall in a barrow. However, what matters is that Honest Tom came to Single-ton. For the Fylde Company, he won his sixth successive R.A.S.E. first prize in 1872.

If one horse can be said to have effected a complete transformation in the quality of cart-horses in an area so big as the Fylde, then Honest Tom did so. Farmers everywhere became enthusiasts, as well they might, for he proved a gold-mine. Within a few years, sheer quality advanced the price of his foals at weaning, from the modest £12 or £15 which breeders had been accustomed to expect, to as much as £100. One of his sons was to realise £600 as a two-year-old. Another, Admiral, bred by John Milner of Kirkham, was bought by Lord Ellesmere and was eventually sold (but only after becoming the first champion stallion of the breed in 1880) to an Australian who auctioned him on reaching home for £1,800. By 1880, indeed, the Fylde had risen to the top – and never since, by whatever method one may reckon, has it been possible to regard it as other than one of the three or four most successful breeding areas. The soil and conditions are perfect, and Fen blood thrived there.

The Cart-Horse Breeding Improvement Company was closed down after about four years, and Miller bought up Honest Tom, whose duties and successes continued unimpaired. By another stroke of genius, he also bought a young horse called Lincoln foaled in 1873, who proved, like Lord Ellesmere's Heart of Oak, in years to come to be one of the seven "foundation sires" of the breed (B.VIII.4). Perhaps the most remarkable thing about Thomas Horrocks Miller is that he not only provided the means to set the Fylde up as a great new home of the heavy-horse, but dealt personally with all the minutiae of affairs concerning his own stud. Even nominations to his stallions went direct to him. He loved handling every detail of the venture, despite the calls of his cotton mills in Preston and his local preoccupations, which included the complete re-modelling of the village and the building of a new house, Singleton Hall, in 1873. (Parson

Wood lived at Singleton Lodge, which former lords of the manor had occupied.) The Hall he filled with many fine paintings by English masters, mostly collected by his father, and many works of taxidermy, the *pièce de resistance* being a stuffed elephant's head, with a tiger clinging to its trunk. Perhaps it was as well that he had no children, by either of his marriages, to be terrified by this. Eventually, he stuffed Honest Tom's head as well, as we shall see.

The parson's early influence on his squire must not be underestimated, for when they first knew each other Wood was thirty-three and Thomas Miller a little boy of six. Wood, in return, owed much to the Millers, who encouraged his intense interest in stock-breeding and agricultural improvement. Earlier Singleton parsons had not been so lucky. In Elizabethan times, when the village was part of Kirkham parish, the unfortunate curate of the chapel, to maintain his family, felt obliged to keep a public house, to the utter neglect of divine service and the cure of souls – a dilemma which was solved by the temporary closure of the chapel. The curate of 1672 turned Congregationalist and practised medicine to support his family, but was excommunicated. The chapel later fell into the hands of Papists, who at last were forcibly ejected by the parishioners in 1745. It was only then that Singleton became a perpetual curacy independent of Kirkham. So Parson Wood's gifts had a better opportunity to thrive under the Miller regime than they could have done in earlier ages: and Miller, without Wood, might never have done the deeds that turned the Fylde men into the keenest of all supporters of the new stud-book movement. (For a further note on Mr. Wood, see section 11 of this chapter. For Honest Tom and Mr. Miller, see B.V.4).

4. WALTER GILBEY AND THE BISHOP'S STORTFORD CO.

It was not often that Walter Gilbey was misinformed. But, in making his way to the Glasgow Stallion Show in 1875, he certainly was. A dedicated Liberal, he was under the same misapprehension as his lordship the Conservative Prime Minister in understanding the Clydesdale to be "a pure breed". Indeed, he had already been instrumental in bringing some Scotch stallions to the Bishop's Stortford district. But he was now organising the neighbouring landowners and farmers into a mood of mutual assistance, and the aim was to obtain the best and purest-bred horse available.

After looking at the animals on show, he selected a fine young stallion for which he was asked £700, a price which hitherto would have been considered outrageous by proprietors of the miserable Essex mares. But his group was going to do nothing by halves so long as he was connected with it. He asked particulars of the breeding, and was told that only the pedigree of the sire could be given. (This was Drew's Prince of Wales, which accounts for the young animal's price and looks.) He declined to buy.

The next year, it was decided to make a business-like arrangement and the Bishop Stortford Agricultural Horse Company was launched in January 1877, with a capital limited to £2,000, for the purchase of two stallions. In fact,

£1,200 was raised – twelve promoter's shares at £50 and sixty preference shares at £10. Each preference share carried with it an obligation to send two mares to the company's stallion at 3 guineas and 5s. the groom, or forfeit these fees. If all went according to plan, everyone would get a full return with interest, and probably a bonus, on the sale of the stallions at the end of a fixed term. Walter Gilbey was the founder, persuader, chairman, and chief organiser. It was typical of him that he should expend so much energy for others on a scheme which would have been much simpler and more profitable to run as a private enterprise for himself. It was also a typical Gilbey touch that the groom's fee was to be twice the usual sum. The existing Clydesdale entires were to be got rid of.

In February £600 was paid for a five-year-old Lancashire-bred horse called Admiral, which they re-named Paragon. A 17-hands whole-coloured dark bay on black legs and very weighty, he was by none other than the Earl of Elles-mere's Columbus. Furthermore, his dam's breeding was known too, her sire being by the Fen-bred British Ensign (foaled 1859), a son of Dack's Matchless. The Company also bought the two-year-old colt Oliver, bred by Henry Coy at Little Downham. The Coy family had bred hundreds of horses on farms between Ely and the Hundred Foot Drain and, what is more, had had a remark-able habit of jotting down the pedigrees of their mares. The farmers of the Essex-Hertfordshire border could now make a real start, actually knowing what they were breeding with.

Since Walter Gilbey and his son, also Walter, are to figure prominently among the leaders of the English cart-horse movement for nearly seventy years, this is perhaps the place to say something of the father. Born in 1831, he was the sixth son of Henry and Elizabeth Gilbey. Henry, a coach proprietor at Bishop's Stortford who sometimes drove the London coach himself, was one of the thirteen children of Daniel Gilbey, landlord of the White Bear at Stanstead. Daniel's forbears had come to the district in Charles II's reign from Lincolnshire, where the family had held land in 1366 and are mentioned, in the Gainsbrough area, in 1209. Young Walter left the grammar school at the age of 15, worked in the office of his cousin, an estate agent at Tring, and then obtained a post at Westminster with parliamentary agents. When the Crimea War broke out, he and his brother Alfred were given jobs in the pay department and served in a convalescent hospital on the shores of the Dardanelles.

On their return home at the end of the war, the brothers were scarcely able to muster twenty shillings between them. Their decision to set up in the wine trade might therefore appear fanciful if it were not for the fact that the family had been previously connected with it, a near relation earlier in the century having been a leading shipper of port (and M.P. for St. Albans and Lord Mayor of London in 1811). They rented a cellar in Oxford Street, worked all the hours that they were able, lived on £2 a week each and, when they saw the advantage of the cheap dues on Cape wines, began to prosper. In 1858, Walter married Ellen Parish of Bishop's Stortford and on the birth of the first of their eight children, Henry Walter, on 1st October 1859, he and his wife were living on less than £4 a week. The firm's prospects could have been ruined when the duty on French wines was reduced from 1s. to 2d., but instead they took advantage of this market, too, and began to sell them cheaper than anyone else. They were joined by their brother Henry and the business expanded exceedingly. The Gilbeys' efforts would have been warmly applauded by Samuel Smiles as a perfect example to match all those he had quoted in *Self Help* – if only their trade had been something different. Mr. Smiles had once written a long article on "Drink" in Eliza Cook's Journal, beginning "The people of Great Britain are a very drinking people. The drinking of intoxicating liquors pervades our entire social system. We drink at births, marriages and deaths. We drink to enhance joy, we drink to drown sorrow" . . . and so on. "In short, one would almost imagine, from all the uses drink is put to, that it is the universal Catholic-con."[5] The long moral which conluded the article brought Eliza Cook a reward in the shape of a handsomely bound copy of *The Teetotallers' Companion*, presented by temperance advocates: but the sentiment of the opening sentences was the Gilbey brothers' inspiration.

It was not so much the size to which the business grew as the speed with which it did so that staggered even the mid-Victorians. The Pantheon, which had begun its existence in 1772 as the first West End theatre and was later turned into the Pantheon Bazaar, became the company's offices, in the very same street where they had begun in a cellar. By the time that Walter Gilbey travelled to Glasgow in his vain search for a pedigree stallion, he was the senior partner in the biggest wine merchants' business in the world, with its main outlets through grocery agencies, and, with the huge tobacco business that was joined to it, employing or engaging the energies of between nine thousand and ten thousand people. As a Liberal, Walter was a strong Home Ruler and the firm lost its Irish loyalist trade: but nationalist orders compensated them three-fold. It was calculated, not much later, that every fourteenth bottle of wine, and every thirty-ninth bottle of spirits drunk in the United Kingdom was supplied by the Gilbeys.

When he ceased to have to live on £4 a week, Walter bought Hargrave Park and took an interest in Jersey cattle. But he sold that and bought a house in Brighton. Two or three years there were enough, and so he was now firmly ensconced not far from where he was born, at Elsenham Hall. Here had lived, before him, George Rush, celebrated balloonist and breeder of race horses. Plenipotentiary, the famous Derby winner of 1834, was buried in the paddocks. And it was here that Walter Gilbey could give free rein to his passion for horses, including hackneys, cart-horses, thoroughbreds, hunters, polo ponies and Shetlands. His other chief interests, apart from fishing and shooting, hunting regularly once a week, and of course the management of his 8,000 acres, were the people who lived round about. Rarely has any man so identified himself with the needs and problems and desires of his neighbours, especially the poor ones: workers' cottages were one of his main concerns. Even that did not exhaust his energies. He experimented in the growing of fruit, lavender and mint and, when he succeeded in what he was aiming at, advertised and made much money out of his jam and lavender water.

Even among the giants of the nineteenth century, he was something of a phenomenon. He is of interest here, however, simply for the fact that he was unsparing of his talents and time in helping to promote the welfare of agriculture in general and horse-breeding in particular. The organisation of his local company for owning cart stallions is typical of all that he was to do in the future, for, although he rejoiced in lavish hospitality, he never attempted to dominate the financial scene, still less to subsidise anything that could be perfectly well supported by the democratic method of everyone contributing a little. When, in due course – thirteen years after the date we are concerned with here – the Prince of Wales presented him with a testimonial portrait of himself in recognition of his services to horse-breeding, there was something symbolic in the fact that it had been paid for by 1,250 people, each subscribing 1 guinea.

As to his appearance, the impressions of a colonial, when this presentation was made in 1891, were vivid. *The Melbourne Argus* reporter told his readers that he "looked like a wicked, worthless and volatile old dandy, and deliberately exaggerated this appearance. Tall, excessively slim, with very small feet and hands, time-worn face of the Voltaire type and scanty black hair carefully brushed to hide his baldness, his small moustache and large rimless eyeglass made him look like a wicked French marquis of the eighteenth century." The only difference between his evening and morning attire was in colour – black at night and russett in the daytime, with bright tie and white gaiters. The boggle-eyed *Argus* man was astonished to find that his manner was genial and unaffected. Those who knew him were well aware also that, as his manner was, so was his nature. *Vanity Fair* described him as "an energetic man with cultivated tastes, embracing agriculture, nankeen trousers, and the fine arts. His pet hobby is the British cart horse". The writer added that "if he were ever cast, destitute of raiment, upon some remote savage strand, and had contrived to save the medals he has won at agricultural shows, at home and abroad, they would be sufficient, if artfully disposed as a necklace, to ensure his admittance at once into the best-dressed circles". He was an abstemious man, and ate little meat. He had four sons and four daughters. All men connected with carthorses, from the Earl of Ellesmere to any groom that he ever had a word with, liked him.

The Hackney Society and the Hunters Improvement Society were to owe much to him, as was the Jersey Cattle Society. He was to serve for years on the council of the Royal Agricultural Society, and to be president of that too. The Royal Agricultural Benevolent Institution was to be indebted to his energetic efforts, as was the Thoroughbred horse, when his persuasiveness resulted in the money given and wasted by the Crown for racing plates being diverted to breeding. He wrote twenty-one books and a host of articles on farming, horse breeding and sporting topics. But these things, in 1877–1878, were still in the future, as were his efforts on behalf of cart-horses and the men who bred and used them.

To return to Paragon, that Lancashire horse of pure Fen blood, his activities up to the time of his purchase by Walter Gilbey require explanation. As a three-year-old, he had been shown at the Glasgow stallion show, where he won third prize before having a season with Scottish mares. At the age of four, he had been in the top five at the same show, and had served the Anglo-Scottish mares in the district of Penrith. And it was to Glasgow that Mr. Gilbey had to travel, once again, the next year to buy him for duty on the borders of Essex and Hertfordshire. His career sums up the alleged "purity" of both the Scottish and the English variety of cart-horse.

The Bishop's Stortford Company was not unique, except in its Gilbeian organisation and éclat. It had been anticipated in 1873 by a couple of Cornish groups of farmers, who bought two Clydesdale stallions at £300 apiece. If anyone came before that, the memory of them has perished. An East Kent Cart-Horse Society was also founded about this time. And so was the South Devon Horse Association, whose secretary, D. R. Scratton, travelled up from Ogwell, near Newton Abbot to Lord Ellesmere's sale and bought a five-year-old son of Heart of Oak, the black-brown Royal Oak for 200 guineas. One observer described this horse as "a thoroughly useful sort, and quite a good country stallion – just the kind to improve ordinary mares".[6] In such outlandish cart-horse areas as South Devon or East Kent or even Bishop's Stortford, there seemed to be no alternative, if one wanted to use a good stallion, to buying one. No one would be silly enough to send a high-class horse there to travel for casual fees. If a few keen spirits could band themselves together and form a company to share the expense, so much the better. But, if the horse died or there was an accident, or when he needed to be replaced in a few years' time by one to cover his daughters, or when farmers could not agree among themselves (stallion-sharing was the first experiment in agricultural co-operation since enclosures had altered the whole atmosphere of farming), so much the worse. Very few companies were to last long, because there was a far better way of doing things – the "Scotch system".

5. MONTGOMERY AND THE SCOTCH SYSTEM

During the time of confusion in England, the chief agents in the steady improvement of the Scottish horse, and especially the notable advance in the standard of the average specimen, had been the local clubs and societies for the hiring of stallions. There was now, in 1874, a network of these co-operative associations, spread all about the areas where breeding was seriously undertaken. Many of them had been running without interruption since the 'thirties.

In mid-century, the societies had selected their horses at local spring stallion shows, but this was wasteful and inefficient. Owners had to hawk their horses round from show to show until they were hired, never knowing whether to exhibit at show A and then make for show B the next day, or go into another district to shows C, D and E. Accordingly, it was agreed in the late 'sixties that the exhibition organised by the Glasgow Agricultural Society should become a central hiring fair, and that local shows should be abandoned. Accredited deputations from societies were given tickets for a special enclosure set apart for them in the judging area, where they had a good view of the horses paraded in the two rings. In return for its efforts and for bearing the financial risk of running the parade, the Glasgow Society claimed first pick of two horses for itself. Any contract provisionally made by an owner with any other association was nullified if his horse was chosen for Glasgow.

The scheme was not without its teething troubles. In the first years, there was no formal entry – horses just arrived. But the Glasgow men had so many stall-fittings to put up in the Cattle Market that they began to insist on horses being entered in advance. No one at first took much notice of this rule and confusion was made worse by the Renfrewshire pirates who used to wait until the Glasgow date was announced and then fix a parade of their own for the day previous. Thomas Dykes in 1871 attended at Paisley and took a few names for Glasgow the next day but, although entries did not close until 10 o'clock at night, a large number of good horses arrived without notice on the following morning, many belonging to leading owners, and were refused entry. But by 1872 the problems were overcome and the Stallion Show was tending to become too big even for the full extent of the cattle market. In 1874, the Glasgow Society was giving a premium of £150 for its selected horses, with £2 service fee and £2 for each foal, compared with only £40 and 25s. per mare less than ten years before.

Every society, on selection of a horse, entered into a formal contract with the owner, but the details varied. Some associations guaranteed a minimum of mares, normally eighty, at a fixed service fee, a further fee being usually payable for each mare that was got in foal. Others offered a premium and reduced service and foaling fees, like Glasgow, but did not guarantee the number of mares. A few hired outright for the season, collecting all the fees themselves, and in these cases naturally a maximum number of mares was agreed.

There was nothing in England to compare with this. Of course, from time immemorial it had been part of the stallion-owner's business to show off his wares at some convenient place just before the start of the breeding season. On a market-day in March or early April, farmers in most districts had the chance of inspecting the dray or hackney or other sorts of stallions that were proposed to travel their neighbourhoods. Here, it might be only one or two; there, a dozen; in some places, twenty, thirty or even fifty. The whole affair was generally quite casual, and often presented a scene as near to chaos as we can imagine today. But gradually some of these parades became organised. The Macclesfield and District Chamber of Agriculture started a show in the yard of the Derby Arms, charging spectators 3d. for admittance, which effectively excluded loafers and small boys. A few agricultural societies, first and certainly foremost Peterborough, began to promote regular spring stallion shows. These attracted the keener spirits, even if the ordinary small farmer was at first disinclined to travel to the county town to see what was to be had.

Of course too, there had been, here and there, local groups who had got together to try to secure a good stallion for service in their district. A group in the High Peak district had got John Chadwick's five-year-old Black horse Sovereign for their use in 1822 by offering a premium. This horse was full of Dishley blood, which is a reminder that many of Bakewell's own stallion-lettings, as his letters to Culley suggest, were to ad-hoc groups rather than to individuals. But in England the practice had never been common and, during the time that the system was being improved and refined in Scotland, did not grow. In any case, this loose sort of arrangement, which was legally little more than the award of a prize of anything up to £100, often failed to work. The local men were sometimes enraged, if the season started slowly, by the sudden removal of the horse to more lucrative parts. Some groups cautiously withheld the premium, or part of it, until the end of the season, but that inhibited the owners from entering in the first place. There was no piece of business more likely than this to be the source of a good row.

The first regular society in "England" for hiring a stallion on the Scotch system was actually a Welsh one. This was the Montgomeryshire District Entire Horse Association, of which Edward Green of the Bank, Pool Quay and John Lewis, Great Weston, were the moving spirits. A prize of £100 was offered in 1876 with a guarantee of 100 mares at £3 each. Nineteen stallions from all parts of the country came forward and the bay four-year-old Marshland Prince, bred and owned by Edward Grundy of Pytchley Manor, Northants, was selected. But Green and his neighbours were not satisfied that this method of choosing a horse was always going to work. Who would send a really good one to Welshpool with only one chance of even earning its return railway fare? And, even if fifty owners took the risk, might not a fifty-first be the horse they really wanted? Accordingly a deputation was chosen to visit likely studs and with power to hire what they considered the most suitable available horse for 1877. They managed to get England's Wonder from Charles Marsters at King's Lynn for 100 mares, the owner to pay the expenses of travelling and to be paid half the £300 fee in April and the rest in July. This was a real capture, for the horse, now six years old, was one of the two most talked of stallions in the country. (See Part B.V.4. The other was Miller's Honest Tom, similarly bred.) *The Mark Lane Express* had already labelled him "the Stockwell of cart-horses", largely on the strength of four of his earliest get, two colts and two fillies having been sold for a total of £1,475 at the age of two. He nicked well with the Montgomeryshire mares, was hired again for the following season and left a lot of extremely good foals. He well earned his affectionate nick-name of the "Old Strawberry", and for many a long year there were good roans of this hue in the county. The Montgomeryshire men's adoption of the Scottish system of hiring by selection committee caused a great stir when it was publicised, and the quick success that attended their efforts played no little part in hastening the movement to form a stud-book society.

The men of Crewe were only a year behind in forming an association, with Lord Combermere as President. They offered a premium of £100 and guaranteed 100 mares at 2 guineas. These terms attracted forty-three candidates, probably because the railway made their centre more accessible than Welshpool. The same year, 1877, a fiasco experienced by Lord Carington at Aylesbury only emphasised the success of the Montgomery method. He offered a £50 prize to which £20 was added by the Buckinghamshire Society. But the local farmers were simply not prepared to pay a reasonable service fee and the winning horse was sold to Lord Camperdown at Shipston-on-Stour without doing anything to help the district.

In 1878, the Norfolk Agricultural Society organised a spring show of cart-stallions at the county town, and announced that prizes would be handed over only at the end of the season if the winners completed their thirteen weeks. But there would be no real success unless the farmers of a locality, or enough of them to make it economic, were keen enough to take an active part in the hiring: nor was the well-intentioned generosity of noble landlords of much use unless, like the Earl of Ellesmere, they were prepared to become heavy-horse breeders themselves.

The Montgomeryshire method, as modified in its second year, was to prove by far the best, both in the selection of the stallion and in the terms of hiring. Choosing the hoped-for sire of one's next-year's foals by means of a competitive show might secure a fine-looking horse, and perhaps even one with a known pedigree, too. But it had two serious drawbacks. Firstly, the judge was, almost inevitably and for obvious reasons, an impartial outsider who would base his choice on ideal characteristics, which were not necessarily those most suitable for the general type of mare in the district concerned. Secondly, pedigree and conformation reveal nothing of fertility. A selection committee, visiting a big stallion-owner, was able not only to choose a horse that they felt would best suit their sort of mares but to ask for evidence of his past record as a foal-getter. As this system became universal, recommendations from other societies became invaluable and, no less important, mutual trust grew between regular customers and the reputable supplier. The annual visit to the stallion-stud was not only a good day out for the club committee, and a hectic catering task for the stallion owner's wife, but an education in itself.

Furthermore, an outright hiring of the horse for the whole season, either exclusively or with a certain number of nominations reserved to the owner, was infinitely more satisfactory than any other arrangement. By collecting its own fees, the local society could ensure that the members, who footed the bill, could be given preference over others, who could be charged more. It could work out its own route for the stallion to walk, subject to an agreed maximum journey per day or distance per week. And it was a simple matter to write into the agreement that a substitute should be sent by the owner if the selected horse fell sick, broke down or was otherwise unable to do his work. The stallion-owner, for his part, could depend on the terms of the agreement being carried out, because the groom, although under the general direction of the society's secretary, was his man. In a wicked world, the Montgomery method was as foolproof and fraudproof as could be devised. But, in 1878, it was on its own. Co-operation, of any sort, between mare-owners was the exception rather than the rule. And many stallion-owners were so blind to the advantages of the new idea that they regarded this "club" business as a sort of sinister threat to free enterprise. It was a threat, of course, to the over-topped sideboned coarse-haired one-guinea screw, but that was a good thing.

6. A "NORMAN" SOCIETY IN THE U.S.A.

The new interest in cart-horse breeding was bound to result in the establishment of official pedigree registers similar to those being already started for several breeds of cattle. But, before any positive action was taken in Britain, a group of Americans actually formed a stud-book society, and this demands consideration here for five reasons. Firstly, theirs was the first register of any breed of horses whatsoever, other than the Thoroughbred. Secondly, their early difficulties were remarkably similar to those experienced by English and Clydesdale enthusiasts and are therefore instructive. Thirdly and more broadly, the Percheron is of particular historical interest because it has some claim to be more nearly related to the medieval war horse than any other modern kind – if pictures of Great Horses resemble any breed at all or have even the slightest resemblance to Great Horses as they really were, they make us think of the Percheron (e.g. especially Paul Potter's well-known painting of about 1652). Fourthly, this breed of horse was destined to loom large in our later story of cart-horse breeding in England. And fifthly, the American society – or, rather, its successor, after it had collapsed – was to be the one horse-breed association in the world which was bigger than that formed for Shires.

The story begins in the old French province of Le Perche, to the west and south-west of Paris and bordering the old province of Normandie to the west and north and Maine on the south-east. In the Dark Ages, it was almost entirely covered by trees and even after much of the land was cleared in the ninth century, splendid forests remained, among them Bellême. The bullying Robert de Bellême, the reader may remember, was he who brought heavy Continental stallions to Powis and Shropshire about 1100. He was unaffectionately known in France as Robert the Devil. His enemy and neighbour Rotrou, Count of Mortagne, Seigneur of Nogent and later Count of Le Perche, and son-in-law of Henry of England, twice fell into his hands after returning from distinguished Crusader service. But fortunately he had the last laugh for, while he was founding the abbey in 1109 which was later to become the celebrated head of the Trappist order, Robert the Devil was howling in the agonies of hell, or at least it was generally hoped that he was. If we are far from the point, we can return to it quickly. Rotrou was buried at Nogent, later named Nogent-le-Rotrou, which for generations has been the very centre, the very Peterborough or Ely, of Percheron breeding. In 1790, Le Perche was carved up into the departments of Orne, Sarthe, Eure et Loir, and Loir et Cher.

Like all European heavy-horses, the Percheron had been a charger in the Middle Ages and an energetic artillery horse and an agricultural horse and all sorts of other horses later. Unlike the English Black horse, he next became a coach horse of the faster type to be found in the days of the new roads and before the railways – an era which in France may be dated between 1800 and 1860. He then had a speed, even over rough ground, of 7½ miles an hour, or 10 m.p.h. if the stages were kind. He stood only about 15.2-hands. When the railways deprived him of this work, he was converted into a heavy draught-horse, in the doing of which mistakes were inevitably made, and in 1874 were still being made. Weight was achieved by crossing and, spurred on by a sudden fantastic demand from the United States, black was becoming now a favoured colour instead of the more correct and more beautiful dappled grey. In addition, the craze for making a dray-horse out of a medium-draught horse within twenty years was leading to elephantine ideas. (About 1885, M. Michel Fardouet, first President of the Percheron Society in France, owned a stallion Malekoff which weighed 21 swt. 68 lb. at the age of five and which had a son, owned by M. Collas of Nocé, which weighed 20 cwt. 15 lb. at the age of two. This was a far cry from the Percheron of 1860.)

Horses which may have been Percherons (and may not) were dispatched to the New World, it appears, on 16th July 1665, on the instructions of Louis XIV to that financial and reforming genius J-B. Colbert. Twenty mares and two stallions were sent to Canada, only eight dying on the voyage. Others followed in 1667, in 1670 and in subsequent years. "These horses, which remained the King's property for three years, were distributed among the gentlemen of the country who had done most to promote colonisation and cultivation."[7] But in Canadian horse-breeding of the following centuries, the Scotsmen over-shadowed the Frenchmen, and it was in the United States that the Percheron found its second great home.

Various legends abounded about French draught-horses imported into America, as they did of English ones, but "The McNitt Horse", which went to Canada in 1816, and later to the United States, is the first that has a name and some sort of history. This is confined to his activities in the New World, which were considerable: about his origin, it is silent, and even though he was grey there is much doubt whether he came from Le Perche. It was Edward Harris of New Jersey who shipped the first recorded true Percherons, in 1839. Only one of four survived the sea crossing and this was a mare. So Mr. Harris returned to Europe and brought back two more stallions and two mares. One of the stallions went blind and was retired from service almost as soon as he started. The other, a horse of about 15-hands, did better and sired about 400 foals before he died in 1856. He was aptly named *Diligence*, a reminder of the earlier and lighter type of Percheron's usefulness in pre-railway times at pulling the old *diligence* on its stages along the roads of France.

However, it was two horses imported in 1851 which really founded the Percheron breed in the United States, even though neither was bought in Le Perche and may not have been 100% true Percherons. Louis Napoleon and Normandy, alias Pleasant Valley Bill, were brought with one other to Ohio. They were certificated by the breeder, Z. Pimont, as *Diligence* colts. Old Bill averaged sixty foals a year for eighteen years, some of them selling for $1,000. Louis Napoleon was for a long while laughed at by the Americans, and was moved from place to place, serving only seven mares in 1859. But his glory came at the last – in Illinois, where his foals out of mares got by the English Fen horse *Samson* were a resounding success. All his colt-foals out of these were left entire and sold for long prices. Owing to infection from unclean mares, he eventually suffered the operation of partial penotomy: but, even then, he somehow got three more foals before dying in 1871.

When the old *diligence* type was superceded by the heavier sort, the Percheron quickly became very popular in the United States, where, by the 'seventies, pure-bred specimens far outnumbered all those of every other European kind. In December 1875, nine gentlemen from Illinois and one from Wisconsin met in Chicago to consider forming a breed society. The following February, a larger meeting at the Transit House in the Union Stock Yards of the same town formed "The National Association of Importers and Breeders of Norman Horses". This name was the first mistake. The meeting emphasised its error by resolving that "the Picardy horse, the Boulogne horse, the Percheron and the Normandy horse are essentially the same race or breed, and should be designated as the Norman horse". The term was, admittedly, generally used in the United States and was familiar in England as a label for this foreign breed. But, if the French were to be permitted a say in their affairs, they would have replied that they knew nothing of the word as a description of this horse. In fact, it was about as accurate as to describe the Suffolk horse as the "Norfolk", the Black as the "Oxford", or the Clydesdale as the "Grampian".

Among those Americans who were disinclined to perpetuate a misnomer was James Harvey Sanders, son of a central Ohio farmer and himself farming in Iowa, whither in 1868 he had brought from his old home a four-year-old stallion called Victor Hugo. (Fourteen years later, the horse was candidly advertised as "sound and hearty, and making a fortune for his owners".) A great student of heredity and breeding, he had started a monthly *Western Stock Journal* in 1869 at his own expense. He lost all his money, and in 1873 became editor-in-chief of *The National Live Stock Journal*. In 1876 he began a register of imported Clydesdale horses, but never completed it. And in the same year he published, on behalf of the new Association, *The Norman Stud Book*, a title he was reluctant to use. A new volume the next year was called, as a compromise, *The Percheron-Norman Stud Book*.

On 14th February 1878 (the day after Lord Ellesmere's sale in England), Dr.

Ezra Stetson proposed that the society, and its horse, should be re-named the Percheron. After somewhat heated discussion, the group became "The National Association of Importers and Breeders of Percheron-Norman Horses". What was done in Chicago on St. Valentine's Day, 1878 was oddly similar to the folly of All Fools' Day the same year in London (Chapter VI.2) and could have served as a warning to English breeders. But this was not all. As a direct result of disagreements at the Chicago meeting, a rival group was started, the "National French Draft Horse Register", and that could have been an admonition to the Clydesdale men (see Chapter VI.11).

It was not until 1883 that Percherons in their native area were favoured with a pedigree register – *Le Stud Book Percheron, publié par la Société Hippique Percheronne, autorisée par le Gouvernement*. Englishmen, Scotsmen and Americans would have been aghast at the notion of their stud-books having to be "authorised by the Government". But they did not have a national stud like the Haras du Pin, which had added heavy draught stallions to its establishment as early as 1808.

7. A REGISTER FOR CLYDESDALES

The setting-up of a Clydesdale stud-book appeared, to Englishmen, as another act of aggression from north of the border. But, for Scotsmen, it was one of self-defence. In the early years of the decade, Thomas Findley of Easter-hill had had talks with Mr. Cockburn, the Glasgow veterinary surgeon, and both were convinced that pedigree registration was essential. Buyers, foreign and English, were dissatisfied with the near-impossibility of obtaining details of breeding. The confusion was made much worse than it need have been by the common practice of new owners changing horses' names and, even more, by the deliberate obstructionism of most of the dealers, who could put jam to their bread if they successfully disguised the fact that the Clydesdales they sold were mostly half, or a quarter, or entirely, English. Obscurantists could do much with a name. Thomas Dykes, for example, was trying to trace the breeding of a colt which went under the name of "Young Sir Walter Scott", which he assumed to be a grandson of the famous Sir Walter Scott, grand-sire of Drew's Prince of Wales. He had a conversation with an informant which went thus:

"He is a son, is he not, of young Sir Walter Scott by old Sir Walter?"
"Na, na, he is naething of the kind."
"Then he was by the old horse himself?"
"You're a' wrong again. In fact, he's nae relation to the auld Sir Wattie at a'. But, you see, ye maun have a guid name if ye want to book mares nooadays."[8]

The colt was subsequently castrated, and so he could be mercifully forgotten, but it was no joke at the time, for Dykes was trying to compile information for the stud-book, to the evolution of which we must return.

As has been suggested, the Highland Society had done more for the Scottish draught-horse than R.A.S.E. for the English, but paradoxically it was the inadequacy of one of its rules that provided the final impetus to the pedigree movement. This rule laid down that entry forms for all young exhibits at its shows must state the pedigree, if known. Less than scrupulous exhibitors soon realised that if they wrote "pedigree unknown", they could select whichever of their colts or fillies were most forward in condition at the time of the show, delaying the decision to the last moment. More innocent men, observing a regulation which was intended to help good breeding without handicapping anyone, were committed to showing the animal they had actually entered, even if it had not come up to expectations, or, if it had "gone wrong", not exhibiting at all. At the show at Aberdeen in 1876 a "pedigree unknown" colt won the two-year-old class. In the autumn, when he was booked for service the follow-ing year, what Dykes described as "an absolutely impossible pedigree" was supplied for him. There was a newspaper controversy and the thing became a scandal. By January 1877 fierce correspondence had fostered an agitation to form a breed society.

The Earl of Dunmore, celebrated as a Shorthorn breeder as well as for his horses, weighed in. He wrote that a stud-book would put a stop to the practice (which he had been given to understand was a very profitable one) of "some Scotch breeders going into Lincolnshire and buying Lincoln mares and re-selling them, or their produce, or both, in Scotland as pure Cyldesdales". He added that he had asked Sir William Stirling Maxwell, Bt., to get a public meeting up in Glasgow during the stallion show. Sir William was unable to do Lord Dunmore's bidding, but J. M. Martin from Dunbarton convened the meeting for the evening of Monday, 26th February.

Unfortunately Lawrence Drew and others who, like him, thought that the Clydesdale and the Shire were the same breed, boycotted the meeting. How-ever, three hundred gentlemen attended and, since (in the words of *The Field*) they were all "eagerly bent on a stud-book", the proceedings were harmonious. Martin, from the chair, suggested that a society should be formed, quite separate from any existing organisation, and that they should be careful not to be too rigorous about insisting on long pedigrees in the first instance: otherwise they would exclude a great number of the most successful prize-winners of recent years. Mr. Jacob Wilson suggested two crosses to begin with – pure Clydesdale sire and dam's sire. An executive committee was appointed to go into these matters. Mr. Hendrie of Larbert agreed to be interim secretary. Lord Dunmore, who said he was astonished that such a meeting had not been called long before and had therefore been happy to travel a thousand miles to attend this one, was chosen as President, and cheerfully accepted office.

Thomas Dykes became secretary later in the year and, the following spring, the first annual general meeting of the society heard that, thanks largely to the enthusiasm and energy of his lordship, ninety-seven life governors had been accepted at 10 guineas each (this was a bargain for the younger ones), together with fifty-seven life members at 5 guineas (an even better bargain) and forty-four annual members. Lord Dunmore had also been instrumental in collecting

PLATES 9 and 10   A Clydesdale and a Shire of the 'fifties. (*above*) Merry Tom 532, a Clydes-dale, won innumerable prizes; (*below*) Kirby 1292, bred in 1850, was two years younger, and of the purest Derbyshire blood. Depicted here as a five-year-old, he is ready to begin his stallion round for Thomas Forshaw of Chorley, Lancashire, father of James. Compare him with Grey Spark (Plate 64).

PLATE 11 Be careful, young lady! Do not be carried away by events! The horse is England's Glory 723, foaled 1851, 17.2 hands, 22 cwt., 1st R.A.S.E. 1859. A g.g.g.g-son of England's Glory 705 (Plate 7), he was grand-sire of The Old Strawberry.

PLATE 12 The Clydesdale stallion Britain, also foaled in 1851, was brought to Windsor in 1856 by the Prince Consort for 240 guineas and won 1st prize at the Royal. Was his groom an exceptionally tall man?

1,400 pedigrees for entry in the first volume of the stud-book, of which he proposed to pay the whole cost of printing and to give a copy to each member. Archibald M'Neilage became assistant secretary. (This was a splendid appointment, for on Dykes' resignation at the end of 1880 he was to begin a period of office as his successor which was to last exactly half a century. No stud-book society executive officer was ever to do more for his breed than he.)

The qualifications of acceptance of horses into the new stud-book were simple enough. All living stallions foaled before 1875, and all living mares foaled before 1877, were eligible if they could be shown to have, at least on one side, what M'Neilage later described as "an unbroken descent from the Lanarkshire fountainhead according to the facts as collected from documentary evidence and the traditions of the older men connected with the horse breeding industry in Scotland". Animals foaled after these dates were to be required to have "a recognised Clydesdale sire and a dam got by a recognised Clydesdale sire". In December 1878, the first volume of the Stud-book was published, and so that hybrid of hybrids, the Clydesdale, whose true heavy carting qualities were derived from England, became somewhat paradoxically the first breed in Great Britain, other than the Thoroughbred itself, to have a pedigree register. Unfortunately this was seriously marred and attenuated by the exclusion of many excellent animals, particularly mares, about whose breeding the Clydesdale Council could get no information from those who alone could have supplied it. The book and the breed were quite inadequate without the support of Lawrence Drew and the two or three hundred men, not a few of them in a big way of business, who shared his ideas.

8. LAWRENCE DREW

With the exception of Robert Bakewell himself, the greatest genius in the history of British heavy-horse breeding is probably another bachelor, the handsome and powerfully built Lawrence Drew. There were indeed many affinities between the two men, though if they had been contemporaries it is likely that there would have been much on which they would have disagreed. But perhaps the most striking similarities were two. Both proved their theories by the practical success they achieved with horses. And the work of each, in the long term, was a glorious failure. We have seen how the achievements of Bakewell were frittered away by the stupidities of the nineteenth century. Drew's efforts were nullified by his early death and the pig-headed obstinacy of other breeders, both Scottish and English.

Drew was born in 1826, the son of Lawrence Drew, an enthusiastic breeder of all kinds of stock, especially Ayrshires, on his farm at Carmyle in Lanarkshire. After leaving Glasgow High School, young Lawrence joined his father, from whom in later years he used to say that he learned almost all he ever knew. At the age of nineteen, he went to Merryton to work for the 11th Duke of Hamilton and was rapidly promoted until he became factor of all his estates in the county. Since both in legend and fact the name of Hamilton runs all through the early history of the Clydesdale horse, it was entirely fitting that his employer should encourage the young man to build up the best stud he could. He first became nationally known to cart-horse men in 1862 when at the great Show at Battersea (a combined Royal and Highland Show in conjunction with the second International Exhibition), he caused something of a sensation with a stallion and a mare. The horse was Sir Walter Scott, which had travelled the Fylde for several seasons before David Riddell[9] saw his merit, and purchased him for use in Scotland. There, as Trotter has remarked, he "effected a revolution. For this act alone the Clydesdale world should be forever grateful to Mr. Riddell."[10] David then sold him to Drew, who of course was acting for the Duke. The mare was called Park's Maggie, but after her success was promptly re-christened London Maggie. However, the Duke died in Paris in July of the following year and his son, only eighteen, did not long pursue stockbreeding. There was a dispersal sale in 1868 and at the age of forty Lawrence left his employment, but was allowed to take a tenancy of the Merryton home farm. Among his foundation stock were Sir Walter Scott and London Maggie.

During the next eighteen years, all his efforts as a breeder (apart from those devoted to his almost-unrivalled Ayrshires) were motivated by his conviction that the English and Scottish horses were essentially the same breed. About this, we shall do best to allow him to speak for himself, the clearest expression of his views being made in a passage he wrote at the end of these years. Earlier (Chapter IV.4) we quoted extensively his belief that it was English mares in their hundreds which had, from about 1850, effected the change in the Clydesdale. This led him to expound his opinion that it was not pedigree but individual quality in a horse, whether English or Scottish, which should be of paramount consideration. "If the horse has merit, that is, if it has all the good points of a first rate draught horse – substance, symmetry, size, weight, bone, sinew, muscle, durability and action, and if it be free from all hereditary disease, you may depend that blood and pedigree are in that horse in a degree sufficient for the purpose of breeding first rate stock or performing hard work. 'Give me five crosses and a good beast rather than a thousand crosses and a brute,' says a writer in *The Breeder's Gazette*, Chicago. 'He who gets in the beast he drives the value of his money can afford to laugh at fashion. Pay nothing extra for any asserted excellence which you cannot see in the animals and their living kindred, and you will be safe, but don't pay a cent for any fancied excellence on paper, which is not a reflection from tangible excellence on four legs. This is the only safe rule, and it is safe from the dangers of fashion.' These are views which breeders and dealers would do well to ponder.

"It will thus be seen that the present breed of horses for agricultural purposes in both countries is due to the blending of Flemish blood with that of the native horse; and, reasoning inductively from effect to cause, we have no hesitation in asserting that the best horses for agricultural purposes, both in England and Scotland, sprang from the same common origin. And they are now so thoroughly mixed and blended together that there is no distinction generically or practically between them.

"It is a remarkable fact that no scientific writer of any note has ever ventured to call this proposition in question. Some men who have neither practical knowledge nor experience of horse-breeding have been airing their views of late in the public prints on this question. They dogmatically assert that the Clydesdale breed of horses is a pure breed, distinct in every sense of the term from the English cart horse, and that it possesses an 'impressiveness', whatever that may mean, to which his English neighbour cannot pretend. They even name certain well known horses which they call pure Clydesdales, and hold them up as instances which, they maintain, demonstrate to a certainty their peculiar views.

"What we, on the contrary, assert, is that the expressions 'Clydesdale horse' and 'Shire horse' are synonyms for the same class of animal, and that they are no more and no less than simply descriptive of the same type of horse ... Whether the sire be English and the dam Clydesdale, or vice versa, if they be properly selected and mated, they breed as true as any horses of the same species can, and transmit to their progeny to the remotest degree all the excellent qualities which they themselves possess."[11]

Drew, holding these views, refused to join the new Clydesdale Society, and so did many other breeders of like mind, including David Riddell, possibly second only to Drew as the Clydesdale expert of his time. They absented themselves from the inaugural meeting, which was a gentlemanly thing to do, as it made the harmony of those who were "bent on a stud-book" quite complete; but, in the long run, it might have been better that they should have been there to put their case and that, in addition, they should have done likewise when the Englishmen, later, had their meeting. Drew and his supporters, who were to number 300 of the Scottish breeders, were to be for some time a crowd of thorns in the flesh both of Dykes and M'Neilage as successive secretaries of the new breed association, and so a Shire historian cannot be more careful to do justice to the Clydesdale Society than by using only these two generous and large-minded gentlemen, and none others (except where stated) as sources of information about Lawrence Drew during the years from 1866, when he set up on his own, to this current year of 1878.

The magnificent stallion Prince of Wales is the best illustration of Drew's methods and ideas. In 1865, General, a son of the Riddell-Hamilton-Drew Sir Walter Scott, and the filly Darling were winners of first prizes at the Highland Show at Inverness. The latter, belonging to J. N. Fleming of Knockdon, Ayrshire happened to be in season and the two were mated on the spot. Next year, the birth of Darling's first foal was difficult and Mr. Fleming sent Willie Greenlees, his page-boy, quickly on horse-back to fetch the veterinary surgeon, Charles Tennant. All was well, unless the colt's funny temper can be ascribed to his awkward appearance in this world. (All through his long life it was dangerous to go into his box, especially when he was feeding.) But nothing stopped him winning at shows for David Riddell, his purchaser, and in six years his success was unbroken except for one defeat at the Dumfries Highland Show by a horse called Rantin' Robin.

In 1870 at Glasgow he was within an ace of being sold to an Australian. Lawrence Drew's elder brother, Robert, happened to be just home from Australia himself and, after a quick consultation, the two brothers intervened and got the horse for £1,500. In Lawrence's hands he soon began to make a name for himself as an even better stock-horse than show-horse, and this intensified the controversy about his breeding. Drew categorically gave it thus:

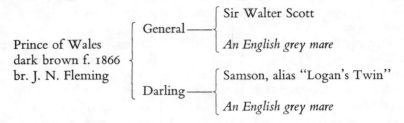

No one disputed that the two grand-dams had come from England. Drew said they were both purchased in Warwickshire, one when she was four and the other when she was two, and were brought to Glasgow and sold to their respective new owners. M'Neilage argued that one of them, General's dam – *Maggie*, alias *Darling*, or "The Wellshot Grey Mare" – had come from Cumberland. Mr. Wilson, farm manager to Mr. Buchanan, her first Scottish owner, had bought her from the dealer William Griffen of Renfrew, who said he had got her in Dumfries. M'Neilage also said she was by Merry Tom, a Clydesdale, which older breeders in the Glasgow area always called "the English horse that came from Carlisle". As for *Darling*'s dam, M'Neilage said this was *Kate*, purchased originally by a Mr. Knox from William Griffen, who said he got her also in Dumfries. He reported the view of some that she was actually bred in that county and was by the Clydesdale Blyth. Apparently *Kate* was quick-tempered, which may be an alternative reason why her marvellous grandson was somewhat difficult to deal with. *Samson*, by whom she was covered to produce *Darling*, occupies exactly the same place in the pedigree of the great Darnley as he does here and is discussed in Chapter VI.11.

However, whether Prince of Wales was two-quarters pure English or three-quarters Scotch did not seem to matter. Drew, who remained adamant about the pure Englishness of the two grand-dams, had no difficulty in persuading men in increasing numbers and at a rapidly-rising fee to put him on English and Scotch mares alike.

A year or so after clubbing together with his brother to find a record sum of money for this cross-bred horse, Drew began purchasing in England on an extensive scale. His breeding programme from 1866 had been somewhat obscure. Dykes states that he was doing a lot of in-breeding, and it would not be surprising if he was quietly using Bakewellian methods to try to fix the types that he admired. Even in 1875, according to Dykes, Young London Maggie (by Prince of Wales and out of the Battersea winner) was in foal to her own sire. But some years later Drew said that in-breeding was "a vice in horse breeding which never ought to be named but to be reprobated". It is difficult to account for this astonishing remark.

Typical of Drew's English-mare and no-pedigree outlook was a very big chestnut mare he bought at Dumfries market as a three-year-old. She was an obvious heavy English type and was in foal, probably to an English stallion. The produce was a colt which Drew sold to as distant a place as possible (the United States). In 1873, his great idea was to get a foal from her by Prince of Wales. But, Dykes wrote, "it did not prove so easy as it would look on paper, for the famous son of General resented with much temper all efforts towards an alliance, and it was only after a desperate strategem that the horse and mare were actually mated". There was a foal – Young Harry, and he won first prize at Glasgow for yearlings. Later at stud, he proved very poor: in which there may be a moral.

Drew in England was like a small boy picking the cherries off the top of a cake. Perhaps, as M'Neilage said, the Clydesdale Young Lofty had been travelling for some seasons in Derbyshire and perhaps some of the mares that Drew bought were by him: but he agreed that "the majority of them were Shire mares". W. R. Trotter related how Drew "drove for weeks round the nooks and corners of Derbyshire, often piloted by Mr. Samuel Wade of Mickleover, who used to tell how Mr. Drew would travel down by the night train from Glasgow to Derby, and drive out to Mr. Wade's place, where he would arrive about four o'clock in the morning, and immediately commence to disturb the slumbers of Mr. Wade by throwing pebbles up to the window . . . On one occasion these two gentlemen secured fourteen choice fillies, nearly all by Lincolnshire Lad, which, of course, Mr. Wade expected would satisfy the cravings of the shrewd Scotchman for some time, but much to his surprise the genial tenant of Merryton returned in about a fortnight for a fresh lot of his favourite sort. This went on for several years, and in the early half of the 'seventies the bulk of the mares and fillies disposed of at Mr. Drew's sensational sales hailed from the Midlands, and those were diffused over the length and breadth of Scotland."[12]

Drew's eyes were open for mares, not pedigrees, and (to quote J. A. Frost, an Englishman) "so keen was his judgment that he would 'spot a winner' from a railway carriage, and has been known to alight at the next station and make the journey back to the farm where he saw the likely animal. On at least one occasion the farmer would not sell the best by itself, so the enthusiast bought the whole team which he had seen at plough from the carriage window."[13] Many of his purchases, as Trotter has mentioned, were daughters of the lean brown-bay horse K or Lincolnshire Lad or Honest Tom, bred at Spilsby in the same year as Prince of Wales. In the end, he bought the horse himself – and this was a very narrow escape for the future of the English cart-horse. If he had seized him for Scotland before 1871, when he covered a Derbyshire mare called Madam, there would have been no Lincolnshire Lad II. And Lincolnshire Lad II's sons and descendants were to be, not only as the sand that is upon the sea-shore, but the whole coast-line of the English cart-horse. While applauding Mr. Drew's judgement, the English must be grateful that he spared K for the most important mating in the history of either breed. On one occasion Drew visited James Forshaw in Nottinghamshire and bought a filly by his famous What's Wanted. This is the only recorded meeting of any length between the rising English expert and, as Dykes called him, "the pioneer of modern draught horse breeding".

In 1875, shortly before the first home sale was held at Merryton that May, Thomas Dykes visited him and "sat and talked in the old back parlour where so many men from so many parts of the world had sat to learn from Mr. Drew". And this Mr. Drew was only forty-nine! Then he went to admire the best mares in the Long Stable. There were thirty-five of them, with young stock in other houses. About the only pearl Drew cast from his wisdom that day was that all the boxes where young stock were kept were bedded with sea-sand, which he had found did not cause sand-crack but produced a naturally-shaped foot by gradually paring away the horn. Visitors to Merryton, like visitors to Dishley a hundred years before, could see all they wished to see, and were treated with the utmost friendliness and hospitality. But they learned as few real secrets from Drew as their predecessors had learned from Bakewell.

Dykes has left us an impression of Prince of Wales, now nine years old and serving mares at the awesome figure of £40 each – a fee never equalled since. "The Prince was looking as well as ever, his grand contour round and sound, well tapered feet and pasterns and characteristic head at once captivating the eye. His hocks are certainly straight" (this was the most frequent criticism made of him) "but his thighs are unusually powerful. The fullness above the hock joints on the insides was visible, but a well-skilled veterinary surgeon who has a great knowledge of the breed at once declared it to be muscle and, as such, a point to be reckoned in the horse's favour. Nor is his action a whit less free than it used to be, for he steps out before like a trotting stallion, and standing behind you can see the soles of his feet clearly every time he lifts." Shortly afterwards, Mr. Fleming sent old Darling over to Drew's, to prove "a breeder's object-lesson when seen in company with her distinguished son. At Merryton she ended her days pulling about meat-coolers, her legs remaining fresh to the last." Her straightish hocks, which she had passed on to Prince of Wales, appeared to do her no harm. (M'Neilage also, praising Prince of Wales, said that his family was "as a rule, characterised by a striking immunity from hereditary disease . . . combined with fine wearing qualities and generally easy action".)

In January 1878, Edward, Prince of Wales, together with the exiled Prince Imperial of France, the only son of Napoleon III and the Empress Eugénie, were on a visit to the Duke and Duchess of Hamilton. (The Duchess was a cousin of Napoleon III.) The party decided, almost on the spur of the moment, to visit the former estate factor's stud. Poor Drew scarcely had time to see that everything was in order, much less to stage a rehearsal. However (our informant is again Dykes) he managed the parade in a fashion that "would have done credit to an Astley or a Hengler". Partly because he now had more young stock then his grooms could deal with, and partly because he thought that a feminine touch would make colts and fillies more tractable, he had recently adopted the unheard-of idea of employing part-time girls. In this he would certainly have found a disbeliever in James Forshaw, and for that matter in most other heavy-horse men, who believed that women were too mistakenly kind to instil the necessary discipline in young and potentially dangerous large animals. However that may be, the appearance of the young lassie grooms in their short gowns and petticoats leading the fillies and colts was a great success with the Prince of Wales. That shrewd judge also complimented his host on his stud and said, "They are a grand lot of mares, Mr. Drew, but I perceive that they are mostly English". The reply he received was, "Aye, and all the better of that, sir."

Drew's chief alarm, after recovering from the initial shock of the unexpected visit, occurred when the stallions were brought out. The five-year-old Lord Harry frisked and gambolled about with a great deal of spirit, and took the eye of the Prince Imperial, who asked if anyone had ever been on his back. Mr. Drew, aghast, replied that no one, to his knowledge, had done such a thing. The next minute, to the astonishment of the company and the horror of the proprietor, the Prince was riding him bare-back, and Lawrence Drew, later, could only say how glad he was to see him safely off and to think what a guid thing it was that Lord Harry and not the auld horse himself that had been chosen for this.

Mr. Drew presented the Prince of Wales with a filly by his namesake as a memento of the visit. The next year she won the Clydesdale Horse Society's cup at the Kilburn Royal Show. But by then, his other royal visitor, the reckless Prince Imperial, was dead. When the Zulu War broke out, he had volunteered for active service and was killed on 1st June. When he heard the news, Drew re-lived his anxiety at the impromptu cowboy antics and, thinking of the two Princes of Wales, put up a full-sized brown and gold painting of the auld horse on an archway leading to the courtyard behind his house.

9. SUFFOLK PEDIGREES

Robert Newton Shaw of Kesgrave Hall, for a short time after the Reform Act of 1832, represented East Suffolk as a Liberal. An old guardsman with a weather-beaten face, he was a leading magistrate, a farmer on a small scale and a well-known breeder and excellent judge of Suffolk horses. In 1840, he urged his fellows to set up a pedigree register. But no one was very enthusiastic, Shaw was growing old and in 1847 he gave up farming. In 1862, N. G. Barthropp of Cretingham Rookery, one of the leading breeders and judges, also retired and decided to do something for those who should come after by compiling his own register. The same year Herman Biddell (who, as already mentioned, had bought one of Barthropp's horses at the dispersal sale simply to prevent it leaving the county) also started collecting information.

Herman was the fourth son of Arthur Biddell (1783–1860) a 1,000-acre tenant farmer, and of Jane, daughter of Robert Ransome, the founder of the agricultural engineering firm. G. E. Evans, who has written charmingly and fully about the Biddell family, well described him as "a man of great strength and versatility of mind. He had all the Biddell family's strain of common-sense and practical application."[14] Mr. Evans comments on his power as a public speaker and as a "writer with a blunt, sinewy style and the gift to coin, on occasion, a particularly memorable phrase". This is no overstatement. Biddell is by far the best writer that the heavy-horse business has ever produced, yet a tiny village school was his only seat of education.

In the November of that year 1862, he assembled at his house a gathering of old stallion-leaders, for the purpose "of recalling facts, histories, and pedigrees which were fast receding into the land of oblivion. To arrest these precious records of history – which had no existence except in the memories of those elderly mèn – notes were taken, and although no special plan was in prospect for utilising the information, the memoranda were all preserved . . . The torrents of fact which the party poured forth was a history in itself, and to have secured it all, the services of a professional reporter should have been employed. That which I did manage to place on record was ample to show that the materials for a Stud-book were in existence, if only means were taken to collect them. Those meetings were repeated, and one was much like another, but fresh histories were forthcoming at every gathering: rich stores of reminis-cence to harvest, with the constant apprehension that much must be lost where each had something to tell, all spoke at once, and only one was present to collect the spoil."[15]

Biddell worked away in spare moments for fifteen years. Then, at a meeting of the Suffolk Agricultural Association at Ipswich on 21st April 1877, Arthur W. Crisp proposed the formation of a Suffolk Stud-book Association. From no one could the suggestion have been more appropriate. He was the grandson of Thomas Crisp of Ufford, from one of whose horses, foaled in 1768, it was shortly to be proved that all true Suffolks were descended. He was the son of Edward Crisp of Rendlesham, a great Suffolk horse man. He was the younger brother of Thomas, who, succeeding their father at the age of nineteen, had become the biggest breeder and exporter of his time, farming 4,000 acres and remaining celebrated until his death in 1869 for his sheep and for his talent in nearly every other branch of agriculture. Arthur himself had given up his own farm at Chillesford in 1873 and was now prepared to devote his energies to a pedigree movement.

On 19th June, a meeting in the Ipswich Town Hall set things going, Crisp and Biddell being appointed joint honorary secretaries. The Earl of Stradbroke, of Henham Hall, who had been President of the county Agricultural Association from its formation as the East Suffolk A.A. in 1831, gave continuity to the new movement by becoming the first Patron. In contrast, the newest recruit to the breed was William Alexander Louis Stephen Douglas, that same 12th Duke of Hamilton who in 1866 had given up the family's historic, or shall we say legendary, connection with heavy-horses in the north. It was no doubt in his capacity as the 9th Duke of Brandon, rather than as the premier peer of Scotland, that he was beginning to buy the choicest Suffolks he could find for his Easton Park estate in that county.

Sadly, Nat Barthropp had died and Biddell wrote of him "Sorely did the county miss that genial face, so ready of wit, so cheerful to the last, so gentle, and yet so full of the man that, when the storms of the world beat heavily on him, he met life as only those can, who are men in heart as well as in name."[16] Barthropp's manuscript of pedigrees never came to light after his death, and Biddel's task, for he was appointed to be solely responsible for producing a retrospective stud-book, was made by that the more onerous.

10. FREDERIC STREET AT THE FARMERS' CLUB

We left Frederic Street preparing his talk for the Farmers' Club meeting in its rooms at the Caledonian Hotel, Adelphi on 4th March 1878 (Section 2). His paper was the 224th to be read since the Club's foundation by members of the Smithfield Club and the then new Royal Agricultural Society in December 1842. It was only the second one to be devoted to cart-horses. The first had been given exactly twenty-five years previously to the very day, by Nat Barthropp, that same well-loved breeder of Suffolks who later had started compiling a pedigree register of his own. In June 1853, three months after Barthropp's paper, Allan Ransome had read a paper "On the comparative advantages of the application of fixed and portable steam-engines to agricultural purposes". The paper presented by Thomas Aveling in February 1878, at the meeting before Street's turn, had been about "Traction engines for agricultural purposes", and was the ninth paper to deal with steam. The contrast illustrates the progressive nature of the Club as clearly as it does the neglect into which cart-horse breeding had fallen.

Much of Aveling's paper was concerned with the legal restrictions on steam engines and the absurd way in which the laws were interpreted – for example, the case of a man who had two road locomotives travelling together and was prosecuted for having only one man precede them with a red flag. On the subject of the frightening of horses, the speaker commented that "Horses incapable of being taught to meet an engine without alarm are a greater danger on other occasions than the engine itself on any. They will shy at a showman's van, a band of music, a wheelbarrow and anything but what exactly pleases their untaught natures." The marvellous imperturbability of modern horses is a reminder of another aspect of breeding and management where in the 'seventies there was much room for improvement. Speaking of practical matters, Mr. Aveling also said that the engineer's task was "to solve the mechanical problem of designing and building an engine strong enough to stand the rough jolting of our rough roads, simple enough to be understood and managed by a farm labourer of ordinary intelligence, and practical enough to be encouraged as a most economical assistant to, or substitute for, the always costly and increasingly costly horse". Before even the breed society had been started, the breed's downfall was being plotted.

The following month, on a fine day with spring-like temperatures, John Brown of March, the chairman, introduced Fred Street on "The Breeding, Rearing and Management of Cart Horses", and said, "Science and steam and machinery have done much for us of late years. I trust they have yet something good in store for us. But we have not yet arrived at a stage at which we can do without that useful animal, the cart horse." Mr. Street's address contained most of the observations that one would expect from an enlightened heavy-horse man, especially one who farmed at Somersham Park near St. Ives where Oliver Cromwell had once been squire. There were also some amusing asides, such as on the usefulness of castor oil for scouring foals – "and then give a dose of diarrhoea mixture: that made by Mr. Goodenough, of Somersham, I never knew to fail". He ranged over the whole practice and economy of breeding, management and feeding. He advocated hiring societies. He commented on the various types of stallion shows. And he fired a broadside at the Royal Agricultural Society for its mean prize-list in comparison with the Highland Society and for constantly chopping and changing its horse-classes.

Mr. Street consistently used the term "Shire-bred" to indicate the breed that he advocated, even though he was a Fenman himself. He praised the great Suffolk landowners for their enthusiastic support of their county's cart-horses and for being willing to exhibit them at shows. "I mention this as I think landowners in other counties do not take that interest in the subject they ought to do." Clydesdales, he said, had been improved, even as to stamina, by the use of Shire-bred blood. "But buyers of Clydesdales do not want to pay fancy prices for Clydesdale blood when in fact they are getting a cross." Hence the Scottish agitation for a stud-book and the formation of the Clydesdale Horse Association.

The Clydesdales were a topic which, in the discussion which followed the paper, introduced some comic relief. Dr. Shorthouse, a visitor from Croydon, could not understand Mr. Street's explanation of the rules the Clydesdale people had worked out to qualify horses to be put in their proposed stud-book. Although the chairman asked him to keep to the point, Shorthouse successfully reached the stage of saying that "Suppose they had a mare of any breed and put her to a donkey, she would have but one cross and the male would come in the stud-book". The chairman's hammer, reminders from others that it was cart-horses they were talking about, and the laughter of the rest were unable to prevent him speaking of the Palmerston Agricultural Association of Ireland, "of which the late Lord Mayo was president". Owners proverbially gave all sorts of fictitious and fanciful pedigrees to their horses. "Directly any horse wins the Derby or the prize at any agricultural show, a yearling from the same stock, or a half-brother, or own brother, is exhibited." Dr. Shorthouse had investigated and published thousands of pedigrees and the point, he said, was almost a hobby of his life. A somewhat irritating guest, he nevertheless had a serious warning to give. When, later, he rose again (members were too polite to groan) it was to remark that, "It would be a vicious system to allow the public at the judging of shows. The judges' decision should not be questioned by the rabble, or by a clique, or by the owners who go and point out the merits of the animals, as they do at the Islington Show." (This was a horse show which was staged on the first Saturday after the Derby by the Agricultural Hall Company. In 1864, when it started, it was the first horse show in England at which saddle horses were actually ridden and jumped, and harness horses actually driven, instead of being shown in hand. Horace Hayes,[17] later, contrasted the Dubliners' enthusiasm for horses as shown at Ball's Bridge with the apathy of Londoners, very few of whom bothered to come: year after year, it was attended only by country people.)

Finlay Dun, the distinguished Scots veterinary surgeon (who as a young lecturer at Edinburgh nearly thirty years before had written his first article for publication – "On the mismanagement of farm horses") praised the Clydesdale. He also said red roan was a terrible colour for a horse. J. K. Fowler of Aylesbury said it was a very good kind of colour. Pickering Phipps, M.P., the Northampton brewer, said this was an important evening not only for breeders but for mercantile men: personally, he preferred a bony horse with little hair, but good big horses were difficult to find, and dear. Professor Pritchard of the Royal Veterinary College, a name to remember in Shire history, stressed the importance of hereditary soundness. George Street of Maulden, Bedfordshire, Frederic's brother, said breeders should make up their minds as to the type they wanted to aim at – "not jumping about from one sort of animal to another, choosing first perhaps the big Lincolnshire horse and then going in for a clean-legged animal".

Captain Heaton's contribution was almost a speech in its own right. Like Fred Street, he criticised the vast number of bad stallions about, the miserable R.A.S.E. prize-list and other disincentives to good breeding. "But I cannot concur with Mr. Finlay Dun about his pet Clydesdales. I must stick up for the Shire breed of cart horses, and I fear that unless something is done our Scotch friends will completely knock our legs from under us . . . Scotch farmers, who are supposed to be able to take care of their money, have paid 20 guineas for serving, and twenty more for a foal. What would an English farmer say if he were asked to pay 40 guineas for the use of a horse?" (Mr. Bell, of Newcastle, said several Northumberland farmers had paid 40 guineas to send a mare to Prince of Wales.) He often had applications from foreign purchasers, and he observed that they generally asked for "a Clydesdale". When questioned, they told him it was because they understood "Clydesdales" were the only pure breed of horses. He always replied that Scotchmen came to England and took away Shire mares by hundreds, and so their horses were half-Shires. "English agriculturalists ought to set up a stud-book as soon as possible, to prevent Clydesdale breeders from claiming purity for their breed over that of Shires."

And that is what Fred Street, in his formal reply, proposed that the meeting should do. But the chairman had to rule him out of order: meetings of the Club could not pass resolutions. Charles Howard said he was pleased Professor Pritchard had mentioned the value of nosebags and suggested that, immediately after the end of the proceedings, a special meeting be held to pursue the question of a stud-book.

This was done, with John Brown again in the chair. Fred Street proposed "that it is desirable to form an Association for the establishment of a Stud-book for Shire-bred horeses". He thought the headquarters should be Cambridge, Peterborough or London, preferably the last. John Fowler seconded him and Henry Heaton supported. Fred Street also proposed, and Major Dashwood (from Kirtlington, Oxon) seconded, that the Earl of Ellesmere should be invited to be President. Fred Street agreed to be interim honorary secretary. The chairman gave permission for another special meeting at the Club four weeks later, and a committee of fifteen was formed to push things forward. Finlay Dun thought a more euphonious name than "Shire-bred" should be chosen.

II. COKE OF DERBYSHIRE AND THE COMMITTEE

Inaugural committees of new societies, especially of those formed in the sort of way that this one was, tend to include a high proportion of men whose enthusiasm evaporates when the real work begins. Some are chosen because they have talked most. Others are included because they are important people, but turn out to have no time or real interest. The new association for cart-horses was fortunate in that exactly two-thirds of the committee appointed from Farmers' Club members who happened to be able to attend the March meeting proved to be stalwart supporters. Of the fifteen, the man who bore the most distinguished name was to prove, in the remaining eleven years of his life, the wisest, the most persuasive and charming, the hardest worker and the most successful as a breeder.

The Hon. Edward Keppel Wentworth Coke of Longford Hall, Derbyshire, was descended from that great exponent of common law, that thorn in the flesh of James I, Chief Justice Sir Edward Coke (1552–1634) of Holkham Hall. Sir Edward's great-great-great-grandson Thomas was born in 1697, was created Earl of Leicester in 1744 and died in 1759. He was pre-deceased both by his son Edward, who left no issue, and by his two brothers and sisters. All of these likewise had been either unmarried or childless except the younger sister Anne, who lived at Longford Hall, one of the family properties. In 1716 she had married Philip Roberts, a Derbyshire man. So their son, Wenman Roberts (1717–1776) succeeded in 1759 to all the estates, though the earldom became extinct. He then took the name and arms of Coke. In 1771, Arthur Young saw and warmly praised the system on the Longford farms, where the carting as well as the ploughing was all done by oxen. They were not yoked but harnessed similarly to horses, except that the collars were narrow-end downwards and could be opened for buckling on. "Mr. Cooke" (Young spelled the name as it is pronounced) "could plough as much land in one day with three oxen in single line as his neighbours could do with four or five horses." Young only ever saw harnessed oxen at two other places, Sir Charles Tynte's at Halswell in Somerset and the Beaconsfield farm of that great Irish master of the English language, Edmund Burke. He also praised "Mr. Cooke" for having "given much attention to the introduction of the Norfolk husbandry in Derbyshire".[18]

Wenman (Roberts) Coke was succeeded by his son Thomas William (1752–1842) who was born in London but spent his early days at Longford Hall, where he developed his passion for good farming. On his father's death, he moved to Holkham at the age of twenty-two and soon became known to all the world as "Mr. Coke of Norfolk". Whether he would have won such immortal fame as an agriculturalist if he had remained, as he was born, Thomas Roberts of Derbyshire, must be a matter of conjecture. By his first wife and cousin, Jane Dutton, he had three daughters. She died in 1800 and after more than twenty-one years' widowhood he married in 1822 Lady Anne Keppel, by whom he had five sons and a daughter. Created Earl of Leicester in 1837, he died at Longford in 1842. His eldest son, also Thomas William (born 1822) succeeded to the title and to Holkham, and the second son, Edward (born 20th August 1824) lived at Longford. He had served as a captain in the Scots Fusilier Guards, had been M.P. for West Norfolk 1847–1852 and had married in 1851. The sort of man who was ideally suited to be the father of a large family, he had no children.

Encouraged by the Earl of Ellesmere, Edward Coke was just now, in his fifty-fourth year, starting on a large scale to breed cart-horses. One of the first fillies he acquired was Cantineer, a brown, bred in 1877 by " – Peat of Belton, Leics". This Peat appears nowhere else in pedigree records but, as Belton is less than four miles from Dishley, one cannot help wondering whether he was of the family of old Bill Peet, Bakewell's long-serving stud-groom.

A note on each of the other first committee members must be brief:

Capt. Henry Heaton was another who was to do great work for the society as a member of the Council for twenty-one years. He was responsible for the success of the Earl of Ellesmere's stud until 1904.

Joseph Martin of Littleport, near Ely, was a breeder on an extensive scale, as the number of "Highfield" mares in future volumes of the Stud-book was to show. He had bred his first outstanding stallion, Golden Ball, in 1854 and another of his own-bred true Fen-type horses was Goliath, foaled in 1876. A stalwart member, he was to serve eighteen years on the Council and often as steward.

James Howard, M.P., of Clapham Park, Bedford had been chairman of the

Farmers' Club in 1870 and was to be a Council member of the breed society until his death in 1889.

James F. Crowther, Knowl Grove, Mirfield owned the Clydesdale stallion Topsman (see VI.10). He had also possessed many fine Shires, including an Honest Tom foaled in 1869, which was one of the best-known sons of Welcher's (or Miller's) great Honest Tom. He was to serve on the Council fifteen years, bred his last Shire in 1891 and died in 1897.

Major F. L. Dashwood of Kirtlington, Oxon, was to serve six years on the Council to 1893 and is to figure much in the story of the next few years.

John Lewin Curtis of Chatteris was another breeder of great Fen horses, and was to continue as a practising member until his death at the end of the First World War. But he was not a man for sitting on councils and talking.

Pickering Phipps, M.P., Northampton, was to serve on the first Council and to remain a member of the society until his death in 1890. He owned geldings at his brewery and bred horses of the heaviest type on his farm at Horton.

Charles Marsters of Saddlebow, King's Lynn, owner of the "Old Strawberry", was another who was a doer and not a talker, though he was to serve on the first Council. He bred his last Shires, Saddlebow Beauty and Saddlebow Darling, in 1888 and lived twelve years after that.

John K. Fowler of Stone, Bucks, had bred his best known horse, Royal George in 1859. He had read three Farmers' Club papers, in 1868, 1873 and 1876. His resignation through ill-health from the original Council on 9th December 1879 was a serious loss.

The Reverend Leonard Wood, who of course must have a few extra sentences, was the only one of the remaining five of the steering committee to be elected to the first Council. He remained Vicar of Singleton until his death, at the age of ninety-two, in 1911. He was always known as "Parson Wood" and no journalist could ever resist calling him "the Grand Old Man of Agriculture". He rarely missed any agricultural show in his area, and was frequently a stock-judge. Mainly owing to his efforts, Lancashire was unique in offering free technical education and a grant of 10s. a week towards students' expenses. The Harris Institute in Preston and the County Council farm at Hutton owed their success largely to his propaganda. He had been an original member of the County Council when it was formed in 1889, was alderman from 1892 and served on every committee connected with farming or the land. At his death he was still chairman of the Blackpool Agricultural Society. One of his grandsons pre-deceased him by twelve years, being killed at the defence of Mafeking: yet the second wife of his old friend and squire lived as lady of the manor and patron of the living until 1941.

Clare Sewell Read, M.P., of Thorpe, Honingham, Norwich, was to be a member of the Society only one year. Chairman of the Farmers' Club in 1868 and 1892, he is described by its historian as "its best speaker and perhaps the best-loved tenant farmer in England . . . and perhaps the strongest advocate for the tenant farmer, both in and out of Parliament, that the Club ever had".[19]

He died in 1905. Robert Leeds of Keswick Old Hall, Norwich, chairman of the Farmers' Club in 1865 and chairman of the directors of the Agricultural Hall, Islington 1871–1890, was also a member of the Society one year. Thomas Duckham (M.P. in 1880 and Chairman of the Club in 1881) and Finlay Dun did not get as far as joining the society when the members' list was opened later in the spring.

CHAPTER VI

1878–1884

The English Cart-horse Society

I. AGRICULTURAL DEPRESSION

HEAVY snow in March 1878 was followed by floods in April. A long hard winter in 1878–1879 wrought havoc among livestock, and was the prelude to the worst year of the century for rain, cold and every imaginable climatic disaster. It was almost certainly worse than 1797 or 1799 and there has not been another quite to match it since. Hay was universally ruined, crops were blighted or rotted, and pastures sodden. The next winter was as bad as its predecessor. The summer of 1880 was another wet and cheerless time. The 1881 snowstorms set the seal on the worst winter in memory. 1882 rivalled 1879 for its seemingly incessant rain, low temperatures and lack of sun. 1883 produced a long drought.

One can understand those who still blamed the deepening agricultural depression upon the weather, but bad seasons ought to make prices rise, not fall. As the 'eighties got under way, the price of wheat followed the example already set by other grain, and sagged under the enormous tonnage of cheap imports, whose cost was kept down by the low freight charges caused by world wide depression. (It was discovered that the cheapest way to send scrap iron from Liverpool to London was to ship it at 1s. a ton for New York, and thence back across the Atlantic.) Farm rents were said to have been reduced in a period of four or five years by nearly £6,000,000: but a countless number in addition were remitted or deferred – a situation which was demoralising to the tenant while he was still in possession, and infuriating if he gave up the struggle and quitted, because landlords could re-let only at a lower rental and on considerably less stringent conditions of husbandry.

Stock breeders and graziers, it is true, still enjoyed a reasonable market – if they escaped the disastrous attacks of pleuro-pneumonia and foot-and-mouth upon their cattle and of liver-rot on their sheep. And cart-horses were a good proposition if they were sound and strong. There was still plenty of work for them on the land, even though less and less of it was ploughed as each year went by. They had ousted oxen, were holding their own against steam and were benefiting from the other forms of mechanisation, like the new sheaf-binder, which were filling such of the gaps left by men going into the towns as needed to be filled. Farms where heavy-horses could be bred, or brought on, could provide enough work for brood mares or young stock to earn their keep, and the ever-increasing need in the towns for sound geldings provided a good market for the five-year-old. There was therefore increased trade all along the line. And, for breeding stock, the export market was beginning to boom in a phenomenal manner. For many years, a good English heavy stallion had been saleable in many parts of Europe, in Russia and across the Atlantic. But now the demand was fantastic, particularly in English-speaking countries and above all in the United States, where the vast new acres under cultivation needed the horses that could be got out of small native mares by European heavy stallions.

2. MAKING A START

Four weeks after Frederic Street's paper, the new association held an open meeting in the Farmers' Club rooms at the Royal Caledonian Hotel, Adelphi, where another paper was due to be read later in the evening. The date was 1st April, and a folly was due to be committed by the forty or so men who were present. Fred Street reported an encouraging response from various gentlemen who approved of the movement and said that Lord Dunmore had written to describe the methods he had adopted in forming the Clydesdale Stud-book Association. John Brown then installed the Earl of Ellesmere in the chair. His lordship began by inviting suggestions for a title of the association.

James Howard made a speech in which he suggested the breed was best known as the "Old English Shire Horse", and he ended by proposing "The English Shire Horse Stud-book". C. S. Read objected, on the ground that there were many good cart-horses that were not Shire horses. George Street agreed with this, and believed that the term "Shire" was known only to a few experts. Fifty per cent of the farmers did not know what it meant, and from 70% to 90% of Englishmen in general had not heard of it. His brother Fred said that 90% of the dealers were perfectly acquainted with the term. The noble President believed the title should be as open and inclusive as possible: otherwise, there could be some misunderstanding among some gentlemen about whether their horses would be eligible.

Only a minority believed that the word "Shire" was well known at all and eventually the suggestions were whittled down to two – 'The Cart Horse Society" and "The Old English Cart Horse Society". The meeting was evenly divided, and his Lordship was unwilling to use his casting vote. After an interval for private bargaining, one party agreed to drop "Old" and the other to add "English". In order that Welsh, Scottish, and Irish breeders should not be excluded, the title at last emerged as "The English Cart Horse Society of Great Britain and Ireland".

(The first literary use of the word "Shire" to denote a breed of horse is ascribed by the Oxford English Dictionary to the first edition of S. Sidney's *Book of the Horse*, 1875. But in 1869, William Wells, M.P., writing the report on the Royal Show, had remarked of Welcher's Honest Tom that he had "grown into a fine specimen of a 'Shire' cart-horse stallion". And Honest Tom was no product of the "Shires". In 1877, both Walter Gilbey in February and Richard Reynolds, in March, used the word in letters to *The Field*.)

It was agreed that life members should pay 10 guineas, and that the annual subscription for others should be 1 guinea. Five new names were added to the committee – William Wells of Peterborough, Townley-Parker of the Fylde group, T. W. Garrett Taylor of Norwich, Henry Overman of Weasenham, Norfolk, and Richard Reynolds, who offered to place his privately-compiled register of 1,000 stallions, ranging in date from 1800 to 1876, at the disposal of the Society.

Later that evening, the Farmers' Club heard Thomas Rose of Melton Magna, Norfolk, speaking on farm work in harvest. The discussion inevitably contained frequent references to beer – whether a wet groat went further than a dry shilling. One member who had let out 200 acres to contract-harvesters at 14s. an acre, including stacking and thatching, said their first action on arrival was to order 400 gallons. The chairman, at the end of the meeting, was happy to report that the cart-horse breeders had now organised themselves. "It must be very satisfactory for us to know that although the new Association forms no part of this Club, it was originated in it, and the Club has been made a sort of nucleus by which that important project has been set afloat." His successful termination of this trying sentence was greeted with loud cheers.

At the next meeting of the association, five weeks later, Charles Dorman of Kingsford, Dorman & Co., Essex Street, Strand was appointed solicitor – a choice that has stood the test of time, for his successors are still the Society's legal advisers a century later. He had served the Agricultural Hall at Islington in this capacity from the time when that project was first mooted in 1860, and had recently, in February, become managing director. He went away to draw up a draft memorandum and articles of association. In June, George Mumford Sexton was selected, after a postal vote, as Secretary at a salary for the first year of £150 and expenses. This was an odder choice, for he had no experience of this type of work, though he was a very able auctioneer and, like other members of his family, had bred some fine Suffolk horses. So the registered office of the new society was neither in Cambridge nor Peterborough, nor even in London, but in his house, Wherstead Hall near Ipswich, in the very heart of the rival breed's territory.

On 11th July the Society was incorporated as a limited company, the word "limited" being omitted by licence of the Board of Trade. The same day, a meeting was held on the Royal Agricultural Society's showground at Durdham Down, Bristol, to complete formalities. The Earl of Ellesmere was unable to attend, but a newly appointed vice-president deputised for him. This was the Earl Spencer, K.G., of Althorp Park, Northampton, proprietor of over 27,000 acres. Now forty-three, he was at this time between two periods of office as Viceroy of Ireland. The committee members had now been transformed into thirty "ordinary councilmen", most of whom had something positive to offer. In some cases, it was self-sacrificing hard work: in others, that influence and prestige which were so essential to the success of any Victorian organisation. The noble President and his deputy contributed handsomely in both ways. The most active new councillors were Walter Gilbey, George Street, and Thomas Brown of Marham Hall, Downham Market.

In accordance with the bye-laws of the Society, two committees were set up. Edward Coke became chairman of the editing committee, of which the other members were Frederic Street (recently elected the first honorary member of the Society in recognition of his position as the founder), Captain Heaton, Major Dashwood, James Howard and Thomas Brown. The finance committee consisted of the Earl of Powis, James F. Crowther, Sir Gilbert East, of Hall Place, Maidenhead, Walter Gilbey, Pickering Phipps and William Wells. The twin tasks of preparing the Stud-book and of acquiring members and money were now vigorously tackled.

3. THE KILBURN ROYAL, 1879

The Royal Show of 1879, a special effort to mark the fortieth anniversary, was staged at Kilburn Park, and lasted seven days. It was therefore the longest ever staged. It was also the most disastrous. The rain and wind were almost continuous. The Prince of Wales, as President, gallantly came four times, in an attempt to bolster sagging morale. Queen Victoria came once, and avoided sinking in the mud by being driven along the sleeper-laid roads and never leaving them. A waiter dropped a tray of crockery, and it had to be dug out of the ooze with a spade. If any one week stands out as a symbol of the real outset of the great agricultural depression, it is the Kilburn Royal.

The English Cart Horse Council had regarded it as an opportunity to bring their breed to the fore. Earl Spencer was asked to use his influence towards having the "Agricultural" classes either restored to their former place at the head of the prize-list, or, better still, re-named "English Cart Horses". His lordship's persuasiveness was considerable, both as a leading light of the R.A.S.E. himself and as the great-nephew of its founder. The 3rd Earl had rescued the Smithfield Club from almost certain bankruptcy when he was President in 1825 and in December 1837 he had made a speech to its members which resulted in the inauguration of the national society. R.A.S.E. was by Earl Spencer out of the Smithfield Club just as surely as the E.C.H.S. was by Frederic Street out of the Farmers' Club.

The 5th Earl could not manage to get the classes re-titled, but they were promoted to the head of the schedule and it was understood that the horses were to be judged as English Cart Horses or Shire-breds (which was, of course, bad luck on anyone simple enough to think that "Agricultural horse" meant what it used to mean). He also succeeded in getting classes for three-year-old stallions and yearling fillies added – highly marketable animals, but rarely exhibited because they were unlikely to be successful when asked to compete against older horses. At the Bristol meeting in 1878, the prize money for all breeds of heavy-horse had totalled only £475, £20 less than that for Shorthorn cattle alone. Now the heavy-horse prizes were almost trebled. (In addition, the Mansion House committee added nearly £600 for foreign breeds, "Percheron", "Norman", "Flemish", and others.) The E.C.H. Council, in reciprocation, presented three £25 champion cups and a fourth was given by the Earl of Ellesmere. He won two of them himself.

The senior stallions' class presented a fascinating confrontation between Lawrence Drew's Lord Harry, which the late Prince Imperial had ridden, and Lord Ellesmere's four-year-old chestnut British Wonder, by the Old Strawberry, and bred by Charles Beart of Stow Bardolph out of a bay mare. The English horse was placed first. Colonel George Morrell of Headington Hill Hall, Oxford, was third with a dark blue-roan five-year-old (later registered as King of the Vale) bred near Aylesbury. A Fen-bred horse, Sir John Falstaff, was reserve for Captain William Betts of Diss: he was by Wiseman's Wonder, perhaps the third best-known sire of the day, son of Dack's Matchless (for which, see B.VIII.1) and owned by the son of old William Wiseman (B.V.1).

The Earl of Ellesmere also won the three-year-old class and a champion cup with Prince of the Isle II, bred by J. Fryer of Chatteris out of an Honest Tom mare, and another of Fryer's breeding was third. Between these stood a horse shown by Richard Towerton of Tetsworth, Oxon, that cannot now be identified. Another champion cup went to Lord Ellesmere for his two-year-old Samson IV which he, or rather his Henry Heaton, had bred, by Samson (1980) out of the Honest Tom mare Honest Lady (who herself came second, at the age of ten, in the senior mares class). Tom Statter's Stand Stud Company of Whitefield, Manchester, great stallion owners and frequent purchasers of Worsley-bred colts, was second with a now unidentifiable colt. Fred Street was third with his own-bred Somersham Samson, another son of Samson (1980). The reserve position went to a recently-joined English Cart Horse member, the Duke of Westminster. The yearling colts' class was won by a Scotsman, James Johnstone of Maryhill, Glasgow, with a Drew-bred colt, turning the tables on Lord Ellesmere, whose *Great Britain* was second. Drew himself was third with a black Lincolnshire Lad colt, whose breeder was listed as "unknown". A thorough Fen animal, Fortrey Samson was reserve for Alfred Richardson of Mepal.

Many of the mares are impossible now to identify. The senior class was won by a seven-year-old brown called *Poppet*, owned by Edward and Alfred Stanford. They lived, of all unikely places, at Steyning and, with Hugh Gorringe of Kingston-by-Sea, were the first Cart Horse members in Sussex. Lord Ellesmere atoned for his lapse by taking 2nd (Honest Lady), 3rd and 4th places. The three-year-olds were headed by Lawrence Drew's *Camilla* (breeder and breeding "unknown"), followed by James Cronshaw of Hulme, John Nix of Alfreton (whose family had been among the most prominent Black Horse breeders in Derbyshire since the days of Bakewell at least, and probably long before that), and Lord Ellesmere. The two-year fillies were owned by William Welcher, James Forshaw (a name was soon to be foremost as a stallion owner) and Lord Ellesmere. John Rowell, T. H. Miller, Lawrence Drew and Henry Pulleine of Selby, the third man in Yorkshire to join the new breed society, had the top four yearling fillies.

The most notable feature of the winning owners' names was that, except for the Scotsmen, they all appeared on the members' list of the English Cart Horse Society. How their animals were kept clean and fit in the 100-acre sea of Kilburn clay and mud is not recorded. Before even the show opened, the incessant rain had turned the Park into a gluey quagmire. Perhaps the greatest equine honours of the proceedings should be accorded not to the show animals but to the hundreds of extra cart-horses (four times the number expected to be required), mostly railway geldings, that were hired in a desperate effort to set up the machinery and other heavy exhibits. They worked day and night. After the seven soaking days of the Show itself, Monday to Monday, the implement section was kept open another three days – during which time it still rained. And then the anonymous work-horses had to pull everything out of what had almost become Kilburn Fen. But it was precisely to improve the conformation and soundness of horses such as these that the breed society was striving.

4. A MEETING IN A STORM

Meanwhile, dissatisfaction with the name of the Society was becoming more and more widespread, and many began to think Street's original suggestion, "Shire-bred", was correct. Whenever the Council met, there were arguments, sometimes pretty warm, but they never occurred in the course of official business. Up and down the country, as new members joined, the rumbling increased. The first Annual General Meeting was held on 7th May 1879 at the Inns of Court Hotel, the excellent new headquarters of the Farmers' Club, and at last Earl Spencer mildly suggested that the title ought to be "more distinctive". The President allowed a discussion in which most of the twelve councilmen and fourteen ordinary members who were present took part, and showed themselves fairly evenly divided between "Shire" and "Cart" supporters. Afterwards, Thomas Spencer of Clavering Hall, Essex obtained the signatures of 112 members to requisition an Extraordinary General Meeting, at which Walter Gilbey was to move that the Society's name be changed to the "Shire Horse Society". (Mr. Dorman had assured the Council that this could be done at the cost of £7 or £8.) This meeting, preceded by a flurry of circulars and propaganda from some individual members to all the others, was held on the Royal showground on Wednesday, 2nd July at 3 p.m.

Buffeted by the winds and drenched with the rain, Edward Coke splashed his way into the tent and, in the absence of the two Earls, opened the meeting. Ninety-nine members were present, together with an uncounted number of gate-crashers who were there merely to shelter from the storm. The Secretary read a letter of apology from the President, who observed that he was opposed on two grounds to changing the title to "Shire Horse Society". In the first place, the only sufficient reason for an alteration would be that the existing name was too narrow, and kept horses out of the Stud-book that ought to be in. He did not think that was so. Secondly, he had never heard a satisfactory definition of the term "Shire Horse" and he believed that, outside a certain limited circle of connoisseurs, few other people knew what it meant either. Indeed, there was a danger that it might be used to confine the Stud-book to horses bred in certain counties or districts. He added that, whatever decision was made, his support for the Society would not be diminished. Lord Spencer, attending Quarter Sessions at home, sent no expression of views, but was known to be on the Shire side.

Walter Gilbey spoke first. He said the term "Shire-bred" had been used by most people in the discussion on Mr. Street's paper and had been a general one for many years. He lived in Essex, and not in the shires, but he called his horses Shire horses. Though show catalogues did not use the term, most entry forms for the Royal had listed the horses in the agricultural classes as Shire horses. Cattle and sheep breeds, however widely distributed, were often known by county names. The term "Clydesdale" for the Scottish draught-horse was exactly comparable with "Shire" for the English type. He moved the resolution. Sanders Spencer, the famous pig man, a controversialist who was always doing battle in the Press, and a neighbour of Frederic Street at St. Ives, seconded without making a speech or comment.

John Treadwell of Upper Winchendon, near Aylesbury, leading for the opposition, was amazed at Mr. Spencer. "One would have thought that, with such a ready pen as he has, he would have been able to use a fluent tongue." Treadwell had to shout louder and louder as he went on, because of the noise of the rain. His main point was that the existing title was appropriate to a national society and that "Shire" would reduce it to a little coterie. He was constantly interrupted, as his rhetorical questions perhaps deserved. "What are we aiming at when we breed stock?" he roared. And a voice roared back, "Profit". Before giving up, he begged for harmony and claimed that an alteration of name would do no good to anyone, but might do a lot of harm to many.

John Coleman, a Derbyshire immigrant, gave a clear exposition of the true aims of the Society. That he did not convince everyone at once was perhaps not surprising, for prejudice or muddled thinking does not always welcome common sense. But in the years to come, his views were to be so universally accepted as to appear obvious. He began by commenting that Mr. Treadwell, in a long speech (which was a sign of a weak argument), had asked what a cart-horse was. Well, a cart-horse was any animal that could draw a cart, and that was not what they wanted a stud-book for. The Stud-book should contain the cream of heavy draught-horse blood, as found in Lincolnshire, Leicestershire, or Derbyshire. This would not be restrictive at all. It would merely set the pattern at which all men everywhere could aim and would at the same time provide them with the pure blood to which they could go to improve their own stock. Furthermore, a stud-book should be restricted not just to excellent types of animal, but to one distinctive type. The Suffolk was distinctive. But even Royal prize-winners in the non-Suffolk classes might represent several different kinds of heavy-horse. They could not all be included in one stud-book, since that would not help breeders to know what they were doing. If this was how the Society was to work, a distinctive title was quite essential. And "Shire" was the only such name he had heard of.

Speaking "a few words on behalf of Ireland", the Hon. Harry de Vere Pery said, "In order to get our foot in Ireland, I think it is very necessary that we should change it to any other name at all rather than the English Cart-horse." Thomas Brown made up for Mr. Pery's terseness. He was diametrically opposed to John Coleman. He wanted the Society to be a national one in the sense that it would include every type of draught-horse, and hoped to see the day when Clydesdales and Suffolks also would appear in the same book. He advocated one house with many mansions, like the Shorthorn Herd-book. "There is no distinctive breed of cart horses. They are all separate classes of the same breed." He claimed that many of those who requisitioned the meeting were indeed dissatisfied with the present title, but were even more opposed to the word "Shire". "Cut it short", someone exclaimed, whereupon he proceeded to discuss half the counties in England, where he knew of members who were opposed to a change.

The next speaker was Frederic Street. And the thunder and the rain were such that he had to stop for several minutes. He told about a horse entered at the Suffolk Show a fortnight earlier. A gentleman had come to its owner and said, "What breed is your horse?" – "An English Cart Horse". – "So is my Suffolk horse. Every horse bred in England is English." When the owner then explained that his horse was Shire-bred he was at once understood. But Mr. Street ended illogically by making the preposterous suggestion that the title should be "The Cart Horse Society of Great Britain and Ireland, excluding Clydesdales and Suffolks".

Charles Howard said that, as an Englishman, he was sorry to find so many gentlemen ashamed of the word "English". He felt that to change the title would be to defraud those who had subscribed to the Society under its present name. He thought it would be better to appoint a small committee than to make a great noise and break up the Society. Joseph Martin, who began by saying he was a man of peace, commented on most of the previous speakers' remarks (some of which he completely misinterpreted), spoke at some length about his milking herd, seconded Mr. Street's amendment "just in order to compromise the matter", and ended by defying anybody to say what description of horse the Clydesdale and Suffolk were. He saw down amid laughter. George Street rose to stress that if the word "Shire" was in any way restrictive it would be unfair to many who had paid their subscriptions and were denied a share of the benefit. Lord Chesham, who was all for a small committee, competed very well with the drumming of the rain, but it is difficult now to judge from the transcript of the meeting exactly what he was advocating, although he also raised a laugh by commenting that Shorthorn breeders who could trace their stock back to Jupiter would always find a black nose.

No other speaker added anything new and finally Mr. Coke put his own views. He understood that the Society had been formed to promote the heavy-boned, silky-haired horses that could be grown in the Shires. The Norfolk horse, with many apologies to his friends in that county, was a sort of degenerated Shire horse, who could be improved by Shire-bred blood. If, on the other hand, the Norfolk horse was a sort of "Suffolk bay", as some claimed, he had no business to be in their stud-book. He looked forward to the day when the Royal Show would have classes for Clydesdales, Suffolks, and Shire horses. Even if the Society was reduced in size by adopting the word "Shire", it should still be done. "I have been laughed at many and many a time when I have been at home" about the expression "English Cart Horse". "I have really felt ashamed of the name." He then systematically demolished any pretence to logic either in the existing name of the Society or in Mr. Street's amendment. If one did not call their horses Shire horses, one would have to call them dray-horses. "They are big, heavy, strong, horses and it is clear from the judging yesterday that the bigger they are, the heavier they are, the stronger they are and the more hair they have got, the more likely they are to win prizes." (That is, the "agricultural" classes this year were in fact for the same type of animal as the old "dray" classes had once been.) "I think many of them are more suitable for the towns of Manchester and Liverpool. It is for those towns we breed them to a great extent and it is there to a great extent we shall find our best customers."

Mr. Coke then said he would take a vote. He hoped that those who were only sheltering from the rain had not been bored, and asked them to step to the rear. He then requested any members who had not paid their subscriptions to do likewise. There was no need for anyone to leave the tent. A show of hands on Mr. Street's amendment proved impossible to count and Mr. Coke asked members to divide by standing on separate sides of the platform. They responded with great good humour. Amid cries of "Shire horses to the right", "Get over, the cart horses", "Steady there, boy" and "Exclude the Suffolks and Clydesdales", noble lords, titled gentlemen, landowners and farmers hilariously sorted themselves out, the short and stout occupying more than their share of space but proving less easy to count than the tall and thin. The platform bristled with beards. There were found to be thirty-six members on Mr. Street's side of it and forty-nine on the other, with fourteen still in their seats. Mr. Gilbey's original motion was then put. On the creaking boards, fifty-two were in support and thirty-three against.

Thomas Brown then claimed that, under the Companies Act of 1862, the name could not be changed unless three-fourths of the votes were for it. A lesser chairman might have faced uproar, but the only member whom Mr. Coke had to call to order was Joseph Martin who, after again saying that he was a man of peace, felt that it was bad taste not to bow, as he had done himself, to the will of the majority. Good or bad taste was of course irrelevant, but no one except Mr. Brown claimed to know the law and the point was not dealt with in the Articles of the Society. Eventually Mr. Coke declared the resolution carried and explained that, if a simple majority was insufficient, the vote would be invalid.

Most members were now free to go out into the rain if they wished, but the Council assembled to thrash out the difficulty. Joseph Martin said it was not at all like an Englishman not to take a whacking and submit to it: Mr. Brown asked him not to harp upon one string so, or he would break it. John Treadwell proposed that legal advice should be taken and it was agreed that Messrs. Coke, Brown and Gilbey should see Mr. Dorman.

Mr. Dorman had no doubt at all. The resolution was invalid. Officially at least, the change of name was not discussed again for four years.

5. PEDIGREES, PEOPLE AND A PATRON

When it was found that the simple majority vote at Kilburn to change the name of the Society was invalid, Walter Gilbey proposed at the next council meeting that "Shire Horses" should be classified separately in the stud-book. It was fortunate that he found no support, because that wedge, if knocked in, would have caused a disastrous split. Thomas Brown's counter proposal was accepted – that the Editing Committee should be authorised to add the words "Shire horse" to those animals in the Stud-book which were entitled to it. When put into practice, this was a more or less meaningless differentiation and therefore did no harm. Owners who were still alive submitted their horses as "Shires" if they personally were in favour of that title. A "Shire" horse of John Coleman would not be a "Shire" if he happened to have been sold to John Treadwell before being considered for the Stud-book. Owners who had been dead a long time would have been astounded if they could have been resurrected to give their opinion. They had never heard of "Shire" horses and would have answered, "Put mine down as a Black (or a Staffordshire Brown, or a Lincoln)". In some of these cases the Editing Committee no doubt tossed a coin. The basic absurdity of the whole business was that the debate had nothing to do with two types of horse, but concerned a choice between two names to embrace several sub-varieties of the same type of horse.

This controversy over names was only a sort of interlude during the hard work of getting the Stud-book launched. No one allowed his individual opinion about the matter to impede the common cause. On the Editing Committee, Shire men and Cart men together spent days at a time examining and sifting pedigrees, some of them very ancient. It had been agreed that the first volume of the book should be restricted to stallions, and to those foaled not later than 1876: that is, it was to be mainly a retrospective register including as many ancestors as could be traced of genuine "English Cart-horses" of the day. It was a tremendous task in spite of the nucleus provided by Richard Reynolds' privately compiled collection of pedigrees, the copyright in which was purchased for 100 guineas. His list was found to contain something like 1,400 horses belonging to about 700 owners, though all these of course needed investigation by the committee, to which Reynolds' name was added. Gilbert

Murray, William Wright and John Nix contributed much information about Derbyshire horses, as did James Forshaw about Nottinghamshire, where he lived, and Lancashire, where he had come from. Probably others offered as much help, or more, but unfortunately every scrap of documentary evidence which the committee acquired was later destroyed.

Reynolds was, incidentally, a "Shire" man and spoke in favour of the change at the Kilburn meeting. It was his proposal, seconded by Frederic Street, that was finally accepted to settle the eligibility of stallions for the first volume. This, simply, was that any animals of the "right type" could be included providing they had no known cross of other blood for at least two generations. In retrospect, this seems very vague. But everyone's very vagueness was the whole reason for needing a stud-book at all.

Meanwhile, the Finance Committee, faced with the task of collecting members at 1 guinea a year or 10 guineas for life, had tried in the autumn of 1878 circularising all recent cart-horse exhibitors at local shows. In this sort of way, progress was slowly made. For example, on 4th February 1879, twenty-nine new members were elected, including the Dukes of Devonshire and Bedford, the Marquises of Stafford and of Exeter, the Earl of Camperdown, Earl Cawdor, Lord Kesteven, two Baronets and an M.P. (The Duke of Bedford was anxious for reassurance that the liability of members was limited.) But the Prince of Wales headed a list of twelve whose election could only be provisional, since their names had not been received in time for the Council to be notified in advance. His Royal Highness was, of course, a special capture, for he had previously dabbled in Suffolks and Clydesdales, as Her Majesty had done. The Council lost little time not just in electing him at the following meeting, but in persuading him to become Patron. And he turned out to be no mere figure-head, but a real enthusiast.

6. THE FIRST LONDON SHOW: 1880

At the Council meeting on 9th December 1879, Frederic Street introduced Mr. J. H. Raffety, a member of the Society, who was lessee of the Agricultural Hall at Islington. This gentleman did not particularly resemble a fairy god-mother in general appearance, but what he came to propose was worthy of one. He offered to stage a Cart Horse Show in the early spring free of all charge and expense, whether for the provision of loose-boxes and stabling and the preparation of the ring, or for anything else. He would also give the sum of £500 from which the Society could allocate prizes. He would provide a further £100 to pay stewards, judges and other officials. And, to cap it all, he would supply free forage, straw, gas, police, staff, printing, postage and advertising. In return he would expect to receive the entry fees for animals exhibited, though the Society could fix these (and did in fact allow members to enter their horses at half fee), admission money at the turn-stiles (though Society members were to be admitted free) and rent for trade stands.

The idea of holding a show had never been discussed or even thought of.

Without Raffety's offer, it would have been impossible to contemplate, because the influx of cash into the Society's coffers was inevitably slowing down to a trickle. Subscriptions were the only source of income and, the keenest spirits having already joined, most other potential members were waiting to see if there would in fact be any positive achievement by the Society, such as the actual publication of a stud-book. So far, all that the outsider was aware of was a prolonged row about the name of the breed.

There was some doubt whether a horse-show was among the proper activities of the Society. The Council, in associating itself with such a thing, would have to rely on a fairly broad interpretation of the four objects for which the Society was established, as set out in its Memorandum of Association. The first of these was "to improve the breed and to promote the breeding of English Cart Horses": the second, "to promote the general interests of the breeders and the owners of English Cart Horses": the third related to the purchase or hire of houses, lands, goods, chattels, and effects, and the disposal of them: the fourth was "to do such other lawful things as may be incidental or conducive to the attainment of the above objects or any of them". Although competitive exhibitions of horses might help to encourage the attainment of the first object and could therefore come within the scope of the fourth, to give money prizes to individual exhibitors might be detrimental to the general interests of the others, which it was the second object of the Society to promote.

The Articles of Association said nothing of horse shows, though they elaborated on publications and pedigrees. Even the bye-laws, though concerned with discipline and disputes, were silent about horse shows. They directed that editing and finance committees should be appointed, but made no provision for any others. Nevertheless, Raffety's proposal was greeted with enthusiasm. A Horse Show committee was immediately appointed and the names of its members – Gilbey, Brown, James Howard and Frederic Street – are a further reminder that Cart and Shire men were working together in the greatest harmony. The date was fixed for Tuesday, 2nd March and the show was to run for three days. They had exactly twelve weeks to plan and advertise it, arrange for railway transport for horses whose numbers could only be guessed until near the time, print a catalogue, reserve hotel accommodation and make all other preparations for a venture in which success was vital, simply because failure might mean suicide. And suicide so early would be entirely unnecessary, because it was surely foolhardy to take the colossal risk of being the first breed society in the world to have its own show, when membership stood at less than 400 (of whom probably more than half were unhappy about the name of the Society), while even the very conformation of an English Cart Horse had been neither defined nor even formally discussed, and before a single volume of a stud-book had been published. But fortune favoured the brave, a cliché the Victorians were as fond of putting to the test as of preaching.

On the Monday afternoon and evening of 1st March 1880, 114 horses arrived at the various London termini and made their way to Islington, where they were met by three men who proved, as they had already done before, that those who talked the most also worked the hardest – Thomas Brown, Joseph Martin and Frederic Street. Their duties as stewards prevented them from attending the monthly meeting that afternoon of the Farmers' Club. With John Treadwell in the chair, the paper was read by Professor Pritchard of the Royal Veterinary College on "Hereditary Diseases in Cart Horses". He began briskly by saying, "I am desirous of arousing the breeders to a knowledge of the folly of carelessly using unsound sires and dams, and of the mischief they bring about." In the discussion that followed his speech, he swept aside both the defeatists, who believed that some such troubles would never be cured, and the optimists, who felt that most of them were not necessarily inherited.

The next day the judges began their work promptly at 11 o'clock – a starting-time that would have seemed like luxury to their successors a few years later. The bad old custom of secret judging, before the public or even the owners were allowed in, had died a well-deserved death at most shows some twenty years since, but in accordance with general custom, the identity of the judges had not been divulged, for it had not occurred to anyone to break the sacred custom of advance secrecy on this point. They turned out to be W. T. Lamb of Welbourn, Richard Reynolds and Samuel Wade. Nor, for their part, did these gentlemen know (officially, at least) who or whose were the horses before them, for as was also customary in shows at that time they were not allowed to see a catalogue. In other respects, the conditions and regulations that were so hastily drawn up would seem remarkably familiar to any exhibitor a century later.

One of these rules was a novelty of the utmost importance. Or, rather, a near-novelty. Hitherto, at any agricultural show (except the Suffolk County), a horse might have a tremendous sidebone, or a ringbone: his feet might be diseased beyond repair: he might have a cataract: he might whistle or roar. But he could win. Not, however, at this show. The Society was determined that its strongest weapon in improving the breed was to be the rejection of any animal, however marvellous otherwise, who would be likely to perpetuate any unsoundness. If a tough attitude could be made clear at the start, then it would soon become an obvious waste of money to bring all the way to London an animal that would not even be considered. And if success in London was ever to become a horse's passport to popularity among breeders, then in due course an increasing proportion of the animals used for breeding would be sound. This is exactly what happened, and it was Professor Pritchard himself who made the start. The only Inspector appointed, he was happy with his brief, that "no animal should receive a prize that was not free from hereditary or other diseases detrimental to breeding sound and healthy stock". No one now can tell how many impressive animals were sent packing from the ring, but a large number of them had arrived as celebrated prize winners. The name of Pritchard stuck in the gorge of more than a few apoplectic owners that day.

A thirteen-year-old horse called Champion won the £40 prize for stallions of five years and upwards, and he was a chestnut. Bred in Rutland, he was shown by Tom Statter's Stand Stud Company which claimed that he had won over £1,300 in his time. No doubt this was chiefly in the form of premiums to travel various districts, but he had several times been second at the Royal Show. He was an enormously heavy and powerful horse, described by Sexton as "a real shaft horse, a tower of strength, with activity and a marvellous constitution". Another chestnut, the five-year-old ex-Ellesmere Samson II, was second – "a long, low horse with bone and hair of the Isle of Ely stamp". Third prize went to an eighteen-year-old, who set an age record for winning a London prize that would never be beaten. This was the rather leggy son of the great Honest Tom, Major, who had spent all his life in the possession of his breeder, Thomas Murfit of Wiggenhall St. Mary, Norfolk. In the years to come, Shire men were to look back almost in disbelief of their memories at the "rough old lot" that occupied the hall at the first Show, and some of the worst were to be found among the sixteen in this class.

First prize for the twelve four-year-olds was only half the value of the senior class, but the winner also won the 50 guinea championship cup. Appropriately, this was Lord Ellesmere's Admiral, also by Honest Tom (1105) and bred in the Fylde. Sexton remarked that he was "a magnificent specimen of a dray horse, a good outline throughout, good limbs and feather, perhaps a bit too high from the ground, with scarcely enough depth of carcase". Behind him, also fittingly, stood a son of the Old Strawberry, shown by Garrett Taylor and bred, like the ancient Major, at Wiggenhall St. Mary, but by James Marston. He appears to have been a different sort altogether – "a really agricultural and general purpose horse, thick, smart, and compact, on short legs of the right quality, with good feather". He was also a good mover. There were twenty-three three-year-olds led by the tall and narrow chestnut Rutland Champion, and fifteen two-year-olds. The latter class was won by another of the President's exhibits, Worsley Wonder. His grand-sire was the Old Strawberry and his dam was by Honest Tom. "How the blood tells!", the secretary was moved to write in his report. And that, of course, was what the Society was seeking to demonstrate. The yearling class of ten was perhaps the best, and the first two places were taken by sons of the Old Strawberry.

More animals were thrown out by Professor Pritchard from the senior mares' class than from any other. In fact, he did not leave many of them in. Lawrence Drew won both the class and the female championship with his six-year-old Topsy. She had wonderful feet and legs, but many thought she was too high off the ground, which was why she had gone north of the border. Of the purest Derbyshire blood for countless generations, she was a perfect sample of those Shire mares which in their hundreds or thousands had been taken to Scotland to make the Clydesdale breed. However, she was an exception in coming south again, for T. H. Miller promptly bought her. The man who bred this first champion mare of the Society is recorded simply as "– Goodall" of Milton, Derbyshire. To be so unknown that others are ignorant even of one's initials or Christian name is somehow depressing, but Mr. Goodall was an instant example of the fact that any man who kept the best mare he could afford and who was fortunate enough to be able to use a really top class stallion stood a chance of breeding a champion. "– Goodall" of Milton stands at the head of that multitude of "small men" who have done just that.

There were only four four-year-old mares, and Lawrence Drew's *Camilla* which had won first prize at the Kilburn Royal eight months earlier was last of the four. The three-year-old class of nine was the strongest – none was rejected and even the last in the line received a commendation card. The first two presented a good contrast between the Shires and the Fens. Edward Coke's *Caprice* represented quality on short legs, beating a filly of great substance and beautiful body, but of rather coarser bone. There were eight two-year-old fillies (Drew, Ellesmere and Coke took the prizes), but not a single entry in the yearling class. This might seem odd in view of the representations made to R.A.S.E. the year before, but there is all the difference for the babies between a draughty London hall in early March and a country show four months later. In a class for geldings of any age, two of the three prizes were awarded – to a six-year-old black owned by Captain W. H. Betts and a nine-year-old horse from P. & R. Phipps' Northampton Brewery. A final class for mares *or* geldings had no entries, though the first prize offered was, at £30, the second highest in the show.

The whole affair was a great success for the famous sires of choicest pedigree. Honest Tom, with eight sons and daughters there, was sire of the champion stallion and four other winners and was dam's sire of four winners. England's Wonder, the Old Strawberry, also had eight progeny on view, and they picked up three prizes. William the Conqueror had a First and Third, and Lincolnshire Lad (1196), long since an exile in Scotland, a third, which was a modest start for the two great foundation sires of later years. A fair amount of business was done in the letting of stallions for the coming season and there was a number of private sales. The Secretary also held an auction, but this did not take place till the day after the show was over, by which time many animals that might have been put on offer had returned home. Even so, thirty-one stallions, two mares and two geldings were successfully transferred to new owners. Stallions averaged 91 guineas, the top price being obtained by Mr. Banyard's own-bred roan British Ore, of Horningsea, Cambs., which had been third in the four-year-old-class, and for which E. Caldecott of Reading paid 200 guineas.

The Prince and Princess of Wales visited the Show on the second day with the Princesses Louise, Victoria and Maud of Wales. And so did the Lord Mayor and Lady Mayoress, the Baroness Burdett-Coutts, Mr. Henry Irving and other notables. But the general public was unaware that this was to be so great an occasion and not enough of them attended. Mr. Raffety could not make money out of the members, who entered free. As it turned out, he made a heavy loss. As for the Society's show account, it was remarkable for its simplicity. Expenditure (prizes £445. 15s., Secretary £25, stewards £21, judges £16, Professor

Pritchard £5. 5s.) totalled £513. This was balanced by "Received from Mr. Raffety, £513".

The Society's funds, left quite intact after these exciting junketings, were now in credit to the sum of £550, a little more than at the end of the year 1879. The accounts, incidentally, were audited by James Harris of Cape & Harris, Old Jewry Chambers, who had been suggested by Walter Gilbey. The two men were friends, and used to ride into the city together, putting up their horses at the same hotel. (The Society has proved no more fickle to its accountant than to its legal advisors, for the grandson of James Harris audits the accounts nearly a century later. Mr. L. M. Gibson Harris understands that in old age Gilbey used to visit his grandfather on Sunday afternoons, "during the course of which a bottle of whisky was consumed, and both were fast asleep by tea-time.")

7. A TRIUMPHANT 730 DAYS

At the Annual General Meeting on the second day of the Show, the eagerly-awaited Stud-book of 2,365 stallions was available. Five-hundred copies had been bound, including a hundred in half-calf, and another 500 were in sheet form, hopefully ready for binding. The bill later presented by Cassell, Petter and Galpin (who three years afterwards were to become known as Cassell & Co. Ltd.) was £447. 7s. – £203 more than the original estimate, owing to the enormous number of changes in the proofs. After much argument, £15 was knocked off the bill before it was paid. The whole affair was a triumph, for the Suffolk book was still not ready.

The simultaneous impact of the show and the Stud-book was remarkable. Sexton, in his report, said that hitherto, "except in a few special localities, and amongst a limited number of men, the English Cart Horse was considered to be a nondescript animal, having not the least claim to purity of lineage but one that might be obtained from the mixture of any kind of blood". The public had thought of him as a ponderous slave, who just appeared on the London stones. Many even of the breeders were astounded to find that Shire-bred horses could be traced back so far. (Elsewhere in his report, he referred rather equivocally to the "old Shire-bred English cart horse". *The Times* correspondent, with no need for diplomacy, wrote of the object of the show being to improve "the Shire or, as they prefer to call it, the English cart-horse".)

It was now time for the Earl of Ellesmere to hand over to his successor, the Earl Spencer. The thirty "councilmen" also, having balloted for the names of the first ten to retire, selected twenty new names from whom the members were asked to elect replacements, and so the still-existing system of providing continuity, and at the same time new blood each year, was put into operation. The first Council had met twenty-two times in two years, apart from the two initial meetings at the Farmers' Club. They met seven times at the Society of Arts, nine times at the Farmers' Club, three times at the Agricultural Hall, twice on the Royal showground, and once at Worsley Hall. Thomas Brown had missed only two meetings, and Frederic Street three. Next were Major

Dashwood who attended seventeen, Walter Gilbey sixteen and George Street fifteen. The President and Vice President had attended twenty-one meetings between them. There were now 376 members of the Society. And the day the first show closed was still only the second anniversary of the paper read by Frederic Street.

In precisely 730 days, the small group of men who had originally intended nothing more than the publication of a register of pedigrees had succeeded in making progress over a much wider front. Indeed, a start had been made in attacking most of those problems which, with hind-sight, it is easy to recognise now but which at the time were not particularly obvious. A sick man does not know he is ill unless he has formerly been well. These problems were eight, and it was the almost fortuitous London Show, rather than the Stud-book, which pointed the way to a solution of many of them:

1. The isolation of breeders from their fellow practitioners in other areas, even in other parishes, was clearly going to be broken down by such an event as a breed show, if it could be held annually. This was particularly important in the case of stock which were spread comparatively thinly across the whole country. There were over 20,000,000 sheep in England and Wales and about 4,250,000 cattle, but not very much more than 1,000,000 working horses of all types on farms – the rest were in the towns. Yet these few horses were distributed over every square mile of the country. A man who attended the show had the unprecedented experience of spending three whole days in the company of other cart-horse breeders and owners, many or most of whom he had never even heard of before. The Lancastrians, the Fenmen, the Derbyshire men and the rest each appeared to the others to talk in an extraordinary, even unintelligible, way. Nothing was so amusing to a Nottinghamshire man as to hear a story told in a strong Berkshire accent. But they turned out to be colleagues and friends to do business with. Perhaps the most notable aspect of the show was the breaking down not of geographical but of social barriers, an achievement which was as extraordinary in 1880 as it has been typical of cart-horse men ever since. There is no branch of horse-breeding, and no other activity either of business or leisure, which has been less subject either to class-consciousness on the grand scale or to petty and absurd snobberies. This show's greatest success lay not so much in the quality of horses exhibited but in its friendly and unpretentious atmosphere.

2. Leadership was no longer a problem. Street had hoped that "more of our chief land-owners will give their attention, as some have nobly done, to the cart-horse; there will be plenty to look after the race-horse. To be the owner of a first-prize cart-horse ought to become as fashionable as the possession of a crack racer."[1] Amazingly, even this was to become a reality in the next twenty years or so. But already an Ellesmere, a Spencer and a Coke, not to mention the heir to the throne, ensured that cart-horse breeding was no longer an occupation

PLATE 13   Young horse off to New South Wales. The roan Iron Duke (1156), just over 16 hands, was only "two off" when he sailed in 1860, but remarkably well furnished. His breeder, George Townsend of Stoney Stanton, Leicestershire, got 200 guineas for him.

PLATE 14   Auld Sir Wattie back home. Ayrshire-bred by George Scott in 1855, rescued from the Fylde by Riddell and sold to the Duke of Hamilton, the great Clydesdale stallion Sir Walter Scott later became Lawrence Drew's own property. He was grandsire of Prince of Wales.

PLATES 15 and 16 Direct descendants of Wiseman's Honest Tom. (*above*) Welcher's Honest Tom 1105, foaled in 1865, was the most celebrated stallion of the 'seventies, first in the Fens and then in the Fylde; (*below*) Lincolnshire Lad II: not a good picture of a not very prepossessing horse—narrow, tall, light-bodied but, for all that, destined to be "the father of the Stud-book". He was foaled in 1870.

that was beyond the pale for a gentleman, and "not quite the thing" for any respectable man. James Forshaw's first great difficulty, when he wanted to buy his first stallion in 1863, had been to overcome the repugnance of his wife at the stigma involved – and they were scarcely in a high position themselves, for it took all the money they possessed to buy this one horse. Nineteen years after generously falling in with her husband's ambition, Mrs. Forshaw was to watch him shake hands with the Prince of Wales simply because he owned the best stallion in England. The cart-horse had returned to its Bakewellian status, and surpassed it.

3. Education received an impetus that was greater than could be achieved by a hundred books. The lack of secretiveness that distinguished cart-horse men from the professionals of the turf meant that a man could learn from listening, or just watching, his fellows. Errors and ignorances and fallacies would wither quicker in the somewhat stifling atmosphere of the Agricultural Hall than anywhere else. Organisers of agricultural shows, too, would learn about the cart-horse and cater for him accordingly. The education that was available at Islington extended even to human behaviour. The standard of deportment, as of horse-care, on the part of many of the grooms would have shocked their successors at the London shows a generation later. But an occasion like this was the finest way to effect an improvement. Many a man gaped to see the Prince of Wales for the first time and many, too, were startled to be visited and addressed by the Earl of Ellesmere. This was the first opportunity of a wider vision of life for many a blinkered eye.

4. Buying and selling horses now at last could be developed into a properly organised affair. The Society had an official auctioneer, and his activities would soon be vastly increased. They would also inspire imitation. It is hard, now, to appreciate the difficulties of buying a good quality horse in days when there were no proper horse auctions and no known (or admitted, or credible) pedigrees. The Worsley Park sale of 1878 had been a unique pioneering effort in this respect. The hiring of stallions, also, could now develop along orderly lines. Some were actually hired at this show but, more importantly, any man or group of neighbours could for the first time look around and note for future reference not only what was what but, of equal value, who was who.

5. Knowledge of pedigrees, obviously, would become within the reach of all, as soon as a volume containing mares was made available. That was the whole point of the Society. But when men could look at one prize-winner and know the breeding, and then look at some others and know they were by the same sire, or were otherwise related, book-knowledge was transformed into practical wisdom and intelligent men could even think in terms of bloodlines and other subtle calculations designed to perpetuate the best qualities and eliminate the worst. Frederic Street, contrasting the situation with that of

Shorthorn cattle, had said, "All must agree that 'Booths' and 'Bates' are both sadly needed in horse-flesh." He added a remark that is astounding in its wisdom and perspicacity. "There are many well-bred mares of the England's Glory breed which ought to be looked up for stud purposes." Bingham's England's Glory, sire and grand-sire of many other England's Glories between the Welland and the Wash, had been dead fifty years. He was a very celebrated horse in his day – in the Fens. Breeders knew his value: all credit to those who used him and who jealously guarded the blood of his sons and daughters. But no man in the Agricultural Hall, not even Street, was aware that Lincolnshire Lad, which Drew had taken to Scotland, was his direct descendant in the male line. Welcher's Honest Tom and the Old Strawberry were both similarly descended. England's Glory or, more accurately, his sire, did more for the breed a hundred years after his death than any other horse. But, such was the confusion that had reigned for half a century that Street assumed something of the status of a prophet, in 1880, when he mentioned him in the same breath as the Bates and the Booths. (The prophet's honour was not to be fully his in his life-time or even afterwards – until now. See Part B.) As for the idea of tracing a mare's ancestry through the female line, back through fifty years, that had been impossible. It was considered enough to say of a mare that she was "by So-and-so": or, more commonly, while studying the pedigree of a stallion, to dismiss the mare's breeding completely on the grounds that a good one "carried her pedigree on her back".

6. The elimination of unsoundness requires no further comment here, except that Professor Pritchard's ruthlessness would have to be maintained for many a long year in order to achieve progress. All kinds of hereditary faults were common. But unsoundness of the bones, such as sidebone, was an insidious menace in the cart-horse. It tended to remain latent in the cart-stallion, for he, unlike his workaday progeny, did not have to thump about on the stony ground of the towns, which was where sidebones grew and unfortunately also took root and did not wither away. Hereditary unsoundness in the Thorough-bred, on the other hand, had already manifested itself during his racing career before he ever went to stud.

7. A consistent standard of conformation, to replace the varying whims of various Royal Show judges, was set by the breed-show system. Curiously, the English Cart Horse Society did so by this means alone. No official printed lists of the points of a stallion or mare of their breed was to be issued until long after the animals had ceased to be of commercial or agricultural importance, after the Second World War. Plenty of statements were to be drawn up by individuals, and some by successive secretaries when requested to write about the breed. But none was apparently issued by the Council (unless one counts A. G. Holland's book in 1929, which was published by the Society and therefore had its authority). Reluctance to do this at the very beginning was, of course, both

natural and wise. Much of the anxiety that was felt about adopting the term "Shire" was based on a fear that the breed would be restricted to a sharply defined standard of conformation. By a model exercise of common-sense and restraint of the tongue and pen, the promoters of the first London Show did much towards including, and nothing to exclude, cart-horses of slightly varying sorts from all over the country.

8. Only in one matter had no progress been made. What was the best name to give this horse over whose pedigree and conformation so much energy was being expended?

8. LONDON SHOWS, 1881–1884

The second spring show, 22nd–24th February 1881, was staged by the optimistic Raffety on similar terms to the first, except that he provided only £100 towards the prizes. The Council, thanks mainly to Walter Gilbey's powers of persuasion, managed after a struggle to obtain donations of nearly £400 to fill the gap. Raffety suggested that Clydesdales and Suffolks should be admitted to the show on special terms "in order that there may be no doubt about the building being filled". This idea was coldly received, but he was allowed, entirely at his own expense, to add three unofficial classes for horses in harness, "singles, pairs and teams, prizes value £67, with silver-mounted whips to the drivers". He lost money, but not as much as the year before.

There were ten official classes for stallions and mares and two for "geldings, any breed". Entries, totalling 146, were thirty-two more than the first year. The champion stallion was a black three-year-old – W. R. Rowland's own-bred Spark from the Aylesbury district, described by Sexton as of "immense substance, fine feet and joints, full of bone and feather". Walter Gilbey bought him at the auction afterwards for 500 guineas. The class for senior stallions, five years and upwards, attracted thirty-one entries, and the top three were a good illustration of the different types of horse on display. Frederic Street's ten-year-old bay Beauchieff was an "agricultural" type of horse and had been bred in Yorkshire. Below him stood two much taller and heavier horses – King of the Vale, Col. Morrell's blue-roan which was 3rd at Kilburn in 1879 and was now seven, and the bay Fen-bred Temptation, five years old, which was the first London winner shown under the Forshaw name.

The seven-year-old champion mare Black Diamond, "a show in herself, as near perfection as it is possible to see", belonged to Lord Ellesmere, who afterwards bought the first prize yearling colt from his exhibitor. The geldings were a terrible lot. And so were most of the non-winners in the breeding classes – if we judge by the standards of only twenty years later. But it is unreasonable to criticise. What, after all, was the Show for, if not to demonstrate by the few good specimens exhibited what the breeder and owner must aim at?

No record remains of how many animals were turned down by the indefatigable Professor Pritchard, whom some exhibitors were unhappy to discover once again examining legs and feet and wind and eyes – a job which he ruthlessly did for the good of the cause rather than the fee which, at about 8d. a horse, was hardly commensurate with his status. The auction was a tremendous success, but no details have survived. Again, the Show was attended by many members of the Royal family, including the Prince and Princess of Wales who were heartily cheered on the streets of Islington as they drove through the snow to the hall. (That evening a thaw began and Mr. Gladstone, arriving at Marlborough House to dine with the Prince, unfortunately slipped in the slush and received a severe blow on the head. He was taken home and spent a week in bed. There was great concern, and the Prince was among the callers, who were so numerous that Downing Street had to be closed for days.)

The Council toyed with the idea of holding the 1882 show at the Bingley Hall, Birmingham or the Pomona Gardens at Manchester, but the terms demanded by Mr. Lythall and Mr. Reilly were worse, or no better, than Mr. Raffety's. Townley-Parker forced the calling of an extraordinary general meeting at the Derby Royal Show in 1881. "I am thoroughly convinced", he said, "that unless the show is held elsewhere than in London for a few years, it will fall to the ground. In London it is not supported by the public." He suggested the covered hay-markets at Liverpool or Preston. But everyone else voted for Islington, and the willing Raffety was not only relieved of providing any prize-money but was also given permission to hold a poultry show in the galleries of his own hall. Whether this actually took place and, if it did, whether it attracted many of those who had been so far indifferent to a display of horses, is now indiscoverable. But the show was a great success, financially and otherwise. Entry fees for exhibits amounted to £297 and the Society, after paying stewards, judges, the veterinary inspector and a bit extra to the secretary, handed the balance of £229 to Raffety. Donations to the prize fund amounted to £561. Of this, £454 was spent on prizes, £26 on printing, £29 to reimburse Raffety for over 6,000 circulars and posters supplied to London carriers, coal merchants and publicans, and 5 guineas to Mr. Dorman for drawing up the agreement. This left a profit of £47. Raffety entertained all the officials and committee to luncheon each day. Later, Sanders Spencer, the pig man, was commissioned at 10 guineas to write a report on the show.

By arrangement with the leading railway companies, cheap trains were run on most lines, which was a very welcome and popular innovation, and marked the start of a long and happy association with some of the railway officials, who set a standard of efficiency both in getting horses to the show and in the more difficult task of getting them away again that was to be for sixty years a marvel. Transport to London could be arranged days ahead, but for the return trip owners were uncertain when they would be able to remove their animals, and all horses sold by auction on the last day would be due for different destinations, possibly on different companies' lines.

A startling feature of this show was that the names of the judges were announced on the prize sheet. Old men shook their heads, having never heard of such a thing before. Even some younger ones wondered what other novelties the new society would have the temerity to introduce next. But it was a good idea, and of course every other show in the country soon copied it. An even more revolutionary innovation was that copies of the printed catalogue were put in the judges' hands when they entered the ring. This broke all the normal rules, for it was supposed to lead to friends and neighbours being favoured.

(When T. F. Plowman at the age of twenty-three succeeded his late father as secretary of the Oxfordshire Agricultural Society in 1867, he was very inexperienced. On the day before his first show, he casually told a steward that he had a special pile of catalogues ready for the judges. His remark was received with absolute horror and he was told that they were supposed to be given manuscript books, listing the animals and their sex and age but omitting all mention of the owner. With voluntary help and by sitting up all night himself, he was able to rectify the omission. If he had not discovered his mistake in the nick of time, everyone would have been thirsting for his blood and judging would have been considered impossible. Over fifty years later, after many years as secretary of the Bath & West Society, he still shuddered at his near escape from crime – and at most agricultural shows, judges still were not allowed to see a printed catalogue! But the Cart-horse Society in 1882 had realised that the mere absence of printed particulars will not turn a biased judge into an impartial one.[2])

The senior stallions (five years old and upward) and senior mares (four and upward) were for the first time divided by height, 16.2- and 16-hands respectively being the maximum for short-legged horses. First prize in the small stallions' class was won by the twelve-year-old Emperor II, bred in the Fens, resident in Suffolk and slyly described by Sanders Spencer as "twice a Shire-bred and once a Clydesdale". James Forshaw's Bar None won the big stallion class, and the championship too. This was an event of double significance. Forshaw and his sons were to become the most consistently formidable challenge to any exhibitors at London shows and, in their sheer professionalism as stallion-owners of the top rank, probably contributed more than any other family to the success of the breed. Bar None was destined to emerge, while the miscellany of English cart-horses was being gradually formed into a true single breed, as the last and youngest of the "foundation sires" of the modern Shire horse, and the only one of them to appear in person at a London Show. (See B.VIII. 5). There is a fitting symbolism in that this magnificent sire, particularly of fillies (it is arguable that no horse ever got better daughters than he did), won the championship in his own right.

As a matter of new policy, there was a different veterinary inspector. R. S. Reynolds was pleased with the marked freedom from hereditary or structural diseases in the senior breeding classes, where he rejected seven out of seventy-one, two for defective wind and five for feet or legs. Of the eighty-one of two and three years of age, he turned down eleven – eight for ring-bone and side-bone, two for diseased hocks and one as a roarer. The situation seemed to be improving, but whether Reynolds was a little less strict, or Pritchard had taught everyone a sharp lesson in the previous years, it is difficult to say. Reynolds did not look very closely at the yearlings, as "signs of hereditary disease are not sufficiently developed at that age" and, at all ages, he was certainly somewhat lenient about defective wind and would not test in-foal mares for this.

The Council planned for the 1883 show in high confidence, for the third one had aroused interest far beyond the circle of members. Cautious men realised they were being invited to participate in a success, and not to support a failure. The suspicious were beginning to think that this new-fangled stunt was the best way of doing business. And indeed there was business done. Walter Gilbey, who had been chairman of the horse show committee from the beginning, arranged to extend the event to four days, with judging completed (hopefully) on the first and the auction on the last. This would leave two clear days for talking and buying and selling and the hiring of stallions for the season. Another advantage, he thought, would appear at the turnstiles, because the general public tended not to be aware of the show until they read the report of the first day in their morning papers. On the first three days, the hall was open until 10 p.m. since "many thousands of business people can only attend in the evening". It was suggested that the show should run from Friday until Tuesday because Saturdays and Mondays were the best days for attracting the general public. But the proposal was mercifully rejected. A long idle February Sunday in a completely unheated and draughty hall might have ended in disaster. The shivering grooms, unable to leave their charges, could only have got hopelessly drunk. And five days in all would have done no good to man or beast.

Admission on the first day up to 4 p.m. cost 5s. and thereafter 1s. Catalogues were produced by the Council, without advertisements, and were sold for 6d. Raffety had previously charged 1s., with advertisements. A new agreement with him put an extra £200 into the Society's coffers. The prize fund was again subscribed, and the champion stallion received just over £100 in cups and cash. This was Spark, the champion of two years before, and his retirement from the show-ring was immediately announced by Walter Gilbey. It was a notable repeated triumph, for the general improvement in standard was shown by the downward placings of Topsy, the 1880 champion mare. In 1881 she had been third. Now she was ninth. And no one could see any loss of form or condition in her. The new champion mare, Mr. Coke's black Chance, combined immense substance with good legs and feet and fine movement. There were 251 exhibits, more than twice as many as at the first show. The Prince of Wales had written to apologise for non-attendance, owing to his being in Berlin for the week. Grooms were given free rail passes home if in charge of horses put up for auction and left unsold. But there can have been few of these, as it was estimated that more than half the exhibits changed hands, either privately or at the sale, during the four days. Professor Robertson, the new veterinary inspector, has left no record of what he did, other than to reject Edward Coke's Certainty for lameness. This stallion was, otherwise, far and away the best of the three-year-olds and had won the E.C.H.S. championship the year before at the York Royal Show (see section 13.)

In 1884, the Society for the first time took over the entire control and direction of the show, renting the Hall for the whole week on terms very favourably negotiated by Gilbey and Garrett Taylor in a five-year contract. There were three reasons for this change. Raffety's Agricultural Agency Company wanted to make changes of which the Council did not approve: it was pretty clear, to judge by the last two shows, that there was no danger of making a loss: and the Society now had a new secretary with a convenient London office. A new committee, meeting annually in the autumn, was for the first time entrusted with the selection of judges and veterinary inspector. For the latter post, they recalled the redoubtable Professor Pritchard. After he had finished, the poor man was not too happy about his own feet and legs, for no less than 359 horses appeared on the scene. The judges sent them to him in batches of ten, and he made a brisk start by rejecting all but two of the first batch of senior small stallions! Still no details remain and it is impossible to put figures to the havoc he wrought. But he certainly rejected comparatively few of the younger horses, which is an indication that the inspections were slowly having their effect. There are few men to whom the breed owes more than to the morally and socially courageous professor. There was only one class for geldings (absurdly, as before, "of any breed" – but who would waste his money sending a Suffolk into the Shires' den?) and he axed more than half of them.

Enterprise of Cannock, Henry Hart's champion stallion, was four years old and probably the best horse yet to appear in London. "His walking and trotting action", wrote Spencer, "is superb; his legs, feet and feather are good; the head well set on and masculine, yet not coarse; ribs well sprung; hind quarters long; and the horse altogether nearly perfect, and shown in the pink of condition". The value of his prizes at the show was £198. 10s. od. – enough to pay and house a shepherd and three carters for a year on a Midland farm. Walter Gilbey had arranged to buy him privately for £1,000, but generously conceded him to Sir Henry Allsopp Bt. of Hindlip Hall, Worcs. The horse was already engaged for the season in Leicestershire, but the following year he would give the Worcestershire farmers an opportunity the like of which they had never dreamed of before. All the lesser cart-horse counties were largely dependent for their progress on the enthusiasm of men like the future Lord Hindlip. Conversely, of course, if he allowed them England's top stallion for a mere 2 or 3 guineas, they might be able to pay him their rent when some good foals came along.

The three-year-old class was won by King of Trent, one of a seemingly endless succession of wonderful colts bred by W. H. Potter of Lockington Grounds, near the Derbyshire boundary of Leicestershire. He had nearly all the qualities a cart-stallion required, including a fine head and crest, marvellous shoulders and deep hind-quarters, but his hocks were a bit full and his action clumsy. He was shown by the Market Rasen and District Cart-Horse Society. This syndicate, formed the previous autumn by Alfred Usher of Wragby on the lines of the Fylde company, was to have an equally short life as a stallion-owning group, lasting only to 1887. It was nearly always discovered that stallion-hiring, rather than owning, was the best activity for a "club". Nevertheless, the members had started by buying a horse that was good enough to be placed first out of seventy-six. This was easily the biggest class yet seen at a London Show, and remained so for an hour or two, until the eighty-five two-year-olds appeared. In 1880, there had been fifteen of these latter; in 1881, sixteen; in 1882, twenty-five; and in 1883, forty-eight. Sanders Spencer, in his report, claimed that eighty-five was a record for any show. "I am aware", he wrote, "that at 'another place' more than one hundred two-year-old stallions have been on show at one time. But there the youngsters were of all or any cross or pure breed, and generally speaking the prize-winners were the result of a very recent if not a first cross with a Shire-bred." Mr. Spencer was always given a free hand to air his own views, but could be depended upon not to grant Glasgow pride of place over London.

The only serious complaint came from P. Albert Muntz, that future apostle Paul of the Shire, whose first-ever exhibit at the London Show was turned down on inspection as being too tall for the small mares class. He later suggested that decisions about the height of an animal were a matter for the Council and not the veterinary inspector. He was sure she had not grown during the journey from Dunsmore to London. As for the general public, over 7,000 of them had now realised that these Shires were something worth seeing, and their attendance enabled the whole show to be run at a cost of only £250, in spite of the fact that for the first time all prize money was paid out of income instead of being begged. The details of the show account are not without interest:

RECEIPTS	£	EXPENDITURE	£
Admission	613	Rent of hall and gas	282
Entry fees (exhibits)	527	Fitting up hall	498
Catalogues (sales &		Printing, stationery	151
adverts)	120	Advertising, bill-posting	174
Implement exhibitions	93	Prizes	477
Half commission on auction	246	Fodder	118
Cost to Society	250	Judges, stewards etc.	62
		Labour, police etc.	87
	1,849		1,849

Financially, the Society was getting on its feet and from its general funds was now able to invest £1,000.

9. STUD-BOOKS AND DISCIPLINE, 1881–1884

If the Editing Committee expected the production of Volume 2 to be a comparatively easy task, they soon discovered otherwise. True, they did not have to search for horses, since the onus was now on their owners to apply. But so many entries, particularly of mares, were vague or muddled that the task of separating the sheep-horses from the goats and of obtaining the signatures of breeders as well as of owners, drove them nearly to despair. How could so many keen cart-horse men be so utterly incompetent in registering the simplest of pedigrees? Only about 400 applications, one quarter, were satisfactorily settled by the closing date, 7th September, which had therefore to be put back. It also became apparent that the enthusiastic owners of hundreds of excellent mares, which had been bought at fairs up and down the country, knew absolutely nothing about their breeding.

Perhaps in the circumstances it was fortunate that a far larger number of men were either too apathetic or too suspicious of the whole stud-book idea to submit their horses at all. The slow response at least prevented chaos. Eventually the text – the pedigrees of 135 stallions and 511 mares, two enormously long essays on breeding and management by Reynolds and the secretary, indices and a list of members – was placed in the printers' hands. Exactly seven weeks later the 364 page volume, marred by scarcely one typographical error, was published at the second London show.

Thomas Wilkinson of Winmarleigh, Lancs, complained that his three mares were only in the appendix of "also-rans", in spite of the full pedigrees he had supplied. He was politely informed that his animals were half-bred Clydesdales and that he should be thankful to see them in print at all. A Wisbech gentleman started collecting pedigrees and cash, submitted to the secretary a statement of monies he held on behalf of the Society, and was sharply told that the Council could not recognise a self-elected agent. There was a certain amount of criticism about the arrangement of the mares which, as in the first Suffolk book, were listed not alphabetically but under their owners' names – a useless system unless it were intended to reprint up-to-date lists every year. Townley-Parker made some suggestions for improvement and the Editing Committee was given authority to do whatever it liked in the future.

Volume 3 was more like the excellent and simple arrangement of the stallions in the first volume, and had good indices. But Volume 4 was a real muddle, which no one liked. So Volume 5, published at the 1884 London Show, appeared in a straightforward form which never had to change thereafter, except that numbers were still not allotted to mares, which was even more confusing than the omission would have been in the case of stallions, because the Beauties, Blossoms and Bonnies were legion. Nevertheless, 1,423 animals appeared in Volume 5, more than twice the average number of those in Volumes 2–4: and their registration was effected with only half the wear and tear on the nerves and temper of the Secretary and the Editing Committee.

In April 1882, the Council was faced with its first disciplinary case. Major Dashwood drew its attention to a stallion advertised by a Buckinghamshire member as "What's Wanted". He said that the horse was really Brown Stout 341 and that the pedigree on the card did not in the least agree with the registered pedigree of the horse. Of the eight Brown Stouts so far registered, this one was bay in colour and eight years old. The card was liable to cause confusion with the celebrated stallion What's Wanted 2332, also bay and now nine years old, owned by James Forshaw. But the point at issue was not whether simple persons would be deceived into thinking the Buckinghamshire horse was a famous sire but whether anyone would be deceived in any way at all.

The matter was referred to the Editing Committee in accordance with the Society's Bye-Law 20, which dealt with "cases of suspected or doubtful pedigrees of English Cart Horses and all cases of alleged misrepresentation relating to them which may be brought under notice of the Society". The committee instructed the Secretary to write to the member, who did not reply. A special committee of three was appointed, according to the rules, consisting of Major Dashwood, John Treadwell and W. Rickford Rowland of Aylesbury, who happened to be the former owner of Brown Stout 341. Interviewed by these three at Witney, the accused member acknowledged that the particulars on the card were altogether wrong and promised that such a thing would not happen again. He later wrote to say that "the horse has been sold into Scotland, so that probably no more will be heard of him in this district". One wonders whether he ever acquired a Clydesdale pedigree. By a coincidence, the famous What's Wanted died during the investigation. The Council made the facts as public as possible in order "to impress upon members the importance of taking active steps to check such unprincipled proceedings". The member's name even appeared in the Press. No doubt this public exposure of crime was a leaf taken out of the book of the R.A.S.E., which in the 'fifties decided on this method of stamping out the false declaration of ages, particularly of pigs, in Royal Show classes.

The President, the Earl of Powis, referred to the case in his speech at a general meeting at the Royal showground at Reading and concluded by saying, "I trust we shall not have a similar disagreeable case occur again". This was too much to hope for, but the following years were to be surprisingly free of roguery at any point where it really mattered. The vast majority of cart-horse men were honest by nature, and the breeders' certificate system required more than one man to fake a pedigree.

10. A BID TO ANNEX SCOTLAND

Some of the best-known English breeders had, in the 1870s, acted on the Drew principles. James Howard had some very good animals by a Clydesdale stallion out of Essex-bred mares. Henry R. Hart, whose Cannock Agricultural Co. Ltd. was becoming a force to be reckoned with at the shows, and whose breeding and selling was on a massive scale, had started with Clydesdale stallions. Thomas Shaw of Winmarleigh had begun in the same way. T. H. Miller's famous Princess Dagmar was partly Scottish, and so was Lord Ellesmere's mare Farmer, one of the best that even he ever had. Charles Tindall had brought a Clydesdale stallion into Lincolnshire in 1875. Col. Sir Robert Loyd-Lindsay, V.C., M.P., had, in Prince Albert, one of the best Clydesdale stallions in

England. (At this time the fame of the Lockinge stud, like its proprietor's elevation to the peerage as Lord Wantage, still lay in the future.) But in the face of
the stud-book movement, crossing with Clydesdales in England was already
being discontinued.

There were to remain, of course, a few isolated Clydesdale studs, most
notably the Marquis of Londonderry's at Seaham, though Sunderland was
virtually Scotland as far as horses were concerned. The descendants of the
Prince Consort's Clydesdales still graced Windsor, but at Sandringham the
Prince of Wales was a breeder of English horses. The Duke of Richmond's
Clydesdales at Goodwood, the Lords Arthur and Lionel Cecil's in Kent, and
Mr. Smith's at Blacon in Cheshire would soon become exceptional.

By about the end of 1882, it was obvious that the English Cart Horse Society
was in a far healthier state than its Scottish rival. In Scotland, there was turmoil.
A large proportion of breeders was solidly behind Lawrence Drew in his belief
that the Scottish and English horses were but two sections of the same breed,
as the Booth and Bates cattle were both alike Shorthorns. The English saw an
opportunity to take over a divided country and to bring the whole cart-horse
industry under one aegis. There was much talk in corners, and much crossing
of the border for discussions with representatives of the old enemy. But it
was Henry Chandos-Pole-Gell of Hopton Hall, Wirksworth, who was rash
enough to raise the matter in public. One of his ancestors, Colonel Pole, had
been highly praised by Arthur Young as "an honourable instance of a change
from war to agriculture. He has long trod the field of Mars with spirit" (he
had been "shot through the head at Fontenoy and twice wounded on the plains
of Minden"): "I have little doubt but he will now sacrifice to Ceres with equal
ardour."[3] Whether his descendant was now treading the paths of war or peace,
it is difficult to judge, but he was perhaps the most suitable man to rise to his
feet, for he had been one of the few Englishmen to attend the Glasgow meeting
to inaugurate the Clydesdale Society, and had not joined the English one until
June 1880.

At the 1883 Annual General Meeting, under "any other business", he took
the plunge. After a few polite introductory remarks, he said "I think we ought
to take some steps to ascertain whether we cannot get the Scotch breeders to
unite with us, and get one stud-book for the whole of Great Britain. Our
country has been drained of its best mares to go to Scotland, and I will undertake
to find one English horse today who has got more prize winning Clydesdales than
any horse in Scotland. I mean old Lincolnshire Lad." (There was laughter and
applause at this. Even two years earlier, Drew himself had written that the old
horse had been the sire of more prize mares at the principal shows in Scotland
during the five years he had been there than any other stallion in the country.)

"Then there is another horse, Topsman. I know many Scotchmen who have
said that if he had only had a little more bloom about him he would have been
a Clydesdale long ago." (More laughter. One must assume the listeners knew
what "Topsman" he was talking about. The *great* Topsman was recognised as

a Clydesdale, having already been allotted the number 886 in the Stud-book. He was bred by William Wilson at Alford in Aberdeenshire out of a mare called Jane, whose dam Peg had been purchased at Glasgow in foal to one Samson, said to have been a Clydesdale but very possibly the well-known English Samson 1918. Samson was bred in the Fens in 1840 but was always known as Bryan's Samson after his owner at Knossington on the Leicester–Rutland border. Drew, however, always said quite definitely that Topsman's dam was "a pure English mare, purchased at Horncastle". This Topsman was a chestnut of great weight and volume and to enquire further into his breeding would lead us into mysteries beyond unravelling. After winning first prize at the Highland Show at Stirling in 1873, he had come into the possession of J. F. Crowther at Mirfield and after a few seasons there figured in a home sale on 11th February 1880 – another example of an Englishman, and an E.C.H. Council member, clearing out his Scottish horses. Alexander Galbraith of Croy-Cunningham brought him back to Scotland for 300 guineas. But there were two other chestnut Topsmans in the English book also, a few years younger. 2172, foaled in 1873 by Nix's *Goliath* was owned by Charles Brookes, who lived at the English Alford, in Lincolnshire! 2173 won at the R.A.S.E Liverpool, like the Scottish Topsman, in 1875. He was owned by Charles Marsters, proprietor of the "Old Strawberry".)

"I had the privilege of attending the Clydesdale Stallion Show, and I may say that one of the best horses there was a half-bred English horse. Its sire was a Clydesdale, and the dam was an English mare and the said sire had a good deal of English blood in him." (His hearers were happy to laugh again. But there is no identifying of this horse at all.)

"Well, gentlemen, I believe there is a large number of breeders in that country who never accepted fully the Clydesdale Stud-book, and I think I am entitled to say this because I was one of the prime movers in establishing it." (Hear, hear.) "If we had a joint stud-book, it would make them prove the purity of their blood and help us to maintain the purity of our own; and if they have got any advantage of our blood they would be obliged to acknowledge it. I have had considerable correspondence with the leading breeders in Scotland, and they say, 'If we could get one stud-book for Great Britain, we could beat the whole world', and I think we could."

After the prolonged applause this remark was designed to evoke, Mr. Chandos-Pole-Gell continued, "I think it would be a good thing if we could get a committee to meet some influential people from Scotland, and see whether anything could be done to make a start in this way. If anything is to be done, the sooner it is done the better. This is just the turning point – when they find that the animals with English blood in them are taking their best prizes – this is just the time when they would be prepared to amalgamate with us in some way. I have had no conversation with the members of the Clydesdale committee, but I have had with farmers connected with the Society, and I find amongst them a desire to unite with us. I do hope that some step will be taken to bring about the amalgamation. If they won't accept it, I could bring forward another proposal which possibly would compel them to come in."

Thomas Brown thoroughly agreed. He had always thought there should be one book for all cart-horses. "Would you include Suffolks?" asked Anthony Hamond. Mr. Brown replied that he cared nothing about Suffolks, and scarcely classed them amongst cart-horses at all. This was a sure signal for more laughter. But Fred Street thought the time had gone by for an amalgamation. There were three good qualities special to the Scotch horse – feet, legs and pasterns: the others were derived from England. "We believe we have got the best animal in the world" (he was interrupted by cries of "hear, hear", and other expressions of enthusiasm) "and we ought to stick to it". The President, the Earl of Powis, thought the matter could be discussed at the York Royal Show, where there was sure to be a number of Scottish breeders.

II. THE SELECT CLYDESDALE SOCIETY

Chandos-Pole-Gell's proposal came to nothing, which was what it deserved. Although the time was right to push forward an amalgamation, the way he tried to do it was tactless and crude. Words which might have been amusing in a private meeting became offensive when reported in the Press, and no self-respecting Scotsman would tolerate the tone of his remarks. Six months later, a very different line of action was taken by the very men who might have responded if the approach from England had been wisely handled by, say, Edward Coke. Equally convinced that two stud-books for the British cart-horse were wrong, Lawrence Drew and his friends prepared to start a third. In August (1883) the Select Clydesdale Horse Society of Scotland was formed, with a registered office in Glasgow and a solicitor, James Dunbar, as secretary. There were six directors, all farmers, of whom Drew was chairman and David Riddell his deputy. Riddell was probably the biggest breeder, dealer and stallion owner in Britain, an expert who knew the types of mares in every district so precisely that he could pick the right stallion for them as well, or better, than any of their owners. The former possessor, as we have seen, of Prince of Wales, he was the present proprietor of Darnley. About the breeding of this great horse, there was less controversy than about Prince of Wales or some others. But, since there are one or two points about him and his immediate ancestry that are of some relevance to the story of the Shire as well as of Clydesdale history, let us consider them. His pedigree is as follows:

| Darnley 222
brown, f. 1872
br. Sir Wm. S.
Maxwell
Keir, Dunblane.
o. (from 1875)
David Riddell | Conqueror 199 | Lockfergus Champion (449)
A *"Galloway Clydesdale"* mare |
| | (187) Keir Peggy
f. 1860 | Samson 741 ("Logan's Twin")
Jean |

Lockfergus Champion was a massive "raw" horse of Kirkcudbright and Wigtown origin. M'Neilage said that the mare to which he was mated was graded up from "native Galloway stock". Their offspring, Conqueror, was as unprepossessing as one might expect. He was undersized, and "walked wide" behind.

Samson really was a twin, and most insignificant to look at. But he was, as M'Neilage called him, "a veritable giant" as a sire – for example, he occupies the same place in the pedigree of Prince of Wales (q.v. V.8) and also of a third outstanding Clydesdale stallion, Old Times. His twin brother, Logan's Lord Clyde (477), was a great show horse and a much inferior breeder. The one real mystery in this pedigree is the identity of the twins' grand-dam. M'Neilage said she was "a chestnut mare bought in Falkirk tryst, and nothing is known of her breeding". Drew stated she was "a pure English mare, having been pur- chased at Horncastle in Lincolnshire by the late James Clark, horse dealer, Glasgow". Jean, to whom Samson was mated to produce Keir Peggy, was a strong, weighty bay mare of great size, and a great prize winner in her young days. She was by the Clydesdale Farmer's Fancy (298) out of a mare descended from old Renfrewshire stock.

The act that resulted in the birth of Darnley was prompted by sheer despera- tion. Keir Peggy, at eleven years of age, was served at every heat, and on several occasions in a heat as the season progressed, by Sir William Maxwell's stock horse. But to no effect. And so, at the very fag-end of the season, in the faint hope of getting a foal out of her somehow – any foal was better than none – the unlikely and somewhat weedy Conqueror was invited to cover her instead. The result was spectacular, but there is absolutely no doubt that no other horse than Conqueror served her in this late summer heat.

The foal, Darnley, was bought at the age of three (by which time he was scarcely beginning to catch up on his late start in life in the high summer of 1872) by David Riddell. M'Neilage has praised his character and his looks, finding serious fault only with his trotting action, which was poor in front but not, like his sire, behind. At any rate he was good enough to be the Highland Show champion three times, at the age of five, six and, in 1884, twelve years of age. Furthermore, he was let for this latter year for £1,000, a fantastic sum for a cart horse stallion, not equalled by any Shire for many years to come. He was already recognised as the most successful sire so far known in Clydesdale history, even though his progeny, like himself, matured slowly.

We must for the time being leave this great horse, in 1884 at the height of his powers. His story provides perhaps the best example of the fact that, in horse breeding more than in the breeding of any other animal, nothing is certain. "The best laid schemes o' mice and men gang aft a-gley." William Cowper, Burns' older contemporary, has also reminded us that "God moves in a mysterious way his wonders to perform". Indeed a sharp reminder to those vain enough to imagine that breeding can be reduced to a mere science was issued over 2,000 years ago, when an anonymous writer pictured the Almighty sarcastically asking Job, "Hast *thou* given the horse his might? Has *thou* clothed his neck with the quivering mane?" Neither Sir William Maxwell, nor Drew, nor Riddell – nor Bakewell, nor Henry Heaton, nor any modern breeder or any geneticist could account for what happened when Darnley was conceived. Or, if they understand, let them try to do it again, with similar materials. And not the least difficult thing to explain is why, of all Clydesdales, this horse, son of the weedy Conqueror, should weigh over a ton.

Of course, Riddell's Darnley, like Prince of Wales, was registered in the Clydesdale Stud-book. And Drew's Lincolnshire Lad 1196 was registered in the English book. But the beliefs and practices of Drew and his friends were going to result in a whole crop of animals that would be eligible for neither book. This was already proving itself to be a practical handicap in the face of the pedigree craze at home and abroad. And so practical considerations as well as theoretical ones lay behind the formation of a third pedigree register for horses which were in reality one breed.

One of the declared objects of the new company was to produce a stud-book "of select horses of a superior type for agricultural purposes and heavy lorry work in the cities". The criterion for acceptance into this book was, either, the winning of a prize at a Scottish agricultural show; or the winning of a stallion premium at Glasgow or selection as a stallion hired to travel in any part of Scotland or elsewhere; or the passing of an "entrance examination" by judges appointed by the directors. "While pedigree will be respected, and will be preserved and easily traced in this stud-book, it will be no factor in the tests of admission, for, while a horse may have a pedigree whose length is lost in the mists of the past, if it suffer from any hereditary disease which is at all likely to impair its usefulness, if, in short, it be not a good, sound horse of the Clydesdale type, it cannot get admission here." For this reason, only living animals were accepted and pedigrees given only as far as the grandparents.

All members were to be life-members on payment of one initial subscription – a guinea in the case of landed proprietors, merchants, manufacturers or other like persons, and only a half-guinea for farmers. Fees for registration were also low – 5s. for a stallion and 2s. 6d. per mare. In six months, there were 303 members, all but six of them resident in Scotland. The exceptions were the Marquis of Londonderry and his manager, R. H. Bryden; James Galbraith, the late Alexander Galbraith's son, who had just started business at Janesville, Wisconsin and was to become the "Mr. Clydesdale" of the western continent; the Montreal Horse Exchange; James M'Kay of Ontario, and Alexander M'Whinnie in Melbourne.

In July 1884, the first volume of the Select stud-book was published, containing 140 stallions and 342 mares, together with other necessary information, and an excellent introductory essay. There was also a group of supporting letters including one from James M'Call, the Principal of Glasgow Veterinary College. He wrote, "You have made out a strong case in favour of the view that our so-called Clydesdales are not only largely related by blood connection to the English Cart Horse, but that the best animals are the result of a cross." The stallions chosen for the book were entered not alphabetically but according to the judgement of the directors. Not surprisingly, no. 1 was Prince of Wales, now eighteen, and "about the most perfect specimen of a horse for agricultural purposes and heavy lorry work in cities that has yet appeared": and no. 2 was Darnley, now twelve, "another of the most perfect type of horses".

Yet, before the book had even gone to the printer, there had been a catastrophe. Lawrence Drew was dead. At the 1884 Glasgow stallion show he had won a triumph by winning both premiums, in competition against 163 stallions, with his Prince of Avondale and Bold Briton. He appeared to be his usual unassuming and amiable self. But he felt terribly ill. On return home, he developed erysipelas and died on Saturday morning, 8th March, in his fifty-eighth year. A great throng attended his funeral, all of them shocked at the premature loss of so able a man, who had become a controversialist only through his beliefs and not by nature.

It was Dykes who was generous enough to be the first to call Drew "the Bakewell of cart horse breeders". He had Bakewell's genius, that gift of seeming never to have acquired his intimate knowledge of horses, but of having been born with it. His crossing of English and Scottish blood appears to contrast starkly with Bakewell's in-breeding. But the difference is more apparent than real. Bakewell started with a much wider cross: and Drew was neither haphazard nor whimsical in his mating of Prince of Wales with English mares or of Lincolnshire Lad with Scottish ones – and, in spite of his condemnation of in-breeding, we must still retain the suspicion that he fixed virtues by practising it at one time. One feels that, had they been contemporaries, they would have understood each other, as other men failed to understand either, even if they venerated them. Both men were bachelors. Both liked to retain their little secrets. But Drew lived in busier times, when communications were quicker and easier. His means of keeping secrets were restricted, though his opportunities for giving help to anyone who asked for it were greatly extended. Trotter referred to him as "a national benefactor". And so he was. The good he had done for the Clydesdale horse was infinitely greater than the temporary damage done to its society by his break-away movement.

12. THE EXPORT MARKET

The only knowledge we have of the identity of individual cart-horses which went abroad before the 1880s comes from a few entries in the first volume of the Stud-book. Among real Fen horses which sailed to the United States were "Astronomer" (88) who won first prize at the Lincoln Royal Show in 1854,[4] and Nonsuch (1657), exported at the age of twelve in 1872 as the winner of £400 English prize-money. England's Glory (737) went from Lincolnshire to Toronto in 1867 when he was two and won fourteen first prizes for John Kemp, never being beaten at a show in his new land. Lyon (1435), a Lancashire-bred horse whose grand-dam was still winning prizes when she was twenty-two, followed a few years later. Sultan (2068), a Fen horse, who won 1st prize at the Royal when two years old in 1854, went to Australia for £200.[5] An Oxfordshire-bred grey horse called *Champion of England* was sold to the Emperor of Russia in the 'forties and several others followed him, including one of James Forshaw's earliest stallions. Another Champion of England (472) went to France in the 'fifties. And so on. Such pieces of information as these form the tip of an ice-berg. It was difficult enough for Coke and company to research the pedigrees of bygone horses without including emigrés.

It was in America where the potential mass market existed and it was a Fenman, J. H. Truman of Whittlesea, who first recognised it. In the 'seventies he had begun paying an annual visit to Chicago to buy beef on the hoof and soon noticed that there were hardly any heavy draught horses worthy of the name. The normal farm animal was a horse or mule of about 16-hands and weighing only 1,100 to 1,200 lb. – scarcely more than half the weight of a good Shire. The shortage of heavy horses for town work was therefore acute. Though men's wages at about 4s. a day were about 25 per cent dearer than in England, horse-food was cheap. So, in 1878, Truman brought out his first shipment of Fed-bred English stallions. He was a man of great energy and integrity and had a vast knowledge of horses, and there was an eager scramble for everything he offered. In February 1883, during his second annual public auction at the Union Stock Yards in Chicago, he heard a whisper or two. He promptly dispatched a letter to the English Cart Horse Council at home explaining that breeders ought to be urged to enter their horses early in the Stud-book since he believed that in the very near future only registered animals would be bought abroad, especially in America. He was soon proved right.

A point he forbore to make in his letter, but which was equally important, was that the English breed's name, or lack of a name, was a severe handicap. We know what he always told people his horses were. He always called them Shires. Only one of those he brought out in those early years was bred on his own farm, and he had been promptly registered as Chicago 3026 ("Shire Horse", naturally). And many were the sweepstakes Chicago won throughout Indiana for Cyrus Moller who bought him.

13. THE ROYAL SHOWS, 1880–1884

Having achieved the distinction of staging the first horse show ever held exclusively for one breed, the Council felt itself in a position to make stronger representations about the ignominious position at Royal Shows of the English Cart Horse, which remained the only one of the three heavy breeds which was not allocated specific classes. In 1880–1882, "Agricultural stallions not qualified to compete as Clydesdales or Suffolks" were put at the head of the prize-list, as were similarly described mares and fillies in the female section. (Each of the two sexes of the three types had three classes, making a total of eighteen, in addition to extra classes provided by the local committees at Carlisle, Derby and Reading. The yearling fillies class had been dropped.) But that was no consolation. It was as if a member of the Church of England were defined as a "Protestant not qualified to be called a Presbyterian or a Methodist". Was he then identical to a Baptist? More important still, the Church of England is Catholic as much as, if not more than, Protestant, just as the English Cart Horse was a dray-horse, not simply an agricultural one.

The R.A.S.E. received the repeated complaints with cautious reserve. The encouragement of pedigree breeding was one of its functions. But it was unconvinced that all the non-Suffolk non-Clydesdale cart horses could be amalgamated into one recognisable breed. In any case, what would be the precise meaning of "English Cart Horse" as a show classification? Impatient at these qualms, E.C.H.S. members at a general meeting held on the Royal show-ground at Reading in 1882 heard some figures which convinced them of injustice. At the previous six Royal Shows, the total entry of 206 Suffolk horses competed for £1,515 prize money – an average of £7.35 a head. 275 Clydesdales had £1,560 prize money – £5.65 a head. But there were 587 "Agricultural" horses sharing £1,730 – £2.95 each on average. As for pedigree or type, no less than 162 of the 184 entries in 1879 were eligible for the Cart Horse Stud-book; in 1880 fifty-eight out of sixty-nine were eligible; and in 1881, sixty-two out of sixty-five.

These figures were eloquently laid before the next general meeting of R.A.S.E., and with immediate success. In 1883, the heavy-horse schedule was headed by "Shire Horses". This was more than anyone had bargained for, because the breed society was still called the "English Cart Horse Society"! As it turned out, twenty-two animals that won prizes or stood reserve in the six "Shire" classes had been registered in or entered for the Cart Horse book as "Shire". (One near-exception was the fifteen-year-old chestnut mare 836 Pink, which had not been labelled "Shire" when registered by John Hopper of Whittlesea in the 1882 volume. But even she had somehow become a Shire mare on being re-registered by Lord Ellesmere in the 1883 book, and now she was reserve in the mare-with-foal class.) Lord Ellesmere, as usual, had tremendous success at the Show, with two Firsts, two Seconds, a Third, and Reserve. Edward Coke had two Firsts, a Second, and Reserve.

So, the first show in the world to provide classes for "Shires" was the Royal, which justifiably had been so much criticised by the cart-horse men in the past. The Council responded by providing a £25 champion stallion prize, won by Coke with his chestnut three-year-old Certainty, bred at Holbeach by Henry Cole Tinsley, who now promptly joined the Cart Horse Society and registered some horses.

Paradoxically, from this time onward the Royal Show tended to decrease in importance to Shire or Cart Horse breeders and owners. It was held at an awkward time of the year and other shows, some of them specialist, such as at Peterborough and Ashbourne, provided better competition, and of course the Society's own London show was pre-eminent. The significance of the Royal lay rather in prestige to the breed in general, and for propaganda reasons it could

THE ENGLISH CART-HORSE SOCIETY

never be ignored. (Since it will not play a great part in the story of the following years, this is perhaps the place to add that after two years, 1883 and 1884, when the "Shire" classification had caused the draught-horse classes to be increased to twenty-four (six extra ones being provided for animals which were neither Shire nor Clydesdales nor Suffolk), the expression "or Agricultural" crept in after "Shire" at Preston in 1885, and the "other types" classes were dropped. This inevitably provoked more strenuous representations to R.A.S.E., which not only omitted the offending words in 1886 at Norwich but also decided not to make any provision for heavy-horses other than those of the three recognised breeds. The local committee did give prizes for just two classes of non-pedigree horses, but for these this was the end of the Royal road. In addition, from 1884 it was accepted that Royal judges should be selected, not in the former erratic and wayward manner, but from approved lists submitted by the Councils of the three breed societies. This prevented any heavy-horse man ever after from winning glory other than in the way the Suffolk or Clydesdale or Shire societies decreed.)

(The senior agricultural society in the country, the Bath and West, had general "Agricultural Horse" classes until 1892. Its Gloucester meeting in 1893 set the future pattern with five classes for Shires and four for "any other agricultural breed". Three of the latter were won by the Lords Arthur and Lionel Cecil from Tunbridge with their Clydesdales.)

14. A NEW SECRETARY AND A NEW NAME

In the first few years, unpaid subscriptions were a nuisance. Mr. Dorman recommended County Court proceedings against those who were three years in arrear, and this would have been justified, since the guineas involved were really shares and not subscriptions at all, as the Society was in fact a limited company. However, action was never brought, saving some embarrassment or favouritism, because the Prince of Wales, who always remembered to come to the Shows, usually forgot his annual payment. In any case, by 1884 the Finance Committee had ceased to care a fig whether a member paid or not. It was easy to strike him off the list, and he was the only loser by that. There was no shortage of replacements.

The Hon. Edward Coke was an ideal choice as third President. He had already taken the chair at nine Council meetings and two General meetings in his predecessors' time and in his own year of office missed only one of eleven sessions. During his year, the constitution was changed to provide for a President-Elect, the term Vice-President being switched to the twelve most recent past Presidents, who were all to retain a seat on the Council until such time as the appearance of a thirteenth – in 1892, if no one died in the meantime – should cause the retirement of the most senior of them. There was some delay over the passing of the resolution, because Thomas Brown pointed out an irregularity in the procedure, as compared with the requirements of the Companies Act of 1862. If Coke uttered a sigh, no one heard it. The error was rectified. A new venture needs its Browns as well as its Streets and Gilbeys. When the year that he made so successful ended in May 1882, Coke resumed his former position as chairman of the Editing Committee, and also headed a special committee to consider some form of reorganisation.

As headquarters, a village near Ipswich was ridiculously inappropriate for a society embracing every county in England except Suffolk. And G. M. Sexton was too busy with his auctioneering, at which he was very good, to do real justice to the secretaryship, at which he was not. For delicacy's sake, Frederic Street became secretary of the special committee and, in no time at all, Sexton was formally appointed official auctioneer to the Society, amid loud applause, and resigned as secretary. Walter Gilbey, who by now had succeeded another first-class and zealous President in the Earl of Powis, knew exactly the man for the job. A reluctant John Sloughgrove was pushed into the post at a salary of £150, with the blessing of H. M. Jenkins, secretary of the R.A.S.E., under whom he had worked since his twenty-first birthday fourteen years before. The new secretary turned out to be one of the most apt appointments ever made.

By the time he took the reins in August 1883, negotiations were nearly complete for renting two rooms from the Medical Society of London at 11 Chandos Street, Cavendish Square, together with the occasional use of a council chamber. Gilbey loaned the furniture, the newly-formed Hackney Society was allowed to borrow a room for a meeting in November, and the premises began to hum with activity. And so the meetings in the Farmers' Club premises at the Inns of Court Hotel in Holborn became a thing of the past. Before disbanding, the special committee recommended that all prize money should come from the Society's funds instead of being badgered out of donors. It also gave up its earlier idea of publishing the Stud-book only in alternate years, with birth sheets issued in the intervening period. This was wise, as even the annual Stud-book, within seven years, was to become three inches thick and to contain 1,158 pages of pedigrees and indices in addition to show reports and results.

Inevitably, the "Shire" and "English Cart Horse" argument was officially resumed before long. A change of name was formally moved at the Council meeting of 5th June 1883 – this time, by Gilbert Murray of Elvaston, Derbyshire. He was seconded, surprisingly, by that self-confessed man of peace, Joseph Martin, who appears to have been converted. William Wells was another convert – a reluctant one, but the number of entries in the Stud-book labelled "Shire Horse" convinced him that this was the name people wanted. (It is odd that he had been the first man to use the word in print.) Edward Coke, naturally, spoke in favour. Walter Gilbey, as President, was temporarily silenced. But John Treadwell was still against a change. Perhaps his name influenced him to crowd his metaphors, for he said he did not like taking a leap in the dark while playing with blank cards. All Buckinghamshire breeders, he claimed, felt as he did. But who was he to talk thus? He had only registered three mares in the Stud-book in four years – and had labelled them all as "Shire"!

Frederic Street thought the existing name not only caused Mr. Coke to be ridiculed at home but made the Society the laughing-stock of the whole world. Did people talk about a Scotch Clydesdale or an English Shorthorn? A Clydesdale, or a Shorthorn, was the same animal in any country. Not only the R.A.S.E. but the Americans also, especially at Chicago, were already using the term "Shire". Many Scotch breeders were held back from supporting the suggested amalgamation of the two societies by the fact that no name had been given to the English horse, and so they had no clear idea what it was really proposed they should amalgamate with. Thomas Brown was gloomy, quoted the Articles of Association, and said there ought to be a pitched battle at a General Meeting, not another fruitless discussion in Council. Major Dashwood was also sad: in Oxfordshire, "Shires" had never been heard of a hundred years before, but they had talked about Cart Horses since 1710. The Duke of Westminster, President-Elect, suggested that the Society might remain the English Cart Horse Society but that its register should be called "The Shire Stud-book". His handsome, fabulously-wealthy, earnest and charitable Grace, the only non-royal Duke to be created in the nineteenth (or twentieth) century, the chief show piece of Mr. Gladstone's party, and proprietor of the Eaton Hall Cart Horse stud, was perfectly serious in this suggestion. He is recorded as having made only one joke in his life, and this was not it. The Council recommended a change of name by seventeen votes to eight.

The subject therefore came before the General Meeting at the York Royal Show, but was not pursued on account of Thomas Brown's bereavement. The following February, Gilbert Murray and Frederick Street proposed an alteration of name once more, and it was at last re-debated at an Extraordinary General Meeting after the A.G.M. at the London Show. Murray and Coke moved the change to "Shire Horse Society". P. Albert Muntz proposed an amendment – "*English* Shire Horse Society". And who would second but Joseph Martin? It was lost, an overwhelming majority supported Murray, and many of those who had opposed him thereupon gracefully said they would support the change when it came up for ratification. The opportunity came four weeks later. Only twenty members attended, there was no discussion and the motion was carried unanimously. Board of Trade sanction for the new name was speedily obtained.

The increasing acceptance of the name "Shire" is reflected by the Stud-book. In Volume 1, the compilers listed only 1,543 stallions (65%) as "Shire Horses". In Volume 2, 510 (79%) of the stallions and mares were so described: in Volume 3, 531 (93%): in Volume 4, 739 (94%): in Volume 5 (February 1884), 1,420 out of 1,423 (99.8%). In this last volume, there were just two odd men out. One was Frederic Clarke of Long Sutton, Lincolnshire, a very precise person who entered six "Shire" mares and two non-Shire, Blossom and Bonny, a nice distinction that is beyond one's wits, after a study of the pedigrees, to see the reason for. The second was F. d'Arcy Newcome of Feltwell Hall, Norfolk, a couple of miles from the Suffolk border, who now began his Shire career by entering the chestnut filly Pink 'Un without a Shire label, as well he might.

Even Thomas Brown had already reverted to Shiredom. In the first three volumes, his five stallions and nineteen mares had been "Shires". In Volume 4 he re-entered some of these with a few new ones – but none was now a "Shire". Now, in Volume 5, Darling and Pet once again, together with Amy and Beauty, Blooming Lass, Broom and Daisy, Fanciful, Matron and Ruth were all once more "Shires", like his nine new mares. Unaware of all this messing about with their status, Thomas Brown's mares were regular and contented breeders at Marham Hall.

A study of the posthumous entries in Volume 1 leaves us wondering upon what whim the term "Shire" was ever applied or withheld. Here are three instances out of very many:

1. Robert Bakewell's G 890 (foaled 1775) from a mare now unknown got a filly foal who in due course was put to Dragon 598 (foaled 1785 in Shropshire) and produced a filly foal who in her turn was covered by Kirby 1286 (foaled 1785, Leics). Not one of these was listed as "Shire Horse", but the foal of this last mating was Kirby 1287, "Shire Horse".

2. Drayman 660 (1868, Cambs) was a "Shire Horse", but Drayman 661 was not. Yet these horses are the same horse, accidentally duplicated owing to his passing from one owner to another.

3. Waxwork 2307 ("Shire Horse" bred at Thorney Fen as lately as 1870) was similarly a duplicated entry for Waxwork 2305, which was not a "Shire".

But all this nonsense was now a thing of the past. Henceforth, the English Cart Horse, if he were not a Suffolk, had to be a Shire horse, or else a horse of no breed at all.

CHAPTER VII

1884–1889

Progress of the Shire

1. PROFIT FROM THE CART-'OSS

FROM about 1885, graziers began to experience the troubles that corn-growers were suffering. Beef, mutton and pork poured into the country from America, Canada, the Argentine and New Zealand, as did cheese, butter and wool. Refrigeration, canning, and faster and inexpensive transport by sea and land were all on the side of the cheaply-produced foreign commodities, while the home producer found his costs steadily rising. He could still sell his produce, but the quality he offered could not command the price it deserved.

Dairy farmers were lucky, and so were cart-horse men. The state of the times and the vigorous and progressive policy of the Shire Horse Society combined to silence those who had scoffed at the idea of a pedigree register for the " 'ole cart-'oss", and to convert many of them into eager supporters. By 1889, the number of work-horses in England and Wales which were listed as engaged solely in agriculture had risen, in twenty years, by 19.7%. Yet the acreage of corn-crops had been reduced in the same period by 19.6%, and of green-crops by 12.6%: and permanent pasture had been increased by 24.6%.

In the light of these changed agricultural circumstances, the fact that the farm-horse population had not merely failed to go down but had so dramatically risen was due to the insatiable demand from the towns for horse-power of all denominations from the pony to the heavy dray and railway shunting horse. A steadily increasing proportion of so-called farm-horses were in fact doing no more than trying to earn their keep while waiting, like so many farmers' boys, until they were old enough to leave the land. If the boys in those bad times mostly found in due course that the London streets were not, after all, paved with gold, tens of thousands of farmers' horses proved that they were.

2. BUILDING ON STRONG FOUNDATIONS

By a coincidence, the first Council meeting under the new name of the Society took place on 1st April, but in 1884 no follies were committed. Indeed, the chief task now was simply to build on solid foundations. In all the years to come, such changes in organisation as had to be made were trivial – for example, the inauguration in 1885 of a selection committee, meeting only in February, to choose a successor to the Presidency and invariably comprising the President of the year, the President-Elect and past Presidents, and the chairmen of the Editing, Finance and Horse Show committees.

In 1885 the new National Pig Breeders' Association was allowed to hold its

annual meeting at the Agricultural Hall during the Shire show, and the follow-
ing week the Hackney Stud-book Society held its first show there, using the
Shire stalls and fittings for the ninety-five stallions and thirty-eight mares on
view. The Hunters Improvement Society in 1887 acquired the services as
secretary of A. B. Charlton who, like Sloughgrove, had been trained at the
R.A.S.E. They were given accommodation in the Shire offices in Chandos
Street for £20 a year, and Charlton became also a part-time member of the
Shire staff. The following year the Hunters joined the Hackney Society in a
joint show, an arrangement that was to continue until the 1920s, with the
Hunters thereafter continuing to appear at the Agricultural Hall as long as it
remained available for its intended purpose. Things were beginning to hum in
the pedigree world, though the Hackney and the Hunter were on the downward slope that was to lead all light-horse breeding to the brink of disaster in
the next thirty years. It was significant that John Sloughgrove, registering a
telegraphic address for the Shire Society, was allowed, quite simply, "Stud
Book London".

The two new light-horse societies joined the Shire men in pressing the railway
companies to extend their cheap show rates to stallions and mares travelling
for breeding purposes from April to June. It was hoped to achieve single fare-
and-a-half for a double journey, with the man in charge going free, but Walter
Gilbey, an enthusiast in all three societies, called on every railway company's
general manager, and managed to obtain single fare plus 10%. This is the first
instance of that co-operation between horse-breed societies which, on the
initiative of the Shire Society forty years later, was to become highly organised.

Shire membership topped the thousand in 1884, and grew ever more rapidly.
But every year many names were struck off for non-payment. A large number
of these were of men retiring from farming, or just giving it up in despair and,
for all the zeal that led them to join in the first place, they thought that to save
a guinea's subscription was a necessary economy. In 1887, price of admission
to the London Show on the first day was reduced from 5s. to 2s. 6d. But the
Society was becoming prosperous. John Sloughgrove's salary was increased to
£250 in 1886 and to £310 in 1889, when he was also allowed an extra £50
to pay a clerk, Frank F. Euren.

3. LONDON SHOWS

Having decided the dates of the 1885 show, the Council somewhat high-
handedly suggested to Archibald M'Neilage that it would be a pity if the
Clydesdale event clashed with it, as had happened the year before. The old-
established Glasgow Show was therefore moved to the first week in March.
In London, perhaps the most notable example of the Society's educational
work over the previous five strenuous years was to be seen in the yearling
classes of twenty-eight colts and twenty-four fillies, which all appeared in fine
condition. Exhibitors had now learned that the Shire judges and the veterinary
inspector, Professor Robertson (who this year had been allowed to appoint two

assistants) did not expect to see a collection of fatted beasts shamble round the ring on pulpy young legs – a sight that had been commonplace hitherto at most agricultural shows, where the prize was frequently awarded to the animal which the stupidity of man had rendered the least likely either to live long or breed well. As to the placing of the young colts, there was some dissatisfaction with the judges, but these hard-working gentlemen, unlike the crowds of unofficial judges who thronged the ring-side and could fortify their opinions with tea or strong drink, had scarcely a moment for relaxation. At the end of the day, their eyes were now dim, their hands insensitive and their perception clouded: all three had already judged 260 stallions since the morning had begun, before being faced with the youngest ones.

In spite of the general improvement in standard, there were the usual loud complaints about the number of animals disqualified on the veterinary inspection. Many believed that the only thing wrong with Mr. Chandos-Pole-Gell's six-year-old Hyperion was that he was temporarily lame after a bad railway journey and the sudden transition from soft ground to hard stones. Rarely has a bad leg been felt by so many unofficial experts in one day. The congestion round all the boxes was indeed fantastic, and it was a good idea of the Horse Show Committee to provide "To be let" and "For sale by auction" notices for those who wanted to display them. This slightly eased the problems of the hundreds of men who for hours a day were hunting for a good horse to start or boost a stud. The best thing that happened at the show was undoubtedly the second appearance of Prince William. His breeder, W. H. Potter, had won the yearling class with him the year before. Now, in the ownership of John Rowell, he was a near-perfect horse with the quality of limb that so many breeders had been striving for. His winning of the championship at the age of two was, even so, a sensation.

At the 1886 show, a new veterinary system was started. Professor J. Wortley Axe was asked to nominate four eminent practitioners, of whom the Council chose two (Professor Pritchard and G. A. Lepper of Aylesbury) to assist him. Only hereditary diseases and unsoundnesses were to count, and were to be specified on a certificate signed by at least two of these officials. The secretary was not allowed to tell anyone, other than the exhibitor, the reason for rejection. The judges, also, were to help by weeding out all horses they considered to be below the highest standard and sending only the best, in batches, for vetting. Those passed sound were to have a certificate signed by two veterinary inspectors – a valuable document to wave before the eyes of mare-owners at home, since duplicates could be supplied, stamped by the secretary, for 5s. For an examination carried out by the most distinguished members of their profession in England, this was a bargain.

In a class of thirty-three yearling colts, the first three were all sired by Premier, and so were those standing fifth, tenth and eleventh. The first, fourth and eighth yearling fillies were also by him. This was a talking-point at the time and perhaps, in retrospect, points out 1886 as the year when all those various types which until so recently had been just "English Cart Horses" were first clearly destined to become one recognisably homogeneous breed, dominated by a few outstanding bloodlines, of which that of Matchless – foaled exactly forty years before and in this instance represented by his great-great-grandson Premier – was by no means the least influential.

This trend is highlighted by a curious little distinction which belongs to the three-year-old Gipsy, who won a highly commended card for Tom Howard of Woodbine Cottage in the village of Bretherton, between Southport and Preston. Not only was she unregistered, but her sire and her dam were both unregistered as well. The swiftly increasing rigour of the rules governing entry to the show make her the last of such a kind. (Her sire, Com'd at Last, did at last get put in the book in 1888 as No. 5740, owned by Peter Wright of near-by Tarleton and bred by his father James. The grand-sire, vaguely given in the show catalogue as "Edmondson's England's Glory", turned out to be Emperor II 697, a Cambridgeshire horse foaled back in 1868 and often known as England's Glory. And who was his grand-sire but Matchless himself? Incidentally, even Gipsy was eventually registered in Volume 10, but by then she was producing English foals in Inverness.)

A gold medal was awarded to the breeders of the champion stallion and mare. R. W. Crawshaw of Staveley, Derbyshire, was the man who had put forward this novel idea. At nearly every English show at this time, scarcely one interested spectator in five hundred had the slightest idea who had bred any of the animals he gazed upon. From the beginning, the Shire catalogue had been exceptional in printing this information, but the notion of actually rewarding, as well as acknowledging, the breeder was especially progressive. No breed society ever did more to bridge the gap – rather, the gulf – between wealthy exhibitor and often obscure and humble breeder. In the years that followed, the practice of giving prizes to breeders was much expanded.

As a result of this show, the Society at last decided to have done with the absurd class for "geldings, any breed". The year before, sixteen had been shown, very obese and old-fashioned. Now there were only five, all equally incapable of anything more arduous than to be transported from show to show and display carcases and rumps that would have watered the mouth only of a French or Belgian gourmand. And yet £30 in prize money was available for them, more than half of what had been allocated to the eighty-five three-year-old stallions ready to go out into the world and influence the breed to the tune of covering 6,000 mares in the next few months. Gelding classes were henceforth temporarily dropped.

In 1887, qualifications for entry to the show were more stringent. Every exhibit had to be eligible for the stud-book, whereas until then any horse got by a registered sire could be shown. This reduced the numbers for the first time (forty-two fewer stallions at 250, but mares exactly the same as the year before at ninety-nine). Quality was certainly up, particularly at the bottom of the scale. Owners of poor to moderate stallions, with no expectation of a prize but hopeful to sell, were beginning to realise that this was an expensive way of going about it, and a poor horse looked worse in close proximity to the best. And this year the best horse, or rather the best and most influential sire, in Shire horse history won the championship. This was Harold, over whom we must not delay here, for he will dominate the whole of our story when we consider bloodlines in Volume 2.

The 1888 show saw entries recover to become the highest yet at 410. That perfection of Shire good looks, Prince William, won the championship again. The burden on the judges was now beoming intolerable, since all three were still required to take part in the examination of every horse, and everything had to be done by 4 p.m. on the second day, for it was unthinkable to keep royalty waiting for the championship judging and presentation of prizes. Even the dismissal of the 254 unfortunates who never even reached the competition proper was not an easy matter, because the gap between the standard of the very worst and the best was now marvellously narrowed. Only nineteen selected animals were thrown out by the veterinary surgeons and 137 returned with certificates of soundness, another wonderful improvement.

There has always been a mystique about judging. It has sometimes been overdone, particularly at local shows, where careful examination of even the veriest weeds is necessary, if only to maintain morale among neighbours and to prevent discouragement. At London such *politesse* was not needed, but the overworked and scrupulous judges must have longed, particularly at the end of the day, to emulate the performance of Peter Crawford of Dumgoyack, Strathblane. This veteran had begun his career as a stallion-leader and, when classes for Clydes were first included at the H.A.S. in 1826, had risen to be stud-groom to the great Samuel Clark. For many years now he had been a stud-owner himself and a very famous one. But he hated judging and it was against all his inclinations that he once agreed to officiate at a county show. The dozen yearlings which formed the first class were only half-way through their second perambulation of the ring and the onlookers were expecting the usual examination one by one – the walk, the trot, the lifting of hoofs and so on – when Mr. Crawford suddenly stepped forward and tapped three of them with his thick oak staff as they passed – "Second – thaird – fairst". None commended. "The rest are trash, a' trash."[1] He was spared from further invitations to officiate. Yet in his memory it must be recorded that this ancient man at his death on 19th December 1891 had never been known to criticise any neighbour's horse nor ever to talk about the 1870 H.A.S. Show at Dumfries when his Rantin' Robin did what no other stallion ever did – had beaten Prince of Wales into second place.

The tenth show in 1889 brought relief to the judges without their seeking it in the Crawford manner. Four were appointed, of whom two were selected by ballot to judge the first class, with one of the others similarly chosen as reserve to give a casting vote if necessary. In succeeding classes, the two pairs took turn and turn about. This was another revolutionary idea. Things had

progressed a long way in the short time since classes at shows had customarily
been decided, by anonymous judges in secret session, before spectators were
allowed in. The method of selecting judges in the first place was also highly
democratic. England and Wales were divided into four districts, and each of the
1,414 members was at liberty to nominate a judge to represent his own area.
From these names, the Council – which had been also democratically elected –
selected their four. The new stystem was at once put to the severest test. In
class 1, for big stallions, Henry Smith of Cropwell Butler, Nottinghamshire,
and John Wills of Exeter (who could have imagined, a few years before, a
Shire judge from *Devon*?) could not agree about the top two horses. Should the
Earl of Ellesmere's Vulcan stand first, or A. B. Freeman-Mitford's Laughing
Stock? Both were so good that everyone knew that whichever was chosen for
the £20 prize would almost certainly also win the cup for the best stallion in
the three classes for four-year-olds and upwards, the supreme champion cup,
a year's tenure of the Elsenham Challenge Cup presented by Walter Gilbey,
and gold medals for his owner and breeder. The other one would win just £15.
John Rowland of Boston and W. H. Potter drew lots, and the unfortunate
Potter had to make the decision. He found that the horses were really quite
inseparable. In the end, he displeased about 50% of the spectators by preferring
Vulcan's jaunty carriage to the muscle and masculinity of the other. As long
as they remained in the hall, the two were judged over and over again by
hundreds proving to their friends that Potter was right, or wrong. (Incidentally,
he was unwittingly responsible for putting the Elsenham Cup out of circulation
earlier than would have happened otherwise, for Vulcan won it again two
years later and so kept it for good. And, by coincidence, the horse he just beat
was Hitchin Conqueror, champion of the intervening year, and the other of
Freeman-Mitford's two first purchases.)

The show brought a wonderful decade to a triumphant end – typified by
the eighty-seven good two-year-old colts, the most so far in any one class.
Of the twenty-seven senior big mares, at least nine were the equal of the
champions at the early shows, when one or two had been far ahead of the rest.
The yearling fillies set a great problem – both in throwing out the least
meritorious two dozen and then in judging the twenty-three that safely returned
from veterinary inspection. Yet this was a class which in 1880 the secretary had
marked in his catalogue "Entry fees returned: not sufficient competition".

The conditions in which those early shows were held are uncomfortable
even to contemplate. Stallions and mares (and, until they were dispensed with, a
few gross geldings) were all housed night and day in the main hall with no
adequate ventilation except draughts. In 1889, 447 pairs of horse-nostrils
blowing in and out competed by day with 4,000 stifling gas-jets and the breath
of even more than that number of half suffocated humans, whose heads seemed
ready to burst as their feet grew colder, for there was no actual heating system.
If there was fog, the air reeked with that also. If there was none, the cigars of
the gentlemen and the pipes of the rest set up a fair imitation of it. It was some-

times impossible to see across the ring, even when it was not full of horse-flesh. At night, the chill was often terrible. After all, it was still February. Horses sometimes died before they could get home, and how many human lives were shortened by old men obstinately insisting on going to the show it would be no less interesting than pointless to discover.

It can be pretty confidently asserted that only one man had the distinction of attending every single Shire Show that was ever held at the Agricultural Hall, from 1880 to 1939. This was James Forshaw's elder son Tom, who knew almost as much about men as he did about Shires, and that was everything. He was also a master of understatement, which is well to remember in reading his recollection of the men who brought the horses to those early shows. "One of the greatest changes that has occurred in my fifty years' connection with the Shire Show", he wrote in 1929, "is that in regard to the grooms and men. There was a time when one's men regarded the Show as an excuse for enjoyment and occasionally, I am afraid, for carousal." (Carousal! Only Tom Forshaw could have called it that.) "Grooms were not always in that clear-headed condition essential to the proper showing of horses in the ring. This often led to indifference and sometimes to careless and even dangerous handling. Unless the master was prepared to give personal attention, his horses, like his men, did not always go into the ring at their best. Men were kicked, and minor accidents were frequent." He added that, "To-day, all is changed. The grooms are sober and acute, and as keen as owners." In defence of the 'eighties, however, it must be admitted that the strain upon the men was enormous. Their masters bartered and exchanged horses from morning till late at night. Foreign buyers took long to make up their minds. The grooms, drunk or sober, were permanently on duty, whereas the masters, in whatever condition they ended each day, did not have to stay in the Hall for four consecutive nights as well and then go home in a box. Skipper, who was regularly employed as foreman of horses, had a terrible time, even with his brother to help him. One boggles at the responsibilities he undertook for a pound or two, and perhaps the absence of fatal accidents should be attributed to him as much as to luck.

In March 1885, just after the Show, Her Majesty was graciously pleased, at the request of the Prince of Wales, to allow the Agricultural Hall to become "Royal". Perhaps, if she had passed a night or two there, instead of an hour or two, she would have changed her mind. In 1886, after a complaint by a Mr. Tewson, smoking was prohibited – only in the boxes and stalls, but this at least reduced the appalling danger of fire. That year also, exhibitors who desired to remove their horses overnight were allowed to do so on payment of a £5 deposit, non-returnable if the horse was not back on time in the morning. Those in the district with stabling to spare did good business with exhibitors who feared for horse or man. In 1888, the Society acquired all its own fittings and compensated J. Sharman, who had previously supplied them, with £25 in view of the short notice that his were not required. He formerly had supplied all hay and straw as well, but this year the contract was given to Nickolls and

Baker at 8s. per horse. This firm kept the contract as long as the London Show lasted.

The biggest step forward towards civilisation came in 1889. The Berners Hall, the third of the subsidiary buildings which, from time to time in its history, sprouted up round the original Hall, was engaged for the better accommodation of the men. It was heated, and the fires were kept up all night. A coffee stall was provided. Two policemen were in attendance at night as well, and even a veterinary surgeon at a cost of 2 guineas. Smoking was prohibited after 10 p.m. By day, Walter Gilbey continued to entertain members of the Council to luncheon in the dining room, a custom begun in 1884 and continued by him and his son until the last London Show.

4. THE LONDON CART HORSE PARADE

The care and management of town horses was still, in general, of a very low standard. If it appeared to be worse in London than anywhere else, perhaps this was simply because there were so many thousands of them, packed, in certain areas particularly, into a comparatively small space. The problem was general, and the reasons three. Firstly, an age that still retained such odd ideas about the rearing of children and the health of women can scarcely be expected to have been very wise about the way to treat the draught-horse which the requirements of industry and commerce had transferred in staggering numbers from green pastures to such unnatural conditions. Secondly, and similarly, if it was an acceptable doctrine that the welfare of working men was subservient to successful trade, that the position of women was secondary to that of men and that children should be seen and not heard, it is not surprising that the horse was for the most part regarded as a mere machine. Thirdly, the horses available were, generally, still of poor quality and prone to all the unsoundnesses which the hard town streets would soon search out and develop, and it was therefore difficult for all but a few owners to set much of a standard.

There were of course, many enlightened proprietors, at the head of whom stood the brewers, who for a century and more had had a reputation for the strength and excellence of their horses: and they were closely followed by most Metropolitan local authorities (the administrative vestries of the larger parishes, and district boards for groups of smaller ones). Some coal merchants and, by now, even certain railway companies were also good horse masters. But they were still out-numbered by stupid, ignorant and callous possessors of lame, unhealthy and worn-out horses that were mishandled by brutish, ill-paid employees. And of course there was every gradation of standard in between. The humanitarian and the horseman alike were concerned to see an improvement. Education in the towns and the breeding of better horses on the farms would be more effective than a tightening of the law.

It was generally conceded that there were more really good heavy horses to be found in Liverpool than anywhere else in the Kingdom, and that the average standard there was much higher than elsewhere. That city's May Parade of town horses was unique in the opportunity it gave to all owners of working horses to show off their animals amid enjoyable carnival surroundings in the very best condition they could get them in, and – irrelevantly but excitingly – decked with flowers in the most fantastic and elaborate way they could devise. Over more than twenty years, the parade had really effected a most marvellous improvement in the town's horses, for a creditable appearance on May-Day could be achieved only by proper care on the other 364 days.

In 1885, the Shire Council felt it was high time a similar effort was made in the metropolis. Though it was agreed that a stud-book society was not the appropriate body to organise such an event, a number of members pushed the idea forward and, at a meeting held during the 1886 show, the London Cart Horse Parade Society was inaugurated, "to improve the general condition and treatment of the London cart horses by encouraging the drivers to take a humane interest in the animals under their charge". No reader can be surprised to find that the chairman was Walter Gilbey. The honorary secretary was W. H. Mole of the R.S.P.C.A. and the committee of twenty-three included the Hon. Edward Coke, James Howard, Frederic Street, William Wells and John Sloughgrove among Shire men; Professors Pritchard and J. Wortley Axe; J. H. Raffety; Herbert Rymill of the Royal City Horse Repository in the Barbican; Thomas Brewis, the coal merchant; and a variety both of practical horsemen and of philanthropists or philohippists. The latter were headed by the original proposer of the whole idea, the Baroness Burdett-Coutts who, as Angela Burdett, had first come into prominence by associating herself and her great wealth with the charitable interests of Charles Dickens.

The first parade was held on Whit-Monday that year at Battersea Park. It was a comparatively restricted affair, but the 1887 parade was open to the drivers of all cart-horses stabled within seven miles of Charing Cross. 383 horses arrived on the scene, with 278 vehicles. The judges were all Shire men – P. Albert Muntz, T. A. Spencer and C. W. Tindall. In 1888 the show was moved to the Inner Circle of Regent's Park and the following year the arrangements set the pattern of things for many years to come, even though wind and rain were terrible throughout the day and reduced the numbers to only 271 horses and 222 vehicles – less than a quarter of the record turn-out of later years. Horses first had to pass the veterinary inspector and then were faced by two sets of judges. First were the three parade judges, who awarded red rosettes and first prizes of up to £1 to all who conformed to their standards – in the early years, about one-third of all competitors, though the proportion steadily rose. There were also blue rosettes for second-prize winners. Every driver not receiving a prize was given a small gratuity. The R.S.P.C.A. gave a diploma to those particularly recommended by the judges. Next, the two Shire judges awarded additional cash prizes for those of the winning animals which were of high quality in themselves, irrespective of what breed they were. Finally, a legacy left by Miss Isobel Constable enabled prizes to be given to those men who could prove the longest service with the same firm, provided that their

masters could testify to their "good conduct and behaviour, and their attach-
ment to, and kind treatment of, the animals under their charge".

The parade judges, like the veterinary inspector, looked for such evils as
grease, lameness, and rein-sores in the mouth, or signs of former sores. They
examined coats and rejected those which bore indication of a fortnight's
brushing after fifty weeks' inattention, or which showed signs of artificial
means of achieving gloss. They expected to find a well-padded and fitting collar,
and harness that was not only clean but also obviously kept always clean. For
this reason, new harness or a new collar was a disqualification, as were all chains
and metal work smeared with black composition, which was regarded as a
probable attempt to conceal rust, dirt and stable slothfulness. Bearing reins and
tight throat lashes were taboo. Horses that had not enough weight or bone for
heavy haulage at four to five miles an hour were also rejected. (There was no
parade for trotting vanners until 1904, when, for the first time, a separate show
was organised for them on Easter Monday.) The ghastly sight of a broken-down
thoroughbred or hackney in a heavy cart designed for a Shire was eventually
banished from the London streets as much by the example and policy of the
parade organisers as by any other means.

The effect of these parades, as they became a regular item on the London
calendar, was cumulative and spreading. The horses gained most, the men gained
much and their families, who had a good day out (including a ride past royalty
and lords and ladies and many dignitaries) gained not a little compared with
how they might otherwise have passed the holiday. At first, support came from
the keenest owners and the keenest men. But as time went on, the suggestion
to take part in the parade might first come from the wives or even the children
of the carters. Eventually the influence of the parade was almost as great upon
those who never took part, and who would have been faulted on all counts if
they did, as upon the regulars. The comments of the public or of neighbours,
who had seen and applauded the best standards, were bitingly directed towards
dirt, disease and delapidation when they saw it in ordinary working conditions.
The parades improved morale and management all round, and on the day
itself, dignity and merriment were added to the cart or dray. Merriment,
combined with decorum, was also the key-note of the committee, officials and
guests when the refreshment interval arrived at 1.30. Walter Gilbey's town
residence, Cambridge House, happened to be in Regent's Park, a highly convenient place for him to entertain them all every year to luncheon *comme il faut*.

5. QUALITY AND PRICE IN TOWN

The best index of Shire prices would be those of sound five-year-old geldings
ready for the town, but it is impossible to work out averages that have much
meaning, at least in respect of the 'eighties. Most animals still changed hands
by private barter at fairs or other places where horsemen met to do business.
The great auction marts at Peterborough, Derby, Crewe, Preston and elsewhere, which in later years offered great numbers of pretty uniformly good

PLATES 17 and 18   The perfect partners. Premier (*above*) and Harold. Harold's progeny out of Premier mares were famous, but Premier (1880–1892) sired equally good offspring from mares got by Harold (1881–1901). So, if he had lived longer he might have shared Harold's monopoly as the male-line ancestor of the vast majority of twentieth-century Shires. Even as it was, most of the best horses of the Harold line had several streams of his Calwich Abbey colleague's blood on the female side.

PLATES 19 and 20 The Drew ideal. (*above*) Castlereagh, the best-bred British cart-stallion of the 'eighties—neither Shire nor Clyde, but both; (*below*) Black Bird, likewise bred and owned by the Marquess of Londonderry. "Found qualified by examination" for Drew's Select Clydesdale Stud-book, he would have been the ideal "Shire" for James Forshaw, whose criteria were "Size—weight—soundness" on short legs.

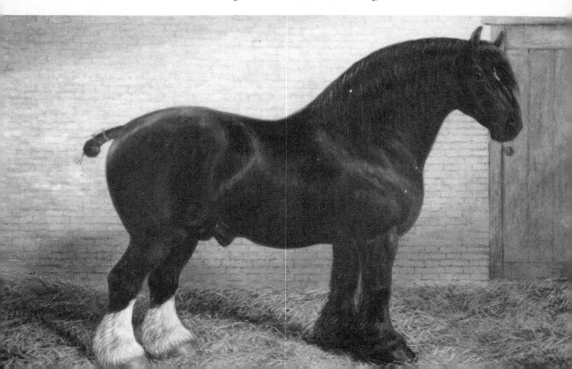

Shires at regular monthly or spring and autumn sales, were not yet in existence. The old repositories, such as Dixon's and Aldridge's in London, dealt in every variety of working horse, and mostly "second-hand": five-year-olds fresh from the country had either to be sought in country markets or were brought in by dealers or professional buyers. In any case, what is the value of any horse, or group of horses, if one cannot go back in time, and see them? Bullocks or sheep or pigs of a certain age, type and weight will vary but little as to value at the same date. They can be nicely averaged. But a horse is bought with an eye to what he is likely to do in the next five or ten years, not on his value for quick slaughter. One Shire gelding might be a bargain at 55 guineas. The next one, just as strong, just as weighty, perhaps with better flesh on him and worth more on the Belgian meat market, would be a disaster at 45 because of some incipient fault of leg or lung. To try to discover the soundness and true draught quality of the 55 guinea horse in, say, 1889 by measuring the work he performed before being worn out is equally useless, unless one knows exactly how well or how badly he was managed.

Nevertheless, buyers for large horse establishments were beginning to admit that more sound and weighty geldings were already becoming available, and they were prepared to pay for them. By 1889, a brewery or other establishment wanting top quality certainly had to go to about £85. For a real matching pair of this standard £200 would not have been unusual, and during the next few years £100 apiece was to become less and less unusual.

The Shire Society's policy of insistence on sound stallions was also just beginning to bear some fruit. There were of course as many bad geldings as before, but their value was decreasing because owners were being educated into a knowledge of what they should be looking for. One example, in the middling range, must suffice us here.

In 1865, the Great Northern Railway had owned 820 horses: in 1888, they had 1,779. The Great Western Railway owned very few in 1865 and about 750 in the later year. The G.N.R. did all its shunting and much of its cartage even in 1865 with its own horse-power, whereas the G.W.R. did not institute a horse department until the appointment in 1881 of Captain James Milne as Superintendent, and even seven years later he was still hiring an enormous number from contractors. Very few horse documents have survived amidst the tons of other railway papers that have been preserved, and therefore fair comparisons are hard to make. However, it is possible to compile a set of figures relating to horses that these two companies disposed of – slaughtered, dead or worn out – in these two years (see table on p. 196).

If these figures fail entirely to support the idea that a £50 horse was a better financial proposition than a £30 one, it is because of their inadequacy. In the first place, there is no reliable record of the sickness rate for these particular horses. In 1865, it was generally about 10% in the G.N.R. – a figure to make a later horsekeeper's hair stand on end: in 1888, it was more like 8%. Secondly, the loads drawn by the better horses were certainly greater or more numerous,

	Number of horses disposed of	Average length of service (years)	Average cost of purchase (£)	Average price obt (dead or alive) (£)	Average capital expenditure	
					Total (£)	Per annum (£)
G.N.R., March 1865	26	3.68	29.57	5.15	24.42	6.63
G.W.R., Jan.–June 1888	40	6.80	55.82	5.59	50.23	7.39

though it is impossible to guess by how much. (In 1886, the G.W.R's own goods cartage horses took an average load outward and inward of 2.04 tons each. S. and E. Leney's, their contractor's, horses took only 1.32 tons.) Thirdly, there is the matter of humanity. This is quite imponderable, but it is certain that railway horses were better treated in 1888 than in 1865 – either because the directors and therefore, at the end of the line, the horsekeepers and carmen, thought they ought to be, or because public opinion was less callous about what it saw in horses which, like the brewers' drays, were very much in the public eye. A little more readiness to put a horse on the sick list; a slight reduction in the number of horses which had worked all day and were sent out again in emergency at night; a small adjustment in the notion of what was meant by "worn-out" – these things constituted a voluntary increase in the cost of horse draught.

In both years, those sold dead or killed fetched from £2 to £3 apiece, and those sold for further labour lower down the social scale normally fetched from £4 to £10. But the 1888 figures include a £17 and £15 horse and few live ones below £7, with a higher proportion slaughtered. In 1865, five G.N.R. horses sold to new owners for £5 to £8 were listed as "used up"; five more, from £4½ to £9, were "used-up – very lame"; a bay mare, "very bad sand cracks", went for £8, a black gelding "very groggy" for £5 and a brown gelding "very foul – bred lice" for £10. (What sort of man bought a very groggy ex-railway horse for £5? Did he have to push it along the road?) The 1888 cast-offs were not quite so lame or groggy. The G.N.R. also was now buying better horses than before. For example, in 1888, 381 were purchased at an average cost of £53. 16s. od. each. (By 1900, the G.N.R. owned 3,011 horses in addition to those used for shunting, and the G.W.R., who had almost done with contractors, about 2,240. The Midland Railway led with nearly 6,000 and the London & North Western was not far behind in second position.)

All this may appear remote from the pedigree fancy. But this is not so. By 1888 there might have been sons of the earliest Shire Show prize-winners – not the best sons, but sound ones – even in the railway companies' ranks, and certainly in the brewery stables or coal yards. The pedigree cart-stallion, though owned by a Duke, was always only one generation removed from the drudgery of the London or Liverpool streets. After all, what was his function, but to beget a thousand sons and daughters either to plod the stones or to breed others to do so?

One extra factor that must not be forgotten in trying to produce the average value of heavy draught-horses at any one date is, in fact, fancy. Many a cart-horse owner has paid an extra tenner for one that pleases his eye, and has rejected a plainer animal that could get his work done just as well. He goes to a dealer, with £50 or perhaps £80 in mind, and sees exactly what he needs. Then he is shown something a little bit special. It may be nothing more than a particularly attractive colour. He would be proud to own it, or perhaps, less logically, he merely falls in love with it. He hesitates, is lost, and returns home guilty and gleeful. In the 'eighties, there were still plenty of horses that had no boards of directors to frown upon such follies. Shades of Blundeville's day and of the "carriars that went with carts who were likewise exquisit in their choyse of horses!"

6. HOME SALES

If it is difficult to suggest an "average price" for the end-product of Shire-breeding, to do so for mares and stallions is impossible. Auctions were held at the London Shows from the beginning. But if five three-year-old stallions were sold, one was perhaps a class-winner and fetched £600, whereas the others were only there for the sale and made £400 altogether. This produces a meaningless "average" of £200. Of the 1886 auction, little detail is known, but ninety-nine were sold for £6,328. 7s., an "average" of £63. 18s. But £577. 10s. was paid for one stallion and £157. 10s. for a mare. The exceptional price illogical though it may seem, is the best guide to the average price. For example, James Forshaw's immensely powerful and very hairy six-year-old chestnut, Royal Sandy, won the big stallion class in 1885 and was then let for the season for £500. This caused a sensation. But the sensation of one season became the accepted feature of the next.

Until life was changed by the events that began in 1914, the "home sale", usually in February but occasionally in the autumn, produced almost all the highest prices ever paid for Shire horses. The Earl of Ellesmere, supreme pioneer and enthusiast, had held a home sale in 1878, as we have already observed. After the formation of the Society, the practice grew, gradually at first and then swiftly. Like a schoolmaster anxious not to award all the prizes to the same boy, the historian, searching for the outstanding home sale during this quinquennium, tries to avoid Walter Gilbey. But in vain. The prize is not for effort but for achievement, for setting up a record that others might beat later, for sheer flair.

More than 2,000 men travelled to Elsenham station on the morning of Thursday, 5th February 1885. Nearly all had in their pocket one of the catalogues that G. M. Sexton had sent out. Seven hundred invited guests, or as many of them as arrived in time to do so, had a look at the forty horses up for sale, and then repaired either to the coach house or to the commodious tent erected alongside, decorated to make an attractive dining *salon*. After what the local paper described as "an elegant and recherché luncheon with an ad lib supply of Moët's choicest champagne", the toasts were drunk. Earl Egerton of Tatton said that Mr. Gilbey had given a stimulus to agriculture all over the world. The company cheered at this. Indeed, they cheered every sentence, and ended with three times three for the whole Gilbey family.

Meanwhile, on the paddocks a quarter of a mile away, the less distinguished were eating and drinking heartily, if not so elegantly, in an enormous refreshment booth. Eventually patricians and plebs joined to make a cheerful throng, some on ground-level and some on the temporary grand-stand or the long line of farm wagons, occasioning surprise and speculation among passengers proceeding to Cambridge in one direction or to Bishop's Stortford in the other upon the adjacent railway line. Mr. Sexton, who had made a very good speech at the luncheon, climbed the rostrum and proceeded to sell all forty Shires. Neither Spark nor any of Gilbey's top show horses was among them except Glow, who the year before had won the yearling filly class at London. Colonel Sir Robert Loyd-Lindsay, V.C., K.C.B., M.P., gave 475 guineas for her – a record price, so far as anyone knew, for a Shire mare. (This was a notable year for the former hero of the battle of the Alma, who was now not only the largest landowner in Berkshire but one of the most influential farming improvers and innovators in England. He became Lord Wantage and a member of the Shire Society the next month and, with Glow, won the junior female cup. Before he left London he paid 1,500 guineas for the magnificent two-year-old supreme champion, the brown Prince William, already nearly 17.1-hands, to lay the foundation of his stud.)

Apart from Glow, this was a draft sale, not a sale of great names. There were twelve stallions, mostly two- and three-year-old colts, and twenty-eight females – six brood mares, three four-year-olds, nine three-year olds, and ten two-year olds. *Coal*, one of the older mares, was of unrecorded pedigree, and realised only 50 guineas. Her six-year-old daughter *Gas* (also black) by Spark made only thirty-five. Yet the total sum was 6,561 guineas – which someone inevitably worked out as an average of £172. 2s. 3¼d., the highest ever recorded at a public sale. It is no wonder that, within a few years, even tenant farmers were bold enough to plan luncheons in tents for the nobility and gentry.

7. LANDOWNER AND TENANT

It has been written that, at this time, there was generally not much contact between "the small family farmers, who had perhaps worked up from the ranks of cowmen or shepherds, and the educated and wealthy men who supported the national and breed societies and the Chambers of Agriculture".[2] But the exception to prove the rule was cart-horse breeding, in which even the biggest man could scarcely form a self-contained unit. From ancient days, the small farmer with a good mare was likely to breed – if he could get the use of a good stallion – a fine foal for someone who could pay a good price for it. Intelligent landlords now saw that, simply by providing the stallion, they could do much to improve both the horse-stock and the income of their tenants. With the depression seemingly a permanent feature of life, their motives need not be philanthropic. Landlords, of course, were rarely suspected of philanthropy. It was the landlords who had inspired the aphorism, much used in these hard times, that "the interests of landlord and tenant were the same". But it was also a landlord who, with more realism than loyalty to his class, added that the interests of the two were as identical as the interests of the butcher and the sheep, for both of whom it was best that the knife should be applied skilfully and quickly. Yet motives do not matter here. If the tenant could breed better foals, both he and his landlord would benefit. And if the latter were going into Shire breeding on his own account, he stood to gain more than the tenant he was helping, by having first pick of the foals.

Lord Rothschild gave 500 guineas at the 1887 London Show for a massive stallion from the Fens, the five-year-old Thorney Tom. His sole purpose was to travel him for tenants and other farmers in the Aylesbury district. The horse could command a 4-guinea fee, but tenants were asked only 1 guinea. It was only after five more years that Lord Rothschild became a Shire man himself, and perhaps the most successful, financially, of them all. For nearly thirty years a local farmer could expect to use a Tring Park stallion on the cheap, though the idea of borrowing one of his lordship's celebrated Shorthorn bulls would have been absurd.

At the same 1887 show, A. B. Freeman-Mitford paid 1,000 guineas for Hitchin Conqueror[3] and 600 guineas for Laughing Stock. The former became London champion and the other would have done so with any luck. Both helped to make the future Lord Redesdale a leading Shire breeder, even if for a regrettably short time. But it is indisputable that the real reason for his starting the stud in the first place, two years after he inherited Batsford Park in north Gloucestershire, was exactly that given eighty years later by the Hon. Mrs. Farrer, one of his daughters – "to try and help the farmers to breed better horses and to have that as an extra side-line". He also founded the Shire Horse Show at Moreton-in-March, at which local men could compete against each other as well as stare at the horses shown (many of them by members of the large house party which always assembled at Batsford for the occasion) in the open classes. A foal prize won there was the passport to an immediate profitable sale if desired. Even in 1906, nine years after he had been compelled to give up breeding, Lord Redesdale retained Hendre Spark, whose service fee was 1 guinea to Batsford tenants, 3 guineas to other tenant-farmers and 6 guineas to everyone else.

William Arkwright's Sutton Scarsdale stud, begun in 1886, was responsible for enormously improving in a couple of generations the horses of the Chesterfield district, which hitherto had lagged strangely behind other parts of Derbyshire in the care given to Shire breeding. He, too, started an annual foal show.

The most celebrated of landlord-inspired shows, one of the earliest, and the longest-lasting, was founded in 1882 by A. C. Duncombe of Calwich Abbey. Long after the disappearance even of Calwich itself, the Ashbourne Shire Horse Society still flourishes under its old name, a title which is justified not only on historical grounds but because of its continued good Shire classes. Originally under the patronage of the Prince of Wales and now of H.M. the Queen, its annual Presidents are a roll of Shire honour – the first three were Duncombe himself, Chandos-Pole-Gell and Coke. For many years, the secretary and treasurer were men on the Calwich Abbey staff.

One more example must be enough. Inevitably, the pioneer of the whole idea, even before the Society began, was Walter Gilbey. His formation of the Bishop's Stortford Horse Company in 1875 has already been mentioned. In 1879 he started the Bishop's Stortford Show. For a few years it was entirely for colts and fillies got by his own and the company's horses, though open classes were later introduced. It was unusual in being held in February or March, a sort of miniature London Show, instead of the autumn. A local committee of management, whose members never changed, gave their services and Mr. Gilbey gave a handsome luncheon at the Railway Hotel. He also gave all the prize-money himself – in 1889, £110 in twelve classes for yearlings, two- and three-year-olds, open and local, colts and fillies, together with one class for four-year-old geldings, which was a little inducement to breeders to keep and use a good working horse until it was ready for the town. That year, the redoubtable Professor Pritchard, acting as judge and veterinary man all in one, said that the horses were "an exceptionally good sample of sires and dams in futurum". And this was in Essex, where, apart from the Suffolk invasion, cart-horses had been, not long before, the roughest and coarsest of any.

8. LOCAL ASSOCIATIONS

Where there were no landowners who cared to take the lead, it was to the advantage of every Shire Society member to be a missionary in his own district. Though the Shire men still lagged behind the Scotsmen, local stallion societies and companies were slowly increasing in number. Of the pioneers already mentioned, the South Devon Horse Association, under its energetic leading light and secretary, D. R. Scratton of Ogwell, has the distinction of being the first corporate body to join the breed society – in the autumn of 1878. It was now flourishing and continued to do so until 1902, when on Scratton's death it fell to pieces. The whole history of the hiring society movement is dominated by personalities. The death of a wealthy and helpful landowner or the breaking up of an estate would call a new society into existence. An old one would extend its operations and perhaps change its name in the process – and then, perhaps, split in two because it was too big. Another society would collapse in financial difficulty, or as a result of some disagreement about the type of horse most suited to the majority of the local mares, and would be replaced by a new one, or perhaps by two new ones serving slightly different areas, and so on. In later times, for example, the Newton Abbot Shire Horse Society catered for the same district as Scratton's former association, and continued to operate until some years after the end of the Second World War.

In 1884, the Warrington District Horse Association, led by Charles Rigby, became the second such body to affiliate to the Shire Society. In 1891 it became the Warrington S.H.S. and showed itself to be one of the durable ones by operating continuously for a further sixty-odd years. The Montgomeryshire Association joined in 1886, ten years after its formation. This was the year that they hired Lincolnshire Lad II for the first of four seasons. He was fourteen now and nineteen when he came the last time, and they paid Walter Johnson of Doncaster £240 for his services on each occasion. This must surely be regarded as the biggest bargain any society has ever made. (See B.V.8.) With slight variations in its name, this Society also lived long and, indeed still goes strong today – the senior hiring society in existence and the true pioneer of the system which was the very making of the Shire horse as a nationwide breed.

Two other "stallion clubs" which affiliated themselves in the 'eighties to the Shire Society were the Kington Stud Co. Ltd. in Herefordshire and the Skidby Entire Horse Company near Hull. Neither lasted long under their first name, but in 1939 Kington Shire Horse Society was operating successfully and the moral successors to the Skidby company were the Cottingham Horse Show and the Brandesburton and District Shire Horse Society, whose stallion was just able to take in the village of Skidby itself.

Most hiring societies did not bother to link themselves to the parent body in this way, but relied on the individual membership of their leading members. Indeed, at this time there was no particular incentive, as there was later, for group membership and in this first decade only four other organisations of any sort became affiliated, and they did so in their role of stallion-hirers. They were the Chester Farmers' Club, which began to hire a horse for the convenience of its members, and the three great county agricultural societies of Leicestershire, Nottinghamshire, and Peterborough. Of these, the last-named was hiring the best stallions that were available in the country. In 1888, they obtained from R. N. Sutton-Nelthorpe of Scawby Hall, Brigg the four-year-old black-brown Weathercock, to serve up to 100 mares for members only. On subscribing £1, they could obtain nominations at 2 guineas each with 1 guinea extra for each foal. Bred by A. C. Duncombe, this horse was by Premier who, since the phenomenal success of his progeny at the 1886 London Show, was now himself serving at ten guineas. More than that, Weathercock's dam was by William the Conqueror, and his grand-dam by Lincolnshire Lad the phenomenal sire of Lincolnshire Lad II.

Competition from a "society horse" was a healthy challenge to those who travelled their own stallions, or who hired them to travel as freelances. But progress in the 'eighties was slow, not only in forming associations but in even recognising any value in them. There were still far too many men who, on finding their mare had come into use, would send the boy with a message to summon the horse next door, whose odd conformation and unsoundness and strangely assorted parentage were faults only eclipsed by the fact that he still retained his testicles. In 1889, there were 1,414 "missionaries" on the Society's membership list, but nearly 224,000 men calling themselves farmers, who owned (if one likes averages) between five and six working horses each.

The London Show remained a great place for society deputations to seek and find a suitable stallion to hire, though the most ambitious associations were learning to make their choice in the previous autumn. The wisdom of being one jump ahead of one's neighbours had, in fact, now brought about the downfall of the Glasgow Stallion Show as the universal clearing-house for the hiring of Clydesdales. The system first began to crack in 1882, when a contract previously made by the Aberdeen Central Society for the hire of Lord Erskine was annulled on his being awarded the £100 premium for the Glasgow District. That autumn, the Aberdeen men, determined to get him, signed a new contract for 1883, containing a condition that he should not be exhibited at Glasgow. Other leading societies followed suit in the ensuing years and the rule which gave first choice to the Glasgow society had to be abandoned. This sensible acceptance of the realities of the position enabled the Glasgow Spring Show to remain a wonderful exhibition of the best Clydesdales stallions, though it became less and less of a hiring mart. Many of the horses shown there were booked for three seasons ahead. It was some years before the Englishmen reached this position or, in proportion to the extent of their horse-breeding districts, had as many local associations as their rivals north of the border.

9. THE SHIRE ABROAD

Of the Shires and other heavy-horses exported for breeding purposes in the 'eighties, it was nobody's business to keep any accurate statistics.

The trade accelerated madly in the second half of the decade. In 1886, H. R. Hart of Cannock sent six top-class stallions to H.I.H. Prince Alfred at the Imperial Land Stud, Brunswick. The following year, nearly 300 Shire colts and fillies were sent to Germany.

However, it was to America that the vast majority of Shires was shipped. More or less simultaneously with the adoption of the title "Shire", the English horse became the craze in the United States. J. H. Truman's forecast in 1883 that pedigree certificates would soon be required for imported breeding horses was correct, and there was a sudden frenetic rush to register stallions in the Shire Stud-book. In 1883, 449 entries were accepted; in 1884, 785; in 1887, 1,145. In 1888, 2,052 stallions were entered and the number exported was over 1,400 – the earliest available figure that is reliable. (Clydesdale exports were 1,149.) Those accepted in 1889 totalled 2,194, easily outnumbering the mares! Over 2,000 export certificates were signed by Sloughgrove that year (compared with 1,040 Clydesdales). Less than half of those that actually crossed the Atlantic are noted in the Stud-book as having done so, because many were registered in hope and kept entire against the arrival of a buyer. Henry Elwis of Sprotborough, near Doncaster, had registered seven stallions and four mares in four years in the early 'eighties, always choosing names beginning with E, including such unlikely ones as Ebbing Tide and Elastic. But in the next four years, abandoning any special initial and pre-fixing all the names with the word "Sprotbro' ", he entered fifteen mares and 134 stallions, and exported the whole lot. Cole Ambrose of Stuntney near Ely staffed his farm entirely with pedigree mares and registered twenty-four which were foaled in 1888: he also registered 156 stallions of the same age, and none of those were meant for the farm. James Crowther at Mirfield registered ninety-five young stallions in 1888, none of which he had bred himself. J. A. Barrs at Nailstone near Hinckley registered forty-two, of which he had bred one. But Stud-book registrations give no idea of what was really happening. James Forshaw later said, "I can truthfully say that hundreds of Shire stallions passed through my hands in two or three years. The Americans did not fetch our best class of horse, but when I once knew what kind of animal they wanted to suit their country, I did not fail to keep some on hand. To buy horses, I travelled everywhere, all over England, never having a day when I was not either selling at home or off trying to buy. You cannot realise the speed with which animals changed hands at that time."

In July 1888, W. Burdett-Coutts, M.P., suggested that the Society should supply the Government with some statistics. But Sloughgrove was told to reply that no one could tell how many were being exported, and any figures he could work out would be so incomplete as to be "of little value for publication by the Agricultural Department of the Privy Council". One of the more curious exports that year was of the roan Great Britain 978, probably the most enormous horse that even the Fens had produced. Bred in 1876 by that stout supporter of the pedigree movement from the very first, Henry Bultitaft of Bedwell Hay, he was a son of the Old Strawberry and out of an Honest Tom 1105 mare. He had won second prize at the Cambridgeshire and Isle of Ely show at the age of seven and numbered among his sons Forshaw's Carlton Blaze whose very short legs made him look, when viewed from behind, like an inverted pear. Thumping about the Ely district until he was twelve, getting heavier and apparently bigger all the time, Great Britain at last joined the great exported, not to impress the mares of America but to amaze visitors to Barnum's menagerie.

An American Clydesdale Stud-book for the U.S. and Canada had been inaugurated at a meeting in Chicago in November 1879 and now, in 1885, the American Shire Horse Association was formed for "the collection, revision, preservation and publication of the history and pedigrees of pure-bred Shire stallions and mares". To help put it on its feet, the Council, prompted by Coke, Chandos-Pole-Gell and Street, made a grant of £50 and a complete set of the six English volumes of the Stud-book. In the fall of the following year, a gold medal was also sent for the best Shire stallion at the Chicago State Fair. And so the first award given by the Shire Society at any show other than London or the Royal went to Galbraith Brothers[4] of Janesville, Wisconsin for their Blyth

Ben (English number 4239), a three-year-old grey bred in the Cambridgeshire Fens and exported by James Forshaw. In 1887, there was no English medal, but Caractacus (3018) won the championship over horses of all breeds. "He is the most remarkable horse of the breed ever seen in an American showyard", said *The Breeder's Gazette* of 17th November. "It is useless to attempt to describe him. Man after man exclaimed, 'From his feet up, he is the best horse I ever saw'." Now four years of age, he was indeed a useful animal, a chestnut bred in Oxfordshire. But he had never won a prize in England either for his breeder, William Way, or for Thomas Shaw of Winmarleigh who bought him as a yearling. And what Shaw did not know about producing winners was little indeed. Nor would he have sold him to Hugh White, from whom he went to the Galbraith brothers, if he could have made much of him here.

Nevertheless, *The Breeder's Gazette's* raptures over the popularity of the Shire were justified. Demands were "unprecedented in the annals of our horse-importing industry, for the impartial historian will record that no breed has ever sprung into popularity so swiftly. That this is due to the inherent merits of the Shire horse, and the success of the cross upon the mares of our country, rather than to any organised efforts on the part of importers to push his claims before the public, there can be no doubt." All American livestock papers filled columns with the Shire horse.

The demand was too great. A breed society only ten years old and faced with a deplorable general standard among draught-horses at home, could not possibly conjure up even a couple of hundred really first-class stallions to spare for others every year, much less ten times that number. Thousands of colts were left entire that by any standard should have been castrated. Furthermore, at this early date, no veterinary inspection was necessary. One well-known stallion could not be exhibited in London because he was a roarer, and leading English Shire-breeders all knew it. But he was sold to America, and his new owner only discovered the unpleasant trick played on him when it was too late. No doubt other rogues played their tricks too, but in general it was no one's fault. Good horses cannot come off assembly lines overnight, and the Shire Society had been formed not for this but to undertake the gradual task of improving English cart-horses. John Shaw of Winmarleigh, one of two cousins that succeeded their uncle, the exporter of Caractacus, who was so ordinary in England but the champion of all breeds in America, later said with his usual terse bluntness, "The horses sent out in those days were all mucky-legged and full of grease". With a great air of superiority, another Shire man remarked that he would receive an order for a stallion weighing at least a ton. "They got the weight and nothing more. It was about as reasonable as ordering a ton or two of books for a library." But it was in no one's power to change the time of the American need, and it is certain that the Shire stallions which filled it gave weight and power to many hundreds of thousands of transatlantic foals when those characteristics were most required. The demand for more, and bigger, and better horses on the farms, not to mention in towns, was fantastic.

The rapid extension of farming to the Middle and Far West is reflected in the production (for example) of wheat – less than 200,000,000 bushels from 2,000,000 farms in 1860 and more than 655,000,000 from 6,000,000 farms forty years later. There was not only more produce, but more of the work was done by horses instead of men – twenty, and sometimes forty, of them forming an enormous team to draw the combine harvester, when it first appeared in the 'eighties, cutting, threshing and bagging seventy to eighty acres of grain in a day: four men doing the work that used to be done by three hundred, and more efficiently.

Yet the farmers found they had to run faster and faster in order to stand still. They were selling in a buyer's market and buying all they needed in a seller's market. The prolonged drought that began in 1886, and was far from finished yet, made things worse. The very men who had ruined the English farmers by producing so much so cheaply, were rushing headlong to disaster themselves. The British agriculturist's interest was at least represented in Parliament: but, at this time, there was scarcely a single farmer sitting in Congress, which cared little what happened on the land, whether it was soil exhaustion and erosion or bankruptcy, as long as food was cheap and plentiful.

10. THE COLLAPSE OF DREWISM

If the Clydesdale Society had found Lawrence Drew a thorn in its side, he too had struggled against difficulties in the last years of his life. His prices had dropped at home and export became difficult, entirely because of the pedigree craze. The fame of the man and the hopelessness of his "select" movement are both illustrated in the extraordinary dispersal sale of his horses on 17th April 1884, just under six weeks after his death.

Only about ten days' notice was given, which was quite absurd. Yet, in spite of that, the number of people who flocked to the Lanarkshire farm that day was surely the largest that had ever attended a livestock sale in the United Kingdom. The oldest and most travelled dealers and breeders were all unanimous about this. Among the vast throng that tried to get near the proceedings were many foreigners, who all said they had never seen such a huge attendance at a sale anywhere in the world. But they had come to stare, not to buy. Almost none of the animals on offer was any longer eligible for inclusion in the Clydesdale Stud-book, and certainly not for the Shire book. There were twelve stallions, and twenty-two Lincolnshire Lad mares with many of their progeny, among the sixty-three head. David Riddell started the bidding for nearly every lot himself and many were knocked down to him at his opening offer. The auld horse, Prince of Wales, as fresh and fit at eighteen as he had ever been, was one of the very few that he did not start, but he joined in at 500 guineas and, after an exchange of 50 guinea advances with Mr. Wallace of Stonelaw, he got him for 900 guineas, 600 less than he received from Drew when the horse was young. But his offer of 500 guineas for Prince of Avondale (by Prince of Wales out of a Lincolnshire Lad mare), which had just won the

Glasgow premium for the second time, was never topped and in this same season he was able to recoup £400 of what he paid. In all, he bought thirty-seven of the sixty-three animals, and paid £6,245 of the £9,584 that the sale realised. An average of no more than £152 to settle up the life's work of the greatest cart-horse expert of all time is a tribute to the strong grip of the pedigree mania.

Sudden death always reveals a few pathetic skeletons in cupboards which their owner, if given warning, would have cleared. Amongst the horses were a few complete weeds, including a stallion that fetched 19 guineas. But the Select Clydesdale movement was really dead even before Drew died, and this sad sale brought mostly the silent ghouls to view its corpse. The genuine mourners, like the brave bidders, had attended the man's funeral five weeks before.

David Riddell became chairman of the directors of the Select Clydesdale Horse Society, which did not survive more than three volumes of its own stud-book. When the organisation folded, the Clydesdale Society accepted the renegades, one by one, into the ranks of orthodoxy with grave and courteous dignity and did everything that was possible to recognise a true and sufficient proportion of "genuine Clydesdale blood" in the horses owned by these new and welcome members.

Even if Drew had lived, his society could not have lasted long, because three stud-books for Clydesdales and Shires were a manifest absurdity. His views either had to prevail, in which case the two "official" books would in some way have to be amalgamated and the "Select" register would immediately become superfluous: or they had to prove unacceptable, in which case the "Select" book could only linger on as long as there were men obstinate enough to produce it. But the immediate and superficial cause of the collapse of his society was, as has already been mentioned, the "stud-book mania" which had been brought on by the suddenly booming export trade. Many of the Americans who were in Britain buying Clydesdales and Shires knew nothing about horses, and were satisfied if what they were offered had a printed pedigree. Probably the sole reason why fewer Clydesdales than Shires went to the United States at this time was the difficulty over the competing Scottish societies. It was safer to buy a Shire. Pedigrees were "manufactured" in scandalous fashion on both sides of the border to satisfy ignorant customers, but a "Select" registration was both difficult to obtain, owing to the inspection-or-prize rule, and also less satisfactory. People buying paper qualifications wanted to prove they had a Shire or a Clydesdale. The last thing they wanted was a cross, whether or not it was a better animal.

With the demise of the Select Clydesdale Society, its second chief tenet, that only sound and meritorious animals ought to be admitted to a stud-book, was also abandoned for good. This, also, was inevitable in any case, because it is impossible in practice to combine in one book a register of pedigrees and a register of animals which are of good conformation and free from hereditary disease. Hereditary unsoundnesses often take several years to manifest themselves and a proper vetting rule would exclude the permanent registration of stallions until they were about six. They might not appear in print, therefore, until they were eight, which would effectively destroy the whole purpose of printing pedigrees at all. Even then, there would be enough late developments to make such a register untrustworthy unless it were reviewed annually. Soundness and good conformation of the individual breeding animal, vital as it was, was a quite separate matter from pedigree. It was a problem that could be tackled voluntarily by the inspection of top-class animals at shows, as the Shire Society had done from the beginning, or compulsorily by the Government if it was thought fit to regard unsoundness as a national problem.

As to Drew's doctrine about cross-breeding, there was now no chance of discovering how it would succeed in the long term, for there were no philanthropists or theorists who were prepared to carry on a breeding policy with animals that would not be eligible for either of the two stud-books. Of all the horses produced in his lifetime along the lines he advocated, one of the last should perhaps be selected here as a memorial to him. Let it be *Castlereagh*, probably the best-bred cart stallion in Great Britain. His pedigree was as follows:

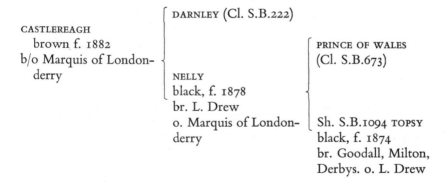

CASTLEREAGH
brown f. 1882
b/o Marquis of Londonderry

DARNLEY (Cl. S.B.222)

NELLY
black, f. 1878
br. L. Drew
o. Marquis of Londonderry

PRINCE OF WALES
(Cl. S.B.673)

Sh. S.B.1094 TOPSY
black, f. 1874
br. Goodall, Milton,
Derbys. o. L. Drew

Topsy, the champion mare at the first London Show in 1880, was by Crown Prince 558 (by Crow's *Crown Prince* – Louth, Lincolnshire: dam by William the Conqueror 2340: grand-dam by Black Legs 142). Her dam was by William the Conqueror 2343, who was destined to be second only to the great Harold himself in his influence on Shire blood-lines.

It was remarked by W. R. Trotter that Castlereagh combined "the blood of the two greatest horses Scotland has ever seen (he wrote in 1889) and the best blood of the whole Shire Horse Stud-book".[5] His breeder, the Marquis of Londonderry, owner of the Seaham Harbour Stud at Sunderland, was an apostle of Drew, being associated with forty-five animals in the first volume of the Select Clydesdale book. As for the personal qualities of Castlereagh, he won first prize at the Newcastle Royal Show in 1887 in a class for stallions not qualified to compete as Shires, Clydesdales, or Suffolks. Second was Thomas Shaw's *The Mikado* ("breeder unknown"). But this was poor competition. Many thought that he should have been first at the Highland Show at Perth where he was "the most typical Clydesdale horse in the ring". As a sire, he appeared to be exceptional, though the fact that he was kept almost exclusively for service in Lord Londonderry's own stud naturally reduced his chances, as also did the fact that he was, according to both breed societies, "without pedigree". At least a dozen of his sons and daughters, nevertheless, won major prizes in 1889, when he himself was only seven. Those out of registered Clydesdale mares were eligible, under the special rule, for the Scottish book, but it would have been useless to use him on pedigree Shire mares, where in fact he would probably have done marvels. The Drew notion was at an end – except in the no-man's-land between Scotland and England.

In Cumberland, and as far south as perhaps Carnforth in Lancashire, the balance was finally and irrevocably tilted the way it had always mainly hung – to the Clydesdale. Now, and for years to come, the Cumberland geldings were first-class, and on the whole it is safe to say that for the next fifty years they commanded the highest prices of any working horses on the market. They remained, until 1939 and beyond, a living tribute to the principles of Lawrence Drew. Absurdly, it was sometimes to be said of them that they lacked "distinction" if left uncastrated. Of course they did, when "distinction" was open only to registered animals of one society or the other. The stallions used were Clydesdales, but the mares were constantly replenished from Shire country further south, including the Fylde. The time was to come when the Royal Lancashire Society dropped the word "Shire" from their gelding classes, in order to allow these fine animals to compete without pretence. The normal name for the cart-horses of northern England, for they had to be called something, came to be "Cumberland Clydes". It is as fair a name as any to describe what were surely but a faint imitation of the type of animal which might have been achieved in Scotland and England by general recognition of the claim that the two kinds of horses were in reality varieties of one breed.

To return to the two great horses that played the leading part in Drew's and Riddell's plans, as indeed they did in orthodox Clydesdale history, Darnley travelled a second and a third season at his record hiring fee of £1,000 in the Rhins of Galloway. Then he died, on 30th September 1886, aged fourteen. Riddell thereupon sent Prince of Wales into the same district for two very successful seasons. The auld horse dropped dead in his stall on 31st December 1888, one day short of becoming officially twenty-three. He had long been kept, in Drew's lifetime, almost exclusively for Shire mares, but in his last five seasons he had got foals, as numerous and good as he had ever got in his younger days, from Clydesdale mares, especially daughters of Darnley. Even before he was dead, it was claimed he had grandsons and granddaughters, and their sons and daughters, in almost every parish of Scotland and every part of the colonies.

As George Culley often thought in his later years of his friend and mentor

Robert Bakewell, so David Riddell was left to remember Lawrence Drew. Like all men, English and Scots, though for more personal reasons, he regretted the premature death of the likeable and unassuming genius. But the real tragedy had been, not that Drew died too soon, but had begun too late. If the Select Book had been published in 1876, it is possible that separate Shire and Clydesdale societies might never have been called into existence.

II. FOUR GREAT PIONEERS

Death struck its first blow at the Shire Society foundation members in the spring of 1887. William T. Lamb of Welbourn, Lincolnshire, was a man ahead of his time in many ways. A true evangelist, he had always been happy to show anyone his account books to prove that, even without breeding, it was possible to work a farm with Shire geldings at the sole cost of their maintenance. He cultivated 350 acres of arable limestone land with ten geldings of three, four and five years (all of which were sold in turn to the towns) plus an old stager to break the young ones in. This economy was the incentive that made many another listen to his modern and scientific ideas of feeding and management. He was the first to adopt the system of naming all his mares with the same prefix. He had served on the Editing Committee from the beginning and appeared as London Show judge for the fourth time – more than anyone else – shortly before he died.

The death of James Howard occurred early in 1889, and in that year William Wells of Holme Wood, Hunts, ex-President and veteran of sixty Council meetings, eighteen of them as chairman, also died. His constant efforts, as a member of the R.A.S.E. council, to get the English breed recognised by that body, were as valuable as any of his other contributions to the Shire. In 1885, after the apparent victory for "Shires" of 1883, the Preston Royal, as already recorded, had reverted to a "Shire or agricultural horses" classification. Wells and Coke managed to have this changed once again, and for good. "To err is human, to forgive divine", as Wells indulgently commented.

Coke of Derbyshire himself was the fourth loss. On 26th March 1889, he attended his 71st Council meeting. There was a vacancy on that body (caused by the election of Chandos-Pole-Gell as President-Elect), and he promptly proposed the co-option of Thomas Brown. It is typical that he should be the first to appreciate the enthusiasm and qualities of the man who, more than anyone else, had been responsible for delaying the adoption of the name which Coke himself said was essential for the success of the breed. But a few weeks later on 26th May Edward Coke died. Thomas Brown was chosen to follow him as chairman of the Editing Committee.

None of these men was irreplaceable. Indeed, the Society was now full of remarkably able people. But Coke, in particular, ought to be remembered as the embodiment of the determination, foresight and courage of the small group who met at the Farmers' Club in 1878. When, amid the storms of Kilburn, he had said to those not entitled to vote, "There is no need to go out of the tent", the truth of his remark was poetic. The Society then had every prospect of failing or becoming a farce, or of developing into a coterie of specialist breeders or – and, this was the most likely – of splitting asunder. But, in ten years, scarcely anyone had "left the tent".

There were now 1,481 members. The names of 2,160 mares had appeared in the last Stud-book that Coke had supervised. 276 stallions had been lately exhibited in London, and even the worst of them was a good horse. All over the world, breeders wanted Shires. And yet the London Shows had been running for only ten years, and the handicap of the "English Cart Horse" label had been removed only five years before. Edward Coke was only one of many who had worked for all this, but if it were necessary to point to just one true "Shire man" as a personification of all that has been best in that human breed, the younger son of "Mr. Coke of Norfolk" would suit very well.

(His stud was dispersed at a sale in October, and Dickie, the manager went off to Sandringham under Edmund Beck. Mrs. Coke died the next year and his younger brother Henry John Coke bred a few Shires at Longford Hall until his death on 12th November 1916 – 162 years after the birth of their famous father. The last Coke foal, born in 1916, was a filly, called Jewel.)

CHAPTER VIII

1889–1900

Size and Substance

I. 12 HANOVER SQUARE

Two cold summers, a drought and a very bad harvest, all in successive years, marked the early 1890s. But only a fool would still try to blame the weather for agricultural misery. After years of retrogression, the resources both of the land itself and of the men who farmed it were now too enfeebled to stand up to foreign competition. In the last years of Victoria's reign, the unfathomable tide did at last begin to turn, but at the time it was not easy to notice it. All this while, the affairs of the Shire Society were on the flood. P. Albert Muntz of Dunsmore evangelised the countryside, proclaiming success for those who bred good heavy-horses. He was almost more certain to be found at a home sale or a club meeting or in those other places where farming speeches and discussions were held than in the chamber of the House. Others followed in his footsteps, preaching the good news.

At the end of 1891, Frank Euren resigned his position as clerk in the Shire office because he was secretary of the Hackney Society as well, and had now taken on the organisation of the London Cart Horse Parade. A. B. Charlton, secretary of the Hunters Improvement Society, was formally appointed part-time assistant Shire secretary at a salary of £60. In addition, W. J. Wickison was employed as full-time clerk at 25s. a week. In 1893, Walter Gilbey, who of course was never paid anything but was worth a king's ransom to the Society, became a baronet. In 1894 membership reached 2,000, Charlton had a £15 rise and Wickison £10. Gilbey and the Duke of Westminster paid £37,000 for Harewood House, the R.A.S.E. moved into it, and the Shire Society took over the remainder of the lease of 12 Hanover Square next door. Nearly £2,000 was spent in modernisation and decoration, which was carried out by those proud owners of the finest Shire geldings, Messrs. Holland and Hannen, at a speed which would be difficult to credit today. The Shire Society celebrated the 5th November by holding a party there in the evening as a prelude to the first council meeting the next day in this elegant and commodious Georgian house (only slightly spoiled by a top storey added by R.A.S.E.). The Hackney and Hunter and Cart Horse Parade societies came along as well as sub-tenants, and offices were also sub-let to the Shorthorn Society, the Sussex Herd-book Society, the Smithfield Club and the British Dairy Farmers' Association. Eight societies under the same roof encouraged the growth of the curious interlocking system whereby a clerk in a large society was often the secretary of a smaller one. One man might be, and sometimes was, the employee of four different societies. But there was still room left, and the Royal Photographic Society was allowed some of it, the remaining corners being eventually allotted to the British Beekeepers.

2. THE STUD-BOOK

Lest we assume that the plebeian English cart-horse was more difficult to incorporate into an efficient pedigree register than other more genteel breeds, a dispute that shook the foundations of the Hackney Society is a reminder that this was not so. When that association began in 1884, it was agreed that, because so few owners could produce any evidence whatever about pedigree, mares could be admitted to the stud-book if on inspection they appeared really to be Hackneys – a method already adopted by the Suffolk Society. Seven years later, many considered that it was time to rely on pedigree only. The heat with which the matter was debated far exceeded the temperature of the controversy about naming the Shire. Walter Gilbey and Anthony Hamond, stout workers for both breeds, were among those who wanted the inspection-method to continue. But "pedigree only" carried the day, amid boisterous scenes. One reporter wrote, "How the Yorkshiremen and the Norfolkers shouted and howled and cheered and waved their sticks, when Lord Londesborough got the best of it on a division! It really looked at one time as if the elegant Mr. Coutts and the sedate Mr. Gilbey were going to have a bout of fisticuffs."

The Shire Society had been committed from the beginning only to pedigree, except for the prize qualification for mares foaled in 1880 or earlier, and even this was now cancelled. Gradually, the conditions of entry to the Stud-book were being made more stringent. The Editing Committee was being required to cope with an ever-increasing stream of applications, and the naming of all these animals was a major problem. It was decided in 1891 that in future, once a Shire had been registered, its name could not be changed. But it was the repetition of the old favourite names that caused the worst trouble. From the earliest days, the Editing Committee had pleaded with owners to play a few variations on these limited themes in order to mitigate the mounting confusion. Accordingly, a system of prefixes and affixes was introduced. Members were invited to apply to have their chosen word officially registered as their distinctive property. A prefix could be used by the owner of a horse, and an affix if he was also the breeder. The first batch of twenty-five applications was considered and twenty-four accepted in April 1892. William Welch of Rauceby near Grantham was granted "Albion" and immediately registered three colts – Albion Premier 13817 and Albion William 13818; and Bar None of Albion 13844, which he had also bred. Lord Hothfield entered a colt, Hothfield Roman, and five fillies with his prefix, and two colts, including Rebel Chief of Hothfield, and twelve fillies with his affix. But since he was a systematic person who used a different letter of the alphabet each year, his animals did not have so many of the old common names – for example, his fillies foaled in 1891 were named Raspberry, Reason, Rebecca, Repeal, Reserve, Rocket, Romance, Rosamond, Rose and Rosetta – all "of Hothfield".

Those who registered the first prefixes and affixes were in fact those least likely to rely on the traditional "Depper", "Bute" or "Darling", and some of them had already been using their village or stud name unofficially. But the idea gradually caught on amongst other members, and the prefix system became an enormous success, and was adopted by other breed societies, for example by the Suffolk Society in 1897. Affixes never became very popular. By the end of 1900, 1,154 prefixes had been allotted, and only 101 affixes. But even that year, thirty-two mares just called Beauty were also registered, as were sixty new plain Blossoms, and eighty fresh young Bonnies. Mares stayed at home and so there was little incentive for small owners to use other than the old familiar stable names. Stallions of course were helped in their travels by distinctive titles, and so in 1900 no plain Champion, Farmer's Glory or Honest Tom was submitted. The one Drayman – the 109th of that name to be registered over the years – was called Drayman XXII because there had for some time been a rule that males with a name used before should have a number added to it.

The first four volumes of the Stud-book were re-issued in abbreviated form in 1891 under one cover. The following year, an index of all the stallions and mares entered in the first thirteen volumes was prepared, and provided an opportunity to allot a number to all the mares, of which there were 13,889. Accordingly, Volume 14 in 1893 continued this practice as a further way of trying to obviate chaos, and the first name in the mare section was 13,890 Abbess. The Index 1–13 contained the names of 27,698 Shires, their owners and breeders, their sire, dam and dam's sire, their colour and their year of foaling. Even without allowing for the appearance of the same animal several times, owing to change of ownership, this involved the inclusion of 55,396 names of men and 110,792 names and registered numbers of horses (less the numerous "blanks" where the pedigree was incomplete). The index comprised 969 printed pages and A. B. Charlton was given a 10 guinea gratuity for all the extra work involved. The clerk, Wickison, received 5 guineas. The book was put on sale at 1 guinea by subscription and 1½ guineas after publication.

All these efforts to cope with the confusion caused by success helped gradually to reduce the number of absurd muddles. For example, a lot of trouble was caused by two mares of Thomas Lowndes of Rolleston Park, Burton-on-Trent. They were both called Mettle and were both by Sweet William 2093. One, foaled in 1872, was registered, and the other was not. In 1891, the latter had a filly foal which appeared in the 1898 volume as being out of 3462 Mettle. But after an enormous amount of correspondence and enquiry, this was corrected in 1890 as "dam: *Mettle* by Sweet William 2093".

Efforts to persuade owners to re-enter horses they bought, to show change of ownership, were largely a failure, even though hundreds did co-operate. As a result, it always has been impossible to know by looking at the Stud-book whether the man who first registered a stallion or mare remained the owner of it for long. Another new idea, in May 1892, also proved largely a failure. This was an obituary-column of stallions. The death or castration of exactly 150 was recorded in the next volume, and the Editing Committee regretted there was not a better response – as they did every year until the scheme finally fizzled out in 1944. Most of the entries in the 1893 volume were of recent date but Robert Cork's Thumper 2113, foaled in 1831 and prominent in the pedigree of some of the best horses of half a century later, is recorded there as dying at the age of nine.

By 1893, the end of the mass-export of stallions to the United States was reflected in the much reduced number of stallions entered in the book. In his report, the Secretary commented that "owners have been compelled to turn their attention to the home demand for geldings, with the result, beneficial to the breed and the breeder alike, that the great majority of colts are now being gelded". He suggested that fewer colts still ought to be left entire. Members were also begged to obtain a breeder's certificate whenever they bought an unregistered Shire. "After a sale has been effected, the late owner loses all interest in the animal, and often fails to satisfactorily answer enquiries addressed to him in regard to pedigree."

During these twelve years the Editing Committee continued to reject many entries as unsatisfactory. The number of faulty ones, or of simply faked ones, that slipped through their fingers will never of course be known. But only fifteen out of nearly 39,000 had to be completely cancelled after once appearing in print, which is a remarkably small number in view of the fact that the breeding and history of a cart-horse for which a pedigree was claimed could rarely be a secret matter and there was always likely to be a vigilant member ready to object to sharp practice. For example, Elmton Majestic 9282, foaled in 1887, appeared in the 1890 volume, his dam being listed as *Bet*, by Majestic 1536. But she was really by a Clydesdale and the entry was subsequently cancelled. Skipper III 13202 was entered in the 1891 book, but on receiving complaints the Committee began to check further. As it happened, J. H. Smith of Alvaston, Derbys, his owner and a member of long standing, had himself been deceived when purchasing the colt. In some alarm, he immediately sent a letter of apology together with a veterinary certificate that the horse had been castrated. The breeder was not a member of the Society and so suffered nothing more than a deservedly evil reputation thenceforward. Much trouble over Burton Peer 11075 was caused by the breeder, E. T. Moore of Beeby, Leicester (not a member) trustingly but foolishly signing the breeder's certificate after inserting only the great name of Harold as sire, verbally explaining to the purchaser, a man who had registered a very large number of animals during the three years he had been a member of the Shire Society, that the dam's breeding was quite unknown to him. Her ancestry had subsequently been invented so far as was necessary to qualify the colt. By the time all the facts had been established, Burton Peer was already at the 1891 London Show. By resolution of the Council, his owner was informed that the registration in the book would be cancelled and that the horse would not be permitted to be exhibited or even to leave his box except to be removed from the Hall altogether. At the next meeting of the Council, the offender's name was unanimously expunged from the list of members.

By far the most important case that arose in this way, either in these years or at any other time, was that of the mare Hale Lofty and her colt foal, also by Harold. Her entry too was cancelled and her owner's name was expunged. (The Council rather favoured this verb.) But no one in 1891 and 1892 knew, or could conceivably have guessed, the gravity of the decision. As it happened, her owner fought the case. He was reinstated and so was she. Had she not been, it is certain that the colt would have been castrated, and there would therefore have been no Lockinge Manners and no Lockinge Forest King. And without Lockinge Forest King the whole development of the twentieth-century Shire would have been different.

In the 'nineties, entries were still coming in for horses foaled before 1880, and were certainly the most troublesome to check. But one stallion that was put in the 1895 volume was an exception. Walter Rawnsley of Well Hall, Alford, a comparatively new member, had come across an old stallion card of "Mountain's Champion" for the year 1860 and sent it to the Society. This horse was the sire of Lincoln 1345 but nothing had previously been known to the Editing Committee about his breeding. Of course this was given on the card and, since Lincoln was the sire of K (or Lincolnshire Lad) 1196 and K was the sire of Lincolnshire Lad II, to whom it was now becoming apparent that so many prize-winners at London could be traced directly back, it was agreed that this Mountain's Champion should be now registered as a matter of historical interest. Accordingly, he appeared inconspicuously in Volume 16 as Champion XXI 15046, foaled in 1857. But the card is in fact the most important piece of historical evidence that has ever been unearthed in respect of Shire pedigrees. It establishes a more remote ancestor, Wiseman's Honest Tom 1060, foaled in 1800, as the chief "foundation sire" of all that is best in the Shire breed of horses. It is not surprising, perhaps, that its significance was not at the time apparent to even the most ardent students of pedigree, because the leading blood-lines in this vast and amorphous mass of animals which went under the name of "the old English breed" were themselves only just becoming gradually clear. But it is odd that the point has remained in obscurity until now.

The enormously weighty volumes of the Stud-book and the accession of nobility and gentry in great numbers to the Shire ranks did not leave the Council satisfied. Three separate campaigns were organised during this period, by circularising the smaller farmers, to encourage more and more people to enter their horses. The first effort of this kind was directed towards Lancashire, the second to the classical Shire areas and the third to the Home Counties. Those who had feared that a "Shire" society might become an esoteric coterie could not have been proved more wrong. In another sense, too, the Shire fellowship was kept as open as possible. A resolution that mares foaled after 1900 should require four registered crosses to be eligible for the Stud-book was almost immediately afterwards quashed: and registered sire, sire of dam and sire of grand-dam remained sufficient.

3. LONDON SHOWS

The Spring Show was nearly asphyxiated by its own success in 1890. As entry-forms poured into the Chandos Street office, John Sloughgrove was at first pleased, then apprehensive and at last thoroughly alarmed. The record 447 horses of the year before had been a "full house". But now, though the number of mares had dropped by five, there were 204 additional stallions. The only possible way to house 646 Shires was to put a couple of hundred in the galleries. When, after feverish sawing and hammering and cursing, these had been refloored and fitted up with separate loose boxes, and the staircase had been converted into an enormous ramp, there was only a day or two's respite before one anxiety gave way to another. The possibility of accidents, even of disaster, scarcely bore thinking of, for there would be more grooms, more owners, more purchasers and certainly more spectators than ever before. Nevertheless, thanks to the strictest discipline (foreman Skipper had been allowed to engage an assistant – his brother – who wondered what sort of mad house he had entered), the worst thing that happened was an accident to a Mr. and Mrs. W. Farrow. The Council, without obligation, later compensated them with a gift of 5 guineas to cover loss of clothing and other expenses, but it is improbable that this good couple ever again spent a day out at the Shire Show.

The cost of preparing the Hall was £1,809, compared with £618 the year before, and entry fees for exhibits brought in only about £400 more. Nevertheless, in spite of all the worry, the show was a resounding success. Of 161 three-year-old stallions, twenty-six lucky ones were selected for veterinary inspection and all returned with certificates of soundness, and so did the twenty two-year-old colts which were chosen out of 134. This was a great achievement especially if compared with the absurd situation only four years before, when in one class so many of those initially chosen were rejected by the inspectors that the stewards had to scour the boxes to bring out again other animals to make up a reasonable number to judge from. Several of the yearlings, both colts and fillies, showed clear signs of being forced. But they received short shrift, and foolish exhibitors were quickly reminded that the London judges were not looking for over-grown hothouse babies with poor joints. However, this year's champion mare, the 17-hand black Starlight, was an example of the fact that not all rejects were doomed for ever. As a yearling filly in 1883, her breeder, Thomas Williamson of Out Rawcliffe in the Fylde, had entrusted her preparation for London to a young fellow called Tom Jackson, who had got her ready with loving care. But young Tom's, and her, first visit to London ended abruptly with the veterinary inspection. Williamson sold her for 120 guineas to Garrett Taylor, and Jackson went to work for Thomas Shaw. Now at the age of eight, she reached the top. Not as wide as she might have been, and higher on the leg than she ought to be, she made up for her failings with marvellous action, splendid feet, flat bone and silky hair – as was to be proved again the next year, and the year after, too. (Tom Jackson also made up for his disappointment. In 1889, he had been in charge of Lord Ellesmere's champion Vulcan. In 1897, he was destined to show the champion stallion for Alexander Henderson and the following year was in charge of his stud when, as we shall see, it swept the championship board. And for yet another employer he was due to exhibit the 1904 champion mare.)

For future years, it was clearly necessary to reduce the number of exhibits, if that were possible (preferably by somehow getting rid of the worst), but at the same time to make adequate arrangements if it were not. The first objective was achieved by requiring every entry-form in 1891 to be accompanied by a veterinary certificate – not of soundness, but of freedom from the hereditary defects of roaring, whistling, ringbone, unsound feet, navicular disease, spavin, cataract, sidebone and shivering. This was only a preliminary passport, because the veterinary inspection at the show itself continued as before. A second rule was that anyone showing more than two animals in any one class had to pay double entry fees for the additional ones. Some people thought mare-classes should be done away with, on the grounds that the whole business was detrimental to the well-being of those in foal, but that proposal was defeated.

At the same time, permanent arrangements for coping with large numbers were made by a new joint agreement between the Shire, Hackney and Hunter societies on the one side and the Royal Agricultural Hall Company on the other. For seven years the latter was to provide everything needed, in galleries as elsewhere, and clear it all away again afterwards for a fixed sum of £1,380 per annum. They also pulled down two adjoining houses, 29 and 30 Barford Street, and erected a building to provide better veterinary accommodation. The net result of all this was that the 1891 show cost the Society no more than that of two years before. (Mr. Raffety's Agricultural Auction & Agency Co. had ceased to be the lessees of the Hall in 1889 and he was now merely the letting agent, a position he filled only until 1892, when he ceased to have any connection with the place.)

As it happened, entries for 1891 were down by 149, though at 497 they were still fifty-one more than in 1889, and use of the galleries was essential. The Elsenham Challenge Cup was won outright. This was virtually bound to happen, as the champions of the two previous years were both again shown by their same owners in top form. The verdict went to Lord Ellesmere's Vulcan over the 1890 champion, Freeman-Mitford's Hitchin Conqueror, and John Sloughgrove recorded (in the place of Sanders Spencer, whose highly individualistic reports were now dispensed with) that "the success of the Worsley Hall stud was most popular, as his lordship was one of the first noblemen to go in extensively and in a most spirited fashion for the breeding and exhibition of Shires. In this most laudable pursuit the Earl of Ellesmere has received the greatest possible assistance from his agent, Captain Henry Heaton, who appears to scarcely know what it is to fail, whether it be in the exhibition of Shires, pigs, or the more pugnacious game fowl."

Among the senior big stallions, there were two particularly interesting horses. One was England's Boast, who had been first shown in London in 1882 when he won the yearling class for his breeder, Charles Beart of Stow Bardolph, one of the original members of the Society. Charles died in 1885 but his son William continued to show the horse, who was now making his ninth London appearance in ten years. He had passed the inspection every time and had only once failed to win an award. This year he was again highly commended and, with eight years' rigorous service behind him as a stock horse, was an excellent advertisement for soundness. The other significant horse was Forshaw's Honest Tom 5123 – "more after the style of the old-fashioned Fen horse. He was very wide and muscular, but his action and style were not exactly such as one looks for at the present time: still, he would prove of great service if mated with those lighter-limbed, free-moving mares which are by no means uncommon in some counties." This is exactly what James Forshaw had him for and, anyway, he won fourth prize. He weighed 1 ton 6 cwt., which makes Slough-grove's comment something of an understatement, for he was no more than 17.2-hands. (That alleged record-sized freak horse, the American-bred Percheron gelding, 1902–1919, owned by Dr. L. D. LeGear, weighed only 73 lb. more – but stood 21-hands high. Even the heaviest horse whose weight is generally admitted to be authenticated, the roan Belgian stallion Brooklyn Supreme, foaled in 1928 and owned in the 'thirties by Ralph Fogelman in Iowa and weighing 1 ton 8cwt. 64 lb., stood 19.2-hands – 8 inches more than Honest Tom.) In the season that followed this show, he travelled the Chester district, and one of the mares he covered was T. J. Dutton's Jeannette. She had been bred in Montgomeryshire and was herself the product of the immense Royal Sandy, who has already been mentioned. She thus represented the half-way stage between the light Welsh mares and the weight of the Fens. Honest Tom completed the transformation in no uncertain manner. The foal born next year grew to weigh 25 cwt., at the same height as his sire. As Sandycroft Tom, he invaded Lincolnshire itself, where in the early years of the next reign he got plenty of heavy-built foals which would have astonished those Montgomery-shire men who had seen only the female line he had sprung from. But his sire, Forshaw's Honest Tom, came of a doughty line. He was by a tough old chestnut horse called Wonder of the West. And who had bred this one but old Charlie Beart again, of Stow Bardolph? He had done it by putting his gigantic prize-winning mare Lioness to that twenty-year-old and apparently inexhaustible celebrity, William Wiseman's Wonder, one of the sons of Dack's Matchless. This legendary Matchless was transforming the English cart-horse, whether through such rugged descendants as these or through the elegant and beautiful What's Wanted and his son Premier. Knowledge of the bloodlines which could achieve these mighty improvements was being disseminated all over

England by the work of the Society. Matchless, long since dead, was becoming a name familiar far beyond the Lincolnshire fens where he had spent all his days, travelling a route that took him through Moulton Eaugate for thirteen successive years.

Among the yearling fillies, Marina won second prize for her breeder, T. H. Miller. Her dam had been covered by two of his young bay stallions, Mohammed and Moloch, and the doubt as to which was the sire placed the conscientious Sloughgrove in some difficulty when trying to work out which stallions had the most progeny amongst the winners. He felt it would be absurd to credit two stallions with half a winner each. So he allotted her to them both, which was equally impossible, if still fair. One Press reporter commented that she had "an embarrassment of blessings, or too much father. She may be a daughter of Moloch, or of Mohammed – either riches or religion. The two benefits are often found in company."

After only one year, the rule about producing a local veterinary certificate to accompany entry-forms for the show was abandoned in 1892. This was wise, for nothing was more calculated to set both veterinaries and exhibitors by the ears, especially with Professor Pritchard on duty as chief inspector for the fifth time. Instead, the fantastic scheme was put into operation of thoroughly vetting every single exhibit before it was passed on to the judges, and four assistant inspectors were appointed. This had never been done anywhere and certainly only fanatics would have dreamed of inspecting 337 stallions and 224 mares with Pritchard thoroughness before beginning to judge them. As it happened, only 487 animals turned up, and the good professor rejected ninety-three, fifty-four of them for sidebone.

Starlight, the ex-reject, won the female championship for the third year in succession – a record. The first time she was owned by R. N. Sutton-Nelthorpe but had then been bought by Fred Crisp at the great Scawby home sale for 925 guineas. Lord Wantage had given a "Lockinge Cup" for champion mares, and Starlight won it the only three times it was competed for. Like Gilbey's Elsenham Cup it became the property of any exhibitor who could win it twice, and so now Crisp kept it for good. It was suggested that champions should not be allowed to compete again at London shows, but that idea was turned down. The top four senior big mares, including Starlight, were all bred in Lancashire: a warning signal to the men of the Fens and the Midlands. Among the yearlings, prizes were replaced by five equal premiums of £10 for colts and four of £5 for fillies. This met with universal criticism. Rules for the auction sale at the end of the show were tightened, particularly with regard to reserved prices, just as they were at this period for other auctions conducted by Mr. Sexton under Shire Horse Society auspices.

The 1893 show was advertised on the "garden-seat" omnibuses of the London Road Car Company, instead of on hoardings as before. Though much smaller than the massive London General (it had only 450 of the 2,210 omnibuses licensed in London and owned 5,000 horses), this progressive company was the ideal choice for modest publicity. It was popular as the pioneer of the penny fare and was this year introducing the novelty of bell-punch tickets.

A sensational decision was made in the stallion championship, made possible only by the Horse Show Committee's abandoning the previous year's unpopular experiment of awarding equal premiums for the best four or five yearlings. The class was judged in the normal way, and so the winner, Lord Belper's Rokeby Harold, went forward as a candidate for the junior cup. And he won it, with another of Harold's sons, Castern Harold, winner of the three-year-old class, as runner-up. Then he beat the senior cup winner as well for the supreme championship. The hall buzzed with the spectators' amazement, and the colt celebrated by getting away from his groom and racing round the ring, making a wonderful show all on his own. Everyone roared approval, which made him go the faster.

The champion mare, the grey fluent-moving Rokeby Fuchsia, had the same prefix as the young horse, and this was a quick illustration of the value of the new idea in naming, for it not only helped to differentiate horses, but also associated them with certain owners. In this case, however, John Parnell of Rugby, who had been one of the first to apply for a registered prefix, had already just disposed of the colt. When his mare won the championship, he cursed his folly. But who would expect a yearling to be supreme champion "stallion"? It had never happened before, and has not happened since.

It was at this show that the success of certain bloodlines first really began to be apparent. There were sixty-five prize-winners and reserved numbers in the twelve classes. John Sloughgrove analysed their pedigrees, and pointed out that forty-one of them could be traced back in direct male line to three horses – Lincolnshire Lad II (twenty-two, including five of the six best two-year-old fillies), William the Conqueror (ten), and What's Wanted (nine). If only he had had a glimpse into the future, and had known about what we can now call the seven foundation sires of the breed, he would have replaced What's Wanted's score of nine by a total of twelve for his great-grandsire Matchless and would have added Heart of Oak, Lincoln and Bar None, whose descendants won seven prizes. So, of the sixty-five, all but fourteen were directly descended from six stallions. But this is a matter of hindsight, which is notoriously easier to practise than foresight.

In 1894, a judges' selection committee replaced the cumbrous system of allowing all members to propose names, and it proved equally impartial. It was decided to close the show at 6 p.m. each evening, which was a relief to horses and grooms. Placards in the hall warned that applause during the judging was strictly prohibited and that offenders would be ejected. This helped the judges' morale even if it left them more doubtful about how unpopular they were with the spectators. A few plain clothes detectives were hired for the Monday before the show opened, and this pleased everyone except the unwelcome visitors who had made a haul in previous years during the confusion of arrival and settling in.

Bury Victor Chief, still only five years old, was supreme champion for the second time and top of his class for the fifth time – a record. He attended no further shows that year, but set out on a busy season at high fees to capitalise upon this fame.

All through the 'nineties, the sons and daughters of Harold, the 1887 champion (son of Lincolnshire Lad II) consistently won more prizes than the progeny of any other stallion. In 1895, thirty-eight of them were at the show. Rokeby Harold, the ex-yearling champion, won the championship again as a three-year-old: Markeaton Royal Harold was the top two-year-old and Ruddington Harold the top yearling: Madge won the two-year-old filly class, and Queen of the Shires the yearling class. Of the 277 Shires in the junior classes, five of the six class winners were therefore by Harold. Others of his sons and daughters won two second prizes, five thirds, a fifth, a reserve and four highly commended cards – a total of eighteen. Even more significantly for the development of the breed along planned lines, seven of these winners (including Markeaton Royal Harold and Madge) were out of mares sired by Premier. A. C. Duncombe did more for the future of the Shire than he ever dreamed when he brought these two contemporaries together at Calwich Abbey. The Harold cross on a Premier mare had now become an almost certain recipe for success and, as a classical blend of different bloodlines, was never to be surpassed. The eighteen Harold winners this year had been bred in nine different counties. Duncombe himself had bred one of the highly commended mares.

A new class for old stallions of ten years and upwards was added and was won by Vulcan, the Earl of Ellesmere's former double champion. Thomas Mott's Pioneer, the reserve, was eleven years old: his sire, Champion of England, had been foaled as long ago as 1869. This class was a marvellous advertisement for continued soundness and good condition in stallions with many years of service at stud behind them. Two classes for geldings were also introduced – not the former "any breed" kind, since the qualification for entry was that they should be by a registered sire and out of a dam by a registered sire. The purpose behind their introduction was to encourage owners to prefer a top-class gelding to a third-rate stallion. The trade in the former was assuming even greater importance: the market for the latter was confined by the restrictions very properly being placed upon imports by the American authorities.

The senior steward, J. Sturley Nunn from Suffolk, was pleased with the way the show proceeded, and the rule about not shouting or applauding during the judging was most sternly enforced. But the hazards of bringing so many horses together in a draughty London hall in February were underlined by disasters that befell some leading exhibits. Minnehaha, the champion mare, home-bred by Mr. Freeman-Mitford, was taken ill at the show and died soon after it. This was a sad blow, for she was probably the best mare seen so far in London – nearly everything about her, from her beautiful bay coat with white points to her perfect feet and feather, and her "laughing water" movement were a joy to look at. Vulcan of Worsley XIII, who won the four-year-old class for

R. G. Heaton of Chatteris, did not recover from a chill and died a week after returning home. Vulcan of Worsley IX won the over-four and under-ten class for big stallions on the Tuesday, was taken ill on the Wednesday and died on the Friday. Whether he would have won another championship for the Earl of Ellesmere is a moot point. The horse who stood second to him in the class was reserve to Rokeby Harold for the greatest honour.

The auction was conducted for the first time by Arthur C. Beck. George Sexton had died the previous spring and the letter of condolence his widow and family received from the Council was no mere formal expression of sympathy, as this representative of a well-known family of Suffolk Horse breeders had served the Shire well for the last fifteen years of his life. His firm – recently renamed Sexton, Grimwade & Beck on the acceptance of young Arthur, brother of Frank (who succeeded father Edmund as agent at Sandringham) – was unanimously elected, on an annual basis, as the official auctioneers to the Society in his place.

In 1896, by the narrowest of majorities, it was decided to reduce the number of judges from four to three. This still gave each of them a respite every third class. Unanimously, a serious attempt was made to reduce draughts as well, and to use more disinfectant. In addition, the latest part of the premises to have sprouted round the original building, the new "Minor Hall", was also utilised. Electric light was now extending its benefits into the main parts of the premises. Hitchin Conqueror, back in action at the age of thirteen after missing a year through an accident, became the second ex-champion to win the old stallions' class. Rokeby Harold won a place in history by becoming supreme champion for the third time at the age of four: he had also been reserve champion when he was two. The most significant innovation this year was an extension of the idea of awards to breeders. For ten years, gold medals had been given to those who had bred the two champions. Now there was £10 for the breeder of the first-prize stallion and mare in every class, and £5 for breeders of second-prize animals and of first-prize winners in the gelding classes, just as Sanders Spencer had advocated in 1886. Every part of the Society's activities was expressly designed to help the "small man". This was wise, for it was upon him that Shire breeding ultimately depended, no matter how many wealthy ones were attracted to it. Simple as it sounds in retrospect, none of the Society's new bright ideas was as revolutionary as this, and few did more good. Lord Rothschild did not really need the £5 he received for being the breeder of the second-prize four-year-old mare. But the vast majority of the twenty-eight men who shared the £205 this first year were very glad of it indeed. Even more, they shared the glory and excitement, not to mention the encouragement, of producing a winner which, for the money's sake, they had been bound to sell, and which they could not have afforded to bring to London on the off-chance of winning, even if they had not. Run mainly by nobility and gentry, the Shire Horse Society was as egalitarian as it could be in the age of Victoria. Mrs. Gill, who lived at Oxlode, Ely, was delighted to receive the £10 due to her late husband as the breeder, eight years before, of Orchard Prince. (Richard Gill had sold this horse as a foal to Thomas Chapman of Orchard Portman near Taunton. But by the time he was five he had caught the eye of that apostle of weight, James Forshaw, and went to Carlton-onTrent. And he had caught that particular eye because he was by Forshaw's own 26 cwt. Honest Tom 5123.)

For the 1897 show, some of the older stallion boxes had to be strengthened, as the partitions between several of them had been knocked to pieces the year before. Stalls under the grandstand were provided with electric light. Sloughgrove became a subscriber to the Royal Veterinary College, so as to entitle exhibitors to send sick horses there during the show. But all passed off without incident. Harold's progeny included the two champions, Markeaton Royal Harold (out of a Premier mare) and Queen of the Shires (out of a Royal Albert mare, whose own dam was by William the Conqueror). The best bloodlines were becoming more and more apparent.

In 1898, excursion trains, with tickets from two to five days' validity, were run by railway companies. A new agreement was signed with the Hall Company. And new arrangements were made for veterinary inspection. It had been increasingly difficult, with entries now regularly topping the 500 mark, to conduct this without holding up the judging. Accordingly, there was a return to something like the old system, the judges starting at 8.30 a.m. on each of the first two days by selecting not more than twenty-five from each class to be dealt with that day. All those not selected for the competition proper could be vetted afterwards. This was voluntary and, of the 459 who actually arrived at the show, only 233 did in fact undergo the veterinary examination – that is, nearly all of them compulsorily. One would have expected, now that the strict standards of soundness demanded in London were well known and consequently no animal came there unsound so far as its owner knew, that owners would have availed themselves of the opportunity of acquiring a certificate from a veterinary professor (the Society's rules insisted that no lesser personage could be appointed chief inspector) for a mere 5s. It would be useful to flaunt before mare-owners in the areas where a real live professor rarely was to be seen. And if the certificate was one of rejection, it was given free: and presumably need not be flaunted anywhere. Alternatively, it is somewhat surprising that the Society did not continue to insist on an examination of even those not selected for final judging, because there would have been time to complete this on the third day. But no doubt owners would have been unco-operative with such discipline as this.

Buscot Harold, two years old, was champion stallion. The young fellow made sage heads nod, for he was by a *son* of Harold out of a Premier *granddaughter*. Without much originality, people all over the hall were saying "Blood will tell". His dam, Aurea, was champion mare. His sire, Markeaton Royal Harold, the previous year's champion, was senior cup-winner and reserve to him for the supreme award. The whole thing was an unprecedented triumph for a family. And Alexander Henderson, M.P., owned, not only all these three, but the winner of the junior mare cup as well, Lockinge Loiret. Such a clean sweep of all four cups, senior and junior, as well as of the supreme awards, has never been known again. The future Lord Faringdon won £315 in cups, cash and medals, including the outright possession of the champion cup because he had won it before. He hardly needed the £10 as breeder of Buscot Harold. Aurea was perhaps the biggest surprise. This was her fourth time in London, and she had been previously commended, reserve and third. Queen of the Shires, still only four, won her class for the fourth consecutive time for Abraham Grandage of Bramhope, Leeds who was probably surprised that, if she was not to be supreme champion, it was Aurea who beat her.

In 1899, entries numbered 586, only sixty less than the never-forgotten night-mare of 1890. Stalls were erected behind the north grandstand and in yet another new area, the curiously-named "King Edward's Hall", which was also now, like most of the rest of the premises, lighted by electricity. A properly graduated circular tan ring with boarded fencing was now at last available for the testing of horses' wind, the former straw ring having long been considered dangerous. One exhibitor removed two of his horses from the ring without permission. He later apologised for his discourtesy. Another exhibited a fourteen-year-old Cornish horse, Premier V 10179 as "Premier Beau 8020" (foaled 1887, and by Premier). It turned out that the fault lay with Lord Ashburton, not a Shire member, who had until recently owned him and whose agent had put him up for sale on the previous 17th December under the wrong name at Tompkins' Repository at Reading, where the exhibitor had bought him in good faith. The prompt admission of error by his Lordship's agent saved the embarrassed exhibitor from disgrace and instant expulsion from the Society. The Prince of Wales picked up £20 as the breeder of the winner of the junior female cup, Victor's Queen, and of the senior cup winner and champion, Dunsmore Gloaming. Both were owned by Sir J. Blundell Maple, M.P., though the Member for Dulwich and holder of a literally household name could not expect to emulate the feat of the new Member for West Stafford the year before.

The twenty-first show in 1900 proved by its sheer uneventfulness that what had been a novelty in 1880 was now merely an annual event. The entry of mares dropped by sixty-eight, chiefly among the brood mares and simply because the show was a week later than usual. Otherwise there was only steady progress, which is always too dull to record. Breeders' prizes of £5 were extended to third prize animals, and altogether the cost of awards was £1,108. Buscot Harold won the male championship for the third consecutive time, a record; and Dunsmore Gloaming was again female champion. Judges came and went from year to year, but some animals were unshakeable, whoever did the selection. The oldest stallions were a remarkable lot. Twenty were entered, sixteen appeared, thirteen were selected, eleven satisfied Professor Penberthy (Professor Pritchard had served for the eighth and last time the year before). All eleven that returned to the ring won prizes and commended cards. Twenty years before, no collection of such ancient dads could have come through all this ordeal. And it was an ordeal, for there was no room for rewarding them purely out of sentiment.

4. COUNTRY SHOWS AND TOWN PARADES

Having from time to time without much success tried to persuade the county and other leading agricultural societies to provide specific Shire classes in the agricultural or cart-horse sections at their shows, the Council decided in 1892 to offer an incentive. The Essex society had in fact asked for a prize for the best Shire in 1885, but this had been refused. In 1890, the Birmingham Agricultural Exhibition Society, which organised shows and sales of Shorthorns, had offered to run a similar autumn event for Shire mares and foals if the Society would offer its patronage. This also was rejected, but when next year the Society offered two gold medals to the R.A.S.E. instead of the cash prizes that had been contributed since 1879, the Tunbridge Wells Association suggested that this medal scheme might be extended to other shows prepared to include Shire classes. The President, Lord Hothfield, came from Kent and he supported the idea. The following year a start was made.

Any county show at which a minimum of £100 prize-money was given in Shire classes was invited to claim a £10 gold medal for the best mare or filly, bred or owned by a resident in the county, and registered in the Stud-book or eligible for it. The only other conditions were that a mare of six years or more must have had a living foal and that no animal could win two medals in one year, unless one was at the Royal. The Derbyshire, Essex, Leicestershire, Norfolk, Nottinghamshire, Staffordshire and Suffolk societies successfully took part, together with the Royal Manchester, Liverpool and North Lancashire, which in 1894 was to be re-named the Royal Lancashire.

County and other shows, if more ambitious, could receive two gold medals, one for each sex, if they were prepared to put up £250 prize-money in at least six open Shire classes: the winning owner, in these cases, was to have been a member of the society concerned for at least six months. There were two participants. One was the Peterborough Society, whose summer show had been long established as the strongest in England for Shires – the Royal, largely because of its peripatetic nature and awkward date in June, not excepted. The Earl of Ellesmere won the mare medal and the stallion one went to John Rowell of Bury in Huntingdonshire, who may be with some justification regarded as the greatest Shire prophet and evangelist among tenant farmers. The other two-medal society was the Moreton-in-Marsh. Mr. Freeman-Mitford's generosity and enthusiasm in creating this and turning it so quickly into such an important affair caused no one to begrudge the fact that he won both medals himself.

The following year, non-county shows could obtain one medal if they offered £150 in prizes. Four more shows joined in – the Ashbourne, Bath and West, Cambridgeshire, and Shropshire and West Midland. As before, no animal could win more than one gold medal in a year, unless one was at the Royal Show.

The gold-medal scheme was so successful that the award of silver medals at other shows began in 1895. This new idea was deliberately designed so as to give the smaller man a real chance of glory. Any little one-day show whose few open classes never attracted any well-known exhibitors, or even a show which had no open classes at all, could participate, provided only that it became a corporate member of the Shire Society for a modest guinea. The winning mare, filly or filly foal had to be registered or eligible for the Stud-book. Further, if at least £25 were awarded for registered or eligible Shire stallions, entire colts or colt foals, a second silver medal would be awarded for the best of them. In order to spread the honours around, no gold medal winner was to be eligible, nor could one animal take two silver ones in the same year. No society was allowed to charge an extra entry-fee for horses competing for these awards. The scheme was announced too late for more than twenty-three societies to participate in 1895, but the following year eighty-two of them claimed ninety-five medals. Many of these, or of the thousands which were awarded in later years, are still treasured in families where the only memory of the circumstances attending the winning of them is that it all happened on the day which first made Grandfather a famous Shire man of his time. More still lie in drawers, unrecognised symbols of the old man's success in one of the very few farming activities that brought much financial reward in those hard old times from which his uncomprehending descendants have been spared.

In 1896, affiliated societies began then to be printed in the Stud-book separately from the list of individual members and their number increased dramatically to the advantage of everyone. The South Devon Horse Association, had been the sole corporate member in 1873. In 1884, there were three: at the end of 1895, thirty-nine; in 1900, 160.

In the towns, a large number of cart-horse parades, mainly on Whit Monday or May Day, were now springing up, modelled rather on London than on Liverpool. In 1899, after enquiries had been addressed to as many local authorities as Sloughgrove thought might respond, silver medals were presented for competition at provincial parades for the first time. Nineteen towns accepted. Three fell by the wayside but the other sixteen were allotted thirty-one medals. Liverpool had three (one being gained by the Lancashire and Yorkshire Railway Company) and so did Manchester (one to the Corporation) and the Royal Lancashire Show. Two were given at Bath (including the Midland Railway), Brighton (one to the Brighton & Hove General Gas Company), Burton-on-Trent (including Bass & Company), Cardiff, Darlington (where the Corporation won both), Eastbourne, Exeter, Plymouth and Swansea. One each went to smaller parades at Bolton, Crewe (won by the Co-op), Croydon and Oldham (Chadderton U.D.C. won this). Local secretaries reported that these medals were much appreciated, and in 1900 the number of medals increased to fifty-one, with twenty premiums of £1. As in London, the awards were made irrespective of whether the winners were Shire, Clydesdale, or Suffolk or even any local

'EACH HAIR IS WUTH A 'SOVREN'

PLATES 21 and 22   A matter of hair. Lockington Beauty, foaled in 1879, had an exceptionally long mane. She was somewhat common-looking, lacked width and weight and had small knees. But no mare produced so many celebrated sons and daughters. The cartoon below appeared in *The Graphic* after the 1889 London Show, and would have been even more appropriate twenty years later.

PLATES 23 and 24   Old William's sons. Staunton Hero (*above*) was the only stallion under 16.2 hands ever to be London champion. He sired only one notable foal. William the Conqueror's line depended solely on Prince William (Plate 26) and, even more, Hitchin Conqueror (*below*) who was first named, absurdly, "Lord Clyde".

type. The pupose was "to encourage the use of a better stamp of heavy draught-horse for town work".

At the London parade in 1900, there were thirty-six Shire medals together with premiums. There were 918 horses, 777 drivers and no one knows how many cheering passengers or densely-packed spectators. Under an unclouded sky, Lady Newton stood for nearly three hours presenting 689 rosettes. "The sleek well groomed appearance of all these horses", commented Frank F. Euren, the secretary and erstwhile Shire Society clerk, "must be a vivid object lesson to the owners of the numerous badly groomed underfed horses that are every day to be seen in the metropolitan area". This was, incidentally, the only year from the beginning until his death in 1906 that Professor Pritchard was not either a judge or veterinary inspector, and he served on the committee twenty years. He worked harder there and longer than he was ever required to do amongst the equine aristocracy at the Shire show, and never received any payment. The honorary veterinary officer this year, W. T. Wilson of Dorset Square, had 3,672 cart-horse feet presented for his inspection, and it is not suprising that he started "at an early hour".

5. THE UNITED STATES

Visitors to the Chicago Show of 1889 saw the largest exhibition of heavy-horses ever assembled together on the American continent. At the request of Alex Galbraith, the former associate of Lawrence Drew, now the leading Clydesdale man in the States and also President of the American Shire Horse Association, the Council offered two extra-large gold medals for competition the following year. And in that next year the Editing Committee met seventeen times especially to examine export certificates for horses whose registration for the Stud-book had not yet been completed. A very large number they refused to sign. Something had to be done about all this, and they made a rule that in future they would grant certificates only for animals already registered in the English book either in their own right or as produce of registered mares. But the pressures were so great that it looked as if they would be unable to enforce it.

However, this little problem was suddenly solved by the transatlantic depression which, for all the warning signs that the late 'eighties had put out, came, when it did come, suddenly and dramatically in 1890, the fourth year of the big drought. Mortgages became impossible to obtain. Stock and crops were sold for less than they cost to produce. Thousands of farmers went bankrupt and hundreds of thousands were brought to their knees in bitter poverty. The climax came in the general panic of 1893, when banks closed their doors, factories shut down, businesses crashed and railroads were bankrupted. Who, now, would buy and ship a Shire horse from Europe? The near-disaster to which the pedigree heavy-horse movement was brought is perhaps best understood by reference to the Percheron men, for theirs was the oldest-established draught breed and was as far ahead of the others in purity of blood as the Suffolk horse had been in the United Kingdom ten years before. Percheron breeders whose animals, taking an average of both sexes and all ages, were worth $500 apiece in 1889 found in a couple of years that they would not fetch $200, if they could be sold at all. Pure-bred brood mares sold for $150 or even $100, and the choicest specimens for $300. Top-class geldings were realising only $50 or $60.

In 1891, there were about 5,000 pure-bred Percheron mares available in the United States, intended as the fountain head of a great tribe of the future. Yet only 4,897 stallions foaled in this whole decade, and a miserable 4,990 mares, eventually (and in many cases very belatedly) found their way into the American Percheron Stud-book. This is an average of less than one foal every five years per mare. Some owners would not breed at all. Others castrated colts which were perfectly fit for breeding. Still more sold valuable mares for town haulage or to other employment from where they were never heard of again. And this was at a time when the American breeders, unlike the English, desperately needed to increase sheer numbers by retaining and breeding from everything that was not actually a misfit. Only 479 mares were put in the book in 1894, 539 the next year and 392 in 1896. In 1898 the breed society went bankrupt and the Stud-book ceased publication.

The ill-effect of the dispersal and scattering of valuable studs of mares was a double one. In the first place 5,000 mares cannot be selectively mated to the best stallions if they are scattered in twos or threes all over so vast an area, and this problem no doubt accounts for the fact that almost as many stallions were registered as mares. By 1900 the mares were in the hands of 547 Illinois breeders, 204 breeders in Iowa, 146 in Ohio, and 124 in Minnesota. There were 367 in Wisconsin, Kansas, Indiana, Michigan, Nebraska and South Dakota. The other 246 owners of pure Percherons were scattered throughout twenty-four other states and territories. Even the Illinois breeders, who probably had over a third of the mares and were far the best placed, were spread over a bigger area than England and Wales combined. The problem of getting a good sound stallion to travel a twelve mile circuit in such a remote area as South Devon was not serious in comparison with this! Secondly, and worse, many carefully-bred mares passed to men who knew nothing about quality, less about bloodlines, and very little even about management or proper feeding. If all these woes befell the Percheron, which had the advantages of being such a good "doer" when there was little to eat, of having clean legs where there was little care bestowed on grooming, and of generally being able to survive in the worst of conditions, there is no cause for wonder that Shire or Clydesdale men suddenly found they could not sell their pedigree stock any longer to the States.

Even if they could, there were now official hurdles to be overcome. A proper veterinary examination was necessary before animals were allowed into the States. That, of course, was warmly applauded by the Shire Council. But the McKinley tariff also put a heavy duty on horses, unless they were accompanied by certificates showing not merely that they were registered in a stud-book, but that "the ancestors have been recorded in a book of record established for the breed for five generations on the side of the sire and four on the side of the dam". This was modified in 1893, when it was required that both parents and all four grandparents should be registered, but for Shire men this concession was more apparent than real. The Shire, still in the process of pedigree-making, was no Thoroughbred. However, if no one can afford to buy one's wares, it does not matter very much about guarantees of purity. In 1892, only 127 Shires were sent to the United States: in 1893, twenty-one: in 1897, three.

James Forshaw had seen the end of the boom approaching and began refusing to let horses go until he had been paid. "I don't mean to say", he later told his daughter, "that I got off absolutely scot-free, but, considering the quantity of horses sold and the money I had handled, I was fortunate. Many large farmers I know went on buying in a reckless manner, and I warned them. But they found their stables full of horses of no quality or marketable value and their pockets full of "I owe yous" for horses already taken. It was many a year before they recovered themselves, and many never did so." Forshaw always saw further ahead than most men, but one good thing that happened to him was pure luck. "Once, in a train, the conversation turned to the Americans and their bills. As it happened, I had one in my pocket book for £400 which was two years over-due. I pulled it out and showed it them and said, to show what faith I had in it, that any of them could have it for five shillings. None of them seemed anxious to accept, so I put it back. When I got home and was looking through my letters, there was one enclosing a cheque for two hundred pounds from this very man, and a promise to send the remaining money very soon. After a short time it came. He also came later in person and began to buy once more. He turned out to be a real good man and we did lots of business together for years after that."

The revival began in 1900, when 159 of the 192 Shires that crossed the Atlantic were for the United States. Under the new regulations, export certificates were precious documents. When George Freir's wife accidentally burnt the paper for Deeping Tom, which her husband had bred on his Deeping St. Nicholas farm four years before, the Editing Committee was reluctant to issue a duplicate and did so only on receipt of her signed statement about the original. J. H. Truman of Whittlesea asked if the Society could help fill the blanks in the pedigree of Scropton Regent, an eight-year-old that he wanted to export: his dam was the unregistered *Poppet* and his grand-dam unknown. But nothing could be done to assist.

For the good of the Shire's reputation, the American Depression had at least created a decent interval between the old times and the new. When business was resumed, it was on an altogether different basis. The United States was no longer a dumping-ground, but another market for the expert breeder. Truman and his two sons, one of whom had settled permanently in the States before the recession, began to flourish mightily, as they deserved to do. Men like James Forshaw were remembered and could do new business. Many others were forgotten, as perhaps some of them deserved also. But to what extent the memory of the coarse curly hair and the grease of so many of the former imports made the task of promoting the Shire in the new century more difficult than it should have been, it is difficult to assess.

6. GOVERNMENT HELP OR INTERFERENCE

The Victorians were sensitive about their freedom both to do what they liked with their own and to succeed or starve according to their ability or their luck. It is, therefore, not surprising that, although suggestions were first made in the 'nineties about state aid for breeders, and the suppression of unsound stallions, nothing resulted except a deal of argument.

W. R. Trotter suggested in 1893 that the Society should subsidise stallion-hiring societies. At about this time, some of these societies were indeed financi-ally embarrassed, but this was due more to inexperience of a still more or less novel idea than to any intrinsic difficulties. Some associations tried to cover too big an area and, although they made up for it by hiring several horses, there were continued upsets because everyone wanted the best one. Others continued to offer premiums to travel their distinct instead of hiring the horse themselves and this resulted in rows with owners of private stallions, the more old-fashioned of whom regarded this co-operative effort as a disgusting manifestation of socialism. And so a number of societies did in fact cease to exist this year. But this was only a temporary set-back for an excellent system – in many areas, the only possible system – for obtaining the use of good stallions.

Frederic Street, in his paper to the Farmers' Club in 1878, had suggested that the money for Queen's Plates designed to improved Thoroughbred stock could be more properly diverted to cart-horses. The point was politely ignored by his audience. But in 1896, the Central Chamber of Agriculture, progressive as always, resolved to urge the Government itself to make a grant for suitable cart stallions. This would have raised the choler of all free men, had there not been a recent precedent for it. In 1888, the Queen's Plates had indeed been superseded and the Royal Commission on Horse Breeding had been distri-buting £5,100 a year (3,200 guineas from Her Majesty's civil list and the rest voted annually by Parliament) in premiums for Thoroughbred stallions. The three heavy-horse societies and the Cleveland Bay men were invited to join a committee to discuss the Central Chamber's idea. But the Shire men resolved "that State aid for the encouragement of Shire or cart-horse breeding is not necessary or desirable". Only the Suffolk and Clydesdale people took part, though of course there were Shire breeders among the Chamber of Agriculture representatives. One of these was a Mr. Beddall, who was a member of the Bedfordshire Shire Horse Society, though not of the Society itself. He thought the Government "should be asked to help those who helped themselves. A grant might be given, not to stallion-owners, but to societies which had a certain number of members and which did not charge more than a certain fixed fee." This compromise was precisely the scheme which was later brought in. But not in the reign of Victoria. The editor of *The Livestock Journal* wrote the last word: "There are only two methods of encouraging the breeding of livestock – one is to trust to private enterprise: the other is to rely on state subsidies. The two systems do not work together, and it has been by private enterprise alone that all advances have been made in this country."

(The Suffolk breeders, as always, were in a better position so far as the availability of stallions was concerned, than the Shire men, whose main concern was for those areas where there were no good ones. No farm in Suffolk was out of a good sire's reach, and they were able to consider the man who could not afford a decent mare. In 1897 they set up their "breeding scheme", which provided a small farmer with a mare of value up to 60 guineas. He paid one quarter the price and an annual 4% interest on the balance. The mare was served free, and the farmer reared the foal, which was then sold by auction. His account was credited with £16. 10s. 0d., together with half the excess over 20 guineas if the foal made more than that sum. This excellent scheme, possible only in a smaller society in a compact area, lasted over fifty years.)

The elimination of unsound stallions was a different matter altogether from the encouragement of good ones. Henry VIII's laws had been concerned solely with size, but no Government had ever thought of sidebones, roaring and so on. J. Wood of Keymer, Sussex, had suggested at the Farmers' Club, the day before the first London Show, that they *should* think of it, and had advocated a system of annual licensing, which would make it an offence for any horse not passed as free from listed hereditary defects to cover any mare not belonging to his owner. G. M. Sexton expressed the same view in Volume 2 of the Stud-book. These were voices in a wilderness, but at last in 1896 the Hunters Improvement Society set up a committee to consider the matter and the Shire Society agreed to co-operate. Messrs. Freeman-Mitford and Rowell and Major Frank Shuttleworth of Biggleswade spent some considerable time in discussion with the Hunter men, but nothing ever came of their deliberations, either in this reign or the next. The whole difficulty, of course, was that there was no way of stopping the unsound stallions, other than by law. If a law were not enacted or (and this was really the point) if even the keenest of improvers believed that interference with the freedom of the individual was a greater evil than any other, nothing at all could be achieved. A stallion with an impeccable pedigree might have every hereditary disease known to man, and yet his breed society was as powerless to interfere with his activities as it would be with those of any other horse of no breed at all. Only if he was presented at a show would he officially be found out and given a certificate of unsoundness. This was of course no impediment to the mare-owner who was ignorant enough to use him, or to his own proprietor, who did not stick the critical document on his stallion's back-side for all to see.

In any case, the Society had plenty of trouble with cases of simple deception. This very year, a stallion was travelling in Nottinghamshire called *Right Sort II*, whose advertisement card was craftily framed with a number and a pedigree which did not in so many words claim to refer to the Shire Horse Society, but which might deceive naïve persons. He might or might not have been unsound, but the Council thought it wise to insert a disclaimer in the local papers. (There was a genuine Right Sort II, but he had been now a long time in Illinois.)

7. DOCKING

It was at this time that the first real argument broke out on the subject of docking. It was a general practice for horses used in harness. But there were three degrees of the operation. The most absurd and drastic was the eighteenth-century Suffolk custom of bung-tailing cart stallions. This consisted of severing the tail right at the rump, leaving the horse with no covering at all and of course with no tail-hairs either. One explanation that was given for this extra-ordinary practice was that the amputation of the tail threw an extra portion of blood and vital force into the other organs of the body – a typical eighteenth-century fantasy. Another reason was that people thought it looked attractive. But even Georgian England seems to have drawn the line at bung-tailing mares – not on the grounds of humanity and protection against flies, but because when in season they would not after all present a pleasing appearance. Geldings were not bung-tailed, because there would be nothing under which to hold the crupper, but nevertheless there were men who managed to drive bung-tailed stallions in harness. These included the celebrated John Julian of Laxfield who about 1815 onwards advertised four famous stallions, Briton, Boxer, Bumper and Bly, for service and, out of season, drove them as a team to a wagon. The best-known of them, Boxer 755, travelled for twenty-five seasons and left an enormous number of foals. He went blind, but his rear end seems to have caused him little difficulty. Perhaps those old-timers of Suffolk were right about the vital force.

John Lawrence, in 1809, called such horses "plug-tails", and explained that the inch-long spigot end was clipped clear of hair. He said that Lord Cadogan, "a fanciful martinet in Queen Anne's reign", did it to all the heavy dragoon horses, but it was uncertain whether his lordship had copied the Suffolk men or vice versa.[1] The French had always after that called a tailless horse-rump "un Cadogan", which was no doubt one way of gaining fame.

A less severe form of "curtailing" was the short dock. This left a number of tail vertebrae, more for the convenience of the driver than of the horse, and was usually accompanied by cutting the tail hairs short, leaving the rump with but little covering and those parts of the skin unprotected which are normally swept by the tail and have no surface muscles to dislodge flies. Common as it was in the 'nineties, not many Shire men would have defended this. But they did regard it as essential partially to dock the working horse, for the protection of the driver, and his team also, from the real danger of the Shire's long tail getting caught up in reins and machinery – especially, on the farm, of mowers and binders.

When, therefore, the Duke of Westminster – a Shire member, but inexperi-enced in driving a cart or practical hay-making – proposed to the Council of

R.A.S.E. in 1892 that docked horses should be banned from exhibition at Royal Shows, there was an outcry and Gilbey, Chandos-Pole-Gell, Anthony Hamond and Garrett Taylor immediately opposed His Grace's fanciful ideas. The Shire Council, when it next met, reacted sharply. Lawton Moore of Brampton Bryan, Herefordshire, said the Society should take steps to ensure that members could "deal with their horses without undue outside interference". It was unanimously resolved that this meddling by R.A.S.E. councillors was "vexatious and unnecessary".

The dispute was prolonged, and in 1898, the R.A.S.E. decided, in spite of the cogent arguments of Sir Walter and Earl Egerton of Tatton, by a majority of four votes that no docked foals should be shown at the 1899 Show, nor any docked yearlings in 1900, and so on. The Shire Council sent them a very strongly-worded letter, pointing out that docking of cart-horses was necessary and that foals were more easily and painlessly docked than older animals. There was a renewed and furious controversy in the correspondence columns of the Press. At the end of the year, P. Albert Muntz managed to re-open the issue in the R.A.S.E. Council and the decision was rescinded by twenty-six votes to twenty-two. Gilbey had proposed that the rule should apply only to hunters and so he got more than he even hoped. After this, the anti-docking men were silent for some years.

8. THE URBAN GELDING

For all the recent and still continuing improvement in the general care of London geldings, it was glanders, that disease which throve on bad feeding, dirty stabling and overwork, which posed the chief problem in the 'nineties. But the paradox is not real. The evil had always stalked the metropolitan streets: only now for the first time was attention really given to the possibility of stamping it out.

Eradication did in fact become feasible, thanks to a Russian veterinary surgeon named Kalning who, impressed by the remarkable effect of tuberculin, had experimented with culture of the glanders organism *bacillus mallei*. In 1891, he proved that an injection of his "mallein" produced local inflammation and a raising of the temperature of every affected horse, whether the disease was in an incipient stage or in a mild chronic form – that is, impossible otherwise to recognise, but highly dangerous to other animals and to man. The following year, (Sir) John M'Fadyean, on his appointment as veterinary officer to Camden Town, introduced mallein to England. In 1894, at the International Congress of Hygiene at Budapest, it was described as "one of the most valuable acquisitions which has ever been added to veterinary medicine".

Unfortunately, the law did not keep pace with medicine. A new Glanders Order in 1892 did almost more harm than good. It rightly defined the disease as inclusive also of "that form of glanders which is commonly known as farcy", or skin-glanders, which inevitably progressed in due course to the real thing. It also empowered local authorities to adopt a policy of compulsory slaughter.

But the paltry compensation (£2 for a carcase if glanders was proved post mortem or, on a higher scale, one-quarter of the value of the horse when fit) was an inducement to sell an affected horse quickly, before the disease became apparent. And the mallein test now enabled unscrupulous owners to do just that. A further order in 1894 was no more effective. Mallein therefore began by doing more to spread the disease than to arrest it. Alexander Cope, the Chief Veterinary Officer of the Board of Agriculture,[2] was driven almost to despair, and his annual reports show a steady loss of faith in man's integrity. It was fortunate that most of the "hot potato" horses went only to other metropolitan owners. In 1900, as in 1890, about 91% of glandered animals were to be found in London. As for the actual number of outbreaks, 555 stables were officially returned as affected by glanders, and 436 by farcy, in 1890: in 1900, after eight years of mallein tests and in spite of the best efforts of the more enlightened men, there were 1,119 affected establishments.

Cope pointed out, at the end of this period, that pleuro-pneumonia in cattle had been rooted out between 1890 and 1898 at a cost of only £282,000. Glanders could have been similarly dealt with more easily and cheaply, for it was less widespread, nor did it require the slaughter of all contacts, since mallein was an infallible diagnostic agent.

(In due course, positive action was taken. William Hunting led a campaign which resulted in the Government officially recognising the test in 1907, when a new Glanders and Farcy Order replaced attempted control by a policy of eradication. The result of the battle was now no longer in doubt. But, if only the authorities had acted sooner, the country would have been free of glanders by 1914.)

To turn from the sad section of the London gelding community to the aristocrats, we find during this decade the demand for the finest specimens still outstripping the supply. We might here allow a contemporary expert, whom we have often quoted already, to comment on the position. This is none other than our Scots friend Thomas Dykes, whose excellent chapter in *Heavy Horses, breeds and management*, the best book[3] ever produced on heavy-horses in general I make no apology for extensively quoting. Dykes' contribution was entitled "The London Work Horse in Street and Stable".

"There are few", he wrote, "except those who are engaged in the trade, or in the superintendence of the larger studs, who really understand the difficulty experienced in getting hold of first-class sound geldings possessing the necessary weight and strength of bone for shifting the heaviest London loads. 'Were I,' said the manager of one of the largest London yards, 'to advertise in the Midland counties for a score of such horses, the chances are that when they were sent up on approval, I should have to consider myself lucky if I got hold of one good working pair. The others would have to be rejected as too light.'

"To those who have visited the Shire Horse Society's shows, since they were first established, this seems somewhat inexplicable. But if the problem were carefully worked out it would be found that, were all the prize and commended stallions stationed out on the cultivable portion of the country where mares are worked for a living when carrying a foal, one would really be astonished to find the amount of ground which has to fall under the mantle of operations of this healthy and useful movement. . . It must also be borne in mind that London, largely through the emulation engendered over the Cart Horse Parade movement, is cutting the old standard figures in the horse ledger, and coming up to the requirements of the times. The increased demand may make the scarcity in this way more real than apparent, but what London is prepared to pay for, and that which it will pay British farmers to supply, should not long be wanting, for granting even that the middleman, as many think, runs away with most of the profit of the business, the farmer-breeder would get a little more all the same.

"If the farmer should wish to breed for the London markets, then he will have to study London requirements, and when he has studied these he may be able, with a full knowledge of his land and how it must be worked at a purely agricultural profit apart from horse-raising, to come to some sound determination. The strength and richness of the pasture will have to be fully considered, for if we do get a little extra bone by using a strong, thick-legged sire, that extra thickness, which is worth £10 an inch under the knee when we bring them to market, may be lost at the mouth. The farmer on stiff, hilly clays or thin lands cannot therefore compete with those who have rich meadows, where the young colts have little to do but eat and grow big and strong."

Dykes writes well about the animals and men employed by the leading heavy-horse proprietors in London. "Many of the best London drivers come up from the country, and though a little 'green' at first, one helps the other, and once knowing the set journeys they are quite as confident as those who have driven on the stones for years. Their sons, as a rule, do not follow their fathers' occupations, the parents always looking out for something superior, as they make better wages as coopers in the breweries, millers in the large mills, or packing box makers in the manufactories to which their fathers are attached.

"In regard to horses and drivers, here is a somewhat typical miller's team, driven by a very able teamsman, one who has won his diploma at the London Cart Horse Parade, also his ornamental cross – though in 1894 he was not in Regent's Park. He has to drive twelve hours a day and do all his grooming and strapping, so that his horses are under his charge in stall and stable, and it is somewhat of a treat to see how he handles them on the street. His horses are hard browns, 16 hands 2 in., or perhaps a little over, with good blue hoofs, little hair on the leg, but well turned joints. They are rare walkers, and come round like a tandem team in the show-ring at Islington, in order that he may get up to the Metropolitan water trough. As he dismounts after the unicorn has quenched his thirst to unslip him and let up the pair, you find that he has just come up from the mills of Mr. F. D. Collen, of Bermondsey, with eighty sacks of flour, in all five and a half tons, and that the weight of waggon, loader and driver will be one and a half tons more, or a load of seven tons. This is his first journey for the day; a second with a similar load he will have in the afternoon in another direction, getting home to supper at 6.30 p.m., having left the yard on his first journey at 6.30 a.m. This from Monday to Saturday every week. The duties of the miller's horses are not of so spasmodic a character, possibly, as those of the brewer's, which are to a certain extent affected by weather, public holidays, and the like. They are out at earlier hours than the others, as bakers are men early at work and can take delivery of sacks of flour long before the cellarmen in some of the large beer public-houses are out of bed.

"Of course, loads and journeys vary in the flour as well as in the beer trade, and some firms have their particular modes of harnessing and yoking. As a rule, the weight is placed next to the wheels, the unicorn horse used being a light, active sort, a hundred-weight and half less than the average of the pair in rear, and worth in the market from £20 to £30 less. His powers are very severely tried at starting, but as soon as a few sacks have been delivered at the different bakeries he steps out with freedom, and if a good walker, as he ought to be, soon carries the team home for second journey at noon, or for supper and rest in the evening when work is over."

Dykes' description of a perfect gelding is also worth reading. "He is a dark brown with black points, eight years old, 17 hands, is well seasoned, and thoroughly knows his business. We go over him as he stands without harness of any kind. His head is broad between the eyes, and his eyes have a mild, full, noble expression, suggestive of a love for his work. His chest is swelling, broad and expansive, and his short legs come to the ground with a very slight inclination inwards. The centre lines of his round, blue hoofs point straight to the front, his fetlocks are bold, firm and prominent, and proportionate to the shapely, muscular knees above.

"Pass round from the front, do not stand too close, and take a good view of him sideways. The head and the neck are well set on, the crest is beautifully arched, and his chin is the proper distance from where his under hame strap would fall if harnessed. The shoulders gently slope upwards to the withers, suggestive of a grand socket for the collar; the withers are not too thin, but formed so that the bottom of the collar, on which falls the strain of draught, shall be well supported at the top. The bones of the legs are flat and clad with silky feather, the pasterns possess that slope at once suggestive of support for his own body and freedom of progressive movement in front of his load. He is deep through the heart; his ribs are round as a well-hooped barrel, and the depth carried well back; his loins are broad and deeply clad with muscle, wave-like from the backbone; his quarters are broad, there is no sudden drooping, but a sabre-like sweep of outer second thighs to the hocks, which are not too wide, but suggestive of leverage without cramping, cleanly chiselled out, and free from all flabbiness; his hind bone flat as in front, and his hind pasterns carried down with medium slope into the best of hoofs.

"Pass in rear of him and you will find great, powerful inner thighs descending with mathematical evenness, all suggestive of power. Have him walked straight away from you and you notice no twisting of hock points out or in, everything being carried straight and free and parallel. As he walks back to you, you observe the same squareness of action in front. Trot him down again and he lifts his hocks cleverly every time like a bit of mechanism till you see the inside of his hoofs; bring him back and you perceive shoulder above and hoof below working as freely and evenly together. Stand to the side and see him walked. Forward he swings, five miles an hour, both ends going together, hind hoof up to old fore hoof mark, and fore-hoof launched out and on again, the pace seemingly being regulated to an inch, and never varying." Dykes showed his Scotsman's love of good action here.

"In regard to colour, dark brown with black points has been chosen, but bays of light or dark shades are equally suitable, and there can be no objection to good hard blacks. Greys when fully ripe, seem to be higher at the withers than others, whilst still retaining their gay carriage, and with the red roans are generally noted for their great weight. Blue roans are very rarely handsome or captivating, but on the average they have more bone than the others, and are great favourites with some London horse owners on account of their hardy constitutions and tractable dispositions. For the hard wharfinger work off the Thames on the Middlesex side, where all is sheer hard horse toil in chains and shafts, they are greatly in use. In and about the mazey wynds, and through the dark arches of Bermondsey you will come across them any hour of a hard working day, each and all walking at a faster pace than is allowed by the managers of brewery studs."

He now moves on to describe a typical city scene before mentioning some of the best London horse-owners. "On London Bridge – this article is written on the eve of the opening of the Tower Bridge, which will greatly relieve the far too congested traffic – it is interesting to watch the apparently never-ending procession passing from right to left, and left to right, each driver, from the drayman who drives his four to the costermonger on the box seat of his donkey-hauled barrow, taking his place and claiming his share of the passage. All this with good humour, though the driver who jogs the lot from the rear (and it is horses' heads to hind boards, and hind boards to heads all the way over), will come in for a good deal of strong language. The study of this moving equine democracy is at all times interesting to those who have a love for work horses. In a short time this picture like many other pictures of old London will be changed, through the lowering of the bascules of the impressing structure further down the river.

"Amongst the best-known work horses which pass over the bridge are those of Messrs. Samuel Taylor and Son, of Tooley Street, the well-known contractors, in whose stud of seventy strong horses there are several very grand teams of blue roans. These horses are put in at a little less price on the top standard than the horses of the larger brewing firms, but the figures run much the same on the average. Horses like the heavy massive greys of Messrs. Lewis Berger and Son, the well-known starch manufacturers, up to 17.2, with weight in proportion, and not falling away below the knee as is sometimes seen in very heavy greys, will command their own prices at any time when ripe for town work.

"This chapter is intended to deal chiefly with the heavier sorts of London horses, and small notice need be taken of those used in the pantechnicon vans, though these are beautiful active horses and well suited for their work, being good, steady walkers when furniture and men are all on board, and equal to trotting home with the empty van at seven miles an hour. The oil distributing people use hardy, square-legged little cart-horses of the Norfolk type, which trot well in front of moderate loads. These horses it would pay farmers to breed on light soils, steep hill-sides, or where there is much green crop cultivation.

"Of what may be styled builder's horses, the heaviest, naturally enough, are those used for heavy stone hauling, and for these the greys and blue roans of Messrs. John Mowlem and Son have long been conspicuous. They must all have weight to shift weight behind. The cement, timber, and glazier and varnish trades prefer smooth-legged horses, upstanding like the Cleveland, or short and cobby, like the Norfolk cart-horses, according to the districts in which they are used.

"Messrs. Watney & Co. possess a grand representative stud of London work horses. Messrs. Courage & Co. of the well-known Horsleydown brewery firm, have been scarcely less noted; indeed, at the outset of the London Cart Horse Parade, the horses of this firm, which are of the low, square-set, blocky type, formed one of the features of the London May Day procession. Messrs. John Watney & Co. of Hammersmith, have magnificent teams, which are rivalled by those of Messrs. Young & Co. of Wandsworth, and the fine turnout of the Mortlake Brewery Company, some of which are equal to the best shown in Regent's Park on Whit Monday. Messrs. William Younger & Son, of Edinburgh, also make a feature with their brewery horses, a good number of which are crosses of Clydesdale and Shire. Messrs. Charrington's horses are very useful sorts; a little light perhaps, one might think, but each and all well suited to the particular loads and particular journeys of the firm. The Burton-on-Trent companies possess many fine teams, but as a rule there is little about them to attract the attention of the Londoner. The harnessing, equipment, and even the set of the build of the waggon are such as to suggest reform to any one who studies the street traffic of the Metropolis. These large firms, however, have in many cases depots in the suburbs attached to railway sidings, so that the long London journeys do not fail to be considered by the stable or stud managers. Of the London distillery firms the most representative horses are undoubtedly those of the Thames Bank Distillery, the leading pairs of which will average 16.3, and this with weight and ample strength of bone. Of course, the small family brewery horses are of the light cobby character, not to be compared to those in the general business."

It was inevitable that Dykes should be drawn into a discussion of the relative needs of Glasgow and London: "Comparisons are frequently made between the work horses of one large city or town and another; these without regard to special conditions of labour, loads, roads, width or narrowness of streets, or length of journeys. Glasgow may well be held as the city where Clydesdale work horses are seen at their best. At any rate, the requirements of the large Glasgow contractors to some extent rule the opinions of the breeders, if not through the showyards, certainly through the purchasers for the fairs and markets. Yet the English dealers for the 'London stones' were in the past always prepared to go a little further at the Rutherglen, Paisley, and Glasgow fairs for a useful half dozen drawn from a string. Possibly against him a Glasgow buyer would bid for a single one, or a pair at most, and get them; but the southern men could not afford to come north and buy them by the 'ones' and the 'twos', and they were no more prepared to accept light weight in the horse market-place than they would do over the grocer's counter. So the Crawfords and many others brought up the heavy Shires to breed with and produce horses of size for the southern markets. Glasgow benefited greatly, as the combination horse exactly suited the Scottish lorry, which is nothing but a Scottish, four-wheeled English waggon, such as is at present to be found in common use by Whitbread's and other firms.

"Messrs. Whitbread have always been partial to the 'pairs' used in front of very neatly built waggons, and horses and waggons one can see very readily match. This, however, being a subject of debateable matter for controversialists on both sides of the Tweed, need not be entered into here. It is argued, however, that the present type of Clydesdale, which is largely a work of showyard and Stud-book evolution, is the best type for Glasgow work, which they say is the most severe work a draught horse can be put to. Therefore they argue this type of horse must be the best for London work also. But the journeys in Glasgow are very short; there are no 'tied' public-houses, and no particular 'monopolies' of the baker business amongst the millers. If we take the horses of the well-known export brewery firm of Wellpark, whose stud is no doubt the most representative one in Glasgow, we find that these single lorry horses carry very light loads of 'stone bottled' ales, packed in barrels, to the docks, there to be shipped to India and the Colonies. In a London or Liverpool sense such horses could not be classed as *brewers'* horses; rather would they be put on the level of the horses of the carmen of the London district and surburban railway stations or the wharfingers of Bermondsey, and the south-east Surrey side of London Bridge. They have frequent short journeys out and home from the docks, but no long tiring ones over heavy roads, and do little feeding from the nose-bag."

The comment of a Derbyshire man, Gilbert Murray of Elvaston, writing the chapter on farm management of the heavy-horse in the same book, adds something to this. "Amongst those who are engaged in the commercial enterprise of the large provincial centres of industry, the Northern horses, though not more weighty, are regarded as more muscular, and are carefully selected for the development of those points which insure free action. Take Glasgow as an illustration of the Northern division and compare it with London as the chief centre of the South. In the former case the average weight of the dray horse is 16 to 18 cwt, whilst in London the best dray horses vary from 18 to 21 cwt. The hours of labour are practically the same, though the loads are widely different. The average load of a single horse on the streets of Glasgow is, inclusive of the dray, three tons ten cwt., whilst in London it is a common occurrence to see two ponderous horses tugging at a load of five tons. Probably the system of yoking double has much to answer for. In this connection it is only fair to say that the average period of the life of a dray horse is greater in London than in Glasgow; this we attribute mainly to the different systems of feeding . . . The usual hours of work of town horses is not less than ten, and this in all weathers."

After this English comment, let our indebtedness to Mr. Dykes end with his account of one of the best-known of all London stables. "Through the kindness of Messrs. Watney & Co. Limited, of the Stag Brewery, Pimlico, and the courtesy of Superintendent Byron, a native of the 'land of cakes', hailing from the county of Ayr, but who has had extensive experience in Liverpool, the writer is enabled to give some interesting information as to their stud, which has won Shire Horse Society's premiums for four years at the London Cart Horse Parades; including leading honours for singles, pairs and unicorn teams in 1894. The full number of horses in this stud is 162; nearly all Shires of the heaviest type. The average price paid for these horses during the past ten years (1884–94) was £84. The Stud-book movement, which commenced in 1877, would seem, therefore, to have had some beneficial effect so far as the supply of geldings of the best types are concerned. Between 1880 and 1884 the Americans raised the price for entire colts which, without an export demand for breeding stock, would have found their way into the shafts. They are purchased when five and a-half years old; guaranteed sound in every way, and no horse with side-bones or ring-bones is ever selected, no matter how superior the animal may be otherwise, as the streets would soon find out the weak spot, and the exigencies of the work would not allow of their standing lame in hospital.

"The first three months are anxious months to the superintendent, as owing to change of climate and stable, they are frequently attacked with a form of catarrh and thickening of the glands. Their first work is generally of a light character – three half-days a week for the first three months on the shorter town journeys; but gradually, as they get accustomed to hard food, which at first consists of chopped bran and a few oats, and there is no risk of feet founder from the effects of such, they are put out on the full journeys of twelve miles out and twelve miles home, or the shorter journeys of six miles out and six home, forenoon and afternoon. The gross loads on these journeys average three tons, waggon, barrels, men, and unloading gear.

"In two or three years they will have put on a full hundred-weight of hard muscle, coming in at 15 cwt. 1 qr. and increasing to 16 cwt. 2 qrs., which is the present stud average. The average service for the past ten years has been six years and eight months, though there were some horses which have exceeded this by two and three years. The cost per horse for veterinary charges is 8s. 11d. per annum, and shoeing £3. 10s.: a fresh set of shoes being required every three weeks. The tear and wear is more severe on the hind shoes than the fore ones, owing no doubt to the heavy friction caused by the leverage of the hocks. The shoeing smiths meet this by using up the old 'pelt' to harden the metal. The average cost to keep a horse per week, bedding included, has for the past three years been as follows – 1891, 17s. 6¾d.; 1892, 18s. 3½d.; 1893, 18s. 5d.

"Those horses which are out on the short journeys consume all their food in the stable, but those on the twelve miles journeys will have to feed from the nose-bag, and each nose-bag is filled with 20 lbs. Such horses are very liable to chills from having to stand in exposed, draughty places to disload, after a hot, sharp pull; and this will possibly evidence itself at night when in stable by feverishness. A strict watch, therefore, is kept upon them, and where the temperature has greatly increased, the superintendent, who must always be close to the yard, is called out at once.

"Naturally enough, such valuable horses are only entrusted to tried draymen, of whom there are six classes: first, 45s. per week; second, 42s.; third, 38s.; fourth, 35s.; fifth, 33s.; sixth, 32s. These draymen mostly come in from Norfolk and Essex, on the introduction of draymen friends working in the yard. The younger men have to work for six years as assistants, or in picking up 'empties', before being allowed to take out a team of their own. The high character of the firm's drivers is shown every year at the London Cart Horse Parade, where they have never failed to secure the diplomas or badges of the Royal Society for the Prevention of Cruelty to Animals.

"In regard to the use of the heavier vans and 'unicorn' teams Superintendent Byron is somewhat against them, and the writer is with him in regard to this. The 'unicorn' horse is often walking idle in chains when the 'shaft horses' are doing all the work. Moreover, at street crossings where policemen give one line of traffic turn about with the other, the extra length of horse causes delay and inconvenience to the public, and yet at the same time, owing to slack chains and their distance from the front axle, they fail to give assistance, exactly when assistance is required, to the horses behind. Pair-horse waggons, with loads to suit, Mr. Byron considers to be preferable; but the horses in these would have to be the heaviest procurable, so that they might always be equal to standing their loads . . . The farmer who can raise such geldings need never be afraid of finding a market for them in London; and at five years and a-half, they ought to yield him a handsome profit."

9. NO NEW BREEDS: AND WHITHER THE OLD?

The various kinds of cattle, sheep and pigs now being fostered by breed societies were many, and the tendency was towards proliferation rather than fusion. The Shorthorn Society, founded in 1875, provides a clear example. It was first divided in 1894, when the Lincoln Red Shorthorn Society was set up (which itself eventually adopted separate dairy and beef classifications in 1946 and a third section, for polled animals, in 1953). Next came the establishment in 1905 of an association to foster the Dairy Shorthorn. Though this was re-united with the original society in 1936, the Northern Dairy Shorthorn Breeders' Society and the Scottish Shorthorn Breeders' Association were to follow. When man controls the breeding of animals he tends to multiply types with special characteristics. When, instead, he crosses them, there is usually some good reason for preserving the original types as well and so a hybrid turns two breeds not into one, but three.

In 1878, it would have been possible to create stud-books for five, six or seven different types of draught-horse, as distinct from each other as the Suffolk from the Shire or Devon cattle from the Hereford – and far less closely related than the Jersey to the Guernsey, or the Shire to the Clydesdale. But it was not done, and by 1890 it hardly could be done. That year, it is true, visitors from the Midlands and the North to the Plymouth Royal Show were much impressed by some fine clean-legged West-Country horses in the agricultural classes. But no one was thinking of making a stud-book for them: the quicker they could be transformed into Shires, the better.

The Cleveland Bay was a valuable farm-horse in Yorkshire and farther north, since for general tillage on light soils he was tough and active. When the breed society was formed in 1884, one qualification for entry into the stud-book was complete freedom from "cart-horse" blood: as it had ever been, the slogan was "neither Blood nor Black". Here was an excellent animal for light draught, but outside his native acres, his ancient blood, when kept pure, was chiefly considered only for crossing purposes. The Vardy Horse or "Northumberland Chapman" horse had virtually been extinguished by the Shire and the Clydesdale. He was a fine animal – strong, hardy, active and clean-legged, a somewhat heavier version of the older and stronger type of Cleveland Bay which had been in fashion in the days when heavy coaches made long journeys on deep muddy roads. At this time Albert Grey of Hawick was trying to revive it, in vain.

As for the towns, there were jobs for about half a million genuine big draught-horses at this time. The full-blooded Shire was too strong, too heavy and too slow for at least 50% of these vacancies. But the "vanners" that filled them were constantly a once-only cross made to produce a gelding of the size, strength and speed required. The Shire, the Suffolk and the Clydesdale between them provided the only pedigree blood for all real draught-horses, whether one wanted an animal to shunt railway wagons or to deliver goods from Harrods. In the mines of South Wales, there was much more head-room than in other pits, and far bigger animals could be used: indeed, they had to be used, because the gradients were exceptionally steep and the bends and twists unusually severe. Some 16,000 or more horses worked underground, and they had a steadily increasing proportion of Shire blood in them. To look at, the best of them were obviously Shires, though the specialist breeders were producing geldings for this job which were about a foot shorter than what anyone in the Midlands would accept as a proper "Sheer". When even ponies are Shires, then the existing breeds have a monopoly.

By the 'nineties, only two serious questions remained to be answered. Would the virtues of the three recognised breeds succeed in reducing the amount of unpredictable mongrel-breeding that was going on? And what would happen to the Shire and Clydesdale now that they were segregated? If the reply to the first was to be "yes", then there was a long way to go. As far as the second question was concerned, a curious thing was happening. The influence of the pedigree movement, and especially of the choice breeding-studs of show animals kept by the wealthy, was causing both breeds to drift in the direction of "quality". But at the same time, the separation of the types since the end of the Drew-movement was already having a greater effect, so that Shire and Clydesdale were more recognisably different than they had been even a couple of generations earlier.

Two very perspicacious commentators, writing independently at the same time in the mid-'nineties, made identical criticisms of each breed. C. I. Douglas said of the Shire, "The improvement is most marked in the mares of all ages, and quality has unmistakably made great strides to the front in all female classes, while an endeavour has also been made to engraft an equal measure of quality on the stallions, and for this reason we find that masculine sires are inordinately scarce. If the Shire horse of the future declines in character it undoubtedly will be due to this cause, viz. a tendency on the part of breeders to use stallions not sufficiently masculine in type, and to lean too much to smartness, cleanliness, and that fatal quality that some applaud, 'prettiness' . . . We would also give a word of warning. Many people are only too apt to believe that what are excellencies in the mare are necessarily also merits in the stallion. No greater mistake could be made. It is essential that the mare should have plenty of depth in her ribs, and general roominess in her middle piece, as her chief function is to carry her offspring during its period of development, and ample room must be necessary for the proper maturing of her progeny. On the other hand, a stallion of this type, viz., with a tendency to excessive middle, is almost invariably a failure at the stud."[4]

Archibald M'Neilage wrote thus: "On the whole, the tendency in the Clydesdale breed during the past ten years has been towards greater elevation of shoulder, roundness of barrel and levelness of top – an influence easily traceable to Darnley and his tribe; and a marked improvement in action and style, as easily traceable to Prince of Wales and his tribe. Aiming at the development of qualities which are enduring rather than temporary, in some localities too much anxiety to produce fancy animals with exaggerated showyard points may have led to the neglect of more solid and enduring excellencies, while there has been a steady determination over all to keep the Clydesdale to the front. The improvement in the female line is greater than in the male line. There is a tendency to overlook the fact that the male must be masculine, and hence a few stallions have appeared which would have secured much greater distinction had they been of the opposite sex . . . That there has been a tendency in the show-yard during the past ten years, to favour 'bonnie' animals rather than strong animals, is not to be denied."[5]

The fashion which made the upper reaches of cart-horse breeding become a gentleman's fancy was responsible for this prettiness or bonniness in stallions, but the good that was done to the whole system by the landed proprietors' studs far outweighed their temptation to forget the precept which James Forshaw, greatest of the English stallion-owners, never failed to print in his advertisements: "Keep the lurry in view".

As for the increasing difference between the breeds, it is probably not unfair to say that it was the Clydesdale that was changing rather than the Shire. And in some respects, this was a reversal, slowly and gradually, towards the earlier type of the 'fifties, entirely owing to its being cut off from fresh infusions of English blood, allowing the differences in soil and climate to have their effect. Lack of bone beneath the knee, lightness of arm, thigh and body; a fine head becoming too fine; good open feet tending to be too open at the coronets and to become a weak white instead of a strong blue; the increasing amount of "daylight" under the body – all these things were both ingrained characteristics and natural to the conditions, in just the same way as it was natural for a Scottish horse to be a late developer, who at three might not be bigger than some Shire yearlings and yet who would grow on until the age of six and live to a great age, whereas the tendency of the Fen horse was to be "soon ripe and soon rotten". It would have been an interesting experiment to transfer all Scottish horses to the Midlands and Fens for a couple of generations, and all Shires to Scotland for a similar period. Even in one generation, it appeared that a Clydesdale bred in England grew coarser and heavier than expected and that a Shire bred in Scotland went lighter and higher. David Riddell always claimed that he could prove that English conditions, particularly Fen conditions, in weight alone could make a 2 cwt. difference to the same animal.

If the Clydesdale had got weight from England, and was tending already to lose it, the Shire men had learned one great lesson from the Scotsmen, to be forgotten only at their peril, that the *sine qua non* of cart-horse breeding was to get the legs and feet right. In the words of a saying that appears to be of north-country origin:

> *Feet, joints, feather:*   (or "feet, fetlocks and feather")
> *Tops may come, but bottoms never.*

A third question, which the Suffolk men were now inclined to ask, was surely of passing concern only. But it did not, for that, make them any less gloomy. In 1878, Fred Street at the Farmers' Club had praised the landowners of Suffolk for supporting their county horse both by breeding and exhibiting, at a time when landowners elsewhere took little or no interest. By the mid-'nineties the positions had been entirely reversed. This support had ceased in Suffolk, while the nobility and gentry all over the rest of England had become Shire men. Herman Biddell was now complaining, "The Duke of Hamilton has a splendid collection of Suffolk mares, and still buys when there is anything of marked value for sale. Mr. Quilter, the member for the Sudbury Division, takes good care to have a Suffolk horse for his district, and has some excellent mares of his own besides: but beyond this there is no great support given to the tenant farmers to encourage the breeding of the horses which have made the county famous, in so far, at least, as active participations in the pursuit is concerned."[6]

The reason for this double *volte-face* was not just that, outside Suffolk, everyone was aping the Prince of Wales and other luminaries. Nor was it entirely that Shire breeding had become a fascinating craze, as Gilbert Murray mildly suggested when he wrote that "the science of breeding is a most interesting and seductive amusement: the uncertainty of the results affords a source of pleasurable enjoyment snatched from the busy occupation of every day life".[7] The pleasurable enjoyment for most men, including the nobility and gentry, came from the good hard cash that town geldings fetched, and there was little uncertainty about the results in that direction. The Suffolk, on the other hand, was suffering from being an agricultural horse, in a time of acute agricultural depression. The drop in rents – either lowered to meet the bad times or simply remitted – caused many Suffolk landowners, especially those who had no income beyond their estates, to give up their studs entirely.

This was a turning of the tables with a vengeance. And the Shire men, one hopes not deliberately or maliciously, took full advantage of it. "The exhibitors of Suffolks", said Biddell sadly, "have an idea that they are treated with scant justice by the Royal Society. Certain it is that year after year the chesnuts are hid in the far, far away of the showyard."[8] And this was the man who had nearly had a row twenty years earlier with James Howard when the latter suggested that favouritism was responsible for the overwhelming success of the Suffolk at Royal Shows in the old days when all the breeds competed together. But this dismal state of affairs was to last only as long as the depression. Biddell was to live till 1917, and see better times come. And if his ghost haunted the Royal Shows of the 1930s, he would have been more than satisfied, for the Suffolks then were certainly not housed in the far, far away.

There was indeed a fourth question which could have been asked in the 'nineties, but it was too preposterous to bother about. Would it be a good idea to import a fourth heavy breed? The Americans had brought in five – the Percheron, the Belgian and three from Britain. The French breed did well there, and in England half-bred Percherons, all imported from the United States, were handy animals for London buses and trams. But the notion of a Percheron stud-book society in England would have given apoplexy to any true Englishman and it is significant that the dastardly act of introducing this excellent breed, with its special virtues, was not done until England had gone half-way to the dogs.

10. PROSPEROUS TIMES

The year 1900 broke all records. The Stud-book prepared then and issued the following February contained 811 stallions and 3,994 mares, a total of 4,805 – 902 more than that of the year before, which itself had been the biggest to date, even counting Volume 11 at the height of the American boom. Exports had recovered and 219 animals had gone abroad, twice as many as in 1899. P. A. Muntz was sure American demand would increase, because "in consequence of the export some years since of crowds of rubbishing culls to that country, the Shire has never yet received a fair trial there". Membership had just topped 3,000, the last 1,000 having taken precisely five years to achieve in spite of the fact that death was naturally removing more members at this stage. Perhaps the best-known names to have disappeared were those of Charles Howard and Anthony Hamond in 1895, and of the Duke of Westminster, whose life was docked in 1899. Possibly the loss of Hamond caused the greatest grief, for he was, in the words of that year's President, A. C. Duncombe, "the kindest man, who seemed born only to do good to his neighbours". He was also a representative of one of the oldest Shire families, for it was his ancestor who in 1790 had bred *Dodman*, whose picture was about the earliest authentic likeness of a cart-horse in existence.

By now 1,154 stud-owners had registered distinctive prefixes. The sum of £1,322 was spent on prizes and cups for the London Show, more than any previous year. The London auction was the biggest so far – 174 animals were sold for £13,872. In the last seventeen years, the total auctioned there was 1,976, realising £139,973. (No records are available for the first four years.) An increasing number of "home sales" was being held every year by the Society's auctioneers, under rules drawn up a few years before. The sale of pedigree and working horses by auction at high-class repositories all over the country was in some respects the most remarkable development of all, and in particular Peterborough, Crewe and Derby had become excellent places for a man to sell animals in ones and twos, or in any number too small to make a sale on the farm. At no less than 158 agricultural shows, twenty-eight gold medals and 145 silver medals were awarded to top-class pedigree Shires, and the Stud-book in preparation contained a list of over 500 prize-winners in open classes at the twenty-four "gold-medal shows" alone. Eighty-seven medals and twenty-five premiums were awarded at twenty different town horse-parades.

In spite of all its activity, the Society made a profit of £1,600 on the year and its reserve fund stood at £8,750. The fine house in Hanover Square had been expensive to adapt and furnish, but, although rent and maintenance cost £735, £696 of this was re-couped from sub-tenants. But there was a hall-porter to be paid, and salaries and wages had risen to no less than £684.

Neither money nor position could obtain special privileges for any members, of whom there were only two categories. The Prince of Wales and Fred Street were one sort. They paid no subscription at all, being honorary members. The other 3,027 men were all ordinary members, annually or for life. The annual subscription was 1 guinea, for which a member received a free stud-book (the one in preparation contained 1,368 pages and two very good photographs of the champions) and could buy back-numbers for half-price or the index to Volumes 1–13 at the original subscription price of 1 guinea. Members could also register animals in the book at half-price – i.e. 5s. per stallion and 2s. 6d. per mare. (In this way, Lord Henry Bentinck saved 12s. 6d., on a stallion and three mares, the Bedford Urban Sanitary Authority 15s., Sir Oswald Mosley £2. 10s. 0d. and Cole Ambrose, in the Fens, £7. 7s. 6d.) Furthermore, a member could enter animals for the London show at half-price and was provided with a free season ticket, admitting him to the grandstand. Life membership could be obtained for 10 guineas, and many had already had double value. One was Alfred Richardson of Mepal, Ely, a member of the original Council in 1878. By the time he died in 1934, he had had a good bargain – unless one takes into consideration all his hard work for the Society, in which case it would be clear that he gave more than he got.

If we analyse the speeches and writings of the chief Shire prophets of that year, we find that, between them, they give ten reasons for all this success. At the risk of repetition, they may be summarised here. Courage at the beginning to have an annual show for just one breed of animal; insistence on strict veterinary inspection (even now, there were objectors to it); the fair and novel system of judging; the generous number of prizes; the unique provision of rewards for breeders, as well as for exhibitors; the auction sales at London shows and the encouragement of pedigree sales elsewhere; the help extended to local shows; the support given to horse parades; good business management of the Society's affairs; and, far from least, the achievement of harnessing such an enormous variety of people to one common cause. A breeder or an owner could participate in the benefits and activities of the Society without even joining it. But if he did, he found a democratic organisation in which everyone had an equal voice. All members elected their Council which, as a result, consisted of practical and active men and not of ancient muddle-heads.

In concluding the business of the Annual General Meeting at the 1900 London Show, the President rose to make a comment amidst tremendous scenes of enthusiasm. "The report submitted by the Council", he said, "is most satisfactory and indicates that the Society is extending more and more every year. I have little doubt but that it will continue to do so." Before the next Show heralded the 1901 season of activities which would prove his point, the little old lady who was his mother had died, and he became King.

CHAPTER IX

1901–1914

The Golden Age

1. PROSPERITY AND THE FANCY

THE first business of the first Council meeting of the new year (or of the new century, if those are right who claim it began in 1901, not 1900), was to resolve a humble address to the new King, Patron and twice the Past-President of the Society. The royal crown now replaced the plume of feathers on the Society's crest.

For farmers, Edward VII's reign was to be a period of slow but notable progress towards more prosperous times. The Almighty issued a sharp reminder in the disastrous season of 1903 that He was ever likely to feed and water the good seed somewhat too liberally, but the general economy of agriculture began to stabilise itself. Shire breeders moved happily from the good times of the 1890s to even better ones, though it became more and more apparent that they would have to rely mainly upon the home market. The Clydesdale men, helped very considerably by increasing success in the export trade, recovered from their two decades of ill-luck and at last reaped the rewards that their genius and enthusiasm merited.

Each of these two breed societies during this time made a serious error in the type of horse it was producing. The Shire became absurdly hairy, and the Clyde went on losing his middle. Both mistakes were caused by paying too much regard to show-yard fancy. Probably, both would have been avoided, had there been only one society and one stud-book to promote the other-than-Suffolk British cart-horse.

2. NORTH OF THE BORDER

Not the Tweed, but a line running from Scarborough due west to Kendal was now more or less the border between the Scottish and the English cart-horse. He who thus re-draws the map, starting 120 miles south of Berwick and ending fifty south of Gretna, will find that he has re-allotted something approaching 4,500,000 acres. Northumberland, Durham and Cumberland were almost wholly lost, except in so far as the expression "Cumberland Clyde" began to denote a rather special sort of horse – a Clydesdale indeed, and having that breed's feet, fetlocks and action, but possessing some of the weight, breadth and power of the Shire: the very model, it may be, of the ideal blend between two extremes of one breed. The North Riding remained much longer a sort of no-man's-land, with the two pedigree societies fighting over the bodies of a kind of draught-horse (quite unlike the descendants of the old Black) that had been so long favoured by the men of those parts. It was in the west, however, where the battle of the breeds was the most exciting, since it was fought by the keenest and most skilful supporters of Shire–Clydesdale blood.

At this time, and for years to come, the greatest joy a stout Shire man from the Fylde could achieve was to take a mare or two up to Kendal, or perhaps only as far as Lancaster, and win a first prize against the Clyde men. But, however loyal the members of each camp were to their own breed, they all knew that if they had some Shire mares and put them to a Clydesdale stallion, they could produce working horses that would find an easy market. The editing committees of both stud-books were watching like hawks, and never scrutinised any breeders' certificates more attentively than they did those of animals bred in such parts as these. So the colts produced by the cross could only become geldings and the price of the fillies was depreciated.

Thomas Shaw, later to become one of the most redoubtable Shire men, had begun his stallion career in 1849 at Ellel, just south of Lancaster, by travelling down into the Fylde two horses got by Samuel Clark's Scottish stallion Clyde. Ten years later he began to go in for English horses only, but never lost his fondness for a horse with style and action. Many a stallion man in Edwardian times and later, however, advertised horses of both breeds. The only one who was wayward enough to register a Shire stallion under the name "Clyde" was Lawrence Wilding of Garstang. "A good server, stands 17.1 hands, stock can be seen", this horse was ten years old at the beginning of the period now under review and had an impeccable Shire pedigree on the side of his sire, who traced back to Honest Tom 1105, What's Wanted 2332 and other celebrated horses that Wilding had used in the 'seventies: his dam's sire was a Fen horse, and a hundred-per-center at that: his grand-dam is not recorded and one wonders whether there was a bar sinister in that last quarter of the chart. However Clyde was fully eligible for the Stud-book because his dam, foaled in 1879, was acceptable under the one-cross rule applicable to mares of that age. His entry form gave John Sloughgrove a mild shock, but no doubt the recording angel could have provided some bigger ones, then and later, had he felt inclined to communicate with creatures here below. (Perhaps Clyde balanced an older stallion which had been registered simply as The Shire Horse in the 1889 volume.)

The Clydesdale Society in 1901 was only just emerging from the difficult times that had first been brought about by the refusal of the late Lawrence Drew and his supporters to join. It is not the business of a southern historian to describe their troubles, but they had also suffered financially by a preponderance of life-members. For example, in 1896, membership stood at 1,358, of whom only 262 paid an annual subscription, compared with 2,151 and 1,469 respectively in the Shire Society: only seventeen new members were elected that year and thirty-seven names removed, whereas in the Shire Society there were 129 new names and seventy-nine dropped out. But now, all this was being changed, and the success of the breed in the export market was remarkable.

Only 167 were sent abroad in 1901, compared with 291 Shires, but in 1903 more Clydes than Shires were exported and so it remained until the outbreak of the war. In those twelve-and-a-half years a total of 11,555 pedigree Clydesdales were sent overseas, and only 5,285 Shires. That is, the Shire had only 31.4% of this market.

The Shire at home and the Clydesdale more particularly abroad were now entering a golden era, when the success of both societies made all their members forget the possible advantages of amalgamation, which hitherto had never been entirely without advocates. Yet it was in this very period that a fusion of the breeds might have prevented the opposite errors that each fell into. So obsessed, particularly in the show-yard, were the Clydesdale men with fineness of leg and smart action that they forgot "middles" entirely, and their horses became light and narrow. Some men, alarmed, attributed this to errors of in-breeding, and claimed (at least, Englishmen claimed) that it was due to the Clydesdale's having been originally a strong carriage-horse ("somewhat of the type of the old Yorkshire Coaching Horse" as one dogmatically expressed it). In the breed arguments that had their periodic public airings in the Press, the Shire men of course asserted that want of substance was inevitable without the contribution that could be made from time to time by English mares, à la Lawrence Drew.

An emigré to New Zealand, presumably from south of the Scarborough–Kendal line, took the trouble to write to *The Farmer & Stockbreeder* that "apart from the want of beast about the present-day Clydesdale, they are so shockingly deficient in bone that to put a good heavy top on such shanks would be out of all proportion, and consequently their knees are small and their hocks likewise. No one can tell the back from the front. And those great foazy frying pans of feet, with no heels, are impossible to any work horse." This sort of letter, and the replies it prompted, was grist to the journalistic mill, whenever the agricultural "silly season" left space in the copious columns of the farming press. (It can be left to a Scotsman to quote the replies that were made to this sort of criticism, but they were no less spirited and reasonable.)

Other correspondents suggested that it was the Shire stallion, rather than the mares, that were needed north of the border. "Would the Scotsman not like one of our stock horses", one of them wrote, "even if his feet and pasterns were considered stumpy and common compared to the sons of Baron's Pride that we saw lumbering round the ring at the last Royal?" Baron's Pride (by Sir Everard by Top-Gallant by Darnley) was foaled in 1890 and died in 1911. Of all the hundreds of prize-winners he sired, Baron of Buchlyvie, foaled in 1900, was the most celebrated. He was for a time owned jointly by James Kilpatrick and William Dunlop, until their friendship turned to animosity. The only thing they could then concur about was that the horse must be sold. It was also agreed that, contrary to usual auction practice (after all, the situation was abnormal), the proprietor of each half should be permitted to make more than one bid for the whole. The sale was held on 14th December 1911. Early in the proceedings, all other bidders dropped out. It was clear that this was a private matter, a struggle to the death between two men. Kilpatrick eventually crushed his opponent at £9,500. This was by far the record price for a cart-horse. (The next best was £5,000 in 1915 for Bonnie Buchlyvie, his son. The highest for a Shire – in the artificial post-war boom that lay ahead and, crazily, for a mare, at that – was 4,600 guineas.) Baron of Buchlyvie lived another two years and three-and-a-half months, dying on 30th June 1914. His purchase price was therefore just over £10 a day. It was fortunate for Mr. Kilpatrick that he was himself the vendor of half this great horse.

We must henceforth allow the Clydesdale to drop out of our story, for its separateness from the Shire, in the eyes of northern and southern breeders alike, was now irrevocable. To write further about the Scottish horses would be both presumptuous and, because any account of them would have to be abbreviated, misleading. This is the place where we must therefore simply mention that the best son of Baron of Buchlyvie, and the best great-great-grand son of Darnley, was foaled in 1908. His name was Dunure Footprint, and he turned out to be probably the most notable horse in the whole history of the Clydesdale breed. (He headed the list of sires of prize-winners from 1915 to 1927 and, at the height of his fame, he was by far the most expensive heavy stallion ever used, for he cost £60 for service and another £60 on the birth of a foal.)

David Riddell's career continued until half way through this period. When he died in 1907, he had been in the Clydesdale business nearly sixty years, and had long been the doyen of Scottish breeders. The changes he had seen since the late 1840s were amazing but, in his heart of hearts, he regretted to the end the missed opportunity of creating one true British cart-horse breed. The Scots and the English together could have produced the super-horse.

3. TOO MUCH HAIR

Lincolnshire Lad 1196 had been taken to Scotland by Lawrence Drew in the 'seventies. At the 1901 London Show, his most successful son, Lincolnshire Lad II, was the direct male ancestor of sixty-four of the 119 winners. The latter's greatest son, Harold, was for the eleventh year in succession the leading sire at the show. But on 2nd April that year, he was destroyed – "by the friendly bullet", as one obituary put it. And that year Prince Harold, the son that only just escaped castration through lack of a pedigree, died too. But there was a two-year-old grandson, the fifth generation from Lincolnshire Lad 1196, who was destined to have an impact on the Shire breed that was more sensational than that of any stallion, his own famous ancestors included. This was Lockinge Forest King. He sired nothing as a two-year-old and died on Sunday, 13th November 1909. So he got all his stock in eight seasons. He won fourth prize at London in 1901 (and first at the Royal and five other major shows) and in 1902 was reserve junior champion at London and champion at the Royal. After that he was never shown again.

"He was barely 17 hands", commented Tom Forshaw, "and was narrow, with not much depth of rib. He had good carriage, and was well made along his top line, and was a straight mover. His bone was of the very flattest and hardest." And he had feather – good feather, but too much of it. The foals which he got in such profusion were magnificent, particularly the fillies. James Forshaw and his sons had tried to buy him as a three-year-old and made no concealment of their admiration for him. But Tom later on criticised the general worship of his hair. "Exhibitors came to believe that if they sent animals with plenty of feather into the ring it did not matter very much how poor the limbs were or how badly made the horse might be. In this way, many horses were bred that did the breed no good, and unless a colt showed feather, however good otherwise he might be, he was likely to be castrated, and I am afraid many good horses were lost." Alfred Clark, possibly the best judge of a mare in Shire history and a London judge more often than anyone else, later wrote "This feather was a great help to some of our clever grooms who are artists, and who can make a bad-shaped leg like a good one. I have seen animals placed in a prominent position, which if they had been waded through a pond beforehand, would not have been looked at." Indeed, was it not Tom Forshaw himself who said, "Give me some hair, and I can make a leg"?

The most immediate result of the hair complex was its adverse effect on the export market. Too many overseas buyers went to Scotland, if they did not prefer France's clean-legged Percherons. A more subtle influence was the neglect, as Forshaw pointed out, of some horses that could have contributed much good to the Shire breed in general. The Hitchin Conqueror strain was one. The descendants of this son of William the Conqueror were short of hair, but in the years to come breeders were to look back with regret that there were none like them available. Girton Charmer, the 1905 champion who went to America, was his grandson: had he been reincarnated twenty years later, there would have been queues to use him. Or would there? Photographs suggest that he had no joints, either fore or aft. Stroxton Tom, the 1902 and 1903 champion, a descendant of Wiseman's Wonder, was another who was ahead of his time. But it is useless to speculate on what might have been done. The paradox is that Lockinge Forest King, and his progeny, were all that was claimed for them and his fee of 20 guineas a mare owed nothing to fancy-points. It was a case of believing that, if all poets are fools, all fools are poets.

Blaisdon Jupiter was perhaps one of the best examples of this error. Tracing to Lincolnshire Lad II in quite a different way, he was the hairiest monster ever to be awarded the London championship, but that was in 1915, a year beyond our chosen period of discussion. In the 1930s, when sanity was prevailing, no one would have wanted him either for the show-ring or the covering-yard. In 1911 was foaled Champion's Goalkeeper. As a two-year-old he became London champion with limbs that were as big as those of any horse a year older. He repeated the feat the next year and became in maturity steadily thicker and coarser. His popularity as a stock-horse could have been disastrous to a breed whose purpose in life was to stand "long days and short nights" and to work hard and feel no trouble. And yet it was not so, for he got some wonderful sons and daughters. The best thing that could have happened would have been that some new Drew should take him to Scotland – in exchange for Dunure Footprint. But here we have strayed too far from our period and, indeed, into realms of heresy. Heretics, like saints, are usually so dubbed only after death. Drew, at any rate, was now a heretic, according to both the Shire and the Clydesdale creeds.

There are perhaps two other trends in this period which merit comment, one beneficial and one not so good. The first was to do with the age at which animals began to breed. The old idea that one should not put a mare to the horse until she was at least four, and ought not to use a stallion before he was five, was now completely discredited. It had now become acceptable that a colt could be given a few mares at the age of two without suffering ill-effects. Whether a filly, covered at that age, would be impeded in her growth and produce a poor foal, was still a matter of debate. But the enormous strides that had been made in the sensible feeding and general management of young stock were now resolving the argument, amongst the more enlightened breeders, into a simple matter of whether the individual filly was herself sufficiently mature. Men had begun to realise that the most regular breeders were the mares that began young. The biggest and heaviest breeds of horse are normally the shortest-lived, and if fifteen can be regarded as an average age when Shire mares cease to breed (though of course some fertile old matrons could go on another ten years) an early start and regular foaling were especially important, particularly as there were those from which a foal was got only in alternate years. The success of Lord Wantage's Lady Victoria did much to convince the cautious. She was the daughter of Prince William and Glow, both of whom were only two years of age when mated, but she was good enough to win the junior championship in London in 1889, and then grew on to become the dam of Lady Marjorie, and therefore the grand-dam of Lockinge Manners, sire of Lockinge Forest King.

Less praiseworthy was the tendency to relieve show animals of all work. The leading stud-owners and stallion proprietors were in a dilemma. The publicity brought by success amidst the increasingly intense competition at the shows was essential: but this success could be secured only by maintaining the potential honours-winner in high show condition. And so the very evil that the Shire Society had in its earliest years tried to stamp out in respect of young stock had spread, though admittedly in a less gross form, to mature animals as well, and to the very specimens that should have done most to improve the next generation. In the old days, before the craze for showing, most even of the best stallions did their share of work on the farm. Nine months' honest work and hard condition had left them in good fettle for their three months on more luxurious, though more demanding, duties. Manners and manageability were also easier to come by if a young horse had been broken to work when too young to know his own strength. But now most of the finest cart-horses had never had a collar on them, and spent three-quarters of the year in a box or a small paddock eating the corn of idleness. The similar treatment of mares was even more dangerous. A stallion's virility and fertility could be expected to revive once he was on the road, even if he approached his first mares in a very sluggish spirit. But mares could much more easily become permanently barren as a result of the various troubles caused by over fatness. One leading breeder, violently opposed to exaggerated veneration of the show system, wrote "It is a matter of no consequence to anyone, save their owners, when second-class horses are laden with blubber: but it is a national calamity when the best animals are stuffed with treacle and drugged with poisons in order to compete successfully with their inferiors. Hence come fever in the feet, diseased livers, and fatty degeneration of the heart, and a host of ailments that often shorten the lives of their victims and always injure their constitutions."

The London Show, of course, was held early in the year precisely to mitigate this danger. The Royal, in early June, was at the worst possible time in all respects for Shire men. The wisest proprietors tended, once an animal had made its reputation with a good prize, not to exhibit it again. In any case, "if not shown, it can't be beat".

All breeders, and not only Shire men, would have done well to take a leaf out of the book of old Smith, "a little farmer at Parham", who owned the Noah of the Suffolk race, a bung-tailed stallion who lived from 1799 to 1813 and from whom all but about six real Suffolks in 1877 were directly descended in the male line. This horse was described to Herman Biddell by an old man who had seen him as "low before, but a wonderful good 'un". And he worked all the year round on the farm, and never left it. He propagated a whole breed by the simple expedient of serving mares only on Sundays, when there were no daily chores to perform. All Smith had to do on his day of rest during the season was to lean on the gate and watch the mares being led from all directions. Daniel Pattle, who was twenty when disaster struck, said, "When the old horse died, that quite broke Smith up, and that year the mortgage was called in". And in this there is no doubt a moral for all of us.

4. IN THE HOUSE

The shows which were organised or supported by the various societies provided excitement and variety enough to compensate the denizens of 12 Hanover Square for an otherwise uneventful life, unrelieved by female company and complicated only by the confusion inherent in a system wherein the assistant secretary of one society happened to be the secretary of another, and its chief clerk organised a third. Over tham all presided John Sloughgrove, rigid and uncompromising in his methods of economy, whether in Shire business or the domestic affairs of the house which were his responsibility.

A reserved man, he appeared brusque and even cold, but the impression was misleading. He was always prepared to give an opinion on any problem that any of the other breed secretaries cared to bring to him, but never offered it either unasked or without the minutest consideration from every point of view. To the society which in the first place he had been unwilling to join, he offered three priceless virtues – common sense, a capacity for hard work, and unwavering loyalty. His second great interest was the London Cart Horse Parade, which his enthusiasm had helped to found and where he was always a steward. He was assistant and then joint treasurer from 1889, which is not surprising in view of the fact that at the age of twenty-one he had been put in charge of all receipts at the 1870 Royal Show at Oxford, and had continued in that duty until he left the R.A.S.E. As time went on, he became first citizen not only of the house but of the whole Square, for he was also honorary secretary of the committee appointed by the occupiers to be responsible for the management of the "enclosed garden or ornamental ground". The Annual General Meeting of this committee met at No. 12 and the Sloughgrove touch was apparent in the perfection with which the communal garden was maintained and in the care which every occupier was obliged to take in not losing his precious key to the gate.

Though born and educated in London, his hobby was his mixed Clock House Farm of several hundred acres at Purleigh, near Maldon in Essex, where he bred a few pedigree Shires. (He had started in 1887, when he bought Farmer's Diamond, an eleven-year-old bay mare from the Fens, whose filly-foal had just been sold to the Prince of Wales. She produced for him five foals in the next eight years, the fillies being registered with his Purleigh prefix.) In 1910, the Shire Council, which had raised his salary regularly over the years, decided that "in the event of his wishing to retire" he was to be paid for the remainder of his life the sum of £200 per annum, £50 more than he received for working when he first joined the Society. But neither he nor they wished any such thing.

When Albert Holland joined the staff in 1901 as a boy from school, this bachelor perfectionist inspired him with great awe. Sir Walter Gilbey, the most frequent member to be seen in the house, was even more frightening at first, with his great height and thinness and his monocle. But no one was anything but kind. Everything connected with the 1902 show was exciting, and the £5 bonus which Albert and his fellow junior, A. J. Gardiner, received was a wonderful thing. (Charlton and Wickison were given £10 extra, and so was T. Skipper, horse foreman as usual.) The more useful he became, the bigger the rise in salary and "if you want to earn a bit extra for your holidays, my boy, you'd better stop late and write out all these export certificates." There was nothing so valuable as a lad with good writing for that sort of job. So it was "Yes, Mr. Sloughgrove". And Mr. Sloughgrove would sometimes invite them all down to his farm, which was another thing to relish. "He was a good man", was Albert's simple memory of him in later years.

There was another annual excitement which began in 1907. Frank F. Euren, the former Shire clerk who was now Hackney and Cart Horse Parade secretary and had attended horse shows in America and several European countries, was appointed by a meeting held in 1906 at 12 Hanover Square to be manager of the proposed International Horse Show. R. S. Summerhays, the historian of that show, describes him as "a fair-haired man of slightly under medium height, unobstrusive by inclination, by no means a dynamic character" but possessed of "great organising abilities, a mercurial temperament and, perhaps more important, a restless imaginative mind".[1] The Agricultural Hall was offered rent free, but Olympia was chosen, and when the show opened on 7th June the following year with Lord Lonsdale as managing director, Albert Holland was one of the officials sleeping on the premises throughout both weeks. A few years later he became collecting-ring steward, which necessitated three changes of clothes during the day, starting with "rat-catcher"and ending with full evening dress.

The show was, to quote Summerhays again, "conceived on lines of such unimagined elegance, that Olympia became at once the centre of fashionable London at the very height of the season" and was "the most famous and exotic show in the world". The best boxes for eight people cost £200. Albert Holland was a steward at every Olympia show (1907–1914 and 1920–1939) and those who have only visited its successor from 1947 at the White City and Wembley can have no idea what it was like. Nevertheless, amidst this glamour, there were draught-horse classes. At the first show, J. Ogden Armour of Chicago, the corned beef magnate, exhibited his famous team of six greys and at Frank Euren's suggestion delighted a bigger but less patrician audience by showing them at the Cart Horse Parade as well. The next year, the International had three classes – singles, pairs and teams – for heavy draught-horses used regularly on the London streets, and offered prizes worth £190. These had been dropped by 1912, but an exhibition that year of representatives of English and other breeds of horses and ponies was a sensational success, remembered for the rest of their lives by all who saw it. For the Shires, Lord Rothschild sent Birdsall Menestrel (London champion 1904 and 1907) and Blaisdon Jupiter (the future rough-legged London champion), J. G. Williams contributed Bardon Forest Princess (winner of the big mares' class at London that year) and Sir Walpole Greenwell brought the champion mare of the year, Dunsmore Chessie – all of them glowingly described in all the best papers and society journals.

Back in 12 Hanover Square, the unfortunate National Poultry Organisation Society had to be given notice to quit at Christmas 1908 in order to house the International. Only twenty months before, the R.A.S.E., in desperate difficulties as a result of the disastrous attempt to make Park Royal a permanent show-ground, had offered Harewood House to the Shire Society and its sub-tenants, but they had all expressed themselves thoroughly satisfied where they were. So it was sold for £45,000 and in 1908–1909 was ornately and hideously rebuilt. Apart from losing their famous neighbours, the inhabitants of No. 12 saw few major changes during these years. Huffer, the porter, who had been part of the general scene for thirteen years, resigned on Guy Fawkes day 1907 and was allotted a gratuity of £25, £5 of which were specially for his wife. The

Council instructed John Sloughgrove to obtain the services of Walter Noble, at that time engaged at the British Linen Bank, at a salary of 52s. 6d. a week and livery. Gardiner, one of the other junior clerks, also left.

One autumn day in 1909, the London County Council men came and fixed a plaque on the wall to inform the curious that from 1818 to 1827 the house had been occupied by Mary Somerville. She had been the most remarkable woman of her time. Born in 1780, the daughter of Vice-Admiral Sir William Fairfax, she married at the age of twenty-four, the son of Sir Samuel Greig, Admiral in the Russian Navy, but was widowed three years later. In 1812 she married her cousin Dr. William Somerville and lived in Edinburgh for four years and then moved to London. Her beauty and charm made people call her "the rose of Jedburgh". While living at No. 12, she wrote a paper for the Royal Society on *The Magnetic Properties of the Violet Rays of the Solar Spectrum*, which was the first of many outstanding contributions to science. Sir Robert Peel conferred on her a civil list pension of £300. Probably her best-known works were *The Connection of the Physical Sciences* (which contained the hint which led to the discovery of the planet Neptune) and *Physical Geography*. From 1838 she lived mostly in Italy for the health of her husband, who died in 1860. She had two daughters and a son, and on the latter's sudden death in 1865 she was unable to conquer her grief by music, painting or needlework, at all of which she excelled, and so settled down (at the age of eighty-five) to write her *Molecular and Microscopic Science* which was published three years before her death in 1872. She would have been surprised to see the name board which John Sloughgrove had put up to identify all the present occupants of No. 12.

As for the Shire men who passed in and out of the great mahogany front door and walked up and down the elegant stairs with more dignity than Frank Euren, who always took them two at a time, there were inevitably some each year who were seen there no more. J. P. Cross of Catthorpe Towers (near Rugby but in Leicestershire) owner of Lockinge Forest King, died on 4th February 1906, a few weeks before he was due to become President. James Forshaw died on 27th March 1908 and could never have been made President (unless he had lived another dozen years at least). Ranking with Bakewell and Lawrence Drew as an expert on the heavy draught-horse, he was liked and respected by all save those who were jealous of his success: but a cross or two of blue blood (or wealth possessed sufficiently long to give a similar hue to it) was needed to make a prospective President in pre-1914 years.

Sir Philip Albert Muntz, Bart, M.P. for North Warwickshire since 1884 and Shire President in 1898, died at the end of the same year, on 21st December. "No man worked harder for the breed than he did", wrote Arthur Beck, the Society's auctioneer. "At every show, at every sale, he was always to be found, and in his forcible way carried conviction to his hearers when insisting on the merits of the breed he loved so well." This preceptor and leader of Shire men had once said, "With a little money and a great deal of intelligence much may be achieved in Shire breeding". He had both, and the fifty-two animals dispersed after his death (forty-one stallions and colts and eleven fillies and young mares) brought in £10,292. 2s. od. He had used to say, "I keep Shires because it pays to do so." This proved his point, for it was a clear-out and not just a sale of selected animals. Twenty-three fetched less than 100 guineas each, and the highest prices were not remarkable – 1,025, 675, 610 and 575 guineas. He had remembered his manager, Tom Ewart, who was given two of the best stallions and at the sale bought four more, to start on his own.

When Earl Beauchamp, President and an enthusiastic breeder of greys, announced at the 1910 Annual General Meeting the name of the President-Elect of 1911, the news was received with acclamation. But this was the second man never to sit on the massive leather arm-chair he had been elected to. Ten weeks later, he did not die, as Cross had done, but succeeded to the throne, and so became Patron instead. Sir Walter Gilbey, on the other hand, who had been President twice already, was now about to drop off the Council because there were twelve more junior Past-Presidents than he. This would never do, and so he was elected Honorary Treasurer in place of E. B. Foster of Foster & Company's Bank, Cambridge who had died seven years before.

Membership of the Society at the end of 1910 had reached 4,000. It had taken ten years and the election of something like 2,300 new men to achieve this fourth thousand, owing to many deaths and some withdrawals. Lest the reader faint with fear at the prospect of over 1,000 more obituaries, let us restrict ourselves to one only. (There should be, even with the greatest economy, two: but the death of Fred Street, oddly, was never referred to, either in council or annual report.) Joseph Martin, of Littleport, "the man of peace" in the early Cart-against-Shire dispute, London steward five times, and a member of Council seventeen years altogether, died in the spring of 1913. His son Heber was a steward himself that year and did that job seventeen times by 1925, more than anyone else. All movements and societies rely much on their Martins.

5. THE STUD-BOOK

By 1901, minimum qualifications for the Stud-book had been fixed much as they have remained ever since apart from a period in the 1920s, when they were made more stringent, and from minor refinements. Mares were required to be at least of seven-eighths registered blood, and stallions had to come from registered sire and dam. But three-quarters blood was sufficient in mares foaled before 1886 and in stallions foaled before 1891. It is somewhat odd that these dates favoured not the mare, but the stallion. There was one other curious exception which was not to be cancelled for fifty years. A colt foal with only seven-eighths "pure" blood could be registered if his dam had already had a filly foal which had been entered in the book.

During this period, two far-reaching proposals were considered and thrown out. The first was absurd in its implications. A Council member urged that mares which had had produce which were eligible for the book should themselves be accepted. If this had been agreed, there would have been a spate of

1. A six-horse team, demonstrating (like all the colour pictures in this book) the modern Shire. Young and Company's Brewery has had more exhibits in the annual Shire Horse Show during the past twenty years than any other proprietor – always of the historically authentic blacks, though before the war they also had bays and browns. They are, incidentally, the only brewery in Britain ever to show an eight-horse team. The Ram Brewery at Wandsworth dates from 1675 and has been in the Young family since 1831 – John Young, who succeeded his uncle, Henry, being the sixth in line to head the business. Both have played vital parts in the recent history of the Shire Horse Society.

2. Young's team of six again, driven by Ernest Critchfield. Breweries are noted for length of service by horse and man, but Young's head horsekeeper record must be unbeatable. John Cornish held the post from 1875 until his death in 1942. Charlie Butler, who had come to the company in 1924 from the Forshaws', then took over, retiring on his 67th birthday, the last day of 1966. A Mortlake pub is now named after him. The third incumbent in 101 years (so far) is Harry Ranson, whose father Fred, a Young's man, was a fine showman in the heavy horse ring. Harry himself was unbeaten for seven consecutive years after the war, when he drove the Young's teams. The company has twenty Shires, which deliver 10,000 tons of beer a year.

retrospective applications going back from one generation to the preceding one and terminating possibly in anything from Shetland pony mares to Suffolks – some of them by that time dead, and impossible to check under the protective clause that "the Editing Committee are empowered to reject or to cancel the entry of any animal of which there is a doubt as to its being of the 'Shire' or Old English Cart Horse Breed". The second proposal came from the Editing Committee itself. It was, quite simply, that mares foaled after 1910 would require a registered sire and registered dam – that is, that the book should be "closed" against new blood. The full Council objected and the idea was abandoned.

A resolution was made in April 1901 to give full publicity to any case where an entry in the Stud-book had to be subsequently cancelled because of some irregularity or a "faked pedigree". Only two months elapsed before the first such case occurred. The pedigree of 28839 Harold's Queen in the 1900 book was proved to be wrong and an advertisement to that effect, including the names of the breeder and owner, was inserted in all the Staffordshire newspapers. This was a pretty effective deterrent.

A requirement was introduced for the 1904 book that, in the case of unregistered dams, a certificate would be required not only from her breeder but from the breeder of the grand-dam also, or that her ancestry should be otherwise satisfactorily authenticated. This gave the Editing Committee much extra work. For example, William Hancorn of Westhide, Hereford wanted to register his 1903 filly-foal bred out of his own-bred eight-year-old *Darby*. The latter was out of *Virgin*, foaled 1879, which he had bought and whose breeder was dead. After investigation, the "proof" that she was by Brown King 4916 was found acceptable and her grand-daughter Westhide Belle was duly registered. Hancorn never repaid all the work done on his behalf by registering any other Shire. Two other members of the family each registered one filly, similarly bred up. None of them ever joined the Shire Society.

In 1908, any man who was expelled from the Society, or from any other pedigree or agricultural society, was put in a worse position than non-members, for it was agreed not to accept his signature on any document at all. It was fortunate that these were rare birds, for the claims of other and highly respectable Shire owners to register horses were invalidated when these miscreants' signatures were required on an application form.

An illuminating example of the thoroughness with which the meticulous Sloughgrove and the Committee did their work is provided by one of the 4,150 registration forms that had to be scrutinised in 1907. The particulars given were these:

Owner: Henry Breedon, Elston, Newark.
Breeder: George C. Harvey, Red Lodge, Screveton, Notts.
Name of mare or filly: Blossom.
Year foaled: 1904.

Sire: Waresley Moonbeam 20141.
Dam: *Blossom* by Albion Prince 10861.
                 Grey, foaled 1892, bred by the late John Cheetham, Orston,
                 Notts.
G-dam: *Blossom* by Welborn Sweep 2315.
                 Grey, aged, bred by the late John Cheetham, Orston, Notts.

The necessary certificates were signed by Breedon, Harvey and twice by John E. Cheetham, Orston Grange, who authenticated the breeding of the unregistered dam and grand-dam by his late father. All this seems straightforward enough, but someone noticed, or knew, that the dam's sire, Albion Prince, was in fact registered in the 1891 volume as foaled in 1889 and out of "*Blossom* by Welborn Sweep 2315": that is, it appeared that he had been mated as a two-year-old with his own dam to produce the Blossom of 1892. Such Bakewellian in-breeding was a rarity amongst Edwardian Shire men, except where it occurred through accident (as was probable in this case) and the committee made a very careful check before registering the grey filly as 53091 Blossom.

But there is a moral to the story. Old John Cheetham had himself bred Albion Prince in 1889 and sold him to the well-known stallion owner William Welch of Rauceby near Grantham, who registered him. His pedigree shows that the breeding of his dam, the first of the three Blossoms, was accurately known – her dam was by Admiral 68 (foaled in 1855 and owned by Thomas Shepherd who was also the owner of Welborn Sweep) and her grand-dam by Dan Howsin's Bang Up 97 (foaled in 1846). So Cheetham could easily have registered her himself back in the 'eighties, which would have saved all the later trouble. But he was neither an S.H.S. man nor did he use the Stud-book himself. Young John Cheetham, however, was otherwise. In any case he was forced to be so. In 1900, he bred a filly called Daisy, a grey which was closely related to the Blossoms. In 1908 she had a colt foal which attracted the interest of the Forshaw brothers. So in the 1911 book he registered her himself as 63366 Daisy II. In the next volume her son appeared as Carlton What's Wanted 29208. For the Forshaws, he won fourth prize in London at the age of four (see section 6, London Show of 1912) and second prize at the age of seven, when he was beaten only by the supreme champion Blaisdon Jupiter, after which he continued to do good stud service for many years: for breeders at large, he became an increasingly major transmitter of Harold blood. When he first won a London award, there would have been a breeder's prize of £5 for John Cheetham if he had been an S.H.S. member. So he promptly joined the Society, picked up the £5 in 1915 and remained a member for fourteen years. To complete the story, we find him registering in the 1913 book a full sister to the Blossom which had caused the doubt in the minds of the Editing Committee. She was one year older and so was ten when her name appeared in print. She too, was grey and had been bred by Mr. Harvey, who had bought the dam from the Cheethams about 1900 and now sold the daughter to John. With a certain lack of originality, this older sister appeared as Blossom III.

The number of people still submitting three generations at once for registration was really amazing, but the Editing Committee could scarcely complain, because it was the clearest possible proof that the pedigree movement was still expanding. A typical example was the receipt in 1909 of applications for the following three animals:

DIAMOND (mare) – foaled 1885, bred by John Bore, Minsterley, Salop.
    Owned by Pryce Davies, Bryndial, Welshpool.
    Sire   – Brown Stout II 6842.
    Dam   – grey, foaled 1878, bred by – Meddings, Worthen, Salop, by
             Pride of Buildwas 2874.

CARBONITUS (stallion) – foaled 1892, bred and owned by Pryce Davies.
    Sire   – Carbonite 11173.
    Dam   – Diamond, (above).

BROWN (mare) – foaled 1905, bred by Pryce Davies.
    Owned by Wm. Jones, Penybywyd, Castle Caereinion, Mont.
    Sire   – Carbonitus (above).
    Dam   – Tip (grey, f. 1897, bred by Francis Bros., Leighton, Welshpool),
             by Corrector III 15058.
    G-dam – Lofty, (bay, f. 1890, bred by R. A. Oliver, Marton, Chirbury,
             Salop), by Aldreth Prince 4204.

The aim of the whole operation was to register Brown. But that could only be done if Carbonitus were registered and, as he was a stallion, his dam must be registered. Was it a coincidence that Diamond was foaled in 1885? If she had been just one year younger, the rules in 1909 required her grand-dam's sire to be registered, and no one alive had the slightest idea who he might have been. After many enquiries – chiefly into what sort of reputation Pryce Davies had amongst his fellow-men, rather than into the unfathomable depths of the animals' pedigrees – the Committee was satisfied, and 60090 Diamond, Carbonitus 27162 and 59651 Brown all duly appeared in the 1910 volume. The wretched William Jones responded to all this help by never joining the Society or breeding or registering another Shire, and 59651 Brown might have been barren for all the good she ever did for the continuance of a pure breed. Perhaps she was.

It may be that the patient reader can bear one more example of what the Editing Committee had too often to deal with. It is chosen because a little mistake seems to have been made. In 1913, John Deakin of Swepstone Fields, Ashby-de-la-Zouch (a non-member – it was they who always posed the problems, and too few joined later in gratitude) submitted five mares all at once – Bonny foaled in 1904 (together with her daughters Princess, 1908, and Blossom, 1911), Mettle foaled in 1907 and Flower foaled in 1908: all these three being out of Flower foaled in 1896, who in turn was out of Flower foaled in 1885. (Note the last date!) This earliest Flower was got by that great progenitor of such a large section of the Shire race, William the Conqueror 2343. He had been listed in Volume 14 as having died in 1883. After much delay and investigation, all five mares were accepted, and we are left to wonder whether to claim a record length of pregnancy or a simple error. The mistake is surprising in view of the hawk-eyed scrutiny these applications received – and of the great number of other applications that were annually turned down on the grounds, not of wrong information, but merely of insufficient or inconclusive evidence. But it is pleasant to have Swepstone Fields recurring in our story, for it is in the same little corner of Leicestershire as Packington and Donisthorpe, where the ancient *Blind Horse* and the *"Donnisthorp" Horse* of the 1760s had hailed from; and "Swebstone" 2079, foaled in 1795, is one of the twenty-five earliest horses in the Stud-book.

The labours of the Editing Committee during this period included the publication in 1905 of an index to Volumes 14–25, price 1 guinea. It comprised 1,440 pages and contained 8,246 stallions and 30,042 mares, with their number, volume, owner, breeder, colour, year of foaling, sire, dam, and sire of dam – 344,052 items to be proof-read by a staff who surely earned the 45 guinea bonus shared between them for this extra work.

From 1909 onwards, the activities of H. R. Burgess were a source of irritation. From an address at Shaldon, Teignmouth – "Hanover House", which was particularly sinister – he kept on sending post cards and entry forms inviting people to register animals in his "Imperial Cart Horse Stud Book". He was still a thorn in the Shire flesh in 1914, and in 1917 the book he published caused confusion to the Irish Department of Agriculture.

6. LONDON SHOWS

The number of farmers coming to Islington for the Shire Show increased year by year. Many a man paid his first visit there because he had been selected as a member of the three-man or five-man deputation from his hiring society anxious to secure a stallion for the season, which ought to have been done earlier than this, but too often had not. Some men came because they were attracted by the possibility of their horse winning them a prize – not the horse they were exhibiting, because they did not go in for that grand sort of enterprise, but the one they had bred. Who but the Shire Society handed out £5 to the small tenant farmer that, two, five or perhaps ten years ago, had bred a good horse? Many a man who had no other holiday in the year now felt that times were a little better. The last week of February was perhaps more convenient than Dairy Show or Smithfield week. His wife and daughter looked forward to the London shops by day and to being taken by Dad to the theatre in the evening.

The 1901 Show, with 667 entries, was the biggest yet, beating the memorable 1890 figure by twenty-one. But high experience and the sprouting habits of the Agricultural Hall enabled the officials to take this number in their stride. The auction sale, also, was the biggest so far. Two hundred and seventeen animals were sold, and the receipts at £19,030 were to remain a record until 1914.

There were now three height divisions for senior mares. The middle one, 16-hands and under 16.2, attracted thirty-nine entries and was won by Lord Rothschild's Alston Rose, a six-year-old who went on to win the championship as well. Tom Forshaw wrote, over thirty years later, "She was just about the sweetest mare that I have ever seen. An ideal brood mare throughout, she was long and wide, and nothing masculine about her. She was a brown, with white face and all white points, well planted on her limbs which had the right texture of bone in them, and her feather was outstanding. If alive to-day she would take some reckoning with." But she only ever had one foal, and that died of joint-ill. She was sold, and won the championship again in 1902.

The gelding championship was carried off, for the fourth time in five years, by Bardon Extraordinary, who originally had been registered as a stallion and had won a London commended card as an uncut colt. In time to come he was generally considered to have been the finest ever to be shown until long after the First World War. He had one unique distinction – as the only gelding ever to be awarded a Shire gold medal at the Royal, in Manchester in 1897. In fact, this was the first S.H.S. medal of any sort to be awarded anywhere to a gelding.

The sensation of the show was Bearwardcote Blaze, whom no one had ever heard of. He was bred and exhibited by two tenant farmers, brothers who had never shown a horse in London before. Placed top of the eighty-six two-year-old colts (Lockinge Forest King was fourth), he won the junior cup against 219 rivals and the supreme championship as well – the best of 335 stallions. *The Live Stock Journal* was pretty cool about it, though admitting he was a "remarkable colt with great substance, good feet, capital joints, good quality feather and particularly full of muscle", and he moved well. But the paper was doubtful if he really was the best even of the young ones, and people who knew what they were about preferred Forshaw's old Stroxton Tom for the championship. However, *The Mark Lane Express* was beside itself with glee. A well known ex-M.P. had told some Essex farmers that Shire-breeding was an industry monopolised by millionaires. Well, the Walwyn brothers had given the lie to *that*. "The very highest honours and the magnificent emoluments of this gigantic industry are not only open to the studs of the titled and rich but to the sons of the soil very generally. The young, plodding, industrious farmer, if he is capable of working with his head as well as with his hands, may climb to the very top of the ladder, despite the superior advantages of the grandees he has to contend with."

The Walwyns may have been industrious, even plodding at times, but they were not all that young. James was fifty-seven and Matthew fifty. Nor were

they the rude peasants that the *Express* would have liked them to be. Their
grandfather, for example, had made something of a name for himself by
cultivating the leading strain of Yorkshire White pigs. But certainly it was the
brothers who put tiny Bearwardcote, between Mickleover and Etwall, on the
map of Derbyshire and of all England. Unfortunately, they did not even come
to the show themselves, for they were ill. Robert Welch, tenant of The Hepnalls,
Etwall, neighbour, friend and newly-joined Shire member himself, brought the
colt to Islington and, immediately the championship was awarded, was offered
£500 for him. He made frantic efforts to contact Bearwardcote Farm to see if
it was all right to sell. It was lucky he did not succeed, because the offer was
doubled. Robert accepted, and spent all the hours until he got home again
worrying whether he had done right.[2] However, all was well. James and
Matthew had gained sudden national fame and a fantastic sum of money
overnight. And the Earl of Ellesmere now owned the finest horse in the land.

The following year's *Live Stock Almanac* featured a picture of Bearwardcote
Blaze – "champion at the London Shire Horse Show. The property of the
Earl of Ellesmere". This was about as far as anyone could go in the pursuit of
snobbery. A Shire review of the previous year, and not even a mention of the
two members who had both bred and exhibited the champion stallion! Only
W. R. Rowland, breeder and owner of Spark (1881) and A. B. Freeman-
Mitford (the champion mare Minnehaha, 1895) had performed the double
feat before then. But, sadly, not much good came of Blaze's sensational success.
He was given a few mares on his arrival at Worsley and got a couple of foals,
a colt and a filly, both of which won eighth prize for Lord Ellesmere at London
when they were three, in 1905. He achieved very little in the next three seasons,
and died of a twisted bowel on 13th September 1904, at the age of five. Back
in Derbyshire, the Walwyns managed to breed a full sister and full brother to
him in 1902 and 1903. The sire, which came from the neighbouring estate, was
Calwich Blaze, one of the most famous sons of Harold. The dam was 27462
Bearwardcote Dorothy, who came of a long line of black and brown mares
bred by the Walwyn family at Osmaston, before they moved to their present
farm in 1895. But the best that either the sister or brother managed to do at
London was a highly commended card for Bearwardcote Champion 22098
in 1905 at the age of two. James Walwyn had then been lying fifteen months
in his Etwall grave but Matthew, the real Shire man of the two, carried on,
always using the best stallions he could get.

In 1902, an idea never heard of at any other show was introduced. A cash
award was offered not only for the prize-winners, but every stallion and mare
recognised by the judges – £3 for reserve placings, £2 for highly commended
and £1 for commended. Breeders' prizes of £5 were also extended, and were
now offered for every prize-winner. The result was an entry of 860 horses –
which staggered even John Sloughgrove. Three tenant farmers, Alfred Clark,
Frederick Griffin and John Rowell – all, somewhat remarkably, from the
Fens – were the judges, and began their work on a dark and gloomy morning

at 8.30 a.m. But the weather soon improved and two sunny and mild days encouraged enormous crowds to attend. 287 horses were awarded either prizes or the new premiums – 124 stallions, 151 mares and twelve geldings. Breeders' prizes on offer were fourteen of £10 (for class winners among stallions and mares) and 105 of £5. The remarkable thing was that only four of the 119 candidates were ineligible on account of their not being members of the Society. The most surprised winner of £5 was probably George Brown of Churston in Cheshire who had bred a colt foal back in 1889 which he had sold to Mr. Hart of the Cannock Agricultural Company. As Hatherton II, it had won commended cards three times in London, then had passed to Abraham Grandage and now at the age of thirteen turned up in the possession of Walpole Greenwell from Surrey to win second prize in the old stallions' class.

Stroxton Tom, whom so many thought should have been the champion the year before, duly won the coveted top award. He became excited by the applause, swerved round suddenly and his hock struck his owner, James Forshaw, a sharp blow just as the King was presenting the cup. The lid went spinning yards away and Stroxton Tom set off in the same direction. He was soon under control again, but by then His Majesty had emulated that high-stepping Hackney secretary, Frank Euren, and covered the distance between the table and the ringside in record time. Three weeks earlier, the Shire Patron had sold five stallions and forty mares for 8,255 guineas, and so February was an exciting month for him. James Forshaw later submitted a plan to the Council to prevent applause, but what it was we cannot know. It is doubtful what could be done except to tie all spectators' hands behind their backs. This show, incidentally, emphasised the predominance of the bay colour in the chief descendants of the Blacks. Twelve of the fourteen class winners among stallions and mares were bay, and twenty-two of the top twenty-eight.

In 1903, remembering the fright he had had the year before, James Forshaw told his son Tom to take Stroxton Tom into the ring. The championship was won a second time and the cup was presented by the future George V and his Queen together. All went peacefully until their Royal Highnesses began to walk out of the ring, when the renewed applause set the horse going at a good pace. Unless he were allowed to go straight on instead of being pulled round, he would inevitably collide with the royal couple, who amid the din were blissfully unaware of what was happening. So he was allowed to go straight ahead, but then suddenly veered towards them. The human Tom in a moment of agony shouted "Heigh-up" (whether to the Prince and Princess or to his horse he was not sure), the Princess put her hand sharply on the Prince's arm and he stopped instantly. Stroxton Tom brushed past his Royal Highness at a hair's breath. So two sons had the same fright that their fathers had had the year before. That year, all four senior stallion classes were won by James Forshaw & Sons and they were paraded by the four sons. "Which is the prouder of the two?" someone asked, "Mr. Forshaw of his winning stallions, or Mrs. Forshaw of her sons?" As for the excitable Stroxton Tom, he was considered by many as the most perfect stallion seen in London up to the war. One enthusiast remembered him thus: "Built on a tremendous scale, a little over 17-hands, with a good ranging neck and head laid into deep shoulders, grand quarters, very wide fore and aft, on short legs, with bones like ivory and bearing a fringe of silky hair, and feet and pasterns like a Clydesdale." Lest the last point be misleading, everyone noticed that the judges had a strong leaning towards weight.

Lord Rothschild won the three-year-old and two-year-old male classes (his Birdsall Menestrel, who won the junior cup, probably being the best three-year-old to have appeared at a London Show) and two female classes. One of these successes was the new champion mare, Solace, who was particularly wide, deep and heavy, but no lady at all. Lord Rothschild had bought her at the Sandringham sale the year before for 575 guineas. (She had had three foals before, but the one she dropped shortly after this Show had to be hand-reared, for she caught a fever and had to be shot. This last of her offspring, Ragged Boy II, turned out to be no more a gentleman than his dam deserved. But he was as prolific as he was lecherous, and long-lived too.) His Majesty, as breeder of Solace, stepped into the ring to receive the gold medal, which he smilingly slipped into his pocket amidst the ringing cheers of all assembled. Solace's success also brought a breeder's £10 cash award to His Majesty, who picked up two other breeder's prizes and three exhibitor's awards, including one for a young mare bred by Sir Oswald Mosley, making a total of £31. At the auction sale which terminated the proceedings, a compulsory reserve price of 50 guineas for stallions, 40 guineas for mares, and 25 guineas for yearling colts and fillies was fixed in order to end the practice, which the Council did not think right, of "sending up screws to be disposed of at whatever price they would fetch". It had the desired effect.

The twenty-fifth show, in 1904, produced the all-time record entry of horses, beating 1902 by two. The idea of 481 stallions, 351 mares and thirty geldings all housed in one building for four days, if suggested now, would induce sleepless nights for any worried secretary or official. But the Edwardian Shire men merely congratulated themselves that "the display of stallions was the best yet seen and that the mares and fillies formed as good a collection as had ever been brought together". His Majesty witnessed the judging of some of the classes and of the championships with evident pleasure. Breeder's prizes on offer now totalled 112. The show cost £4,250, of which just over half was spent in prizes and almost £1,300 to rent and fit up the hall and for gas and water. There was a loss of £985 – normally, the more numerous the entries, the greater the loss. But who worried about that? There was still a profit on the year of £113 and a reserve fund of £12,000, even though the prizes given at country shows now numbered 914.

However, never again could such numbers as these come to Islington. After the Show, the Royal Agricultural Hall Company politely called attention to the fact that the Society had broken the "very stringent regulations" of the

London County Council, particularly by blocking up gangways with the excessive amount of provender that some exhibitors, distrusting what was officially provided, had brought with them. (Actually, what was supplied by Nickolls and Baker at a charge of £244. 14s. 4d. was the very best. It had to be, and a partner in the firm personally went every year to make his selection on home counties farms. No one wanted Mr. Sloughgrove coming across to 18 Mortimer Street to complain.) The Hall Company very mildly passed on the L.C.C.'s instruction that the maximum number of horses in future should be 700. Having referred this problem to the Horse Show Committee, the Council adjourned "till Tuesday of Derby week". It was eventually decided that no exhibitor could show more than fourteen horses, or more than two in any one class. If necessary, gelding classes would have to be cancelled.

In 1905, entries were just nineteen less than the permitted maximum. Someone had suggested separate classes for tenant farmers to show yearling colts and fillies, but the idea was turned down – not only because it would send entries up too high, but because everyone remembered the Walwyn brothers. Instead, there was a further restriction. All mares of five years and upwards had to be either in foal or to have had a foal the year before. This regulation was also extended to mares competing for gold medals at country shows. A new award board owned by the Hunter Society was hired for £5 and a telephone was installed so that it could be operated speedily.

The 1906 Show was reduced in numbers to a mere 593, but the general standard was without doubt the highest so far achieved. If they paid 5s. extra, exhibitors could add the words "For sale privately" or "To be let" in the catalogue. Similar notices were again available for hanging in the boxes, and so were "Sold privately" cards for horses entered for the auction but disposed of beforehand. Turmoil was gradually being reduced, grooms were reminded that if they wanted to smoke after 6 p.m. they must retire to the special room provided or leave the Hall, to which they must return by 12.30 a.m. One exhibitor was called before the committee for smoking in a horse box. The Forshaws had specially invited the breeder of their Present King II to join the Society, but he had not done so. When the horse was made champion stallion, this Mr. Phillipson dashed to the secretary's room with his application form. But the Council refused to award him the gold medal and £10 prize, and returned his form and his money. He did join in January the next year and Present King II was second in his class the following month, which brought him in £5. He paid four annual subscriptions, the horse was not shown again and he ended the whole transaction 16s. and four volumes of the Stud book to the good. Sir Albert Muntz, after the 1906 Show, urged that it really was vital to "suppress clapping and the noisy demonstrations likely to excite the horses". Rather feebly, the Council decided to put up extra notices.

The year 1907 saw Lockinge Forest King first head the list of winning sires. In 1908, he had an outstanding success. Every one of the first six two-year-old fillies was by him, and so were the first three four-year-old mares. He had fifty-one sons and daughters at the Show and they won twenty-four prizes (including four firsts), two highly commended and seven commended. Anyone under suspension by any other Society (and there was one) was barred from exhibiting, at this or future London Shows. Yearling colts and fillies were exempted from veterinary inspection. The Society provided canvas to cover the fronts of stallion boxes. There was a new class for barren mares of five years and upwards, but they would not be eligible for the championships. A mare that was not in foal but had had a foal the previous year could be entered either in this or the appropriate ordinary class. No mare could compete in it a second time until she had produced a living foal. Someone asked whether a mare which was in foal to an unregistered stallion could be entered, for the purposes of the show, in this new class, since she would not be eligible for the ordinary classes. The answer to this absurd question was, not surprisingly, in the negative. At the risk of being repetitive, it is probably true to say that the general standard of the exhibits was higher than that of two years before. A new seven year agreement with the Hall Company also provided an enlarged judging ring, more seating for members, much new stabling, and a lower rent.

The 1909 Show opened in an appalling fog, but was more memorable for the fact that Lord Rothschild, having won one of the two championships in each of the preceding six years, now won them both. These eight championships involved seven different horses, and if his 1901 champion, Alston Rose, is added (she was champion in 1902 for her new owner), he owned eight different winners of nine championships in nine years. It should not be assumed that he entirely bought his way into this. The two champions this year had not done remarkable things in the show ring before coming into his possession. Halstead Royal Duke had appeared once in London – in 1907 as a yearling, when he was highly commended: and Chiltern Maid's previous appearance the year before as a three-year-old had brought her a fifth prize in her class. Lord Rothschild's advantage lay partly in employing Tom Fowler, who could both spot a likely horse in early life better than most men and bring it out in the finest condition, and partly in being able to indulge his employee's fancies in this respect. Without a man of Fowler's genius, his lordship would have wasted his money: Tom Fowler could not have achieved his success without his employer's resources. But, while both deserve praise – not least for the benefits they brought to cart-horse breeding at its more humdrum and utilitarian level – their triumphs emphasise the extraordinary achievements of James Forshaw, whose every error or misfortune had to be paid out of profits made in the hazardous business of stallion-keeping.

A little mare that Lord Rothschild had sold the year before and that won the under-16-hands class for H. S. Leon of Bletchley Park, brings a sad touch to the record of this show. She had been bred by the Walwyn brothers, but Matthew had now followed his brother to his Etwall grave. He was fifty-eight when he died on 14th September 1908. His sister Frances could not, according to the rules, be awarded the breeder's prize of £10. A. C. Duncombe of Calwich

Abbey, now in his sixteenth year as Chairman of the Editing Committee, made a plea on her behalf, explaining the interest she had always taken in the activities of the farm and her devoted work in helping to manage it. But it was her brothers, and not she, who had been Shire members and to break the rule might become an embarrassing precedent.

This year a rule prohibiting the use of resin, soap or any other substance "designed to give an artificial appearance", or of sawdust above the knee, or cording, was at last strictly enforced by the appointment of an inspector whose duty it was to look at the horses before they entered the ring. His brief was an extension of a regulation that had been introduced a few years before, but had been more often broken than observed. Sawdust had spread in the 'eighties from the legs to the back so that it was sometimes difficult to know even the colour of a horse. Bandaging and pulling and clipping the joints came later, and now resin had been for some years plastered on to such an extent that one could hardly distinguish white legs from black ones. Alfred Clark had judged at seven London shows and in 1908 his clothes were almost ruined by all this stuff, so he cheerfully agreed to be the first inspector.

The most popular event at the first show of the new reign in 1911 was the choice of Pailton Sorais as champion mare. This beautiful daughter of Lockinge Forest King was now eight years old. She had been reserve champion for three years in succession for Max Michaelis, being beaten each time by a different opponent. No rules could stifle the loud and enthusiastic applause that greeted the decision which saved her from being the best Shire mare never to win the championship. Another popular choice enabled King George V to get quickly off the mark as a stud-owner. His seven-year-old Hoe Forest King (whose sire is not difficult to guess) won the small stallion class, having been Highly Commended and third in previous years when his exhibitor was Edward VII. The class for barren mares was dropped, after only three years, owing to lack of support. It had never attracted more than six entries.

The next show, in 1912, was notable for producing probably the best group of Shire stallions all of the same age ever seen together in the history of the breed. They were four-year-olds, and their class attracted fifty-one entries. Certainly the first half-dozen, taken together, were as magnificent in their size and substance as in their supreme quality, and all contributed magnificently to the breed as stud horses. Twenty or more years later, with the exception of the sixth in the line, they were just the horses that most Shire men, trying to eliminate superfluity of hair, would have wished to see reincarnated. Unexciting as it may be to list them, this is a necessary tribute to possibly the finest example of what a breed society had been able to achieve in just over thirty years. That they were not just a freak coming-together of exceptional animals is indicated by the fact that the reserve champion came from the over-four-year-old class (Blusterer, aged six, bred by Lord Rothschild and exhibited by H. H. Smith Carington, Ashby Folville, Leicestershire). The highest position that each occupied at any of the London Shows is indicated in parentheses:

1 WARTON DRAUGHTSMAN 27895, bay, by Tatton Friar 21953
  Breeder – James Bullock, Draycott-le-Clay, Sudbury, Derbyshire
  Exhibitor – The Duke of Devonshire, Chatsworth, Derbyshire
  (Supreme champion this year)

2 EATON NUNSUCH 27301, brown, by Lymm Champion 22562
  Breeder and Exhibitor – The Duke of Westminster, Eaton Hall, Chester
  (Second this year)

3 RICKFORD COMING KING 27709, brown, by Ravenspur 22709,
  Breeder – the late Lord Winterstoke, Blagdon, Somerset
  Exhibitor – Robert Heath, Biddulph Grange, Staffs.
  (Supreme champion, 1918, for J. Forshaw & Sons)

4 CARLTON WHAT'S WANTED 29208, black, by Southgate Honest Tom
  16984
  Breeder – J. E. Cheetham, Orston Grange, Bottesford, Notts.
  Exhibitors – James Forshaw & Sons, Carlton-on-Trent, Newark
  (2nd in his class to Blaisdon Jupiter in 1915)

5 BABINGLEY NULLI SECUNDUS 26993, brown, by Calwich Blend 17226
  Breeder – E. W. Betts, Babingley, King's Lynn
  Exhibitor – Lord Rothschild, Tring Park, Herts.
  (Junior champion in 1911)

6 BLAISDON JUPITER 27051, bay, by Montford Jupiter 18940
  Breeder – Tom Stelfox, Walden Court, Newent, Glos.
  Exhibitor – Lord Rothschild
  (Supreme champion 1915)

The fourteenth horse in the line was one Lockinge Hengist – never heard of thereafter, for the simple reason that he went abroad: with what astounding success, we shall see in due course.

In 1913, the two-year-old Champion's Goalkeeper won the stallion championship, less than a fortnight after fetching the sum of 4,100 guineas at Lord Rothschild's latest home sale. This has turned out to be the record price ever paid for a Shire stallion. His purchaser, Sir Walpole Greenwell of Marden Park in Surrey, also won the female championship for the second year running with his Dunsmore Chessie, the only chestnut ever to become breed champion. So he became the fourth man to win both championships at a London Show.

One of the best mares of all time returned home unhonoured this year. William Thompson junior of Kibworth Beauchamp, Leicestershire, was now inspector under the soap-and-resin rule and had occasion to warn her groom, who ignored repeated instructions and led her into the ring. She was in fact judged and placed first in the four-year-old class and reserve to Dunsmore Chessie both for the senior cup and for the supreme championship before the Horse Show Committee stepped in and disqualified her completely. Bought as a foal by Lord Rothschild from Thomas Green of Welshpool and registered as Lorna Doone, she had been first as a yearling and also at two years, being reserve for the junior cup the second time. She was then sold privately to the brothers W. & H. Whitley, who had been making expensive purchases for their choice Primley stud at Paignton since 1907, and who were attracted by her name as well as by her looks. For them, she had been second as a three-year-old.

In 1914 Lorna Doone came into the ring unresined, and won the championship. Champion's Goalkeeper won the other championship for the second time – and was still only three years old. Both were bred in the same county. This was the fifth year this had happened, but this occasion was something a little special. They were the first champions not bred in England, and Powis Castle and Thomas Green's farm were about as close to each other as they could be. There was something special, also, about Hollywood, the champion gelding. He was exhibited by Mawers Ltd. of the Fulham Road, and was the first representative of genuine commercial users of heavy town geldings to win the supreme honour, though his trade is somewhat surprising for his owners were house-furnishers. W. G. Mawer, head of the firm, had been a member of the Society for twelve months and was delighted with his success.

This Show offered 216 cash awards for 163 stallions (fifty-three actual prizes, with the same number for breeders, the remaining 110 being awards for Highly Commended and Commended animals), 229 awards for 173 mares (fifty-six, fifty-six and 117) and seventeen prizes for eleven geldings (eleven for exhibitors and six for breeders). Twenty-two of the 115 breeders' awards could not be claimed, as five were dead and seventeen were non-members. The total value of prizes was £2,230. This was also the last show under the existing seven year agreement with the Agricultural Hall, and a serious proposal was made to transfer to Olympia in 1915. There had been a similar suggestion prior to 1907, but since the International Horse Show did not bring glamour to the place until that year, it had been premature.

R. G. Heaton, managing director of Olympia Limited was a great breeder of hackneys. But he also had Shire links, as befitted a Heaton of Chatteris. He had joined the Shire Society in 1889 and from his Ferry Hill stud took part in the last three years of the exporting boom – registering fifty-two stallions and six mares, only one of which he had bred, but nearly all of which were sent abroad. From the 1894 volume onwards, a total of eleven stallions and nineteen mares had now been connected with his name – several of them bought from Henry at Worsley and others sold to that famous stud.

The Royal Agricultural Hall's managing director was a Shire member of long standing. This was Charles W. Tindall, who in 1910 had succeeded another Shire man, the late Garrett Taylor, one of the original E.C.H.S. Councilmen. (Taylor had followed Charles Dorman in 1901. The chairman was none other than Sir Walter Gilbey.) Tindall had joined the Society in February 1879 and was now serving his twenty-second year as a Council member. He had judged once – in 1894 with Henry Heaton as one of his three colleagues and R. G. Heaton as a steward. From 1881 to 1893, he had been manager for R. N. Sutton-Nelthorpe at Scawby, Brigg, and during the last twenty years, since settling at Wainfleet, had entered thirty-four stallions in the Stud-book, and five mares. In this year, 1914, he sold one of the last Shires to go to East Prussia before that market was suddenly closed. His stallions bore resounding names like Crossbar, Running River, Rustnot, Roadmender and Grand Compounder. Sutton-Nelthorpe's horses were perhaps named with more flair than any Shires, but whether Tindall had been responsible or whether he merely caught the spirit, it is difficult to say. Certainly his successor at Scawby, G. P. Tyrwhitt-Drake, had continued the tradition.

Mr. Heaton, of course, offered the lustre associated with the International Horse Show. He could also provide a bigger ring (eighty-four feet by 324, as compared with seventy-seven by 255 at Islington), and a grandstand seating 2,500, as against 1,500. Olympia had about the same ratio of boxes to stalls, totalling 700, as the Hall, but they were palatial in their splendour. Its promenade was nine feet wide and went all round the ring: the R.A.H. promenade was ten feet wide, but only on three sides. His shops were under the grandstand, instead of in front of it. But Mr. Tindall had a few advantages, too. He had entrances to the ring at both ends, instead of only one, and the ramps from the gallery deposited horses at the clear end of the hall, instead of the busy entrance end. Mr. Heaton wanted a seven year agreement at £2,000 a year for the three weeks of horse shows, or £2,070 if the agreement was for only five years: Mr. Tindall asked £1,800 for five or seven years.

A meeting was held at Hanover Square on 7th May 1913, attended by representatives of the Shire, Hackney, Hunter and Polo Pony societies. The two directors were called into the Council chamber in turn, and they offered all sorts of extra inducements. Dazzled by the aristocratic splendour of I.H.S., the thirteen representatives resolved to report to their Councils in favour of Olympia. The Shire representatives then said their view was only a personal opinion, whereupon all the others hastened to express the same reservation also. The four secretaries, John Sloughgrove, A. B. Charlton (his assistant in the Shire Society, but present as Hunter Secretary), the quick-footed Frank Euren, and F. H. Badge of the Polo Ponies then went away to draw up the recommendations for their respective Councils. Mr. Tindall followed up later with a better offer. Eventually he won the day. The Shire Council decided, on 9th June 1914, to accept a five-year agreement to continue at the Royal Agricultural Hall, the other societies having also agreed to place loyalty before glamour.

7. THE GOVERNMENT SCHEME

A suggestion that all travelling stallions should require a certificate of soundness was made in 1903 by the President, Sir Alexander Henderson. Captain

W. H. O. Duncombe and the Earl of Verulam, in support, urged that the Board of Agriculture should be approached with a view to the necessary legislation being considered. But Sir Walter was strongly "against any government interference, on the grounds that all benefits accruing to horse-breeding had arisen from voluntary effort": and in any case it would be impossible to obtain uniform vetting by district inspectors. Sir P. A. Muntz, A. C. Duncombe and Lord Middleton were entirely in agreement with him, and the matter was dropped.

Six years later, the Worcestershire Chamber of Agriculture resolved to press the Board to initiate such a scheme, and to include stallions standing at home as well. The Shire Council sympathised this time, but felt quite unable to join them in asking for compulsion. An ordinary member, J. P. T. Jackson, of Chorley, advocated a different approach. At the A.G.M. (1909) he proposed that after 2nd August 1911 (when entries for the 1912 volume would close) no animal should be eligible for the Stud-book unless its sire had been certified free from hereditary unsoundness during the season prior to its birth. The Editing Committee considered this to be impracticable, and did nothing. So Jackson, at the next A.G.M., moved that unless the Council took some action the Secretary would be required to conduct a poll of members. The Duke of Devonshire, Lord Hothfield, Lord Middleton and the President (Earl Beauchamp) were among those who rose to their feet and explained the difficulties of the scheme. Only three members voted for it.

A year later, John Morris of Wrockwardine, supported by Goodwin Preece, a fellow Salopian, suggested yet another solution. He proposed a second stud-book to which stallions and mares from the ordinary book could be elevated at the age of six, if they were then passed as sound. The Editing Committee, in reply, succinctly pointed out the basic error of this and similar proposals. "Both these gentlemen," they reported, "seem to overlook the cardinal point that all established stud-books are simply records of pedigrees, and that entry therein must necessarily be based on breeding. The problem of ensuring soundness must therefore be sought outside their pages."

However, even before Mr. Morris had made his proposal, the Board had announced its own scheme. It was entirely voluntary and would begin at once – in time for the 1911 season. It was confined to stallions of three years or over, which were entered or accepted for entry in recognised stud-books. Owners could apply to have them examined by a veterinary officer appointed by the Board, free of cost, unless the service fee exceeded £10, in which case there would be a charge of two guineas for the first examination and one guinea on subsequent occasions. If the stallion was passed, a certificate of registration would be issued, valid until 31st October, when it had to be returned either with a request for re-examination for the following year or an intimation that it was to be cancelled. The essential requirements were stated both in general and particular terms. "A stallion will not be registered nor retained in the register unless it is certified to be sound and suitable for breeding purposes and is free from the following diseases and defects: cataract, roaring, whistling, ringbone, sidebone, bone·spavin, navicular disease, shivering, stringhalt, defective genital organs." The last of these may appear to be a distinctly non-hereditary unsoundness, but many rigs are fertile and pass on their defect. That these listed diseases were not to be regarded as the only disqualifications was emphasised by the rule that "if the report of the veterinary surgeon shows that the stallion is suffering from a disease, defect, or deformity, which in his opinion renders it unsound or unsuitable for breeding purposes, the owner will be so informed". The regulations provided suitable channels of appeal, reserved the Board's right to inspect registered stallions at any time and ended with the threat that if an owner was detected in fraudulent practices in connection with the scheme, "all his stallions will be liable to be struck off the register and he may be debarred from obtaining any further benefit thereunder".

The Shire men at their A.G.M. passed a unanimous vote of thanks to the Board of Agriculture & Fisheries for instituting the plan and then more or less ignored it. Ninety-seven stallions of three years and upwards had just passed the strict London Show inspection and a further nine, not shown in London, were similarly successful later at country shows before being awarded Shire medals. The Board's list comprised only ninety-six, of which seven were successful London animals and therefore already rigorously vetted that year. Abraham Grandage of Bramhope, near Leeds, was the only "big name" who really supported it. His Gaer Conqueror, London champion for the second successive year, and two others had Shire certificates: with the Board he registered nine – one of the London winners and eight others. The only other stallions registered by any well-known Shire men were a few which were due to travel in districts where the local farmers specifically asked for a certificate. Thirty-one of the stallions on the Board's list were owned in Devon. With Cornwall (eight) and Somerset (four), the south-west accounted for forty-three. There were twenty in the western and Welsh counties, twelve in Yorkshire (thanks to Mr. Grandage) and nine in Norfolk. This left only twelve in the rest of England – Cambridge having two, Lincolnshire one, and Leicester and Derby none at all.

The Devon thirty-one are worth further analysis. They were owned by twenty-three different men of whom only nine were S.H.S. members. Some of the stallions owned by these "small men" were locally bred, though they all traced back in only one or two generations on both sides to Fen or Midland blood, and mostly blue blood. Others had been bought from famous studs – for example, three originally owned by the late Albert Muntz at Dunmore, and the four-year-old Bury Pointsman bred by John Rowell. The County Livestock Adviser had done good work in interesting the Devonians in the scheme. These stallions, unlike those of the Forshaws or other great proprietors, were not destined to travel far beyond their own locality, and so between 2,000 and 3,000 mares were covered in the county that year by entire horses of known pedigree and certified soundness. However, the historian must give the credit for these Devon sires not to the Board which approved them, but to the Shire

Society whose efforts had produced them. Thirty-one years earlier, thirty-one well-bred Shire stock-horses in the county of Devon would have been an impossible dream.

Members of the other breed societies, both heavy and light, were similarly slow to support the scheme, and the Board was disappointed. But in 1912 there was an improvement. Two hundred and forty-seven Shire stallions were vetted and passed. In December of that year, Lord Lucas, Parliamentary Secretary to the Board, presided over a meeting of representatives of all breed societies. He emphasised that he wished to work amicably with them. There was, indeed, one point on which everyone present agreed. Although not one of the societies had their own schedule of hereditary unsoundnesses, all were happy with the Board's list, which had already been approved also by the National Veterinary Association. But all the delegates objected to the idea of the referee, to be appointed in cases of dispute, being nominated by the Board. They wanted to be able to provide their own. The societies took unanimous exception also to Lord Lucas' view that a stallion, rejected in one year, would be ineligible for all future years. After much fierce argument, he gave way to the extent of allowing a second chance, provided it were in the year immediately following rejection. Archibald M'Neilage, for the Clydesdale Society, received strong support from all the others in his proposal that, if a horse was passed sound every year from the age of three to eight, he should then have a free certificate for life, on the grounds that if there was any hereditary disease about him it would be apparent by then. But Lord Lucas was adamant in refusing this concession. J. T. C. Eadie and Alfred Clark had been instructed by their Council to say that the Shire Society would not accept the Board's certificate at the London Show. Lord Lucas was both amazed and angry. But Mr. Eadie forebore to enrage him further by pointing out that a Shire certificate bore the name of a veterinary *professor* and was a document devised more than thirty years before the Government had interested itself in the matter. Instead he mildly replied that a Government certificate might be dated in early November and would be four months old by the time of the Show, which was too long in the case of a three-year-old.

In 1913, the number of Shires on the Board's list rose to 388, still less than one-sixth of the pedigree stallions available for service. They belonged to owners spread over forty-two counties, as compared with nineteen in the first year. Devon, with thirty-four, was still near the top, but Norfolk had thirty-eight and Yorkshire, if one puts all the Ridings together, forty-seven – and this was without the help of Abraham Grandage, who had just transferred his stud to Alderley in Cheshire, where twenty of the twenty-two Board-registered stallions were his. A few other "big men" had now joined him in supporting the scheme – the Forshaws with twenty-four stallions, Lord Middleton with eleven, F. W. Griffin (seven) and A. H. Clark (six), and J. B. Brooks at Finstall near Bromsgrove (seven). But most of them still believed that, though the thing was a good idea, it was for other people. The Shire Council magnanimously agreed this year that medal winners at country shows need not be examined if they held the Board's certificate. But, though the Board agreed to accept the Shire certificate, the Council would not countenance any reciprocal concession for London.

On 1st April, thirty-five years to the day after the "English Cart-horse Society" was formally launched, the Council first had to consider a second piece of Government "interference" – one that was very helpful to the "smaller men" and, indirectly, to the leading stallion-owners also. This was the "Improvement of Live-Stock Scheme", for which £40,000 was made available from the Development Fund. It was designed to subsidise clubs and societies wishing to hire pedigree bulls, boars, or stallions of heavy draught breeds. (In the case of bulls, private owners could also be helped if they were prepared to allow neighbours to send cows, since cattle-breeding hardly lent itself to the club-system.) So far as heavy-horses were concerned, preference was to be given to new societies specially formed as a result of the scheme, and many new ones instantly sprang up. But existing clubs could benefit if their rules were made to conform to requirements. Those paying a dividend or bonus, or those owning a stallion, were not eligible, nor were those charging a service fee to members of more than 3 guineas or hiring a stallion not on the Board's register. A society accepted under the scheme would receive a direct grant of £40, and up to a total of £40 in assisted nominations. Bona fide farmers whose holdings did not exceed 100 acres were eligible for one of these each year, the society being reimbursed in each case with not more than half the normal fee. Therefore, a society whose horse served at 3 guineas could charge half-fee to as many as twenty-five members, or two guineas to thirty-eight members, according to the number eligible to benefit. The Board issued a little booklet containing all the regulations, together with model rules for a hiring society and a model agreement for the hiring of a stallion. This had to be done on one of three principles: a fixed inclusive fee, an inclusive fee variable according to the number of mares served, or a fixed premium with further payment for each mare served and, if desired, for each mare proving in foal.

A problem which neither a breed society nor a Government board could successfully cope with was that of infertility. A barren mare brought sad loss to her owner, especially if he had only one or two, but a sterile stallion was a disaster to the society which had hired him. The matter was discussed at length by the Shire Council in June 1914 at the instigation of John Nix, the third-generation owner of the Outseats stud at Alfreton, Derbyshire, which had been famous for Blacks or Shires for over 100 years. Trying to drive a wedge into the problem at one of the more obvious cracks, he proposed that, at the London Show auction, all stallions offered over three-years-old must have a guarantee of their fertility. But it was eventually decided, inevitably but reluctantly, that a stud-book society could not deal with this matter. Somewhat inadequately, it was resolved that a warranty of soundness, at all sales under Shire rules, should not be held to be good if a stallion "is found to be ruptured or if both his testicles are not down". But had not the unruptured Rokeby Harold won the supreme

London championship when nine months old in 1893? And had not his testicles duly come down and, at the age of three had he not been supreme champion again – and had then begotten but four or five foals? And once more, when he was four, he was champion a third time – but never managed to "stop" another mare, for all his grand appearance. This was still a sore point. Neither a stud-book, nor a London inspection, or a Board of Agriculture veterinary certificate, nor even a red-white-and-blue champion's card, was a passport to fertility.

8. IN THE COUNTRY

The Society's first new idea at the beginning of the new reign in 1901 was to extend breeder's prizes to the affiliated country shows. The breeder of every gold medal winner, provided that he was a member of the Society and that the dam of the winner was in the Stud-book, received £5. Twenty-four such prizes out of a possible twenty-eight were awarded. From 1903, those who had bred silver-medal winners were also rewarded, with a £1 prize. That year 194 such medals were presented, and 137 breeder's prizes. (In twenty-five cases the winner was out of an unregistered mare and in twenty-five the breeder was a non-member. The breeders of the remaining seven winners were dead.)

As an encouragement to the "small man" to keep a good mare instead of a common one, and to use a pedigree stallion, this was money well spent. A congratulatory letter from the Shire Horse Society enclosing £1 had an effect on the recipient that it is impossible for us now to appreciate. Occasionally, the breeder was the "big man" and the exhibitor a person of humble status. Lord Llangattock received £2 as breeder of two mares that won the silver medals at Coleshill and Congleton shows. He owned sixty times the acreage that each of the mare-owners farmed as tenants, but these exceptions did not destroy the principle. In 1904, the two gold-medal schemes were merged: any society could claim one gold medal if its Shire classes carried £100 in prize money. In county shows, a resident or occupier of agricultural land in the county was eligible: in other cases, members of the agricultural society concerned could qualify.

This increasing involvement of the Shire Society with agricultural societies, great and small, brought about a number of knotty problems. It is surprising that there were not more. There was a row over the disqualification, on veterinary grounds, of the apparent winner of the silver medal at the Leek Show. At the Welsh National Show a gold medal was offered, but who was entitled to claim it was a nice point. A county society suspended two of its members for fraudulent practices in a Shire class, and the Council resolved in 1907 to suspend them from the Shire Society as well. It is remarkable that this was in fact the first occasion on which the Council had to bring into operation the full machinery set up by its Bye-laws – the appointment of an investigatory sub-committee, the calling of a special meeting at which the accused member was invited to attend with his witnesses, and so on. One of the members was censured and the other expelled, nemine contradicente. (One councillor abstained.) This punishment was serious enough for a stallion-owner in a big way of business, but worse was to follow. No prize could be awarded to any horse either owned by him or sold by him to a new owner. County societies banned this person from showing Shires at their shows. Entries submitted by him for the Stud-book were not accepted, nor were export-certificates. The member was later reinstated but, whether he was guilty or innocent, the whole affair was a sensational warning to others.

There can be absolutely no doubt that if we could see the worst couple of thousand cart-horses in 1914, we would find them very much superior on average to their predecessors of 1880, or even 1901, just as the best thousand or two were infinitely sounder and better shaped than those of twenty or thirty years before. But it was a slow business. Farmers in general still paid only a quarter of the attention and intelligence to breeding from their cart mares that they gave to their sheep and cattle. "For sale. A big, heavy wide SHIRE STAL-LION. 17.2 hands". "Entire cart colt for sale, 2 y.o., immense bone, splendid hair". "Big weighty stallion, plenty of bone and hair, 17.1, 8 years. Reason of selling – giving up the farm. Price moderate". Whatever defects lay behind such advertisements as these, it scarcely mattered to many intending purchasers if the horse was cheap enough, virile and tough.

There were far too many men like the Warwickshire carrier who made his deliveries with a pale chestnut entire heavy-horse whose unbeauteous outlines baffled any attempt to guess his parentage. The inspiration that replaced an unprofitable gelding by this creature on the daily round put butter on the carrier's bread and a little jam as well. It was really surprising, he said, how often he was asked to take the horse out of the shafts and earn a timely half-sovereign. Even five bob would send both on their way rejoicing. And there were too many men, also, like the Essex farmer with a small Thoroughbred mare which had produced several weedy foals to a blood stallion. He took the trouble to consult a knowledgeable neighbour, who advised the use of a good strong Hackney horse, to add size to her quality. But it was a Shire stallion, whose fee was in inverse proportion to his weight and hair, that happened to come along at the right time and the farmer, thinking to get more from a smaller outlay, was amazed a year later to be presented with a fiddle-headed foal with a great body, slender legs and feet like soup-plates.

Perhaps idiots got what they deserved. At the other end of the scale, intelligent men were in a far better position, however small their resources, to improve their cart-horses, and even have some ambitions in the pedigree way, than they had ever been before. To counterbalance the Essex fool and his fiddle-headed foal, an example might be quoted from that county. Any tenant of Major-General Sir Henry Ewart of Felix Hall, Kelvedon would be well repaid if he had a few good mares, for his landlord always kept a 5-guinea horse which he could use for exactly one-third of that fee. In 1902, for example, he had the four-year-old Sweldon King, which he had bought after winning sixth prize at London the year before. This horse was a good mover, had good feet and flat bone, and was a bargain for those on the estate at 35s.

Landlords of this kind were destined soon and suddenly to be in trouble themselves, though in August 1914 they could scarcely be expected to foretell the fate in store for their secure world. But already the self-help system of hiring societies was gathering a momentum which received a tremendous boost from the Board of Agriculture scheme in 1913–1914. Yet the help of landlord or Government for the ambitious small breeder, though it enabled him to produce commercial stock of the highest quality and value, was still insufficient to put the Hampshire or Surrey or Carmarthen man on level terms with even the smallest breeder in Leicestershire, Lincoln or Derby. Most landlords, even if they kept two or more stallions, allowed a reduction on only one. However good he might be, he was not necessarily right for the specially good mare that Mr. A or Mr. B possessed. Well, there was no actual *compulsion* for A or B to use the landlord's horse. But even though the mare might be extra special and the expense of sending her away (and losing her work as well) seemed worth it, another point to be taken into consideration was what the landlord might say about a presumptuous tenant. If the squire's valuable prize-winning horse was not good enough for him, he must be better off than he should be – a matter to be looked into. Mr. C and Mr. D, farming in a different county, where most people bred good Shires as a recognised part of their farming operations, would have a generous choice of five, six or seven travelling stallions, all good ones, to choose from: some "small men" were even lucky enough to live within a day's walk of a big stallion stud.

Similarly, the selection committee of the hiring society did not necessarily comprise the most intelligent horsemen, or, even if it did, each member of it would vote for the horse which he thought would suit his twelve mares, not the one mare owned by young E. The great Shire breeding areas would never be overhauled by the lesser ones in producing numbers of prize-winning horses. Nevertheless, the most notable achievement of the Shire Society in thirty-five years had been the improvement in the backward districts. Relatively, it was greater even than that shown in the old home of the Black.

To end this country survey at the most exalted level, the R.A.S.E. continued its somewhat less than helpful attitude by dropping the class for yearling fillies at the first of the three Park Royal shows in 1903. At the premier agricultural show of the country, held in June, one of the most awkward months of the summer, this had been perhaps one of the most useful and sensible classes of all. So the Society provided all the prizes to ensure its reinclusion and in 1907 also gave the money for foal classes, additional to that for mare-with-foal. The total cost, a mere £70 a year, nevertheless represented the net value, less Stud-books, of 100 members' subscriptions. Finally, John Sloughgrove, that jealous guardian of the Society's purse, appears in 1910 to have had a bad dream, in which every winner of a gold medal (and there had been 490 of them in "county shows" alone) arrived simultaneously on the Hanover Square doorstep to exchange it for £10. In case this ever really came to pass, the Council decided that these things would be henceforth irredeemable, like the silver ones.

9. HOME AND REPOSITORY SALES

In the month that followed the death of Queen Victoria, five big home sales were held. In the Fens, Alfred Clark and his neighbour Fred Griffin sold fifty mares and fillies for £5,600: next day, Joseph Topham, another neighbour, sold forty-one Shires, every one of them home-bred, for £3,601. The following week Lord Wantage's sale of fifty-one geldings brought in £4,539 and Sir Blundell Maple's first-ever sale fetched £9,058 for forty-seven animals. Having travelled fiom Wantage to St. Albans that week, keen sale-goers still had Dunsmore to visit a week later still, when fifty-two lots brought in £9,720 for Sir Albert Muntz. Seven days later, the London Show opened.

The peak year for these sales came the next year, when there were no less than fourteen major ones, at which 583 of the choicest specimens of the breed were sold. Perhaps the most notable was the Sandringham sale in February, when 8,255 guineas were given for five stallions and forty mares. Among them was the eight-year-old Solace – at 575 guineas, a bargain for Lord Rothschild, as she won the London championship the next year at the age of nine. Prices often threatened to become unrealistic, but never in fact did so. After all, 500 guineas for a cart mare was much more likely to be recouped than the enormous sums laid out on race-horses. She had only to breed a couple of really good foals to a horse of top rank to cover her cost. If she bred a couple more which ended as geldings hauling beer or coal, they would be profit. And she might of course breed something as good as herself or better.

After 1902, the number of home sales declined steadily, though some of those which were held were spectacular enough – Lord Rothschild's in 1908 (seventeen stallions and eighteen mares for 8,890 guineas); in 1909, the post-mortem sale of Sir Albert Muntz (forty-one stallions and eleven mares – 9,802 guineas) and the Lockinge sale of forty Shires all sired by one horse, Lockinge Forester, own brother to Lockinge Forest King; another post-mortem sale in 1911 at Tatton Park, of Earl Egerton of Tatton (only sixteen stallions and six mares making 9,346 guineas); and, also in 1911, Max Michaelis' record total of 15,110 guineas (twenty-two stallions, sixty-two mares). Perhaps the grandest of all was Lord Rothschild's 1913 offering of twenty stallions and twelve mares, which fetched 13,839 guineas, including the all-time record of 4,100 guineas for Champion's Goalkeeper, actually only a two-year-old colt. But Clark and Griffin and Matthew Hubbard of Eaton and other outstanding tenant farmers ceased to invite the nobility and gentry to their homes: and, among the wealthy, Sir Walpole Greenwell, whose stud at Marden Park in Surrey first came into real prominence after the turn of the century, and who won five of the ten championships in ten years, never had a home sale at all. In February 1914 no one had one, but it is impossible to know if any proprietors had had it in mind to hold a sale in October.

For most Shire men it was much more convenient to sell a dozen or half-dozen at frequent intervals, rather than wait until all the blood needed renewing. And this is what the new Peterborough Repository enabled Sir Walpole and many other leading breeders, new and old, to do. Formerly in that city, there had been frequent sales in the yard of the Wagon and Horses in Bridge Street, but these were of little more importance than those held in a score of other breeding centres. However, on Friday, 11th March 1898 Messrs. Sexton, Grimwade and Beck had opened their splendid new premises on the Lincoln Road, only five minutes' walk from the Great Northern Railway station and close to the cattle market. Good advertising and the fact that the proprietors were also the official Society auctioneers combined to ensure the biggest gathering of prominent Shire men ever seen at any sale other than a home sale or London Show auctions. The large company partook of an excellent free luncheon and then Mr. Beck moved to the shining new rostrum with commendable punctuality to begin a catalogue which realised £2,700.

Every month there was a sale, with March and October the special occasions for top-class breeding stock. For example, the March sale in 1901 began on Thursday, 21st, with a sale and letting of Shire stallions: on the Friday, Shire mares, fillies, yearling colts and geldings were offered: the Saturday was devoted to Hackney and harness horses and on the same day the Peterborough Agricultural Society's annual Stallion Show was held – Thoroughbreds, Hackneys and Shires. Sometimes, in a special "combination sale" the repository took over the exact position of the old joint home sale. That held for H. W. Kearns and William Richardson in January 1909 is an example. The former sent a large number of brood mares from Lancashire and the latter's contribution from Cambridgeshire was fifteen stallions and colts. But the ordinary February sale of 1914 illustrates better how the repository was operating. B. N. Everard of the Bardon Stud near Leicester, the last owner of Lockinge Forest King, was giving up and his eleven stallions were offered there. Sir Berkeley Sheffield of Normanby Park, near Scunthorpe, sent a consignment of thirteen females and ten young stallions and colts. Sir Walpole entered six females and a yearling colt.

Crewe, favoured by its railway communications and well placed for the western Shire breeders, was second only to Peterborough for high-class breeding stock and, in sheer numbers sold, was outstanding. Henry Manley & Sons had sold over 6,500 horses of all types at their monthly sales in 1900 and in March 1901 opened their new repository with a three-day sale of 750, a 15 guinea prize being offered for the best cart-horse. A special train-load of geldings for London left at 5.20 p.m. on the heavy-horse day, the Friday, and reached Euston at 9.20 p.m., with stops at Stafford and Rugby to detach boxes destined for elsewhere. Also at Crewe, Frank Lloyd & Sons held great regular sales at their "Cheshire Repository", Frank himself being a prominent Shire Society member living at Eyton House, Wrexham. At his "North Wales Repository" in his home town, the Great March Sales in 1901 disposed of nearly 1,000 horses in three days – two days for heavy town geldings and mares and light lurry, parcel, van and tram horses and the third for registered Shire stallions, mares and fillies, with three classes for choice geldings.

At Preston, Edward Hothersall was the man who ended the old-fashioned method of selling horses. Vendors used to put them all on offer in the market, which was in the centre of the town, and would run them up and down the Lancaster Road for the benefit of potential customers. The chaos, and the utter uncertainty about what one was buying, began to come to an end in 1897 when the Corporation built a new cattle market and adjacent hotel. Hothersall, an ex-farmer who had begun the business of selling while licensee of the Plungington Hotel, took over as tenant of both. In 1906 he bought a piece of land adjoining and erected his own repository with accommodation for 300 horses and twenty-four loose boxes in addition. The old way of selling now died, even on Fair Day. At some of his sales, practically every horse sold had been bred in Lancashire, especially the Fylde.

Derby sales, begun in the 1880s by Andrew Smith, a Quaker and a member of the well-known Essex milling family, succeeded so well under his calm and scrupulously honest management that at the turn of the century, Sexton, Grimwade & Beck forced him to sell out by the simple process of threatening to open in opposition. He was thereupon appointed manager.

These centres were the chief ones, with Peterborough always offering the largest quantities of blue blood. All were either built or first became prosperous during this period. But there were, of course, many others. At March, Frederick Grounds was surrounded by large arable farms, all working enormous numbers of Shires and Shire-types and – in addition to those he sold at his weekly sales in the cattle market and the large special sales of heavy-horses – possibly sold more Shires at dispersal sales on Cambridgeshire farms than any other firm was ever called upon to do on the retirement or death of their clients. At Grantham, Escritt & Barrell usually claimed that their geldings – about 100 sold a month – were a "grand lot": and so they were, in spite of the fact that the frequent sales at Melton Mowbray, only sixteen miles away, were of superior class. Warner, Sheppard and Wade's Leicester repository was even then mostly devoted to light-horses and later was destined to be the last horse repository left in England, but it was here that Mr. Freeman-Mitford's Shires had been disposed of in 1897. The York Repository, first opened in 1884, due to last three-quarters of a century as a centre for bloodstock sales, and, allegedly, one of the ugliest buildings in Europe, also had its annual Spring Shire and Cart Horse Show and Sale all through the 1901–1914 period. Even at unlikely Wimborne, T. Ensor & Sons' great annual spring and autumn sales (chiefly town mares and geldings at the first, and vast numbers of yearlings and foals at the second) was not to be despised either by the dealer, the buyer for a large town user or the budding local breeder. Horses bought at these sales could easily be transported all over the country, as Wimborne was on the L.S.W.R. and also on the joint Somerset and Dorset-Midland Railway line.

Tompkins of Reading sold all sorts at their three day sale the week following the Queen's death. But was it not this firm which had been honoured, four years before, with the task of selling twenty-one horses, surplus to Her Majesty's requirements, at Windsor? Admittedly, they were of the somewhat unimproved type. The Orphan IV, a five-year-old, went to James Forshaw for 65 guineas. The twelve-year-old Wide Sarah made 31 guineas. Somehow, it is difficult to associate Wide Sarah with Her Majesty, for she had been bred at the Rose and Crown, Thorney, and her only recorded son had been sold to the Reading Urban Sanitary Authority. *Blossom*, unregistered though by a pedigree sire, was bought by Harrod's for 53 guineas. There were a couple of Clyde/Shire yearling crosses (a filly, 19 guineas, and a colt who would have to be castrated, 17 guineas) and a Clydesdale mare (29 guineas). This had been the sort of thing Her late Majesty had had. The Shire Society had done as much for her son, it appears, as for John Doe, Richard Roe – or Matthew Walwyn.

In contrast with the newer repositories, some of the town marts, at which "second-hand" horses of every description were offered, had a considerable history. Cave's of Birmingham was established in 1799. In London, Beevor's was founded in St. Martin's Lane in 1753 and later became Aldridge's. After the death of Stewart Freeman (a Shire member from 1886) in 1907, it lost much of its cart-horse trade to the Barbican, where Mr. Stollery in 1899 had succeeded Herbert Rymill, that staunch supporter of the Society from the earliest times – he had been elected in June 1878.

The newest repository on the scene in the metropolis was the Elephant and Castle, started in 1895 at the instigation of Richard Tilling as a cheaper way of disposing of 500 unwanted horses every year than by paying an auctioneer's fees. But amongst the "second-hand" horses, and many of them bus horses at that, we are far from the Shire market, especially those "fresh from the farm". However, in view of the urgent need that suddenly arose in 1914, we should not omit to mention the American and Canadian horses that were sold at the American Horse Repository in Liverpool and the Canadian Horse Repository in Lamb's Conduit Street, Holborn. A fair proportion of these were heavy draughters. This was a case of Europe "getting her own back". All these repositories were, indirectly, the descendants of the great Smithfield Friday horse fair that we heard about for the first time in the twelfth century and, for the second time, in 1724. From Sexton, Grimwade & Beck at Peterborough to the Elephant and Castle, none of the modern repositories lasted so long as Smithfield.

10. THE SHIRE ABROAD

At the beginning of the century there were 13,537,000 horses on the farms and city streets of the United States, and the number was rapidly growing. An American writer has estimated that at least half of them contained "from 10 to 50 per cent of Great War Horse blood".[3] The assertion would be as difficult to deny as to prove. The Shire men of England had every hope that in adding more weight and strength to the 7,000,000 with some Percheron, Belgian, Shire, Clydesdale and even Suffolk blood in them already, and in introducing some true European weight to the other 7,000,000, their own breed would play an ever expanding part. By far the most influential agent in attempting this was John G. Truman, son of the J. H. Truman of Whittlesea whom we have already several times met.

Born in 1865, young John first went to America at the tender age of seventeen, and there rented a livery barn at Avon, Illinois. Here, he was to handle the horses sent out by his father. Then he acquired a place at the little town of Bushnell. A disastrous fire put him out of business, and for a while he earned his living as a commercial horse dealer. But a citizen of his adoptive town loaned him $10,000 to buy Shires and from there he did not look back. He became a director of the American Shire Horse Association in 1890 and President in 1902, an office he was to hold for twenty-two years. During the period now under review, he employed twenty men at Bushnell and another half-dozen who were perpetually on the move selling stallions. This was a more complicated business than in England, for these were almost always sold not by auction or completed private sale but on the instalment system over two to four years. He also had a branch barn at Billings, Montana, with one of his brothers in charge. Unlike most importers, he brought in not only stallions for the endless task of grading-up but mares as well, and was indefatigable in helping anyone who had the wish to set up a stud of pure-bred horses. Of the 3,907 pedigree Shires which migrated to the United States in 1900–1917, he imported 1,032, over 26%. In 1909 it was 200 out of 466. He was particularly interested in buying and breeding greys, then at their lowest ebb of popularity in England but the most acceptable colour in America largely owing to everyone's being so accustomed to the Percheron. At once the Forshaw and the Muntz and the Gilbey of the American Shire, he founded the Bushnell Horse Show in 1908, which a crowd of 15,000 attended on the 15th and 16th of October. In 1911, this show had 641 entries. At the sale, he disposed of fifty-four Shire mares and fillies which made a total of $49,760. The top price was a record $6,200 and three others went for $4,500, $4,000 and $2,700. These were figures that no other draught breed in America had ever touched.

John also imported Percherons, and Belgians too, both in ever-increasing numbers. His brother in England, H. H. Truman of March, who was a veterinary surgeon and spoke fluent French, travelled constantly on the Continent buying horses for him and, with his father all this while acting as his Shire agent, the flow of pedigree English, French and Belgian heavy-horses to Bushnell was strong and fast. Oddly, it was John Truman who exhibited the first pure-bred Percherons that many men in England had ever seen. At the International Horse Show of 1912 he paraded his stallion Intitule (which he later sold for $10,750) and the Chicago International champion mare Hysope. Little did the English admirers of Birdsall Menestrel, Blaisdon Jupiter, Dunsmore Chessie and Bardon Forest Princess on that great occasion think that this breed would so soon come to stay.[4]

In 1902, the Percheron Society of America was formed, taking over from the former bankrupt association the old pedigrees and records. Fortunately, although he had been paid no salary since some time before the collapse, the

former secretary had continued to file data. With the recovery, just one benefit
was found to have accrued from the dispersal of studs of choice mares in the
early 'nineties. That was, the number of new men brought into the business.
In 1890 there were 593 owners of pure Percherons. In 1900 – though this was
discovered only when the new society had really got on its feet – there were
1,634, each of them of course owning far fewer on average than their predecessors in 1890. Less happily, the new society in 1904 was troubled, like the
old one, by unwelcome competition from a rival faction, the Percheron
Registry Association. But this gracefully faded out in 1911. Membership stood
at 3,000 in 1910, at 6,420 in 1914, and by 1920 was nearly 11,000, which made
the P.S.A. the richest and most powerful horse breed society in the world.

However, with Shire prospects in America there was already something
wrong. It can be stated in one word – "Hair". Exports to the United States
had risen from 159 in 1900 and 229 in 1901 to 504 in 1910. But they had then
dropped to 300: now, in 1912, only 231 were sent, and in 1913, 185. These
figures quite startlingly reflect how the growing fad in England for profusion
of feather was totally contrary to what Americans wanted.

By 1914, other explanations were being given. John Truman himself said
that "one of the greatest drawbacks to the progress of the Shire in this country
is not the horse, but unscrupulous dealers in England, who make a practice of
quoting prices so ridiculously low that the prospective buyer makes up his
mind that, if that is all they are worth in England, he had better raise the
Percheron or Belgian horse. A leading Illinois breeder was offered a Shire
stallion delivered in New York for 800 dollars, and represented to be as good
as any in England."[5] Fortunately, this man knew Truman and knew what a
Shire was. He came to England and paid 340 guineas for a good one at Peterborough. Of course, a few bad hats could still spoil the market, if they could
get a pedigree weed through the American veterinary inspection. Others claimed
that the Percheron was taking what should have been the British share of the
market because it was *cheaper*. Certainly a really useful Percheron stallion could
be bought in France for far less than a horse of equal position in the British
rankings. For every man who could afford a good British horse, there were five
who could afford only a Percheron (so the argument ran). The Percheron's
service fees were inevitably lower, because he had cost less. Five Percheron
stallions would therefore have much more than five times the number of mares
that came to the one Shire or Clydesdale in the district. It followed that next
year there would be six or seven times more men with half-bred Percheron
foals to sing the praises of.

One of the biggest Percheron importers, and certainly the most flamboyant,
was Frank Iams, the "Peaches and Cream" salesman. He had begun business in
1880 and, before trade ceased in the 'nineties, had offered British horses as well.
But now it was only Percherons or Belgians. Every year the Wells Fargo
Pacific Express laid on a special train to take 200 of these stallions from New
York to St. Paul, Nebraska. He claimed he sold stallions "so good and big at

$1,000 and $1,400 (few higher)" that it was pointless to buy a dearer one. His advertisements warned "Don't be buncoed by con-salesmen, grafters or knockers".[6] Yet it was not Iams, but too much hair, which they did not want to clean and which produced the abhorred grease if they didn't clean it, that really knocked the Shire in the States.

As has been suggested, the Clydesdale was also in trouble in America, though not to so great a degree. Alexander Galbraith, still maintaining the principle of Lawrence Drew, was now President of the American Clydesdale Association. (We last met him as President of the American Shire Horse Assocation: Chapter VIII.5.) He was in no doubt about the reasons. When he first started business in the west, he found that the Clydesdale's legs and action produced a far better cross on under-sized and light-boned native mares than the Percheron, which was stout-built but had inferior legs. As years went on, however, and heavier horses were demanded, the Clydesdale lost weight and substance, whereas the French horses were gaining in these respects. The real answer was a good-quality Shire. He believed that "but for the excessive hair on their legs especially in more recent years, the Shires would have held a place in American opinion alongside the Percheron". He bitterly deplored the loss of size and substance in the Clydesdale caused by the show-yard fashion in his native Scotland of concentrating on good "underpinning". If anyone in the heavy-horse business knew what he was talking about, it was Alex Galbraith.

From 1902, the Shire Society offered two gold medals at each of three North American Shows – the International Horse Show, Chicago (which had been founded in the year the Civil War ended) and Winnipeg and Toronto. The mare medal at Winnipeg could not be awarded for the absurd reason that the "winner", Brandon Georgina, was not in the English Stud-book: nor, being Canadian-bred, could she be entered, since under the Society's Bye-Law 36 no animal could be registered unless bred in the U.K. It had occurred to no one, in drawing up the rules for gold medals, that sooner or later a pure-bred foal would be produced abroad worthy to win an award. The rule was immediately changed so that animals registered in the American or the Canadian Shire Stud-books could be eligible, but this was too late for Georgina. The two Chicago winners (the first since the 1893 offer) were bred at Southgate and Enfield. In 1904, "Mr. Clydesdale", Alex Galbraith himself, won the Winnipeg Shire stallion medal with Rockingham II, a Derbyshire-bred chestnut.

King Edward and Lord Rothschild in 1906 sent a consignment of Shires to the United States for exhibition, in the hope of arousing more interest in the breed. They included the latter's 1905 London champion stallion, Girton Charmer, who was chosen for his moderation of hair and high quality, and Blythwood Guelder Rose, reserve champion mare in 1903 and at the head of the 16.0–16.2 class in 1905 at the age of ten – a mare of great wearing quality which in the days of her youth could get no higher than Highly Commended. Both these stayed on as settlers. In 1908 the Wisconsin State Fair was allotted two gold medals. In the following year Iowa, Minnesota and Calgary had one

each. In 1910 Brandon was offered one medal and Illinois two, making nine
shows altogether. Gold medals, silver medals from 1911 and, by 1913, gold
cups valued at £50, were being sent round the world in an endeavour to achieve
the popularity that an excess of hair on the legs was much more effectively
denying the Shire horse.

The most interesting of the American winners of Shire awards was the
recipient of the 1912 Chicago stallion medal. This was Lockinge Hengist,
bred at Lady Wantage's stud in 1908. He was by Lockinge Forester, a full
brother to Lockinge Forest King and one year younger, and was out of a mare
by Markeaton Royal Harold, the 1897 London champion. At the Lockinge
sale of Forester's sons and daughters on 13th October 1909, he was sold to John
Byron of Beckingham (Gainsborough) for 72 guineas. Mr. Byron showed him
as a four-year-old in London, where he stood fourteenth and won a commended
card and £1. John Truman bought him and showed him in November at
Chicago, where he was grand champion Shire stallion and S.H.S. gold medal
winner. He then sold him to George J. Stoll of Chestnut, Illinois, for $11,500,
which remained a record price for a Shire in the United States. It was not just
the wizardry of John Truman that brought about this astonishing rise in
Hengist's fortunes, nor even the lower standard of competition then to be
found on the other side of the Atlantic. There were two other reasons. In the
first place, the 1912 four-year-old class in London was the best ever seen, as the
reader may remember – Hengist could have been a class-winner if he had
appeared in, say, 1892. Secondly, Lockinge Forest King's full brother did not
get his foals quite so hairy, and Hengist was certainly deficient in that respect
in the eyes of the London judges. A London man's commended was a Chicago
man's champion – and, it may be added, by the time he walked into the Union
Stock-yard in that city he had lost even some of the hair he had possessed
before. (Lockinge Horsa, incidentally, by the same sire and of the same age,
was bought at the same 1909 sale by S. Weller of Tiverton, for 50 guineas.
His maximum success was to become champion of Devon.) At the next
Chicago show, there were 116 Shire stallions and fifty-eight mares competing
for the £50 gold cups. A Cornish-bred two-year-old, Bocadden Hereford,
won the stallion cup, and the nine-year-old roan Coldham Surprise from
Wisbech took the cup for mares.

Argentina's "John Truman" was Ernest Drabble of Buenos Aires, whose
whole-hearted efforts to popularise the Shire there were acknowledged in 1904
by his being elected an honorary member of the Shire Society – the first since
Edward VII. The Argentinians had their own Shire stud-book and in the seven
Palermo shows (1908–1914) for which gold medals and, later, gold cups were
sent from London, only two of the fourteen winning animals were English-
bred. It is pleasant to find Shires with such names as Merlin de la Guardia.
Very many of the exhibitors who won these awards were members of the
English society, as well as of their own. M. A. Martinez de Hoz was frequently
in London and he won the first stallion gold medal at the Palermo Show with

an Argentina-bred horse bearing the traditional Fens name Honest Tom. B. G. Paz joined as a life member in 1908 but, when the gold cups came along in 1913, it was his executors who took the mare cup two years in succession. Carlos Olaguer was another very successful Shire man who joined the original Society as a life-member. Ernest Drabble himself and his brother also did well, but they gave their horses, *anglicé*, such names as Drabble Model, or Drabble Charming Lad. At the 1912 show at Palermo (1912 was a significant year everywhere) one stallion was sold for £628. In 1913, thirty-five stallions and four mares competed for the Shire Gold Cup, and in 1914, thirty-one stallions and nine mares. Between 1901 and 1914, 628 pedigree Shires were imported from England. Uruguay and Chile between them imported a further eighteen to South America.

The fourth and last country to have its own stud-book for Shires was Australia, where the great horse States were Queensland, New South Wales and Victoria. But imports were really very few during this period, except in 1911 and 1912, when they numbered sixty-three and sixty: in the other twelve years up to the war they totalled another sixty-eight only. However, in the past – that is, twenty or more years earlier, when no records were preserved – there had been a steady stream of immigrants. Importers had generally retained these in studs in order to propagate more or less pure strains for entry in the stud-book: thence in greater numbers their progeny had performed the task of adding weight to the local horses. The Society gave gold medals in 1912 to the Royal Agricultural Societies both of Victoria and New South Wales, the former being offered the splendid new gold cups in 1913–1914. In the 1913 Victoria show, a Derbyshire-bred stallion beat thirteen others and a Fen-bred daughter of Lockinge Forest King won the cup in a field of seven.

A gold medal offered to the R.A.S. of Tasmania in 1914 was won by Quarrington Chatsworth for Lewis Oppenheim of Latrobe, and the same horse continued winning the Shire medal until 1921. It was the boast of all keen horse-men in the north-west of the island that Oppenheim's fine horse had been bred by one Sir Joseph Quarrington of Chatsworth Park, England. They were unaware that someone else occupied this property. It was in fact the Duke of Devonshire himself who bred him, in 1910. As Victor Cavendish, M.P., at Holker Hall, Cark-in-Cartmel, he had also bred the sire and dam. The horse had been sold as a foal to Fred Ward and his son Walter at Quarrington, near Sleaford, whence came his name.

(As it turned out, he was the last pure-bred Shire stallion ever imported from England into Tasmania, since post-war imports were all Clydesdales, resulting in a genuine blend of the two varieties in the 'thirties. But he did well, living and covering mares until 1935. And his best son, *Dictator* (out of an unregistered Shire mare) was used, until his death in 1947, as a stock horse by Clayton Pegus of Mount Hicks, in the Burnie district.)

Tasmanian and other Australian heavy-horses in the last years before mechanisation presented a curious and fascinating blend of bloods, from which the New Zealanders had drawn in their turn. For example, in the 1901–1914 period, there was a large number of "Shires" in New Zealand descended from *King of the Ring*, reputed to be the best Shire stallion in Tasmania before being sold to cross the sea for 1,000 guineas. And he had been sired by an old horse called *Bay Thumper*, who had come from Warwickshire in the 'seventies, and did service near Melbourne before sailing across the Bass Strait. The Australian daughters of a *Lincolnshire Hero* (which *Hero*, it is impossible to tell) were also sold in some numbers to become the basis of New Zealand stock.

The Boer War of 1899–1902, for which 70,000 horses were bought in the United Kingdom, had seen a large number of Shires, in teams of six, drawing heavy guns. In 1912, the Hon. Sir David Graaf, Bart, Minister of Public Works, ordered eighteen Shire stallions for service in the Union. This was a flash in the pan in a curious year when everything seemed to happen, for South Africa was scarcely suitable territory for the breed. Much more permanent appeared to be the steady trade with Russia, which in 1903–1914 took 266 pedigree Shire stallions, and Germany, which imported 307 between 1897 and 1914. The Germans were interested in short-legged, thick horses up to 16-hands, and paid moderate prices. The end of this trade came soon, and had nothing to do with hair.

From 1903–1914, to the chagrin of the English breeders, Clydesdale exports were regularly more numerous than those of Shires. But in the last few years both began to drop alarmingly, owing to narrow tops and feathery bottoms respectively. The Shire men contented themselves with arguing that the home market was large and safe, which it still appeared to be, while the foreign demand was fickle.

One branch of the export trade, however, which Shire men viewed with disfavour was that involving old and worn-out horses for slaughter on the Continent. In 1898 a deputation from the R.S.P.C.A. had waited on the President of the Board of Agriculture. As a result, an Exportation of Horses Order had come into operation on 1st January 1899. This made it unlawful to export any horse which owing to age, infirmity, illness, injury, fatigue or any other reason could not be conveyed without cruelty. It also laid down a standard of fittings and accommodation in the ships. However, it had been comparatively ineffective and in 1910, the Shire, Hunter and Polo Pony societies urged the Government to do something about it. Unfortunately there was a public uproar as a result, which some described as "morbid and senti-mental" on the grounds that the road journey to hunt kennels in England was as bad as the walk to the docks. It was also claimed that farmers could ill afford to lose the £5 or £6 that continental buyers offered. But neither of these arguments was to the point, whereas the conditions of the sea-journey were. However, nothing more was done. In 1913, 26,051 of these aged and decrepit animals were sent to Belgium, and 17,886 to Holland.

In the same year, Germany imported from England of all breeds fifty-four stallions, 1,517 mares and 2,575 geldings. These were neither decrepit nor aged, and were intended for purposes which were soon to amaze the innocent exporters.

II. THE AUGUST SUN

Like Aaron in the wilderness with his golden calf, the Shire men had fashioned four hairy legs and said "These be thy gods, O Israel". However, lest their idolatry should have assumed too prominent a place in the narrative of these golden years, we must conclude by emphasising the enormous progress made in orthodoxy as well – the freedom of the best breeding stock from hereditary disease and of the ordinary working cart gelding from unsoundness; improved conformation, more weight and size; and better management in country and town. The expansion of the methods by which these things were encouraged is best summarised in the table which follows at the end of this chapter.

Light-horse breeding, meanwhile, was now even deeper in the mire than it had been at any time since it had first ceased to bring a profit, in the last two Victorian decades. Motor cars were now something more than a mere threat, and the motor-bus and taxi were steadily following the electric tram in cutting off the market for the misfits. There were mares, but no one would breed from them. Even the army was buying mostly American "range-bred" horses, the product of natural and indiscriminate matings on the great pastures of the new world. They were so cheap that dealers made a fat profit when selling them at £40 to buyers from the Remounts Department, who often did not realise that they were taking animals that the U.S. cavalry would not touch. What attraction was there for farmers, even if it were decided to subsidise them, to breed for a market which needed only 1,500 to 2,000 remounts a year? The light-horse seemed doomed, whereas the chief menace to the heavy one seemed to be the steam lorry.

One other point is worth making. Though the number of nobility and gentry who actively supported the improvement of the cart-horse was still growing, it is possible to detect already, in the composition of the Shire Council, a broadening of the basis on which the Society rested. Affairs were no longer completely dominated by the great and the wealthy, and many more working farmers, mostly tenants, were playing a leading part. It would be invidious to examine the individual pedigrees or status of the thirty elected members of the Council in 1901 and of their successors in 1914 to prove it, but there had been a shift. It was but slight, for in addition to the ex-officio twelve most recent past-presidents, the Duke of Devonshire, Lord Middleton and Lord Hothfield were all in 1914 ordinary elected councillors. Yet they were no mere Shire-proprietors. The enthusiasm of the first was phenomenal. And the two barons, both born in 1844, would have been successful Shire men even if they had both been sons of tenant farmers, perhaps finding difficulty in persuading Dad to become a pedigree man, instead of one a Willoughby and the other a Tufton, and both Etonians. Lord Middleton once went to watch a pair of his horses

3. Major and Royal, black Shire geldings weighing one ton each and standing 17.3 hands high. These two, aged five and six, won first prize in the Pairs class at the National Shire Show in 1975. The horse tradition at Daniel Thwaites and Company of Blackburn lapsed in 1927. It was re-started in 1960 by David Kay, later to be the youngest-ever President of the Shire Horse Society. When David Clarkson (shown here alongside the coachman, Eric Longson) was taken on in 1965, he had never driven a horse. Yet he became coachman in 1970 and, in 1975, head horsekeeper – at 33, probably the youngest in the British Isles.

4. Watney Shires, Command and Sovereign, photographed in 1974 outside their stables at West Bergholt, near Colchester. The record of one of the constituent companies, Mann, Crossman and Paulin Limited, at the Shire Shows in London before the Second World War, when A. E. Leech was Stables Superintendent, was outstanding. (See page 689.) In 1975, Watney Mann Limited disposed of their horses, which were purchased by Mr. Leslie E. Mills of Barretts Farm, Dedham, Essex. John Peacock (driving in this picture) remained with the brewery, but Richard Wright, also pictured, joined Mr. Mills as head horseman. With two other ex-Watney geldings, Royal and Majestic, they won the Pairs turn-out class, at the first attempt, at the 1976 National Shire Horse Show.

ploughing stubble, and remarked to a boy he saw there that they were fine specimens. The boy, just taken on to the staff, agreed with this obviously earnest stranger, but when the latter said he was proud to say he owned them, he warned him, "By gum, mister, Lord Middleton would kick thy arse if he heard thee say that". And it was not the farm-boy who told the story later at a dinner.

In 1914, old Frederic Street had been dead these four years. Latterly in his life, he had been howled down more than once at meetings of that same Farmers' Club where he had first proposed an association for Shire-breds. Members objected to his asking what was going to happen about food in England "when a European war comes, as it is sure to come".[7] Of all Shire members, he would have been the least surprised that eventually John Slough-grove with a sigh picked up a patriotic pen and expunged from the list of corporate members the name *Verband für die Zucht des schweren Arbeitspferdes in der Provinz Sachsen*, Kaiserstrasse 7, Halle a Saale.

Comparative table of
MEMBERS, REGISTRATIONS OF MARES, LONDON AND OTHER SHOW STATISTICS
in 1891, 1901 and 1914

	Ref. to notes	1891	1901	1914
No. of paid-up members		1,791	3,029	4,199
No. of affiliated socs.		9	160	305
STUD-BOOK				
No. of mares, latest volume	(a)	2,578	3,994	3,418
No. of mares to date		10,909	34,518	73,164
LONDON SHOW				
No. of classes: s. – mares – gldgs		6–5–0	7–7–3	7–7–3
No. of entries	(b)	475	667	719
Value of awards (excl. challenge cups)		£854	£1,537	£2,195
No. of animals winning prizes		47	103	347
No. of other animals H.C. or C.		103	144	13
total	(c)	—— 150	—— 247	—— 360
Breeder's prizes: £10 and g. medal		—	—	2
£10		—	14	12
£5		—	44	101
total	(d)	—— —	—— 58	—— 115
Auction: no. of horses sold		136	217	165
Auction gross receipts (S.H.S. took 5%)		£10,159	£19,030	£21,612
Trade stand receipts		£186	£278	£331
Gate receipts (gen. public)		£496	£395	£523
Gross expenditure		£2,411	£3,197	£3,577

	Ref. to notes	1891	1901	1914
ROYAL SHOW				
Prizes for foals and yrlg fillies		—	—	£100
Gold medals		2	2	2
£5 breeders' prize to g.m. winners		—	2	2
ROYAL ULSTER SHOW		—	—	£10
OTHER BRITISH SHOWS (1891–1901–1913)	(e)			
Number receiving S.H.S. medals		—	168	281
Gold medals awarded		—	26	44
£5 breeder's prizes	(f)	—	22	35
Silver medals awarded		—	159	248
£1 breeder's prizes	(f)	—	—	158
OVERSEAS SHOWS (1891–1901–1913)	(e)			
Number receiving S.H.S. medals		—	—	23
£50 gold cups		—	—	8
gold medals		—	—	12
silver medals		—	—	20
TOWN CART HORSE PARADES				
Number receiving S.H.S. awards		1	15	19
Awards (s.m. or premium or both)		20	75	87
SOCIETY'S RESERVE FUND	(g)	£4,743	£9,958	£18,998

NOTES

(a) The number of stallions registered (500–811–891) is obviously a less reliable guide to progress than the number of mares.

(b) In 1914, absentees kept the number below the 700 L.C.C. maximum.

(c) These totals are the figures to remark. Their increase was not due to more money being allowed for prizes. On the contrary, the standard required to achieve a commended card was higher in 1901 than in 1891, and in 1914 than in 1901.

(d) These figures show the prizes offered. Those actually awarded were fewer, owing to the breeder being dead or a non-member.

(e) In 1914, many August and autumn shows were cancelled. For fair comparison, the 1913 figures have been used.

(f) The breeder's prizes *offered* corresponded to the number of medals. These figures show those actually awarded to breeders who were members of S.H.S. in the year of award.

(g) 1914 figure is nominal. Funded property had depreciated since purchase. Real value only about £14,960.

CHAPTER X

1914–1920

The Great War Boom

I. 1914: CARNAGE AND THE IMPORTANCE OF PEDIGREE

ON August Bank Holiday, 1914 at the Meynell Hunt Show, Rea Queen of the Forest won the Shire gold medal for Arthur Sanders, of Stenson, home of that celebrated stallion owner of long ago, Mr. Stych. The normal weekday inhabitants of 12 Hanover Square were out and away, enjoying the brilliant sunshine. The Royal Agricultural Hall, in its off-season, was deserted. The British Army owned 25,000 horses.

Two days later, the 11th County of London Rifles took over the Hall and, on village greens and in hotel yards all over the kingdom, motley collections of horses were assembled for inspection by military buyers, who worked so fast that in twelve days they had acquired 140,000 animals. No one who saw, or took part in, these biggest and most sudden sales of all time, in which every horse-owner in the land was potentially a compulsory vendor, ever forgot the day they were held in his parish. Otherwise, however, apart from the activity at the recruiting offices, and the news a fortnight later that the Expeditionary Force had landed in France, there was little outwardly to suggest in those glorious late summer days that this was a war to end the old way of life, that almost 1,000,000 tramping men from Britain and its Empire were to be killed, that 500,000 toiling horses bought by the British Army would meet a violent end or die prematurely or be mercifully put down to end their suffering. A few of the autumn agricultural shows were cancelled, but many were held. The Rifles left the Hall again to go to France and the usual round of shows there was able to re-start. The first shipload of horses purchased by the Remount Commission, which had been sent to America immediately on the declaration of war, docked in October.

In November, Sir Walter Gilbey died. He was mourned by the Hunter men, the Hackney men and the R.A.S.E., as well as by the Shire men, for he had been President of all four societies. He was mourned by the thousands who took an interest in the Cart Horse Parade, which he had founded, and indeed by men everywhere. But still he was eighty-three years of age, and when better for an old man to die, than at the beginning of the end of the old order of things? And was there not a new Sir Walter, his eldest son, on whose enthusiasm and support all the horse societies could count, as before? Except that he was now, in 1914, only fifty-five, one could say that the change would hardly be noticed. However, the war was suddenly grim. The British lost 12% of their animals by the end of December, chiefly in the retreat from Mons, the battle of the Marne and the first battle of Ypres. This was equivalent to an annual loss of 36% per annum. If the carnage had continued at that rate throughout the war, it would have been utterly impossible to replace horses at the speed required. The military effort would have completely collapsed because, although the opportunities for cavalry, important as they were, turned out to be very few, every other operation of war depended on light and heavy draught-horses, and this remained the case until the end, in spite of the rapid development of motor vehicles.

The finicky activities of a pedigree society might well have seemed irrelevant in those desperate circumstances. When horses were wanted in hundreds of thousands, what mattered their ancestry or their finer points? Yet all the draught-horses, English, American or Canadian, however plain, owed something to the work of the breed associations over the past thirty-five years. It was the Percheron, Shire or other pure-bred stallions who had got the vast majority of them and whose blood in some measure was to be found in the rest. If the civilised nations had decided upon such a war as this in 1880, instead of 1914, they could not have achieved it – they had enough men available for slaughter, but could not have supplied the horses. So now the hard work of the stud-book societies had at all costs to be continued. They had bred for peace, and their horses were being used for war. If the work of years was not to be wasted entirely, the effort had to be redoubled. The casualties of war must not be replaced by inferior stock: and, when the war should end, the world would no doubt look to Britain for the finest foundation mares and stallions to re-build its studs.

It was not to be regarded as a trivial matter, therefore, when Ratcliffe Friar 29772 was shown to have a wrong pedigree. He was not out of 50131 Farnfields Princess, but out of another *Princess*, a two-cross mare. He had no right to be in the Stud-book. Yet it was a little late to cancel his entry. He was now four, and had covered a large number of mares whose innocent owners thought they were using a pure-bred Shire stallion. So he was allowed to stay. And the breeder and owner escaped punishment only because it proved impossible to lay the blame on either of them for what appeared to be a genuine mistake.

2. 1915: ALARMS AT HANOVER SQUARE: THE AMERICAN DRAFTER

The King and Queen visited the Spring Show as usual. For the first time, there was no President to receive them. Sir Berkeley Sheffield had been on active service for seven months, and so Lord Northbourne, the President-Elect, deputised. He was also appointed as Shire representative on a R.A.S.E. committee to assist French and Belgian agriculture when the war ended. The Shire Society donated 250 guineas to the fund. The Bath and West Society only managed 100.

The Shire men very nearly lost their home this year. The International Horse Shows Limited had of course abandoned any thoughts of Olympia, and many of the splendid horses that had last appeared there in June 1914 were now officers' chargers or doing other military duties. But an office had to be maintained, and the directors were not enamoured of their position as sub-tenants of the Shire Society. They gave notice in March that they would quit at the end of September. It must be confessed that the Shire men had done well out of the arrangements. The house had rarely cost them more than £120 a year, and in 1913 rent and maintenance was only £843, and rents received had amounted to £1,014. Even after paying the hall porter, this left them rent-free masters of the house.

But by now the Shire Council was not so happy either. The British Dairy Farmers' Association had quit the third floor at Christmas 1913 and it had been impossible to find suitable new tenants, because the R.A.S.E. had put on a restrictive covenant that the house should be used only by "kindred societies". If now the International left, the Hackney Society and the Cart Horse Parade Society would have to follow. Even Frank Euren, who was secretary of all three, could hardly trot from one house to another to attend to his various business. And the Guernsey Cattle Society would go too, because their secretary was on Euren's staff. This would reduce rent contributions to £370.

What was to be done? Even if R.A.S.E. waived their restrictions on its use, the house was scarcely suitable for business purposes. There was no lift, the sanitary arrangements were inadequate for anything but a sort of family-life and there was the problem of the hall porter. Any business house would expect to remain open until 6 or 7 in the evening. One porter could not manage the extra time and on security grounds the front door could not be left open and unattended. Sloughgrove, with the approval of H. H. Smith Carington, the new chairman of the Finance Committee, gave all the other tenants notice to quit and an emergency committee decided to ask the R.A.S.E. to cancel the sub-lease. After considering the possibility of all the societies migrating en masse to a new home, it was decided instead to search for a suite of offices for the Shire and Hunter societies and their associated smaller friends.

Meanwhile, committees and councils of the other large societies met in frantic haste. The small ones, such as the Sussex cattle, the Southdown sheep and the Large Black Pigs, could merely wring their hands and look on. What-ever species they represented, they would all be forced like little lambs to follow Mary. However, the folly of moving at all soon became apparent. On 4th May, at a meeting attended by twenty-four delegates and the five most important secretaries, they all decided to remain for at least five years, but under new conditions. The Shire dictatorship was done away with. A House Committee of four, representing the Shire Society (whose delegate was to be chairman), the Shorthorn Society, the Hunter and Pony group and the International and Hackney group was to administer affairs. The Shorthorn Society took over most of the vacant third floor as well as the second, and was to pay £300 a year; the International and Hackney were to pay £225; the Shire and the Hunter and Pony group each to pay £150. Of the smaller societies, the Guernsey rent was fixed at 11 guineas: the Sussex and the Southdown each

£10; the Large Black Pigs 9 guineas; the Cart Horse Parade 7 guineas; and the miscellaneous (who they were, it is now doubtful) were to pay £1. 13s. od. If anyone suspected the Shire Society had used its fat rents to send silver medals to Manawatu or Macleod, or to reward the cart-horses of Bolton or Bootle, he could now be content. A separate banking account under the control of a joint committee pleased everyone, and life went on much as before. The Hackney share of their group's £225 was £80, and included the 8 guineas usually paid for a little bit of freehold property owned by the Shire Society at the rear of the house, and this was to be passed on by the committee to the Shire men.

The most successful of all Shire exhibitors, Baron Rothschild of Tring, died on 31st March but in death he did almost as much for the breed as in life, for the dispersal sale on 21st October scattered his marvellous animals all over England. The prices, it is almost superfluous to mention, set up a record. Forty-seven animals (thirty-two males and fifteen females) made an average of over £564, even though eighteen of them were untried colts and six were half-grown fillies. Tom Fowler, the genius of a manager who had made the stud such a success, had not been forgotten. He took over as tenant, and among the horses that went to him instead of being put up for sale were old Birdsall Menestrel, London champion in 1904 and 1907 and reserve champion no less than four times, and his daughter Cattlegate Rose, a great brood mare. By an odd coincidence, Tring was to remain as famous in the Shire world as it had ever been because of another stud which had fast been coming into prominence, at the other end of town. J. G. Williams at Pendley Manor and his manager, Harry Bishop, had an entirely different philosophy, and kept only mares, but the stud was soon to be as formidable in the show-ring as Tring Park had ever been.

Horses and mules from America were now pouring into England at the rate of 15,000 a month. The British Remount Commission, trading only with well-known and reputable dealers, was faced with a gigantic task in delivering the animals they bought. From the sale yard in, say, Des Moines or Kansas City horses had to be collected in a nearby depot where they were malleined for glanders and otherwise sorted out into "shippers" and the unfit. When a train-load of from 300 to 600 had been assembled, off they would go. The U.S. authorities allowed no horse to travel continuously for more than thirty-six hours, so there would be a wait of a day or two along the line at another specially constructed depot. Here the consignment was examined again, after which most would proceed and a few would be held back. At last, after a week or more, the majority arrived at the embarkation point. At some stage on the train journey, at least 70% contracted "shipping fever", a sort of influenza which frequently led to pneumonia or other lung troubles. The disease was caught in dealers' yards or from the railway vans, which all became so infected that real sanitation became impossible. The illness was apparent at once in some cases, but only after weeks in others. In order to avoid the disaster of its spread on board ship, all horses were kept at the embarkation depot for a minimum of seven weeks before sailing. At last, the readiest thousand or so at the last halting place began the close-confined sea-journey in dark and stifling conditions. Their eventual release from their ammonia-reeking quarters was a blessed escape for both animals and men. Then began the process, all over again, of recovery, feeding-up and veterinary attention in England. Ultimately came the final short sea-journey at dead of a moonless night.

Of the animals' toughness there is no doubt. American cavalry or other light-horses – at least, those available for purchase – were scarce and, for the most part, highly unsuitable. It was the draughters which were the success, and their numbers seemed inexhaustible. Though all were the result of the crossing of heavy European stallions on light American mares, there were three official categories. The light artillery horse was from 15.2- to 16-hands and weighed about 1,200 lb.: short in the leg and back, and strong. The best were chiefly from Iowa and Illinois, half-bred Percherons being more numerous than all the rest together. Heavy artillery horses comprised the other two classifications, with minimum weights of 1,400 and 1,500 pounds. Amongst these, the Percheron-type again predominated, the heavier ones having three-quarters blood, and the Shire-type came a rather poor second. Of really heavy-horses there was a great scarcity, though more were available in the later years. For these rarer creatures Iowa and Illinois were again, with Canada, the best centres.

The ubiquitous Percheron-type gained tremendous popularity with those who used them in France. In the first cross, it was the produce of small western mares weighing only from 800 to 1,000 lb. It was generally considered that, if fed and reared as they would have been on English farms, these young animals would mature at 1,400 to 1,500 lb.; but they were just allowed to grow naturally on native pastures and normally finished at no more than 1,200. The mares among them, put again to Percheron stallions, produced three-quarter foals which grew to about 1,300 to 1,500 lb. The natural robustness of the Percheron, his power to stamp his qualities on his progeny (similar to the prepotency, among light-horses, of the Arab), the hardiness of the little non-descript dams and the conditions under which their progeny grew, all contributed to an amazingly uniform strength and fortitude in the face of every conceivable kind of misery. They had no beauty, but they were not bought for their looks. By the end of the year they formed a high proportion of the 660,000 horses and mules that were on the books of the British Director of Remounts.

In England, as many mares as could be bred from were put to the horse, though no one really expected the war could last until 1921, when the first crop of war-time foals would reach the age of five. The task of the breed societies was to see that pedigree stock and intelligent breeding were kept up in the confusion of the times and, furthermore, that eligible animals actually were registered. In both respects, the Shire Society did well. Seven hundred stallions and 3,409 mares were registered during the course of the year – only

264 and 200 fewer, in spite of all pre-occupations of the breeders' minds, than the average for the preceding three years. Shire medals were given at the few shows held, including the Royal – gold ones at nine shows and silver ones at sixty-two, compared with forty-one and 241 in 1913. Just two Cart Horse Parades took place, at Bolton and Oldham. John Sloughgrove lost two of his staff, Roche and Tilley, to the army and struggled on with Messrs. Charlton, Wickison, Holland and a junior. By the end of the year, 315 new members had joined the Society since the outbreak of war and only 266 had dropped out. Even more encouragingly, 228 mare-owners had applied for a prefix in the same seventeen month period.

3. 1916: THE DEATH OF SLOUGHGROVE: ARMY HORSES: THE FRENCH BREED

So many stallion-leaders now had horse jobs in the army that urgent representations were made by the Shire Council to Lord Derby's Committee for the temporary release, from April to the end of June, of as many as possible. Some men were freed, but not enough, and the stallion-owners were in great difficulties. Gold medals were given at seven shows and silver ones at forty-three. But these were the last that John Sloughgrove administered. On Friday 3rd November he was knocked down by a cab in Oxford Street. When he regained consciousness in Bart's Hospital, his first enquiry was whether he could attend the Council meeting the following Tuesday. In thirty-three years and three months this originally unwilling recruit to the Cart Horse Society had never missed one such occasion. He died on the Monday and his great friend and assistant, A. B. Charlton, recorded in rather grisly fashion that this enabled him to maintain his 100% record.

Sloughgrove was a man who despised publicity, believed absolutely in the superiority of the Shire over all other horses, and strove only to perfect the work of the organisation which he served. One President, at the end of his year of office, had described the Society as "a democratic institution under a benevolent autocracy". Others, less elaborately, had said that S.H.S. stood for "Sloughgrove's Horse Society". It was appropriate that its official representative at his funeral was the new Sir Walter Gilbey, son of the man who had bullied John into the job in 1883. Charlton, assistant secretary since 1891, took over and was allowed to continue as secretary of the Hunter organisation also, but resigned as National Pony Society secretary in favour of F. H. Badge, one of his Hunter staff.

316 new Shire members, 216 new prefixes, Stud-book entries of 830 stallions and 3,528 mares (130 and 119 more than the year before) suggested that the pedigree movement was not suffering, after all, from the war. But owing to the paper shortage, all the information was going to have to be crammed into 788 Stud-book pages compared with the 1,224 page volume that had appeared early in the year. Frederic Babbage of Mornington Crescent, who had photographed the champions since 1899, died in the spring, soon after the show.

797,174 horses filled the register of the Director of Remounts, who since March had been supplying animals to the Belgian army as well as to Empire troops in France. The idea of actually allowing the veterinary service to have any say whatever in the management of horses in war had never occurred to anyone before 1914, and the results of this innovation were now clear. In the Boer War, the annual mortality of horses on the British side was 55%. In 1912, when there was no war, the total wastage was 14.8%. From the outbreak of war until December 1916, in spite of the numbers involved having been multiplied by thirty-two, and of enemy guns, hazardous sea crossings and the general conditions of warfare, the wastage was less still, at only 13%. On the Western front alone it was just under 10% (9.47% in 1916). In West Africa it was 9.09%. In France and Flanders, the most serious troubles were mange, respiratory diseases and ophthalmia, together with galls, bad shoeing, and simple exhaustion and starvation.

The British public had no idea of the amazing achievements of those concerned with the management and welfare of army horses, but Lloyd George came under fire in the Commons about the sale of unfit animals, particularly in the East. Colonel Lockwood (Epping) said that those who subscribed £150,000 to the R.S.P.C.A. appeal fund for the care of sick horses would not be pleased to know that, having been nursed, they were often sold. But the Minister of Munitions (this was just before he became Prime Minister in the Coalition Government) managed to turn away wrath, adding that he had had a letter from an old lady who reminded him that, when he departed this life and applied to enter the celestial regions, it would be a good thing for him to have the support and suffrages of all the broken down horses he had saved from suffering. "Hear, hear", cried pious members of the Lower House. From then on, there was increased care to slaughter unfit horses, and none at all were allowed to be cast and sold to oriental gentlemen for civilian work: only in Western Europe could that be done.

Towards the end of the year, there were plenty of stout Shire men who frightened their wives by a sudden roar of anger and dismay at what they read in the agricultural Press. "While we're fighting the damned Hun, they're going to bring in a bloody French horse." Indeed they were. The part-bred Percheron from the States had so captured the hearts of many on active service, that it was proposed to import a couple of pure-bred Percheron stallions and a few mares from France itself. The thing was ominous, for it was not as if this country, like America, was full of hundreds of thousands of little no-breed mares that were good for nothing except to be graded up. This was only the second instance, since the formation of stud and herd and flock books, of a foreign breed of animal being imported. Hundreds of thousands of "Dutch" cattle – a term as vague as the "Flemish" horse – had been imported during the nineteenth century to supply some of the milk requirements of a growing population. But imports had been prohibited since 1892 owing to pleuro-pneumonia on the Continent. However, a shipment of pedigree animals was arranged by the five-year-old British Frisian Cattle Society in 1914, and arrived only three days before the war. Now, during the war, this further affront to British pride was deliberately organised – and by Lord Lonsdale, of all men!

4. 1917: A FRENZIED YEAR

On the first day of the new year, the Food Production Department of the Board of Agriculture was formed, and so farming, after all, was now only two years behind other industries of national importance in achieving any sort of status or priority. The Board had been originally set up only to cope with the negative task of controlling pests and diseases, of administering tithe, and so on, but now at last was enabled to formulate and even enforce a proper farming policy. The farmer faced increased calls upon his productive capacity with depleted staffs and horses, and, equally incommoding, in face of a great shortage of civilian blacksmiths, wheelwrights, harness makers and other ancillary tradesmen. A bewildering number of authorities now controlled his working life. The Minister of Munitions decided what machinery and implements he could have: the Minister of Food dictated the feeding-stuffs supply: replacement labour was controlled by the War Office, the Home Office or the Ministry of National Service, dependent on whether it consisted of soldiers or prisoners, interned aliens, or civilians. But at any rate the farmer was now given a channel of communication, through local Executive Committees and the Food Production Department, with these strange overlords. That was a help. Yet the first "help" given to agriculture in 1917 was the calling-up of 30,000 farm workers.

Another war-time body, the Railway Executive Committee, withdrew cheap rates of travel for horses before the Shire Show but promised to get animals to the London termini as best they could. They supplied no cartage facilities and Charlton at short notice had to improvise a system of his own to get grooms' boxes to the Hall. In this, he had the willing help of A. J. Baker, the forage man. At the Annual Meeting, the second absentee President was elected in the person of the Prince of Wales, who could not be prised away from the front, though those responsible for his safety would have preferred to see him incongruously seated in the leather armchair at No. 12. Ten days after the Show, the death of H. H. Smith Carington deprived the Society of a worthy successor to the first Sir Walter as Finance Committee chairman and general Shire enthusiast. His Ashby Folville stud had been his chief hobby and in recent years he had given enormous prices for Shire stallions – for example, 3,950 guineas for three at the dispersal sale at Tring Park and 3,000 guineas for Norbury Menestrel at that of Leopold Salomons three months later. He paid gladly because he hoped they would bring a benefit to his part of Leicestershire, and particularly to his own tenants. At the age of sixty-five, his loss may be regarded as particularly severe and premature. Apart from his two years, the finances of the Society were guarded for sixty-two years by the elder and, from now on, by the younger Gilbey.

In March, the Royal Flying Corps took over the Hall. John Buchan, the manager (unrelated to the novelist) had had little to do in the past twelve months because so many regular shows there had been cancelled. But, now that he was made secretary to the company as well, he was able to fill in part of the otherwise completely empty days by running all over London from one Government department to another trying to discover some official who was important enough to pay the rent. He occupied some of the rest of his time by being editor, publisher, advertisement agent, chief reporter and sole salesman of the *Islington Volunteer Gazette*. (He was Company quartermaster-sergeant.) He had to give up his gazette when he could obtain no more paper, but getting the rent was an absorbing occupation. Aeroplanes came in and out of the Hall by the dozen every day.

Stallion-leaders were even more difficult to find this year, as were men competent to foal down mares, though a few were reluctantly released for a few months by the army, which was having its own troubles. Lieutenant H. C. Harper (in peace time, managing director of the Crystal Palace horse show and honorary secretary since its formation in 1904 of the London Van Horse Parade Society) wrote *Hints on Horses* for the benefit of the increasing number of emergency transport drivers whose sole previous experience of animal care had been confined to their dog, cat or canary at home. The supply of horsemen of military age had dried up.

In May the Society, together with the Shorthorn men, pointed out to the Board of Agriculture that the indiscriminate ploughing up of pastures would be disastrous, since their function was to feed fat bullocks and grow horses. (The Government aimed at ploughing up an extra 2,000,000 acres or so, which meant extra horse-work, with less space to grow young ones on.) At the same time, the London Cart Horse Parade Society, though otherwise of course inactive, speaking in the name of the Borough Councils, Corporations and principal horse-users of the metropolis, called upon the Government to do much more to encourage horse-breeding, since the shortage of heavy-horses for civilian use was alarming. The R.A.S.E., backed by every stud-book society, condemned the cessation of horse-racing as a threat to breeding, though the Prime Minister was no doubt surprised to find all the cart horse men among the complainants. In June an Order by the Food Production Department, prohibiting the sale of agricultural horses except under special licence, caused real dismay. In conjunction with the Clydesdale Society, very warm representations were at once made and Sir Arthur Lee, the Director-General, as well as the President of the Board himself, Mr. Prothero, were not slow in exempting both pedigree and other valuable horses and foals. For more ordinary horses, they promised that, where justified, licences would be promptly given by local committees. Though they could not absolutely withdraw the Order, it was far from their intention to hamstring the normal processes of horse-rearing, from "sucker sales" to the transfer of five-year-old geldings to the towns.

Army buyers were not now allowed to impress a farmer's horse, but this did not much matter because, after 1914, compulsory purchase had rarely been resorted to. Nor were they allowed to offer a farmer more than £75 for a voluntary sale. The Remount Department was now in fact handing over considerable numbers of semi-fit heavy-horses to the Board of Agriculture to try to make up the grave shortage on the land, and so for the first time in history the Government was the owner of horses, other than military ones. Whether they had ringbone, sidebone, chronic laminitis or anything else, they all had something. Yet they all managed to shuffle or skiffle across the fields of England. In addition, convalescent horses were transferred on loan for use in prisoners-of-war ploughing camps. When fully fit and conditioned again, they were taken back for service in France and replaced by others. At the bottom end of the scale, horses cast at home by the army for incurable lameness, blindness, broken wind or other debilities were finding a ready sale. Early in the war, they had fetched only knacker's prices. Now, even the slaughterer could give more because there was a market for their meat and a demand for their hides. And dealers were surprised by what they could sell for further work.

The British were full of admiration for the German veterinary arrangements, and the French asked why their own could not be organised like the British, which was placed in the hands of one man. They were thinking no doubt, of Colonel John Moore, Director of Veterinary Services, B.E.F. The French veterinary surgeons (who of course claimed that they were the best in the world) alleged they were subordinated to "useless parasites of so-called horse-men looking for a soft job and the glory of being an officer". However, as far as France is concerned, it is the excellent horse from Le Perche that worries us here, not the adequacy or otherwise of that country's army veterinary arrangements.

In America, the horse supply seemed inexhaustible. The activities of Captain John Blakeway at Columbia, Tennessee, were typical of the work done by the British buyers. Between 15th September 1916, when he arrived there, and early May 1917, when he left, 16,388 horses and mules had been bought at the stockyards, assembled in the concentration corrals and shipped to England, or else were ready to go. His first shipment of mules, 880 in number, had all been unloaded off the *Parisienne* in excellent shape. His last loads were twice that number of mules and a final batch of horses. The only contretemps in eight months, during which he and his wife had become extremely popular temporary citizens of Columbia, occurred just before he left. With a large force of men, he was driving 500 horses from the stockyards to the corrals when they stampeded in that sudden and simultaneous manner that is a speciality of their species. South High Street had never before been put in such confusion on a Saturday afternoon. However, when all was over, he still had 499 alive and only Alex McKay, a stockman, got hurt. This was a lucky escape, for the animals were a valuable lot, averaging $200 each and containing many of seven-eighths pure heavy blood, weighing 1,700 lb. to 1,800 lb. His next job was to buy as many as he could in a few months' stay at Kansas City, Missouri. And they would surely be needed, because now that the United States were entering the war, the British began handling horses for them also. By 1st October the British Army in France and England alone had lost 225,856 horses killed, missing, died or destroyed, with a further 30,348 cast. The French Army at home had lost the services altogether of 541,714.

On the domestic scene, the Royal Show had gone to the wall, but gold medals were given in March at the Peterborough Stallion Show and the Spalding and Montgomeryshire Shows in the autumn, and silver medals at twenty-six other shows, including pale shadows of the former great Peterborough and Royal Norfolk summer shows. A telephone extension was put in from the Hunter to the Shire offices, so that Charlton could be in both places at once. The staff was insured against air-raids at 10s.%, and received a 10% war bonus. The Articles of Association were altered so as to increase the elected members of Council to thirty-six and ensure a more uniform county representation. During the year, 259 prefixes were allotted to new men who had enough brood mares to make such a distinction worth while. 526 new members were elected, mostly tenant-farmers – a record, resulting in a net increase of 371. Stud-book entires, still increasing in spite of every difficulty, were up by twenty-three stallions and 461 mares, and the paper to print them all was bought a year in advance. The photographs of the champions were taken for the first time by G. H. Parsons of Alsager. The Secretary confidently reported that "The prosperity of the Society is an index to the well-being of the breed generally. As long as breeders continue to produce the heaviest and best of draught horses in the shape of the modern Shire, there will be little reason to fear the competition of the motor, the Percheron, or any other mechanical or foreign element." But, if those at home had only known, the British horse losses in France and Flanders were now again verging on the disastrous – 28% in the year and 10% in the last three months alone, chiefly owing to the heavy fighting at Vimy Ridge and Paschendaele and to night bombing. At the latter rate, if it had been the same in other theatres, it would have been necessary to buy a third of a million horses every year, just for British forces alone, which would have been impossible.

5. 1918: TRIUMPHANT CONCLUSION

Now that Islington was no longer available, Peterborough and Crewe repositories, and even Birmingham, were considered as sites for the Spring Show. But when Tattersalls offered the Park Paddocks at Newmarket to the four societies exiled from the Agricultural Hall, Mr. Prothero, President of the Board of Agriculture, advised that the Minister of Munitions and the Railway Executive Committee would be less likely to object to the shows being held at all if they were out of the way of the main munitions centres and if all the societies shared one allocation of timber, which was extremely scarce. So the offer was accepted and restricted shows for stallions only were arranged – the Shires on two days in the last week in February and the Hunters and Polo

Ponies, followed by the Hackneys, the following week. The two big societies paid £100 rent each and £225 towards alterations and reinstatement, and the Hackney Society paid £100 altogether.

A Shire Show, even a makeshift one, and even in the bleak days of February 1918, was of great national interest. The emaciated *Daily Sketch*, "the premier picture paper", next day devoted more than half the back page to six pictures of the Shire Show – "Mr. T. Forshaw with Rickford Coming King, winner of the Gold Challenge Cup": "Harboro' Nulli Secundus, reserve to him for the senior cup": "Speckington Victor Chief, a three year old, was led in by a soldier": "Lord and Lady Middleton attended" – of course, as he was President: "the little daughter of Mr. Richard Marsh, the King's trainer": and finally, a local stallion, who did not win a prize and appears to have caught the photographer's eye only because he was completely out of control. Most of the front page was taken up with "The Latest Outrage on the Red Cross" – the sinking of the *Glenart Castle* in the Bristol Channel, yet one more of the "unspeakable atrocities" and "crimes against humanity, for which the Huns must pay a heavy reckoning." Twenty-nine people saved and 153 missing and feared drowned. There were six photographs.

The rest of the news crammed into the remaining paper-allowance puts into perspective the prominence given to the Shire Show. "Germans again try to bridge the Yser" (foiled). "Surprise – 1,200 yards into the Hun positions". "Khaki mesmerises the Sinn Feiners" (bands and banners as 1,200 people ploughed the lawns at Lord Listowel's mansion). Litvinoff, the Bolshevik "ambassador" turned out of his "embassy" in Victoria Street by his landlord, who was commander of a special police division and had been hoodwinked into letting it to him. Amateur theatricals at Cambridge in aid of the Red Cross. The Land Girls' Club in Upper Baker Street. Mrs. Lloyd George at a working men's club concert at Kew. A picture of the King's meat card. Little Belgian refugees waiting, women teachers protesting, the Guernsey Light Infantry training. "Buy your fish at Liptons". "Make your hair beautiful with McClinton's Colleen Shampoo" (2d.). "Beat three ounces of margarine with milk, add a tablespoon of cornflour and spread it on your bread". "*The Silence of Elinor Grey* – begin this charming new love-story to-day". Railway companies were providing rope halters for their horses in London so that in an air-raid they could be taken out of the shafts and tied to a wheel. A millwright, on being fined £3 at Newcastle-on-Tyne for losing 190 hours of work in thirteen weeks, attacked the magistrate who "promptly threw him with a ju-jitsu trick", and had him handcuffed to a policeman, whereupon two bottles of beer were discovered in his pockets. It was rumoured that the price of whisky would be fixed by the Food Controller at 8s. 6d. a quart. Standard boots would be on sale on Monday. A Manchester chief inspector was missing, perhaps because he had lost his memory after falling from the top of a tram-car while arresting a notorious criminal. The chief duty of "The Man in the Street" column was to keep British spirits high. So he began thus: "Peeps at Jerry are highly interesting

just now. The bags he used to get from Bradford are right gone in the hinter-
land, and he has had to resort to paper trousers. Paper collars for thin necks are
selling in Berlin at 2/6 to 3/0 per collar." This was the sort of thing, with the
Shire Show, that gave everyone heart to win the war in a year that no one
could expect it to end.

George Young at Nocton Fen bought five Shire geldings, paying from £100
to £120 apiece. On over 8,000 acres, his full strength was 254. A friend of his
bought 120 for the army at the same time. The whole consignment, off Lincolnshire farms, was shipped to France within five days, put to work at once and
almost immediately wiped out. Not one survived. In spite of inevitable losses of
this nature, the average annual mortality from injury and disease of all horses
and mules with the British forces at home and in France and Flanders was less
than 14% throughout the war. This was an impressive achievement, but the
horror of the situation is only apparent when one considers that this means
425,000 animals killed or shot. If one adds the French losses and those of the
British in other theatres of war, the figures pass 1,000,000 without calling on
the wastages of any other army, whether of the Allies or of their opponents.
At sea on ocean routes, losses of horses and mules in freight ship transports were
under 1% for the whole war – that is, only about 7,000 died or were drowned
at sea. This was an astounding achievement in the face not only of the difficult
conditions generally but of the actual sinking of shipping, which amounted to
a total loss by the British Empire alone of over 7,500,000 gross tons during the
war. Something like 40% of the ships carrying horses from America docked in
England without a single mortality among 1,000 to 2,000 animals. It is difficult
to know whether the greatest credit should be given to the judgement of the
buyers in the first place, the efforts of all personnel at the various depots, the
shipping authorities, the naval escorting ships, the men in charge of the animals
at sea, or the toughness of the horses and mules themselves. In 1918, 196 crossings were made from Canada or the U.S.A. and seventy-six of these were
completed without losing a single horse or mule.

Once again, the Shire Society requested the release of stallion-men for the
season and the authorities did their best to oblige. But their own troubles were
now severe, as is shown by the unemotional official report: "Owing to the
necessity of releasing from remount squadrons at home all personnel fit for
more active service and their replacement by men of low category, inferior
physique and generally without previous knowledge of horses, the work of
training and conditioning horses and maintaining the rate of output became
one of increasing difficulty. The turnover of men was continuous during the
last two years of the war. During the six months 1st January to 30th June 1918,
2,534 of all ranks were transferred to other units and 816 were released for coal
mining, shipbuilding etc. – i.e. the personnel was changed at the rate of some
40% per annum."[1] In June, 22,000 more skilled farm workers were called up.
The few agricultural shows held the year before still manfully continued, and
Oldham had its horse parade.

By late autumn, provision of feeding-stuffs was a matter of desperate concern. There were enough in the country to maintain the existing livestock only until 25th January. The Chief Livestock Commissioner hurriedly summoned a meeting at the Ministry of Food on 1st November. All the breed society representatives agreed that there were two priorities – the continued production of milk, and the preservation of pedigree stock as a national asset after the war. Horse breeders were in a better position than cattle, sheep and pig men because they were assured of cereal rations by orders already issued by the Controller of Horse Transport, who was also responsible for long hay. Shire stallions, for example, were allowed 2 lb. of bran a day.

On 5th November, the Shire Council solemnly discussed a suggestion that all the occupants of 12 Hanover Square should contribute to a fund for putting the house in order when the lease expired – in March 1941. Learning that two men had sent foals to Peterborough sales with incorrect pedigrees, they decided to ask Sexton, Grimwade & Beck and other auctioneers to print in their sales catalogues the name and address of the breeders of all unregistered animals offered. They expelled a member of the Society for the false pedigree of a mare and they debated, not for the first time, the case of another member who had been ejected from the R.A.S.E. and from the Kent and Romney Marsh Sheep Society. Lord Middleton was praised for sending circulars to all the farmers in Yorkshire extolling the advantages of pedigree Shire-breeding, but the Council decided that, since the demand for Shires was so far ahead of supply, a more general publicity drive was inappropriate in the middle of the war.

But suddenly, a week later, it was no longer the middle of the war. The shooting stopped, and in no time at all the owner of a Shire stallion could buy 4 lb. of bran for him instead of two, every day. Arrangements were made for Australian soldier farmers to visit Shire studs. Peace had come, if no Utopia.

Looking back, the Council somewhat smugly congratulated itself on having watched over the interests of the breed in very difficult circumstances, on having done its best to help individual members in cases of hardship, and on having maintained the Society's leading position among stud-book associations. 747 new members had joined in the year, a net increase of 620. In addition, E. Somerville Tattersall was elected the fourth honorary member in the Society's history, for his generous help in enabling the Spring Show to be held. In the last twelve months 434 prefixes had been allotted to new breeders. The number of entries for the volume of the Stud-book in preparation was easily an all-time record – 911 stallions and 5,483 mares. They were all crammed into 729 pages, and any information which was not absolutely vital was omitted. Even so, incessant applications and cajolery were needed before the Paper Controller would release the 5½ tons of paper required.

6. 1919: INSULTS AND PROSPERITY

The sale of surplus Army horses began soon after the armistice, starting with those for slaughter and followed by those over twelve years old. By the middle of March, 42,138 British-owned horses had been sold alive in France, and 8,779 mules: in England, 62,520 horses and 1,478 mules: in Egypt 1,184 horses, 4,448 mules, 19,179 camels and 10,559 donkeys, and so on in Mesopotamia, Salonika and Italy. In America, 11,877 horses and 5,488 mules had been awaiting shipment when the war ended and were disposed of there. The average price was £26 for horses and just over £30 for the mules. If slaughtered animals are included, the total number disposed of by the British all over the world at that date was just over a quarter of a million for £7,600,000.

In England, ex-army heavy draught-horses were in the greatest demand. From March, younger horses also became available and average prices were £55, with good ones making over £100. To take one week's sales only, on Tuesday 25th March 120 Superior heavy and light draught-horses were offered at Tompkins' Repository, Reading and, at the Ormskirk Remount Depot 100 Staunch heavy draught-horses, 200 light draught vanners and fifty riding and driving animals, smart cobs and carriage horses; on Wednesday, at the Holywell Stables, Oxford, fifty Very Active heavy and light draught-horses: on Thursday, in the Old Brewery Yard, Banbury, fifty Upstanding draught-horses: on Friday, Tompkins' again, with 120 Very Powerful draught-horses; on Saturday, at Leicester Repository, 125 High Class Specially Selected draught-horses and at the Raven Repository, Shrewsbury, 150 Grand army horses. Every horse was provided with a coupon entitling the purchaser to obtain the forage ration of his class. The auctioneers were confident that sales would prove a great attraction to Borough Councils, Breweries, Town Carmen, and Coal Merchants and also for those requiring Smart Trotting Vanners. They did, even though it was only in the eye of the auctioneers that they were Grand, Staunch, Upstanding and Selected. Most of them would make a Shire man weep. So it was very irritating that a pure-bred American Percheron gelding, which had somehow got included in the sale list and was offered at Tattersalls, made the record price of 250 guineas. Could this have been a crafty trick to win publicity for the foreign breed?

Meanwhile at the Agricultural Hall, John Buchan's chief pre-occupation was now no longer to obtain the rent or to engineer its resumption whenever a reorganisation in the Civil Service interrupted the monthly payments. That had been difficult enough, one gentleman even asking him if there were any old cheques that he could have a look at, presumably to satisfy himself that the Hall existed and that the Government had sometimes paid to occupy it. Buchan's task now was to get the R.A.F. out. They were only using it for a public exhibition of captured enemy aircraft. The Shire Society lent him its considerable weight, but without success. Charlton reported that "all efforts failed to move the military authorities from the position in which they were entrenched. Even the suggestion that the show of aircraft, which they contemplated holding, however interesting and remunerative it might be in itself, was not of such national importance . . . as the series of horse shows, had no effect upon them." Sadly but gratefully, Mr. Tattersall's invitation to hold a second

group of truncated Shire, Hunter-and-Pony and Hackney shows at Newmarket
was accepted.

The *Daily Telegraph* report of this 1919 Shire stallion show was the crowning
insult in a stream of abuse which had been directed at the Shire ever since the
end of hostilities. The Shire horse, it was said, had been unable to stand the
strain and hardship of modern warfare. His condition was delicate, his stamina
poor. He could not battle against the draughty conditions of army stabling.
If he had to stand all night in mud up to his knees with no firm place to lie
down, he got grease and other leg ailments or respiratory troubles. On poor
quality and inadequate rations, he was a bad "doer". In fact, he was of no use
at all. The Shire men, whose ranks were swelling every day, had shrugged off
these arguments as part of the usual game. But never had any newspaper
produced such a report on a Shire Show (and this was the fortieth) as that which
infuriated all true Englishmen on 27th February. Who was this Special Correspondent, this traitor, this rascal who dared to disparage the King's own favourite breed? It was pretty generally felt that the culprit was Captain Sidney
Galtrey, joint Secretary of the new British Percheron Horse Society and a
frequent singer of the French breed's praises.

He began thus. "The great English cart-horse, known as the Shire, was not a
conspicuous success as a war horse, but he nevertheless remains pre-eminent
among British breeds of heavy draught horses. His ponderous bulk, his comparative lack of activity, inability to combat exposure and the diseases brought
about by exposure and service in mud, and his proneness to debility when the
limited ration and out-of-door conditions told on him – all these considerations
fought against him on active service. But now, with thoughts turned again
solely towards the peaceful pursuits of agriculture and industry, in country and
town, he reassumes with becoming dignity the part he played before the war.
He is essentially the horse of peace and prosperity, and to see him as he was
yesterday at the Shire Society's Show at Newmarket is to know him quite at
his best."

Purple-faced Shire men found the next paragraph comparatively innocuous,
but the third and fourth renewed the risk of seizure: "Shire breeders do not
need to be reminded that the chief criticism directed against the big horses during
the last four or five years has been on account of the mass of 'feather', or long
hair, on the legs. It has been the curse of the horse on active service, the har-
bourer of 'grease' and other leg ailments, the cause of serious wastage in
horse-flesh, and directly responsible for the introduction to this country of the
Percheron breed of clean-legged draught horses from France and America. In
recent years this 'feather' development has gone beyond being merely a
fashion and a simple characteristic of the breed: it now amounts to a craze, and
even many of the breed's greatest admirers are becoming alarmed, and wondering how the evil can be checked. Unquestionably this mass of hair on the
leg helps to suggest size and great weight. It also suggests a certain massiveness
and grandeur of outline, and yet its advantages are nil. The soldier with heavy

batteries or heavy transport abhors it; the farmer, especially he who has to cultivate heavy land, hates it. The latter, however, has to use the Shire because up to the present time there has been no horse of sufficient weight to take his place.

"As I looked at all these great cart horse stallions yesterday, I wondered how any change in this direction, any abatement in the orgie, could be brought about. Unquestionably the evolution from a little to a lot of hair has been spread over many years, and it will take a long time to eliminate. The show ring is to blame, and not until the society come to a belated decision on the point will there be any move towards reform, for it is quite correct to say that an owner who dared to bring in a horse with a minimum of 'feather' would be snubbed by having it studiously ignored. The society claim that the Shire is the finest heavy draught horse in the world. Let them set about removing, or even reducing, the ridiculous 'feather', and all the world will concede their claim. For when it comes to moving a great load, this great fellow, with the big bone and muscular development and the big spread of feet, may well be pre-eminent."

The writer had left himself little space to describe the horses, which he did in lukewarm terms. Blaisdon Draughtsman, winner of the senior class, was "a great hulking fellow". Of the champion, Generosity, "I suppose he had no superior in the show" and his feather was straight and fine, "such as is not common to most Shires." Of the two-year-olds, "Obviously their condition to-day is not due either to wartime or armistice rations. They have been 'forced' like some exotic, nourished on soft foods, maybe even milk when it has been available, with plenty of chopped hay."

When the gravity of the insult was privately pointed out (by Sir Walter Gilbey), the editor was abashed at what his paper had done. A long article by the Agricultural Correspondent on 26th March compensated by explaining the grand qualities of the Shire horse and its sterling work throughout the war. "Many of the earliest heavy horses sent to France and Belgium were either Shires or Shire-bred stock. Some of them are still out there, and not a few of them have struggled through the mud and morasses from Mons to Mons again." They did not lie down and die of pneumonia by the roadside. Their hairy legs were never a nuisance, because they had a close crop with the military horse-clippers. In all transport lines, the star turn was a pair of Shires. In Divisional supply trains, field ambulances, and first line transport, they were magnificent, in just the same way as, in peace-time, they had been supreme as workers and as the tenant-farmer's financial sheet-anchor. The writer significantly began his piece with the words "Unaided by any Government grant, and built up entirely by the private enterprise of English and Welsh farmers" – a reminder that the French Percheron was the only heavy breed to be semi-officially supported by a traitorous British government.

Others, too, sprang to the ramparts. The Shire had come out of the war, not as a failure, but with great éclat. Only a fool would try to use him as a jack of all trades: he was a heavy draughter. In R.A.S.C. and R.E. haulage, he was superb. Second Lieutenant Edmund Beck wrote to *The Live Stock Journal* that "amongst the Yanks are some nice light compact horses, but the bulk of them are a plain-headed long-backed bad type. These horses have served their purpose when no others could be had, and that is all that can be said for them." Every battery commander he had ever met agreed with him. However, Mr. Beck was scarcely less partial than Captain Galtrey. After demobilisation, he was to succeed his father as one of the best Shire auctioneers that there have been, and a doughty champion of the breed. It is significant that, in his counter-attack, he was even prepared to admit that the few Clydesdales he had come across were "very good on the whole". There is no better cure to end a family row and make all relations close their ranks than the interference of a stranger. When times or seasons were slack, the Shire and Clydesdale and Suffolk men used to amuse themselves by slanging each other. "A Clyde might manage to pull an owd hen off her nest" . . . "The Suffolk would be a good horse if it had some feet and legs – and if it hadn't got such an ugly top and head" . . . "The Shire people get a horse with four great gummy brushes on its legs – and then call it 'feather'." And so on. But this was serious. Even the tight little Suffolk Society had cause to fear, since it was no longer the only clean-legged heavy breed in the country.

Charlton – as Sloughgrove would have done – pointed out that the un-paralleled prosperity of the Shire Society was "the best possible answer to the small body of malcontents, who have recently been extolling the merits of the foreign horse at the expense of our native breeds". He granted that other men's horses had their uses, but not in England. Shire men "deprecate the foreign invasion, because they consider it to be totally unnecessary and because it casts an unmerited slur on our native horses at a time when all the world is expected to flock here to buy our incomparable livestock". A little booklet was issued free to all members and anyone else the secretary could think of, containing reprints of the chief pro-Shire articles and letters in the press.

As the busy season came on, the argument died down. Prices went on rising. The Duke of Westminster had started the post-war home sale ball rolling in February with twenty-three stallions and seventeen mares which fetched 13,805 guineas. Hiring societies offered more and more money for stallions – booking them in many cases at 1,000 guineas, and for a year ahead, or two years if they could not get the ones they wanted at once. The Royal Show was held again and the Society gave an extra £100 for five first prizes in mare classes, to compensate for their absence at the Spring Show. There were seventeen other gold medal shows and each was given an additional £10 for the best mare, and at 144 silver medal shows a special £5 was given. Offers to shows abroad were still restricted to silver medals, but two each were offered at eleven different centres. Cart horse parades in general had no time to organise themselves as early as Easter Monday or May Day, but Manchester and Salford managed one, as well as Oldham.

Many of the ex-army horses owned by the Board of Agriculture (which this year became at last a Ministry) had been sold by the end of March, but its horse-scheme was not brought to an end until 30th September when the 10,000 retained for the harvest started to be sold off, like their 4,200 tractors. They made an average price of £60. With each animal, a second-hand set of plough harness – collar and hames, bridle, backband, chains, plough lines and nosebag – was offered for £2. The army reduced its horse strength to 210,090 by August and to 150,000 at the end of the year. Messrs. Tindall and Buchan at last found a General at the War Office who was prepared to get the R.A.F. turned out of the Hall, which he did as a debt of gratitude for the help he had received from Buchan when, as a less senior officer, he had taken the premises over in the first place.

Throughout the summer and until the regular shows could start up again, the Hall was turned into a huge auction mart for ex-army lorries, cars and motorcycles, with a roaring trade at bargain prices. But in due course there was a Dairy Show again, and then Smithfield, which was the show for which the premises had been built in 1862. This was followed by the World's Fair, that popular Christmas entertainment, at which in the old days many a monkey had escaped for a few days into the rafters and Blondin had made many an omelette as he swayed on his 384 feet of rope, throwing the empty egg-shells among the 3,000 spectators. The circus this year was a gold-mine. There was a great hunger for entertainment and plenty of money to spend on it.

The Shire Society was prosperous and gave 500 guineas to the Agricultural Relief of Allies Committee. This may not appear much, but A.B.C., trained by John Sloughgrove, was well aware that, in a non-trading organisation, this sum represented the subscription of 500 members. He reported that the "campaign of calumny" appeared to have died out, "probably because it did the breed more good than harm. It certainly had the effect of arousing the honest anger of Shire men, who proceeded to enrol within a few months more than 700 new breeders, as a mild demonstration that the Old English horse still holds the sway in this country and is not easily to be ousted by any foreign importations." Membership was in fact within four of 6,000 and there were probably about 5,000 other breeders who were members of their local hiring societies. Entries submitted for the Stud-book, though 202 less than the year before, were nevertheless the second highest ever achieved. The work of preparing the volume was made difficult by the fact that the preceding one, which should have been ready by February of this year, did not appear until September owing to staff shortages at the printers and in Hanover Square. Temporary clerical assistance was brought in to help clear the back-log.

7. 1920: THE ALMIGHTY GUINEA

Like the circus-goers who had waited for the treat of seeing the World's Fair once again, the Shire men were looking forward eagerly to the first post-war London Show. Three weeks before this, however, many of them had a wonderful old-fashioned day out at Tring. J. G. Williams had sold his Pendley stud to John Measures and his former manager, Harry Bishop, and they were to finance the venture by a home sale. Enormous crowds rolled up, wondering what the prices would be. No stallions had ever been kept at Pendley Manor and so it seemed doubtful whether the sums obtained at the Rothschild sales of 1913 and 1915 at the other end of the town would be approached. But the thirty-two mares and fillies, together with two colt foals (or, rather, yearlings, for it was thirty-five days into the new year), were as choice a collection of cart-horse flesh as could be imagined. Hardly had a couple been sold before the majority of men realised their cheque books would have to remain in their pockets. Leaving out the one stallion offered (not a Pendley horse), the thirty-four, of which nineteen were still only about eight or twenty months old, realised 23,745 guineas, an average of £733 10s. 0d. and an all-time record.

Edmund Beck, lately second lieutenant Army Service Corps, suffering from war injuries that were eventually to be fatal to him, was jubilant at this testimony to faith in his beloved Shire. Pendley Footprint, one of the colts, made 2,300 guineas, a record for a yearling. Snelston Lady, nine years old, realised 2,200, a record for a mare (but easily beaten three weeks later). Seven of the mares made 1,000 guineas or over. The long queues waiting patiently to get into Tring station afterwards realised they had been present at a cart-horse event the like of which had never been seen before. They were not to know that it would never be seen again, and so in a glow of optimism they were prepared to put up with the terrible running of the trains on their homeward journey. The over-used and under-maintained rolling stock also posed a few problems for those who had bought expensive mares at the sale.

Sir Eric Geddes, the first Minister of Transport (who had taken office in October 1919) did his best to ruin the London Show. Railway rates were increased by 60% and the old concessions – half-rate for horses returning from shows and free travel for the men in charge – were not available. Only five days beforehand, Charlton learned that there would be absolutely no cartage facilities, either. It was as bad as 1917, and we had won the war fifteen months ago. The Royal and country shows were also affected by the cost and difficulty of transport, and entries were disappointing. But, to compensate, many local one-day events had record numbers of exhibits. The Society awarded forty-six gold medals at thirty-eight shows, 231 silver medals at 224 shows – and nineteen abroad at nine shows, the only part of the programme that had not assumed its pre-war scope. However, only London, Liverpool and four other cart-horse parades were held, including of course Oldham. For the first time, awards at these were available only to horses of "Shire type". Altruism in encouraging town users to use a good kind of horse was all very well: but it would be going too far if a Shire medal were given to a Percheron. Owing to the increasing cost of silver, all affiliated societies had to subscribe 2 guineas this year, instead of one.

Inflation was affecting everything. A 25% rise in office staff salaries replaced a war bonus. Entry fees for the Stud-book were doubled to 10s. for stallions and 5s. for mares (non-members 40s. and 20s.). The old guinea annual subscription was not increased, but new members had to pay a joining fee of 1 guinea. The London Show had cost £3,742 to stage in 1917, including £835 for rent and fittings: now it was £5,491, with rent and fittings accounting for £1,208. So charges were all put up – 3 guineas for members to show a stallion and 2 for a mare, a rise of 1 guinea each, and non-members paid 6 and 4 guineas. About the only item left unchanged was the admission of the public at 2s. 6d., and 1s. on the last day. The decreased value of money partly accounts for the high prices in the Shire trade, whether for Pendley aristocrats or the humble dray or cart horse that it was their task to improve the shape of. But scarcity and strong demand played its part.

Newark Shire Horse Society had wanted to hire the Forshaws' March King, but were unlucky, as the Crewe Society had already booked him for 1,000 guineas. So they reserved him for 1921 at 2,000 guineas. The Montgomeryshire Society offered a 1,500 guinea premium, and William Cumber's Theale Lock-inge won it. Crewe S.H.S. promptly engaged him for the next year to follow March King, at 2,000 guineas. These two hiring fees were, and are, a record.

Spring sales at all the repositories saw enormous numbers of animals changing hands. Sellers at Peterborough included nearly all the "big names" in the Shire world, with Manley's at Crewe not far behind. Lloyd's sales in the same town were some of the biggest they ever held. The gelding trade, whether at these great centres or at innumerable sales all over the country, appeared to be as usual the stout back-bone of the industry. William Barrs, possessor of an illus-trious Shire-breeding name, sold fourteen non-fancy working pedigree mares at his Measham farm in Leicestershire for sums up to 350 guineas. At one farm sale, someone bought a Shire mare, with no pretensions to show-ring qualities, for 920 guineas. Everyone thought he was crazy, and he probably was.

The army was still selling thousands of surplus horses. Aldridge's in St. Martin's Lane included a large number every time among the 300 work horses, light and heavy, that they sold each week. Autumn foal sales in most cases resulted in a clear-out of everything available, though it was noticed that, except for the very best, the inflated prices of 1918 and 1919 were not forth-coming for these.

At the end of this greatest of the boom years, 684 new members had been elected, a net increase of 432, and membership stood at 6,328. 418 prefixes had been issued. The Stud-book now in the printer's hands set an all-time record with 923 stallions and 5,656 mares, beating the previous best two years before by 165. One or two criticisms were being made about other breed societies in 12 Hanover Square. For example, the Shorthorn Herd-book was behind-hand and the volume listing animals calved in 1917 was nearly two years late. Light-horse breeders were still in the doldrums. But the Shire and the rest of the heavy brigade all seemed to be making rapid headway, and the Percheron, though it shared the success, appeared little more than an irritation which had distracted the attention of a few erstwhile Shire supporters. The year ended with good

news also in veterinary affairs. Joint-ill or joint-felon (or polyarthritis, rheu-
matic-arthritis, navel ill, or omphelo-thrombo-phlebitis, to give it some of the
other names under which it then went) had long been a scourge, particularly in
heavy-horse foals. After years of investigation in Scotland and England, supported by the Clydesdale and Shire Societies, a vaccine was announced in
December. The Royal Veterinary College had also studied abortion for several
years, and now offered a simple blood test to determine contagious forms, and
was prepared to give free advice on this other hazard in breeding horses.

8. SPRING SHOWS

In 1915, the President was absent on active service. Lord Rothschild and the
brothers Whitley, who won the championships with the hairy Blaisdon Jupiter
and (for the second time) Lorna Doone, were absent ill. It was decided that the
King would not therefore present the cups himself. His only duty, with the
Queen, was to bow and smile as everyone cheered their patriotic devotion.
Entries of horses were down to 527, which everyone, including His Majesty,
agreed was not bad in the circumstances. The auction was likewise a smaller
affair, but demand was brisk, and the average price the second best so far
recorded. There were fifty new boxes for mares, which reduced the number
housed in draughty open stalls, and catering arrangements had been extended.

Exactly the same number of horses was entered for the 1916 show, which the
King and the Queen and Princess Mary, like everyone else, agreed was not only
a remarkable coincidence, but really better than not bad. It was only the second
public appearance of His Majesty since his accident in France. The horses, who
did not know this, were somewhat upset and excited by the continued rounds
of deafening hurrahs which greeted his arrival, and the vigorous and earnest
rendering of the National Anthem, followed by renewed and prolonged cheering. Now that Lord Rothschild was dead and his stud dispersed, J. G. Williams
upheld the honour of Tring by winning a prize with every animal he exhibited.
He won in every female class – yearlings, second and third; two-year-old, first;
three-year-old, fourth; four-year-old, second; senior mares under 16-hands,
first; under 16.2, first; and 16.2 and over, second. Even as an example of the
judgment of Harry Bishop, in selecting for exhibition exactly those animals
that would win, this unique achievement was almost incredible. His Snelston
Lady, second in the big mares class, was reserve for the championship and so
the King had a chance to congratulate owner and manager as he presented the
gold medal. The mare championship was once again won by Lorna Doone.
John Rowell, who had shown the champion stallion of thirty-one years before,
the superb Prince William, received the champion cup for Bury King's Champion, bred on a little north Somerset farm by George Edwards, former head
man to the late Lord Winterstoke of the Wills tobacco family of Bristol.
George had also bred (though not in his own name) the winner of the big
stallions' class and this older horse, Rickford Coming King, was destined two
years later to bring him a distinction no other man has ever achieved. Second in

this class was the one-eyed Champion's Clansman. (The other eye had suffered from a cataract and had been removed.) Sir Arthur Nicholson had bought him at the Tring Park dispersal and sent him to London only after seeking a ruling from the veterinary inspector, Professor Penberthy, as to his eligibility. The judges obviously shared the Professor's view that a stallion does not require two eyes to serve a mare. In this class Blaisdon Jupiter, who seemed coarser and hairier than ever, was only third. The 1910–1911 champion, Gaer Conqueror, did well at the age of eleven to be reserve to Bury King's Champion for the championship. W. G. Mawer again came before the King to receive the gelding cup, this time for his black Caractacus, a better horse altogether than the ungelded chestnut of the same name which had been the sensation of all America in 1887. The auction produced a new record average and its own new record price – £1,680 for Forage Conqueror, second in the four-year-old class.

In 1917, Champion's Clansman's missing eye[2] did not prevent him becoming supreme champion and Sir Arthur Nicholson became the fifth man to win both championships the same year. His mare, Roycroft Forest Queen, just beat the redoubtable Lorna Doone, both in the senior big mares' class and for the senior cup and the supreme championship. So the latter, disqualified in 1913, still came within an ace of a quadruple championship for the Whitley brothers. The gelding championship was awarded to an animal which was later objected to, and a special committee came to the conclusion that the exhibitor had too hastily jumped to conclusions as to its breeding. The horse was undoubtedly a Shire and he was certainly unable to do any damage by propagating any error that might lie in his documentation. But rules must be kept, and three months later the class prize and cup were awarded instead to the previous year's winner, Mawers Limited's Caractacus. At this show, for the first time, the groom in charge of each first prize winner was given a sum of money and a certificate. The Council felt that such a proof of ability to bring out Shire horses would be an excellent testimonial for use in a man's future career. Even amid all the difficulties of this desperate year of the war, entries still dropped only by twenty-seven to 500 exactly. At the auction, a new record average price was again set, and the amount of business done privately was exceptional, including the last minute hiring of stallions by committees which had been unable to travel round the studs so easily as before.

At the open air show at Newmarket in 1918, the weather in the last week of February was kind. The 168 stallions found they had plenty of room in the excellent loose-boxes, which had never before housed such creatures as they. For the first time, animals belonging to the same owner were placed in adjoining boxes, owing to the shortage of grooms, instead of being allocated places according to their class. The large area of grass adjoining the sale paddock was turned into a judging ring with a circumference of 450 feet, and was covered with rushes. It had a little judges' tent in the middle. Spectators, in the sale paddock, had litter to stand on and a canvas roof over their heads. The gravel road between arena and spectators was covered with tan and used for trotting the horses. There was a canvas shelter for waiting horses, a veterinary yard was set up in the Lower Paddock, there were facilities for private examination of stallions, the auction was held in the Tattersall sale-room, and Newmarket station, built with horses in mind, was ideal. Meals could not be provided, nor living quarters for grooms, but these were only a few minutes' walk away in the town. A night watchman and a veterinary officer were the sole humans in charge at night. Admission for spectators was 2s. 6d., and 1s. for the auction on the second day.

There were only four stallion classes, instead of seven, the yearlings being dropped and all the senior horses put in one group irrespective of height. The ten-year-old Rickford Coming King won the championship for the Forshaw brothers. He appears in the records as having been bred by the late Lord Winterstoke, but the credit was due to George Edwards who thus became the only man so far who has had the distinction – in his own name or of his employer – of breeding two supreme champion Shires. It is an admirable illustration of the fact that, however concentrated among a comparatively limited number of men the ownership of the most valuable Shire horses tended to be from 1880 until 1939, their breeding was extremely broadly based. Few noticed Edwards' unique achievement and he was not the man to draw attention to himself. He did not win the breeders' gold medal and £10 prize because what he had done in 1907 and again in 1908 to bring the horse into the world was officially the work of Lord Winterstoke. And he was dead, so nobody won these awards. George, nevertheless, enjoyed the show and went quietly home to his Somerset farm on the edge of that district where Daniel Defoe had noticed such huge horses, but which in Shire times had been so backward in this respect. Rickford Coming King, 1 ton and 2 cwt. on short legs, was hardly backward.

The next year, the Forshaws won the championship again, this time with the Montgomeryshire-bred Generosity. This turned out to be an unfortunate thing for the Forshaws, the breed, and the show system in general. The difference between Rickford Coming King's great powers as a stock-horse and those of Generosity was as great as the change of weather for this second Newmarket show. February was filling the dykes and it was only by the continual supply of extra rushes that the ground was prevented from becoming a quagmire. The judges needed their little tent and the spectators their awning.

If we were to treat poor Generosity with the kindness due to his name and nature, we would forget him. But his story must be told. When he was a yearling in 1916, J. Downes Evans, then seventeen years old, bought him for £58 – the very first purchase he had ever made on his own. But, like father, like son, and that experienced Shire man Morris Evans thought he could not have done better himself. That autumn, the son joined the 1st Life Guards and the father was in poor health, and so he sold the colt in 1917 to Edgar Appleby of Rugby for £750, a 1,228% profit. He was a beautiful animal and, in the Peterborough Spring Sales in 1918, the Forshaws gave 1,500 guineas for him. So, when he won the championship this year, those mare-owners in East Lancashire who had hired him as a three-year-old were awaiting their foals. They were disappointed. In spite of looking everything that a young Shire stallion should be, he was almost useless. One or two, perhaps three, foals were about the sum total of his achievement. Some people had hard words to say about him. George Linney, who travelled horses for the Forshaws for many years and was (though he would have been embarrassed to hear it said) the very model of what a stallion-man should be, put it more gently. "I think he was one of the most perfect stallions I ever saw. But, you know, every horse has its fault – the same as we have. And Generosity had a fault, too. He just couldn't manage to get his mares in foal." (A possible reason for his deficiency was the illness he had contracted the year before, when he very nearly died during the season. It certainly accounts for the disappointment of the Lancastrians this year, and probably for the fact that this coming season he was as infertile as he was virile.)

The supreme championship being won this year by an almost sterile horse was an ironic coincidence, because the Council had paid great attention to the possibility of framing some rule for the auction sale to deal with younger horses which, after purchase, turned out to be unable to get foals. But such a provision proved to be beyond wit or wisdom to devise. Only thirty horses were in fact sold, but once again a new record average price of £474 was set up. Perhaps the most memorable feature of this show was the exceptional number of horses weighing well over 1 ton. But, in spite of what the *Telegraph*'s Special Correspondent might think, the top prizes were not awarded to hair and bulk alone – Sundridge Coming King was the heaviest (now five years old, he was over 24 cwt.), but was placed only sixth in his class.

A thick fog was at its densest at 8.30 in the morning when, in 1920, selection of the stallions for veterinary examination began at the eagerly-awaited first London Show since 1917. The suggestion that a film should be made had been turned down, which is a pity. Massive horses jerking along with Charlie Chaplinesque rapidity in the swirling gloom would have made a wonderfully unrealistic record of the most notable Shire Show of all time. The fog lifted at midday, then descended before judging was finished, and on the second day it was almost impossible for spectators and reporters to make out the numbers worn by any of the mares. Even the judges were confused.

Five-hundred-and-twenty-one animals had fumbled their way to the Hall, all travelling at the full new inflated railway rates both ways, and so this was not bad. Farmer members were there in vast numbers and in places stood twelve deep round the ring. It is a wonder that the 5,000 or more members of the public who rolled up were able to get in at all. The most notable feature of this memorable show was the quality of the mares, which seemed to have improved out of all knowledge in the three years that they had not been shown at all. William Dunlop, the celebrated Clydesdale breeder from Dunure Mains, Ayr, won the yearling class with Pendley Vanity that he had paid 1,500 guineas for three weeks earlier. Another filly which fetched 700 guineas at Pendley was Highly Commended. Pendley Princess IV (1,300 guineas at the stud sale) was third for Sir Edward Stern in the two-year-olds, the King winning the class with his own-bred Maid Marion 2nd. In this class, ex-Pendley fillies which had been sold for 875 and 725 guineas were eighth and eleventh. Indeed, the fifty-two two-year fillies were the most costly lot of young females ever shown together. Medlar Bella was another ex-Pendley success, winning the four-year-old class: she had cost 1,800 guineas.

Snelston Lady, that had so recently become the most expensive Shire mare in England, was beaten into second place by a five-year-old which only a few remembered from 1917, when she took second prize in her class. This was Gleadthorpe Seclusion, now a most beautiful mare in perfect condition. And when she was selected as supreme champion there was not a man in the Hall who disagreed with the judges. The farmers chortled more than anyone. All these expensive purchases, and every one of them trounced by a "farmer's mare"! Her owner, A. R. Grimes, was actually a veterinary surgeon from Warsop, Notts, and belonged to a family of great Shire enthusiasts. She was bought at the auction by David Davies, M.P., to go to Montgomeryshire for the record sum of 4,600 guineas – 500 guineas more than Champion's Goal-keeper, the most expensive stallion ever bought. But money does not buy success. She had a colt foal on 26th May and was served on 7th June by Norbury Menestrel, sire of the foal. She was second at the Royal a few weeks later, died of a ruptured diaphragm on 21st November and went to the kennels. But Montgomeryshire had an ace up its sleeve. A grey mare bred by William Vaughan had stood modestly in fifth place in this same London class of 1920. Her name was Erfyl Lady Grey and in due course her beauty was to be sung all over England, and Scotland too, as well as Wales.

Quaintly, amidst the great wealth of mare perfection this year, there was no reserve senior champion. Halstead Royal Duchess, placed top of the 16–16.2 class, was selected for this position but eventually did not fulfil the foaling condition. John Bradley, her breeder and owner, had won innumerable prizes with her including the junior cup in 1912 when she beat Lorna Doone. (She was by Lockinge Forest King out of the third of his "Halstead Duchesses".) But John was now dead. His executors sold her to R. W. Carson for 1,850 guineas. (In 1921 she really did win her class, and really was reserve champion. The following year at the age of thirteen she won the class again.)

Their Majesties and Princess Mary arrived in the Hall just as the judges were choosing the King's own-bred three-year-old Field Marshal V as winner of the junior cup. A great roar of cheering and applause seemed for the moment to shift some of the thick fog which, having once penetrated the building, was, as always, reluctant to leave it. A little while later, Field Marshal was preferred to Blaisdon Draughtsman, the senior cup winner, for the championship. Another roar greeted this somewhat unexpected decision – unexpected especially to Percy Toone, the auctioneer from Hinckley who was so taken with the senior horse that he made himself somewhat conspicuous by shouting out and applauding in his favour. Everyone felt rather sorry for F. W. Cope from Cheswardine in Shropshire, because his horse had been reserve champion the year before, as well. But even a republican among the spectators (if one can imagine such a person at a Shire show) could not have argued against the young horse's stylish carriage, good bone and fine forehand, and Draughtsman was a bit slack in his back, as Mr. Toone could not deny. The King was the first man since those tenant farmer brothers, the Walwyns in 1901, to be both breeder and exhibitor of a Shire champion of either sex. Amid scenes of great excitement, he went into the ring and received the gold cup from the President, Sir Arthur Nicholson. This was appropriate, for Sir Arthur's one-eyed Champion's Clansman was the sire of His Majesty's horse. Peering through the mists, as they had all day, the crowd perceived Mr. Cope shaking hands with his royal conqueror. Then they saw the King congratulating Mr. Grimes and presenting him with the mare cup. Next, he seemed to be talking for an unusually long time to some grooms. Finally he shook hands very heartily with the three judges. Not surprisingly, perhaps. But one cannot imagine three men less likely to give the verdict to a champion king when their sole business was to select a champion horse. They were Tom Fowler, formerly manager for the late Lord Rothschild, R. H. Keene, formerly manager for R. W. Hudson (and both now stud-owners themselves), and James Forshaw, younger of the brothers. Oddly, in this most outstanding of Shire shows, the greatest stallion-owners and the greatest mare-owner could not compete – the Forshaws because James was judging, and Harry Bishop because he had promised purchasers at the Pendley sale that he would not show against them. At last, looking as pleased, someone remarked, as a dog with two tails, the King left, to renewed cheering, and the royal party groped their way home to the Palace.

London Show auctions dealt normally in "useful" rather than outstanding horses, and only five mares ever made four-figure sums there. All of these were in 1920. And of the twelve stallions reaching 1,000 guineas or more at these sales, four were sold this year – including Ansty Forest Clansman, third in the two-year-old class, for whom J. J. Stubley of King's Lynn paid 2,500 guineas. Rievaulx Friar, who was fourth among the three-year-olds, made more money for Robert McGowan of Ingatestone in Essex than Generosity had done for the Evans family or for Edgar Appleby. Robert had bought him as a two-year-old colt in poor condition for £200, and now sold him within the year for £2,300 to J. H. Hughes of Fenny Compton. He was to prove a steady prize-winner for the next five years, as these pages will show. But as a sire, at any rate of London prize-winners, he was to achieve almost nothing (see 1925 Show). Roycroft Coming King stood twenty-third in the three-year-olds – and the Forshaws paid 1,600 guineas for him.

William Dunlop took Lincoln Footprint, first in the yearling class, to Scotland for 400 guineas. Perhaps he liked the name as much as the colt, for he had tried to buy Pendley Footprint at the Bishop and Measures sale three weeks before. Had he not bred Dunure Footprint, greatest of Clydesdale stallions, son of Baron of Buchlyvie and great-great-great-grandson of Darnley? And what was Mr. Dunlop doing now? He was reducing his Clydesdale stud, and taking English horses to Ayr, three of them from Pendley. He had become a Shire member in November 1919 and had just been elected to the Shire council. There were some on both sides of the border who were getting that old idea which a few men of an earlier generation once had – that the Clydesdale and the Shire would gain by an amalgamation. William Dunlop could have become the new Lawrence Drew.

9. THE STUD-BOOK

Something has been said in the synopsis of each year about entries for the Stud-book and the increasing difficulties of actually producing the volumes. Somehow, the office staff and the Editing Committee maintained their hawk-eyed scrutiny of all applications in order to reduce simple errors and fraudulent claims to the minimum. Before the 40th volume was published, seven months late, in September 1919, it was calculated that it had occasioned between 1,000 and 1,500 letters of enquiry. Some of the mistakes were absurd. Two foals, by different sires, were bred by different men in the same year out of the same mare. Each breeder happened to re-enter his mare to show her produce and this made the error immediately obvious, and clearly showed that, whichever breeder was wrong, at least he was innocent of any crime. But few mares were thus re-entered and if the foals had merely been entered in their own right under their own names, only an accident or a particularly keen memory would have shown that there was something to investigate. Hitchin Conqueror 4458 (foaled in 1883) was quoted in a pedigree, when Hitchin Thunderer 18094 (foaled in 1897) was intended. That was an easy one to detect, and was a mistake by a not very scholarly breeder: had it been an attempt to improve the pedigree by including a famous sire, it would have been too crude. Mr. A. bred a filly foal out of a dam which – someone just happened to know – he had sold to Mr. B. four years before. That was an odd one.

The Suffolk Society kept track of its horses by publishing each year a list of pedigree animals in the possession of each member and a list of transfers effected during the twelve months. But what could be done by the men of Suffolk was clearly out of the question for a society whose books now contained over 36,000 stallions and nearly 100,000 mares. Nevertheless, the Editing Committee was determined to do something, and therefore in 1919 proposed a system of registration and transfer certificates. The former would provide owners, between the time of acceptance for the Stud-book and its publication, with a proof of registration. If the animal concerned were sold, the purchaser would naturally expect to receive the certificate as well. A transfer certificate would be completed by a vendor and handed to the purchaser, who would lodge it with the Society. No colt or filly would be accepted for registration unless the breeder was the same man who had registered the dam, or unless he possessed a transfer certificate for her. Of course, the scheme could not absolutely prevent deliberate fraud, but the committee believed that the amount of work involved in the office would be offset by an enormous reduction in the number of queries. It would pay for itself, particularly if a 1s. fee were charged for each certificate. Furthermore, it should increase membership of the Society, which would be immediately brought in contact with new owners of horses. There was a great number of men who purchased pedigree Shires and scarcely knew even the address of the Society. There was no intention to publish the transfers in the Stud-book, as even this part of what the Suffolk society was able to do would have been too big a task.

In its earnest recommendation of the scheme, the Committee argued that "the sole object is to ensure accuracy in the Stud-book by securing actual knowledge of the owners of all registered stallions and mares at any given time. Under the present system, which is the same now as it was forty years ago, errors are discovered through the very absurdity of the mistake made, or they are detected by the experience or intuition of the trained members of the staff. But the errors which cannot be detected by these crude methods must be innumerable, although we must hope that they are all accidental and none fraudulent. Whether it is now desirable to institute a system which will tend to greater accuracy in recording pedigrees, or whether it is better to continue the present uncertain and defective system, it is for the Council to decide."

The Council did decide. After long discussion, they rejected the scheme by a substantial majority. Among those disappointed by this unaccountable decision were Alfred Clark and A. C. Duncombe, the successive chairmen of the Editing Committee during the time it had worked on the idea, and the secretary. To them can certainly be added anyone who tries to write the history of the breed.

At the end of this same busy year, the Committee resurrected the proposal, made three times in the past thirty years, that the Stud-book should be confined to animals of which both parents were registered. (Oddly, the American Shire Stud-book was "closed" in this way.) But the Council still felt it should be kept open to some extent, and a compromise was reached. Mares foaled in 1922 and after would be required to have four registered crosses – registered sire and registered sires of dam, granddam and great-granddam – instead of three. That is, they would have a minimum of fifteen-sixteenths registered blood. A committee recommendation to which the Council did agree in 1919 was to permit foreign-bred Shires to be registered (see section 10). An index to Volumes 26–40 had been proposed, but not enough members expressed their willingness to subscribe 3 guineas each to make it economic. This no doubt pleased the office staff as much as the decision not to introduce transfer certificates had disappointed them.

As for the spectre of fraud, which always haunts pedigree societies, there was one case where the law, somewhat surprisingly, solved a little problem. A certain gentleman in Cambridgeshire had long been suspected of inventing fanciful ancestries, but the Editing Committee had found him clever. However, in November 1920, they learned with pardonable pleasure that he had been convicted of selling an animal with a false pedigree and was beginning a term of imprisonment.

IO. THE SHIRE ABROAD

Thanks to the persistence of one member of the Society, Edward Goodwin Preece of Shrewsbury (the same who had supported the idea of a second stud-book of stallions certified sound), the Council devoted much time in 1916 to proposals for Shire propaganda abroad. Preece advocated advertisements and editorial matter in the foreign Press, the exhibition of geldings in gears, ship-ments of selected colts and fillies for exhibition and sale, and refusal to issue export certificates except for animals passed sound by veterinary surgeons ap-pointed by the Society. He believed that these things would be of far more value than gold cups or medals.

The British societies undoubtedly were at a disadvantage in comparison with the Belgian and Percheron breeders, who were virtually part of a nationalised industry supported by all the funds and facilities of their respective Govern-ments. The Shire Society was in fact actually prohibited by its Articles of Association from engaging in trading enterprises. Even to send six top-class geldings to the United States for exhibition purposes (assuming it could be done in war time) would involve an enormous expense to a Society which was designed to do no more than support itself. Tom Forshaw produced an estimate which is of interest as an example of costs at that time.

	£	s.	d.
Six geldings at £140 each	840.	0.	0.
Expenses finding them	12.	0.	0.
3 months keep to get into condition for shipping, @ 25s. per horse per week	97.	10.	0.
Man to take full charge @ 25s. per week	16.	5.	0.
Shoeing for 6 horses, 3 months	6.	0.	0.
Railway charges in England, say	15.	0.	0.
Insurance of horses @ 6%	52.	8.	0.
Shipping @ £12 each (probably an under-estimate)	72.	0.	0.
Feed on Ship	10.	0.	0.
Duty in U.S.A. (non-pedigree-breeding stock @ 33.1/3% of value of horses)	279.	6.	0.
	£1,400.	9.	0.

This sum left nothing for veterinary attention, or for wagon and harness and travel expenses in America, which was costly, nor for a man in charge from the time of leaving England. Not surprisingly, with the worsening war situation, foreign propaganda became more and more remote from reality and the matter was dropped. It was impossible to send even gold medals out of the country.

However, in the summer of 1919 John G. Truman, still President of the American Shire Horse Association, was in England and met a committee of the Society. He brought with him a request from the Canadian Society that there should be prizes for "grade" animals, by pedigree sires out of non-pedigree

PLATE 25 Markeaton Royal Harold, champion in 1897 and reserve to his young son Buscot Harold for that honour the next year. But he stands here as a typical representative of Harold's 101 best sons.

PLATE 26 Prince William, son of William the Conqueror and Lockington Beauty (Plate 21). Champion at the age of two in 1885 and again three years later. Here he is, after eighteen years of service, still handsome, though his feet are killing him. He has served about 1500 mares, many of them twice or more.

PLATE 27 "We aren't very big, but to-day we won a rosette in Regent's Park, and have just got home. We are not aware, of course, that we are traitors, pulling this stuff, or that our firm will become 'Esso'".

PLATE 28 "This is my V.H.C. card in the competition for best gelding, Liverpool Parade, 1901. Behind the guv'nor is Mr. Reynolds, the great vet. He often smokes a pipe, and has more hair on his face than I have on my legs."

dams. This was agreed, and the English society provided 20 guineas in prizes at three shows in Canada and three in the United States. The Society also provided a collection of news items, photographs and articles on the breed, and a grant of £500 to the American society, and of £100 to the Canadian society, for general publicity to counteract "the flamboyant notices issued by other breeds".

In 1920, John Truman was very pleased at the results, particularly of the prizes for grade Shires. He wrote, "At the Iowa and Illinois State Fairs they brought out the best classes of the show, and the class of grade Shire geldings at the International (Chicago) will be the largest ever shown there. At Illinois, the Shires were superior in numbers and much superior in quality to any other breed, and you will, I am sure, be pleased to know that in the grade gelding and mare classes in competition with the Clydesdale and Percheron breeds, Shires were very successful. In no class did the Percheron stand ahead of them, and in only one or two classes the so-called Clydes. In competition for your special grade prizes, the class was extraordinarily strong." He looked forward to a six-horse team of grade Shires coming for exhibition one day so that the breed "may be shown in its true light, as the actual facts are that the Clydesdale people rob the Shire of his just dues by calling the cross-bred Shire horses Clydesdales". The Americans and Canadians did so much to add to the English sponsorship that the Council decided to renew the publicity scheme, which had cost £825 in 1920, for a second year.

It had also been agreed, during John Truman's visit, that animals eligible for the American Stud-book should be eligible also for the English one. Since the conditions of entry for the American book were more stringent than for the English, this was merely a matter of rescinding Bye-Law 36, that "no horse shall be entered in the Stud-book unless bred in the United Kingdom". But the agreement was not very fruitful. Only in Volume 42, prepared in 1920, was there an "American section", by which was meant a section of the Stud-book for American-bred Shires living in England. It contained five mares, all owned by Truman's Pioneer Stud Farm, Whittlesea, Peterborough. One had actually been bred in England and had already been registered in Volume 38 before being exported, and so, now that she had returned home, it would have been more logical and correct to re-enter her (and the only point of doing this seems to have been to list her prizes at American shows) in the ordinary part of the Stud-book. The others were bred by four different Illinois men, the four dams and four sires all being English-bred. The two most valuable were Eureka Pearl, foaled in 1914 and Royal Tulip foaled in 1913, Grand Champions at the Chicago International in 1917 and 1918. This reciprocal situation was slightly odd, because mares could enter the English book if they were seven-eighths "pure" (fifteen-sixteenths from 1922), whereas in America they had to be entirely pure-bred – unless already in the English book. One of the five, Truman's Duchess 2nd, would not have been eligible for the American book in the first place if her dam, Maryshall Duchess, had been bred in America, for this

Maryshall Duchess, bred at Hose, Leicestershire, was a bay mare with two only crosses of registered blood.

11. THE BRITISH PERCHERON

Before the war, that extraordinary and terrifying person, the 11th Duke of Bedford, had brought two pure-bred Percheron stallions from France to Woburn. They were probably the first ever to come to England, other than those shown by French owners on such special occasions as the Kilburn Royal Show in 1879 or by Truman at the 1912 International Horse Show. These stallions were no doubt an admirable addition to his collection of European bison, Père David deer and Przevalsky horses from the Gobi desert, but the Duke did not want them for stud purposes, not yet for publicity. As his grandson has written, he "lived a cold, aloof existence, isolated from the outside world by a mass of servants, sycophants and a eleven mile well."[3] He used his Percheron stallions for carriage work.

For several decades, however, half-bred Percherons had been one of the commonest sights in London: they had been imported in their thousands from the United States to horse the buses and for other light draught work. Many had been purchased from the omnibus companies for the artillery in the Boer war, at the end of which a Royal Commission on horse-breeding found that 90% of London bus horses were purchased either in America or at Liverpool on landing from that country, and were the progeny of Percheron stallions out of common American working mares.

The vast numbers of such animals acquired from 1914 onwards by the British Remount Purchasing Officers in America, their amazing activity and hardiness, and their good temper and fortitude either on sea or rail journeys or in conditions of war, have already been mentioned. The Engilsh were impressed, in addition, by the notable uniformity of the progeny got by pure Percheron stallions out of nondescript mares of all types. This prompted Major-General Sir William Birkbeck, Director of Remounts, in 1916 to send Colonel T. R. F. Bate R.A. and Lieutenant-Colonel Sir Merrik R. Burrell, Inspector of Remounts, to study the pedigree stallions at the French Government haras. They reported enthusiastically and at Sir William's suggestion R. E. Prothero (Lord Ernle), President of the Board of Agriculture, obtained the permission of his French counterpart to bring two pure-bred stallions and twelve mares to England. Since neither the Army nor the Board could become horse-breeders, Lord Lonsdale and Henry Overman of Weasenham in Norfolk agreed to purchase the animals.

By a coincidence, Overman's father had been one of the first twenty members of the committee which had set the English Cart Horse Society in motion in 1878. His contribution to Shire pedigrees had been slight – he had bred Honest Tom III 5124 in 1876 and two of his sons Norfolk Tom and Weasenham Tom 5420, both in 1880, with another Weasenham Tom 2515 coming between, in 1878. But that is all, though he remained a member until his death. But his son was to do much more for the French breed. Armed with the necessary papers of authority, he went to Mortagne in October 1916 and joined the French officials who were selecting stallions for purchase by the Government studs. His presence was flattering, for no Frenchman thought the day would come when the English would ask permission to buy Percherons. The age of the animals he chose is reflected by the initial letters of their names. There were eight three-year-olds – Navrante, Ninette, Niobe, Neva, Nodale, Nicoline, Nive, another Neva, and the stallion Nonius; two four-year-olds, Mesnière, and the stallion Misanthrope; one aged five, Limoselle; and two of six years, Irène and Kalidaca. Nonius and six of the females went to Lord Lonsdale at Barley Thorpe, Oakham while Overman had the other six mares and Misanthrope, who was already on his way to 21 cwt., a fine specimen of great quality and with grand action.

The following spring, owners of mares in the Oakham and Kings Lynn-Swaffham districts almost fell over themselves in their eagerness to get nominations to Nonius and Misanthrope, while pedigree Shire men were aghast at what was being done. Shades of Richard Parkinson who had written in 1808 that the Rutland horses were "of all shapes except real good shapes" and of Edward Coke who in 1878 in the Kilburn tent had described the Norfolk horses as "a sort of degenerated Shire-horse, who could be improved by Shire-bred blood"!

The Board of Agriculture thought they would like more of these horses and in October Overman was accompanied by six others, including Burrell and Birkbeck himself on the trip to Mortagne. This time money had been advanced by the Treasury, and twelve stallions and thirty-three mares were divided among Lord Lonsdale, Overman and nine others. In the meantime, Lord Lonsdale had managed,somehow, to buy the six-year-old stallion Lagor privately.

Though the intention had been to provide a means for the production of half-bred Percherons in this country, it was of course desirable that pure-blooded stallions for this purpose should be not merely imported but actually bred here, and this was why, from the start, mares had also been brought in. Therefore, it was essential as soon as possible to set up a register – the first pure-bred foals from the original batch of twelve mares would be due in 1918. So, on Wednesday, 16th January 1918 a meeting was called after lunch at Lord Lonsdale's town house, 14 Carlton House Terrace. There were sixteen men present, of whom exactly half were civilians. Considerable preparatory work had already been done and, before the meeting broke up, not only had the British Percheron Horse Society been formally inaugurated but a draft Memorandum and Articles of Association and all other necessary legal and organisational formalities approved and settled. In these matters, it was of course possible to take the procedures of the Shire Horse Society as a model, even to the appointment of Russell, Harris, Gardiner & Co. of Old Broad Street, as auditors. Likewise the Council members were to retire in rotation, one-third each year, and the President (the Earl of Lonsdale) was to be succeeded after only one year by the President-Elect (Henry Overman). The Shire Society was imitated also in that the twelve most recent Past-Presidents were to serve *ex officio* on the

Council. Lord Lonsdale was in addition elected honorary Treasurer and Captain Sidney Galtrey, the most junior serving officer present, was picked to be honorary Secretary. Shortly afterwards A. W. Hewett was appointed auctioneer and joint honorary Secretary, taking over the latter duties entirely in April 1919, when Captain Galtrey had to resign owing to pressure of his other duties.

If organisation was modelled on existing societies, the Stud-book regulations were entirely different from those with which any of the three native breed societies had begun their operations forty years before. The new society was not attempting to sort out a mass of existing animals whose ancestry, known and unknown, pure or mixed, lay for generations or centuries in this country. It could ensure that all blood was 100% pure and, furthermore, could insist, in the case of imported animals, on a high individual standard. Therefore, an imported stallion or mare was required to have been already entered in the register of the Société Hippique Percheronne de France, or of the Percheron Society of America, or of the Canadian Percheron Horse Breeders' Association: in addition, the animal had to be passed by a veterinary officer appointed by the Society as free from hereditary disease and also to be further certified by an inspector of the Society as of sufficiently good conformation and type. These last individual requirements were, of course, a very sensible precaution against the private importation, when the war should be over, of foreign breeders' pedigree misfits and weeds. (It could hardly be foreseen at that time, of course, that the day would soon come when a vast number of pedigree Percherons would be bred in their native country with no thought of any qualities but those required for meat. Huge tops would delight the butcher: but, when accompanied by heavily sideboned bottoms, would not be exactly what were required for draught.)

Animals bred in the British Isles would be eligible for the new Stud-book if both sire and dam were already registered in it or were entered in one of the three books abroad: that is, the Stud-book was "closed" from the start against "graded-up" animals. (It was to remain so until the next war.) Finally, in order to keep out "throw-backs" as far as colour was concerned (a freak colour would of course be likely to have a disproportionate influence in a breeding group whose numbers were limited), no imported mare and no stallion at all would be admitted unless either grey or black. One extra rule was an innovation in this country. All pedigree foals intended for entry in the Stud-book were to be branded on the neck before weaning, the branding irons being supplied by the secretary. There were those who knew of the difficulties other breed societies had experienced – for example, the Shire Society's very first disciplinary case in 1882 when a "Brown Stout" had been advertised as "What's Wanted". But this branding was to last only seven years as a compulsory rule.

The Shire Council, in April 1918, considered the publicity that had attended the formation of the British Percheron Society, but decided "to take no action at present". It is difficult to imagine what action could have been taken other than to march to the French Embassy or Lord Lonsdale's house and break the windows. The furore over the *Telegraph* report of the 1919 Shire show, suspected of having been written by Captain Galtrey, has already been described. By now, the end of the war had facilitated the importation of more Percherons, and Henry Overman helped to buy three more stallions and twenty-eight mares in France. They were sent to Sir Merrik Burrell's farm at Knepp Castle, Horsham where they were auctioned to those members of the society who had subscribed to the guarantee fund for their purchase. Prices reflected the inflation of the times, the stallions realising 1,600, 600 and 350 guineas, and the top mare 2,200, with three others reaching four figures. The thirty-one head totalled 20,485, an average of 660.8 guineas. Among those eager to make their own selection in France was Mrs. Emmet of Moreton Morrell, Warwickshire. Her stallion Rhum and mare Messalline were cunningly chosen purchases.

Everything in the Percheron garden seemed lovely, except for a little hornet's nest which threatened the ears of the Council when it opened a register for foals got by Percheron stallions out of "approved mares", and proposed a supplement to this register, to contain a list of such approved mares suitable for mating with Percherons. However, this was of minor importance. No one suggested that the Stud-book itself should be opened to graded-up stock. Twenty years were to elapse before there was any way of obtaining registration except by having a registered sire and a registered dam.

The 1919 Royal Show at Cardiff had three classes for Percherons, judged by the celebrated French expert, A. Ollivier, who described the occasion as one "of the greatest importance for the horse industry of France". Overman's Misanthrope won the stallion class by a mile: Lord Lonsdale's Kalidaca was first among mares with foal: and Lord Stalbridge's beautiful Pigeonnette had no real rivals among the barren or maiden mares. Shire and Suffolk men looked on in puzzled fascination. A second official auction, of twenty-five mares, was held in November, the top price being 370 guineas. At the end of the year, the Society had 185 members.

In 1920, there were sales in May and June at Tattersall's. The Royal at Darlington provided five classes for Percherons (ten for Shires). The Royal Norfolk had two classes for the breed, as for Shires, at its Spring Stallion Show and four (as against nine for Shires) at its Summer Show. The Bath and West and the Royal Counties also each furnished two classes, and seven for Shires. A batch of registered Percherons was imported from America and another from Canada. These were followed in the autumn by forty-five mares and fillies from France, selected by Overman and Sir Merrik Burrell, who had succeeded him as President. All were sold at official auctions under the hammer of A. W. Hewett. But these were not enough to supply the demand. The French, pleased as they were at the popularity of their horses here, urgently needed to re-build their own stock and were compelled to set a rigid limit on exports. The adverse rate of exchange with America and the high cost of freightage, which was out of all proportion to the pre-war rates, made North American horses uneconomic:

and, whereas half-bred Percherons had been plentiful and cheap, the value of top-class pedigree breeding stock was as high in America and Canada as it was in Europe. Consequently, the society's activities were stunted simply because intending members could not get horses. By the end of the year, membership had in fact dropped by eighteen to 167, just for this reason.

12. STALLION LICENSING: AND FERTILITY

The Improvement of Live-Stock Scheme, begun in 1913, made good progress during the war. In 1918, grants were made in respect of 122 stallions, which served a total of 12,281 mares for members of the societies concerned. Two thousand, one hundred and sixty-five of these were on assisted nominations. But hiring was becoming a more and more expensive business, and societies found it difficult to keep the service fee at the maximum 3 guineas permitted under the scheme, without resorting to inferior stallions. At last, in 1919, the Board responded to repeated requests and raised the maximum to 4 guineas for service and 400 guineas for the hire of the horse for the season.

The Board's voluntary scheme for vetting the soundness of pedigree heavy stallions in general also made headway. In 1918, no less than 1,429 passed the test in England and Wales, and were certified sound. In 1919, the number rose to 1,725. In Scotland, the Clydesdale men, who had previously had no veterinary inspection at all for horses entered at the Glasgow Stallion Show, introduced one during the war but, unlike the Shire Society, were prepared to exempt those animals which already held a Government certificate.

However, the number of certificated heavy stallions was still only something like a third – or a quarter – of the total number. Perhaps it was even less than a quarter. No one knew. There were 8,257 "stallions being used for service" on English and Welsh farms in 1916, according to the agricultural returns, but these included entire horses of every breed and type. Mr. Prothero made it public, at the end of that year, that the Board intended to introduce legislation. His plans had nothing to do with pedigree. Otherwise, in principle, the proposed Bill was similar to the idea advocated by Sir Alexander Henderson (now Lord Faringdon) when he was Shire Society President in 1903. But the Shire Council's first reaction was cautious. It expressed the view that "as private enterprise had built up the breed, so private enterprise would in the end eliminate the unsound stallion, and incidentally the unsound mare". This was no doubt true in the higher reaches of horse-breeding but, as long as careless or ignorant people were allowed to possess horses, it was otherwise a pious hope. In any case, Mr. Prothero was clearly determined. So throughout 1917 the Council maintained close contact with the Clydesdale men. The two societies were particularly anxious about four points – that compulsory examination should apply only to stallions travelling for service, and not to those standing at home; that, if continuously licensed up to the age of six, a stallion should then have a permanent licence without further inspection (a system which worked well in New Zealand, where inspection ceased after the age of five); that there should be a satisfactory appeal system; and that there should be uniformity of practice throughout the United Kingdom.

It became apparent that the Earl of Derby, Secretary of State for War, and a bigger gun than Mr. Prothero, was behind the Bill, which had really originated in the urgent need for improving the supply of horses for the army. There was therefore no chance of its being fought, except in detail. Anyhow, most of the objections that the breed societies had been putting forward were due to suspicion rather than opposition to the basic idea. Mr. Prothero would not budge on the matter of exempting senior stallions, and the most that was ever wrung from him was an undertaking that an aged horse which had been previously licensed regularly would not be rejected for wind alone. This wind testing was a matter of some anxiety and the Council rather envied the Clydesdale Society which had persuaded the Scottish Board to agree to a uniform gallop for wind, of 100 yards out and back, and to make special provisions for horses which roared merely because they were suffering from strangles or a severe cold, and other reasonable gives-and-takes. Eventually, the Horse Breeding Act, 1918 was passed in respect of stallions "travelling for hire or exhibited in public places or markets or shows", and became effective in 1920. The voluntary scheme was now superseded and, naturally, a special inspection of stallions for whom application was being made to participate in the Heavy Horse Breeding Scheme was now unnecessary. On the other hand, acceptance of the Society's London Show certificate by the Ministry was impossible under the new Act. But the first complaint over that matter concerned a horse which Professor Penberthy and his colleagues rejected at London in 1920 and was passed by the Government inspector in 1921.

The extent to which the pedigree movement in general had advanced by 1920 can perhaps be indicated by the relative number of licences granted to pure-bred and to other stallions in England and Wales during this first year of the Act's operations. Similarly, progress towards soundness can be gauged by the number of licences refused:

PEDIGREE STALLIONS				NON-PEDIGREE STALLIONS			
Licences refused			Licences granted	Licences granted		Licences refused	
%	No.					No.	%
10.4	262	Shires	2,258	172	Shire-type		
13.8	46	Clydesdale	286	10	"Clydesdales"		
5.9	12	Suffolks	193	4	"Suffolks"		
0.3	1	Percherons	33	9	"Percherons"	35	12.3
				54	Other heavy stallions		
			———	———			
			2,770	249			

3,019

But how misleading are these figures? It depends upon another figure, which no one knew in 1920, and certainly cannot be computed now – the number of stallions which their owners did not propose to travel for hire or exhibit in a public place, and for which licences need not be applied. Most of the entire horses standing strictly at home were non-pedigree, and largely nondescript also. How free they were from hereditary unsoundness is even more a matter of guesswork, but inevitably they must have been worse than those for whom a licence was sought. They served less mares than the others, mostly neighbour's mares, but there is no doubt that the owners took a chance here and there and hurried them along the lanes when required. After all, even if they were spotted, what policeman could prove that they were travelling for hire, unless he followed them and peeped over the wall to disprove the tale he had been told about the reason for their being on the road? And, even if he saw what he thought he might see, could he expect to see money being passed, to prove the hire? His task was harder than that of spying after hours on the local pub and proving that the landlord was not just entertaining his friends to a private party. It was more reminiscent of the problem of proving, in the time of Henry VIII, that an owner had "willingly suffered" his mare to be covered by a horse below the legal height. In spite of the Shire and Clydesdale Societies' representations, the Horse Breeding Act of 1918 should have made inspection and licensing compulsory for every entire horse. But that would have involved an unwarrantable intrusion into a man's private business which, in 1920, no one could stomach, because the refusal of a licence, in that event, would inevitably entail an order to castrate. And we had not fought the war with the object of giving a Government department the power to force a man to geld his horse. That was certain.

The Act required that stallion-leaders should carry the horse's licence with them, and not a few little comedies were enacted when police officers or Ministry officials, observing a stallion proceeding along a public highway, or exhibited on premises not in the occupation of his owner, or otherwise out and about, asked to see the paper. The report for the first year mildly stated that "the necessity for having the licence available for production by the groom did not seem to be generally understood at first". Leaders, waxing heavily sarcastic, were wont to enquire if the policeman would also like the horse to wear number-plates fore and aft.

It was something of a shock to the Council that over 10% of the pedigree Shires examined were refused licences. From the first furious onslaughts upon unsoundness by Professor Pritchard in 1880, the Society had done everything it could in every sphere to tackle the problem. The Act just showed how inadequate any voluntary system must be. Of the 262 unsound stallions, seventy-four roared and seventy-three whistled; fifty-seven had a sidebone, fourteen a ringbone, and four had bone spavin; there were nineteen with cataract; six were shiverers and two had stringhalt; one was "lame", another was of "defective conformation"; ten had defective genital organs and one was "immature". Yet in 1917, when the Bill was being argued with Mr. Prothero and the Board, the Council had claimed that the unsound stallion was "less troublesome than the weedy nondescript one and the non-foal-getter". The nondescript weed would now have to stay at home, because he could be disqualified as being of defective conformation, so that was all right. But what of the sterile horse?

In 1916, that very progressive group, the North-West Anglesey Shire Horse Society, had asked the Council to devise a way of obtaining from all societies a return of mares served and foals obtained by hired stallions, and to make the figures available for inspection on payment of a small fee. This excellent and, one would think, obvious idea for checking fertility had to be rejected under the pressure of war difficulties. The Society never was able to deal with this matter, but the Ministry of Agriculture, in the years to come, did collect some figures, though only in respect of stallions subsidised under the Improvement of Livestock Scheme, and it published these only for the foaling years 1925–1937, and not very systematically at that. Though this is beyond the period of our present chapter, these foaling returns show so little variation from year to year that they can be assumed to be applicable to 1920 as well as to any other time.

Surprise, surprise! The Shire Council need not have been so concerned. The Generosities of the breed were the exceptions. In spite of all the drawbacks to conception that the travelling system entailed, the Ministry's Report in 1932 said, baldly and dogmatically, that "draught-horse breeds, with 59% fertility, are more fertile than light-horse breeds, with 54%".[4] In the thirteen years for which figures are available, heavy stallions in the Ministry scheme only once left less than 58% of their mares in foal (57.4% in 1936), and in four seasons (1925–1928) fractionally just over 60%. Separate figures for any of the individual breeds are extant only for 1935–1937, in which years Suffolks led with 68.1, 67.2 and 66.0%: Shires achieved 58.6, 59.1 and 60.0%; and Clydesdales 52.4, 53.0 and 51.6%. But comparisons are invidious. There are as many reasons for taking glory from the Suffolks, which travelled only their own and two neighbouring counties, as for not criticising the Clydesdale. And success is comparative. Horse breeding was, is, and ever will be, a frustrating affair. As one of the Reports observed, "If these figures applied to other stock, breeders would have reason to be dissatisfied with the results."[4]

CHAPTER XI

1921–1924

A Sudden Rain of Blows

I. THE DEPRESSION

SURVEYING the havoc of the year 1921, A. B. Charlton waxed biblical. Furious at the publicity given by the Press to the sudden collapse of Shire prices, he suggested in his report that "an enemy hath done this". Grimly, he pointed out that "the cessation of trade in Shires is but symptomatic of the unprecedented depression which is being experienced in all branches of the country's business". He was right, of course, but a vicious vicar, a burglarious bank manager or a drug-addicted doctor must expect more publicity than other men. For over forty years, Shire horses had been the most dependably profitable enterprise on any farm: it was not without good reason that they had been dubbed "the rent-payers". It was a compliment to the status of the Shire that the London papers should take a grisly pleasure in constantly quoting low prices and lack of buyers.

In June 1921, 2,171,288 of the would be workers of Great Britain – that is, 17.8% of those covered by unemployment insurance – had no work to do. In the countryside, high taxes and death duties were breaking up big estates. Harman Brothers of Holborn in August advertised many properties "to be sold cheap with possession owing to the railway strike and drought, which may not occur again for a century". In Hertfordshire, 200 acres were offered for £4,000, with good farm house, buildings and cottages. "One of the best farms in the county", 430 acres with two farm houses, two sets of buildings and cottages, could be had for £9,500. In Cambridgeshire "400 acres, £6,000; good old manor house, wants restoring: grand buildings and cottages". Professor C. L. Mowat has instanced a firm of auctioneers which claimed to have sold enough land in twelve months to form a whole county. He added that "*The Times* published an article in 1922 entitled 'England changing hands', mentioning one firm with 79,000 acres announced for sale in its advertisements."[1] Some of the purchasers were new men who had no roots in the countryside and these included war profiteers. Others were the existing tenants who, confused by the novel experience during recent years of being praised and encouraged by the Government, were now just about to be told to go to the devil again. In October 1919, Lloyd George had promised the farmers he would guarantee their prices, and the Agriculture Act of December 1920 had confirmed what he said. But in August 1921, the Corn Production Acts (Repeal) Act threw all these promises out of the window, together with the Agricultural Wages Board, and "turned adrift the farmer, the farm labourer, and the whole state of farming."[2] This volte-face engendered a bitterness and distrust of Governments among the farming community which the next ten years did much to exacerbate and which remained deep rooted for twenty.

Statistics showed the agriculturist not to be so badly hit as some others. For example, the Board of Trade index numbers of wholesale prices of all articles show a drop in the two years 1920–1922 from 313.9 (based on an index of 100 in 1913) to 158.8, whereas similar Ministry of Agriculture figures show a decline in prices of agricultural produce only from 292 to 169, against which the cost to the farmer of feeding stuffs fell from 268 to 151, though fertilisers had actually risen from 215 to 220. These figures by no means comforted a tenant farmer suddenly faced with a sale, and the choice of quitting or buying. A Shropshire farmer, writing to *The Mark Lane Express*, put the position clearly. He had decided to buy his 100 acres. He had to put up one-third of the purchase money, to find which he was forced to sell stock he needed on the farm, at ludicrously low prices. On the other two-thirds he had to pay $6\frac{1}{2}\%$, which was greater than his rent had been. "I have ruin staring me in the face."

The appalling outbreaks of foot and mouth disease in each of the three years 1922–1924 were for many the last straw. John Moore's account of the atmosphere of those years as they affected his home town of Tewkesbury is only thinly disguised as fiction. He too is scriptural. "It was like the plague that walketh at noon-day." Farmer Jeffs drove down the High Street, encountering the vicar and demanding to know why he didn't pray. "If thee be any good, get down on thy knees: that's what we pay thee for, out of the tithe." With a final admonishment to the parson "Earn they keep", Mr. Jeffs drove his mare home – to be greeted by his cowman asking him to come and look at a calf which was drooling saliva. The normally jovial Mr. Jeffs looked grey and old when they came to slaughter the herd he had taken twenty years to build up.[3]

2. SHIRE SLUMP

If, from John Moore's Tewkesbury, you follow the Severn downstream through Gloucester and take up a position at some convenient place such as Minsterworth or Stonebench, on any one of a hundred or more days of the year, but especially at the spring tides and, above all, at the vernal or autumn equinox, you see an amazing sight. A huge tide-wave rushes in the contrary direction over the top of the river which, in a second or two, is not only flowing backwards but is apparently out of control. The level has risen several feet and the banks are submerged. The Shire men in 1921 likewise watched the circumstances of their business instantly and spectacularly changed. If it had merely been a matter of the general depression, their difficulty might be likened to any ordinary tidal river. It was turned into a Severn bore by two special factors – a sudden glut of horses and an equally sudden drop in demand.

These reversals of the previous trend of course affected the other breeds also. The Suffolk, primarily an agricultural horse, and the Clydesdale, of which so many were exported, perhaps suffered less. The Percheron men, hampered at the beginning by the difficulty of acquiring enough stock, were now suddenly near to being overwhelmed by the new adverse tide, at the same time as prices were largely maintained in France by the meat trade. But we must speak here in terms of the Shire, which is our concern.

The glut had two causes. Firstly, from the earliest conceivable moment in 1915 onwards, as many Shires as possible had been bred in order to meet the desperate demand for increased production on the land at home and for the army. The very first war-time foals reached the age of five and were therefore ready for work off the land in – of all years – 1921. Cart-horse breeding is the longest-term enterprise on any farm. The seed sown today comes to full fruition only in six years' time. Since it would be unreasonable to expect that Shire men should have been any more clairvoyant than Lloyd George was in 1920, we must not be surprised that in 1921 there was also an unusually high number not only of two to four year olds but yearlings and foals as well.

Secondly, the allied armies had not only ceased, quite abruptly, to want any more horses: they started sending back to civilian life all those they already had. The enormous number purchased in America never returned there. They stayed in Europe (where they were needed) or were sold in Britain (where, under sensible planning, it would have been recognised that most of them were not). By the end of 1921, the number of army horses, fit for work, which had been sold on the open market in this country alone was 141,000. Many were "rubbish" – mere apologies for horses. They did little good for the reputation of the horse against the motor-engine. But they were cheap. And now, in 1921, anyone who wanted a horse had perforce to think of the pennies and pounds in a way he had forgotten during the past seven years or so.

The sudden drop in demand for horses was due to the development of the internal combustion engine during the war. Long before 1914, the car had been challenging the light-horse, but the heavy one had been safe. Now, it was realised that the motor-lorry on the streets and the motor-plough and tractor on the farm threatened the cart-horse with extinction. As it happened, things did not turn out so badly as the pessimists among the breeders expected. The towns had to wait for another world war before the motor's long and convincing lead on points, slowly built up over twenty years of combat, was suddenly converted into a knock-out victory. In the country, the motor proved, during those same twenty years, to be not so much a rival to the horse as an assistant, and only that on the farms of the wealthy. Nevertheless, the carpet-sweeper manufacturer hardly raises a cheer when he hears that someone had invented a vacuum cleaner.

The immediate effects of the collapse were grisly enough, though they can best be appreciated through the eyes of individuals, of whom it will be sufficiently painful to quote only three. The Forshaw brothers, Thomas and James, had followed their father in confining their business at Carlton-on-Trent entirely to Shire horses and can be described, without offence to others, as the greatest of the professionals. One of their stallions, bought for £1,600, they estimated in 1923 as being worth £250 – and he was still only seven years old, in his prime. But they could not get that for him, because no one offered to buy. The tax inspector refused to believe any of their figures. (Possibly this was the first time that anyone in the world had not accepted the word of the Forshaws.) He wanted to allow only the usual percentage reduction for depreciation. They argued and appealed, apparently in vain. Meanwhile, they had bought some Frisian cattle, merely as a means of keeping going. It was their only alternative to selling up the best-known stallion stud in England. They attacked their new enterprise in typical Forshaw fashion, importing a bull, Carlton Overwinnaar, in 1922 and aiming at big, well-fleshed cows with a high butter-fat record and at producing good young bulls for dairy-farmers. But that is by the way, except to show that their idea of a true Shire influenced their outlook on cattle. Eventually, having told the tax-man that they would carry their appeals to the House of Lords if they could, simply because it would be cheaper than to pay his demands, he saw that they were telling the truth.

On 30th September 1921, Henry Hobbs made a valuation of the Shires that with his brother Robert he had on the family farms at Kelmscott, Little Faringdon, Bampton and Meysey Hampton in Gloucestershire. There were ninety-seven of them – two stallions, thirty-four mares, twenty-six geldings, twenty-eight yearlings (an equal number of each sex) and seven foals, all pure bred and in their quality reflecting not just the brothers' devotion, but the skill and care of their father Robert since 1882 and of their grandfather Charles before him. Their horses were as famous as their Oxford Down sheep and Gloucester Old Spot pigs, and almost as celebrated as their Dairy Shorthorns. Writing down what they were worth in that depressing year was a gloomy business. Henry put the home-bred three-year-old stallion Kelmscott Centre Half (by Champion's Goalkeeper) at £600 and the other, of the same age, at £400. Among the mares, Minion's Chum he valued at £200, Kelmscott Clansmaid at £150 and Kelmscott Duke's Petal at £100. He made the total £5,564. Excluding the two entire horses, this worked out at an average of just over £48. He doubted whether the tax-man would believe this: but also doubted whether in fact, if he wanted to sell, he could get any price at all. The following year's valuation showed ninety-eight horses, totalling £4,173. The two stallions, which would normally have appreciated, he listed at £400 and £200, but these were paper figures. (In 1920, £1,000 would indeed have been a fair price for a four-year-old of the Kelmscott Centre Half quality – indeed, his own brother Kelmscott Centre Forward had been sold at Peterborough that year for 1,000 guineas.) The average, without the entires, was £37.2. The seven yearling colts of the year before had been castrated, and the three colt foals of 1921 likewise. There was no point in waiting to see how they would turn out. He had nine new foals but the only animals sold had been disposed of at Stow Fair. They were as follows:

1920 valuation approx. £1,240

1921 valuation

Kelmscott Movement aged 14, home-bred dam of seven foals	40
Kelmscott Fashion, 13 (three foals)	45
Halstead Duchess VII,12 (3rd in London for Lord Rothschild, sold to J. G. Williams in 1913 for 825 guineas. Had never bred)	50
Kelmscott Rosy Morn, 11 (two foals)	40
Kelmscott Modish, 9 (five foals)	50
Kelmscott Model Maid, 8 (two foals)	35
Kelmscott Blue Bird, 7 (one foal)	40
	£300

1922: Sold at Stow Fair £82. 9s. od.

Four years later, Henry Hobbs moved to Woburn to start the Duke of Bedford's Shire stud. It was almost fifty years later that he turned up the little black cash book again. On the cover appeared the words "Cirencester Laundry. Mrs. R. W. Hobbs. Kelmscott. Maids' initials F. R. and R. N." Inside was this record of how the slump affected one great farming family's Shires.

Our third illustration is a memory from the auctioneer's viewpoint. S. T. Parker of Derby, one of the best-known sellers of Shires in England and still on the rostrum at the Derby foal sales, fifty years after the period in question, has commented, "I have often told some of our young auctioneers, when they come to me and grouse about having a poor trade, of my experience as a young salesman in 1923, standing up to offer for sale a catalogue of 175 horses, including a class of over 50 town geldings and mares, four years old and over, and only selling one horse in this class, the prize-winner, at 50 guineas. Shire-bred grazing foals were virtually unsaleable, and could be bought for as little as five guineas. A buyer could have the pick of the yard for fifteen."

To quote "average prices" in these years is more misleading than ever, since they do not take account of the enormous number left unsold at every sale. But the following list of *highest* prices recorded in 1921–1923 will perhaps be sufficiently revealing:

	1921		1922		1923	
	£.	s.	£.	s.	£.	s.
Brood mares	1,155.	0.	525.	0.	231.	0.
3-year-old fillies	761.	5.	262.	10.	210.	0.
2-year-old fillies	840.	0.	262.	10.	178.	10.
Yearling fillies	577.	10.	178.	10.	126.	0.
Filly foals	336.	0.	315.	0.	115.	10.
Yearling colts	336.	0.	157.	10.	135.	0.
Colt foals	194.	5.	147.	0.	96.	12.

It must be borne in mind that, even in time of depression, there are always likely to be a few men with resources at their command who will bid against each other for the best. If these, then, are the prices for the best of all, it requires little imagination to understand the dilemma of the man wanting to sell a "sound and useful" gelding in these years. Ought he to accept a low offer simply because he might not receive another?

When this depression is translated into terms of the horse population, the figures are remarkable. The third census taken by the Board of Trade for the War Office shows that the total number of horses, of all kinds, in Great Britain in June 1920 was 2,081,457: by June 1924, when the fourth census was taken, it had dropped by 9.09% to 1,892,205. Quoting now in thousands, we find that agricultural horses decreased from 775 to 754 (a reduction of 2.7%); mature town draught-horses, light and heavy, from 411 to 374 (9%) – of these, heavy ones dropped from 193 to 176 (8.8%). The biggest decrease was in young horses, under three years – heavy types from 225 to 150 (41.2% reduction on 1920) and light types, excluding Thoroughbreds, from 90 to 62 thousand (31.1%). The Ministry of Agriculture returns show a similar pattern in respect of foals, though of course in exaggerated form. In 1916, the first war-time breeding resulted in 109,807 foals of all types; in 1920, there were 97,298; mares covered in 1924 were so many fewer that the 1925 crop was 44,875, a drop of 53.9% on 1920.

Over supply and lack of demand were not the only troubles that afflicted the Shire men in these brief few years. The roads were being made too slippery. Some people wanted to bar horses from the town streets because they impeded traffic. The docking question came up again. There was a row with R.A.S.E. about judging at shows. The Government stopped its grants to stallion societies. There was a move to prohibit the export of old or surplus horses. The export market for pedigree breeding stock, that pipe-dream of the war-years, vanished. And, finally, there was a need for self-examination. Had the Shire been developed on the right lines?

3. SOCIETY AFFAIRS

An extraordinary thing was done in February 1921 by the Past-Presidents and the other select few whose duty it was to choose the next President-Elect. As if to show that the war really had turned everything upside down, they picked a tenant farmer.

John Rowell, of Manor Farm, Bury, in Huntingdon, had joined the Society at the very beginning. And many a fine and weighty Shire had he and his father before him bred, earlier than that. In 1849, John senior owned the good bay colt foal Major, son of England's Glory (717) and grandson of the legendary Seward's Major (1447) – all of the finest Fens blood. In 1859 he had bred that celebrated Black, Heart of Oak (1005), which eventually went to the Earl of Ellesmere's and became one of the eight foundation sires of the modern breed: and he had bred the dam, too, also by England's Glory 717. Then there was

Samson (1952) bred in 1861 by Thomas Mott, a familiar Littleport name. John, the father, who owned him, weighed him once, and he was 1 ton 8 cwt.

John the younger had had his first home sale in 1889 – somewhat peculiarly, in the month of June. The total receipts were nearly £5,000 for fourteen mares, thirteen fillies, fifteen three-year-old stallions and eighteen colts – an average of just over 77 guineas, which was a good thing in those days. Lord de Ramsey of Ramsey Abbey had been there in person and bought three of his tenant's Shires – Bury Rose for 50 guineas and two two-year-olds, *Bury Mettle* and Bury Drayman, for 63 guineas and 80 guineas. The Prince of Wales had been represented too, and Bury Lassie, a yearling, was bought for Sandringham at 200 guineas. One of the company there that day turned, very genially, to Mr. Morrow (who represented the U.S. Department of Agriculture) and said, "Could the head of a Republic do better than this?" The Argentinian purchasers thought it was a good joke, too, when they heard about it. Four years before, in 1885, John had shown Prince William, the outstanding London champion, and sold him to Lord Wantage for 1,500 guineas. That very year of the sale he bred Bury Victor Chief and sold him two years later to Joseph Wainwright for 2,500 guineas, and he was twice London champion. Much more recently he owned the 1916 supreme stallion, Bury King's Champion.

John had been elected to the Council in 1880 and eight further times since, making twenty-seven years' service. In 1890, the only year when the number of votes cast for each candidate was divulged by the scrutineers (who were normally secretaries of other societies inhabiting No. 12) he easily topped the poll. He had been chairman and vice-chairman of the Horse Show and Editing Committees. He had judged London five times, and had officiated in every county in England and at every show of any consequence. But it was for none of these things that he was chosen President. Even less was it because anyone thought that a representative of the tenant farmer interest would be sound politics or a publicity gimmick. Even in 1921, the Lords Middleton and Northbourne, the Earls Bathurst and Beauchamp and the other selectors would not do anything so uncouth as that. He was chosen simply because he was liked and respected, always full of hope and enthusiasm for the breed, always ready to work for it, always ready to help anyone else. A picture of the King's Field Marshal V was selected to advertise the Shire horse on the Society's posters: if they had wanted to advertise the Shire man, most members would have picked John Rowell.

But in choosing him as President, they were too late. He died on 15th March 1922 and at the April Council meeting, when he should have taken office, they stood instead in his memory. Sir Walter Gilbey, the retiring President, referred to his sterling character and spotless integrity, and said "We may not see his like again". His daughter had written to say that he had felt a deep and sincere pride at having been elected. She had found, amongst his papers, some notes of the remarks he had intended to make at this meeting. They contained the words "My aim in year of office, to hearten Shire men in their work. Present slump will pass and good times come again. Up to younger men coming on to keep their courage up and their heads level." He had been a old man and none can live for ever. But the twenty-eight gathered in the Council room, from His Grace of Devonshire to the head clerk, W. J. Wickison, were all near to weeping.

The Selection Committee had already and hastily done their work a second time. In tribute to John, they deliberately chose another tenant farmer and Fenman, Alfred Clark of Moulton Eaugate. Careful though the Society had always been to nominate only true supporters to the Presidency, the men who filled the office during these testing four years – Gilbey, Clark, the Duke of Devonshire and Sir Bernard Greenwell, son of Sir Walpole – were as strong a quartet as ever were appointed in succession.

Other good and well-loved men who died in these gloomy times were Lord Middleton in 1922, and John Eadie in 1923. The latter had joined the Shire Society, with his father James, in 1892. They were brewers who kept a large breeding stud at Barrow-on-Trent. John was best remembered for that outstanding gelding Bardon Extraordinary and the other, hardly less extraordinary, Barrow Farmer. He had sold them both for a then record price of 200 guineas each. But there were many men who had bought a mare or two from his stud and set out on a successful Shire career – and this was the thing which gave him simple pleasure to think about.

In April 1923, the slump had so seriously affected the Society's finances that Charlton was told, amongst the economies, to cut down on office and clerical expenditure. Almost immediately, Wickison died, which was not the sort of economy anyone had thought of. Times were hard and, since he had received an advance of the second quarter's salary, the Council were unable to make any further token of gratitude to his wife Mabel. This was not a happy time. The four men who were left to run the office closed their ranks. Charlton was receiving £850 per annum. The ex-junior A. G. Holland, was now appointed assistant secretary at £375. M. R. Leather, £230, and A. E. Sparrow, £220, completed the team, though – in accordance with the Hanover Square custom – they had irons in the fires of other rooms. A sum of £300 a year was budgetted for casual clerical assistance at A.B.C's discretion.

Wickison's experience over more than twenty years was missed, particularly in the matter of vetting stud-book entries. But the 1923 volume had been issued at the normal time, during the London Show, and at last the confusions and delays caused by the war had been overcome. The Editing Committee's most regular appeal to members was now that they should make more effort to describe the markings of animals fully and accurately. Too many were vaguely putting "three white legs", without saying which legs, and there had been not a few cases of disputed identity owing to the actual markings being different from those in the book, and others where the mention of a small piece of white at the time of registration would have saved an argument later. One very successful exhibitor, who had been presented to the King at the beginning of this period, was expelled from the Society at the end of it, for substituting mares at a show and for showing a horse as his when it was in fact another horse belonging to someone else.

Another disciplinary case, a curious one, was the most boring and regular item on the Council's agenda from the middle of the war until the end of 1922. The member concerned had committed no offence against the Society's rules but had broken those of two other societies and, in accordance with the principle of all acting in concert, he had been suspended from the Shire Society. He started a civil action, but eventually withdrew it. Counsel then advised the Society that to expel him for conduct "derogatory to the character and prejudicial to the interests of the Society" would be very difficult (*Young* v *Ladies Imperial Club 1920* must be borne in mind), in view of the fact that he had really prejudiced only two quite different societies. Finally, to rid itself of a gentleman whom it did not want but who took crafty care to see that his subscription never failed to arrive punctually, the Council had the brilliant idea of telling him it would institute a formal enquiry unless he was prepared to resign. A formal enquiry into what, was left vague. But mercifully there must have been something to do with his Shires as well, for he did resign. The Shire Society has been very fortunate to have had few cases like this.

In 1921, another difficulty arose, this time over a Shire prefix being identical to a word used outside Shire-breeding circles. It was inevitable that it would happen, sooner or later. George Gosling in Staffordshire had been granted the prefix Rickerscote in 1919. Subsequently, C. & E. Stephenson Limited of the same place had registered the same word as a trade-mark and, in doing so, had claimed to have used it since 25th March 1913. Fortunately, the thing was easily solved – Gosling had not used his Shire prefix, and Stephensons had used their trade-mark only for other kinds of livestock. The Council had to request Gosling to choose another word, and suggested Silkmore. Gosling did nothing about it, and Charlton had to send his 10s. back. Stephensons paid 10s. to have the Rickerscote prefix for Shires, and used it to name three mares in the 1924 volume, but this is all either party ever managed.

Financially, this was the most confusing time the Shire men had passed through. The period began with the owners of 12 Hanover Square offering to sell it, together with 289/291 Oxford Street, for £20,000. (Twenty years of the R.A.S.E.'s lease had still to run.) Neither the Society itself nor the joint house committee representing all the societies was prepared to risk this. They were then offered alternative premises in Portland Place, if they cleared out. They refused to do this, too. The 1922 Show receipts were down by £1,112 compared with 1921: but the net loss involved in staging it was only £754 more, because costs were beginning to fall. 1922 was in fact a weird year, for the Society had a working loss of £869, and yet the balance sheet showed an improvement because the value of invested funds had risen by £1,615 – "a fine example", A.B.C. called it, "of the silver lining which appertains to every cloud". These invested funds soon had to be drawn upon, for the urgent

TABLE A. MEMBERSHIP, REGISTRATIONS, LONDON SHOW ENTRIES, ETC.

	Averages 1917–19	1920	1921	1922	1923	1924
New members joining	636[1]	684	449	252	159	115
Net gain/loss	+470	+432	+163	−114[2]	−513	−611
Annual members[3]	3,620	4,403	4,545	4,453	4,115	3,618
Total membership 31st December	5,409[4]	6,328	6,491[5]	6,377	6,023	5,527
New prefixes allotted[6]	313	418	259	135	89	69
Stud-book[7] – new stallions	860	923	663	431	312	242
new mares	4,616	5,656	4,140	2,660	2,453	1,860
	(Av. 1912–14)					
London Show entries – stallions	376	287	309	258	183	154
mares	290	213	261	215	187	159
geldings	35	21	19	27	32	53
	701	521	589	500	402	366
Commercial horses[8] – no. of entries					52	73

[1] 747 new members joined in 1918 – a record.

[2] The first decrease ever recorded.

[3] The number of *annual* subscribers is the surest guide to the health of membership. The rest were life members, and two or three honorary members.

[4] Membership on 31st December 1919 was 5,896 – an increase of 1,411 in three years.

[5] This was the peak year.

[6] *Total* number of prefixes would be meaningless. They were usually left on register, as a reference-guide, long after a member's death.

[7] Figures relate to *year of registration*, not publication. (Horses registered e.g. 1921 appeared in 1922 volume.)

[8] i.e. singles, pairs, teams etc. It is impossible to work out the number of different horses – some appeared in two or more classes, wearing different numbers. Nearly all were geldings – in 1923, three were mares, in 1924, five.

TABLE B. SELECTED COSTS ($£$)

		1913	1920	1923	1924
i	Salaries and wages	1,101	2,010	1,684	1,625
ii	Printing of stud book	1,068	3,076	1,643	1,215
iii	Offices (rent, etc.)	NIL	196	237	228
		(140 profit)			
iv	Publicity	NIL (see vii)	748	1,040	313
v	Rent and fittings of Hall, Spring show	598	1,208	1,551	1,279[1]
vi	Prizes, medals etc., Spring show	1,834	2,542	2,551	2,037
vii	Prizes, medals etc, other shows	1,724[2]	1,513	1,492	1,252
viii	Profit/loss on year's working	+919[3]	+2,057	−2,496[4]	−625

[1] For 1924, the Agricultural Hall Co. agreed to cancel existing agreement and substituted a basic rental of £1,200 for 500 boxes or stalls, and £4 per horse over 500.

[2] Unusually high for pre-war (average 1910–1912 was £1,161) owing to £400 in gold cups, overseas, etc.

[3] Unusually low owing to gold cups, and the new Corporation Duty (£176).

[4] The seventh loss and the largest (the others in 1880, 1886, 1894, 1895, 1905, 1919).

FORAGE. In 1910–1914, Nickolls and Baker contracted for this at 6/9, 6/9, 7/6, 7/6 and 7/– per horse. In 1920–1924, 17/–, 15/–, 12/–, 11/–, 10/9.

necessity to encourage the breeding and showing of good Shires in discouraging times, and an all-out effort to publicise the breed in America and Canada, forced the Council to sell £3,250 of National War Bonds in April 1923. There was a big economy campaign at the end of the year and the policy of old John Slough-grove of saving against the seemingly unlikely arrival of a rainy day was soon to prove of great benefit. (The attached tables give some indication of the way that outside influences upset the equilibrium of Shire affairs during these four years.)

4. GOVERNMENT GRANTS

A canny, or perhaps merely distrustful, representative of the Swindon Shire Horse Society asked, at the Annual General Meeting in February 1921, whether it was the Government's intention to continue grants under the Heavy Horse Breeding scheme. There had been a strange dearth of paper emanating from Whitehall. But in April forms flew in all directions and ninety-two societies were helped.

On 16th August, Sir Eric Geddes, lately the first Minister of Transport, was appointed to head a Committee on National Expenditure to examine the estimates and recommend economies. The Ministry of Agriculture in November warned the hiring societies that the grants for 1922 might be revised or cancelled. This was a little late. By now many societies reckoned to have arranged for their next year's horse. How would they know whether they would be able to afford it? The East Devon society did its best to kick up a fuss about this absurd uncertainty. In spite of repeated enquiries by the Shire Society itself, there was no information even on 23rd February, the date of the A.G.M. However, on 10th February, the Geddes Committee had published its first two reports recommending savings of £75,000,000, additional to the £75,000,000 already axed in the 1922 Estimates. Its third report was published on 24th February, and recommended a saving of a further £11,000,000.

Eventually on 6th March, the Ministry informed the Society that it was compelled to abandon the Heavy Horse scheme. E. B. Shine, Assistant Secretary, concluded his letter with the hope that the societies "which were established under the Live Stock Scheme will continue to operate successfully". Poor man, he was a good friend to the Society and of course was personally very sorry about it. The Government saved approximately £7,000 on heavy-horse breeding, roughly 0.0043% of the new national economies. All this may appear very trivial, but for several thousands of small farmers it was serious. A week later, an emergency Council meeting decided to appeal to the Prime Minister (Lloyd George), the Chancellor of the Exchequer (Sir R. S. Horne) and the Minister (Sir Arthur Griffith-Boscawen). The latter met a Shire deputation on 24th March. The Suffolk men had desired to be represented, but their letter had been delayed in the post and arrived only on the morning of the meeting. (What *was* the matter with the post-war Post Office?) Sir Arthur could not budge. He was sorry. He must continue the new milk-recording scheme, and the grants for bulls and boars. Yes, he was sorry. But, more brightly, he added that actual help for breeders was now less necessary than when the scheme first started, because the Horse Breeding Act made it compulsory for all travelling stallions to be vetted. Grinding their teeth at this example of ministerial logic, the Shire men retired defeated and wrote a letter about it to the men of Suffolk.

The decision to stop the grants was more sensible than the Minister's explanation of it. There were too many heavy-horses in the country, and people should not be encouraged to breed now. But, for the Society, the damage was out of all proportion to the money involved. Strenuous efforts had been made, for more than forty years, to improve the cart-horse – not only the choicest purebred specimens but the ordinary workers. Furthermore, the geographical range of the Shire-bred had been steadily extended throughout this period. In the new areas, the use of a good pedigree horse, instead of any old scrub stallion, had depended upon the grants. Many societies in the newer districts now promptly folded up, and the work of years was likely to be undone.

It is difficult now to realise that a few pounds could make so much difference. But a hiring society had to work on a basis of 100 mares per horse, all located within a manageable radius. Enthusiastic members had always to be supplemented by men who would not join at all unless the fee could be brought down almost as low as the price they would have to pay for an inferior horse. If the removal of the direct grant and of the half-fee subsidy available to those farming less than 100 acres caused a number of the members to drop out, the cost to the keener ones would rise beyond their means.

In a southern or western county, the collapse of the local hiring society almost inevitably meant that there was no good stallion available in the district. A stallion-owner in the Fens was not likely to be happy about the gamble of sending a valuable horse to Dorset or Kent to pick up what trade he could, in a time of depression. It was the old problem again, which the Ministry scheme and the consistent efforts of the breed society had come so near, until now, of solving – the problem caused by the fact that good Shire breeding was quite unlike the breeding of any other farm stock. It could not be done on one's own, but needed the co-operation of neighbours.

In, say, Leicestershire or Lincolnshire, there were still plenty of stallions, privately travelled. Owing to the few mares being bred from in these years, owners were only too willing to let them serve at what the small horse-owner could afford. So the situation, for the small man, was not so bad: but it was hardly a happy one for the stallion-owner. And it was the owners of good stallions (whether wealthy land-owners or hard-working men undertaking a risky living by buying just one or two to travel), and their willingness to play fair with the farmers of the district where they sent their horses, who had done most to improve and increase the cart-horse.

In sharp contrast to the winding-up of many of the poorer and smaller societies, the Crewe, Montgomeryshire, Newark and other well-established associations continued not only to operate, but in some cases to pay very high hiring fees. But, if they had formerly hired two or three horses, it was the cheapest (which had come just within the maximum hiring fee stipulated under the grant scheme) which was now in jeopardy: and their least wealthy members, who most needed encouragement, suffered from this. The quality of cart-horse breeding was dealt a blow which was quite disproportionate to the meagre £7,000 involved. The National Farmers' Union sent a questionnaire to branches and every one replied urging that pressure be brought on the Government to think again.

Noel Buxton, the first Labour Minister of Agriculture, generously agreed that the Conservatives had made a mistake. On 19th February 1924, in reply to a question in the House, he said, "I am satisfied that the withdrawal of the grant has discouraged co-operation among farmers in the hiring of stallions and has otherwise proved detrimental to the heavy-horse breeding industry." He immediately restored it (at £40 per society) without, however, providing for assisted nominations. But the societies which had collapsed could not be revived in time to operate that season.

5. ANTI-DOCKING

The docking argument had been more or less in abeyance since, at the end of the last century, the Society had persuaded the R.A.S.E. to rescind its resolution to ban docked horses from its shows. In 1913, it is true, there was a move by a small group of persons to promote a Bill, but a short salvo from the Shire Council effectively discouraged further action, and the idea was dropped. But now, in 1921, as if horse users were not already in enough of a mess, it raised its tail once again – and, incredibly, none of the interested parties saw it happen.

In the afternoon of Friday, 8th April, A. B. Charlton was sitting in his office, preoccupied with the week-old miners' strike and wondering whether the transport workers and the railway men would decide to come out as well. The telephone rang. Did he know that a private Bill, presented by Colonel Burn, to prohibit the docking of horses, had passed its second reading in the House? He certainly did not. He had never even heard of it. He forgot the strikers, and reacted with speed. He obtained a copy of the Bill and found that it made docking an offence which incurred a maximum penalty of £25 or one month's imprisonment, with or without hard labour. The only exemption lay in cases where a member of the Royal College of Veterinary Surgeons certified the operation as necessary for surgical treatment, or "otherwise for the benefit of the horse". To his surprise, he found a Shire member among its supporters (just as the Duke of Westminster had been in favour of the R.A.S.E. ban, over twenty years before). This was Lord Henry Cavendish-Bentinck, Member for South Nottingham, and a member of the Society since 1896. He had a stud at Underley Hall, Kirkby Lonsdale. (A son of General Bentinck, he was half-brother to the 6th Duke of Portland.)

On enquiry, Charlton discovered, to his even greater amazement, that neither Mr. Shine nor anyone else at the Ministry of Agriculture had any idea of what was happening. He bought thirty more copies of the Bill, had some letters prepared and addressed them to the President and the members of the Horse Show Committee, of which John Rowell was the chairman. Among these, surprisingly, was a prominent Member of Parliament. (This was David Davies, Liberal member for Montgomeryshire since 1906. In 1916 he had been recalled from command of the 14th Welsh Fusiliers to become Parliamentary Private Secretary to Lloyd George, and was dismissed the next year for criticising the conduct of the war. He was now absorbed in the greatest of all his many interests, the League of Nations Union. A life member of the Shire Society since the age of twenty-four, he had bought the record-priced Gleadthorpe Seclusion for his Llandinam estates, but she was now dead. He also at this time owned the Percheron stallion Prescient and nine mares, and was awaiting some foals. The very day Charlton's letter arrived the first of them was born.)

The new President, installed only three days before, was just the man for an emergency. It was Sir Walter Gilbey. He told A.B.C. to call an emergency meeting of the Council and to write to every other breed society concerned. On the following Monday, he button-holed all the most influential Members he knew. Later in the week, while the Government was calling up reservists, requisitioning vehicles for food distribution, turning Kensington Gardens into an armed camp and appealing for volunteers to join the Defence Force, he met the Minister himself. The latter confessed that he was totally unaware of this anti-docking Bill, but agreed that it was absurd and unnecessary. Sir Walter was relieved when he heard this: and so was the Minister, when the news came through that the General Strike was averted and, with it, the possibility of civil war.

By 3rd May, the Clydesdale, Suffolk and Percheron societies had joined in the Shire dissent. So had R.A.S.E., the Hackney, Hunter, National Pony and New Forest Pony societies, the County Polo Association and the London Cart and Van Horse Parade societies; the Central National Farmers' Union and its Aylesbury, Lancashire and Berkshire branches; from Shropshire, the County Council Agricultural Committee and the Chamber of Agriculture; the Fareham & Hants. Farmers' Club, the Lancaster Agricultural Society and the Land Agents' Society. This assorted group of militants fired off various protests in all directions. "The continual interference with the liberties of the horse-breeder and owner in the conduct of his business" was the chief objection – and was of a type that earned more sympathy in 1921, when the freedom of the citizen still had some appeal to the hearts and minds of the nation, than it would fifty years later. The practical arguments against the prohibition of docking were many. Every cart horse on the farms was docked. If that were not allowed, there would be more accidents, especially to drivers of mowers and binders, when tails became entangled in reins and machinery, and the horses ran away. Indeed, in all driving, whether of heavy-horses or of the hackney, docking was essential for safety reasons. Even in polo, the swishing of tails was dangerous to pony and rider, and would add "an artificial difficulty" to the game. Docking was now governed by the Animals (Anaesthetics) Act of 1919 and so there could be no cruelty.

The dock healed within a week, whereas to pull the hair by force, which would be the only alternative, was less humane because it would have to be repeated throughout an animal's life. In town, docking also protected the public from disease caused by tails becoming too big, or, if the horse were sick, filthy. In the country, the harassed farmer would have to devote much of his time to plaiting his horses' tails after all his men had gone home, because Parliament had recently reduced the working week. Finally, why not prohibit the cutting of lamb', tails? Or – it needed only one more logical step to achieve a *reductio ad absurdum* – why no Bill to forbid the castration of horses, cattle and sheep?

The third reading was due in June, but Colonel Burn and his friends could not withstand this fire, and it was announced on 31st May that the Bill was withdrawn. The miners' strike ended on 1st July.

6. NATIONAL HORSE ASSOCIATION

Docking arguments were not the only vertebrae of contention at this time. The regulations which governed the shipping of worn-out or misfit horses for slaughter in Holland and Belgium were not working as satisfactorily as they might. During the war the thing had been forgotten, and the trade had virtually ceased anyway. But in 1921 a Bill was originated in the House of Lords containing a proposal to impose an export duty on all horses sent to the Continent. The Minister of Agriculture (Griffith-Boscawen) refused absolutely to countenance the idea, and the Shire council vigorously supported him. However, cruelty to animals was annually becoming a more and more explosive subject and the Shire men thought it advisable in May meticulously to define their position. "No member of the Society would support anything in the nature of cruelty to animals, but a tax would tend to keep unsound and worn-out horses in the country for breeding and working purposes which would otherwise be cleared out, to the country's advantage. The slaughter of shiverers and other unsound horses was more humanitarian than to tempt owners to retain and work them sub rosa. More supervision at the ports was essential, and prosecutions should be enforced against all who brought for shipment animals in an unfit condition."

The Bill was abandoned before it reached the Lower House and instead the Minister made an Exportation and Transit of Horses, Asses and Mules Order which came into force on 1st February 1922. This considerably strengthened the rules. Horses had to be examined before being entrained for the coast, and at the ports. Rolling stock had to be disinfected. Animals must not be carried in the winter months except under a permanent deck cover. A ration of food was compulsory if the voyage was more than six hours. A humane killer had to be provided for use on any horse injured so seriously that the master of the vessel believed it would not be disembarked without cruelty.

However, it was the docking scare which brought the horse breed societies together at last. In November 1921, a joint meeting of most of them unanimously decided to form a permanent committee to watch the industry's interests in Parliament. But there were many other matters also which could best be tackled by united effort and, in the following January, Sir Walter Gilbey suggested to the Shire Council that a national association ought to be formed, similar to those already in existence for cattle, sheep and pig breeders. In April he was accordingly asked, with A. H. Clark, the new President, and David Davies, M.P., to put the idea to the other bodies concerned. A meeting at the Royal showground in Cambridge on 4th July, attended by delegates from fourteen societies, formally inaugurated the National Horse Association. Gilbey, inevitably, was elected chairman. Charlton was honorary secretary and took the minutes. Next week, he gave them to R. A. Brown, a young man on his staff in the Hunter office, to type out. Fred Griffin replaced David Davies as one of the three permanent Shire representatives and, by October, the twelve horse and pony breed societies, together with fifteen other interested bodies, were members. The Shire Society provided the initial funds in the form of a £100 grant.

There were plenty of problems to discuss. The imposition of entertainments tax at agricultural shows had to be fought, and this was effectively done. (The Shire Society had been fighting it since 1920 – on behalf of others, since the London Show was exempt.) Railway rates for horses attending shows were also reduced, after much strenuous importuning, from 218% of pre-war charges to 150%. But much remained to be done, particularly in the fares for mares visiting the stallion and for travelling stallions whose territories were awkwardly shaped and involved short hops by rail between the steady plodding of most of the week. Slippery roads must be made safer. The moaners who claimed horse traffic was congesting the streets must be answered. The advantages of the commercial horse over the commercial motor must be advertised. And the talk about a possible tax on betting must be monitored, to ensure that, if it came about, it would be horse-breeding that benefited and not merely the general national purse.

One controversy which might have been tackled by the Association, but which it studiously avoided, was the single judge argument. In 1920 the modernisation of agricultural shows was being widely discussed and Sir Gilbert Greenall took the opportunity of advocating that only one judge should be appointed for each breed. He claimed that a single opinion would ensure more uniformity of type among the winners at any one show. "Much valuable time often spent in argument", followed by the "unsatisfactory" calling in of the third man as referee, would be saved. There would be more top-class judges available for the late summer and autumn shows if the available supply had not been over-used, and these shows would then get better entries. Furthermore, "under the single system every man will have to render an account of his stewardship and it will soon be known who are the soundest judges". Finally, a single judge would be cheaper. The only argument, he said, which could be used against his proposal was that "two bad judges are better than one, a dogma to which few will subscribe".

The Shire men totally and vigorously disagreed with him. It was doubtful if two bad judges were *worse* than one. But the point was that two judges were unlikely to share the same foibles or (alas for the frailty of human nature!) the same favouritisms. As far as Shires were concerned, though everyone always grumbled if placed lower than he would place himself if he were judge, no one had ever grumbled on the grounds of bias at London Shows or at any others which employed the dual system. This was a matter of the utmost importance, for the whole fashion and trend of pedigree breeding depended on a form of competition decided entirely by personal opinion, not by performance.

Sir Gilbert, nevertheless, had produced some points which were difficult to answer. And he was not a man to be ignored. Chiefly known as a specialist in Hackney horses and ponies and as an authority on hunter stallions, he had been Master of the Belvoir since 1896, was the unpaid director of the Royal Shows for twenty-five years, and had been twice President of R.A.S.E. His Large and Middle White pigs were celebrated. He had recently, in 1919, bought all the Large Whites belonging to that great Shire leader the Earl of Ellesmere, who had died in 1914, and he now had the best herd in the world. But all branches of the livestock industry received his untiring support. At his Cheshire home, separated from Warrington by the Manchester Ship Canal, his model stables for fifty horses adjoined his private riding school, his covered driving-school, where eight horses could be broken to harness at the same time, and his museum of all types of vehicle which he had crammed into his coach-houses. He was head of the brewery firm of Greenall, Whitley & Co, and what Sir Walter Gilbey did not do for livestock societies, he did. If Gilbey could be called "the carter's friend", Greenall was certainly known as "the vanman's friend" and did not miss a London Van Horse Parade for thirty years. He always kept Shire, Thoroughbred and Hackney stallions for the use of farmers in the Belvoir country at a nominal fee. (Sir Gilbert had succeeded his father, also Sir Gilbert, in 1894. He was later (1927) created Baron Daresbury. He died on 24th October 1938.)

We have digressed, but not irresponsibly, for we must not allow Shire bias (and a historian is, after all, a single judge) to inhibit us from admitting that Sir Gilbert and Sir Walter would have made a perfectly efficient National Horse Association on their own, except that here was a case where the third judge, as referee, would have been necessary. It was not until 1924 that Sir Gilbert's suggestion was acted upon by the R.A.S.E., which proposed for the following year to appoint only one judge at the Royal, with a younger man as "assistant" to learn from him. Charlton, on the instructions of the Council, wrote to R.A.S.E. that the Shire Society would give its usual prizes for the Royal only if the normal judging system was maintained. After some very formal and frigid correspondence, the R.A.S.E. secretary wrote – inappropriately, on Armistice Day – that the four classes from which the Shire Society had withdrawn its prize money would not be included in the 1925 schedule: and in addition, as this Society was not contributing, the details of the remaining classes would not be submitted for approval. His letter ended, like his previous ones, with the request that Mr. Charlton submit a list of recommended judges, from which R.A.S.E. could select one, and a list of younger men from whom an assistant judge might be chosen. Charlton countered, as he had done in his other letters, by offering to submit the names which appeared on the panel of Shire judges which, for the first time, had been drawn up this year for the use of any affiliated society which wished to consult it. (Previously the Society had always refused to nominate possible judges, even when specifically asked for advice by agricultural societies. It was decided to compile a list this year only because so many new shows had sprung up in 1920, whose organisers, particularly in "non-Shire" areas, really did need guidance.)

Alfred Clark brought the matter before the National Horse Association in December. But opinions were divided among the horse societies, and many of the Shire men's allies came from the breed societies of other livestock. So no action was taken. Eventually, early in the new year, the Shire men suddenly climbed down and agreed to give financial support for the Chester Show on the usual terms, upon a pledge being given by R.A.S.E. to review the situation before the 1926 Show. The R.A.S.E. thereupon appointed Fred Griffin as judge, with the son of his lifelong friend and neighbour, Alfred Clark, as assistant. The new Clark, who had the same Christian name and initials as his father, was always listed as "Capt. A.H.", to differentiate them. He was scarcely in 1925 a learner, but it may be assumed that he realised that the R.A.S.E. did not expect him to argue with Mr. Griffin.

(The rest of the story takes us beyond our little period, but as there is not much to tell, it may as well be told here. In June 1925, the Shire men called a conference in Hanover Square, with Lord Harlech in the chair, at which thirty-eight breed societies – horses, cattle, sheep and pigs – unanimously objected to the "assistant judge" idea. R.A.S.E. gracefully abandoned it and in 1926, and for ever after, appointed one judge only. The Shire men dare not go on strike for two. The Suffolk and the Percheron men, unhampered by the expense of a great London show, were filling the Royal basket with many eggs, and it was essential for the Shire men not to get at loggerheads with the national society. Indeed the 1926 Royal at Reading provided a sharp lesson. Liberal subsidies of the prize money by the Suffolk society resulted in an entry of 103 of that breed. There were only eighty-eight Shires, and fifty-eight Percherons and eighteen Clydesdales. This was the first time that Shires had been outnumbered at the Royal Show since 1882, which was the last year when they were merely amongst the "agricultural stallions, mares and fillies" – and oddly enough Reading had been the venue for that show too. In point of fact, the Royal was at a very inconvenient time of year and, within the Shire ranks, the Peterborough Show in July and, increasingly, the Royal Lancashire Show also, were recognised as the chief summer competitions for the breed. But the prestige of the Royal had to be taken into account for publicity reasons. The last shot in the judging war was fired in 1931. The Suffolk society was once again making representations to R.A.S.E. for the resumption of dual judging, and invited the support of the Shire society. The Council was in an acid if not sour mood and resolved that "the Suffolk Society be informed that the Society had decided to adhere to the rules of the Royal Agricultural Society of England.")

The chief concern of the National Horse Association, at its birth and until it reached maturity, was the commercial horse and, in due course, the harness horse in general. In 1924 another organisation was formed, with the object of improving the standard of riding. This was the Institute of the Horse, which put its early emphasis on the training of riding school instructors. However, by the end of 1924, the senior of these bodies, the National Horse Association, was a somewhat ailing child. Too many of its constituent breed societies were giving too little active support. They had got accustomed over many years to the habit of leaving things to Uncle Shire, the biggest and wealthiest of them, and of allowing a Gilbey, either father or son, to fight their battles for them.

7. THE TOWN STREETS

Slippery roads, and the difficulty of devising a surface that was suitable for both motor and horse traffic, engaged the anxious attention of the Shire Council from 1920, and was the first problem passed to the National Horse Association two years later. But it was not a new one, and the needs of the motor car had only complicated it.

In the London of the 1840s, when streets in the city were mostly paved with stone setts and those in the west-end were macadamised, a form of wood-paving was tried, disastrously. In the 'seventies a different kind of wood block was tried, with some success. Asphalt, introduced in the 'eighties, caused an outcry. On 15th February 1889, a meeting of horse-owners at the Royal City Repository, Barbican, called by Herbert Rymill, proprietor of that establishment, expressed alarm about the slippery roads, especially wood and asphalt. It was decided to form a "Horse Accident Prevention Society (Unsafe Pavements)". On 12th March following, a further meeting brought in some influential men – W. Burdett-Coutts, M.P., as President, supported by John Blundell Maple, the well-known furnisher and for the past two years M.P. for Dulwich. They re-named themselves the Society for Promoting the Safety of Horses. The Press of course now took an interest, and painted gruesome pictures of slipping and struggling horses, frightened and falling, with broken bones and cruel lacerations, as an everyday sight in London. Unfortunately, this was not an exaggeration.

Walter Gilbey the elder had been unable to get to the meeting, but *The Sunday Times* naturally consulted him. He would not join the general condemnation of the asphalt. The essential thing, for that, or wood, or granite, or even for some ideal surface, if such a thing could be invented, was to keep it clean and well sanded.

The New Yorkers thought they were not far off achieving the perfect pavement. In London, rock asphalt, a limestone, was used and consequently soon became polished by hooves and tyres but they had experimented with Trinidad asphalt which was based on artificial sandstone. They issued some startling figures. In Madison Avenue, 61,493 vehicles were observed passing over a stretch of Sicilian asphalt: there were 233 accidents to horses, including 143 complete falls. In the same period and over a similar gradient, 71,831 vehicles had passed over Trinidad asphalt: there were only four accidents, and no complete falls.

But all this was a matter of history. In 1920, County Councils in various parts of the country were making tests. Some of them had tried a larger size of grit spread thicker on the tar, and S.H.S. warmly recommended this as giving not only a better foot-hold for horses but a longer life to the road surface. In July 1921, Charlton, representing the breed societies, attended a meeting at the Ministry of Transport of the Slippery Road Surfaces Sub-Committee. It rather feebly came to the conclusion that any road surface able to withstand modern traffic was liable to be slippery, and remembered that the old untreated water-bound granite also became perilous when there was greasy mud or ice about. The committee thought that improved shoeing was needed. So R.A.S.E. encouraged private experiments to invent and market a really serviceable non-slipping shoe.

A far more sinister menace to the town horse – or rather, in this case, to his owners – was the beginning of allegations that the congestion in London streets (which in 1919 had been described as intolerable by a Select Committee on London Traffic) was mainly due to horses. The summer of 1923 produced quite a crop of these complaints, and they had to be taken more seriously than the old pre-war grumbles from fussy people who had campaigned on the grounds that horses made the streets "insanitary". It had been possible then to offer a frivolous or ribald answer. Now, it could be a matter of the horse being told to get out of the way. This was about as logical as to complain that in the crowded streets of Oxford the university people got in the way of car-workers and their wives from Cowley who were trying to do their shopping. But the horse was more vulnerable to banishment than the undergraduate.

The London and Home Counties Traffic Advisory Committee, created in 1924, was a potential enemy to the horse-owner, and indeed in March of that year the London County Council had looked with favour on a proposal to restrict horse traffic. The Shire Society and the National Horse Association countered with the argument that congestion was caused by motor buses, which kept stopping at awkward places, and by motor lorries. When there were strikes and no buses, there was no obstruction. Someone counted the traffic passing Conduit Street on two separate days and found a ratio of fifty-three motors to two horses the first time, and fifty-four motors to one horse the second. Between Grafton Street and Piccadilly, he found sixty-three motors to every one horse going west. He appears to have chosen his times with some cunning but his point was naive and self-defeating. The horseman's real argument was the contrary one. Horses were more economical. They were far more efficient within circumscribed areas. They were therefore returning to popularity. As one newspaper headline proclaimed, "Leading London Grocer saves £3,000 a year by going back to the horse".

A special committee of the Shire Council addressed enquiries to railway companies, coal merchants, metropolitan borough council surveyors and others. One council had replaced its motors after two or three years' use and horses were now saving it 5s. a ton on the removal of domestic rubbish. A coal merchant with 400 heavy-horses and seven motor lorries was emphatic that the latter were an unprofitable investment. Another compared the cost of a 2-ton petrol lorry with a pair-horse van and announced the lorry was far too expensive. The Clydesdale men, in particular, were delighted with the result of a Glasgow Corporation enquiry which showed that, whether costs were reckoned per day, per hour, per ton or per load, the horse was 50% cheaper.

The Shire men quoted America, where Harry N. Taylor, President of the Trucking Corporation of New York City, the largest drayage company in the world, said he used over 1,200 draught-horses on the streets there, and they were more economic than his motor-lorries for all short hauls. A motor-truck cost 6 cents a minute, doing no more work than a heavy dray team at 2 cents a minute. The Mayor of every town in England received a leaflet from A.B.C. entitled *Economy by Horse Usage: striking facts for British Corporations*. It was an account of the operations of the Bureau of Street Cleansing, Department of Public Works, City of Buffalo, N.Y. Wm. F. Schwartz and H. C. Tenjost were very proud of their 450 heavy-horses and forty-two mules, which had removed 1,165,390 cubic yards of material during the year ended 30th June 1924. Street refuse had cost 62 cents a cubic yard, ashes 68 cents and garbage $2.57. The average working life of a gelding was ten years. What was true in the States was true also in England. Horses were, and are, cheap. What makes the difference is the cost of men. In 1924, after their brief taste of high wages, men were again getting cheap. And motor-lorries now, compared with the thousands which had been bought up after the war almost at scrap prices, were becoming very expensive.

8. PUBLICITY FOR GELDINGS

Throughout the first forty years of the Shire Society, heavy-horses had enjoyed an economy which was nearly perfect in its balance. The Creator continued to ordain the birth of about 100 colts for every 100 fillies, but man's ingenuity modified His work and made of these one stallion, ninety-nine geldings and 100 mares. Those who bred Shires did their farming work with mares: others used young stock, every year buying more and selling the matured ones at a profit: the town haulier used the geldings. Back again in the country, there were always other small farmers, neither breeding nor rearing, who required only the cheapest form of traction, and so the gelding which had grown somewhat elderly for urban life but was too useful to slaughter could always find a position with them.

The geldings had required almost no selling. The town proprietor had always preferred them. They were docile and reliable at all times, whereas the mare, though a wonderful worker, was too often in the spring and summer subject at her intervals to those restless stirrings which she no doubt imperfectly understood but which were sufficient to make her irritable and erratic in her behaviour. In buying a mare from the country, there was also the possibility that she might be in foal. For example, Mr. Wright in Beresford Street, Camberwell Gate had bought a couple of really good ones in the autumn of 1920. But the following February, he found they were both in foal and he had to set about finding someone to buy them, though he liked them so well that he was anxious to buy them back in due course. Not far away, a haulage contractor was in exactly the same difficulty and advertised "two weighty wagon mares, which have proved in foal, six years, warranted reliable workers in shafts and chains. Reasonable offer accepted for immediate disposal, or owner would exchange for two horses, or mares not in foal, suitable for city work." It really was better to buy geldings. A crafty man selling a mare to a town proprietor in the autumn was always able to get the better of the bargain if his customer had to sell again in the early spring and, in buying back, probably through a third party, he was not only saved winter keep but obtained two for the reduced price of one.

Before the war, Mr. Myers of Burntwood Lane, Wandsworth Common, had been caught out four times in one summer. He had bought a lot of horses for his contractor's work, and among them were "four big, weighty, wide, Shire-bred cart mares, 16 to 17.1 hands". But he had to sell them all and advertised them at £20, £30, £50 and £50, aged five to eight years. "They would pay anyone well who could foal them down. They are worth nearly double the money if not in foal." The odd thing in this case was that he had not been caught out by a dealer of the shady type, but was able to discover the facts. The sire was a registered Shire. "Farmers or gentlemen" who cared to answer his plea to "come to Wandsworth Common Station on the L.B. and S.C. Railway" could have got a bargain. What had halved the value for him would enhance it for others.

Such accidents or surprises, but not the deliberate deceits, account for the occasional appearance in the Shire Stud-book of some large commercial or industrial companies as breeders. The British Dyestuffs Corporation had enough money to arrange the foaling down on a farm near Huddersfield of a lovely mare they had bought, and are therefore recorded as the breeders of Gunthwaite Victor 2nd 38251 in the 1922 volume. The dam had been eligible for the Stud-book and had been covered (more successfully than was thought) by a registered stallion. (Such involuntary pedigree Shire breeders were of course out-numbered by those urban organisations, such as town councils and co-operative societies, which had their own farms and bred Shires as a policy.)

In this balanced economy prior to 1920, the Shire Society could afford to concentrate on improving one stallion and 100 mares and to leave the ninety-nine geldings to sell themselves. But the problem now was not merely a diminishing market for the breed, in competition with the motor. If the town demand were to contract faster than the country one, there would be a serious imbalance. It looked as if this would happen. And, in 1925–1939, it did happen. The motor lorry could begin to supersede the horse in the town with much less difficulty than the inefficient tractor in the country with its woeful lack of versatility. What would happen to the surplus geldings? The English were averse to eating them, as they ate the surplus and castrated males among all other farm live-stock. Therefore, the Shire Society was forced to make unprecedented efforts to demonstrate their virtues for haulage. One aspect of this was to point out their economic advantages, as has already been discussed. The other was to do everything possible to improve their quality. In a sellers' market, too many bad ones had still been produced during a period of forty years when the best breeding stock had steadily improved. Now, during the sudden breeding slump, many potential young stallions had been castrated and were the élite of the geldings on offer. The aim of the Society was to bring the standard of the ordinary Shire-bred working gelding as near to this as possible.

A start was made at the 1922 Royal Show at Cambridge. At previous Royals, the Shire gelding classes had been poorly filled, and of unexciting quality. Now, at a cost of £250, a special "gelding committee" subsidised the appearance of selected animals. The resultant class of seventeen created a sensation, and was one of the most notable features of the whole show. First prize went to Elma Darkie, a five-year-old black who had been second at London for his breeder George Kendrew, of Northallerton, and was now owned by B. A. Cleminson of Rawcliffe Manor, York. He was a beautifully proportioned horse of 1 ton 16 lb. and his photograph in all the papers did more for the Shire gelding trade than a million words of propaganda. Milton Schofield of Alkrington, Lancashire bought him for the astonishing price of £500. Two others in the class sold for £200 each.

In 1923, efforts were intensified. The Society offered to pay three-quarters of the railway fares to the Royal of all Shire geldings exhibited, and subsidised also a class for three-year-olds. Elma Darkie, now re-named Alkrington Darkie, won the senior class again. A scheme was also instituted for geldings at country shows, similar to the gold and silver medals for mares and, at the biggest shows, for stallions. Any affiliated show offering prizes of £10 or more in a separate class or classes for "cart horse geldings" could claim a bronze medal, to be won by the best animal got by a registered Shire stallion, exhibited by a member of the Society, and certified as a good and quiet worker. Including the special offer, not repeated, of a gold medal at the Royal Lancashire (won by Alkrington Darkie), these new awards were made at thirty-nine shows, and in 1924 at fifty.

The year 1923 also saw the introduction at the London Show itself of classes for commercial horses "of Shire type" yoked to a vehicle. The normal classes for geldings in hand required that they should be by a registered sire, but in point of fact, five of those aged five and upwards which received prizes or cards this year were also out of registered dams – including Alkrington Darkie, who

PLATES 29 and 30   The youngest champion stallion, and the oldest. (*above*) Rokeby Harold was nine months old at the 1893 Show, and celebrated by breaking free and rushing round the ring on his own. Here he is at 18 months; (*below*) Stroxton Tom, possibly the best stallion of all time, was eleven in 1903, and nearly knocked the future King on his face (having just missed the present one the year before). Rokeby Harold was a failure at stud: Tom transmitted Matchless blood to thousands.

PLATES 31 and 32   The Forshaws' whole-page advertisement (*left*), in *The Livestock Journal*, February 27, 1903, speaks for itself. So does the weighty creature (*below*), identity now unknown, which they went on using in advertisements until 1921.

won the gelding championship; so were six of the nine four-year-olds that were rewarded; of the three-year-olds all nine were pure bred, no doubt reflecting the high proportion of promising colts that were castrated as the slump settled on the trade. Prizes for these in-hand classes were increased compared with any previous year. But in the new commercial classes no enquiry was made into their breeding, any more than was done at town horse parades which, until now, had been the only occasions at which Shire Society prizes had ever been given for horses in harness. There were three classes, for singles, pairs, and teams of three or four. No one really won, because ten equal premiums of £4 and five premiums of £7 respectively were given in the first two classes, the driver receiving £1, and three premiums of £10 in the third, with £2 for the driver. Mann, Crossman & Paulin won six premiums, together with a champion gold medal for their team of three bay geldings, their pair of greys being the reserve for this. Only thirteen firms shared the thirty premiums or commendations. All were London horses except one belonging to the Gas Light and Coke Co., and he came only from Ilford Gas Works. Forty-eight horses in these successful exhibits were geldings, as against three mares.

In 1924, provision for geldings was greatly extended. There was an extra class for two-year-old show geldings, and the new classes for "commercial horses" were increased over the previous year. Premiums were replaced by prizes of up to £12. The value of these, together with payments to drivers and carters, three gold medals, a silver cup and a silver medal, totalled £216. No less than ninety-three commercial horses, eighty-eight of them geldings, won prizes or cards of commendation. The champion gold medal was again won by Mann, Crossman & Paulin's same team of bays, with Liverpool Corporation's single horse turn-out reserve. Three other provincial competitors won prizes. This year there were also singles and pair classes restricted to road transport contractors, cartage contractors and carmen, the champion silver medal being won by J. Moon & Sons from Cardiff. The Moons also won a class for single horses, without harness or vehicle, regularly worked in town for two years, and Liverpool Corporation a similar class with a minimum of five years' regular work. A champion gold medal for these two classes was awarded to the Moons.

Finally, a class for a team of four horses that had regularly worked throughout the previous year and up to the very week of the show was a real test of quality, because they, too, had to be shown without harness or vehicle. Mann, Crossman & Paulin's teams came first (silver cup), third and fourth out of four entries, Liverpool Corporation being second. The sixteen geldings in this class then brought the whole meeting to a triumphant conclusion by standing in formation and then turning slowly and together to give the impression of a huge revolving wheel. This was a magnificent sight, calculated to make any owner of a smelly motor-lorry hurry away and sell it at once.

9. INTER-BREED RIVALRY

A spate of pamphlets issued soon after the war, each designed to prove that the Clydesdale, the Suffolk or the Percheron was the best breed of heavy-horse, took the Shire men somewhat aback. Until the sudden assault in 1919 on their horses' war record, their jaunty supposition that the Shire was incomparably the best appeared to require no proof. Even in the face of that attack, their calm was but little ruffled, for membership continued to grow at a rapid rate. It was only on the collapse of the horse trade that they realised there would be a fight for survival, with four breeds instead of three competing for a dwindling market. But they were somewhat slow in doing anything about it. For example, their financial assistance to those exhibiting geldings at the 1922 Royal Show was prompted only by the disgrace of 1921, when the Clydesdale gelding class had fifteen entries, and the Shire class four. And the Royal that year had been staged, of all places, at Derby!

A comment on the rival breeds might well begin with the newcomers. The Percheron Society rented an office in April 1921 at 27 Cavendish Square, and in June 1922 published the first volume of its Stud-book. This contained 162 stallions and 440 mares, all numbers being prefixed by "B" to denote the British book. The names of the first President's horses were listed first and so Lord Lonsdale's Lagor became B 1, with B 1 Orglandie heading the mares section. The second President's outstanding stallion became Misanthrope B 5. Sixty-five studs were represented in the book.

As if to correct the somewhat aggressive attitude that Captain Galtrey had shown, Sir Merrik Burrell wrote in this first volume that those who had intro-duced the Percheron to England had not done so "with any desire to injure those fine breeds of heavy draught-horses already existing in the country, neither did they import the horses with the view of making any money out of them". Even so, the Percheron men were banging their drum with all the enthusiasm of a Salvation Army convert. They were even exporting a few from England, and made plenty of capital out of that. Mrs. Emmet sold several to a man in New South Wales, and he asked for three more mares in 1923, provided they were all in foal to her own horse. David Davies, M.P., was a Shire man, but had a few Percherons at Llandinam. He put his French-bred B 66 Nature to Prescient, and bred a colt foal on 12th April 1920. This animal, Dinam Bijou, sailed on S.S. *Chepstow Castle* in October 1922 for Natal, at a price of £100. (His full brother, a year younger, Dinam Espoir, was the colt which had been foaled the day his owner received A.B.C.'s docking letter: he was castrated at the age of four and went to the G.W.R. as a five-year-old for £52. A full sister one year younger again, died from scour at a day old. The mother went to a knacker at the age of ten for £2. But no breed society advertised these aspects of the slump.)

Who were these breeders of Percherons? Only a few, like David Davies, faced both ways. Most of the leading supporters were new to pedigree heavy-horse breeding. Not many were deserters from the Shire ranks, though there were one or two notable defections. At Buscot Park, home of so many great Shires in the past, the last to be bred there was Buscot Cissie in 1920. Lord

Faringdon lived to the age of eighty-three in 1934, but his son Lieutenant-Colonel the Hon. H. G. Henderson had a Percheron stallion and eight mares by 1922. Chivers & Sons Limited, of Histon, which under the leadership of John Chivers had bred over fifty pure-bred Shire mares and fillies before the war, had five Percheron stallions and twenty-two mares in 1922 and phased out their Shires, the last being Histon Lioness 3rd, foaled in 1925. Herbert Whitley at Primley in Devon, owner of those pre-war celebrities Dunsmore Fuchsia, Tatton Dray King and Lorna Doone, acquired a Percheron stallion and five mares and for a time had both breeds, but was to finish Shire breeding when in 1934 he sold Primley Statesman, foaled in 1926, to Thomas Balderston.

(There were to be a few more deserters yet. In 1932, the 11th Lord Middleton became President of the British Percheron Society, whereas his uncle, the 9th Baron, had been twice President of the Shire and one of its greatest evangelists. R. S. Hudson, Minister of Agriculture from 1940, became the Percheron President in 1946, and the nearest he had come to being a Shire man was to enjoy the joke of pretending to allow Albert Holland to "convert" him: yet his father, R. W., had won twenty-eight prizes at London shows in 1898–1907. The Sneath family, who have done so much for the Percheron breed in recent years, is represented in Shire history by many members from 1884 onwards. Of the "dual personalities" perhaps the veterinary surgeon J. G. Runciman – breeder and last owner of the quadruple Shire champion of the 1930s, Bower Winalot, and Percheron President in 1959 – was the most outstanding.)

As time went on, there developed a type of Percheron man which was distinct from the Shire man. It is perhaps absurd to generalise at all, but the contrast, in the very broadest terms, can be summed up as the difference between Chapel and Church, or between the cup that cheers and the other which, if taken to excess, can also inebriate. There have been, of course, many staunch Methodists or Baptists and many total abstainers amongst Shire men, including leading enthusiasts of the breed. And there are examples in the contrary direction. But a funny story, of the Englishman-Scotsman-Irishman sort, would have it all wrong if it were about an encounter between a teetotal Shire man on his way home from chapel and a Percheron breeder calling at the Black Horse after morning service at church.

The breeders of Suffolks were now gaining an advantage which logically they were entitled to. Any farmer who thought that the town market was not now worth bothering about might well be advised seriously to consider taking up this breed whose virtues, and they were considerable, were almost entirely displayed on the land. The breed society began to organise September sales in addition to those which had been held for many years in spring and summer. It boasted that there were 150 Suffolk breeders in Norfolk, many more than ever before, and that the Punches were spreading far beyond their home county. The Shire men countered by special grants of money to the Essex, Royal Norfolk, Yorkshire and other shows in "vulnerable areas" so as to increase the Shire class entries. In 1923, when the slump was driving some small local agricultural societies to the wall, there were more shows receiving gold and silver medals for their Shire classes than in any other year, before or since, and others were accepting the new bronze medals for geldings. One gold medal was found in a train by a G.W.R. inspector, who sent it to the Society. He received £1 reward, but no one ever claimed the medal. (After 1925, special grants to shows in areas threatened by Suffolk invasion had to be stopped for reasons of economy, but the Society tried to compensate by allowing prize-money in gelding classes to count towards the £100 total needed to qualify for a Shire gold medal.)

Breed arguments were conducted in lively fashion in the Press. Someone claimed the Percheron could "kill the Shire in any kind of work, and is harder and sounder". Sir Walter Gilbey responded by issuing a challenge in the *Live Stock Journal* at £100, or £200 if preferred, the winner to give the money to the Agricultural Benevolent Institution. He suggested practical tests with one, two, three or four horses of each breed, for weight and distance. *Country Life* thought the Shire would win easily, and diplomatically suggested that if the Suffolk competed he would do well at the weight because he was so determined: the Clyde too would be a worthy opponent in the distance test. Unfortunately, no one accepted Sir Walter's challenge.

An unfortunate misprint in a letter from Edmund Beck, as it appeared in the *Live Stock Journal*, added to the fun. He had written about Shire foals, but the expression appeared in the paper as "Shire fowls". Supporters of the other breeds chortled in glee. "What is the difference?" asked one of the wits. "They each have feathers up to their navel." Mr. Beck was filled with rage, especially when the editor of the paper added insult to injury by quoting him shortly afterwards as having said he had sold 167 foals at Peterborough at prices varying up to 20 guineas, whereas he had actually stated that this number *averaged 22* guineas.

The well-known London veterinary surgeon, W. S. King of 264 Burdett Road, E.14, was one of those who gave the Shire view – though, of course, like everyone else, he was completely unbiassed. He had been associated with cart horses for twenty-five years and was now (in 1924) responsible for supervising between 4,000 and 5,000 of the four heavy breeds. In the war, he had had to deal with thousands more, mostly Percherons. "In recording briefly my experience from a commercial draught point of view, I wish it to be borne in mind that I hold no brief from any particular breed", he wrote to the *Live Stock Journal*. Percherons, he said, were very susceptible to break-down of the check ligament and flexor tendons, and he could prove it from his case-book. They were also prone to azoturia, a painful sort of spasm and paralysis of the hindquarters, a result normally of high feeding in conjunction with lack of exercise and work. He had seen eighteen cases in one day after a bank-holiday in 1921. Suffolks soon developed contracted and brittle feet, arthritis of the fetlock joint and the various forms of exostosis (i.e. ringbone, sidebone, splint and spavin). Clydesdales were better than both of these, but the very length and obliquity in the pasterns caused trouble, especially ringbone and navicular disease. The

Shires were by far the best. With proper management, they did not get grease, even if overfed with old beans. Mr. King would show anyone, by appointment, as many large stables of Shire-breds as he pleased where there was absolute freedom from the trouble. Scorning even to mention sidebone or other leg and foot troubles in connexion with the Shire, he pointed out that their working life averaged eight to nine years in many big firms and that, previous to the Great War, it was quite common to do a fifteen hour day – "a truly remarkable achievement, especially when one takes into consideration the almost unsur-mountable difficulties which many of these animals had to overcome." Triumph-antly, he pointed to the fact, and this was undeniable, that the vast majority of the heavy town horses were Shire-bred, as one could see by looking at the 800 or 900 entries in the London Cart Horse Parade. The three hundred in the Liverpool parade were all Shires.

The contests between Shire and Clydesdale supporters were more fascinating than others, because the breeds were so closely related and yet, during the past forty years, had grown farther apart. It was the exaggerated differences between them that attracted at once the greatest derision and the secret envy of the rival supporters. The Clydesdale men (it was argued in the south) were not satisfied unless their horse could imitate Blondin on a tight-rope: the Shire men (the north retaliated) were too easily satisfied when theirs hid his defects under a lot of hair. At the Royal, the Shire men had no idea what they were striving after, as they put two cumbersome hirsute dray-horses first and third, with a "quality" horse in between: in the Clydesdale ring, judging was a funereal mystery, an esoteric ceremony of legs where tops were forgotten.

These battles were somewhat reminiscent of the antics of the quaint rhinoc-eros, among which ferocious fights are frequently a prelude to mating. The Shire and the Clyde societies secretly wanted to mate. The Clyde mare covered by a Shire stallion would produce the true cart-horse that was in danger of being lost in the pursuit of oblique pasterns and super-fine bone: the Clyde stallion on a Shire mare would get something which had manageable legs and yet was still a true cart-horse. The two crosses, put back again, the first to a Clydesdale stallion and the other to a Shire, might produce exactly what the new age required. Where the first-cross progeny was a male, it had been demonstrated for years that, castrated, he was a highly marketable animal. Lawrence Drew had shown that the first-cross female could be bred from with success, contrary to generally-accepted theory.

What was William Dunlop doing, praising the Shires – and not only praising them, but buying them and taking them to Scotland? Whether Clydesdale versus Shire skirmishes would result, rhino-like, in a mating or merely in the expenditure of useless energy was a matter that was worth watching.

10. WEIGHT-PULLING TESTS, 1924

Competing not only against the motor but against the other heavy breeds of horse which were also fighting for survival, the Shire men now at last felt obliged to put an end to futile argument by actually proving that the old English cart-horse was not only the most beautiful of them all, but the strongest. And so tests were organised at the 1924 London show, not by inviting others to join a competition in the way Sir Walter had so recently suggested, or even in the manner of the old barbaric Suffolk drawing matches of the eighteenth century, but more after the style of the enterprising Mr. Banks at the beginning of the nineteenth. This gentleman had bet that an ordinary cart-horse could pull 36 tons a distance of six miles along the Surrey Iron Railway, which ran between Wandsworth and Merstham. A horse taken at random from the timber yard of a Mr. Harwood did the thing with ease at just under four miles an hour, in spite of four stops to demonstrate a start from a dead rest. After winning his bet in the presence of a numerous party of gentlemen, Mr. Banks added four extra wagons and fifty labourers, which made a total final load of 55 tons 6 cwt., 2 qrs., and the horse moved along again with the greatest unconcern.[4] However, Mr. Banks' aim was to demonstrate the advantage of a railway line, not the power of a horse.

The Shire trial in 1924 was the first carried out at a British show, and was promoted by Sir Walter, with the assistance of T. Eaton Jones the Liverpool Corporation veterinary superintendent, A. J. Baker the forage man and that totally unbiassed supporter of the Shire, W. S. King. Ordinary working dock geldings, owned by Liverpool Corporation, were used, and drew an ordinary Liverpool dock-side 2½ ton lorry without springs, eighteen-and-a-half feet long and seven-and-a-half feet wide. Sir William Nott-Bower, Commissioner of the City Police, and Lieutenant-Colonel Percy Laurie, Assistant Commissioner of the Metropolitan Police, were the umpires. The first test was held on the Monday afternoon before the opening of the Show, on the granite setts of the Liverpool Road outside the Hall. The conditions were nearly as bad as they could be. The surface was slippery with sleet and turning room was restricted by an incline which had to be negotiated by the shaft horse. Nevertheless two horses, shod in Liverpool style – with caulkins (heels) and toe pieces – started and moved away easily with a total load of 18.5 tons.

The second and third tests were carried out in the presence of the King on the Wednesday afternoon, immediately after he had presented the champion cups. His Majesty had expressed himself somewhat uneasy, owing to the attempts of a certain horse-protection society to interfere with the programme. But the Shire men assured him that the lurking watch-dogs would have nothing to complain about and His Majesty assured them, in his turn, that of course Shire breeders could never be associated with cruelty, and in any case Laurie and Nott-Bower were sound fellows. So they began. In the ring, the layer of loam had been very heavily rolled when first laid before the show, and the top layer of tan was again rolled, but the surface presented a pretty formidable task. Two horses started and took a load of 6 tons, and the weight, announced through a megaphone, produced a loud cheer. Then the favoured few repaired to the corridor at the rear of the grandstand. Here, on the worn wood blocks, the two horses had an unnecessary difficulty, for it was too narrow for them to pull to one side and then to the other in the customary way of getting a start with a heavy load. Nevertheless, they moved off with 16.5 tons. The megaphoned final result brought an even louder cheer. The horse-protectors went home discomfited but everyone else was very happy, including His Majesty. The tests were repeated, with the same loads, for the public on the following two days.

On 1st April, the Council politely considered a suggestion submitted by a Mrs. Walters for a weight-pulling contest between two Shires and two oxen. But they came to the conclusion that this was scarcely a progressive idea. There might be those who wanted horses off the city streets, but none was thinking of oxen as replacements, even on 1st April.

On St. George's day, the British Empire Exhibition was opened at Wembley by His Majesty – the greatest show in Britain since the Great Exhibition of 1851. The Shire Society made a grant to Liverpool Corporation to stage another weight-pulling test and this duly took place during Civic Week of the Exhibition in September, against the background of a West African stucco fort, a mock Taj Mahal and a mountain of Australian butter. This time, they pulled against a dynamometer made by Salter & Co., and attached to an immovable object. One horse exerted a pull equivalent to a starting load of 29 tons, in Liverpool shoes, and 12 tons in flat shoes. A pair, shod Liverpool-style, easily pulled the maximum register of the instrument and the draught was considered equal to a starting load of 50 tons. Among the 17,000,000 who passed through the turnstiles of the Exhibition before it closed on 1st November, there were no doubt during Civic Week a few horse-savers eager to witness some form of cruelty. But nothing was heard from them.

The Society capitalised on the tests by telling the world what these Liverpool horses were accustomed to do in their normal working life at home. "A common load along the line of docks – which are uniformly level – and on the granite setts of the Liverpool streets is from 5 to 8 tons, drawn by a single horse: from 7 to 12 tons drawn by two horses; but much larger weights, according to the density of the packages, are often moved with ease. Recently a boiler weighing 18 tons was easily moved by a team of two horses, and a load of over 25 tons on a waggon was moved for a distance of 300 yards by two horses.

"The roads leading from the docks rise from the river and represent various inclines, some of which are extremely steep, while others, although not so steep, are of greater length. For the negotiation of these inclines and for the transport of loose material such as excavation work, sand, gravel, setts, macadam, stones etc., two-wheeled carts are used. For single horses, the carts weigh from 21 to 26 cwt., and a common load placed on the cart is from $2\frac{1}{2}$ to 3 tons. The carts for pairs of horses weigh from 25 to 30 cwt., and the loads placed upon these vary from 4 to 5 tons.

"In this class of cartage the weights do not look to be heavy, but it must be remembered that in many cases the cartage is finally done upon unpaved and soft ground. The grip upon the various roadways traversed is obtained through the use of very heavy shoes with long heels and toe-pieces attached."

The Society also publicised the results of similar tests held that year at the Iowa State Fair and at the Canadian Regina Show, since the *Nor'-West Farmer* had claimed a world record at the latter. The adjoining table gives the essential figures, and it remains only to be said that, whereas in America pulling contests have been and still are a popular feature of the draft-horse year, there has never been a Shire test since.

WEIGHT-PULLING TESTS
(Pairs of horses except where stated) .

ISLINGTON	($2\frac{1}{2}$ ton Liverpool dock lorry)	
	On tan over loam	6 tons
	On wood blocks	16.5 tons
	On granite setts	18.5 tons
WEMBLEY	(dynamometer on immovable object)	
	One horse recorded 29 tons in Liverpool shoes	
	One horse recorded 12 tons in flat shoes	
	Two horses pulled maximum register of dyna-	
	mometer, considered equal to	50 tons
IOWA	(dynamometer on vehicle)	
	Equivalent to load on granite setts of	17.39 tons
REGINA	(dynamometer on vehicle)	
	Equivalent to load on asphalt pavement of	16.4 tons

						Measurements (inches)		
							fore	rear
				Weight	Heart-	loin-		
Horses used (all geldings)		*Age*	*Height*	(lb.)	girth	girth	cannon	cannon
Islington & Wembley – SHIRES :								
	Theobald	9	17.0	1,708	84	88	$11\frac{1}{2}$	$12\frac{1}{2}$
	Umber	8	16.3	1,764	82	89	12	14
	Varzy	7	17.2	2,100	92	91	12	13
	Vedas	7	16.2	1,785	83	84	12	13
	Verdict	8	$17.1\frac{1}{2}$	2,072	91	94	$12\frac{1}{2}$	$12\frac{1}{2}$
	Vesuvius	8	17.2	1,764	88	91	12	13
	Vulcan	8	$16.2\frac{1}{2}$	1,894	87	89	12	$12\frac{1}{2}$
Iowa – PERCHERONS :	Dan	12	$16.2\frac{1}{4}$	1,810	81	83	$9\frac{3}{4}$	12
	Tag	7	$17.1\frac{1}{2}$	1,850	83	84	10	$11\frac{1}{2}$
Regina – BELGIAN								
GRADE :	Jumbo	8	$17.2\frac{3}{4}$	1,860	88	85	$10\frac{1}{4}$	$11\frac{3}{4}$
	Barney	8	$16.3\frac{1}{2}$	1,840	86	84	10	$11\frac{1}{4}$

11. LONDON SHOWS

At the London Show of 1921, the buoyant atmosphere of the year before had already been replaced by that certain sinking feeling that the Bovril advertisers knew and loved so well. There were £2,800 in prizes this year including those for breeders, men in charge of first prize horses, and so on as before. The Ministry of Transport allowed horses to travel at half rate on the return journey with free provender. The grooms went free. Though the basic rates were high, this was a pleasant old-time gesture, and even cartage was once again available to and from the London termini. But the Postmaster-General refused to provide the usual telegraphic facilities, because the Society would not guarantee him against loss. A very strong protest was made about this. The Fox News Company took some film, of a sort, of the show. There was no fog.

The King's horse, Field Marshal 5th, won the championship again, and poor Cope's Blaisdon Draughtsman was once more the reserve. There is something peculiarly frustrating in being adjudged the owner of the second best horse in England three years in succession. But anyone who had not seen the Sandringham horse, and perhaps imagined that in 1920 the judges wore the rosy spectacles of patriotism, was now reassured by the renewed verdict of three different judges. Had these gentlemen possessed any doubts at all, they would have been excused for thinking that enough was sufficient and for recognising the Gloucestershire-bred horse at last. But like all those who knew their business and had seen the horses, they had no doubt that His Majesty had won fair and square. Rievaulx Friar, the £200 two-year-old which had been sold for £2,300, stood second to the King's horse in the four-year-old class.

Undeterred by their great clearance-sale the year before, Harry Bishop and John Measures came back to win three firsts for females – two-year-olds and two senior classes (under 16-hands, and 16.2 and over). Their filly, Bignell Sister Superior, won the junior cup, the King's home-bred Maid Marion 2nd, winner of the three-year-olds, being reserve to her. Marden Evelyn 2nd, their big mare, won for Pendley its first supreme championship.

Another winner of three first prizes was Robert Ludwig Mond, who had now won forty-three prizes or commendations at the Spring Show in eight years. Like Lord Hothfield, also in Kent, the Greenwells in Surrey and, among practical farmers, the Luckins in Sussex, he was considered to have effectively disproved the old myth that proper Shires could not be reared south of the Thames. Indeed, he favoured the heaviest, deepest and widest stallions that one can imagine. He went one better than many, in keeping a stallion for his tenants' use entirely free of charge. His three-year-old Sundridge Nulli Secundus (by Babingley Nulli Secundus and bred by Allan Holm, who produced many fine Shires at Tilton in Leicestershire) had been Reserve in 1920 to the King's horse for the junior cup. This year he won it, since his rival, now four, was classed as a senior.

Robert, son of the great chemist and naturalised Briton, Ludwig Mond, was born in 1867 and was a little more than a year older than his brother, Sir Alfred. The latter is best remembered as Lord Melchett, chairman of Imperial Chemical Industries, though at this time he was First Commissioner of Works, a post he had held since 1916. (Two months after this show he became Minister of

Health.) Robert had assisted his father in chemical research, particularly in the discovery of new carbonyls, and was honorary secretary of the Davy-Faraday Research Laboratory. But he contributed no less to the sum of knowledge as an archaeologist, particularly in the Middle East, than as a chemist. More to the point of Shire history, he had been applying scientific methods since 1910, not long after his father's death, to farming at Combe Bank, near Sevenoaks. He was especially interested in pioneering pure milk production, and in his massive Shires.

It was therefore a great blow to the Society that, a few months after this show, he gave up the Combe Bank enterprise, at the age of fifty-four. In the remaining years of his life (he was knighted in 1932 and died in 1938) a continuation of his experiments would have been invaluable to the breed. It would have been of particular interest to have seen whether the great weight and substance he so much admired could have been maintained over several generations on Kentish soil without recourse at any time to old-fashioned Fen blood, and whether perhaps great bone could have been successfully combined with diminished hair.

Mond's stud was dispersed at a home sale on 19th October, and Sundridge Nulli Secundus made 3,100 guineas. This is the highest price paid since 1920 for any Shire, and was partly caused by his having been already let for 1922 at £1,200 to the Great Eccleston Society, those doughty supporters, even in difficult times, of the best breeding. The purchaser was John Q. Rowett of Frant in Sussex, who also acquired this great horse's massive sire Babingley Nulli Secundus, now thirteen, for 600 guineas. Altogether, Rowett bought seven lots for 5,945 guineas, and these were the basis of his new stud. Even more importantly, he acquired the services of Mond's stud manager, Alf Millen. At this time, Mr. Rowett was financing what was to prove the last expedition of his friend and Dulwich College contemporary, Sir Ernest Shackleton. Had he known his friend would die, he might have acted otherwise. But there were two other things he did not know, either – the immediate future of heavy-horse affairs and his own early fate.

If Babingley Nulli Secundus had a tremendous influence on the breed, Childwick Champion proved greater still. Over 45% of the stallions that were being registered, within twenty years, were to be descended from Harold through him. He was bought at the Combe Bank sale by a farmer who had long coveted him and now at last could buy this outstanding old stock-horse – he was now eighteen, and Fred Ibbotson gave 775 guineas for him. Other prices ranged, as befitted the surrounding gloom, down to the ridiculous. Sundridge Coming King, seven years old and a son of Babingley Nulli Secundus, went for 26 guineas. First, second and third at previous London Shows, this elephantine stallion had proved a great stock-horse, but now had gone all wrong and the price he fetched was scarcely more than 1 guinea per cwt. Mares covered by Sundridge Nulli Secundus went for 800, 84, 190 and 35 guineas. Jos. Holland of Edingale, who left Tamworth on the 2.27 train in the morning to get to Sevenoaks in time for the sale, did not buy, as he intended. He could have had Sun-dridge Hero, three-year-old son of Childwick Champion pretty cheaply, because there were no offers for him even at 20 guineas.

The 1922 Show really proved that all things were upside down. The hall was packed as it had never been before, from floor to galleries. On the Wednesday afternoon enthusiastic, perhaps even hysterical, cheering greeted the arrival of Their Majesties and Princess Mary. Yet the talk was all of the slump. If, when they met the year before, old friends feared the worst, now they knew the Government really had forgotten them. Farmers had been useful to win the war. Now they could go back and sit in their corners. "Farmers Face Bank-ruptcy" was a common newspaper headline. But the King was a good man. Three cheers for the royal Shire man! Having won the gold championship cup outright the year before, he had given the Society a new one. But it was a perpetual cup, and so the Council still had to buy a cup for competition on the usual terms, that any competitor winning it twice could keep it. Yet, incredibly, what was his duty this year, but to present these new trophies to a *lady*?

Mrs. Stanton of Snelston Hall, near Ashbourne was no mere remote pro-prietor of many acres, but personally controlled everything that happened upon them. If Lady Wantage had won the stallion championship, it would have been, with all due respect to her, a different matter. After her gallant husband's death in 1901, the Lockinge stud continued, but what it achieved with her permission and whole-hearted support was done by the little man of the prominent sandy eyebrows, her stud manager, C. H. Eady. In any case, Lady Wantage herself had now recently died, too. But Mrs. Stanton was everything at Snelston Hall, and her stud-groom just a stud-groom. Her eight-year-old Harboro' Nulli Secundus, a son (like the young Sundridge Nulli Secundus, who now won the four-year-old class for his new owner J. Q. Rowett) of Babingley Nulli Secun-dus, had done pretty well at Spring Shows all his life and now he came right to the top in no uncertain manner. The King gracefully handed her all the gold and silver she had so convincingly won, but a comment he made before he left the hall suggests that he had not forgotten the two previous years when he had won the honours himself. Discussing the art of breeding, he remarked that almost anyone could buy a champion Shire: personally, he bred them. Lest it may be considered tactless to quote his unguarded observation, the historian must claim necessity. Nothing else can so clearly demonstrate His Majesty's intense pride in his Sandringham Shires. But the implied criticism, if it could be referred ungallantly to Mrs. Stanton, would have been a little unfair. She had owned the horse since 1916, when he was two. Only skill could produce him six years later as the best Shire of all England. And if it was easy, it is odd that no other lady has ever exhibited a Shire champion, before or since.

Harboro' Nulli Secundus was a horse which will be vividly recalled as long as anyone lives who ever came in contact with him. Contact was painful. Those who are charitable would describe him as high-mettled, on the ground that a sullen vicious stallion will let you get near him, and then attack, whereas he made his intentions plain without subterfuge. But the majority of his acquaintances prefer to call him a really nasty horse, a pig of a horse, whose box it would be utter folly for any stranger to attempt to enter. A fascinating photograph exists wherein his groom wears the countenance of a man who has been asked to hold a time-bomb for a few moments. At this 1922 show, he was led by the head man, J. H. Knight, whose outlook on life could not be described by anyone as of the soberest or steadiest or daintiest. When the championship decision was made, he recklessly in his excitement threw the leading rein over the horse's neck and let him go. Fortunately all creatures present, human and equine, survived the risk, but there was a terrible row about the whole incident.

This fearsome stallion had some ability to transmit wickedness. One of his sons, Blurton Secundus, won fourth prize as a three-year-old at this same show. A few weeks later he began his first season, on hire to the Kettering Society, but became savage after serving his first mare. He was utterly unmanageable and was eventually destroyed in July. The Kettering men had all been afraid to send any mares to him and this led to a dispute with his owner. The Council was appealed to, but could not intervene, for the horse had not broken the contract, only the nerve of anyone who went near him. There is no easy redress in law for those who get more than they pay for.

Second to Harboro' Nulli Secundus in the big stallion class was Rievaulx Friar. Third, on his first and only appearance in London, was one of the most influential stallions between the two wars – and, some would say, the best. This was the dark grey, six-year-old massive horse of 17.2-hands, March King, exhibited by the Forshaw brothers. He had been bred at March by Dr. H. H. Truman, son of J. H. and brother of John T. the "American Truman" of Bushnell, Illinois, and was a grandson of Lockinge Forest King. Possessed of a tremendous span of bone and full of spirited action and energy, his claim to celebrity at this time was that he had been hired the year before by the Newark S.H.S. at 2,000 guineas, a record fee. But his remarkable pre-potency has given him a truer fame than that. He was the chief agent of an astounding increase in the percentage of grey horses in the Stud-book in the next twenty years. Perhaps the most remarkable feature of his career is that it was so short. It lasted only four full seasons, for in April 1923, standing at home at a fee of 15 guineas (it had been 25 the year before) he died of a twisted bowel. If he had lived twice as long, like his sire King of Tandridge (who had completed nine seasons before a twisted bowel had finished him, too) or four times as long like Childwick Champion, who was now still on duty and lived to do nineteen seasons, one wonders whether he might have turned the hair of the whole breed as grey as the Percheron.

A notable feature of the show was the exceptional standard of the females, among whom the champion was Crossways Forest Maid, a grand-daughter of Lockinge Forest King. Her owner, Owen Williams of Cowbridge, Glam., was the first man to take a championship out of England since Lawrence Drew had done so at the very first show of all, though two stallions and a mare, with six championships between them, had been Montgomeryshire-bred.

The railways actually reintroduced special trains with excursion fares for the Show this year. But the Postmaster-General was still obstinate about a guarantee for telegrams, and so A.B.C. engaged Boy Scouts to run to and from the local post office. The Shire Council, not surprisingly, refused to accept applications for trade-stand space from motor-car and tractor manufacturers. The London County Council produced far more stringent regulations about staircases, barriers and seating than they ever used to do before the war. The Horse Show Committee decreed a £1 fine on every exhibitor who failed to put his horse in the grand parade, but abandoned any attempt to enforce it. All Highly Commended animals were listed this year for the first time in an order of merit, so that they could no longer be regarded as equal. A new agreement with the Hall company caused the Society's share of the rental and fittings to rise from £1,263 to £1,553. The slump is most clearly indicated in the auction sale. In 1920, 110 horses were disposed of for £47,772 (average £434): in 1921, seventy-seven for £20,005 (£260): this year, fifty-four for £7,538 (£140).

In 1923, the stallion and mare championships were both a repeat of the previous year, which meant that the Society had to find 150 guineas to replace the challenge cups. It says much for the judges that, in spite of the previous year's incident, they stuck to their task of judging horses, not behaviour, and selected Harboro' Nulli Secundus again. His five to nine-year-olds class was generally considered one of the best groups ever seen at Islington, rivalling the famous four-year-old collection of 1912. The Forshaws' bay Wyresdale Draughtsman, a typical representative of their Carlton stud – wide, deep and massive on big hard legs – stood second. Sundridge Nulli Secundus was third, and fourth was Rievaulx Friar. Of thirty-six entries in the class, no less than twenty-five won prizes or were commended. Ten stallions, aged ten and upwards, were entered, all appeared and all were vetted sound. Old Rickford Coming King, now fifteen, won the class for the Forshaws. And so, although their classes were reduced to six by the abolition of the height division among the five to nine group, this may perhaps be called stallions' year, as 1922 had been mares' year. It could equally well be labelled geldings' year owing to the increased prizes of the normal in-hand classes and the introduction of commercial classes, as already described. It was also Boy Scouts' year again, for they did well with the telegrams. It could even be called railways' year, with the new grouping of the old companies into four great ones trying to set a standard of service which until 1939 was remarkably high, whatever the idiosyncracies of horse-removal that they were asked to cope with.

In addition, this was Canadian year, as will be explained. And it was certainly Lady Elizabeth Bowes-Lyon's year. Only recently engaged to the Duke of York, this young lady of twenty-three was the object of all eyes when she appeared at the Hall, with the King and Queen and the Duke. It was the year of Alfred Clark's presidency, and perhaps one might find excuse in marking the commencement of modern times, or certainly the end of the old order of things, in recording that the first tenant farmer Shire President had the duty of welcoming the first future commoner Queen Consort of this country, though it is only right to point out that the one was scarcely a mud-spattered forelock-toucher and the other was descended from Elizabeth of York, and lived some of the year in Glamis Castle. At this visit to the Shires, she exercised, as usual, her extraordinary gift for putting everyone at their ease. The President's future daughter-in-law, who was vague about the Shires but keenly interested in this intriguing visitor, asked him what she was like. "Oh", he replied, "she was a nice little thing." He was more than once reminded of this when the nice little thing's husband became King. Among those whom the Duke of York met on his first introduction to a world in which his father was so much at home was W. T. Hayr, grazier upon land that only Leicestershire could produce, member of the Editing and Horse Show Committees, and winner again of a gold medal as breeder of Harboro' Nulli Secundus. A genial and well-loved Shire man, he set out to put the Duke at his ease, and said, "I was sorry to hear your father lost that good filly he had." The Duke was equal to the occasion and replied, "Yes, it was sad. And thank you for your sympathy."

To whom the 1924 show belonged, there is no doubt whatever. It was as if one were to go to a beauty contest and, without warning, Helen of Troy walked in. Everyone gasped. Who was this creature? And from where had she sprung, so unexpectedly? Her name was Erfyl Lady Grey, and she was nine years old. Sometimes a child who is not especially graceful, or a girl who is not obviously pretty, becomes in maturity a woman of consummate loveliness and charm. Lady Grey was one of these. She was bred on the hill farm of Hafod, Llanerfyl, by William Vaughan. William and his brother John were born there, but John had taken Llyssun farm and both had joined the Shire Society in 1901. (John married a daughter of Edward Green, one of the most celebrated of the early Montgomeryshire Shire men, but on her death had joined his father-in-law at the Moors, Welshpool. He then married the other daughter and on Green's death in 1915 took over that farm.) Adjoining the Moors was the Bank, Pool Quay, where Thomas Green, half-brother to Edward, had bred Lorna Doone herself.

The pedigree of Erfyl Lady Grey stands as a tribute not only to the Montgomeryshire men but as an illustration of the breed society's patient policy which now, at the very time that all its activities were being threatened by the possible redundancy of the cart-horse, had come to full fruition:

88450 ERFYL LADY GREY, bred 1915 by William Vaughan. Grey, stripe down forehead, little white on four legs. By Moors Kitchener 25443 (bred 1906 by Edward Green. By Moors Drayman 21664 out of 45798 Moors Victoria by Moors Regent 17492).

dam: 88451 ERFYL LADY WHITE, bred 1908 by David Thomas Evans, Penrhydd-

lan, Llandinam. Whole white. By Moors Chief 22594 (bred 1903 by Edward
Green. By Moors Regent 17492 out of 36681 Moors Ruby by Moors Zealot
15731).

She was not registered until 1918 volume, where she appears next to her
daughter. In 1912 she had bred a black filly foal who also appears in this same
volume as 87672 Brimaston Bloom, by John Vaughan's Llyssun Champion
27507: in 1913, a black colt (by another John Vaughan horse), castrated: in
1915 Erfyl Lady Grey: in 1917, bay colt, full brother to her, castrated.

g-dam: 32940 LOFTY, bred 1894 by Evans. Grey. By Country Fashion 12951
(a grey son of Lincolnshire Lad II).

g-g-dam: a brown mare, bred 1888 by David Morgan, Neawdd, Mochdre. By
A 1 6596 (a bay, bred 1883 by Wm. Davies of Newtown, and of west-country
and Radnorshire blood).

g-g-g-dam: a brown mare bred 1875 by Morgan. By King Dick 1213, hero of
many a tale, true and imagined, and deserving of a book to himself.

In 1919, William Vaughan died, and there was a sale. Among the Shires
offered was the four-year-old Erfyl Lady Grey – standing at the back, uncon-
sidered, just a young grey mare, one among many. John Anwyl of Preston
Brockhurst, Shrewsbury, spotted her and yet suppressed his excitement and
bought her for about £300. He showed her at the Montgomeryshire show and
she was good enough to win the Gold Medal, but as there were no open classes
at this great county show from 1904 to 1923, not much notice was taken by the
generality of Shire men. In 1920, she stood moderately fifth at the London
Show in the big mares class, but there seemed nothing about her to catch the
eye. (Most people thought in 1924 they were seeing her for the first time. And
it is not often that a Shire man forgets things like that.) Chivers & Sons Limited
then bought her and later registered her first foal, born that spring, as Histon
Lucky King 38858. The next year, 1921, she bred another colt foal to that other
Montgomeryshire-bred celebrity, Champion's Goalkeeper, and at March in
July won the mare and foal class and another gold medal as best mare exhibited
by a member of the March Shire & Hackney Horse & Foal Show Society. Her
foal was registered as Histon Goalkeeper 39218. In 1922 she was barren, but at
the March society's show was entered in the pairs class with 67652 Lioness. They
stood only fifth, but that was not Lady Grey's fault, for she beat the winner of
the mare-with-foal open class to win the Shire gold medal again. She still
managed to remain more or less unheard of, but George Foster of Anstey Hall,
Trumpington had now had several good mares beaten by her, so he stepped in
and took her, together with Histon Goalkeeper, to the other side of the city of
Cambridge. He kept her dark in 1923 and she spent months preparing to be,

what she eventually was, the sensation of 1924. She was the champion of the year as soon as she came into view. Mr. Foster created a record by the fact that a second mare belonging to him, Gunby Autumn Tints, shown in the same class, was reserve champion.

Thomas Forshaw once commented that Erfyl Lady Grey was "a beautiful mare in every sense, and was considered by Shire connoisseurs to be the best ever seen. How wonderfully and majestically built she was, with limbs of the quality that would wear for ever, feet, joints, feather ideal, and gay in her movements!" Following the London show, she dropped a grey filly foal to Histon Menestrel; it won first prizes at March, Tring and the Great Yorkshire and was registered as 117880 Bower Lady Grey.

Reluctantly, we leave the grey lady for a while. The stallion championship was won by the five-year-old brown Herontye Buscot, who was not a surprise at all, as he had won the junior cup in 1922 and was reserve champion in 1923. By Champion's Goalkeeper, he belonged to James Gould of Lymm, but was bred near East Grinstead by Andrew Devitt, who dearly wanted the glory of the gold medal. Unfortunately, his membership of the Society had lapsed in 1920 but he was allowed to pay four years' subscriptions to be reinstated and the medal was his, a worthy memento of the first Shire champion ever bred in Sussex (and, to the time of writing, the last). Second to Herontye Buscot, both in the class and in the competition for the senior cup and the supreme championship, was Sundridge Nulli Secundus. But his owner J. Q. Rowett died later that year at the age of forty-eight, nine weeks older than his friend Shackleton had been when struck down by angina on the island of South Georgia. Rowett's stud was one of the shortest-lived of any of those which heavy expenditure bid fair to bring to the top. (Sundridge Nulli Secundus then went to Mrs. Stanton's stud to replace Harboro' Nulli Secundus who had to be destroyed in June. Alf Millen went back to Kent in charge of Sir Bernard Greenwell's Marden stud. The name of Rowett lived on in the Rowett Institute of Research in Animal Nutrition attached to Aberdeen University.) Third was Rievaulx Friar. The class for aged stallions was merged with the five – nine year olds, which allowed the under 16.2 small horse class to be reinstated.

The Boy Scouts ran about again. The railway companies made very co-operative arrangements to unload all horses at either Maiden Lane or King's Cross. The geldings were a feature of the show (section 8) and many men carried away a lasting memory of those sixteen workers revolving like a wheel. But the overwhelming impression was the glory of Erfyl Lady Grey. As for the rest of her triumphs, they must be held over for the next chapter. Meanwhile, to quote Thomas Forshaw again, he remarked years later that, "Her equal will be hard to find, but one never knows what perseverance can do. And without perseverance you won't go far to-day."

12. PETERBOROUGH ACTIVITIES

The stallion show in March, the agricultural show in July and the foal show in

September (or, after the war, in October) had long combined, with Sexton, Grimwade & Beck's regular sales, to make Peterborough the centre of the Shire world. The importance of the sales has been mentioned already. A brief review of the three great seasonal events in the city is appropriate here. It will give an opportunity to see the effect of the slump on the most aristocratic end of the Shire social scale, and the attempts made to counteract it.

The parade of stallions had a history which stretched far back into the mists of many years; indeed, of many centuries, before the Peterborough Agricultural Society came into existence in 1797 and eventually transformed it into an organised competitive show. There were four classes for Shires and in two of them, for three-year-olds and for senior horses, the winners were required to serve mares in the Peterborough area during the season and actually to stand in the city for part of one day each week. The requirements were of the strictest. Though stallions might arrive with London Show veterinary certificates issued only a month previously, they were not only re-tested but were galloped pretty severely for their wind, which the Shire Society had always objected to in the case of old horses. The agricultural society was frequently subjected to criticism on this point by owners, but selection for service at Peterborough set the seal upon a stock horse's fame. On the strength of it, his lettings were assured for years to come.

For the 1923 show, on Saturday 24th March, twenty-eight Shires altogether were entered, but only eleven came forward. The Thoroughbred stallion section had to be completely abandoned for lack of support. (At the Norfolk stallion show on the same day, there were twelve Shires and ten Suffolks – a decline for the second year in succession. But there were no less than twelve Percherons, three more than the year before. Not content with being the ancient battle-ground of the two English breeds, the individualists of Norfolk were determined, like the Athenians of old who had intrigued St. Paul, to spend their time in nothing else but to tell or hear some new thing. But even they could muster only one hunter sire and a handful of hackneys this year. The other great stallion show in the county, the King's Lynn and West Norfolk, under royal patronage, was in danger of folding up completely.)

For Shire men, the Peterborough summer show was the star fixture of that part of the year, its permanent site helping to make competition even fiercer, and consequently the glory even greater, than at the Royal itself. One of its most attractive classes was that for a pair of mares or geldings. Most men, asked to name their outstanding memory of Shires they had seen in that city, would have mentioned something in connexion with these pairs. There were too many, in 1924, who were tempted to look back from the hardships of the time to the good old days: which is, perhaps, an excuse for us briefly to do the same. Geldings had been first admitted to the class in 1895, but only twice did any stand in the top three positions in twenty years. James Eadie won third prize in 1898 with Bardon Extraordinary, the quadruple London champion, who was shown with Barrow Farmer, the 1900 London champion. Mann, Crossman &

Paulin were now third in 1924 with Albion Wonder and Albion Perfection. Otherwise, mares always swept the board.

Any man who had been to Peterborough shows for thirty or forty years would almost certainly have named four daughters of Harold as his pick of these pairs classes. In 1896, Sir Albert Muntz had shown the six-year-old Dunsmore Gloaming (the future 1899–1900 London champion) and Melody, then eight (bred by A. B. Freeman-Mitford out of a Premier mare). Both were bay and touched 17.2-hands, massive in limb and body, and almost identical except for Gloaming's two white feet. The other never-to-be-forgotten pair of Harold mares came in 1900. Queen of the Shires, the 1897 London champion was then six and Southgate Charm was four. Fred Crisp, who had bred the latter, had in these two a pair which were as tall as the others, somewhat longer, and yet with legs and pasterns which would have delighted a Clydesdale breeder. They too were as alike as could be, even to their sire's peculiarly rich brown, except that Queen of the Shires had white markings whereas her partner was a whole colour.

If Shire breeding had not been primarily a business and only secondarily a matter of producing things of beauty, there would have been no need, in 1924, to look back with regret into the past. It is not difficult to guess why. Erfyl Lady Grey was there. With Lanes Darling 2nd, a bay aged eight, acting as no mean partner, she won the pairs. And she inevitably won the open mares' class as well, with Crossways Forest Maid, her predecessor in 1922–1923 as London champion, second. Third was Pendley Lady, London reserve champion in 1922, but really a "summer mare" with not enough hair for Islington in those days.

In the autumn, only Tring (in August) and Ashbourne (then in September) rivalled the Peterborough October foal show. The Shire sales immediately after the 1922 show were as dispiriting as they could be. Eighty-one filly foals were entered for auction, and sixty-eight came forward. One made 300 guineas, one was withdrawn at 270, one made 140 and one 100. The next best prices were 94, 88, 84, 76, 74 and 70 guineas. Eight went for from 50 to 54 guineas: six from 40 to 44; four from 30 to 39, twenty-two were sold for 21 to 29 guineas; seventeen from 10 to 19, and one made 9 guineas. And this was the leading foal sale in England, the mecca of Shire men! The slump in breeding and in the gelding trade made colt-foal prices far worse. Of 111 entered, the top price was 140 guineas and many were sold, if they were sold at all, for 7, 6½ and 6 guineas – sums which in some cases were no more than the cost of getting them conceived. The next day at the sale of older animals, Sir Berkeley Sheffield's Gunby King, four years old, highly commended at the London show the year before, and holder of a current Ministry stallion licence, was sold for 18 guineas – at least ten times less than he would have made, even if gelded, eighteen months earlier.

However, Edmund Beck, out of the army and full of keenness, and Fred Griffin, who had been running the famous Boro' Fen stud for thirty-five years, had already thought up a new idea, which was enthusiastically taken up by

Robert Bibby, the Peterborough A.S. secretary, and his council. Stallion-owners had been invited in 1922 to nominate sires for a "produce stakes" the following year at a subscription of 7 guineas each horse. By the end of the year, when nominations closed, forty-four proprietors, including the King, had submitted the names of fifty-eight stallions. In October 1923, thirty-six colt foals and thirty-two filly foals were duly entered for the stakes, and thirty-three and twenty-seven respectively, sired by thirty-one of the nominated stallions, actually appeared on the showground. Top prizes for filly and colt foals were £40. (The biggest prize in any London class, even for mature breeding stock, was £30.) There were also awards of £20, £10 and £5 for the sires of the first three foals in each class. These were the first cash prizes awarded at any show to Shires not actually judged, or even present, themselves. They were really the only feature which made the Stakes very much different in principle from the normal practice at most local foal shows, where owners – both of hiring society or "club" stallions and of those travelled under private enterprise – usually gave special prizes for the best foals got by their own horses. In fact, the small prizes for sires at the Stakes in comparison with those given for the foals indicate that the main attraction to owners who nominated their stallions was the publicity to be gained by the success of the foals they got.

Arthur Colclough of Sandbach, Cheshire, had the honour of winning the colt foals' class in this first stakes in 1923. He had one or two Shires in the Stud-book in previous years, and now promptly completed an application form for membership of the Society, and was elected in December. Here was a recruit that would never have joined without winning the £40 windfall. Sir Arthur Nicholson, who owned the winning sire, Pendley Footprint, bought the foal, registered him as Leek Victor 39523 and won fifth prize with him in London the following February. The winning filly-foal was bred by Fred Griffin and the winning sire was his own Rowington Recruit, that he had bought in 1919 at the age of three. As the foal also won the ordinary open class and the local radius-class as well, Mr. Griffin collected £80 by showing her that day. As Boro' Melody, she was later third for him in London as a two-year-old.

These first foal stakes were such a success that it was possible to reduce the stake money for the 1924 show to only 5 guineas per stallion. The whole scheme did much to strengthen the normal classes, local and open, and to increase the attendance of buyers at the usual foal auction that Edmund Beck conducted in the afternoon, and at his sale of older horses the next day. With additions, these stakes were a major interest at Peterborough until another war eventually intervened.

13. THE GLORIOUS CANADIAN FIASCO

The Shire men had looked forward to the resumption after the war of the export trade. They had also expected to find new customers in the war-torn areas of Western Europe. Both hopes were misplaced. France and Belgium were not in such a bad way that there was any temptation to experiment with British breeds. Ex-army horses filled their immediate requirements for working horses, and the straitened stocks of pedigree Percheron, Belgian and other breeds were given time to recover. All that the Shire Society got from Europe after the war (apart from the Percheron invasion, which it did not want) was a piece of paper. In recognition of the 750 guineas donated to the Agricultural Relief of Allies Committee, there arrived at No. 12 a diploma of "témoinage de reconnaissance du Gouvernement Belge à la Shire Horse Society pour sa participation à la reconstitution agricole de la Belgique". As for the Russian market, it had gone for ever, and the German one was virtually dead.

In the United States and Canada, as already mentioned, £825 was spent on publicity in 1920 and the campaign was renewed in 1921, when it cost £750. The result was depressing. Hardly anyone in all that vast area sent to England for a Shire. In 1922, a sum of £300 was voted for United States advertising, on condition that the American Shire Horse Association spent a similar sum. Yet Americans, though they read articles about Shires, did not import more than one or two. Canada was almost given up in despair, as these figures show:

Pedigree horses	Imported into Canada		Registered in Canada	
	1911–14	1919–20	1911–14	1919–20
Clydesdales	3,405	112	14,191	6,107
Percherons	1,681	1,332★	2,936	2,734
Belgians	375	385★	478	591
Shires	268	23	612	140
Suffolks	95	6	252	31

★ from U.S.A.

However, the Duke of Devonshire, on his return to England after five years as Governor-General of the Dominion, argued that the best publicity was by demonstration rather than mere propaganda. The Council knew he was right. So Thomas Forshaw, Alfred Clark and Edmund Beck were instructed to purchase, if they could, five horses for £1,000, to be presented as a gift to the Canadian government. This was not too difficult in view of the collapse in prices, and was made easier when Forshaw himself and Sir Bernard Greenwell offered the pick of their stables for this sum. The three selectors had in mind maximum weight, size and power, which was easy enough: and minimum hair, much less easy to find in 1923. When they had chosen their five, Mrs. Stanton presented an extra one to the Duke of Devonshire to add to the contingent. The story of the sensation they caused in the Dominion is worth recalling as a relief from the gloom of this period of depression. The horses were:

MARDEN JUPITER 34960, bay 7-year-old, from Sir Bernard Greenwell. Bred by his father, Sir Walpole. By Champion's Goalkeeper out of a Lockinge Forest King mare. 6th in London as a 4-year-old.

SNELSTON TOPPER 38528, bay 4-year-old, presented by Mrs. Stanton. Bred at Sandbach, Cheshire by C. W. Lowe. By Harboro' Nulli Secundus. 10th in London as 2-year-old; highly commended (13th) as 3-year-old.

HAWTON CARLTON 38846, brown 2-year-old, from the Forshaws. Bred near Newark by Ben Farrow. By Quenby Teamster 35017, the stallion hired from the Forshaws in 1920 by the Newark S.H.S. and serving members' mares at 6 gns.

102996 ESSENDON JET, black 8-year-old from Greenwell. Bred at Hatfield, Herts., by Samuel Wallace. By Coleshill Forester 24149 (foaled 1905, by Lockinge Forest King).

102419 COXALL DAY DAWN, brown 6-year-old from her breeder, J. Goodwin Finney, Coxall, Bucknell, Salop. By Shopnoller Drayman 30915.

109178 MOULTON HOPEFUL, bay 3-year-old from Sandringham. Bred by Alfred Clark and sold to the King at 2 years. By Horning Mimic 34048, who was in the Moulton stud.

The five horses bought by the Society were paraded several times at the London Show. Teddy Walters from Marden took Jupiter round the ring, and he went like a hackney. (Amongst the stock he left in England were four geldings owned by Eady Robinson of Higham Ferrers, who considered them the best group by one horse that anyone ever had: and if anyone is able to be a judge of that, it is Mr. Robinson.) The King presented the horses on the Wednesday afternoon, 21st February to the Honourable Duncan Marshall, Canadian Commissioner of Agriculture. E. S. Archibald, Director of the Dominion Experimental Farms, and George Rothwell, his Chief Animal Husbandman, were also there. During the presentation Queen Mary turned to Alfred Clark and asked, typically of her interest in such matters, "Do the owners get a profit when you buy horses from them?" The President was equal to the occasion. "Not always, Ma'am," he replied, "but His Majesty did on the one we bought from him." Her Majesty seemed pleased, but it is doubtful whether she was aware that it was from Clark himself that the King had bought the mare in the first place.

Fred Jordan, an experienced Shire groom, had been suggested by the Forshaws as the right man to look after the horses, which, accompanied also by George Rothwell, were embarked at Glasgow on 4th April. The next day they set sail. Marden Jupiter had a cold and was off his feed. For the first nine days he did not show much life and the two men were worried. However they were more worried afterwards because, on regaining his spirits, he developed a consuming ambition to annihilate Snelston Topper, two stalls away. He had to be watched day and night and, in spite of Mr. Rothwell and Fred taking turns, a

serious accident was only just prevented on the eleventh day. By now they
were also worried about Coxall Day Dawn, who had been due to foal on the
14th. They docked at St. John on the 18th, were delayed a couple of days by
lack of transport, but eventually reached the government's central experimental farm, Ottawa on Saturday, 21st April – Day Dawn still carrying her
foal and Jupiter still thwarted of his evil intentions. However, the following
Tuesday, the party was increased by a strong filly foal. (The sire was Bowland
Dray King, a Lancashire colt. A. B. Charlton was immediately sent papers so
that the newcomer could be registered in the Canadian books.) Rothwell was
sure Essendon Jet was also in foal: Fred Jordan was equally certain she was not.
A week later, they were all fairly fit, except that Moulton Hopeful had a cold
and young Hawton Carlton was slow to recover from the journey. Snelston
Topper had been quite unaffected by the trip, and his would-be assassin was
beginning to round out.

"These Shire horses have most assuredly created a furore amongst the horsemen of Canada to date", wrote Rothwell to Charlton nine days after they
reached Ottawa. He was being inundated with visitors and letters. Many of the
latter were to the effect that the whole project was ill-advised – but they were
all from individuals who had not seen the horses and who knew nothing of the
breed. Everyone who had come to look at them was, he said, "of the opinion
that up to the present time we have not seen Shire horses in Canada. They
admit they may have seen some horses that were called Shires. I might state
that my time has been very largely taken up with showing off these animals to
horsemen, Members of Parliament and visitors generally, who have come here
with the express purpose of looking them over. There has not been a farm
periodical in Canada that has not had a go at them in one way or another. One
of our large Toronto dailies is badgering me at the present time for photographs." But he was naturally reluctant to allow this until they had all regained
their form and weight.

"It so happens", continued Rothwell, "that my father, who runs a large
establishment within a few miles of this farm, owns what is considered to be one
of the best studs of Clydesdales in Canada at the present time. He has looked
over these horses pretty carefully and, although he is a careful man in the statement of his opinions, has expressed his complete satisfaction and admiration
concerning them. He says that Coxall Day Dawn was about the type of Clydesdale mare that he used to see in Scotland when he was importing in 1880 and
thereabouts."

The five horses given by the Society were in due course sent on to their final
destination, the Government experimental station for Central Alberta at
Lacombe, about midway between Edmonton and Calgary. They arrived on the
morning of 16th May, and F. H. Reed, the superintendent, was delighted with
them. "We were expecting something extra good in this shipment", he wrote
to Charlton, "and I assure you that our highest expectations have been more
than fulfilled. I have seen quite a number of Shire horses at exhibitions in

Canada and the United States, but these are of much better type than anything which I have ever seen before in this country." He then explained his plans for Jupiter. "At this station we propose breeding this year five pure-bred Clydesdale mares to him. There are also in the Lacombe district about 20 pure-bred Shire mares, and two breeders of Shires in other districts have stated that they propose sending in about ten of their best mares." Jupiter was also expected to do good work on the numerous grade-Clydesdales in Central Alberta for the production of top-quality commercial horses. Imported stallions were often not too sure in their first season and, though Mr. Reed hoped for some good foals the next spring, he did not anticipate the best results until the 1925 crop. For this reason, he would not ask the colt, Hawton Carlton, to assist Jupiter until the following year.

Mrs. Stanton's gift of Snelston Topper had been something of an embarrassment to the Canadians, as his services would have been superfluous in Alberta. Consequently, it was decided to leave him in the east and he was sent to the Lennoxville experimental farm, Quebec. For him, a groom of Fred Jordan calibre was found, on the advice of the Forshaws, in the person of Frank Oxley, as great a Shire enthusiast as any. Frank had emigrated from the Newark district to Western Canada but gladly came east to look after this fine horse. All through the exceptional heat of the summer, he was up at three o'clock every morning to exercise his charge in the cool hours, and was able to keep him in top condition to meet his mares.

George Rothwell was delighted with both horse and man, and wrote after the season was over that "Topper has done more to popularise horse breeding than any other single factor for a number of years in that particular district. He has been bred to some fifty-five mares, which may not look a very large number from the Old Country standpoint, but represents nevertheless, I can assure you, a very fair season's work when it is considered that there was no time to advertise this horse, and he went to a section where, temporarily at least, there is not much interest shown in horse breeding, although its proximity to Montreal should make it a breeding centre for draft horses. We had anticipated moving the horse away from Lennoxville for next season, but the public are so anxious to have him retained that we have decided to leave him another year. We have had an excellent opportunity of studying fully how a horse of this type will impress himself on the ordinary farm mare. He has been a centre of attraction at all the farm excursions, demonstrations, etc." (And it turned out that, far from being affected by the new climate, he left all but three of his mares in foal, which was an eye-opener to everyone in the district.)

Meanwhile, in the west, the first disaster struck on the afternoon of Friday, 10th August. About three o'clock, the three mares were seen by one of the men from the cattle barn, and they were all right. But when Fred Jordan went out at four o'clock he found Moulton Hopeful, the three-year-old Clark-Sandringham mare, very badly bloated and practically suffocated. He led her gently and slowly about fifty yards to the barn and the veterinary surgeon, W. J. Brandewie, was there in less than ten minutes. He used two trocars without success. Within half an hour of her trouble being first noticed, Hopeful was dead. The post-mortem showed a misplacement of the caecum and a number of small constrictions along the intestines. But the prime cause of the sudden and fatal large formation of gas was one of the mysteries of horse-management. Essendon Jet and Coxall Day Dawn, whose foal was doing well, were both now in foal to Jupiter, who had been used more extensively during the previous twelve weeks than had been anticipated. Hawton Carlton was developing in a most impressive manner.

The following February, Rothwell attended the annual meeting of the Shire Horse Association of Canada, at which there was a long discussion about the discrimination against the breed on the Western Canada show circuit. Most of the larger shows had eliminated the Shire entirely from their schedules. Rothwell gave a glowing account of the London Show the year before. He told his hosts that, though he had expected to see a wonderful lot of horses, it was far beyond anything he had dreamed of. But he had been impressed most by the organisation, and the quiet, business-like way the judges and stewards had gone about their work. There was nothing in the United States, or Canada itself, to equal it. His audience boggled at the thought of 400 Shires in one building, all as good or better than Jupiter, Jet and company, and they went into raptures at his description of the studs he had been able to visit. They promptly elected George Rothwell as Honorary President of their Association.

On 24th March 1924, Marden Jupiter and Hawton Carlton were exhibited at the great Calgary Show. Jupiter, who won the champion medal, now weighed nearly 1 ton 3 cwt. (2,485 lb.). He was paraded in the arena on three nights with a very good Percheron, a good but rather small Clydesdale, a Belgian and the King's Hackney, Will Somers. The first night they only walked, but on the Thursday they were trotted, and Fred Jordan kept Jupiter towards the middle of the arena. The Hackney and the Shire put up such a show that the ring steward made them go five times round. The big horse moved his knees and hocks as well as the "professional", and the crowd cheered. This excited Jupiter and he performed even better. Everyone just stood up and yelled. It was the sensation of the show. The following day, E. D. Adams, secretary of the Clydesdale Breeders' Association and President of the Alberta Horse Breeders' Association, told F. H. Reed, the Ottawa experimental farm director, it was the most wonderful performance ever seen at a Calgary Horse Show. Norman Weir, Clydesdale President, with a dozen horsemen round him, added, "In my opinion, that is the best draft horse of any breed that ever stepped in a Calgary show ring." Reed expected to see a consignment of twenty-five to thirty mares shipped from England as a result of all this.

Joined by Essendon Jet, Marden Jupiter appeared at the Royal Agricultural Winter Fair at Toronto, which was claimed to be the biggest show of its kind in all America. Both received Grand Champion honours, and Jupiter had the opportunity of making 10,000 people roar at more performances of his Hackney trot on the tan bark in the evenings.

Finally that year, they both repeated their triumph at the International Live Stock Exposition, Chicago, in competition with Shires from the United States. The Chicago *Daily Drovers Journal* reported that Jupiter "is a whale of a horse any way you take him. He is the largest stallion representing any breed at the 1924 International. Weighing close to 2,500 lb., he is one of the cleanest-legged big horses ever seen at Chicago." The official report of the show said that he was "a horse of tremendous scale, balanced in body proportion, stood squarely on his legs, and had big, shapely feet. He went straight in front, working his pads close together and well beneath him, a great specimen of size and quality." Of Essendon Jet, the report described her as "big, broody, and full of muscle. She could tramp away at the walk and trot to please anyone." Several breeders said, "We have never before seen real Shires at Chicago until now."

Coxall Day Dawn had produced her second foal on Canadian soil, a colt by Jupiter, but had died not long after. Now Essendon Jet contracted a chill at the Chicago show and succumbed also. All those gift mares had gone in little over twenty months. By the end of the next year, Jupiter and Hawton Carlton were also dead. Death dispelled the dream of converting Canada from Clydes. And so the whole project turned out a glorious failure.

Somewhat perversely, the extra horse that had caused some embarrassment to George Rothwell continued to thrive. Snelston Topper was moved to Lacombe in 1926 and the next year pure-bred Shire, Clydesdale and Percheron mares were sent to him, not to mention a crowd of grade-mares of all three types, from a distance of 100 miles in all directions. One of his foals out of a registered Clydesdale mare was regarded as the finest ever born at Lacombe. In hard breeding condition, at which Frank Oxley kept him well, Topper was usually just under the ton at about 2,200 lb. but in show order he went to 2,375 lb. Prizes for his foals were offered by the Government at Calgary, Edmonton and Lacombe and George Rothwell remarked that he was a splendid Shire advertisement in the province of Alberta. He lived to the tolerably respectable age of eleven-and-a-half and one of the most successful of his sons, Innisfail King, bred by Tom Rawlinson, was engaged for several years in the 'thirties serving 100 mares a season, leaving a steady 70% in foal.

Frank Oxley, who had joined the parent Shire Society from Lacombe in 1928, came home to England in 1933 and settled at Belchamp St. Pauls, near Clare in Suffolk. He never bred any Shires of his own, but remained a member until 1939. As for Fred Jordan (who unlike Frank, had only gone out to Canada to take Shires), that is another story and another time.

This fiasco, splendid though it was, represents the only occasion that the Shire Horse Society ever purchased any Shire horses. And it was followed by the abandonment of hope, between the wars, for a thriving, if modest, export market. There was a consignment to Australia in 1925 and in ones or twos pedigree Shires went elsewhere, but export now ceased to be of significance in the economy of the Shire.

14. 1924: TOWARDS STABILITY

Even while the shock of the depression was still comparatively fresh, there were signs, at least by the autumn of 1924, that all was not completely lost. In the towns, there was some disillusion with the motor-lorry, and many were seeing it rather as a challenge to the railways for medium distance hauls than as a replacement on local work for the horse, which was in this sphere both economical and manoeuvrable. The petrol driven delivery van was a greater danger to the van-horse than the heavy lorry was to the Shire. The purchase price of good sound geldings, which had driven many men to try the novelty of modern motor traction in 1920, had dropped amazingly, and the slump itself was now in the horseman's favour. After several years of depression in industry and trade, many men could not afford to replace their first worn-out motor lorry, which they had bought at a knock-down price from the army. And the cost of labour, which is always a prime factor in the economics of horse as against motor haulage, was dropping steadily. On the farms, it was quite clear that the same arguments applied to an even greater degree. In addition, the tractor could not travel on a road, nor do half the jobs that horses had been expected to perform.

The lack of breeding during these three or four years, and the gradual disappearance of the ex-army horses which had formed such a high proportion of the glut, were now beginning to enhance the value of the horses available. Sound geldings were once more in demand at from £50 to £60, and it was no uncommon thing for a man to ask £200 for a five or six-year-old show gelding, or for one which would make people think what a fine brewery or coal merchant it was who possessed him. In fact, a really good gelding could command as high a price as he would as a second-rate stallion. The law of supply and demand was now beginning to operate in conditions of sanity, if of somewhat gloomy sanity. A man would not be a fool at all if he made a resolution, on New Year's Eve as 1924 was fading away, to put a good number of his mares to the horse again next season. It was, of course, a gamble. Who could tell what the foal would be worth, in 1931, as a staunch puller of heavy loads on the town streets?

The close of the year marked the end of the craziest decade in the history of heavy-horse breeding. The one thing that the Shire is unsuited to is lunatic or erratic behaviour. He thrives best in a steady atmosphere. He was not really a 4,000 guinea animal: but he was worth more than 5 or 10 as a baby, or 40 when mature.

CHAPTER XII

1925–1929

Good Breeding in Bad Times

1. THE PROPHET OF DOOM

RUIN and misery, disaster and disillusion were the lot of the farmers. This was the theme Sir Walter Gilbey never ceased to preach and, in his endeavour to shake the Government into action, he followed the example of Ezekiel, Jeremiah and the other prophets of old who symbolically acted out in their lives their warnings of doom. That is, he sold his Elsenham estate in 1926, and made political capital out of his enormous financial loss. This well-known property, well-advertised, realised only about £8 an acre, a farcical price for the land itself, not to mention the fine buildings that stood upon it. He then gave the sale the fullest publicity, and he had no mean ability in that direction. Whenever he spoke, he made certain that reporters were there to listen. All the papers quoted him, and *The Spectator* praised him.

Year after year he hammered away at Mr. Baldwin. In 1929, Ramsey MacDonald, in opposition, was saying that nationalisation of the land was the only solution, and Sir Walter called down the divine wrath upon him, too. "We have the best farmers in the world", he told the Press, at the 1929 Shire Show luncheon (at which, as usual, he entertained the Council), "and if they cannot make a paying proposition of farming, does Mr. MacDonald think that an army of officials in Whitehall is going to do so?" Every year since the depression had started, Sir Walter also reminded His Majesty that the Show which he favoured with his presence was almost entirely a gathering of farmers, struggling unaided to feed the mouths of the people and earn an honest living in the process. This year, serious illness prevented the King from coming: but the Prince of Wales, his deputy, was not left unaware of the position by the persistent Sir Walter. In point of fact, in February 1929, prices had been more or less stable since 1926. Four months later, Mr. MacDonald's second Labour Government was given a second chance to see what it could do, but before the year was out a second world-wide slump had begun.

2. HORSE AND MOTOR

Internal combustion engines took the place of horses more rapidly in the towns than on the farms. This created a greater difficulty for Shire-breeders than for any others, for two reasons. Firstly, the Shire had been developed in sheer size and strength as primarily a town horse, able and willing to haul all the goods that the industrial and commercial activity of the country required. Indeed, since the coming of the railways, he had had to pull many of the vastly increased number of loads twice, both to the rail depot and from it again. Secondly, as has been observed, a market for five-year-old geldings which contracted more rapidly than that for mares or younger geldings resulted in a large proportion of the former either being slaughtered at knacker's prices or being retained for farm work, involving the farmer in the use of draught-power which depreciated in value instead of paying for itself.

An extra source of confusion was that, throughout the inter-war period, mechanisation in the towns did not proceed at a regular pace, but by fits and starts. It was impossible to guess, at the time a mare was ready for the horse, what the demand for the foal, if there was to be one, would be in six years' time. Looking back, one may reasonably ask why this was so. If, thanks to the progress stimulated by war, the tractor and motor-lorry were both available in 1920, why did they not replace the horse promptly and completely on both farm and street?

Let us consider agriculture first. Restraints upon the speedy adoption of the tractor were of two kinds, practical and economic. Its practical shortcomings in the 'twenties comprised a restricted sphere of operations, unreliability, and the lack of implements suitable for motor traction.[1]

If the wheels had metal strakes (and they nearly all did), tractors were not allowed on public roads and did serious damage to private ones. So, unless the wheels were changed, the tractor could not be used for both haulage and cultivation. Wheels of smooth iron or with solid rubber or the early type of pneumatic tyres all slipped on wet surfaces or immobilised the tractor in mud. The iron or solid tyres badly compacted heavy land. And yet it was on heavy land that the power of the tractor would have been most useful, if it had not been for the fact that this was just the sort of land that was now under grass instead of the plough.

Unreliability stemmed from the chain-drive, an unguarded and frequently choked carburettor and the use of metals which may have been suitable for a motor-car on smooth roads but were inadequate for heavy and prolonged running on the farm. Service stations were too few and the number of manufacturers, and consequently the variety of spare parts required, too many. In ploughing, the tractor might need between twenty and thirty gallons of clean water for cooling: and the only water available at hand in those days was in the horse-pond.

Without purpose-built tools, the farmer who sat on a tractor had to pull a horse-implement behind him, instead of walking behind both. The plough or hoe was difficult to control, even with a second man to guide it, and the task was almost impossible in the case of crops sown in rows. Furthermore (here to quote Miss Whetham verbatim) "a tractor going over a bump pulled the implement either out of the ground or into it, giving in turn uneven cultivation. Horses stopped with any check to the implement but the same blockage might break a tractor-drawn implement or pull the tractor over backwards, a common cause of fatal accidents. Ferguson's three-point linkage was invented about 1920, but only became common a decade later in conjunction with the hydraulic lift, which allowed the implement to adjust to the changes in the angle of the tractor to the land surface being worked by the tool."[2] Reversing was almost impossible, and turning was uncertain and wide: where space to manoeuvre was confined, many gateways and entrances were too narrow.

The second group of objections to the tractor, that of economy, was naturally based in part on the first. It is uneconomic to use a machine which is inefficient, unreliable and restricted in its application, when the horse was versatile, reliable and efficient. Even when the tractor, in years to come, overcame all three handicaps, it never was and never can be preferable to the horse on these grounds, except when sheer power is required. The good horse does better work than the best machine, and can be depended upon to have the extra advantage of knowing how to do it and of where to put his feet. To succeed, the motor had to be cheaper than the horse or, in some other guise than the simple tractor, to perform something new that horses could not achieve. Until such time as it could supplant him almost entirely, the tractor was feasible only on the big farms and only when the new machine and a reduced number of animals and men, together, cost less to buy and maintain than the original number of horses and men. On small farms, this was an impossibility and, with the steady reduction of the area of land under tillage all through the long depression, there was a decreasing proportion of those operations which the machine of that time was best fitted to do.

As to specific items in the relative economy of the horse and the tractor, there were so many variables that any set of figures truly reflecting the position on one farm would not necessarily apply to any other. The initial cost of a tractor was about the same as a pair of horses with their gears. A tractor's useful life at that time could be estimated at only four to five years, whereas depreciation on a pair of good young geldings could be spread over, say, ten years. Therefore, a tractor, it would appear, ought to replace four horses in order to justify the capital expenditure. However, as we have observed throughout the Shire story, the purchase of good young geldings and working them until they could work no more was the worst, not the best, form of horse-economy. Provided the town market did not collapse, horse-power on farms where the animals were bred or brought on should involve a capital gain, not a loss at all. On other farms using up older horses, it was possible to buy many more than four for the price of a tractor: and depreciation on each of them, though they lasted only two or three years, was less.

When the calculation is made in the more realistic terms, not of length of service, but of hours of work per annum, amount of work per hour, power obtainable, and so on, every man had to work out his own sums. For many or most jobs (until they were done in a quite different way – as, for example, harvesting by a self-propelled combine), the engine was likely to be over-powered. It could do more work in an hour. It could work for more hours in a single day, unless it broke down – in fact, it could operate for the full extent of the man's working day, whereas a horse needed his time at the beginning and end of it. It could do more in a single week, more in busy periods or more in a time of urgency against a change in the weather. But, for all this, it might be actually required to work less in a whole year than the horse. It was only on the largest farms that these comparative advantages and drawbacks of the two forms of traction could be combined in a partnership of both. The tractor did not do much even to solve the difficulty that more horses were needed at some periods of the year than at others, because on well-organised farms surplus or maturing stock was disposed of precisely when the busy time was over. Where horses were not working, they still had to be fed. But even idle tractors slowly rusted away, since farmers were never the men to expend much care on their machines. Few could be found, of a Sunday morning, polishing their tractors with the loving devotion lavished by the surburban householder to his family car.

All these points would have sounded over theoretical, if they had been put to the ordinary farmer in the 'twenties and 'thirties. In retaining his horses, he simply saw himself as following a system which involved the least expense. Farming just was not an industry into which the practitioner put capital. Some of the old landlords had done so, but they were going or gone. The farmer could not afford a tractor, and that was the end of the matter.

But it is not the end of the historian's argument, for we have not yet touched upon the two most important factors in the relative economy of the horse and the motor – the cost of fuel or fodder, and the cost of human labour. Both are applicable to the town horse and motor-lorry also, the first in a lesser degree but the second equally. Not only in the five years immediately under review but throughout the inter-war period, the food that a horse consumed was cheap – cheapest on the mixed farm which grew it all, but in the heart of London and Birmingham cheaper than petrol or diesel oil. Labour, also, was cheap in town and country. If horse-traction required more men, their employment was not a decisive element in the cost of using horses.

The strongest arguments in favour of the horse throughout these two decades were that this animal created a market for the produce of the British farm and employment for the British worker. Both arguments appeared indisputable on patriotic grounds and remained valid for reasons of self-interest in the eyes of the coal merchants, the haulier and the railway companies, as well as of the farmer. It was of course crazy that, in a starving world, in a largely mal-fed Britain, it should be accounted a good thing that 1,663,088 horses in 1924 and 1,129,281 in 1934 should eat up the product of 3 acres each (half in grazing and half in cereals) of British soil. In 1929, there were 300,000 heavy-horses in commercial undertakings, and they cost at least £40 each to feed and bed – a total of about £12,000,000, a large proportion of which went into the needy farmers' pockets. But, within a crazy civilisation, it was logical that this should be done, if no one else was able to afford to eat it up, either in the form of bread or beef. In a world ordered by sound sense, it ought to sound equally crazy that a thing should be good because it makes extra work. But we shall not be in a position to be so loftily critical of this until we have found a means whereby machinery and automation enable us all to have a fair share of the privilege of earning increased leisure and play.

Slippery roads were a continuing problem to the horse-owner. Trying to make a joke of his difficulties in a hilly country, a farmer at Alderley in Gloucestershire advertised in the *Wotton-under-Edge Gazette*: "Wanted, man to teach horses to skate. Urgent." In the towns, to add insult to injury, the public often reacted to slips and falls as if they were the owner's fault. One haulier was prosecuted in 1925 for cruelty in expecting his horse to pull too great a load when, in fact, the surface of the street was alone to blame for the difficulty in starting. In court, statistics of the London Show weight-pulling tests were quoted, and he was acquitted. But between the objectors to the horse on the one hand and its zealous protectors on the other, this man and his fellows had a difficult time.

Many streets, particularly in the provinces, were in fact equally dangerous for motors, and investigations by a special committee of the National Horse Association were supported by the Automobile Association. But the possibility of the town horse becoming redundant or of constantly falling down appeared less likely than that of his being forbidden. The campaign, started in the first years of the 'twenties, developed into a serious proposal in 1924 to ban horses from certain streets in London. The attack was smartly stepped up early in the second half of the decade. In June 1925 it was proposed in the House of Lords that all horses in London should be licensed and that, as each died, the licence should not be renewed for a replacement. The National Horse Association vigorously opposed both this and other suggestions aimed at the banning of horses from street work, but its arguments were not helped by a fantastic traffic jam which paralysed all movement on Blackfriars Bridge for two hours. Newspapers, particularly, fanned the flames of dispute whenever there was nothing else to excite their readers. Someone suggested that coal and rubbish carts, which were pretty generally horse-drawn, should be allowed to work only at night, which was absurd. Other reformers proposed the compulsory provision of car parks by big shops, restrictions on parking in the street, or the removal of ground floor shop-frontages so that pedestrians could walk in an arcade while horses and carts or other slow vehicles could drive on the pavement. But the popular Press chiefly adopted the slogan "Millions lost through cart-horses".

Those responsible for transport and haulage were not so anti-horse as the Press. The Commercial Motor Users' Association was told in February 1925 by its president, Mr. Shrapnel Smith, that, in thousands of instances, the horse was irreplaceable. He was himself a big user of horses. He ridiculed the idea of eliminating them. On 4th November, the President of the Society of Motor Manufacturers and Traders told members of the Association of Retail Distributors at Olympia that "the horse is again being resorted to by some London firms". Selfridges discovered that horse traction was cheaper by 3d. a mile. One Manchester firm worked out that the delivery of cloth cost them 0.852d. per piece by horse and 2.454d. by motor.

In 1926, although the General Strike caused the postponement of the London Cart Horse Parade from Whit Monday to August Bank holiday, over 500 horses turned up, as if to prove the point. In 1927 the National Horse Association issued hundreds of thousands of stickers, stamps and other propaganda material. But it was the figures produced by town councils that were seized upon with most alacrity by the horsemen, because they involved the rate-payers' money. A new study by Glasgow Corporation was a god-send. Its costing of horse-drawn vehicles incorporated wages based upon an eight-hour day, insurance, fodder and its preparation, depreciation of horse (over eight years at £100 per horse, which was a high estimate in that year), saddlery, shoeing and veterinary, stabling, and depreciation of cart and repairs. The figures for motor-vehicles were calculated on the equivalent items together with £6 per annum for licence. Comparative expense was as follows:

	Horse-drawn vehicle (3 loads, or 5.2 tons, per day).		Mechanical vehicle (3.2 loads, or 8 tons, per day).	
	s.	d.	s.	d.
Cost per day	18	8.75	40	11.00
Cost per hour	2	4.09	5	1.375
Cost per load	6	2.91	12	9.44
Cost per ton	3	7.22	5	1.375

Prior to 1914, the Shire breeder had depended upon prosperity in trade and industry in his efforts to persuade men to use better and more expensive horses and to prove that sound well-bred animals were an economy, even though they cost more to buy. But in the inter-war years, it was hard times in industry and trade that kept open the market for the town horse. The horses which were least quickly displaced in urban areas were those worked by "small men" who had not the capital to mechanise; those in trades requiring much waiting about, and starting and stopping in deliveries; and the heaviest and strongest Shire types used on short hauls, for they were highly manoeuvrable in congested yards and narrow entrances, which in any case had been built for horses. Coal delivery, railway cartage and railway shunting, and constructional work involving the moving of materials such as sand, soil or stones in awkward places were essentially horse jobs. By the end of 1929, horse traffic, so far from showing much noticeable reduction since 1924, appeared to have increased. Outside the towns, there were one or two jobs on which even the most enthusiastic horse advocate would not have opposed their retirement in favour of the motor engine – for example, the haulage of timber from the woods. Even though a motor might pull it along the road, it was horses only, often in teams

PLATES 33 and 34 Rothschild types. (*above*) Belle Cole, the champion mare of 1908, with her 1907 foal. Named King Cole VII, he grew to be one of the finest and most prolific stock-horses of all time. Drowned in the Welland when still only nine, he left behind him a legion of offspring and of legends; (*below*) Halstead Royal Duke, London champion in 1909, when Lord Rothschild won both championships.

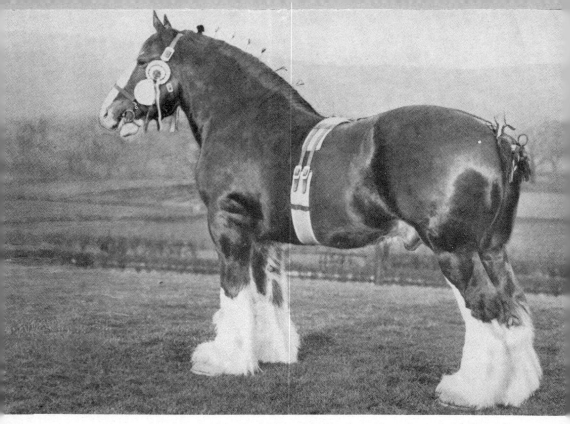

PLATES 35 and 36 Patrician and plebeian. (*above*) The Duke of Devonshire's Warton Draughtsman, champion of champions in the great year 1912 and (*below*) one of the 377 other stallions he defeated. This unidentifiable horse's lone admirer is John Burns, one of the first Labour M.P.s in 1892 and the first working man ever to enter the Cabinet (1906–1914). His famous straw hat of the dock-strike days has now been graded-up into a pedigree tile fit for a Shire Show.

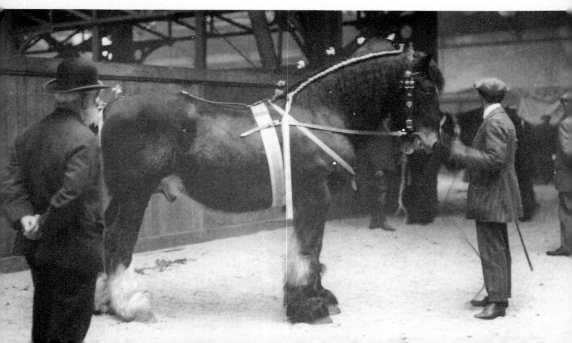

of eight or ten, which could compete with the initial removal. Able as they were at this work, and grand as was the sight they presented, toil which was hard enough to reduce their effective working lives often only to two years was more appropriate to elephants or tractors.

All through these dismal years, the number of mares put to the stallion had steadily decreased. But by 1929 it was at last generally realised that not only was the heavy-horse not superseded in the towns, and certainly not in the country, but that the market for them was once again good – in fact, very good, since cost of production, and not just the price obtainable, was now based on depression values. It was also noticeable that it was only the soundest and best specimens which commanded the good prices. Second-rate animals continued to be largely unsaleable, which was of course a good thing. This year, for the first time since 1921, the number of licences issued by the Ministry for travelling stallions showed a slight rise compared with the year before, though the bare figures are their own commentary on what had happened during these eight years – not only the overall slump, but the percentage decrease of Shires as against Clydesdales, whose clean legs were sought after for gelding-production, and Suffolks, which, as farm rather than town horses, were less affected:

England and Wales only

	Total Licences	Shire	Clydesdale	Suffolk	Percheron	Others
1921	3,099	2,463	280	237	39	80
1928	1,033	720	120	132	38	23
1929	1,089	760	133	129	41	26

(These figures include both pedigree and non-pedigree animals in the same column.)

The number of draught-horse foals conceived showed only a slight increase. In 1930, there were 37,907 living foals – 324 more than in 1929, and 66,098 less than in 1919. Nonetheless, it was the first time in ten years that the number had not fallen.

Several new stallion-hiring societies were being formed, or revived under new names and with slightly different areas of operation, depending on where the interested farmers were located. The country market seemed secure. Any slight contraction was due rather to the reduced amount of work to be done, with the continued reversion of arable land to grass, than to its being done by tractors. And if the horse was really going to be "knocked out" in the towns, surely it would have happened by now?

3. THE INFIRMITY OF THE N.H.A.

R. A. Brown, the young man who typed the first Minutes of the National Horse Association in April 1922, had joined the Hunter staff under A. B. Charlton in 1920 and the following year had also become assistant secretary of the National Pony Society. In 1923, in addition, he had been given his first post of sole responsibility as secretary of the London Van Horse Parade Society whose Easter Monday turn-out was, in sheer number of animals, a bigger affair even than the older Cart Horse Parade. In 1914, 1,259 horses had been present, belonging to general carriers, grocers, butchers, bakers, laundrymen, dairymen and so on – from big firms like Tillings, the Army & Navy Stores, Harrods, W. H. Smith and Carter Paterson down to the one-horse greengrocer. Even in the 'twenties, young Brown had to organise about 800 vehicles.

Now, in March 1925, he took over from Charlton the secretaryship of the National Horse Association. His work on behalf of the joint breed societies ranged from negotiations about entertainment tax at shows and concessionary railway fares to the bigger issues of the state of the roads and the proposals to ban horse traffic. He had also to scrutinise a succession of Bills designed to restrict the export of worn-out and misfit horses. One was abandoned in 1927, but another was soon promoted. N. W. Smith Caringtou, second son of the 1908 Shire President who had been such an enthusiastic proprietor of the Ashby Folville stud, was a useful watch-dog in the Commons. As in other matters of animal welfare, proper precautions against suffering were increasingly likely to be exaggerated into misguided restrictions upon reasonable trade and management.

One of Brown's first tasks on becoming N.H.A. secretary had been to organise a conference on the growing and highly alarming problem of abortion in mares. Many well-known breeders of all types of horse were invited to give their views. At the conclusion, apropos nothing in particular, Lord Mowbray and Stourton suggested that the Association should accept individual members. This did not come about at once, but later in the year the scare about a town streets ban brought into membership other bodies, outside the breed societies, which were concerned for the future of the commercial horse – the National Farmers' Union, the Master Saddlers' Federation, the Amalgamated Society of Farriers and Blacksmiths, the British Hay Traders' Association, and so on.

In May 1928, the Shire Society, somewhat dissatisfied with the lines on which the Association was moving, proposed that it should be entirely re-constituted, and an open meeting was held. The result of this was a resolution, not only that individuals should be accepted as members, but that they should also be represented on the council, along with one delegate from each of the breed societies. Unwittingly, the Society was therefore responsible for the fact that within a very few years the Association became dominated by interests which were not necessarily in accord with those of the Shire, and in one instance very certainly opposed to them.

This divorce of aims was yet to come in 1929, but at the beginning of that year there were already 192 private subscribers, compared with seventy-six affiliated societies and organisations. (It was in 1929, incidentally, that the five-year-old Institute of the Horse, the riders' organisation, inaugurated the Pony Club.) What was really needed, from the Shire men's point of view, was a "National Heavy Horse Association". But the competition between the four potential members of such a grouping was too fierce to allow them to co-operate except in the generalised and somewhat wishy-washy atmosphere of the N.H.A. or, on rare occasions, in circumstances where it was obvious that none of them could possibly gain an advantage over the other.

4. SOCIETY AFFAIRS

Domestically, this quinquennium began sadly for the Shire men with the death, two days before the 1925 London Show, of A. C. Duncombe of Calwich Abbey. A member since March 1881, he had been twice President and was responsible, as chairman of the Editing Committee, for twenty-seven of the forty-six volumes of the Stud-book published so far. The amount of work this involved can scarcely be imagined now. Volumes were left ever open on his study table for constant reference. At certain times of the year, a day had rarely passed without his writing to John Sloughgrove, or, later, A.B.C. He had owned both Harold and Premier, whose blood when mingled made the greatest combination ever known in Shire horse history. He, and they, had made the Ashbourne Show one of the greatest events in the Shire year. Most of all, he was beloved by all who knew him. His was the second human portrait to be hung in the Council room and no one doubted that, if there were to be just two, he and the first Sir Walter were the right choice amongst so many great Shire men now dead. Of horses, there were more than two pictures, and Harold and Premier were among them.

Shortly after this Show, A. J. Baker also died. Officially the merchant from whom forage and litter had been bought for the London Show since 1888, and supplier also to R.A.S.E. and the International Horse Show, he was unofficially one of the best friends the Society, and particularly its stewards, had ever known. In thirty-eight years, no one had ever complained about the quality or the prompt and fair distribution of hay. When in difficulty, as in the absence of cartage during and after the war or in trying to cope with the strange surroundings of Newmarket, Sloughgrove or Charlton knew they could always turn to him. As if to emphasise that the old order was passing, the deaths occurred the following year of Lord Hothfield, a member since 1882, and of C. W. Tindall, one of the few pre-1880 survivors and managing director of the Agricultural Hall since 1910.

Among the living, the Presidents of these five years were a particularly interesting series. Lord Harlech could have held office at any time in the Society's history. But the choice of Fred Griffin to succeed him emphasised that the 'twenties were indeed egalitarian times and that there had been no freakishness in the election of a tenant farmer four years before. He was followed by Mrs. Stanton, the first lady President of any horse society in the world. This choice would appear to suggest that the Society either was determined to be the first in every innovation or that it believed in the equality of the sexes. One rather doubts the latter, because there has never been another Lady President since then, just as a lady has never since owned a Spring Show champion. Her selection proves only the singularity of Mrs. Stanton. It can also be interpreted as a fitting gesture to that part of Derbyshire from which her neighbour, the late A. C. Duncombe, also hailed.

Fred Griffin, in his term of office, had persuaded a number of his friends and acquaintances, in the Fens and elsewhere, to join the Society as supporters and Mrs. Stanton followed his example. She managed to coerce the Duke of York, Prince Henry (Duke of Gloucester), and a large number of hunting people whom she felt should do something for the farmers in return for the privilege of riding over their land. The Prince of Wales, forgetting that he was already a member (as absentee President in 1917), sent her his subscription like a gentleman. This sudden little influx of non-practising members included a number of ladies. However, one of the lady-members who had joined a year or two before was far from being non-practising. This was Miss Gwen Webb-Peploe, who in 1927 created a sensation by actually showing a Shire herself in the ring. The next year, she showed two, and two again in 1929. She had bred these fillies herself. Many an older groom wondered what was happening in the Shire world. But they need not have worried, for Miss Webb-Peploe was unique in her way, as Mrs. Stanton was in hers.

As to who ought to succeed Mrs. Stanton, there was no doubt in any minds, because this was the Golden Jubilee year and show, 1928–1929. But there was a little practical difficulty. Sir Walter no longer had any Shire horses, having recently sold his estate. Although, in these crazy times, there might be a few new Shire members who were not really Shire people, it was unthinkable that the Jubilee-year President should be horseless. He sought the help of William Cumber of Theale near Reading, who kept his Shires in Wiltshire at Yatesbury and was now a very prominent man in the breed's affairs, as he was in other branches of farming. Cumber bought three for him, kept them and arranged to show them. And they did very respectably. Tilton Clansman II was second in the yearling class out of twenty-five: Tilton Hiawatha was seventh and Brockhill Miracle reserved (eleventh) out of thirty in the two-year-old class. Mr. Cumber's own Shires won second, third, fourth and fifth prizes in various classes.

Just before this Jubilee show opened, Shire men mourned Sir Arthur Nicholson, who had exhibited both the champions in 1917 and the stallion champion of 1925 and 1927: but fortunately this staunch Shire man from Leek left a son to carry on. Among the last new members elected in the period 1925–1929 were Sir Gomer Berry (the future Lord Kemsley), Worcester Corporation, the Duke of Wellington, the visiting Committee of the Lancashire County Mental Hospital, and Canon F. H. Webb-Peploe. The Duke had just bred a colt foal out of a new mare. It was named Ewhurst Gay Lad, but his gaiety was soon cut short, and he never became a stallion, and that was the end of the Duke as a pedigree Shire man. As for the Canon, there have been many reverend Shire breeders, but he was not one of them. In any case, the garden of Christ Church Vicarage, Cheltenham, that pillar of the Evangelical wing of the Church to which the family belonged (his father was Prebendary H. W., a prominent opponent of High Church practices in his day), was scarcely suitable for breeding cart-horses. It was Gwen, not her father, who was the round peg in the square hole of a genteel vicarage. She was happier at Ilmington, near Stratford-on-Avon, putting her prolific mares to the stallion calling at Folly Farm, than teaching in the Sunday School, as the parson's daughter was still expected to do in the 'twenties. The Canon had joined the Society only to acknowledge and support her remarkable achievement of being the second and last lady to be elected to the Shire Council.

Meanwhile, the last of the varied group of Presidents in this strange five years had now taken office. This was A. Thomas Loyd, son of a cousin of the late Lady Wantage and her successor at Lockinge in 1920. (Lady Wantage had taken an active interest in the estate during the nineteen years of her widowhood but if anyone had suggested she took the Presidential chair once filled by her illustrious husband, he would have been accounted mad. So different were the ways of 1907 or 1917 from 1927.) In true Lockinge style, Mr. Loyd at the Jubilee Show in 1929 a month before being installed as President, won eight prizes including three firsts, and his Lockinge Ridgeway Rose had carried off the mare championship for the second successive time. The lovely Rose, which had come to live where that ancient highroad of prehistoric man, the Ridgeway, ran through the estate of the Loyds, showed that the Shire world was not perhaps so curiously new after all, and it was clear that neither England wholly nor Lockinge, even partly, had gone to the devil.

Irresistibly, one is drawn to the horses and the men who bred, owned and showed them, but, before considering the London Shows of the period in more detail we must at least refer to the gloomy subject of the Society's struggle to provide the maximum encouragement for Shires in the form of prizes and medals at London, the Royal, country shows and parades, while at the same time exercising the most rigid economy where possible in the face of a diminishing income. Special committees constantly were appointed. The London Show was reduced to only three days in 1926. Small sums of money became of great value. The entry fee of 1 guinea for new members, imposed in the recent boom times, was done away with at the end of 1925. The Lichfield Shire Horse Society was charged only 1 guinea subscription instead of 2 in 1927. A donation of 100 guineas was made towards the rebuilding of the Royal Veterinary College. £1,500 of funded property was sold in 1925 and a further £1,173 in 1928. Nevertheless, brainless critics and certain jealous members of less provident and business-like societies accused the Society of hoarding its funds. But a £30,000 reserve in 1920 had now become £23,000, and that was not hoarding, except in the eyes of those who failed to see the bad times becoming worse before they got better.

Other critics made jokes about the Shire Society's interest in the proposals to establish the Tote, which they presumed (correctly) to be stirred by the hope of getting something out of it. For over twenty years, the Gilbeys, father and son, had been agitating for the introduction of the Totalisator. Sir Walter, senior, had made enquiries in France about their pari-mutuel and found that in 1901 (when only 7% was deducted) 4% went on expenses, 2% to public charities and 1% to horse breeding. Even the 1% had brought in £90,383, as a result of which a horse show in Paris was able to offer £12,000 in prizes and the French army was in a fair way to being able to provide itself with thousands of horses at a moment's notice, if required. In 1906 Gilbey père had conducted a campaign to introduce the pari-mutuel on British race-courses: he thought £300,000 could easily be provided for hospitals and horses. Ten years later, in the middle of the war, hundreds of breeders, owners and trainers had signed a petition in favour of it. It had been adopted in most European countries, in India, South Africa, Australasia and America and "it is surely absurd that what is considered good enough for the Colonies should not be thought worth considering for the Mother Country".

Now at last in 1927 it seemed about to become a reality. Charlton, as always, reacted quickly. Albert Holland, his assistant, praising his alertness forty years later, said, "There was another case: always on his toes. He saw the chance of it there, you see. As secretary of the Shire and Hunter, he said, 'We'll get in there quick.'" And they did. A deputation representing all the societies met the Chancellor on 15th March. Mr. Churchill listened with some sympathy and told them that "If, at any time, the totalisator were legalised and became an important feature in racing in this country", that would be the moment for the societies to press their claims for a share "in whatever was left over after the Government had taken what, no doubt, would be recognised as its prior due." The following year, the Tote was introduced, and the Racecourse Betting Act established the Racecourse Betting Control Board, which was to keep back a proportion of the proceeds for the benefit of horse-breeding. But the enormous cost of operating the totalisator made any hope in the foreseeable future of the cart-horse profiting from it pretty forlorn. So, to the wit who enquired whether Sir Walter was going to set up a Shire Horse racing association, the answer was a despondent "no". Even if he was, the idea would not have been new. In the eighteenth century, cart-horse races were quite common, the rules sometimes stipulating that the owners had to exchange mounts and that the prize should go to the slowest.

As the Jubilee Show of 1929 approached, various forms of decorous publicity were adopted, such as posters for display by affiliated societies, stickers for use on letters and special advertisements in the Press. A.B.C. was asked to write a jubilee history of the society. But, as Sexton had been a good auctioneer and a poor secretary, Charlton, a magnificent secretary, was no great hand at this, a matter of regret both then and now.

The table which follows may be compared with that in XI.3.

	Average 1922–1924	1925	1926	1927	1928	1929
New members joining	175	113	190[1]	137[1]	116	114
Net loss	413	274	218	260	291	179
Annual members	4,062	3,377	3,162	2,916	2,652	2,478
Total membership 31st December	5,976	5,253	5,035	4,775	4,484	4,305
New prefixes allotted	98	53	37	45	43	30
Stud-book – new stallions	328	193	195	175	253	200
new mares	2,324	1,494	1,428	1,099	1,168	783
London show entries – stallions	198	123	123	122	114	139
mares	187	141	142	141	120	110
geldings	37	37	60	57	40	65
total	422	301	325	320	274	314
produce groups[2]					81	92
commercial horses[3]						
entries	62	58	50	71	37	59
no. of horses[4]		?	?	70	33	50

[1] F. W. Griffin and Mrs. Stanton, Presidents, canvassed members. Many of them were not active breeders or Shire owners.

[2] See Section 5 (Stallions and mares, four year old or under, already counted in breeding class above).

[3] Nearly all geldings. 1925, 4 were mares: 1926, 4; 1927, 3; 1928, 0; 1929, 3.

[4] Prior to 1927, it is impossible to work out. One entry might be a team of four: but some individual horses figured in two or more classes and only from 1927 onwards did they retain the same catalogue number in each class.

5. LONDON SHOWS

Herontye Buscot sank to the tan with a sudden attack of colic during the judging of the big stallions in 1925. With him collapsed Andrew Devitt's hopes of winning a second gold medal as breeder of the champion. For his owner, James Gould, this was just another London Show misfortune. In his earlier days he had experienced more than one piece of bad luck which would have dis-heartened a less determined character. Lincoln What's Wanted 2nd won the class for the Forshaws, with Sundridge Nulli Secundus breathing across his neck. Rievaulx Friar, making his last of six London appearances, in which he had never won his class but had never stood lower than fourth, was third. (Incidentally, the only London prize-winners he ever sired were three mares which were Highly Commended, ninth and fifth, the last being in a class of "middle-sized" mares in 1929.)

The supreme honour went to a four-year-old bred by Fred Doble in Wilt-shire. This was Cowage Clansman which had two eyes and was exhibited by Sir Arthur Nicholson. The Forshaws' horse was reserve champion. If only Erfyl Lady Grey had also had colic (nothing less would have prevented her from being the mare of the year again), Sir Arthur would have won both championships, as he had done with three eyes in 1917, because his home-bred Leek Pearl, who won the four-year-old class, was reserve to her.

Entries, excluding the commercial classes, dropped from 366 in 1924 to 301. Financially, this was a blow. But the standard was so good now that it was just as difficult to win any sort of prize as it had been in 1904 when there were 862 entries: to be placed really high in a class, it was more difficult. Superabundant hair was at last no longer being regarded a sine-qua-non for success and it was only the economics, not the quality, of breeding that was in the doldrums. Thirteen breeding and four gelding classes offered £2,200 in prizes, and the commercial classes provided £300. Among the latter, special prizes were also awarded for "the cleanest and best appointed horses and gears", not only in the open singles, pairs and teams classes but also in the restricted classes, in which coal merchants, as well as cartage firms, could now compete. There was also a new class for Shire-bred barge horses, but there were only four entries, all from the Regent's Canal and Dock Company, whose horses were supplied on con-tract by Thomas Tillings'. So they won all the prizes and the class was never held again. To avoid misunderstanding or sharp practice, it was now made clear that, in all the commercial classes, horses must have worked regularly in the six months prior to the show. This year George Gotheridge of Romford, who was one of the best known gelding men in the country and had supplied top-class animals to almost every leading commercial proprietor in the south, was appointed as special judge for the gelding and commercial classes. Two of the three breeding-class judges acted with him in rotation. Lieutenant Colonel Percy Laurie, who had helped to see fair play at the weight-pulling the year before, judged the appointments and gears. Anything acceptable to his eagle eye was of guardsman standard. (Curiously, he was re-appointed in 1926 and in 1927 – the only judge of anything at a London show to officiate in consecutive years.)

Economy dictated the non-employment of sandwich-board men to pub-licise the show. A proper heating and ventilating system had now been installed in the Hall, but it was decided not to use it. However, Boy Scouts continued to rush to and fro with telegrams. Minimum reserve prices were fixed for the auction at 25 guineas for yearlings and 40 guineas and 50 guineas for the females and males.

A rule was changed to enable a mere M.R.C.V.S., instead of a Professor or at least a Fellow of the College to be selected as Chief Veterinary Inspector. But the chosen official was in fact T. Eaton Jones, F.R.C.V.S. He had joined the staff of R. S. Reynolds, that pioneer of Shire pedigrees, at Liverpool Corpora-tion at the age of twenty-four and was appointed to succeed him in 1901. He was still only thirty years old then, and grew a beard in order to acquire a more mature look. He took his F.R.C.V.S. when he was forty, and his teenage daughter helped by studying with him. She later married T. Baker Marsh, son of George Marsh of Speke – whose initials symbolically were G.G. and who was the Gotheridge of the North, in supplying many of the best geldings that went to Liverpool. T. Eaton Jones who was also Secretary of the Liverpool

Parade, became the senior veterinary officer at Aintree and was consultant to the Royal Lancashire society for forty years. His son-in-law was later to be Royal Lancashire show director for many years – and a future Shire President. (Professor Penberthy officiated as Chief Veterinary Inspector in 1926 for the last time. Thereafter, Eaton Jones was appointed every year as long as the London Shows lasted.)

In 1926 Erfyl Lady Grey had her third championship partner. Lincoln What's Wanted II turned the tables on Cowage Clansman who now was of age to compete with him among the senior big stallions and stood second to him in the class as well. Leek Pearl also had to compete in the same group as the eleven-year-old celebrity and was second for the female championship, the senior cup and in the class. The class-winners were owned by a pretty formidable collection of older and younger Shire experts, of whom the Forshaws won three male classes (their yearling colt Co-operation was bred by Scunthorpe Co-op at their Winteringham farm) and Mr. Foster headed two female classes. Two outstanding female champions of the future made a promising debut at the show. Kerry Clanish Maid was third in the three-year-old class for William Cumber and Lockinge Ridgeway Rose was second among the yearlings for A. T. Loyd.

The number of days allotted to the show was reduced from four to three. For many years, judging had occupied the Tuesday, Wednesday and the morning of Thursday, ending in a parade, and the auction sale had occupied the Thursday afternoon and Friday. But even with the addition since 1923 of the commercial classes, reduced entries had now resulted in wasted time and unnecessary expense to exhibitors. The plan to complete all the judging in two days, leaving the Thursday morning free for the sale and the afternoon for the commercial horses, proved popular, particularly as all animals not entered for auction were allowed to leave the hall after 6 p.m. on Wednesday. An attempt to interest the Suffolk and British Percheron men in each having a show of their own on the Friday and Saturday, prior to the preparation of the Hall for the Hunter Show the following week, did not succeed. It would have been a useful Hanover Square type of arrangement to sub-let the Shire week in this way, but perhaps it was not surprising that the other two Societies were somewhat suspicious of the invitation to become fleas on the broad back of the Shire, tempting as it was to consider the publicity to be obtained by a London Show. Even so, the net cost to the Shire exchequer was reduced from £2,169 in 1925 to £1,589 by the reduction to three days.

Sir Walter presided over a splendid lunch for members of the Press on the first day. The King could not visit the show this year, but the Prince of Wales, who did come, arrived in unorthodox fashion on the first morning and so the cups were presented next day by Lady Harlech. Tom Skipper, now seventy-two, was still responsible as horse foreman for getting animals into the ring, as he had been doing for forty-three years. He had long since become a professional at the job and was in requisition at nearly every big show in England. In recent years, attempts by a succession of stewards and officials to persuade him to be presented to Royalty, which always failed, had become almost a form of competition. Great would have been the renown of him who trapped Tom into such a meeting. But he was too crafty, as well as too shy. When the King, or the Prince, was around, the white side-whiskers, glasses and hard hat of this remarkable and efficient servant were nowhere to be seen.

The year 1927 gave a championship opportunity to other mares, because Erfyl Lady Grey was not competing. But the unfortunate Leek Pearl, making her fifth London appearance (first and junior cup at the age of two and three, reserve to Lady Grey in all things at four and five), once again scored a near miss. Wick Lady Clansman performed a real Lady Grey trick. She also was six years old, but had come to London only once before, when at the age of two she had been put among a mass of "commendeds". Now, in the ownership of William Cumber, she went straight to the top of all the females and, to add insult to the surprise, was in the same class as Pearl who therefore completed a hat-trick as reserve champion mare without even winning her class.

Since Cowage Clansman, the 1925 stallion champion, took advantage of the absence of Lincoln What's Wanted II to take over the title again, 1927 was remarkable for the fact that the two champions were bred by two Dobles, brothers, Fred and Sam, in Wiltshire. This rivals – or does it beat? – George Edwards' effort in being the only man to breed two London champions, in 1916 and 1918. The King seemed for some reason to take more interest in the reserve champion stallion, Morris Belcher's Eaton Premier King, than in Cowage Clansman himself. Ominously for their rivals, Lockinge Ridgeway Rose moved to first place in her class, and won the junior cup, and Kerry Clanish Maid, now owned by Major J. A. Morrison of Basildon Park, Reading, also moved to the top of the four-year-olds. (Major Morrison was in process of taking over as proprietor of the Pendley stud.) Second was Pendley Gracious Lady, owned by Cumber and bred at Pendley: third was Dalbury Diamond, owned by Morrison. The year before they had been in the order third, first and second. This was the year when Gwen Webb-Peploe amazed everyone by exhibiting a Shire herself. She won ninth prize with her own-bred yearling Remembrance of Arden.

An extra commercial class was provided this year for single horses yoked to a vehicle, open only to metropolitan borough councils. The intention was to encourage the trend shown by local authorities towards reverting to horse-power for much of their work. Twenty-two geldings were entered and eighteen received some recognition. Stepney won three gold medals, including the first prize. Bethnal Green won a gold medal, two Highly Commended cards and one Commended. Westminster won a gold medal and a reserve. Bermondsey and Kensington each won three Highly Commended or Commended cards, Lewisham two and St. Pancras one. The judging of the seven commercial classes was entrusted to the three main judges instead of to a special "gelding judge" (which was in any case contrary to the Society's normal policy and had come in for much criticism) and they acted in pairs in the usual way.

The next year, 1928, provided the explanation of the King's interest in Eaton Premier King the year before. This horse, now five, was of age to join the senior big stallions' class. Here he beat Cowage Clansman into second place, won the senior cup (with Clansman as reserve) and the supreme championship as well, the reserve to him in this being the junior champion, yet another of Sir Arthur Nicholson's horses, Stretton Broadside. His Majesty, having presented the gold cup to his owner, said, "Belcher, I do want to have a special look at your horse. He reminds me so much of my own." The King had had many horses, but he had no need to explain that he was referring to the one which had made him so proud in 1920 and 1921, Field Marshal V. They walked over to the horse and talked so long that everyone wondered what they had to discuss. But if Morris Belcher did not already appreciate His Majesty's knowledge of the points of a Shire, and how to breed for them, he found it out when he stood before his King, like some latter-day Robert Bakewell displaying the merits of the Black Horse to an earlier Farmer George in 1785.

The standard of exhibits was considered by many to have been the best that they could remember, and the competition was fiercer than ever, with several winners of the year before being pushed down the line. But entries were down by forty-six to 274. The commercial classes dropped alarmingly to thirty-seven entries, represented by only thirty-three horses, due to the current depression combined with the high standard required to win anything at Islington. These were times when it was too costly to exhibit any horse that was not outstanding.

Lockinge Ridgeway Rose won the mare championship, though she was still only three. Gwen Webb-Peploe took a commended with a new yearling, Gracious Lady of Arden, and came back in the very next class with Remembrance of Arden, which this time was highly commended.

One of the most notable classes was that of the short-legged brigade, the under 16.2 senior stallions. The winner, Dunsmore Special, was owned by one of those ex-managers that were succeeding, in the bleakest of financial climates, as proprietors – Thomas Ewart, who had brought Sir Albert Muntz so much success in the years gone by. William Todd's remarkably attractive grey, Ponton Pioneer, was second. He was always a great favourite with the London spectators but never big enough to go right to the top. Leek Secundus for Sir Arthur and Modest Prince for F. W. Cope (that regular runner-up in the years of the King's triumph) made a quartet of real "farmers' horses" that could hardly be bettered, and there were many more below them, of great weight and with as big a top as any taller horse, all of the finest quality.

The short-leggers' class had been instituted in 1882, but only three members of it had ever won any recognition outside its confines. The last had been, in fact, a Muntz horse – Dunsmore Bounding Willow, who was once reserve for the senior cup to John Rowell's supreme champion Bury Victor Chief: and that was in 1894. Nailstone Spartan, owned by the great John Adcock Barrs, had done the same thing in 1892 as reserve to Alfred Clark's massive Extraordinary for the senior cup. And way back in the mists of time, one Staunton Hero in this class had actually been made champion stallion in 1886, when he was exhibited by an owner with exceptionally long legs, one Walter Gilbey. Capstone Harold, son of Harold, won the class four years in succession for James Forshaw in 1901–1904, but was never seriously considered against his taller rivals, and he was a mighty weight indeed.

However, the outstanding feature of the show was yet another innovation, the produce class for groups of three animals from the breeding classes, four years old or under, by the same sire. There was no entry fee, but the onus was upon stallion-owners to persuade those who owned their best progeny to exhibit them at the show. The President herself won the gold medal as owner of Seedsman, sire of the winning group – Pendley Harvester (first yearlings for Major Morrison), Lockinge Faith (first yearling fillies, entered in the name of Mrs. Loyd) and Pendley Sylvia (third yearlings, Major Morrison). Seedsman died the following August at the age of only five – a severe loss to breeding. The silver medal went to the Forshaws, whose ex-champion Lincoln What's Wanted II was the sire of Lockinge Ridgeway Rose, the new champion mare, Black Bertha (sixth, three-year-olds, for Cyril Alderson, Lower Leighton, Welshpool) and Blurton What's Wanted (eighth, three-year-olds for W. H. Holdcroft, Norton-in-Hales, Salop.) These sires were followed by Cumber's Basildon Clansman, easily the leading sire of the show, with nineteen of his progeny among the prize-winners or commended animals, though many were too old for the produce group – including those ex-champions Cowage Clansman (second in the big stallions' class at the age of seven, and reserve for the senior cup) and Wick Lady Clansman (also seven and now senior cup winner and reserve for the championship), not to mention the five-year-old Kerry Clanish maid, working her way towards the top year by year. There were no less than eighty-one young animals in these produce groups altogether, and a fascinating task they presented for the judges, both official and at the ringside. More gloomily, the show cost £2,314 net to run owing to reduced receipts from all departments, including the auction sale, where the charge for horses offered but not sold was reduced from 2 guineas to 1 guinea, to help the unfortunate owners.

The idea of these groups had originated with Fred Griffin and others at Peterborough, where the Produce Stakes had quickly established themselves in the past five years. There had been some doubt whether it would be best to introduce them there or in London. As it happened, they were begun in both places in 1928, and at Ashbourne as well. (The groups continued to be a popular feature at London, Ashbourne and Peterborough until the war. The Shire Society offered gold or silver medals for them to any affiliated show in 1929 and Bakewell, Leicestershire and the Royal Norfolk joined in, but only for one year. In the 'thirties, Lincolnshire had group-classes at five shows and the Royal Counties at seven. It was obviously an idea which was suitable only for the few really large competitions attracting entries from a very wide area.)

Most "new" ideas have had a precedent somewhere at some time in the past. The first group-class that appears to be traceable was held in 1878 and was for Suffolks. Charles Frost of Wherstead, known as "The Evergreen", claimed never to have given more than five and thirty pounds for a cart-horse in his life and yet owned what were said to have been the three best Suffolks ever bred by one man. He sold Cup-bearer II, a six-year-old stallion, to an Ipswich brewer, Mr. Catchpole, for 330 guineas. This was in 1876. The next year the horse died, and Frost immediately posted a refund of £100. Not to be outdone in gentlemanly conduct, the recipient instituted "The Catchpole Challenge Cup, value £100" for the best stallion shown together with two of his foals. It was won for Richard Garrett, the celebrated maker of drills and horse-hoes at Leiston, by Cup-bearer III – a son of Cup-bearer II, and bred by Frost. The next year the same stallion won again with two new foals, and this entitled Garrett to keep the cup. And that was the end of that experiment. And this must be the end of this digression, though it is worth pondering what might have been the outcome if, in the 1920s, the Shire men had insisted on the sires of competing groups coming to the show in person and being judged with them. There might have been some surprising results.

In 1929, everyone made a special effort for the Jubilee Show, and entries were up a little in spite of the worsening times. The weather was bitterly cold and attendance of spectators was somewhat disappointing. The show retained all the recent additions and the "old stallion" class for horses of ten years and upwards was reinstated after a five year gap. (In that time 130 prizes and commended cards had been given in the "under 16.2" and "16.2 and over" classes for stallions five years and upwards, but horses aged ten or more had managed to win only nine of these, by far the best effort being by the Duke of Westminster's Dollar Dictator which at the age of twelve had actually come top of the small stallions' class in 1924.) It was won by Pendley Footprint, who was exactly ten. He was one of the three stallions to do very well for the Leek stud whose owner, Sir Arthur Nicholson had died just before the show. Stretton Broadside was reserve champion at the age of four and Cowage Clansman, the ex-champion, was second in his class to Eaton Premier King.

Eaton Premier King and Lockinge Ridgeway Rose won the two championships for the second successive year, though their cups were presented by a novice at this particular duty. The Prince of Wales of course had been to the show before, and now was deputising on the correct day for the Patron, still recovering from his serious and prolonged illness. The King was always at ease among Shire men, because he was one himself: his eldest son was at home with them because they were the sort of earthy and unaffected people he liked. On return home, he was able to inform His Majesty that the Sandringham horses had had only a moderate success this year – a third, a sixth and a highly-commended card. He probably also reported that Miss Webb-Peploe had been in the ring again. Lady Distain of Arden, the latest yearling, and Remembrance of Arden, now three, were both highly commended.

From this show onwards, the short-legged group were allowed an extra inch, as the small stallions aged five to nine were now defined as "under 16.3". Another new thing was the appointment of an honorary medical officer, an idea which was somewhat overdue especially in view of the obstinate persistence of many old men in travelling to the show, when their wives and common-sense told them that in February they should stop at home. The doctor, whose practice was in Surrey, was one of the four Forshaw brothers. A highly-commended yearling filly appeared in the name of this Dr. William H. Forshaw, and he had also bred the fourth prize-winner in the small mares' class. William Cumber had for three years shown more horses at the show than anyone else, but this year owing to being responsible for the horseless President's entries, he had only eight, the same as Tom and James Forshaw and Fred Griffin, but one less than Pendley (Major Morrison), whereas Mrs. Stanton had ten.

The appointments and gears of the commercial classes were judged by a couple of Major-Generals, one of whom was Sir John Moore, formerly Director of the Army Veterinary Services. The President gave championship cups for the open and restricted commercial classes, and these were won respectively by Mann, Crossman & Paulin Ltd., with a bay pair and Charles Franklin (the coal merchant from Bedford) with his black Major. There were now five champion-ships – the King's perpetual cup and Society's gold cup, for stallions: the Society's gold cup, for mares: Mr. Stanton's perpetual cup for geldings, first presented the year before to supersede a society cup; and these two commercial cups. In addition, there were the senior and junior (under four years) cups for stallions and mares.

The female classes were a triumph for Wantage and Pendley, each having three first-prize winners, leaving only the two-year-old class for others to win. But even there Major Morrison was second (to T. M. Watson of Blackpool). The big mares' class was won for Pendley by Kerry Clanish Maid, who had now risen to be reserve to Lockinge Ridgeway Rose for the senior cup. Second to her, after a two year absence, was none other than old Erfyl Lady Grey herself, now fourteen years of age. The reason for her non-appearance in 1927 and 1928 was not that Mr. Foster had decided three championships to be enough. She had not foaled since 1925, and so was ineligible. But now, after being covered several times throughout the previous season, she appeared to have conceived at the last moment – on 15th August 1928 – to Bower Black Prince. Alas, the hopes were false. She was not in foal at all and, some weeks after the show was over, she had to concede her second prize to Fenny Misty Morn, a mere five-year-old and yet another mare from Pendley.

Erfyl Lady Grey was *the* mare of the 'twenties, as Lorna Doone had been the Venus of the decade before, and Kerry Clanish Maid was to be the great modern type of the 'thirties. All three were bred near Welshpool, and it was a Montgomeryshire man who, on first seeing Lady Grey, broke spontaneously into verse:

Ceffyl glas, du-las, o deulu,
Cofra lle cefaist dy fagu;
Stwffio'th groen nes mynd yn gry
A bwyd o Hafod y Beudy![3]

Though life is brief and beauty briefer still, this grey lady, more than any other, left a memory which has remained fresh as long as men are alive who saw her. Thomas Forshaw's remembrance of her majestic build and gaiety of movement, has already been quoted. Her vivacious action is the more remarkable in view of her enormous size. She stood 17.1½-hands and Holland recorded her measurements at this, her last, show. Her girth was 9 ft.; forearm 23½ inches; thigh, 22½ inches; bone, 12½ inches below the knee and 13 inches below the hock; fore-feet 9 inches across the bare foot. Never again would there be another Shire mare like her, even for size alone. Her weight was 22½ cwt., but it was the manner in which she carried it that was her glory.

6. SHIRE AND CLYDESDALE

In 1880, the English and Scottish varieties of the cart-horse were remarkably similar, for the simple reason that a large proportion of their ancestry was identical. Even though the stud-book societies tended to fix the distinctive points of each, and the interchange of blood ceased among registered animals, nevertheless in 1900 the two varieties could have become almost indistinguishable – if their respective breeders had been striving after the same ideal. But they were not, and the next twenty years saw them grow apart to such an extent that by 1920 it was more reasonable to call them two "breeds" than it had been at any time since, say, 1840, when one could have spoken of one Scottish and four or five English cart-horse types. Many years of prosperity had enabled extravagances to go unpunished.

No better or more impartial summary of the differences between the two in the 'twenties has been, or could be, written than that offered by Professor J. A. S. Watson and J. A. More at the beginning of the next decade: "The Clydesdale is similar in height to the Shire, the stallion being 17 hands or over and the mare about 16.2. The general build, however, is less massive, the legs being proportionately longer, and the body neither so deep nor so wide. The head shows more quality and refinement, the eye being larger and the muzzle finer. The neck is rather longer and more crested, the head more gaily carried, and the shoulder has on the average more slope. The back is more frequently faulty than in the Shire, being sometimes too long, sometimes hollow, and sometimes rather bare of muscle. Flatness of rib and shallowness of heart or belly are commoner faults. The quarters are usually longer and more level, but narrower when viewed from behind. The arms and gaskins are not so large and are shorter in proportion to the length of the cannon. The bone of the Clydesdale is much smaller, but is harder, flatter, and cleaner, and the feather, which is more silky in quality, is confined to the back of the leg. The pasterns are longer and have more slope, the feet are relatively larger and wider, but with a more frequent tendency to flatness. The Clydesdale, as a breed, is very free from leg troubles like grease, side-bone, ring-bone, navicular disease, etc., and the average working life, particularly when tested against other breeds on paved streets, is exceptionally long. The breed is also remarkable for its straight, free, and close movement, and shows great ability and cleverness in handling loads.

"In general it may be said that the Shire excels in weight and strength, and in endurance; while in speed, agility, and wearing qualities the Clydesdale is pre-eminent. The temperament of the Clydesdale is more mettlesome and nervous than that of the Shire; he is more troublesome to break, and requires more horsemanship on the part of his driver. Another point of difference is that the Shire matures at a much earlier age than the Clydesdale, so that the difference in weight is far more marked at the yearling or two-year-old stage than in aged animals. Clydesdales are of all the ordinary colours, bay and brown predominating, while chestnut and grey are rare. White faces and legs are almost constant features, and splashes of white on the belly, or white hairs irregularly mixed throughout the coat, are becoming increasingly common."[4]

By 1925 it was perfectly clear on both sides not only that mistakes had been made but that each breed, in a time of trouble, was likely to pay dear for them. It was also not difficult to see that the imperfections of each could be corrected by the strong points of the other. The proof of such a mixed pudding lay in the gelding, for many a breeder on both sides of the border had been producing the best sort of commercial heavy-horse imaginable by a judicious cross in either direction. There were those who still said that, whereas the first cross might be a success, its progeny into the third and fourth generations would be sure to be a nondescript failure. This nonsensical argument was prompted by the memory of forty years of inter-breed rivalry, and ignored the generations of inter-breeding and mixing that had preceded them.

There were, however, precedents enough for a fusion of the two bloods. For example, the Hackney as found in Yorkshire had in years past been a lean-necked good-shouldered horse, but with a tendency to become leggy and narrow-chested, and dishy in his action. In Norfolk, he had been short and thick in the neck, with shoulders steep and heavy, round barrelled and inclined to roll in his gait. In both counties he was of mixed origin, the extremes ranging from a considerable amount of Thoroughbred blood in Yorkshire and of Punch-type blood in Norfolk. Yet the two, combined by human genius, became the modern Hackney. The Dales and Fell ponies presented an even more recent picture of confusion similar to that existing between the Clydesdale and the Shire in the time of Lawrence Drew. A certain mare, bred in the Fell district, by a Fell stallion out of a Fell mare, was rather too tall for her breed but was able to win a cup at the London Pony show – as a Dales mare. At the same show, Lord Lonsdale exhibited, as one of a Fell group which won first prize, a stallion whose full brother was in the Dales Stud-book. The two sorts of Hackney had grown together. The Fell and Dales ponies, originally indistinguishable, were growing apart. The cart-horse breeders knew in their heart of hearts that the crisis was imminent. Which example should they follow?

The Scotsmen had for some years been plagued by the scourge of grass-sickness, the dreaded symptoms of which were loss of appetite, saliva flowing from the mouth and a clear discharge from the nostrils. Some had believed that this discharge transmitted the disease, others that it was due to the infection of food. The mortality rate in infected animals was rarely below 80%, and at times 90%. When in 1921 Professor Gaiger, who had been investigating it at Glasgow, announced that the sickness was Borna disease (first discovered in the Saxon district of Borna in 1894) or Enzootic Meningoencephalitis, no one really cheered. He said that the trouble lay, not in the abdomen, but in the brain, and that research might eventually produce a preventative. The disease had struck England seriously only in Northumberland and the north-east coast – which, horse-wise, was Clydesdale country anyway. The Scottish breeders believed that English horses were more largely immune and the Shire had some added attraction for them for that reason.

The Englishmen were particularly concerned about the export market. The Clydesdale were now dominating this and, the longer the situation lasted, the more difficult the export of Shires became, even if only because of stud-book difficulties. Canada and Australia, in so far as they had British breeds, were almost wholly Clydesdale territories. (Shire men could be forgiven the impression that all, and not just many, Canadian farmers had emigrated from Scotland.) A Shire stallion in those parts could scarcely find any mares out of whom his progeny would be eligible for a stud-book, whereas a Clydesdale could. However eager they were to produce saleable working horses, the breeders there were certainly not encouraged if they could not register what they were breeding in any pedigree register.

William Dunlop had alarmed his fellow Scotsmen in 1920 by taking home those choice Shires he had bought. James Kilpatrick, his rival and probably the most influential Clydesdale breeder of all, motored down from Craigie Mains and bought two Shire fillies from William Cumber's Yatesbury stud. Cumber also sold Wick Brigadier (seventh at London in 1925 as a two-year-old for her breeder, Fred Doble) to a syndicate of breeders in Aberdeenshire early in 1926. Many other Scotsmen had made similar purchases. Conversely, many Clydesdale stallions were travelling much further south than they had been wont.

Though talk about some form of amalgamation became common in 1926, it was the speeches at the dinner of the Peterborough Agricultural Society after the 1927 foal show that brought the whole topic into the open and, on the Shire side, showed who was for, and who against. Fred Griffin, chairman of the Peterborough society, started the discussion by saying that one of his members, who was unable to be present, had written to suggest that each breed society should accept cross-bred animals into a new appendix to its stud-book, as a start to a possible, but not inevitable, merging of the two registers.

Mr. Griffin was cautious and so was Alfred Clark. William Cumber was less so. He told the company that he intended to bring the matter before the next Shire Council meeting. He did not necessarily press for an appendix, and certainly not for a combined stud-book, but "I see no harm in half a dozen men sitting round a table trying to find something useful". The two chief opponents of the idea were absolutely forthright. Edmund Beck, the auctioneer, said that Shires were the best horses, and if the Scotsmen wanted them, they could come and buy them. James Forshaw echoed his words, and most certainly expressed the view of his brother Tom as well.

Later in the month, Cumber's proposal for a small committee to confer with the Clydesdale men was put to the Council, and rejected. He and Griffin had lost the first round. But the second one opened at the very next meeting in December (the Council always met in both Dairy Show and Smithfield weeks) when a letter from the Highland and Agricultural Society was read. It announced that at the 1928 show, at Aberdeen, the classes formerly labelled "Draught Horses" would be re-named "Clydesdale Horses" but that the committee was prepared to consider the inclusion of extra classes for Shires, if assurances could be given that they would be adequately filled and if a contribution were made to the prize fund. The Beck-Forshaw supporters, no less than the Griffin-Cumber men, welcomed the idea, if with different motives. After all, the R.A.S.E. had first given separate classes for Clydesdales at Royal Shows in 1869, and had done so ever since. It was about time that the Highland Show should reciprocate. Unanimously, the Council set up a special committee, with power to spend £200.

In the negotiations which followed, both the H.A.S.S. and the S.H.S. did all they could to please. The Shire men protested that the choice of a judge was entirely a matter for the Highland men and they "would be quite satisfied if a Scotchman should be selected". Not to be out-done, the Highland Society, in conveying the thanks of the directors for the cordial co-operation of the Shire Horse Society, wrote that Mr. J. Morris Belcher of Tibberton Manor, Salop, had been invited to judge the Shire classes as he was to be at the show in any case, as a judge of Shropshire sheep.

Three classes were arranged, with prize money of £117. The Shire Society was to contribute 40% of this and also to pay the entry fees of seventeen selected animals and half their transport costs. Eventually there were eight entries in each class. Fred Griffin's Brockhill Padre won the £20 prize for stallions, followed by another of his horses (£15), then one of Alfred Clark's (£10), and William Cumber (£4), who also had a Very Highly Commended and Highly Commended. The winner among yeld mares or fillies was a certain thirteen-year-old who brought the crowd to its feet. This was none other than Erfyl Lady Grey herself. How Lawrence Drew's heart would have warmed at the sight of this English grey mare! The gelding class was won for H. T. L. Young, the Wandsworth brewer, by Bower King John, once registered as a stallion by G. R. C. Foster and recently reserve champion gelding at London and R.A.S.E. champion. Before a highly critical crowd, the English horses gave a striking display.

Perhaps this was the greatest of all Erfyl Lady Grey's triumphs. Welshmen had broken into song at the sight of her, and Englishmen were stirred to enthusiasm, but a spontaneous ovation from Scotsmen as she joined the parade was the finest tribute of all, for they were not only cunning connoisseurs of a draught-horse but confident that theirs were the best. A vast crowd in the stands and at the ring-side roared approval at her majestic beauty. The following October, not a few Shires left the Peterborough sale for North Britain.

The experiment was repeated at Alloa in 1929, when the Duke of Devonshire won the stallion class with Cippenham Friar, which had won the junior cup at London in 1923 and his class again the following year when he was four. The current Shire champion, Lockinge Ridgeway Rose, won the female class. The judge was Tom Forshaw, and it is odd that the Highland men had chosen, in him and Morris Belcher, the two men who were, and always would remain, the least likely in all England ever to consider or countenance in their own Shire breeding even the possibility of adding any Clydesdale blood for any purpose whatsoever. They gladly accepted their invitations and courteously carried out their duties, but regarded themselves not as negotiators towards an alliance but as demonstrators of what a true heavy cart-horse really was. As for William Cumber and Fred Griffin, there had been many who assured them that it would be impossible to win over Archibald M'Neilage, the Clydesdale secretary, to the idea of a synthesis of the stud-books. But that remained to be seen.

7. IN THE HOUSE

At the end of 1928, for the second time in eight years, the Society was offered the freehold of 12 Hanover Square and of 289/291 Oxford Street. The asking price in 1921 had been £20,000. When the breed societies had turned it down, the Great Western Railway had bought it. In March 1928, the lease on the double-fronted Oxford Street premises had expired, and the tenant, F. Chaventré, had signed a seven year agreement to continue his high-class coiffeur's establishment at the more realistic rent of £2,000 per annum. The R.A.S.E's lease on No. 12 now had only twelve years to run. Accordingly, the G.W.R. now proposed to ask something between £50,000 and £60,000 for the two sets of premises. (David Davies, that keen Liberal Shire man who was to be President in 1930, was a director of the G.W.R.) The Oxford Street frontage could probably have been resold for about £28,000.

The dilemma facing the House Committee of the eighteen societies in general and, in particular, the Shire Horse Society (as sub-tenants of the R.A.S.E.) was whether to buy their house for what would amount to a net sum of between £25,000 and £28,000 and thus secure themselves in 1941, or continue to enjoy the advantage of paying a ridiculously small rent for another thirteen years and to face the realities of life at the end of that time. The other societies were not interested in buying and the Shire men, who prior to the war would probably have been very happy to exchange some of their steadily accumulating funded property for this piece of real estate, were now forced to turn it down. If one is living partly on capital, the purchase of property is not a sensible proposition.

Nine weeks after the Silver Jubilee Show and the issue of his book dealing with the fifty years' activities of the Society, on 27th April 1929, A. B. Charlton died suddenly. If the reader has failed to perceive any difference between the régime of John Sloughgrove and that of his successor, the blame does not lie entirely with this account of their work. Apart from the fact that Sloughgrove enjoyed a smooth passage throughout his career, whereas Charlton had a rough ride through the war-time years of unhealthy boom and immense practical difficulties, and then onwards into the years of depression, their ways were very similar. Both were immensely capable of hard work. Both showed impeccable efficiency not only in minutiae but in the broader issues involved in a breed society. Each grasped the essential points of a matter quickly, though one would usually not reveal the fact at once because he never gave any but a well-considered reply, whereas the other was likely to astound others by moving to the next matter in a flash. Each gave unswerving loyalty to their successive Presidents and Councils. Both expected a similar response from their subordinates and both received it, in ways that accorded with the difference of their personalities. Sloughgrove had been reserved and utterly fair, and courteous. Charlton was "a jokey man", who took his juniors into his confidence and valued their opinions. John, who loved his farm, solemnly believed that the Shire Society was the best in the world: A.B.C., whose great hobby was playing bowls, untiringly chaffed those who praised any other type of horse (except, of course, his Hunters). He was less good at receiving banter than handing it out, but his staff forgave him that, except perhaps the Hunter junior clerk, George Hayes, who was very keen on the stage. Charlton used to make play with this until young George retorted that there was more to acting than sitting on a horse and chasing a poor fox. A.B.C. did not like that very much. But that had been a long time ago, and George was now a famous actor currently on tour in the United States with the New Shakespeare Company, playing the parts of Hamlet and Shylock.

Charlton, like Sloughgrove, had been trained at the R.A.S.E., of which his uncle was secretary. He came to the Chandos Street offices in 1887 as secretary of the Hunters Improvement Society and had edited its stud-book for forty-two years. He was also immediately appointed to the Shire staff, and from 1891 was assistant secretary until Sloughgrove's fatal accident in 1916. When the National Pony Society moved to 12 Hanover Square in 1898, he had become secretary to that, too, until 1916, and also of the County Polo Association from 1899. The Advisory Council of Horse Breeding was set up in 1911 and he was made joint secretary. He had succeeded Sloughgrove as honorary treasurer of the London Cart Horse Parade and, as we have noticed, handed over to R. A. Brown his office with the National Horse Society in 1925.

His sudden death bequeathed to the Shire men a lesser problem than might have been the case in such circumstances. Albert Holland, the assistant secretary, had been with the Society twenty-five years, half of that time observing how Sloughgrove did things and during the latter half learning from Charlton. He had also been secretary of the Sussex Herd-book Society since 1913. His outside interest happened to be, not farming or bowls, but cricket, but that was not particularly relevant. He knew the work at least from A.B.C. to S. Between T and Z lay the hazards and horrors which the 'thirties might have in store, and no one could be yet experienced in those.

M. R. Leather stepped up a place to become assistant secretary. (He was also secretary of the Large Black Pig Society.) The rest of the staff consisted of a clerk and a typist and, in view of the fact that Charlton's other work, including the hours he had devoted to his historical researches, had taken up so much of his time in recent years, it was not considered necessary to add to their number. Times were hard and there was no reason why everyone should not work harder.

F. H. Badge who on the death of Sloughgrove in 1916 had succeeded Charlton as National Pony secretary, now stepped up a place to fill his shoes as secretary of the Hunter Society, on the staff of which he had already served for twenty-five years. But a third vacancy left by Charlton's death was naturally filled by Holland. As representative of the senior breed society in the house, he now became the third Shire man to be secretary of the Hanover Square residents' association. The inhabitants of the Square had first set up a committee of management on 5th June 1858 and the secretary had always been drawn from R.A.S.E. (which had moved into No. 12 in 1842) until they left the Square in 1906. Since then, meetings had reverted to No. 12. In 1926, the *Daily Telegraph* (17th April) had held the gardens up as "an example of what it is possible to achieve in the planning of these small open spaces". When A.B.C. died, the perfect expanse of turf (not far short of the standards required for bowls), the flower beds at various levels, the rockeries, a sunken garden, a sun-dial, and a bird-bath were as neat and tidy as ever. He was proud of the charm and atmosphere of rest in this square in the very heart of the West End, even though the upper-class residents were being steadily superseded by business establishments and their elegant houses by motley and generally ugly rebuilding.

So it was now Albert Holland who had the task of collecting from each occupier of the Square his annual 2 guineas for a key to the garden. One of the members of The Oriental Club at No. 18, who lived at Tunbridge Wells, often brought some new and exotic shrub for the gardener to plant. The ghost of Mary Somerville might raise a refined eyebrow when Revells, the ladies' fashion firm, photographed some of their models there. But really it was all very decorous and polite in the Square, and very quiet.

CHAPTER XIII

1930–1939

Recovery and Refinement

1. A BREAK IN THE CLOUDS

BAD times became worse in 1930. Sir Walter's voice was loud in the land. In particular, he poured scorn on the Agricultural Land (Utilisation) Bill – "tens of thousands of unemployed, who know nothing about agriculture, to be taught by the very people who have been engaged in it all their lives and who, through lack of legislation to help them, have been unable to make it pay". In 1931, little or nothing was going well. High production costs and low market prices painted a dismal picture which looked even darker in the wet and sunless summer. Hay and harvest were a long struggle and root crops expensive to clean.

The threat of national bankruptcy, before which Ramsay MacDonald's second Labour cabinet crumbled rather than collapsed, was staved off only by the King's intervention in persuading the Prime Minister to stay and head an all-party Government. As they struggled with the harvest, the farmers thanked heaven for a Shire sovereign, a great man for common-sense coalitions. (Had he been on the Shire Council, perhaps he would have used his favourite political theory to solve the Anglo-Scottish cart-horse dilemma.)

The National Government was barely a month old when Britain was forced off the gold standard, but a change of policy from free trade to a protective tariff gave the wretched agriculturist some hope. Even before the year was out, the prophet of doom could begin to see better times coming and the end of foreign "dumping". In addition, marketing organisation, regulation of home grown products, subsidies and price insurance, and miscellaneous other forms of assistance – for improved water supplies, agricultural education, research, and so on – were all either started or greatly increased. 1932, in short, saw the end of an agricultural "laissez faire". The wheat acreage increased from 1,200,000 in 1932 to 1,700,000 in five years, and production from 1,000,000 to 1,500,000 tons. Farm produce in general expanded by one-sixth.

Jeremiah had once hidden his girdle in a hole and dug it up again after many days, filthy. Isaiah had walked naked three years to symbolise the fate of the Egyptians when Assyria should come and lead them away with bare buttocks. Ezekiel went through the pantomime of poking a hole in his house and carrying his stuff out through it in the night-time. Sir Walter had sold his estate, and made that a symbolic act, too. But as the first glimpse of light spread over the horizon in the 'thirties, he began to act the different pantomime of Rotten Row. In June 1932, the newspapers gleefully headlined a

"World Storm over Rotten Row Dress Critic". By October it had become "The Battle of Rotten Row". In 1933, he spied a woman rider in a pullover, and his new season's campaign began with "Atrocities in Rotten Row: Sir W. Gilbey's Attack". Every paper fanned the flames. One man wrote in *The Evening News* that Sir Walter Gilbey's hat was an atrocity and ought to be put in the British Museum. He had his unique curly-brimmed billycocks specially made for him and they were caricatured almost as often as Sir Winston Churchill's more variegated headgear.

In 1935, he attacked shorts and sloppy youths, and the repercussions were even louder. *The Philadelphia Inquirer* devoted a whole page to crabby old Sir Walter tongue-lashing the riding cuties. "The Victorian Gin King shudders at bare legs, rubber boots and sweaters, but just wait until he meets Central Park's lady centaurs." In 1936, the Gilbey season (which never opened until the Shire one was safely launched) began when he remarked that London would be a wilderness of slouch hats, were it not that so many men were too slovenly to wear any at all. *Punch*, on 29th July, reported that during the heat-wave a cart horse had been seen near Hyde Park wearing a pink sun bonnet, but that the news had not yet been broken to Sir W. G. In April 1937, it was announced at the hatters' dinner that his curly bowler was to be preserved in the Victoria and Albert Museum. In another way it was made immortal when Battersby & Co. used it as the inspiration to create the Homburg.

This hilarity symbolised somewhat more cheerful days for farmers and Shire men. The prosperity was of course relative. Compared with the 'twenties, the farmer could slightly smile: compared with any time since, he was still having a very bad time of it.

2. THE HORSE IN THE COUNTRY

Amid the universal gloom of 1930–1931, the British horse-breeder thought he knew the cause, or one of the main causes, of the troubles. His reasoning may have been superficial, but it was logical, and there were others who agreed with him. The U.S. Department of Agriculture estimated that its horse and mule population had decreased, in ten years, by over 6,250,000. Consequently, 18,000,000 acres which had been required to maintain them were now used for the production of crops for which there was no market. Canada, Australia, Argentina and Russia, the other exporters of wheat, were producing more and more also. Production even in Europe had increased. And, everywhere, better seed selection gave a heavier yield per acre.

So Britain suffered from "dumping". Our farmers could not possibly compete with this vast tonnage of cheap grain and therefore grew less and less cereals. Land which was superfluous for grazing lay idle. As a result, fewer horses were required. In our towns, every new motor-lorry consumed foreign fuel, whereas the horse it superseded had eaten three acres of home-grown food. It was the tractor on the American farm and the motor in the British town which did the damage. If only dumping were stopped, British farmers in general and horse-men in particular would see their way to recovery. If, in addition, the Americans would only revert to horses, they too and all the world might be saved.

When the economy did at last in 1932 cease to go backwards, and in 1933 begin to move forward and then accelerate almost continuously until 1939, it is a remarkable fact that cart-horse breeding in Britain did all these things absolutely pari passu. As an index of the general recovery of the 'thirties, the increasing prosperity of the Shire-breeding industry is absolutely reliable. Protective tariffs and government aid helped the farmers, who needed more and more horses for their new cultivations, and these horses had to be fed. In the towns, the demand for draught geldings continued better than it would have done either if trade had not recovered at all, or if it had become so prosperous that everyone could afford a motor, or if successive Chancellors had not been tempted constantly to seek revenue from the motor-users, or if there had not been enough unemployed (10.5% of insured workers in 1929, 22.2% in 1932, and still 10.8% in 1937) to keep wages down and cheap carters and vanmen plentiful.

Throughout the 'thirties, the relative costs of horse and tractor were being continually worked out. Wayne Dinsmore, the Percheron man, now also secretary of the Horse Association of America, said in 1931 that a middle-west farmer could feed a horse for $40 a year, and all other items, including harness and shoeing, cost only another $20. Horses worked about 1,000 hours a year on well-managed farms. Therefore they cost only 6 cents an hour and a six-horse team could plough six, disc thirty or harrow sixty acres a day for $3.60. The Department of Agricultural Economics at Oxford University put the cost of a tractor at 2s. 10d. per hour in a year of 740 hours: two horses cost 10d. an hour doing half the work. Figures evaluated by the Department of Economics at Wye College showed a greater difference still. An hour's horse work was 4¾d., and so a pair would do the same work in two hours for 1s. 7d. as a tractor achieved in one hour for 3s. 0d. To quote only one more example, A. J. Marval and P. J. Jones in the *Ministry of Agriculture Journal* gave the costing of horses at Lord Wandsworth College farm during seven years ending March 1937. Average hours worked were 1,562 (almost exactly thirty per week) nearly one-third of it in ploughing. Annual cost was £34, of which fodder accounted for 57%, labour (in "attendance" only) 18%, depreciation 12% and harness depreciation and repairs, shoeing and veterinary fees 13%. Cost per hour was therefore about 5¼d.

The efficiency of the tractor during the decade was enormously improved, particularly by the introduction of heavily treaded pneumatic tyres, which made them acceptable on public roads and effective on the land in all conditions. The three-point linkage and the hydraulic lift revolutionised the driver's control and manipulation of his instruments and machines. Tractors could work successfully even among roots, potatoes and vegetables. They could at last do most things, and the only real objection was the initial cost. By

1939, small farms were still largely tractorless, and the others were far from horseless. Not every new thing was against the horse. The tax on fuel was always more likely to rise than fall: Philip Snowden's 1929 budget had increased it and he had done so again in his National budget of September 1931. 1932 saw the introduction not only of two new tractors running on diesel (cheaply, yet not so cheap as the old paraffin ones) but on pneumatic-tyred wheels for carts. The Dunlop land tyre enabled a horse to pull and manoeuvre a load of seed, manure or produce over soft and cultivated land where even he could not have done so before. And the low loading-line was a wonderful saving of labour. This invention was imitated by many a handy improvisor who fitted old car wheels to a trolley.

So, in 1932 the trade for foals and geldings was a little better than it had been. In 1934, it was much better, because old horses now comprised an increasingly large proportion of the workers and more were wearing out, in town and country, than in any one year for over a decade. The five leading Shire auctioneers in the country were unanimously cheerful about their year, and on enquiry from Albert Holland commented thus in turn: 1. Trade certainly improved. Chief difficulty – shortage, especially of heavy geldings fit for town work. Up to 75 guineas. 2. In October, Shire geldings made 80 guineas (twice), a matched pair 140 guineas and the best thirteen averaged £75. 15s. od. Autumn foal sales realised best prices for ten years: almost every one changed hands. 3. Unabated improvement throughout the year. Prices from 39 to 60 guineas according to age and quality. Five-year-old gelding from North Wales made 72, quite a few 60 to 70 guineas. "Young horses, two and three years old, have been a wonderfully good trade – good entries at each sale and an excellent clearance at 25 to 50 guineas." Commercial foals – good advance in numbers and prices. 4. Foal trade exceptionally good. Omitting the best potential breeders, useful grazing foals were 22 to 30 guineas at October sales, with most of the 250 on offer sold. 5. Values considerably increased – especially for three- and four-year-olds which ranged from 45 to 76 guineas, and all sold. (At one farm sale, where two Shire working mares each made 76 guineas and a third 80, three motor lorries made £17, £16 and £14, but one must assume that the lorries were such that the mares were used to pull them away.)

This same year, the number of licences issued in England and Wales for travelling heavy stallions, which had sunk to its lowest ebb in 1928 (1,033, of which 720 were for Shires) had climbed to 1,433, including 962 Shires. Even so, the demand upon them was unexpectedly heavy. Many of those let to hiring societies for a maximum of 100 mares – a target not reached in most cases for some years – ended by covering far more than that number.) One, with his owner's permission, covered 140, and another 147. Lower in the social scale, many a privately-travelled stallion owned by the one-horse man who led him was called upon to perform amazing feats which were good neither for his present or future well-being, but put unexpected cash in his delighted owner's pocket. But of exact figures we unfortunately must remain as ignorant now as the tax-inspector probably was then.

The approved hiring societies had received an unexpected boost in 1930, when the direct grant from the Ministry was increased from £40 to £60 and the maximum hiring fees which would qualify the societies to benefit was raised to 400 guineas, and the maximum service fee to 4, as it had been in 1919–1921. The formation of new societies, or the resuscitation of old ones, noticeable in 1929, was thus further encouraged. But the following year Government economies forced E. B. Shine to write, gloomily, to say that the grant had reverted to £40 again. (In 1933, the ever-courteous and helpful Mr. Shine retired, to the regret of all Shire men who had ever had dealings with Whitehall, and he was elected the fifth honorary life member of the Society. Though he also received a great honour as Companion of the Bath, he was no less appreciative of the respect of his old customers.)

However, it was not at this middle level of pedigree breeding, and certainly not at the topmost level (the really expensive stallion standing at home or hired by wealthier societies with sufficient keen members to hire a "best" horse as well as another which came within the Government scheme), that the two main problems of the 'thirties lay. The Shire and other breed society men were chiefly worried by the number of non-pedigree stallions still licensed annually and by the unsoundness of those which were not licensed at all.

In the matter of soundness, there was no happy mean. The Ministry's veterinary officers had often been criticised for the severity with which they tested old stallions, particularly for wind. It was claimed that some had been galloped so hard that, instead of being passed sound, they had gone lame and, in one or two cases, had died. If they were sound at eight or ten, they were sound, for hereditary purposes, at twelve or fourteen. The Ministry at last agreed to be more reasonable about this. But why were they content that the Horse Breeding Act of 1918 did not extend to stallions standing on farms or other private property? An unsound or ill-shaped horse could beget a bad foal as certainly at home as he could in the yard of the Black Bull or at a country cross-roads. And were inspectors so numerous that they could pounce upon the owner of an unlicensed stallion that received a message from the farmer next door to step along the road and oblige a mare that had come into use? Wenvoe and District S.H.S. raised the matter with some vigour in 1934. But nothing was done. Eventually, in 1938, the National Horse Association took it up and asked the Shire Council's opinion. The latter was in a mood of disgust with the Association on the question of docking, as we must shortly see. So Holland wrote direct to the Ministry urging that the Act should be extended to all uncastrated horses and coldly sent a copy of the letter to the N.H.A. Shire men welcomed the proposals in this direction framed by the N.F.U. But nothing was done before the war.

The other source of concern, the number of non-pedigree entire horses, was a double one – the number of heavy draught stallions of no particular breed still licensed each year: and the number of licensed Shires (as of Suffolks and other breeds) which were not in the pedigree register. Heavy stallions that were neither Shire, Clydesdale, Suffolk, Percheron nor good red herring mustered seventy-one licences between them in 1936. Stallions of the four heavy breeds, licensed in England and Wales, numbered 1,498 pedigree animals and 206 non-pedigree. Of the 1,188 Shire stallions licensed, no fewer than 170 were not in the Stud-book. They were undoubtedly Shires, otherwise the Ministry would not have classified them as such. Many, or all, may have been full of the purest blood. But, as the Society tried to explain to everyone who would listen, "apart from the fact that foals got by non-pedigree sires must be more or less an unknown quantity as far as blood is concerned, there is unfortunately the further point that owners of mares sometimes accept the services of these stallions in the belief that, being licensed by the Ministry of Agriculture and Fisheries, they must of necessity be registered horses. The result is that not infrequently entries are tendered for registration in the Shire Horse Stud-book which have to be returned to disappointed owners who then realise for the first time that they have made use of a non-pedigree sire. For divers reasons members of the Society are most unlikely to be misled in this matter, but they would do well to impress upon their non-member friends the fact that both pedigree and non-pedigree licences are issued, that the groom in charge has to carry the licence with him, and that a mere glance at this document will instantly disclose whether it refers to a pedigree or non-pedigree horse."

In 1938, 160 of the 1,210 Shire stallions licensed were unregistered. The breed society, not unnaturally, continued to grumble. But there was some satisfaction in reflecting that this was at least a proof of the good work done by the Society over so many years. These horses, however they had been bred, were absolutely sound: and they were, in conformation, unquestionable specimens of the Shire breed. And that is more than could have been said, sixty years before, even of some of the Royal Show champions themselves.

3. THE TOWN GELDING

Although the commercial horse was displaced faster than the country one, the motor engineers of the 1930s in certain respects had less success in producing a lorry that could compete with the horse for cheapness and versatility than they had in developing the all-round usefulness of the farm tractor. Where mileage made speed and power important, motorised lorries and vans were of course a great boon. For example, the four great railway companies began to use them for much of their country cartage and were able to offer a door-to-door service, even to the most remote farms, of a frequency and standard that had been hitherto impossible. (This was a development not untinged with irony, for one of the prime considerations in the whole development of the railway system had been the siting of stations and depots at points which were within daily horse delivery distance of the farthest places which each had to serve.) But for real town work, especially over short distances and with frequent stops and long waits, the heavy-horse was more efficient and cheap, as he still is. In addition, many warehouses and other premises, even many streets, were almost impossible for motors to negotiate, whereas the half-lock of the horse lorry permitted a complete right-angle turn. Finally, a good horse knew his job, which simplified and speeded the carter's work. Many a Shire took his man safely home when the latter was incapable of driving or even walking, though that was not an argument in favour of the horse that employers liked to consider necessary.

Two big Liverpool firms in 1935 sold their motor lorries and bought extra horses, as being cheaper and handier in narrow streets. In Oxford, the railway companies, for town work, and the Co-op increased their horses, while at the same time the Corporation disposed of all theirs. In 1936 in London, Capon & Sons Limited, the road transport contractors, decided to retain nearly 200 heavy draught-horses as they had so much work within a four mile radius. J. Reece Limited had to keep sixty-six horses for delivery from railways and docks to the London market, owing to congestion and to certain warehouses with awkward entrances. Barnett Joel Limited had reduced their 200 horses as far as possible but had to have thirty for fish transport, since Billingsgate and the railheads were so inconvenient to work otherwise. In 1937, Chepstow U.D.C. thought of acquiring a motor dust-cart but found it would cost £650 to buy and £3 8s. 2d. a week to run (in all, a 3d. rate), and so accepted a tender of £64. 5s. 0d. for two horse-drawn vehicles. In 1938, Sir Edward Mann said, "A horse costs 17 shillings a week, and a motor about three times as much. As long as I have anything to do with my firm, I shall see that horses are used." They were all Shires. "I have tried others, but they have all been found wanting." In Greater London there were well above 40,000 commercial draught-horses at work, over half of them heavy ones. That there were not even more in the towns was due partly to prejudice and the desire to present an up-to-date image (Selfridge's still were unabashed with sixty-five light vanners, but a horse-drawn van with "Jones: Bristol's Modern Store" painted on the side tended to promote mirth) and partly to the constant threat that horse traffic would be partly or wholly banned from city streets.

The London Traffic Advisory Committee pondered in 1930 whether to suggest that Oxford Street should be barred to all slow-moving transport, both equine and mechanical, and in February 1931 the Minister of Transport, Herbert Morrison, drew up some Oxford Street Draft Regulations. This was quite unfair. The horse-vehicles hugged the kerb and were in no one's way, though they were frequently held up by stationary buses. Slow motor lorries were not so courteous and held up taxis and cars. The horse-owners were in an uproar, not because they wanted to use Oxford Street (most of them instructed their men to avoid all main thoroughfares where possible and to use collateral streets where progress was unimpeded by motorised traffic), but as a matter of principle. Never in history had the horseman's liberties been so infringed. The

Shire Society suffered with dignity the extra insult in that Oxford Street was a thirty-seconds' walk from 12 Hanover Square. The new Road Traffic Act and the novel Highway Code were watched with care and concern by the National Horse Association, which also sent a deputation to argue the Oxford Street case. Major-General Sir John Moore, the former Director of Veterinary Services, was a great ally of the horse-owners, and as willing as Sir Walter to come from his Hampstead home and stand on street corners and count the number of buses causing obstruction. Only one vehicle in ninety-seven proceeding along the Strand was horse-drawn. More horses passed over Tower Bridge than anywhere else, and that was the least congested district of all. Herbert Morrison, answering a question in the House, admitted, "There can be no question that, as a matter of sheer transport economics, for short distance journeys, with frequent stoppages, the horse is still more economical."

The fifth and last census of horses in Great Britain was taken in May 1934. In ten years, total numbers had fallen from 1,892,205 to 1,278,341. In round thousands, agricultural horses had decreaseed from 754 to 653 (a reduction of 13.4%) and town draught-horses from 374 to 147 (60.7%). Among these latter, heavy-horses dropped from 176 to 80 (54.5%). Of young horses under three years (omitting Thoroughbreds), the numbers of heavy types declined from 150 to 93 (a drop of 38%), and of light types from 62 to 39 (37.1%).

There was a great surge in the battle in 1935. Sir John said that in the provinces horse-traffic was only 8% of the total, and in London only 5%. The *Daily Express* conducted a major anti-horse campaign. Sir John wrote pro-horse articles for any paper that would accept them. The Metropolitan Drinking Fountain and Cattle Trough Association took a census of the horses drinking from sixty-six of their troughs in central London and found that from thirty-eight of them more horses drank than in previous years.

Leslie Hore-Belisha, the new Minister of Transport in Baldwin's National Government, June 1935, lost no time at all in proposing to ban horses during certain hours from Regent Street and adjacent roads. He also told the House on 24th July, that it was desirable to free the streets from horse-drawn vehicles and he would therefore consider any proposals from local authorities. He was also approaching the principal users of horses in London to try to persuade them to substitute motors. Sir Walter said the horseman was being subjected to a monstrous tyranny. Tha National Horse Association produced a list of sixty major horse-owning contractors whom Mr. Hore-Belisha had not had the courtesy to include in his enquiries, and said that all he had done was to twist the arm of the railway companies. Sir John found that every time he travelled in a taxi, it was delayed by buses and, if he travelled in a bus, it was snarled up by taxis and cars. But the inventor of the Belisha beacon was a tougher nut than some of his predecessors and during his two years' office began to wear away the horse-owners' outer defences. A massive deputation which waited on him in October 1936 tried to prevent him making further gains in this street fighting, and, after courteously congratulating him on his promotion to the

Cabinet, pointed out that it was "a grave encroachment on their rights and liberties that horse-owners, who were rate-payers, should be arbitrarily banned from any highway in order to meet the supposed convenience of rival forms of transport which are entirely responsible for the congestion which has arisen". They drew his attention to the fact that men would be thrown out of employment, small traders would be ruined, the price of coal would go up, and milk would take longer to deliver. Furthermore, did he realise that the working-horse population represented a capital value of at least £10,000,000 and consumed at least £8,000,000 of home-grown agricultural produce every year?

When Neville Chamberlain formed his cabinet in May 1937, horsemen were glad to see the back of Hore-Belisha, and they thought he would be a great success as War Minister. Oddly enough, a month after war actually broke out, the ban on horses in certain central London Streets during certain hours of the day was entirely lifted.

In spite of all difficulties, the market for heavy draught geldings remained so good throughout the 'thirties that the English breeders and farmers with five-year-olds for sale soon began to suffer attacks from a completely different quarter, in the form of foreign competition. Until the end of Victoria's reign, French and Belgian horses had been a common sight in the London streets, and in the 1890s some thousands of American-bred horses (by exported Shire and Clydesdale stallions) came over every year. There just were not enough British geldings to go round. But the breed societies had so improved both the numbers and quality of home-produced horses that transport operators were glad to forget the foreigners. The Continental ones were compact and heavy, but sluggish and particularly subject to side-bone and contracted feet, and their hoofs were shelly. Those from America were generally soft in condition. Their legs went, and in the English climate they got chills and catarrh. There was a $33\frac{1}{3}\%$ import duty on British geldings landed in America, but none on foreign ones arriving in Britain, and so these cheaply-produced and cheaply-transported horses were usually bought by small town operators who were too ignorant or too poor to avoid making a bad bargain.

However, in the 'twenties these imports had tailed off, simply because there was no market for them: good home-bred horses could be had for a song. But from about 1933, they began to come in again. Belgian horses were the greatest competitors of the Shire-breds. Sixty-eight were imported in 1933: 158 in 1934: 2,954 in 1935; 3,208 in 1936. They were no more beautiful than before – mostly chestnuts with plenty of white, with bunched-up heads and small feet. But, as with the Shire, their soundness had been immeasurably improved in forty years. A Whitbread, a Mann or a Young would have been horrified at the thought of using them. But in the meat market or other such places, a horse could look as ugly as sin, but still be welcome if he was a good worker. The imported Belgians, big, hard and tough horses, certainly were that, and their clean legs required little attention. Many were sold every week at the Elephant & Castle repository and, as Albert Holland remarked, "This man who brought the Belgians over, he got a lot of trade from the I-bought-one-and-he-was-all-right sort of recommendation. They were cheap, and a chap would have a friend who was a carter, *he'd* go and see, and this man would say he'd be bringing some more next month, and they'd wait for him."

In 1934, the Shire Society, the N.H.A. and the N.F.U. began to press for an import duty on these Belgians, and on the Dutch and Percheron geldings also coming in. After all, English horses sent to France, Germany, Spain, Italy and elsewhere were subject to a tax of between £5 and £10. The Suffolk Society made approaches to the Import Duties Advisory Committee in 1935. The Suffolk breeders indeed, had greater cause to worry, because 407 of the Belgians imported that year were mares. They were alleged to be destined only for town work but, used for breeding instead, they could cause confusion in Suffolk ranks if their progeny fell into unscrupulous hands.

Before starting on the catalogue at the 1936 Peterborough March Sales, Edmund Beck proposed a resolution asking the Government to put a heavy duty on foreign horses. James Forshaw seconded, and the motion was carried with loud acclamation. In October 1937, Morris Belcher told the Council he was certain that some of the imported mares were being used for breeding. Captain Louis Gryspeerdt disagreed with him. (He and his brother at Croydon, like their father before them, were among the best-known dealers of high-class draught-horses in the country, and were also the chief importers of the best Belgians.) There was the unusual spectacle of what the *Daily Dispatch* happily described as "quite a breeze" at this meeting and, at the following one (Smithfield week), Albert Holland was told to find out what the leading Shire auctioneers had to say, and also to check with the Suffolk men. In an argument between Captain Gryspeerdt and Sir Edward Mann at the 1938 A.G.M., the former said that there were still not enough heavy-horses being bred in England, and if the source of supply from Belgium were cut off, transport contractors would be driven willy-nilly to mechanical power. The latter replied that this was nonsense. The auctioneers bombarded Holland with figures and comments about their sales in 1938. Typical of them was the report of Harrison & Hetherington of Carlisle, selling mostly Clydesdales and Clyde crosses: "The percentage of seasoned horses which were passed out of the ring unsold at our last sale was very considerably higher than usual, and we have not the slightest hesitation in attributing this entirely to the importation of heavy-horses." Henry Manley & Son at Crewe reported in June 1938 that compared with the first few months of 1937 their turnover was £5,000 down. "It is difficult to say to what extent the importation of horses has affected this state of affairs. We have resolutely declined to sell drafts even of Canadian, as well as of Argentine, Belgian and Polish horses." (The total imports of all types of horses from all sources in 1937 was 17,557.)

The N.F.U., N.H.A. and the Shire and Suffolk societies continued their efforts to achieve an import duty on horses right into 1939, but a slackening of this trade in 1938 put the Minister of Agriculture less on their side. In the end, of course, this matter, like the banning of horses from the streets, was resolved in an unwelcome way.

4. ANTI-DOCKING AGAIN

After the battle of 1921, the docking war was confined for many years to a series of small skirmishes. But both sides were watching each other with care. A Shire member took the trouble to make a census at the 1935 London Cart Horse Parade and found that 189 horses were undocked and 485 (72%) docked – some very short and some moderately. Tails now came to the fore again, as a subject of dispute if not literally, at about this time and in 1936 the Blue Cross (Our Dumb Friends' League) was insolent enough to submit an advertisement for insertion in the London Show catalogue containing the plea "Will you please help us to put a stop to the cruel and unnecessary practice of docking horses' tails?" Albert Holland refused to accept it.

In 1938, a new Docking of Horses Bill came before the House, and the National Horse Association took steps to oppose it. But this body was no longer an association of breed societies or even of "professionals". Individual membership far outweighed all other representation. An outcry arose from a large number of these subscribers, demanding that opposition to the Bill be withdrawn. Many of them resigned in protest at the action already taken. As a result, its council instructed R. A. Brown to proceed no further.

The Shire Council accepted with more sorrow than anger this unfilial act by the foal it had sired. Had it not been the very question of docking that brought the societies together to conceive the Association sixteen years before? Those Shire men could be excused who darkly suspected that in the lull since membership had been thrown open to individuals in 1928, the self-appointed friends of the dumb had been stealthily infiltrating its ranks.

Among M.Ps, ignorance about horses was of course more widespread in 1938 than it had been in 1921, and the Society found that it was necessary to spell out the reasons why docking should not be prohibited. It was not a matter of vanity, nor of showing and exhibition, but of practical necessity. The "rein under tail" danger, for example, was particularly grave in the case of ploughing horses, which were controlled by a man on the ground, too low to minimise the risk, and using long lines: and winter ploughing in the Fens was not so simple as the summer ploughing matches, which were all that some M.Ps might have seen. Perhaps, too, Members did not realise the misery inflicted on undocked horses by irritation and soreness caused when mud and grit was picked up by long tails. And did they realise that a tail could not be cleaned until it were dry, which in most cases meant the next day? They must remember that lice bred in uncleaned or badly cleaned tails. And was it reasonable to expect a man to clean tails properly, and perhaps bind or braid them as well, which might take half an hour each, when economic reasons necessitated his looking after eight horses?

PLATE 37   Blue blood. Stallions in the ring at the 1913 London Show. Altogether there were 383 of them, with 280 mares and 22 geldings.

PLATE 38   Tom, Dick and Harry. Working geldings on holiday at the London Cart Horse Parade on Whit Monday, 1913. Only one of the 772 horses examined was rejected, which was a record. (The one that failed was too small for his job.)

PLATE 39   Fruitful mother. Dunsmore Chessie was the only chestnut of either sex to be London champion. Here she is with her colt foal in 1913.

PLATE 40   Father of thousands. Childwick Champion (1903–1924). Over 45% of the stallions registered in 1939 were descended in the male line from him. Sire of the record-priced stallion and mare.

Most of the opposition to docking was based on the idea that it prevented the poor horse from protecting himself against fleas. But in proper docking only the tip of the tail, on which the very longest hairs grew, was removed and this left a perfectly effective defence against smaller flies, whereas the chief enemy was the horsefly which no tail, however long, could remove. Members unfortunate enough themselves to have been bitten by this creature would know how very tenacious it was and how difficult of removal, short of killing it.

Both M.Ps and the public daily saw many docked horses in the city streets without realising that they were in fact docked – because they associated the operation with the "short-dock" and the removal of most of the hair, now a very uncommon practice. Many persons thought that a tail could be clipped or plucked instead. But clipping was an expedient which deprived the horse of any defence at all against any flies, and plucking was so painful as to make it exceedingly risky to the person attempting it and was also the cause of sore docks. Severance of the end vertebrae, on the other hand, could only legally be done by a veterinary surgeon and therefore proper supervision assured a quick heal. So ran the arguments put forward by the heavy-horse men, with the additional warning that, if docking were permitted only on veterinary advice when necessary for the welfare of the horse, there would be sure to be unscrupulous persons who would deliberately cause a tail injury in order to get it done.

The best ally of the Shire Society was now clearly that organisation to which the majority of its members belonged, now numbering 140,000 and still growing, the National Farmers' Union. William Cumber, President-elect of the Shires, appropriately proposed co-operation with that body, and in the autumn a letter from the Union thanked the breed society for its support in once again staving off the threat to the horse owners' right to manage their affairs as they thought fit. And so it happened that, in spite of a number of Shire men having served as President (James Forshaw, Sir Edward Mann and Cumber, in addition to Sir Walter in the first year), the National Horse Association grew apart from the Society which had brought it into existence.

5. CLYDESDALE AND SHIRE

Dumfries was the venue of the 1930 Highland and Agricultural Show. It was agreed to delete the Shire stallion classes, since owners were reluctant to send them north so soon after the breeding season, but there was a good entry of mares and geldings, subsidised by the Society and judged by James Gould of Lymm. Marden Unity (three-years-old and fourth in London) won for Sir Bernard Greenwell. Mann, Crossman & Paulin Limited took the first two gelding places with perfect examples of brewers' horses – Lancaster, the seven-year-old current London champion, and Norman, six years of age and a future double champion.

On both sides of the border, it now seemed as if some sort of interchange of blood was about to be officially recognised. But suddenly the English opponents of the idea, led by Tom Forshaw, managed to scotch the plan. The Council voted by a narrow majority against any formal talks with the Scottish breeders, and did not even record the fact in their minutes. Sponsorship of Shires at the 1931 H.A.S. Show at Edinburgh was axed in a new economy drive. However, three classes were provided by the Highland men who actually increased Shire prizes by 50% and anonymous Shire members provided out of their own pockets enough money to subsidise a total entry of just ten horses. The judge was a Clydesdale man, John Wilson. One of the suggestions that had been made when negotiations had seemed likely to succeed was that the two breeds should exchange judges, and this is a rare instance of the idea being half-put into practice.

Early this year, Archibald M'Neilage had died suddenly. At their February meeting, the Shire councillors stood silent in memory of a remarkable man who had just managed to complete half a century, from 1st January 1881, as Clydesdale secretary, and had thirty months' apprenticeship as assistant secretary from May 1878, before that. Even among breed-society secretaries, famous for their indestructibility, this was something exceptional.

Later in the year, Fred Griffin also died. He had been a leading Shire man for thirty-four years in succession to his father, who had won a prize at the first London Show of 1880. Though early cart-horse breeding is singularly ill-documented, it seems pretty clear that their forebears, at least as far back as Thomas Griffin of Peakirk in Elizabethan times, had all been breeders of mighty horses. Perhaps the most remarkable thing about the last of the Shire Griffins (the tradition was now being carried on by his son-in-law Will Smith) was that, at the end of his life, he should have been one of the two most prominent advocates of a union with the Clydesdales. In assessing him, it is immaterial whether he and his supporters were right or wrong. He was an old man and had bred as many true old Fens-type heavyweights as any, and more than most. That the fitting place to record his death is here, in a discussion about a new policy towards the Clydesdales, and not at the Peterborough shows or elsewhere, is sufficient testimony to the fact that, right to the end, he worked and planned for the future and was content to let past triumphs lie.

It would be ludicrous to assume that other Shire men, and Clydesdale men, too, who did not think as he did, were living in the past. The Forshaws, particularly, had been for generations the most supremely successful of the "professional" English cart-horse experts because, living constantly for the present and future, they were usually a jump or two ahead of other people. In arguing that the Shire breed had the material, within its own ranks, to "clean up" the legs, they were absolutely right. And so, too, were those Clydesdale breeders who insisted that weighty commercial types were available north of the border and could influence the breed, provided only that show judges were prepared to favour them. But the modification of each breed, if restricted to its own resources, would be slow. Time was not on the side of the horse.

The stud-book societies had done wonders in improving the quality and soundness of cart-horses and in ensuring that predictable types of animal could be bred by means of studying pedigrees. But the rejection of a bridge between the two was a failure to recognise that breeders who wanted to produce cart horses they could sell at commercial prices would do so in the way they thought fit, whatever the pedigree societies might decide. It was, essentially, the error of believing the means to be more important than the end. Shire classes at the Highland shows now fizzled out because the Shire Society willed that it should be so.

In 1934, the Society spent a large part of its dwindling income in sponsoring its troops to do battle with the Suffolks at the Royal Show, which that year was at Ipswich. At the time of course, it appeared important not to let that admirable agricultural horse get away with a numerical triumph, which would be certain to be well publicised. But in retrospect it appears somewhat futile as compared with what might have been achieved, if not in seeking a link with the Scotsmen, at least by doing the opposite in persuading some of them that the Shire was the better horse. The real enemy was the auld enemy, if he were not to be the true friend and cousin.

In this same year, an old-fashioned slanging match in public enlivened the columns of the agricultural Press, correspondents out-doing each other in extravagant praise and libellous abuse of each of the four breeds and of any reasonable cross that could be produced from them. This was quite harmless, and was good clean fun. More earnest was the silent battle of wits that went on between breeders north and south of the Tweed from about this time onwards. Plenty of clean-legged two-year-old Shires that were exactly of the type required to produce a "modern" Shire were snapped up at sales to go to Scotland instead, to make a re-built Clydesdale commercial animal. Other animals travelled in the contrary direction. In 1936, the Ayrshire Agricultural Society suggested that an exhibition of Shire teams at their centenary show would be a good idea, but the Society did not respond. Even when the Clydesdale Society, which was staging a display of horses at the Empire Exhibition in Scotland in 1938, offered facilities to show Shires, a warm letter of thanks was returned, with a polite refusal. The frontier was officially closed. North of it, and in one or two districts to the south, grass sickness was still taking its toll: in the summer of 1936, between 1,200 and 1,500 horses (it was impossible to be more precise) had succumbed. The Clydesdale men, now easily the chief heavy-horse exporters, sent 127 pedigree animals abroad, and, in 1937, 129 – sixty-two to Australia, fifty-two to Canada, six to New Zealand, five to South America and four to the U.S.A.

Nevertheless, in spite of all the difficulties and missed opportunities, a steady movement towards the clean-legged Shire horse went on all through the 'thirties. One could see it first in the foal stakes at Peterborough, then gradually creeping up through the age-groups in London. Slow as the process is of modifying any characteristic in a breed of horses, the material was available. Everything depended on the judges.

As a class, stock judges have acquired the reputation of living in a dream-world totally unconnected with the practical requirements of the market that the animals they scrutinise are supposed to serve. But the Shire Society's judges, chosen always from the ranks of men still actively engaged upon the business of breeding, responded right nobly. It was noticeable from year to year that the cleaner-legged animals tended more and more to head the line, while the old-fashioned "rough 'uns" brought up the rear. The Forshaws and others, such as Colonel Nicholson, did not fail to preach that a stallion should be big, masculine and comparatively coarse, if the breed was not to become over-refined. But even their counsel was one of caution and common-sense, and not in any sense an obstinate longing for the Shire of their youth.

The result of all this doubt and self-examination was that the best pedigree Shires of 1939 were at a high peak of perfection – perhaps the highest peak. As 1879 had been the last year of absolute confusion, and 1919 saw the breed at its hairiest and grossest, so the example set by the leaders of London fashion in 1939 was one of cleanness and action, still combined with weight, in a blend that had not been achieved before and has certainly not been regained since.

6. THE STUD-BOOK

The first thirteen volumes of the Stud-book were printed by Cassell, but from 1893 they had been the responsibility of William Clowes & Sons Limited, a firm associated in the minds of many with such other respectable works as *Hymns Ancient and Modern* (from its first edition in 1861), *Brassey's Naval Annual* and the *Armed Forces Year Book*. When Volume 51 appeared in 1930, they had printed 34,742 pages of it, a number which would have been considerably higher if the old pre-war lavish scale of production had been maintained. But in the economy drive of 1930, A. G. Holland suggested obtaining an estimate from a different firm. Volume 52 was entrusted to W. E. Baxter Limited of Lewes, which had had a long agricultural connexion.

John Baxter had begun business in 1802, but the first record of his early activities is a brief reference by that famous, or infamous, radical writer William Cobbett. This self-taught son of a Surrey labourer walked into Baxter's shop in the morning of Thursday, 10th January 1822 and was shown "a farmer's account book, which is a very complete thing of its kind."[1] (The night before, Cobbett had been involved in a pretty rowdy meeting of farmers and landowners, followed by a dinner, at which he had quoted from his *Weekly Political Register* to prove that he was the friend of the farmer as well as of the labourer. "Born in a farm-house, bred up at the plough-tail, with a smock-frock on my back, taking great delight in all the pursuits of farmers, liking their society, and having amongst them my most esteemed friends, it is natural that I should feel, and I do feel, uncommonly anxious to prevent, as far as I am able, that total ruin which now menaces them".[2] He would have felt something oddly familiar about the year 1930 and it would be interesting to see what sort of a partnership he would have made with Sir Walter. No doubt in 1930 he would also have been struck by the continuing prettiness of the Lewes girls – their "round faces, features small, little hands and wrists, plump arms and bright eyes".[3])

John Baxter eventually retired to a small farm outside the ancient town, but the family business prospered. In 1879, they printed the first volume of the Sussex Cattle Society's Herd-book and since then had accumulated their responsibilities in that line, taking on in turn the pedigrees of English Guernsey Cattle, British Friesian Cattle, the National Pony Society, the Arab Horse Society, Aberdeen Angus Cattle, the Dairy Shorthorn Association's Year Book, and now in 1930 the British Percheron Horse Society. But in suggesting them, Albert Holland was not taking a leaf out of the Percheron men's stud-book. As secretary for the past seventeen years of the Sussex Cattle Society, Baxter's first pedigree-book customers, he was recommending from experience. Just as he had started at the bottom of the ladder himself, so had W. B. Reynolds in 1921 begun as a Baxter apprentice, and was eventually to end his career as managing director. He and his colleagues gave "Dutchy" Holland, as he was known in those parts, good service. The 1931 Shire volume was printed quicker, better and more cheaply than ever before, though Clowes' standard of accuracy would have been impossible to surpass.

Two ideas, which might have been thought useful long since, came into the limelight at this time, and as quickly disappeared from it. The Royal College of Veterinary Surgeons suggested that a uniform system of listing the markings of animals should be adopted. The Society had always had, and continued to have, trouble over persuading breeders to describe their animals fully and accurately. But the proposition was turned down. And then at the 1930 A.G.M. a member suggested that it would be an advantage to draw up an official standard description of the breed. He was invited, as members raising points at general meetings always are, to put his ideas on paper. This he did, and the Council decided to take no action. It is perhaps odd that all the "Points of a Shire Horse" that had ever been printed or lectured upon were in fact unofficial, though the set of standards summarised by Charlton in his jubilee book the year before had inevitably acquired some sort of imprimatur. In 1930, as now or in 1880, the Editing Committee was "empowered to reject or cancel the entry of any animal of which there is a doubt of its being of the Shire or Old English Cart Horse breed". What that breed should look like, everyone knew, but no one could yet with the Society's authority say.

In 1932, the qualifications for mares were relaxed to what they had been prior to 1923. That is, only three registered crosses were necessary. This was sensible. It still provided that a registered mare should be of seven-eighths "pure" blood: but it also recognised the practical difficulties of obtaining breeders' certificates for the great-granddam. However, side by side with the determination by the Council to keep the Studbook still truly "open" (in

1938, yet another proposal to close it against all animals whose parents were not both registered was firmly turned down), was the problem, and it was a growing one, of dealing with unscrupulous persons. In January 1937, Tom Forshaw and Colonel Nicholson complained bitterly of animals sold by auction as non-pedigree but which had later been submitted for registration, backed by forms purporting to be signed by the respective breeders. Nothing could have been more indicative of the real revival in heavy-horse breeding than this re-appearance of the enterprising "pedigree-makers", those curious individuals who offered, on payment of their expenses, to obtain the pedigree of a horse that had just been purchased. The Society issued a warning to members. "It can be taken as reasonably certain that if a horse has a pedigree the vendor makes this known at the time of sale. Some certificates reputed to bear the breeder's signature have been found, on investigation, to be false."

In January 1939, the Ministry offered to allow its Livestock Officers to report any apparent irregularities that came to their notice on their rounds. In April it was proposed by William Cumber, seconded by Colonel Nicholson and agreed that the Council "be at liberty to include reports made to them by any officer of the Ministry of Agriculture & Fisheries . . . among the sources of information as to any suspected failure by a member in the observance of any rule, regulation or by-law made by the Council."

But this sort of snooping was not very satisfactory. The Stud-book depended too largely on the integrity of those who used it, and some stricter rules were inevitable. Alfred Luckin of Orfold in Sussex had already proposed that the registration of foals should be permitted. George Fitzpatrick, the Liverpool wholesale fruit salesman, who owned magnificent Shires, suggested that registration within a month of birth should be compulsory. But it was felt that non-acceptance of all horses until they were yearlings was necessary, owing to the impossibility of knowing what the permanent coat-colour would be until that age.

The solution adopted eventually, in April 1939, was based upon the fact that, of the 1,038 new mares entered in Volumes 59 (1938) no less than 272 were from unregistered dams (i.e. from two-cross mares): of the 292 new stallions, forty-four were out of dams which had to be entered in order to make their sons eligible. This continuing grading-up, still going on after all these decades of pedigree activity, may appear surprising, but it was nevertheless welcomed. However, the Council determined that it should now be better supervised and controlled. It explained matters tactfully to members: "The Council have now deputed a Special Committee to go thoroughly into the whole procedure of Stud-book registration with a view to so amending the present regulations as to preclude the possibility of any animal being included in the Stud-book of which there is the slightest doubt of its ancestry. It is not suggested that in the past there has been any attempt to get into the Stud-book animals other than pure bred Shires, but it has become abundantly clear that the less stringent conditions of registration in force in connection with horses as opposed to cattle, have resulted in a lack of care on the part of breeders to keep a reliable record of their own breeding operations. Indeed, it is an unfortunate fact that in very many cases the breeder's memory is solely relied upon so that sooner or later it is inevitable that there shall be no records available at all, and it is when this position is reached that attempts are made to build up a pedigree from scraps of information gleaned from outside sources. Such methods can but result in inaccuracies, and it is felt that after sixty years of Stud-book registration the open nature of the book should be modified."

The recommendation of the committee, adopted by the Council in April 1939, was to institute a Grading-up Register, in two parts. Register A was open to all living mares and fillies got by a registered sire – provided, of course their dams were recognisably of "correct Shire type". If someone put a Percheron mare or a Suffolk, or for that matter a Shetland pony, to a Shire stallion, he could not reasonably claim to put the produce in the Register, even though there was no provision for inspection before acceptance. Should he try to do so, the only remedy was a complaint by someone else to be followed by an investigation. Register B was open to mares and fillies out of a dam entered in Register A and got by a registered sire. Somewhat illogically, fillies could be submitted for the Grade Registers while still foals, though for the Stud-book proper it remained necessary to wait until they were yearlings. Filly-foals by registered sires out of Register B mares would become eligible for the Stud-book. The fee for entries in the Grade Register was fixed at only 2s. 6d. to members and non-members alike, in an attempt to interest the "small man" and eventually to recruit him to the Society.

The existing rules and provisions of the Stud-book, whereby a three-cross-mare could be entered together with particulars and certificates relating to her dam and grand-dam, were to continue unchanged for two years and of course would have to be used in cases where the unregistered dam or grand-dam of a filly proposed for the Stud-book itself were no longer alive. But, after 1st October 1941, the use of Grade Registers would be compulsory: that is, the Stud-book would be open only to fillies whose dams were either registered themselves or in Register B. Furthermore, a filly could not go in Register B unless her dam were in Register A of an earlier volume, and so on. As far as stallions were concerned, it would then be necessary to drop the quaint old rule under which the dam need not be a registered mare if she had had other produce (i.e. a filly) already entered.

In the short time available between the announcement of the scheme in April, and October, when entries for Volume 61 closed, the response was very good. One hundred and thirty-three mares were accepted for Register A and thirty-eight for Register B, and a few well-known pedigree men were among those who gave support – for example, Sir Bernard Greenwell (three A mares with the Marden prefix), Lieutenant-Colonel T. W. Daniel (A.85 Mettingham Beauty), Morris Belcher (A.117 Tibberton Ann). Other names were new – such as Miss Susannah and Miss Frances Wilkins whose first registrations (they also joined the Society) were A.128 Wiggs Bonnie (1926) and her daughters B.34 Wiggs Belle (1936), B.35 Wiggs Dolly (1933) and B.36 Wiggs Flower (1934), all bred by themselves on their farm at Weston-on-Trent. A couple of entries evoke a curious reminiscence of the days when breeders were not required to sign certificates to authenticate pedigrees and, as a consequence, their initials were often unknown. The form for A.21 Cholesbury Duchess was signed "Mr. Dowson" and for A.22 Cholesbury Whitesocks, "Mr. Marks", to support George Brown's entries.

Perhaps the most encouraging entry in the Grade Register was made by the Timberlake family of Hastoe Farm, Tring. On the death of Lord Rothschild in 1915 the family had re-registered in their own name a number of his old mares, some with famous associations, such as Lockinge Princess William, Folville Choice, and Danesfield Fashion. But nothing had ever been registered from Hastoe farm since 1921. Now, there appeared A.60 Hastoe Bess (foaled 1921) and her daughter B.13 Hastoe Bess 7th (foaled 1939). These Grade Registers were a symbol of a re-birth.

7. SOCIETY AFFAIRS

From time to time in the course of fifty years, the method of election to the Shire Council had been queried, and a new batch of suggestions was considered at the A.G.M. of 1930. But once again the old system prevailed. Most members were satisfied that a form of procedure which had been copied by many of the younger breed societies was adequate to safeguard democratic principles. Shire men had always been particularly sensitive to the right of a tenant of fifty acres to have equal voting power with the proprietor of five thousand. Accordingly, nomination forms were issued as usual the following November to every member, but the usual apathy over such matters resulted in there being no candidates for eight counties, which meant that these areas' representation on the Council would fall well below that to which their proportion of the membership entitled them. The Council therefore exercised its power to nominate candidates itself for these counties, and to reduce the other nominations to sixteen. From these twenty-four, members were entitled to vote for not less than six nor more than twelve, to fill the twelve vacancies caused by the retirement of one-third of the Council. The only non-democratic aspect of it all was that the Council was increased from the elected thirty-six to a possible forty-eight by the fact that the twelve most recent Past-Presidents were ex-officio members. Of these, Mrs. Stanton had unfortunately just sold her stud and retired from the Shire stage.

Of more serious concern was the financial position. If its funded property continued to be eroded as in the years 1925–1929, the Society would be penniless in less than twenty years. Its investments had been reduced from £26,000 to £19,500 and of course in the years ahead dwindling interest would accelerate the downhill run. In 1930, the London Show made a record loss of £2,519, which the Society's share of the auction sale only reduced to £2,414.

(A mere nineteen horses were sold, for £1,874, of which Sexton, Grimwade and Beck received £35 and the Society £105. In 1920, 110 had been sold for £47,772: in 1902, 241 for £18,419.)

An economy investigation was instituted, but in the end made cuts amounting only to £700 in an annual turnover of nearly £10,000, because the Council felt that all the affairs of horse-breeding and of farming were at a crisis. It would be better to carry on for a couple of years, by which time there would either be universal ruin or the prospect would have brightened, in which case any panicky action, such as the abandonment of the London Show, would be bitterly regretted. Holland suggested a Derby sweepstake among members, as was conducted by the National Horse Breeding Society of India, or the setting up of a special donation fund for the London prizes, as had been done in the early days. But since 1884, when this had become unnecessary, every activity of the Society – with the exception of champion cups customarily replaced by exhibitors successful enough to have won them outright – had been financed by the modest 1 guinea annual subscription and the charges made for Stud-book entries, show entries and so on. Even now, that remarkable record was broken only by the making of one experiment, which in any case turned out an almost total failure. In early 1931 the President, David Davies, arranged for the wide distribution of a quarto brochure of eight pages, extremely well printed on good quality paper and containing six excellent half-tone pictures. It was issued "in the belief that thousands of men and women in Great Britain not directly connected with agriculture would desire to assist in saving the Society from the danger of gradual extinction . . . English men and women have always been lovers of the horse." Eighty English lovers of the horse subscribed £163 (and ninepence) between them, and earned the right to come to the London Show free, for ever. This was the only appeal to the public that has ever been made by the Society, and even that was scarcely a cry for charity, because if anyone cared to arrive at the Spring Show today with proof that he, or she, is one of the eighty, no doubt the promise would be honoured, though perhaps with some surprise.

Complete ruin never came, and by the end of 1939, thanks to the control of affairs by able men of business, the Society's activities had been continuously maintained without curtailment. And the invested funds had dropped in ten years only from £19,500 to £15,337. Nevertheless, there appeared at first to be a very real danger that the London Show would have to be abandoned after 1935, when the current agreement with the hall company expired. In 1931, Thomas Loyd, the President, met Hunter Society representatives to enquire about the fifty-fifty sharing of rent and costs, since the two old friends' mutual agreement allowed for adjustments to be negotiated if one party met unusually bad times. Unfortunately, the Hunter men were in even worse case, for on the very morning of the meeting, 4th August, they had learned that the Light Horse Breeding grant of £30,000 a year from the War Office was to be withdrawn under the new Government economies. The Honourable

Alexander E. Parker, who had become Managing Director of the Hall in 1926 on the death of Charles Tindall, did everything he could to help the societies and in 1933 was even prepared to reduce the tenancy from three weeks to two. But, to allow time for setting up and dismantling, this would have involved condensing the Shire, Hunter and Pony Shows into six days, which was quite impossible. And so he allowed £200 off the rent instead.

Early in 1934, a year before the agreement ran out, a saviour appeared, in the unlikely guise of the Wholesale Furniture Trades Exhibition, which wished to rent the hall in 1935–1937 during the time when the horse shows were normally held. Accordingly a three year contract was signed, whereby the Shire Show was to be held in the last week of January and the Hunter and Pony Shows in March. (The Shire men had been asked to consider putting their show back to mid-March, but there were four objections to a late date – it would affect the brood mare classes, it would be too close to the beginning of the stallions' season, it would clash with the Peterborough spring sales, and it might reduce attendance, since farmers would be busy with spring sowing.) The exhibition organisers paid generous compensation and also met the additional expense of setting up and dismantling the horse boxes twice instead of once. All this helped to reduce the cost to the Shire Society of rent and fittings from £1,373 in 1934 to £987 at the January show in 1935. In 1936 and 1937 the Show was actually held in the first week of February, and there was no trade exhibition in 1937. In 1938 the furniture men finally removed themselves from the scene, and the three horse shows made a five year agreement with Mr. Parker to come together again for their old dates in the last two weeks of February and the first in March.

The mid-'thirties saw another scare about the occupancy of the house. There had been minor changes over recent years. The International Horse Show was now gone. Frank Euren, the erstwhile Hackney secretary, was dead: one wonders if he took the stairs to heaven, where he surely went, two at a time. The British Percheron Society had even come into the house – and left it again. (This was in 1930, when A. W. Hewett resigned as honorary secretary. Edward Ashby, a member of the Hackney group staff, was appointed at a salary of £60. And so the Percheron men had held their council meetings in the Shire chamber for twelve months, at the end of which Ashby was appointed English Jersey Cattle secretary, with the result that they had to follow him to 19 Bloomsbury Square.) But the real dilemma came at the end of 1935, when the Shorthorn Society intimated that it would probably be vacating its offices. This put the Shire men in a quandary, because there was only a little over five years of the lease unexpired and a new tenant would be difficult to find. The Shorthorn accommodation comprised 2,174 square feet, over a quarter of this being storage space, and they paid £548 a year. All the other societies occupied 3,898 square feet, of which two-fifths were storage, paying £754 between them.

Had the Shorthorn men any right to give notice and walk out? No legal agreement had ever been drawn up when the joint House Committee had been formed twenty years before, and no clarification of the position was afforded by the Minutes of either society. Discussions were in danger of becoming a little heated. Sir Walter, chairman of the House Committee, thought the cattle society had a moral obligation to stay. (He was also Shire treasurer.) Major Yates, the Shorthorn President, questioned the validity of the joint committee and thought it was merely a convenient method whereby the Shire Society, which after all was the sole legal sub-tenant of R.A.S.E., kept its accounts in order. Loyd and Cumber eventually suggested dropping the claims about moral obligation, and Yates and Briggs responded by not pressing their innuendo. The mutual good-will of over fifty years' living in the same house was soon restored.

The house was occupied in this way:

1. the Shorthorns (with the Romney sheep) on the second and third floors, with much of the basement;

2. the Shires (with the Sussex cattle, Kerry cattle and Large Black pigs) on most of the first floor, with storage space elsewhere, including separate premises at the back;

3. the Hunters (with the National Ponies, N.H.A. and Van Horse Parade); the Hackney and Cart Horse Parade; and the Guernseys and Dairy Farmers in four ground-floor rooms, most of the fourth attic floor, and storage space elsewhere.

The main difficulty was that the house was crammed full of furniture, people, and the records and papers and books of fifty years. Many of the storage rooms could not be used to their fullest advantage, and shelving was restricted to the walls, simply because of the danger of the whole place falling in ruins if the beams gave way. Yet if the Shorthorns left, money would be short. A special Council meeting considered once again the possibility of moving altogether. More commodious offices were available at 7 Park Lane or Central House in Upper Woburn Place. But the Duke of Devonshire said there were many practical as well as sentimental reasons for staying in the house, and he would bitterly regret any move.

By September 1936, all was settled. The Shorthorns left. The Guernseys (with the Hackneys) moved from the ground floor to occupy the whole of the second, and paid £200 extra. The Hunters (and their colleagues) expanded to occupy more of the ground floor than before and much extra storage behind the house, at £250 extra. The third floor was let to R. H. Brine and H. D. King, quantity surveyors, at £150, and the back part of the ground floor was taken by F. D. Sheridan & Co., estate agents, at £200. The Shire Society's net rent expenditure in 1934 had been £209. In 1936, it was £230; in 1937, £218.

One cannot but admire Sir Walter and his colleagues, and appreciate R. A. Brown's recollection that, when the National Horse Association was run by Shire men, it was an extraordinarily business-like body. The only other things that happened relating to the house during these years was that "Stud Book London" was relinquished as the Society's telegraphic address at the end of 1938, and that all sorts of discussions took place about what to do when the lease expired in March 1941.

One of the Gilbey dreams of thirty years finally became a reality at the end of the 'thirties. Cart-horse breeding was to be assisted by the Tote. The Racecourse Betting Control Board, established in 1928, had long been pregnant and at last in 1936 gave birth to the Racecourse Totalisator Charity Trust. But this mountain in turn brought forth a Shire mouse. A miserable £500 was allocated of which £300 had to be used for increasing the prizes at the next London Show and £200 for similar purposes at the country shows. Feeling like a small boy who hopes for cash largesse from uncle to spend on what he likes, and receives instead a useful pair of shoes, the Shire men said "thank you very much" and did as they were told. First prize in each London class was increased in 1938 from £15 to £20 and others in proportion, including breeders' prizes. The second year's grant was £750 and so in 1939 first prizes were raised to £25. The third annual grant was £1,000: but it was now too late for spending on shows.

The following figures show the state of some of the Society's affairs at the lowest ebb of the 'thirties and in 1938 (not 1939, when membership, etc., was upset by the outbreak of war), compared with 1920, the last of the boom years.

	1920	Lowest in 1930–1939	1938
New members joining	684	92 in 1932	193
Loss/gain in year	+432	—242 in 1932	+16
Annual members, total	4,403	1,796 in 1934	1,979
Total membership	6,328	3,525 in 1934	3,672
Stud-book* – new stallions	923	192 in 1930	304
new mares	5,656	743 in 1933	1,102
London Show: total entries†	521	253 in 1935	306
Heavy stallions licensed – total	3,019	1,087 in 1930	1,868
– Shire (all)	2,430	752 in 1930	1,210
„ (pedigree)	2,258	704 in 1931	1,050

* Published the following year (1921, 1939, etc.).
† Excluding commercial classes (none in 1920).

8. THE KING, AND OTHER MEN

The choice of two M.Ps, David Davies and N. W. Smith Carington, as successive Presidents was not without special significance or value, in 1930–1931. However, the former had given up his seat before taking office, in order to have more time for international politics and his plans for an international police force. The latter, like Sir Walter three years before, was now horseless but did not buy any to mark the occasion. When he died eighteen months after his year of office, the Society lost an enthusiastic and influential campaigner and an exceptionally popular member. His successor, Thomas Forshaw, was received with the loud and prolonged applause that his and his family's Shire renown and integrity deserved.

Sir Edward D. Stern, to everyone's regret, became the fourth President who never was, for he died on 17th April 1933 at the age of seventy-eight and never occupied the chair. The Jersey and Shire societies were both deprived of a connoisseur of choice pedigree animals and his beautiful Fan Court estate at Chertsey was sold later that year. A Hackney man before joining the Shire Society in 1903, his best-known cart-horse was probably Danesfield Stonewall, bought from the breeder R. W. Hudson as a three-year-old in 1907. He won London prizes with him every year from 1908 to 1911 before selling him to F. E. Muntz, but Stonewall's value was as an exceptional stock-getter, which Sir Edward made sure that every farmer in his part of Surrey could afford to use. His stallion at the time of his death was the home-bred Fancourt Dandy. The Fan Court dispersal included also a two-year-old colt bred at home, Fancourt Ajax, and eleven females, seven hunters and thirty-nine breeding Jerseys.

A. T. Loyd was called upon to fill Sir Edward's place, and no one had been President twice within so short an interval. His position among men, his abilities and his enthusiasm made him an obvious choice in an emergency. It was certainly a decision that delighted Albert Holland who, like any secretary, was in a special position to judge his bosses. The Duke of Devonshire broke the record by being elected for a third time in 1934, and was somewhat startled at the acclamation with which he was greeted. But if he had only been vain enough to reckon up all he had done for the Society since first holding that office in 1901, or to consider the effect upon morale of his single-minded enthusiasm for the old English cart-horse, he would not have been surprised at all. Sir Edward Mann in 1935 was another popular but at the time a somewhat novel choice. A member of the Society for over half a century, he was personally responsible for ensuring that his horses were the finest possible advertisement that the breed, and his brewery, could possibly have. He was, in fact, the first President who was not a breeder but a proprietor of geldings.

During Mann's year of office, the Society suffered the loss of its Patron. Like not a few of its other members, the King had been a model squire and, as observers have often remarked, the sureness of touch with which he transformed this "ordinariness" into kingship amounted almost to genius. Certainly his common-sense and lack of pomposity endeared him to all Shire men, perhaps most of all on those never-forgotten occasions when he had raised his hat to two successive Presidents and received at their hands, with almost naive delight, like a schoolboy winning a prize, the cup won by his home-bred stallion.

At his death on 20th January 1936 (and where should that occur more fittingly than at Sandringham?) many a Shire man cast his mind back to some of the animals he and his father had bred – especially, perhaps, to Anchorite, that son of Harold foaled in 1896, Benedick, son of Harold's son Prince Harold, Dunsmore Gloaming the 1899–1900 champion mare, Solace the champion of 1903, and of course Field Marshal V himself.

At the London Show two weeks after his death, the home-bred Appleton Binder was fourth in the four-year-old stallions' class and so King Edward VIII, as his new owner, appeared in the prize-list. But that was the beginning and end of His Majesty's active Shire career. He had been an absentee President in 1917 and on 8th April of this year accepted the position of third Patron of the Society. But he had already decided to terminate Shire and other horse-breeding at Sandringham which (*The Times* obituary commented thirty-six years later) "caused circles enjoying much influence to fear for the soundness of the King's judgement in matters of moment. He also set in train measures of economy in the royal estates which caused hard feelings among his old retainers." Be these things as they may, all old Shire men who had had the pleasure of meeting him would regard it as typical of his courteous interest in ordinary people and their activities that, many years later, a sick and dying man, he took the trouble to reply promptly to an enquiry about the Sandringham stud addressed to him, with some hesitancy, for the purposes of this present record. Apologising for his inability to contribute "anything worthwhile" to this history, he wrote, "Time unfortunately has dimmed my recollections of my brief association with this interesting breed of horses. However, I recall my father's stud at Sandringham, of which he was justly proud." In somewhat shaky writing he signed his letter "Edward, Duke of Windsor" and initialled the envelope. It was dated 24th April 1972 and he died on 28th May, mourned by Shire men who had forgiven his impulsive reaction against squiredom thirty-six years before.

Arthur C. Beck's retirement followed the death of his royal squire, and the removal of this staunch man, no less a Shire supporter than his auctioneer nephew or royal employer, enabled strange things to happen at Sandringham. In 1937 four Suffolk mares were purchased and when, in accordance with the breed society's rules, transfer certificates were applied for, Raymond Keer, the secretary, Sir W. E. Cuthbert Quilter, the President, and all the Suffolk Councilmen were full of joy. Shire men wagged their heads at the misguided ideas now prevailing where for over fifty years there had been right-thinking policies. One of the mares, Harkstead Emerald 6th (whose ancestry in tail female was recorded to the 10th dam), dropped a whole-colour red chesnut colt foal a little later, on 9th May, and when he was registered as Sandringham Standard 6868 two breeders were listed, as was the customary Suffolk Stud-book procedure – "mating breeder H. R. Winch: foaling breeder,

Sandringham Estate". A cart-horse bred by "Sandringham Estate", indeed! In the old King's days, it was unthinkable that the breeder of a cart-horse at Sandringham should be recorded as "The Estate": it was always none other than H.M. the King himself. Let it be noted also that if this foal had been a Shire he would have been given the number, not 6868, but 42761; or, more correctly (since Shires, unlike Suffolks, could not be submitted for registration until they were yearlings), in the 1939 volume as 43043, pushing Saundby Goldfinder up to the next number.

In 1938 the other three mares had foals, and three more were purchased. King George VI now became Patron, not only of the Shire Society which he had thus honoured in 1937, but of the Suffolk as well. One hopes that his father, who had once remarked that some people bought Shire champions, but that he bred them, lay easy in his grave. Sandringham Standard, forsooth! And Sandringham Saturn, Safety and Sapphire, all bred by "Sandringham Estate"! Shire men could have wept for Field Marshal V, "owner and breeder, H.M. the King" – or even for Appleton Binder, that last of the royal squire's stallions, and a proper old brown one. This horse, offered at the Peterborough March Sales in 1936 soon after winning his fourth prize in London, had been bought by the Forshaw brothers, for they likewise were believers in weight, legs and feet. At the very time all this nonsense was starting at Sandringham in February 1937, he was shown again, and moved up a place to third, among the four-year-olds. The catalogue of course recorded him as bred by "His Majesty the late King George V".

9. PETERBOROUGH AND EDMUND BECK

Seventy-seven stallions, the best in England, were nominated for the 1930 Produce Stakes by thirty-two different owners (the Forshaws entering thirteen, Belcher and Cumber eleven each and the Duke of Devonshire four). The foal show itself attracted entries which were not only more than the year before (twenty-seven colts and forty-five fillies in the Stakes; twenty-one and thirty-two in the open classes; thirteen mares with foal; twelve groups of three) but the second highest in the show's history, which was one of the few encouraging aspects of 1930 anywhere. Edmund Beck's grievous war sufferings still failed to impair his cheerfulness, in spite of the fact that another operation meant that he conducted the auction afterwards minus not one leg now, but both.

Disaster, however, was lurking round the corner of the repository. By the time of the next foal show, Messrs. Sexton, Grimwade & Beck felt unable to keep it going any longer in those bad times and offered either to sell it complete to the Shire Society for £6,000 or to let it for £200 a year exclusive of rates and repairs. This rent would have excluded the two shops on the front, the flat above and the hall over the entrance, but would have provided ninety-six loose boxes, seven small boxes, twenty-six stalls, iron stable and a large separate building, formerly used as a gun park but at that time let to

Messrs. Barford and Perkins. The Society could not contemplete either suggestion. But it was vital to maintain the Produce Stakes and the March and
October pedigree sales. (These were conducted under S.H.S. rules, the ordinary
monthly sales being in accordance with the auctioneer's own rules.) So a
subsidy of £100 a year was provided. As it happened, by that time the worst of
the troubles were over, the firm's commission having increased by £1,000
over 1930, and after 1934 the subsidy was no longer needed.

However, in 1935 Arthur Beck and Frank Grimwade sold the repository to
Messrs. John Thornton, Hobson & Company of Victoria House, Southampton
Row. The first of these names had long been associated with Shorthorns. (In
1857, John Thornton joined Mr. Strafford, the leading shorthorn auctioneer and
proprietor of Coates' Herd Book. He founded his own firm in 1868 and after
operating for many years from 7 Princes Street, Hanover Square, he died in
December 1908.) Actually, nothing was really changed, since Beck personally
continued to conduct all Shire sales and the Society merely had to elect as its
official auctioneer "Edmund Beck, Peterborough" instead of "Sexton, Grimwade
& Beck, Colchester & Peterborough". The sale following the Produce Stakes
and Foal Show of 1935 was the first engagement under the new name.

The Spring Sale in 1936 reflected the revival of Shire affairs. One hundred
and forty-six stallions in particular met a remarkable trade. By the end of the
first day ninety-four animals had been sold for 8,528 guineas. They included
five from G. R. C. Foster, who also sent sixteen mares, as he had sold some of
his farms (a few weeks later he himself was dead), and five which were part of
the late J. G. McDougall's stud. One of the latter, the London reserve junior
cup winner, Whittlesea Coming King, was bought for 675 guineas by Fred
Parsons in Somerset, who recouped £300 within a few months, as he was
already let to the Peterborough Society. Appleton Binder came from
Sandringham to mark the end of Shire affairs there and the Forshaws paid 300
guineas for him. (In 1919, the Spring Sales had lasted four days and over 700
Shires had been sold for £70,000. But that was another age.)

In 1937, the Peterborough Agricultural Society stallion show was given up,
owing to entries having become so few. But this was not really any cause for
despair, but rather an indication of progress. The elaboration of the show
system in general and of the Society's involvement in it, the organisation and
recent revival of the hiring societies and the visits of their selection committees
to the various stallion studs, the working of the Horse-Breeding Act which
controlled the soundness and conformation of the travelling stallions and
consequently their numbers, all combined to produce in the average owner of
even a couple of mares an awareness of "what was about". He did not really
need, as in the old days he had needed, to go to a parade and fuss around
feeling legs and listening to tales, in order to make up his mind which was the
one he wanted to use. So the passing of the Peterborough Stallion Show, as of
other like parades, was not so sad an affair after all, except to the nostalgically
inclined.

In July 1938, Edmund Beck, the brave and cheerful, died. The terrible progress of gangrene had now taken an arm and, before death released him, he had been in danger of losing the other. He ought chiefly to be remembered, perhaps, for his skill at his life's work. He was a compelling and brilliant salesman of a horse. His familiar "I can't dwell" and his "Quick" made everyone take notice of what was happening. Trivial things, however, remain in the memory. S. T. Parker of Derby started work in the period when Derby Auctions was owned by Sexton, Grimwade & Beck and, not unnaturally, was solemnly impressed by anything the great man said. In the hot summer of 1921 Beck commented that Owen Webb of Cambridge, who was his maternal grandfather, used to say, "Port wine is the warmest drink in winter and the coolest in summer." This remark was still lodged in the Parker memory in 1971. Perhaps it was not profound, but, for that matter, why should anyone remember that Gladstone once said, "I do *not* eat nuts"?

Of three different men, asked to describe Beck in the fewest possible words, one said, "A grand chap and a great auctioneer." Another replied that he was "A man who was out to keep the Shire Society together". The third simply remarked, "A hundred-per-cent Shire man." Beck himself once wrote, "As a schoolboy at Christ's Hospital, I was taken by my uncle" (of Sandringham) "to see my first Shire Horse Show, and I vividly remember seeing Markeaton Royal Harold win the championship." That was 1897. Two years before his death, he wrote, "It is very easy, and there is a tendency as one grows older, to think that the old times were the best, but we must all agree that the best horses of today are fully equal to, if not better than, those of thirty years ago." Questioned in the 'twenties and 'thirties about the future of the Shire, he loved to sum up his views with the reminder that "threatened men live long". Would that he, too, had done so.

The Spring Sale, one of the two main events of the year at the repository, was conducted in 1939 by Harry Hobson. It shows how, for those who wished to buy or sell the best pedigree Shires by the auction method, Peterborough had now almost entirely superseded the London Show. Compared with the mere four he sold at Islington, Hobson had a catalogue of thirty-seven stallions of four years and upward, forty-four three-year-olds, thirty-three of two years, and ten yearling colts; twenty-nine older mares, nineteen three-year-olds, eight of two years and eight yearlings; not to mention pure-bred geldings, five Clydesdale fillies and some odds and ends.

"The Shire event of the summer", as the Peterborough Agricultural Society always and without exaggeration described its main show, was also the last great Shire event of the days of peace, with the possible exception of the Royal, held the following week. Colonel A. F. Nicholson, son of Sir Arthur (but people had now after ten years ceased to think of him just in those terms), and John Belcher, son of Morris, were the judges. White Gate Clanish Maid, aged two, won the S.H.S. gold medal for Richard Cambidge of Wheaton Aston, Staffs, who had bred her. Woburn Dustman, a yearling, won the stallion's medal for Messrs. Reinhold & Freshney of Little Milton, Oxon (in practice it was T. H. B. Freshney, whose Shire ancestry stretched back through many generations in the Fens). He had been bred officially by the Duke of Bedford and actually by his manager Henry Hobbs. These two Shires had each been second in their London classes.

The fifty-five sires which were nominated for the Produce Stakes due to be held in the autumn can be regarded as the very cream of sixty years' effort by the breed society. Numbers had decreased because to get a winning group of three sons or daughters was just about the most difficult task in the Shire world. William Cumber had nominated twelve stallions, Morris Belcher eight, the Forshaws seven, and James Gould five; Enoch Bostock only one – but that was Kirkland Mimic; Colonel Nicholson one – but it was Edingale Blend; J. G. Runciman one – Bower Winalot himself who, between nomination and show, had become the first quadruple champion in London.

If Fred Street could have come alive to see what his idea had achieved, he would have been satisfied. But would he have made himself unpopular, in the 'thirties, by once again forecasting that "War will surely come"? When war did come, the Peterborough Foal Stakes were held, though Ashbourne and others were cancelled, and Raans Record Wave (Reinhold and Freshney) was sire of the winning filly and of the winning produce group. The story of one of these three foals points the moral of all the breed society's work.

Stephen Rains of Nether Farm, Alton, in the parish of Kirk Ireton, Derbyshire, was encouraged by his schoolboy son in the early 'thirties to aim for pedigree breeding from their mares. For the first year or two, they could not get any of them in foal at all, and began to think they never would. But in 1936 they picked up a pedigree two-year-old filly for 27 guineas and that same year put her to Messrs. Belcher's celebrated Lechwyche Clansman, a great sire now fourteen years old. Most of their friends and critics said they were soft in the head to use such an expensive stallion. But they got a colt foal, and he was sold to become registered as Blackbrook Clansman 1st. Their mare missed the next year but, still soft in the head or softer, they had her covered in 1939 by Harboro' Goldfinder himself. She bred a filly foal and they entered her for the Bakewell show on 10th August 1939. A chap they knew, who was very good at getting foals ready for showing, promised to help, but let them down. So young Rains had a go. They won first prize with her, beating two other Harboro' Goldfinder fillies among nineteen others! This was the most memorable thing that had ever happened.

In 1970, old Stephen and a visitor to his little house had a tremendous search through hundreds of catalogues, pulled out of cupboards and drawers and hidey-holes, for the Bakewell catalogue of 1939. Every show held in Derbyshire from 1920 onwards, and many before that, seemed to be represented, but not that one. "Yes, but it doesn't matter, you see, because I've brought the Shire Book specially, and it gives the results. There it is. First prize, definitely, to S. Rains for filly foal by Harboro' Goldfinder 41177. Dam,

Longford Daisy." Longford Daisy? Good heavens, how did she get that name? Was she bred by the ghost of Edward Coke himself? Alas, no. We know nothing of any Mr. Coke. (It was only a fancy, anyway.) She came from Mr. Barker, who died. That is why she was sold, for 27 guineas. (Sure enough, another Shire Book tells us that 127840 Longford Daisy was bred by E. J. Barker of Daisy Bank in the same village as Longford Hall.)

In spite of that Shire Book, which records that Longford Daisy's foal beat W. H. Appleby's that year at Bakewell, and Mr. Gould's as well (and seventeen others), the missing show book became an obsession, as if to find it would make her materialise, there in the very sitting room, for any visitor to see. Or, if Mrs. Rains had still been alive, she could have proved the whole thing, instead. She did all the writing connected with these matters. It's a funny thing, but the memory of going to far-off Peterborough in the October was clean gone. Someone must have taken her, for the Shire Book says she was second there, and was one of the three that won the Stakes for Harboro' Goldfinder. But that doesn't matter. At Bakewell, she won.

What happened, then, to this foal that won Bakewell? Was she sold? No, it would be against nature to sell her. She became petrified in the memory, like some female Peter Pan, working away on the farm through the war, year after year, never growing up, always remaining the filly that won Bakewell. A brown filly she was, like her mother. A bit of white on the off fore-leg. Mr. Belcher's Harboro' Goldfinder, he was dark brown as well. Stephen's son went off to the war. The war brought confusion everywhere, long before old age brought it to Stephen Rains.

In 1971, a few months after the search for the missing show book, the old man died, his catalogues still in a muddle. Mrs. Rains had never registered the filly, and he had never been a member of the Shire Horse Society. And that is why he never had a copy of the Shire Book – 61st Volume, published January 1940, recording for all the world to see, as long as time lasts, that on 10th August 1939, Longford Daisy's filly foal by Harboro' Goldfinder beat all nineteen others at Bakewell, to win the £10 prize for her breeder, Stephen Rains. (It also records that on 4th October she really had gone, somehow, to Peterborough, and won £6 second prize.) A proper share of honour in history belongs to S. Rains and to thousands, such as he, who hold a simple faith – that a Shire is the one animal in the world you can spend hours remembering, thirty years later, and bringing back to life, and explaining to strangers, if only you can find the show book.

10. SOME ROYAL SHOWS

The gold, silver and bronze medal schemes continued in 1930 to flourish at those shows which had not collapsed owing to the bad times. At thirty-three shows, gold medals were awarded to thirty-nine horses, and the breeders of twenty-seven of these, being still alive and members of the Society, also received prizes. One hundred and sixty-two silver medals were awarded at sixty-one shows, including eight overseas, with the breeders of 122 winners being entitled to prizes. There were sixty bronze medal shows. At eleven horse parades, sixty-nine silver medals and many cash prizes were presented.

So few mares were being put to the horse in that time of woe and doubt, that the rule for gold medal shows was relaxed. In 1931, a mare became eligible for this award provided that she had foaled that year or in either of the two preceding years. Owners, like breeders, now for the first time had to be members of the Society in order to qualify for gold and silver awards, though not for the bronze ones. At the same time, the special grants and donations to some country shows towards their Shire classes were axed as an economy and in order not to give offence to others.

The Royal Welsh Society's show was one of only four with a class open to senior stallions (the others being the Royal Lancashire, the Yorkshire, and the Tunbridge Wells and S.E. Counties) and they all did well to attract seven or eight entries each at such an awkward time as July. In 1931, for their Llanelli show, the Royal Welsh attempted to grapple with the problem of the entire horse which was more capable of winning prizes than getting foals, and enquired whether there would be any objection to a rule that stallions of four years and upwards must be proved stock getters. Holland was told to reply that the Shire Society "had no wish to interfere in any matter in which it had no concern", which was of course perfectly reasonable. But it might have been more happily phrased, because this has always been a matter of the gravest concern in relation to the show system.

The Welshmen carried out their intention. They gave first prize to that black stock-horse *par excellence*, the nine-year-old Ledwyche Clansman who had come more or less hot-foot from a busy season in north Herefordshire. As if to provide a sample of what he could do, a son of his, Lugg Side Clansman, won the yearling colts' class. But it was the sire who was chosen as champion stallion. Morris Belcher owned them both. Ledwyche Clansman had been bred by J. T. Green, Wootton, Ashbourne and sold to Edward Howells, Lower Ledwyche, near Ludlow. Belcher had bought him in 1928 and immediately let him to Bishop's Castle S.H.S: then for seven successive seasons 1929–1935 he was hired by North Herefordshire S.H.S., by which time he could not find many mares to serve which were not his own daughters. From 1936–1938 he was let to the West Staffs S.H.S., though in the last two years he stood for them in a Stafford stables on Saturdays only, serving mares at his own home on the Lillehurst farm on other days. He was eighteen when his career finished. He was never shown in London until 1931, when he was fourth in the big stallions' class, and did not go there again. Young Lugg Side Clansman was one of his numerous North Herefordshire progeny, bred by Samuel Goodwin of Ivington Court, Leominster out of Lugg Side Darkie, whose sixth dam was Worsley Alberta bred in 1890 out of an unregistered mare which belonged to the Earl of Ellesmere and traced in the male line to *A Grey Horse* owned by one Ivens of Eydon in Northamptonshire in the early eighteen-twenties. This grey stallion was a noted horse in his day and was not without considerable influence in the formation of the Shire breed.

(David Davies, the 1930 Shire president, had resuscitated the collapsed Royal Welsh Society in 1922, and served it continuously as chairman until his death in June 1944, the last twelve years as Baron Davies of Llandinam. Some of the other domestic debts that his country owed him were better known than this. He spent large sums on housing estates and on the Presbyterian church, and in 1911 had given £150,000 to launch a campaign which, before his death, had halved the tuberculosis mortality rate in Wales. But the revival of the agricultural society was itself no mean offering.)

However, it was the Royal Agricultural Society of England which produced the real excitement, particularly in 1934. The Royal Welsh asked for a little grant that year, but the Shire men felt unable to break their new rule, to subsidise only the R.A.S.E. For the latter, they suddenly increased their donation, now normally about £120, to £500. After years of economy, it was folly, but it was fun. It all began the previous autumn when Sir Walter Gilbey and Tom Forshaw told the Horse Show Committee that for the 1934 Royal the Suffolk men were really going to town – because the town happened to be Ipswich. With the prospect of the chesnut men making a tremendous effort when it came to the county town of East Suffolk, the very heart of the county breed, the supporters of hairy legs had to make a gesture. Prizes in all classes were increased and four new classes added – two and three year old geldings, and harness classes for singles, pairs and teams. Sir Walter in addition gave a silver cup for the best team. Travelling expenses were also offered in some cases. There was an entry of 121 Shires, and nothing like it had been seen for twenty years. In particular, the daily parade of the teams was a tremendous success, with a vast crowd crammed round the ring and an atmosphere suggestive of a football match. Mann, Crossman & Paulin and Young & Company, among brewers, supported the show in great style, as did Charles Franklin the Bedford-based coal merchant.

The only fly in the ointment of that wonderful but expensive week was that, as could be expected, every other breed society made a special effort too and, though the 107,001 visitors had a glorious heavy-horse treat the like of which has never been repeated, it is doubtful whether all the money poured into publicity converted a single man present from one breed to another. But even a churl had to admire the home team's performance. Their classes for "best feet" (which, of course, Shire men argued had never been necessary for the Old English horses because that vital appendage had never been a breed weakness) attracted thirty-one stallions and sixty-one mares. There was a total of 265 Suffolks – more than any breed of any species of animal in the show. On the second day, all their horses were allowed, as a unique privilege, to parade in the large ring on their own. There would not have been room for the Shires and others, in any case. The climax of their display, however, was on the last day when twenty-four single-horse Suffolk turnouts were judged.

The sun shone continuously all the time the Show was open and, although the colour has always been unpopular in Shires, there are few more attractive sights in sunshine than gleaming chesnut coats of varying shades. The President of R.A.S.E. that year was the Earl of Stradbroke, son of the very man whom the Suffolk Horse Association, as it was originally named, elected as their first Patron in 1877.[4] Swelling with county pride, he said, "Suffolk people are like Punches. When they put their shoulders to the collar, something has got to move." Their beautiful six-year-old champion stallion Martlesham Beau-Ideal was owned by A. H. Huddlestone at Methley, near Leeds but had been bred, as his name suggests, near Woodbridge. The Shire champion stallion (classes up to three-year-olds only) was Raans Clansman, shown by the Forshaws and bred by William Clark at Amersham. How Herman Biddell and Fred Street would have loved all this. And what an argument they would have had – with Thomas Brown to interject "O, I care nothing about Suffolks, I scarcely class them amongst cart horses", as he had done at the 1883 meeting, to make everyone laugh. All in all, there has never been anything since, like the Ipswich Royal 1934.

In the second half of the decade, the Royal continued the popular new classes for teams. The Shire Society started giving a little financial help once again to a few county shows, but as usual the smaller breed societies were able to make effective sallies in a manner that the Shire men, with heavy financial London Show commitments, could not do. It was very irritating, for example, to learn that Suffolk classes were to be provided in 1938 at the Shropshire & West Midland and that the breed society was not only subsidising them heavily but refunding the entry fees to all members who cared to compete. Ironically, R.A.S.E. agreed to accept London Show veterinary certificates for the 1939 Royal – at last, sixty years after the Cart-horse men had first determined to be extremely strict on matters of hereditary soundness, so as to avoid the absurdities that were happening at Royal Shows, where prizes were awarded to sidebones and defective wind.

The 1939 Royal, the centenary show, was held in Windsor Great Park under the Presidency of the King. It bid fair to be Ipswich all over again. Indeed, as far as livestock in general was concerned, it surpassed all records – 4,548 entries for horses, cattle, goats, sheep and pigs as against 3,997 at the golden jubilee show, also at Windsor (in 1889) and 3,534 at Ipswich. But draught-horses were fewer than at either of these. There were ninety Shires (167 in 1889), fifty Clydesdales (ninety-three), 168 Suffolks (105) and 109 Percherons. There were no non-pedigree draught-horses (fifteen in 1889) and no asses (seventeen). Total horse numbers, however were up compared with 1889, from 989 to 1,428 – largely accounted for by riding classes (161 hunters) and jumping (315), neither of which was on the 1889 schedule at all. Holland had warned members what would happen. "It is certain all breeds will do their utmost to ensure their classes being well filled on this unique occasion, and it is sincerely hoped that Shire enthusiasts will see to it the superiority of England's Premier Draught

Horse is amply demonstrated at England's Premier Agricultural Show." (Premier agricultural show the Royal certainly was, and is, but the real settlement of the horse argument was that, of the 1,699 heavy stallions licensed for England and Wales that summer, 1,092 were Shires: that is, all other breeds combined could muster only 36% of the total.)

Chenies Mavis won the Shire gold medal for W. J. Thompson. (The story of her breeding by William Simpson must be left for another time.) James Gould won the stallion medal with Lymm Coming King, bred near Leek by C. R. Harrison. Gardden Connell won a special prize as reserve, for Reuben Haigh, and how Stephen James spotted him and recommended him to Mr. Haigh is also another story for another occasion. But who won the glory? Possibly, this is the point at which a biassed commentator should shirk responsibility and with it escape the charge of prejudice. So we quote instead Professor J. A. Scott Watson who considered that the outstanding feature of the heavy-horse section was not the breeding classes but the display of four-horse teams in harness. "The Suffolk was most largely represented, though many horsemen thought that the first-prize Shire team, of four really magnificent greys, was the most remarkable of all. On the other hand, it was one of the Suffolk teams, parading in old-time harness with its full complement of brasses and bells, which was the favourite with the ring-side crowd."[5] The greys had been sent by Sir Edward Mann from Mann, Crossman & Paulin's famous brewery stable. Young & Company's four black geldings were second: but as they had beaten M.C. & P. in the pairs class, domestic honours were even. Perhaps best of all was a non-competitive parade of teams of six organised by these breweries and by Fremlin's, who also had greys. The Centenary Royal was indeed a great occasion. But a couple of months later this sort of amusement came to an abrupt end.

11. LONDON SHOWS

Entries for the 1930 Show were only 43% of the number in 1921. There were 117 stallions, ninety-one mares and forty-six geldings (exclusive of the commercial classes). The largest class was the three-year-old stallions, of whom there were thirty, and it was possible to deal with all these in the ring without a preliminary "weeding-out". So operations began on the first day at 10 a.m. instead of 8.30.

Thirty years before, in 1898–1900, Buscot Harold had won the stallion championship three times in succession. Now, Eaton Premier King became the second horse to do so. Among the mares, Lockinge Ridgeway Rose was the fourth to achieve the same feat. *The Farmer and Stockbreeder* remarked that the odds against this double-triple win "are so long that even the youngest adherent of the Shire is unlikely to live to see such a coincidence again". It was very difficult to fault Morris Belcher's stallion at all. His character, power and sheer size gave him a majesty above all others and yet his freshness of limb and joints enabled him to move with the precision of a much smaller and lighter animal. He was one of the supreme specimens, in all time, of his breed. Thomas Loyd's mare was considered by some to be a little lacking in the thighs, but she combined old-fashioned weight and power with a comparative cleanness and correctness of limb which breeders in the coming decade were to strive for more and more.

If there had been a pairs class for human beings on the basis of the popular class for mares at Peterborough and elsewhere, the proprietor of Lockinge and the Shropshire farmer, universally respected and liked, would have taken some beating. There was certainly no pair whom the office staff or any other servants of the Society would have placed higher in regard. Two outbursts of cheering, which in 1930 a throng of staid and steady country men were still uninhibited enough to produce, if sufficiently moved, was a judgment of the owners as well. Thomas Loyd in addition became the fourth President in office to win a championship. The Earl of Ellesmere had done it in 1880, Lord Rothschild in 1906 and Sir Walpole Greenwell had won both the top awards on that memorable occasion in 1913. In the absence of any member of the royal family, Mrs. Loyd presented the cups. As her husband also won first prize in three other female classes, owned the sire of the winning produce group and two of the three members of that group as well, and had provided special extra breeder's prizes for each of the ten cup-winners and reserves, this was Lockinge year.

The Forshaws won three of the six stallion classes. In the "regular workers" class among commercial horses, John Mowlem & Company Limited, staunch supporters of the London Cart Horse Parades from the earliest days, did well to win a card with Snip, aged sixteen. Sir Gomer Berry, proprietor of the Amalgamated Press, the *Daily Sketch, Daily Telegraph* and others, had just become the fourth owner of the Pendley stud in ten years, and Harry Bishop gave him a good start. The very first of eleven Pendley animals sent into the ring, on the Tuesday afternoon, was a two-year-old gelding called Sunny Jim and he won the class.

It was Pendley's year in 1931. Sir Gomer, who had presented a 100 guinea stallion cup to replace that which Morris Belcher had won outright, now proceeded to win first prize in every female class except yearlings, in which he did not compete, and which William Cumber won with Theale Joan 2nd. Pendley Marceline won the two-year-olds: Llynclys Lady Loue the three-year-olds (she had won her class for Cumber the year before): Pendley Lady Luck, the four-year-olds: Pendley Choice under 16.2: and Kerry Clanish Maid the big mares. When the championships were due to be decided, a staffing problem was posed and so young Denis Berry, Sir Gomer's second son, now nineteen, pleaded with Harry Bishop to be allowed to lead one of the mares, and was given Llynclys Lady Loue. The big mare won the senior cup with Lady Luck her reserve. Marceline won the junior cup with Lady Loue reserve. Then the judges created their own sensation by placing the two young mares above the others for the championships. But they were unanimous, and

Marceline of the elegant legs became the second two-year-old filly to beat them all at London.

Marceline was born in the parish of Slyne, the most southerly point in Lancashire reached by travelling Clydesdale stallions. Indeed, the border between the breeds was marked there years before, by two adjoining farms. At Throstle Grove, R. Thompson kept Clydesdale mares and at Williamsland, W. Fox had his Shires. But Slyne's claim to fame derives from the Ancliffe Hall stud run by William Newhouse. Shires had been bred at Ancliffe by his father Edward since the latter part of the nineteenth-century, but it was between the two world wars that they really came to the fore. Two mares shown individually and as a pair at northern shows and ploughing matches were Chance, bred in Lincolnshire in 1912, and Ancliffe Bessie, bred in 1914 by Margaret Stuart, widow of John, who had managed Earl Egerton's stud. Both were good hard browns. Chance was slightly wider and lower-set than Bessie, but they formed an impressive pair. It was Bessie, however, who brought glory to Ancliffe through her daughter Ancliffe Winnie that William Newhouse bred in 1920. By the Forshaws' Warrior Carlton, she was one of the quality mares of her time, with limbs as strong and clean as any judge could desire and with that straight and silky feather that breeders strove so hard to obtain. One of her offspring was a filly by Darley Wild Wave in 1929 that inherited her marvellous legs. Harold Burrow, a young veterinary surgeon on the Birmingham Corporation staff, went home on holiday and visited the Ancliffe stud. The veterinary surgeon, O. A. Ducksbury, was about to dock the foal but allowed the young man, who was his future son-in-law, to "have a go" because in his first job he never had occasion to do the operation. The filly was hardly a suitable "practice animal" for, after being sold, she became Pendley Marceline.

When Sir Gomer came up to receive four cups, three of which he could keep, from the Duke of Gloucester, everyone cheered again as they had the year before. He was too new to be cheered for himself, but everyone was excited by the marvellous mares he had collected and full of admiration for a man prepared to be so enthusiastic as he obviously was in such a dark farming and economic year. There was some doubt whether all this excitement was for the good of Sir Gomer's health. A. G. Holland vividly remembered that "he was so elated that it sort of overcame him".

The new champion stallion had been bred, like Marceline, in Lancashire. This was Kirkland Black Friar. Still only four, this formidable character had already had four owners – W. H. Wildman his breeder, Robert Stuart who named him, Mrs. Stanton (who paid 800 guineas) and now E. W. Webb (310 guineas) of Etchingham in Sussex. His old-fashioned black colour made him a popular champion, but he was a massive, ill-tempered and almost uncontroll-able horse whom it was expedient to delegate three men at a time to cope with.

Bill Raby, never ill in his life and apparently still fit as a fiddle, dropped dead in the hall on the first morning. Horses had perished at London shows, but men never, which was surprising. For many years Bill had been stud-groom to S. E. Thompson, a Shire member since 1904, who occasionally brought along a filly from his Westby farm in the Blackpool district for the auction sale. Westby Nathalie, a yearling, was the third such in twelve years. Standing sixteenth in a class of twenty-four, she won a commended card, but a man cannot take much interest in things like that when he loses an old friend and servant in such a shocking manner. (Lieutenant-Colonel T. W. Daniel bought the filly for 36 guineas, showed her in London two years later, when she was third, and sold her for 78 guineas to a new member from the Chesterfield district, F. A. Parker. The late Bill Raby's boss moved to Buckinghamshire in 1932.)

Only twelve animals, including Westby Nathalie, were sold at the auction, for £1,240, because no one had any money to spare. Edmund Beck, in a wheel-chair, was as cheerful as ever, and as hopeful of better times to come. But his work was over in an hour, and there was nothing for visitors to do on the third day except eat, drink and talk between 11 a.m. and 2 p.m., when the commercial classes started. These were generally thought to be the best collection of heavy harness horses ever brought together. Sir Walter Gilbey, presiding at his luncheon as usual, commented as usual on the state of agriculture. "Owner occupiers trying to carry on, but landlords all over England receiving notice from their tenants . . . God help the Government, the farmer and the taxpayer!"

Thirteen days before the 1932 show a great home sale at Pendley cleared out all the prize-winners of the past two years. Twenty-two females and three colts averaged £101. (The sale there exactly twelve years earlier had averaged over £721 a head, but it would be difficult to decide which was the better collection of the two.) Consequently, only Raans Record, which had been withdrawn at 420 guineas, won Sir Gomer a prize at the Show – third in the three year olds. This class was won by Bower Winalot, a horse which had started life almost at the top. As a foal in 1929 at Peterborough he was shown by his breeder, J. G. Runciman, the well-known Cambridge veterinary surgeon, and was beaten only by F. W. Griffin's Boro' Padre. He was then bought by G. R. C. Foster of Erfyl Lady Grey fame and the London Show confirmed their relative placings. In 1931 he had won his class, and the junior cup as well. Now he did both these things again and won the supreme championship as well, beating the senior cup winner and previous year's champion, the savage Kirkland Black Friar.

Among the females, the move from Hertfordshire brought Kerry Clanish Maid, who had been climbing steadily over the years, to the very top at last, at the age of nine. Her new owners, the brothers J. and W. Whewell, of the New Bridge Chemical Works at Radcliffe, Lancashire, made one of the best bargains ever achieved among Shires when they bought this mare of the perfect feet at the Pendley sale for 170 guineas, and their success was a pointer towards things to come from them, particularly in the 'sixties. Kerry Clanish Maid was one of three purchases that William Whewell made at Pendley, with the idea of being a breeder as well as an owner of geldings. He paid 520 guineas altogether and people who had never heard of him were saying, "There's a chap in Lancashire who's gone mad." But within a few years the chap in Lancashire had become "Bill" and, so far from calling him mad, it had become a cliché to say, "He has a wonderful eye for a horse", as if that explained him away.

Pendley Marceline won the junior cup but her new owner, Charles Franklin (who had paid only 250 guineas – for a filly good enough to be London champion at the age of two!) had to be content with reserve for the supreme honour. Gwen Webb-Peploe made the last of her six annual appearances in the ring this year and her first exhibit in 1927, Remembrance of Arden, now six, came back to win fifth in the class for small mares. Gwen had exhibited nine mares and won fifth, sixth, ninth, Highly Commended four times and Commended twice – a 100% record. What is more, she had bred them all herself and showed them personally. All this took some doing in a man's world, where standards had never been higher, nor would be again. Sir John Gilmour, Minister of Agriculture, visited the Show and saw her mare.

The South Wales Colliery Owners' Association had arranged to give a fifteen minute show each day of their pit horses. These were the shortest of the short-legged Shires in existence, thick-set and up to 15.2-hands or a little more, but none the less real Shires for all that, and they worked in the only pits with enough headroom underground to accommodate them. In all other coalfields, ponies had to be used: but of the 11,500 employed in the South Wales mines at this time, less than 10% were ponies. Some had been shown at the 1931 International Horse Show. But now the colliery owners thought better of repeating the venture in those miserable times, and so the little demonstration was cancelled.

The 1933 Show was widely regarded by many as the best over-all exhibition of quality ever assembled under one roof. And there were many who were in a position to know. Tom Forshaw and Alfred Clark, for example, who between them knew all that was known about judging stallions and mares, had been attending London Shows since 1880. Bower Winalot and Kerry Clanish Maid were the champions for the second successive year. But, if anyone were to think that the winner of one year had only to put in an appearance in order to win again the next, he would learn his mistake unless he used to the full the months, one might say twelve whole months, of planning and care that are needed to produce a horse in perfect condition on the right day. The Forshaws, as so often when they were not right at the top, were only one step behind Winalot with their Carlton Royal Duke, who was unfortunate enough to be in the same age-group as his rival and so was second to him in all things. He provided a typical instance of Forshaw astuteness. His breeder, Albert Wadsley, had failed to win a prize with him at any show and gave up exhibiting him, saying "We won't get anything with that bugger." One of his neighbours recalled that "He was so poor his ribs cracked in his flesh." But Tom Forshaw bought him and in less than a year this dizzy eminence was achieved. Raans Record, one of the greatest sires, had to stand third.

Kirkland Black Friar, terrifying as always, won the big-horse class (with the Forshaws' Bradgate Premier and Colonel Nicholson's Edingale Blend just below him.) His owner, E. W. Webb had a good day, since his own-bred Etchingham Solace, three-years-old, won the junior cup and was reserve to Kerry Clanish Maid for the top honour of all, and he also won first in the four year mares. That regular favourite, William Todd's marvellous little grey Ponton Pioneer, was as fresh as ever at thirteen to come fifth in the small stallions class: the winner, Forshaws' Gay Albert was ten, but he was the only competitor who was not less than half Pioneer's age.

If, in 1934, Kerry Clanish Maid had not gone lame just before the show, she might have been champion again, in which case the extraordinary 1930 coincidence of both champions simultaneously completing a hat-trick would have been repeated and *The Farmer & Stockbreeder's* prognostication confounded, for Bower Winalot did his half of that tremendously difficult task. Now that he was five, he had to compete in the same class as Kirkland Black Friar, who had not been beaten in London for Mr. Webb. The black horse snorted menacingly at him from the next position not only in the class but in the senior stallions' cup and the championship line-up as well. Webb's more peaceful and manageable exhibit, the four-year-old Etchingham Solace, became champion mare in place of Kerry Clanish Maid, but perhaps it is the mare who took advantage of the latter's absence to win the senior big mares' class that deserves a special mention. This was E. J. Holland's Thurvaston Rosebud, who was also reserve for the senior cup. (The reserve champion was Marden Abbess, the three-year-old junior cup winner – a typical home-bred quality product of Sir Bernard Greenwell's.) Rosebud, now five, was making her first and only visit to the metropolis. She was a real working mare for Jos. Holland. "She ploughed the fields and sowed the wheat", he recalled many years later, "and then I took her to London and won with her". (This remarkable man, fatherless at the age of two in 1891, completed sixty years of farming and breeding horses on his own account in 1971, when he still had twenty Shires, and in 1975 was still successfully exhibiting.) It was the Joscelyn Hollands of the Shire world who, as much as the Rothschilds or the Gomer Berrys, made the breed what it was and, much more than they, kept ever the ploughing, and the "lurry", in mind.

Carting operations in the towns and from the docks, at any rate in Liverpool, owed hundreds of its best workers to G. G. Marsh and his son Baker. And so it was a good advertisement for the breed in general that this year their seven-year-old Wonder won them the gelding championship for the third time in a period of eleven years. Young & Company's brewery won the commercial classes' gold medal championship, for the fourth year in succession

– in 1931 with Bower King John, aged seven; in 1932, with Wandle Jonathan, seven, and in the last two years with both of them together, as they won the pairs class and were put above the singles for the championship.

There had been a few surprise champions at London over the years, but 1935 produced the biggest sensation of all. J. G. McDougall, a new member of the Shire Society, bought in 1934 a couple of filly foals by Raans Record from Pendley. One he called Margaret of Chippinghurst and the other Marina of Chippinghurst. He also bought one by Radium 5th from Allan Holm at Tilton and called her Milady of Chippinghurst. He entered them all for the London Show. Margaret won the yearling filly class, Milady was fifth and Marina, sixth. Mr. McDougall therefore won first prize with one of the first – and last – three Shires to step into the London ring in his name. This show was the only one that has ever been held in January and therefore particularly handicapped the yearlings, who in real age were only about eight or nine months old. In spite of this, Margaret was selected as winner of the junior cup in preference to G. R. C. Foster's own-bred Bower June Rose (by Bower Winalot) the two-year-old winner, and Tilton Lady in White (by Radium 5th) who won the three-year-old class for her breeder, Allan Holm. Then, she beat all the senior winners (which included the 1934 champion Etchingham Solace) to become the first and only yearling supreme champion mare in London.

Tom Fowler of Tring, one of the judges, said "Don't show her again this year, and then she can't be beat." So they didn't. And they couldn't – at least in the name of McDougall for, by the time the summer show season opened, he was dead. Margaret is recorded as "bred by Sir Gomer Berry, exhibited by J. G. McDougall", but it would be more correct to state that she was created by the genius of Harry Bishop, and selected by the unerring eye of Tom Freshney, McDougall's manager. Though bought as a foal, she had been longer with Harry than Tom. So both can be said to have prepared her for her astonishing win.

These two men were of course supported and encouraged by the wealth of a newspaper proprietor and a flour miller. But the new champion stallion was a real farmer's horse. His dam's origin can be traced back to 1899, when James Guilford of Normanton House, Thurlaston in Leicestershire bred a filly he called *Brisk* out of a mare whose generations stretched back heaven knows how far in the district. From her in 1905 he bred *Bonny*. Her foal in 1910, with three crosses of registered blood, was eligible for the Stud-book. It was H. R. Guilford who entered her in the book as 71821 Normanton Brisk, and she bred him a succession of good foals over the years on his Muswell Leys farm, Lutterworth. One of her last was Muswell Leys Royal Carnation, in 1923. Carnation had a colt foal in 1931, and he was shown at the Leicestershire show by Harold Guilford. He was standing second when Morris Belcher's son John, who had been judging Shropshire sheep, spotted him. Disagreeing with the judges' verdict, as any man is entitled to do, he got into quick communication with his father-in-law, W. T. Hayr, who was Shire steward. The result was that, before the colt left the ring, he had changed hands for £50. The Leicestershire show was in June, so Hayr bought the dam too, and put her in one of his best pastures: one of *his* best was just about the richest in England, and it killed her. So the foal was brought up on the bottle, but this did not prevent him winning the Foal Challenge Cup at Ashbourne. (This had been competed for since 1900, when Victor Cavendish, later the 9th Duke of Devonshire, won it: but no one had yet won it twice. Hayr had done so in 1908 and Belcher in 1922. On winning it again in 1931, Hayr owned it outright. On his death in 1939 it came to his daughter and so has remained ever since in the Belcher family. The thirty-one different names upon it represent most of the greatest men in thirty-two years of Shire history.) Registered next year by Mr. Hayr as Harboro' Goldfinder, the colt first appeared in London in 1934, and won the junior cup. Now, a year later, shown by Morris Belcher, he was champion of all, and Harold Guilford was entitled to the first of three breeder's gold medals. (As if clairvoyant of what was to happen, he had in 1932 – after breeding fifteen pedigree Shires from his one or two mares in eighteen years – joined the Society at last.) Goldfinder was by that outstanding sire of the 'thirties, Kirkland Mimic.

The redoubtable Kirkland Black Friar was not there to challenge for the supremacy again, because he had been found dead in his box a few days before the show. There were dark suspicions all round, and lighter hearts in some quarters, but after a thorough investigation the Royal Veterinary College experts reported the cause of death as acute auto-intoxication. A few days earlier another of Mr. Webb's Shires, Black Bertha, a big ten-year-old who had won three third prizes in London, had died of similar symptoms but the affair was attributed to a gruesome prank of coincidence.

A final remarkable thing about the 1935 show was the increase in attendance. It may have been due to the January date. Or it may have symbolised that in 1935 the farmers at last felt themselves to be not quite the depressed class that they had been. A night or two at say, the Norfolk Hotel (9s. 6d., or best rooms 12s.: 18s. to 20s. if the missus wanted to come too) was more of a possibility than it had been for years. But the slight average improvement in the farmers' lot did not help everyone. Kirkland Mimic's Fen breeders failed this very year and Chapel Hill Farm at Whaplode Drove was taken over by George Ivatt.

In 1936 Harboro' Goldfinder was again champion, and Raans Clansman (bred by William Clark & Son at Amersham and owned by the Forshaws) was still just one place behind him, as he was in each of the three years they had been shown – in 1934 as reserve junior champion and now for two years as reserve champion: being the same age, Clansman had also taken second prize in the class each time. Old House Conquering Mimic, another son of Kirkland Mimic, was junior champion. Margaret of Chippinghurst, shown by Tom Freshney for McDougall's executors, duly won the two-year-old filly class, and the junior cup. But nothing could ever be taken for granted when Sir Bernard Greenwell was represented. Almost incredibly, a four-year-old called Marden

Blanche, home-bred, rose from eighth place in 1935 (her first appearance in London) not only to the top of the class but to win the senior cup and then to beat Margaret for the championship as well.

This was the last Show for three famous Shire studs. King Edward VIII, as has already been mentioned, won fourth prize with Appleton Binder before selling up. Pendley with four entries won three third prizes, including Raans Record and his son Raans Record Wave, aged four, but in September Sir Gomer also sold up. Harry Bishop, that animal genius whose skill was not confined to Shires (he once sold a wire-haired terrier to the U.S.A. for £1,000), then took over the farm on which Pendley had always bred pigs – and there he bred pigs. G. R. C. Foster entered two sons and six daughters of Bower Winalot and won a first, second, two fourths, a seventh and Reserve, and also showed two other mares (second and fifth), but his death nine weeks later brought his stud to an end. He was, as his enthusiasm deserved to make him, the only man who had ever had a stallion and mare which each won the championship three years in succession. He had also been blessed in having an exceptional head man in William (or "Jack") Johnson. Jack had learned his trade, as so many first-rate men had done, on the Forshaw staff, but was possessed in addition with a unique flair for showing horses. Some people believed that, if given time, he could make a donkey look like a Shire.

Of all the geldings which ever appeared in London, probably this year's champion (making his sixth appearance) was, and deserves to remain, the best-known, both for his beauty and the riotous temperament which enforced the early removal of his masculinity and which took long to desert him even after that. His name was Pendley Warrant, but his association with the place whose name he took (though not to begin with, for he was formerly called Royal Warrant) was brief and eventful. He cannot be ignored here, as he never could be ignored in his lifetime, but his story must wait for the Shire biography of Charles Franklin, the Bedford coal merchant. It was he who had bought the 1931 champion Pendley Marceline at the same time in 1932.

Among the commercial horses, the class restricted to rural or borough councils was deleted this year. (In 1935 only Liverpool Corporation, which had won first prize the last four years, had entered, Finsbury, Stepney, Bermondsey and the others having dropped out.) But the class for teams of four was revived after a three year interval. The other open and restricted classes flourished, with a new rule brought in for geldings "certified as regularly worked in any city or town for three or more years". This was the result of an unfortunate and thoughtless piece of judging the year before, when a prize had been given to a five-year-old which, as Liverpool Corporation (in the person of T. Eaton Jones) pointed out, had had no business to have been working in a town for three years. So the words "seven years old and upward" were added.

Another and more pleasing fact to which Mr. Eaton Jones drew attention, this time in his capacity as Chief Veterinary Inspector, was that of all those horses entered in the breeding classes which were old enough to be subject to veterinary examination (142) only one had been rejected, a three-year-old colt for whistling. This, he said, "undoubtedly proves that the Shire breed of horses is the soundest in the world". Old Professor Pritchard, that scourge of the early shows, would have been pleased.

On the suggestion of the Gloucestershire & District Agricultural Valuers' Association, a judging competition for members of Young Farmers' Clubs (a movement which had begun in 1921) and for sons of members was first held this year, in imitation of the stock judging contest first begun at the 1930 Royal Show. Forty competitors under twenty-five had a go on the Thursday morning at judging five mixed mares and fillies and were marked for correct placing (140 points), publicly explaining their decisions in not more than four minutes (80 points) and their general style of examination (20 points). The ringside was packed with spectators, and it is difficult to imagine a more terrifying ordeal. The winner was W. J. Cumber junior with 229 marks, beating the runner-up easily. This was presumably a proof of the value of pedigree. In one other respect, the show saw the revival of a very old idea, never before applied to London. There was a special class to select a stallion to travel the Isle of Man for the government in the 1937 season at a premium of £200. Hundreds or thousands of hiring agreements must have been privately entered upon at the London Show over the years, but never before had it been turned into a hiring competition.

Perhaps the most conclusive evidence of the strong position that heavy-horse breeding had now regained was that horses were not allowed to leave the hall, as they had been permitted to do during the past few years of depression and rigid economy, until the end of the third day. In spite of this, the entries were more than for some years. The human congestion in the hall, also, took many a mind back to the old times. Sir Edward Mann, the retiring president, said "It is many a long day since I have seen such crowds and such enthusiasm. It is a fitting climax to a much more prosperous year". The President-Elect, Christopher Barker, added that, during the past year or two, Shire foals had paid the rent of many small farms in his county of Yorkshire.

In 1937, 'flu and colds caused some absenteeism among horses and men, since the weather was too mild for health. As if fate knew there were only three more chances in which to prove that anything could happen at a London Show, a coal-mare's unexpected son became champion stallion. Enoch Bostock, man of few words and simple-living, who farmed at Gibbett Hill, where Warwick University now stands, received his King George V cup from the Earl of Feversham, a distant cousin of the late revered A. C. Duncombe, after lunching – it was his normal habit, and why should he change now? – on a pork pie and a glass of beer. And William Newhouse renewed his vow that he would never sell an apparently barren mare again without a more careful check.

What had happened requires some explanation. We remember Newhouse as the breeder of Pendley Marceline, whose dam Ancliffe Winnie had the dual

5. Hull Brewery geldings at Egton Show, with Bill Edwards, horse-box driver *(above)*, and Pat Flood *(below)*, formerly of Thwaites'. After Major R. W. Gleadow retired as Chairman and Managing Director in 1974, the horses were given up. Pat joined Messrs. Cammidge and Robson, Flower Hill Farm, North Newbald. Baron and Bob you will see again.

6. The Courage show team, driven by Jim Lockwood, seen at Maidenhead Thicket outside the Shire Horse Inn – formerly the Coach and Horses, a well-known inn by the London to Bristol road. It was re-named when the adjacent Courage Shire Horse Centre was built, and opened to the public in 1975. In the first year, over 80,000 visitors came to see the horses, which are in the charge of foreman Peter Riseborough. The timber-built stables, coach house, foaling box (there is an intention to breed Shires in the future), farrier's shop and display and harness room would have been considered a mad extravaganza ten years earlier: now it is already an accepted part of the pattern of Shire revival. Courage's Brewery in former days used Clydesdales, but some of the breweries which were incorporated in recent years into the present firm (such as the Bristol Brewery, Georges and Company Limited) had always been "Shire people".

task of producing foals and of competing against all other Shires in north Lancashire. She particularly had to beat the mares of another man of Slyne, John Hoggarth of Manor Farm. John was related to William and so the battle, being a family one, was a serious matter. Poor Winnie had died in 1932 of a twisted gut. So William went off to the Peterborough sales and bought Harcourt Belle, a five-year-old bred in Derbyshire.

Her main job was to prevent John Hoggarth from overwhelming William, particularly with Cote Stones Betty, a mare which inherited not only the exact markings of her sire Harboro' Nulli Secundus but also his temperament. She was impossible to break to harness and never did a day's work in her life. But she was a consistent winner at north country shows. It was absolutely essential that William Newhouse should have something to beat her with, and Harcourt Belle ought to be able to do it. Next year, before the show season, William was inspired to send her to Enoch Bostock's Kirkland Mimic. But as for winning at shows, she rubbed off most of her feather and was a non-starter, after all, to beat Cote Stones Betty. So William, doubting if she was in foal anyway, sold her to W. A. Tipping, the Birmingham coal merchant. However, she had conceived after all. Fortunately Mr. Tipping was a member of the Shire Society, and did not immediately get rid of her, as most town-users would have done. So the foal was born in a Birmingham coal-yard. At least, that is the saying: less dramatically, it may be that he first saw the light of day at Holly Bank, Kings Heath. Enoch Bostock the ungarrulous, owner of the sire, heard about him, came to Birmingham, bought him, had a glass of beer and perhaps a pork pie, took him back to Gibbet Hill, and named him Old House Conquering Mimic. And so it was that the Ancliffe stud of William Newhouse did not give its name either to Pendley Marceline or to Old House Conquering Mimic. The only Shire ever "bred" by W. A. Tipping in over thirty years' membership of the Society was supreme champion of the breed. His dam, continuing to rub the feather off her legs, pulled coal round the Birmingham streets and never again saw another stallion as long as she lived.

Though he had to stand down in the final test in this year of 1937 in favour of young Old House Conquering Mimic, Harboro' Goldfinder won the senior cup and was reserve to him as champion. Even so, he had some difficulty against the reserve for the junior cup, the yearling Wootton Mimic bred and shown by J. T. Green of Fold Farm, Wootton, near Ashbourne – yet another son of Kirkland Mimic. The latter, not surprisingly, won the produce group once again with Old House Conquering Mimic, Wootton Mimic and (since Harboro' Goldfinder was too old, at six) Culcliffe Mimic, fourth in the two-year-olds. For the fourth successive year a Raans-bred horse stood one place below Goldfinder, only this time it was not Raans Clansman but Raans Record, who was second in the senior big class and reserve for the senior cup for "Reinhold & Freshney", as Tom Freshney's enterprise, originally started for the late J. G. McDougall, had become. His late Majesty's Appleton Binder stood third, for the Forshaws. There was a division of opinion about him, for he stood second to begin with. The third judge, as umpire, did not like his abundant hair, and moved him down.

The Forshaws won the short-leggers' class with The Dean, bred by Stanley Dean at Heaton, near Bolton, for the fourth year in succession, and this weighty but active character was now nine-years-old. (The class during the past ten years had still failed to win any of the championship placings, in spite of the extra inch allowed it from 1929, and the last to be honoured outside its confines was therefore still Dunsmore Bounding Willow, in 1894. The Forshaws, those believers in great weight in the smallest circumference had produced the winner of the class no less than twenty-nine times in forty-nine years. This outstanding record is perhaps one of the most noteworthy achievements in the history of Shire horse shows.)

Sir Bernard Greenwell produced another home-bred filly to take the supreme female championship. This was the grey Marden Daphne, only three. Like Marden Blanche the year before, her triumph was unarguable, but nevertheless unexpected and sudden, because she had been only Highly Commended (eleventh) as a yearling and fifth the year before as a two-year-old. This was another Greenwell record, for no one else had ever won successive championships with two different mares, both home-bred. The achievement was made even more remarkable by the fact that the two were comparatively unrelated.

Pendley Warrant won the gelding championship again, this time for his new owner, Percy Surridge. Later in the year, after an unbeaten show season, including appearances at the Suffolk, Sussex and Peterborough shows, he was handed over to farmer Percy's town brother and partner to join the 185 Shire geldings – all pure-bred, and not one less than 17-hands, as an absolute minimum – working in the name of F. W. Surridge, and available for dust-hauling for the Lambeth or Finsbury Borough Councils or on general cartage work. The Surridge method of working was perfection, and ought to have its memorial in due course. Now that Pendley Warrant was nine, it was time that he settled down at last, and so after this he was put on more regular work than the show-circuit had permitted.

The Young Farmers' competition was repeated, with the maximum age reduced to twenty-one. The Council opened the competition to girls. No budding Gwen Webb-Peploe emerged yet, though Mary Lawton from Alfred Clark's (taught by her father Jim, the head-man) had already shown at county shows that no one is unique. J. W. Bucknell won and, like John Cumber, he came from Berkshire. There was also a class for teams of three this year, and the Berkshire County Council team won that, too, with the Somerset federation second and Cheltenham third. This time they had to judge two rings, of four mares and four geldings. The rules about speaking distinctly so that judges and spectators could all hear, and not reading verbatim from their notes, were hard on these young people. If their elders always had to explain their work lucidly to an audience afterwards, there would have been a severe shortage of judges at the 150 shows where pedigree Shire classes were held.

In 1938, there was no 18-hands Old House Conquering Mimic. He had been found ill in his field the previous autumn and never recovered. This was almost as severe a loss to other breeders as it was to Enoch Bostock himself. Mimic had stood second in a show-ring only once – at Ashbourne. Otherwise, he was never beaten in his class. More importantly, his first and only few foals suggested he might have become a great stock horse like his sire. With him no longer among the living, Harboro' Goldfinder had little difficulty in regaining the stallion gold cup for the third time – the second in eight years to be won outright by Morris Belcher. (Oddly, the winner of the yearling class was Harboro' Goldfound, Peterborough foal champion the previous autumn, for Mr. Hayr, by Goldfinder; and second was Old House Conquering Mimic II for Bostock – inevitably by Kirkland Mimic.)

Raans Record, now nine, and two years older than Goldfinder, was again second in the big five-plus class and reserve for the senior cup. This completed a wry record for the Raans horses, for it was the fifth successive year that a stallion bred by William Clark & Son had been just one place down from the junior or senior cup, and on two occasions for the championship – without even winning his class! Tom Freshney, fortunate in his head man (Fred Croft, late of Cumber's and Pendley) was also in a unique position this year in owning three generations of stallions all let to leading societies – Raans Record (Winslow & District S.H.S. for the second successive season), his son Raans Record Wave (aged six, Welshpool Society) and the latter's son Raans Wild Wave (three-years-old, and about to do his first season, for the Welbeck Society). All three were bred by William Clark. Perhaps the grand-sire's greatest achievement was that he was the only horse to have won the challenge cup outright for being the sire of the winning group of foals at Peterborough two years in succession – and this, by the age of five years. He had been six when his yearling daughter won the London championship. And he was only a two-year-old colt when mated with Permanent Wave, as was his son when covering Raans Wild Rose. (The grand-parents of sire, son and grand-son were each descended in the direct male line in the proportion of three to one from Harold and William the Conqueror, respectively the chief and second chief foundation sires of the breed.)

Since the previous show, Morris Belcher had bought Wootton Mimic, who now won his class again, together with the junior cup and, in addition, was reserve champion stallion, so making his owner one of the few who have shown the top two stallions at a London show. Belcher, about to take over the Presidency, also won the four-year-old class. Culcliffe Mimic rose from fourth place in 1937 to top for E. W. Webb and was also reserve for the junior cup.

The judges ought to be mentioned this year, because it was apparent that – even if any two of them inevitably disagreed on points of detail and had to call in the third several times as umpire – they were unanimous and consistent in preferring animals with comparatively little feather. Whenever a horse appeared to be placed lower in the line than might have been expected, a glance at the legs provided the reason. Thomas Forshaw, James Gould (junior) of Lymm and John Vaughan of Welshpool clearly set the seal on the "new Shire" this year. In the case particularly of Forshaw, this was significant because, as ever, he was the apostle of weight and power and for ten years or more had argued that it was possible to retain this while at the same time reducing the hair, without recourse to negotiations with the Clydesdale breeders. Incidentally, his ineligibility to exhibit allowed someone else – Cumber, with Theale Camrose – to win the "short-legs" class for the first time in ten years. And Camrose, who started down the line and was moved up several times, appeared to do so chiefly on the strength of his "modern" clean limbs.

Among the mares, Marden Daphne, who won her class, had to give way for the championship to the previous year's runner up, Leek Beauty. The junior cup was won by William Milner of Callaughton with his Wenlock Rosebud, a really hefty three-year-old with minimum hair. Milner was as uncompromising in his views as the Forshaws, and here was a mare to exhibit their idea of "the modern Shire" – but Vaughan and Gould were the judges for the class and had no need to call upon their colleague to place her.

The grant from the Racecourse Betting Control Board enabled a greatly improved prize-list this year, and an extra class for geldings. The cup was won by Mann, Crossman & Paulin with their winner of the four-year-old class, Lincoln. (He was by Pave Lane Friar, a horse whose name and place of origin take the mind to one of the earliest known names in Shire breeding – Mr. Handley of Pave Lane, Salop, in the later years of the eighteenth century.) Amongst the commercial horses, the off-side leader of Mann, Crossman & Paulin's second-prize team of four (Young's were first this year) was none other than the fifteen-year-old Norman, attending his twelfth consecutive London Show. He had been champion gelding in 1932 at the age of eight, and again the following year. After that he had appeared in the commercial classes, in 1934–1936 winning first prize in the single-horse regular-worker without-harness-or-vehicle class and now in the last two years as one of the brewery team.

A pair of Field-Marshals, Lord Birdwood and Lord Milne, judged "cleanest and best appointed horses and gears" in the four commercial-horse classes and gave first place to Liverpool Corporation's matched pair of eight-year-old bay geldings, Jumbo and Jubilee. By a coincidence, a "Mimic Field Marshal" was at this time giving the Editing Committee a certain amount of trouble. He was a grey colt foaled in Pembrokeshire in 1935, who with his dam Queen (foaled in 1921) and grand-dam Black Jewel (1916) had been submitted the year before for the stud-book. Black Jewel was all right but it had been alleged that her daughter was not by Castlecenlas Chief (fifteen-years-old at the material time and a typical "old 'un" such as abounded in West Wales) but by a son of his which went under the name of *Star Chief* and was not only unregistered but in fact ineligible. However, the doubts were eventually all resolved and the allegations turned out to be a little bit of malice, and so Queen and her son were accepted a couple of months after the show. Mimic Field Marshal was as genuine as Lords Birdwood and Milne, and his name derived only from the fact that he was by Gardden Mimic, himself a son – it is not difficult to guess – of that stallion of innumerable issue, Kirkland Mimic.

A girl competitor, Miss J. S. Holland[6] with a score of 310 out of 360 in the Y.F.C. competition was only one point behind Charles Bucknell, who kept the gold medal in the family and helped Berkshire to win the team event once again. The biggest crowd for many a year attended this show and a good proportion of them enjoyed judging the judges' judgment of the efforts of these Shire judges of the future.

A special surprise was provided in 1939 by a famous old horse. When G. R. C. Foster died in 1936, Bower Winalot was officially seven-years-old, and actually only a few weeks less. He was not only the triple London champion of 1932–1934, but had won the last Peterborough Produce Stakes with a filly foal (bred by Foster himself, who thus won the Foster cup) and was sire of the winning group (all filly foals). In addition, he was already second only to Kirkland Mimic (twenty-one) in the number of his progeny (nineteen) which had won prizes at gold medal shows throughout the country in 1935. After Foster's death, he stood at a farm in the Newmarket area for a fairly modest 7 guineas (tenant farmers only 5 guineas) and 5s. the groom. The Forshaw brothers had a mind to buy him. But it was not to be so. The terms of his sale as a foal had included an agreement that his breeder was to have the first option if ever he were re-sold. So now he went back to James Runciman and in 1937 stood at Grange Farm, Girton, for 6 guineas to all comers. If he had created no sensation at the beginning of his show career (simply because he won prizes from the start), he compensated by doing so at the age of ten, for now he returned to London after a five years' absence and won his class, the senior cup and, for the fourth time, the championship – the first horse ever to do such a thing as this.

By now, old Kirkland Mimic was dead. In his last season, fourteen years of age, he had stood at Bostock's Tocil Farm at 8 guineas, over 18-hands high and still implanting, as ever, with his marvellous prepotency his great qualities, even to that rich brown coat and white socks, on nearly all his progeny. So the world lay at Bower Winalot's feet. But it was all rather odd, really. That he was a remarkable horse, cannot be denied. But for the future of the breed – certainly as the judges of 1938 had seen it – the resurrection of this old champion was not the most progressive step. His hair was more abundant than many were looking to find. Nor was his bone so flat and hard as would certainly have been required in a new younger champion. But there it was. And no one could say that the championship was won by the artistry of "Jack" Johnson, for that creator of feet had gone into Essex on Foster's death to manage a Percheron stud. And who are we, now, to wonder why the judges did not look to new blood? A horse of such magnificence and power who moved his enormous weight with such agility and accuracy after many seasons at show and stud probably deserved any reward that came his way. Only Stroxton Tom, who was eleven in 1903, had been an older male champion than he, and only Rickford Coming King in 1918 had been as old. Both were Forshaw horses. He was certainly a tribute to his veterinary owner who was the only man to breed a champion and then buy him back, though many a poor tenant farmer had often longed for enough money to be able to re-purchase a wonderful stallion that he had bred but could not keep.

Perhaps the oddest thing about Bower Winalot was his sire, Lucky Dog, bred in 1922 by Alfred Luckin in Sussex and owned by the King. His successes, both as a show horse and stock getter, do not take long to tell. He won the second prize as a yearling and fifth prize at two years for the King, in London. A daughter of his, Briony, won a London fourth prize as a yearling for His Majesty and was reserve (eighth) next year. There was also another daughter called Woburn Romance foaled in 1928. She was bred by Edward Betts and at three years of age had a colt foal which rose to the dizzy heights, after being castrated, of winning a second prize at the age of four in London and of being reserve (sixth) two years later for the Duke of Bedford. And there was Bower Winalot – a full brother, one year younger, to Woburn Romance: but his breeder ("foaling breeder") was Runciman because Betts had died during the year. And that is all that Lucky Dog, or his progeny, or his daughter's progeny, ever achieved. In using him a second time at the age of six, old Edward Betts was breeding by pedigree and not by past performance. It is a pity that this celebrated man, tenant of Sandringham, a Shire member for the past thirty years, who bore a name well known long before that in the breeding both of English Cart-horses and Suffolks, and who could not be forgotten if only for his breeding of Babingley Nulli Secundus in 1908, could not guess what he was doing at the very last. But his royal landlord did at least live long enough to see the first three triumphs of what his blue blooded but feeble Lucky Dog had got in a rare moment of inspiration one spring day in 1928.

Kirkland Mimic's, and Belcher's, Wootton Mimic won the junior cup again, but whereas he had very properly stood reserve to the older Kirkland Mimic – Belcher horse for the championship in 1938, it was a little hard on them all, not to mention John Green his breeder, that he had to bow before old Bower Winalot for the supreme championship this year. Yet he was young, and there was always another year. But, unfortunately, not another show.

Batty Grace Darling travelled from Yorkshire to become champion mare – the first to do so since 1897 and only the second in the history of the show: but even she had been bred in Lancashire. The junior cup-winner, and reserve champion, was a daughter of Bower Winalot.

The Young Farmers of Collingham, near Newark, had an overwhelming win in the judging competition, as was right and proper. What business had

Somerset to be even second, though they did have a Golledge and a Withers in their team? Two well-known faces were, alas, missing. There was no Edmund Beck, whose place was taken by Harry Hobson, of the firm that had bought the Peterborough Repository. But he had precisely four animals to sell – two geldings, a filly and a colt, which made a total of £240. 9s. od. For ten years, the auction had out-lived its usefulness, and indeed its popularity had been waning fast even in the 'twenties, when 110 horses sold in 1920 had dropped to twenty-six in 1929. Peterborough repository had become the mecca of those who wanted to buy, and it no longer made sense to bring a stallion or mare to the London Show simply in order to sell it. A few top horses there did change hands, it is true, but as the result of private deals. The London auction was continued only as a service for anyone who cared to make use of it, and several times during the past decade the Council had been on the point of discontinuing it. Mr. Hobson's real business in Shires was done in the country.

There was no G. H. Parsons, either, to turn the air blue with his frustration when the horses would not stand as he wished for their photographs. He had decided the time had come when he must cease to travel from Alsager for the occasion. His talent for animal photography amounted almost to genius, which perhaps excused his excitability about it: but since he had an almost equal talent for touching up pictures that he did not approve, it was really a mystery why he caused such agony in the first place. A missing leg could always be painted in and, if so, could be depended upon to look better than the other three. In true Shire style, he had paid his annual subscription to the Society since 1917, when he had promptly joined on his appointment as official photographer on the death of Babbage. Nor had he always been content with the camera alone. Before the war he had bought and registered a couple of mares.

There had been a hope that the King would come to the show, but it coincided with his tour of the northern counties, so there was no opportunity to remind him that a real cart-horse looked different from a Suffolk. But Sir Reginald Dorman-Smith, who had become Minister of Agriculture only the previous month, was there – and, glory be! he was a real farmers' man, too. Had he not been President of the N.F.U. in 1936–1937? And the new Duke of Devonshire, Under-Secretary for the Dominions, was present, as well. (His yearling Chatsworth Royal Match won fourth prize: Thomas James was third in the big stallions class: and Batty Naomi was third in the three-year-olds. His Grace's father "the Old Dook" would have been moderately pleased.) But who were these he had brought with him? It was the Emir Feisal of Saudi Arabia, the Emir Khalid and Sheik Hafiz Wahba. This was a ridiculous thing to happen at a Shire Show, but at least they were clothed as a proper Sheik or Emir should be. Everything new in history has been done before, and some people remembered the time when the Maharajah of Bwnonuggur had arrived at the London Cart Horse Parade (it was 1893) with a fine head-dress, black coat and shabby brown trousers with stripes – a sorry contrast to the Prince and Princess of Wales, the Princesses Victoria and Maud, the Duke of York and

Princess May, the Duke and Duchess of Teck, Mr. Chandos-Pole-Gell, the new baronet and Lady Gilbey, Baroness and Mr. Burdett-Coutts and Superintendent Beard of the Metropolitan Police. Now, in 1939, the second Sir Walter, attending his 58th Shire Show, noted the eastern potentates' style of dress with approval. Tom Forshaw was attending his 60th Shire Show. He had been at the first one as a boy of fourteen and never missed one since. He noted that the Shire of 1939 was, in general, an animal to be proud of. As the family's advertisements had regularly stated for a couple of generations, "Breed the best, if you breed at all. Size – weight – soundness."

12. THE END OF AN ERA

The last two years of this period deprived the Shire ranks of some of their best leaders. Apart from Edmund Beck, a notable trio died in 1938. First, "The Dook" himself. As Victor Cavendish, he had joined in 1893, first served on the Council in 1897 and was President in 1901. After succeeding to Chatsworth, he was President twice more. This unique distinction alone serves to inform us of his love of Shires, and their breeders' respect and affection for him. Robert Whitehead of Hargate Hall, near Buxton joined in 1899 and was President in 1916. His last entry in the Stud-book was Peak Christabel foaled in 1935, by Peak Vandal out of Peak Christina. Lord Harlech began in 1914 with two fillies bred by the Duke of Sutherland at Lilleshall in 1913, and named them Brogyntyn Aconite and Brogyntyn Aster, and then followed next year with Brogyntyn Begonia, Bergamot and Bramble. He was the 1925 President. Of these three, only the Duke had a Shire-supporting successor, but it was to Brogyntyn Farm that John Suckley moved at the end of the next war and became one of the staunchest modern Shire supporters.

Three more outstanding men were removed in 1939. Sir Bernard Greenwell had continued where his father left off in 1920, and was President in 1924. His vast knowledge of financial affairs had been of great benefit to the Council during difficult years, but his loss was really lamented entirely for personal reasons. The Marden stud continued under his son Sir Peter. The Moulton Shires had been managed by Alfred Clark junior for some years before the death this year of his father, who since 1880 had judged London more often and served on the Council more often than any other man. He was not only the first tenant-farmer President but had been responsible for ten volumes of the Stud-book. The death of W. T. Hayr was a reminder of the disgraceful agricultural policy of successive governments between the wars. There was no justice when a man of his shrewd judgement and abilities, occupying some of the richest pastures in all England, had no means of escape from the general disasters of these years. And the very geniality and likeability of such men as he perhaps made even sharper the suspicion with which the farming community looked upon Governments for many years to come. The Harboro' prefix would resound no more, but his daughter had married Morris Belcher's son, an excellent Shire alliance.

Before the 1939 Annual General Meeting, an extraordinary general meeting was called, in order to change the name of the Society again. But, in contrast to 1878 and 1884, this was a mere formality. There was no suggestion that the title should revert to the "English Cart Horse Society". Nor was it proposed, as any canny forecaster might justifiably have expected ten years earlier, that some such name as "British Cart Horse Society" should symbolise the amalgamation of Shire and Clydesdale. It was simply that by calling themselves, in publications and correspondence, "The Shire Horse Society", instead of using their full legal title, members were breaking the law as laid down in the Companies Act 1929. (At the mention of this, there were some who thought they saw the ghost of old Thomas Brown sitting on that vacant chair, ready to do verbal battle with John Coleman, Frederic Street and Edward Coke, and to quote from the Companies Act 1862.) The whole thing took only a couple of minutes. Henceforward, The Shire Horse Society of the United Kingdom of Great Britain and Ireland was to be short-docked, and would be simply, The Shire Horse Society.

At the Annual General Meeting immediately following, it was Sir Walter who moved the vote of thanks to the retiring President. Mr. Belcher, he said, was a pillar of the Shire industry, and the well-being of the breed was in large measure due to him. Thomas Forshaw, seconding, spoke also of Sir Walter, whose whole life had been spent in hard work on behalf of the horse generally and of the Shire in particular. Morris Belcher said that, with William Cumber as the new President, and Colonel Nicholson to follow, the Society would be in excellent hands. Cumber was confident he would have everyone's continued full support during his year of office. He needed this support more than he realised, for it was to be seven years, not one, before he could hand over responsibility.

CHAPTER XIV

1939–1947

The Horse-world Turned Upside Down

1. MECHANISING FOR VICTORY

THE two great patriotic arguments of the 'twenties and 'thirties in favour of using draught-horses were killed stone dead by the war. The fact that horses provided employment for British workmen and a market for British farm produce suddenly ceased to be praiseworthy. Instead, it made them unthrifty and wasteful. Similarly, the individual's own private arguments for not investing in motor power, whether on the town streets or on the farm, were invalidated. The Government, which had ignored the farmer so long, was now willing to help him overcome the problem either of lack of capital or of getting a reasonable return upon it. The urban horse-user now faced worries and difficulties over the stabling of animals in towns liable to be subjected to bombing. And the increasing cost and scarcity of labour affected town and country alike.

In 1936, the Government had begun seriously to make some plans for feeding the population in the event of a war. These had to be based on a complicated set of calculations, taking into consideration the relative merits of growing food for direct human consumption as against crops for conversion into food *via* meat and milk; an anticipation of what sort of things could be bought overseas and of what would be hard to obtain; an estimate of possible shipping losses; the relative bulk of different commodities; manpower difficulties; and the possible progress and duration of a war. After these matters had been weighed, it was estimated that, on the outbreak of hostilities, 1,300,000 acres of permanent grassland would have to be ploughed. But between 1936 and 1939, a further 600,000 acres slipped back from arable to grass, and so when the time came to begin the programme, it had to be considerably increased. The target was in fact fixed at 2,010,000 extra acres, almost 10% of all grassland. The task was made infinitely more difficult by the fact that, in comparison with 1914, the land was in less good heart, buildings were more dilapidated and the farmers poorer and less resilient. In some districts there were men whose fathers had ploughed in their day but who themselves possessed neither the machinery nor even the knowledge and experience of growing cereals.

What was the power available for these cultivations? What were the relative numbers of living and mechanical horses? It is perhaps somewhat ungracious to dispute with the official agricultural historian of the Second World War, Mr. Keith A. H. Murray, from whose researches the facts and the figures in these paragraphs are gratefully derived. However, one of his statements has unfortunately proved liable to mis-interpretation. "Between 1931 and 1937", wrote Mr. Murray,[1] "the tractor surpassed the horse as a source of power, and by 1939 accounted for almost two-thirds of the total draught power used on farms". This remark has already been quoted uncritically by another eminent writer, in such a way as to be misleading, and so there is some danger that a general misconception may arise about the position at the outbreak of the war. Mr. Murray's figures do not mean that in 1939 there were more tractors than horses, or even that tractors were doing more of the farm work. They were doing much less. Actually, there were 649,000 farm work-horses and 56,200 tractors. The latter represented a total of 1,075,000 h.p.: that is, each was on average a machine of 19.1 h.p. But it is quite certain that no farmer in England was able to dispense with 19.1 horses if he bought a tractor. If, in practice, a tractor replaced two horses, the ratio in 1939 was 112.4 thousand mechanical horses to 649 thousand real ones. If a tractor replaced four horses (and it could not do this everywhere), there was an equivalent of 224.8 mechanical horses for every 649 living ones.

It was clear that the work of ploughing up and cultivating over 2,000,000 additional acres, should war break out, would have to be done by mechanical power. Accordingly, in April 1939, the Minister of Agriculture, Sir Reginald Dorman-Smith, was given authority to buy and store 3,000 to 5,000 tractors, with implements, at a cost of £1,250,000 to £2,250,000. He was also allowed to offer a subsidy of £2 for every acre of permanent grass ploughed up between 3rd May and 30th September. The first few months of war itself produced confusion in the manpower situation. 42,000 regular skilled men and another 8,000 casual workers left the land to join the forces or for better paid war work, just at a time when it was estimated that over 80,000 extra ones were really needed. But the Ministry of Labour coped with the situation by persuasion and the raising of farm wages and, later, by compulsion. In addition, the Women's Land Army soon reached a membership of 10,000. In May 1940 Sir Reginald was made Governor of Burma and R. S. Hudson (a Percheron man!) became Minister of Agriculture. The Ford Motor Company, which had been originally directed to produce 100 tractors a day, was now switched partially to armaments. The Ministry began to buy binders and threshers for allocation, like their tractors, to the War Agricultural Executive Committees.

By the middle of 1944, the "War Ags" alone operated 10,660 tractors and nearly 50,000 other pieces of machinery, employed 11,000 men and 24,500 women, and farmed 390,000 acres. The Minister, through his agents, was therefore the largest agriculturist in England, with holdings that were nearly as extensive as the whole of Hertfordshire. The other farmers of Great Britain between them had 173,370 tractors, considerably more than three times the number they had just before the war. Even so, the situation was becoming desperate. For example, recruitment to the W.L.A. was stopped in order to draft women to munitions, and the ploughing-up campaign had got to a point beyond which it seemed impossible to progress, not only because of the worsening labour shortage but on account of the dangers of continuous cropping on certain lands and of the imbalance likely to be created between livestock and crops. Nevertheless, the farmers did their job. On a total agricultural acreage which had shrunk since 1914–1918 by 10% or 3,250,000 acres (even during the war, 800,000 acres of arable land were lost to aerodromes, factories and so on), production in 1943–1944 exceeded that of 1917–1918 by 14,788,000 tons, and the national dairy herd numbered 4,040,000 compared with 3,030,000 in 1918. If we remember the distressed circumstances of the farming community in 1939 compared with 1914 and the prolonged duration of the all-out agricultural war effort, which lasted six full years, whereas in the earlier war it had been necessary only for the last two, these figures are astounding.

Mr. Murray has summed up the agricultural revolution during this war in these words: "Without such an increase in tractor power it would have been impossible to carry out the task of increasing the arable areas by some six million acres. The time for ploughing and preparing the land, both in the autumn and spring, was far too limited to have permitted such an expansion even if horses had been available. The tracror's ability to cover the ground faster and, given relays of drivers, to work ceaselessly day and night was essential. Moreover there were many jobs, such as ditch digging, land clearing, levelling and deep ploughing which could not have been tackled by horse labour."[2] He added, "By the end of the war, British farming was claimed to be the most highly mechanised in the world. Though this assertion might require some qualification, it is certainly true that there had been yet another agricultural transformation; what was achieved within a period of six years might well have taken decades in time of peace."

The contribution made by draught-horses to the war effort, if viewed as a percentage of all farm work and cultivations, diminished at a headlong rate. But the actual number of horses, and their total work-hours, decreased slowly. In 1939, most men were primarily operating a system of horse-husbandry. During the six years of war, such was the hectic round of daily life for a dwindling labour-force of men, that there was no time to re-model the operations, much less the buildings and lay-out of the farm, to suit the motor engine. Therefore, it is possible still to regard the vast army of new tractors and tractor-ploughs as assisting rather than superceding the horses. The Government, therefore, from the beginning of the war to the end, was prepared to allow fodder for working horses.

The relative claims of various species of large animals to be kept alive in war-time presented a confusing problem which was eventually resolved in July 1941. Under the system then put into operation, farmers with beef cattle, sheep and young stock of any sort could keep for themselves whatever feeding stuffs they produced on their own land, but were allowed to buy none. Pigs, poultry, dairy cows and work-horses were put in a rationing scheme. Keepers of poultry and pigs were allocated sufficient for less than one-sixth of the number they had maintained pre-war. (It was reduced still more in 1943.) Dairy farmers had to provide from their own resources for the maintenance of each cow and the production of the first half-gallon of milk per day, beyond which point rations were available. In the case of draught-horses, the owner had to prove that he could not provide enough grain of his own growing. Of course, in the towns he could not grow any. An early dilemma occurred with the increasing shortage of oats for pit ponies and urban horses, because there had been a gentleman's agreement that the Ministry of Food would not take feeding stuffs from farmers by compulsion. To meet the crisis, shipping space had to be found for the importation of 64,000 tons of maize. In the four years 1941–1942 to 1944–1945, cereals allocated under the rationing scheme amounted to 16,000, 19,000, 15,000 and 12,000 tons for horses; 33,000, 34,000, 37,000 and 33,000 tons for dairy cows and calves; and 40,000, 33,000, 37,000 and 45,000 tons for pigs and poultry, including domestically owned animals and birds.

The following table gives some indication of the relative numbers of horses and tractors, and the ploughs that each used, together with the acreage of arable and grass land, during the successive years of the war.

		Average per annum of 1937–9	1940	1941	1942	1943	1944
(a) Arable acres (inc. temp. grass) G.B. (millions)		11.87	13.20	14.99	16.18	17.39	17.94
Permanent grass, acres ,, ,,		17.33	15.90	14.07	12.75	11.42	10.81
		29.20	29.10	29.06	28.93	28.81	28.75
(b) New tractor-drawn ploughs, U.K.	home produced		8,680	10,495	8,929	8,307	9,738
	imported		14,529	18,424	13,751	12,090	6,423
	total		23,209	28,919	22,680	20,397	16,161
(c) New tractors[1]	home produced	1,333	19,316	24,401	27,056	25,059	23,022
	imported	1,337	5,960	8,677	8,003	6,278	6,103
	total	2,670	25,276	33,078	35,059	31,337	29,125
(d) New horse-drawn ploughs, U.K.	home produced	1,289	14,492	14,162	14,485	10,939	13,963
	imported	155	321	200	0	0	0
(e) No. of horses on farms,[2] England and Wales only	agricultural	555,321	541,394	564,301	484,782	520,108	485,181
	all	853,758	819,569	823,614	783,159	744,687	707,913

[1] These of course represent only part of the picture of mechanisation. E.g. they ignore the increased number of vans and lorries used by farmers.

In 1937–1939, 14,940 (average 4,980) tractors were manufactured in U.K. but it was estimated that all but about 4,000 were exported. 4,010 were imported during this time.

[2] "Agricultural horses" means actual working horses, including brood mares; therefore excluding young stock as well as light horses, etc. (1942 figures of agricultural horses are certainly wrong – they should be about 70,000 more, and "other horses" reduced by the same number, i.e. the total is correct.)

2. DOWN IN THE DENHAM DUMPS: 1939–1941

However small and inadequate a country's professional standing army may be in time of peace, and however antiquated its equipment, no one would suggest it be done away with in war time simply because the volunteers and conscripts who are enlisted happen to be ten times, or a hundred times, as numerous. That is why working horses were kept alive by the Government. But the same Government in 1939 had no interest whatever in breeding more of them.

In the First World War, the first heavy-horses bred specifically to help the national cause were foaled in 1916 and were therefore only two when hostilities ended. Even if the Government wished to increase the number of horses in the second war, the first crop of such foals would not reach the age of four until 1945. The struggle was not expected to last so long. The British Army would not need heavy-horses, though the Germans had a use for them. At home, all expansion of the agricultural industry clearly depended on the motor engine. A double blow was therefore aimed, in the nation's interest, at those who kept stallions or bred from their working mares.

In October 1939, the Ministry grants under the Heavy Horse Breeding Scheme were suspended. This saved the country the princely sum of nearly £10,000. The Shire Society, led by William Cumber and assisted by Sir Walter Gilbey's usual active lobbying, protested loud and long. Hiring "clubs" and War Agricultural Executive Committees supported the Society, and many addressed urgent pleas direct to the Minister, who was deaf to their cries.

The second blow was far more deadly to pedigree interests. Breeders were deprived of the right to any fodder that they could not produce themselves. Many men with Shire studs lent, or actually gave, even their best mares to farmers who could feed and work them. Stallion owners, if they did not have too many and if they had enough acres, could "lose" them amongst the rest of the stock. But the biggest men suffered more than any. The most dramatic effect of this prohibition occurred at Carlton-on-Trent and Yatesbury, the two largest stallion studs in the country.

James Forshaw had started keeping entire horses on his own account in 1863. In 1939, his two sons had seventy-five stallions which were licensed by the Ministry, with young stock coming on. The animals were worth about £15,000. The Forshaws had only 180 acres and so feed always had to be bought in. Now they were faced with immediate disaster. In the tradition of their father, they refused to "mess about" and sent a large number for slaughter at once. One train alone carried away twenty-three stallions. Their breeding epitomised the sixty years' work of the Shire Society. And Tom, the elder brother, had shared this progress from the very start, for he had been taken to the first London Show as a boy and had not missed one since. The price the stallions fetched was £3 a head, from the knacker. Within a few months, the rules regarding horse-flesh for human consumption had been changed and the animals, at £6 per live cwt., would have fetched about £120 each. The finest stallions to the knacker. Eighty years of Forshaw genius to the horse-butcher. The modern age had begun.

William Cumber at Yatesbury was perhaps more realistic, though he had farms also at Theale to cope with the feeding problem. He had sixty licensed stallions in the 1939 season. They did not go to the knacker. Instead, he castrated the majority of them. Fifteen were gelded in one day. Eleven were broken to work in a week – ten by Friday, leaving one for the Saturday morning. Westminster City Council bought some at £100 apiece, and two were sold for £500 as a matched pair. A matched pair! Where was the greater lunacy – in the heart of the man who fancied a matched pair in those dark days, or in humanity itself which condemned the best breeding stock, the fruit of many centuries' work and effort, to the castrator's knife?

The Frithville stud, four miles north of Boston, had forty-four stallions in 1939. They were valued on 5th April at £5,660. Twelve were let and sixteen travelled; they produced a gross income of £3,604. The stud had been started by Benjamin Balderston when he bought his first cart-stallion in 1867, paying £65. 10s. od. to Mr. Key of Glentworth for Wiltshire Champion (2351), fourteen years old. Benjamin had become a Shire member in 1879, but his son Tom, scarcely out of boyhood, had run affairs from 1880 and the old man had died two years after that. In 1939 Tom Balderston, an immense and heavy figure of 19-hands, was one of the best-loved Shire men in England, still unconscious of the need ever to say anything but exactly what he thought and to dress exactly as made him happiest, even to wearing Wellington boots at the Peterborough Foal Stakes dinner. Unlike Cumber or the Forshaws, he was fortunate enough to be able to feed most of his stallions. And he had had many hundreds since the day when, a young fellow in his early teens, he had had the task of putting down old Bang-Up 101, who had been with his father ten years and had served 1,000 mares in four seasons. Many years later he wrote in his horse book on the Bang-Up page, "Could not travel and had him killed after the season. Poor old boy." If he had been forced now, in 1939, to put down most of his beloved horses, or else watch them starve, he would surely have died of grief.

The war of course had a sudden effect also upon other parts of the Shire Society's activities. September shows in 1939 were mostly cancelled, the most important of these, for Shire men, being Ashbourne, followed by Altrincham, Cheshire, Montgomery, and Thame, and also the Tarporley Hunt and Winslow shows. But the Peterborough Foal Show and Stallion Produce Stakes were held, as has been already noted. The usual flood of late entries for the Stud-book was reduced to a trickle and the year ended with 238 new colts registered, compared with 304 in 1938, and 956 mares, as against 1,102. The new Grade Register, which had been announced only in April, therefore had a difficult start.

The *News of the World* Darts Championship Finals which had been held at the Royal Agricultural Hall in May turned out to be the last event ever held there. The Bakers' Exhibition, which was due to open the new season after the summer recess, had been all fitted up ready for 2nd September but, since war was certain to be declared the following day, the bakers cancelled it. The Shire Society decided that, even if the hall were available the following February, the Government would not permit a Spring Show, and so plans for this were abandoned. As it turned out, the War Office took over the Hall in March 1940, and put gun limbers in the gallery. They filled the ground floor with a vast mass of sandbags.

On the 19th March 1940, the Shire men held their Annual General Meeting for the first (and last) time in Hanover Square. It was followed by an Extraordinary Meeting which ratified arrangements to postpone all elections and general meetings for the duration of the war and to place the entire management of the Society's affairs in the hands of a Special Emergency Committee. This all-powerful septemvirate consisted of William Cumber (who now faced the prospect of remaining as President until the war ended), Colonel A. F. Nicholson of Leek (President-elect), Christopher Barker (1936 President), Sir Walter Gilbey, A. Thomas Loyd of Lockinge, Morris Belcher and Tom Forshaw. Considerable amendments and additions to the Articles of Association were necessary to enable all affairs to be thus completely controlled by a junta. For sixty years, the right of a tenant farmer with two pedigree mares and eighty acres, to speak and vote on equal terms with His Grace at Chatsworth or any other grand person had been jealously preserved. But now the members were happy to sign away their free and democratic privileges in the Society while they were preoccupied with the needs of a greater democracy and freedom.

In the almost total absence of shows (though there was a Royal Norfolk Society stallion show at Norwich in March as usual), foal premiums were proposed – a small grant for every foal got that year and actually entered in the Stud-book on its birth in 1941. But the Committee decided to use the period of inactivity to try to recoup the financial losses of previous years. A hundred guineas was given to the Red Cross Agricultural Fund. Tom Forshaw suggested that members should club together to buy a Shire Horse Spitfire for the R.A.F.

The Peterborough Foal Show was held again. At the sale afterwards, twenty colts, eligible for the Stud-book, made miserable prices ranging from 10 to 32 guineas. W. J. Thompson of Crowland sold up his stud at this sale. A Shire member since 1901, he owned about 1,000 acres which were now managed by his nephew Maurice Riddington. It was in 1938 that the stud had come top of a London class for the first time, with Chenies Mavis, a two-year-old who was also reserve for the junior cup. This had been the work of Reg Nunn, who on the death of G. R. C. Foster in 1936 came to Thompson's as head man and bought the filly from her breeder, Bill Simpson of Chenies on the Duke of Bedford's estate. But all the Crowland land was now being ploughed up, and it had to be done with speed. There was no place for perfection, or the Shire.

Reg took care that Mavis did not go into the sale. With her foal, a real ugly duckling which later grew into an elegant swan called Heaton Lady May, she went with him to his new job at Billy Whewell's in Lancashire. It was in this county that the most successful of the few local foal shows this year was held – the Great Eccleston Society's wonderful crop got by its 1939 horse, Belcher's mighty Harboro' Goldfinder.

The Hanover Square lease now had only six months to run, and the search was intensified for other worthy premises to act as "Breed Society House". A property in Harley Street seemed ideal: in fact it was better and cheaper than No. 12. But the Hunter Society's secretary had been called up, and so they had requested that Holland should temporarily take over his duties. There was little Hunter work to do, anyway, and even less money available for rent. Then came another blow – the decision of the Large Black Pig men to desert the côterie. The Shire Emergency Committee discussed the problem in an air-raid and were worried about the non-arrival of Morris Belcher, who had telephoned that he was on the way. Was he alive? Yes, but if his journey from Shropshire was fruitless, so were the rest of the committee's deliberations.

Another air-raid settled the argument by bringing the tenancy of No. 12 to a premature end. John Lewis' store in Oxford Street was on fire, and much of the water that was poured on the place found its way into the cellars of the house behind. It was three or four feet deep. Hundredweights of old letters, tons of various breed society documents and books and many thousands of pictures of Shire horses were submerged. When the waters decreased Holland and his assistant secretary, M. R. Leather were able to peer down the steps at a sodden mess. Everything was ruined. The records of all the past were now a pulp. Conditions were intolerable. New premises were hastily rented, at 5 Broadway East, Denham.

Denham! 5 Broadway East! What an address! A shop on a new estate! What would Lord Ellesmere have thought of *that*? Its only distinction was its proximity to the film studios, but there is something ironic in that thought. In the old days, if anyone had wanted to set up a film studio in Hanover Square, such a cheapening of the neighbourhood would have roused the choler of the Shire leaders. The front of this plebeian 5 Broadway East had been blown out, but a local builder was engaged to brick it up and put in some small windows. Holland and Leather carted the furniture down in several lorry loads, and left R. A. Brown, secretary of the National Horse Association, of the London Van Horse Parade Society and of the National Pony Society, alone in the old house. Soon he also moved out, went on war work and wrote a few letters occasionally in his spare time just to prove that his societies were not dead, but only hibernating.

The local builder did a remarkably poor job on the front of the shop. "Honestly", as Holland said (and when did he speak otherwise?), "you could actually see through some of the brickwork." Whenever the electricity was cut off, the flames of the candles were blown about by the wind whistling eerily between the bricks. "But asbestos boarding made a good partition, you know." So they could have a secretary's room and an assistant secretary's room. Or they could have a general office and an inner office. If they wished, they could even have a Shire office and a Hunter office, and both could trot from one to the other to keep warm. There was also a vast amount of storage space. It was useful for unwanted furniture, but there were no papers and books and photographs to put in it. These were growing fungus in Hanover Square.

What *would* the Earl of Ellesmere have thought of 5 Broadway East? It had no decorated plaster ceilings. There were no ornate marble chimney-pieces. (The one in the old music room had been magnificently carved all over with stringed and wind instruments.) There was no noble staircase with fluted columns, no doors of mahogany from the West Indies. There was no porter. Callers were few, but those who were ribald enough to open the door and cry "Shop" were answered by Holland himself, or Leather. However, these two were at least spared the pain of seeing the railings removed from the Square, and of watching the elegant garden, which for so many years successive R.A.S.E. and Shire secretaries had supervised, degenerate swiftly into a wilderness where rubbish could blow and remain. But this was a negative sort of consolation. And it did not compensate for the loneliness. Perhaps the ghost of Frank Euren, trotting up and down the stairs of the deserted No. 12 two at a time, felt lonely, too. Or did he talk to Mary Somerville?

By the end of the year, Shire subscriptions were down from £1,899 in 1939 to £1,644, and those of affiliated societies from £350 to £165. But the lack of anything to spend money on had made the Society nearly £3,000 better off. One hundred and sixty-two colts had been registered in the year, and 553 mares.

The year 1941 opened in gloom, but the pedigree season began surprisingly with a defiant, if minor, flourish. The Forshaws' business had been hit for six and their horses decimated by the lack of fodder. But this family had travelled entire horses in the Fylde ever since the year of Waterloo, if not before. In 1859, when James had left his Goosnargh home at the age of nineteen, he did not intend the tradition to be broken. He set up his own stud (with one colt) in 1863 and in due course, especially after his father's death, regularly sent horses back to his native area. And so in March 1941, in spite of all the set-backs, his sons Thomas and James did not see why the 126th season should not be observed, and duly dispatched three horses to parade before the season in a Preston yard. Surprisingly, there were no less than twenty-two other heavy stallions on display in the town that month.

In London, the Salvage and Disposals department of the Ministry of Supply took over the Hall from the R.A.F. and used it to sort out old clothes and equipment. The Shire Emergency Committee was affected by a sort of torpor, and Holland had trouble with his draughts at Denham. Nevertheless, it was arranged to offer prizes for foals at autumn sales which were to be held at

Peterborough, Crewe, Derby and Menai Bridge. In the Fylde, the Great Eccleston men, under the leadership of the hiring society chairman T. P. Stuart, member of a great Shire family, and R. G. Thompson, chairman of the agricultural society, held that autumn a marvellous foal show which attracted many who had been starved of Shire activities. At a lunch at the Black Bull, Morris Belcher's health was drunk: his Harboro' Goldfinder had been retained for a fourth season. A toast was drunk to Tom Fowler, too, the Lancastrian who had made the Rothschild stud the wonder of the breed. "To my knowledge", he said, "there have been five or six London champions bred within five miles of where we are sitting." Everyone was jovial, though the members were somewhat peeved that Shire prizes had not been allocated to the Preston foal sales.

3. A MINI-BOOM: 1942–1946

In 1942, the Government suddenly played a new tune. Stallion grants were resumed. Rations were also allocated to them, and even extra rations during the thirteen weeks that they were covering mares. Tom Balderston died. Poor old boy. Or was he? He had sixty-two years running the Frithville stud, coinciding exactly with the life of the breed society. It was the right time to go. For more than another thirty-two years and, one hopes, for many more still to come, the mere mention of his name has evoked a smile from those lucky enough to have known him.

The idea of holding a spring stallion show this year had been proposed, but was rejected after Tattersall's at Knightsbridge had been inspected and the police had objected, and after one or two Midlands venues had been considered. But a show of geldings was promoted at Hall, Wateridge and Owen's horse repository at Shrewsbury in co-operation with the senior partner, F. A. Phillips, and in conjunction with their regular March sale of heavy-horses. (They held main sales for these in March, April and October.) In spite of somewhat poor publicity, a vast and enthusiastic crowd turned up, and there was difficulty in moving spectators back to allow animals to be paraded before each class. A Lancashire horse won each of the three classes, with R. G. Thompson's dark bay three-year-old taking the championship. He was by Hendre Broadside out of a Clydesdale mare – "a most successful example of the fusion of the two heavy breeds with the Shire on top" as one journalist expressed it. (The rules said that exhibits simply had to be "by registered Shire stallions".) He was sold for 186 guineas, more than had been given for a gelding at Shrewsbury for over twenty years, which was also true of those which went for 182, 180 and 172 guineas.

The sale at the Peterborough repository the same month by John Thornton, Hobson & Company is of historical importance because it was the last ever held there. It was requisitioned soon after and only the loss of the Islington hall was more grievous. This last effort was a one-day sale, with eighty-nine Shires and one Clydesdale entered by sixty-two exhibitors, Mr. Loyd's four-year-old

Lockinge Reaper making top price of 340 guineas. In the very good old days, the March Shire sale had occupied four days (in 1919, 700 animals totalled £70,000) and, in the 'thirties, two days.

Also in March, M. R. Leather, a loyal servant for twenty-three years, suddenly died, leaving Albert Holland practically desolate in his draughty shop, for everyone else had been called up. Mrs. Leather, whose son was in a R.A.F. hospital, was immediately paid a full quarter's salary in advance, £93. 15s. 0d., and received a gift of £250.

At this time, some heterodox proposals were brought forward to mix Clydesdale with Shire blood. It is not the place to discuss these here. But it was clear that, after two-and-a-half years of inactivity, the full Council must at last meet. Draughty Denham was singularly inappropriate and so, in August, William Cumber, as Chairman of the Farmers' Club, welcomed himself and the other Councillors as guests. This was the first time since 1883 that the Council had re-visited the Club where Fred Street had brought the Society into being. Apart from Scottish blood, another urgent item on the agenda was to consider some sort of substitute for the Peterborough Spring Show and Sale.

A stallion-show in 1943 was accordingly held in Derby cattle market. Geographically the venue was ideal and, in practice, these were about the only suitable premises which had not been requisitioned. The Ministry of Agriculture stipulated that a maximum of thirty stallions should be entered "for show only": all the rest must be for sale also. Albert Holland showed that a suburban exile had not impaired his perfectionist efficiency at running a show. The scene was one of great enthusiasm. There were three classes, and three classes for mares were added as an extra. William Whewell won the championship with Tabley Grey Duke, shown by Reg Nunn. Thirty-two stallions were sold for £4,974, and these excluded most of the prizewinners, which largely came from Lancashire and were not for sale. Twenty-one mares increased the proceeds to £7,202.

The second Shrewsbury gelding show was a greater success than the first in all ways. William Whewell won the championship at this, too. His horse, and the reserve champion (exhibited by a newcomer to the show-ring, Harry Ashcroft of Scarisbrick, between Ormskirk and Southport) were both out of Clydesdale mares. Harry Holderness, perhaps the greatest Shire reporter of all time, writing in The Preston Guardian, probably the best agricultural paper in the country, commented that the judges were not so influenced by weight as they had been in pre-war years. "They went all out for the modern type, and it may be added that they set a standard for the breed which will undoubtedly be followed at other shows."

Silver medals were offered this year for Shires at the increasing number of shows organised on behalf of the Red Cross Agriculture Fund. William Cumber was awarded the M.B.E. With Peterborough out of the reckoning, prizes were allotted for autumn foal shows and sales at Preston, Welshpool and Hereford, in addition to the three which the Society had supported since 1941.

In 1944 there was a repetition of the previous year's shows. At Derby, where hundreds of enthusiasts crowded the ring, William Whewell again won the stallion championship, with a different horse, Bradford Diagram, aged six. Crimwell Modern Boy, two-years-old, owned by William Brock of Crimwell Pool, Whitley near Warrington, was one of the few prize-winners offered for sale. In *The Preston Guardian*, Harry Holderness significantly reiterated his comment of the year before, in stronger terms: "There was far less hair to be seen in the wrong places. The horses were of a cleaner type altogether." Some journalists suggested Crimwell Modern Boy had Clydesdale blood, but it was a bad guess. Whatever he looked, his breeding was purely English, as we shall see. He was a colt whose action was particularly crisp compared with the heavy, almost lumbering gait of some of his rivals at the show. The honorary veterinary officer, Professor Harold Burrow, has recollected that "Perhaps it was his hock-action which attracted most attention. He flexed his hocks almost like a Hackney, so much so that some ringside observers suspected that he was suffering from double stringhalt or that perhaps he was a shiverer." Professor Burrow put him through every test to detect either of these unsoundnesses, and indeed repeated the tests rigorously, but the colt gave no sign that he was otherwise than sound in every way. G. H. Bowser, who also kept Percherons (and became President of that society in 1952) bought him for 860 guineas.

At Shrewsbury, J. B. Brown of Retford paid 370 guineas for the champion gelding, a seven-year-old bay standing 17.2-hands, by Ponton Woldsman and shown by R. N. Bramley of Firbeck, a few miles into the West Riding. He deserves notice, for the price he fetched was the highest for a Shire gelding since 1922, when Alkrington Darkie was sold for £500. No one, two or three years before, could have dreamed that any sort of cart horse could fetch a sum anything approaching the boom figures of 1920. (Later, at the age of eleven, after he had won innumerable prizes, he was described by a commentator as a "massive gelding, fresh as paint, springy on his great frontal columns, and notable for his terrific depth and powerful shoulders".) The reserve champion also broke a price record. At 300 guineas, paid by Mr. Middleton of Bromsgrove, Whewell's black of 17-hands set a new ceiling for three-year-old geldings.

The Suffolk breeders held a stallion show which attracted eighty-seven entries in four classes, an all-time record for them and only three less than the Shire Show. Twelve premiums of £25 boosted the two-year-old class to forty-three. At the two-day-sale, 111 horses were sold. The Percheron people had fifty-eight stallions in four classes at their show at Histon, Cambridge, and ninety-three animals were bought at the sale, including a seven-year-old mare for 125 guineas paid by R. S. Hudson, the Minister of Agriculture. Shire silver and bronze medals were awarded to fifty-two different exhibitors at fifty shows organised for the benefit of the Red Cross Agriculture Fund, which early in the year had passed the £4,000,000 mark. (The first £1,000,000 had taken twenty-six months to raise and the fourth, four-and-a-half months.

Special sales had raised £1,500,000 of this, "rural pennies" £1,380,000 and, among many more supporters, pedigree stock breeders £76,504.)

In April, the Great Eccleston Agricultural Society called a meeting to see if the enormous gap left by the ending of the Peterborough Foal Show and Produce Stakes could be filled. Under the chairmanship of R. G. Thompson, and with John Hothersall of the Preston auction mart as secretary, an organisation was formed which on 16th October held the "National Pedigree Shire Produce Stakes". It was an enormous success. Thirty stallions were nominated and there were over a hundred entries competing for £300 in prizes. Enthusiasts attended from all over the country and stood four and five deep round the ring side. An excellent cinder track enabled the foals to display their paces to the best advantage. Lancastrians thought that others could show the same initiative and believed the Shire Emergency Committee was afflicted by paralysis. So Hothersall was instructed to request an Annual General Meeting of the Society the following spring and a quick return to normal working, but this was rejected as premature.

At the Society's 1945 stallion show, the familiar and well-loved figure of A. Thomas Loyd of Lockinge was missed. His death the previous November at the age of sixty-two had been a blow and a shock to Shire men. This third Derby show was the best of the war-time series, with 103 entries in three classes. Again, there was emphasis on the "modern" Shire. "If the world at large wanted to know what is happening to the breed, Derby supplied an impressive answer", wrote one reporter. "The horses were massive, deep and broad, as champion weight shifters must be, but in almost every instance it was made apparent that fashionable limbs must be clean as well as powerful, with flat bone and feet of really enduring quality. It was a wonderful collection of the highest quality that paraded before the judges, who were quick to interpret 1945 ideas of what a Shire should be." It was of note that the championship went to Grey Spark, a four-year-old shown by the Forshaws, who had always been regarded and are still erroneously remembered as obstinately "old-fashioned" and unwilling to revise their ideas of a Shire. The winner of the three-year-olds, and reserve champion, was Bradgate Grey King, who had only escaped castration as a colt because a swelling on the groin delayed this operation in the first place. He was exhibited by his third owner, Morris Belcher, the last man in England who would consider following new "crazes". (Bradgate Grey King was by Lymm Grey King, a relatively small horse, massive neither in height nor depth nor weight. He carried a moderate amount of feather, but it was of the right kind – straight, fine and silky: and the underlying bone was flat and hard. Lymm Grey King deserves a place among the more prominent sires of the century for his ability to transmit to his off-spring all the qualities most to be desired in the modern true Shire, and it is sad that so many of his descendants were destined for destruction or impotence. He was bred in 1932 by George Roberts of Creswell, Derby., and was by Carlton Grey Kingmaker, also somewhat lacking in substance, but a sparkling mover.)

On 11th April 1945, Sir Walter Gilbey, father figure of the Shire Horse Society, and indeed of every organisation formed for the welfare of horses and the men who bred and owned them, died at the age of eighty-five. He had not misssed a Derby since 1875, nor a London Cart Horse Parade since his father had founded it, and very few London Shows. As in the 'twenties and 'thirties he had acted out the woes of the agricultural community like a prophet of old, so even his death was a symbol. The passing of this indefatigable man, kind and uncompromising, charming and hospitable, a man as able in the Society's finances as in the arts of publicity and persuasion, who did for Shire men all that his father before him had done, marked the end of an age. In less than five weeks, the war in Europe ended, and this was to herald the real end of the horse age at last. He would not have wished to live beyond it, though he would have liked to see some post-war Derby days.

Fifty-six Red Cross and other shows were awarded Shire medals and rosettes, the Preston National Pedigree Shire Produce Stakes was held again, as were the foal shows that the Society had supported during the war, and towards the end of the year arrangements were made for restoring the old organisation.

In 1946 the Shrewsbury gelding show was held for the fifth time. 450 guineas was given for a brown gelding. And, amid much rejoicing, the first Spring Show since 1939 took place. This latter event had its origin in a conversation between S. T. Parker and Harold Burrow. Stanley Parker in 1915 had come straight from school to work for Andrew Smith, horse auctioneer of Derby (at that time, as manager for Sexton, Grimwade & Beck who had bought him out in 1900 and were to sell the business back to him in 1921) and secretary of the Derbyshire Agricultural Society. In 1925 he had succeeded Smith. The Lancastrian, Harold Burrow, after serving under the great Brennan De Vine at Birmingham, had been veterinary officer to Birkenhead Corporation and then to Derbyshire County Council, but, tiring of being "nationalised" in 1938, had gone into private practice in Derby in 1942 and was now Professor of Veterinary Medicine at the Royal Veterinary College. He was also veterinary officer to the Derby stallion shows. At a meeting of the stallion hiring committee of the Derbyshire A.S., these two men hit on the idea of using the Derby racecourse for a "London" Show. A return to the Royal Agricultural Hall was clearly out of the reckoning. It had suffered only minor damage during the war, but the Post Office, which had shared the premises with the Ministry of Supply during the later years, was now in serious difficulties owing to the loss of Mount Pleasant – parcels were all being sorted at the London railway termini, and losses, owing to lack of proper supervision, were heavy. There seemed no possible chance of getting the Post Office out. (In fact they were still there almost thirty years later.)

Harold Burrow went to see Major W. H. Wortley, the officer commanding the military depot occupying the racecourse, in civilian life a Bungay veterinary surgeon and a fellow-examiner to the R.C.V.S. With Parker, they worked out the possibilities, and Albert Holland was full of enthusiasm. One area was cleared and thoroughly disinfected (the Army had a large number of sick horses there), and so on Thursday, 7th March occurred the first of thirteen post-war Spring Shows in accommodation designed for the aristocracy of horseflesh. As Holland mused many years afterwards, "They'd got such wonderful boxes. 12 feet square, mangers, drains, herring-bone what-you-call-'em. Marvellous."

In a mood of great euphoria, an enormous crowd assembled to see the 167 stallions and mares that were entered. Lillingstone What's Wanted, bred and owned by H. Eady Robinson of Higham Ferrers, Northamptonshire, became champion stallion and Crimwell Quality, bred at Eaton, Leicestershire by Fred Hubbard, son of that doughty old Shire man Matthew, and shown by D. K. Steadman from Montgomeryshire, was champion mare. It was a mixture of old times and new. Tom Fowler of Rothschild memory and James Runciman, the veterinary breeder of Bower Winalot, judged the stallions. T. H. Balderston, son of old Tom, and William Brock from Lancashire judged the mares. Two Johns, sons of Morris Belcher and William Cumber were the stewards, and Professor Harold Burrow was the honorary veterinary surgeon.

The evening before this show, the Society at last returned to peace-time operation. At the Midland Hotel, Derby, the first A.G.M. for seven years heard the names of the successful twelve candidates who were to replace the eight survivors of the twelve who had been elected, to serve three years on the Council, in 1937. At the next Council meeting, William Cumber was at last after seven years able to hand over the Presidency to Colonel Nicholson. He had attended every one of the thirteen Emergency Committee meetings, and Morris Belcher and Tom Forshaw had missed only three between them. Colonel Nicholson had been on active service and had attended none. It was a remarkable coincidence that had thrust upon the broad shoulders of W. J. Cumber the unique responsibility also of being chairman, likewise for seven years, of the "sire" of the Shire Horse Society, the Farmers' Club. This was a period of perhaps the Club's greatest strength and service, as a reminder of which he received magnificent presentations subscribed by the members. The portrait of William J. Cumber will no doubt continue to gaze down the Club's staircase long after there are any to remember why he should be thus honoured. (He died in 1974.)

It was quite like the old days this year. The London Cart Horse Parade was revived, though it was held later – on August Bank Holiday. The Gas Light and Coke Company, the L.M.S. Railway, Lambeth and Hammersmith Borough Councils, coal merchants big and small, and the brewers won Shire rosettes. Twenty-one special prizes were given at "gold medal" shows because gold medals could not be had. There were sixty-nine silver medal shows, also with prizes for breeders. There were twenty-nine shows with bronze medals for geldings. The National Pedigree Shire Foal Stakes removed from Preston to Haydock Park racecourse. One hundred and fifty-six new members joined the Shire Society, making nearly 850 new recruits since the outbreak of war, though total membership had dropped from 3,641 to 3,518 during this time. Amongst the losses by death were those of Sir Edward Mann, E. W. Heading-ton of the Cippenham stud at Slough, George Marsh the best-known name in Shire geldings, Fred Parsons of Speckington in Somerset, and Thomas P. Stuart. The Society's funds had increased from £14,900 to £23,716, prizes and medals during the war years having cost only £3,000. Eight hundred and seventy-nine stallions and 3,294 mares had been registered by Holland in five years at dismal Denham.

The second show on the Derby Racecourse Paddocks, in 1947, had to be postponed a fortnight because of that severe and prolonged winter's snow and cold, which made the showground impossible and the roads impassable. When it was eventually held, the spectators could appreciate all the improvements made, in conjunction with the owners (Truman, Hanbury, Buxton & Company Limited), since the army had left. Commercial classes were added for the first time since 1939, and there was a total entry of 129. Spectators could pretend, for a few hours, that it was quite like old times, even though Derby Racecourse was not the Royal Agricultural Hall. But 1947 was a year, not of joy, but of death, despair and destruction.

4. THE STUD-BOOK AND THE CLYDESDALE

The Grading-up Register was issued in 1940 and 1941 as a little booklet, and several requests were made to bind it in the Stud-book. The Emergency Committee refused, being cynical enough to believe that some unscrupulous owners of Grade B or Grade A mares would describe them as "registered in the Stud-book". Instead, it produced the 1942 Volume with a pocket inside the back cover. So the Register could be kept *with* the Stud-book, but was not *of* it. The rule laid down in 1939 that, from 1941, mares could be graded up only *via* the Register was rescinded, and throughout this time the Register was a voluntary matter of convenience only.

A bombshell arrived in the post during November 1941, from George Heywood, secretary to the Newcastle (Staffs) and District S.H.S. He had been instructed to enquire whether, to speed the process of obtaining cleaner-legged Shires, the progeny of a Clydesdale stallion out of a Shire mare could be considered for the Stud-book. The Emergency Committee promptly decided that the state of the nation had not quite reached that point of gravity. However, there was a general feeling that an acceleration of the change towards less hair was desirable in an age when there was not the time to care for shaggy legs in the old manner. The following May, Will Smith of Thorney, a council member, made precisely the same suggestion as the Staffordshire society. It was accordingly resolved by the Emergency Committee to call the Council together for the first time since the war-time arrangements had been put into force.

Those who could not attend the meeting submitted their views on paper.

Twenty-six did attend. Will Smith opened the discussion by saying that "We only want a dash of the Clydesdale limbs to do away with the hair." William Cumber, in the chair, observed somewhat tartly that the first-cross he had proposed was 50%, which was more than a "dash of blood". He forebore to remind the meeting that he himself, with Will Smith's late father-in-law Fred Griffin, had expended considerable time, energy and money only twelve years earlier on a scheme for some form of rapprochement with the Clydesdale Society and that it was the Shire Society which had vetoed it.

Tom Fowler, who had produced those vast and classically hairy Shires for Lord Rothschild, agreed with Will Smith. So did Alfred Clark, son of Fred Griffin's old friend and neighbour. But James Forshaw said they could not be called the Shire Horse Society if they allowed this idea. Enoch Bostock felt the same way, though the first-cross gelding made a better commercial horse than either breed. R. G. Thompson said the day had passed when there could be two sorts of Shire, one for the commercial market and one for the show-ring. Morris Belcher claimed it was absurd to say that a lot of hair had not been done away with during the previous ten years. "We have a horse with power, grit, limbs and feet. What more can we desire? There are good Clydes about, but they have not the depth of rib or foot." R. H. Keene remembered the Shires of fifty-four years ago, and the breed had improved. James Runciman thought the Ministry should be asked not to grant licences to hairy-legged horses. "They have been examining horses for unsoundness for years, yet they have never cast one for conformation."

Tom Forshaw suggested that the first-cross filly foal, by a registered Shire stallion out of a registered Clydesdale mare, be admitted to Appendix B, instead of Appendix A, of the Grade Register. William Cumber was as astounded as anyone at what the old opponent of fusing the breeds had said. Concealing his amazement, he said he thought this was good. "It would merely put the Shire/Clyde filly one step higher than the man who puts a Shire on, say, a Forest pony". He then revealed that he had had a personal communication from the Clydesdale men only a few days before, asking for advice about organising a Grading-up Register, which they had not got. He believed the Forshaw idea opened the way for reciprocal action. "The Clyde people are not satisfied with their animal. No one has yet found the perfect horse."

A couple of guns were fired, from an important quarter, in favour of Shire purity. Percy Surridge, the London haulage contractor, reminded the Council he had been using their products for thirty years. "Only one horse does our job, the Shire. I think you all know what we people need – weight, feet, depth and constitution. I cannot get labour now to clean the hair, but you gentlemen who breed horses must be careful not to sacrifice the weight." Sir Edward Mann, as buyer of his brewery's horses, said "We have used Shire horses ever since I can remember" (he had been a member of the Society since 1882) "and during that time I have seen many ideas, and many faults, in the breeding of your horses. I am not a believer in a lot of wool round their legs, but I am a believer in constitution, good limbs and good feet. My opinion is, if you jump from one thing to the other you will get trouble whatever you do. There is no short cut to fixing the type of an animal." This was the wisdom of a very old man near the end of a long life. He was the first to mention by name the dreaded word *grease*, that curse that embraced the hairy leg. "I was prevailed upon some years ago to have a few Clydes. The very worst specimen of grease I ever saw in my life was one of them, on all four feet, too." Grease lay not in a breed but in an individual, and in the care of it. But, if they talked of breeds, "the Shire is the best draught horse in the world".

The discussion ended in a unanimous vote in favour of Tom Forshaw's suggestion as a basis of negotiation with the Clydesdale Society, in the hope that the latter, if they started a Grade Register, would reciprocate. Before the meeting broke up, Alfred Clark moved that the Ministry should be asked to refuse to license any stallion with grease or thick legs. Someone suggested that might create the risk of "putting the breed into the hands of vets, or perhaps a racehorse trainer". So he hastily changed his resolution, and it was unanimously agreed to press that "*all* horses used for breeding purposes shall be licensed in the same way as bulls." The Ministry later acknowledged the request, which would be borne in mind. The Clydesdale Society also acknowledged Albert Holland's letter, but did not, as promised, communicate further. Eventually they said that the whole matter had been deferred until after the war. The Emergency Committee then resolved to admit the female produce of the Shire/Clyde cross into Register B.

Few realised the significance of the new rule. If the fullest possible advantage of it were taken, one could achieve in six generations a registered Shire mare that was proportionately more Clydesdale than Shire. If any reader happens to be non-mathematical, he may find the table overleaf of use:

† In column 7, for the sake of simplicity, a "registered stallion" has been regarded as 100% pure, and a "registered mare" as possibly the progeny of a registered stallion out of a "B" mare and therefore 75% pure Shire and 25% Clydesdale. However, the registered stallion in column 2 is not pure, but has $20\frac{1}{4}$ parts Shire and $11\frac{3}{4}$ parts Clydesdale blood out of 32: the B mare is 11 parts Shire and 21 parts Clydesdale. Therefore, if all the animals in column 7 also contained blood in the same proportions as those in column 2, and if the registered Clydesdales in column 7 were 100% "pure", the registered "Shire" filly in column 1 would be only $1,285\frac{3}{4}$ parts Shire and $2,810\frac{1}{4}$ parts Clydesdale in 4,096. That is, she would have a little less than 31.4% Shire blood, but just over 68.6% Clydesdale blood. It is of course possible to refine these calculations *ad infinitum*, each time reducing the proportion of Shire blood. But the exercise, already theoretical, becomes somewhat academic! Nevertheless, the permitted influence given to the Clydesdale was greater than Tom Forshaw probably calculated.

As for the time factor, if all the mares in column 7 were foaled in 1943 and

1	2 Parents	3 G-parents	4 G-g parents	5 G-g-g parents	6 G-g-g-g-parents	7 G-g-g-g-g-parents	Proportion of Blood (a) SHIRE (min.)	(b) CLYDE (max.)
Registered Filly	Registered stallion	Registered stallion	Registered stallion	Registered "s"	Registered "s"	Registered s × registered m	1¾	¼
					Registered "m"	Registered s × "B" m	1½	½
				Registered "m"	Registered "s"	Registered s × registered m	1¾	¼
					"B" mare	Registered s × registered Clyde m	1	1
			Registered mare	Registered "s"	Registered "s"	Registered s × registered m	1¾	¼
					Registered "m"	Registered s × "B" m	1½	½
				"B" mare	Registered "s"	Registered s × registered m	1¾	¼
					Registered Clyde m	2 registered Clydes	0	2
		Registered mare	Registered stallion	Registered "s"	Registered "s"	Registered s × registered m	1¾	¼
					Registered "m"	Registered s × "B" m	1½	½
				Registered "m"	Registered "s"	Registered s × registered m	1¾	¼
					"B" mare	Registered s × registered Clyde m	1	1
			"B" mare	Registered "s"	Registered "s"	Registered s × registered m	1¾	¼
					Registered "m"	Registered s × "B" m	1½	½
				Registered Clyde mare	Registered "s"	Registered s × registered m	1¾	¼
					2 registered Clydes	4 registered Clydes	0	4
	"B" mare	Registered stallion	Registered stallion	Registered "s"		Registered s × registered m	1¾	¼
						Registered s × "B" m	1½	½
				Registered "m"		Registered s × registered m	1¾	¼
						Registered s × registered Clyde m	1	1
			Registered mare	Registered "s"		Registered s × registered m	1¾	¼
						Registered s × "B" m	1½	½
				"B" mare		Registered s × registered m	1¾	¼
						2 registered Clydes	0	2
		Registered Clyde mare	2 registered Clydes	4 registered Clydes	8 registered Clydes	16 registered Clydes	0	16

Parts in 64: 31¼ | 32¾
or †Parts in 4,096: 1,285¾ | 2,810¼

were covered successfully at the age of two, the animals in column 6 would be foaled in 1946. If, thereafter, every filly produced a foal at the age of three, the eligible filly in column 1 could be foaled in 1961. If every "Shire" breeder in England did exactly the same thing, starting at the same time and proceeding at the same rate, every female in the Stud-book proper would be more Clydesdale than Shire, within twenty years. If such females (that is, those like the filly in column 1) were covered by stallions containing blood in the proportion similar to the stallion in column 2, the progeny would be $3,877\frac{3}{4}$ parts Shire and $4,314\frac{1}{4}$ parts Clydesdale. If they were colts, they would be eligible for the Stud-book. Mated to a filly of Column 1 proportions, such a colt's produce would be only $6,449\frac{1}{4}$ parts Shire and $9,934\frac{3}{4}$ parts Clydesdale. By that time, therefore, even registered Shire stallions would be less than 40% Shire, and more than 60% Clydesdale.

It is time to return from arithmetical fantasy to reality. However, our academic digression does serve as a reminder of the reason why the Scottish horse, in the nineteenth century, became so like the English and illustrates how easily the English one, in the twentieth, could be made to resemble the Scottish, even within Stud-book rules. If the two "breeds" had been as different as the Suffolk or Percheron is from either, chaos would have resulted. But they are, as they always have been, two varieties of the same British cart-horse.

At the end of 1945, Will Smith had another go, proposing to the Council that the produce of a registered Clydesdale stallion out of a registered Shire mare should be eligible for Register B, on equal terms with the other cross. This time, Fowler sided with Tom Forshaw in opposing the new idea, which was thrown out. Smith raised the subject again when an Annual General Meeting was at last held in 1946 and William Brock, Christopher Barker, W. J. Cumber and R. G. Thompson were among those who strongly opposed him. That was the end of the proposal.

Unfortunately, it was neither the beginning nor the end of the use of Clydesdale stallions by some breeders who wished to speed the cleaner-legs campaign in their own way and who found it hard to resist the temptation to fake certificates of breeding to gain entry for the produce into the Stud-book. Most people believed that cases had been occurring for some time, but it was a new member who had the hardihood to put the allegations on paper and demand that the Society take some action about it. This was Flight-Lieutenant Reg Kilby, who had taken the Home Farm at Tring Park and whose stud relied heavily upon the advice of Tom Fowler. Perhaps the R.A.F. dives in where the cart-horse man fears to tread. A special committee's investigations were not very revealing as, indeed, they could not be. Let anyone try to do better who thinks that he can decide with the aid of only quasi-judicial powers, which mare was served by what horse on which dates several years ago: and if he can do that, let him decide which of two or more services by different horses was the effective one. It is not proposed to pursue that matter here, simply because the extent to which any allegations were true is utterly impossible to determine: and even a sample enquiry cannot be reported both with clarity and without libel.

This sort of suspicion was, of course, damaging to any movement which inevitably has to rely largely on the honesty of those who support it. And allegation is difficult to refute, even when entirely unfounded. Let us end by quoting just one example of the harm that can be done by seeing fire every time there appears to be smoke. The reader may remember the crisp-moving Crimwell Modern Boy, which won the two-year-old class at the 1944 Derby stallion show for William Brock and was sold for 860 guineas after two inspections by Professor Harold Burrow. This, and the very name of the horse, makes him of some significance. *The Farmer and Stockbreeder* said he was "the very type that Shire men should aim at". Harry Holderness of *The Preston Guardian*, wrote, guardedly (and without the italics used here), "He is a bay, powerfully quartered, growthy, beautiful in limb and conformation, and coupled with links of steel. When he moved he gave us plenty of chance to see his great plates and *in the cleanliness of his limbs he indicated the proximity on his dam's side of Clydesdale blood*." Perhaps the only rubbish Holderness ever wrote.

First, let us look at the Stud-book claims:

Grading-Up Register 2 (1941): A172 KITTY, bred 1927 by W. Sharpe, Morley House, Bicker, Boston: o, E. A. Sharpe and Sons, Rectory Farm, Barrowby, Grantham. Sire: Deeping Fearless 39872 (bred in 1923 by George Freir).

Her daughter (in same register): B52 FLOWER, bred 1935 by E.A. Sharpe and Sons: o, William Leadenham, Spittlegate Farm, Grantham. Sire: Burcot Bulwark 40228 (bred 1927).

Vol. 65: CRIMWELL MODERN BOY 43919, bred 1942 by William Leadenham: o, William Brock. Sire: Horbling What's Wanted 42940, bred in 1936, and owned by J. H. Owen and Sons, Kirkby Langthorpe, Sleaford: dam, B52 Flower. (This volume repeats the breeding of Flower and Kitty, with a curious mistake, saying that the latter was bred by E. A. Sharpe & Sons. Grading-up Register 2 was right – she was bred by the uncle, W. Sharpe.) Crimwell Modern Boy was eligible for the Stud-book because a younger full sister, 133138 Crimwell Flower, foaled in 1940, was already registered.

Bill Rastall could tell us whether these particulars were true or false. Born in 1890, he went on the land after leaving school, became a wagoner for J. T. Lord at Hough Grange in 1919, and travelled stallions for William Todd of Ponton 1923–1924 and for the Grantham Society 1925–1935. Bill led Burcot Bulwark in 1931–1943, in the last of which years one of his get was B52 Flower. His comment on this horse thirty-five years later was "He was all

right, but I shouldn't pass him sound. Never did. He had three sidebones."
From 1936, Bill Rastall led "against the Grantham Society" for Owens of
Horbling. In 1941 he had Horbling What's Wanted. "He was the best getter I
had with Owen. Leadenham's colt was the best of his get. They said there was
some Clyde in him but there wasn't. He was out of Leadenham's mare by
Burcot Bulwark, out of Sharpe's little rough-legged mare. Came out of the
Fens somewhere. He was a good colt. His only fault, he was light in his colour.
He got his clean legs from What's Wanted's dam's sire, Boro' Blue Blood."
(This horse, 32134, was bred in 1913 and was a son of King of Tandridge, the
most influential son in later years, through his own sons, of Lockinge Forest
King.) "Brock bought him at 18 months for £60 and sold him as a two-year-
old at Derby for 860 guineas after winning his class. He was decent enough to
give Leadenham the prize."[3]

If Bill Rastall knew anything about "a bit of Clyde" in Crimwell Modern
Boy, he would have said so. And what he did not know about what was going
on in the part of England where he moved about, is not worth recording.

Whatever the rights and wrongs of all this, the breed was certainly changing
rapidly. One old stager, asked by a friend at an agricultural show whether he
had seen the Shires, replied, "No, I haven't seen any Shires. But I saw some
giraffes walking round."[4]

5. THE MASSACRE OF 1947

"You can pin-point the thing, you know. 1947. War Ended. Things settled
down. Then, wham. All collapsed over-night." In a conversational style worthy
of Alfred Jingle, a certain former London horse-contractor reminisced about
the end of the working-horse trade. "Wages, of course. And prosperity. People
struggled on all through. Little change in their arrangements. But war alters it
all in the end. People re-equipping. Couldn't get new vans anyway. So they'd
wash their hands of it all. Dealers, repositories, forage merchants, harness
makers – the lot. Can't think of a dealer who didn't end up broke: or bust."

How many tons could be hauled by a horse – per man? That was the
question that everyone asked in 1947. Robert Deards, the transport contractors, did not carry out a detailed survey of relative costs. No one did, then. It
was left to two breweries, much later, to surprise everyone with the figures.
How many tons *per man*? Well, 2. That was simply it. A motor engine could
haul 20 – per man. At the Elephant and Castle, "the world's largest horse
auction", founded by Tillings and others in 1895, the auctioneer Alfred Harris,
resplendent as ever with shiny top hat and buttonhole, was obliged to sell
second-hand motors, as well as second-hand horses. Cave's of Birmingham,
established in 1799, used to sell 140 to 200 horses a week. Now they too had to
try motor auctions. But old Mr. Cave was very old and Mr. Jagger, his
assistant, retired. In the end they closed down. This was not quite yet. But in
1947 the repositories were empty or emptying. The knackers' yards were full.

In March 1947, William Cumber reminded the Shire A.G.M. that, in agriculture, there were "only 20% less horses now than in 1939, in spite of mechanisation". The horse was the most economic way to cultivate the land, and so on. Before the year was out, he had to sing a different song. If a horse's working life was ten years, it would need 44,000 to be bred each year to arrest the drop in numbers. In 1946, there had been only 16,000 live foals. At least 15% of these foals were killed, as foals, for food. One man had nine mares with foals. A dealer offered £28 each for the foals – for slaughter: the old knacker's price had always been £5 per full-grown horse. The slaughter included vast numbers of breeding animals, too. "There will soon be no mares to breed from."

The Shire Society wrote to Tom Williams, the Minister of Agriculture. He passed the letter on to the Minister of Food, John Strachey. The reply was that "The Ministry does not control the slaughter of horses for food and the steps which they have taken for regulating the trade in horseflesh are limited to the fixing of maximum prices, the licensing of wholesalers, the prohibition of the use of horseflesh in any manufactured meat product or compound article of food, and certain other minor matters. The introduction of measures to limit the number of horses slaughtered for food would involve the introduction of new and additional restrictions." Maximum permitted prices "are at a level which does not encourage the sale of fit horses for slaughter for food. Such horses would normally fetch a substantially higher price than they are worth as meat, and it is felt most unlikely that owners would dispose of their horses for slaughter as long as a genuine demand exists for working or breeding animals." Of course. But there was no genuine demand.

In the House of Commons, Lieutenant-Colonel Bromley-Davenport asked if the Minister of Food was aware that unlicensed slaughterers were doing an extensive trade at high prices. Dr. Edith Summerskill replied that he was not, and that such a traffic in horseflesh would constitute a breach of the regulations. In 1948, she said the Knackers' Yard Order would come into effect on 19th December. Owners of such yards would have to obtain licences from local authorities and from the Ministry of Food and would be obliged to keep records of the number of animals slaughtered. But these records are a couple of years too late to reveal the brisk trade in death during 1947. Statistics for that year are in fact non-existent. Colonel Stanley Bell, one of the few Lancastrian Presidents of the Shire Society, probably got as near the truth as anyone – and he could talk only about Rochdale. He said that 2,600 horses were slaughtered there during the twelve months. In the country as a whole, it is a conservative estimate that 100,000 were put down, and at least another 100,000 in 1948. And it is pretty safe to say that 40% of these were under three years of age.

Mechanisation of transport in the towns had of course been continuing at an accelerating rate for something approaching thirty years and the sudden rush at the end was a noisy finale, like the last of the water running out of a bath. It was on the farm where the change was sudden. A variety of causes combined to bring it about. Farm workers continued to leave the land. Those who

7. Haven't we met before, somewhere? Yes, it's Bob and Baron again (see 5), now working for Wadworth and Company Limited, the Devizes brewers. When Hull Brewery gave up horses, Wadworth's were just one of those re-starting horse deliveries. So they were just what was wanted, and are pictured here with their driver, Ken Percey – formerly of Thwaites. Malcolm Searle, his assistant, is just coming up to half his age. Bob and Baron, now (in 1976) aged six and seven, have clearly taken to the West country. Perhaps you, dear reader, would feel as sleek and healthy in the atmosphere of the brewery yard! This pair deliver beer to pubs within a mile and a half of the town.

8. Some of Whitbread and Company Limited's staff on holiday and full of *joie de vivre* on the hop farm at Paddock Wood. When Samuel Whitbread founded the brewery in 1742, he went in for great Shires, though nobody knew them by that name in those days. (A sample of these dray horses, exactly fifty years on, can be seen in black and white Plate 5.) By 1900, Whitbread's had nearly 400 Shires. The company has horsed the Speaker's coach on ceremonial occasions since 1839, and the Lord Mayor's coach, with six greys, from 1954. Colonel W. H. Whitbread was President of the Shire Horse Society 230 years after his ancestor bought his first horses. Soundness and good conformation are easier to come by today.

remained cost more to pay in relation to the rise in agricultural prices. Their minimum hours were reduced, and this particularly affected the cost of horse operations, in view of the carter's or ploughman's "non-productive" hours at the beginning and end of each day, and in the middle of it too, in the care and baiting of his horses. As the war-effort slackened off from its headlong intensity, the available machines could cope with the work, without the horses. The farmers themselves were in a vastly improved financial position. Their share of the national income had risen from 1.2% in 1938–1939 to 2.4% in 1944–1945. By 1947, they had satisfied themselves that, whatever might happen in the future, they were not going to be "kicked out and forgotten" as they had been in 1921. Engines and machines had improved out of knowledge, as they do in the urgency of war. Many of those who had gained experience of machinery under the "War Ags" went into the service trades which increased on a scale that, before the war, was quite unknown in the farming industry. The capital was available, or could be borrowed, to reorganise a farm's machinery so that it formed a planned and inter-connecting whole, instead of a collection of items that did not belong together, as perforce it had been during the war when the farmer was allocated all sorts of things that would not go with the Fordson tractor he had been given in the first place. More than that, the farmers could reorganise the very farm itself to fit the machinery that would work it.

K. A. H. Murray has summed it all up. "Whereas in many other industries the war often entailed the sacrifice of peace-time plans and ambitions, in agriculture it offered an opportunity such as it could never have been given in peace-time to apply new knowledge and to revive the productivity of the land."[5] As our horse-contractor said of the London trade, this happened suddenly. "War ended, things settled down. Then wham."

The year 1947 was the real year of the new age, and even the farmers could not quite believe it. Adrian Bell caught the atmosphere well when he wrote of the man with 100 acres, a tractor and, still, two horses. "One horse is useful for occasional carting of hay, straw, and fodder to the cows, for horse-hoeing and raking and pulling the light seed-harrows. What about the other? He is young, he is frisky, and needs plenty of regular hard work to keep him in order. But there is only work for him sporadically; and that is bad, because, though he is frisky, his muscles are not hard, and after half a day's hard pulling he is like a fat man who has run a mile to catch a train. Why then does the farmer keep this second horse who costs £1 a week for his keep? To be quite truthful the farmer keeps him for just the same reason that one touches wood: this is a transitional age, and he has an uneasy feeling that there might come a freakish season when the tractor would not operate on the land, so he could still plough with his horses. A sort of "you never know" feeling. It is difficult after centuries of horse work to feel quite sure that the horse is dispensable. Talk to any farmer and the chances are he will tell you he has at least one horse that hardly does three weeks work in the year."[6]

CHAPTER XV

1948–1975

To the Brink, and Back Again

IF THE Shire horse were now extinct, the final stage of its long journey would be a simple affair to narrate. But it is not, and it does not appear in the least likely to become so. Its history, still being enacted, is impossible for a contemporary, without clairvoyance, to interpret. Seeming triumphs may be mere flashes in the pan, and disasters turn out to be disguised blessings. The heretics of today may be revealed as the pillars of tomorrow's faith, friends may be misguided, foolish men shown to be wise, and important ones of no lasting account. So, these last pages are confined chiefly to simple reporting of what facts seem to be relevant to the topics that have gone before. That is, to tying loose ends. As far as possible, the names of individual horses or men are omitted. It will be the duty of some later commentator to select and praise the great ones of our present time.

I. NEAR TO DEATH: 1948–1962

Colonel T. W. Daniel of the Mettingham stud remarked to the Council, "We should not only go into the question of getting publicity, but also of how *not* to get it." He had in mind Harry Ferguson in particular, who was firing broadsides pretty regularly at horse-husbandry. Of all the cultivable acres in the British Isles, said Ferguson, 40% were wasted. Over 1,000,000 power animals were needlessly kept. On a ten acre farm four acres had to feed the horse and the farmer had to work for 1,000 hours to cultivate his land: with a Ferguson tractor he could do it in 200 hours, decrease his costs, keep more hens or extra pigs or cattle, and at the same time save his country (either the U.K. or Eire) from economic strangulation and ultimate, or possibly imminent, ruin. The Newton Abbot and District Heavy Horse Society, doughty successors to old Scratton's South Devon Horse Association which had joined the English Cart Horse Society in 1878, protested that his brochures contained "detrimental references to the horse". They did indeed.

The Society set up a propaganda committee, and G. T. Burrows, retired editor of *The Livestock Journal*, was appointed publicity officer. He died in 1949 and was succeeded by J. E. Hargreaves of *The Preston Guardian*. It was all a desperate business. At the 1950 A.G.M., Sir Stanley Bell referred to the continued slaughter. The horse population had decreased by 27% in two years. Liverpool members complained that the local licensing authorities were stipulating that hauliers wishing to purchase an additional motor vehicle must produce evidence that they had dispensed with three horses – if, of course, they had owned any. This was reported to the Ministry of Agriculture, which was worried by the state of affairs and had set up a Heavy Horse Committee comprising all interested bodies, including three representatives of each of the breed societies, to evolve schemes for encouraging the use of horses. In 1951, the Suffolk Horse Society's "mares scheme" for small farmers had to be ended and the last Society mare was sold. (G. E. Evans has selected this as the chief "farewell year" of the draught-horse on many farms in that county.[1]) The Shire Society spent hours debating a motion by Chris Catterall that its funds should be spent liberally and urgently over five years rather than allow them to remain "until such times as the position of the Shire horse is beyond help". His proposal was carried but, as William Cumber remarked, giving doles was of no use, whatever form they took. "The only thing that will encourage breeding is a market for horses."

In 1952, an illustrated booklet, *The Heavy Horse for Farm Work and Transport*, was published by the British Horse Society (see below). This was one mouse to which the Ministry's mountain of a Heavy Horse Committee gave birth. A film extolling heavy-horses was another. Holland publicised with considerable glee the fact that three days of incessant rain had turned the 100 acre site of the 1952 Isle of Thanet ploughing match into a quagmire. "While the fourteen two or four horse teams plodded on regardless of conditions, all completing the course, a large proportion of the machine-drawn ploughs floundered in the swamp and bogged down." In the class for champion ploughmen, "twenty-two started, but by the time the match was concluded a dozen tractor engines were silenced". However, except at this ploughing match, the air was increasingly filled with the roar of machines, and it is pointless to follow in any further detail the annual decline in horse-breeding throughout this period. The slaughter rate declined only because there were less horses left to kill.

We turn therefore to some points of detail concerning the breed and the Society.

a. *The British Horse Society*

The docking scare of 1921 had brought the National Horse Association into existence. It was the 1948 Olympic Games which transformed it. The Institute of the Horse, founded in 1924 to promote riding, had been accepted as the authority to represent Great Britain at international horse events but, with the games due to be contested in this country, it believed that a strong united organisation was required. Accordingly, in January 1947, it had approached the N.H.A. with a view to an amalgamation. After many matings, the produce of the two was the British Horse Society, formed in November. Reg Brown of the N.H.A. was appointed secretary and in truly Gilbeian style the first President was a Shire man, W. J. Cumber. Sir Walter would have been pleased about this.

b. *London Office again*

Albert Holland managed to escape from the Denham wilderness in April
1948, for accommodation was found in a house rented by the British Dairy
Farmers at 17 Devonshire Street, somewhat fittingly during the presidency of
the son and successor of "the old Dook". So the Council, for the second time
in its history, ceased to require the unfailing hospitality of the Farmers' Club
for its meetings and the Shire offices moved back from dreadful Denham into
the West End, bringing the Hunters with them. But they were no longer
masters of a house, or even a shop.

c. *Stallion licensing*

The request made to the Ministry during the war that the licensing scheme
should be applied to all stallions, and not merely to those which travelled or
stood in public places, was repeated soon after the war at the instigation of the
Llandyssul Heavy Horse Society. All breed societies were unanimous about
this, and welcomed the Horse Breeding Act 1948, which came into effect the
following January. Part 2 made the licensing of all entire horses compulsory.

d. *Docking*

In 1949, the attack on docking was resumed, after an interval of eleven years.
There had recently been rumblings of renewed trouble when the R.S.P.C.A.
and other bodies tried to persuade the R.A.S.E. to refuse docked horses at
Royal Shows, as has been proposed in 1892. Now a Private Bill to prohibit the
practice actually reached the committee stage of the Second Reading without
the knowledge of anyone affected by it. 1921 was repeating itself. Holland
reacted as vigorously as Charlton had done twenty-eight years before. The
Council engaged parliamentary agents to oppose the Bill and mobilised its
three sister-societies. Major Harry Legge-Bourke, member for the Isle of Ely,
led a deputation to Major Younger at the Home Office, and proposed an
amendment to the Bill allowing the Minister to grant authority for docking in
respect of agricultural horses. But, this time, the heavy-horse men had no other
allies, except the National Farmers' Union. Some influential bodies that
promised support were afraid of public opinion, which was entirely ignorant
of the facts of the case: the British Horse Society was of course afraid of its
own members, as its predecessor, the N.H.A., had been in 1938. The Shire,
Clydesdale, Suffolk and Percheron secretaries sent out questionnaires to all their
members, who totalled about 9,000, and received replies from only twenty-
four who were in favour of the Bill.

It was all in vain. The Bill was passed, without amendment, and the
Docking and Nicking of Horses Act 1949 came into force on the first day of
the following year. Docking, like the useless practice of nicking, was entirely
prohibited except where a Member of the R.C.V.S. certified it to be necessary.
A second section of the Act forbade the importation of docked horses from 1st
January 1955, exemption being possible only in exceptional circumstances,

when the horse was required for breeding and no undocked substitute was available. In 1952, the Council asked the three other Societies if they were interested in trying to get the Act repealed: in 1955 the Royal Highland Society, whose attitude was very different from the R.A.S.E., were prepared to back the Clydesdale Society in trying for an amendment to exclude heavy-horses. But it was a lost cause. An old Shire breeder said "They're going to look queer things with long tails." Yet it had to be.

e. *Government grants*

E. B. Shine, who had been such a friend of the Shire Society prior to his retirement as Assistant Secretary at the Ministry, died in the autumn of 1952, leaving John G. Truman of Bushnell, Illinois as the sole honorary member. Shine would not have been happy with what occurred in the next few years. By the end of 1954, there were few stallion societies which had not collapsed. Some had tried amalgamating with neighbours, but an enlarged area and few mares made the old-fashioned walking route virtually a thing of the past. It was a matter of a motorised box all the way. J. E. Jones, the Montgomeryshire breeder, suggested that the Government grants should be given to stallion owners instead of to societies: otherwise no one would want to keep a stallion at all. The Clydesdale Society was also in favour of this. In November 1955, they suggested that a subsidy of £250 for a travelling stallion and £150 for one which stood at home would cost the Government only about £25,000. (The year before, 212 stallions of the four breeds had been licensed in England and Wales, and fifteen other heavy ones. But it was a reasonable estimate that the real onus of maintaining all four heavy breeds fell upon only about 100.) In March 1957 the Minister, Derick Amory, in spite of intense pressure, solved the whole problem by stopping the grants altogether, and for good.

Albert Holland wrote to Robert Jarvis, the Clydesdale secretary, "Although I am not a Socialist, I do not think Mr. Tom Williams would have taken such a drastic step to save so little." To Albert Vyse, Percheron secretary, he wrote that "the amount involved is so ridiculously small that it is difficult to understand the mentality of the Minister in his statement that he had to save funds". He did not write to Raymond Keer, for the Suffolk men had tried to plough a lone furrow in asking for the retention of grants to societies instead of allocating them to stallion-owners. But he did address a letter of thanks to Major Legge-Bourke who, as in the docking case, had done his best. "It is a pity", wrote Holland, "that the Minister could not have been at Derby to see the Shire Horse Show. He might have changed his views when he had before him 91 Shires of all ages, being judged before a crowd of between two and three thousand enthusiasts. At the sale the following day, every lot was sold and the demand for work horses was greater than the supply." The few remaining hiring societies were very bitter, because the grant was withheld a month before the season started, and long after hiring arrangements had been made. By 1962, only eight hiring societies were still active.

f. *The Tote*

The Racecourse Totalisator Charity Trust, on the other hand, continued to help, though there were almost annual alarms about its intentions. Grants were resumed after the war at £500, and rose to £2,000 by 1949. In the mid-'fifties the Shire, Clydesdale and Suffolk societies were receiving £1,800 each and the Percheron Society £1,400 out of a total of nearly £600,000 Tote profits, the main portion of which was of course allocated to racing. Since the Shire was the only society with London headquarters, the co-ordination of the four organisations' efforts to persuade the Trust to continue its grant fell upon Albert Holland, and it was a task he performed with persistence and great skill, his statement in 1956 being a masterly effort. However, it was rather sad that the heavy-horse societies had to form their own little independent group to fight for themselves, because it was precisely for this sort of thing that they had formed the National Horse Association years before.

By 1961, the grant to the Shire Society had shrivelled to £700, though a bonus of £300 was given when the Racecourse Totalisator Charity Trust was wound up that year. Under the organisation set up by the new Betting Levy Act, Field Marshal Lord Harding, chairman of the Horserace Betting Levy Board, continued the grants but, in spite of all Holland's persuasive powers, they continued to shrink. In 1963 separate grants to the hiring societies were cut off and the Society's grant, which had to cover the gap, was down to £500.

g. *Spring Shows*

If the Spring Shows failed to reflect the growing misery of these years, it was simply because so many staunch members obstinately averted their eyes from the escalating cost of sending heavy-horses many miles for exhibition without compensation in the form of lucrative trade. Herein lies a further reason for refraining from discussing the best horses of this period. It was the owners that had no hope of winning their class, and yet loyally brought their horses along, who kept things going. There can be no champions and no class-winners without losers to make them so – and no show either. And, without its show, the whole structure of the breed society might well have collapsed in the late 'fifties. Tempting as it is, therefore, to dilate on the Whewells' Althorpe Trump Card of 1947-1948, Richard Sutton's The Bomber in 1949, George Richardson's Grange Wood Clifford's What's Wanted in 1953-1955 and R. A. S. Pleavin's Manor Premier King at the very end of this period, or to point to Morris Belcher and Eady Robinson with two champions each, it is premature, now, to do so. These, and other great horses and their owners may perhaps be accorded justice at a later date in a separate account of them. It is those who came and were beaten by them that we now salute.

The last show at which all animals were compulsorily inspected, was 1949, and Professor Harold Burrow's last as Honorary Veterinary Inspector. In 1950, a whole class could be inspected, but only if the judges wished. In 1952, admission still cost spectators only 2s. 6d. A man could park his car, enter the Show, buy a catalogue and have a good day out for 7s. 6d. A member, of course, could enter free. But in 1953 non-members were asked to pay 5s.

The depths were plumbed in 1955. Proceedings opened in steady rain, carried across the ground by a cold wind. A very poor class of two-year-olds began to churn the ring into mud: there were only four of them. In the whole show, only twenty-six stallions, twenty-eight mares and fillies and fourteen geldings were forward. But the weather improved, and a fine class of brood mares cheered everyone up. The next day, at S. T. Parker's auction, sixty-four horses were offered and forty-two sold. The top price was 60 guineas for a five-year-old mare – a skewbald! In 1956, eighty-five animals were entered for the 75th anniversary show. Albert Holland worked out that during three-quarters of a century, 28,897 horses had appeared in the Spring Show judging ring, and had been awarded £105,260 in prizes. That was an interesting but melancholy piece of research. At the present rate, it would take 400 years to do it again.

Breeders' prizes were cancelled in 1958, which, after many previous scares, really was the last year on Derby Racecourse. The beautiful brick stables were then demolished and the Paddocks became a housing estate. If it had not been for the Percheron breeders, the show might well have been transferred in 1959 to the Shropshire and West Midland showyard at Shrewsbury. It was very suitable, and the location would have been a just reward for the special loyalty of the Lancashire and Montgomeryshire Shire men. But a shrinking exhibition meant a dwindling attendance, and the Racecourse Betting Control Board had to be somehow impressed. The Suffolk and Percheron societies had been approached with a view to combining in a "National Heavy Horse Show". The latter accepted, but could not go to Shrewsbury, since their members were mostly in the Cambridgeshire area. So the Peterborough A.S. showground was chosen, and the westerners had farther to travel. The Shire entries were down again – eighteen stallions, twenty-six mares, ten geldings, and ten commercial turn-outs. This was the lowest ever. But the Percheron section with twenty entries, and four turn-outs as well, helped to make it look better. The Percheron Society, which forty years before had been the great enemy, now became and remained the friendly colleague and partner of the Shire Society. The Suffolk Society, for geographical reasons, unfortunately was unable ever to turn the event into a really national English show. Shire entries in 1960–1962 were eighty-six, seventy-six and eighty-three, which represented sheer determination to keep things going. But only Albert Holland knew how he had to persuade and cajole the members to exhibit.

h. *Foal Stakes*

The Lancastrians' successful war-time effort to replace the Peterborough Foal Show and Stakes led to a certain difference of opinion between the promoters and the Council itself. The latter felt that a show calling itself the "National

Pedigree Shire Foal Stakes" ought to be broader-based in its management and should have a formal link with the breed society itself: the former tended to regard this as a "take-over" attitude by the official body, which had been too sleepy to organise the thing in the first place, as it should have done. There was a somewhat uneasy liaison, but the autumn show played an almost incalculably valuable part in providing a competition and mart for foals.

After Haydock Park in 1947, the Show transferred to Derby and, in 1952–1953, to Crewe. Six members of the Shire Council now served on the Foal Stakes Council. A complication arose when the President of the latter happened to be disqualified for angrily leaving the ring with his horse at a Spring Show when he disagreed with the judges. (This was the first disqualification at a Spring Show since 1896.) In 1954 the Stakes were back at Derby, and had far outgrown "foal" status, with classes for older animals. In 1955, they actually were taken over by the Society and the foal society now nominated members to the S.H.S. Foal Stakes Committee. There was an entry of forty-eight foals and thirty-two mares and fillies: thirty-three stallions were nominated for the stakes, and prize-money amounted to £346, with six challenge cups. In 1959 the event moved, like the Spring Show itself, from the Derby paddocks to Peterborough showground, where in five years it fizzled out. However, a "Midlands Shire Foal Society" was formed, also in 1959, in order to cater for and foster interest in the central and west Midlands. It held shows in Derby cattle market and, under the direction of keen supporters who were as determined as the Great Eccleston men had been during the war, was strong enough in 1963 to be ready to fill the gap left by the collapse of the Foal Stakes. Among the leaders were members of the Yates family, especially Gwendoline, of Champion Farm, Quarndon, who shortly became President.

i. *Affiliated shows*

The Spring gelding show continued at Shrewsbury, but in 1949 Hall, Wateridge & Owen combined it with their Special April Prize Sale. The cost to the Shire Society of prizes at country shows in 1948 was £1,585: by 1963, it was only £291. Support was still given to the declining London Cart Horse Parade, sole survivor of such organisations. Even the Liverpool May Day Parade had not re-started after the war.

As the heavy-horse became rarer, so it became more popular amongst the spectators at shows. For example, seventeen four-horse teams of the four breeds, parading together, were a tremendous success at the Cambridge Royal Show in 1951. Turnouts were acclaimed at smaller shows. Heavy-horses displayed at the International Horse Show and the Horse of the Year Show sent people into raptures. At the latter in 1952, pairs of Shires, Clydesdales, Suffolks and Percherons were harnessed to harrows and gave a perfect demonstration of maze marching. "They were skilfully handled", observed Holland, "and gave a performance without a hitch at the end of each session of the Show. The climax was reached when amidst tremendous applause a single

Shetland pony, harnessed to miniature harrows, appeared and walked off behind the majestic pair of Shires." This sort of pretty thing, accompanied by tremendous applause, was a sure sign that the heavy-horses were not actually wanted for their real work.

j. *The Stud-book*

Dark suspicions about the use of Clydesdale stallions prompted William Faulkner of Dalbury Lees, Derbyshire, to suggest in 1948, that, when Shire and Clydesdale stallions travelled in the same box during the service season, no produce of that year reputed to be by the Shire should be accepted for registration. It was scarcely possible to do this, but the Council circularised members about the matter, and also warned them against stallions of two different breeds travelling the same route in alternate weeks. More positively, it was decided that the birth of all foals likely to be registered must be recorded and lodged with the secretary within twenty-eight days, showing pedigree, colour and full markings, together with a sketch card in duplicate, one copy of which would be returned to the breeder on acceptance. Only foals thus recorded would be eligible for entry in the Stud-book as yearlings. One minor relaxation in respect of the B register was occasioned by the delay in registering mares in the Clydesdale book, for which they were accepted only after they had produced a foal. So a filly foal would now be received for Grade B if its dam were "*eligible* for the Clydesdale Stud-book".

Early the following year (1949) it was realised that the recording of foals within four weeks could not be put into operation effectively after all. Many of those who registered horses were not members of the Society and the Council decided that a large proportion of these could not be reached even by Press announcements, "as it is well known that many of the smaller farmers in Wales and other outlying districts never see a copy of the agricultural journals". Instead, it was decided that, from 1950, all animals must be actually registered, whether in the Stud-book or Grade Registers, within the year of birth – i.e. by December 31st.

In 1951, the Society issued its own service books to each stallion owner and hiring society. These contained counterfoils in triplicate, with the usual spaces for dates of each service, signatures of mare owner and stallion groom and so on, and also required the name, colour and precise markings to be supplied of any mare which was not already in the Stud-book. One copy was for retention by the mare owner, one for the stallion owner, and one was to be sent to Holland. As the latter informed members, "the close co-operation of stallion owners and hiring societies is essential to the project being as near foolproof as possible. Circumstances have compelled the Council to take this action in order to tighten up the system of entry into the Stud-book."

At the beginning of 1953, the four-week rule was finally brought into operation, but on stricter terms even than envisaged in 1948. Filly foals had to be not merely recorded, but actually registered within thirty days of birth. In the case of colt foals, the dam had to be re-entered in the Stud-book within thirty days and the foal (not necessarily named) listed as produce: if he was to be registered, it must be as a yearling. No other application would be accepted. If the foal was not actually bred by the owner of it, he had to supply the name and address of the breeder but not a breeder's certificate, which would be obtained by the secretary of the Society. Finally, the Council resolved that "the Editing Committee is empowered to reject or cancel the entry of an animal at its discretion and shall not be required to give any reason for such rejection or cancellation and shall have power to call for any further evidence which it shall in its own absolute discretion think fit, as to the identity, pedigree, or otherwise, of a foal."

The President of 1950, H. T. L. Young, had remarked that he was worried, as a user of commercial horses, about the state of Shire breeding. "It is all legs, with very little middle. We are sacrificing weight for activity, which is not required in the job for which the Shire gelding is used." Two years later, Colonel Nicholson put it more bluntly at the Annual General Meeting: "For some considerable time now I have been wondering where we are wandering and I have no doubt that amongst this large gathering tonight, there are quite a number who are also wondering. Is it not time that the breeders in this Society pulled up their socks and made a determined effort to let us get back to where we were about 10 or 12 years ago? I do not want to move any resolution or anything of that sort tonight, but I do want to ask you breeders to think on these things and see whether during the next 12 months we can't get back on to that straight path and produce the pure bred Shire and so strengthen our Stud-book."

Amid these dark and confusing days, the Society tried valiantly to produce its Stud-book annually. (The Percheron Society, from the start, had issued volumes at irregular intervals – the first appeared in 1922 and only seven appeared in the first twenty-one years.) Printing, paper and staff difficulties during the war had increasingly delayed their publication and Volumes 67 and 68 appeared under one cover, but each contained all the old information appropriate to its year, including the leading show results. Two more pairs were issued, and then Volumes 73–75 all appeared together. There were then two more "threes", and in the last volume of the last group the Grading-Up register was bound in, instead of being issued separately. Volume 82 was issued in loose leaf form, bereft of all information except the actual registers, and there was a binder to contain the sheets. Somewhere along the line, partly because of the new rule about early registration, the numbering of the series had become disjointed. After having been behind hand during the war, Holland got ahead of things, so that the Volume published in 1963, containing animals foaled in 1962, appeared as No. 86. It should have been Volume 84.

k. *Conformation*

Shire secretaries had never been afraid to describe the points of a Shire horse when asked to write an article about them for the Press. And leading breeders had often done so, too. But, oddly, it was not until 1947–1948 that a standard of conformation for stallions, mares and geldings was formally drawn up, reviewed and finally adopted by the Council itself.

l. *The Honourable Roll*

Inevitably, some of the greatest names in Shire history were removed during the period. Harry Bishop, who had made his name with the Pendley stud, and James Forshaw died in 1952. Colonel Nicholson in 1954. Tom Forshaw (who had still attended every Spring Show that had taken place) and Milton Harris, one of the best-known gelding men, in 1955. Norman R. Lloyd of Chirbury in 1956, Alfred Clark II in 1958, Morris Belcher in 1963. Shire-biographies of these would admirably illuminate many facets of Shire history. But perhaps H. T. L. Young of the Ram Brewery, who died in 1957, should be an exception to this chapter's rule against the praise of individuals in recent years, for he took on the mantle of the Gilbeys: and this, in such difficult times, required singular enthusiasm and stout heartedness. His death during sleep thirty-six hours after attending the Foal Stakes was a staggering blow to the Shire men.

Holland wrote in the 1957 Report, "For 25 years our esteemed friend and colleague maintained a stud of the finest Shire geldings, and his magnificent team of blacks is acclaimed throughout the horse world. He must be given most of the credit for the introduction of the heavy horse teams, a feature at all the principal shows. Mr. Young devoted much time to the administration work of our Society, and his appointment as President on four different occasions has never been excelled during the Society's existence. He attended most of the big shows, always accompanied by Mrs. Young, who shared her husband's great admiration for the Shire Horse. We feel with this dear lady in her great sorrow." H. T. L. Young was a typical Shire man of the true sort.

m. *The Secretary*

Albert Holland worked for the Society for exactly sixty years before officially retiring on 30th September 1962. But even then he served another nine months unpaid, after which he was made an honorary member with a permanent seat on the Council. The bachelor John Sloughgrove had found relaxation on his Essex farm. Charlton had been addicted to bowls. Holland hardly ever missed a Saturday's play at Lords: otherwise, he devoted his life, from the day he left school, to horse-society work. He was a remarkable man, if only because his enthusiasm and efficiency were as unfailing at the end as they had ever been: and his had been the most difficult and disheartening task of all the Shire secretaries. Perhaps, in a history full of coincidence, it is appropriate that he at last relinquished his task in the year that Morris Belcher died. It was Belcher who was mainly responsible for giving him his chance on the death of Charlton in 1929. And they both remained stout pillars of the Society through more lean years than fat ones.

2. THE SEVEN SNEEZES: 1963-1975

When the works of man threaten with extinction such creatures as the tiger, the elephant or the rhinoceros, it is his duty to save them if he can, or enough of them to conserve the species, for he did not create them and has no right to destroy them. But the Shire horse, unlike these, is the product of man himself. Without any further use for it, he would presumably be at liberty to cease his careful breeding and to allow it to become extinct.

Thou must not kill, but need'st not strive
Officiously to keep alive.

But is the cynic's interpretation of the sixth commandment, even in this case, the whole duty of man? Surely not. Though created for substance and strength, the Shire has both a majesty and beauty that in no other horse are to be found in such combination. The generation which cast away this work of centuries would certainly be regarded with contempt by posterity, as would an age which allowed Salisbury Cathedral to fall into ruin.

The Shire men certainly strove, and a dwindling band of them was still striving, even though they had permitted some of the size and substance and, with it, some of the beauty and majesty to fade. But in 1963 their breed did face extinction. The first and decisive step along the path to destruction would have been the collapse of the Stud-book society. It was an unvoiced fear, but most thought that this was imminent. It would occur, perhaps, in a couple of years or so. And then doom would follow. Perhaps within twenty years a few specimens might be put in a Longleat or a Woburn Park, to do nothing but stand idle and be gazed at. But where would be the glory of Salisbury if it were to become no longer a temple of God but a Gothic museum?

Albert Holland, that doughty striver, that Londoner through and through, that cheerful defender of the faith, had left the scene. Roy W. Bird was invited, with the kind permission of the council of the Peterborough Agricultural Society, to take his place. (After leaving the army in 1947, he had joined the late Robert Bibby, secretary of the Peterborough A.S., the following year and had succeeded him in 1957.) He took up his additional duties on 1st June 1963 and it was generally considered that these would consist of providing a home of rest for the moribund horse society for perhaps a couple of years, and then of superintending the funeral rites. Peterborough would be a decent place to die. Fred Street himself had suggested that his proposed society should be housed in London or Cambridge or Peterborough. Cambridge was now the headquarters of the Percheron, whose English branch would presumably expire there. London was only for the young and vigorous.

"Yes", said one haulage contractor that summer, "we still have a horse. Just one, with one old man looking after him. When you take the horse out of the shafts, you have to be careful he doesn't fall down: but if we took the horse away from old Joe, *he* would fall down. It's sentiment, really." Sentiment would not save the dray-horse nor prevent his extinction. As W. J. Cumber had said in 1951, "the only thing that will encourage breeding is a market for horses".

The funeral of the Shire Society never took place. Had it done so, it is impossible to imagine a more inappropriate undertaker than the Society's dynamic and ebullient new secretary. Instead, the market slightly revived. Slowly but miraculously, people wanted Shires again: not old obstinate people striving officiously to keep alive, but new ones and many young ones. Of this new life, Roy Bird and a succession of very modern and able Presidents, two at least of whom were absurdly youthful when judged by the standards of the past, were not only the symbol or the symptom but perhaps, more than they would admit, the actual cause.

When Gehazi with the staff failed to tap new life into the Shunammite's son, it was the active breath, literally the inspiration, of Elisha that made the child sneeze seven times and live again. Except that he was no bald-head, David Kay became the Elisha of the Shire. Born on 26th April 1935 in the little village of Balderstone about six miles from Blackburn, he had joined the staff of Thwaites Brewery at the age of seventeen. Three years later, he began to suggest that his company should employ one or two horses in local delivery. At first, his suggestions were flatly rejected: he was a young upstart who did not know what he was talking about. Thwaites had last used horses in 1927 and had therefore lost not only its horse-tradition but also its stables, harness, drays and even its horse-records. Eventually his importuning bore fruit and in 1959 he was told he could have a couple of horses if he could organise the thing himself. The firm's estates department suggested that they could be accommodated in "Shaw's Yard" near the brewery. The gate had been nailed up for years, but he and the foreman carpenter hammered it open with a big mallet and went in. The place was knee-deep in weeds and full of old fireplaces, barrels, bits of machinery and broken bicycles. It was an absolute tip and the buildings were dropping to pieces. The one they chose for the stable had three walls and a leaking roof.

On 1st May 1960, David Kay had a working lorry, a show lorry, a stable and yard that were ship-shape, two bay geldings and two men. One of them was Harry Crossland, who had led the last old horse away from Thwaites' in 1927 and who now brought in the first new one in 1960. The other was the horse-foreman, Patrick Flood, who had spent a number of years in a family carting business before joining a Birmingham brewery, where he had stayed until the stables were closed down. Kay bought a show gelding from William Whewell. He was called Drayman and he was black. In 1963, Thwaites had a pair of blacks. In 1964 they had a team of them. By 1967, Flood had a stable staff of seven. Two years later he was succeeded by Kenneth Percey, who soon gathered round him a group of carters whose most noticeable characteristic was firstly their youth and secondly their quiet way of dealing with their charges. The latter quality they learned – as they had learned all they knew about horses – from Kenneth himself. Perhaps the real revival of the Shire as an occupation fit for young men of the second half of the twentieth century is illustrated best of all in Mrs. Percey's shopping before the staff departed on a few days' showing. Her husband developed the habit of giving her an enormous list of foodstuffs and of sending one of the young carters to fetch all the purchases back from the supermarket. One day, just before a holiday week-end, an assistant there asked her "if the boy-scouts were off camping again".

When heavy-horse carters are mistaken for scouts, it is a symbol that the Shire is no longer dependent on old men and sentiment. And this is true of the only other name that can be mentioned here. David Clarkson joined the staff in 1965, having never driven a horse in his life. In 1970, at the age of only twenty-eight he was appointed coachman and drove Thwaites' four-horse team in a show-ring for the first time at the Shire Show, where he won first prize. Within four years he became foreman in succession to Ken Percey, who in 1974 took charge of the stables of yet another brewery reverting to Shires – Wadworth's at Devizes.

We have not finished yet with David Kay. Perhaps the most amazing, and certainly the most enlightened thing that the Shire Society hierarchy has ever done was to elect this young man as President in 1967, an office he took up six days after his thirty-second birthday. He was indeed the representative "modern man", for he was not merely young: he really was new. Even the election of the aged tenant farmer, the beloved John Rowell, in 1922, was not so revolutionary as this. Among the targets Kay set for 1968 was 100 Shires at the Spring Show, which had not been achieved since the early 'fifties. The entries actually numbered 113. To celebrate this and to mark the Society's ninetieth anniversary, he organised a marathon drive from Peterborough to Buckingham Palace. It was started by the Duchess of Gloucester, performed by five teams of Shires and their drivers and one President, in stages, and occupied two-and-a-half days. An address of loyal greetings to Her Majesty was delivered at their destination, tantamount to an intimation from the Shires to their royal Patron that they were not dead or dying after all. Indeed, a new generation of Shire men had the reins in their hands and an advancing team before them. Perhaps the most foolhardy thing a historian can do is to presume to judge the present, and to think he can select, of all contemporary names, those that will remain the most significant in years to come. But David Kay began to preach the gospel of the Shire at the age of twenty in 1955, when young men with cart-horses were laughed to scorn, and old ones pitied. In less than two decades, pseudo-sophistication was left behind, and young men, and young women too, could boast about Shires rather than apologise for them.

John A. Young, the first "modern" President, holding office for two consecutive years in 1963–1964, also then became treasurer. He effected a complete, even ruthless, reorganisation of the Society's finances. Had it not been for him, the revival of the breed would have been impossible, simply because the breed society would have become bankrupt.

Albert Holland died on 20th November 1971, happy that his life's work had a lasting result after all. Where would the new young Shire men be, but for the doggedness and devotion of the old ones? Three years before his death, 12 Hanover Square was utterly demolished, to be replaced by a modern office block. Yet his memorial, and that of the vast company of men for whom he had worked for over sixty years, would never have been a building or a decorous garden in front of it, but a breed. At the very time he died, his energetic successor was reporting that "the amount of post which pours into the office each morning is almost unbelievable – enquiries from those who want to start breeding horses, from those who have been breeding horses in the past and now want to return to them, and of course many well-wishers overseas. The number of new members in the last three years is quite staggering. It is only a matter of eight or ten years ago that the Society was interesting fewer than ten members each year. Articles appearing in the national and regional press are continually referring to the use to which horses are now returning in both industry and agriculture, and the great revival of interest." The work that this involved was phenomenal and it became necessary to have an assistant secretary. The appointment of a lady to the office was in accord with the modern image of the Society as re-drawn by Messers. Young, Kay and Bird: the choice was also singularly appropriate, for Mrs. Pat Wakefield had already played a large part, since 1963, in bringing new vitality to the Society's daily business and in charming those great individualists, the Shire men, into willing co-operation, one with another and old with young, in the new pattern of things essential to any organisation's success in the 1970s. The Society was exceptionally fortunate also in that the whole of the East of England staff "adopted" the Shire. Not since the early days of John Sloughgrove has youth so dominated the administration.

Now follow a few somewhat random facts and figures to mark the recovery of the heavy-horse in general and in particular of the Shire, from weakness near to death.

a. *Membership*

Morris Belcher died in 1963, but this is not the place to recite the rest of the faithful departed. The living were now required to pay a subscription of 2 guineas – the first time in the Society's history it had been raised. There were only ten recruits. Total membership, at 1,079, was 32% of what it had been in 1947. Annual subscriptions (these best reveal the state of affairs, for declining life membership depended only on the death rate) numbered 349, 18.7% of the 1947 figure and less than 8% of the peak year of 1922. In 1964, total numbers dropped by 12% on 1963, with new members in single figures. Membership dropped a further 17% in 1965. In 1966, it reached its lowest point – 803, including only 210 annual and 593 life members. In the five years 1969–1973, there were 555 *new* members – 260% of the *total* annual membership of 1966. In 1968 the Society's offices moved, with Roy Bird, from 12 Priestgate in Peterborough to the new Alwalton Showground. The Peterborough Show became the East of England Show by incorporating its neighbours.

b. *The Stud-book*

The rule of 1953 about registering filly foals, and colt foals as produce under their dam, within thirty days, were found to be too harsh. Entry within the year of birth for both sexes was substituted. Later registrations were also accepted in special circumstances, on a sliding scale of charges which rose in 1969 to £30 for animals aged three or over. Numbers rose gradually – in 1963, twenty-five colts and forty-nine fillies were registered; in 1968, twenty-nine colts and eighty-three fillies, and, in 1973, seventy-seven colts and 133 fillies.

In 1970, it became compulsory to use a registered prefix. In 1971, further changes were made, including two reversals of all former S.H.S. policy.

The first was an inspection rule, under which animals tendered for registration out of their year of birth could be accepted only after inspection by a member of the Editing Committee and a member of Council. A revised *Standard of points for Shires*, issued in 1973, provided firm guide-lines, though of course it was primarily intended for show judges. Colour was specifically mentioned for the first time – for mares (and geldings), black, brown, bay, grey, roan and chestnut: for stallions, the first four only. A stallion "should not be roan or chestnut": and "no good stallion should be splashed with large white patches over the body". That is, no good pure-bred *Shire* stallion. There was also specific advice that, whereas a great characteristic of the breed had formerly been the wealth of hair on the legs, "to-day the demand is for a cleaner-legged horse with straight fine, silky hair" – with the added comment "not too much".

The second innovation was that animals bred outside the United Kingdom were acceptable provided that both parents were already in the book: or perhaps it was not quite an innovation, since in 1921 the abortive "American section" of Volume 42 contained five mares. Subject to confirmation by the American Clydesdale Society, fillies by a pedigree Shire in the English book out of a pedigree Clydesdale in the American book were also made eligible for Register B.

Perhaps the greatest strength of the Shire Stud-book now, and for the future, is that it is still published every year and is available, as of old, by the time of the Spring Show.

c. *Stallion licensing*

The abolition of compulsory Government licensing was advocated by some horse breeders in 1969. For example the National Pony Society was in favour of replacing the licence by a scheme to be operated by the stud-book associations themselves. A meeting was called by the Ministry. Representatives of eleven breed societies, the British Veterinary Association, the British Equine Veterinary Association and the British Export Council strongly supported the retention of licensing, on the ground that the reasons for which it had been introduced were still valid. The result was that the Ministry, with some modifications, decided to retain the system, no doubt to the general good of horse breeding in this country.

d. *Stallion premium scheme*

The Horse Race Betting Levy Board continued its annual grant at £500, of which £200 was spent on helping the eight surviving hiring societies, and increased it to £750 in 1969. But one of the major obstacles in the way both of improvement and of the wider geographical spread of breeding was the fact that stallion-owning had now become an expensive undertaking which brought little financial compensation. Consequently, too many good colts were being castrated which for the good of the breed should be left entire. So the Council determined to organise the first stallion premium scheme ever to be operated by the Society. A cogent case was submitted to the Board, which allocated the sum of £3,000 for 1973. A donation from the President and a contribution from Society funds increased the cash available to £5,000. With this money, it was possible to offer premiums of £100 for two-year-old stallions and of £150 for older horses, conditional upon their being paraded for inspection at the Spring Show. Thirty-seven applications were received, and thirty-three premiums awarded. In 1974, the Horse Race Betting Levy Board offered £10,000, conditionally upon the Society adding another £2,000.

e. *Hiring societies*

Seven of the eight societies which managed to survive until 1962 were still alive twelve years later, and the eighth was not defunct, but re-juvenated and re-named. First among these is that old pioneer "club" of 1876, the Montgomeryshire District Entire Horse Society, which is now the doyen of all cart-horse societies in Britain, the four breed societies themselves not accepted. Appropriately its chairman since 1935 has been John Downes Evans, son of one of the earliest members, Morris Evans. This family's fame in national pedigree records may be said to have begun, though modestly enough, in 1884 with a five-year-old roan mare which was reserve number (fourth) at the London Show: "Exhibitors, Morris and Edward Evans, Wernllwyd, Berriew: breeder, William Evans, Wernllwyd, Berriew." And why was this 1243 Berriew Venture a roan? Simply because she was by England's Wonder, the Old Strawberry himself, the society's horse in 1877 and 1878. But her dams, and a long line of them, had probably been in the family during the two hundred years that, to William Evans' knowledge, his forebears had been breeding horses. The prefix that the Evans later adopted, "Powisland", will inevitably take the reader's thoughts back to those who were unfortunate enough to have to put up with Robert de Bellême in order to benefit from his stallions.

If the Montgomeryshire society merits a book of its own, so do the others in this surviving group. But here it must suffice to do little more than list them. The Mobberley and District S.H.S. was founded in 1910 as a direct result of the death of Lord Egerton and to fill the gap left locally by the dispersal of his nationally famous Tatton Park stud. The Lichfield S.H.S. began in 1911, and has had only two secretaries – F. D. Winterton until 1958 and R. F. Scoffham since then. The Wisbech S.H.S. is said to have been founded in 1917, but if all its records had survived it would be shown to be older than that: the 1918 financial statement shows a balance of £630. The reason for the historical doubt is that the members of this "club" have run it under several names, including the "Wisbech Stallion Society". As early as 1902, it became affiliated to the parent body as the "Wisbech and District Horse Society". The Great Eccleston S.H.S. was founded in 1918. The High Peak S.H.S. (like the now defunct Pentrich, Shottle and District S.H.S.) began in 1930. The hiring committee of the Derbyshire Agricultural and Horticultural Society was set up in 1932, to fill gaps left by the demise of earlier societies in the county and the dispersal of Mrs. Stanton's stud.

The odd one out among these eight societies is the Rotherham and District Heavy Horse Society, survivor in 1962 of fifteen hiring associations operating in Yorkshire in 1939. It crumbled in the 'sixties, rather than collapsed, since its members got into the habit, as individuals, of using S. G. Garrett's stallions. But it has been replaced by the Yorkshire S.H.S. formed by W. H. Chambers of Swanland-dale, North Ferriby, in 1968. This is the first post-war foundation of its kind, but at the time of writing apparently not the last.

f. *Spring Shows*
In the first five years of this period, entries at the Spring Show were eighty-three, eighty-four, ninety-six and eighty, the drop to within four of the 1961 all-time low of seventy-six coinciding with the move to the Peterborough society's new showground outside the city at Alwalton. The Percherons enabled the muster of animals to top three figures. However, the following year, 1968, was a landmark in the recovery, with 113 Shire entries, the highest for fifteen years. In spite of a bitterly cold night preceding the show, as those who had to spend it on the ground will remember, and two or three inches of snow to greet the horses and men in the first couple of classes, the attendance and gate money showed a sharp rise over recent years. In 1973, Shire entries for the Spring Show numbered 116 including thirty-seven stallions seeking the new premiums. These latter formed the largest group of animals in a Shire ring since the 1946 Spring Show, when there were thirty-seven entries in the three-year-old class and forty-two in the senior mares. In addition, there were eleven singles, seven pairs, and three teams in the turn-outs. These figures were equalled in 1974, when the fifteen-year Spring Show liaison with the Percheron Society came to an end, and "The National Heavy Horse Show" became "The National Shire Horse Show". The fact that

the Percheron men were now strong enough to venture their own exhibition was the clearest possible indication of the reviving strength of cart-horse breeding.

g. *Percheron, Clydesdale and Suffolk*

When the joint show was first held in 1959, the Percheron section comprised twenty entries. At the new separate British Percheron Horse Show on Cottenham racecourse on 25th May 1974, there was a muster of almost three times that number. The ring was occupied from ten o'clock until after five by classes or demonstrations that were all solely concerned with Percheron horses and all proceeding without delay or haste. An explanatory running commentary maintained the unflagging attention of even the most ignorant spectators: and, since the ring-side was crowded three and four deep, there must have been many of these. On a cold and sunless day, nothing could have better indicated the general revival of interest in the heavy-horse. Of the twenty-six females in the breeding classes, twelve had been imported from France. Truly beefy types these were, and presented to the beholder that now rare sight in England, a docked tail. Percheron breeders had an advantage over Shire men in being thus able quickly to supplement their numbers of brood mares to meet the increased demand.

The quality of animals exhibited and the recognition of the need to interest, inform and educate the casual spectator gave the British Percheron Horse Society maximum points in the inter-breed contest for the year. Yet this society had so recently come even nearer to collapse than that of the Shire men. It was first rescued, and then revived, not by gimmickry or any other trick, but simply by the determined enthusiasm of a new generation of farmer-breeders. Albert Vyse, the secretary, attempting to divert attention from the organisation which lay behind the finest old-fashioned "day out" that any lover of heavy-horse flesh could be treated to, said, "This is a true revival, and it is due entirely to farmers. I just happen to be in the middle of it all." As if to illustrate the fact that the old animosities had been driven out of the door by the new spirit, one of those who did much to help the success of the day, though practically unseen, certainly unsung and, to the general public, unknown, was Denys Benson of East Hanningfield in Essex, Shire horse breeder and one of the staunchest and most hard-working members of the Shire Horse Society through the darkest years and on into the new dawn.

Meanwhile the Clydesdale spring show at Glasgow awaited a similar revival. The stallion show organised by the Glasgow Agricultural Society first came into our story in the 1860s. In 1974, the entries at Scotstown numbered only three senior stallions, three two-year-olds and eleven yearlings, with thirty-four mares and fillies and five geldings. Among them light roans predominated and all were judged with traditional Scots deliberation. The Suffolk Horse Society, also, looked for the breath of life. But the Suffolk horse itself, already in 1878 the most ancient of the British breeds in its purity, retains the essential glory – an unchanged conformation. Of all those who have maintained for posterity the true Suffolk, the name of William C. Saunders of Hoxne would spring first to mind. The animals bred by others as well as by him would have rejoiced the heart of Herman Biddell and his friends. All four societies in Britain can still learn from each other and all have much to contribute to the heavy-horse scene in the spirit of friendlier but still healthy competition that now prevails.

h. *Midlands Shire foal show*

The society which began in Derby in 1959 grew steadily in strength and influence after 1963, under the continued presidency of Gwendoline Yates. In 1964, before the revival was apparent elsewhere, there was an entry of seventy-eight – twenty-six colt foals, twenty-four filly foals, and twenty-eight in other classes. By 1971, the average price for filly foals had reached £200, which was reminiscent of 1920. The venue was moved first to the new equestrian centre at Hazelwood near Derby, then back to Derby itself (where a new cattle market had replaced the old) and, in 1973, to Hazelwood again. Upon those who ran the show and sale and annual dinner fell the mantle of Peterborough Foal Show, a mantle which had been picked from the war-time mud by the Lancashire men of Great Eccleston and worn by them through long and difficult intervening years.

i. *A miscellany of shows*

At the beginning of 1971, the Southern Counties Horse Ploughing Association was formed. Within eighteen months it had 263 members, many of them very young indeed. The youngest of all was Richard Ashford, aged thirteen, his great desire being to become a good horse ploughman. To this end, his farmer father bought him a pair of yearling Shires to grow up with him and maybe take part in matches in a few years. And these colts were purchased from E. J. Holland, who was born in 1889, lost his father at the age of two, and took over the responsibility of the farm entirely from his mother and elder brother in 1912. Mrs. Holland would have liked her husband to retire in his eighties, so that they could travel. But her sacrifice will no doubt enable Richard Ashford, perhaps about the year 2040, to tell his grandsons without boasting or exaggeration how his first Shires were bought from old Joscelyn Holland, the owner of the famous Edingale stud in Staffordshire, that ranked with the best in all England for sixty solid years.

Another thirteen-year-old Shire man in 1972 was Mark Morton, who helped his elder brother Andrew, a full sixteen-years-old, and their father Geoff on their 138 acre farm at Holme-on-Spalding Moor in the East Riding. This was run entirely with horses, which worked in teams of up to four or five for ploughing and six for disc harrowing. When the new Southern Counties Horse Ploughing Association held its first great match at Windsor Great Park in the October, there was father Geoff to demonstrate to a crowd of farmers from a wide area the way to do four acres a day with a four-horse team and a two-share John Deere gang plough. The following year, when he held two "open days" on his farm, nearly 6,000 people came to look.

Through the doubtful 'sixties, Hall, Wateridge and Owen continued to include Shire classes in their April horse shows and sales. Even the London Cart Horse Parade had survived by amalgamating in 1966 with the younger Van Horse Parade to form the London Harness Horse Parade. Then new things began to appear amid old surroundings. Young's eight horse team at a Royal Show was thought to be the first exhibited in England. Some agricultural shows re-introduced Shire classes for the first time for many years. Perhaps the innovation which would most have astonished George V or any other great breeder of the 'twenties was that Southern British Road Services Limited in 1974 sponsored Shire classes at four shows. The Essex, Kent, South of England and Suffolk shows catered for areas where, even fifty years earlier, the Shire was weakly supported. If the breed were to die, it would have perished there long since.

In 1974, the death of W. J. Cumber at the age of ninety-five was another token that the old order was passing. Born in the year when Fred Street addressed the Farmers' Club about his idea of starting a stud-book society, he could vividly remember the day when, as a teenager entrusted with his first task to be done entirely on his own, he had taken a mare six miles to be served by a local celebrity called Wokefield William. For seventy years precisely he had been a member of the Shire Horse Society. It was well over half a century since he first had those two great stallions Theale Lockinge and Basildon Clansman, representatives of the two supreme bloodlines of William the Conqueror and Harold. But it is unwise to assume that any great name disappears for ever from the Shire scene. The reader will feel some familiarity with the New Bond Street wine merchants J. R. Parkington & Company Limited, who in the year of Cumber's death sponsored the first "Parkington Golden Guinea Shire Horse of the Year Championship", with the finals held at the Horse of the Year Show in October. The name of all four directors of this company happened to be Gilbey.

j. The United States

Over the years of depression, the American Shire-breeders, such as there were of them, had become long-lost cousins. But in 1966 Roy Bird informed members of "a farmer from the U.S.A." who intended to visit England in July to search for a couple of Shires and for some acquaintance with breeders here. Twelve months later, Jim's Chieftain 45261 bred by J. B. Cooke of Deeping High Bank (ancient Shire ground, this – and a black yearling colt it was, too) left home to travel by sea to join his new owner Arlin Wareing at Blackfoot, Idaho. He withstood the crossing well, did not like the overland journey, but settled down well in his new home.

The interest that this aroused was reminiscent of the Canadian venture of

1923. Yet the sequel is different. This was no fiasco, but the beginning of a revival of the Shire in the United States (in 1968 the first National Shire Horse Show was held since 1949) and also of a relationship between American and English breeders that is closer and more understanding than at any time in Shire history. In 1970, forty American heavy-horse breeders led by Maurice Telleen, editor of *The Draft Horse Journal*, attended the joint show of Shires and Percherons at Peterborough and visited the stables of Young & Company, Watney Mann and Whitbread and Company, the Harness Horse Parade in London and the Cole Ambrose Limited farm in the Fens, where more pedigree Shires have been bred than on any other farm in England. They also made Suffolk and Clydesdale contacts and visits. A return trip by British breeders to the western and mid-western States cemented the new relationship. This was led by Anthony D. Crossman, another young President in the modern image, and was a success from the moment the party's cavalcade of eight cars, all decked with Union Jacks, arrived at its first stopping place, Waterloo, Iowa, to find a welcome spelled out in electric lights to the "Draft Horse Party from Britain". A second tour to England in 1971, again organised by Telleen, included a visit to R. J. Brickell's farm at Enstone in Oxfordshire (another young farmer operating with Shires) and A. W. Lewis' at Tanworth-in-Arden, together with a Shire Horse Society open week-end at Warwick University and Stoneleigh. A lecture and demonstration of Shire horse judging by H. Eady Robinson at the National Equestrian Centre before an enthusiastic audience of young and old from all parts of the country was arranged in conjunction with this second American visit. Shires began, as a result of all these things, to travel to the United States in increasing numbers: for example, four were bought by Nelson Brinkerhoff in 1972 and eight by Arlin Wareing on behalf of other breeders. Fred Street would have been charmed by the fact that Shire-breds were in some cases not just crossing the Atlantic, but flying over it. Geldings also went to the Eichoff Brewers in Switzerland.

k. *Modern Presidents*

For some years, one of the highlights of the Horse of the Year Show has been the Musical Drive by pairs of heavy-horses from the stables of five breweries – Young and Company, Courage, Daniel Thwaites and Company, Watney Mann and Whitbreads. In that order these companies, from 1963, also supplied the first Presidents to hold office for two consecutive years. In this, the historian and the general body of Shire men have satisfaction – the former, because from the very beginning of real Shire history it has always been the brewers who have been the foremost owners of the finest dray-horses, which is what the Shire in his day has primarily been: the latter, because each of these five has been given a difficult challenge by his predecessor in the finding of some new way to promote the welfare of the Society. This may be exhausting for Presidents, but it has been a Shire tradition from the time of Lord Ellesmere onwards, and it is for the good of ordinary members to whom their leadership is given.

l. *The farmers*

Since the prime town employers of the great black horse have always been the brewers, it is appropriate that the Society's recovery has been directed by a line of Presidents drawn from their ranks. But the Shire's prime breeder, from time immemorial to the time of Ellesmere, was the working English farmer. Although, as we have seen, many big landowners, both those of ancient line and those who had made new wealth in commerce or industry, contributed inestimably to the improvement and spread of pedigree stock during the forty years from 1878, it must be pointed out that, as we have also seen, most of these lost interest when, in the 'twenties and later, the heavy-horse ceased to be a good business proposition. At Chatsworth and Lockinge and elsewhere we have observed and praised some of the honourable exceptions. Nevertheless, the credit for the fact that the breed did not die out and that, from the 1960s it began again to flourish, we are indebted solely to working farmer breeders, as of old. It is to be hoped that, in the years to come, all those who gaze with delight upon Shires will know that this is so. These great and beautiful animals are the product not, like the Thoroughbred, of wealth, but of native genius.

m. *The future*

Arlin Wareing of Blackfoot was invited at the 1972 A.G.M. to say what sort of animals the modern American Shire men chiefly wanted. His simple reply was that they required horses of real substance and size. Any English breeder or owner, invited to say what sort of horse is most saleable in England, can reply, equally briefly, that it is a black one. If these things remain so, the ghost of the men of old time, from Bakewell onwards, need not haunt us, in spite of the troubles of the recent past. The modern Shire, needing convalescence and recuperation to build himself up to his former strength, perhaps requires only a course of good Fen treatment, as advocated by Sir Edward Verney to his son in 1635.

PART B

THE SEVEN LINES OF BLOOD

CHAPTER I

Volume One of the Stud-book

I. THE FINGER OF GOD

NOT a single word have the members of Edward Coke's first Editing Committee left behind them to tell us how they worked in compiling the first vital volume of the Stud-book. Every scrap of evidence which they used was later destroyed. We do not even know how many meetings they held. Herman Biddell, on the other hand, who was given sole responsibility for the retrospective Suffolk book, wrote a complete account of his labours. This is instructive, because it gives us an insight into the immeasurably more daunting task that faced Coke and his company.

The first Shire volume, therefore, on which all future volumes and of course all pedigree breeding were to depend, can best be understood – that is, its virtues can best be appreciated and its shortcomings explained – by comparing it with the Suffolk book, which was the simplest of the three to compile, rather than with the Clydesdale one, where the difficulties were more akin to those facing Coke and his fellow-workers, though on a smaller scale. For this reason, it is proposed in this chapter to use the Suffolk book throughout for purposes of comparison.

When the Suffolk Stud-book Association was founded in 1877, Biddell expressed himself willing to prepare a first volume, to contain pedigrees of animals foaled prior to 1879. He devoted the whole of his time to this task for two and a half years, entirely without remuneration. His expenses were paid, but not always claimed. In the course of his visits to all parts of the county, he spent long hours in railway trains and sometimes longer ones on draughty stations, but he often did not write down the fare, especially when the journey in search of someone who might be able to help turned out to be fruitless. He received some clerical assistance, but much of it was from muddle-headed persons who succeeded only in mixing up the jigsaw pieces he was trying to fit together. He had publicity too, amongst breeders, but this was received with suspicion by the more backward and unenlightened. (Suffolk did not have more than its fair share of those who looked askance at a new-fangled idea like a Stud-book. But even a fair share was plenty.) He had, as a basis, the results of his fifteen to twenty years' private research as a part-time pedigree historian, but unfortunately the late Nathaniel Barthropp's manuscripts, which would have been nuggets of pure gold, never came to light.

To his task he brought two precious assets. He had a keenly analytical and disciplined brain, activated by dogged determination. He was also a master of vivid and often pungent prose. These qualities all too rarely go together. That a grizzle-headed, nineteen-stone 19th century Suffolk farmer, standing 18.3-hands high, educated only at a little school in the village of Grundisburgh, should have possessed them both is a marvel. He is said to have been as effective with his tongue as with his pen, and one wonders what he might have achieved if he had chosen another career than farming.

His main sources of information were of five kinds. First were the old stallion cards that began to flood in upon him in ones, twos, handfuls and hundreds from all quarters. Among these were a few scarce and old ones "sent by the Secretary of the English Cart Society, picked up in far away corners in his search for records of another breed". One collection of 120 from Otley had been found in a beam and, "to judge from their cob-webbed faces and stable smell, had been there for many a year." Some of these cards were as frustrating as others were illuminating. For example, Andrew Blake's Everitt (which Biddell entered in his book as No. 173) was foaled in 1778 and travelled for several years at a fee of 18s. 6d. The advertisement said, " 'Tis too tedious to mention his stock, as 'tis well known in the neighbourhood, colts sold as high as 50 and 60gns each at two years old." A later advertisement said, " 'Tis needless to mention his pedigree as 'tis too well known." Biddell commented that this was "a fact patent enough in the year 1778 no doubt, but exactly a century afterwards it took the editor a week's search through ten volumes of musty papers to ascertain". Samson (109, foaled about 1796) was out of a mare "from the well known stock of Mr. Otterwill". In some irritation, Biddell observed that "the editor has not elsewhere met with an allusion to the well known stock of Mr. Otterwill".

In the second place, he waded through the files of *The Ipswich Journal*, which were complete from the year 1725. He also searched all through *The Suffolk Chronicle*. By *The Norwich Mercury* and *The Bury and Norwich Post* he was sent extracts, "all the more welcome after the charge of half-a-crown a volume paid for the right of search in a paper of another county, where little was hoped for, and less found". Thirdly, there were the bound catalogues of the Suffolk Agricultural Association's shows from 1847, when the first printed one was issued. These belonged to his brother Manfred and were the only complete set in existence. In addition, he worked through the catalogues of Royal Shows from the beginning. Fourthly, he used all the sale catalogues that he could lay hands on. And last, but far from the least important, were the further particulars obtained from grooms and stallion leaders, similar to those he had got twenty years before, but this time gleaned by travelling about the county instead of calling local meetings at home. In general, these old men responded magnificently, and Biddell wrote glowing descriptions of more than thirty who had been the most helpful. Where else but in the world of the heavy-horse can one imagine a prosperous mid-Victorian going out of his way to pay tribute in print to other men's humble servants, or even to his own? His pages on this topic are surely unique.

When all was done, he had only three regrets. The job should have been tackled at least fifty years before. "We commenced too late", he wrote, simply. He deplored, too, the delay in publication, for the book was originally intended for distribution at the Kilburn Royal Show in 1879, but did not appear until twelve months later. And he was sorry that he lacked another year at his labour of love, to try to fill in the blanks. "For the errors in the work, I make no apology whatever. They need neither apology nor explanation. I have no anxious fears of their existence, nor sanguinary (sic) hopes that there are none to be found. All they require, is to be corrected, for which, blank pages are inserted at the end of the volume."

Biddell's heavy labours were child's play compared with those that Coke's committee undertook. Suffolk embraces about 948 thousand acres, whereas the districts where the "English Cart Horse" were most likely to be found cover an area about fifteen times that size, even if Yorkshire and seventeen other counties, not to mention Wales, are completely ignored. Furthermore, Suffolk Horse breeding in the fifty years prior to 1878 had been becoming steadily more organised and close-knit, whereas the breeding of Shires had been dissipated over a vaster area than ever and the blood, except in a very few districts, had become mixed and distinctions blurred. Anyone who cared to attend the Suffolk county shows could meet all the stallion owners. Very few Leicestershire men even knew the names of their fellows in Staffordshire.

Edward Coke and Frederic Street, Captain Heaton and Major Dashwood, James Howard and Thomas Brown – did ever a committee of six compile a bible so swiftly, or by methods so unfathomable? One can, by reading Biddell's book, almost share and re-live the joys and frustrations of his research, and the patient piecing together of the fragments. The committee's book, on the other hand, is like the tables of testimony, those tables of stone written apparently with the finger of God, who alone knows what Richard Reynolds, Gilbert Murray, William Wright, John Nix and James Forshaw actually did to help. George Mumford Sexton, playing the part of Moses, emerged with the finished article, ready-written on the one side and on the other, from his incongruous Mount Sinai, the flat land of East Suffolk.

2. PEDIGREES AND THE TABLES

Copies of the English Cart Horse Stud-book were available to members at the Annual Meeting on 3rd March 1880, the second day of the first London Show. The Suffolk Stud-book was ready the following June. An analysis of what each contained is illuminating.

a. *The general text*

The E.C.H. book is a fat octavo volume of 744 pages, containing a "History of the English Cart Horse", by R. S. Reynolds (17 pages – barely 6,000 words), and two prize essays (59 pages) on "The Breeding, Rearing, Feeding and General Management of Farm Horses" by W. R. Trotter from

Northumberland (who did not join the Society until 1881) and Frederic Street himself. Professor Pritchard added a few comments on Trotter's essay. If we bear in mind that the first people to join a pedigree society are those who are already experts, we cannot but conclude that most of what both essayists had to say was absurdly elementary for their readers, unless the general standard of practice at that time was even lower than we have estimated.

The Suffolk book was a quarto volume of 722 pages, including the eight blank ones. Biddell had written several essays totalling almost exactly 100,000 words and one dare not skip even those passages whose interest has been dulled by a century of time, for fear of missing a gem either of expression or information. He had pieces about the growth of the stud-book movement in the county; about the "points" of the Suffolk according to various experts; about the history of the breed, including the various elements of outside blood that had been incorporated; and about some outstanding breeders of the past. He was blunt about the faults of animals that were no longer living, but was never unkind about a man. He attended to detail, but was never trivial. He was accurate without being pedantic. And his sheer ability to express himself in plain and vibrant English is singular amongst practical horsemen and a thing to enjoy. He also added a list of all prize-winners and judges at the County Shows from their beginning in 1832, of winners at Woodbridge Stallion Show since its reorganisation in 1871, and of Suffolk R.A.S.E. winners since the commencement of Royal Shows in 1839. (Alas, the E.C.H. book could do nothing like this. What *was* an English Cart-Horse?) Biddell also included well-reproduced full-page drawings of seven stallions and seven mares.

b. *Pedigrees*

(i) *Register of Stallions*. The E.C.H. book contains stallions only, arranged alphabetically, horses of the same name being placed in chronological order. They were numbered 1–2381. There were two late insertions (1572a and 1982a), but eight numbers were not allotted. There were also six accidental duplicated entries which were cancelled in the errata of Volume 2, and a further four at least which were never cancelled or further commented on. (Confusion over date of foaling etc. may well have caused further duplicates which no one will ever now discover.) The actual number of stallions in the Volume has therefore to be taken as 2,365. The words "Shire Horse" were added in many cases but (as the Preface explained) "it was not to be inferred from the absence of these words that the stallions are not true Shire horses". Owing to the row about the name of the Society, it had been resolved "to leave it to the opinion of individual owners to use the term or not". As some individual owners had been dead a century, one wonders how the editors obtained their opinions. The distinction was in fact entirely whimsical.

The Suffolk book contains 1,236 stallions, arranged under their owners' names, which were given in alphabetical order, each owner's horses being also arranged alphabetically. This necessitated the same horse being entered as many times as he had known owners, which was cumbersome. To make it absurd as well, such stallions were allotted two, three or more different numbers, according to the number of owners they had. (For example, Crisp's Cup-bearer 416, foaled in 1864, one of the greatest Suffolk sires, appears in the book also as Garrett's Cup-bearer 565.) The horses were numbered 1–1411, but, if we subtract 204 of these duplicates and add twenty-nine insertions (e.g. 14a, 1341a and 1341b) the actual number of animals is 1,236. So the E.C.H. book contained less than twice as many horses as Biddell's, which indicates the comparative completeness of his work. It should have had at least seven times as many. One curious feature of the Suffolk book, due to Biddell's thorough-ness, is that it includes some horses which were never in fact used as stallions. Earl 1209, "a light-built colt with small weak forelegs" foaled in 1866, never had any progeny. Sheldon's Rufus 1082, foaled 1860, was hurt in the back and never sired a foal. Captain 1375 (f. about 1841) had a few mares as a two-year-old but went into Messrs. Bullard's dray the next year as a gelding. One would think that the inclusion of such as these was not of much guidance to breeders seeking to establish the ancestry of horses alive in 1880.

Both books give as much information as possible about owner, breeder, prizes won, and pedigree. The Suffolk book in addition has notes, often very copious, in which Biddell not only told all he knew about a horse, including pithy comments on its conformation and character, but also drew attention to any improbabilities or impossibilities which, even after the most exhaustive research, still remained in the pedigree as stated. The E.C.H. book is not only far less accurate, but leaves obvious mistakes (such as the two in the pedigree of Matchless 1509, q.v. VIII.1) unacknowledged. Another E.C.H. weakness, stemming also from lack of time, was a frequent failure properly to link up horses figuring in pedigrees. For example, the dam's sire of Admiral 69 (who was later to figure in the pedigree of the mighty Lockinge Forest King) appears just as "Seward's Major", but in reality he was the celebrated Major 1447.

The E.C.H. book was provided with adequate cross-references in the shape of an alphabetic index of owners and breeders and a chronological index of horses. The Suffolk book had no cross-references at all. (Basically, the E.C.H. book's pattern has never had to be changed to this day. The Suffolk book required only indices to become, as it soon did, a model of its kind. Naturally, a smaller society was later also able to add such refinements as lists of transfers and complete lists of pedigree animals in the possession of each member. The Shire Society, dealing with vast numbers, could not cope with such a thing as this, to the distress of a breed historian.)

(ii) *Appendix of stallions.* The E.C.H. book included an appendix of sixty-five unnumbered "pedigrees not deemed eligible for the Stud-book". The reason for this was not explained and it appears to be no more logical than a directory of non-subscribers to the telephone. But its purpose was really to act as a sort of consolation prize and as an encouragement for the future – and perhaps as a warning.

The Suffolk book also had an appendix, and a very odd thing it was. There were only eight horses in it. Six had already been entered, complete with Stud-book numbers, in their correct place under the name of their owners, but were repeated here because "some were of mixed origin, others of an entirely different breed". Two were here merely because their owners were unknown and they could not be put anywhere else.

(iii) *Register of mares*. The E.C.H. book contained no mares: they were first entered in Volume 2. The Suffolk book had 1,125 mares, set out in the same way as the stallions.

c. *Genealogical tables*

Coke's committee was well aware that Biddell's book would contain horses foaled from about 1760 onwards, and that he would also be able to trace whole tribes and families descended from one or more horses of this early date. The E.C.H. men were therefore in a quandry. Very little could be ascertained, especially in a short time (they had begun far later than Biddell and were determined to publish before him), about eighteenth-century Shires or Lincolns or Blacks or Browns. In fact, their knowledge was more or less confined to the descendants and relations of one Leicestershire stallion, *The Packington Blind Horse*, who was serving mares about 1755–1770. Of the excellence of this family no proof is required now, other than its still being so well remembered then. It would be foolish to decry the legend of this horse. But he was not, as Crisp's Horse of Ufford was going to appear in the Suffolk breed, the Abraham of Shires. He was only the Joseph or Benjamin – if he was that. To be truthful, there was not a man alive who could point to any good horse which was known to be directly descended in the male line from him. If that was due simply to the disheartening ignorance that prevailed about pedigrees as a result of the confusion of the years 1820 onwards, then of course the discovery of information and its publication would put *The Packington Blind Horse* in a place of honour and would be of help to breeders. But if it was due simply to the fading away of whatever excellences that horse's line had possessed, then to exalt him too high would be merely a vainglorious search for antiquity for its own sake or, rather, for the sake of not being out-done by the Suffolk men.

Someone unearthed a genealogical table, compiled over forty years before, in 1834, of some of the descendants of this *Packington Blind Horse*. Who this was, we can now only guess. It was most probably Gilbert Murray of Elvaston, a good and true Shire man, who had collected pedigrees of a great number of stallions that had travelled north Leicestershire, south Derbyshire and south Nottinghamshire from 1818 onwards. His contribution towards the Editing Committee's work was of great value, second only to Reynolds' collection. But it is just possible that John Nix of Alfreton or William Wright of Wheston Hall (see II.2) was responsible. Our ignorance of how the English Cart-Horse book came into being is grievous.

PLATE 41 (*above*) The one-eyed winner. Sir Arthur Nicholson's Champion's Clansman, the best son (both as show horse and sire) of Childwick Champion (Plate 40). Champion in 1917.

PLATE 42 (*left*) Sir Walter Gilbey the Elder. From the portrait painted by W. Q. Orchardson, R.A., which was presented to Sir Walter, by the (then) Prince of Wales, in 1891.

PLATES 43 and 44 Field-Marshal 5th was bred and owned by George V and twice won the London championship. Here he is (*above*), soon after his first success, in 1920; (*below*) His Majesty receives the gold cup the next year from A. C. Duncombe, the President. A. B. Charlton looks on.

The committee, in its haste, bound into the Stud-book this "table of the more immediate descendants of *The Packington Blind Horse*" together with dates, shown clearly as either "ascertained" or "inferred". It measures 17 inches by 17½ inches and runs to eight generations in all – two sons and three daughters; three grandsons and two grand-daughters; sixteen animals in the fourth generation; twenty-five in the fifth; thirty-two in the sixth; forty-eight in the seventh; and thirty-eight in the eighth. It is utterly useless. It does not include the Stud-book numbers of the stallions it quotes, which makes identification often impossible. Where such a link can be made, the table makes claims that the Stud-book itself does not make . . . and so on. In fact, at times the two documents correspond only a little more closely than the story of Adam and Eve resembles the six-day creation in Genesis. The Editing Committee was really very foolish to print this genealogy without making the slightest attempt to link it to its own researches, the results of which appear under the individual early horses scattered throughout the register itself. (For an example of the muddle of the table, see the next section.)

Of course, this family tree has some tradition behind it. But if the entries in the Stud-book mean anything at all, they must be accepted as the only authentic information. Apart from those which also appear in the confusing *Packington Blind Horse* "family", only eight stallions in the E.C.H. book dated back to before 1800. With inter-breed rivalry at its height, this no doubt seemed a serious matter at the time. But a century later, its importance somewhat dwindles. One of the horses foaled in the very year 1800 was Honest Tom 1060. He has become everything, as eventually will appear, and the others nothing. His seed was multiplied as the sand which is upon the sea-shore. Coke and his colleagues, in inserting the "P.B.H." table, were entirely concerned to prevent the Suffolk people from having a monopoly of the ancient genealogies. At the time, this was harmless enough, but they have misled all students of pedigree who have followed after.

The Suffolk genealogical tables, in contrast, are splendid affairs, and link up perfectly with the Stud-book entries. That of Crisp's Horse of Ufford and his 761 direct male descendants in up to seventeen generations was so big that it had to be issued separately from the book, on rollers. It is ten and a half feet long and one foot high. (Anyone seeking to buy a copy of Biddell's book now will be very lucky to find one with table and rollers still accompanying it.) A shortened version was printed in the text, and so were tables of the male descendants of all those "heads of families" referred to below.

3. THE CONFUSION CONFRONTING COKE'S COMMITTEE

Lest Edward Coke and his Editing Committee be criticised over-much for the muddles that there are in their work, it is salutary to apprise ourselves of the sort of problem they faced. Four examples will suffice.

(*a*) According to the Genealogical Table of 1834, various celebrated horses called "Tinker" were descended from *The Packington Blind Horse*. But the editors could find no proof of this, and their evidence of these horses' relationship was quite different from the Table:

Genealogical Table	Stud-book
1 Packington Blind Horse, sire of	
2 Oldacre's Old Kirby, sire of	
3 Bulstrode's Bald Horse, sire of	
4 R. Horsefield's Tinker (1788?)	(Not mentioned)
sire of	
5 Thos. Horsefield's Tinker (1795?)	T. Horsefield's *Tinker* of Knot Mill,
sire of	Lancs. sire of
(a) Raingill's Tinker (1809?)	TINKER 2148 (1800) b and o Parker Raingill, Chorlton-on-Medlock sire of
(b) Barnes' Tinker (1805)	TINKER 2149 (1805) o
	(i) Barnes of Lawton
(c) Hulme's Tinker (1810)	(ii) Hulme of Halebank
	sire of
(d) Rathbone's Tinker (1817)	TINKER 2150 (1817) b and o Rathbone, Helsby, Ches.

Reasonable guesses based upon age are of course less easy to make in trying to distinguish or identify generations among horses than they are in human genealogies. A twenty-year-old stallion could cover his own g.g.g.g.g-daughter, provided that each of his descendants in the female line had been obliging enough to produce a foal at the age of three.

(*b*) Stud cards, those documents essential to people compiling first volumes of stud-books, provided many a headache. Taking one at random, we find a card of Major's Ploughboy, foaled in 1865, giving a male-line pedigree thus:

sire: "Young Major, late the property of Mr. R. Watson, Dogdyke."
g-sire: "Old Major, late the property of Mr. R. Watson, North Kyme."
g.g-sire: "Mr. Tewson's horse Major, of Terrington."
g.g.g-sire: "Mr. Steward's Old Major."

And so on. In this instance, the Editing Committee which entered Major's Ploughboy as 1475 seem to have missed out a generation. Perhaps they had not seen this particular card. But the card itself, printed at Driffield, betrayed Yorkshire ignorance of the famous proprietor of Major (1447) – a Fenman would have known better than to call Mr. Seward "Steward". There are twenty-seven Majors in Volume 1, and Seward's was the great one. (See V.4.) He was, in fact the ancestor of all the rest, except perhaps one. The youngest was Major 1472 (foaled in 1874), a g.g.g-son. Major 1471 (foaled 1872) was a g.g.g.g.g.g-son.

(*c*) A card for Simon Pure (2018), foaled in 1868 gives this:

sire: "Young Sampson, late the property of Mr. C. Lister" . . . etc.

g-sire: "That wonderful horse Sampson, the winner of many prizes, the property of Mr. W. Gant, Alford" . . . etc.

g.g-sire: "That justly celebrated horse Sampson, the property of W. Saberton Esq. Witcham."

g.g.g-s: "That unequalled and famed horse Sampson, the property of Mr. Henry, of Norman Cross."

In this instance, the Editors agreed except about the spelling, and added an extra generation. The g.g.g.g-sire was Nix's *Samson*. There are seventy-six different Samsons actually registered in Volume 1. Fifty-three belonged to four separate families. The rest are miscellaneous singles and groups. No less than five Samsons foaled in 1866 were actually registered later in Volume 1.

(*d*) The farther a horse travelled from the place of his breeding the more likelihood of confusion there was. The great Bulstrode of Leicestershire had many horses. Sometimes just "Bulstode's Horse" was quoted. It is conceivable that there was a horse, or horses, simply called "Bulstrode" after him. But "Brown's Bulstrode" appearing in the pedigree of Walker's Horse 2239 (foaled 1802), is suspect. It could so easily be "Bulstrode's Brown". If this seems far-fetched, a card of Young John Bull (1180), foaled in 1863, contains a precisely similar error. It says John Bull's grand-dam was by "Mr. Gee's Old Nanbury, which was allowed to be the best horse in England". He was not quite the best horse. And he was Mr. Hanbury's *Old G*, not Mr. Gee's Old Nanbury at all.

4. THE PURITY OF THE STALLIONS

a. *Conditions of entry*

The conditions laid down by the Suffolk Association (Biddell being the sole arbiter of a horse's conformity to them) were that stallions and mares were eligible, either if they were claimed to be Suffolks, and no outside cross was known to exist in the pedigree: or, if they had been accepted as Suffolks by any Agricultural Show, even if a "taint" of other blood was known to exist.

The E.C.H.S. rule was similar to the first Suffolk one, though less stringent – "no outside cross for at least two generations". The second Suffolk rule did not enter into the matter, since no Agricultural Shows had ever had classes labelled "English Cart Horses", much less "Shires". The editorial committee was responsible for selection.

In practice, there was a strange discrepancy of interpretation. Biddell was in general far more accurate, as, with his advantages, he should have been. But, obsessed as he and every other good Suffolk man was with the purer blood of their horses, he invariably carried his registrations back one generation further than his terms of reference strictly allowed. The E.C.H. editors, on the other hand, were more cautious, and the earliest known ancestor of nearly every horse, famous or otherwise, was not actually registered, even though they could have done so without breaking the rules.

b. *Pedigrees in male line*

Simply as regards dates, the Suffolk book contained a higher proportion of early horses, and therefore there was more likelihood of continuous pedigrees over many generations being ascertainable.

	Suffolk		*E.C.H.*	
	No.	%	No.	%
Foaled before 1800	102	8.3	33	1.4
1800–1819	135	10.9	175	7.4
1820–1839	152	12.3	340	14.4
1840–1859	322	26.0	868	36.7
1860–1878	519	42.0	949	40.1 (to 1876 only)
Doubtful*	6	0.5		
	1,236	100.0	2,365	100.0

*Actually, 130 of the Suffolk stallions are undated in the Stud-book. In all but six cases it is possible to make a guess that is accurate enough for these broad divisions of time.

As far as continuous pedigrees are concerned, the Suffolk Society was immeasurably better off. In fact, virtually all its living and recent stallions could be traced back in the male line to one single horse. The following table shows this:

Suffolk horses in Vol. 1 – descent in direct male line. The figures do not tally with those quoted by Biddell in his text (pp. 20 ff.) which are rounded, but they accord with actual Stud-book entries:

a. CRISP'S HORSE 404 of Ufford (foaled 1768)
   (one of "the old breed")
   and 761 descendants, all via Smith's Horse of Parham (f 1799)   762
b. BLAKE'S FARMER 174 (foaled 1760)
   (a Lincolnshire trotting stallion)
   and 131 descendants
   (only one or two surviving in 1879)   132
c. WRIGHT'S ATTLEBOROUGH FARMER'S GLORY 1396 (foaled 1796)
   (probably by Lincs. cart-horse out of Suffolk mare)
   and 122 descendants.
   (three surviving in 1879)   123

d. WINTER'S STORMER 1329 (bay f about 1790)
    (a trotting horse of great substance, got by a blood horse)
    sire of
  BARBER'S PROCTOR 58 (foaled about 1793)
    (out of chesnut mare)
    and 25 other descendants ("the Shadingfield stock")
    (extinct in male line by about 1855)   27
e. J. CLAYDEN'S SAMSON 324 (foaled about 1835)
    (Suffolk, but pedigree lost. Possibly a branch of c.)
    and 23 descendants ("the Linton Samsons")
    (extinct in male line in 1879, unless in Cambs. or Essex)   24
f. 28 stallions, pedigree unknown
    (all, except two, probably "Suffolk")
    and 54 descendants
    (none surviving in 1879)   82
g. 86 horses of unknown pedigree
    no known descendants   86

            1,236

Only five or six Suffolk stallions in 1878, therefore, claimed descent from any other foundation sire than Smith's Horse of Parham, foaled as recently as 1799. The eighty-six horses in (g) were of antiquarian interest only. Those in (d)–(f), and to a large extent those in (b) and (c) were of practical concern to the breeder in 1878 only in respect of the pedigree of contemporary mares.

An equivalent analysis of E.C.H. male-line pedigrees is impossible to make. Even if it were not, it would occupy a dozen pages filled with small groups, and would be no less absurd than tedious.

As already suggested, Biddell admitted horses which his terms of reference did not strictly allow. The Lincolnshire trotting stallion, Blake's Farmer (b) in the Table above, and Winter's Stormer and his son Barber's Proctor (d) are obvious examples. So is Farmer's Glory (c), whose story illustrates the point in respect of the others. He was owned by J. Wright, a dealer, of Attleborough in Norfolk. Chesnut in colour, he was probably half Fen horse and half Suffolk. An old man who remembered him told Biddell "He looked like a Lincolnshire: he had a little white and was a little hairy." Many of his sons and descendants were noted for their size. Mumford's Champion 891 (foaled about 1830), one of his g.g.g.g-sons, was 18-hands and weighed a ton. Hercules 87, g.g.g-son of Mumford's Champion and foaled in 1848, was a dark chesnut with coarse and hairy legs. At the age of ten this Hercules won his first prize, at Bury St. Edmunds. "But I fancy" (wrote Biddell) "his owner was aghast at what (the judges) had done." He ended his days in Westmorland.

Martin's Boxer 868 was foaled in 1813 and has some claim to being the worst horse in the book. He was supposed to be a Suffolk, but was in fact a rough-legged bay horse, belonging to a timber carter, out of a black brood mare, and was bred by a Mr. Wainwright of Leiston. "How he came to look like a Suffolk," commented Biddell, "no one seems able to explain." He was also a bad tempered brute which eventually at the age of nineteen was taken in hand by a new leader, John Alexander, who cannot have been much older than the horse, for he was still farming in 1880. When John went to fetch him, Boxer five times seized the leg of his pony and knocked him off. The final contretemps was witnessed by an old woman, who valiantly offered to help, but John said, "No, thank'ee Mum, I'll try and get on alone." Boxer was fit, fresh and fertile. He went on travelling regularly until he was twenty-five and served a tremendous number of the very good class mares in his district, for reasons which would be unfathomable to any modern breeder. However, there was little trace of his blood in the horses selected for the Stud-book fifty years later. Biddell, anxious to prove the potency of pure blood, commented, "It seems as if the blood thus introduced was so foreign in the original stock, that the parent stem rejected it, repelled it, refused to allow it to mingle with the ancient family strain, upon which it was for twenty years persistently grafted." (Incidentally, how long Boxer would have gone on covering mares no one can guess. He was stopped only by an accident on a four-horse threshing machine.)

In about 1780, a Mr. Newstead hired a black stallion from Robert Bakewell and foolishly travelled it under the name *Dishley* in the Stowmarket area where he lived. Naturally, Biddell did not put it in the book, but he did include anonymously, as "Horse 905", a stallion that was foaled about 1780, owned by another Mr. Newstead of Hundon, even though he suspected that it also was a Black horse and not a Sorrel at all. The eighty-six horses of unknown pedigree (g), in contrast, appear to be perfectly in order. If one knows nothing of an animal's breeding, it can have "no known outside cross".

Compared with the few Black or hairy intruders that penetrated Suffolk, an enormous number of Suffolk horses had spread over the other counties of England, to the confusion of all. Nevertheless, the E.C.H. editors seem to have been more successful in their attempts to keep out extraneous blood. Detective examination now reveals only one horse in the E.C.H. book with a definite Suffolk connection. This is Heart of Oak 1001, a bay, bred in Essex in 1850. All that is recorded of his pedigree is that his sire was Pledger's *Heart of Oak*. The latter is undoubtedly Pledger's Heart of Oak 958 in the Suffolk book, got by a pure (but un-named) Suffolk horse out of a Shire-bred mare.

So Heart of Oak 1001 (E.C.H.) may have been only one-quarter Suffolk, if his unknown dam was all right, whereas his sire, a registered Suffolk, was half Shire. The other "howlers" of the E.C.H. editors seem restricted to simple internal blunders and muddles, though these are numerous enough. Coke and his colleagues were so scrupulous as to omit all horses of which they did not know, at least approximately, the foaling date, and usually the name. For this reason, the sire of Wiseman's Honest Tom 1060, direct ancestor of all Shires now alive, still remains unregistered as *Milton and Colley's Brown Horse of*

Bassingham, and the dam's sire of his son England's Glory 705 is outside the pale as *Odam's Horse of Thorney Fen*. There are innumerable examples of what were clearly good old Fen or Black or Brown Horses which they did not register. Even *The Packington Blind Horse* himself is not in the book.

c. *Pedigrees in tail female*

It is obviously part of a stud-book's function to enable pedigrees to be studied in tail female, but the chances of doing so in any detail in 1880 were very limited. All that people usually knew about an English Cart Horse or a mare was that he or she was "by So-and-so". If anything was known at all of the breeding of the dam, it was probably just that she likewise was "by Such-and-such". It was a comparatively rare case when the parentage of the g.g-dam was known.

The Suffolk book is infinitely superior in this respect (as it ought to be) but, here again, Biddell included some horses which the E.C.H. editors, in his place, would have excluded on the grounds that the dams patently had "other blood". To take one example, Barlow's Traveller 71 of Hasketon, foaled 1848, was directly descended from the old stock in the male line, but he was a bay horse with black legs and his grand-dam seems to have travelled across the North Sea. Nor had he qualified himself for the book by having been accepted as a Suffolk at any agricultural show. (One may presumably take it that only a misprint makes the pedigree of Porter's Boxer 976, foaled in 1846, appear suspect. His dam was "a chesnut mare" and his g-dam was "by Mr. Edwards of Framlingham".)

d. *Pedigrees in E.C.H. appendix*

Many of the sixty-five stallions in the E.C.H. appendix have far more complete tail-female pedigrees than most of those actually in the book. For example, *Short Legs*, bred in Durham in 1845, could be traced back to the sire of his g.g.g.g-dam, and so could *Black Robin*, a Yorkshire horse foaled in 1856. This is farther than all but two or three of the accepted stallions can be traced in the female line. Though the evidence on which the editors formed their judgement has been totally destroyed, the objections to their registration can be guessed pretty accurately in most cases:

a. Clydesdale blood.	9.
b. Bred in Durham/Northumberland (Clydesdale or Vardy blood)	19.
c. Bred in Yorkshire (Cleveland Bay blood?)	9.
d. Bred in N. Lancs. (Clydesdale blood?)	3.
e. Suffolk blood	11.
f. Flemish blood	4.
g. Impossible to guess.	10.
	65.

They were indeed a mixed bag. One, *Lofty* (f 1876) owned by the Earl of Ellesmere, was own brother to Mr. Lawrence Drew's celebrated *Countess*. One was called *Vardy* (and he claimed Bakewell's G in his ancestry). Another was called *Border Ranger*. One *Samson* was "bred by the Duke of Rutland: dam, a Flemish Mare"; another *Samson*, bred by the Rev. S. Terry at Odiham, was by *Samson* out of *Violet* by Terry's *Vaverley*, g-dam by Terry's *Wanderer*, g.g-dam by Brown's *Bloomer*. *Champion* was by *Goliath* out of *Lightsome* by *The Suffolk Champion*.

CHAPTER II

Some Famous Men of the Old Time

VOLUME I placed all breeders, in 1880 and thereafter, under an enormous debt to Richard Reynolds and to Edward Coke and his committee. But the historian's curses are heaped on the heads of those who allowed the subsequent destruction of every irreplaceable morsel of evidence on which these gentlemen had based their knowledge. We lament, too, that no other county but Suffolk produced a Herman Biddell, and so we have only the dimmest idea of those men who in the reign of George III fixed the several varieties of the future Shire breed. Nevertheless, we must pay what poor tribute we can to some of the great men of bygone times.

For reasons of space, it is necessary to concentrate on those counties which led the breeding of real Black or Brown horses in the eighteenth century. But brief reference to one or two people who lived and worked in areas which bordered on these chief regions increases the number of counties mentioned to twenty-one.

Horses marked * are eighteenth-century animals which appear among the descendants of the *Packington Blind Horse* listed in the next chapter, to which the reader is referred. Men marked † are referred to in more detail under the county appropriate to them.

I. LEICESTERSHIRE

Six days after the death, on 6th July 1716 at the age of seventy-three, of the first of the Robert Bakewells to be tenant at Dishley, an inventory of his stock was made. It included "Seven mares with three foles – £70-00-00". One wonders what they were like, and what the famous grandson thought of their descendants. As a little boy he may even have seen the actual foles as adults, for they would have been nine years old when he was born. However, of Bakewell the Great we must say nothing here, since his influence has been discussed in Part A and the next chapter contains a note on his horses (III.2).

Bakewell was unique in many ways, but not in the attention he gave to breeding heavy-horses, which was a Leicestershire obsession. William Pitt began the horse-section of his county review with the words, "From many curious anecdotes related from one generatiom to another, from extraordinary facts preserved in the archives of some of the oldest families, and from certain old parochial registers, Leicestershire seems to have been always eminent for a useful and beautiful breed of black horses." He gives one example of this enthusiasm. "By an agreement amongst the occupiers of lands in the parish of Wimeswold" (Wymeswold, north of Loughborough), "it was made unlawful for any man to bring a mare into their common fields: stallions being thought more grand, and therefore the only beasts that were fit for the Wimeswold farmers to use. The farmer's chief pride was in his team of horses, and it frequently carried him into very blameable lengths. He very often bestowed that expense and attention upon his horses which, by the immutable laws of nature, belonged to his family and children; and many instances might be collected of families being entirely ruined by this false pride and preposterous folly."[1]

Pitt thought that John Monk, who had written the draft report in 1794, had overestimated the number of Black horses in the county. But even his own more cautious calculation is impressive enough. Compared with 2,000 "blood-horses or hacknies" and a further 2,000 young blood-horses and "miscellaneous horses of all denominations", he computed that there were 24,000 Blacks. There were, he believed, at the end of each year 19,200 working and breeding horses and young stock of two-years-old: 2,400 foals (2,400 having been already sold out of the county in the autumn); and 2,400 yearlings, the residue of a crop of twice that number the year before. Even if one makes no allowance for land occupied by towns or otherwise not farmed, this works out at one horse on each twenty-two acres. It was big business. The cart horses sold out of the county each year were worth about £75,000.

Amongst the fanatics of Leicestershire, pedigree history must begin with the shadowy figure of Mr. Hood. R. S. Reynolds, upon what evidence we cannot now know (for reasons already deplored), was inclined to identify "Hood's Horse of Packington" with *The Packington Blind Horse* which appears to have flourished within the period 1755–1770. Many of this celebrity's sons were owned by a Mr. Oldacre of "Peatland Lodge", presumably Peatling, in the parish of either Peatling Magna or Peatling Parva.

Oldacre was said to have been both a noted cart-horse breeder and a considerable importer of Flemish stallions. His life's work is remembered now by the name of six horses only. *Old Kirby**, foaled in 1773, was said to be a son of the *Blind Horse* (or perhaps a grandson). *Mansetter**, foaled perhaps about 1766, was sire of Kirby (1286)* foaled 1785, which in turn was sire of Mansetter (1476)* alias Bald Horse, foaled in 1790. The last that Oldacre bred appears to have been Blaze (189) in the year 1800, of which the sire was either Bakewell's G (890) or one of its sons. The sixth horse, bred in 1802 (by whom, it is not recorded), Brown George (301), was owned by "Oldacre of Castle Donington", but whether this was the same man is a matter of guess-work.

The sire of Brown George was Bald Horse (93)* and he was bred in 1778 by another cart-horse man celebrated in his day, Mr. Bulstrode of Isley Walton. He travelled this famous stallion fourteen seasons, and in the later years charged 3 guineas for service. This is the only one of his horses registered in the Stud-book, but old pedigrees and stallion-cards constantly mention his name, usually in the phrase "Bulstrode's Horse" which one hopes was clearer to contemporaries than to those of us who live after.

Mr. Hart deserves mention here, for one of his horses is the earliest that Edward Coke and his committee actually registered. This is his own-bred Blaze (183)* foaled in 1770 – a son of Oldacre's *Mansetter* and used by Bakewell. Hart's address is given simply as "Culloden", which does not mean that he lived in Inverness, but suggests that his farm had been constituted in 1746, the year of the battle.

One of the sons of this Blaze was Swebstone (2079)* bred in 1795. He was owned about the turn of the century by Joseph Wild, whose name appears in rustic spelling as Wiles, Wyles, Wyeld and every possible variation. For thirty years or more he was proprietor of a famous stallion stud on the north side of Market Bosworth – on the road to Barton in the Beans and, about four miles further on, to Swepstone, where this horse was presumably born, with Packington two or three miles beyond it. With the new century, we emerge into the light of day because, although only eight others of his animals are listed in Volume 1, they offer a picture of a great stallion-owner replenishing his stud in exactly the same way as his successors in the twentieth century – searching for promising colts got by his own stock-horses, purchasing them and bringing them on in the hope that one out of every dozen or so would grow into a worthy recruit to the staff. These are the other eight:

DERBYSHIRE 577, brown, bred in 1800 by Hall of Swepstone. (Was it he who also bred Wild's earlier horse?). This stallion is the earliest example, in the Stud-book, of what was later to be the classic cross of Fen and Midland blood. His sire was the great Fen horse Caswell's Honest Tom (1062). His dam was by a *Brown Horse* belonging to Stych†, Wild's Derbyshire counterpart. Derbyshire was the direct male ancestor both of the sire and of the dam of William the Conqueror himself (see VII.1).

BLACK LEGS 142, black, bred in 1804 by Pickering of Thurlaston Field, about six miles to the south east. Son of Derbyshire 577, and g.g.g-sire of William the Conqueror's sire and dam.

BROWN COLT 294, bred in 1804 by Smedley of Bradley, near Ashbourne. By Oldacre's Mansetter (1476)*.

LEICESTERSHIRE BALD (or LEICESTERSHIRE BOY) 1318, brown, bred by Wild himself in 1810. He was by Derbyshire 577, above, and after serving four seasons was sold into Derbyshire. He did nine seasons for James Ward of Dronfield and eight more for William Mellor† of Calow, Chesterfield, and died at about the age of twenty-five.

BROWN COLT 295, foaled in 1810. Like Brown Colt 294, bred by Smedley. By Black Legs 142, above. Later owned by William Mellor†, Derby.

KING CHARLES 1203, brown, bred in 1816 by Blount of Sutton. By Brown Colt 295. Blount had bred the dam, by *Wylde's Blaze* – one of the otherwise forgotten Wild horses.

MARSTON 1491, black, bred in 1824 by Johnson of Marston Hall, Hartington,
   Derby. By Black Legs 142.
DERBYSHIRE 579, brown, foaled in 1826. Another of Hall's breeding, like
   Derbyshire 577. The dam was by a Stycht† *Brown Horse*. The sire was Black
   Legs 142.

So great was Wild's business that he not only travelled his horses in many
parts but supplied many other stallion keepers all over the Midlands. If a
register of his animals ever came to light, they would fill a book.

On the other side of Leicester, to the east, Mr. Berridge of Frisby on the
Wreake (a name reminiscent of the Frisians and their black horses) became
between 1820 and 1860 a proprietor almost as well known as Wild had been,
though only four of his horses found their way into the pedigree records,
together with two owned by Berridge of Ingarsby. Nothing but grey and
black appear to have interested this staunch pair as they looked round each year
to choose some promising colts that their stallions had left behind them.

With F. T. Bryan of Knossington, with whom this survey must end, we are
on the border of Rutland, a county whose horses Richard Parkinson had
described in 1808[2] as "the most unprofitable sort I ever saw for sale, considering that they are chiefly raised in enclosed grounds". He said he hardly saw a
good brood mare, except at Mr. Chapman's, and even his would not do for a
dray. The Rutland horses were "of various colours, and of all shapes, except
real good shapes". Bryan flourished from 1840 to the mid-seventies and he,
too, had horses of all hues – blue-roans, chestnuts, bays, and almost every
colour except black. He owned and dealt in hundreds of stallions. Ten were
eventually included in Volume I, no less than six of these being winners of
eight first prizes at the Royal between 1842 and 1851. He sold an enormous
number of horses to the North of England, not a few to Scotland, of which
Prodigy (1825) in the early 'fifties was perhaps the best, and some abroad, such
as Sultan (2068) to Australia for £200. He did much to improve the horses in
the "Horse-shoe Shire" of Rutland, but Oldacre, Bulstrode, Wild and the
Berridges would not have approved of these rainbow colours travelling
Leicestershire, whether or not the Scotsmen or the colonials wanted them.

2. DERBYSHIRE

Very old men, in 1879, were unanimous that in the days when their
grandfathers were alive and their fathers were young chaps, Joseph Webb had
been the most noted breeder in the county. Edward Coke had no hesitation in
registering Ruler 1905, bred by this famous Webb in the year 1773 – the
second-earliest horse that was allotted a place in the Stud-book. But nothing
was recorded in 1879 of the tales that the old fellows had heard, and nothing
preserved of written evidence or printed stallion card to tell us about Ruler's
sire *Bumper* or even where Webb lived, except that it was at "Marston". Since
he is occasionally referred to as "of Staffordshire", it was presumably either at

Marston Montgomery or further east and south at Marston-on-Dove, both places being near the county boundary.

Webb also bred King Tom 1260 (owned later by Mr. Handley†, Salop) and his two most famous sons Marston 1486* and Bulstrode 348 (both owned by John Chadwick†, Staffs.). The last of Webb's horses to be found in the Stud-book – there are just five! – is Farmer's Glory 808 (see Chadwick again). The historian owes an apology to Joseph Webb, perhaps a deeper one that is possible to realise, for treating him as a cross-reference to others, but that is all that can be done.

William Mellor of Calow (Chesterfield) was another mighty man in those days. No less than thirteen of the horses he bred or owned were put in the book, the first foaled in 1790, and the last in 1823. Two had been owned by Joseph Wild† (Leics.). A whole forgotten chapter of Black horse breeding lies in the pedigree of Merryman 1553, which he bred in 1810. The sire was *Whitehead's Horse* of Flentham: the dam, which Mellor bred, was by *Gibson's Horse*, of Whissendine; the g-dam, by *Hurd's Horse*; the g.g-dam by *Shuttleworth's Horse*, of Scalford. All these men are long-forgotten. The last-named horse could have been foaled as recently as 1798; but it is a sure guess that he came into the world nearer 1760 than that.

It is also sure that the mare that he covered was bred by Mellor – how else would so long a pedigree in tail female be recorded? Many Mellors in the county of Derbyshire have bred Black and Shire horses, but to study even those of William would take us all this section, and we must leave him.

What can we say of Thomas Hudson of Rowland? Nothing, even though he also was a great man in his day. His memorial consists just of seven horses standing in his name in the book. Here they are ("b" showing that he was the breeder, and "o" the owner):

```
(b/o)            (b)
Champion   —   Sovereign
375            2034
  f 1820         f 1817←┐
                        ┊                      (o)              Bakewell's
                        ┊               ┌ The Stretford G 2110 — G 890*
                   ┌(b/o)               │    f 1800
                   │ G 892           ┤
                   │ f 1810          │ (b/o)
                   ┘                 └ black mare
       (b/o)       ┐                                          ┝(o) Bakewell'
       G 895       │                     (o)                   Blaze 184*
         f 1827    │ b/o               Regulator 1852
                   └ black mare——— f 1807
```

All these horses were black, except G 890 and his son, which were black-brown. (There is also a Stretford G 2067 in the book, foaled 1805, but this entry is a doublet of 2110.)

John Sims of Stanton-by-Bridge was another notable man, represented in the book by horses foaled 1790–1834. And so were Richard Shaw of Monsal Dale (stallions 1780–1803), William Cockayne of Walton (1799–1812) and Richard Gibbs of Tissington Wood (1796–1842). All these were farming when in 1794 Thomas Brown of Luton wrote his draft report on the county, noting that every agricultural operation was done by horses, chiefly the brood mares of the strong cart kind, "excellent stock for breeding waggon and dray horses, which are in such request in every part of the kingdom. . . . In brood mares, great improvements have certainly been made, and I trust will continue to go on, from the conveniency of the pastures, and the fair field they open for extending and improving the breed of draught horses." Mr. Bakewell's stallions had been heard of, it seems, only by the bigger men. The dairy farmers kept eight brood mares to do the work of four geldings, and from their four or five foals each year made enough money nearly to keep them all, as well as having an extra team at hand at critical times such as turnip sowing. Mr. Brown begged leave "to conclude with remarking that, from the civilities I received in Derbyshire, I have no apprehension of anything uncivil from any of its inhabitants in their marginal remarks."[3] Three families whose members were all very civil gentlemen indeed, and famous breeders in several generations, must now engage us.

First, the Stych family of Stenson. *Stych's Brown Horse*, foaled about 1790 or a little earlier, appears in a number of high-class pedigrees which have survived, and his colour is easily explained by his having been bred in Staffordshire, some of the old cards mentioning him as "descended from the Ingestre Stud" (Summerland†, Staffs.). He is particularly to be noted by the historian as sire of dam of Wild's Derbyshire 577, (†Leics), from whom were descended both parents of William the Conqueror 2343 (VII.1).

The first horse of a younger Stych to be honoured by posthumous Stud-book entry was one of his two best – Bang-Up 94, which he bred in 1834 out of an ancient mare that came of Bakewell's old stock. Bang-Up was grey, a colour which would have astonished and probably disgusted Stych senior, but already by that time the mixing of colours was producing the incalculable effects that have marked Shire breeding ever since, pure though the old county colours had been not long before. He was grey because his sire Sancho 1993 was grey, but about Sancho's breeding there is a muddle. The younger Stych was a typical stallion-owner, always on the look-out for a good colt by one of his own horses, and five of the best of Bang-Up's appear in the Stud-book. All are brown. Stych had a brother-in-law, Thomas Hinckley, at Colton near Rugeley in Staffordshire, and the two of them were constantly exchanging horses. One such stallion, a son of Bang-Up, was Invincible (1140). He was more commonly known, when in Staffordshire, as Derbyshire Hero, but when he won first prize at the 1845 Shrewsbury Royal at the age of six, he was given the name Shropshire Friend. For a later son of Bang-Up, a different method was adopted. When travelling for Stych or let by him, he was Derbyshire Hero (588): in Mr. Hinckley's hands he was Staffordshire Hero. This horse, like the scores of others they owned, travelled many a distant circuit in the 'fifties.

Perhaps the best stallion ever owned by the brothers-in-law was Champion 419. Like Bang-Up, he was grey. He was bred in 1855 by Kilbey of Bodicote Fields, in Oxfordshire, but within a mile or so of the Northamptonshire border. The canny Stych recognised his worth and his sons were regarded as the leading Derbyshire sires throughout the 'sixties. Indeed, most Midlands men regarded Champion as quite in the class of Dack's Matchless 1509 (foaled 1846 – VIII.1) or Major 1447 (foaled 1838 – V.4) the two greatest names of the previous two decades and both true Fen horses. Even Welcher's (or Miller's) Honest Tom 1105 (f 1862, g.g-son of Major) who carried on the tradition of ensuring that the most talked-of stallion in England at any one time should be a Fen horse, was thought by many to be inferior to Stych's Champion. To what extent Champion was to stamp his mark permanently upon hundreds, and then upon thousands, of future generations, an examination of Harold's pedigree will reveal (see VI.2, which gives Champion's pedigree also).

The Wrights of Wheston Hall, near Tideswell, made a very special contribution to Shire history. In the first place, there were three generations of them – Joseph (to 1810), Anthony (to 1835) and William, whose last horse was foaled in 1872. (Joseph subscribed ten guineas in 1789 to help rescue Bakewell from bankruptcy.) Secondly, they owned an enormous number of stallions, all of the choicest sort: fifty-six were registered by Coke's first committee, far more than those selected from any other nineteenth-century stud. And thirdly, the story of their business, their buying and selling of stallions, and of their relationship with other specialists in Derbyshire, Leicester and Stafford, tells all that is best of the history of the Shire, other than in the Fens, during the eighty years of change and confusion that separated the death of Bakewell and the birth of the stud-book movement. Precisely for this reason, we either have to build the whole of this chapter round the family and its stallions, which would be absurd (man for man, and horse for horse, none of them was greater than others in our narrative), or we must abandon the attempt to discuss their horses at all, because even the most patient reader, possessing but ten fingers to keep between the pages, would be daunted by the cross-references to all the other men in our selected roll of honour.

Let us content ourselves with two horses – Joseph's first recorded stallion, and William's last:

Blaze 187* was black, bred in 1799 by William Cockayne. His sire was The Blind Horse 192*, bred by Summerland† (Staffs.). His dam was by "Bustrode's† Horse" (possibly Bald Horse 93*, Leics.). His g-dam was by the *Packington Blind Horse*. That alone is enough to show us the class of stallion-owner to which Joseph Wright belonged.

John Bull 1187 was grey, and was bred in 1872 by Ralph Buxton at

Chelmorton, four miles away across the river Wye, using William's Merryman 1572. Although Wheston Hall and Chelmorton are both about 1,100 feet above sea level and although William Wright, like his father and grandfather, was associated with every well-known breeder *except* those in the Fens, it was in the Fens that John Bull's family tree was rooted. His pedigree shows breeding closely allied to the two greatest bloodlines of the breed, those of Lincolnshire Lad I and II (Chapter V) and of William the Conqueror (VII.1) and to that of another great "foundation sire" also, Royal Albert (VIII.3). This was more clever of Ralph Buxton than we might give him credit for, unless we remember that he was not following established bloodlines but unknowingly helping to create them:

1. G-sire: Drayman 640, descended in male line from Fisher's† Black Horse (Fens), as was William the Conqueror.
2. Dam of sire: a mare whose sire, dam and g-dam were all descended in the male line from Wiseman's† Honest Tom 1060, as was Lincolnshire Lad.
3. Sire of dam: William Wright's Iron Duke 1153 (bought from his breeder near Buxton) by John Bull 1169, one of the first stallions that William Wright had after the death of his father. (He sold him, but later got him back when he came across him in the possession of some gipsies, but that is another story.) John Bull was the g.g.g-sire of Royal Albert. Iron Duke's dam was by Matchless 1506, as was the dam of Lincolnshire Lad II.
4. G-dam: not recorded.

William Wright gave so much help, from his vast store of personal and inherited knowledge, to the first Editing Committee that, too old to join the breed society as an active member, he was belatedly given a presentation copy of Volume 1 in May 1884.

The Outseats stud at Somercotes, near Alfreton, comes last only chronologically, because John Nix, the end of his line, lived to 1927. His grandfather had at one time owned Lily Street Farm a mile or so to the west of Somercotes and there, like the Nixes before him for many a generation, had kept Black stallions. About 1820, he moved to Somercotes and built his first house there. Alas, not a word has been preserved of his horses, and his son Thomas, who was born in 1812, owned the first Nix stallion which has been put in the Stud-book. He bought him from Anthony Wright – it was Luck's All 1426 bred in 1837 and prominent in the pedigree of Royal Albert (VIII.3). The next to be later honoured by the Editing Committee was Ben 120, bred at Outseats Farm in 1840 out of a mare purchased from John Chadwick† (Staffs.). How many stallions he owned at any one time is somewhat uncertain, but it was usually between twenty and twenty-five.

A two-year-old he acquired in 1847 had no name, and he consulted his little four-year-old orphaned nephew John, whom he was bringing up. And that was how Uncle Tom (2198) got his name. In 1866 at the age of fifty-four, Tom Nix died and young John, now twenty-three, took over the business. Thirty-four Nix stallions foaled prior to 1877 are in the Stud-book and both John and Uncle Tom have earned the gratitude of later students of pedigree by using a different name for all their horses, instead of repeating old favourites over and over again. The names are refreshingly distinctive, too – Attila and Armadale, Beauchieff, Birkland and Brumby K: Great Rocks, Silverhill, and so on. John joined the Society at the beginning, at the age of thirty-five, when there lay ahead of him almost another half-century of stallion-owning. Like other men's, his career had its ups and downs. One of his biggest 'downs' was when he lost seven horses, uninsured, in the sinking, during a terrible storm, of the ship in which they were travelling to the United States. But these things are part of modern history, and have no place in this review.

With bachelor John's death in September 1927, a symbol of the good old days vanished too. Immaculate in dress to the last, upright and dignified, punctilious in his habits, a staunch churchman, the last Nix in the Shire business was a Victorian in the classic mould. He forbade flowers at his funeral, which was of the utmost simplicity. But in a downpour of rain, a vast throng of people attended at Alfreton church, to which his body was borne on a "J. Nix" farm wagon drawn by two of his last horses. He left behind him a reputation summed up in a certain oft-repeated saying. If a stallion developed a fault it used to be said that "the Forshaws would shoot him, John Nix would cut him and —— would use him". Mr. —— was another Derbyshire man who began business too late for inclusion here.

3. STAFFORDSHIRE

Some of the cleverest breeders in the history of the Shire will figure in this note. This is mildly surprising in view of the fact that William Pitt of Pendeford in his 1794 survey did not exactly enthuse over the cart-horses of his own county and certainly thought less of them than those he described in his General View of Leicestershire. "There is nothing very remarkable in our breed", he wrote, "though we have a sufficiency of good stout horses for the use both of the carrier and the farmer. The colour is most generally black or brown, each being equally esteemed, and equally useful: and indeed, as the old proverb says, 'a good horse is never of a bad colour'. Some respectable stallions are kept of each colour. But in respect to the breed of horses, I think this county must yield the palm to the neighbouring ones of Leicester and Derby. And, indeed, breeding horses is by no means a main object here, and carried little farther than to supply the county, and also the neighbouring fairs, with a few. There are some considerable shows and fairs, when a great number of excellent colts and horses are offered to sale, particularly at Stafford and Burton."[4]

If we except the Gallemore family whose stallions had to be hidden away from Bonny Prince Charlie in the '45 (A.III.1), the story of the Brown Horses of Staffordshire can be picked up only in 1778 when the long-established Mr. Summerland of Ingestre, in the valley of the Trent a few miles east of Stafford, paid Mr. Hambleton, twenty miles away at Calton Moor near the beautiful Manifold river, the sum of 350 guineas for *Sweet William*. This was a fantastic price for a cart stallion, but these gentlemen allowed no half measures either in quality or weight, and wanted something better than "respectable". Summerland had a stallion named *Drayman* which had reached its twenty hundredweight by the time it was four, and even a Fenman could not have complained at that. A few years later his *Wiltshire Blind Horse* achieved a tremendous reputation as a stock-getter and its name crops up in countless pedigrees, though of its own not one jot nor tittle is known. The cunning J.S. knew where he had got it from and it was enough for others to know what they could get from it.

Indeed, he appears to have been something of a Brown-horse Bakewell. For twenty years or more after he had ceased business about the end of the century, other men boasted that their mares were "by Summerland's Brown Horse of the Ingestre Breed, by Bakewell's G", or "by Stych's Brown Horse descended from the Ingestre Stud" or just "descended from the Ingestre breed". If one dealt with Summerland, one was shown no mere collection of individuals but a whole special race, as at Dishley. Unfortunately for us today, this has resulted in the great Summerland being represented in the Stud-book by only one horse, just as only three stand even in Bakewell's name. This is Blaze 192, which he bred in 1795 and sold to Thomas Gillman of Sheen near the Dove. It was, oddly, black, but this is accounted for by the fact that the sire was Hart of Culloden's Blaze 183*. His *alias*, The Blind Horse, is more difficult to explain. Was it just a coincidence about the old *Wiltshire Blind Horse*? or about *The Packington Blind Horse*? But perhaps, without further evidence, it is unfair to suggest any undesirable hereditary traits in this stud.

As for Hambleton who received 350 guineas for *Sweet William*, a whole world of Staffordshire Brown Horses is summed up in the little we now know of one of the three horses appearing in his name in the Stud-book, for the names of its sire and g-sire unmistakably hark back to the old Gallemores of the Croxden Abbey estate:

SWEET WILLIAM 2084, brown, bred in 1800 by Apsley, Dunston, nr. Stafford
          owned by 1) T. Hodgkinson of Swinscoe (2 miles
          from Calton)
                    2). Hambleton of Calton
Sire: GALLEMORE 904*, foaled in 1790, by Gallemore 903*, foaled 1780
Dam: a mare possibly bred by Apsley
      D-sire: Summerland's *Sweet William*
          (i.e. the one he bought from Hambleton in 1778).

A couple of miles to the east of Calton, over the Manifold, lived William

Massey of Ilam. He, and other members of his family, had a strain of horses which had their origin in Leicestershire. The Masseys' considerable breeding activities are hinted at in the only horses now standing to their name in the Stud-book:

MANSETTER 1479, brown, bred (in 1813) and owned by William Massey
  Sire: MANSETTER 1477, brown, bred in 1807 by William Massey
        G-sire: MERRYMAN 1548, bred and owned in 1800 by Massey of
           Birchall Moor (by Oldacre's Mansetter 1476)*
  Dam: bred by William Massey (by Blaze 192*, Summerland's second
  Blind Horse).
        G-dam: bred by William Massey (by Farmer's Glory 807* f. 1790)
                G.g-dam: "William Massey's Mare that was bar-
                ren only two years out of twenty."

William Massey travelled this brown colt at the age of two years.

John Chadwick of Grindon, if the whole truth were known, should probably be regarded as the greatest name in the history of the Shire horse prior to 1880. His little village is near the Manifold river, about four miles north of William Massey's home, and three from Hambleton's Calton. He had inherited the stallion business from his father, and it would be a reasonable guess that it had been in the family for many generations. John was without any doubt the most extensive stallion proprietor in all England prior to the Forshaws and one or two others of modern times. But he was much more than that. Like James and Tom Forshaw also were to be, he was known and trusted everywhere for his judgement of a cart horse. Furthermore, his knowledge and business connexions extended far beyond the confines of his county, which was the case with but few men of his day. He had brown horses and black horses. In the latter, we can always see Leicestershire or Derbyshire blood – often contributed directly by the sires themselves. Twenty-four stallions in Volume 1 belonged to him – fittingly, more than those in the name of any one other man. Nineteen were foaled between 1790 and 1820, and a comment about these may do something to indicate the importance of their owner. (Since the three earliest appear in the table given in the next chapter, their breeding is not indicated here.)

  1. DRAYMAN 603*, black, f 1790. The sire, Chadwick's *Packington*, was
     probably owned by John's father.
  2. MARSTON 1486*, brown, f 1791. Sold for 500 guineas either by Webb at
     the age of two, and therefore to Chadwick, or by Chadwick at the age
     of ten to someone unknown. There is a muddle in the evidence.
  3. PACKINGTON 1703*, black, f 1796.
  4. BULSTRODE 348, brown, f 1801. A full brother to No. 2. In 1806 he was let

to W. Cockayne† (Derby.) for 100 guineas, and again the next year for 150 guineas.

5. FARMER'S GLORY 808, black, f 1801. Like Nos. 2 and 4, bred by Webb† (Derby.). By Gallemore 904*. Webb bred the dam, which was by another early Chadwick horse, *Old Tom*. The g-dam was by Bulstrode's Bald 93* and the g.g-dam by Bakewell's G 890*. Four of the greatest experts of the eighteenth century took part in the breeding of this horse.

6. FARMER'S GLORY 809, black f 1805. By Chadwick's *Old Tom*. John Chadwick bred him and his dam which was by No. 2.

7. MARSTON 1488, black, f 1805. By No. 2. Dam by Farmer's Glory 807*.

8. PACKINGTON 1704, black, f 1807. Bred by Chadwick; by No. 3. Chadwick bred the dam, by Bald 93*.

9. LITTLE JOHN 1399, black or brown, f 1808. Also known as Kirby. By Oldacre's Kirby 1286.

10. KIRBY 1288, brown, f 1810. Bred by Chadwick. By Kettle's Kirby 1287*. Chadwick bred the dam, by No. 4.

11. ROBIN HOOD 1863, brown, f 1812. Bred in Staffs. By No. 9.

12. VICTORY 2219, brown, f 1812. Bred in Cheshire. By No. 2. Dam by Bald 93*.

13. BROWN BOBBY 289, brown, f 1814. Bred by Chadwick. By No. 9. Dam by Bald 93*.

14. INVINCIBLE 1138, chestnut, f 1816. Bred by Chadwick. By *The Berkshire Grey Horse*. Dam, bred by Chadwick, by Stych's *Old Chestnut Horse*.

15. INVINCIBLE 1130, chestnut, f 1816. By Dumpling 679, bred in 1810 and owned by Stych† (Derby.) by *New's Brown Horse of Chaddleworth Mills*, Berks.

16. SOVEREIGN 2034, black, f 1817. Bred by Thos. Hudson† (Derby.). By G 892, a horse whose antecedents on both sides seem to have been in Hudson's hands for generations. Sovereign won a premium for travelling the High Peak district.

17. KIRBY 1289, brown, f 1818. Of identical breeding to No. 10, possibly a full brother.

18. LITTLE JOHN 1401, brown, f 1818. All the breeding is of pure Derbyshire origin, except that the dam's sire was "descended from the Ingestre stud".

19. DRAYMAN 611, black, f 1820. By No. 15. Dam by No. 8. G-dam by No. 2.

With these horses, we have paid all the tribute we can to John Chadwick. Other members of the family, especially William of Totmonslow in the 'twenties and 'thirties, were also well known. But there was never another like John. The last horse owned by a Chadwick of this line was said to be Lord Byron 351, foaled in 1870, who on the death of his proprietor was bought by a tailor and then sold to a cloth hawker. The story may be apocryphal, but it is a fitting allegory which symbolises the truth that, while we expect our horses to go on becoming better and better, this principle does not work out for their human owners.

By the 'forties and 'fifties it was the name of Hinckley, not Chadwick, that was best known in Staffordshire. To him we have already referred in connection with his brother-in-law, Mr. Stych, in Derbyshire.

4. SHROPSHIRE, CHESHIRE AND LANCASHIRE

The further west or north we travel, the more we find ourselves among breeders whose stock-horses were derived from the districts already commented on. Mr. Handley of Pave Lane, for example, owned King Tom 1260*, bred in 1786 by Webb† in Derbyshire. This horse must have been no inconsiderable sire, to judge by his two sons which brought a small fortune to John Chadwick† (Nos. 2 and 4 in the list of his early horses in the foregoing section), but all his other sons and daughters are lost in the anonymity which now effaces the Shropshire cart-horses of those days. Handley, too, is heard of no more. A century and a half later, a Handley led stallions for Morris Belcher, the most famous Shropshire Shire man of modern times. Who knows but what in the eighteenth century an early Belcher may have led stallions for Handley?

Mr. Kettle of the Marsh, whoever he was, is known today only for his Kirby 1287* (sire of John Chadwick's Kirby 1288 – No.10 in the list referred to). He bred him himself in 1800 but the sire was Oldacre's Kirby 1286*. The dam was by Dragon 598* bred in 1785 by "Dutton of Chapel House", a horse got by *Stone's Brown Horse of Coalbrook*, and the grand-dam was by Bakewell's G 890. Kettle bred them both. Reynolds knew that Kettle sold his Kirby for 525 guineas on the 25th March 1811. But he does not say who paid this enormous price and, all the evidence having been destroyed, we shall probably never find out. This is all that need be said of the Shropshire horses. Where they were of native origin, they had little part to play in the future of the breed. They became of significance only in so far as blood was imported from further east.

Cheshire was supplied with heavy stallions by Summerland, Chadwick and other Staffordshire men, and between 1825 and 1860 some of the Masseys† (Staffs.), notably Thomas and Daniel, kept a large number of stallions at Acton, near Nantwich. The Derbyshire owners also sent horses into Cheshire. Those which were locally owned were scattered in ones and twos amongst what the eastern Midlands breeders would have regarded as "small men". At their head, so far as date goes, is Ploughboy 1719 bred in 1785 by Occleston of Bollin Hall: and his sire was Summerland's *Wiltshire Brown Horse*. The black Truemould 2196 was bred at Sale by Jonathan Renshaw in 1797, the result of a visit from Staffordshire by one of Summerland's horses.

The first Lancashire-bred horse to get into the Stud-book is listed simply as Brown Horse 326*, bred in 1780 by one Fray of Halliwell near Bolton, a horse tracing on the dam's side, if not the sire's also, to *The Packington Blind Horse*. Richard Reynolds, as soon as he became the Liverpool Corporation veterinary officer in 1867, talked to many an ancient Liverpudlian and learned that there had been a large number "of the heaviest description of stallions" imported into industrial Lancashire seventy and more years before – as working horses. They sometimes divided their duties and some of them became noted as sires. But "their pedigrees were not so accurately ascertained as if bought for stud purposes". This is a polite way of saying that few men really knew anything at all about the ancestry of any horses thereabouts and, as long as they were huge and heavy, cared even less. Gradually, however, selected strains began to show their worth. Joseph Battersby of Winwick, near Warrington, bred the black Blaze 191 in 1803, which was got by Handley's King Tom 1260* from Pave Lane, and he thereafter became famous for his black stallions, which were more successful at getting good foals than any of the old dock horses had been. A Mr. Jackson also became celebrated for his dark iron-greys, and "Jackson's breed of Altcar" became favourites. Two, both whimsically named "Farmer", were put in the Stud-book. One, 776, foaled in 1819, was by "*The Liverpool Grey Horse*" and the other 779, foaled in 1825, was by "*A Grey Horse from Liverpool*". These creatures no doubt had a lot to do with some of the future Liverpool horses, but had absolutely no effect on pedigree history. Thomas Horsefield of Knot Mill had a black-grey horse called *Tinker* in the 1790s, son of another Horsefield *Tinker* that was supposed to have been by Bulstrode's Bald 93*. From this horse was descended a whole number of *Tinkers*, three of them (foaled 1800–1817) registered in Volume 1 (see I.3). G 893 (foaled 1819, owned by Durning of Bickerstaffe) combined Battersby's black Blaze 191 with Tinker blood in an incredibly fertile combination.

From about 1815–1840, H. Hulme of Halebank and Joseph Heaps of Chorley travelled dray-stallions in the districts between Liverpool and Manchester. Peter Leather of Stretton, Warrington, brought a large number of really heavy stallions into the same area between 1830–1870, most of them bred in Derbyshire and Stafford. Reynolds, of course, saw the later specimens and commented that Mr. Leather's interests were "good feet, plenty of bone, hair and muscle. Quality and activity, if unaccompanied by the former desiderata, were with him very minor considerations." George Wilson of Liverpool did the same from about 1850, and stallions thumped into his Wood Lane premises at Little Woolton from all parts of the Midlands and the Fens.

Further north, from 1815 at least, the Thomas Forshaws, father and son, of Eccleston, supplied many a horse to the Fylde, and the family also kept stallions at Chorley. In 1857, Thomas the younger moved to Goosnargh and it was only two years afterwards that his severity drove his nineteen-year-old son away from home to seek freedom and fortune elsewhere. And it was with the likes of young James, not with his slave-driving father or any other of the Fylde breeders of those days, that the development and improvement of the dray-horse lay. The Fylde had to await its T. H. Miller, as the south of the county had to wait for the Earl of Ellesmere, before it did much more than produce muscle, bone and hair, together with the all-too-frequent occurrence of the "Liverpool coat-of-arms", in the form of sidebone, in a pretty generous and plentiful manner, and without any idea of system or planned improvement. By then, of course, stallions had long been replaced by geldings as movers of great weights on the streets and at the dockside.

5. NOTTINGHAMSHIRE

Topper (2169) foaled in 1792, is the one Nottingham-bred stallion of the eighteenth century to find his way into the Stud-book. He was bred by a Mr. Butler of Rampton, and was by Wink's *Topper*. But who was Wink, or where he lived, or what was his *Topper*, are mysteries today. Mr. Peck had a brown horse at Hayton, north of East Retford, and in 1804 won a premium with it for the best dray stallion to travel the Retford district. This horse was by a renowned sire belonging to Mr. Ashton of Fenton, over the county boundary in Lincolnshire. In 1818 a premium was won at Southwell by Mr. Whitehurst of Arnold with his six-year-old black Drayman (606), which was descended from the best-known Leicestershire horses. Six years later, this prize went to Mr. Hill's Farmer (777) a four-year-old brown, which was by *Cockin's Brown Horse* of Grove, out of a mare whose dam was by Wink's *Topper*. A Hill and a Cockin are as good as a Wink to a blind historian, for his material is nothing but snippets.

When he wrote his survey of the county in 1794, Robert Lowe observed that nearly all farm work was done by horses, but he was not much impressed by them. Those bred in the Trent valley were "chiefly a middling kind of black cart horse, though the breed begins to be improved by Leicestershire stallions". In the clay district, "most farmers raise a foal or two every year, but of a middling kind of black horses, which calls for improvement." When he summed up the county in brief, he again used the expression "a middling sort".[5] And, indeed, even in the years which followed, it is difficult to form any clearer picture of the Nottinghamshire horses, which remained comparatively without distinction. Perhaps this is because the best-known suppliers of stallions all imported from neighbouring counties. W. H. Challinor of Shireoaks brought in stallions from Derbyshire, Yorkshire and elsewhere between 1802 and 1856, as well he might, being situated in the Worksop area. William Hudson, of the same parish, from 1840 to 1875 supplied the northern parts of the county with a fairly mixed bag of stallions – good in themselves, but varying in type from the clean legged Yorkshire sorts to Midlands blacks, with not a few Fen horses as well. (Incidentally, he was one who lived long enough to be a member of the breed society for its first ten years.) Joshua Booth of East Markham brought in more Fens blood than anyone else, though over a limited period (1840–1860), while S. Bell of Sturton-le-Steeple on the Lincolnshire border got many of his from Yorkshire. All this was due to the county's geographical position which caused it to remain, right until the formation of the breed society, a sort of no man's land of cart horses, a fixed or recognisable type being difficult to achieve.

One man, however, during the crucial years from 1830 to the late 'sixties, towered above the rest as an owner and a connoisseur of stallions. This was Dan Howsin of Bathley, a few miles north of Newark. Fifteen horses stand to his name in Volume 1. The earliest was a Fen horse *par excellence*, Oxford 1683, foaled in 1826, which won prizes till he was sixteen years old. He bought his stallions in many different areas and so, here, we must either say less about him than he deserves, or extend the Nottinghamshire pages farther than the county merits by examining a confusing variety of unrelated pedigrees. Unlike Challinor, Hudson, Booth and Bell, he would not buy a colt from Yorkshire, for he loved a true heavy-horse. But his eagle eye spotted a good one in many a distant place. He even picked up a useful recruit in Dorking – the roan Lion (1375) foaled in 1840. There is no doubt that, had he been born fifty years later, Dan Howsin would have been a man to rival James Forshaw, whose migration from Lancashire eventually ended in the 'eighties at Carlton-on-Trent, only two to three miles away. The difference between the men lay chiefly in the times in which they lived, for Howsin was hard put to it to ascertain much about the breeding of a horse that caught his fancy and, furthermore, found immense difficulty in the middle years of the century in discovering stallions that were free from faults that he would not tolerate. A little tribute to the old man was paid by young James Forshaw when he first moved into Nottinghamshire in 1873. He bought a fine brown stallion of exceptional weight and substance which was bred near Retford. This seemed to him a superb animal, and so he named it Dan Howsin.

6. NORTHAMPTONSHIRE, SOUTHWARD AND POINTS WEST

In the book of the Recording Angel, though not in that compiled by the Editing Committee, there stands a vast array of cart-stallions credited to the Law family of Thenford. Now Thenford is at the opposite end of this long county from that which looks towards Peterborough and the Fens. It was remote, too, in the old days from Leicester. It looks rather to Banbury and Oxfordshire. In 1702, and probably before, Richard Law owned heavy stallions and Joseph, born in 1740, continued the family business by keeping five or six at a time. As he had five sons, this was convenient, for they each travelled one of them in the season. But the only Law horse prior to Joseph's death to be included in the Stud-book is Drayman (605), which he himself bred at the last in 1808. The reason for its inclusion is that, unlike his others, it was by a Fen horse, and a famous one at that – Honest Tom 1062 (see William the Conqueror, VII.1).

The eldest and youngest sons never became stallion-owners themselves. The fourth son, Thomas, moved over the county boundary and kept some at Milcombe, but none of these appear in the Stud-book. The second and third brothers, Joseph junior and John, continued their father's business in partnership until 1820, when John took all the entires a mile away to Middleton Cheney, where he was a stallion-owner for almost forty years. Joseph did not have any stallions of his own until 1843, when he bought a yearling from its breeder, Reeve of Fawsley. This was Champion (387), which became a very famous sire indeed. The first of all John's horses to be put in the book, curiously, was of exactly the same age – Merryman (1563), bred by Taylor of Thorpe Mandeville. One other, locally bred in 1852, stands in the book in John's name. And so, of all the horses owned by the three brothers, their father and his father before him, only four were included by Coke's committee.

The reason is not far to seek. The type of horse that they had and that was bred in this district was neither the Leicester nor the Fen type, though of shaggy hair on the legs they seemed not to be lacking. A marvellous Law stallion of about 1800, called *Waxwork*, had a completely white belly, but was otherwise black. For thirty years or more his descendants, particularly in the Towcester area, were similarly marked. In 1805–1820, the Laws' *Dumplings* and *Captains*, their favourite *Goldfinder*, which they would not sell for 200 guineas, their *Eagle* and their two *Staffordshires* were wonderfully celebrated. But to put them in the Stud-book sixty years afterwards was another matter.

The Wilsons of Moreton Pinkney were famous for their cart-stallions as well as for other farm stock in the late eighteenth century, but their contribution to pedigree history is precisely nil. Ivens of Eydon is, on the other hand, a name that occurs in many illustrious pedigrees as the owner of a *Grey Horse*. This stallion, with one of his sons, Farmer's Glory 818 (foaled in 1825, grey, and owned by Ivens), is the earliest traceable ancestor of the great Bar None 2388 (q.v. VIII.5), as he is also of the celebrated Stych's† Champion 419 (Derby.). One other grey Ivens horse is in the Stud-book – Champion 376, also foaled in 1825, and bred by Ivens himself. But it is only from about 1850 that horses belonging to men in these parts were accepted into the book in any numbers. A second John Law, for example, who set up at Moreton Pinkney, where the Wilsons had had their stallions, inherited the great Champion 387 from Joseph junior, and there are ten others of his horses in Volume 1.

The same story repeats itself further afield. The name of Manning was one of several which had been familiar in the stallion business in the Northampton-Wellingbrough-Kettering area, but it is only John Manning whose name occurs in Volume 1, which has twenty-one of his stallions in the 1850–1875 period. Over the Warwickshire border at Rugby, where the great horse-fair was still one of the most important markets in England, the Hipwells were extensive stallion men. But it is W. J. Hipwell who is credited with the majority of their twenty horses (none of them before 1850) which appear in this first volume. He lived to be a Shire society member for thirty years, to 1909.

To the west and south, the tale is similar. Before and after 1800 in Oxfordshire, Beere's horses of Neithrop (Banbury) were highly esteemed. None of them was put in the Shire book, and it was not until 1847, the time of William Butler of Hanwell Fields, that horses harking from these parts were accepted by the Editing Committee. Seven of his are entered.

If we move from Oxford into Berkshire, we notice in the early days a concentration on the growing-on of draught-horses for the towns, rather than on breeding. "The Berkshire farmer", wrote William Pearce in 1794, "considers his profit from horses no inconsiderable part of his farming and this, in some degree, accounts for the unnecessary number of horses we see kept in every part of the county. Some breed their own stock, and others buy in suckers, which they put to work very early; and after using them for two or three years, sell off, to the brewers in London, and the stage waggons, at such high prices, as to make eight or ten pounds per annum of each horse; considering his work equal to the expense of his keep."[6] (He thought the introduction of the Norfolk plough would save a third of the 12,000 heavy horses in the county. In turn that would save 3,500 acres, on which enough wheat could be grown to feed thousands and enough barley to provide as much beer as poor labouring men, however thirsty, could ever dream of.) Of Berkshire breeders of any particular note, there was none. Stallions travelled there from further north, and a reminder of it is a horse, bought up as a colt by Ivens, which was probably got about 1810 by one of his own horses travelling in the far west of the county – yet another grey one, going under the name of the *Berkshire Grey Horse*. It figures as sire of John Bull 1161 in the pedigree of William the Conqueror. Significantly, the dam of John Bull was by *Percey's Grey Horse* of Idstone. Idstone is a stone's throw from Wiltshire – but Percey's stallion headquarters were at Northampton. We can reasonably assume that Summerland† sent stallions from Staffordshire to Wiltshire, which would account for his "Wiltshire" stallions.

We might conclude our brief survey of this area by turning to Buckinghamshire. At the end of the eighteenth century, no oxen were used for work, but the horses, "of the heavy black kind", were nearly all "brought in at two or three years old . . . The slowness of their motion is an objection to them."[7] Within a generation or two, the Vale of Aylesbury became recognised as an area second only to the Fens in ability to grow horses of exceptional size and weight. Among the first to realise this were members of the Watts family of Claydon and, until the breed society was formed, they were the best-known Buckinghamshire men in the business, though only eight of their horses are now in the book, dating from 1830. One of them, foaled in 1838, was called Activity (61). Perhaps this indicates that the Watts had taken note of the objectionably slow motion of the earlier Buckinghamshire specimens. His pedigree is hopelessly vague: he was by "John Law's Horse". In heavens' name, which one? His dam was by *Beere's Conqueror* – a sad consolation for the Neithrop breeder who is not otherwise represented.

Perhaps Claydon is a good place to terminate this erratic journey. Was it not from there that Sir Edmund Verney in 1635, doubtful of the Vale's potential, had told his son to send away as many cart horses as possible to gather flesh at an easy charge – in the Fens?

7. THE FENS

Those who produced their draft county surveys for the Board of Agriculture in 1793–1794 were somewhat critical of horse management in these areas. Speaking of the Lincolnshire Fens, Thomas Stone said black cart brood mares were used for farmwork and "as they generally produce a foal every year, which sells for 10 or 12 pounds, they are undoubtedly profitable". Colts rising two made from £18 to £20. But he thought breeders ought to sell off their ageing mares instead of continuing with them until worn out. He also remarked that horses were sold for town work absurdly young. "Being driven hard about the pavements in London, and kept in hot stables, they soon give way in their feet, and they become foundered and useless." He thought they should be kept in the country until six or seven, and suggested that, since "the horse is an impoverisher of the land he depastures upon in the same ratio that sheep are the contrary", they ought to be kept in confined situations and fed upon tares and lucerne in the summer. More useful than this advice to his contemporaries is his reminder to later ages of the vast extent of the commons still remaining at that time. On Wildmoor Fen horses wintered out with neat cattle and were driven "to such distress for food that they eat up every remaining dead thistle, and are said to devour the hair off the manes and tails of each other, and also the dung of geese".[8] Arthur Young had observed that Long Sutton, "one of the most famous tracts of land in this country and extending to 3500 acres, annually had 30,000 sheep, 1000 horses and 300 beasts upon it."[9]

George Maxwell, writing of Huntingdon, commented that in the Fens every farmer worked brood mares and bred as many foals from them as possible, selling the colts off at two years and all the fillies that could be spared. In higher parts of the county the same general management applied, though not so many were bred.[10] Another survey of this county was made by Stone, who said it was "not famous for any particular breed. The farmers' horses are of the heavy black kind, and they do not generally look forward to the advantage that might be derived by selling them off for more valuable purposes when mature." [11]

On Cambridgeshire, Charles Vancouver was quite derogatory. "Nothing in the county of Cambridge is replete with more error and abuse, or more capable of reform, under the present circumstances of the county, than the feeding and working management of farm horses." Then, having glowingly reported the Norfolk method, he added "The scarcity of pasture ground, the want of proper attention to the raising of green food for soiling their horses in summer, and the great neglect in the culture of artificial grasses, all conduce to an expense in supporting the farm horses in the upper parts of this country that is absolutely enormous. They are kept in the stable throughout the year, each horse is fed with a peck of corn per day, with as much chaff, chopped straw and hay, as they can eat, and work but one journey in the day; which seldom exceeds seven hours, but never eight; except in the neighbourhood of Leverington, Parson-drove, and Thorney, where two journies a day are not unusual, ploughing from seven to twelve, and from two in the afternoon until night; or when the day will admit of it, till seven in the evening, doing about an acre each journey."[12]

It was at Thorney, in 1791, that R. Fullard had a big sale of black horses, and one of them was bought by Mr. Cork. This is the first beginning of our knowledge of any individual Fen horses that appear in modern Shire pedigrees. The Corks, of Tydd St. Giles, continued owning stallions for another fifty or sixty years and four of Robert Cork's, foaled between 1830 and 1850, are in Volume 1. They are three Honest Toms and a Thumper, names that were always favourite in his and many other Fen families. Like all his horses, their breeding was looked to with great care, and he knew the antecedents of the dams and g-dams pretty thoroughly. The Cork's friends, the Fullard family of Thorney Fen, went on breeding Shires until the First World War.

Near Spalding, also in the 1790s, a member of the Fisher family owned a horse which he called *John Bull* but which was usually referred to as *Fisher's Black Horse of Weston*. This stallion was a great celebrity in his time, but the Fishers are represented in Volume 1 by a solitary horse – the black Sweep 2082, bred in 1866 by T. Fisher. There was nothing particularly remarkable about this animal. There were, and had been, hundreds like him, though only a handful have been recorded, and there had been, and were, thousands of their brothers which were castrated and sent to the great towns to move the heaviest loads that a modern industrial community could shift in no other way. But Sweep's breeding, though typical of the jealous care with which the purity of Fen blood was preserved (by a host of breeders who were nearly all "small men") in those years of confusion elsewhere, is also of great historical interest, as far as his earliest traceable ancestors are concerned. In the male line, it reads thus (** denoting that the dam was certainly bred by the same man: otherwise, it is doubtful):

Sire: LINCOLNSHIRE SWEEP 1366, black, bred 1853 by Lake, of Deeping**

G-s: SWEEP 2081, black, bred 1847 by Scrimshaw of Parson Drove**

G.g-s: DRAGON 600, grey, bred 1843 by Maxwell, of Boro' Fen

G.g.g-s: DRAGON 599, black, bred 1834 by William Nix, of Somersham**

G.g.g.g-s: PHENOMENON 1712, bay, bred 1823 by Parnel, of Thorney Fen

G.g.g.g.g-s: PHENOMENON 1711, brown, bred 1812 by Johnson, of Whittlesea

G.g.g.g.g.g-s: *Fisher's Black Horse*, of Weston.

Dragon 599 was out of an old mare by Honest Tom 1060 (see below). There is an element of confusion about his sire in the Stud-book, which erroneously inserts an extra Phenomenon (1713) in the pedigree.

Sweep 2082's dam had been bred by Fisher, and this was her ancestry in the male line:

Sire: CHAMPION 391, brown, bred 1845 by Wiles, of Manea**

G-s: HONEST TOM 1073, brown, bred 1831 by Andrews, of Elm
G.g-s: HONEST TOM 1067, (unknown), bred 1826 by Goodman, of
               Tholomas Drove
G.g.g-s: ENGLAND'S GLORY 705, brown, bred 1841 by Larmet, of Gedney
G.g.g.g-s: HONEST TOM 1060, (unknown), bred 1800. Owned by Wiseman,
               of Fleet

The g-dam of Sweep had also been bred by Fisher:

Sire: COMPETITOR 514, black, bred 1839 by Clarke, of Long Sutton
G-s: HONEST TOM 1071, brown, bred 1830, by Warth, of Walsoken
G.g-s: HONEST TOM 1066 (unrecorded), bred 1824, by Green, of
               Upwell Fen
G.g.g-s: HONEST TOM 1061 (unrecorded), bred 1805. Owned by Thorpe,
               of Holbeach
G.g.g.g-s: *Townsend's Honest Tom.* Townsend lived at Fleet.

If Sweep himself was nothing out of the ordinary, his remotest traceable ancestors were. The two earliest stallions to which his sire and his dam can be traced form the very foundation on which the whole modern breed of Shires was based. Honest Tom 1060 is the primogenitor of the greatest Shire line, and Fisher's Black horse is the earliest discoverable ancestor in the male line of William the Conqueror 2343, whose line is the second greatest. The history of Shire horse breeding is the story of how these lines dominated all others.

There is something singularly appropriate in the fact that Honest Tom 1060 was foaled in the year 1800, for it is only with the turn of the century that the fogs and mists lift off the Fens and the enquirer can begin to see what was happening. Indeed, it was only then that the completion of their proper draining was in sight. Even so, the breeders and their horses – perhaps because both were so numerous – do not stand out in sharp perspective for many years to come.

The Johnsons, scattered over an area from Whittlesea through March to Burwell on the eastern perimeter of Cambridgeshire, were accounted notable men in the first half of the century. Drage Camps of Haddenham began some time before 1825, when he bred the brown Farmer (778) by the mysterious Ireland's Brown Horse of Manea (1150) out of a mare he had bred himself as a very young man. He continued as a well-known name until very late in life. In 1878 he bred a black colt foal (Black Draught 2395) a week or two before joining the new pedigree society. He did not breed his last until 1888, and was still a member of the Shire Horse Society when he died in 1896. The Porters, Robert and Hugh in succession, also of Haddenham, were well-known breeders in the middle fifty years of the century. The Richardsons in the Chatteris area had been notable breeders from time immemorial, though the earliest of their horses in the Stud-book is Farmer's Glory 823 bred in 1830. Alfred Richardson of Mepal was the last of the line, and attended the jubilee London Show in 1929. Stephen Bradley of Tydd St. Giles owned, and bred, stallions for the first forty years or so of the century. And how many stallions the four members of the Eno family had, at Long Sutton and Sutton St. James, is beyond discovery. The Taylors, in the Ely and Wisbech areas, were great names in mid-century, as were the Coys, especially those in and around Downham, and the Flanders family, mostly in the Littleport district. The Goldens, round Ramsey in Huntingdon, lived to become Shire members, but John Hemmant of Thorney Fen, Adams of Landbeach, and Ingle of Doddington were part of history before the Society began. The name of Seward became immortal through two horses of prime historical importance. Seward of Quadring owned Honest Tom 1062, foaled perhaps in 1796 – another son of *Fisher's Black Horse*, and founder of the William the Conqueror line. Seward of Chatteris in 1838 bred and owned Major 1447 (V.4), one of the greatest descendants of Wiseman's Honest Tom.

The great Matchless 1509 (VIII.1) brought, in his day, almost greater glory to the name of Dack of Tydd St. Mary. By 1878 there were no Sewards and no Dacks to reap the rewards of the great contribution they had made to the making of the Shire. But John Rowell of Bury, breeder of Heart of Oak 1005 (VIII.2), had a son who was to become the great doyen of the tenant-farmer Shire breeders and who, sadly, died before becoming the first Shire president drawn from their ranks in 1922.

This list must be halted before it becomes impossibly tedious to the reader, for by no means can it be made complete. As Fred Street once remarked, "Cattle or sheep are well, in the way; but to a Fenman nothing is of so much interest as his horses. They are his special pride. Young fellows of twenty will tell you the best points, and pick out the worst, in a horse or mare, and have the pedigrees of their own-bred horses at the fingers' ends." Let us finish, therefore, with two brothers from Fred's own parish of Somersham, equals both in skill and honour with the Derbyshire branch of the Nix family.

William Nix of Somersham, born in 1792, was in his 'teens when he first saw Wiseman's Honest Tom. He thought he was the best horse in the district. As an old man of eighty-seven, his opinion had hardened. He believed Honest Tom was the greatest he had ever seen. And he himself had owned hundreds and seen thousands. One he had both bred (in 1838) and owned was Captain 358. This horse, generally known as the Old Mill Horse, travelled nearly thirty years round Somersham, and the mind boggles at the number of foals he got in this time, for William Nix took a bit of care with his stallions. In his young days he and his brother John and Mr. Moseley (Fred Street's predecessor at Somersham Park) promised thirty mares at 2 guineas each to one of the horses of Mr. Wood of Elm, the last owner of Honest Tom 1060. But Wood's horses had too many mares. Out of these thirty they got only one foal, which was sold as a two-year-old by John Nix for 175 guineas. The Nix brothers never forgot this lesson, and would never allow their stallions to have too many mares. As a result, they earned a great reputation for the fertility of their stock.

William Nix would be as delighted as William Wiseman to know the supreme position that the researches of the 1970s have accorded Honest Tom. He lived just long enough to see the Cart Horse Society founded: and his younger brother was a member of it for over twelve years, the last foal he bred being a black colt in 1888. This old-fashioned looking animal was by his home-bred black Gordon 4424, whose chestnut dam *Onyx* was one of eight foals he had got in eight successive years out of the chestnut *Pink*. And he had bred old *Pink* in the days when he and his brother, like many men all over the Fens, were struggling, amid confusion, to keep alive the tradition of the Fishers and Corks and the men of long ago.

8. FROM BEDFORD TO BEVERLEY

If we loop our way eastwards and north from where we left off before studying the Fens, the account of our journey will be short, for there is little of significance to recite. In Bedford, as in Hertford, the use of Black horses was most noticeable, but not the breeding of them. Yearlings and two-year-olds were brought from the Fens and grown on, via farm-work, to duties in the big road teams which hauled produce to London and returned laden with town manure: others went to London only once and never came back, except perhaps to light duties when old or lame.

However, as the nineteenth century wore on, there was more breeding done, and Thomas Cleaver of Toddington Mills near Dunstable may be singled out as the man, stallion-owner pure and simple, who supplied nearly every good horse that ever covered a mare in a big part of the county between the years 1830 and 1870. He bought them either in the Fens or in the Vale of Aylesbury, and on occasions he would find a good colt sired by one of his own horses in Bedfordshire itself. By 1880 he deserved thanks for most of the better heavy-horses in the county. There were plenty of very bad ones.

Of Essex horses, the less said the better. They were as mixed in type, but as uniform in their inferiority, as its sheep and cattle. Suffolk, of course, was unique and had its separate race of horses. Norfolk had indifferent ones – except where they were Fen horses in the west, or Suffolks in the south. The mixture of the two, which was the commonest "breed", was not a desirable experiment. The men of this famous agricultural county would have done better to have kept to their own ancient individual variety – a sort of bay or brown version of the Suffolk. This had virtually disappeared by the mid-eighteenth century, though by the middle of the following one the "bay Suffolk", with perhaps a little token tuft of hair below the ankles, was back again, owing to a reversal of the earlier trend – the increasing use of Suffolk stallions instead of Black ones, owing to the railways, which had obviated the need for heavy road-teams to take farm produce long distances. One is reluctant to dismiss this marvellously progressive agricultural county as ruthlessly as (Shire-wise) it deserves, because though the breeding of horses was nondescript, their management, in all its aspects, was outstandingly good. Nevertheless, it must be done. Otherwise, how shall we not speak of every county in England, which would be absurd?

If we leap over the Wash and land in the Lincoln Marsh, we must pause only to pay tribute to the Gants – Emmanuel of Bilsby Field near Alford and William of Thurlby (the little Thurlby two miles from Bilsby Field). Great stallion-owners were these two from about 1825 onwards, with twenty-seven of their best horses named in Volume 1. Emmanuel even lived to become a Cart Horse Society man. His last entries were Cowbit Tom, bred in 1879 near Spalding, as his name suggests; Major IV, bred almost next door at Sutton-on-Sea in 1882 by "– Chatterton" (old Gant kept forgetting to find out the initials); and Briton Still, exported to the Galbraiths in Wisconsin at the age of five in 1887. This horse was bred, also next door, by John Mountain – who, using a Gant horse, had bred in 1857 a certain "Champion" which is a vital link in the pedigree of every Shire horse alive in the late twentieth century, as must be discussed later. The last Shire that Emmanuel Gant ever bred was 2973 Black Bess in 1883. He sold her to a young farmer called Alfred Clark at Moulton Eaugate who got from her one of his early stallions, and the first he had bred himself. This was Headlight in 1888. Clark became a household name wherever Shires were bred. Of Gant, few had heard outside his native county. But who is to say which was really the better man?

Over all Kesteven and Lindsey, as in the Fens, there were few really outstanding Black Horse men in the old time, simply because there were so many able ones. If we move westward from Alford through Horncastle, that great collecting area and mart for the heavy-horse, to Lincoln and then take the main road south, we can visit Welbourn to see an example of this – and a pleasant one, too, for it was said to be the prettiest village between Grantham and Lincoln. In this parish of less than five hundred souls, there were several mighty men. Thomas Shepherd, born in 1792, was a farmer-butcher, as his father and grandfather had been before him. He kept stallions almost from his boyhood and when at last he grew too old to see to them he stayed at home to help mind the shop while Young Tom travelled one horse and Bill Padgett the other. The Shepherd class of stallion is shown by the fact that Lincolnshire Lad 1196 himself was one of theirs for a time. The best of Old Tom's earlier stallions had been Lively Lad 1416, bred in 1826 by Joseph Burtt of the same parish, a member of a family that had farmed thereabouts since at least 1630. Joseph in 1818 had bred David 565 (see pedigree of William the Conqueror, VII.1) a fine son of Honest Tom 1062. When Tom Shepherd the Younger died, the Burtts took his farm and continued to prosper exceedingly, to the extent of 2,700 acres, while the descendants of the two Tom Shepherds live in a Welbourn council house. Robert Hall, his son John (born in 1738) and grandson John (1763) were all Black Horse men, as was Thomas (1795) of the next generation. Late in the eighteenth century, the second John owned a famous Black stallion, which everyone just called *Hall's Horse*. The Hall of the fourth generation from Robert lived next door to William Lamb, that great enthusiast and evangelist of the English Cart Horse Society (see A.VII.1). Lamb lived and died before

PLATE 45 Start of the day. G.W.R. horses coming down the ramps from their "dormi-tories" at Mint Stables, Paddington, one fine morning in 1922. Part of St. Mary's Hospital now occupies the site.

PLATE 46 End of the road. The last shunting horse at Paddington, 14th August, 1925. The scene shows High Level Goods, demolished five years later.

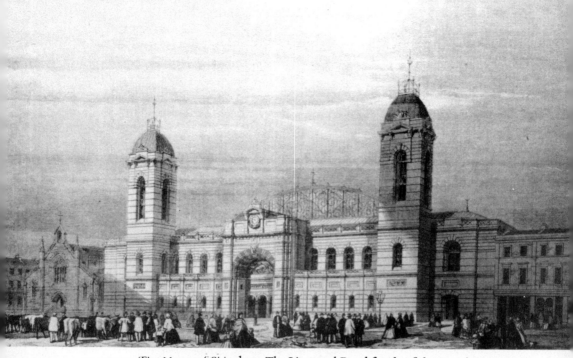

PLATE 47 The Mecca of Shiredom. The Liverpool Road façade of the Royal Agricultural Hall in Islington always looked much the same as in this artist's impression of 1862, when it was under construction. Behind this front, many changes and expansions occurred over the years.

PLATE 48 The Holy of Holies. A. B. Charlton sorting out some papers before a meeting in the Council Room at 12, Hanover Square. The house no longer exists.

his time and Hall fell upon evil days, and went out of farming. And what shall we say of Henry Minnitt? Nothing here, but a whole Shire book could be written without travelling as far from Welbourn Old Farm as any of the Shepherd's old stallions used to do.

We really must hurry north. In the eighteenth century, Black horses crossed the Humber into the ideal flat lands of Holderness and from there, and from Howden also, they crept north. William Marshall, of course, would have stopped them at Beverley. He was sorry to see the "Howden mack"[13] (or *make*) of Blacks "worming their way" into the Vale of Pickering, for in his prejudiced eyes they were as great a pest as the plague of grey rats. He wrote in 1788, and did not mince his words. "A breed of horses better calculated for eating than working, and whose main tendency is to render their drivers as sluggish as themselves, are ill adapted to the present rents of the Vale. Norfolk has already experienced the evil consequences of encouraging that breed; and I hope this county will not suffer by the same indiscretion. It is laughable enough to see a slender half-bred mare, who perhaps a few years ago received the embraces of Jalap or his offspring, bending under the weight of a cumbersome animal, whose very legs, in all their admired roughness, are nearly equal in size to the body of her former gallant. No wonder that monsters, having not their likeness in nature, should be the produce of such unnatural amours." [14]

Monsters were replaced in due course by good cart horses. But the East Riding, a century later, was not among the quickest areas to be converted to the pedigree movement. Where the blood was purest, it was generally Anglo-Scottish. In the early 'seventies one of the best-known stallions travelling the Beverley district was *Lord of the Manor*. Bred in 1866, his sire was Lincolnshire 1355 (winner of first prize at the Newcastle Royal in 1864, and at the Great Yorkshire at Howden, Wetherby and Beverley in 1864, '68 and '69): his dam, as his card proudly claimed, was "*Flower*, a celebrated Black Clydesdale Mare purchased by Mr. Strickland to breed from". His proprietor asserted that he was "undoubtedly descended, as his pedigree testifies, from the best and *purest breed of Cart Horses*, so that his Stock is sure to be first-class animals."

In 1888 – ten years after the pedigree movement had begun north and south of the border – John Ellerington of Hen Gate, Beverley, was advertising "The Powerful Black Cart Stallion, *BLACK PRINCE*, a beautiful black, with immense bone and superior action." His dam was by Black Douglas (a well-known Clydesdale prize-winner). The usual stud-card details concluded that "From the above, it will be seen that Black Prince is a pure-bred Carting Stallion". Indeed he was, but only Lawrence Drew would have put him in a stud-book, and Drew and his movement were dead.

Nevertheless, even though in years to come there were great Shire studs dotted like oases in the more southern districts of Yorkshire and fifteen Shire stallion-hiring societies operated in the county right through to 1939 (mostly, but not all, in the southern parts), Yorkshire remained a land where Clydesdale and Shire met and mingled. The Shire was commonest in the East Riding and south of a line from York to Keighley in the West Riding, and the Clydesdale elsewhere. The Clydesdale in Yorkshire tended to be heavier-boned than in Scotland, and the Shire lighter than in the Fylde or the Fens. Outside pedigree circles, the vast majority of farmers, following the example of those who used *Lord of the Manor* or *Black Prince*, could not have cared less whether what they bred was Clydesdale, Shire or a cross in any proportion whatever. But this is all another matter. If by "men of old time" we principally mean those living in the reign of George III, then Black was Black and Clydesdale nowt.

CHAPTER III

Two Leicestershire Lines that Faded

I. THE PACKINGTON BLIND HORSE

Our knowledge of *The Packington Blind Horse* is dim indeed. This is not so disappointing as our total ignorance about the antecedents of two Lincolnshire horses, Milton and Colley's *Brown Horse of Bassingham* and Fisher's Black Horse, *John Bull*, for they, as the sires respectively of Honest Tom 1060 and Honest Tom 1062, are the true ancestors of the whole modern breed of Shires. The importance of the *Blind Horse* has, in fact, been exaggerated by reason of two circumstances:

1. Compared with information about early Suffolk horses, details of early Shires were pathetically sparse. It is a historical accident that this horse and his descendants had men not only to remember them, but actually to write down pedigrees. By 1834, when the genealogical table was compiled, 150 known members of his line were indeed known, and had been well-known. But between 1834 and 1880 their influence waned rather than increased. Yet the record remained, and it was largely in a spirit of useless rivalry with the Suffolks over purity of blood that this family tree was included in the Stud-book. Unfortunately, it has always been assumed since then that his is the one name that matters in the early origins of the Shire.

2. The first Editing Committee was not to know, in 1879, which were the most important horses of those they were proposing to enter in the book. They naturally gave emphasis to the one illustrious line which was moderately well documented. The two Honest Toms, as primogenitors of Lincolnshire Lad II and William the Conqueror, became of supreme importance only *after* 1880. It could not be otherwise. The whole purpose of the Stud-book and the London Shows was to discover and then use the best blood-lines, not to forecast them.

Nevertheless, the *Packington Blind Horse* is of interest to the historian. He was clearly the great sire of his day in Leicestershire and Derbyshire, and the best-known sires for many generations afterwards were descended from him. And did not even Bakewell – who scorned to use Fen horses because of their roughness – condescend to mingle his blood with his Frisian mares in the attempt, frittered away later, to produce the perfect cart horse?

Here follows, therefore, a table of those of his descendants whose names have survived. It is cut short at the foaling year 1799 simply to avoid confusion to reader and writer alike. Unfortunately, the Stud-book itself and the Genealogical table are quite irreconcilable on numerous points, and the only evidence in choosing between them is internal.

DESCENDANTS OF THE PACKINGTON BLIND HORSE

(to 1799 only), according to the Stud-book

1	2	3	4
			LITTLE JOHN 1398 (1796)[a]...........
			BLAZE 187 (1799)[b]...
			PACKINGTON 1703[c] see 3[c]............
LOCKWOOD G[a] 1418 (1799)........	MARSTON 1486 (1791)[a]..........	KING TOM 1260 (1786)[a]..........	Webb's Brown Horse[d] mare[e]............. Ball[f]...............
		mare[b]...........	
			HAWKSWORTH'S HORSE 994 (1790)[g] FARMER'S GLORY 807 (1790)[h] ...... SIMS' HORSE 2019 (1795)[i]...........
	CLUBFOOT 497 (1785)[b].........	PACKINGTON 1703 (1796)[c] BLAZE 184 (1790)[d].	BLAZE 185 (1785)[j]...
		G 890 (1775)[e]...... SWEBSTONE 2079 (1795)[f]......... BLAZE 192 (1795)[g]. BLAZE 186 (1797)[h].	BLAZE 183 (1770)[k]...
	BLAZE 187[c] see 4b.		
	GALLEMORE 904 (1790)[d].........	GALLEMORE 903 (1780)[i]......... MANSETTER 1476 (1790)[j]......... mare[k].........	KIRBY 1286 (1785)[l]..
BLACK LEGS[b] 141 (1798)	mare[e]............. Oldacre's Little John[f]		

{RULER 1906 (1783)[a]......... {RULER 1905 (1773)[a].... Bumper[a]

{mare[b].................. BALD HORSE 93[b] see 5h

mare[b]..................... un-named horse[c]......... The Packington Blind Horse[c]

{THE BLIND HORSE 192[c]

{ = 3g .... Bulstrode's Horse[d]

mare[d]..................... mare .... The Packington Blind Horse

BROWN HORSE 326 (1780)[e] mare[e]................. The Packington Blind Horse

mare[f]..................... Donnisthorp's Horse[f]...... The Packington Blind Horse

.... Merryman[g] .... The Packington Blind Horse

Bulstrode's Horse[g]

BALD HORSE 93 (1778)[h].....

Oldacre's Old Kirby[h]...... The Packington Blind Horse

Oldacre's Mansetter[i]..........

N.B. 1. Horses marked * are also mentioned in the relevant part of Chapter II, as are breeders marked †.

2. No attempt has been made to correct or ascertain names and addresses, where vague.

NOTES TO PAGES 550 & 551

1a LOCKWOOD G 1418, brown: b Grinders, Lockwood, Staffs.: o Fallows, Booth Hall, Derby.

b BLACK LEGS 141, black: b and o Joseph Wright (Derby.).†

2a MARSTON 1486, –: b Webb (Derby.):†* o John Chadwick (Staffs.).†*

b CLUBFOOT 497, brown: o C. Hutton, Sutton Scarsdale, Derby.

c See 4b.

d GALLEMORE 904, –: b and o Perkins, Whitgreave, Staffs.*

f *Little John*, unidentifiable.

3a KING TOM 1260, brown: b Webb (Derby.).†* o Handley (Salop).†*

c PACKINGTON 1703, black: b Clarkson, Breedon, Leics: o John Chadwick (Staffs.).†*
Same horse as 4c, which shows dam's breeding.

d BLAZE 184, black: b R. Bakewell (Leics.). (See section 2.) o Thos. Hudson (Derby.).†

e G 890, bl-br: b and o R. Bakewell (Leics.). (See section 2.)

f SWEBSTONE 2079, –: oWyldes (Wild), (Leics.).†*

g BLAZE 192, alias THE BLIND HORSE, black: b J. Summerland (Staffs.):†* o Thos. Gillman (Staffs.).†* Same horse as 5c.

h BLAZE 186, –: b Seleby, Snibson, Derby. (unidentifiable): o Brown, Broughton, Derby.

i GALLEMORE 903, –: b and o Moore, Winshill, Derby.
Who his sire really was cannot be determined. The editors of the Stud-book admitted defeat in 1886. Presumably an earlier *Kirby* owned by Oldacre.

j MANSETTER 1476, alias BALD HORSE, –: b and o Oldacre (Leics.)†* (see also Massey, Staffs.†*).
Cannot have been the son of Kirby 1286 if the dates are right.

k This pedigree seems highly suspect.

4a LITTLE JOHN, 1398, black: b and o R. Gibbs, Tissington, Derby.†

b BLAZE 187, black: b W. Cockayne (Derby.):†* o Joseph Wright (Derby.).†

c See 3c.

d Webb's *Brown Horse* – (i.e. Derby.).†

f *Ball*. Stud-book gives sire as "Bustrode's Horse". Gen. table definitely gives as Bulstrode's Bald Horse – i.e. Bald Horse 93 (5g).

g HAWKSWORTH'S HORSE 994, black: b Hawksworth, Stanton Dale, Derby.: o W. Mellor (Derby.).† His dam was by *General*, "brother to Mansetter".

h FARMER'S GLORY 807, –: b Sims, Stanton-by-Dale, Derby.: o Shaw (Derby.)†* (see also Massey, Staffs.).†

i SIMS' HORSE 2019, black: b Sims (as h): o Mellor (as g).
His dam was by *Faulkner's Old Horse*.
BLAZE 185, alias BALD HORSE, –: b Ashby, Eckington, Derby.: o Radford, Little Eaton, Derby.
Ashby bred the dam, which was by *The Sinfin Old Horse*. Radford was a member of the Dishley Society.

k BLAZE 183, –: b and o Hart (Leics.).†*
There is much doubt about the date of this horse – if 1770 was right, he is the earliest

registered Shire horse. It is more than likely there was a second Blaze, a son, foaled about 1790, which was the sire of 3 f-g-h.

l KIRBY 1286, –: b and o Oldacre (Leics.).†
  Here too, the date is wrong if the two Gallemores are right. Possibly the sire of Gallemore 903 was really Old Kirby (6h).

5a RULER 1906, –: b Chatterton, Ashbourne: o Wagstaffe, Atlow, Ashbourne. Dam also bred by Chatterton.

c THE BLIND HORSE 192. Same horse as BLAZE 192 (see 3g).

e BROWN HORSE 326, brown: b and o Fray, Halliwell, Bolton, Lancs.†*
  The sire was *P. Grundy's Horse of Hulton* (Lancs.).

f This mare is stated to have been bred by "Donnisthorpe of Packington"! (See 6g.)

g *Bulstrode's Horse.* See 6d.

h BALD HORSE 93, –: b and o Bulstrode (Leics.).†*
  He was a travelling stallion for fourteen years, and at the age of ten Bulstrode was charging three guineas for service. His importance in many good pedigrees suggests he was one of the greatest 18th-century stallions. Bulstrode bred his dam, but she cannot have been by Gallemore 903 (3i) as the Stud-book preposterously claims.

i Oldacre's *Mansetter.* Leics.†*

6a RULER 1905, –: b and o Webb (Derby.).†

6 Bulstrode's Horse. This is not very illuminating, for he had scores of them.

f Donnisthorpe is a village near Packington. Surely this should be "The Donnisthorpe Horse"?

g *Merryman.* Unidentifiable. Gen. table calls him "Old Merryman", foaled about 1770, and states he was a son of P.B.H. There were a "Massey's Merryman" (*c.* 1793) and a "Harp's Merryman" (*c.* 1795) both said to be son of Oldacre's *Mansetter.*

h Oldacre's *Old Kirby.* Leics.†*

7a *Bumper* is untraceable.

c *THE PACKINGTON BLIND HORSE* (Leics.).†* Tradition held that he was owned by a Mr. Hood. He appears to have been serving mares first about 1755 and is last heard of about 1770. He was active in Leicestershire, Derbyshire and Warwickshire. It seems that he was black, with white face and markings. He stood about 16.2-hands and was described as having a broad breast, thick and upright shoulders, low forehand, well sprung ribs, thick forearms and thighs, short legs, and good feet and pasterns. His blood ran, in several streams, in the veins of William the Conqueror 2343 (see VII.1).

In compiling the table, two fairly safe assumptions were made:

(*a*) that the Stud-book entries, in spite of some gross errors, are on the whole more accurate. The Editing Committee rightly tended towards caution, and preferred to omit any horse it was not confident about. Its very errors are plain to see, and no attempt was made to "fiddle" with dates, even when patently wrong.

(*b*) that the Genealogical table was compiled from memory. Though we know that old breeders' memories were incredibly good compared with those which in a modern age are cluttered up with so many extraneous interests, and though it was written forty-four years before the Editing Committee set to work, memory is less reliable than printed or written matter and is liable to become muddled when there are two, three or four horses with the same name, belonging to the same man and either descended from each other, in which case the confusion is of comparatively little importance, or else quite unrelated, which makes all the difference in the world. The dates in the Genealogical table are mostly given as "approximate", which causes suspicion that they were made to fit the pedigrees. As classical scholars, faced with a corrupted text, were wont to say, "lectio difficilior potior". The less expected version is more likely to be the true one.

The chart on pp. 550–551, therefore, was compiled from the Stud-book itself. The only concession made to the unknown compiler of the Genealogical table is to accept that Oldacre's *Mansetter* was a son of his *Old Kirby* and that both the latter and *Merryman* were sons of *The Packington Blind Horse*. The Stud-book does not say they were, simply because the Editors did not actually enter these three horses, but only listed them as sires of some they did register. But if it were not so, it would be incredible that the legend of *The Packington Blind Horse* should have grown at all.

N.B. For completeness, the other eighteenth-century horses in the Stud-book (only eight) are commented on in section 3.

2. THE DISHLEY BREED

Bakewell's secrecy about the breeding of his stallions, added to the fact that the names, or letters, of so few of them have survived (every Bakewell horse was, to the outside world, not so much an individual as a representative of the "Dishley Breed" in general), put the Editing Committee in a quandary, for they tried strictly to observe their rule about not admitting known crosses of other blood. In the end they accepted two true Bakewell horses and one "dud".

(i) G 890 (see 3e in the table in the preceding section). Bakewell's own brief account, in a letter to Culley, of his taking this horse to London, where he was admired by the King and the Prince of Wales, has been given in A.III.4, and need not be repeated here. Others have also referred in print to G, but the fullest particulars are those supplied by William Pitt, who speaks of "the famous horse Gee, the noblest, and most complete and beautiful creature of his kind that had been seen in Europe. How far his elegant points were adapted for the labour that horses of this sort are principally designed to perform, is a question perhaps undetermined; be this as it may, beyond all controversy, he was strong and handsome, and commanded the admiration of all who saw him; for a time he was the first subject of conversation, and almost the wonder of the day; he was taken to Tattersall's, and shown there to the nobility and gentry, with great approbation; and Mr. Bakewell had the honour of showing him personally to his Majesty: he is said to have been very quiet and docile, and Bakewell in describing his points, invited his Majesty to touch him, which was, I believe, declined. He was killed by lightning in his pasture; a son of his was afterwards sold to Mr. Inge, of Thorpe, for a large sum."[1]

(The Inges of Thorpe Hall, near Tamworth, long remained faithful to the Shire-bred horse. When William Inge died in 1903, his wife took over and kept the Shires going until her death at the age of ninety-four, when she had been widowed over half a century. For years a M.F.H., she was a great rider across country until late in life, and a noted enthusiast of old English breeds such as dual purpose Shorthorns, Shropshire sheep and, naturally, Tamworth pigs. A wonderful picture survives of four of her Shire teams in 1933.)

Unfortunately, we know nothing of the son of G that Mr. Inge bought. But five, or rather four, stallions which appear in Volume I are stated to be by him. Firstly there is Clubfoot 497. His claim seems perfectly valid, though his name does not sound prepossessing to a careful breeder. (He appears in the foregoing table: 2b.) There is something definitely wrong about the pedigrees of the rest. G 891 (owned and bred by Massey, Staffs.†), Merryman 1552 (owned by Stych, Derbys.†) and Stretford G 2067 (owned by T. Hudson, Derbys.†) are all recorded as having been foaled in 1805. It is a test of our credulity that all these were, by a coincidence, procreated when G was twenty-nine years of age! The fifth "son" did not really exist, because "The Stretford G 2110" is an accidental duplicate entry of Stretford G 2067 (except that the foaling date is given as 1800).

A daughter of G appears in the Stud-book as the dam of the black Nelson 1609, foaled in 1803. She seems reasonably genuine. This Nelson, incidentally, was mated to his own daughter to sire Nelson 1613 in 1811 and Nelson 1616 ten years later. If Mr. Taylor of Whitemeadow really did organise this, perhaps he was acting under the influence of Bakewell's ghost. An alleged grandson of G, known as *Durning's G*, was head of a whole tribe of Blacks in Lancashire.

(ii) Blaze 184. This is the only other true Bakewell horse that was put in the Stud-book. Nothing is now known about him except what is given there. (See 3d in the table in the foregoing section.) Typical of the utter confusion which immediately assails the mind of him who is rash enough to compare the genealogical table of Volume I with the actual Stud-book registrations, is the fact that the table claims five famous sons for this Blaze, whereas the Stud-book ascribes three of them to other Blazes. Only William Mellor's Blaze 190, foaled in 1802, and Hudson's Regulator 1852, foaled in 1807, seem to be really his.

(iii) The "dud" Bakewell horse remains to be disposed of. This is Big Ben 130, a brown stallion foaled in 1813, eighteen years after Bakewell's death. His owner, Smith of Castle Donington, in claiming that he was bred by "Mr. Bakewell of Dishley" was either deceived or deceiving – unless he counted Robert Honeyborn, the great man's nephew and successor, as "Bakewell". Why the E.C.H. Editing Committee accepted this patently absurd pedigree is unfathomable. To make the whole affair more ludicrous still, Big Ben's sire was Dumpling 679, bred in 1810 and owned by Stych* of Derbyshire.† Even over Bakewell's dead body, one can scarcely conceive of one of his mares being covered by a two-year-old colt who had already earned a name like that.

In just two other pedigrees in the Stud-book does the name of Bakewell occur:

(i) K 1191, black, foaled in 1820. He was bred by P. Wright of Spilsby, Lincs., who had been a member of the Dishley Society.

Sire: "Bakewell's B." Even if B was bred in the last year of Bakewell's life, he would be twenty-four in 1819. We might be inclined to accept this, were it not for the claim about the dam.

Dam: mare, bred by Wright, by "Bakewell's K". The famous K is the only Bakewell stallion other than G of which we have any description. Marshall's account of him has been quoted in Part A (III.5). K was foaled in 1766 and died in 1785. If he really was the sire of the dam of K 1191, then she could not have been less than thirty-four years of age at the time K 1191 was foaled. We suspect a little latitude on the part of Mr. Wright in making this claim.

(ii) Welton 2330 (black) foaled in 1826, bred in Northumberland.

Sire: Brinkburn 253 black, foaled in 1866, bred in Northumberland.
         g-sire: *Royal George* (by Thompson's *Black Horse of Picknell*, Yorks., out of "a Derbyshire mare").
         dam of sire: by *Bakewell* out of a mare by Orpeth's *Small Tail*.
Dam: by *Watton's Horse of Matfen Moorhouses* (Northumberland).
         g-dam: by *Price's Horse*, by *Old Bakewell*.

In this pedigree there lies a hint of the Bakewell Blacks let to his pupil and friend George Culley. It is also a reminder of the diffusion of Dishley blood all over England, and into Wales and Scotland. It is perhaps appropriate that the recorded information about Bakewell's horses becomes more chaotic the more one tries to examine it, for it was to chaos that the breeders of the following three-quarters of a century reduced his work and achievements. For the foundation of the Shire breed, when it was at last systematically laid, the materials had therefore to be sought in the Fens. Bakewell refused to use Fen-bred horses, which were not in his opinion of a useful form at all. They were better than the Suffolks, but that was all that he could say for them.

3. OTHER STALLIONS PRIOR TO 1800

The only horses listed in the Stud-book as foaled prior to 1800 which the table in Section 1 does not contain are:

Samson 1914 (1780) black: b Collis, Marchinson, Derby. (unidentifiable. Marchington, Staffs?.): o Shaw† (Derby.).
    Sire: Bulstrode's *Mansetter*.
    The genealogical table lists a "Shaw's Samson" foaled about 1793, by Old-acre's *Mansetter*.
Ploughboy 1720 (1795) brown: b and o Toplis, Shottle, Derby.
    Sire: *Barker's Horse* of Houghton Field.

Ploughboy 1719 (1785) brown: o Occleston, Bollin Hall, Cheshire.

Truemould 2196 (1797) black: b and o Jonathan Renshaw, Sale, Ches.*

Sire of both: Summerland's *Wiltshire Brown Horse*.

Topper 2169 (1792) –: b and o Butler, Rampton, Notts.

HONEST TOM 1062. Fens horse. Stud-book gives as foaled 1806 but almost certainly 1796. See pedigree of William the Conqueror (VII.1).

Drayman 603 (1790), black: b Meakin, Staffs: o John Chadwick (Staffs.).†*

Sire: Chadwick's *Packington* (obviously not Packington 1703 – 3c in section 1 table).

Dam: by Marston 1486. Clearly a muddle here, for Marston was foaled in 1791 (see 2a in the table).

Dragon 598 (1785) –: b and o Dutton, Chapel House, (sic) (Salop).*

Sire: *Stone's Brown Horse* of Coalbrook.

CHAPTER IV

We are Seven

I. DESCENT IN MALE LINE

In the breeding of blood stock, the importance of the individual is paramount. The value of one outstanding animal may be astronomical, and that of an ordinary specimen very little. The female line must be therefore studied as carefully as the male. The stallion is of more importance than the mare only in so far as he can procreate many offspring in a season, and she can produce just one. But among Shire horses the striving towards perfection in quite this manner has been inhibited by two factors.

Firstly, no one in 1880 really knew much about the pedigree of any but a few mares, whereas the ancestry (the *male* ancestry) of the best stallions was known through many generations. The one branch of knowledge could therefore never catch up with the other. Furthermore, the Stud-book started by being "open" and, though the requirements for a mare's eligibility have been made more rigorous, has remained so ever since. Consequently, the male ancestry of any foal born in 1974 is bound to be traceable to some date prior to 1878. But the pedigree, in tail female, of a filly might stop short at a g.g-dam (possibly herself foaled only nine years ago) whose name or breeding, or any other particulars at all, it is not incumbent on anyone to record.

Secondly, cart-horse breeding is essentially an exercise in mass-production, or the nearest approach to it that can be achieved in a species where the female has one offspring in twelve months. The purpose of the Stud-book Society was the improvement of the general average standard of soundness and conformation among thousands or tens of thousands of horses, not the creation of a few marvellous ones. A railway or a coal company or a town council was not looking for a Shire that could dash along the dock-side or sprint from the stable a second or two faster than any other horse, or even for one that could pull a hundredweight more. But it did want ten, or a hundred, or a thousand, that were all hardy, strong, willing, well-mannered, and able to work and live long in an unnatural environment and on unnatural surfaces.

Shire brood mares, both before 1880 and after it, "doubled" as farm workers. Many or most of them were descended from mares that had been on the same farm through generation after generation. If, in 1900, one looked at a random-choice selection of a thousand "Shire" mares in all parts of the country and were able to check back on their g-dams and g.g-dams, one would find that an enormous proportion of them had been scarcely recognisable as "Shires" at all, which is not surprising, for they were not. The vast mass of the breed was made by constantly putting genuine Shire stallions, true descendants of the old Blacks, upon these local varieties of mare and then by putting other genuine Shire stallions upon their daughters. Far into the twentieth century, even a top-class registered stallion would cover ninety, or even ninety-five, "ordinary" mares for every five or ten pedigree ones he received.

The emphasis on the sire has therefore always been immense, and accounts for the fact that many a man who, without difficulty or recourse to reference books, could rattle off a horse's male line of pedigree through the generations until he ran out of breath or was halted by the listener, would be reduced to silence if the female ancestry were enquired into. "Out of a So-and-so mare" might be as far as he would get, perhaps adding, as if that settled the matter, "Came out of the Fens somewhere", or "She was bred in Wales". For a Leicestershire man, perhaps Wales was foreign parts, and a Montgomeryshire mare was a creature unknown: but a stallion bred there, Champion's Goalkeeper for example, could become everyone's property.

That is not to say that there were not men who did not, even in the earliest days of the Society, study carefully the mares they proposed to breed from and, so far as they could, select from the choicest female lines. Even in the days of mid-nineteenth century confusion, men had done that in the Fens and parts of the Midlands, but only they knew these dams and dams of dams. With the aid of the new Stud-book they could do it better. And they were joined – and out-done – by wealthy landowners who joined the Shire ranks as a craze or to make even more money, and who could, and did, begin to study the female line as carefully as they would in breeding Thoroughbreds. This nicety of selection was extended over an ever-widening circle of breeders as time and education went on, until the tenant farmer, when he wanted some new mares, was able to vie with the Duke of Westminster or Lord Rothschild or any other of the great ones, in discrimination if not in money.

Until the whole pattern of life, of the economy and of the structure of the cart-horse trade was knocked by the First World War utterly out of shape, the cost of a choice brood mare, out of an immaculately-bred dam, had been growing steadily to be far in excess of the cost of a working animal. But the acid test, always, of the value of a Shire was the current market price of heavy town geldings. Consequently, taking the breed as a whole, the function of the finest mares in England was not essentially to breed a colt or filly foal good enough to be a London champion, gratifying as that might be to its owner, but to breed the perfect *colt* foal that could go out, after a few years, around the countryside and beget hundreds of foals, out of ordinary mares, most of them only partially Shire mares, and very few indeed of them in the Stud-book; foals that would be better than their dams.

J. G. Williams went so far in his perfection of breeding that he would keep no stallion on his stud farm at Pendley, chiefly because the presence of one might offer a temptation to use him on a mare which, after careful study by his Harry Bishop, was considered best suited to a particular stallion a hundred miles away. His stud did an enormous amount of good to the breed. But, as far as the ordinary breeder and the ordinary horse were concerned, this benefit was only conferred when the produce of one of these exotic matings was a colt-foal, and that colt eventually travelled for the Such-and-Such hiring society. If the produce was a filly, she would remain with Mr. Williams or be sold to some other great person, until she had a son of her own, one day, to walk the lanes of Devon or Cardigan or Kent or, of course, Leicester or Derby.

Having made this apology on behalf of that most matronly, and lovable, and charming, of all creatures, the Shire mare, we must now turn to the stallions and concentrate on one particular horse who has eventually proved to be the daddy of them all.

2. THE FOUNDATION SIRES

Everybody sought to hire or use those stallions which had won a London prize. Success at some of the great agricultural shows of course brought kudos. But nearly all of these were held either during, or too soon after, the breeding season to make the exhibition of a busily-occupied stock horse a welcome or even logical proposition. The breed's own show was of paramount importance. A good result there was essential if a young stallion was going to start his active life at a high fee and stand a chance of his progress as a sire being watched by all the experts. So far as stallions were concerned, show success was essentially, even solely, measurable at the Royal Agricultural Hall.

Within fifteen years of the inauguration of the London Show, it was becoming clear that the majority of prize-winners was descended in the male line from a handful of stallions, one or two long dead and others recent. John Sloughgrove began to tabulate these lines of pedigree as best he could. His efforts were not very systematic, but that was not his fault. He was a secretary, not a prophet of how the breed was to develop in years yet to come. Sometimes he traced a number of the winners to Vulcan 4145: on other occasions he traced a group instead to Heart of Oak 1005, the g-sire of Vulcan, because there were winning horses which were descended from him through other sons and g-sons than Vulcan. Some years, he quoted Matchless 1509 as the ancestor of several winners but occasionally he listed What's Wanted 2332 or Honest Tom 5123 (both of whom, through different sons, were grand-sons of Matchless). In his time, he offered 19 different "foundation sires" of this sort, and even Charlton who succeeded him was unable to be consistent from year to year.

However, with the benefit of hindsight, it is a simple matter to discover that there were only seven or eight foundation sires of any real significance. Seven – or eight? The dilemma is whether to list both Seward's Major and Lincolnshire Lad separately, or to replace them by Wiseman's Honest Tom, who was the male ancestor of both. The latter appears logical, though no Shire breeder could have known of this link before 1896 and, in fact, very few of them knew it (or, if they did, thought it was worth bothering about) even after that. The table which follows is based on logic and so, as Wordsworth's cottage girl remarked,

"We are seven". By the 1870s, two of these in the church-yard lay, like the little maid's sister and brother: the other five still lived.

This table requires a few words of explanation:

(*a*) It covers only the years 1893–1924. By 1893, a pattern of successful blood-lines had begun to develop. By 1924, the trend was so obvious that it would be tedious to continue the figures further.

(*b*) The years 1918–1919 have been omitted, because the Newmarket shows

| | | | I HONEST TOM 1060 b via LINCOLNSHIRE LAD | | | | | | | | | | |
| | Total no. of prize-winners | a via MAJOR | i via Linc. Lad II α Harold | β Others | ii Others | 2 Total | WM. THE CONQUEROR | 3 MATCH-LESS | 4 HEART OF OAK | 5 RYL. ALBT | 6 LIN-COLN | 7 BAR NONE | All others |
Year													
1893	65	—	16	6	—	22	10	12	2	—	1	4	14
1894	65	5	11	4	2	22	9	9	3	7	3	9	3
1895	80	—	19	10	1	30	8	17	6	2	—	8	9
1896	80	4	25	8	1	38	9	12	4	3	2	5	7
1897	83	4	31	4	1	40	7	16	—	3	3	5	9
1898	92	5	30	8	—	43	14	11	4	6	4	2	8
1899	92	2	30	10	1	43	14	17	4	2	5	5	2
1900	98	—	35	8	—	43	18	15	5	4	4	5	4
1901	119	6	51	13	1	71	15	13	5	6	3	—	6
1902	128	2	53	13	2	70	21	16	3	5	7	6	—
1903	125	1	51	14		66	25	18	4	3	5	4	—
1904	135	2	54	18		74	33	15	5	3	2	3	—
1905	128	5	41	19		65	28	11	7	4	7	4	2
1906	127	2	50	23		75	24	15	4	2	3	3	1
1907	132	—	62	21		83	26	9	—	2	3	6	3
1908	137	—	68	20		88	25	11	—	4	3	5	1
1909	132	1	73	19		93	28	7	1	—	—	1	2
1910	133	2	67	15		84	27	12	2	2	4	2	
1911	133	3	64	13		80	37	6	2	2	6	—	
1912	134	2	72	5		79	41	9	—	2	2	1	
1913	129	3	69	7		79	36	7	—	—	5	2	
1914	134	1	77	6		84	41	1	—	—	6	2	
1915	133	1	84	9		94	35	1	—	1	2	—	
1916	134	2	77	9		88	40	2	—	1	3	—	
1917	130	—	81	7		88	33	4	—	1	3	1	
1918/19													
1920	131	—	92	5		97	29	2	—		3		
1921	132	—	86	5		91	40	1	—		—		
1922	132	1	92	3		96	34	1	1		—		
1923	128	—	90	5		95	32	1			—		
1924	133	—	104	1		105	26	1			1		
			1,755	308									
			2,063		9								
	3,534	54	2,072			2,126	765	272	62	65	90	83	71

were incomplete, being restricted to stallions. This means that the table contains exactly thirty shows.

(c) The first column gives the total number of prize-winners each year –
stallions, mares and (from 1895, when classes for them were re-introduced)
geldings. By "prize-winners" is meant those animals which won cash awards
and also the reserve in each class. Highly commended or commended animals
are not included.

(d) Columns 1–7 show the number of winners directly descended in the male
line from each of the foundation sires. Column 8 shows how many other
winners there were.

(e) Column 1, Honest Tom, is subdivided into the two lines through Major
and Lincolnshire Lad. In addition, the lines descending from the latter are again
divided, because his descendants through Lincolnshire Lad II did overwhelm-
ingly better than those through any other sons. Similarly a further and final
subdivision has been made, because the line through Harold was far more
successful than through any other sons of Lincolnshire Lad II.

As the table shows, 1909 was the last year that any prizes were won by horses
not descended in the male line from one of the foundation sires. There were
two that year, and it is perhaps fitting before we move on to the main theme,
to commemorate these last, and to see what manner of breeding produced them:

GREYLAKE PILOT 25245 (bay, four years old) was seventh in his class of forty-nine
for Warner Barrs of the famous Nailstone stud, Nuneaton. He was bred in
Cornwall by W. S. Ward of Greylake, Borton, Camelford. His sire, Parkside
Pilot 20794, traced in six generations to Gloucester 942, bred in 1853 by
Thomas Hibbard of Bishopstone (the one on the Swindon-Wantage road,
just inside the Wilts. border). Hibbard was a very well-known and extensive
cart-horse breeder and stallion-owner. Gloucester was by Wirdnam's *Grey
Horse*, now unidentifiable. George Wirdnam, who is credited with a black
and brown stallion in Volume 1, farmed at Wanborough, three miles nearer
to Swindon than Hibbard.

45516 LEEK CHANCE (black, six years old) was fifth in the class for senior mares
under 16-hands, for Sir Arthur Nicholson, Leek. She was bred by Arthur
Critchlow (Stanley Farm, Stockton Brook, on the main road from Leek to
Stoke-on-Trent), out of a mare by Bold Harold (son of Harold). Her sire was
Girton Meteor 19649. This stallion, out of a Harold mare, was by the 1894
London supreme champion stallion, Bury Victor Chief, which traced in
seven generations to Champion 380, grey, bred in 1835 by Lord St. John,
Melchbourn Park, Beds., and owned by T. Cleaver of Toddington Mills
(mentioned in Chapter II.8). This Champion was by Chibnall's *Champion*, a
horse that cannot be identified: Chibnall farmed at Bromham (Beds.)

3. A DADDY TO THEM ALL

The table in section 2 showed the increasing dominance at the London shows of horses descended in the male line from Honest Tom 1060, who was foaled in the year 1800. By 1924, 105 prize-winners out of 133 were thus traceable to him. Of these 105, all except one were descended through one single stallion, Harold, foaled in 1881. By 1939, Honest Tom 1060, via Harold, not only dominated the London shows but *the entire Stud-book*. Of 238 colts registered that year, 217 were directly descended from Harold, and the remaining 21 from William the Conqueror. The next two chapters are therefore devoted to the Honest Tom 1060 line, particularly its main line *via* Harold.

However, before we pursue this theme, it is worth noting that the other six foundation sires listed in Section 2 also had Honest Tom 1060 blood in their veins. The extent of it, as far as it is known, is shown by the following table. In particular, Heart of Oak and Matchless should be noticed. The dams of both were directly descended in the male line from Honest Tom, and Matchless was, in addition, himself descended in this way from a grand-daughter of Honest Tom. Lincoln got his Honest Tom blood through Heart of Oak, one of whose daughters was his dam. Royal Albert and Bar None traced to Honest Tom in five and four ways respectively. William the Conqueror owed the least to this old Fen horse.

In column 11, Farmer's Glory 816 (marked†) was by Drayman 607 and the three stallions and three mares marked* were by England's Glory 705. Drayman and England's Glory were both sons of Honest Tom 1060. The pedigree of these two and their relevant sons and daughters will be found in section V.3.

In examining this table, it should be borne in mind that, the pedigrees of all foundation sires being so incompletely known, there may be many other links of which we are ignorant, as we shall see.

HAROLD.. **LINCOLNSHIRE**
3703　　　**LAD II** 1365....
(f. 1881)　　(f. 1870)

K (alias
LINCOLNSHIRE LAD)....
1196 (f. 1866)

LINCOLN
1345.......

MOUNTAIN'S
CHAMPION
Diamond.......

mare........　　mare........

Madam.................................

MATCHLESS
1506.........

MATCHLESS
1509..........
(f. 1846)

LINCOLN
1350......　　*Star*..........
(f. 1873)

**HEART OF
OAK**
1005.......
(f. 1859)

HEART OF
OAK 1003....

mare ....

WILLIAM THE CONQUEROR..mare.........
2343 (f. 1862)

mare........

BROWN
GEORGE
309...........

**ROYAL
ALBERT**...
1185
(f. 1872)

JOHN BULL..
1183

JOHN BULL
1180

WARWICK..
2246

JOHN BULL
1169.......

mare........

MATCHLESS
1506.........

mare..........

mare ....

ABRAHAM
NEWLAND
12.........

ABRAHAM
NEWLAND
10...........

mare........

ROYAL
ALBERT
1881.......

ABRAHAM
NEWLAND
10..........

**BAR
NONE**
2388 ...mare..
(f. 1877)

GREAT
BRITAIN....
973

GREAT
BRITAIN
972

GREAT
BRITAIN....
968

JOHN BULL
1169.......

mare...........

MATCHLESS
1526...........

mare........

mare...........

mare........

mare ....

HONEST TOM
1075.........

MAJOR 1447 (f. 1838).......⎫
          HONEST   HONEST
         ⎬ TOM 1073.... TOM 1067*
(i.e. 15046) ......HONEST TOM
      1085...........⎭
LINCOLN LINCOLN 1328... OXFORD   FARMER'S
  1334........   1683.......... GLORY 816†
  mare.........COMPETITOR HONEST
      514............ TOM 1071... mare*

                OXFORD   FARMER'S
....   1683......... GLORY 816†

⎧ ACTIVE 29..................... FARMER'S
⎪   PROFIT
⎨   873.......... mare*
⎪ mare......... STAFFORD
⎩   2049.......... HONEST   HONEST
               TOM 1073... TOM 1067*

mare........................... HONEST TOM
              1071........ mare*
ENGLAND'S MAJOR   HONEST   HONEST
  GLORY 717.. 1447........... TOM 1073... TOM 1067*

BANG-UP   TRUE   TRUE
  95.......... mare........... BRITON   BRITON
               2180........ 2179*

.... HONEST TOM
                 1069*

.... OXFORD 1683 FARMER'S
                    GLORY 816†
LUCK'S ALL   FARMER'S
  1426........ mare........... OXFORD 1683 GLORY 816†

mare........................... FARMER'S GLORY 824..mare*

mare........................... FARMER'S GLORY 824..mare*

.... HONEST TOM
                 1069*

.... OXFORD
             1683......... FARMER'S
                  GLORY 816†
LUCK'S ALL
  1426........ mare........... OXFORD
             1683......... FARMER'S
                  GLORY 816†

.... HONEST TOM
                 1069*

The Wiseman's Honest Tom Line

I. WILLIAM WISEMAN AND HONEST TOM 1060

IN the spring of 1800, when Honest Tom was foaled, William Wiseman, son of John Wiseman, was a young chap of twenty. That he, or perhaps his father, bred the foal, is nearly certain, but not quite. A year or so later, young William took 74 acres of lowland grazing in the parish of Fleet, a couple of miles to the east of Holbeach. It was there that he kept the colt that was to turn out to be the head of the Shire breed. W. Wiseman of Fleet he called himself, but none of his early stud cards survives.

Of Honest Tom's dam, we know nothing at all. His sire was Milton and Colley's *Brown Horse of Bassingham*. This parish, south of Lincoln, is not far short of forty miles distant from Fleet. Neither Milton nor Colley appear in the registers there, though there were Colleys in the neighbouring parish of Carlton le Moorland. Of them and their Brown Horse, cart-horse history has nothing to say. So Honest Tom's sire is a shadow-horse, a legendary creature belonging to almost legendary men. All that recent study has revealed is that his name, also, was *Honest Tom*, and that his great son was also a brown (see section 7).

William was a go-ahead young man. He married early, by farmers' reckoning. In 1804, his first son, also William, was born. In 1806, he sold Honest Tom to W. Wood of Elm, the other side of Wisbech – for the staggering price of 400 guineas, some said. (Or was that Honest Tom's most famous son that fetched such a sum? Memory muddles these things.) Perhaps it really was 400 guineas. As has been mentioned already, Wood seems to have over-used the horse, perhaps to try to recoup the money. It was really a pity that William sold at all. He was now doing well. He had farms at Moulton, Whaplode and Weston, and was always the first to pay his tithe to the rector, Richard Dods, on those 74 acres 0 rood 24 perches at Fleet. In 1810, he was a member of the Spalding Gentlemen's Society, then celebrating its centenary. In 1811, he had high hopes of a new *Honest Tom*, a son of his old one, and travelled him as a three-year-old.

The following year he issued this card: "To cover this season, 1812, by Subscription (by Desire of several Gentlemen) a light brown cart horse, called Young Honest Tom, the Property of W. Wiseman, of Whaplode; One Hundred Mares at Two Guineas each Mare, and Half-a-Crown the Man (own Mares excepted). He was got by Old Honest Tom, the Property of W. Wiseman, which Horse was well known in this Neighbourhood. *Young Honest Tom* was bred out of a Mare, the Property of Mr. J. Measures, of Whaplode, which Mare was got by Mr. Fisher's noted brown Horse, of Weston. W.W. leaves the

Merits of this Horse to those Gentlemen who well know him; and those who wish to subscribe are requested to specify the Number of Mares they wish to subscribe for. He will travel a small Circuit for the Accommodation of his Friends." This horse's small circuit and many mares may have produced some grand horses but, alas, we know nothing of any of them. And he himself was never given a number by Coke and company. All we know about him appears on Wiseman's gentlemanly advertisement.

Time passed, and William prospered further. John and Henry, his second and third sons, were born. William, junior, married Ann Maria Holland in 1835. He himself by now had lost his wife but married again in April 1845, to Mary, sister of Richard Everard of Great Hale, gentleman. She produced at the end of the year his fourth son, Richard Everard Wiseman. In 1856, now seventy-five, a man of means and a Trustee for the Moulton poor he lived then at Fengate with his young wife and son, while William junior and John lived at Weston Hills and Henry at Whaplode. Young William's wife died that year, but old William bred a marvellous colt foal. How many he had bred or owned in over half a century, there is no telling, but this one was fit to class with the original Honest Tom of long ago. His breeding was typical of W.W. The sire was the great Dack's Matchless. The dam was by Eno's Honest Tom (1071) of Long Sutton (who was out of a mare by England's Glory 705, the best son of William's old original Honest Tom 1060), by Green's Honest Tom (1066) of Upwell Fen, by Thorpe's Honest Tom (1061) of Holbeach, by Townsend's *Honest Tom* of Fleet, a contemporary and neighbour of Honest Tom 1060. The old man gave this new colt a name to fit him, and called him Wonder. The Editing Committee later entered him as No. 2357, and Reynolds has reported that Wiseman's Wonder was still serving mares successfully and travelling a full season on a wide circuit in the late 'seventies when he was over twenty years of age. A wonder he was, and no Shire breeder in England who knew his business would have ranked any stallions but those two descendants of Honest Tom 1060 himself, Welcher's Honest Tom and the Old Strawberry, or perhaps Stych's Champion, above him as stock-horses. And time proved them right, for Wonder was the sire and grand-sire of many a London winner of the Matchless line. These four were the great names of the 'sixties and 'seventies.

But the old man had died in May 1867, at the age of eighty-seven, in the middle of another busy season. He was described by J. R. Jackson, the Vicar of Moulton, as "ripe in years, childlike in faith and a steadfast member of the church". He was revered "for his manliness of character and for his kindliness of heart". If we add that Honest Tom 1060 was his, and Wonder was his, what else can one say to praise him?

After only nine months, William junior, who took over Wonder, followed his father (and his wife, who had been dead eleven years) to the grave. He left one of his surviving sons, John Joseph, to farm at Weston and to arrange for Wonder to continue his travels for the 1868 season. But the family could not keep up the standard set by the old man. Perhaps the four sons and the numerous grandsons were just too many, and perhaps the depression hit hard at their thinly spread resources during the next twenty years. By 1900, the Wisemans had come down in the world. Some of them still occupied Bridge Farm at Moulton Eaugate, but there it was Alfred Clark, not the Wisemans, who had become a nationally known Shire man. The last Wiseman in Shire breeding took over St. Lambert's Hall, Weston, in 1903, joined the Society and re-registered under his own name seven mares bred and owned by the late William Ward of that place. But the only pedigree Shires he bred were out of these mares. He sold all their foals as young ones, and a filly foal in 1915 was the last. She went to George Ford of Cuckoo Road, Spalding and became 104734 North Drove Pansy. All seven old mares were dead by the end of the war.

There have been no Wisemans farming round there for many a year now, but those who seek a memorial to old William and the horse that most nearly approximates to the ancestor of the whole breed of Shire horses will find two of them, suitably modest and inconspicuous. Over the Holland there is a little crossing still called Wiseman's Bridge, and branching off the A16 there is a little road known as Wiseman's Gate. But if you ask people thereabouts to tell you the reason for these names, few could tell who Wiseman was and none could say why we should account him a famous man.

2. THE TWO GLORIES OF WILLIAM BINGHAM

Of the sons of Honest Tom 1060, only two are of historic importance, for it was through them alone that he is the great ancestor of the Shire breed. Both were got some years after the old horse had been sold to Wood of Elm.

The brown Drayman 607 was bred in 1813 by Allen of Whaplode, who made no other contribution to Shire history than this. He must have been a sensible man, for he would not sell the horse to anyone, and kept him as a wonderful earner of fees for many years. But Drayman's fame rests on just one son, bred in 1823 by someone unknown, out of a mare which is now also unknown. This was Farmer's Glory 816.

England's Glory 705, also brown, was one year junior to Drayman and was bred by one Larmet of Gedney, out of a mare he had also bred himself, got by *Odam's Horse of Thorney Fen*. And that is all there is to be said – a misty, unsatisfactory picture, somehow given reality by the succession of later horse-breeding Odams, most notably Walter, who bred pedigree Shires from 1896 until his death at the beginning of the Second World War, and also by the fact that a young member of another branch of the family, John Odam, was chairman of the East of England Show at the time these words were written. England's Glory passed on the magic of his sire through three sons and three daughters, as will be shortly described.

William Bingham bought this England's Glory in 1816. In 1824, he bought Farmer's Glory, son of Drayman. And so he owned both horses through which old Honest Tom lives today. Having achieved this distinction, which can be in any case only a posthumous one, he died, on 14th August, at the age of sixty-nine. Twenty-five years older than Wiseman, and a gentleman farmer, he had long hunted the fox in the Sleaford area. His home, Bingham Lodge, Holbeach Marsh, was actually about twenty-six miles distant from Sleaford and as near to the Wash as anyone can farm. He had bought it in 1803 from his neighbour, John Reckerby. His wife was the fourth daughter of Francis and Elizabeth Holliday, who lived at Leaden Hall, also in Holbeach Marsh, most of which they owned.

He died childless, and there was a sale of the live and dead farm stock the following year, 4th April 1825. This included twenty-four "superior-bred horses of the nag and cart kind" – but not the eleven-year-old England's Glory nor his young "nephew" Farmer's Glory. Mrs. Bingham was not going to sell these. That very year the two-year-old Farmer's Glory began his work promisingly by siring Oxford 1683. In fact it was the best thing he ever did, for it was only through this son that his line was continued, to contribute to Lincolnshire Lad, Royal Albert and Bar None. Mary Bingham outlived her husband by over 25 years, dying in 1850 at the age of eighty-three. One other faint echo of her husband's judgement of a cart-horse is found in Bingham's *Samson*, foaled perhaps a year or two earlier than the younger Glory, but known now only in the pedigree of Royal Albert.

If there were a posthumous award for the man who owned the two most influential stallions in the history of the Great Horse or Black or Shire Horse, the prize would go to William Bingham. A. C. Duncombe, owner of Harold and Premier, must be the runner-up. The measure of Mr. Bingham's glory is that he bought England's Glory and Farmer's Glory over half a century before there was such a thing as a stud-book. The whole of England was Duncombe's parish: Bingham was confined between Sleaford and the Wash.

3. SONS AND DAUGHTERS OF GLORY

This table is a resumé of what has been already said. It shows the whole extent of the known pedigree of Honest Tom 1060 and of his two chief sons (columns 3–5, a pathetic fragment), and also indicates the four horses and three mares of the next generation (column 2) and the seven horses and one mare of the following generation (column 1) through whom the 'foundation sires' can be traced back to William Wiseman's original horse. The left-hand margin recapitulates the foundation sires, according to which of these g.g-sons or g.g-daughters of Honest Tom appear in their scantily known pedigree.

The notes which follow the table give as much additional information as is known about the pedigree of those in columns 2 and 3. (Men marked † are mentioned in Chapter II.)

PEDIGREE OF WISEMAN'S HONEST TOM AND OF HIS TWO CHIEF SONS: SHOWING ALSO THEIR MOST INFLUENTIAL DESCENDANTS

Descendants	1	2	3	4	5
LINCOLNSHIRE LAD LINCOLNSHIRE LAD II (twice) ROYAL ALBERT (twice) BAR NONE (twice)	OXFORD 1683 (f. 1826)	FARMER'S GLORY 816 (f. 1823)	DRAYMAN 607 (f. 1813)	Wiseman's **HONEST TOM** 1060 (f. 1800)	Milton and Colley's *Brown Horse of Bassingham* (*Honest Tom*) *Odam's Horse* of Thorney Fen
WILLIAM THE CONQUEROR	TRUE BRITON	TRUE BRITON 2179 (f. 1817)	TRUE BRITON 2180 (f. 1826)	mare	
ROYAL ALBERT (twice)	FARMER'S GLORY 824 (f. 1830)	mare			
LINCOLNSHIRE LAD HEART OF OAK LINCOLN	HONEST TOM 1071 (f. 1830)	mare			
MAJOR (son) LINCOLNSHIRE LAD (g.g.g-son) MATCHLESS LINCOLN HEART OF OAK	HONEST TOM 1073 (f. 1831)	HONEST TOM 1067 (f. 1826)	**ENGLAND'S GLORY** 705 (f. 1814)		
ROYAL ALBERT BAR NONE		mare HONEST TOM 1069 (f. 1826)			
BAR NONE	HONEST TOM 1075 (f. 1832)	mare			
MATCHLESS (g-son)	FARMER'S PROFIT 873 (f. 1833)	mare			

NOTES TO PAGE 570

All the horses noted below were Fen-bred, except 2f. Three of the men, in addition to Wiseman, were connected with the parish of Fleet.

1a OXFORD 1683, brown: b Fairchild, Deeping: o Dan Howsin (Notts†).

b TRUE BRITON 2180, brown: b and o Thacker, Canwick, Lincs.

c FARMER'S GLORY 824, brown: b and o J. Grebby, Croft Marsh, Boston.
  Sire: *Jake's K* (unidentifiable).

d HONEST TOM 1071, brown: b Warth, Walsoken, Norfolk: o E. Eno (Lincs. See Fens†).
  Sire: Honest Tom 1066 (b 1824; o Green, Upwell Fen, Wisbech).
  G-sire: Honest Tom 1061 (f 1805; o Thorpe of Holbeach).
  G.g-sire: Townsend's *Honest Tom*. C. Townsend farmed at Fleet.

e HONEST TOM 1073 (alias Phenomenon), brown: b Andrews of Elm, Wisbech: o Purrant of Elm and Mudd of Wisbech.

f *Mare*, the dam of John Bull 1169: breeder not recorded.

g HONEST TOM 1075, bay: b and o J. Wainman, of Fleet.
  Dam, bred by Wainman, by Marden and Fisher's *Brown Horse*.

h FARMER'S PROFIT 873, bay: b Jarvis Wilder, Holbeach Marsh: o Dack, Tydd St. Mary (see Fens†).
  Sire: Howard's *Farmer's Profit* (unidentifiable).

2a FARMER'S GLORY 816, –: Bingham's.

b TRUE BRITON 2179, brown: b Savage, South Moulton: o Cooper, Fleet Bank.
  Dam by Honest Tom 1063. This horse "foaled about 1810" was owned in turn by Townsend of Fleet and Abrahams of Fleet. No pedigree is given at all.

c *Mare* bred by Grebby (as 1c).

d *Mare* bred by Warth (as 1d).

e HONEST TOM 1067, –: b and o N. Goodman, Tholomas Drove.

f HONEST TOM 1069, –: b Bell, Figgins Burn, Yorks.: o Leake and Drury, Grimsby.
  Dam bred by Bell, by Honest Tom 1063 (as 2b).

g *Mare* bred by Jarvis Wilder (as 1h).

4. SEWARD'S MAJOR AND HIS DESCENDANTS

The brown Major was bred in 1838 at Chatteris by William Seward, to whom two other stallions in the Stud-book are credited, one of them a son of this one. Major's fame in his own day is illustrated by the fact that of the 27 Majors in Volume One, he was the first and, in fact, the ancestor of all the others, with one possible exception (see I.3). Here is his pedigree:

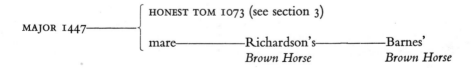

MAJOR 1447 ⎰ HONEST TOM 1073 (see section 3)
          ⎱ mare————Richardson's————Barnes'
                    Brown Horse   *Brown Horse*

Seward had bred the dam. For the Richardsons, see II.7: this one is probably James, of Chatteris. There was also a number of Barnes in the Fens, and further north in Lincs., but which one owned this *Brown Horse* it is impossible to determine.

Our interest in Major is chiefly concentrated on two of his descendants, Welcher's Honest Tom 1105 and Marsters' England's Wonder 761 (the Old Strawberry), and there are two reasons for this. Firstly, they were the two stallions which were uppermost in the minds of those who began the Stud-book. With Stych's Champion and Wiseman's Wonder third and fourth, they were to be both an example for breeders and a means to imitate it. Secondly, their own ancestry shows why they were such marvellous horses. Their breeding was purely Fen breeding, and largely in-breeding at that. They were, therefore, the main links between the good old days, before the times of mid-century confusion, and the new age of system and pedigree.

An examination of the table of successful blood-lines in IV.2 may not appear to support the pinnacle on which contemporary breeders, and the historian a century later, have put them. It may look as if they were of more use as an

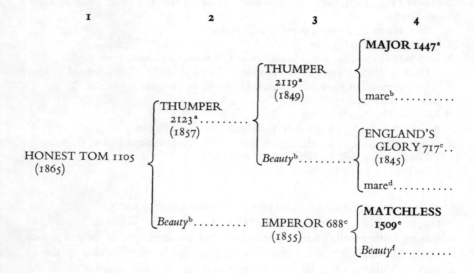

Notes:
1   Breeder: William Welcher, Snare Hill, Watton, Norfolk.
    First R.A.S.E. 1867–1872 inc. Total prizes valued £526. 15s. od. Height: 17-hands.
2a THUMPER 2123, bay: b and o John Tibbett, Doddington, Isle of Ely.
    Six horses in Vol. 1 are associated with Tibbett.
 b *Beauty* was bred by Welcher. Many prizes Cambs. and Norfolk; second R.A.S.E. 1871.
3a THUMPER 2119, brown: o Ingle of Doddington (Fens†).
 b *Beauty*, bred by Tibbett. First prize R.A.S.E. 1847.
 c EMPEROR 688, bay: b Gedney, Cowbit, nr. Spalding. (Gedney really was a man, as

example than as a means to copy it. But this is illusory. The overwhelming success and popularity of the other branch of the Honest Tom 1060 line, through the Lincolnshire Lads, caused breeders more and more to use a top-cross of that division of the blood: to some extent a different line altogether, that of William the Conqueror, was also more used. Yet all the best horses of the sixty glorious years to 1939 had an immense proportion of Welcher's Honest Tom and Marsters' Old Strawberry blood in their veins, acquired through all the stallions and mares that contributed their share to the descendants' ultimate conformation. Something must be written to their glory here.

HONEST TOM 1105. His purchase by T. H. Miller and the impetus he gave to Shire-breeding in the Fylde has already been mentioned (Part A, V.3). Honest Tom made the Fylde cart-horse, and his blood flowed back from there to all parts of England where men wanted the best – including the Fens where all his ancestors had been bred. And it must be remembered that he had four good seasons in his native place before ever leaving for Lancashire.

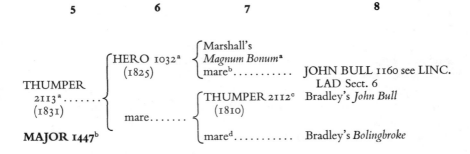

	5	6	7	8

THUMPER 2113[a] ...... (1831) — HERO 1032[a] (1825) — Marshall's *Magnum Bonum*[a] / mare[b] .... JOHN BULL 1160 see LINC. LAD Sect. 6

mare .... — THUMPER 2112[c] (1810) Bradley's *John Bull* / mare[d] .... Bradley's *Bolingbroke*

MAJOR 1447[b]

THUMPER 2113[c] as above

PLOUGHBOY 1734[d] .... Dupear's (1839) *Brown Horse*

well as a place). o Fryer Richardson and later John Hemmant (Fens†).
Emperor won a host of prizes, including first R.A.S.E. 1859.
4c ENGLAND'S GLORY 717, bay: b W. Laxon: o R. Brown, both of March.
Laxon also bred Thumper 2117 in 1846, of identical breeding to Thumper 2119 (3a above) and winner of 2 firsts and a second R.A.S.E. 1857–1859. His third horse in Vol. One is England's Glory 722 (by England's Glory 717) f 1850.
Brown also bred Samson 1922 in 1843 – a celebrated chestnut which won first prize R.A.S.E. the three years 1845–1847.
England's Glory 717 himself was first R.A.S.E. at Windsor 1851.
N.B. For pedigree of his dam, see Heart of Oak 1005.

  d *Mare* probably bred by Tibbett.
  e One of the "foundation sires".
  f *Beauty* was bred by (or at) Gedney.
5a THUMPER 2113, bay: b Dearlove, Leverington: o Robert Cork (Fens†).
    Dearlove also bred this horse's dam.
  d PLOUGH BOY 1734, bay: b Beeston of Weston Hill: o Sharman of Spalding.
    Sharman bred two other horses in Vol. I.
6a HERO 1032, bay: b B. Ewen of Tydd St. Giles, who also bred his dam.
7c THUMPER 2112, –: b Dearlove: o Stephen Bradley (Fens†).
    Mr. Bradley was keen on colts got by his own horses.
8 His *John Bull* appears in the pedigree of Lincolnshire Lad 1.

In 1880, eight of Honest Tom's sons and daughters were shown at the first London Show. Five won prizes, including Admiral 71, the champion stallion, described by Sexton as "a magnificent specimen of a dray horse, a good outline throughout, good limbs and feather, perhaps a bit too high from the ground, with scarcely enough depth of carcase, a fault that is often seen in the sons of Honest Tom, though curiously enough about the reverse of this may be said of his daughters." Another man spoke of his grand set of hard flat legs and flash hair. Later that year, at the age of four, Admiral suited his deeds to his name and sailed the high seas to begin a new life in Australia, to the great advantage of Lord Ellesmere's bank account.

Four prizes in 1880 went to progeny of Honest Tom's daughters. During the season that followed, the old horse had sixty mares, other than Miller's own – a modest number that would have surprised old Wood, who had so over-used the old ancestral Honest Tom 1060. But Miller strictly limited the nomination cards that he always signed personally, even though he charged only 5 guineas a service. (We may now say "only": but many men expected to get a good horse for a couple of guineas, and most would never consider paying more than one guinea, even to cover really good mares.)

At the beginning of the 1882 season, 144 of his sons and daughters had been or were being registered for the Stud-book – far more than any other horse could boast. Rising 17, he was now limited to 20 mares, other than Miller's, at the increased fee of seven guineas, and stood at Grange Farm, Singleton where John Haslam, one of Miller's tenants, was in charge.

On 25th February 1885, a few weeks short of his 20th actual birthday, Honest Tom died. A telegram was dispatched to the Agricultural Hall where Miller was exhibiting at the 6th London Show. He telegraphed back "Bury body Park grounds. Send head and neck taxidermist." Miller, it may be recalled, was a great one for stuffing animals and it was generally believed at Singleton that the whole of the old horse would have been so treated had he not suffered at the last with grease in one leg. So the headless body was laid to rest and to this day a tombstone marks the spot. The verse inscribed upon it is scarcely the finest poetry, but the sentiment was hearty:

Great Honest Tom lies here,
At rest after a life of fame.
The laurels o'er his grave attest
He carried a Champion's name.
The brave horse sleeps –
But on our lips
His praise will never tire.
No scion he leaves can o'er eclipse
Their grand and honest sire.

Tom's neck and head, with a wisp of hay in his mouth and wearing stable bridle and check-rein, were installed in the billiards room of the house. A wild stroke once shot a ball through the glass case and the whole thing was sent for renovation, during which a Preston admirer deprived him of a few hairs. When the contents of the Park were eventually sold up, the famous head was not included. Instead, it was carried by four men into Derby House, Preston as a gift to the Royal Lancashire A.S. No door within was wide enough to admit the case, which remained in the vestibule leading to the garden, upon which Tom seemed timelessly to gaze – alertly, as if out of the top of a loose box door at the sound of someone coming down the yard. But now he watches over the cattle and their purchasers at the Preston premises of Messrs. Hothersall, who in their thriving horse-repository days sold many of his descendants.

ENGLAND'S WONDER 761. His breeding was very similar to that of Honest Tom, most of his ancestors hailing from the same parts of the Fens.

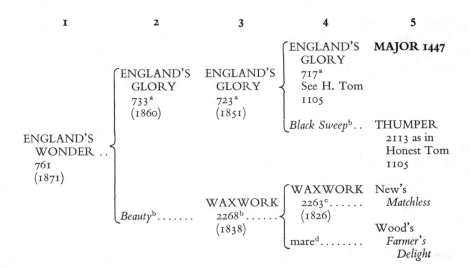

1	2	3	4	5
			ENGLAND'S GLORY 717[a] See H. Tom 1105	MAJOR 1447
	ENGLAND'S GLORY 733[a] (1860)	ENGLAND'S GLORY 723[a] (1851)		
ENGLAND'S WONDER .. 761 (1871)			Black Sweep[b]..	THUMPER 2113 as in Honest Tom 1105
		WAXWORK 2268[b]...... (1838)	WAXWORK 2263[c]...... (1826)	New's Matchless
	Beauty[b].......		mare[d]........	Wood's Farmer's Delight

NOTES TO PAGE 575

1 ENGLAND'S WONDER 761, strawberry roan: b Charles Winearls, Tilney-cum-Isling-
                                               ton, Norfolk.

                                           o Charles Marsters, Saddlebow, King's
                                               Lynn.

    Third R.A.S.E. 1873: Six prizes 1874–1876.

2a ENGLAND'S GLORY 733, bay: b Samuel Fyson, Warboys, Hunts.

                                  o Edward Winearls, Marham, Downham Market,
                                      Norfolk.

    Fyson appears in Vol. 1 as breeder also of Farmer's Friend 803 (f 1862) by the
same sire.

    This horse won many first Prizes at Hunts. Peterborough and Cambs. county shows.
An extant picture of him fails to suggest why.

  b *Beauty* bred by Charles Winearls.

3a ENGLAND'S GLORY 723, bay: b J. Woolsey, Newton, Wisbech.

                                  o B. Taylor, Peterborough, who lated moved to the
                                      Wisbech area (Fens†).

    This horse was first R.A.S.E. 1859; first six successive years at Peterborough, etc.

  b WAXWORK 2268, roan: b R. Norman, Cottenham, Cambs.

                              o T. Farrow, Downham Market, Norfolk.

    Both men appear only here.

4b *Black Sweep*, bred by Woolsey.

  c WAXWORK 2263, roan: o Woods of Cottenham.

  d Mare bred by Norman.

    Compared with Honest Tom, England's Wonder suffered under one great
handicap – his colour. Many men were prejudiced against that aspect of "The
Old Strawberry". But Charlie Marsters, having bought him, was not fool
enough to sell him. Richard Reynolds considered him the best stallion alive in
1880. *The Mark Lane Express* called him "the Stockwell of cart-horses". Fred
Street said he would rather use him than any horse in the kingdom. The new
Montgomeryshire hiring society (as described in A.V.5) paid £300 for his
services in 1877 and again in 1878 and he turned the draught-horses of that
county from nothing to 'the tops'. At the first London Show, Marsters exhibited The Coming Wonder (2678) in the yearling class and won first prize.
He had been bred at Welshpool, and was a chestnut. But another son of the
same age, another Coming Wonder (3039), stayed in Wales and travelled for
many years, leaving a vast number of strangely coloured progeny behind him.
He was a bay roan. The Old Strawberry himself left roans of many hues, and
chestnuts, all with or without white legs and white patches, and even varieties
of skewbald. In Montgomery and west Norfolk it was years before this tendency to oddity of colour died out. It was generally unpopular; without it,
there is no knowing how vast the demand for this marvellous stallion's services
might have been.

    The last London winner of a first prize to trace direct descent in male line
from the old strawberry wonder was old Rose. This venerable matron did

good to all who had to do with her. She was bred in 1902 by Joseph and William Wild of Moss Farm, Farnworth (Bolton) – by Insurgent, g.g.g-son of the Strawberry, out of a mare of long Wild ancestry. She won prizes all over Lancashire, was sold, and sold again, and at last finished up at Pendley Manor, the greatest stud of mares in the country. She won first prize at London in 1909, and William Wild at once joined the Shire Society to collect a £10 breeder's prize. He bred as many as he could out of her dam and registered them all. Rose won the first prize again in 1911, 1913 and 1916. In 1920, when J. G. Williams retired and Harry Bishop, his manager, took over in partnership with John Measures, there was a great sale. The last to be sold was old Rose, now eighteen. She stood a bare 16.1-hands, and her massive body was set on nearly perfect short legs, whose movement and elasticity had been little impaired either by age or by the many foals she had bred, year after year without fail. She was sold for 200 guineas and Edmund Beck, the auctioneer, invited a cheer for the old lady as she made her way out. As her white hind legs disappeared from public gaze, the last obvious relic of the old Strawberry vanished. Rose died a couple of years later and William Wild's name was heard no longer in pedigree breeding. Times were hard then. But the Strawberry's blood was continued in less direct parts of the pedigree of many among the breed which he did so much to create.

5. WHO WAS MOUNTAIN'S CHAMPION?

As the 'eighties ended, it was becoming clear that the sons and grandsons of Lincolnshire Lad 1196 were a force to be reckoned with as sires of horses fit to win London prizes. A few years later their prominence was obvious to anyone who had some knowledge of Shire pedigrees. But this Lincolnshire Lad's own forefathers remained somewhat vague. When Volume 1 was compiled, his sire had been given as "Lister's Lincoln". Perhaps Coke and company had not tried too hard to be more precise, for the Lad was already then in the possession of Lawrence Drew and was busy covering Clydesdale mares in Scotland, whence he would never return. In Volume 6 (1885) the errata column had identified this "Lincoln", for the benefit of pedigree students, with Lincoln 1345 in Volume 1. But that did not shine a particularly piercing light on his ancestry, for Volume 1 gave the sire of Lincoln 1345 merely as "Mountain's Champion", and no one seemed to know who this horse might be, which was very odd, for he could not have been foaled much before 1845 at the very earliest.

Walter Rawnsley's discovery, in June 1894, of an old travelling card of this Mountain's Champion and his alertness in sending it to the Editing Committee has already been mentioned (Part A, VIII.2). The Council accepted the committee's suggestion that this long-dead horse should be registered in Volume 16, but it was done in the most unostentatious manner possible. He was quietly inserted, in his proper alphabetical place between Chaddleworth 15045 and Charlcotte Laddie 15047 (where few would notice him) as Champion XXI 15046, with a note that "This Stallion is the sire of Lister's Lincoln (1345), and the above particulars respecting him have been taken from his travelling card for the season 1860, kindly placed at the Society's disposal by Mr. W. H. Rawnsley." Since only the errata column of an intermediate volume had definitely identified Lincolnshire Lad's sire with Lincoln 1345 (Lister had any number of *Lincolns*), it was still not clear to any but the most persistent respecters of pedigree that this registration – if noticed at all – laid bare the whole male line of Lincolnshire Lad, from whom at the 1895 Show (with which the publication of Volume 16 coincided) no less than thirty of the eighty prize-winners were descended.

Perhaps the significance of the whole thing was academic. It was sufficient for most people to know that a horse was a son or grandson or great-grandson of Lincolnshire Lad. If Lincolnshire Lad himself could be proved to have been found in some bull-rushes or to have arrived from Mars, perhaps it would have been immaterial. But one would have expected *someone* to point out that the newly published facts revealed his close relationship to Major and his direct descent, like Major's, from Wiseman's Honest Tom. No one did. But now, when the point is certainly academic rather than practical, perhaps justice should be done.

If the Editing Committee had tried to puzzle even the keenest readers as to the breeding of Champion's dam, they could not have succeeded better than they did. But let us look at the full pedigree as it really is, for a note on it will explain this.

1	2	3	4	5	6
CHAMPION XXI 15046 (1857)	HONEST TOM[a] 1085.. (1844)	HONEST TOM 1073[a], g.g-son of **HONEST TOM 1060** see sect. 3			
	mare[b]...	Hewison's Champion[b]			
		mare[c]......	K 1194.. (1842)	K 1193[a].. (1830)	K 1191[a] see III.2 (f. 1820)
				mare[b]....	*Abraham Newland*[b]

Notes:

1 CHAMPION XXI 15046. No colour or breeder's name was given by the card. Owner was J. Mountain, Saleby, Alford. This was probably John Mountain, who sold a lot of colts and stallions to the U.S.A. in the 'eighties. Many Mountains were breeding Shires in Lincs., but none ever joined the Society. S. Mountain of Coveham bred the nicely-named King Mountain 7504 (by Sir Garnet 4037 out of *Mrs. Carill.*)

2a HONEST TOM 1085, bay: b Tiggardine, Tholomas Drove, Wisbech.

o Emmanuel Gant, Alford (Fens†) and Williamson of Sutton Marsh.

Tiggardine is unknown to us. Williamson had also owned Champion 378 (f 1878).
3b Unidentifiable.
 c The Stud-book, quoting the stallion card, merely states "a K mare, the property of
   Mr. Harrison of East Keal, Spilsby". This could mean anything, but the errata of
   this Volume 16 has a correction about K 1194 (without acknowledgment to
   source) which must be more than a coincidence.
4 K 1194, black. Entered in Volume 1 as foaled in 1831 and by K 1191. Now corrected.
 b Abram of Wainfleet: o Kirkby, Croft, Boston.
5a K 1193, black: b William Stubbs, Bratoft, Lincs.
        o Joseph Lea, Burgh-in-the-Marsh.
   One would have expected him to be foaled in 1831, in view of the muddle about
   the missing generation. But a year's error was frequent in compiling early pedigrees,
   since it was only after the beginning of the pedigree movement that 1st January
   became official "birthday" of every horse.
6a K 1191. For this horse, bred by a member of the Dishley Society, see III.2 (Bakewell).
 b *Abraham Newland.* This horse could be one of many which were optimistically named
   after the Chief Cashier of the Bank of England, who lived at Highbury and left a
   fortune of £200,000. (See also re Matchless 1509.)

6. LINCOLNSHIRE LAD 1196

The longer one contemplates, from the vantage point of posterity, that
bay-brown horse variously called K or Lincolnshire Lad or (with customary
lack of originality) Honest Tom, the more one is inclined to ask whether it is
logical to single him out, from the line that runs from Honest Tom 1060
through nine generations to Harold 3703, as a "foundation sire". He was, of
course, the sire of Lincolnshire Lad II. But, other than that, we must consider
whether he was any more important than any other father whose contribution
to affairs is made vicariously through a son.

He was bred in 1866 by J. Bassitt of Willoughby, south of Alford. William
Whetton of Sutton Scarsdale took him to Derbyshire and then sold him to
Thomas Shepherd at Welbourn (see II.8). After two or three years with this
farmer-butcher, he went back to Derbyshire again before the 1871 season, to
J. Burrows at Risley Park Farm, between Derby and Nottingham. About this
move there is something of a mystery. The friendly but inscrutable Lawrence
Drew seems to have been behind it and it is highly probable that he was in fact
the real owner from now on. Be that as it may, one of Lincolnshire Lad's earliest
deeds on settling for a second time in Derbyshire was to go to Fred Ford's at
Locko Park, a mile or so away, and serve a mare called *Madam.* Another thing
he did was to win first prize at Ripley and Derby shows. The next year, *Madam*
produced a grey colt foal. Mother and son won first prize in that class at Derby:
father won first prize at Ripley again. These are the total show successes of both
Lincolnshire Lad 1196 and his son Lincolnshire Lad II.

Overleaf is the pedigree of 1196. Bassitt bred his dam, and probably his
grand-dam and g.g-dam. In other cases, dams were bred, or probably bred,
by the breeder of sons unless it is stated in the notes to be otherwise.

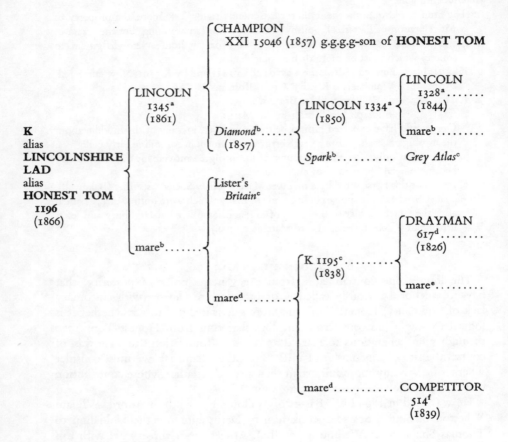

CHAMPION
XXI 15046 (1857) g.g.g.g-son of **HONEST TOM**

LINCOLN
1345[a]
(1861)

Diamond[b]......
(1857)

LINCOLN 1334[a]
(1850)

LINCOLN
1328[a]......
(1844)

mare[b]........

Spark[b].......... *Grey Atlas*[c]

K
alias
**LINCOLNSHIRE
LAD**
alias
HONEST TOM
1196
(1866)

Lister's
Britain[c]

mare[b]......

mare[d]........

K 1195[c].........
(1838)

DRAYMAN
617[d].......
(1826)

mare[e]........

mare[d].......... COMPETITOR
514[f]
(1839)

Notes:

2a LINCOLN 1345, bay: b J. C. Young, Alford: o Henry Lister, Saleby.
    Both were near neighbours of J. Bassitt.

3b *Diamond*: b Waterhouse, Clayworth Fields, Rugby.
    Young bought her as a yearling and she won many prizes for him.

  c Lister's *Britain*. Unidentifiable. There were many Listers breeding cart-horses, in
    Lincs. and Derbyshire, but it may of course have been Henry Lister (2a).

4a Lincoln 1334, bay: b J. W. Barnes, Branstone, Leics.: o J. Nix (Derby.†).

  c K 1195, black: b Watson, o Thomas Key, both of Billinghay, Sleaford.

5a LINCOLN 1328, bay: b Weightman, Stoke, Notts: o Howsin (Notts†).

  d DRAYMAN 617, chestnut: b Gilbert, Branstone: o Howsin.

  f COMPETITOR 514, black: b J. Clarke, o Joseph Eno†, both of Long Sutton (Lincs.).

6 7 8 9

1060. See sect. 5

⎧ OXFORD 1683[a]
⎨   (1826) g.g-son of **HONEST TOM 1060.** See sect. 3
⎩ mare[b] . . . . Hooten's *Loveden Lad*[a]

PLOUGHBOY 1726[c]
(1818) . . . . Dixon's *Waxwork*[b]

⎧ JOHN BULL 1160[d] . . Pacey's LAME
⎨   (1816)   HORSE 1702[c] . . . . . *Marfleet's Horse* of
⎩   Somerton Castle[a]
  mare[e] . . . . *Hall's Horse*
                       of Dunston[d]

⎧ *Stephenson's K*[f]
⎨   Boor and Bonner's
⎩ mare[g] . . . . *Farmer's Glory*[e]

                    ⎧ HONEST TOM   HONEST TOM   Townsend's
                    ⎨   1066[f] . . . .   1061[b] . . . .   *Honest Tom*[a]
HONEST TOM   ⎨   (1824)   (1805)
1071[h] . . . . ⎨
(1830)   ⎩ mare . . . .   ENGLAND'S   **HONEST TOM**
                                      GLORY 705   **1060**
                                      See sect. 2

                                ⎧ PHENOMENON   *Fisher's Black Horse*
                MAGNUM   ⎨   1711[c] . . . .   of Weston (*John*
                BONUM 1439[g] ⎨   (1812)   *Bull*)[b]
mare[i] . . . . (1824)   ⎨
                                   ⎩ mare[d] . . . .   Bradley's *John Bull*[c]

    6c PLOUGHBOY 1726, brown, b and o Musson, Waltham, Leics.
      d JOHN BULL 1160, chestnut: b Abrahams, Scothern, Lincs.
                        o Nicholas Brumby, South Carlton, Lincs.
           He won first prize at five successive Lincolnshire shows.
      f Stephenson's K. Probably Stephenson of Frampton, a mile or two from the Wash,
           owner of England's Glory 706, a son of England's Glory 705 himself.
      h HONEST TOM 1071. See Sect. 6.
      i *Mare* bred by Moses Cubley, Swaton, Lincs.
    7a Hooten and his *Loveden Lad* are both unidentifiable.
      b Dixon's *Waxwork*. See Sect. 7.
      c PACEY'S LAME HORSE (alias JOHN BULL) 1702, –: b and o Pacey of Bassingham.
      d *Hall's Horse*. Dunston is only 10 miles from Bassingham (c) and Somerton Castle (8c).

  e Boor and Bonner were partners at Bicker a few miles from Frampton (6f). They owned England's Glory 707, a son of 705, and the same age as Stephenson's England's Glory 706.

  f HONEST TOM 1066, –: b and o Green, Upwell Fen, Wisbech.

  g MAGNUM BONUM 1439, –: b and o Marshall, Parson Drove, Wisbech.

8b HONEST TOM 1061, –: o Thorpe, Holbeach.

  c PHENOMENON 1711, brown: o Johnson, Whittlesea.

9a See Section 3 – 1d.

  b Fisher's *Black Horse* stands at the head of William the Conqueror's pedigree (q.v.).

  c Stephen Bradley lived at Tydd St. Giles. This *John Bull* was sire also of Thumper 2112 (f 1810).

The bay-brown sire, whose efforts hitherto had resulted in more or less unremarkable produce, had a wonderful crop of foals in 1872. Lawrence Drew had known exactly where the right mares for him were to be found. No doubt, had *Madam*'s foal been a filly, it would have been whisked to Scotland with scores of others. This was a lucky escape for the English, but the following year Drew either finally bought (or, as we may suspect, formally took over) Lincolnshire Lad and removed him, more or less permanently, north of the border where in five seasons he begat an amazing number of foals. He died in 1878 and in 1883 Henry Chandos-Pole-Gell (as already observed, A.VI.10) made Englishmen laugh by saying he had sired more prize-winning Clydesdales than any horse in Scotland. But the remark was too near the truth to be genuinely funny, from either the Scotch or English point of view.

Of 1,400 mares in the English Stud-book, volumes 2–4, there are nine by the horse that Bassitt bred: there is also a handful of stallions by him. Of the 342 mares selected by Drew for Volume One of his Select Clydesdale book, 23 are his daughters. Herein lies the clue to this horse's significance. If the Scottish and English Stud-books had been combined, as common sense dictated that they should have been, Lincolnshire Lad would have taken his place, with the Scottish Prince of Wales, as one of the two great bridges between the two. As always, Drew was right. Just as he saw in the Anglo-Scottish Prince of Wales the horse to produce the perfect blend, so also he recognised in Lincolnshire Lad a pure English horse whose English daughters were ideal for mating to the best Scottish stallions, and who himself could get better foals out of Clydesdale mares than any horse either side of the border. As it was, the collapse of the movement for amalgamation resulted in this great stallion falling between two stools, if such an undignified metaphor can be permitted. The Scottish historian, if he wishes, can largely forget that this horse ever came north: the English one must view him mainly as the sire of one son, with two or three lesser ones in the background of the picture.

Apart from Lincolnshire Lad II, the only Lincolnshire Lad sons, of the few registered, which had any impact on the breed's future were two. All prize-winners at London between 1894 and 1902 which were descended from Lincolnshire Lad, but not through Lincolnshire Lad II (there were nine), traced to them.

(a) HYDRAULIC 1130, chestnut: bred 1872 by Powers, Barkstone, Grantham. Sold to Charles Brooks, Alford, and then to Thomas Shepherd, early owner of the sire. Two of his sons did very well in 1884. (Hyperion 3155 was first in the under 16.2-hands class for Chandos-Pole-Gell and Commodore 2413 was second for Shepherd in the big stallions' class.) Several daughters were to be found in Scotland.

(b) NOBLE 1641, brown: bred 1874 by Thomas Newham, Etwall, Derby. Owned by J. Bullock, Egginton.

By an odd coincidence, the last direct descendants of each of these horses to win a London prize both appeared in the four-year-old gelding class in 1902. *Bonny Captain* (black) g.g.g-son of Noble, was second for Sir Oswald Mosley. *Duke* (bay), g.g-son of Hydraulic, was fourth. He was bred by the Bedford Urban Sanitary Authority at their sewage farm.

7. ONE OF THE MISSING LINKS

One August day in 1971, five men were sitting in a farmhouse in the Leicester-shire village of Plungar, in the northern tip of the county, within a mile of the Nottinghamshire boundary to the west and three miles from Belvoir Castle and then into Lincolnshire in the east. The host was Frank Kirk. His father Tom, who had come across from his modern bungalow, had farmed the land before him, as his family had for generations. The only other member of the group who was of significance was Frank Dixon Goodson, retired farmer of Eastwell, three miles to the south, but now living hard by at Branston.

The aim of the conversation was to build up a picture of Shire breeding in the district in Edwardian times, mainly by the aid of Tom Kirk, who could remem-ber every stallion that walked through Plungar, and the name of his owner and, in most cases, the man who travelled him as well. That fascinating afternoon's test of memory is irrelevant here. What is pertinent to the ancestry of the whole breed of Shire horses is that Mr. Goodson had with him a handbill, printed in 1824, of a horse belonging to Frank Dixon, his great-grandfather and one of his predecessors at Eastwell. The stallion turned out to be, in fact, Dixon's *Waxwork* (7b, in Section 6).

The 1970's are, naturally, less favourable to those who would fill the gaps in old Shire pedigrees than the 1870's. The county record offices do not contain such material as this, and all depends on little privately-owned collections of papers, usually to be properly interpreted only by those who own them and who are old enough to understand the nature of days gone by.

A man who can remember 1904, or even 1924, can attune himself to what his ancestors did and tried to do in 1824 in a way altogether unfathomable by a man who cannot remember before 1944. Nevertheless, though old men with memories are fast being lost and, in many cases, their precious little notebooks or cash books or old papers destroyed, it is far from impossible to rescue some of those facts which Coke and company, if they had been Biddells and the Shire world was twenty times smaller, could and would have discovered and noted. It would be tedious and laborious to read an account of every such conversation which has resulted in pedigrees being more complete in 1974 than they were in 1874, but Dixon's *Waxwork* and the horse which succeeded him may justifiably stand as an example of them all – an outstanding one, because Tom Kirk's visitors in August 1971 had no idea that Frank Goodson's maternal ancestor was Frank Dixon. Where in England does one start to search for a Dixon that possessed a *Waxwork* in 1817? One finds him only by such an accident as this.

The handbill announced *Waxwork* as a Noted Brown Horse ready to cover mares at One Pound each, payable at mid-summer, and one shilling the groom, payable of course on the spot. He travelled a three-counties route. Starting from home on Mondays, he went north into Notts to stay the night at Whatton, from where he moved north-east across the northern point of Leicestershire on Tuesdays to Long Bennington in Lincolnshire, and then north again to Balderton (Notts) for Wednesday night. Then he walked back into Lincolnshire and gradually south through Foston (Thursday nights) and Great Ponton (Friday nights) before doing the ten miles or so back to his home quarters on Saturdays. If Waxwork's route remained the same from 1817 to 1824 (and it probably did), it is very likely that Mr. Musson of Waltham (on the Wolds) put his mare to him some time on a Saturday afternoon that year of 1817 when Ploughboy 1726 (Sect. 6 6c.) was conceived.

One of the company in Frank Kirk's house eagerly waited to see what the breeding of Dixon's *Waxwork* might be. But the handbill was utterly silent. Not a word about it was given. All that was revealed that was not known before, was that *Waxwork* was a brown horse, and was still alive in 1824. In such disappointments as these there is consolation only in feeling some sort of kinship with one's painstaking and patient mentor from long ago, Herman Biddell.

Frank Dixon was thrown from a horse and killed outright not long after the handbill's 1824 season. To prove it, the company in 1971 stared somewhat gloomily at the coroner's certificate, dated 5th August. What happened to *Waxwork* is totally unknown, but another of Dixon's stallions, "the Brown Horse Wellington, ten years old", was advertised for sale by auction on Monday, 17th January 1825 "at 11 o'clock in the forenoon in Mr. Bawderson's yard, the King's Head Inn, in Melton-Mowbray". The little group in Frank Kirk's house speculated as to whether the auctioneer was Thomas Bonsor, great-grandfather of Tom Kirk, his predecessor at Pastures Farm, and friend of Dixon, just as the two descendants were friends. Bonsor did quite a bit of auctioneering and was a meticulous keeper of accounts (he always wrote down the cost of taking his wife into Melton, Nottingham, or Leicester), but no selling records are entered for this year. The pedigree of *Wellington* was given on the auction notice, and this seemed to add insult to injury – what historian can really care much about him? He appears in the ancestry of no horses of importance and has no more significance than hundreds of contemporary stallions of whom we have never heard.

But there was a surprise. *Wellington* was by "that noted brown horse Honest Tom, the property of Mr. Wiseman of Moulton, which covered by subscription at 2 gns. a mare, and when six years old was sold for 400 gns". This was indeed Honest Tom 1060. It was news that he was brown and if it had only come to light earlier that Mr. Wiseman of Fleet and Mr. Wiseman of Whaplode was also Mr. Wiseman of Moulton (as also of Weston), it would have saved time in tracking the all-important but ubiquitous W.W. to his right parish. But more than this, the g-sire was given – "that capital brown horse Old Honest Tom". So this was the name of Milton & Colley's *Brown Horse of Bassingham*! And who was he got by? The sale notice failed to say.

One is left to wonder why Wellington was never registered in Volume One. Had they never heard of him? Perhaps not. But perhaps they, too, had seen such a notice as this and grown suspicious, for his dam was "a capital Sorril Mare (the property of Mr. Carter) which when a yearling was sold for 60gns". (This may have been John Carter of Dunsby, well known as a stallion-owner some years later). She was got by "that noted Sorril horse Robin Hood, late the property of Mr. Cook of Pinchbeck, which he sold, when the season was over, for . . ." The rest of the bill is defaced, and leaves us wondering about this Sorril business, for the Suffolks were mostly called Sorrels in those days. One only hopes that, if *Robin Hood* was a Suffolk, "Cook" was not actually Cox. (More violent twists of name are not uncommon among compilers of early stud cards.) If so, one hates to see this horse near the head of William the Conqueror's pedigree (VII.1).

Tom Kirk's little group discussion in 1971 ranged from Bonsor and Dixon in George IV's reign to an expensive modern riding school where "you want to be careful, sending anyone. You'd buy the 'oss in two hours' lessons". At the end of the afternoon, he produced a big old envelope in which he had written down the information for which the meeting had really assembled. It contained the name of every horse that had walked through Plungar in Edwardian times, just as *Waxwork* had done in 1824 on Mondays about mid-day. There were "Club horses" and free-lance horses. The names of the owners of the latter numbered fourteen and the name of horses and grooms filled the paper, at all angles, before exhaustion had called a halt. Six weeks and six days after the talk, Tom Kirk was dead. The most patient research has failed to trace any possible flaw in his memory. Almost his last words on that August afternoon were "There were some good mares about in those days." There were some good men, too, and fortunately, there still are.

8. LINCOLNSHIRE LAD II

A tall, narrow, grey horse with very flat bone, carrying a great covering of hair. That was how old James Forshaw, to his dying day in 1908, remembered the famous son of the first Lincolnshire Lad. Actually he stood 17-hands, but looked more, because of that narrowness and a remarkable lightness of his middle piece. Most people thought he was all right along the top, but were far from entranced about the want of body. Nevertheless, many a good stallion has been so: better that than the rotundity essential to a mare. Of muscle, he was not particularly possessed. As to his hair, it was remarkable. "It hangs and grows", wrote Douglas, "all down the front of his shins and fetlocks right over his feet, giving at first sight the impression that he is wanting in joint; but turn this hair back, and the mistake is at once apparent."[1] He did once win that prize when shown with his dam at Derby, but no one thereafter ever had the temerity to submit him to the judges again.

His offspring were uniformly excellent in their pasterns, where he appeared not to be outstanding. All the hair on the shin re-appeared only in isolated animals – notably in Lockinge Forest King, his renowned and prolific g.g.g-son. All his sons and daughters appeared to be good-looking, while no one would ever claim that he was: nevertheless, they all bore some strange resemblance to him, especially in the head, which made them not difficult to recognise. The pedigree, and the personal appearance, and the progeny of Lincolnshire Lad II, are a wonderful text for a geneticist's sermon.

John Whitehurst of Markeaton, who manipulated a more graphic turn of phrase than most stallion-owners, used to describe him, only 25 years after he had covered his last mare, as "the Father of the Stud-book", or sometimes, as "the tap-root of the Shire breed". Indeed so, but his ascent to this position began inauspiciously, if not dismally. Fred Ford (who only ever bred one other Shire that was registered) sold him as a foal to William Harriman of Wilsthorpe (Derby). Then he came back to Locko, in the ownership of William Clarke, before moving a few miles north to J. H. Kyte at Smalley. In his last season in the county of his birth he covered a mare for a Mr. Potter of Spondon. That was in 1880. The next year at the age of eleven he was bought by Captain Heaton for Worsley. He had several years there, but appeared to get nothing of much note from Lord Ellesmere's mares and had little opportunity to serve any others, though he did visit Chatteris. Heaton and his employer were not sorry to receive an offer from Walter Johnson of Hatfield and gladly sent him off to the Doncaster area. No one up there was very interested in paying even a couple of pounds for his services. But the following year, 1886, those crafty men of genius, the members of the Montgomeryshire society, hired him for £240 – £20 less than for his partner, and namesake (he himself was sometimes called Lincoln) Lincoln 1351, from T. B. Freshney of Louth. (They had paid Thomas Shaw, Garstang, £250 to hire Adam 65 and James Forshaw £275 for St. Ives 2919 in 1883; £275 for King of Bucks 2815 (Forshaw) in 1884, and £575 to Forshaw for Royal Sandy 3993 in 1885.) Now sixteen, he was said to be "as active as a four-year-old", and was re-hired for the same sum the following year, when his first crop of Montgomery foals turned out a marvellous lot. The third year, the Welshmen cheerfully paid a modest £10 increase in the hiring fee. He came back a fourth and last time at the age of nineteen in 1891, but no record of the fee survives.

The old Lad could now do no wrong. Most of his sons and daughters were late developers – including Harold, who resulted from the mating with Potter's mare at Spondon; and it was only after he came into Johnson's hands that his Worsley foals became prominent. (One of these, Carbon 3523, was actually his assistant in Montgomery in 1887. Then owned by Colonel Henry Platt at Bangor, he was four that year and proved one of the best sires that Association had ever hired, and was engaged twice more.) The Lad's fee had now increased to 5 guineas and, about Christmas-time 1894, he was bought by Fred Crisp of the White House Stud Farm at New Southgate, North London, where he served at 10 guineas. He died there on 27th June 1895, aged twenty-three years.

(Walter Johnson deserves a special mention, as owner at some time of three of the seven foundation sires of the Shire breed. He bought Royal Albert as a foal (see VIII.3) in 1872, Bar None as a three-year-old straight from farm-work in 1880 (VIII.5) and Lincolnshire Lad II as an apparent near-failure at the age of fifteen in 1885.) Lincolnshire Lad II's pedigree is given overleaf.

The old grey horse sired the London champion mare of 1886 (Scarsdale Bonny) and the champion stallion of 1887 (Harold himself). He had a host of beautiful daughters but, if he is judged on the basis of the sons through whom with rare prepotency he transmitted his latent talents to tens of thousands, then those should be mentioned who were themselves the sires or forefathers of London Show winners. These are listed on page 589 in order of age, by which the slow development of his abilities is well illustrated.

PEDIGREE OF LINCOLNSHIRE LAD II 1365

1	2	3	4	5	6	7

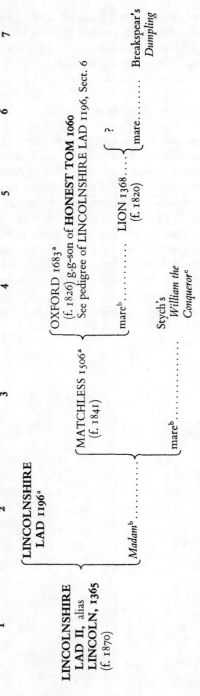

**LINCOLNSHIRE
LAD 1196**[a]

**LINCOLNSHIRE
LAD II,** alias
LINCOLN, 1365
(f. 1870)

MATCHLESS 1506[a]
(f. 1841)

Madam[b] . . . .

OXFORD 1683[a]
(f. 1826) g.g-son of **HONEST TOM 1060**
See pedigree of LINCOLNSHIRE LAD 1196, Sect. 6

mare[b] . . . .

mare[b] . . . .

Stych's
*William the
Conqueror*[c]

LION 1368 . . . . . .
(f. 1820)

mare . . . .

?

Breakspear's
Dumpling

Notes:

2b *Madam* must have been grey, giving her colour to her son.

3a MATCHLESS 1506, grey: b Mead, Brill, Bucks: o Dan Howsin (Notts†).

4c Stych (Derby:†).

5   LION 1368, chestnut: o Archer, Ickford, Bucks.
    Sire not recorded.

7   Where does one look for a *Dumpling* owned by a Breakspear?

Name of son	Year of Foaling	Age of L.L. II at Service	No. of prizes won by descendants winning at London 1893–1924	Breeder
WARRIOR 2689	1878	5	9	H. T. Hanbury, Willsthorpe, Derby.
HAROLD 3703	1881	8	1,755	(John) Potter, Spondon, Derby.
LINCOLNSHIRE BOY 3188	1881	8	15	William Goodall, Mackworth, Derby.
CARBON 3523	1883	10	45	Earl of Ellesmere, Worsley Hall.
HANDCUFF 4437	1884	11	3	Earl of Ellesmere.
PAXTON 4604	1884	11	15	Earl of Ellesmere.
LANCASHIRE LAD II 6031	1885	12	31	Earl of Ellesmere.
DUNSMORE BARRIER 13010	1889	16	1	Alfred Tanner, Shrawardine, Salop.
POTENTATE 12086	1889	16	152	Wm. Humphreys, Evenall, Oswestry, Salop.
NAILSTONE SALOPIAN 12226	1889	16	1	John Green, Baschurch, Salop.
REGINALD 14242	1889	16	1	J. Marshall Dugdale, Llanfyllin, Mont.
*PRIDE OF HATFIELD 13103	1890	17	1	George Smales, Gowdall, Selby, Yorks.
EASTOFT LAD 14019	1891	18	1	Wm. Milman, Thorne, Yorks.
ERCALL WYNN 14620	1892	19	13	Richard Wainwright, Sweeny, Oswestry, Salop.
YORKSHIRE LAD V 15947	1894	21	2	Cockayne Bros, Sheffield Lane Paddocks, Sheffield.
Prizes won by Lincolnshire Lad II's own progeny			18	

2,063

* Originally registered as Gee Whoa Hoy. Name changed by special permission when bought by Walter Johnson.

CHAPTER VI

They All Go Back to Harold

1. HAROLD'S LIFE AND TIMES

IF his sire had made a slow and uncertain start, it was only a piece of pure luck that enabled Harold to start at all, at least in England. His breeder, John Potter of Spondon, kept him a couple of years, but, not being a Shire member, did not bother to register him in the Stud-book. (Volume 1 contains a horse bred by his father in 1838 – Gallemore 907 by Elsome's *White Legs* out of a Potter-bred mare by Doar's *Valentine*. This stallion, entered by Coke's committee on the strength of his having been owned by Anthony Wright of Wheston Hall, had hitherto been the sum total of this branch of the Potter family's contribution to pedigree breeding.) In 1883, when Harold was two, Charles I. Douglas, "of Toronto and 13 Radstock Road, Liverpool" toured the Derbyshire farms and bought him up, with a score of others, for export to the United States.

Harold was the pick of the bunch, and Douglas decided to show him in London the following February. Any success there would add a tenner, or perhaps much more, to his value in the States. The young brown horse did well. In a class of seventy-six three-year-olds, he managed to collect a "commended" card. In those days, only the prize-winners and reserve were placed in actual order of merit, so it is impossible to say where he stood: but he cannot have been lower than fifteenth, or higher than twelfth. Douglas did not know, or could not remember, the breeder's Christian name, so the records show him as " – Potter."

Sir Henry Allsopp's purchase at this show, for a thousand guineas, of the champion stallion, Enterprise of Cannock (by Heart of Oak 1009, a son of Welcher's Honest Tom) has already been mentioned (A.VI.8). But, since his tenants would have to wait a year for his services because he was under contract to do a season in Leicestershire, Sir Henry was on the look-out for another. He had a liking for Harold, and Douglas cheerfully parted with him. After all, the horse was perhaps a bit too good for the Americans, who at that time were mostly being fobbed off with rubbish, and if Sir Henry was willing to pay a little over the odds, then it would save the expense and risk of shipping him. So Harold and a black horse purchased from James Crowther's Mirfield stud went to serve the Worcestershire mares, which were scarcely such as to make the name of any horse as a sire of champions. Sir Henry registered him, but by the time the volume containing his name was published, Harold was four years old. The breeder was still given as " – Potter", whom no one had really heard of.

But his owner was now created Lord Hindlip, and everyone had heard of him.

Harold continued, throughout his second season of 1885, to do what he could for the tenants of Hindlip Hall and the other farmers round about, and during the year developed marvellously. So he was entered, together with Enterprise of Cannock, for the 1886 show. The result was amazing. Both were in the five-years-and-over class for horses of 16.2-hands and upwards. Harold won first prize, and the ex-supreme champion was fourth. Sanders Spencer reported that Harold's "great size and substance on short legs, plentifully covered with silky hair, his splendid shoulders, well sprung ribs and grand movement caused him to be a favourite not only for the chief prize in his class, for the still greater honour of champion". He did not achieve that, for the heavyweight Staunton Hero, the winner of the other senior class, under 16.2-hands, beat him for senior cup (open to all horses of four and upward) and was also made champion. This was the first and only time in sixty years of London shows that the male champion came from the "small stallions" class. The champion mare, by a coincidence, was very closely related to Harold. She was by Lincolnshire Lad II, as he was; and out of a mare by Stych's famous Champion (of Stenson) as he was; and was bred about the same distance from the centre of Derby as he was. Her breeder was Arthur Tomlinson of Stenson to the south, whereas Spondon is to the east.

At this show, A. C. Duncombe released Harold from his bondage to the Worcester mares by paying 550 guineas for him at the auction, and taking him to join Premier at Calwich Abbey under the expert care of John Green, who had been there since 1870. But before considering Harold's life at Calwich, let us spare a thought for poor Enterprise of Cannock. The elegant ex-champion had not fared well in Worcestershire. There had been much dispute over him, even in 1884. Some claimed he was too "tasty" and not masculine enough, that he had too little hair, that his knees were too small and that his forelegs were lacking in substance: others had said his walking and trotting action and spirit, together with his fine head, his feet and feather and his sheer beauty outweighed all defects. But now, after a couple of years in rustic obscurity, he seemed to have lost all the hair he had, and lacked all his old freedom and elasticity of movement. He was lucky to be even fourth. During the year, Lord Hindlip died, and the horse was put up for auction at Hindlip Hall. He went back to his former home at Cannock. The following winter James Galbraith bought him to go to Wisconsin. This was an ironic substitution for the destiny of Harold. But he never reached even New York. One of the most violent storms ever encountered in the Atlantic killed him, together with many more Shires on their way to a new home in the west.

Harold came right to the top in 1887, when he won the championship for Duncombe. His breeder, too, now at last blossomed out as John Holland Potter, winner of a fifteen-guinea gold medal (this was the second year of breeders' prizes) to remind him of the great day. But even this did not tempt John to become a Shire Society member. Tom Forshaw, who was then twenty-one, and attended every Spring Show from the beginning until 1939, wrote that Harold was "a beautiful dark brown, with broad, white face and white hind legs to the hocks. Standing 17.2-hands, he was a majestic horse in carriage and movement, and would weigh about 21 cwt." The casual observer was inclined to suggest he was rather short of joint, but this was an illusion, for he wore his hair down the front of his shin, like his father. His strongest asset of all was his complete masculinity at every point and in all his outlook. In his action, he looked most impressive of all from behind.

In 1888 he was shown again, and was placed 5th (reserve for a prize). The winner of the class, champion of 1886 and now also champion once again, was Prince William, two years younger at the age of five. This horse turned out to be one of the two sons through whom William the Conqueror was to become, and remain, the second great foundation sire of the whole breed. And who bred him, but another member of the Potter family? This was W.H., of Lockington. By a coincidence, Hitchin Conqueror, also five, the other son by whom William the Conqueror achieved immortality, was also in the class. He received a highly commended card but, following Harold's footsteps, was destined to come to the top later. And his breeder, George Shepperson, was another Lockington man. This senior class of 1888 probably gave rise to more argument than any other at any show before or since. But what none of the spectators realised, nor the judges, was that in Prince William, Harold and Hitchin Conqueror, though only one won a prize, they were gazing upon the three stallions from which, within fifty years, every single pedigree Shire in the country, thousands of non-pedigree Shires, and a mass of mere useful "cart-'osses" were to be directly descended in the male line. If there is one show above all others which the modern lover of Shires might choose to attend, could he be transported back through time, he might well select this unique occasion – especially if he were privileged to retain his knowledge of the subsequent importance of the three animals while listening to the contemporary arguments.

Of great interest to the modern visitor to the 1888 show (if the time-machine allowed him to linger a little longer) would be the first-prize winner out of sixty-one in the three-year stallion class. It was All Here 4829, bred by the late Lord Hindlip and exhibited by his successor. This was Harold's earliest prize-winning son. He does not figure among his great ones, and in fact died in September of the following year.

Harold never appeared in London again, and perhaps it was a pity he had come in 1888. From now on, his life was entirely devoted to the begetting of a vast number of sons and daughters, the most remarkable thing about which was their amazing uniformity. Some horses seemed to get better sons than daughters, or vice versa. Harold's progeny were always good. Anyone owning a Shire got by him had only to drop a hint, and customers would queue up. The contribution made to this success by Premier, one year older than Harold and the greatest of the Matchless line, must not be overlooked in this connexion. In these two horses, Duncombe owned if not the best two stallions ever in the possession of one man (William Bingham's Glories probably have that honour, if only we knew the circumstances), yet certainly the most perfect partners in the history of Shire-horse breeding. Harold on a Premier mare was the perfect combination. Premier put to a Harold mare was almost as good. Yet these two each served mares for only 10 guineas apiece. Unhappily Premier died on 28th April 1892 but a vast proportion of the Shire breed was built up by crossing and re-crossing the descendants of Premier with Harold blood. The story of these two partners is an explanation, also, of the fact that the Matchless line appeared to die out, whereas the Harold line waxed wider and greater. In most of the best Shires directly descended in male line from Harold will be found one, two, three or more streams of Premier blood somewhere on the female side.

The year before Premier's death, he had been paraded with eighteen of his sons and daughters at a Calwich Abbey sale. Though these included a number of foals, they made an average of £273 each. The top price was 1,100 guineas for the six-year-old Chancellor 4959. To celebrate this four-figure sum, a tree was planted on the spot where he stood at the sale. The next year Premier was laid to rest at one side of it. Nine years later, on 2nd April 1901, Harold was rescued from the infirmities of old age by the "friendly bullet" and was buried on the other side. As long as the Duncombes lived, and while Calwich Abbey existed at all, this was hallowed ground and, guarded by railings, lovingly preserved. Harold, with his partner, had "made" the great Ashbourne Show and at this, seventy years and more after the death of the greatest of all Shires, Herbert Bury, assistant and later successor to John Green, never failed to wear his tie-pin made from one of Harold's teeth.

Before turning to the sons of Harold, a tribute must be paid, however brief, to his daughters – "and what big, roomy dams they proved", wrote one enthusiast, "unexcelled as breeders." Tom Forshaw wrote of the best of them, many years later (and he never allowed words to run away with him), "perhaps two of his best daughters were Dunsmore Gloaming and Queen of the Shires, both of them London Champions. These were very big mares, each close on 17.2-hands, and good mares, too, although they varied very much in type. Dunsmore Gloaming had big limbs, rather of the stallion type, yet was a well built mare, with good head, neck, shoulders, back and quarters. Perhaps to some critics she was not straight enough in the hind legs, whereas Queen of the Shires was equally as big in height, a shade longer, yet well made, and she had the legs that would carry her right to the top of the big mare class at any show today. Her limbs were beautifully turned and perfectly set on the pasterns, with the quality of bone to suit the most fastidious Scotsman.

"At Peterborough Summer Show you see some extraordinary pair classes, but I doubt if we have seen anything to equal two of the Shows I well remember, when Dunsmore Gloaming and Melody in one case, and Queen of the Shires and Southgate Charm in the other, headed the line. They, in my opinion, are outstanding winners as pairs, each pair being so much alike, both in size and quality. These four mares were all by the famous Harold."

Harold was all things to all men, and to all mares too. Had he been foaled in 1481 instead of 1881, the men of those days, having recovered from their amazement at the mere idea of such a great and grand creature, would no doubt have found in him the perfect war-horse, indomitable in courage and terrifying in his fire and spirit. But in the hands of the gentle Duncombe, the quiet Green and the canny stud groom Johnny Rankin, he was a beloved creature of peace, whose death Lady Florence Duncombe, no less than these men, mourned with a sentiment that may seem alien and even embarrassing today, but which was genuine.

2. THE FLOWER OF FLOWERS

Harold had been dead almost five years when his dam (who had been dead nearly twenty) was registered in the Stud-book. This posthumous recognition by the Editing Committee (of which A. C. Duncombe himself was serving his thirteenth consecutive year as chairman) was dictated solely by the difficulty that exporters faced in providing the United States authorities with the statutory length of pedigree to accompany the numerous sons and grandsons of Harold, and grand-daughters too, that were in constant demand across the Atlantic. The trade there, after its almost complete cessation in the 'nineties, was now of a very different class from that for which Harold himself had been considered too good in the 'eighties. Good-quality animals alone were acceptable, and of registered pedigree on both sides to the third generation. When Harold was registered in 1885, the Stud-book qualification was simply 'registered sire and dam's sire' and so Sir Henry Allsopp had only to quote Lincolnshire Lad and "dam by Champion 419". But a pedigree that was still good enough for His Majesty or any other English breeder was not sufficient to gain admission to Chicago, Wisconsin or Illinois.

By 1906, when the by-gone matron was registered, J. H. Potter had moved from Spondon to Stanton-by-Dale and from there to Rolleston, where Sir Oswald Mosley, at the Hall, had been a keen Shire man some dozen years. Potter was now, in fact, on the point of moving once again, to retirement at Ashby-de-la-Zouch. He readily agreed to become the only man ever to have a mare entered in the Stud-book gratis – and there are now more than a hundred and forty thousand of them. He stated that she was called Flower, scarcely an unusual name. In the previous twenty-six volumes, there had been 714 Flowers, and she was one of twenty-nine in this one. The rule now was that an ancient matron foaled before 1886 could be entered if her sire and dam's sire were registered, but Potter could not conform to this. So she was allowed to appear under the old easier rule, which had been abolished in 1897, that a pre-1881 mare was eligible if either her sire or her dam's sire were registered. The information he supplied was printed thus:

47962 – FLOWER
  Owner: John Holland Potter, Rolleston, Burton-on-Trent
      Black, blaze, four white legs, white patch under belly. Foaled 1870.
Breeder: late Joseph Potter, Spondon, Derby.
Sire: Champion (419)
Dam: *Flower* (chestnut, bred by late Joseph Potter), by Ploughboy (Porter's).

To provide even this much, J.H.P. had to crystallise his memory. Fifteen
years earlier, in 1891, when someone wanted to register a grand-daughter of the
black Flower, all that he had ventured about her age that she had been foaled
"*about* 1870". It is also a pity that Porter's *Ploughboy* is now unidentifiable.
Presumably it was a horse belonging to one of the Porters of Haddenham (see
Fens) Robert or Hugh, but Edward Porter of Wendy in Cambridgeshire, and
Richard Porter of Sowerby, Lancashire, both had stallions in the 1860s, and so
no doubt did other Porters also.
  Harold's pedigree, as far as it will ever be known, was therefore "completed"
in 1906 like this:

Sire: LINCOLNSHIRE LAD II

		CONQUEROR	CONQUEROR—CHAMPION—FARMER'S GLORY—Ivens'			
		531	529	379	818	*Grey*
		f 1847	f 1843	f 1829	f 1825	Horse
	CHAMPION	alias				
	419	Champion	mare a			
Dam:	f 1855		prizewinner			
47962		mare———	CONQUEROR 529———as above			
FLOWER						
	Flower——Porter's *Ploughboy*					

Champion 419 was none other than Stych's Champion (see Derbys: II.2).
He was grey, like all his known immediate sires. His breeder, Kilbey of Bodicote
Fields, also bred his dam, his sire and his g-sire. Champion 379 was bred forty
miles away on the eastern edge of Northants, by Backall of Woodford. Farmer's Glory was owned, if not bred, by Ivens on the Oxfordshire side of the
county at Eydon. (For Ivens and his grey horses, see II.6).
  The white patch on Flower's belly, uncharacteristic of true Shires, tempts
one to speculate whether she had some blood in her of that marvellous stallion
belonging to the Laws of Thenford, about 1800, called *Waxwork*, who was
completely black except for a completely white belly – a peculiarity that had
lasted in his descendants for thirty years or more (II.6). Did that white on the
belly reappear once again in 1870?
  Little as is really known of Stych's Champion's pedigree, the inbreeding that
produced him surely accounts for his success in general and, more particularly,
for the fixing of qualities which old Flower, when mated to Lincolnshire Lad II,

transmitted to Harold. Even in a stallion's world, as that of the Shire was, Harold's amazing pre-potency must be attributed in large measure to his much-neglected dam, who should be regarded as the Flower of all Flowers of the Stud-book.

3. THE 101 BEST SONS OF HAROLD

No one knows how many sons and daughters Harold had. Here, we must omit the daughters, having paid faint honour to four of his best (section 1). Of his sons, some lived in obscurity, though they remained entire and covered mares all over England on the strength of their famous father's name. Many, of course, were castrated, and a vast proportion of these devoted their lives to pulling drays and lorries around the town streets. (An average of at least 90% of the mares which even the most illustrious of Shire stallions covered were unregistered and unregistrable. Therefore the male produce of such matings was *ipso facto* ineligible for the Stud-book.) An uncountable number, a host in themselves, went abroad.

Here we consider only the 98 sons which achieved passing fame as London prize-winners themselves or more lasting glory as the sires or direct male ancestors of London prize-winners, together with three more who never did either of these things but who are worthy representatives of all the rest who likewise never reached the Agricultural Hall in person or by proxy. One of these three is Hendre Harold, which won first prize as a yearling at the Royal Show in 1895. Another is a colt that so delighted James Bucknell when he brought him from Derby to Somerset and won the county show with him in 1890 that he registered him as Harold II. After all, he did more to increase the breed in Somerset than the Lancashire colt out of Cronton Hasty that was castrated and never registered (no. 29 in the list below). Third is Calwich William, which won first prize in the tenant farmers' class for colt foals at Ashbourne itself in 1896.

They are listed below in alphabetical order. The casual reader who finds the catalogue unattractive and indigestible can easily skip it. The more determined searcher may be rewarded by some interesting comparisons – for example, among those bearing the Rokeby prefix, registered by that doughty enthusiast, John Parnell of Rugby. He will also notice that the son who passed on Harold's qualities to a greater number of descendants than any other – to almost as many as the rest combined – never won a London prize. However, in order to make the facts tolerably concise,

(a) only the *highest* London prize won by each son has generally been mentioned.

(b) the successes won by them as *sires*, g-sires etc, of London winners have been restricted to the years 1893–1924, to link with the tables given in IV.2 and section 5 of this chapter.

N.B. Those marked* are out of Premier mares – the direct classic cross.

Name of son	Where and when bred	Highest London prize	Descendants at London Shows 1893–1924	
			No. of Prizes	No. of Shows
1. ALL HERE 4829	Hindlip '85	1st of 61 in 1888		
2. AMBUSH 18475	Derby. '98		2	1
3. ANCHORITE 16488	Norfolk '96	3rd of 36 in 1901 (b Prince of Wales)	1	1
4. BARDON HAROLD 15463	Leics. '94		2	2
5. BARROW ADVANCE 17751	Derby. '98		3	3
6. BARROW SIR JAMES 17142	Derby. '97	4th of 44 in 1898	4	4
7. BOLD HAROLD 16005	Derby. '95		4	4
8. BRACKNELL HAROLD 13895	Derby. '91		4	4
9. BURGUNDY 12862	Staffs. '90	3rd of 54 in 1892		
10. BURY BLOOD ROYAL 15522	Hunts. '94	1st of 45 in 1898	4	3
11. BURY PREMIER DUKE 16575*	Hunts. '96	Reserve Champion in 1900 (2nd of 263) Reserve Senior Cup in 1901 (2nd of 115)	5	3
12. CALWICH BLAZE 14544	Staffs. '92		11	10
13. CALWICH BLEND 17276*	Staffs. '97	3rd of 16 in 1912 (age 15, shown by the King)	107	19
14. CALWICH BRIDEGROOM 16040	Is. of Man '95	C in 68, in 1898 (and 1904)	3	3
15. CALWICH CAPTAIN 16041	Staffs. '94	3rd of 8 in 1908		
16. CALWICH COMBINATION 11118	Derby. '89	Reserve Senior Cup in 1895 (2nd of 117)	19	16
17. CALWICH CONQUEROR 14545	Derby. '92		1	1
18. CALWICH GENERAL 13936	Staffs. '91		1	1
19. CALWICH GUARDIAN 15038	Derby. '93		3	3
20. CALWICH MARKSMAN 12873	Derby. '90	3rd of 39 in 1895		
21. CALWICH TOM 16042*	Lancs. '95		3	3
22. CALWICH WILLIAM 16587	Staffs. '96	(see above)		
23. CAPSTONE HAROLD 16590	Leics. '96	1st in 1901–1904 (of 24, 28, 27 and 36)	3	3
24. CASTERN HAROLD 12898*	Derby. '90	Res. Jnr. Cup in 1893 (2nd of 155)	4	4
25. CATTHORPE MERRY BOY 12903	Derby. '90		1	1
26. CHIEFTAIN HAROLD 17251	Lancs. '94	C in 45, in 1898		
27. CODNOR HAROLD 17266	Derby. '97	3rd of 12 in 1907		
28. COLLEGE DON 11236	Leics. '89	2nd of 20 in 1900 (b W. H. Potter)	2	2

Name of son	Where and when bred		Highest London prize	Descendants at London Shows 1893–1924	
				No. of Prizes	No. of Shows
29. Colt out of 6071 Cronton Hasty	Lancs.	'93	HC in 33, in 1894 (not reg.)		
30. CONQUERING HAROLD 15558	Staffs.	'93		162	22
31. COPENHAGEN 19512	Lancs.	'99	C in 43, in 1906		
32. COTGRAVE BONNIE BOY BLUE 17276	Notts	'97	C in 63, in 1899		
33. COTGRAVE HAROLD 16077	Notts	'95	C in 66, in 1897		
34. COTON 7060	Derby.	'87		1	1
35. DELAMERE HAROLD 15576	Staffs.	'94		1	1
36. DELAMERE SURPRISE 17929	Ches.	'97	4th of 44 in 1903		
37. DEVON HAROLD 12983	Devon	'90	C in 20, in 1900		
38. DUNSMORE FIELD MARSHAL 15589	Derby.	'94	C in 63, in 1896		
39. DUNSMORE MASTERMAN 12874*	Calwich	'90	4th of 54 in 1892 as "Calwich Masterman"	17	9
40. DUNSMORE STERLING HAROLD 17986	Derby.	'98	HC in 53, in 1899		
41. EAST ANGLIAN 14017	Derby.	'91	4th of 20 in 1901	4	4
42. ELY HAROLD 11367	Notts	'88	C in 134, in 1890 as "Cronton Harold"	2	2
43. ETHELWULF 16667	Norfolk	'96	(b Prince of Wales)	4	4
44. GOWNSMAN 14648	Notts	'91	5th of 46 in 1893	1	1
45. GRAFTON 9461	Leics.	'88	HC in 134, in 1890		
46. GRAFTON II 13120	Derby.	'90	5th of 75 in 1893		
47. HARMONY 13145	Derby.	'89	C in 102, in 1892		
48. HAROLD II 13146	Derby.	'89	(See above)		
49. HAROLD HAREFOOT 13147	Herts.	'90	2nd of 39 in 1891	5	4
50. HAROLD'S DRAYMAN 18785	Notts	'99	C in 120, in 1902		
51. HAROLD'S LAST 20541	Staffs.	'01	C in 121, in 1904		
52. HAROLD'S PILOT 11564	Derby.	'87	(Formerly Blagdon Pilot 6749)	8	6
53. HAROLD'S RIVAL 15619	Herts.	'93	4th of 32 in 1898	10	6
54. HENDRE HAROLD 15630	Staffs.	'94	(See above)		
55. HENDRE SWELL 15631*	Calwich	'94		1	1
56. HERALD 11601	Derby.	'89		10	9
57. HINDLIP CHAMPION 9584	Leics.	'88	2nd in 1890–1891 (of 134, and 113)	35	19
58. HOLDFAST 18808	Norfolk (P. of Wales)	'99	HC in 54, in 1900		
59. HORBLING HAROLD 15647	Notts	'94	HC in 32, in 1895 as "Cotgrave Harold"	3	3

Name of son	Where and when bred		Highest London prize	Descendants at London Shows 1893–1924	
				No. of Prizes	No. of Shows
60. INTAKE ADVANCE 18822	Yorks.	'99	C in 86, in 1901	1	1
61. JOLLITY 19729*	Derby.	'00	5th of 61 in 1905		
62. KENNETT 13206*	Hunts. (W. H. O. Duncombe)	'89	Res. (5th) in 39, in 1895	10	7
63. LIMECROFTS HAROLD 15203*	Staffs.	'93		1	1
64. LULLINGTON HAROLD 15705	Derby.	'94		2	2
65. MARKEATON ROYAL HAROLD* 15225	Derby.	'93	Res. Jnr. Cup in 1895 (2nd of 124). Champion in 1897 (1st of 319.) Sen. Cup, Res. Champ. in 1898 (2nd of 300)	83	20
66. MARMION II 9885	Glos.	'87	1st of 58 in 1891	19	14
67. MERRIE ANDREW 18208	Staffs.	'98		1	1
68. NAILSTONE HAROLD 15254	Leics.	'93	2nd in 1894–1896 (of 33, 51 and 41)	4	3
69. NAILSTONE PHILANTHROPIST 15257	Derby.	'93	5th of 51 in 1895		
70. NAILSTONE ROYAL HAROLD 15746	Leics. (W. H. Potter)	'94		1	1
71. NOTTINGHAM HAROLD 16296	Notts.	'94	3rd of 74 in 1897		
72. OLD WARDEN ROYAL HAROLD 16300*	Calwich	'94	HC in 63, in 1896	2	2
73. PELHAM 15278	Leics.	'93	HC in 41, in 1896		
74. PRINCE HAROLD 14228	Lancs.	'90		704	26
75. RALEIGH 13489	Norfolk	'90	6th of 75 in 1893		
76. RATCLIFFE ROYAL HAROLD 16910	War.	'96		3	3
77. REGENT II 6316	Hindlip	'86		54	24
78. ROCKS HAROLD 14822	Derby.	'92	5th of 34 in 1893		
79. ROKEBY EARL 13518*	War.	'90		2	2
80. ROKEBY EGBERT 16928	Derby.	'96	C in 55, in 1897		
81. ROKEBY FRIAR 14827	War.	'91	3rd of 46 in 1893	283	26
82. ROKEBY HAROLD 15313	Bucks.	'92	Champion 1893, '95–6 (1st of 294, 241, 263)	3	3
83. ROKEBY HERMIT 12169	Leics.	'89	HC in 51, in 1894		
84. ROKEBY PORTLAND 15898	Staffs.	'94	Res. Jnr. Cup in 1896 (2nd of 153)		
85. ROKEBY RAJAH 13520	Derby.	'90	HC in 40, in 1894		

Name of son	Where and when bred		Highest London prize	Descendants at London Shows 1893–1924	
				No. of Prizes	No. of Shows
86. ROYAL HAROLD 13530	Leics.	'90		I	I
87. RUDDINGTON HAROLD 15813	Staffs.	'94	1st of 32 in 1895		
88. RUDDINGTON PREMIER 16944*	Notts	'96		I	I
89. RUFFORD HAROLD 12212	Derby.	'87	C in 29, in 1896 (orig. Leake FitzHerbert 7551)	I	I
90. SAXON HAROLD 15337	Essex	'93	3rd of 51 in 1895		
91. SCALFORD BARON 19107	Leics.	'97		I	I
92. SCALFORD BANKER 16964	Leics.	'96	C in 55, in 1898		
93. SCROPTON BOUNDER 16388	Derby.	'95	HC in 49, in 1896		
94. SELF HELP 15832	Herts.	'94	HC in 29, in 1900		
95. SHEEN HAROLD 15834	Derby.	'93		7	7
96. TATTON HAROLD 15386	Staffs.	'93	HC in 51, in 1895	I	I
97. THE COLONEL V 10617	Lincs.	'88		4	3
98. WARWICK IV 14414	Leics.	'91	HC in 51, in 1892	I	I
99. WATNALL WARRIOR 20147	Notts	'00	C in 46, in 1901		
100. WITHAM PRINCE 10815	Lincs.	'88	4th of 51 in 1889		
101. WORCESTER 6587	Worcs.	'85	HC in 22, in 1889		

	1,641
Prizes won by these sons of HAROLD HIMSELF	114 (17)
	1,755

4. HOW PRINCE HAROLD ESCAPED CASTRATION

In 1888, on Houghton Tower Farm at Hale in Lancashire, Thomas Charnock's bay mare Hale Lofty had a colt foal by his own-bred Lancashire Lad 6030, one of Harold's first sons. But it was dead. The next year he had her covered by Harold in person, and a black colt foal, with star and white hind legs, was the result in 1890. At Ashbourne Show, they won first prize for best brood mare and foal in the open class and the colt won the thirty-guinea cup for the best Shire foal sired by any of A. C. Duncombe's stallions. They also won the champion cup at the Wirral and Birkenhead Show. The foal was sold to Peter Blundell of Weeton (five miles inland from Blackpool sands) who had just completed a term of service on the Shire Council. Charnock hastened to register the dam in order to enable Blundell to enter the colt in the Stud-book.

The following February, Hale Lofty duly appeared in Volume 12. The particulars were of the briefest kind – bred in 1880 by Thomas Charnock: sire, Cromwell 2415. Had she been even one year younger, she would not have qualified. All mares foaled in 1881 or later were now required to be by a registered sire out of dam got by a registered sire – that is, three-quarters registered blood: and Charnock did not know the breeding of her dam. In June, Blundell showed the yearling colt at the Doncaster Royal and was awarded a prize. Thomas Shaw of Winmarleigh, a few miles away, the owner of Cromwell, immediately raised an objection. The nature of this is now not absolutely clear, but it could have rested on one of two possible grounds – either that Hale Lofty was not by Cromwell at all or that, alternatively, if she was by him, she could not have been foaled earlier than 1881. (Cromwell himself was only two years old in 1879, and Shaw would have known perfectly well which outside mares he had been allowed, if indeed he had had any). Either way, the substance of his claim was that Hale Lofty was not entitled to be in the Stud-book and her son was therefore ineligible to compete at the show. But in fact his objection must have been based on Cromwell's not being her sire at all: the year of her foaling was a technical point and he was not in a position to know that Charnock could not produce evidence about the dam which would satisfy the requirements for mares foaled in 1881 or later.

The R.A.S.E. secretary immediately dispatched a letter across the showground to John Sloughgrove, requesting an investigation. The Editing Committee was in any case due to meet that day at the show and Tom Brown, the chairman, requested Shaw and Blundell to attend for interview. This was an embarrassing situation for Blundell, even though clearly he was not personally at fault. Less than four months previously, he had been a judge at the London Show for the second time, and only six other men so far had been given this responsibility and honour more than once. At the end of the month, a full report of the investigation into Hale Lofty's breeding was presented to the Council. Charnock had been summoned to appear and, after he had been heard, it was unanimously resolved "that Mr. Charnock's name be removed from the list of members of the Society under Bye-law 10", which dealt with "conduct derogatory to the character or prejudicial to the interest of the Society." He showed Hale Lofty at a couple of Lancashire shows later that summer and she won first prize in the cart-mare class. For some reason now obscure, John Parr of Nottingham, a member of the Editing Committee, was asked to continue the investigation into Hale Lofty's pedigree and his report caused the Council in November to pass a resolution which, in view of the precipitate expulsion of Mr. Charnock, appears somewhat guarded. It was agreed "that the entry of Hale Lofty in its present form cannot be accepted, the date of birth not being in accordance with the evidence elicited by the committee." The wording is odd, because she had been accepted already, and the point at issue was whether her entry should be cancelled. But this is what the resolution meant and Sloughgrove was instructed to write to R.A.S.E. "stating that the mare Hale Lofty was disqualified, and consequently her produce Prince Harold is not eligible for the Stud-book." (Readers who have not examined the list of Harold's best sons need to be informed that 40% of the London prizes won in 1893–1924 by descendants of Harold were destined to be gained by those which traced their ancestry through this Prince Harold.)

Mr. Charnock did not act like a guilty man. Having honourably bought back the colt from Peter Blundell, he wrote asking permission to come to London and examine the original entry form he had submitted for Hale Lofty, and on 9th December the Council agreed. On 2nd February (1892) it was stated that he had made a further application on behalf of the mare, "adducing fresh evidence". The Council felt that the case should be re-opened. The Editing Committee reported back, at the next meeting (25th February, during the London Show), that it was a very unsatisfactory case, but that the balance of probability was in favour of the mare being by Conqueror 3042, and not Cromwell. They therefore recommended that she should be re-entered in the Stud-book. (Volume 13, containing her cancellation, had been issued that very day.) That summer, she won a number of prizes at leading county shows. It was not until December that Thomas Charnock was unanimously re-elected a member of the Society, which was the least the Council could do if it was to accept the mare after all.

Volume 14 duly contained Hale Lofty again – as 14883 Hale Lofty, because mares were now at last being given numbers. Still 'foaled in 1880', she now appeared as by Conqueror 3042, a brown horse which was bred in the Fens at Moulton and which spent his life at Heckington Fen. (Shaw's Cromwell, a bay, was also Fen-bred, at Holbeach.) But the real surprise is that she also was now listed as being *bred* in the Fens, by William Hand at Donington, and not by Charnock at all.

The re-acceptance of his dam had saved Prince Harold from almost inevitable castration. He could have been travelled, of course, as a non-pedigree stallion, but it is highly unlikely that Mr. Charnock, having shown such determination over the eligibility of his dam, would have accepted a course of action which would have been tantamount to an admission of his own guilt. He would certainly have gelded the horse and sent him to pass his life in front of a Liverpool dray. But now, all was well and Prince Harold 14228 appeared, like his dam, in Volume 14. But, before it was published, the young horse had been sold again – and the purchaser, of all men in the Shire world, was A. C. Duncombe! His interest in a colt by his own Harold was natural. But, as vice-chairman of the Editing Committee he could have done nothing more calculated to vindicate Mr. Charnock.

In 1895, Prince Harold moved again, and it was said that Lord Llangattock paid 2,500 guineas for the privilege of taking him to his 6,100 acres at the Hendre, Monmouth. If so, Mr. Duncombe hardly suffered for his faith in man and horse. In October 1900 a home sale at The Hendre, of six stallions and thirty-eight mares, made an average of £226. 1s. 8d., the highest up to that time in a Shire sale. Among them were a few sons and many daughters of Prince Harold, but there were still plenty of them left at home when in 1901 the horse died unexpectedly, not long after the shooting of his sire. Everyone sympathised with Lord Llangattock at the premature loss of his great stallion, one of whose personal claims to fame was allegedly that he had more bone below the knee than any horse in England. But he had not done too badly with him. The sale of four sons and a daughter, to the tune of 3,750 guineas, repaid the purchase price with 50% interest, without help from all the others his lord-ship bred and sold, or from the 10 guinea service fee for a horse which, but for Charnock's persistence, would not have been worth twopence as far as pedigree breeding was concerned. Between 1896 and 1914, Prince Harold's progeny won seventy-four prizes between them at London Shows, including the cham-pionship (Princess Beryl in 1906). Among these was Lockinge Manners whose best effort was seventh prize, but who compensated by siring Lockinge Forest King.

By way of postscript, something should be added about three important characters in this story. Cromwell, the non-sire of Hale Lofty, after winning many prizes and serving many mares for Shaw, ended his days in Australia, whither he emigrated at the age of twelve to become the stock-horse for a Mr. Gedney of Melbourne, whose family were late of the Fens. Thomas Charnock continued to appear in the records until 1913 as "elected 1892", whereas in fairness it should have been given as 1884. Twenty-one of his horses won prizes or commended cards in London. By far the best were Calwich Com-bination (son of Harold – see list in section 3), three times winner of second prizes as well as reserve for the senior cup, and his son Seldom Seen, reserve to Rokeby Harold for the championship in 1896. Honest Freddy Bent, whose own family took the tenancy of Houghton Towers farm in 1922, remembered the Charnock horses of the 'nineties, when he was a boy. Six or seven were loaded every year for the London Show on a Sunday night at Ditton Junction. That was a special night of the year round there, and over seventy years later the scene remained vivid. "What a clatter", he wrote to say, "through the village of Hale!"

As for Peter Blundell, who never had the prize for Prince Harold at the 1891 Royal Show, he continued as a Shire man until his death in 1906, and left a family to carry on. By an odd coincidence, at the same time as the Prince Harold trouble was being sorted out, he had his own problems with a black mare called Topsy's Gipsy. He had bred her in 1881; Joseph Smith of Preston had won third prize with her in London in 1883 ("a thick square filly, with lots of timber"); Walter Gilbey had bought and registered her in Volume 5 (1884), as by Honest Tom 1105; A. H. Smith-Barry, M.P., of Marbury Hall, Northwich, acquired her in 1885, in-foal. In 1892, someone eventually raised the question as to whether she really was by Honest Tom. Volume 14 therefore saw her appear again, as by "Honest Tom 1105 or Cardinal 2407", the latter horse being another Thomas Shaw stallion and, like Cromwell and Conqueror, Fen-bred. Her first foal, perhaps appropriately, had been named Topsy Turvy.

5. EIGHT SONS DOMINATE THE LONDON SHOW

If we look now to see which of Harold's sons were chiefly instrumental for the success of his descendants at the London Shows, we find that their number steadily reduces as time went on. For example, compare the year 1901 with 1924. In the former year, Harold was still alive. (Actually, he was destroyed a month after the Show.) For the first time, the number of his descendants winning London prizes topped the fifty-mark. There were fifty-one of them: eight were his own sons and forty-three were descended from no less than twenty-one of his sons. In 1924, the number of his prize-winning descendants had more than doubled, to 104: but they traced to him through only five of his sons.

In the 1870s, very few breeders were really aware of any good bloodlines. They would have laughed to scorn any suggestion that one stallion could have a significant influence on the future breeding of the general mass of tens of thousands of cart-horses, of all different shapes and sizes and sorts, that filled the land. In the 'eighties, the notion did not appear so mad after all, and the likeliest candidate was Lincolnshire Lad II. By the mid-'nineties, Harold in particular was a good bet. As to which of his sons would do the most good, most people would have chosen the triple champion Rokeby Harold. He was described by one observer, who only voiced the view of everyone, as possessing "all the qualifications of the typical Shire stallion, as he has size, colour, substance, bone, hair and perfect action, besides showing throughout perfect masculine character – likely to perpetuate the characteristics of the true Shire horse". Tom Forshaw remembered him as the best yearling he ever saw, growing later into "a marvellous horse who had splendid carriage, was wide and deep, with extraordinary limbs planted truly, and well feathered. He had good feet and was a clever mover." But he was an almost complete failure at stud. He got four mares in foal (perhaps one or two more) when he was three, in 1895. His failure-rate the next year and as long as he was persisted with thereafter was 100%.

The perfect stallion, even if bred according to the dictates of the geneticists and by the inspiration of genius, cannot be guaranteed to be prepotent to the third and fourth generation of them that succeed him – or even potent in the begetting of one generation. If he could, the gentlemen connected with the turf would find their business as dull as that of car-racing, where the vehicle is predictable and the element of sport is retained only in the unpredictability of the driver and his mechanics. But it is a bad thing for everyone, and not only his owner, when a stallion which is perfect in the beauty of his every point, the product of patient thought, skilful planning and sheer luck, turns out to be sterile. One might well weep for the mighty Rokeby Harold who possessed in abundance everything else but the ability to produce those tiny live spermatozoa.

In the following table, the fading of the lines through Markeaton Royal Harold, Regent II and Hindlip Champion, as time moved on, is apparent, and it was permanent. The seeming lack of success of the Marmion II line is delusory,

London prize-winners descended in male line from sons of HAROLD

Year	London prize-winning progeny of HAROLD HIMSELF	1 from PRINCE HAROLD	2 from ROKEBY FRIAR	3 from CONQUERING HAROLD	4 from CALWICH BLEND	5 from MARKEATON ROYAL HAROLD	6 from REGENT II	7 from HINDLIP CHAMPION	8 from MARMION II	9 from other sons	Total (including sons of HAROLD)	Number of HAROLD's sons represented in columns 1–9
1893	10						3	1	2		16	3
1894	6						3		1	1	11	3
1895	14						3			2	19	3
1896	15						4	1	1	4	25	7
1897	10	3	1			1	5	2		9	31	13
1898	8	5	1			1	3	3		9	30	11
1899	7	3	1	1		3	2	2		11	30	16
1900	12	6	1			4	1	2	2	7	35	13
1901	8	9	1	1		9	2	2	2	18	51	21
1902	8	11	3	2	2	7	4	4	1	14	53	16
1903	7	7	1	5	2	4	3	2	2	21	51	25
1904	3	15	3	3	2	6	3	1		18	54	22
1905	1	15	2	7		3	3	4	1	7	41	13
1906	2	16	2	6		6	3	1	1	11	50	18
1907	1	26	2	8		9	2	2	1	12	62	18
1908		41	4	7	2	4	2		1	7	68	12
1909		44	6	7	2	6		1		8	73	15
1910		41	5	9	2	4	1	3		3	67	10
1911		37	5	6	3	4	1	1		5	64	12
1912	1	45	9	10	3	3	1	1		8	72	11
1913		37	12	10	3	5		1		3	69	10
1914		49	14		6	1	1	1		2	77	8
1915		46	18	3	6	2	1	1	1	3	84	11
1916		47	18	3	6		1			2	77	7
1917		46	17	6	5	1	1			5	81	10
1920	37		31	12	11		1				92	5
1921	33		28	14	9				2		86	5
1922	33		36	11	10				1	1	92	6
1923	25		37	11	15					2	90	6
1924	27		42	13	21					1	104	5
Total	114	704	283	162	107	83	54	35	19	194	1755	

as will be seen later. But special attention is drawn to the Prince Harold line, vastly more successful than all the rest until and during the first war years, but beginning to lose ground afterwards.

1. Prince Harold has already been discussed in section 4. He was never shown in London, and had only 9 full seasons, dying in 1901.

2. ROKEBY FRIAR 14827 was bred in 1891 by John Parnell of Rugby (who, as the prefix suggests, also for a short time owned the handsome sterile Rokeby Harold). His dam was by the Derbyshire John Nix's Gay Lad, a horse of Derbys-Leics. origin. H.C. at London as a yearling, he was then bought by Arthur Nicholson, Highfield Hall, Leek. His 3rd prize the next year was the first London success of the Leek stud. Nicholson was knighted in 1908: Rokeby Friar was put down by "the friendly bullet" in 1909.

3. CONQUERING HAROLD 15558 was bred in 1893 by John Williamson of Cheddleton, Staffs, and was bought as two-year-old by Thomas Charnock, who thus deserves credit for his connexion with two of the important sons of Harold. Dam by Marquis VIII, a Stafford-bred horse whose sire was Fen-bred, by Heart of Oak 1005. Never shown in London, his brief career ended after the 1900 season.

4. CALWICH BLEND 17226 was bred in 1897 at Cheddleton, like Conquering Harold, but by William Sergeant. Dam by Premier. Bought by Duncombe as a foal: later went to Sandringham. A photograph exists of him held by Frank Beck (later killed at Gallipoli), who wrote on the back "Calwich Blend, taken by Her Royal Highness the Princess Victoria". In 1912, on his only London appearance, Blend was 3rd in the old stallions' class for the King. Died, or put down, at the beginning of the following season.

5. MARKEATON ROYAL HAROLD 15225 was bred in 1893 by John Smith of Ellastone, Staffs, out of Sensible, a Premier mare out of Nellie Blacklegs (see IX.2). Bought as a foal by John Whitehurst, the well-known stallion owner of Markeaton, Derby, who consistently refused to sell him in spite of importuning approaches by the Buscot Park stud groom, the agent (Walter Crosland) and finally Alexander Henderson himself. His answer each time was "I bought him for my own smoking". When Henderson at last wrote and asked him to name a price, he thought he would finish the matter by reply "£1500", a fantastic price for a yearling. The cheque arrived by return of post, so he had to part with the colt. An outstanding show animal for five years, he was succeeded as champion for three successive years by his son Buscot Harold, which he had sired when only two years old – a promising start. Markeaton Royal Harold, not counting this 'practice' year, had fifteen years as a stock horse before being put down in January 1911. (Henderson was M.P. from 1898, Baronet 1902, 1st Baron Faringdon 1916).

6. REGENT II 6316 was bred in 1886 by Lord Hindlip, after whose death later that year the foal went to Calwich to join his sire. He was a full brother to All Here, Harold's first prize-winning son, who was one year older. Their dam was by No. 1, a Worcester-bred stallion whose pedigree fades out in Buckingham-

shire in the middle of the nineteenth century. His career was almost literally cut short by an accident while attempting to serve a mare in May 1897.

7. HINDLIP CHAMPION 9584 was bred in 1888 by F. B. Champion of Ashby-de-la-Zouch. His dam, of a long line of Champion-bred mares, was by Simon Pure who had two generations of Alford-district blood and, prior to that, an ancestry rooted in the Huntingdon fens. Bought by Allsopp as a yearling, was twice second in London, but met a premature end on 17th October 1893, after only three full seasons.

8. MARMION II 9885 was bred in 1887 by A. B. Freeman-Mitford at Batsford Park, Glos., out of that astonishing matron Lockington Beauty (IX.2). He was sold as a two-year-old to William Arkwright, Sutton Scarsdale. He was 1st as a 4-year-old at London, and was then sold for 1,400 guineas to Fred Crisp. A horse with marvellous limbs and feet, he was said many years later by Tom Forshaw to be "one of the finest movers that ever entered a ring." He dropped dead in October 1903.

6. UNTO THE THIRD AND FOURTH GENERATION

The London Show of 1921 is of special significance. It was the very last event of the war-time boom. The uneasiness in some hearts when the Shire men gathered at the Agricultural Hall on 15th February was forgotten when they cheered the King and his Field Marshal 5th. But by the end of the year even supreme optimists could not delude themselves that winning the war had brought back the golden age.

The prize-winning horses of 1921, though they were the product of the good days now passing, were to set the pattern of pedigrees in a quite different age. It is therefore appropriate to choose this year for a closer examination of the progress of the Harold line. The table in Section 5 shows that, of his eight originally most successful sons, three had now ceased to be represented among the prize-winners – Markeaton Royal Harold, which is surprising: and Regent II and Hindlip Champion, which is less so. Descendants of all the other sons of Harold not among the "top eight", were appearing less and less among the prizes every year: this year there was none at all.

Prince Harold's descendants this year won more prizes than those of any other of the five, as had happened for twenty-four years. But it was to be for the last time, for the Rokeby Friar line would come to the top the next year. Conquering Harold and Calwich Blend followed after, as they had done for some years. Marmion II appeared to have a pretty tenuous hold on pasthumous glory, through one single descendant.

The following table takes us in detail to the g.g.g-sons of Harold, the last column indicating the number of prize-winners in 1921 that had been sired by them or by their sons. For the sake of completeness, the other male lines of blood which produced prize-winners have been added in abbreviated form. In columns 1–5, figures in parentheses show number of prize-winners descended from the horse in question.

DESCENT OF THE 132 PRIZE-WINNERS AT THE 1921 LONDON SHOW

1	2	3	4	5	6	
		PRINCE HAROLD...... (33)	LOCKINGE MANNERS (33)	LOCKINGE FOREST KING (31)	L.F.K. himself	1
					BARDON RULER	1
					BARN KING via son	1
					CLUMBER F.K.	3
					COLESHILL FORESTER	2
					HALSTEAD B. BLOOD & 2 sons	7
					HALSTEAD R. DUKE & 1 son	2
					KING FOREST	1
					K. of TANDRIDGE & 3 sons	5
					MOULTON VICTOR K.	1
					PALTERTON F.K. via son	1
					RATCLIFFE CONQ KING	1
					RATCLIFFE F.K. & 1 son	2
					REDLYNCH F.K. via 3 sons	3
				SCARCLIFFE MANNERS		1
				WOODFOLD LORD OF THE VALE		1
		ROKEBY FRIAR......... (28)	CHILDWICK MAJESTIC.... (28)	CHILDWICK CHAMPION (28)	Ch Champ himself	3
					CHAMP' CLANSMAN & 2 sons	8
					CHAMPION'S COUNTERSEAL	1
					CHAMP. GOALKEEPER & son	12
					CHAMP' GOVERNOR via 1 son	1
					EATON ABBOT	1
					MIMMS CHAMPION	2

Pedigree tree (read left → right, descendants with numbers at right):

HAROLD (86)
- CONQUERING HAROLD (14)
  - TATTON FRIAR (12)
    - FRIAR JOHN....
      - T.F. himself — 6
      - F. TUCK IV & 2 sons — 1 — 2
  - LYMM LION.. (2)
    - WARTON DRAUGHTSMAN
      - W.D. himself — 1
      - BLAISDON DRAUGHTSMAN — 2
      - BORO' DRAUGHTSMAN — 1
    - LYMM CHAMPION.... EATON NUNSUCH & 1 son — 2

LINCOLNSHIRE LAD II (91)
- CALWICH BLEND (9)
  - BABINGLEY NULLI SECUNDUS (8)
    - B.N.S. himself — 2
    - CHAMP' COMBINATION — 1
    - HARBORO' N.S. — 2
    - MOORS N.S. — 1
    - SUNDRIDGE COMING K. — 0
    - (SUNDRIDGE N.S.) — 1
    - WAYDALE N.S. — 0
    - (PENDLEY FOOTPRINT) — 1
    - BROWN PRINCE XIV
- ROYALIST COUNT ....
  - SOUTHGATE H. TOM..... CARLTON WHAT'S WANTED — 2
- MARMION II.... (2)

CARBON.. (3)
- MONTFORD JUPITER (3)....
  - BLAISDON JUPITER II — 1
  - GAER CONQUEROR — 2

POTENTATE (2)
- MOORS ZEALOT.......
- MOORS POTENTATE..
  - DUNSMORE JAMESON... WAINGROVES JAMESON — 1
  - SEVERN MASTERMAN .... WARE COMING KING — 1

WILLIAM THE CONQUEROR (40)
- HITCHIN CONQUEROR (31) see VII.6
- PRINCE WILLIAM (9)

MATCHLESS (1) via his g.g.g-son PREMIER see VIII.1

Others (0)

The process of selective elimination, which had reduced the effective sons of Lincolnshire Lad to one only, Lincolnshire Lad II; and had confined Lincolnshire Lad II's influence to Harold (the Carbon and Potentate lines still gradually fading out) and Harold's sons to eight and now five, was still at work, as may be seen (for example) among the descendants of Lockinge Forest King. This selection was natural rather than planned. Hoe Forest King at the age of seven won the senior under 16.2-hands class in 1911 for the new King: Marden Forest King won his class twice, in 1910–1911, for Sir Walpole Greenwell. Neither horse and neither owner can therefore be called obscure. So it was not for want of effort by Shire breeders that these two horses did not appear, in 1921 or afterwards, as sires and grand-sires of an ever-improving breed. Of the thirteen Lockinge Forest King sons which do appear in the table, Halstead Royal Duke had the best opportunities of all of founding a famous line, for he was the 1909 champion. But natural selection thwarts man's artificial attempts to turn breeding into too exact a science.

A brief biography follows of Lockinge Forest King, Childwick Champion and Babingley Nulli Secundus. If the choice of the last-named appears questionable, the answer is that his influence was due to grow enormously as the 'twenties progressed, and it is more sensible to discuss him now than later. The Tatton Friar strain was due to be continued only through Friar Tuck IV and it is therefore more convenient to postpone a comment on him (to section II).

7. LOCKINGE FOREST KING, 1899–1909

The sensational stallion of the new century had been Lockinge Forest King. Because he was responsible for starting the craze for superabundant feather that later proved to be an unwanted nuisance, he has already been described in the general survey of 1901–1914 (A.IX.3), as has his show-ring career, which ended at the age of three when he was reserve to the junior cup winner in London. But the question remains to be answered why a smallish narrow horse, not very masculine in appearance, with a light middle, who was never better than second best among the young ones at the Shire Show, and who would probably have been placed nowhere had he ever been exhibited as a mature animal, should start a craze like this. It was not in imitation of himself but simply because of the foals he left. In this he was a reincarnation of his g.g.g-sire Lincolnshire Lad II. His own assets were bones of the very flattest and hardest, and perfectly shaped hind legs. These he transmitted, together with qualities that were not apparent in himself. And of course he handed on that hairiness. The result was that all Shires, good, bad, and indifferent, had to be hairy, too, even if they possessed neither the blood nor the bone of Lockinge Forest King.

He was bred in 1899 by a little man with feather of his own, in the form of protruding sandy eyebrows, C. H. Eady, stud manager to Baron Wantage, K.C.B., V.C., on the 12,000 Berkshire acres of the Lockinge estate. On 12th February 1901, there was an astonishing sale of 51 home-bred Shire geldings at

PLATE 49   Erfyl Lady Grey. The only picture of this great beauty is not flattering.

PLATE 50   Grey ladies in five generations. Trimmer (20), Bonny (15), Jewel (9), Queenie (5) and Princess Marina (0), in 1934. Percy Cottrell, like his forebears at Abbots Bromley, Staffordshire bred all his own horses from good stallions but never registered one. Jack Brown worked over fifty years for the family. The two young men in the picture "lived in".

PLATE 51 "Keep you hat on, Griffin. I shall not mind." The President in 1927 (almost hidden) had not been well, and the King was solicitous. Morris Belcher receives his gold medal for reserve champion stallion. Charlton in attendance.

PLATE 52 Eaton Premier King was champion, not just reserve, the next three years. "Belcher," said His Majesty in 1928, "I do want to have a special look at your horse. He reminds me so much of my own". (See Plate 43).

Lockinge. Lord Wantage failed to act the part of host, but that was simply because the old hero lay on his death-bed, and died soon after. Eady then sold the two-year-old colt for Lady Wantage to J. P. Cross of Catthorpe Towers. When Cross also died in February 1906, the stallion was not retained by his son, but was bought by William Everard of Bardon Hall, Leicester, who had already made considerable use of him. On 23rd October the next year, he held a home sale jointly with Matthew Hubbard of Eaton, who contributed 32 horses. Fifteen of the thirty offered by Everard were young fillies by Lockinge Forest King and they made an average price of £222. Since the best two (460 and 440 guineas) did not unduly falsify the average, this was something amazing.

It was at Bardon, which, once he had arrived, he never left, that the horse was really set in breeding motion, for, like Harold and others of his line, he made a slow start as a stock-getter. In four years of service there, a constant succession of the most beautiful foals were begotten, as if on the production-line of some highly systematised factory. He had some great sons, but it was daughters in which he specialised. The whole thing must remain as great an object of astonishment now as it was then, for it was all over by the end of the 1909 season. W. T. Everard died that year and Charlie McKenna, the stud groom, could not – or perhaps he would not – persuade the son B.N. to keep him going, and the life of Lockinge Forest King ended in November. No one but Charlie and other employees had actually seen him for long before that. Lockinge Forest King's exceptional hair had brought its own retribution: he was grievously affected by grease or, more bluntly put, "greased up to his eyes". One could bring mares to him, but no one was never allowed to see him serve them. Mr. McKenna had to be trusted that it was the king of sires himself that attended to their needs. In most cases, the proof was plain a year later. It would have been almost safe for the Bardon stud to offer "money refunded, if not absolutely delighted".

To recite his best progeny would be tedious. Even at the 1908 show, all the first five two-year-old fillies were his daughters. In 1909, he was the sire of the champion stallion, champion mare, reserve champion mare, two other first prize winners, sixteen other prize-winners, seven "highly commendeds" and twelve "commendeds". So his sons and daughters won forty awards out of 292, excluding geldings – or forty out of only 245 if one excludes animals that were too old to be by him. Eleven others of his progeny were also exhibited. This fantastic performance was nearly equalled in 1910, when thirty-eight of his fifty sons and daughters at the show were rewarded. The eight-year-old champion of 1911, Pailton Sorais (the produce of one of his very first encounters with a mare, for he was given none as a two-year-old) was sold by Max Michaelis to Nicholson for 1,200 guineas, which remained a record for mares until the brief post-war boom.

John Bradley, a tenant farmer at Halstead, Leics., did as well from Lockinge Forest King as anyone ever did with one mare. His Halstead Duchess III was by Menestrel, a famous g-son of William the Conqueror. From her L.F.K. got

Halstead Royal Duke in 1906, and he was the London champion for Lord
Rothschild in 1909: in 1908 he got Halstead Blue Blood, third out of 107
two-year-olds in 1910, also for Lord Rothschild – this horse was to prove one
of the three L.F.K. sons who perpetuated his line; and in 1909 he got Halstead
Royal Duchess, winner of the junior cup in 1912 and of the 16–16.2 class in
1914 for Bradley himself: after Bradley's death she was the disqualified reserve
champion of 1920 (she failed to foal) and the winner of her class in 1922 when,
at thirteen, she was the oldest mare present. In the quality of Bradley's mare lay
the secret of her success when mated to this horse – if what is obvious can be
called a secret. Similarly Lockinge Forest King's own success is to be found in
the perfect judgement of the blend which was used in the breeding of his dam.
It is worth studying his pedigree briefly, if only to honour some of those other
foundation sires which the overwhelming popularity of the Harold line, used
as a top-cross, tends to leave in obscurity:

Sire: Lockinge Manners 16780: bay, blaze, four white legs. (By PRINCE HAROLD)
              bred 1896 by Lord Wantage.
   Sire's dam: 15079 Lady Marjorie: bay, blaze, white hind legs
                    (by Lord Arthur 9834, g-son of PREMIER: MATCHLESS line).
                    bred 1891 by Lord Wantage.
                    Once described as "a nearly perfect mare from a family of
                    nearly perfect mares."
   g-dam: 5085 Lady Victoria: bay, mottled face, one white hind leg
                    (by Prince William 3956 by WILLIAM THE CONQUEROR)
                    . bred 1886 by Lord Wantage.
   3rd dam: 2427 Glow: bay, (by Spark 2497, double London champion)
                    bred 1883 by Walter Gilbey.
   4th dam: 260 Carol: bay, (by Honest Prince 1058)
                    bred 1879 by Richard Wardle, Weston Underwood, Derby.
   5th dam: unrecorded.
Dam: 4470 The Forest Queen: brown, white hind legs. (By ROYAL ALBERT)
              bred 1885 by W. W. McGibbon, Rangemore, Staffs.
G-dam: 3436 Madam: brown, (By Hercules 1032)
              bred 1875 by Thos. Lowndes, Castern Hall, Ashbourne.
3rd d: *Mare* (by Sweet William 2093, g-son of MATCHLESS).
4th d: unrecorded.

There is a number of points worth considering which are not shown by the
short pedigree offered above:
   (i) Three of Lockinge Forest King's g.g.g-parents (that is 3/16 of that generation) are entirely unknown. Seven of the preceding generation (7/32) are
unknown: 32 of the previous one (32/64), more than half of the one before
that (65/128), and from there a rapidly increasing proportion.
   (ii) in spite of (i), Honest Tom 1060 was not only his progenitor in the male

line, but appears no less than 40 times altogether, even in the known pedigree.

(iii) Matchless appears four times in the known genealogy and Major three times.

(iv) As well as the recognised foundation sires, other celebrated names appear in the pedigree – e.g. Bakewell's G 890. And Hercules 1032 (who forms 1/8 of L.F.K.'s ancestry), though he contributed no known blood from the foundation sires, was descended in the male line from Ivens' *Grey Horse* (who manages to appear somewhere in all the best circles), and was out of a mare by Stych's Champion.

(v) In addition to (iii) and (iv), other ancient stallions, no doubt carefully bred and much prized in their day, though nothing is discoverable about them now, dimly appear – for example, Vawser's *Brown Stout*, about 1840; *Edmunds' Horse of Crick*, c. 1830; *Buck's Horse of Deeping*, c. 1825; Beckford's *Frolic* and Nutt's *Honest Tom* (one wonders how many Honest Toms there have been) about 1820; and so on, back to the eighteenth-century *Bodsley Gravel Horse*, who is an enigma indeed.

In such a way, then, by studying pedigrees, by hoping the gaps therein would not produce something odd, and by mysteries unfathomed, was Lockinge Forest King produced. In the next parish the same year, a man could try to form the same pattern, and be lucky to get something to make a railway gelding.

Lockinge Forest King's own sons had sons and daughters in plenty. But the three which effectively and prepotently carried on his branch of the family were not themselves the darlings of the show-ring, any more than he was:

(a) KING OF TANDRIDGE 24351 bred in 1905 by Max Michaelis, Tandridge Court, Oxted, Surrey out of the blue-blooded Rokeby Vesta. He won first prize at Reigate as a yearling and 3rd RASE: 5th at London 1907 and first (and reserve for junior cup) 1908. For four seasons he covered some of the most expensive mares in England. Michaelis then gave up his stud – on 26th October 1911, twenty-two stallions and sixty-two mares were sold for 15,110 guineas at Brook Farm, where most were kept. Many of the young animals were by King of Tandridge and seventeen of the mares had been covered by him that season. The London, Brighton and South Coast trains to Oxted, and those of the South-Eastern and Chatham railway too, were full of Shire men that day. King of Tandridge, sold for 1,600 guineas, did not have far to go – only a few stations along the S.E. and C.R. line from Godstone to Dorking, where he joined a similar stud owned by another amateur enthusiast, Leopold Salomons. He repaid the money twice over when let to Louth S.H.S. in 1912–1914 and to Crewe S.H.S. in 1915, quite apart from the succession of foals he got at Dorking. But Salomons died·in 1915 and the Shire stud was sold on 19th January the following year. The nine stallions and twenty-eight mares realised 11,796 guineas, of which Norbury Menestrel (the greatest agent of the day for the transmission of the William the Conqueror line of blood) made 3,000 guineas and King of Tandridge 2,000. These were remarkable prices, since the William the Conqueror representative was twelve and the Harold horse eleven. Later in the year, the whole of the magnificently beautiful 1,000-acre Norbury Park estate was sold and the death of Salomons, like that of Lord Rothschild, also in 1915, marks the end of an era when wealthy men often liked to be Shire fanciers. Lest one is tempted to criticise these unfairly in comparison with the practical breeder and farmer, it should be emphasised that King of Tandridge had been actually bred at Tandridge and Norbury Menestrel at Norbury Park. These men did not buy their way into Shire success by purchasing animals: they did so by employing such men as John Bastin who ran the Salomons farms, and Thornton, the Michaelis stud groom. King of Tandridge, unfortunately, did not repay his purchase price this time. After a second season at Crewe, which brought in a 1,100 guinea fee, he died in February 1917 of a twisted bowel, whereas Norbury Menestrel carried on until just before the start of the 1921 season.

(b) HALSTEAD BLUE BLOOD 27397 has already been mentioned. He came into Lord Rothschild's possession as a yearling, being bought from Bradley under the name "Halstead Sign of Riches". He was let to the Winslow SHS in 1911–1912 and 1914–1915, with the intervening year at home, and at the Tring Park dispersion sale, Edgar Appleby of Long Lawford, Rugby bought him for 1,550 guineas and had six seasons' use of him. His full brother, Halstead Royal Duke, more famous as a show horse, had developed a thick hock and went for 575 guineas.

(c) REDLYNCH FOREST KING 23626. Bred in 1904 by John Harper, Lilbourne Lodge, Rugby, who had to register the dam hastily in order that Percy Taunton of Redlynch, Wilts, the purchaser, could register him. His highest prize in two London appearances was seventh in 1905. Sold to Sir William Cooke, Wheatley Park, Doncaster that year, and to Sir Arthur Nicholson in 1908. His premature demise in November 1912 was a blow to all Shire men. Even in his short career under the care of the perfectionist head man at Leek, George Croft, he sired more prize-winners than all stallions in Shire history except these eight – Harold: Lockinge Forest King: Childwick Champion, his son Champion's Goalkeeper, and his g-son Basildon Clansman; Babingley Nulli Secundus; Norbury Menestrel, of William the Conqueror descent; and Dunsmore Jameson, g-son of Potentate, son of Lincolnshire Lad II. Had he lived even to the modest age of twelve, he might have become the greatest sire after Harold; or perhaps the greatest of all.

8. CHILDWICK CHAMPION, 1903–1924

This marvellous horse deserves a biography for three reasons. Most importantly, it is through him much more than through Lockinge Forest King that the modern Shire is descended, as will be seen. Secondly, he was the sire of both the stallion and the mare which made the record prices in Shire history. Thirdly, it is quite certain that more money changed hands in respect of him, either by sale or letting or fee, than any other Shire that has lived.

1903. He was bred by A. W. Richman at the stud farm of Sir J. Blundell
Maple, the upholsterer, near his home, Childwickbury, St. Albans. His sire,
Childwick Majestic, stood 17 hands on very short legs, had immense bone and
good quality feather, was said to leave 85% of his mares in foal, and served at
10 guineas (5 guineas to tenant-farmers). His dam, Blythwood Laurel was by
Ercall Wynn (by Lincolnshire Lad II). Maple died that same year, aged fifty-
eight.

1904. At the dispersal of the Childwick stud he was bought by Lord
Rothschild. His arrival at Tring Park was vividly remembered nearly seventy
years later by Arthur Gutteridge, retired shoesmith but in those days on the
stable staff at Tring. "Now in 1904 a particular thing I remember, was having to
go to Tring Station one Saturday afternoon to fetch a couple of young horses,
both from Childwick. One was a yearling colt and the other, a two-year-old
filly, and all I thought about at the time was worrying if they'd be all right to
lead together. But they were as good as gold. The filly was called Childwick
Girlie, and she turned out a real plain one, and never did much good. The
other was Childwick Champion, and he looked a tough little bugger – a real
rough 'un with all hair hanging down over his belly. Never would have
thought he'd have grown so big. When he was mature, he was a beauty – a
real good big 'un. And as quiet as a lamb. He was a wonderful stock getter.
Never a better horse lived, probably. And to think all I cared about was
whether he behaved himself on the way home and then, when I saw him,
I thought what a funny little devil he looked. Still, when you are 18, you don't
know everything. The next Saturday I had to go and fetch two more, two
fillies, and I can't even remember what they were. But it was 67 years ago."
Childwick Girlie was also by Childwick Majestic.

1905. First at London, Peterborough, Royal Lancs., and R.A.S.E. (where he
was reserve for championship). Served one or two mares at home.

1906. First and reserve for junior cup, London. Let to R. W. Hudson,
Danesfield, Marlow for limited number of mares. (Hudson had just succeeded
Rothschild as S.H.S. president.) Now grown into a heavy and hirsute sort
that Rothschild, Richardson Carr his agent and Tom Fowler his Shire
manager, loved to see. He was somewhat coarse-limbed but had wonderful
feet.

1907–1908. Let to Montgomeryshire S.H.S. Left an outstanding crop of
foals. The verdict on him was that he did as much good as Lincolnshire Lad II
and Carbon, 1886–1891. One foal got in 1908 was Lorna Doone for Thomas
Green. Fowler purchased her as a foal, and sold her to the Whitley brothers at
Paignton, for whom she was champion mare 1914–1916. C.C. himself was
reserve London champion in 1908.

1909. Let to Welbeck Tenants S.H.S. At home, he sired Champion's
Clansman, the one-eyed champion.

1910–1912. Let to Montgomeryshire S.H.S. In 1910 (second S.H.S.), he got
Champion's Goalkeeper for the Earl of Powis. Tom Fowler in 1911, scouring

the area of his previous year's visit, as usual, bought Goalkeeper as a foal, and as a yearling, 1912, he was reserve champion at the Royal.

1913. Let to Welbeck Tenants' No. 1 Society. (At the Tring Park sale of young Shires, up to three years old, on 14th February, the two-year-old Champion's Goalkeeper was sold for 4,100 guineas, which has for ever after remained a record price for a Shire stallion. The buyer was Sir Walpole Greenwell, whose chief rival, C. R. H. Gresson of the Edgcote Shorthorn Co. near Banbury, gave up at 4,000 guineas. The excitement at the sale was intense. "Up the ring he came", a spectator recalled, "a type of the Shire one seldom sees, except in dreams. Weighty and massive, yet full of wonderful quality, with the action of a hackney and the force and power of a mature stallion." He was London champion twelve days later and again the next year, 1913–1914, but developed over the years a coarseness that in no way helped the breed. He died in 1928 still at Marden Park, in the possession of Sir Walpole's son, Sir Bernard. At the 1913 Tring sale, three yearling colts and three other two-year-colts by C. Champion made a total of 1965 guineas.)

1914. Let to Fred W. Ibbotson, Langwith, Notts, who until the previous year had been a member of the Welbeck Tenants' association. When they decided to change to another horse, Ibbotson resigned and hired him personally. Among the foals he left this year was Gleadthorpe Seclusion for Tom Kay (member of a Sheffield haulage family) at Cuckney, Mansfield. Tom Kay died and she was bought by Arthur Grimes of Gleadthorpe, one of three great Shire brothers in the area. (After she had become champion mare at London in 1920, she was sold at the Society's auction for 4,600 guineas to David Davies – the record figure for any Shire, including stallions. She was in foal to Norbury Menestrel and duly produced Hafren Invincible on 25th May. She was served again on 7th June, but died of a ruptured diaphragm on 24th November, aged five. By way of compensation Invincible, her only living produce – she had had a foal, born dead, in 1919 – served one thousand and fourteen Pla Dinam and other Montgomeryshire mares in 1923–1931.)

1915. Sold after Lord Rothschild's death at his dispersal sale for 2,300 guineas to R. L. Mond, Combe Bank, Sundridge, near Sevenoaks, who also bought Babingley Nulli Secundus (q.v.). Fred Ibbotson would dearly have liked him – but what farmer could match that price? So he gave 600 guineas for Friar Tuck IV – see section II. (Champion's son, Champion's Clansman the one-eyed horse, having, as one commentator put it, "forged his way through the living alley into the ring", was bought for 1,900 guineas by Sir Arthur Nicholson – a long and deep horse of 17.3-hands with limbs, feet and joints of the finest quality, as was his silky hair. He became London champion in 1917). Champion himself was already under contract to travel the Market Harborough district for Mr. Fernie's Hunt Shire Horse Committee.

1916. Stood at his unfamiliar Kent home.

1917–1918. Back to Market Harborough.

1919. At home.

1920. Market Harborough S.H.S.

1921. Market Harborough again. On 19th October 1921, Mond prematurely gave up his short-lived but famous stud and at the dispersal Fred Ibbotson at last got the horse he had used often, hired once and long coveted. He had to pay 775 guineas, Champion was now eighteen years old, and prices had started to tumble at the beginning of the disastrous slump. But he was satisfied.

At the sale, descendants of Champion fetched varying prices which reflect as much the anxious times as the eternal chanciness of horse-breeding. Of his sons, a four-year-old made 34 guineas, a three-year-old attracted no bids and a yearling made 320 guineas: a two-year-old daughter made 800 guineas and a yearling 255 guineas. A stallion and a mare out of two of his daughters made 300 guineas each. Five Shires, of which two of his daughters were the g-dams, made 700, 180, 150, 70 and 40 guineas. He himself travelled happily to Nottinghamshire, the perfect type of the old-fashioned heavy breeding stallion.

1922. Once again to Market Harborough. (He was already under contract to return there when Fred Ibbotson bought him.) The old stalwart successfully completed his season, and so the hiring fee of £1,000 repaid his purchase price, his keep and a little bit over.

1923. He stood at home.

1924. Childwick Champion died at the last. Almost no details of his letting fees have survived, but the horse must have brought his four owners at least £10,000 in hire and service, as well as about 3,300 guineas the three times he was sold.

9. BABINGLEY NULLI SECUNDUS, 1908–1924

This horse, the youngest of the three, actually belonged to an 'earlier' generation, since he was a grandson of Harold. He was bred in 1908 by Edward Betts of Babingley, near King's Lynn. The Betts family, in various parts of Norfolk, can be traced back in connexion with heavy horse breeding to the 1790s, when one of them, of Forncett, was advertising a Suffolk stallion. Over the Suffolk border one Edmund Betts bred a "Suffolk bay" called Turnstile in 1804. Captain W. H. Betts of Frenze Hall, Diss in 1877 bought a two-year-old Suffolk colt called Indian Prince, which according to Herman Biddell, "at the Diss meeting of the Norfolk A.S. went amiss" and was thereafter used as a gelding on the farm. Then Capt. Betts turned to Shires and bought Sir John Falstaff, Waggoner and Wonderful Tom: in 1879 he also bought a young son of Marsters' England's Wonder. Like father, like son: he was named Strawberry Wonder.

It is therefore not surprising that young Edward should follow the example and set up as a Shire man, though perhaps the real incentive was the fact that he was a tenant on the Prince of Wales' Sandringham estate. He made the name Babingley known all over the Shire world, but it was Babingley Nulli Secundus which sealed his fame. The horse's breeding gives some reason for his success:

Sire: CALWICH BLEND, now owned by the King.
dam: 40775 Babingley Violet (bred by Betts, 1902)
       by Premvictor 19947 (one of Edward VII's most famous stallions),
       son of Bury Victor Chief, 1892/4 London champion.
g.d. 27415 Babingley Regina (bred by Joseph Grimes, Palterton, Chesterfield,
       in 1897) by REGENT II.
3rd dam: 24472 Palterton Quality (bred by T. A. Smith, Coton-in-the-Clay,
       Staffs in 1894)
       by Newton Ranger 13391 by ROYAL ALBERT.
4th dam: *Mettle* (bred by G. L. White, Egginton, Derby. in 1886)
       by ROYAL ALBERT.

Babingley Nulli Secundus picked up a few minor prizes in 1908 as a foal with his dam, and also as a yearling, after which he came under the divining eye of Tom Fowler, that genius who could look at a colt and see a stallion. So E. W. Betts soon had a cheque from Lord Rothschild instead of his brown horse.

Fowler was right. As a three-year-old, Babingley N.S. was taken to London and won his class and the junior cup, and was reserve to the champion. He was let to Spalding S.H.S. that year. The next year, he was fifth in that most amazing of all stallion classes (mentioned in A.IX.6), placed just in front of the future champion Blaisdon Jupiter and Betts' own-bred Babingley Forest King. That was the last of his show appearances. After standing at Tring that year, he was let to Mr. Fernie's Hunt in 1913–1914 and to the Montgomeryshire Society (which comes into the life of every best horse in the land) in 1915. His success there was phenomenal, almost equal to Childwick Champion's, but he was never to return. At the dispersal of the late Lord Rothschild's stud, R. L. Mond, to set up his own new one, paid 5,450 guineas for just three cart-horses – 2,300 guineas for Childwick Champion, 2,500 guineas for Babingley Nulli Secundus and 650 for the yearling Champion's Combination 33096. The latter was indeed a fine combination, being by Babingley N.S. out of a Childwick Champion mare, bred not at Tring but by Arthur Whittle of Great Glen, Leics: he took first prize the next year in London.

So B.N.S., now an enormous horse of tremendous width and depth and bidding fair to become the heaviest stallion in England (and not the least rugged and rough) continued his partnership with Childwick Champion, though most of his active service was spent on behalf of the members of the Melton Mowbray S.H.S. for whom he put in five seasons (1916 and 1918–1921, with one year at home).

When Mond gave up his stud in 1921, six years almost to the day after the dispersal sale at Tring Park, Childwick Champion and Babingley N.S. at last parted company. The old horse cost Ibbotson 775 guineas, and J. Q. Rowett paid 600 guineas to take the thirteen-year-old B.N.S. into Sussex. (Their joint-production, Champion's Combination, was bought by the Atherstone Shire Horse Society for 300 guineas – a reasonable risk, for they had hired him in

1919 and 1920 and he was due to come to them again the following year in any case.) John Rowett, as has been mentioned, bought a number of Mond horses to begin his new stud, including Sundridge Nulli Secundus, the son of B.N.S. He also took over Alfred Millen, Mond's head man.

B.N.S. impressed his enormous weight for a couple of seasons on all the mares sent to him in Sussex. But he got ready for the 1924 season with such zeal that he became afflicted with paralysis and had to be destroyed. His ex-colleague Childwick Champion died the same year. And in the October John Rowett died too, and that is the end of the story.

As a postscript, we select, from all Babingley Nulli Secundus' manifold progeny of superlative quality, those two sons through whom the magic of Wiseman's Honest Tom, the Lincolnshire Lads and Harold was to be chiefly perpetuated. (Their importance becomes apparent in the 1939 table in section 11.)

HARBOROUGH NULLI SECUNDUS 33231, foaled 1914. Bred by W. T. Hayr of Tur Langton, Leics. Sold to the Whinnerah brothers of Warton, Lancs. Seventh prize as a yearling and in 1917 reserve for the junior cup. Sold to Mrs. Stanton, and was reserve champion in the next year. "High-mettled" or "a dangerous old sod", according to one's choice (character is in the eye of the handler), he carried off the championship in 1922–1923 (A.XI.10). Not long before the 1939 war, Tom Forshaw said that "He has helped to improve the quality of the Shire of late years. He was a horse I always greatly admired. Plenty of size, 17.2-hands, grand dark brown colour, with white face and white legs, limbs of wonderful quality, feather like silk, and a gay, high courage." His gaiety, increasingly boisterous, was not always shared by those who had to deal with him, in some of whom regret was not unmixed with relief when he had to be put down and the bull-staff they found it prudent to lead him by could be laid aside, in June 1924, three months after his sire. Had he lived in an earlier age, he would have terrified the King's enemies. An interesting example of how bias, either against a horse or its owner, can occasionally cloud both the judgement and the memory was provided by the man who insisted in later years, and could not be persuaded otherwise, that Harborough N.S. was "useless as a sire. For all his randiness, he never bred a bloody donkey".

SUNDRIDGE NULLI SECUNDUS 36952. Bred in 1918 by Allan Holm of Tilton, Leics. Stood 17.3-hands. First prize 1920–1921 for Mond, winning the junior cup the second year. Bought by Rowett for 3,100 guineas at the sale. First, third, second and reserve champion 1922–1924. Bought by Mrs. Stanton on Rowett's death, to succeed Harborough N.S. Second, fourth and fourth in 1925–1927. Even in the dark days of 1927, his fee was 10 guineas and the Peterborough A.S., hiring him the following year, charged 10 guineas to non-members and £6 10s. od. to members. At the Snelston dispersal in January 1930, he was bought by Sam Foster of Church Broughton, Derbys. for 200 guineas. His great days were now over, but he could still be justifiably advertised in the way he had always been — "Rare breeding! Size! Weight! Constitution! Activity!"

10. TOM FOWLER AND THE LORD

If Lord Rothschild had bought up winning horses at top prices it would not have been surprising, though he would still have needed his Tom Fowler to maintain and produce them at their best. But he did not do that. He generally bought young animals, which needed a foreseeing eye such as few possess, though of course it must be admitted that Fowler could afford to make more mistakes than would have been comfortable if he were relying on his own resources. But he did much more than pick out future prize-winners. By some sort of sheer genius, he selected just those colts that lived to become not only great sires, but even more than that, those which were to become the chief fathers of all succeeding generations. And these ancestors of the modern Shire were all at Tring Park together. Since this is undoubtedly the most astonishing achievement in the whole history of the breed, and was of its very nature one that could not be appreciated until long after the event, it must be recorded here.

When Lord Rothschild's death ended his stud, there were ten senior stallions for disposal. If we add another which had dropped dead of heart failure two years earlier, we find among these eleven the following:

1. Halstead Blue Blood, aged seven, bought as a yearling. One of the three sons of Lockinge Forest King which proved most successful in the long term.

2. Childwick Champion himself, aged twelve, bought as a yearling.

3. Champion's Clansman, the best breeding son of Childwick Champion, bred at Tring Park.

4. Babingley Nulli Secundus himself, aged seven, bought as a yearling.

5. Friar Tuck IV, the most successful breeding grandson of Tatton Friar. Aged six, he was the only one not bought young. But in fact he started his career very late, and was not registered until the age of four, coming to Tring the next year.

6. Birdsall Menestrel, now aged fifteen, bought as a yearling (sire of Norbury Menestrel), and

7. Blythwood King Maker, foaled 1899 and aged fourteen when he died, bought as a yearling. These two were the most successful sons, again as far as prepotency is concerned, of Menestrel and Blythwood Conqueror respectively: the two latter were the chief breeding sons of Hitchin Conqueror: and he was the most pre-potent son of William the Conqueror.

If the reader will look at the 1921 show table in section 6, he will find that the first five horses among these seven were the ancestors of forty-nine of the eighty-six Harold winners: the other two were the ancestors of twenty-five of the forty winners belonging to the William the Conqueror line. Of the stallions registered in 1939 (section 11), 158 of the 217 in the Harold line, and eighteen of the twenty-one in the William the Conqueror line, were descended from these. That is, of the 238 Shire stallions registered only twenty-four years after the end of the Tring Park stud, 176 were the direct descendants of these six horses.

Beside this uncanny knack of having chosen, virtually at babyhood, the very colts of the new century which would become the forefathers of almost all modern Shires (and it must be remembered that eight or nine hundred pedigree colts a year were being registered in those days), the ability of being able to spot mere prizewinners, even mere champions, pales into insignificance. Blaisdon Jupiter, bought as a two-year-old, and Halstead Royal Duke (Halstead Blue Blood's full brother), bought as a yearling, were two others among the ten stallions at the 1915 sale. Both, like Birdsall Menestrel, were London champions. But what are three London champions in the same stud, compared with six with the magic seed that was potent to the third and fourth generation? It was as if God had looked upon Nathan Rothschild at Tring Park, much as upon Jacob at Bethel, and chosen these stallions to multiply their seed more than that of any others. Old employees of Tring Park tended to refer to their master as "the lord" – for example, the present writer has been told that "the lord always came round to the stables on his cob on a Saturday morning". Though confusing, the term seems to have some point.

11. SIRES OF THE NEW GENERATION

It may be remembered that the majority of those present at the first London Show in 1880 (and they were mostly horse men, for the general public was more or less unaware of it) expressed themselves surprised that there was any such thing as "pedigree" in the common English cart-horse. By 1939, the Society had not only proved that there was, but had contrived to narrow all the lines of breeding to just two, of which one proved so popular and successful that 91% of all the new stallions of the year traced directly to him. This had been achieved in one life-time. Indeed, Tom Forshaw of Carlton-on-Trent had literally seen it all happen, for he had been present at every single one of those sixty Shire Horse Shows.

If therefore, instead of looking at those choice creatures of beauty which were paraded at the sixtieth and last London Show, we examine the breeding of all the colts which their owners submitted that year for registration, we shall obtain a more accurate picture of the position which the pedigree movement had reached. These colts duly appeared in Volume 61 in February, 1940. Alas, too few remained entire and served their quota of mares. But that is irrelevant.

In connexion with the table overleaf, a few points are worth emphasis:

(a) The 238 stallions are all descended directly from ten which were foaled between 1899 and 1908 – a single decade only thirty to forty years before. In the twelve volumes in which the registrations of these ten are scattered, no less than 11,595 stallions altogether were entered. On the face of it, one would have expected the 238 to trace to more than ten of these.

(b) Of the 238, 135 were foaled in 1938, 70 in 1937, 26 in 1935–1936, three in 1930–1934, and four in 1925–1928. The delayed registration of the oldest seven, in particular, was partly caused by the aftermath of the bad times in 1922–1934, when breeding, and registration, were neglected by many. These older horses were entered now in order to enable their produce to qualify.

DESCENT OF THE 238 STALLIONS REGISTERED IN VOLUME 61

I	2	3	4

PRINCE HAROLD...... (26)   LOCKINGE MANNERS.....

ROKEBY FRIAR......... (109)   CHILDWICK MAJESTIC.....

LINCOLNSHIRE LAD II (217)   HAROLD (217)

CONQUERING HAROLD (23)   TATTON FRIAR*...... (15)
LYMM LION*... (8)

CALWICH BLEND (32)   BABINGLEY NULLI SECUNDUS... (32)
—

MARMION II .... (27)   SOUTHGATE H. TOM......

—   —

—   —

—   —

WILLIAM THE CONQ. (21)   HITCHIN CONQUEROR (18)
PRINCE WILLIAM (3)

—Others (0)

5   **6**

      —
      —
      —
      —

LOCKINGE   HALSTEAD BLUE BLOOD   2
FOREST   —
KING   —
(26)   KING OF TANDRIDGE   23 [a]
       —
       —
       —
       REDLYNCH F.K.   1

—
—

CHILDWICK   CHAMPION'S CLANSMAN   38
CHAMPION   —
(109)   CHAMP' GOALKEEPER   18
       —
       EATON ABBOT   22 [b]
       MIMMS CHAMPION   31 [c]
       —

FRIAR JOHN …   F. TUCK IV*   15
—   —
            —

LYMM
CHAMPION…   EATON NUNSUCH*   8

CHAMP' COMBINATION   5
HARBORO' N.S.   14
—
SUNDRIDGE N.S.   11
—
PENDLEY FOOTPRINT*   2
—

CARLTON W.W.   LINCOLN W. WANTED II*   27

Notes
   [a] 16 via his son MARCH KING*
   [b] All via his g-son SEEDSMAN*
   [c] All via g-son KIRKLAND MIMIC*

(c) The numbers in Volume 61 were reduced by the outbreak of war in September 1939, causing late entries to be neglected. But the overall picture is not distorted.

(d) Among the descendants of Harold, the Prince Harold line via Lockinge Forest King has shown the usual narrowing-down. And it has been outstripped by the Rokeby Friar line via Childwick Champion. (This is perhaps not altogether surprising, for L.F.K's best progeny were the fillies.) The Tatton Friar branch of the Conquering Harold line has been narrowed down to one g-son only. The Calwich Blend line has done well through Babingley Nulli Secundus. Marmion II's line, which appeared to have such a tenuous grip on life, has flourished exceedingly, through one single branch. Of other direct descendants of Harold, or of his sire Lincolnshire Lad II, there are none. (For convenience, some details of the two lines from William the Conqueror have been given also.)

N.B. Most of the stallions which appear here have been already commented on, in sections 7-9. The following notes, of somewhat skeletal nature, about others marked * complete the ancestral picture, but should be read in the knowledge that many other wonderful horses than these were bred in the 'twenties and 'thirties, some of which, as individuals or as sires, have a bigger claim on our attention. A few have received some small tribute already (Part A) but unfortunately some magnificent examples of what the pedigree movement produced will not appear on these pages at all. We here concentrate, as before, on prepotency through several generations.

MARCH KING 34955 had a short life. Bred in 1916 by Dr. H. H. Truman at March, he was grey, out of the grey Abingworth Gipsy. (For his grey antecedents, see Appendix 10d.)

Bought as yearling by the Forshaws, he grew to be 17.2-hands with a giant framework, a tremendous span of bone and a somewhat funny temper to go with it. He was described by a rapturous beholder as "perfect for all his mighty frame in proportion to build. He stands on splendid feet, with legs of magnificent bone and muscle, and moves with a grand action full of energy and spirit. He is masculine enough in character to satisfy any critic of present-day stallions." He was let in 1920 to Crewe S.H.S. for 1,000 guineas, and the Newark & District S.H.S., which had been angling for him for eighteen months, secured him for 1921 at 2,000 guineas, the record fee for a Shire stallion – on condition that he was not shown in London.

This most expensive of all travelling stallion routes started from March King's own home at Carlton-on-Trent, for the Newark Society operated in the Forshaws' own country. On Monday mornings he left for Baines' yard in Newark, where he arrived at 10.15. From there he went on to Coddington and Beckingham, and then retraced his steps to Barnby Manor, where Mrs. Platt, following her late husband's example, was a great supporter, financial and otherwise, of the Newark Society. On Tuesdays, he took the bridle road to

Claypole and on to Long Bennington to stay the night at the chairman's, W. B. Bingham. From there on Wednesday he would walk to Staunton, Cotham and Hawton, where he had a three-hour stop at Ben Farrow's to bait before going back into Newark to meet the mares on market-day. On Thursday, he was out again to Kelham, Rolleston and through field and by-way to Hockerton. Fridays took him via Knapthorpe, Caunton, Norwell (baiting at the secretary's, Everitt Brown) and on to the Forshaws'. On Saturday he made a short day-trip, to Crow Park Farm, Weston, and back. By the time he finished his three months' walking, and Hardy had been paid his usual £2 gift by the members, there was something obviously wrong with prices. When a great crop of marvellous foals was dropped the following year, the slump was really on, and the stout men of Newark failed to get the reward that their initiative in breaking a record had merited.

One of the Long Bennington men, R. T. Sumner, said[1] of the matter almost fifty years later, "Yes, I remember March King. When Newark had him at a big price I wouldn't use him – too expensive. Lord Middleton used to send two round in them days and I used one of them, it was less money. They used to send the best one up round Stragglethorpe and then swop him with ours for the last week of the season. The Horncastle Society came to Tom Forshaw and said they wanted a grey and wanted one with hair. Tom brought March King out for them to see and he had hair all over his toes and they said, 'We're having that bugger, never mind the cost.' "

But it was not to be. In 1922, the horse stood at home, at a fee of 25 guineas a mare. That year he made his first and only London appearance, being placed third in the big stallions' class, behind Harborough Nulli Secundus, the champion, and Rievaulx Friar. The latter, as has been observed (A.XI and A.XII), had a long and successful show career, but did almost nothing to further pedigree breeding, and absolutely nothing to improve the Shire breed. It is ironic that March King should stand below him on the one occasion they were judged together. Owing to the slump, the Forshaws advertised him for 1923 at 15 guineas. But he died at the very commencement of the season, of a twisted bowel. So he had only four seasons of service – two years less even than Redlynch Forest King.

The full extent of the influence this magnificent creature might have exerted on the breed, had he lived even to a moderate age, is impossible to guess: but the transmission of his grey colour provides a ready check on the potency of his brief exertions. From 1884 to 1920 the number of greys among Shire stallions had dropped steadily from 12% to 2.4%: grey mares had fluctuated rather more, but a general overall decline reduced them from 9% to 3.2%. In the 1939 volume of the Stud-book, 69 out of 304 stallions (22.7%) were grey, as were 129 of 1,102 mares (11.7%). The peak was reached in 1944 – 38.5% grey stallions (76 of 197) and 25.5% grey mares (207 of 815). And this was simply caused by the short-lived March King, mainly through his sons Ponton Pioneer and Elwyn March King, and his grandson, Carlton Grey Kingmaker via Grey

King Carlton. (For Carlton Grey Kingmaker's son Lymm Grey King, see A.XIV.5.)

There is a postscript. Ben Farrow, at whose place March King baited on Wednesdays, was a great friend of Tom Forshaw, who used to say that he was the best judge of a foal in England. As a result of one of March King's visits, he got a nice grey colt out of an unregistered mare. In 1925 it won the London gelding championship for George Marsh and his son Baker, of Speke. The gelding was appropriately called Uncle Ben, because by then his breeder had died, prematurely like March King, at the age of forty-six. And that was not all, for Tom Forshaw's son was killed in a car accident with young Rowland Farrow.

SEEDSMAN 39589, like Kirkland Mimic (below) was owned in his early days by Robert Stuart of Kirkland in the Fylde, a shrewd picker of a foal. Bred by W. & J. Sumner of Fulwood, Preston, in 1923, he was by Hadlow Prince William (surely the hairiest horse of the century) by Eaton Abbot, the latter being one of the innumerable stallions bred and retained by the Duke of Westminster. Seedsman was bought by Mrs. Stanton for 1,050 guineas after he won 3rd prize in London, 1926: he was second in 1927. He was well-named, for he achieved all his success as a sire in three brief seasons, dying in August 1928. He is another of the great "might-have-beens" in sire and Shire history.

KIRKLAND MIMIC 39739 was by Horning Mimic, by Mimms Champion, who was foaled in 1907. Mimms Champion never appeared in London and devoted all his life to producing hundreds and thousands of fine foals – he was still doing so in 1921 long after his breeder Daniel Crawford of Hatfield, Herts, was dead. But it was only through one son, and this one grandson, that pedigree stock was to continue and increase. Kirkland Mimic was bred in the Fens by Frank White and his sons at Chapel Hill, Whaplode Drove in 1924, their first year at this farm. His dam was 83629 Aldwick Queen. (Foaled in 1915, she was by the outstanding stock horse King Cole 7th 26351, which Tom Dibble had taken to Shopnoller in 1911 on the death of Lord Winterstoke and would not let out of the county of Somerset until 1916 – and then with a fatal result, for the horse was drowned in the Welland while pursuing his duties for the Peterborough A.S. Aldwick Queen was bred by H. J. Dibble of Aldwick Court Farm, Wrington, Somerset (no relation to her sire's owner) and was from a long line of brown mares owned and bred by W. L. Roe and his father before him at Rexworthy, near Bridgwater. So, on the female side, Mimic's ancestry was pure Zummerzet.)

The Whites sold their foal to Robert Stuart at the Kirkland Stud Farm, Garstang, who also baptised (if that is not the wrong word) the wild Kirkland Black Friar. He in turn sold him to A. W. C. Butler of the Finstall Stud Farm, Bromsgrove, Worcs, for whom he won first prize and the junior cup in London in 1927, and was then let to the Crewe & District S.H.S. In 1928 he was hired by the Carmarthen society and in 1929 by the Atherstone Hunt & District S.H.S. When the Finstall stud finished in 1930, he was bought by Enoch

PLATE 53 Plastered with mud. Hauling timber in February 1931, near Hildenborough, Kent. This was one of the worst jobs Shires were called upon to do, and the working life of those regularly employed in the trade was short.

PLATE 54 All spruced up. In the 'thirties, cleanliness, fitness for the job and general management were judged as rigorously as ever in Regent's Park—but the vehicles were not so heavy-laden as in the old days with brothers, sisters, aunts, uncles, cousins and kids.

PLATE 55 Liverpool Dock Horses. Two horses often pulled 12-ton loads on the level dock-sides. Much more was within their power as the tests in 1924 had proved. Note the typical broad wheels.

PLATE 56 The day Birkenhead won. At the Hoylake Show in 1934, the Corporation team of six beat Liverpool, for the first time in memory. Veterinary Superintendent Harold Burrow is just visible on the right of this special celebration photo.

PLATES 57 and 58   The Peterborough scene. (*above*) Filly foals at the Shire Stallion Produce
Stakes in 1930. Their dams wait patiently while they are judged; (*below*) Autumn sunshine
and lengthening shadows at the Repository during the sale following the show.

PLATE 59 A perfect gelding. There were many but Norman is chosen here, not because he won the London championship twice for Mann, Crossman and Paulin but because he appeared at twelve consecutive Shows (1927–1938) transferring in 1934 to the "commercial" working classes.

PLATE 60 Mares moving house, from Bletchingdon, Oxfordshire to Shropshire. Norman's unrecorded dam was bred in Oxfordshire and was no doubt such a mare as these.

Bostock who let him to the Warwick & District S.H.S. in 1931–1933, to the Derbyshire A.S. in 1934–1937 and finally to the Newcastle (Staffs) & District in 1938, in which year he died. His two outstanding sons were Harborough Goldfinder and Old House Conquering Mimic, who monopolised the London championship 1935–1938.

The most successful sire of the 'thirties, in temperament he was the very reverse of the fearsome Kirkland Black Friar. He was as kind to mare or groom as he was prepotent, and stamped his best qualities on the great majority of the foals he sired. He was slightly bent over at the knees and some of his progeny inherited that peculiarity but, unlike him, they invariably straightened up as they reached the yearling stage. If ever a horse's memory was revered by those who had to deal with him, it was that of Kirkland Mimic.

TATTON FRIAR 21953 was bred in 1900 by John Ball of Shortwick, Cheshire out of a mare by a grandson of Honest Tom 1105. Earl Egerton of Tatton took him the 26 miles to Tatton Hall and registered him rather late in life. He won three London prizes, the best being in 1907 when he was reserve champion. He was sold in 1909 for 1,100 guineas to Sidney Grimes of Scarcliffe Grange – a return to the land of his mothers, for Henry Grimes, who had died the year he was foaled, had bred his grand-dam in 1887. But Tatton Friar had only one season in the Bolsover district before rupturing a blood vessel in March 1910. (Tatton Friar was the dam's sire of Harborough Nulli Secundus (section 9) and of the one-eyed 1917 Champion, Champion's Clansman son of Childwick Champion (section 8). He was also sire of the 1912 champion, Warton Draughtsman.)

FRIAR TUCK IV 31447 began very late in life. He was four when sold in 1913 by his breeder, Herbert Lees of New House Farm, Warwick to Sir Herbert Leon, Bletchley Park, who registered him in the 1914 volume. He was then sold to Lord Rothschild and at the 1915 sale to Fred Ibbotson for 600 guineas. His useful career terminated with a twisted bowel in September 1918.

LYMM LION 18892 was bred in 1899 at Arley in Cheshire by James Whitlow, and taken up the road to Lymm as a foal by James Gould. He never went to London, for in those days Gould was still busy building up his business with a stallion or two to travel. Then came a few mares, then a move to a bigger place in 1906. Only after that, slowly and in spite of disheartening bad luck, grew the fame of the Shire breeder who, perhaps more than any, fitted the description of "not going in for talking, only for thinking". But Lymm Lion had died of a chill contracted in a wet spell during his travels in June 1909.

EATON NUNSUCH 27301 may have come out of The Nun, but he was an unholy terror. To describe him politely, he was a pig of a horse. He was bred in 1908 by the Duke of Westminster, and was third and second London 1911–1912. When he was let to the Wem & District S.H.S., the man in charge of him walked out after a week, valuing his life more than his wages. So a boy, George Chubb, went down to travel him for a week until a replacement could be found. Then, after a while, the second man gave up abruptly and, to judge from his language, was subject to nightmares for some while afterwards. John Crowe (one of four brothers who had come from Scotland to manage different English studs) sent for young George again. But George refused. Eventually they got to the root of his objection. "I won't go on a boy's wages, to do work that two men couldn't do. I'll only go if you give me man's wages – *and* if you let me finish the season out as well." He had his way. He was about the only employee at Eaton Hall who did not sigh in relief when the furious horse's career was terminated in August 1915. Nunsuch was by Lymm Champion by Lymm Lion.

PENDLEY FOOTPRINT 37728 was bred in 1919 at Pendley Manor, Tring by J. G. Williams, whose successors, Harry Bishop (his former manager) and John Measures, at their great 1920 sale splendidly publicised this colt. Someone waxed literary, quoting George Borrow – "the best colt in Mother England". Perhaps the Scotsmen thought so, too, for there were several at the sale specially to bid for him. But the business was over in no time.

"What shall I say for him?" asked Mr. Beck.

A still, small voice on his left said, "2,000".

A few people laughed nervously. Some applauded.

"2,200", said another voice on the left.

"Three hundred". This was the Shire President, Sir Arthur Nicholson, who in his time had spent a lot of money at Tring, and had recently lost Champion's Clansman of the single eye just as his stock were making a name.

Everyone whose fond ideas of possessing Footprint had vanished now looked forward to watching some fun. But there was no further bid. As the near-perfect young Shire passed out of the haze of smoke on his way to Leek, Mr. Beck said "And I hope Sir Arthur has the best of luck with him". He deserved to, for this was the highest price ever paid for a yearling colt in Shire history. And this "yearling" was eight months old to the day, for he had not been foaled until 4th June.

Sir Arthur entered him for the 1921–1923 shows, and won fourth prize in 1923. He re-appeared in London in 1929 and won first prize in the old stallions' class. But the one-time apprentice in the firm of Brough, silk manufacturers of Leek, had died ten days before at the age of eighty-six, and his son, taking on the great stud, decided to sell the horse, which had put in seven wonderful seasons. He went to Tommy Mott of Littleport, son and grandson of famous Fen breeders. (One can glimpse their contribution by looking at the pedigree of Samson 1952 who weighed 1 ton 8 cwt. – bred by Thos. Mott of Littleport in 1861; dam bred by John Mott of Littleport.) And to whom could the old horse go with more assurance of being better tended, than to Thos. Mott, manufacturer of horse and cattle medicines?

LINCOLN WHAT'S WANTED II 35812 was the best show horse in the group. Bred in 1917 by Thomas Baxter of Freeford, Lichfield, he was bought by John Measures and then, after being seventh as a three-year-old, was sold to the Forshaws. Increasing success in the show ring ended with the 1926 championship at the age of nine. Only three older horses have ever won the Shire championship. Like March King, he was let to the Newark society, but at only a fifth of March King's fee. This is no disparagement of the horse: it merely reflects the economics of the country in general and Shire breeding in particular in 1928 and 1931, compared with 1921. He died in 1933.

12. BASILDON CLANSMAN, 1918–1931

This horse does not appear in the table given in the foregoing section. In 1939, he was just one of the three sons via whom 38 colts out of the 238 claimed descent from Champion's Clansman. And he appeared to be the least of these three. Eleven of the colts were descended from him, thirteen from Leek Clansman 35792 and fourteen from Ansty Forest Clansman 37072. However, there are two particular reasons why it is that he demands a special mention.

Firstly, it was through him much more than the other two that Champion's Clansman was soon to survive as a direct male ancestor of Shire stallions. Indeed (as the table in the next section will show) by 1974 it was through him alone that any colt could claim descent from old One-Eye. Even more than that, he was destined to top the list of between-the-wars horses via whom all modern Shires, if pure-bred, trace to Harold.

Secondly, the story of Basildon Clansman is a story with a moral, a story with several morals. His life sums up the changes and chances, the luck, the wisdom and the perpetual surprises that are inevitably and always associated with horse-breeding. His must be the last biography in this book of any stallion of Harold's line, for we must stop somewhere. And as an example of the eternal fascination of the search for the perfect horse or for the super-sire of horses, as an epitome of the whole history of Shire-breeding from Bakewell onwards, the dark brown Basildon Clansman 36277 is ideal.

The Stud-book tells us that he was bred in 1918 by Major J. A. Morrison of Basildon Park, Reading. In fact, he first saw the light of day at Yatesbury in Wiltshire, for William Cumber had agreed to look after the mare while her owner was away at the war. This mare was Tandridge Choice, bred by Max Michaelis in Surrey, by Shamrock of Tandridge out of the great London Champion of 1911, Pailton Sorais. In 1918, Tandridge Choice was seven years old and had come to Basildon Park via Lord Poltimore in Devon and Alfred Barclay of Compton, Berks. Major Morrison had done all he could to get the best possible foal out of her, for she had been covered by old One-Eye a few weeks after he won the London championship.

However, when Morrison first saw her produce as a yearling in 1919, he did not like the look of him at all, and made up his mind to castrate him. Cumber was strongly averse to this idea. What was Morrison to do? He had provided himself with a string of professional advisers for the several kinds of pedigree livestock which he kept at Basildon Park and had long been pressing his neighbour (Cumber lived at Theale, though his stud was at Yatesbury) to fill the last vacancy by acting as his Shire consultant. W.J.C. had as long refused to accept the rôle, on the grounds that it would put him in an embarrassing position when they competed against each other at shows. Morrison now suggested that Cumber should back his opinion by buying a half share in the rather sorry looking colt for £100. The deal was done, on the understanding that they would exhibit him in London jointly as a two-year-old.

In January 1920, Cumber reported that it would be a waste of time and money to take Clansman to the Show. With an air of "I told you so", Morrison cheerfully disposed of the other half of the animal for another £100. The two-year-old stayed at home, and all he did that spring and summer was to cover a filly and a young mare which were presented to him to see what he could do. What he did was amazing.

The filly was two years old, like him. Her name was Nolands Poppy and she belonged to Sam Doble of Cowage, on the Yatesbury doorstep. Next year she had a colt foal which Sam registered as Cowage Clansman. He showed him in London in 1923, when he stood sixth in the two-year-old class. Then Sir Arthur Nicholson bought him and took him to Leek. He won the three-year-old class the next year, and the Junior Cup as well. In 1925, he won the four-year-old class and became supreme champion. The following year he was reserve to the Forshaws' Lincoln What's Wanted II for the championship, but he was champion again in 1927.

The young mare, Wick Bluebell, was four. She belonged to Sam's brother Fred, at Berwick Bassett. She had a filly foal the next year and Fred registered her as Wick Lady Clansman. She stood fifth out of fifty-eight as a yearling in London and was highly commended in 1923. Later, W. J. Cumber bought her and, at the age of six, she came suddenly to the top, by winning the senior class for big mares, and the supreme championship.

The whole thing is almost romantic. A two-year-old colt, not fit to be shown in London, covering two fillies that belong to two brothers and begetting foals which, at the age of six, are simultaneously male and female London champion. Anything else young Basildon Clansman might do must surely be an anticlimax. To complete the fairy-story, he ought either to have dropped dead at once or else to have won the championship himself. He did neither. It is true that he went to London as a three-year-old, when he was ninth out of sixty-five, and at the age of six he was fourth in the senior big stallion class. But it was as a stock horse that he proved the power of pedigree.

When he was three, he continued at home and once again covered Sam Doble's young Nolands Poppy. Their foal, Cowage Dalesman, was brown, like his brother. He had no chance of achieving Cowage Clansman's show success, for he injured his shoulder as a foal and it was not surprising that on his one London appearance at the age of two, he could get no higher than highly commended (15th), while his older brother was winning the junior cup. Cumber bought him and let him in 1925–1928 to Sir Bernard Greenwell. Many a prize-winning foal with the famous Marden prefix was got by him – Traitor and Teresa, Tilly, Topsy, Trinket and Tulip, foaled in 1926; Ulysses, Umpire, Unionist and Upstart, and Undine, Unice (how did she get among the

U's?), Unity and Ursula in 1927; Solitaire, as a result of a special visit by her dam, in 1928; and Dalesman, Vizier and Vulcan, and Vanity, Venus, Verbena and Viola in 1929. Sir Bernard was paying £1,000 a year for his services, which appears ridiculous in the depth of a slump, but he admitted he was satisfied: and Surrey farmers were more than satisfied, as they had every call to be with the generous enthusiasm of the owner of Marden Park for the improvement of the Shire.

In 1922, when he was four, Basildon Clansman was hired by the Montgomeryshire society. The slump had started and he did not fill up his nominations. However, many members made surprisingly good prices from the foals he left and his one season in Wales is memorable for the result obtained when he covered Ben Alderson's Kerry Blossom. The foal was Kerry Clanish Maid, whose name has so constantly recurred in our story of the 'twenties and early 'thirties (A.XII and A.XIII). The mare with the perfect feet, she climbed steadily up the London hierarchy until she became champion in 1932–1933. She was truly the modern ideal of the 'thirties, as Erfyl Lady Grey was the beauty of the 'twenties.

Basildon Clansman was hired by the Oswestry District S.H. Society in 1923–1925. In 1926–1929 the Market Harborough and Melton Mowbray S.H. Society paid £1,000 each year for his services. In the depressed circumstances of the time, such a fee (paid by a "club", not by a wealthy enthusiast like Sir Bernard) was really more astonishing than the record £2,000 received by Cumber for Theale Lockinge and by the Forshaws for March King a few years earlier, at the end of the boom period. Of all the sons and daughters Clansman begot before his death after the 1931 season, we must confine ourselves to the mention of three.

Leek Masterman III was foaled in 1928 and was exhibited as a two-year-old in London by Colonel A. F. Nicholson. He did not think much of the colt's chances and was amazed to see the judges apparently preparing to put him at the top of the class. His incredulity was shared by those who stood near, until someone suggested that the old practice of sending away all the also-rans, as used to be done in the days of huge classes, was being re-introduced, and that the Leek colt was going to have the honour of being the first to be thrown out.

"What you need now", said a friend, "is some b-f to come along and offer you £200 for him."

"I wish they would," said Nicholson.

William Cumber chipped in. "All right", he said, "I'll be the b-f."

So the deal was done on the spot. But Leek Masterman was indeed being chosen, not as the first reject, but for the first prize. The colonel was still able to laugh, even when it was pointed out to him that the £20 prize was really Cumber's. To complete his loss, the breeder's prize of £5 was not payable. His father, Sir Arthur, had been still alive when the colt was born, and so, according to the records, was the breeder.

The colt became a stallion of evil habits, but did yeoman service for the

Yatesbury stud. He was let that year to Ernest Headington at Slough to serve a few mares, and then put in two seasons at Lechlade for the United Hunts Society, two for the Bath Heavy Horse Society, two for Bridgwater S.H.S. and one for Launceston S.H.S. At the age of eleven in 1939 he was still on duty, having paid for himself many times over. It was only the war that cut short his career as a stallion. As for his crimes, he never killed a man, like other wicked ones did, though many a leader said his prayers with special fervour. The most spectacular thing he did was to seize a heifer by the neck and shake her until she died. Of his sons, Theale Perseverance, bred in Cornwall in 1936, took after him and indeed surpassed him. Cumber, who wished he had never bought him, certainly named him wrong. At the age of four he achieved the distinction of being the only Yatesbury stallion to be shot as utterly beyond human control.

In the last five seasons before the Second World War, Basildon Clansman was well represented by his sons in the Yatesbury stud. Altogether, 128 stallions appeared on the Cumber books during that half-decade. Some of them, of course, were ending their careers in 1935 and others just beginning in 1939. Fifty-nine of them were descended directly from Basildon Clansman – ten sons, thirty-two grandsons, sixteen great-grandsons and one g.g-grandson. Five had been bred by Cumber and the rest were bought in from the district, where their sires had travelled. Among them were the two horses via whom eighty-two of the 228 stallions registered in Volumes 93–97 claim descent from Champion's Clansman (as will be seen from the table in the next section):

Theale Richard 40179, black, bred in 1926 by Richard Richards, Llynclys, Salop. He was let to Lichfield S.H.S., Winslow S.H.S., Crewe S.H.S., the Pentrich, Shottle and District Heavy Horse Association and the North-West Anglesey S.H.S. and continued in the Yatesbury stud to the age of twelve.

Theale Tilton 40430, brown, bred in 1927 by Allan Holm, Tilton, Leics. Colonel Nicholson hired him as a two-year-old for one or two Leek mares, and the societies he helped as an older horse included Dinas Powis, Wenvoe District, Haverfordwest, Kingston, East Devon and Winchcombe. His Yatesbury career finished at the age of eleven.

It is now impossible to know or guess how many good geldings and mares, from Launceston to Liverpool and the Isle of Man to London had Basildon's Clansman blood in their veins by 1939. Of these, inevitably only a few were well known. Not many had pedigree names. A large number in the towns had no official name at all, but were known by a number on the hoof or in a ledger. By 1949, a vast crowd of them had been slaughtered. As to William J. Cumber, who was born less than nine months after Fred Street had made his speech to the Farmers' Club in 1878, he died just before these words were written in 1974. His lifetime had seen the foaling of a g.g.g.g.g.g.g.g.g.g-son of his Basildon Clansman and therefore of a g.g.g.g.g.g.g.g.g.g.g.g.g.g.g-son of Harold. And even Harold was over two years younger than W. J. Cumber of Theale.

13. HASTINGS REVERSED

When Lincolnshire Lad II mounted that stout old matron Flower in the spring of 1880, it seemed a matter of very ordinary routine, for at this particular time any reasonable Derbyshire mare was welcome to his service at a modest fee. Although he was now eight years old, he was not particularly famous and had to aim at taking something like ten mares a week. Flower's owner, John Potter, certainly did not have a copy of the just-published Volume I in his hand at the time the thing was done. Indeed, he did not become a "pedigree man" for another nineteen years. So the resulting foal, Harold, can scarcely be called a product of the Stud-book movement. Instead, the whole of the Stud-book has now become the product of Harold.

With Albert Frost's somewhat unoriginal statement that the Battle of Hastings resulted in a victory for William the Conqueror over Harold, our investigation of Shire history began. It ends with Harold (3703) utterly vanquishing William the Conqueror (2343) in the battle of pedigrees. We have examined the year 1939, the last in which the world of the Shire was recognisably similar to what it had been for generations past, and have seen the extent of the supremacy which the Harold line achieved in a mere sixty years. If one now looks at the 228 colts foaled in the years 1969–1973 which are registered in Volumes 93–97, it will be found that, according to the pedigrees given, every single one of them can claim descent in direct male line from this richly brown London champion of 1887. William the Conqueror has now faded out of the picture, and so have the other foundation sires. It is all Harold. His 101 best sons, reduced by 1921 to five, are now only three. Marmion II is still represented by a single line of descent, Prince Harold is there via two sons of March King and, towering above them both, stands Rokeby Friar via three sons of Childwick Champion. The Conquering Harold branch of Harold's line has died and so has that of Calwich Blend, that great product of the classic Harold-Premier cross, whose descendants, through that redoubtable old wide-fronted warrior, Babingley Nulli Secundus, seemed to flourish so exceedingly in 1939. The last stallions claiming direct descent from Calwich Blend appear as sires of a few of the dams of these colts in Volumes 93–97. This is so also of William the Conqueror himself. One or two dams of these colts trace back directly to him via Hitchin Conqueror, but that is all.

Fifty-one different sires were responsible for getting these 228 colts, as is indicated by the following table, which is modelled on the lines of those for 1921 and 1939 (see sections 6 and 11 in this chapter for Lincolnshire Lad II and Harold, and VII.1 for William the Conqueror), except that, to save space and to allow for two extra generations to be named, the sons of Harold are moved from column 3 to column 1.

In these recent volumes there are some horses of which Harold is the seventeenth sire, and Wiseman's Honest Tom 1060 therefore the twenty-sixth. If you, dear reader, were in a stud-book, your twenty-sixth sire would probably have

1   2   3   4

DESCENT OF THE 228 STALLIONS REGISTERED

PRINCE   LOCKINGE   LOCKINGE   KING OF
HAROLD .....   MANNERS..   F. KING....   TANDRIDGE .
(62)

                                                      ⎧ CHAMPION'S
                                                      │   CLANSMAN ..
                                                      │   (82)

ROKEBY   CHILDWICK   CHILDWICK   │
FRIAR ....   MAJESTIC...   CHAMPION ⎨   CHAMPION'S
(144)   (144)   GOALKEEPER
                                                        (35)

CONQUERING
HAROLD
(0)
                                                      │ MIMMS
CALWICH   │   CHAMPION...
BLEND   ⎩   (27)
(0)

MARMION II....   SOUTHGATE
(22)   H. TOM.....   CARLTON
                                    WH' W.....   LINCOLN
                                                      WH' W. II.....

ALL OTHER LINES
(0)

5   6

IN VOLUMES 93-97 (foaled 1969-1973)

MARCH KING
　　　　GREY KING CARLTON
　　　　(all via his g.g.g.g.g-son
　　　　EDINGALE COMMANDO II)
　　　　　　　　by 6 sires   32

　　　　PONTON PIONEER
　　　　(all via his g.g.g-son
　　　　RATBY MAJESTIC)
　　　　　　　　by 6 sires   30

BASILDON
CLANSMAN
(82)
　　　　THEALE RICHARD
　　　　(all via his g.g.g.g.g-son
　　　　POLWARTH SPELLBINDER)
　　　　　　　　by 2 sires   5

　　　　THEALE TILTON
　　　　(all via his g.g.g.g-son
　　　　HIS EXCELLENCY)
　　　　　　　　by 14 sires 77

PENDLEY
　RECORD ..... CIPPENHAM RECORDER
　　　　(all via his g-son
　　　　RAANS RECORD WAVE)
　　　　　　　　by 10 sires 35

HORNING
　MIMIC .... KIRKLAND MIMIC
　　　　(all via his g.g-son
　　　　NEWTON FIELDS
　　　　AMBASSADOR)
　　　　　　　　by 9 sires   27

TILTON
　WHAT'S W.... EDINGALE WHAT'S
　　　　WANTED II
　　　　(all via his g.g-son
　　　　ALNELAND DELEGATE)
　　　　　　　　by 4 sires   22

been procreating your twenty-fifth about the time when King John was signing
Magna Carta or importing Flemish stallions.

But there is another way of considering the matter. In the twenty-sixth
generation of the ancestors of any man or horse, there are 67,108,864 individuals, half of them males. All modern Shires therefore trace back to between
33 and 34 million stallions foaled about the year 1800. Honest Tom 1060, all on
his own, must comprise many millions of these. But a million or more places
in this vast assembly will be occupied by that other Honest Tom – Caswell's
and Seward's 1062, son of *Fisher's Black Horse of Weston* and direct ancestor of
William the Conqueror. The millions of forefathers still remaining in the 26th
generation will be horses such as *Townsend's Honest Tom*, *Clayworth's Horse of
Candlesby* and Gallemore 904; or *Marfleet's Horse of Somerton Castle*, Oldacre's
Mansetter; *Summerland's Brown Horse* of the Ingestre breed, Blaze 183, and the
Sinfin Old Horse; or Bradley's *John Bull*, Bulstrode's Bald 93 or Bakewell's *B*;
or *Ivens' Grey Horse*, John Chadwick's Marston 1486 and all the rest of them –
including of course the *Packington Blind Horse* and the sire of Joseph Webb's
Ruler 1905, that mysterious breederless, ownerless, placeless and timeless
Bumper.

CHAPTER VII

William the Conqueror's Line

I. THE SUDDEN CELEBRITY OF OLD WILLIAM

IN 1862, a certain mare had a colt foal. What her name was, or what her colour was, we do not know. Where the foaling took place, we do not know, for she belonged jointly to Henry Barrs of Repton Park and John Kyte of Smedley, and their farms were about twelve miles distant from each other, with Derby in between. They were pleased with the colt, which was brown, and called him William the Conqueror. This was not really a very original name, because the dam was by Thomas Nix's William the Conqueror, which was likewise brown and was himself by Yeoman's brown William the Conqueror.

Mr. Kyte and Mr. Barrs kept the colt to use as a stallion. They kept him nineteen years, during which time he led a busy and highly profitable life. In his younger days, they won second prize with him at the Derbyshire Show and when he was sixteen he also took first prize at Ilkeston Show and first prize at Moor Green. He was a remarkably fertile and steady stock-horse and there was no trouble at all in getting mares for him. Sometimes he served them in Mr. Barrs' district and sometimes in Mr. Kyte's and, altogether, he usually had more than a hundred a year. He always left excellent foals, and not many barren mares. His satisfied customers called him Old William, but his fame was confined to the Derby area.

Edward Coke and Gilbert Murray knew of him, because they lived in the southern part of the county themselves. And so, when Old William was seventeen and the first volume of the Stud-book was being prepared, it was decided to put him in. Unfortunately, no one made a proper check of the details. Henry Barrs was misprinted as 'Barr', and was given no initials. He was also inadvertently transferred to the wrong county. No enquiry was made about the dam's name, but perhaps that is not surprising, for in those days it did not seem to matter. His sire was given as "Domber's *Leicestershire*", but neither Mr. Domber nor his *Leicestershire* was explained, so the information was really quite useless. The main point was that William the Conqueror himself was to go in the book as No. 2343, which would mean that his progeny could also be registered. As he had now covered something approaching two thousand mares, and looked as if he could continue to serve indefinitely, this was important. It turned out later (five years later), that Domber's *Leicestershire* was the same horse as Taylor's Leicestershire which had already been registered, like his son Old William, in Volume I, and was number 1317. This correction was printed in Volume XI but it was not explained who Domber was or how long he possessed the horse.

However, as we do not know anything about Taylor either, except that he was a Wirksworth man, perhaps that is not surprising.

In 1881, the Royal Show was at Derby, through which Old William had travelled for so many years to get from Mr. Barrs' to Mr. Kyte's or from Mr. Kyte's to Mr. Barrs'. A couple of his sons were exhibited there by Robert Ratcliff of Newton Park, the brewer. These two geldings created a sensation, and everyone went into raptures over them. One was Samson, a four-year-old bred by John Lee of Newton Solney: the other was, and is, anonymous. They were in fact typical examples of what Old William had been procreating these past fifteen years or more. The Earl of Ellesmere, through Henry Heaton, turned Old William's sudden recognition by the outside world into national fame by buying the old stallion for service at Worsley. His limbs and joints and feet were still in wonderful shape in spite of all the miles he had walked in his nineteen years and in spite of the strain to which his massive weight had subjected them in mounting, and then dismounting, the countless mares he had been asked to serve. His gait was still free and swinging and Edward McKenna, the stud groom at Worsley, said many times in the years to come, with a touch of awe in his voice "It was a treat just to hear him walk down the yard."

Miraculously, everyone in England suddenly learned that Old William's stock were marvellous animals and they were searched out and bought up in their hundreds, though no doubt the cunning Lawrence Drew had already taken scores of his earlier daughters away to Scotland, and kept quiet about the source of supply. Henry Barrs and John Kyte lost no time in joining the English Cart-Horse Society.

The next year, 1882, was to be Old William's first full season at Worsley. But it was back to his old stamping-ground that he was sent by the combined wisdom of Lord Ellesmere, Henry Heaton and Edward McKenna. There, in the parish of Lockington (over the Leicestershire border) at the age of twenty he served the two mares through whom alone his tremendous influence on the whole Shire breed was exerted. These were George Shepperson's Flower and W. H. Potter's Lockington Beauty. When their foals were safely delivered the following year, Old William was back again under the care of Mr. Kyte. And it was there that he died that summer.

John Kyte has the singular distinction of having owned the two chief progenitors of the Shire, for he was also at one time the proprietor of Lincolnshire Lad II (See V.8). So perhaps he should go to the top of the "doubles" table, above Bingham with his two Glories and Duncombe with Harold and Premier. Fate allowed him another nine years as a Shire Society member. Henry Barrs lived one year longer, until 1893, by which time John Adcock Barrs of the great Nailstone stud had already made the Barrs name famous.

Old William's pedigree, given below so far as it can be accurately discovered, is remarkable in three respects. Firstly, both his sire and his nameless dam trace back in the direct male line to *Fisher's Black Horse* of Weston, *John Bull*, which was a neighbour and older contemporary of Wiseman's Honest Tom 1060.

Both of the main-blood lines in the Shire breed therefore stem from a similar origin. Secondly, even the skeletal facts that we possess shows a noticeable degree of line-breeding. And thirdly, he is the only one of the foundation sires who had a significant amount of blood deriving from the *Packington Blind Horse* line. He may be looked upon as the supreme example of the judicious blend of the Leicester-Derby type and the Fens type.

In the table overleaf, a dam printed in capitals as MARE was certainly bred by the same man who bred her son. (In other cases, this is only probably so.)

2. STAUNTON HERO, 1881–1891: A DEAD END

Before we turn to the foals bred by George Shepperson and W. H. Potter, we should mention one that was born slightly earlier – five weeks, in fact, before Old William achieved instant fame by means of the Royal Show of 1881 and his purchase by Lord Ellesmere. This was a brown colt foal that he got out of the fifteen-year-old Black Duchess belonging to J. W. Chappell of Breaston. (This mare had been bred by Richard Potter of Draycott. Wherever one looks, on enquiring into the breeding of famous horses of this time, one sees a member of the Potter clan.) Chappell registered him as Staunton Hero 2918 and then sold him as a two-year-old in 1883 to Douglas for export to America. Harold, of exactly the same age and in the same year had likewise been sold to Douglas for the same purpose. But, like Harold, Staunton Hero was reprieved. In his case, the purchaser was Walter Gilbey. Three years later, he became the supreme champion stallion at London, and, from that day to this, and presumably for all time, he has remained the only stallion under 16.2 hands ever to achieve the top honour of all, whether at London, Derby, Peterborough, or anywhere else the Shire Show may be held. The red, white and blue card at London was the passport to the best mares in England, but it was not Staunton Hero that made the Old William line the second most potent in the history of the breed. The sons of George Shepperson's *Flower* and W. H. Potter's Lockington Beauty also became London champions, as we shall see, and it was through them that the old horse influenced the Shire of the future. Compared with them, Staunton Hero's own progeny of the first generation met with little London success:

	No. of seasons at stud	No. of London prizes won by progeny
Staunton Hero	8	5 (1886–1890 shows)
Hitchin Conqueror	13½	69 (1889–1908 shows)
Prince William	20	43 (1888–1909 shows)

Staunton Hero's prizewinning sons and daughters were as unimpressive as they were few. Glime was highly commended as a yearling filly for her breeder, Walter Gilbey, and was sold at the age of three to the Prince of Wales. Saucebox 5328 and Silverwood 5336 were both commended when shown as three-year-olds by their breeder John Skelton of Carlton Grange, Newmarket in 1888.

THE PEDIGREE OF WILLIAM THE CONQUEROR 2343

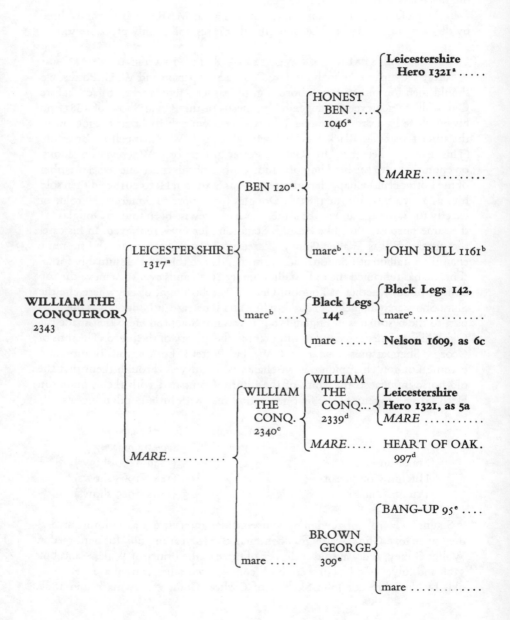

1	2	3	4	5

WILLIAM THE CONQUEROR 2343

LEICESTERSHIRE 1317[a]

BEN 120[a]

HONEST BEN .... 1046[a]

Leicestershire Hero 1321[a] .....

MARE...........

mare[b] ...... JOHN BULL 1161[b]

mare[b] ....

Black Legs 144[c]

Black Legs 142, mare[c] ....

mare ...... Nelson 1609, as 6c

MARE...........

WILLIAM THE CONQ. 2340[c]

WILLIAM THE CONQ. 2339[d]

Leicestershire Hero 1321, as 5a
MARE ....

MARE..... HEART OF OAK. 997[d]

mare ..... BROWN GEORGE 309[e]

BANG-UP 95[e] ....

mare ....

6   **7**   **8**   **9**   **10**

Black Legs 142[a] . . . .
{
  DERBYSHIRE 577[a] . . . .
{
    HONEST TOM 1062[a] . . . .
{
      John Bull (Fisher's Black Horse of Weston)[a]

      MARE . . . .   Cox's Robin Hood

    MARE . . . .   *Stych's Brown Horse*

  MARE . . . .   BLAZE 183 *g.g-son of P. Blind Horse see* III.1

MARE . . . .
{
  Arnold's Brown George mare . . . .   CONQUEROR. 524[b]   STAFFORDSHIRE HERO 2056[b], *g.g.g-son of P. Blind Horse* (?)

VICTORY 2219[b] . . . . . .
{
  MARSTON 1486 *descended from P. Blind Horse*

  mare . . . .   BALD HORSE 93 *g-son of P. Blind Horse*

mare . . . .   PACKINGTON 1704 (?)[b] . . . .
{
  PACKINGTON 1703 *g.g.g-son of P. Blind Horse*

  MARE . . . .   BALD HORSE 93 *g-son of P. Bl. Horse*

{
The Berkshire Grey Horse (Ivens')

mare . . . . *as 6a*   *Percey's Grey Horse of Idstone, Berks*

Nelson 1609[c] . . . . . .
{
  BLAZE 188[c] . . . . . .   SWEBSTONE 2079 *g.g.g-son of P. Blind Horse*

  MARE . . . .
{
    G890 *g.g.g-son of P. Blind Horse*

    mare . . . .   BALD HORSE 93 *g-son of P. Bl. Horse*

Campion's Waggoner[d]
DAVID 565[e] . . **HONEST TOM** 1062, *as* 8a

{
BANG-UP 94[f] . . . .
{
  SANCHO 1993[d]

  MARE . . . .   DUMPLING 679[c] . . . .   *New's Brown Horse of Chaddleworth Mills*

mare . . . .   TRUE BRITON 2180[e] *g.g-son of* **HONEST TOM** 1060 *see* V.3

Black Legs 144, as 4c

In the following notes, all eighteenth-century horses descended from *The Packington Blind Horse* are omitted, as they have been commented on in B.III 1 and 2. Breeders or owners marked † are referred to in B.II.

2a Leicestershire 1317, brown; f 1857. In the pedigree of William the Conqueror in Stud-book Volume 1, given as Domber's *Leicestershire*. Corrected in Volume 6. Owned and bred by Taylor of Wirksworth, who is not otherwise represented in the Stud-book.

3a Ben 120, –: f 1840. Bred by Thos. Nix (Derby.†): o John Chadwick (Staffs.†).
 b Mare bred by Richard Gibbs of Tissington Wood (Derby.†).
 c William the Conqueror 2340, brown: f 1844. b Smith, Kidsley Park, Derby.: o Thos. Nix.

4a Honest Ben 1046, brown: f 1833. b and o John Chadwick.
 b Mare bred by John Chadwick.
 c Black Legs 144, black: f 1822. o and b Richard Gibbs.
 d William the Conqueror 2339, brown: f 1835. b Collins, Osmaston, Derby.: o Joseph Yeoman, Pennymoor Hay, Staffs.
 e Brown George 309, brown: f 1850. b and o Hazard, Melbourn, Cambs.

5a Leicestershire Hero 1321, also known as Old Leicestershire, brown: f 1820. b E. Gent, Hinckley, Leics., o John Beard, Hazelwood, Duffield, Derby.
 b John Bull 1161, grey: f 1818. b Percey, Northampton: o J. Lister, Pentrich, Derby.
 c mare b Kirkham of Egginton, Derby.
 d Heart of Oak 997, brown: f 1821. b Joseph Burtt, Welbourn, Lincs.: o Lister (as 5b) and Lambert of Wath, Yorks.
 e Bang-Up 95, brown: f 1844. b Ely, Hill Top, Derby.: o Stych (Derby.†).

6a Black Legs 142, black: f 1804. b Pickering, Thurlaston, Leics.: o Joseph "Wyldes" (Leics.,† q.v. for the horse also) and Bowmar of Osmaston, Derby.
 b Victory 2219, brown: f 1812. b S. Jones, Poulton, Ches.: o John Chadwick.
 c Nelson 1609, black: f 1803. b Harrison of Ashbourne: o Wagstaff of Atlow, Ashbourne.
 d *Waggoner*. Possibly o Campion of Edale, Derby.
 e David 565, –: f 1818. b Burtt as 5d: o John Caswell, Wigtoft, Lincs. This brings us, for the first time in the pedigree, into the Fens.
 f Bang-Up 94, grey: f 1834. o and b Stych.

7a Derbyshire 577, brown: f 1800. See II.1 (Wild) for this horse.
 b Packington 1704. See II.3 (Chadwick).
 c Blaze, alias Bald, –: f 1800. o Knowles, Nailstone, Leics.
 d Sancho 1993, –: f 1829. b and o Sir H. Crewe, Bt., Calke Abbey, Derby. A muddle in the Stud-book makes his sire impossible to determine.
 e True Briton 2180. See V.3.

8a HONEST TOM 1062 alias Old Tom, alias Little David, alias Old David 1062, chestnut: f 1796(?), b Elstone of Swarby, Lincs: o John Caswell of Wigtoft (as 6e) and Seward of Quadring, Lincs. This celebrated horse was bought by Caswell for £300 at the age of five. Unfortunately, the Stud-book gives him as foaled in 1806 which is almost certainly wrong, even though it accords with the date of David (6e) and the fact that he covered by subscription at 3 guineas a mare in 1814. It does not fit in with the foaling of Derbyshire (7a) and, in fact, most nineteenth-century stallion owners who had horses that they traced back to Caswell's Honest Tom (as he was

PLATES 61 and 62   The last London Show. (*above*) J. Downes Evans (the same who, at the age of seventeen, bought the future 1919 champion stallion for only £58) leads his winner of the two-year-old class, Powisland Bold Chief, at the head of the line; (*left*) Bower Winalot, photographed outside the Royal Agricultural Hall immediately after his "come-back" triumph when, at the age of ten, he became the only Shire of either sex to win the championship a fourth time.

PLATE 63 Five men look back. From left to right: Tom Forshaw, Col. A. F. Nicholson, William Cumber, Christopher Barker and J. Morris Belcher at the Shrewsbury Show of Geldings in March 1942. They had little to smile about.

PLATE 64 One horse looks ahead. Grey Spark, foaled in 1939 and now, in 1945, champion of the breed. He is held by Richard Forshaw, son of James and nephew of Tom. Compare this last Carlton champion with old Kirby (Plate 10).

usually known) dated him as 1796. Elstone, the breeder, appears only here in Shire history. There were several Caswells owning heavy stallions in the Spalding area at this time. For the Sewards see II.7.

The pedigree of some other descendants of Honest Tom 1062 has been clarified, and some obvious mistakes in the Stud-book corrected, by a stud-card found under a beam at Church Farm, Legsby near Market Rasen in 1954. Mrs. Vickers was kind enough to send this card, which is for *Young Comet*, the property of W. Bruntlett of Covenham, in the 1857 season, when the horse was three. Though it is irrelevant here, it is pleasing that beams in old houses can still give up their treasures, as they did for Herman Biddell in 1879.

b Conqueror 524, black: f 1810. b Hambleton (Staffs.†): o Joseph Edge, Albion Hotel, Westhoughton, Lancs.

c Dumpling 679, brown: f 1810. b and o Stych.

9a *John Bull*. See II.7 (Fisher).

b Staffordshire Hero, brown: f 1800: b and o Hambleton (Staffs.†). His sire was *Hean's Horse*, by Bald Horse 93, g-son of the *Packington Blind Horse*. Hean is a mystery man.

10 Cox was a not uncommon Shire name in various parts both of the Fens and Midlands. This owner of *Robin Hood* was probably one of the Littleport farmers called Cox.

King Henry 7499 was also bred by Skelton: for Gilbey he won second prize as a four-year-old in 1889 and was highly commended the next year. But that is the total of the Hero's achievements, other than honest plodding progeny.

The same difference is shown in succeeding generations. In 1904, for example, William the Conqueror was the foundation sire of 33 of the 135 horses which were prize winners or reserve numbers. Twenty traced to him *via* Hitchin Conqueror and twelve *via* Prince William. Even the "odd one out" was not *via* Staunton Hero. It was a four-year-old gelding called Wimbledon Prince, by Dunsmore Willington Boy 13021 by Duke of Normandy 4359, by William the Conqueror.

Staunton Hero contributed virtually nothing to pedigree history. And why was this? We can blame neither the inconvenient shortness of his legs, nor the languor induced by a sleek and fleshy show condition. Many a stallion in those days which attended a constant round of shows, as Staunton Hero did over the eastern counties, inclined with the passing years to imitate Narcissus rather than Priapus. But not those at Elsenham Hall. Mr. Gilbey believed in keeping his horses really hardy, and they were all wintered out, by day and night. Hero's failure was not an inability to procreate, but the roughness of the seed-bed – those terrible Essex mares, to whose service he was permanently confined. He had plenty of sons and daughters, all a little better than their dams, but none very good. Good old Walter Gilbey! He was determined to devote Staunton Hero's energies to the same purpose as that for which, ten years before, his Bishops Stortford company had been formed. Hitchin Conqueror and Prince William were fashionable horses, the very dean and archdeacon of Barchester among stallions. Staunton Hero was commissioned willy-nilly as a missionary among the barbarous females of Essex.

However, in 1889, at Gilbey's second home sale on 12th February, the Hon. Cecil Parker, who was there with Lord Egerton, gave 500 guineas for him on behalf of his uncle, the Duke of Westminster. The horse had already won more than that sum in prizes – £543, and, only the year before, the Gold Medal at the Brussels Show. So off he went to Eaton Hall. The next year he won £20 for His Grace, as the best of thirty-two senior stallions with short legs in class II. In addition, he now enjoyed the somewhat more comfortable mares of Cheshire. For His Grace himself, he sired six filly foals that were later put into the Studbook. But alas, he died after the 1891 season. His life was less than half as long as his old father's and, having left his native Derbyshire at the age of two, he had never had the privilege of walking from Mr. Barrs' place to Mr. Kyte's, and then back from Mr. Kyte's to Mr. Barrs', serving the best mares in the land as he went. And, sadly, none of his Cheshire daughters ever won a London prize or produced sons or daughters that did so.

One daughter alone brought credit to old Short-legs. And this, after all, was 4113 Glime, that had been born in 1885. Out of her, the Prince of Wales had bred a filly in 1890 which was sold to P. A. Muntz and registered as 14655 Dunsmore Gloaming. In the hands of several different owners, she met with increasing show success until in 1889 and 1890 she was the champion mare of all for Sir J. Blundell Maple. She also had the unique distinction of being sold twice at Dunsmore home sales, the first time for 1,010 guineas and the second for 780 guineas. This lovely Dunsmore Gloaming has already been eulogised (see VI.1). But why was she such a beauty? Because her dam was by Staunton Hero? Or because she herself was by none other than Harold? Or for both reasons?

Staunton Hero had been the product of a typical 'routine' mating of Old William with a Derbyshire mare. The oddest part of the whole story is that Hitchin Conqueror and Prince William, also, were the product of exactly similar matings – the like of which, ever since William had been old enough to serve a mare, had occurred hundreds of times in the district. His sudden popularity and his instantaneous transfer to the dizzy heights of being on the pay-roll of the Earl of Ellesmere were quite irrelevant. The two sons by which he was destined to influence the whole Shire breed were got, not because his lordship bought him, but because he had the good sense to act as if he had not.

3. HITCHIN CONQUEROR, 1883–1899

George Shepperson sold his bay colt foal out of Flower to Alexander Crawford, four miles away at West Leake (Notts), who, with a somewhat warped sense of Scottish humour, registered him as Lord Clyde 3825. The colt did indeed "show a bit of daylight" under his body at that time, but when Arthur Ranson of Hitchin bought him as a two-year-old, he very properly made all haste to register him under a different name. This change was then permissible but, for some reason, perhaps to destroy the memory of Crawford's little joke, the horse was also given a new number. He was now lighter in colour than had been anticipated. So the brown Lord Clyde 3825 officially died and the bay Hitchin Conqueror 4458 was born, celebrating the occasion by winning first prize at the Herts Show.

At the age of four, Hitchin Conqueror stood 17.1-hands on legs that were, after all, far from long, and he was as near the ideal of Shire massiveness as anyone could hope for. He was reserve to the London prize-winners that year and A. B. Freeman-Mitford bought him privately for £1,000. The next year he was highly commended. After a year's rest from show training and excitement, he reappeared in 1890 to win the supreme championship – a marvellous horse both in joints and bone and action. It was bad luck that Lady Mitford's illness prevented her enthusiastic husband from being present at this triumph and receiving the awards from the Prince of Wales, for his animals had twice been runners-up to the champion.

When joint-ill brought about the end of the Batsford Park stud in 1897, Hitchin Conqueror had already left for his fifth and last home – W. & J. Thompson's at Desford, Leics. For them at the age of thirteen he won the old stallions class. The next year, 1898, he was let to the Peterborough A.S. which in the two previous years had hired his sons Menestrel and Blythwood Conqueror, and twelve months later on 26th June 1899 died of a ruptured stomach.

(There is something of a mystery about Hitchin Conqueror's dam. When he won the championship in 1890 she was stated to be – as the Stud-book had already said – "Flower – by Honest Prince 1058". But from 1891, and always thereafter, she was given as "Flower – Sutton-Nelthorpe's (Vol. 11")"; that is, 3876 Flower. This mare was bred in 1879 and had already been registered in Volume 8 as "Bonny – Pountain's" by Honest Prince 1058, and bred by " – Fletcher, Derbyshire". Colonel Pountain, of Barrow Hall, Derby, who registered her, listed three filly foals he had bred out of her in 1884–1886: the first of these, Barrow Belle, was by William the Conqueror – almost the last foal the old horse ever got. R. N. Sutton-Nelthorpe, who re-registered her as Flower in 1889 (Volume 11, 1890) listed another filly foal he had himself bred from her in 1889, by Will-o'-the-Wisp 6574. It seems inconceivable that in 1885, when Hitchin Conqueror's registration was submitted, his dam George Shepperson's *Flower* was in fact producing her second foal as Pountain's Bonny. Pountain's Bonny, alias Sutton-Nelthorpe's Flower, joined Freeman-Mitford's stud at Batsford Park in 1890, after the London Show, and obliged him with a filly foal the next year. He thought he had acquired Hitchin Conqueror's dam. Perhaps he had, because, if he had got the wrong Flower, one would have thought George Shepperson would have corrected his mistake, for he at last in December 1888 had become the fifth Shepperson to join the Shire Society. At any rate, whether there were two Flowers or one, it does not matter, because all we can ever know about the breeding of either or both is that her, or their, sire was Honest Prince 1058. He, incidentally, was owned by none other than Mr. Kyte of Smedley.)

The massive Menestrel 14180, bred by Freeman-Mitford out of a Premier mare in 1891 (died December 1909,) was his most influential son – *via* one son Birdsall Menestrel (f 1900, destroyed August 1917), London champion in 1904 and 1907.

The second most prepotent son was Blythwood Conqueror 14997, bred in 1893 by James Blyth at Stansted, Essex, out of a Harold mare. His influence was exerted through Blythwood Kingmaker 18534 (f 1899, died of heart failure May 1913).

(The two Somerset-bred champions of 1916 and 1918, for whose breeding George Edwards was responsible, were of the William the Conqueror line. Bury King's Champion was by King Cole VII by Birdsall Menestrel; and Rickford Coming King was by Ravenspur 22709, by Blythwood Kingmaker.)

Blaisdon Conqueror 15989, bred in 1894 by Peter Stubs at Blaisdon in Gloucestershire, on the eastern edge of the Forest of Dean, is the third chief son of Hitchin Conqueror. He was out of a Lancashire-bred mare by Garnet 2787, whose male ancestry leads us back to Dack's Matchless. One of the mares in this line is recorded as having been "Purchased at the Barbican Sale: by Whitfield's Black Horse". The latter was no doubt Whitfield's Horse 2335, bred in 1838 and later acquired and travelled with great pride and éclat and no small profit, by Mr. Whitfield all round the Chesterfield district. Blaisdon Conqueror, who stood 17.2-hands high, died on 22nd October 1904 of enteritis. (See section 5 for what happened to him then and where he is now.)

4. PRINCE WILLIAM, 1883–1905

Of Lockington Beauty, the dam of W. H. Potter's bay colt-foal by Old William, we need say nothing here, for her career is related in Chapter IX.2. Potter called the colt Prince William. He took him next February to London, won the yearling class of thirty-nine with him, and sold him. He returned home with £15 prize money and £252 from John Rowell. Sanders Spencer described the colt as having "capital feet and pasterns, silky hair, flat bone, forehand good and quarters lengthy: but he is slightly flat-sided". The next year Rowell exhibited him in superlative condition and well furnished, and he won his class and the junior cup, and the supreme championship as well. He was not only the best of the 288 entire horses on parade but possibly the best two-year-old ever seen. Lord Wantage promptly gave 1,500 guineas for him as the foundation of the Lockinge stud. Potter, of course, did not even get a medal, as the awards to breeders had not then been started. Prince William again won the junior cup the next year and, after a year's rest, the supreme championship for the second time in 1888. In 1894, Lord Wantage had a home sale of fifty-one Shires of all ages and sexes, every single one of which was bred at home and was by Prince

William: they averaged 112 guineas. (His Lordship's fifty-one varieties became famous when exactly the same number of geldings was sold at Lockinge four years later.) The handsome bay horse outlived the Crimean hero, and died in 1905.

5. A SHOW OF DRY BONES

At the request of Richard Lyddeker, Lady Wantage in 1905 donated the skull and left-side limb bones of Prince William to the British Museum. She also presented the feet and malformed limb-bones of an unnamed Shire colt from Lockinge. Peter Stubs gave the skull and limb-bones of Blaisdon Conqueror. The two stallions were marked by an exceptional development of the splint-bones, which (especially in Prince William) were long and stout, and ended in a triangular piece inclining noticeably outwards. Lyddeker used these bones as clear examples of the vestigial remains of the second and third toes possessed by the forerunners of the modern horse. This peculiarity was exceptionally notice-able in the colt. Indeed it was a deformity, and had been the reason for his being put down. His splint-bones were really lateral toes in a high degree of develop-ment, the constituent bones being separately identifiable: the outer toe actually terminated in a little fully-formed hoof. (Of course, there have been many greater "freaks" than this. For example, a pure-bred Shire gelding owned by Sir Garrard Tyrwhitt-Drake had two feet on its near front leg. The 'spare' one was the size of a pony's foot and did not reach the ground. This leg also poss-essed a highly-developed third toe. In spite of its owner's interest in showman-ship – he was the only man ever to present a circus at the Albert Hall – the gelding spent a long life on ordinary farm work and successfully did his share of cartage along the hard roads.)

The mounted head of Starlight (1882-1899), the triple London champion of 1890-1892, was also donated to Mr. Lyddeker by the widow of Fred Crisp. But this was required merely to demonstrate what a Shire beauty's head ought to be. The display items of all this material, which included also the limb bones of that great Thoroughbred, Stockwell (1849-1876) were eventually moved to Tring Park when, following the bequest of Lord Rothschild, it became part of the British Museum (Natural History) in 1938: the other osteological material remained in London.

6. OLD WILLIAM'S DESCENDANTS IN 1921 AND 1939

The tables which follow overleaf show the descent from Old William of forty of the 132 winners at the London Show in 1921 (Table A) and of twenty-one of the 238 stallions registered in Volume 61 (Table B). They may be compared with the similar tables showing descent from Lincolnshire Lad II and Harold in VI.6 and VI.11. There is no table for William the Conqueror's direct descend-ants in Volumes 93-97 (comparable with that in VI.13) simply because he has none.

TABLE A: DESCENT OF THE 132 PRIZE-WINNERS AT THE 1921 LONDON SHOW

1	2	3	4	5	6	
WILLIAM THE CONQUEROR (40)	HITCHIN CONQUEROR (31)	MENESTREL......	BIRDSALL MENESTREL (20)	KING COLE VII (3)	KING'S MESSENGER	2
					LONGFORTH KING COLE	1
					N.M. himself	7
				NORBURY MENESTREL (15)	MARDEN JOHN & 1 son	4
					MENESTREL OF SUNDRIDGE	1
					NORBURY CORONATION	1
					RATCLIFFE MENESTREL	0
					THEALE LOCKINGE	1
					THEALE MENESTREL	1
		BLYTHWOOD CONQUEROR..	BLYTHWOOD KINGMAKER (5)	ROYAL OAK XIV		
				SNOWDON MENESTREL		1
				BARN KINGMAKER		1
				LUNESDALE K-M..	WELDON	1
				RAVENSPUR......	RICKFORD COMING KING	1
				SLIPTON KING	NORMANBY BRIAR KING	1
				TOP SAWYER IV		
				RELIANCE VI		0
	PRINCE WILLIAM (9)	BLAISDON CONQUEROR..	MONNOW CONQUEROR..	MONNOW DRAYMAN (6)	M.D. himself	3
					SANDSIDE SENSATION	1
					TARNACRE ROSEWOOD	1
					WYRESDALE DRAUGHTSMAN	1
		BRITISH FLAG III......	BOXTED FLAG II	DRAYMAN XXIII (9)	TATTON DRAY KING	8
					and 2 sons and 2 g-sons	
		LOCKINGE......	STARBORO' CORONATION..	TANDRIDGE RELIANCE	FOLVILLE DRAY KING	1
		ALBERT.......				0
HAROLD (86)	CARBON (3)	See VI.6				
	POTENTATE (2)					
LINCOLNSHIRE LAD II (91)						
MATCHLESS (1)		via his g.g.g-son PREMIER see VIII.1				
Others (0)						

TABLE B: DESCENT OF THE 238 STALLIONS REGISTERED IN VOLUME 61

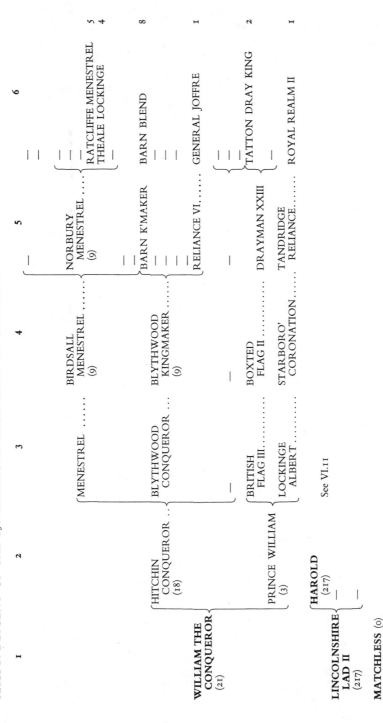

1	2	3	4	5	6	
WILLIAM THE CONQUEROR (21)	HITCHIN CONQUEROR (18)	MENESTREL	BIRDSALL MENESTREL (9)	NORBURY MENESTREL (9)	RATCLIFFE MENESTREL	5
					THEALE LOCKINGE	4
		BLYTHWOOD CONQUEROR	BLYTHWOOD KINGMAKER (9)	BARN K'MAKER	BARN BLEND	8
				RELIANCE VI......	GENERAL JOFFRE	1
	PRINCE WILLIAM (3)	BRITISH FLAG III	BOXTED FLAG II	DRAYMAN XXIII	TATTON DRAY KING	2
		LOCKINGE ALBERT	STARBORO' CORONATION	TANDRIDGE RELIANCE......	ROYAL REALM II	1
HAROLD (217)	See VI.11					
LINCOLNSHIRE LAD II (217)						
MATCHLESS (0)						
Others (0)						

It is possible that nothing could have prevented the gradual eclipse of the William the Conqueror line, in the direct male descent, by that of Harold. But it could have been at the very least slowed down if it had not been for the fact that his great son Hitchin Conqueror, *his* son Blythwood Conqueror and their descendants were in general short of hair. In the boom years of 1914–1920, profusion of feather was a fetish and Hitchin Conqueror blood was as a consequence studiously neglected. By the 'thirties, this folly was recognised, but it was then too late to cry, "Come back, all is forgiven."

CHAPTER VIII

The Other Five Lines

I. DACK'S MATCHLESS

THIS horse was once described by old James Forshaw as "the sire of all time". Foaled in 1846, he travelled a round which led him through Moulton Eaugate, which the Clarks were later to make famous, for thirteen consecutive seasons. Towards the end of his career, it was also claimed that thirty of his sons were serving mares in the Fens in the same year. No horse was valued higher by the Fenmen of the 'fifties and 'sixties and, if they had only kept better records, we would have a clearer idea of the immense proportion of his blood that very many of the best horses from 1878 onwards had in their veins.

Six stallions are credited to Dack of Tydd St. Mary in Volume 1, and two to his widow, Blanche. They were bred between 1833 and 1867 by eight different men, all in the Wisbech-Holbeach district. Three of them appear in this pedigree of Matchless himself (mares in capitals being known to have been bred by the same man as bred the son).

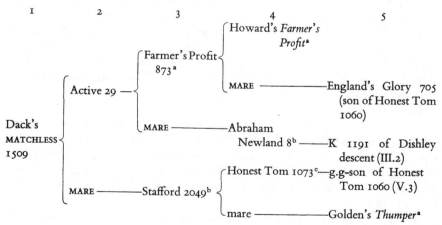

1 MATCHLESS 1509, bay: f 1846. b Lindsey, Pinchbeck: o Dack. Lindsey appears nowhere else in Shire records.
2 Active 29, brown: f 1841. b Sharp, West Walton, Norfolk: o Dack. Sharp also appears only here.
3a Farmer's Profit 873, bay: f 1833. b Jarvis Wilder, Holbeach Marsh: o Dack. This is the only one of Wilder's horses we know about.
  b Stafford 2049, –: f 1838. b J. Infield of West Fen, March (see also section 4, Lincoln): o C. Coverley, Castle Bytham, Lincs.

4a Howard's *Farmer's Profit*. Impossible to identify, but possibly the owner was a Howard of Long Sutton.

b Abraham Newland 8, black: f 1826. b Gask of Wrangle: o Israel Brice of Risby, Market Rasen. Gask bred one other black horse in Volume 1. Brice appears in connexion with six stallions, 1825-1853. (The Stud-book wrongly inserts an extra generation – Abraham Newland 10, foaled in 1840. The muddle is scarcely surprising – there are nine Abraham Newlands in Volume 1, seven of them (1831-1868) descended from Abraham Newland 8 and the eighth probably so. See also V.5 – the pedigree of Mountain's Champion.)

c Honest Tom 1073. A similar Stud-book error occurs here, an extra generation (Honest Tom 1079) being wrongly interpolated. Both the sire, 1073, and the son, 1079, were also known as Phenomenon.

5a Golden's *Thumper*. Perhaps one of the Goldens owning stallions at March. But there were other Goldens in the Ramsey district.

In 1931, someone found an old stud card, dated 1878, of an "England's Glory" which, in a long article in *The Livestock Journal*, he wrongly identified with England's Glory 720. The horse in question was actually the ten-year-old Emperor II 697, bred and owned by Richard Hopper of Whittlesea, who frequently called him England's Glory. Hopper claimed that his stallion had got 100 foals in one season a couple of years earlier. How many mares had he required to achieve that? Emperor II was out of a mare by a son of Matchless and is just one example of how Matchless dominates the unknown regions of many pedigrees. John Whitehurst, that acute and articulate stallion owner of the early years of the present century, remarked in 1920 that Matchless was "one of the greatest of all the noted sires of bygone days, and belonged' to a noted tribe which was famous in Lincolnshire many generations before the birth of the Stud-book. Strains of this blood are scarce and very valuable in a breeding animal." It just so happened that he owned a couple of stallions descended from him. His partiality was, nevertheless, justified.

There are two or three main lines of descent from Matchless:

(i) via his son Wiseman's Wonder 2357 (see V.1), his g-son Wonder of the West 2371 (chestnut, bred 1876 by Charles Beart of Stow Bardolph) and his g.g-son Honest Tom 5123 (bay, bred 1884 by Thomas Mott of Littleport), sire of the great 1902-1903 champion, Stroxton Tom, which would have been popular had he lived in the 1930s, but which was ahead of his time through a shortage of hair.

(ii) via Matchless Junior 1544, Bold Lincoln 231 and What's Wanted 2332. What's Wanted was bred in 1873 by J. Ashmore of Darlton, Notts out of a mare by Oxford 1683 of the Honest Tom 1060 line via Drayman. James Forshaw purchased him and travelled him seven seasons in Lancashire where he not only proved extraordinarily prolific but passed on his superb quality, bone and feet, long silky feather and gaiety of action to his progeny, which were seized upon by buyers all over England and Scotland. His celebrated son Premier 2646 (who had more Honest Tom 1060 than Matchless blood in him) was bred in Lancashire by John Fisher of Layton Hall in 1880, but had not quite the size and dash of his sire. James Forshaw bought him as a foal and later sold him to A. C. Duncombe. What's Wanted died prematurely of heart disease on 22nd May 1882, and Premier on 28th April 1892. (For some observations about Premier at Calwich Abbey, see VI.1.)

(iii) via his g-son Thumper 2136, an iron-grey celebrity bred in 1868 by John Griffin of Boro' Fen. When a rupture finished his career on 16th March, 1885, he left innumerable descendants all over the Fens and became the ancestor of many a man's family of mares.

2. HEART OF OAK

Famous already when the Earl of Ellesmere bought him at the age of eleven in 1870, his influence was enormously extended by his activities at Worsley during the next eight or nine years. See Part A.V.2.

Bred by John Rowell senior in 1859, he was a true Black and his ancestry, as far as can be ascertained, was rooted in the Fens:

Sire: Heart of Oak 1003, black, bred 1852 by R. Taylor of Soham.

    G-sire: Glory 940, brown, bred 1845 by Taylor: by Glory 939, brown, bred 1837 by R. Johnson of Haddenham: by K 1192, bred by J. Grebby of Croft Marsh, Boston – by his *Grey Horse* (one of several – but which one, is a matter of guesswork) out of a mare by *Clayworth's Horse of Candlesby*, which he often used.

    Dam of sire: bred by Taylor, by Honest Tom 1071 (descended from Townsend's *Honest Tom* and Honest Tom 1060 – see B.V.3).

Dam: bred by John Rowell, senior.

    Dam's sire: England's Glory 717, bred 1845 by W. Laxon of March (by Seward's MAJOR 1447) out of his mare by Lincoln 1326, bred 1837 by Hutchinson of Gedney – tracing to Cawood Robinson's *Stafford*, Marshall's *Magnum Bonum* (of Parson Drove) and John Bull 1160, the direct-line male ancestor of Royal Albert.

Heart of Oak blood was transmitted to the modern Shire very largely through his grand-son Vulcan 4145, Lord Ellesmere's 1889 champion stallion (from whom, incidentally, the champion mares of 1901–1902 and 1910 were descended). Vulcan was the first horse ever to be let for £1,000, which the men of Montgomeryshire paid for his services in 1892. An old member of that society, nearly forty years later commented, "He did not leave anything very great, but they were quite good sorts with the right class of leg. But most of his stock were on the small side." He died of a twisted bowel on 8th August 1903, aged twenty.

3. ROYAL ALBERT

This richly brown horse of 17.2-hands was bred in 1872 at Hatfield (Yorks) by one Charles Marsden who sold him as a foal to his neighbour, the well-known cart-stallion specialist Walter Johnson. Johnson owned the sire, the grey John Bull 1183, and Marsden's father William had bred the black dam, which was by the black Nottinghamshire-bred Royal Albert 1881. Johnson used to say he was "an upstanding, leggy, narrow horse, but he had wonderful limbs, particularly the hind legs".

In his pedigree there are seventy-four known names extending over thirteen generations. For reasons of space, it cannot be reproduced here – even though our knowledge does not extend to the other 8116 animals! The table below shows the remotest of his known ancestors.

G-sire (John Bull) **1180** **descended** **from**	i John Bull 1160 (see V.6) by Pacey's Lame Horse 1702 (f 1811 at Bassingham) by *Marfleet's Horse* of Somerton Castle ii Honest Tom 1060 (via Honest Tom 1069 – see V.3) iii Honest Tom 1060 (via Matchless 1506 – see V.8) iv Luck's All 1426 (f 1837 at Navenby) by *England's Glory* alias *The Poynton Horse* v Honest Tom 1060 (via Oxford 1683 – see V.3) vi Ivens' *Berkshire Grey Horse* & *Percey's Grey Horse* (via John Bull 1161, see VII.1) vii Two Bakewell horses *B* and *K*, via K 1191 (see III.2) viii Wilmott's *Primrose* ix As i x Hanbury's *Old G*
Dam of sire **descended** **from**	i Turner's *Active* ii Honest Tom 1060 (via Oxford 1683 as above) iii Vipau's *Waxwork* iv Challoner's *Shireoak*
Dam	bred by William Marsden, father of Charles. No other details are officially recorded, but Johnson said she was a black cart mare of great size and weight, "with the broadest, flattest and most correct hind legs I ever met with".
Dam's sire **descended** **from**	i Two Bakewell horses as above ii Honest Tom 1060 (via Farmer's Glory 824, see V.3) iii Grey's *Waxwork* iv Bingham's *Samson* (i.e. Bingham of Holbeach Marsh – see V.2)

G-dam – unknown. One cannot resist thinking of the possibility that Royal
Albert's quality – and, as a cart-horse, his defects – stemmed from
light Yorkshire blood in this quarter.

Royal Albert stayed in Yorkshire, serving mares always at 2 guineas only, until he was eleven. Then he went, via George Naylor of Newhaven (Derbys) to Cecil Salt, Willington. His seven seasons in Derbyshire were by far his most successful, for he suited the "old-fashioned mares" admirably. His fee then was 10 guineas. He died in 1890, and at the London Show that year his sons and daughters won two firsts, one second, two thirds, one fourth and one fifth prizes, one highly commended and two commended – far more than any other sire. His stock were generally very tall horses of "quality", with good ribs and excellent hind-legs, especially in the breadth and flatness of the hocks: the forelegs were their worst feature. His blood became increasingly a connoisseur's item, the experts discovering that a top cross of Lincolnshire Lad II blood "nicked" extraordinarily well, the coarseness blending marvellously with the refinement. Royal Albert mares (who were always better than his sons), when put to a Lincolnshire Lad II horse, produced wonderful daughters, but sons (with the outstanding exception of Lockinge Forest King; VI.7) tended to procreate less good stock. A second cross of Lincolnshire Lad II blood produced excellent breeding stock of both sexes.

It should be borne in mind that, although the Royal Albert male line died out as time went on, thoughtful breeders were taking greater and greater pains to find mares which had a high proportion of his blood.

4. LINCOLN

It is not easy to decide whether this horse owed his fame and influence to the fact that he was brought to join T. H. Miller and Honest Tom 1105 at Singleton Park (see A.V.3) or whether Honest Tom was lucky in having such a partner. They certainly proved a fine combination both in Miller's stud and in the Fylde generally, and Miller did well to get him from John Mayer of the Market Hotel, Derby, to whom he had gone from his Huntingdon birthplace, and who appears to have called him Hercules.

He had $13\frac{1}{4}$ inches of bone below the knee, according to Miller, and was serving mares in 1880 at 3 guineas, while Honest Tom cost 5 guineas. Compared with what the Scotsmen were prepared to pay for the use of their best stallions, these were bargain-basement fees. He died at the age of twelve in 1885, the same year as the twenty-year-old Honest Tom. Since the latter's epitaph in Singleton Park has already been quoted, perhaps Lincoln's should be given also, excruciating though it is as a piece of verse:

> He got a chance and by chance got a name,
> Which added vastly to his own great fame.
> But by mischance he hurt his poor dear toe
> Which caused him to be placed down here below.
> Lincoln lies here –
> A horse renowned for bone,
> A fact commemorated by this stone.

It is difficult to explain why Mr. Miller did not have at least his poor dear head stuffed, like Honest Tom's.

His breeding is as follows:

LINCOLN 1350, bay, bred 1873 by Infield Jones of Great Bentley, Essex who had moved his stud there from Wimblington, Cambs.

Sire: Samson 1952, the 28 cwt. horse bred by Thomas Mott of Littleport in 1861 and owned by John Rowell.

G-sire Samson 1925 (ches., bred 1847 by W. T. Saberton, Witcham) by Samson 1917 (bred 1840 by Saberton) by Nix's *Samson* and out of a mare tracing back to *Fisher's Black Horse of Weston.*

Dam of sire: by Waxwork 2268 (bred 1838 by R. Norman of Cottenham) tracing to New's *Matchless* and, on her dam's side, to Wood's *Farmer's Delight.*

Dam: Star, a black prize-winning mare bred by Infield Jones by HEART OF OAK 1005. (Infield Jones, then at Wimblington.)

G-dam: by Thumper 2113 (bred 1831 by Dearlove of Leverington) descended from Marshall's *Magnum Bonum*, Bradley's *John Bull* and Bradley's *Bolingbroke.*

(Bradley of Tydd St. Giles).

   G-g-dam: by Jones' *Little John*
      G.g.g-dam: by Honest Tom 1098 a descendant of Honest Tom 1060 and other Fen celebrities. This horse is recorded as being bred by J. Infield of West Fen, March, as was the dam's sire of Matchless. It is possible there is confusion about "J. Infield" and "Infield Jones".

The 1883 and 1885 champion mare Chance, one of the best, or *the* best, mare in the nineteenth century, was a daughter of his. A full brother of Chance, four years younger, was owned by Miller, who named him Mastodon 5203 – a reincarnation of the 28 cwt. Samson! Bury Victor Chief, the champion of 1892, was Lincoln's grandson. Erfyl Lady Grey, the Venus of the breed, was Lincoln's g.g.g.g.g.g-daughter.

5. BAR NONE

This was the only one of the foundation sires (unless we supersede Honest Tom 1060 by Harold) to appear at the London Show. Like Royal Albert, he was bred in the unlikely county of Yorkshire – by Thomas Holmes of Fenwick Hall, near Doncaster, in 1877. Like Royal Albert, too, he was acquired by Walter Johnson, who bought him "out of the plough" when rising three. He used him for a season and then sold him to James Forshaw, then still at Blyth, near Worksop, who in 1882 won the stallion championship with him. Spark, the champion of 1881 and 1883, was an old-fashioned somewhat coarse type: but Bar None, though big, was "all quality" – flat, hard bone: silky, straight hair, perfect joints, pasterns and hind leg. He would have been ideal for the

1930s. He wore so well that Forshaw nearly showed him again at the age of thirteen, but decided to keep to his resolve that to show a London champion a second time was to risk all in order to gain little or nothing.

He stood at Blyth and then Carlton-on-Trent for twelve seasons and Forshaw calculated that he sired 1,000 living foals during this time. Most were conspicuous for flat bone and silky feather, in an age when round cannons and coarse curly hair were still the Shire's unwanted hall-marks. When he died on 6th October 1892 of heart disease, James and his elder son Tom sat down to work out how much his sons and daughters were worth. Even by calculating the prices for which, to their sure knowledge, some of them had been sold, and omitting guesses at anything else, they reached the sum of £100,000, which was pretty fair for cart-horse flesh in the 'nineties.

He was outstandingly pre-potent, his stock being easily picked out, by anyone who knew something of him and of them, by their 'classy' legs and beauty of movement. His daughters were uniformly good, if somewhat lacking in weight and size. Indeed, there probably never was a better sire of well-formed fillies in the early history of the breed. More important still, they seemed to cross well with nearly every good strain of blood, from Lincolnshire Lad II or William the Conqueror to Heart of Oak and Lincoln. It is precisely for this reason that his name appears to fade from the honours lists, since in Shire pedigrees the male line is always quoted.

Most Shire men believed that his own qualities came mostly from his sire. As far as colour is concerned, that is demonstrably true, for although his dam, her sire, and her grandsire were all roans it is impossible to find a single one of his sons or daughters of that colour: almost all, like Bar None himself, were bay.

Sire: Lincoln, alias Merryman, 1348, brown: bred 1866 by Enoch Goodson of "Muston Goss" (presumably Muston Gorse, just outside the Leics. boundary with Lincs.). His direct male ancestor was Ivens' *Grey Horse*, which appears in so many leading pedigrees (See II.6).

G-sire: Other early stallions appearing in the pedigree are Goldby's *Conqueror*, *Thomas Law's Horse of Milcombe* (II.6), James's *Farmer's Glory*, and William the Conqueror 2340 (dam's sire of William the Conqueror 2343).

Dam of sire: All known lines from her lead to elements of the *Packington Blind Horse* tribe, to Summerland's *Brown George* (Staffs.†), Stych's *Brown Horse* (Derby†), Massey's *Brown Horse* (Staffs.†) and the like, as well as to more or less untraceable creatures such as Taylor's *Grey Horse of Gotham*.

Dam: Her g.g-sire was Great Britain 968, full brother to the g.g.g-sire of Royal Albert. In the rest of her pedigree nearly all the leading names not listed above occur, including Honest Tom 1060, as well as less identifiable ones such as *Bulmer's Colt*.

Like William the Conqueror, Bar None, though Yorkshire-bred, was a classic blend of the best Fens and Derby-Leicester blood.

CHAPTER IX

Tail Female

I. A FEW EARLY MATRONS

THE senior mare in the Stud-book is 4372 Roany, foaled in 1840. An unfortunate colour! She appears to have been "without father bred", and without mother, too. Her breeder, Edwards of Marston (Swindon) appears to have possessed no Christian names. She had a red-roan colt foal in 1846. He was called Washburn's *Drayman* and won first prize at the Worcestershire Show in 1848, but was not selected for inclusion in Volume 1. She herself was put in Volume 8. The next oldest mare is 4839 Diamond, born in 1848. She was a strawberry roan by a horse called *Regulator* out of a mare by a *Brown Stout*. She was registered in Volume 9 forty-four years after her birth by Robert Lewis of Stapleton Castle, Presteigne, Radnorshire, who wanted to enter her chestnut son Stapleton 6444, produced when she was ten.

The mares with the longest recorded pedigree in the female line of all those foaled before 1880 were two (presumably) full sisters – 4426 Harrold's Smiler, a chestnut foaled in 1869 and 4346 Pride of the Valley, a brown of 1872. They were bred by Robert Clarke at Padge Hall, Hinckley, and the sire of every generation to the g.g.g.g-dam was given in Volume 2, each being a horse registered in Volume 1. The earliest of them was Black Legs 142, foaled in 1804. Pride of the Valley, incidentally, had a filly-foal called *Winkey* when she was eighteen.

Among those who crept into the book without pedigree at all were 2095 Frankham's Blossom, "bred in Lincolnshire" in 1876: 5241 Ops, "foaled about 1877"; 5130 Luna, "foaled 1873, bred by – Dovill"; and 1951 Butler's Tidy, a Fylde mare who was "aged" in Volume 5 (she began her breeding career with foals in 1874 and 1875 by Honest Tom 1105). Among many more in this pedigreeless category was Joseph Flintham's 400 Diamond, but she differed from most in two respects. Firstly, she resided at Aldeburgh, in the heart of the Sorrel county. Secondly, Mr. Flintham took the trouble, in registering her in Volume 2 (she was born in 1856) to list the fifteen foals she had between 1862 and 1877, the only year she missed being 1875. The last of those without pedigree, who were registered on the strength of their prize-winning, appeared in Volume 10. There were thirteen of them there, from Jackson's Beauty, foaled in 1880 (whose daughter Beautiful Bells also won a prize), through Spencer's Diamond ("bought at Rugby Fair") and Richardson's Jenny ("bought at Kendal Fair") to Wigmore Stout, dam of Daffodil.

William Way of Wheatley, Oxon knew a lot about the breeding of his

Bowler when he registered her in Volume 5. She was foaled in 1871, by Black Prince 166: "dam *Violet*, by *Southam's Horse*: g-dam, *Smiler* by *Guntrip's Horse*: g.g-dam *Flower* by *Archer's Horse*". These three gentlemen can all be identified as Buckinghamshire owners of stallions. Mr. Way put Bowler in the book because she had a filly foal in 1881 by *Young Shakespeare*, that "famous prize cart stallion" by Old Shakespeare (2000). Both Shakespeares were owned by William Gosling Rowles of Kidlington and travelled daily from home in an eight-mile radius. Rowles, born in 1848, was seventeen when his father died. He was a keen Shakespearean scholar, played a silver cornet and won a silver cup for jumping over 21 feet. Old Shakespeare lived till the age of at least twenty-three, and the "beautiful silver roan" *Young Shakespeare*'s two fore-hoofs still serve as door-stops for Coriolanus Rowles of Kidlington. To handle and gaze at these gives some reality to old Bowler, but does not, unfortunately further illuminate her pedigree.

2. TWO FOUNDING MOTHERS

Something has been said, in discussing the importance of the male line in Shire-breeding (IV.1), by way of apology for the neglect in our story of the mares. Unfortunately, this discourtesy is unavoidable. Very few famous show mares were also great brood mares. There may be two reasons for this. In the first place, whereas after the London show the stallion had time to get into breeding condition before his season began and was rarely or ever shown again that year, the show mare was likely to be kept in luxurious form all through the spring and summer, and there was a temptation not to breed from her as soon as was really desirable. She was then more likely to prove a difficult breeder than her less august sisters. Secondly, the show mare was also likely to be the big mare, and the biggest well-bred cart mares are usually the least prolific: it is almost as if nature were anxious to set a limit upon size by inhibiting fertility at a certain point. Consequently, a study of female lines throws up comparatively few famous names. Most of the celebrated Shire mares owed their reputation either to their prizes or their progeny, but not to both.

However, there are two old dames which can well stand as the female counterpart of the foundation sires, about whom so much has had to be written. They were born at the time the Stud-book was being planned. Let a short tribute to them apply vicariously to the 140,000 or more registered mares that have succeeded them and to all those wonderful brood mares before their time that not only did their daily work on the farm with patience and skill but also conceived, carried, brought forth and suckled every Great Horse, Black Horse, English Cart-horse and Shire that ever lived.

(i) 800 NELLIE BLACKLEGS, brown, was bred in 1878 by John Smith of Ellastone, Staffs and, for her day, her pedigree is well recorded:

sire – Bestwick's Prince 2717 (7th sire, Ivens' *Grey Horse*)

dam – *Poppet* by Heart of Oak 1002 (4th sire, Wild's *Brown Colt*, by *Black Legs*)
g-d – *Mettle* by Brown George 305 (6th sire, Oldacre's *Mansetter*)
g g-d – *Black Mare* by Black Legs 144 (5th sire, *John Bull*, i.e. *Fisher's Black Horse of Weston*.)

John Smith died in 1879, but his son, also John, bred the following five from her in five years, every one of them by A. C. Duncombe's Premier himself.

HYDROMETER 3744 (brown) in 1883. Sold as a foal to A. C. Duncombe and, as four-year-old, to James Forshaw. Fourth, second and finally in 1889 first in small stallions, London. Then sold to Duke of Marlborough. At the dispersal of his stud in 1893, the Warwick S.H.S. paid 600 guineas for him. A great stock horse, he alone made Nellie Blacklegs' descendants legion.

NORTHWOOD 4593 (bay) in 1884. Sold as a foal to A. C. Duncombe and as three-year-old to Lord Middleton, for whom he had eight prolific seasons before injuring his hind leg on 10th September 1895. Among his last crop of foals was 22925 Birdsall Darling, dam of the great 1904 London champion, Birdsall Menestrel.

CHANCELLOR 4959 (bay) in 1885. Sold as a foal to A. C. Duncombe after winning the President's cup at Ashbourne. Bought in 1891 (after winning third prize in big stallions' class, but on the strength of his progeny so far) by Fred Crisp of New Southgate, London N, for 1,100 guineas, which appears to have been then a record. Crisp let him to Peterborough A.S. in 1892 for £500.

SENATOR II 6381 (bay) in 1886. Sold as a foal to A. C. Duncombe, and in 1891 sold again for 350 guineas. Castrated at the age of eighteen after his final season in 1904. Progeny innumerable.

8815 SENSIBLE (bay) in 1887. Her greatest achievement was, when put to Harold, to breed a colt foal in 1893 which John Smith sold to John Whitehurst. As Markeaton Royal Harold he was champion stallion in 1897 for Alexander Henderson and, as we have seen, his progeny won eighty-five London prizes (see VI.5).

CALWICH TOPSMAN 8959 (bay) in 1888. Sold as a foal to A. C. Duncombe, and in 1891 re-sold for 500 guineas. The least successful of the family, though he got some foals for the Prince of Wales in 1893.

(ii) 1686 LOCKINGTON BEAUTY, black, was bred in 1879 by " – White, Alderwasley, Belper", according to her first owner, W. H. Potter of Lockington Grounds, Leics. He named her in hope and on account of her unusually long mane rather than in truth, for she was really a common-looking mare with small knees and lacking in weight and width. She was by Champion 457 (4th sire, Matchless) and her dam, *Beauty*, was by Warrior 2245 (8th sire, via Drayman 607, Honest Tom 1060).

She had eight foals in eight years of which five were outstanding:

PRINCE WILLIAM 3956 in 1883, one of the two greatest sons of William the Conqueror (VII.4).

3011 BLUE RUIN (bay) in 1884 (full sister to Prince William). Sold as foal to R. N. Sutton-Nelthorpe who loved to choose odd names for his horses. First in big mares class twice before her death in foaling in 1889. Foal registered as Blue Blazes 12810: he was chestnut.

PREMIER PRINCE 5270 (bay) in 1885 (by Premier). First in London as a yearling: sold to John Rowell: in 1888 sold to J. T. Power for whom he won Royal Dublin Spring Show twice. Covered hundreds of nondescript mares in County Dublin before his death early in his sixth season there (29th April 1893).

Colt foal in 1886 (by Premier). Born dead.

Lockington Beauty was then sold by Potter to A. B. Freeman-Mitford, Batsford Park, Glos.

MARMION II 9885 (brown) in 1887 (one of Harold's eight chief sons). See VI.5.

MARS VICTOR 9889 (bay) in 1888 (by Hitchin Conqueror). Second in London as yearling: sold at two years to Walter Gilbey for £1,500 (after his sire won London championship). Won four-year-old class 1892; second in big stallions (he was of unusual size) in 1893.

MOMUS 11877 (brown) in 1889 (by Laughing Stock 4516 – Mr. Freeman-Mitford's own horse). Won prizes at London (including second as yearling) until he was seven.

Madge Wildfire (bay) in 1890 (by Laughing Stock). Died before she was registered.

Lockington Beauty had foals also in 1892 (18594 Merveille of Batsford, bay, by Hitchin Conqueror) and 1895 (22286 Peeress of Batsford, bay, by Menestrel – sold to the Earl of Verulam and later to Walpole Greenwell to become one of the foundation mares of his stud). She died at the time Mr. Freeman-Mitford had to sell up owing to joint-ill in 1896.

3. RECIPE FOR SUCCESS IN THE 'THIRTIES

If we examine the female ancestry of the last half-dozen London champion mares, the whole history of the pedigree movement for Shires is summed up without any comment being required:

		Breeder
1934:	ETCHINGHAM SOLACE. f 1930	E. W. Webb
	by Lincoln What's Wanted II (4th sire – Harold)	
dam:	99467 Northlands Solace. f 1918	John Pearman,
	by Northlands Apollo 34203 (5th sire – Harold)	Warnham, Sussex
g-d:	68037 Normanby Royal Girl. f 1910	Sir B. G. D. Sheffield
	by Halstead Royal Duke 25255 (4th sire – Harold)	

Breeder

3rd dam: 53509 Country Girl. f 1906   Lord Rothschild
by Blythwood Kingmaker 18534 (3rd sire – W. Conq.)

4th dam: 41397 Childwick Girlie. f 1900   Sir Blundell Maple
by Childwick Majestic 17254   (g-sire – Harold)

5th dam: 27133 Twycross Star. f 1890   R. A. Haywood,
by Albert Edward 5467   (by Royal Albert)   Twycross, Leics.

6th dam: 8672 Princess. f 1887   (g-sire – W. Conq.)   John Haywood
by Prince Arthur 5278

7th dam: *Blossom* by Samson 1975   (g-sire – Hathaway's   (John Haywood?)
                                           King George I)

8th dam: by W. Conq.   (John Haywood?)

1935:   127882 MARGARET OF CHIPPINGHURST. f 1934   Pendley Stock Farms
by Raans Record 40796   (7th sire – Harold)

dam: 123133 Llynclys Lady Loue. f 1928   R. W. Richards,
by Basildon Clansman 36277   (5th sire – Harold) Llynclys, Oswestry

g-dam: 108829 Llynclys Queenie. f 1920   R. W. Richards
by Blaisdon Draughtsman 32113 (4th sire – Harold)

3rd dam: 75121 Llynclys Heiress. f 1911   John Richards
by Childwick Champion 22215   (3rd sire – Harold)

4th dam: 45575 Llynclys Brown Lady. f 1903   John Richards
by Llynclys Baronet 19772   (3rd sire – W. Conq.)

5th dam: 42547 Llynclys Gipsy. f 1897   Edward Evans,
by Eardiston Lad 14014   (by L.L. II)   Llynclys, Salop

6th dam: 31231 Brown. f 1894   (g-sire – W. Conq.)   Edward Evans
by Excellent II 14030

7th dam: *Brown.* f 1889   Edward Evans
by Brown Stout 5602   (3rd sire – Vevers'
                                Brown Stout)

8th dam: *Diamond.* f 1883   Edward Evans
by Meredith's King of the Vale (4th sire – Sancho
2839   1993)

1936:   126226 MARDEN BLANCHE. f 1932   Sir Bernard Greenwell
by Marden Valiant 40766   (7th sire – Harold)

dam: 121058 Marden Thistle. f 1926   Sir Bernard Greenwell
by Champion's Goalkeeper   (4th sire – Harold)
30296

g-dam: 102161 Chatley Fluff. f 1919   J. and W. Bourne,
by Marden Peter 33356   (5th sire – Harold) Norton St. Philip,
                                                    Somerset

3rd dam: 84308 Chatley Queen. f 1915   J. and W. Bourne
by King Cole 7th 26351   (4th sire – W. Conq.)

4th dam: 50341 Bluebell. f 1901   Mrs. Sarah F. Bourne
by Calwich Prince 15531   (g-sire – Harold)

5th dam: 26451 May Blossom. f 1892   W. E. Budgett,
by Hydrometer 3744   (5th sire – Matchless) Stoke Bishop, Bristol

6th dam: *Silverlocks II.* f 1889   W. E. Budgett
   by Premier 2646 (4th sire – Matchless)

7th dam: 4391 Scarsdale Silverlocks. f 1879 — Wingfield,
        (by L.L. II) Ambaston, Derby.

8th dam: by Devonshire 594 (6th sire – Ivens' (Wingfield?)
        Grey Horse)

9th dam: by Bang-Up 95 (g-sire – Sancho (Wingfield?)
        1993)

1937: 127872 MARDEN DAPHNE. f 1934 Sir Bernard Greenwell
   by Theale Josh 41311 (8th sire – Harold)

dam: 124746 Marden Wendy. f 1930 Sir Bernard Greenwell
   by Stretton Broadside 39985 (5th sire – Harold)

g-d: 85662 Marden Ladyship. f 1915 Sir Walpole
   by Champion's Goalkeeper (4th sire – Harold) Greenwell
   30296

3rd dam: 67780 Marden Forest Lass. f 1910 Sir Walpole
   by Lockinge F. King (3rd sire – Harold) Greenwell

4th dam: 36143 Hendre Beryl. f 1900 F. W. Barling, Ross,
   by Prince Harold (by Harold) Herefs.

5th dam: 23003 Bodenham Beauty. f 1892 Henry Medlicott,
   by Dunsmore Hydro 13020 (6th sire – Matchless) Bodenham, Herefs.

6th dam: 5119 Lively. f 1882 E. T. Goodwin,
   by Honest Tom III 3736 (5th sire – Major) Hampton Bishop,
        Herefs.

7th dam: 4645 Bonnie. f 1879 E. T. Goodwin
   by *Prince of Wales*

8th dam: *Lester*   (Goodwin?)

1938: 126937 LEEK BEAUTY. f 1933 Col. A. F. Nicholson
   by Leek Blend 2nd 40962 (8th sire – W. Conq.)

dam: 124698 Leek Mimi. f 1930 Col. A. F. Nicholson
   by Lincoln What's Wanted (4th sire – Harold)
   2nd 35812

g-d: 119855 Leek Coral. f 1925 Sir Arthur Nicholson
   by Pendley Footprint 37728 (3rd sire – Harold)

3rd dam: 112124 Leek Pearl. f 1921 Sir Arthur Nicholson
   by Champion's Goalkeeper (4th sire – Harold)
   30296

4th dam: 85505 Leek Destiny. f 1915 Sir Arthur Nicholson
   by Coronation 7th 29263 (5th sire – Harold)

5th dam: 51487 Leek Dainty. f 1905 Sir Arthur Nicholson
   by Girton Meteor 19649 (3rd sire – Lincoln)

6th dam: 42494 Leek Maud. f 1902 Edward Heath,
   by Leek Monarch 17446 (g-sire – W. Conq.) Baddeley Hall, Staffs.

7th dam: *Jolly.* f 1896 Edward Heath
   by Paxton 4604 (by L.L. II)

		Breeder
8th dam:	*Kit.* f 1888	H. Durber,
	by What's Wanted 4176 (5th sire – Ivens'	Silverdale, Staffs.
	Grey Horse)	

(All nine generations were bred in Staffordshire. *Kit* was brown. One can picture a continuous ancestry running back to the eighteenth century Staffordshire Brown horses.)

1939:	126610 BATTY GRACE DARLING. f 1933	Robert Jemson,
	by Edingale Blend 40272 (6th sire – W. Conq.)	Batty Hill, Cockerham, Lancs.
dam:	114876 Mill House Brock. f 1922	John Jemson (a)
	by Burscough Ironclad 37194 (6th sire – Harold)	Mill House, Cockerham, Lancs.
g-d:	92880 Eskham Queen. f 1916	John Jemson (b)
	by Bedford 3rd 29065 (4th sire – Harold)	Eskham House, Nateby, Lancs.
3rd dam:	55088 Rington Primrose. f 1906	William Jemson,
	by Lockinge Manners 16780 (g-sire – Harold)	Holme House, Carleton, Lancs.
4th dam:	46101 Rington Mary. f 1901	J. and T. Hull,
	by Harold William 18070 (g-sire – Harold)	Preesall, Lancs.
5th dam:	12155 Dinah. f 1886	Thomas Bee,
	by Fen Champion 3085 (3rd sire – *Wade's Horse of Stonton*)	Stalmine, Lancs.
6th dam:	by King Alfred 2442 (g-sire – Matchless)	

This line of mares was entirely Fylde-bred. One wonders if the 7th dam was possibly an Honest Tom 1105 mare.

4. THE MARES OF STUNTNEY HALL

The Shires of Stuntney Hall, a mile and a half from Ely Cathedral, like Cole Ambrose who registered the majority of them, demand their own biography, but here it must suffice to say that the farm has two unique claims to fame. Firstly, more Shires have been registered from here than from anywhere else. Secondly, it is the only stud which was breeding pedigree animals before the Society was founded and which still continues to do so today, under the same family's control.

Cole Ambrose was born in 1841 and began farming on his own account at the age of fourteen on his father's 'practice farm', where a housekeeper looked after his domestic affairs. He was still under twenty years of age when he moved to Stuntney, where eventually he owned 1,600 acres (as well as 2,000 acres elsewhere). On his death in 1921 he was succeeded by his second son Owen Seaber Ambrose (1882–1967). Cole Ambrose Ltd. was formed in 1967, and is under the management of David Morbey, great-grandson of Cole Ambrose and great-nephew of Owen Ambrose.

The following table, showing the number of Stuntney Shires, is restricted to animals actually registered by Cole Ambrose and his successors: that is, it omits those bred there and sold before registration. Until the First World War, Ambrose produced a tremendous number of home-bred stallions, and bought even more, for export to Europe and the U.S.A. His son's policy was to have none at all. He relied on the horses hired by the Wisbech Society, as is still done today.

SHIRES REGISTERED BY MESSRS. COLE AMBROSE

| | Stallions | | Mares | | |
	Home-bred	Others	Home-bred	Others	Totals
Prior to 1878	4	—	21	2	27
1878–1900	248	304	82	270	904
1901–1914	259	3	301	1	564
1915–1920	2	—	123	—	125
1921–1939	1*	—	210	—	211
1940–1963	—	—	131	—	131
1964–1973	3†	—	24	—	27
	517	307	892	273	1,989

* Stuntney Flamingo 40417 brown, f 1927.

† Three colts bred in 1973. One reason for the first Stuntney entire horses being registered for over forty years was of course the sudden demand for more Shire stallions in the country at large. A second reason was the stricter requirements of the Society, making it advantageous and more economical to register animals in their year of birth.

The Stud-book (Volumes 1 to 97, 1880–1973) contains 45,576 stallions and 140,298 mares – a total of 185,874 animals. Of these, no less than 1,989, or 1.07%, have been registered from Stuntney Hall. No other place can claim any number even remotely approaching this.

The registrations in the year 1973 consisted of three colt foals and three filly foals. In addition, two colt foals of that year were sold to J. R. Suckley of Brogyntyn Farm, Oswestry, who registered them with the Stuntney prefix and name that they had been given at home. All eight were by the Wisbech Society's horse, Hainton Wonder 45391, bred in 1969 by F. Cosgrove and Son, North Walk Farm, Hainton, Lincoln and hired from them in 1972. In tail female, their pedigree shows an unbroken succession of Stuntney breeding lasting nearly a century:

140264 Stuntney Beatrice, 10th dam 4411 Smart, bred by Cole Ambrose in 1882; 11th dam 1919 Stuntney Smart (chestnut) bred by Charles Day, Prickwillow, Ely in 1878, and 0 by Cole Ambrose; 12th dam by Samson 2491 (chestnut bred in 1856 by W. H. Nix, Somersham, Hunts.).
140265 Stuntney Beryl. 10th dam 13574 Stuntney Cordelia bred by Cole

Ambrose in 1890, 11th dam 4403 Short, bay, bred 1883 by John Martin, Southery, Norfolk; 12th dam by Farmer's Friend 798 (bred 1851 by Newton of Methwold, Norfolk).

140266 Stuntney Brenda. 8th dam 5447 Stuntney Short II, bred by Cole Ambrose in 1885; 9th dam 1901 Stuntney Blossom II, roan, bred 1871 by John Hopkins, Middle Fen, Ely, by Matchless (or Matchett) 1526 bred in 1860 by T. Coy, Needingworth, St. Ives, Hunts.

Stuntney Alexis 45558. 10th dam 11013 Stuntney Blossom III, blue roan, bred 1881 by Cole Ambrose; 11th dam 1901 Stuntney Blossom II (9th dam of 140266 Stuntney Brenda above).

Stuntney Andrew 45559. 10th dam 18945 Stuntney Cicely, brown, bred 1891 by Cole Ambrose; 11th dam 3723 Welcome Princess, bay, bred 1884 by Ezra Chivers, Rampton, Cambs.: 12th dam by Matchless 1538 bred in 1873 by T. Coy as above.

Stuntney Augustus 45560; 8th dam 110176 Stuntney Princess Amie (7th dam of Stuntney Beatrice above); 13th dam as 12th dam of Stuntney Beatrice.

The two colts sold to J. R. Suckley were:

Stuntney Adam 45556: 3rd dam 137525 Stuntney Fine Lady (4th dam of Stuntney Andrew above); 11th dam as 12th dam of Stuntney Andrew.

Stuntney Alexander 45557. 9th dam 13581 Stuntney Geraldine, brown, bred by Cole Ambrose in 1890; 10th dam 5450 Stuntney Violet, bay, bred 1878 by William Cole Ambrose (elder brother of Cole Ambrose), Quy, Cambs., o by Cole Ambrose; 11th dam by Emperor 692 (chestnut, bred 1864 by Morley Beart, Welney Wisbech, Cambs.) g-son of Dack's Matchless 1509.

Here's Fens breeding! Our only regret is that none of these foals happens to trace back to the very earliest of the mares that appear in Cole Ambrose's name as breeder-owner – old 1896 Stuntney Beauty, a chestnut foaled in 1868. She was by the same Samson who sired the filly who became the 12th dam of Stuntney Beatrice and 13th dam of Stuntney Augustus. But perhaps there is sufficient satisfaction in reflecting that these foals trace back to 1879, the very year when Edward Coke and his committee were compiling Volume 1. It was then that Stuntney Beatrice's g.g.g.g.g.g.g.g.g.g-dam first came from Prickwillow to Stuntney. In that same year William Cole Ambrose of Quy sold to his younger brother the filly who now appears as the 10th dam of Stuntney Alexander. It is doubtful if any breeder of any kind of horse can claim so long a line of pedigree mares bred by his family on the same farm.

If it is fitting to conclude our long story with the homely matron rather than with the flaunting stallion, which has perhaps too much claimed our attention, then there are no mares more significant than these. When the yearlings Smart and Violet walked over from Prickwillow and Quy, "the English cart-horse was considered", as George Sexton remarked, "to be a nondescript animal not having the least claim to purity of lineage". So far as the Fens were concerned, this was mere ignorance on the part of the outside world. Nevertheless, whatever was the case then, there is a certain purity of lineage now, and it is recorded in the Stud-book for all to see.

So far as anyone can now tell, the 10th to 12th dams of Stuntney Beatrice were not by stallions descended directly from any of the great sires that have figured so largely here. But her 9th dam was a descendant in direct male line of Matchless, via Premier: the 7th and 8th dams trace similarly to William the Conqueror, via Hitchin Conqueror: the 3rd to 6th dams, her grand-dam, her dam and she herself are all by sires descended directly from Wiseman's Honest Tom 1060 via Lincolnshire Lad II and Harold – three via Prince Harold and Lockinge Forest King, three via Rokeby Friar and Childwick Champion, and one via Calwich Blend and Babingley Nulli Secundus. And, for the most part, this has been done without the mares having ever to step outside the farm where they were all born.

5. BACK TO THE BEGINNING

Our story began in Shropshire at the end of the eleventh century, in the days when the Great Horse was new in the land. The earliest Shropshire-bred horse in the Stud-book is Kirby 1287 bred in 1800 by "Mr. Kettle of the Marsh", and sold, at the age of eleven on 25th March 1811 for the fantastic sum of 525 guineas. Kettle was a selective breeder. The horse that got his fine colt was Kirby (1286), bred and owned by the celebrated Leicestershire stallion man Oldacre and a son of his famous *Mansetter*. Kettle had bred the dam, too, and she was by Dragon (598), bred in 1785 by Dutton of Chapel House and a son of *Stone's Brown Horse of Coalbrook*. Furthermore, he had also bred the grand-dam, using Robert Bakewell's G (890).

Of the great grand-dam and the mares from which she sprang, we now know nothing, and never shall. But we can reasonably guess that, like the Cole Ambrose mares of recent times in the Ely district, they had wandered but little over the generations. It may be that the blood ran in their veins of old Morel Lestrange, who stayed in Shropshire covering mares in 1314 instead of going to fight at Bannockburn. Perhaps there was even a Kettle mare whose 100th sire was one of the stallions brought to the Bridgnorth area by Robert de Bellême in 1098. This is an idle fancy. But one thing is sure. Robert has the distinction of remaining the only nasty character that has been raked up in the whole of this history of the Shire-Horse men.

London Champions, 1880–1939

BLOODLINES are indicated in this way:

Animals descended in male line from HONEST TOM 1060,

via Lincolnshire Lad II, Harold and Prince Harold, thus:	P. Harold***
via Lincolnshire Lad II, Harold and Rokeby Friar, thus:	R. Friar***
via Lincolnshire Lad II, Harold and Conquering Harold thus:	Conq. H.***
via Lincolnshire Lad II, Harold and Calwich Blend, thus:	C. Blend***
via Lincolnshire Lad II, Harold and Markeaton Royal Harold, thus:	M.R.H.***
via Lincolnshire Lad II, Harold and Marmion II, thus:	Mar II***
via Lincolnshire Lad II, Harold and Bardon Harold, thus:	B.H.***
via Lincolnshire Lad II, Harold and Calwich Blaze, thus:	C. Blaze***
via Lincolnshire Lad II and other sons:	L. L. II**
via Major 1447:	Major *

Animals descended in male line from William the Conqueror 2343:	W. Conq.
Animals descended in male line from Heart of Oak 1005:	Heart of Oak
Animals descended in male line from Lincoln 1350:	Lincoln
Animals descended in male line from Matchless 1509:	Matchless

Animals descended in some other line: the name of the remotest known male ancestor shown thus: Crow's *Crown Prince*

Where an animal's name appears a second or subsequent time, the Stud-book number, name of breeder and bloodline are not repeated.

The address of breeder or exhibitor is not repeated after first entry; e.g. in the first list (of stallions) A. B. Freeman-Mitford owned the 1890 champion and his address is given: in the *second* list, his address is not given even for the earlier year, 1885.

(A)	Champion Stallion and Breeder	Age	Bloodline	Exhibitor
1880	ADMIRAL 71 John Milner Kirkham, Lancs.	4	Major*	Earl of Ellesmere Worsley Hall Manchester
1881	SPARK 2497 W. R. Rowland Creslow, Bucks.	3	Wirdnam's *Grey Horse*	William Rickford Rowland
1882	BAR NONE 2388 Thomas Holmes Fenwick Hall, Doncaster Yorks.	5	Bar None	James Forshaw Blyth, Notts

(A)	*Champion Stallion and Breeder*	*Age*	*Bloodline*	*Exhibitor*
1883	SPARK	5		Walter Gilbey Elsenham Hall, Essex
1884	ENTERPRISE OF CANNOCK 2772 Thomas S. Minton Montford, Salop	4	Major*	Cannock Agricultural Co. Cannock, Staffs.
1885	PRINCE WILLIAM 3956 W. H. Potter Lockington Grds. Leics.	2	Son of W. Conq.	John Rowell Bury, Hunts.
1886	STAUNTON HERO 2918 J. W. Chappell jn. Breaston, Derby.	5	Son of W. Conq.	Walter Gilbey
1887	HAROLD 3703 J. H. Potter Spondon, Derby.	6	Harold***	A. C. Duncombe, Calwich Abbey Ashbourne, Derby.
1888	PRINCE WILLIAM	5		Lord Wantage Lockinge Park, Berks.
1889	VULCAN 4145 John Whitehead Medlar Hall, Kirkham Lancs.	6	Heart of Oak	Earl of Ellsmere
1890	HITCHIN CONQUEROR 4458 George S. Shepperson Lockington, Leics.	7	Son of W. Conq.	A. B. Freeman–Mitford Batsford Park, Glos.
1891	VULCAN	8		Earl of Ellesmere
1892	BURY VICTOR CHIEF 11105 John Rowell	3	Lincoln	Joseph Wainwright Bowden Hall Chapel-en-le-Frith Derby.
1893	ROKEBY HAROLD 15313 A. C. Rogers Prebend House Buckingham	1	Son of Harold***	Lord Belper Kingston Hall, Notts
1894	BURY VICTOR CHIEF	5		Joseph Wainwright
1895	ROKEBY HAROLD	3		Lord Belper
1896	ROKEBY HAROLD	4		Lord Belper
1897	MARKEATON ROYAL HAROLD 15225 John Smith Ellastone, Staffs.	4	Son of Harold ***	Alexander Henderson Buscot Park, Berks.
1898	BUSCOT HAROLD 16576 Alexander Henderson, M.P.	2	Son of M. R. H.***	Alexander Henderson, M.P.
1899	BUSCOT HAROLD	3		Alexander Henderson, M.P.

(A)	*Champion Stallion and Breeder*	Age	Bloodline	*Exhibitor*
1900	BUSCOT HAROLD	4		Alexander Henderson, M.P.
1901	BEARWARDCOTE BLAZE 18501 J. and M. Walwyn Bearwardcote Etwall, Derby.	2	Son of C. Blaze***	J. and M. Walwyn
1902	STROXTON TOM 15871 C. R. Lynn Stroxton, Lincs.	10	Matchless	James Forshaw & Sons now Carlton-on-Trent, Notts
1903	STROXTON TOM	11		James Forshaw and Sons
1904	BIRDSALL MENESTREL 19337 Lord Middleton Birdsall House, Yorks.	4	W. Conq.	Lord Rothschild Tring Park, Herts.
1905	GIRTON CHARMER 20515 Fred Crisp Girton, Cambs.	4	W. Conq.	Lord Rothschild
1906	PRESENT KING II 19948 Joseph Phillipson Hainton, Lincs.	7	L. L. II**	James Forshaw & Sons
1907	BIRDSALL MENESTREL	7		Lord Rothschild
1908	TATTON DRAY KING 23777 William Whitehead Forton Hall Garstang, Lancs.	4	W. Conq.	Earl Egerton of Tatton Tatton Park, Cheshire
1909	HALSTEAD ROYAL DUKE 25255 John Bradley Halstead, Leics.	3	P. Harold***	Lord Rothschild
1910	GAER CONQUEROR 25218 Peter Stubs Blaisdon, Glos.	5	L. L. II**	Abraham Grandage Bramhope, Yorks.
1911	GAER CONQUEROR	6		Abraham Grandage
1912	WARTON DRAUGHTSMAN 27895 James Bullock Draycott-le-Clay, Staffs.	4	Conq. H.***	Duke of Devonshire Chatsworth, Derby.
1913	CHAMPION'S GOALKEEPER 30296 Earl of Powis Powis Castle, Mont.	2	R. Friar***	Sir Walpole Greenwell, Bt Marden Park, Surrey
1914	CHAMPION'S GOALKEEPER	3		Sir Walpole Greenwell, Bt
1915	BLAISDON JUPITER 27051 Tom Stelfox Walden Court Newent, Glos.	7	L. L. II**	Lord Rothschild
1916	BURY KING'S CHAMPION 32190 G. H. Edwards Wadley Farm Blagdon, Somerset	3	W. Conq.	John Rowell

(A)	Champion Stallion and Breeder	Age	Bloodline	Exhibitor
1917	CHAMPION'S CLANSMAN 29221 William Roberts Radmanthwaite Mansfield, Notts	7	R. Friar***	Sir Arthur Nichsolson Highfield Hall Leek, Staffs.
1918	RICKFORD COMING KING 27709 Lord Winterstoke Combe Lodge Blagdon, Somerset	10	W. Conq.	J. Forshaw & Sons
1919	GENEROSITY 34773 J. T. Ward Pentrehilin Churchstoke, Mont.	4	P. Harold***	J. Forshaw & Sons
1920	FIELD-MARSHAL 5th 35627 H.M. The King, Sandringham, Norfolk	3	R. Friar***	H.M. The King
1921	FIELD-MARSHAL 5th	4		H.M. The King
1922	HARBORO' NULLI SECUNDUS 33231 W. T. Hayr Tur Langton Manor, Leics.	8	C. Blend***	Mrs. Stanton Snelston Hall, Derby.
1923	HARBORO' NULLI SECUNDUS	9		Mrs. Stanton
1924	HERONTYE BUSCOT 37494 Andrew Devitt Herontye E. Grinstead, Sussex	5	R. Friar***	James Gould Crouchley Hall Lymm, Cheshire
1925	COWAGE CLANSMAN 38767 S. J. Doble Cowage, Calne, Wilts.	4	R. Friar***	Sir Arthur Nicholson
1926	LINCOLN WHAT'S WANTED II 35812 Thomas Baxter Freeford, Lichfield, Staffs.	9	Mar. II***	J. Forshaw & Sons
1927	COWAGE CLANSMAN	6		Sir Arthur Nicholson
1928	EATON PREMIER KING 39486 T. E. Pleavin Gwastad Farm Cefn-y-bedd Wrexham, Denb.	5	Conq. H.***	J. Morris Belcher Tibberton Manor, Salop
1929	EATON PREMIER KING	6		J. Morris Belcher
1930	EATON PREMIER KING	7		J. Morris Belcher
1931	KIRKLAND BLACK FRIAR 40320 W. H. Wildman Borwick Carnforth, Lancs.	4	Conq. H.***	E. W. Webb Ketchingham Farm Etchingham, Sussex

(A)	Champion Stallion and Breeder	Age	Bloodline	Exhibitor
1932	BOWER WINALOT 40672 J. G. Runciman, MRCVS 15 Downing St., Cambridge	3	C. Blend***	G. R. C. Foster Anstey Hall Trumpington, Cambs.
1933	BOWER WINALOT	4		G. R. C. Foster
1934	BOWER WINALOT	5		G. R. C. Foster
1935	HARBORO' GOLDFINDER 41177 H. R. Guilford Muswell Leys Lutterworth, Leics.	4	R. Friar***	J. Morris Belcher
1936	HARBORO' GOLDFINDER	5		J. Morris Belcher
1937	OLD HOUSE CONQUERING MIMIC 42065 W. A. Tipping King's Heath War.	3	R. Friar***	Enoch Bostock Gibbett Hill Coventry, War.
1938	HARBORO' GOLDFINDER	7		J. Morris Belcher
1939	BOWER WINALOT	10		J. G. Runciman

(B)	Champion Mare and Breeder	Age	Bloodline	Exhibitor
1880	1094 TOPSY "Goodall Milton, Derby."	6	Crow's Crown Prince	Lawrence Drew Merryton, Hamilton
1881	93 BLACK DIAMOND "Lamburn Herdwick, Bucks."	7	Iron's King of the Valley	Earl of Ellesmere
1882	1087 THURSA Langton Bennett Boycott Farm, Buckingham	5	Belcher's Emperor	Garrett Taylor Trowse Hall, Norwich
1883	262 CHANCE William Lawrenson Preesall, Lancs.	3	dau. of Lincoln	Hon. E. Coke Longford Hall, Derby.
1884	1419 CZARINA E. and M. Williams Blakesley, Northants	3	Belcher's Emperor	Hon. E. Coke
1885	CHANCE	5		Hon. E. Coke
1886	4386 BONNY Arthur Tomlinson Stenson, Derby.	7	dau. of L. L. II**	Arthur Tomlinson
1887	2068 BLACK BESS Joseph Scottorn Wilford Hill, Notts	5	Nix's Samson	T. H. Miller Singleton Park, Lancs.

(B)	Champion Mare and Breeder	Age	Bloodline	Exhibitor
1888	1281 BLOSSOM II John Hopper North Side Whittlesea, Cambs.	8	Howard's Farmer's Profit	Earl of Ellesmere
1889	BLOSSOM II	9		Earl of Ellesmere
1890	10982 STARLIGHT Thomas Williamson Hales Hall Out-Rawcliffe, Lancs.	8	Howard's Farmer's Profit	R. N. Sutton-Nelthorpe Scawby Hall Brigg, Lincs.
1891	STARLIGHT	9		Fred Crisp White House Stud Farm New Southgate, N. (and Girton: see 1905s)
1892	STARLIGHT	10		Fred Crisp
1893	15507 ROKEBY FUCHSIA W. H. & J. Spalton Denby, Derby.	6	L. L. II**	John Parnell Rugby, War.
1894	ROKEBY FUCHSIA	7		John Parnell
1895	12989 MINNEHAHA A. B. Freeman-Mitford	6	Fisher's Black Horse of Weston	A. B. Freeman-Mitford
1896	19593 CATTHORPE NAXOS T. E. Hewer Knighton Hungerford, Berks.	4	L. L. II**	J. P. Cross Catthorpe Towers, Leics.
1897	20686 QUEEN OF THE SHIRES John Blunt Breedon-on-the-Hill, Leics.	3	dau. of Harold***	Abraham Grandage
1898	13951 AUREA Thomas Walsh Thornton, Lancs.	7	Matchless	Alexander Henderson, M.P.
1899	14655 DUNSMORE GLOAMING H.R.H. The Prince of Wales	9	dau. of Harold***	Sir J. Blundell Maple, M.P. Childwick St. Albans, Herts.
1900	DUNSMORE GLOAMING	10		Sir J. Blundell Maple, M.P.
1901	21218 ALSTON ROSE (Exors. of) John Mercer Alston Hall Preston, Lancs.	6	Heart of Oak	Lord Rothschild
1902	ALSTON ROSE	7		R. W. Hudson Danesfield, Marlow, Bucks.
1903	24787 SOLACE H.M. The King	9	Matchless	Lord Rothschild

(B)	*Champion Mare and Breeder*	*Age*	*Bloodline*	*Exhibitor*
1904	44710 DESFORD COUNTESS George Bass, Bagworth Park, Leics.	5	B. H.***	W. & J. Thompson Barron's Park Desford, Leics.
1905	44795 DUNSMORE FUCHSIA G. G. Atterbury West Haddon, Northants	2	L. L. II**	Sir P. Albert Muntz, Bt, M.P. Dunsmore Rugby, War.
1906	29761 PRINCESS BERYL Sir Henry Ewart Felix Hall Kelvedon, Essex	10	P. Harold***	Lord Rothschild
1907	52340 STOLEN DUCHESS William Harpham Corringham, Lincs.	6	Mar. II***	James Forshaw & Sons
1908	44091 BELLE COLE William Snalam Fir Tree Farm Crossmoor Kirkham, Lancs.	5	Conq. H.***	Lord Rothschild
1909	50678 CHILTERN MAID Walter McCreary Bilton Park, War.	4	P. Harold***	Lord Rothschild
1910	53825 EUREKA F. J. Olver Bocaddon Lanreath, Cornwall	4	Heart of Oak	Sir Walpole Greenwell, Bt
1911	45919 PAILTON SORAIS J. L. Harrison Pailton Fields Rugby, War.	8	P. Harold***	Max Michaelis Tandridge Court, Surrey
1912	60183 DUNSMORE CHESSIE J. and M. Hewitt Monk's Kirby, War.	4	L. L. II**	Sir Walpole Greenwell, Bt
1913	DUNSMORE CHESSIE	5		Sir Walpole Greenwell, Bt
1914	64248 LORNA DOONE Thomas Green The Bank Pool Quay, Mont.	5	R. Friar***	W. and H. Whitley Primley Farm, Paignton, Devon
1915	LORNA DOONE	6		W. and H. Whitley
1916	LORNA DOONE	7		W. and H. Whitley
1917	75832 ROYCROFT FOREST QUEEN F. S. Hawthorn Roycroft Lodge Uttoxeter, Staffs.	5	P. Harold***	Sir Arthur Nicholson
1918	(Stallions only)			

(B)	Champion Mare and Breeder	Age	Bloodline	Exhibitor
1919	(Stallions only)			
1920	84986 GLEADTHORPE SECLUSION (Exors. of) Tom Kay Hatfield House Cuckney, Notts	5	R. Friar***	A. R. Grimes Gleadthorpe Grange Warsop, Notts
1921	85659 MARDEN EVELYN 2nd Sir Walpole Greenwell, Bt.	6	R. Friar***	Pendley Stock Farms (H. W. Bishop & J. Measures) Tring, Herts.
1922	102484 CROSSWAYS FOREST MAID F. Farnsworth & Sons Shawswell Cirencester, Glos.	4	Conq. H.***	Owen Williams Crossways Cowbridge, Glam
1923	CROSSWAYS FOREST MAID	5		Owen Williams
1924	88450 ERFYL LADY GREY William Vaughan Hafod Llanerfyl, Mont.	9	Lincoln	G. R. C. Foster
1925	ERFYL LADY GREY	10		G. R. C. Foster
1926	ERFYL LADY GREY	11		G. R. C. Foster
1927	113355 WICK LADY CLANSMAN Fred Doble, Winterbourne Bassett, Wilts.	6	R. Friar***	William J. Cumber Theale, Berks.
1928	119877 LOCKINGE RIDGEWAY ROSE W. G. & E. H. Roberts Great Hope, Leighton Welshpool, Mont.	3	Mar. II***	A. Thomas Loyd (Lockinge)
1929	LOCKINGE RIDGEWAY ROSE	4		A. Thomas Loyd
1930	LOCKINGE RIDGEWAY ROSE	5		A. Thomas Loyd
1931	124090 PENDLEY MARCELINE William Newhouse Ancliffe Hall Slyne, Lancs.	2	C. Blend***	Pendley Stock Farms (Sir Gomer Berry, Bt)
1932	118409 KERRY CLANISH MAID Ben Alderson Glanmeheli Kerry, Mont.	9	R. Friar***	J. and W. Whewell Radcliffe, Lancs.
1933	KERRY CLANISH MAID	10		J. and W. Whewell
1934	124549 ETCHINGHAM SOLACE E. W. Webb	4	Mar. II***	E. W. Webb
1935	127882 MARGARET OF CHIPPINGHURST Pendley Stock Farms (Sir Gomer Berry, Bt)	1	R. Friar***	J. G. McDougall Chippinghurst Manor Cuddesdon, Oxon
1936	126226 MARDEN BLANCHE Sir Bernard Greenwell, Bt	4	C. Blend***	Sir Bernard Greenwell, Bt

(B)	*Champion Mare and Breeder*	*Age*	*Bloodline*	*Exhibitor*
1937	127872 MARDEN DAPHNE Sir Bernard Greenwell, Bt	3	R. Friar***	Sir Bernard Greenwell, Bt
1938	126937 LEEK BEAUTY Col. A. F. Nicholson	5	W. Conq.	Col. A. F. Nicholson
1939	126610 BATTY GRACE DARLING Robert Jemson Batty Hill Cockerham, Lancs.	6	W. Conq.	C. & M. Barker Stilton House Helmsley, Yorks.

(C)	*Champion Gelding and Breeder*	*Age*	*Bloodline*	*Exhibitor*
1880– 1894	No champions			
1895	ELFORD CAPTAIN Charles Coxon Elford Park, Staffs.	3	W. Conq.	Charles Coxon
1896	HENDRE PREMIER Richard Messinger Norton, Northants	5	Matchless	William Thompson Celyn Farm, Leeswood Mold, Flint.
1897	BARDON EXTRAORDINARY (late 14496) W. T. Everard Bardon Hall, Leics.	5	W. Conq.	W. T. Everard
1898	BARDON EXTRAORDINARY	6		James Eadie Barrow Hall, Derby.
1899	BARDON EXTRAORDINARY	7		James Eadie
1900	BARROW FARMER G. H. Spraggon Stocksfield, Northumb.	6	Matchless	James Eadie
1901	BARDON EXTRAORDINARY	9		O. R. Ward Noon Sun Farm Great Warford Mobberley, Ches.
1902	LOCKINGE EBONY Thomas Brown Middle Hulme Leek, Staffs.	4	Son of R. Friar***	Lady Wantage
1903	REDLYNCH DUKE F. Cole Dodford Chippenham, Wilts.	7	Matchless	Thomas Edwards Spring Bank Litherland, Lancs.
1904	MIDDLETON HERO Thomas Parker Upper Rawcliffe Garstang, Lancs.	5	W. Conq.	John Hulbert Home Farm Middleton, Lancs.

(C)	*Champion Gelding and Breeder*	*Age*	*Bloodline*	*Exhibitor*
1905	OLDFIELD DUKE T. Simpson Jay Warren Farm Wimbledon, Surrey	5	W. Conq.	A. C. Sparkes Oldfield Altrincham, Cheshire
1906	SHUSTOKE JUMBO Mark Alcock The Hill Farm Shustoke, War	3	M. R. H.***	Mark Alcock
1907	OLDFIELD DUKE	7		A. C. Sparkes
1908	OLDFIELD PLOUGHMAN Arthur Dodd Chester Lane Farm Marton, Cheshire	3	Conq. H.***	A. C. Sparkes
1909	MIDLANDS BOSS J. B. Gardner Kinoulton, Notts	4	W. Conq.	Peter Davies Midlands Farm Warburton, Cheshire
1910	HUMPTY DUMPTY II G. H. Harris Longmoor Farm Aston Abbots, Bucks.	4	M. R. H.***	G. H. Harris
1911	MIDLANDS SQUIRE Edwin Armstrong Scarcliffe Lanes, Derby.	5	P. Harold***	Peter Davies
1912	Midlands Squire, as LYMM DRAYMAN	6		Joseph Palmer Holly Bank Lymm, Cheshire
1913	Midlands Squire, as LYMM DRAYMAN	7		Joseph Palmer
1914	HOLLYWOOD Hamer Towgood Saintfoins, Little Shelford, Cambs.	7	W. Conq.	Mawers Ltd. 223 Fulham Road London S.W.
1915	TRAVELLER Sir Berkeley Sheffield, Bt Normanby Park Scunthorpe, Lincs.	4	W. Conq.	R. I. Swaby and Son Westfield Park Scunthorpe, Lincs.
1916	CARACTACUS Thos. Dare Poling, Sussex	6	P. Harold***	Mawers Ltd.
1917	CARACTACUS	7		Mawers Ltd.
1918	(Stallions only)			
1919	(Stallions only)			
1920	DOGDYKE PREMIER J. and J. W. Bee Sedgbrook, Lincs.	4	P. Harold***	S. Leggate & Son Dogdyke, Lincs.

(C)	Champion Gelding and Breeder	Age	Bloodline	Exhibitor
1921	BROTHERTOFT FENMAN Mary Potter Treswell, Notts	7	C. Blend***	Henry Vere & Sons Thornton Grange New York, Lincs.
1922	COMRADE (formerly Elmton King) W. T. Cocking Elmton Grange, Derby.	6	P. Harold***	G. L. Hardcastle Long Knowle Hilton Lane Prestwich, Lancs.
1923	ALKRINGTON DARKIE (formerly Elma Darkie) George Kendrew Elm House Northallerton, Yorks.	6	W. Conq.	Milton Schofield Moss Farm Alkrington, Lancs.
1924	CAPTAIN F. C. Bush Marston-on-Dove Derby.	5	W. Conq.	George G. Marsh & Son Mount Pleasant Speke, Lancs.
1925	UNCLE BEN Ben Farrow Hawton Grange, Notts	3	P. Harold***	George G. Marsh & Son
1926	ALBION VICTOR A. A. Naylor Barton Fields Church Broughton, Derby.	4	R. Friar***	Mann, Crossman & Paulin Ltd. Albion Brewery Whitechapel Road, E.1
1927	CAESAR R. T. Owen Dwygir Rhosgoch, Anglesey	5	L. L. II**	J. W. Warburton Oaklands Farm Hale Barns Altrincham, Cheshire
1928	SAXON JACK Sir Walter Gilbey, Bt	7	W. Conq.	E. J. Wythes Copped Hall Epping, Essex
1929	CAESAR	7		J. W. Warburton
1930	LANCASTER Christopher Fox Bank End Glasson Dock, Lancs.	7	C. Blend ***	Mann, Crossman & Paulin Ltd.
1931	HASELEY BRIAR Milton Harris Little Milton Manor Oxon	4	W. Conq.	G. G. Marsh & Son
1932	NORMAN Milton Harris	8	R. Friar***	Mann, Crossman & Paulin Ltd.
1933	NORMAN	9		Mann, Crossman & Paulin Ltd.
1934	WONDER R. C. Price Broughton, Salop	7	R. Friar***	G. G. Marsh & Son

(C)	*Champion Gelding and Breeder*	*Age*	*Bloodline*	*Exhibitor*
1935	SOLOMON R. P. Wareing Poulton Hall Farm Poulton-le-Fylde, Lancs.	4	R. Friar***	C. & M. Barker
1936	PENDLEY WARRANT (formerly Royal Warrant 40612) Bibby Bros. Coat Green Farm Carnforth, Lancs.	8	Mar. II***	Charles Franklin 10 Bank Buildings Bedford
1937	PENDLEY WARRANT	9		Percy Surridge Great Lake Farm Horley, Surrey
1938	LINCOLN John Dargue Burnside Hall Kendal, Westmorland	4	Conq. H.***	Mann, Crossman & Paulin Ltd.
1939	ALBION SURPRISE David Powell, Lower Kimbolton, Herefordshire	4	R. Friar***	Mann, Crossman & Paulin Ltd.

Leading Sires, 1880–1939

(*a*) ANNUAL LIST

Column (i) lists the sire with the largest number of winning sons and daughters at the London Show – that is, winners of prizes, or highly commended or commended cards, and how many.

Column (ii) lists the two sires with the largest number of sons and daughters winning prizes, or H.C. or C. at London or R.A.S.E., or prizes (but *not* H.C. or C.) at "Gold Medal" shows. This list begins only at 1899, when for the first time there were sufficient Gold Medal shows to make it significant. N.B. This column does *not* show the sires whose progeny won most *prizes* (which would be meaningless) but those with the largest number of different sons and daughters winning prizes in the relevant year.

Bloodlines are indicated (once only and in column 1 where possible) in the same way as in Appendix 1.

(i) LONDON SHOWS
Leading Sire and no. of winning progeny

1880	HONEST TOM 1105 Major*	5
1881	ENGLAND'S WONDER Major*	3
1882	WHAT'S WANTED Matchless	4
1883	{ LINCONSHIRE TOM Major*	4
	{ LINCOLN Lincoln	4
1884	WHAT'S WANTED	6
1885	LINCOLN	6
1886	PREMIER Matchless	11
1887	PREMIER	10
1888	PREMIER	14
1889	{ PREMIER	5
	{ HAROLD***	5
1890	ROYAL ALBERT R. Albert	10
1891	HAROLD	9
1892	HAROLD	11
1893	HAROLD	10
1894	HAROLD	17
1895	HAROLD	18
1896	HAROLD	28
1897	HAROLD	24
1898	HAROLD	15
1899	HAROLD	10

(ii) LONDON and GOLD MEDAL SHOWS
Leading Sires and number of winning progeny

| HAROLD | 25 |
| PRINCE HAROLD*** | 21 |

(i) LONDON SHOWS *Leading Sire and no. of winning progeny*		(ii) LONDON and GOLD MEDAL SHOWS *Leading Sires and number of winning progeny*		
1900	HAROLD 19	HAROLD	38	
		PRINCE HAROLD	17	
1901	HAROLD 15	HAROLD	30	
		PRINCE HAROLD	18	
1902 {	HAROLD 12	M. R. HAROLD	25	
	MARKEATON ROYAL HAROLD*** 12	HAROLD	17	
1903	DUNSMORE JAMESON L. L. II** 10	M. R. HAROLD	17	
		D. JAMESON	17	
1904	D. JAMESON 15	D. JAMESON	28	
		M. R. HAROLD	20	
1905	D. JAMESON 18	D. JAMESON	39	
		LOCKINGE FOREST KING	23	
1906	D. JAMESON 28	L. F. KING	42	
		D. JAMESON	41	
1907	LOCKINGE F. KING P. Harold*** 28	L. F. KING	44	
		D. JAMESON	44	
1908	L. F. KING 33	L. F. KING	56	
		D. JAMESON	49	
1909	L. F. KING 40	L. F. KING	75	
		D. M. JAMESON	31	
1910	L. F. KING 38	L. F. KING	64	
		TATTON FRIAR	25	Cong. H***
1911	L. F. KING 24	L. F. KING	45	
		TATTON DRAY KING	21	Wm. Conq.
1912	L. F. KING 21	L. F. KING	37	
		REDLYNCH F. KING	23	
1913	REDLYNCH F. KING P. Harold*** 22	REDLYNCH F. KING	37	
		L. F. KING	24	
1914	REDLYNCH F. KING 20	REDLYNCH F. KING	30	
		NORBURY MENESTREL	26	
1915	NORBURY MENESTREL Wm. Conq. 17	N. MENESTREL	22	
		CHILDWICK CHAMP.	20	R. Friar***
1916	N. MENESTREL 17	N. MENESTREL	24	
		CHILDWICK CHAMPION	22	
1917	N. MENESTREL 17	N. MENESTREL	18	
		CHILDWICK CHAMPION	13	
1918	BABINGLEY N. S. C. Blend*** 8	—		
1919	BABINGLEY N. S. 5	N. MENESTREL	16	
	CH. CLANSMAN R. Friar*** 5	CHAMPION'S CLANSMAN	16	
	CH. GOALKEEPER R. Friar*** 5			
1920	CHAMPION'S GOALKEEPER 13	N. MENESTREL	32	
		CH. GOALKEEPER	27	
1921	N. MENESTREL 17	CH. GOALKEEPER	39	
		N. MENESTREL	30	

(i) LONDON SHOWS
Leading Sire and no. of winning progeny

Year	Sire		No.
1922	CH. GOALKEEPER		19
1923	CH. GOALKEEPER		13
1924	CH. GOALKEEPER		16
1925	CH. GOALKEEPER		15
1926	CH. GOALKEEPER		20
1927	SUNDRIDGE N. S.	C. Blend***	13
1928	BASILDON CLANSMAN	R. Friar***	19
1929	BASILDON CLANSMAN		12
1930	SUNDRIDGE N. S.		14
	HEIRLOOM III	C. Blend***	14
1931	MOULTON HARBORO'	C. Blend***	10
1932	HEIRLOOM III		13
1933	STRETTON BROADSIDE		12
		C. Blend***	
1934	STATFOLD N. S.	C. Blend***	11
1935	KIRKLAND MIMIC	R. Friar***	10
1936	BOWER WINALOT	C. Blend***	13
1937	K. MIMIC		14
1938	K. MIMIC		12
1939	K. MIMIC		11

(ii) LONDON and GOLD MEDAL SHOWS
Leading Sires and number of winning progeny

Sire	No.	
CH. GOALKEEPER	37	
N. MENESTREL	24	
CH. GOALKEEPER	42	
HARBORO' N. S.	24	C. Blend***
CH. GOALKEEPER	39	
HARBORO' N. S.	25	
CH. GOALKEEPER	36	
MARCH KING	22	P. Harold***
CH. GOALKEEPER	42	
SUNDRIDGE N. S.	23	
BASILDON CLANSMAN	26	
SUNDRIDGE N. S.	25	
B. CLANSMAN	27	
SUNDRIDGE N. S.	20	
B. CLANSMAN	29	
SUNDRIDGE N. S.	21	
SUNDRIDGE N. S.	24	
LINCOLN W. W. II	17	Mar. II***
B. CLANSMAN	19	
SUNBRIDGE N. S.	18	
HEIRLOOM III	16	
SUNDRIDGE N. S.	16	
EDINGALE BLEND	12	W. Conq.
EATON PREM. K.	12	Conq. H.***
KIRKLAND MIMIC	17	
E. BLEND	16	
K. MIMIC	21	
BOWER WINALOT	19	
B. WINALOT	24	
K. MIMIC	18	
B. WINALOT	23	
K. MIMIC	20	
K. MIMIC	23	
TILTON W. W.	19	Mar. II***
K. MIMIC	24	
TILTON W. W.	23	

(*b*) THE "TOP FIFTY"

There is no way, of course, of discovering the 'best sires'. If one means by this the most potent, the quest is hopeless because a very large proportion of the progeny of every cart-horse stallion is lost for ever in anonymity, especially of his sons among the town geldings. If one means those that transmitted the highest quality, then much depends on the sort of mares they were required to serve. If one means pre-potency, even that issue is clouded by the emphasis on the male line. Harold and some of his sons, and William the Conqueror, clearly stand out: but the characteristics passed on by some of those horses whose virtues were particularly found in their daughters (Premier and Bar None are notable examples) are impossible to quantify.

The sort of consideration which affects the value of the following list is illustrated by such random examples as these four:

(i) Only two of Harold's sons, Prince Harold and Markeaton Royal Harold, qualify as sires in their own right to appear in this list.

(ii) In the immediate pre-war years, King Cole VII 26351 foaled in 1907 (of the William the Conqueror line), was regarded by many breeders as the horse they would chiefly wish to use. He sired 31 winners at London Shows, including the 1916 champion stallion – not enough to get him in any list here. Much of the enormous good he did to the breed was achieved in Somerset: if he had moved in more fashionable circles earlier (he was drowned in the Welland six weeks after his son won the championship) he might have appeared near the top of the list.

(iii) Lymm Grey King 41462, foaled in 1932 (a descendant of Lockinge Forest King) was a late starter, like many of his line. His progeny had four wins at the 1938–1939 shows. But he was the leading sire at each of the first three post-war shows in 1945–1947, in which he had 25 winners.

(iv) Lucky Dog 39250 sired only one London prize-winner – Bower Winalot, the only pre-war quadruple champion. How does one rate him?

The "top fifty" have been selected numerically on the basis of London Shows. They are listed in order of their age. Those foaled in 1873 or earlier, and those foaled in 1922 or later, have here been given a special advantage. The former were too old to have much chance of having as many winning sons and daughters at London Shows as younger sires: the latters' progeny were competing at a time when the prize list was reduced and, of course, some of them were too young to get on a list of stallions whose sons and daughters won fifty or more London prizes.

	Year Foaled	No. of Prizes H. C. & C.	Years	Bloodline
A. Nine horses too old to have a fair chance of recording fifty or more winners at London among their progeny (one notable exception)				
1. William the Conqueror 2343	1862	32	1880–1896	
2. Honest Tom 1105	1865	16	1880–1890	Major*
3. Thumper 2136	1868	19	1880–1893	Matchless
4. England's Wonder 761	1871	23	1880–1891	Major*
5. Hydraulic 1130	1872	23	1880–1890	son of L. L. 1196*
6. Lincolnshire Lad II 1365	1872	58	1881–1905	
7. Royal Albert 1885	1872	46	1883–1897	
8. Lincoln 1350	1873	24	1881–1888	
9. What's Wanted 2332	1873	24	1881–1891	Matchless
B. Twenty-seven horses with progeny winning more than fifty London prizes or H. C. or C.				
10 Bar None 2388	1877	74	1884–1904	

		Year Foaled	No. of Prizes H. C. & C.	Years	Bloodline
11.	Premier 2646	1880	66	1886–1906	Matchless
12.	Harold 3703	1881	228	1888–1912	
13.	Hitchin Conqueror 4458	1883	61	1889–1908	W. Conq.
14.	Bury Victor Chief 11105	1889	56	1894–1914	Lincoln
15.	Prince Harold 14228	1890	74	1896–1914	son of Harold***
16.	Menestrel 14180	1891	67	1898–1913	W. Conq.
17.	Markeaton Royal Harold 15225	1893	85	1897–1913	son of Harold***
18.	Dunsmore Jameson 17972	1898	162	1902–1915	L. L. II**
19.	Lockinge Forest King 18867	1899	261	1904–1922	P. Harold***
20.	Birdsall Menestrel 19337	1900	70	1904–1921	W. Conq.
21.	Tatton Friar 21953	1900	68	1906–1921	Conq. Harold***
22.	Childwick Champion 22215	1903	149	1908–1926	R. Friar***
23.	Redlynch Forest King 23626	1904	99	1908–1923	P. Harold***
24.	Norbury Menestrel 23543	1904	163	1909–1930	W. Conq.
25.	Tatton Dray King 23777	1904	94	1909–1925	W. Conq.
26.	King of Tandridge 24351	1905	70	1910–1923	P. Harold***
27.	Babingley Nulli Secundus 26993	1908	103	1913–1930	C. Blend***
28.	Champion's Cransman 29221	1910	53	1915–1929	R. Friar***
29.	Champion's Goalkeeper 30296	1911	152	1916–1935	R. Friar***
30.	Harboro' Nulli Secundus 33231	1914	61	1920–1931	C. Blend***
31.	Theale Lockinge 35246	1916	52	1920–1933	W. Conq.
32.	Monks Green Friar 35891	1916	67	1921–1932	Conq. Harold***
33.	March King 34955	1916	53	1922–1934	P. Harold***
34.	Lincoln What's Wanted II 35812	1917	62	1926–1937	Marmion II***
35.	Sundridge N. Secundus 36952	1918	93	1922–1937	C. Blend***
36.	Basildon Clansman 36277	1918	107	1922–1939	R. Friar***

C. Fourteen horses too young to have fair chance of recording fifty winners at London among their progeny (two notable exceptions)

37.	Heirloom III 39510	1922	59	from 1927	C. Blend***
38.	Seedsman 39589	1923	34	from 1928	R. Friar***
39.	Eaton Premier King 39486	1923	38	from 1928	Conq. Harold***
40.	Moulton Harboro' 39559	1923	31	from 1929	C. Blend***
41.	Kirkland Mimic 39739	1924	62	from 1931	R. Friar***
42.	Stretton Broadside 39985	1925	43	from 1930	C. Blend***
43.	Statfold Nulli Secundus 40170	1926	31	from 1931	C. Blend***
44.	Pendley Harvester 40368	1927	39	from 1932	R. Friar***
45.	Edingale Blend 40272	1927	27	from 1932	W. Conq.
46.	Tilton What's Wanted 40637	1928	26	from 1934	Marmion II***
47.	Bower Winalot 40672	1929	46	from 1933	C. Blend***
48.	Raans Record 40796	1929	35	from 1933	R. Friar***
49.	Ridgeway Renown 41030	1929	32	from 1934	Marmion II***
50.	Theale Josh 41311	1931	20	from 1935	R. Friar***

Principal Exhibitors, 1880–1939

(a) THE "TOP FIFTY"

Of the studs which won prizes between 1880 and 1939 at London Shows in the largest numbers, most were owned by men of wealth. But not all. The Forshaws, who easily top the list, were pure Shire "professionals". William Cumber, the Barrs and A. H. Clark support them to ensure that four of the nine most successful exhibitors were practical farmers and horsemen.

In the list which follows, awards in the "commercial horse" classes, introduced in 1923, have not been counted, but in-hand gelding classes, from their reinstatement in 1895, have been included. Indeed, the tenth name on the list is there entirely on the strength of gelding prizes.

In reckoning the number of winners, "highly commended" and "commended" cards have been included, as well as actual prizes, and each award has been counted as one unit. If the value of the prize were taken into account (for example, twenty points for a champion, seven for a fourth prize, two for highly commended and so on), there would be some changes of position in this roll of honour, though not among the leaders. Lower down, Sir Edward Stern, Fred Parsons and Sir Berkeley Sheffield would have dropped a few places, and Sir Alexander Henderson, Mrs. Stanton and J. P. Cross would have gained some. But it has seemed fairest to allot the greatest honour to those who brought to London the most horses which were recognised by the judges, to greater or less degree, as meritorious.

Where son (or nephew or other heir) followed father, the successes of each have been added together. This favours the Forshaws and others; but is unavoidable, because it would be even more impossible now than it would have been at the time to decide at what point the credit should cease to go to father and be bestowed upon son – as in the case of the Clarks. Similarly, where a manager himself became a proprietor on the death of his employer, his successes under his own name have been added to those of his predecessor, for it was he who was responsible for all. Such men include Tom Ewart, Tom Fowler and Harry Bishop.

Some men, like Hamer Towgood or Earl Egerton, had no successor to carry on their glory. The latter was particularly unlucky, and so are the Stuarts. John Stuart was his manager, and there never has been a better Shire man than he. But he died before his guv'nor. The very last horse he bought was Tatton Friar, foaled in 1900 and destined to grow into one of the finest stallions the breed has ever had. But when the colt arrived in the yard, John, still only 38 years of age, was on his death bed. He sent his wife Margaret to go and look, and give her opinion of the young animal. She and her family, and his brother and their families, won forty-seven London awards between them, but none of these can be counted here.

Fred Griffin, Lord Middleton and others spanned a long period as exhibitors. For some, unfortunately, the Shire Shows started too late. Edward Coke does not appear on this list, even though in the ten years to 1889 he had thirty-nine awards – more than anyone except the Earl of Ellesmere and Sir Walter Gilbey. For others, alas, the London Shows ended too soon – for men such as Lt.-Col. T. W. Daniel and Enoch Bostock, who had each won thirty-five awards by 1939.

This table does not claim to be a list of the greatest Shire men. It contains the 9th Duke of Devonshire, whose animals won 109 awards and who would sit up half the night or longer in the harness room until he was content that a mare was safely delivered of her foal. It does not mention Cole and Owen Ambrose (who registered 1,831 pure-bred Shires with the Stuntney prefix in this period) because they hardly ever exhibited at London where their success was confined to a "highly commended" card for Childwick Lottie (not one of the 1,831) in 1910. But it does record and honour the names of those who sent to that stuffy Islington hall in February the greatest numbers of the most beautiful draught-horses – looking as handsome as good feeding and good management all the year round, and infinite pains in preparation for the show itself, could make them.

NOTES. In this list, the date of an exhibitor's death is given only in the case of those who died in 1939 or before.

"Number of shows" refers to those at which an exhibitor actually won an award.

Similarly, "Period" gives the first and last shows at which the exhibitor won, not the total period during which he exhibited. The symbol "j" followed by a numeral indicates the number of shows in the period at which the exhibitor or a member of his family or his manager was a judge, and he was therefore ineligible to compete. The Forshaws would have probably won something like thirty-five more prizes had they not judged, between them, at six shows.

"s/m" denotes breeding classes (stallions and mares).

"g" denotes gelding classes.

Exhibitors	No. of Shows	Period	s/m	g	Total
1. JAMES FORSHAW AND SONS, Carlton-on-Trent, nr. Newark, Notts: (until 1887 Blyth, nr. Worksop). As James Forshaw to 1900. James d. 27th March 1908. Sons, Thomas and James. (Omitting another son, Wm. H. Forshaw, F.R.C.S., Slythehurst, Ewhurst, Surrey, seven awards 1920–1929.)	53	1881–1939 Jas j 1 Tom j 4 Jas jnr. j 1	308	1	309
2. THE DUNSMORE STUD. SIR P. ALBERT MUNTZ, (BT 1902) (M.P. from 1884), Dunsmore nr. Rugby. d. 21st December 1908.	24	1885–1908	175	0	255
TOM EWART (ex stud manager) d. 1930; J. A. Ewart in 1931.	21	1909–1931 j 1	80	0	
3. SIR WALPOLE L. GREENWELL, (BT 1906), Marden Park, Surrey, 112 awards, d. 24th October 1919. SIR BERNARD	41	1896–1939	224	7	231

Exhibitors	No. of Shows	Period	Number of Awards		
			s/m	g	Total
E. GREENWELL, BT (son), 119 (d. 28th November 1939).					
4. WILLIAM J. CUMBER (C.B.E., 1943), Theale, Berks. (stud at Yatesbury, Wilts.) As "W. J. Cumber and Son" (John) from 1938.	24	1914–1939 j 2	161	10	171
5. TRING PARK, Herts. 1ST BARON ROTHS-CHILD OF TRING (Nathan Meyer Rothschild), d. 31st March 1915.	22	1893–1915	146	1	166
TOM FOWLER (ex stud manager) at Stud Farm, Tring.	16	1917–1939 j 5	12	7	
6. LOCKINGE PARK, Wantage, Berks. COL. SIR ROBERT LOYD-LINDSAY, V.C., K.C.B., M.P. (1ST BARON WANTAGE 1885), twenty-six awards, d. 1901. LADY WANTAGE, twenty-five awards, d. 1920. A. THOMAS LOYD, O.B.E., D.L., J.P., M.A. (M.P. 1921–1923), ninety-two awards.	42	1885–1939	126	17	143
7. SIR ARTHUR NICHOLSON J.P., (Kt, 1908) Highfield Hall, Leek, Staffs, 109 awards, d. 1929. COL. ARTHUR F. NICHOLSON T.D. (C.B.E., 1936) (son), twenty-four awards.	39	1893–1938 A.F. j 1	133	0	133
8. JOHN ADCOCK BARRS, Nailstone, Hinck-ley, Leics., seventy-two awards, d. 1897. MRS. J. A. BARRS, ten awards. From 1904, WARNER BARRS (son) forty-two awards. d. 1915. The Nailstone Stud had existed since before 1800, when owned by Knowles. When J. A. Barrs died, only that other great stallion man, J. Forshaw, had had more awards (seventy-nine) than he. W. Barrs was followed by McKenna and Young to 1925 (see under Bardon Stud, No. 31) and then C.A. (to 1937) and then F. H. Parkinson. (Omitting another son, William Barrs, Odstone Hall, 2 miles distant, five awards 1891–1914: bred his last Shire 1932.)	29	1888–1915	124	0	124
9. A. H. CLARK, Moulton Eaugate, Spalding, Lincs. As "A. H. Clark and Son" (A.H. Jnr.) from 1920, d. 1939.	37	1882–1938 A.H. j 9 A.H. jr j 2	117	5	122

Exhibitors	No. of Shows	Period	s/m	g	Total
10. MANN, CROSSMAN AND PAULIN LTD., Albion Brewery, Whitechapel Road, E.1. Sir Edward Mann (Bt, 1905) had attended London Shows from 1880.	16	1923–1939	0	121	121
11. PENDLEY, Tring, Herts. (HARRY W. BISHOP manager or proprietor throughout).					
J. G. WILLIAMS: Pendley Manor, retired 1920.	10	1908–1917	56	1	
H. W. BISHOP and JOHN W. MEASURES (Pendley Stock Farms) from 1920 (Measures won also fifty-one awards from Dunsby – see No. 47).	3	1921–1926 Bishop j 2 Measures j 1	11	0	
MAJOR J. A. MORRISON, D.S.O. (P. Stock Farms) from 1927. Had won ten awards 1923–1927 from Basildon Park, Reading. d. 1934.	2	1928–1929	18	0	115
SIR GOMER BERRY, BT (Lord Kemsley) (P. Stock Farms): stud dispersed September 1936.	7	1930–1936	27	1	
H. W. BISHOP (Park Hill Farm).	1	1939	0	1	
12. J. MORRIS BELCHER, Tibberton Manor, Newport, Salop.	25	1912–1939 j 2	111	1	112
12. F. W. GRIFFIN, Boro' Fen, Peterborough, 109 awards, d. 1931. His executors, 2 (1933, 1938).	34	1892–1938 j 6	111	1	112
14. THE 9th DUKE OF DEVONSHIRE, K.G., Chatsworth, Bakewell, Derby. (until 1908 as Victor Cavendish, M.P., Holker Hall, Cark-in-Cartmel, Lancs.), 107 awards, d. 6th May 1938. The 10th Duke (son) 1939, three awards.	39	1897–1939	110	0	110
15. KNOTTINGLEY STUD FARM, Smallages, Sykehouse, Yorks., WILLIAM JACKSON (The Hall, Knottingley), twenty-nine awards, retired 1906. JOHN C. JACKSON (The Grange, Askern), 64, retired 1931.	27	1899–1926	103	0	103
16. G. R. C. FOSTER, Anstey Hall, Trumpington, Cambs. d. 1936.	17	1920–1936	101	0	101
17. ABRAHAM GRANDAGE, Bramhope, near Leeds; from 1913 as "A Grandage Ltd.", at Monks Heath, Chelford, Cheshire. (Bramhope premises taken	25	1894–1921	97	2	99

	No. of		Number of Awards		
Exhibitors	Shows	Period	s/m	g	Total
by Denby Collins, two awards, 1916.) Stud closed after conjunctivitis.					
18. The 3rd EARL OF ELLESMERE, Worsley Hall, Manchester. Ninety-seven awards, d. 13th July 1914. The 4th Earl, one award.	21	1880–1915	98	0	98
19. H.M. THE KING, Sandringham, Norfolk. EDWARD VII (as Prince of Wales to 1900) forty-one awards, d. 6th May 1910. GEORGE V, fifty-four awards, d. 20th January 1936. EDWARD VIII, one award, sold stud 1936.	37	1891–1936	95	1	96
19. SIR WALTER GILBEY, (BT 1893), Elsenham Hall, Essex, ninety-three awards, d. 1914. SIR WALTER GILBEY, BT (son) three awards (1929), gave up farming 1926.	24	1881–1906 1929	92	4	96
21. The 9th BARON MIDDLETON, Birdsall House, E.R., d. 1922.	31	1888–1922	86	5	91
22. "H. & R. AINSCOUGH", Burscough Mills, nr. Ormskirk, Lancs. (S.H.S. members: R. Ainscough 1886–1920, Thomas 1893–1927, John 1922–1938).	40	1890–1937	89	0	89
22. H. H. SMITH CARINGTON, Ashby Folville, Leics. Sixty-nine awards, d. 4th March 1917. Sons F. H. and N. W. (M.P. from 1923) as "Ashby Folville Stud". Twenty awards, gave up breeding: N.W. d. 1933.	23	1900–1924	88	1	89
24. The 2nd BARON EGERTON OF TATTON (1st EARL EGERTON 1897), Tatton Park, Knutsford, Ches., d. 1909.	22	1887–1909	81	0	81
24. WILLIAM WHITLEY, Primley, Paignton, Devon (with brother as W. AND H. WHITLEY from 1908; as HERBERT WHITLEY from 1921).	14	1907–1928	81	0	81
26. ERNEST W. HEADINGTON, Cippenham Court, Slough, Bucks.	30	1908–1939 j 1	62	15	77
27. HENRY R. HART, Longhouse Stud Farm, Cannock, Staffs. (1882–1883 as "Patent Urban Manure Company"; from 1884 as "Cannock Agricultural Co. Ltd."; from 1900 likewise and also as H. R. Hart), d. 26th December 1906.	26	1881–1906	76	0	76

Exhibitors	No. of Shows	Period	s/m	g	Total
			Number of Awards		
28. The 1st DUKE OF WESTMINSTER, K.G., Eaton Hall, Chester, nine awards, d. 1899. The 2nd DUKE (grandson) sixty-five awards.	24	1881–1924	73	1	74
29. JOHN ROWELL, Manor Farm, Bury, Hunts., sixty-five awards, d. 15th March 1922 (Edward P. from 1923, d. 1929).	32	1884–1927 j 5	73	0	73
30. LEOPOLD SALOMONS, Norbury Park, Dorking, Surrey, d. 1915.	14	1901–1915	72	0	72
31. THE BARDON STUD, Stanton-under-Bardon, Leics.					
WILLIAM THOMAS EVERARD (Bardon Hall), thirty awards, d. 1909. B. N. EVERARD (son), twenty-three awards: dispersal sale 11th February 1914.	13	1893–1913	52	1	} 70
CHARLES E. MCKENNA (ex manager, Bardon Stud Farm); from 1915 as MCKENNA AND YOUNG; from 1918 at Nailstone Stud (succeeding Barrs q.v.). Sold out 1920. (John W. Whitehurst took Bardon tenancy in 1917, but did not show in two years there. He and his sons had thirty-four awards from Markeaton, Derby., 1894–1907, and Branston, Burton-on-Trent, 1920–1921.)	7	1914–1920	17	0	
31. R. W. HUDSON, Danesfield, Great Marlow, Bucks.: gave up breeding 1908.	9	1898–1907	28	6	} 70
ROBERT H. KEENE (ex-manager) took over land (Westfield Farm, Medmenham).	16	1909–1932 j 5	35	1	
33. SIR EDWARD D. STERN (Kt, 1904), Fan Court, Chertsey, Surrey, d. 17th April 1933.	26	1904–1933	69	0	69
33. "W. AND J. THOMPSON", St. Leonard's Works, Leicester (Barron's Park Stud Farm, Desford).	14	1895–1908 Wm. jnr. j 2	67	2	69
35. JAMES GOULD, Model Farm (from 1906 Crouchley Hall) Lymm, Cheshire.	24	1904–1935 j 5 Jas jnr. j 1	65	2	67
35. SIR BERKELEY SHEFFIELD 6th Bt. (M.P., 1907–1910 and later), Normanby Park, Scunthorpe, Lincs.: dispersal sale 8th February 1922.	16	1906–1921	67	0	67

Exhibitors	No. of Shows	Period	Number of Awards		
			s/m	g	Total
37. F. E. MUNTZ, J.P., D.L., Umberslade, Hockley Heath, War. d. 25th November 1920.	12	1904–1917	65	0	64
37. F. W. (FRED) PARSONS, Speckington, Ilchester, Som.; from 1921 as "F. W. Parsons & Son" (2nd son HUGH): from 1927 "Sons" (6th son PERCY).	22	1899, 1913–1939	59	5	64
39. E. W. WEBB, Ketchingham Farm, Etchingham, Sussex.	12	1928–1939	56	7	63
40. MAX MICHAELIS, Tandridge Court, Oxted, Surrey. Dispersal sale 26th October 1911.	10	1901–1911	62	0	62
41. SIR ALEXANDER HENDERSON (Bt, 1902; M.P., 1898–1906 and later, the 1st BARON FARINGDON 1916), Buscot Park, Faringdon, Berks.; ceased showing 1909, d. 1934.	14	1894–1909	56	1	57
42. ROBERT N. SUTTON-NELTHORPE, Scawby Hall, Brigg, Lincs.: ceased showing 1916, d. 1937.	22	1884–1916	55	1	56
43. MRS. STANTON, Snelston Hall, Ashbourne, Derby. Dispersal sale 22nd January 1930.	16	1910–1929	53	0	53
44. J. P. CROSS, Catthorpe Towers (near Rugby), Leics., forty-eight awards, d. 4th February 1906. J. L. CROSS (son) from 1907, four awards at four shows.	21	1887–1913	52	0	52
44. W. H. O. DUNCOMBE, Waresley Park, Sandy, Beds., ceased showing 1907, d. 6th January 1917.	12	1892–1906	52	0	52
44. JOHN PARNELL, Rugby (builder: stud farm at Woolscott), d. 1904. (Omitting WILLIAM HOWKINS, ex-manager, whose six awards from Hillmorton Grounds began only in 1921.)	16	1887–1904	51	1	52
47. JOHN W. MEASURES, Dunsby, Bourne, Lincs. (retired owing to blindness). N.B. Figures exclude awards won also from Pendley 1921–1926, see No. 11.	22	1902–1929 j 2	51	0	51
47. WILLIAM H. NEALE, Bacon's End (from 1917 Priory Farm, Shustoke) Coleshill, Birmingham.	28	1896 1904–1937	48	3	51
47. SIR EDWARD E. PEARSON (Kt, 1918), Brickendonbury, Hertford, d. 1925.	20	1904–1926	49	2	51

Exhibitors	No. of Shows	Period	s/m	g	Total
50. JAMES EADIE, Barrow Hall, Barrow-on-Trent, Derby., thirty-six awards, d. 1904. JOHN T. C. EADIE, (Grange Farm): gave up breeding 1912.	13	1897–1912 J.T.C. j 4	41	9	50
50. The 1st BARON HOTHFIELD (Henry James Tufton), Hothfield Place, Ashford, Kent. Gave up breeding 1921, d. 1926.	29	1890–1921	50	0	50
50. HAMER TOWGOOD, Saintfoins, Little Shelford, Cambs., d. 1913 (executors 1914).	16	1895–1914	46	4	50
RES. No. H. W. KEARNS, Baxenden House, Accrington, Lancs. (Brooklands, Cheshire from 1914) with stud at Millers Dale, Derby. Gave up breeding 1923.	16	1901–1915, 1922	47	0	47

(*b*) THE "SMALL STALLIONS"

The most outstanding record of consistent success at Shire shows – and, arguably, at any horse shows anywhere – surely belongs to the Forshaws for their achievement in the "small stallions" class over a period of forty years. No exhibitor of any stock is ever likely to equal it.

"Small" is misleading. Certainly, from 1882, when the class was instituted, until 1928, competing animals had to be under 16.2-hands: and from 1929, under 16.3. (Until 1894, the class was open to horses of five years and upwards. From 1895, there was an upper age limit of nine, all older stallions being in one class irrespective of height.) But these horses, and especially the winners, were not *small*. There was no shortage of size and substance of bone or body. Indeed, particularly in earlier years, the low wither-height merely accentuated the massive ponderosity of the leading competitors. The Forshaws indeed were, more than anyone else, the unfailing apostles of weight. (Once, when Tom was showing his wares to a deputation from a hiring society, and expatiating on their several virtues, the group at last came to a great hairy monster whose praise even he, its owner, found hard to sing. So they passed on, Tom merely murmuring, more to himself than to his guests, "Weight . . . weight . . . weight", as one intones a creed.)

The list of results below shows increasing Forshaw dominance of this specialised class, which (as discussed in Part A.XII.6) nevertheless produced only one champion stallion of the breed:

1882	Sir Richard Wallace, Bt	Emperor II 2769 (12 years) (James Forshaw 3rd)
1883	Frederic Street	Somersham Samson 2496 (6) (J.F. 2nd)
1884	H. Chandos-Pole-Gell	Hyperion 3155 (5)
1885	The Earl of Ellesmere	Esquire 2774 (5)
1886	Walter Gilbey	Staunton Hero 2918 (5) – supreme champion
1887	Henry Freshney	Sir Garnet 4037 (5)
1888	Walter Gilbey	Staunton Hero (J.F. 2nd)
1889	James Forshaw	Hydrometer 3744 (6)

1890   The Duke of Westminster   Staunton Hero (J.F. 2nd)
1891   T. H. Miller   Mohammed 6173 (6)
1892   J. A. Barrs   Nailstone Spartan 11956 (5) – res. senior champion
                                   (J.F. H.C.)
1893   J. A. Barrs   Nailstone Spartan (J.F. H.C.)
1894   P. A. Muntz, M.P.   Dunsmore Bounding Willow 13013 (5) (J.F.
                                   reserve – 5th)
1895   William Hollins   Scarsdale Rocket 12249 (6) (J.F. 2nd)
1896   James Forshaw   Downham Ben 12992 (8)
1897   James Forshaw   Downham Ben
1898   P. A. Muntz, M.P.   Dunsmore Bounding Willow (J.F. 3rd)
1899   James Forshaw   Yorkshire Ben 16479 (5)
1900   Lord Rothschild   Vulcan VII 14400 (9) (J.F. ineligible – judging)
1901   J. Forshaw & Sons   Capstone Harold 16590
1902   J. Forshaw & Sons   Capstone Harold
1903   J. Forshaw & Sons   Capstone Harold
1904   J. Forshaw & Sons   Capstone Harold
1905   J. Forshaw & Sons   Raydon Duke 18302 (7)
1906   J. Forshaw & Sons   Raydon Duke
1907   Lord Winterstoke   Ravenspur 22709 (5)
1908   J. Forshaw & Sons   Glen Royal II 21466 (7)
1909   J. Forshaw & Sons   Yorkshire Lion 23885 (5)
1910   J. Forshaw & Sons   Royalist Count 22743 (7)
1911   H.M. The King   Hoe Forest King 24321 (7) (Forshaws Res – 5)
1912   Abraham Grandage   Bramhope Emperor 25976 (5) (Forshaws 2nd)
1913   J. Forshaw & Sons   Warmington Boss 27893 (6)
1914   H. H. Smith Carington   Ivy Victor Chief 25310 (8) (Forshaws ineligible
                                   – Tom judging)
1915   Sir Berkeley Sheffield, Bt   Harboro' Royal Duke 29458 (5) (Forshaws
                                   2nd)
1916   J. Forshaw & Sons   Blackthorn King 29105 (7)
1917   J. Forshaw & Sons   Blackthorn King
1918   (No height classes)
1919   (No height classes)
1920   E. J. Wythes   Copped Hall Menestrel 31342 (8) (Forshaws
                                   ineligible – James judging)
1921   Sir Arthur Nicholson   Hall Place Champion 34003 (6) (Forshaws 3rd)
1922   J. Forshaw & Sons   Colney King 2nd 34657 (6)
1923   (No height classes)
1924   The Duke of Westminster   Dollar Dictator 32302 (12) (Forshaws ineligible –
                                   Tom judging)
1925   J. Forshaw & Sons   Bridgford Forest Clansman 38069 (5)
1926   J. Forshaw & Sons   Dogdyke Jonathan 38785 (5)
1927   J. Forshaw & Sons   Bridgford Forest Clansman
1928   Thomas Ewart   Dunsmore Special 38183 (9) (Forshaws ineligible –
                                   Tom judging)
1929   J. Forshaw & Sons   Maryshall Hero 39269 (7)
1930   J. Forshaw & Sons   Lymm Thumper 2nd 39919 (5)

1931	J. Forshaw & Sons	Boro' King Cole 39644 (7)
1932	J. Forshaw & Sons	Gay Albert 39885 (9)
1933	J. Forshaw & Sons	Gay Albert
1934	J. Forshaw & Sons	The Dean 40628 (6)
1935	J. Forshaw & Sons	The Dean
1936	J. Forshaw & Sons	The Dean
1937	J. Forshaw & Sons	The Dean
1938	W. Cumber & Son	Theale Camrose 42128 (Forshaws ineligible – Tom judging)
1939	J. Morris Belcher	Litchfield Robin 41717 (6) (Forshaws 3rd)

There were fifty-five shows with height classes for senior stallions, but a member of the Forshaw family was judging on six occasions. So, out of forty-nine possible shows, they won first prize for "small" stallions twenty-nine times, with eighteen different horses. (From 1896, twenty-eight times out of thirty-five.)

(In the same fifty-five shows where there were height classes, the Forshaws also won more first prizes for big stallions than anyone else – thirteen. But twenty-five other exhibitors also topped the class – Morris Belcher on seven occasions and Lord Rothschild on five.)

County Championship, 1880–1914

THE following table lists the number of successful London Show horses bred in each county during the first thirty-five years. It gives no real indication of the progress of the Society's chief work, which was the improvement of cart-horses in general throughout the country. But it does show where the best specimens were being bred. Of these, the stallions in particular improved the general standard elsewhere but good mares also increasingly tended to be bought by ambitious farmers in the "lesser" counties.

Shire breeding was essentially a co-operative enterprise in so far as the ordinary farmer depended upon a large number of his neighbours having the same interest as himself. Consequently, the very best stock for the most part continued to be bred in those counties where the type of farming, the soil and climate, and tradition had always favoured their production. These figures in the table tend to disguise that fact, and Surrey may be taken as the outstanding example. Its thirteenth place is surprisingly high until one discovers that this was largely due to a very few large landowners' studs. Of the 183 successful Surrey-bred horses in 1880–1914, 107 were crowded into the years 1911–1914, and of these no less than ninety were bred by those enthusiastic and wealthy amateurs Max Michaelis (forty-three), Sir Walpole Greenwell (thirty-one) and Leopold Salomons (sixteen): and even the remaining seventeen owed their success mainly, or even entirely, to their breeders' proximity to those gentlemen's studs.

A further reservation must be made. The table cannot be taken either as proof or disproof of the old allegation that good Shires could not be bred outside their original areas. The fact that a few prize-winners were bred in Devon or Cornwall (not on the whole, by big landowners) means little, of itself. Where had the sires and dams been bred? Was it possible in those counties to breed a prize-winner from animals descended from generations of local or naturalised stock? The acid test would have to repeat the Clydesdale "experiment". It is possible that thirty or forty years' deprivation of replenishment from the Fens and Midlands fountain heads might have led to similar differences to that produced by the isolation of Clydesdale and Shire after the establishment of the separate Stud-books. The Michaelis, Greenwell and Salomons studs did not really help to answer the question, because their home-bred Shires were the produce of expensive purchases from outside, or of their immediate descendants.

Even in later years, seeming exceptions are delusive. Sir Bernard Greenwell's 1937 champion mare was of the fourth female generation bred in Surrey and had at least four generations of Herefordshire-bred mares (hardly more "classical" than Surrey) in her pedigree before that. But she was got by Theale Josh, bred in Leics.: her dam was by Stretton Broadside (also Leics.-bred): her g-dam was by Champion's Goalkeeper: and so on. See B.VIII.3.

The table includes all those animals which won prizes or were highly commended or commended at London shows – stallions and mares from 1880 onwards, and geldings from 1895. Seven horses successful in 1880 and 1881 have had to be omitted because there is no way of discovering where they were bred.

1. LEICESTERSHIRE	653	29.	SOMERSET	45
2. DERBYSHIRE	638	30.	SUSSEX	32
3. LANCASHIRE	625	31.	DEVON	25
4. LINCOLNSHIRE	457	32.	MIDDLESEX	24
5. WARWICKSHIRE	404	33.	RUTLAND	22
6. NOTTINGHAMSHIRE	354	34.	SUFFOLK	18
7. YORKSHIRE	330	35.	ANGLESEY	17
8. CAMBS. & ISLE OF ELY	307	36.	WESTMORLAND	14
9. STAFFORDSHIRE	305	37.	CORNWALL	11
10. CHESHIRE	287	38.	DENBIGHSHIRE	9
11. NORTHANTS & P'BORO	275		FLINTSHIRE	9
12. HERTFORDSHIRE	237	40.	GLAMORGAN	7
13. SURREY	183	41.	CARMARTHENSHIRE	6
14. MONTGOMERYSHIRE	174		CAERNARVONSHIRE	6
15. ESSEX	163	43.	HAMPSHIRE	5
16. BUCKINGHAMSHIRE	158		PEMBROKESHIRE	5
17. BERKSHIRE	155		RADNOR	5
HUNTINGDONSHIRE	155	46.	BRECKNOCK	4
19. NORFOLK	153		DORSET	4
20. SHROPSHIRE	126		DURHAM	4
21. GLOUCESTERSHIRE	92	49.	ISLE OF MAN	3
22. HEREFORDSHIRE	78		NORTHUMBERLAND	3
23. MONMOUTHSHIRE	74	51.	CARDIGANSHIRE	2
24. BEDFORDSHIRE	66			
WORCESTERSHIRE	66		(SCOTLAND)	2
26. KENT	62		(IRELAND)	2
27. WILTSHIRE	55			
28. OXFORDSHIRE	53		UNKNOWN	7
			TOTAL	6,976

Affiliated Societies

(*a*) THE NUMBER OF CORPORATE MEMBERS

Most, if not all, of the organisations which became corporate members of the Shire Horse Society did so in order to qualify for the Society's medals. The table which follows shows such membership on 1st January of selected significant years.

The gold medal scheme began in 1892. The silver medal scheme was started in 1895 but too late in the year. Some shows were actually over before the offer was made and the schedules of most of the rest had already been prepared. Therefore, corporate membership at the beginning of 1896 (column 1 in the table below) includes only the first twenty-one silver medal societies, together with those qualifying for a gold medal. Column 2 shows the progress made by the end of Victoria's reign, and column 3 the further advance (helped by the offer of prizes to the *breeders* of gold medal winners from 1901 and to the *breeders* of silver medal winners from 1903) up to the outbreak of the First World War.

Corporate membership at the beginning of 1924 (column 4) was the highest in the Society's history. This may appear surprising, in view of the tendency for less affluent shows to "fold up" at that time, but was due to the offer of bronze medals for geldings from 1923. The decline in the next fifteen years to 1939 (column 5) reflects the collapse of many smaller shows, rather than any reduced proportion of those which included good Shire classes. Similarly, 1954 (column 6) is indicative of the post-war euphoria of those keen to run local shows in general, for the figures run counter to the sudden and widespread cessation of Shire breeding, which is illustrated rather by the 1964 figures (column 7). Column 8 clearly reflects the revival of interest in Shire classes, because by 1974 there were no societies whose Shire subscriptions were paid purely out of sentiment.

	Corporate membership on 1st January							
	1	2	3	4	5	6	7	8
	1896	1901	1914	1924	1939	1954	1964	1974
(i) Agricultural, etc., Societies	15	105	199	224	124	166	62	
(ii) Mare & Foal, and other Horse Shows	9	35	78	77	21	22	2	
(iii) Stallion Shows			1	1				
(iv) Stallion Hiring Societies	15	20	26	31	56	31	6	
(v) Abroad (Germany)			1					
	39	160	305	333	201	219	70	61

The division between the above categories is in many instances difficult to make. For example,

(i) "Agricultural, etc., societies" include Ashbourne Shire Horse Society, which began as a foal show, was never (in spite of its name) a stallion-hiring society, and became and still remains an agricultural society. This category also includes many farmers' clubs, tenants' associations, and such miscellaneous organisations as "horse, cattle and cheese show", "horse, foal and athletic association", "horse and poultry show", "sports and social committee", and so on. (R.A.S.E. was, and is, the only society assisted by the offer of S.H.S. awards without having to become a member. Prizes were offered at Royal Shows 1879–1890, prior to the gold medal scheme.)

(ii) Many "mare and foal shows" and the like, were actually organised by stallion hiring societies. But hiring societies more often supported the local agricultural show (if it was held in the autumn) with classes for mares and foals belonging to their members, and for foals got by their stallion of the previous year. Some of the S.H.S. members in this category were ploughing associations which included classes for mares and foals in their day's programme: others were shows devoted only to horses, but horses of all kinds.

(ii) There was no incentive for organisers of stallion parades and shows to join S.H.S., because silver medals were restricted to mares and fillies, unless a show was big enough to qualify for two, in which case only the second medal could be given for stallions. The 1914 member was the Caerphilly Entire Horse Parade and Show, which oddly had mare classes as well, and qualified for one medal. The member in 1924 was the Carmarthen Entire Horse Show which was affiliated to S.H.S. for three years. On the other hand, gold medals were awarded at two stallion shows organised by agricultural societies – Peterborough A.S. until 1925, and the Royal Norfolk A.A. until 1939.

(iv) Comparatively few stallion-hiring societies were members, because there was nothing to be gained – until, in recent times, the grants from the Horserace Betting Levy Board were conditional upon membership. Such "clubs"were usually called "Shire Horse" societies, "Heavy Horse" societies, or "Entire Horse" societies or occasionally, if operating in two spheres of interest, by some such name as "Shire and Hackney" society. Usually the chairman, and perhaps one or two leading members, of a hiring society was an individual member of S.H.S.

(v) Until expunged by Sloughgrove on the outbreak of hostilities.

(*b*) GOLD MEDAL SHOWS, 1892–1896.

These were the first societies to participate in the Gold Medal scheme:

R.A.S.E. – 2 medals from 1892.

ASHBOURNE – from 1893.

BATH and WEST OF ENGLAND – 1893, 1895, 1896.

BELPER – from 1894.

BURTON-ON-TRENT – from 1896.

CAMBS. AND ISLE OF ELY – 1893, 1895, 1896 with Suffolk.

DERBYSHIRE – from 1892.

ESSEX – from 1892 (two medals from 1893).

ROYAL LANCASHIRE – from 1892 (two medals from 1893): (as "Royal Manchester, Liverpool & North Lancs." in 1892–1893).

LEICESTERSHIRE – from 1892.

LINCOLNSHIRE – from 1894.

MORETON-IN-MARSH – from 1892* (two medals for first three years).

NORFOLK – from 1892.

NOTTINGHAMSHIRE – from 1892 (two medals from 1895).

PETERBOROUGH – from 1892: stallion show in March; also at Summer Show.

SHROPSHIRE & W. MIDLAND – from 1893.

STAFFORDSHIRE – 1892, 1894.

SUFFOLK – 1892, 1893, 1895, 1896 with Cambs.

YORKSHIRE – from 1894.

   * Founded by A. B. Freeman-Mitford who won both the first two gold medals, with Minnehaha and Menestrel.

(c) GOLD & SILVER MEDAL SHOWS, 1913

This was the biggest year to date in the medal scheme. GOLD MEDAL shows are listed in capital letters. (A society offering a minimum of £100 in prize money for Shires was eligible for a gold medal: a society offering £250 or more could claim two.)

Silver medal shows are printed in lower-case type. (Any affiliated society could offer a S.H.S. silver medal. Any such society offering not less than £25 in prizes for males could claim a second one.)

National and Regional Societies.

R.A.S.E. (2)
BATH AND WEST
North Wales
ROYAL COUNTIES

ROYAL ULSTER (2)
United Counties
WELSH NATIONAL

Other societies, listed in alphabetical order of counties (beginning with the county show: if no county show, the county is printed in italic within parentheses).

Anglesey.

Bedfordshire (2), Bedfordshire S.H.S.

(Berks.) – EAST BERKS., Newbury, North Berks., South Berks.

Brecknockshire, Hay.

(Bucks.) – Chiltern Hills, N.W. Bucks., R. & C. Bucks., R.S. Bucks., Winslow.

(Caernavon) – Conway.

CAMBS. AND ISLE OF ELY, Cottenham, Haddenham, Littleport, March, Wisbech.

(Cards.) – Lampeter, Llanilar, Talybont.

Cheshire (2), ALTRINCHAM, Cheshire Foal, Mid Cheshire, S. Cheshire, WIRRAL AND BIRKENHEAD, Wirral Farmers.

(Cornwall) – Camelford, Launceston.

Denbighshire and Flintshire, Abergele, Chirk, Old Colwyn.

DERBYSHIRE, ASHBOURNE, Bakewell, Belper, Chesterfield, Ripley, Shottle, Wirksworth.

Devon.

(Dorset) – Dorchester, Melplash.

ESSEX (2), Great Chesterford, Romford & S. Essex, S.E. Essex, Tendring Hundred, Tolleshunt D'Arcy.

(Glam) – Caerphilly, Cardiff, Lisvane, Pontardulais, Pontlliw, Swansea.

(Glos.) – Berkeley Hunt, Lechlade, MORETON-IN-MARSH, W. Gloucester.

(*Hants*) – Fareham, Romsey, R.I. of Wight.

Herefordshire and Worcs (2), Harewood End, Herefs. Horse, Kington (See also Worcs).

Hertfordshire, Harpenden, Royston, TRING, WALTHAM CROSS.

HUNTINGDONSHIRE, Gransden, THORNEY.

Isle of Man.

(*Kent*) – Ashford, Capel, Chiddingstone, East Kent, Mid Kent, TUNBRIDGE WELLS, Westerham Hill.

ROYAL LANCASHIRE, BLACKPOOL, Bury & Ramsbottom, Darwen, Garstang, Goosnargh, Great Eccleston, Great Harwood, Lancaster, Lytham, North Lonsdale, Ormskirk, Prescot, Rochdale, Rufford, Warrington, Whalley, Worsley.

LEICESTERSHIRE, Ashby-de-la-Zouch, Loughborough, Lutterworth, Market Bosworth, MARKET HARBOROUGH, MELTON MOWBRAY.

LINCOLNSHIRE (2), Alford, Billingborough, Boston, Bourne, Corringham, Crowland, Friskney, Frithville, Gainsborough, Gosberton, Grantham, Harmston, Haxey, Horncastle, Louth, Mablethorpe, Messingham, North Thoresby, Saltfleet, Saxilby, Scunthorpe, SPALDING, Spilsby, Stamford, Stickney, Tattershall, Wainfleet, Winterton, Wragby.

(*Mon.*) – Abergavenny, Bedwellty, Chepstow, Monmouth Farmers.

MONTGOMERYSHIRE, Gregynog.

ROYAL NORFOLK, East Norfolk, King's Lynn, North Walsham, Waveney Valley, Wymondham.

NORTHAMPTONSHIRE, Brackley, Daventry, Kettering, Pytchley, Thrapston (2), Woodford Halse.

NOTTINGHAMSHIRE (2), Bassetlaw, Blyth, Charborough, Collingham, East Markham, Greasley, Kingston, Mansfield, Newark, Newcastle Estates, Norwell, Rampton, Welbeck.

OXFORDSHIRE, Banbury, Bicester, THAME, Woodstock.

Pembrokeshire, North Pembroke.

PETERBOROUGH (2) (See also Hunts.)

Radnorshire.

Rutland.

SHROPSHIRE, Acton Burnell, Bishops Castle, Bridgnorth, Craven Arms, Ludlow, Market Drayton, Newport, Oswestry, Rea Valley, Wem, Wenlock, Whitchurch.

Somerset (2), Banwell, Mid-Somerset, N.E. Somerset.

STAFFORDSHIRE, Alrewas, Brewood, Hallam and Eccleshall, Keele, Knighton, Leek, Meynell Hunt (at Tutbury), Uttoxeter, West Staffs.

SUFFOLK, Eye, Framlingham, Hadleigh, Halesworth, Mutford, Stowmarket, Wickhambrook.

(*Surrey*) – East Surrey, GUILDFORD, REIGATE AND REDHILL, Oxted.

SUSSEX, Arundel.

WARWICKSHIRE, Ansley, Atherstone, Coleshill, Henley-in-Arden, Monks Kirby, Perry Bar, Warwickshire Hunt.

Westmorland, Burton, Milnthorpe and Carnforth.

Wiltshire (2).

(*Worcs*) – Alvechurch, Madresfield, Ombersley, Worcestershire S.H.A. (See also Herefordshire)

YORKSHIRE, Beverley, Brandesburton, Bridlington, Bubwith, Doncaster, Driffield,

Eastrington, Goole, Harrogate, Harthill, Hornsea, Howdenshire, Hutton Cranswick, Maltby, Market Weighton, Monk Fryston, Normanby, Northallerton, Norton, Ripon, Ryedale and Pickering, Selby, Sheffield, Sherburn-in-Elmet, Snaith, Stokesley, Thirsk, Thorne, Tong, Wetherby, Wharfedale.

(*d*) LATER MEDAL SHOWS

Only in 1922, when 286 shows were involved, and in 1923 when the number of shows offering S.H.S. medals reached the record of 288 (owing to the introduction of bronze medals for geldings), were the 1913 figures surpassed. By 1928, the number of medal shows had declined to 207; by 1938, to 145; by 1948, to 126. (At twenty-nine of these last, special prizes were awarded, instead of the old gold medals, and at ninety-two, silver medals. Sixty-three shows received bronze medals for geldings, but fifty-eight of these were also in one of the other two categories.) In 1973, the Shire revival entailed the award of fifty-eight silver spoons, which had superceded the medals, and special prizes at other events.

(*e*) OVERSEAS SHOWS, 1902–1939

A gold medal scheme for Shire classes at shows overseas was first regularised in 1902. In 1911 silver medals were introduced, and in 1913–1915 eight gold cups were also offered annually. From 1916, the awards had to be confined by government regulation to silver medals. The following shows participated:

Show	From/to	No. of shows	No. of S.H.S. medals
U.S.A.			
1. CHICAGO INTERNATIONAL, Ill.	1902–1939	30	60
2. Oregon	1913–1931	19	38
3. Iowa	1909–1923	15	29
4. Illinois	1910–1921	10	20
5. California	1913–1926	10	18
6. S. Dakota	1912–1923	9	15

Also Nebraska, Wisconsin, Bushnell (Ill), and St. Joseph (Mo.) at three shows; Washington, Forest City, and Minnesota, at two shows; and Indiana, Montana and Galesburg (Ill.), one show each. A total of 114 shows and 217 medals.

Show	From/to	No. of shows	No. of S.H.S. medals
Canada			
1. TORONTO, Ontario	1902–1923	22	45
2. Calgary, Alberta	1909–1931	22	37
3. Edmonton, Alberta	1916–1931	14	25
4. Winnipeg, Manitoba	1902–1914	13	20

Also Brandon (Manitoba) at six shows; Regina (Saskatchewan) at five; Vancouver (B.C.) and Victoria (B.C.) at four; Lethbridge (Alberta) and New Westminster (B.C.) at three; and Macleod (Alberta), St. John (N.B.) at two. A total of 100 shows and 161 medals.

Show	From/to	No. of shows	No. of S.H.S. medals
Elsewhere in America			
Argentina (Sociedad Rural)	1908–1939	28	44

Also Argentina (Rosario), two shows; and Panama – Pacific International – and San Joaquin (Bolivia) one show each. A total of thirty-two shows and fifty medals.

Australia	*Show* *From/to*	*No.* *of shows*	*No. of* *S.H.S. medals*
Tasmania	1914–1923	9	15

Also R.A.S. New South Wales and R.A.S. Victoria, three shows each. A total of fifteen shows and twenty-seven medals.

New Zealand

At Christchurch and Manawatu, on two occasions each, a total of eight medals was awarded.

Cart–Horse Parades to 1939

THE general scheme, under which silver medals were offered for competition at town gelding parades, began in 1899. Prior to that, the only parade at which S.H.S. awards were made was the London one, whose inauguration was largely due to the Society or, rather, to its leading members. Silver medals were given to 1936, and silver or bronze from 1937.

As the table below shows, many parades failed to re-start after the First World War. After the Second World War, the London parade was the sole survivor and at this rosettes were offered, as they still are at its successor.

For the first twenty years, awards were open to outstanding animals of "any breed", but from 1920 the stipulation was that they must be of "Shire-type". No popery, and no percheronry!

The number of medals awarded was determined by the total number of horses at the parade. In this table, parades are placed according to the number of years they qualified for them, not according to their size.

Eighteen of the fifty-six different organisations concerned were in Lancashire. Two hundred and twenty-five separate parades at which medals were given were in Lancashire, as against 314 (or 268 if London is omitted) elsewhere. Again, if London is regarded as a special case, 717 medals were sent to Lancashire towns, and only 583 to other provincial towns.

	No. of Parades	Span of Dates	No. of Medals	
1. LONDON	46	1888–1939	1,581	Cancelled 1910 (death of King) and 1915–1919
2. LIVERPOOL	36	1899–1939	299	Founded 1863 or earlier
3. OLDHAM	36	1899–1934	72	The only parade to continue in the war
4. CARDIFF	34	1899–1934	101	
5. BOLTON	23	1899–1939	38	Not 1916–1933
6. MALTON	20	1900–1928	20	Not 1915–1923
7. ST. HELENS	18	1907–1931	37	
8. SHEFFIELD	18	1903–1925	36	
9. SALFORD*	17	1923–1939	36	See also MANCHESTER & SALFORD
10. DERBY	16	1924–1939	29	
11. MANCHESTER & SALFORD*	15	1919–1939	74	1919 and 1926–1939. See also MANCHESTER; also SALFORD
12. BRIGHTON	15	1899–1914	72	
13. EXETER	15	1899–1914	44	
14. GLOSSOP	14	1903–1928	26	1903–1914; 1927–1928
15. LEWISHAM	14	1901–1914	25	

	No. of Parades	Span of Dates	No. of Medals	
16. BELFAST etc.	14	1900–1936	14	N. Ireland 1900; B'fast 1923–1929; R. Ulster 1931–1936
17. SWANSEA	12	1899–1910	35	
18. PRESTWICH	12	1903–1914	24	
19. MANCHESTER*	11	1899–1931	54	1899–1900; 1903, 1908, 1925–1931. See also M. & SALFORD
20. DARLINGTON	11	1899–1909	32	

	No. of Parades	Dates	No. of Medals		No. of Parades	Dates	No. of Medals
21. RADCLIFFE	10	1905–1914	10	30. FELIXSTOWE	6	1902–1907	9
22. BURNLEY	9	1900–1908	18	31. BRIDGEND	6	1905–1910	6
23. WARRINGTON	9	1902–1932	16	BURY	6	1904–1910	6
24. BARNARD CASTLE	8	1902–1911	16	LEIGH	6	1930–1937	6
25. WEST BROMWICH	8	1928–1939	9	34. R. LANCS. A.S.	5	1899–1924	15
26. LINCOLN	6	1923–1928	18	35. WORTHING	5	1900–1904	10
27. CAMBRIDGE	6	1908–1914	12	36. BOOTLE	5	1909–1913	5
DONCASTER	6	1924–1929	12	37. NORTHAMPTON	4	1900–1903	8
29. CREWE	6	1899–1904	11	38. ROCHDALE	4	1900–1913	4

Two Parades: 39. Bath 1899–1900 (5 medals); Burton-on-Trent 1899–1900 (5); 41. Salisbury 1911–1912 (4); 42. Chorley 1907–1908 (3); Croydon 1899–1900 (3); 44. Haslingden 1913–1914 (2); Nantymoel 1908–1909 (2); Plymouth 1899–1900 (2); Richmond (Yorks) 1905–1906 (2).

One Parade: 48. Acton 1914 (2); Hyde 1920 (2); Huddersfield 1904 (2); Winchester 1914 (2); 52–56. Colchester 1936, Eastbourne 1899, Newton 1935, Poynton 1932, Reading 1930 (one medal each).

Spring Show Champions, 1945–1975

THE address of breeder or exhibitor is not given if it has already appeared in the 1880–1939 list (Appendix 1).

(A)	*Champion Stallion and Breeder*	*Age*	*Exhibitor*
1945	GREY SPARK 43426 W. H. Spikings Gorefield, Cambs.	6	J. Forshaw & Sons
1946	LILLINGSTONE WHAT'S WANTED 43774 H. Eady Robinson	5	H. Eady Robinson Higham Ferrers, Northants
1947	ALTHORPE TRUMP CARD 43873 J. R. Glew Trent Side House Althorpe, Lincs.	5	J. and W. Whewell
1948	ALTHORPE TRUMP CARD	6	J. and W. Whewell
1949	THE BOMBER 44039 J. Kirkland Broadholme House Belper, Derby.	8	Richard Sutton Moor House Longton, Lancs.
1950	BRADGATE SUPREME 44257 J. T. Appleby Home Farm Allestree, Derby.	6	J. Morris Belcher & Son
1951	LILLINGSTONE BRANDMARK 44514 T. H. B. Freshney Berryfield Farm Aylesbury	4	H. Eady Robinson
1952	SUNDERLANDS STEROPE 44632 W. and J. Sumner Shire Bank Farm Fulwood, Lancs.	3	J. Morris Belcher & Son
1953	GRANGE WOOD CLIFFORDS WHAT'S WANTED 44559 William Beresford Clifford Wood Stone, Staffs.	5	George Richardson Frogmore Farm Moreton-in-Marsh, Glos.
1954	GRANGE WOOD CLIFFORDS W.W.	6	George Richardson
1955	GRANGE WOOD CLIFFORDS W.W.	7	George Richardson

(A)	*Champion Stallion and Breeder*	*Age*	*Exhibitor*
1956	NANTWICH SUPREME 44617 A. E. E. Vaughan Red Hall Wistaston, Ches.	7	Vaughan Bros Nantwich Shire Stud Farm Wistaston, Ches.
1957	HIS EXCELLENCY 44674 T. H. B. Freshney	7	James Gould
1958	LILLINGSTONE LAKES SUPERIOR 44829 Alex Findlay Lakes Farm Cardington, Beds.	6	H. Eady Robinson
1959	LILLINGSTONE LAKES SUPERIOR	7	H. Eady Robinson
1960	LILLINGSTONE LAKES SUPERIOR	8	H. Eady Robinson
1961	MANOR PREMIER KING 44948 R. A. S. Pleavin	6	R. A. S. Pleavin Shordley Manor Hope, Flint.
1962	MAIDENWELL BOLD CHIEF 45099 E. L. Wright Kenwick, Louth, Lincs.	3	Charles Clark Maidenwell Louth, Lincs.
1963	MANOR PREMIER KING	8	R. A. S. Pleavin
1964	CARR COMING KING 45059 S. G. Garrett	6	S. G. Garrett Manor Farm Carr, Maltby, Yorks.
1965	ALNELAND DELEGATE 45080 J. R. Suckley	6	J. R. Suckley Brogyntyn Farm Oswestry, Salop
1966	LADBROOK WHAT'S WANTED 45178 George Richardson	3	Arthur W. Lewis Little Ladbrook Farm Tanworth-in-Arden, War.
1967	GRANGE WOOD WILLIAM 45226 J. K. Finney Calton Lees Beeley, Derby.	2	E. J. Richardson (Frogmore Farm. Now Tithe Farm Boundary, Woodville, Derby.–Leics.)
1968	GRANGE WOOD WILLIAM	3	E. J. Richardson
1969	GRANGE WOOD WILLIAM	4	E. J. Richardson
1970	GRANGE WOOD WILLIAM	5	E. J. Richardson
1971	ROYSTON HAROLD 45335 W. H. Chambers Trinity House Farm Swanland Dale N. Ferriby, Yorks.	3	C. C. Etches Brookfield Farm Mickleover, Derby.
1972	LAYSTON CONJURER 45393 E. J. Richardson	3	J. Russell Church Farm Barnsley, Glos.
1973	ROYSTON HAROLD	5	C. C. Etches

(A)	*Champion Stallion and Breeder*	*Age*	*Exhibitor*
1974	WOODHOUSE FOOTPRINT 45442 L. Fountain	3	L. Fountain Woodhouse Farm Marston Montgomery, Derby.
1975	HILLMOOR ENTERPRISE 45392 T. E. Moss	5	T. E. Moss Hillmoor Farm Eaton, Ches.

(B)	*Champion Mare and Breeder*	*Age*	*Exhibitor*
1945	(Stallions only)		
1946	133744 CRIMWELL QUALITY Frederick Hubbard Lings Farm Eaton, Lincs.	5	D. K. Steadman The Maesydd Pool Quay Welshpool, Mont.
1947	CRIMWELL QUALITY	6	Chris Catterall The Breck Hambleton, Lancs.
1948	CRIMWELL QUALITY	7	Chris Catterall
1949	CRIMWELL QUALITY	8	Chris Catterall
1950	136703 LECKHAMPSTEAD SHEILA O. Lester and Sons Leckhampstead, Bucks.	4	W. Cumber & Son (Theale) Ltd.
1951	LECKHAMPSTEAD SHEILA	5	W. Cumber & Son (Theale) Ltd.
1952	LECKHAMPSTEAD SHEILA	6	W. Cumber & Son (Theale) Ltd.
1953	137421 GREAT HAYWOOD LADY LINCOLN Thomas Marsh	4	Thomas Marsh Tithe Barn Farm Great Haywood, Staffs.
1954	137937 BURNHAM FASHION G. W. Gladwin	3	G. W. Gladwin Burnham Grange Barton-on-Humber, Lincs.
1955	137850 STRETE MELODY W. P. Mingo Strete Farm Whimple, Devon	5	Colin McKie Village Farm Milton Ernest, Beds.
1956	138192 CRESSWELL GREY PRINCESS Fred Moss	4	Fred Moss Cresswell Farm Betchton Rode Heath, Ches.
1957	CRESWELL GREY PRINCESS	5	Fred Moss
1958	CRESSWELL GREY PRINCESS	6	Fred Moss
1959	138498 LILLINGSTONE LUCKY CHANCE H. Eady Robinson	6	H. Eady Robinson

(B)	*Champion Mare and Breeder*	*Age*	*Exhibitor*
1960	139184 CULCLIFFE MODERN MAID E. T. Lowe Glebe Farm Ratcliffe Culey, Leics.	2	John H. Frank Horton, Northants
1961	CULCLIFFE MODERN MAID	3	John H. Frank
1962	CULCLIFFE MODERN MAID	4	John H. Frank
1963	139080 BELLE VUE AMY J. W. Widdowson	6	J. W. Widdowson Belle Vue Farm Nether Handley, Derby.
1964	139247 BARTON PEARL 2ND Andrew Bros. Grange Farm Barton-on-Humber, Lincs.	5	J. W. Widdowson
1965	139199 GRANGE WOOD SUNSET E. J. Richardson	7	E. J. Richardson
1966	GRANGE WOOD SUNSET	8	E. J. Richardson
1967	139682 LAYSTON SUNBEAM J. Russell	4	E. J. Richardson
1968	LAYSTON SUNBEAM	5	E. J. Richardson
1969	139538 BURNHAM BEAUTY G. W. Gladwin	8	W. Salt & Sons Quixhill Farm Denstone, Staffs.
1970	139854 BURFORD LADY IN WHITE H. Sutton	3	H. Sutton Burford Lane Farm Lymm, Ches.
1971	BURFORD LADY IN WHITE	4	H. Sutton
1972	139514 SLEIGHTWOOD MISS FASHION J. T. Henton & Sons Emu Lodge Farm Barnby-in-the-Willows, Notts	9	T. Yates Hall Farm Windley, Derby.
1973	BURFORD LADY IN WHITE	6	H. Sutton
1974	139920 WHEELTON ROSE J. W. Pooley Spout House Higher Wheelton, Lancs.	5	Ll. Joseph & Sons Grove House South Cornelly, Glam
1975	139950 GRANGE WOOD SELENA E. J. Richardson	5	T. W. Critchlow Manor House Farm Cubley, Derby.

(C)	*Champion Gelding and Breeder*	*Age*	*Exhibitor*
1945	Stallions only		
1946	Stallions and Mares only		
1947	No gelding championship		
1948	BIRKWOOD CLAREMONT Edward Cottam Belmont Farm Slyne, Lancs.	5	Fl/Lt R. J. Kilby Rose and Crown Hotel Tring, Herts.

(C)	*Champion Gelding and Breeder*	*Age*	*Exhibitor*
1949	HEATON WARRANT R. Moore and Sons Outerthwaite Farm Allithwaite, Lancs.	6	J. & W. Whewell
1950	GLOBE WARRANT (late Kytes Warrant) W. Cumber & Son (Theale) Ltd.	4	T. Marsden & Sons Globe Mills Midge Hall Preston, Lancs.
1951	GLOBE WARRANT	5	T. Marsden & Sons
1952	HEATON SILVER LAD Harry Francis Ganaraw, Mon.	5	J. and W. Whewell
1953	COPPER M. Hutchinson Priory Park Ulverston, Lancs.	5	Offiler's Brewery Ltd. 7 Ambrose Street Derby
1954	PRESTON WARRANT J. Moorhouse Gilpins Farm Levens Westmorland	6	Offiler's Brewery Ltd.
1955	PRESTON WARRANT	7	Offiler's Brewery Ltd.
1956	HEATON GAY LAD J. T. Appleby	5	J. and W. Whewell Ltd.
1957	HIGHLIGHT T. H. B. Freshney	3	T. H. B. Freshney
1958	HEATON TRIMINAL H. Bielby Ash Row Farm Sherburn-in-Elmet, Yorks.	5	J. and W. Whewell Ltd.
1959	WANDLE MAJESTIC G. Caley New House Farm Burstwick, Yorks.	5	Young & Co's Brewery Ltd. Ram Brewery Wandsworth S.W.18
1960	PARK HOUSE EXCELLENCY Thomas Marsh Tithe Barn Great Haywood, Staffs.	3	J. E. Crosland Park House Farm Aberford, Yorks.
1961	BELLASIZE MAJESTIC J. Martinson Bellasize Grange Howden, Yorks.	4	J. & W. Whewell Ltd.
1962	BELLASIZE MAJESTIC	5	J. & W. Whewell Ltd.
1963	BELLASIZE MAJESTIC	6	J. & W. Whewell Ltd.
1964	BELLASIZE MAJESTIC	7	J. & W. Whewell Ltd.
1965	BELLASIZE MAJESTIC	8	J. & W. Whewell Ltd.

(C)	*Champion Gelding and Breeder*	*Age*	*Exhibitor*
1966	HEATON KING WILLIAM W. Sudell Lower Park Head Plumpton, Lancs.	4	J. & W. Whewell Ltd.
1967	HEATON MAJESTIC J. B. Cooke Cowbit House Deeping High Bank, Lincs.	3	J. & W. Whewell Ltd
1968	HEATON MAJESTIC	4	J. & W. Whewell Ltd.
1969	HEATON MAJESTIC	5	J. & W. Whewell Ltd.
1970	HEATON MAJESTIC	6	J. & W. Whewell Ltd.
1971	HEATON MAJESTIC	7	J. & W. Whewell Ltd.
1972	HEATON MAJESTIC	8	J. & W. Whewell Ltd.
1973	WHITLEY SUPERMAN Arthur Wright Farms Ltd.	5	Arthur Wright Farms Ltd. Village Farm Daresbury, Ches.
1974	COWERSLANE DAVID C. Walton Bassingham, Lincs.	3	T. Yates
1975	ST. VINCENT'S KING WILLIAM E. Coward Ltd.	5	E. Coward Ltd. Bluebell Farm Thorney, Peterborough

The Stud-book: Conditions of Entry

(a) THE PEDIGREE SYSTEM

There are two ways of deciding whether an animal is a Shire (or a Suffolk or Arab or Dachsund or Siamese). The first is pedigree and the second is appearance. With two exceptions, the Shire Society has always used only the former. That is, if the parents of a horse are "Shires" it is clearly a Shire, whatever curious tricks heredity may have played; on the other hand, however obviously a horse appears to be a Shire, it cannot be accepted as such unless the parents pass some sort of test concerning their ancestry.

Of the two exceptions, one was brief-lived. During the first ten years of the Society, a mare (but not a stallion) could be registered as a Shire if she had been recognised as a Shire by a judge at a reputable agricultural show, and awarded a prize as such. The second exception occurred nearly a century after the Stud-book was opened, when a new rule was introduced whereby any man who wanted to register his animal as a Shire but failed to do so while it was still a foal, had to submit it for inspection. Though this appears to be a radical break with tradition, it was not so much a change of principle as a matter of policy. The pedigree system would still have been sufficient, were it not for the frailty of human nature, whereunder even the most elaborate system of authenticating pedigrees sometimes fails to eliminate the fake.

Since the "Shire" in 1878 was scarcely a breed at all (what was an "English Cart-horse"?) one might well expect approved conformation to have been regarded as a vital qualification for entry into the proposed Stud-book. But the Society decided otherwise and the breed was developed almost solely by the system of gradually tightening the rules for pedigree. Some of the steps taken along this path have been discussed in Part A of this book, and here they are summarised in tabular form.

After the first few years of somewhat hurried decisions, the Shire Council announced each new hardening of the rules a couple of years in advance, and retrospective changes were made more gradually than those for the future. For example, in 1939 it was still possible to register a stallion foaled in, say, 1878, on the same terms as applied in 1896. At no stage, and not even now, after nearly a hundred years of pedigree-recording, has the Society ever "closed" its book so as to admit only the daughters of animals already in it (and it completely closed even the stallion section only after seventy years): occasionally, such a course has been proposed, but has always been rejected. The nearest that the Society came to demanding absolute "purity" was in December 1890, when the Editing Committee moved that for Volume 14 (1893) a stallion or mare foaled in 1881 or later should be accepted only if its sire and dam were both registered. But the Council turned down the proposal the following February. In October 1899, the Editing Committee recommended that mares foaled after 1900 should have a minimum of four registered crosses, i.e. 15/16 registered blood. This, too, was refused (though this near-purity was demanded in the 1920s). Later Editing Committees' proposals that the Stud-book should be "closed" after 1910 and again after 1920, were also rejected, as was an individual proposition in 1938.

In studying the slow progress towards purity as summarised in the following table, the reader may with advantage bear in mind that the Society, even though so many of its leading members for the first forty years or so were wealthy men, consistently recognised that it was primarily acting for the good of people producing work-horses. That is, it never forgot that the Shire was a variety (though an improved one) of the "common cart horse" which common men did their daily work with. There may have been malcontents in Edwardian times who begrudged a Rothschild, a Muntz or a Greenwell their success (stupidly, because their efforts benefited every breeder in the land), but the Shire Society remained ever realistic on this point. However much the show-system may have tended towards a "fancy", its leaders never withdrew from even the humblest breeder the opportunity of converting their homely mares into pedigree Shires by the simple process of using a top-class stallion, available through the local hiring "club" at a cheap rate. Hundreds of prize-winning Shires were thus produced after only a couple of generations of grading-up. If these fine horses of unsung ancestry in the female line were sold to become pampered darlings of the rich, there was no harm in that: indeed there was a lot of good in it, because it was the hard-up breeder who, relatively speaking, gained the most.

Perhaps the Stud-book rules of the British Percheron Society illustrate by contrast, the difficulty that the Shire men had in forming their breed in the first place. They also show, by comparison, the difficulty of rigidly adhering to a policy of continual striving after purity and perfection if times were hard. When the Percherons came first to England, demand for work horses was high and the breed society could call its own tune. Whether bred at home or abroad, Percherons (mares as well as stallions) were accepted for the Stud-book only if 100 % "pure" – that is, by a sire and out of a dam entered in the Stud-book of the British Percheron Horse Society, La Société Hippique Percheronne de France, the Percheron Society of America or the Canadian Percheron Horse Breeders' Association. The Stud-book was therefore "closed" from the start. There was, in addition, a colour rule: home-bred stallions, and all imported animals, must be grey or black. Thirdly, there was a conformation rule for imported horses: they must be certified by an inspector appointed by B.P.H.S., as being of sufficiently good conformation and type and must be passed, by a veterinary officer nominated by B.P.H.S., as free from hereditary disease. Fourthly, in order to prevent any roguery, it was required that, before being weaned, all foals intended for registration had to be branded on the neck with irons supplied by the secretary. (The French society had been doing this since 1889.)

With such a purist start, one might expect no change in the future, for surely it would be a matter of continuing to breed Percherons of untainted blood, both for perpetuating the breed and for producing cross-breds or improved working stock. But by the beginning of the 1939 war, the Percheron Society, too, had its Supplementary Register. It was more stringently kept than that for Shires – Register A mares, eligible when three years old and got by a pedigree stallion, had to be passed for appearance (grey or black, not under 16-hands, inspected and passed as of suitable conformation) and certified sound by a veterinary certificate which was not more than one month out of date. A mare in Register B represented the second pedigree cross. Her daughter, 7/8 pure, was acceptable for the Stud-book, but she had to be distinguished by an asterisk, as did all future progeny. So, the first stallion to appear in the book under this scheme would be 15/16 "pure", but the asterisk would reveal his taint to all. Even his progeny, out of a pure-bred mare and therefore 31/32 pure, would still be labelled with the asterisk. This damning mark could not be dropped except by a three-quarters majority decision at a meeting of Society members, of whom only those were entitled to vote who possessed animals of which over 50% were of pure stock. (In the 1960s the use of the Percheron grading-up register lapsed and was only resumed in the 'seventies.)

(b) THE RULES, 1879–1952

In the following tables,

(i) "Year of registration" means the year in which the breeder submitted the necessary application: "Volume Number" therefore relates to the volume bearing the date of the following year, when the pedigree was published.

(Owing to delays in 1939–1945 and to confusion reigning about 1960 the numbering of Stud-books became out of joint. E.g. Volume 97, dated 1973, and containing the Spring Show report of 1973 and foals born in 1973, ought not to have appeared, under the system operating from 1880–1939, until 1976 and should contain the show report and foals of the previous year.)

(ii) The fraction of required registered blood as quoted in this table is of course an absolute minimum, and is theoretical rather than actual. It is not suggested that a 3/4-bred Shire (by a registered stallion out of a dam by registered stallion) was in practice as much as one-quarter anything else: the final quarter was itself in most cases fifty or more per cent real Shire, and occasionally completely Shire. Shire men have always been better at breeding horses than registering pedigrees and many a good-looking cart-horse lacked only the necessary papers to prove that it was what it appeared to be – a Shire.

OPERATIVE FROM			STALLIONS	LESSER REQUIREMENTS FOR "OLD-TIME" STALLIONS	
Year of Regn.	Vol. No.	Year of Foaling	MINIMUM *Registered Blood*	Year of Foaling	MINIMUM *Registered Blood*
1879	1	Before 1877	"No known cross for two generations"		
1880	2	Before 1879	"No known cross for two generations"		
1881	3	Before 1881	"No known cross for two generations"		
1882	4	Before 1882	"No known cross for two generations"		
1883	5	1881 plus	3/4: reg. sire, reg. dam's sire	Before 1881	1/4: reg. s. *or* d.s eligible
1885	7			Before 1881	3/4: reg. s. *and* reg. d.s. (*see a*)
1887	9			Before 1881	1/4: reg. s. *or* reg. d.s.
1889	11	1881 plus	3/4: reg. s. reg. d.s. (*see b*)		
1894	16	1893 plus	7/8: reg. s. reg. d.s. reg. g.d.s. (*see c*) or 3/4 (*see d*)	Before 1881 / 1881–1892	1/4: reg. s. *or* reg. d.s. / 3/4: reg. s. *and* reg. d.s.
1896	18	1891 plus	7/8 or 3/4 as above (*see e*)	Before 1891	3/4: reg. s. *and* reg. d.s. (*see e*)

OPERATIVE FROM		STALLIONS		LESSER REQUIREMENTS FOR "OLD-TIME" STALLIONS	
Year of Regn.	*Vol. No.*	*Year of Foaling*	MINIMUM *Registered Blood*	*Year of Foaling*	MINIMUM *Registered Blood*
1898	20	1891 plus	7/8 or 3/4 as above (*see f*)	Before 1891	3/4: reg. s. *and* reg. d.s. (*see f*)
1900	22	1891 plus	2/2: reg. s. *and* reg. d. or 7/8 (*see g*)		
1945	67			Stallions foaled before 1891 not now accepted	
1950	73	1950	2/2 ONLY (*see h*) FOALS ONLY (*see i*)		
1953 etc.			Subsequent changes in regulations were only matters of detail – see section c		

Notes

a For entry into Volumes 7 and 8, the requirement for stallions foaled before 1881 was made the same as for young stallions, but was then relaxed again.

b A certificate, signed by the breeder of the stallion, was now required. In 1886, James Forshaw had asked for a ruling on who was the breeder of any colt or filly. The Council unanimously decided that it was the owner of the dam at time of foaling. This is all very well, but when it is a matter of giving a certificate, a man who has bought an in-foal mare has no more proof than anyone else about the identity of the stallion that covered her last.

c If the dam was not a registered mare, her age, colour and breeder were now to be stated: similar particulars were also required of the grand-dam, if foaled in 1881 or later and if not registered.

d The third cross (registered sire of g-dam) was not necessary if the dam had produce (i.e. a daughter) which had been registered in an earlier volume. That is, in these circumstances the qualification for a stallion was no more stringent than for a mare (q.v.).

e Stallions foaled in 1891 or 1892 were suddenly subjected to stricter conditions than would have been imposed, had their entry forms been submitted when they were younger.

f If the dam was not a registered mare, a certificate signed by her breeder was now also required, unless she had had produce already registered in an earlier volume. (This certificate was not required in the case of stallions foaled before 1881.)

g The dam need not be a registered mare, if she had had produce registered in an earlier volume. That is, in these circumstances, the conditions continued to be no more stringent for a stallion than for a mare (q.v.).

h At last, the facility for registering a colt on the same terms as his elder half-sister was withdrawn.

i It was now made a rule that colt foals must be registered in the year of their birth. But see section c.

OPERATIVE FROM Year of Regn.	Vol. No.	Year of Foaling	FILLIES AND MARES MINIMUM *Registered Blood*	"OLD-TIME" MATRONS Year of Foaling	MINIMUM *Registered Blood*
1880	2	Before 1878	1/2: reg. s. – *or* 0/2: prize rule (*see a, b*)		
1881	3	Before 1879	1/2: reg. s. – *or* 0/2: prize rule (*see a, b*)		
1882	4	1877–1881	3/4: reg. s. *and* reg. d.s.	Before 1880	1/2: reg. s. *or* 0/2: prize rule (*see a, b*)
1883	5	1881 plus	3/4: reg. s. *and* reg. d.s.	Before 1881	1/4: reg. s. *or* reg. d.s. *or* 0/2: prize rule (*see c*)
1889	11	1881 plus	3/4: reg. s. *and* reg. d.s. (*see d*)		1/4: reg. s. *or* reg. d.s.
1894	16	1881 plus	3/4: reg. s. *and* reg. d.s. (*see e*)		
1896	18	1891 plus	7/8: reg. s. reg. d.s. reg. g.d.s. (*see f*) or 3/4 (*see g*)	⌠Before 1881 ⌡1881–1890	1/4: reg. s. *or* reg. d.s. 3/4: reg. s. *and* reg. d.s. (*see h*)
1898	20	1891 plus	7/8: reg. s. reg. d.s. reg. g.d.s. (*see h*)		
1901	23	1886 plus	7/8: reg. s. reg. d.s. reg. g.d.s.	Before 1886	3/4: reg. s. *and* reg. d.s. (*see i*)
1903	25	1886 plus	7/8: reg. s. reg. d.s. reg. g.d.s. (*see j*)		
1923	45	1922 plus	15/16: reg. s. reg. d.s. reg.g.d.s. reg.g.g.d.s. (*see k*) or 7/8 (*see l*)	⌠Before 1886 ⌡1886–1921	3/4: reg. s. *and* reg. d.s. 7/8 (*or* 3/4) (*see l*)
1932	54	1886 plus	7/8 (*or* 3/4) as prior to vol. 45 (*see m*)	Before 1886	3/4 (*see m*)
1939	61	1886 plus	7/8 (as above, *or* reg. s. × "B" mare) (*see n*)		
1945	67			Mares foaled before 1886 not now accepted	
1950	73	1950	7/8 (equiv.) reg. s. × "B" mare (*see o*) FOALS ONLY (*see p*)		
1953			Subsequent changes in rules were only matters of detail – *see* section c		

Notes

a For Volumes 2–4 there was an additional compulsory qualification – that mares must have produced a living foal. However, for Volume 4, fillies could be accepted on the strength of the new $\frac{3}{4}$-blood rule instead. This accounts for the apparent confusion of dates in this table. The rule about having produced a living foal was scrapped altogether from Volume 5.

b The prize rule for older mares was an alternative to the pedigree qualification. For Volumes 2–5, a mare so qualifying, or her produce, must have won a prize as an "English Cart Horse" at a recognised agricultural show. For Volume 6, if it was her produce that thus qualified her, such colt or filly must have been a winner as a yearling or older, not as a foal. For Volume 7, the rule stipulated that the qualifying prize must have been won in open competition, not in a local class. From Volume 11 onwards, the prize qualification wss cancelled.

c This backward step was caused by the difficulty of obtaining enough mares for the Stud-book, compared with stallions.

d A certificate, signed by the breeder of the mare, was now required.

e If the dam were not a registered mare, her age, colour and breeder were now to be stated.

f Similar particulars were to be given for the grand-dam, if she were not registered.

g The third cross (registered sire of g-dam) was not necessary if the dam had had produce registered in an earlier volume.

h In the case of mares foaled 1881 and onwards, a certificate signed by the breeder of the dam was now also required, if the dam was not registered and if she had not produce already registered.

i A certificate signed by the breeder of the dam was required now, as under (h), even for mares foaled before 1881.

j A certificate was now required from the breeder of the g-dam (if unregistered and if she had not already figured in a registered pedigree). If he was dead, some other authentication could be accepted.

k A certificate signed by the breeder of the g.g-dam was now required.

l The fourth cross could be dispensed with if the g-dam had already appeared in a registered pedigree. Similarly with the third cross for older mares, as before.

m Owing to the difficulties of the 'twenties, when so little breeding was done and records were badly kept, the qualifications were relaxed, after nine years, to what they had been before.

n There was of course no difference between a Register B mare and a non-registered mare with two crosses of registered blood. But when the Grade Registers were introduced in 1939, it was intended that their use should be compulsory after October 31, 1941 – i.e. no graded-up mare could be entered in the Stud-book after that date, in the old way, showing the details of three crosses. Her dam would have first to appear in Register B, and her g-dam in Register A. However, this rule was not enforced owing to the war.

o The use of the Grade Register was now compulsory. Since the female produce of a registered Shire stallion and a registered Clydesdale mare had been since 1943 eligible for Register B, it would be folly here to apportion the minimum fraction of registered Shire blood necessary to qualify a mare for the Shire Stud-book.

p As with colts, fillies now had to be registered in the year of birth. See section c.

GRADE REGISTER "B" MARES AND FILLIES

Year of Regn.	Vol. No.	Age	Qualification	
1939	61	Living	3/4: reg. s. × "A" mare	Voluntary scheme (1941 – compulsory scheme postponed)
1943	65	Living	{ 3/4: reg. s. × "A" mare or reg. s. × reg. Clyde mare*	
1950	75	Foal	{ 3/4: reg. s. × "A" mare or reg. s. × reg. Clyde mare*	Compulsory scheme
1953 etc.			Subsequent minor rules: see section c	

GRADE REGISTER "A" MARES AND FILLIES

1939	61	Living	1/2: reg. s. × mare of "Shire type"	Voluntary scheme (1941 – compulsory scheme postponed)
1950	73	Foal	1/2: reg. s. × mare of "Shire type"	Compulsory scheme
1953 etc.			Subsequent minor modifications: see section c	

* For a discussion of the effect of giving preferential treatment to Clydesdale mares over half-bred Shire mares, see Part A.XIV.6.

(c) 1953–1974

From 1st January 1953, fillies for the Stud-book or for Grade Register B had to be registered within thirty days of birth. Colts had to be "recorded" within thirty days – that is, the dam had to be re-entered to show him (not necessarily named) as produce: if it were then desired actually to register the colt, he had to be entered within twelve months. The fee was still 5s. for fillies and 10s. (now in two equal instalments) for colts. There were two other new regulations. Firstly, an official sketch card had to be completed, showing full particulars of the foal's markings. Secondly, if the owner was not also the breeder, it was the Society's secretary, and not the owner, who was responsible for obtaining the breeder's signature on the requisite certificate of breeding. In the case of fillies, any failure to comply with the new regulations would cause her to be acceptable only for Grade Register "A", instead of Register "B" or the Stud-book itself: in the case of colts, of course, rejection was absolute.

In 1955, the fee was raised to £1 both for colts (5s. and 15s.) and fillies, and in 1969 to £2.

In 1969, Shires tendered for registration out of their year of birth were again formally accepted – under protest, in the form of a £10 fee for yearlings, £20 for two-year-olds and £30 for older animals.

In 1970, it became compulsory for all animals submitted for entry in the Stud-book to have included in their name a registered prefix (for which the fee was now £2.)

For 1972, two changes were made that were contrary to classic Shire Horse Society practice (though none the less sensible for that: indeed the first could be reasonably regarded as long overdue):

(i) animals entered for the Stud-book out of their year of birth could not be accepted until they had been inspected by a member of the Editing Committee and a member of the Council. An inspection rule, though common enough in other breeds, was a revolutionary change for Shire men – even though, year after year, the reminder was printed in successive volumes of the Stud-book that "the Editing Committee are empowered to reject or cancel the entry of any animal of which there is a doubt as to its being of the 'Shire' or 'Old English Cart Horse breed' ": these words had been changed in Volume 73 (1951) to "as to the correctness of the pedigree".

(ii) animals bred outside the United Kingdom were now eligible for the Stud-book, provided that both sire and dam were in the S.H.S. book. Furthermore, mares became eligible for Grade Register "B" if by a stallion in the S.H.S. book and out of a Clydesdale mare entered in the American Clydesdale Stud-book, just as if she were in the C.H.S. book in Scotland. (There had been four Illinois-bred mares in the abortive "American Section" of Vol. 42 in 1921. All were by exported registered stallions out of exported registered mares.)

(In 1972, Grade Register entry fees for females registered out of their year of birth were raised to £5.)

1973 saw the introduction of a revised standard of points for the conformation of Shires, in order to strengthen the hand both of inspectors appointed under the new rule of the previous year, and of judges at shows. The Council report commented that consideration had had to be given to "the suggestion that blood from other breeds was creeping into Shires other than as provided by the Stud-book regulations". This new standard of conformation is printed in Appendix 9.

For 1974, a long-standing difficulty (a solution of which was rejected by the Council in 1919—see A.X.9) was resolved by a new rule that made it compulsory to re-enter a stallion or mare in the Stud-book upon its changing ownership. The fee for this was to be £4, and failure to comply would make the animal ineligible to compete at the Society's Show or for any of its awards elsewhere.

This year also, Stud-book fees were raised – from £2 for colt (total fee) or filly, to £7 which entitled the breeder to a free copy of one volume of the Stud-book. For second and subsequent registrations in the same year by the same breeder there was a £2 discount. For registrations out of the year of birth the fees were increased to £30 (yearlings), £40 (two-year-olds) and £50 for older animals. Entries for the Grade Registers were increased to £10, irrespective of age. (Membership subscriptions were increased to £4.)

Gone were the days – and these lasted until after the Second World War – when a member could join for 1 guinea a year, inclusive of Stud-book, and register his animals for 5s. and 10s. apiece, and half-a-crown for the new-fangled Grade Registers. £50 for a three-year-old mare's registration is twenty thousand per cent of the old "five bob".

Conformation

THE famous fifteen properties of a good horse as put forward by Wynkyn de Worde in 1496 are not altogether irrelevant to our interest:

"*Of a man.* Bolde, prowde, and hardye.
Of a woman. Fayre-breasted, faire of haire, and easy to move.
Of a foxe. A fair taylle, short eers, with a good trotte.
Of a hare. A grate eye, a dry head, and well rennynge.
Of an asse. A bygge chynn, a flat legge, and a good hoof."

The modern Shire breeder might object to the short eers and the bygge chynn, and of course the points are inadequate for a distinctive breed. He would certainly object to Blundeville's dictum in 1580 (A.I.6) that, provided a horse had deep ribs, a large belly, strong legs, good feet and courage "it maketh no matter how fowle or evill favoured he be".

Two centuries later, George Culley's ideal horse was the image of his friend and mentor's ideal. Bakewell's views have already been discussed (A.III.5 q.v.) and so his pupil's interpretation of them is perhaps worth quoting here:

"His head should be as small as the proportion of the animal will admit;
his nostrils expanded, and muzzle fine;
his eyes chearful and prominent;
his ears small, upright, and placed near together;

his neck, rising out from between his shoulders with an easy tapering curve, must join gracefully to the head;

his shoulders, being well thrown back, must also go into his neck (at what is called the points) unperceived, which perhaps facilitates the going much more than the narrow shoulders." (He added in a footnote, "Whoever has observed a greyhound or a hare will perceive how very wide they are made at the upper part of the shoulders, and there are few animals that move with so much ease and swiftness.")

the arm, or fore-thigh, should be muscular and, tapering from the shoulder, meet with a fine, straight, sinewy, bony leg;

the hoof circular, and wide at the heel;

his chest deep, and full at the girth;

his loin or fillets broad and straight, and body round;

his hips or hooks by no means wide, but quarters long, and tail set on so as to be nearly in the same right line as his back;

his thighs strong and muscular;

his legs clean and fine-boned, the leg-bones not round, but what is called lathy and flat." [1]

As to the Shire himself, Fred Street, a century later still, was the first to offer a list of points. He produced them at his speech to the Farmers' Club in 1878, wrote them down in the Livestock Almanac of 1879 and perfected them in his essay printed in Volume 1 of the Stud-book. Since the latter gave some official authority to his views, we quote them here:

"The feet should be firm, deep, and wide at heel; the pasterns not too long and straight; flat bone; short between fetlock and knee. A stallion should not measure less than 11 inches below the knee, and girth from 7 ft. 9 ins. to 8 ft. 3 ins.; should not stand more than 17 hands; should have a wide chest; head big and masculine, without coarseness; eyes prominent and kindly; the head and eyes together should denote intelligence and good temper; shoulders well thrown back; full flowing mane, short back; well-arched ribs; deep middle; large muscular development of the loin; long quarters with tail well set on; the lower part of the rump wide and well let down; good big second thighs; large, flat, clean hocks; plenty of long, silky hair on legs; or, to sum up in a few words, a horse should in form be long. low and wide; and in constitution thoroughly free from all hereditary disease. A main point is action. He should, above all, be a good mover in the cart-horse pace – walking: and, if required to trot, should have the action of a Norfolk cob or a Percheron."

Oddly, the Society did not proceed itself to issue an official standard of conformation. Prominent members frequently lectured about the Shire, or wrote in the agricultural press about it. Of course, they all spoke with the same voice when they attempted to describe the breed, though naturally they emphasised different points as the need arose. The Scotsman, Thomas Dykes, gave as good a description as any of the perfect town heavy gelding (A.VIII.8). But it was not until the publication of Albert Holland's jubilee book in 1929 that official recognition can be claimed for any formal list of points – and that is only by tacit admission, on the grounds that the book was actually published by the Society. This standard proved useful amid the conflicting claims of the 'thirties – a period of mixed progress and misgiving, of which the views of a symposium of eleven prominent breeders in 1937 is typical. Christopher Barker, the President, emphasised a good second thigh and a height of only 16.3–17-hands. Norman Lloyd of Chirbury wanted activity; Colonel Daniel clean leags, heavy stallions and quiet mares; Tom and James Forshaw great *weight*, and docility. Colonel Nicholson said, "no foot, no horse". Captain Clark said, "no head, no horse", because at that end of the animal are the brain, eyes and ears. Enoch Bostock said the ideal horse was the one he hoped to exhibit at the next London Show. And so on.

The war and the 'fifties did at last move the Council to produce a standard of conformation – identical to Holland's. In 1973, there appeared a new version which was first publicly printed in the catalogue of the Spring Show. The text follows, italics being used to show additions or change from the Holland text which, where superseded, is given in parentheses (except that minor differences of wording are ignored):

STALLIONS

Colour: *Black, brown, bay or grey. No good stallion should be splashed with large white patches over the body. He should not be roan or chestnut.* (1929: "Predominating colours bays and brown, then blacks and greys.")

Height: *Minimum 16.2-hands and upwards. Average about 17.2-hands.* (1929: "16.2 to 17.3, average about 17-hands.")

Head: Long and lean, neither too large nor too small, with long neck in proportion to the body. Large jaw bone should be avoided. (1929 adds "Forehead broad between the eyes.")

Eyes: Large, well set and docile in expression. *Wall eye to be avoided at all cost.*

Nose: Nostrils thin and wide; lips together and nose slightly Roman.

Ears: Long, lean, sharp and sensitive.

Throat: Clean cut and lean.

Shoulder: Deep and oblique, wide enough to support the collar.

Neck: Long, slightly arched, well set on to give the horse a commanding appearance.

Girth: The girth varies from 6 ft. to 8 ft. in stallions of from 16.2 to *18 hands.* (1929: "to 17.3")

Back: Short, *strong* and muscular. *Should not be dipped or roached.* (1929: "slightly arched".)

Loins: Standing well up, denoting constitution (*must not be flat*).

Fore-end: Wide across the chest, with legs well under the body and well enveloped in muscle, or action is impeded.

Hind-quarters: Long and sweeping, wide and full of muscle, well let down towards the thighs.

Ribs: Round, deep and well sprung, *not flat.*

Forelegs: *Should be as straight as possible down to pastern.*

Hind legs: *Hocks should not be too far back and in line with the hindquarters with ample width broadside and narrow in front. "Puffy" and "sickle" hocks should be avoided.* The leg sinews should be clean cut and hard like fine cords to touch, and clear of *short* cannon bone.

Bone Measurement: Of flat bone 11 inches is ample, although occasionally $12\frac{1}{2}$ inches (1929 "12 inches") is recorded – flat bone is heavier and stronger than spongy bone. Hocks must be broad, deep and flat, and set at the correct angle for leverage.

Feet: Deep, solid and *wide* (1929: "and not too wide with thick open walls.") *Coronets should be hard and sinewy with substance.*

Hair: *Not too much, fine,* straight and silky. (1929 has "long" and "heavy when lifted".)

The 1973 text states he "should stand from 16.2-hands upwards, and weight from 18 cwt. to 22 cwt. when matured, without being overdone in condition. He should possess a masculine head, and a good crest with sloping, not upright, shoulders running well into the back, which should be short and well coupled with the loins. The tail should be well set up, and not what is known as "goose-rumped". Both head and tail should be carried erect. The ribs should be well sprung, not flat sided, with good middle, which generally denotes good constitution. A stallion should have good feet and joints; the feet should be wide and big around the top of the coronets with sufficient length in the pasterns. When in motion, he should go with force using both knees and hocks, which latter should be kept close together, he should go straight and true before and behind.

"A good Shire stallion should have strong character."

1929 sums up: "Of majestic size and bearing, striking action and courage. 'Each link in the chain one strength' – that is a beautifully balanced horse, one whose whole body moves in unison with great ease – and without friction, embodying all the fine points above mentioned, and attracts even people who are not horsemen."

MODIFICATION OR VARIATION OF STALLION STANDARD OF POINTS FOR MARES

Colour: *Black, brown, bay, grey, roan and chestnut.* (1929: "Bays and browns predominate, then blacks and greys.")

Height: *16-hands upwards.* (1929: "16 to 17 hands")

Head: *Long snd lean. neither too large nor too small, long neck in proportion to the body, but of feminine appearance.* (1929: "Lean and sensitive. Forehead wide between the eyes.")

Neck: Long and slightly arched, and not of masculine appearance.

Girth: 5 ft. to 7 ft. (matured) according to size and age of animal.

Back: *Strong and in some instances longer than a male.* (1929: "Slightly arched and a little longer than a male.")

Legs: Short, with short cannons. (1929 adds "Arms and thighs long, big and full of muscle", and "loins thick and full of muscle".)

Bone Measurement: *9 to 11 inches* (1929: "10½ to 12 inches") of flat bone, with clean cut sinews.

A mare should be on the quality side, long and deep with free action, of a feminine and matronly appearance, *standing from 16-hands and upwards on short legs*: she should have plenty of room to carry her foal.

MODIFICATION OR VARIATION OF STALLION STANDARD OF POINTS FOR GELDINGS

Colour: *As for mares.* (1929: "Bay, brown and grey are the favoured colours, and an occasional chestnut and roan.")

Heights: *16.2-hands and upwards.* (1929: "16.1 to 17.3")

Head: (1929: "lean and intelligent")

Girth: From 6 ft to 7 ft. 6 ins. (1929 adds, in respect of geldings, "wide from shoulder-point to shoulder-point, but not wide between the forelegs".)

Bone Measurement: *10 to 11 inches* (1929: "10½ to 12") under knee, slightly more under hock and broadside on, of flat hard quality.

A gelding should be upstanding, thick, well-balanced, very active and a gay mover; he should be full of courage (1929 adds "yet has no vice"), and should look like, and be able to do a full day's work. (1929 adds "without the least distress – to which work is a recreation"); *Geldings weigh from 17 to 22 cwt.*

To be sure, this is long enough, and its detail contrasts with the attempts of some who have tried from time to time to sum up the essentials of a Shire in an alliterative phrase – for example, that the stallion should be Coarser and more Compact than a mare, and should have Courage and Constitution; or that the mare should be Long, Low and Lusty. The breeder's virtues, on the other hand, should be those of Patience and Perseverance, for after all he is seeking Perfection. And on that point, Tom Forshaw once said (and he was then an old man who had known all the best horses of half a century), "I have no fear but that we shall produce even better Shires than we have seen in the past. With careful selection and judicious mating, great results can be obtained."

This must be the creed to which a breed society holds, even though there may have been periods when its members have erred and strayed, and followed too much the devices and desires of their own hearts. Perhaps, if hair was at one time over-much desired, the attempt later to reduce it led to a worse mistake. That great Shire-man veterinary surgeon, Professor Harold Burrow, has said

> "So long as the feather is silky and straight,
> For heaven's sake leave it alone,
> Since when you get rid of the feather,
> You also eliminate bone."

Excessive hair on the legs, especially if coarse or curly, is highly undesirable. Nevertheless it seems to be proved that a reasonable amount of straight silky hair is essential to the maintenance of true weight and Shire character. Perhaps that is the reason why those who were accustomed to such stallions as Champion's Clansman or Rickford Coming King would scarcely accept the present-day breed as true Shires.

Colour

(a) AN ANALYSIS, 1770–1970.

About the colour of his horses, "the Shire-bred man is in no wise particular", once wrote Herman Biddell.[1] "Watching the ring at the Royal, one sees black, brown, grey, bay and chesnut; with or without white, whole-coloured, blotched and sandy roan. The breeders of these fashionable horses on this point are totally without prejudice and, stopping short of sky blue or emerald green, they appparently claim all shades as the 'true colour' of the Shire-bred proper." He of course spoke with total prejudice, for he was a true Suffolk man. " 'Chesnuts all, and all chesnut, with white facings as few as possible' is his creed, and right bravely is this idea carried out."

The proper reply to Biddell is that any fool can breed chesnuts if he uses a chesnut horse and a chesnut mare. Meanwhile a spirited answer had already been given by Sanders Spencer, reporting on the 1885 London Show and answering another who had quibbled about the diversity of Shire colour. "I would class with Shire-breds the many-hued or coloured Shorthorn, and then ask him what two breeds of animals, and the crosses from them, are half as extensively bred all over the world, or can nearly approach them in usefulness and grandeur."[2]

It had not always been thus. In 1800, a 'Shire' that was not black or brown was as rare as a Suffolk that was bay. The following tables give some idea of the rate at which other colours appeared and increased, and also of the manner in which, partly through breeders' selection and partly through genetical inheritance the proportions of the various colours has fluctuated. By 'selection' is meant chiefly the typical Shire man's avoidance, when he can, of chesnuts and parti-colours and his varying reactions to grey, which was as unpopular in 1900 as it was popular fifty years later. The colour factor in heredity is so complicated a subject and, in the case of Shires, so unpredictable, that breeders have been restricted to such rough-and-ready rules as 'two chesnuts always make a chesnut' and 'to get a grey you must have a grey'. (More scientific principles would require knowledge that the breeder does not have – and cannot have. Full brothers and sisters are rare among Shires: not many mares have had three foals all by the same sire. Because of this, one cannot assemble information about the colour genes of a horse or mare; the impossibility of forecasting a colour is made complete by the fact that the Shire Stud-book is not 'closed'.)

Table A below shows the colour of the 2,902 stallions, subsequently registered, which were foaled between 1770 and 1876 – the years covered by Volume 1. 548 of these were registered, not in Volume 1, but in Volumes 2-12. (There are only one or two early horses in subsequent volumes and these have been ignored.) The period has been divided into five ten-year spans followed by a large span of 26 years, and a final ten-year span. The earliest decades suffer from the fact that percentages are based upon low total numbers, and also from the high proportion of animals whose colour has not been recorded. However, it is unlikely that the 'unknowns', if we could find out about them, would seriously distort the relative proportion of the colours: if it altered it at all, it would probably be in favour of the most orthodox hues of the day. It is unimaginable that Blaze 183, foaled in 1770 was anything but black, or possibly brown, or that Blunston's Horse 226, bred in the heart of Derbyshire in 1830 (all we know is, "by Brentnall's Blaze" – presumably Isaac Brentnall of Risley) was a chestnut, roan or piebald, for this oddity would surely have been recorded: indeed, the absence of information suggests that he was not grey, either, or even bay.

Table B shows the colour of mares foaled in selected specimen years to 1970. It begins with the periods 1841–1866 and 1867-1876, to provide a comparison with the stallions of those same periods in Table A. (They have been taken from Volumes 2-13, after which time the registration of early mares had practically ceased.) The table continues with the years 1906, 1921, 1936, 1951 and 1961-1970; these are reasonably spaced intervals, ending with the decade prior to the rule of 1973 that the permitted colour of mares should be "black, brown, bay, grey, roan and chestnut". Mares have been chosen because their colours tend to show more accurately what is being actually bred, rather than what the prevalent general 'fancy' is. The owner of a colt whose colour was unpopular would see little demand for his services, unless he was of exceptional quality otherwise, and would be likely to castrate him. But the decision whether or not to register a mare was less likely to be made on the grounds that she was of a "good" or "bad" colour: one of a bad colour could be registered late if she happened to produce a good foal (especially one of a good colour) that was worth putting in the book. In particular, no one in high Edwardian days would be likely to register a stallion of a really "wrong" colour, such as piebald or

TABLE A. COLOUR OF STALLIONS, 1770–1876

	1	2	3	4	5	6	7
Year foaled	1770–1800	1801–1810	1811–1820	1821–1830	1831–1840	1841–1866	1867–1876
Volume No.	1	1	1	1	1	1–12	1–12
No. of Horses	48	72	112	177	172	1,223	1,098
Colour Unknown	24	14	16	46	28	181	32
Known Colours	24	58	96	131	144	1,042	1,066
	%	%	%	%	%	%	%
Black	54.17	46.55	33.33	29.01	20.14	13.44	12.85
Brown	45.83	48.28	41.67	33.59	40.28	35.03	28.05
Grey		3.45	14.59	22.14	13.19	15.07	9.01
Chestnut		1.72	8.33	4.58	8.34	6.81	8.44
Bay			1.04	4.58	13.19	18.52	30.58
Roan			1.04	5.34	4.86	11.04	11.07
Parti-coloured [i]				0.76			
White [ii]							0.09
Dun							

[i] Piebald. Everett's Horse 770, f. 1825, b and o Everett of Broughton, Lincs. By *Holmes's Horse of Edwalton*, Notts.

[ii] Devonshire 594, f. 1860. b Rains of Castle Donington, Leics. By Stych's Champion 419 (grey); dam by King David 1211 (chestnut). This horse must surely have been really a grey.

dun. But seven such mares appear in the 1906 book. In this volume, only forty-eight stallions of the unpopular chestnut colour were registered – 5.13 % of 935. But there were 258 chestnut mares – 8.9% of 3,188. In 1936, there were only two chestnut stallions (0.63%) out of 319, compared with 23 chestnut mares out of 904 (2.55%) As the table shows, the percentage of chestnut mares has fallen steadily from pre-Stud-book days, but the trend has been a step or two behind the decline in chestnut stallions.

In 1906, grey was at the height of its unpopularity. Only 19 stallions, of 935 registered that year, (2.03%) were grey; but there were 140 grey mares out of 3,188 (4.39%). By 1936, grey was in favour. There were no less than 55 grey stallions out of 319 (17.24%); but the number of grey mares, lagging behind, had risen only to 76 out of 904 (8.41%).

In these tables, where the colour is difficult to allocate, the lighter hue has been chosen. E.g. "black-brown" has been counted as brown: "black-grey", as grey; "brown-bay" as bay. The roans include every variety that it is possible to imagine, but the earlier animals of this type were usually registered simply as "roan".

In each column, mares originally entered in an earlier volume and now reregistered to show change of owner, prizes, produce etc., have been ignored.

If one reads Table B in conjunction with Table A (making allowance in columns 6 and 7 for the "time-lag" in the colour of mares) it will be seen that black decreases continuously from 1770 to 1931, but continuously rises thereafter. The percentage of greys rises from 1801 to 1830, falls almost steadily to 1921 and then rises and falls again suddenly. Chestnut reaches alarming proportions in mid-Victorian times (when much Suffolk blood was intermixed) but has gradually and with difficulty been almost eliminated in Stud-book times. Bay becomes more and more common until 1931, since when the numbers have fallen and then tended to level out. Roans reached their peak just before the Stud-book was founded (a high peak in the case of stallions – many colts were left entire with a view to getting a supply of roan geldings, which were very popular in many city stables) but have dwindled steadily thereafter.

TABLE B. COLOUR OF MARES, 1841–1970

	6	7	8	9	10	11	12	13
Year foaled[i]	1841–1866	1867–1876						1961–1970
Volume No./date[ii]	2–13	2–13	1906	1921	1931	1936	1951	85–94
No. of Mares	104	1,884	3,188	5,652	800	904	210	632
Colour Unknown		12		1	1			
Known Colours	104	1,872	3,188	5,651	799	904	210	632
	%	%	%	%	%	%	%	%
Black	18.27	15.81	12.05	10.70	8.75	12.28	19.52	24.52
Brown	23.07	22.70	24.97	28.10	29.04	29.20	20.48	23.89
Grey	9.62	9.56	4.39	2.87	5.01	8.41	24.76	9.97
Chestnut	13.46	10.58	8.09	4.87	1.63	2.55	1.44	0.16
Bay	29.81	34.46	47.33	51.86	55.19	46.90	33.33	40.99
Roan[iii]	4.81	6.78	2.95	1.54	0.38	0.55	0.47	0.47
Parti-coloured[iv]			0.09	0.02				
White	0.96	0.11				0.11		
Dun[v]			0.13	0.04				

ⁱ To correspond with the stallions (columns 6–7) the year of foaling has been taken in the first two columns. In columns 8–12 the date of the Stud-book (one year after registration) seems to give a fairer picture. In column 13, the date of the Stud-book corresponds to the year of foaling. Only one mare foaled earlier than 1841 is in the Stud-book – a roan. See B.IX.I

ⁱⁱ In 1921, and in 1931, there were incomplete particulars in respect of one mare, and these were never supplied.

ⁱⁱⁱ The most famous *roan* in Shire history is a stallion – the Old Strawberry himself, Charles Marsters' England's Wonder 761 f. 1871. Considering his fame and fertility, and that he got several sons and daughters of really odd colours, the fact that roan diminished so fast amongst registered Shires from his time onwards is a clear indication of the general disapproval of these varieties of hues by breeders, even though roans were popular with many town carters.

^{iv} *The parti-colours.* In the middle of the nineteenth century a certain Mr. Colvin of Pishobury near Sawbridgeworth had a family of piebald English Cart-horses which he carefully bred for colour. But his fancy was unique, and perished with him: nearly every other breeder attempted to avoid what he was trying to achieve. At Holker Hall, before the time of Victor Cavendish, the future 9th Duke of Devonshire, there had been a family of peculiar roan skewbalds, but under his management this died out.

There is one parti-colour mare in the 1921 volume – 104957 Pickworth Beauty, f. 1916, "brown and white body, white face, four white legs". Her half-sister in the same volume, 104958 Pickworth Blossom, though listed as a brown, had enough white on her body almost to bring her into the same category. The dam of both was the unregistered *Violet* (chestnut and white), f 1908, which was got by Cottam Captain 19514 (piebald), bred in 1898 by William Stafford Brown of Cottam, near Newark. This stallion was bought by James Forshaw who in 1907 re-sold him to Buenos Aires, where his colouring was more prized than at home.

His half-sister 47544 Cottam Smart (a skewbald, but recorded as "piebald – white and bay patches") is one of three parti-coloured mares in the 1906 volume. Both she and Cottam Captain were out of 23146 Brisk (piebald) f 1886, g-dam *Flower* (piebald) bred in 1873 by Thomas Brown of Long Bennington. The colour is impossible to trace further, our knowledge of *Flower*'s breeding being only that her sire, Drayman 675, was grey. (It is possible that all those in the family listed as piebald were really skewbald.)

The other two parti-colours in the 1906 volume are 49618 Tilney Flash, "roan and white, white face, four white legs", whose antecedents on both sides had a lot of white on the face and legs, though more on the body, and were in many cases roan: and 49710 Venture, "skewbald, lot of white", whose grey and bay parents and grandparents appear sufficiently orthodox to make us wonder why, if Venture turned out a skewbald, thousands of other Shire mares were not like her. But colour inheritance in horses is so intricate a branch of genetics as to be unfathomable in cases where pedigrees are as brief and inadequate as in the Ventures of the Shire world.

(In 1960, there was just one mare, out of 62, which was neither black, brown, bay nor grey. This was 139313 Decoy Silver Cloud – "grey dun, white face, fore legs white to knees, hind legs white to hocks, white patch on belly and flecked with white hairs." Whence came she? Via the grading-up register. Her g.g-dam is as undocumented as any cart-mare had been in the days before the breed society was founded.)

v *The duns*. George Street had something to say about a dun cart-stallion at the Farmers' Club meeting in 1878 when his brother made his famous speech which resulted in the foundation of the Society. This horse "was used in our district, and nearly all its stock were of one colour, a yellowish bay with a brown mark down the back and sometimes down the shoulders also. I have been told that the horse was bred from a nag or half-bred mare, but have been unable to trace its pedigree any further back. If the horse had been in a stud-book, it would have been interesting to discover the origin of that distinctive mark which had been reproduced in successive generations, but perhaps the owner would not have entered him". No one ever did, nor any of the progeny either. But if George did not know the immediate cause of the markings, the original cause is clear: it was a reversion to the colouring of the most primitive forms of Equus caballus.

The two duns in the 1921 volume were mother and daughter, bred in the Aberystwyth area – 101333 Bertha Queen (f 1919) and the oddly-named 101922 Brown (f 1909). The latter was out of the dun *Jewel* (f 1900), out of the grey *Brown* (f 1893), beyond which point our knowledge of the breeding fades out. No trace of dun colouring is apparent in the male lines.

There is no evidence by which to explain three of the four duns in the 1906 volume. For example, the fourteen immediate progenitors of 48921 Nottingham Norah consisted of 7 bay, 6 brown and a black, and her g.g.g.-parents (which included Harold, William the Conqueror, What's Wanted and Royal Albert) were 4 grey, 3 brown, 2 black, 2 bay – and five whose colour is lost amidst the mists that lie beyond the Stud-book. The ancestry of Tangmere Belle and Wallington Rosebud is similarly uninstructive. However, the fourth merits more comment. 47946 Florrie, bred in Anglesey by William Jones in 1901, was "dun, black streak along back". Her dam, 25696 Corwen (Evan Evans, 1896) was "dark buff, black stripe from shoulders to tail, black below knees and hocks". The g-dam was *Seren* (buff, 1891) and g.g-dam *True* (buff, 1881).

Here, we are dealing with something more deep-seated than simple inheritance of coat colour, just as we were in the case of the great Prince William's legs. (See B.VII.5.) The black dorsal stripe on the dun Florrie and her dam does not take us back as far as Hipparion and other three-toed Equidae, but it does revert to the markings on the most primitive form of the modern horse, which we can see today in some zoos as "reconstituted" specimens of *Equus przevalskii*.

(b) BREEDING TO COLOUR

Gregor Johann Mendel published his work on the natural laws of heredity, based on his experiments with garden peas, in 1866. He submitted it to the chief scientific societies all over the world, and it was ignored by all of them. The good Abbot died in 1884, and it was not until 1900 that his laws began to be taken seriously, and their immense value to animal and plant breeding at last recognised.

It would be idle to speculate whether his discoveries, if generally accepted earlier, could have benefited the Cart-horse men. In the first place, the laws governing the inheritance of colour are extraordinarily complicated, and are by no means fully agreed upon even today. Secondly, the Shire Stud-book has remained "open". If one cannot be certain about colour inheritance in Thoroughbreds, whose pedigrees have been recorded for so much longer and for which the Stud-book is closed to all except those animals whose parents are both registered, there can be no hope for the Shire-bred.

It must suffice here to say that the Mendelian Laws have done little more for the Shire-breeder than give scientific support to what he and his fellows had already learned, not from genetics, but from careful observation. And this is limited to two or three facts:

1. Chestnut mated to chestnut can result only in a chestnut foal, since the colour is recessive and therefore pure.

This fact makes life easy, colour-wise, for the Suffolk breeder. Herman Biddell had nothing to boast about. Shire men could have turned their breed entirely chestnut, had they wished to do so.

2(i) Grey mated to grey nearly always produces grey. Nearly always, but not inevitably. (It is possible that the offspring of such a mating will escape what Federico Tesio[3], suggested was not a "colour" at all but a "pathological discoloration", and so will be either genetic "bay" or chestnut, according to what colour it inherits from its "disguised" parents.)

This fact makes it nearly as simple for the Percheron breeder to fix grey as the colour for his breed as it has been for the Suffolk man to fix chestnut. Shire men could turn their breed grey more quickly than they could turn it chestnut, though not with such certainty of reaching 100% success in a measurable time.

(ii) A grey cannot be produced unless at least one of the two parents is grey. That is, it can only be transmitted directly from parent to offspring: it cannot skip a generation. (Tesio drew attention to the existence, among the many thousands of greys that have appeared in the General Stud-book, of forty-four seeming exceptions to this rule. But he quotes I. B. and C. H. Robertson who, writing in *The Breeder's Review*, 1914, showed that all these cases are probably erroneous: one at least of the parents, although originally registered as a "bay" or chestnut foal, turned out to be grey afterwards, but the registration was for some reason never corrected – possibly because the horses concerned were insignificant as far as racing interests were concerned. There are apparent exceptions among Shires also, but the Shire Stud-book is so inaccurate that there is no difficulty in accepting that similar errors occur here also.)

This fact would make it more simple to eradicate grey from the Shire breed than to do away with chestnut.

(N.B. All that is written here about grey applies equally to roan.)

"Bay" (if we use this term genetically to include what practical men call both bays and browns, and perhaps even blacks) may be either pure or hybrid "bay": but it is more or less impossible to tell if a "bay" stallion is pure until he has sired perhaps hundreds of "bay" progeny without ever throwing a chestnut one. It is quite definitely impossible to tell if a "bay" mare is pure, simply because she cannot have enough foals in a lifetime to prove the point, though of course she would prove herself at once to be of hybrid colour if at any time she produced a chestnut foal.

Nevertheless, it is pretty clear that the Shire breed contains a much greater proportion of pure "bays" than it did in the muddled period of the 1870s, because chestnut has been almost eliminated. If the Stud-book had been closed, and if chestnut had been banned, it would be possible eventually to achieve a breed whose members were all pure "bay". But chestnut mares are not banned and, whereas chestnut is not now (since 1973) recognised as a proper colour for stallions, the fact that a stallion's dam might have entered the Stud-book via the Grading-up Registers constantly increases the chance that he might be, if not actually chestnut, a hybrid "bay" capable of getting chestnut foals out of either chestnut or hybrid "bay" mares.

In differentiating between the various shades of the genetic "bay", from darkest to light there is no help from the Mendelian Laws. If the Shire man wanted to restore black as the main or only colour of his breed he could do so only by trying to ensure that only the very darkest specimens, the black ones, were used for breeding purposes, in the hope that the animals most richly endowed with pigmentation would pass on that quality, as they would transmit other qualities not subject to the Mendelian Laws. After all, the Frisians are all black and, in Bakewell's day, the Shires were Blacks. No doubt it could be done.

In spite of a century of Stud-book registration, the modern Shire is not so pure as he was in the eighteenth century. He may be a better horse, but we cannot judge whether even that is so, since none of us has ever seen the cart-horse of the early Georges, or even a reliable picture of one.

(c) THE CHESTNUT IN HAROLD: DUNSMORE CHESSIE

Here is a chart of the coat-colours of Harold's immediate antecedents. It is pointless to carry it back beyond his g.g-parents: five even of these are unrecorded as to colour. The chart reveals that, just as Lincolnshire Lad II failed to transmit his greyness to Harold, so had that other great sire, Stych's Champion, failed to pass on greyness to Harold's dam. Another point of interest, and one we shall pursue, is that the great horse's g-dam was chestnut in colour.

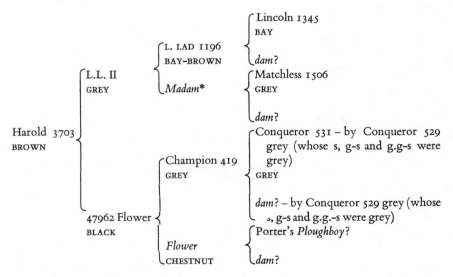

* Colour not recorded, but was clearly grey.

Now follows a table showing the colours of Harold's "101 best sons" as selected in B.VI.3. That his colour was genetically a hybrid, not a pure, "bay" is revealed by the fact that he was capable of begetting chestnut foals out of bay mares:

HAROLD'S "101 BEST SONS"						THEIR DAMS	
Black	Brown	Bay	Chestnut	Grey	Bl-Roan		
5	4					Black	9
4	11	10				Brown	25
6	10	27	4			Bay	47
		1	2			Chestnut	3
	1	1		2		Grey	4
	1				2	Blue-Roan	3
		2				Other Roan	2
1	3	2	1	1*		Unrecorded	8
—	—	—	—	—	—		
16	30	43	7	3	2		101

* The dam of this one must have been grey, but it is impossible to work out the colours of the other seven.

The only chestnut Shire ever selected as supreme champion of the breed was that great mare Dunsmore Chessie. Her very colour proves her magnificence to those of us who never saw her, because it was a drawback that no Shire judge would overlook unless excellence in every other aspect forced him to do so. And she was chosen as champion mare not once, but twice: that is, by six judges. Whence came this chestnut coat? Immediately, from her mother. Ultimately, it would appear, from the brown Harold. Of her 32 g.g.g.g-parents, none was chestnut. Of all the sixty-two animals in these five generations, there are three chestnuts, as follow:

A.1. Her sire: Dunsmore Raider 21367 (bay)
  2. His dam: 28410 Dunsmore Combine – chestnut
  3. Her dam: 14655 Dunsmore Gloaming (bay)
  4. Her sire: Harold 3703 (brown)
B.1. Her dam: 39317 Jewel's Eve – chestnut
  2. Her sire: Puckrup Prince Harold 18294 – chestnut
  3. His sire: Prince Harold 14228 (black)
  4. His sire: Harold 3703 (brown)

There may have been others among the sixty-two, of course, which had the recessive chestnut lurking beneath their actual coat-hue. But, on the face of it, the colour which came to light in Dunsmore Chessie seems to have been derived from the latent chestnut in Harold himself.

(d) THE ORIGIN OF MARCH KING'S GREYNESS

If the appearance of chestnut was frequently unaccountable by the honest breeder of Shires, the birth of a grey one was always to be easily explained. One had only to look at sire or dam, for one of them was inevitably grey. Of all the descendants in the male line of Harold, March King was the most outstanding in one particular way – his prepotency in begetting good grey offspring. Yet this quality, inevitably, was the one virtue (if it was that) that he could not possibly have inherited from Harold, simply because Harold himself was not grey. How he did obtain his colour is shown by the following list of his grey antecedents. Back to the fifth generation, and also in the seventh, the line of grey-inheritance is absolutely clear, because in each case only one of the two parents was grey or roan. But in the sixth and eighth generations, the unrecorded mares may have had grey hairs, for all we know.

MARCH KING 34955, dark grey, f 1916
1. His dam: 59031 Abingworth Gipsy, grey, f 1908.
2. Her sire: Sussex Menestrel 23700, grey, f 1904.
3. His dam: 40352 Sussex Bluegown, grey, f 1900.
4. Her dam: 22556 Sussex Bluebell, blue-roan, f 1894.
5. Her dam: 4820 Depper, roan, f 1879.
6. Her sire: Gay Lad 3665, roan, f 1874.
    (Her dam is unrecorded.)
7. His dam: Unrecorded, but may have been roan or grey.
    (His sire was bay.)
8. Her sire: Drayman 625, roan, f 1842.
    (Her dam is unrecorded.)
9. His sire: (Clarke's *Plumper*) and his dam are not of recorded colour, but one or the other must have been roan or grey. (His dam was by Hipwell's *Brown George*, which does not help, except to eliminate him.) It is here that the pedigree fades out.

APPENDIX II

The Old Favourite Names

CART-HORSE names have ever been plain, though not necessarily unoriginal. At Holkham in 1719, Thomas Coke had an *Ashborn Black*, a *Longford* (which likewise came from Derbyshire, from his younger brother Edward's place) a *Pye Bald* and even a *Cripple*. But he loved to call his horses after friends and relatives. *Walpole* commemorated his stepfather, Col. Horatios Walpole, who had died two years before. *Wyville Clumsey* reminded him of his brother-in-law Sir Marmaduke Wyvill, Bt, who departed this life in 1716. And so on. Thomas' great-nephew and namesake, "Coke of Norfolk" himself, preferred traditional names. The nine teams of cart-horses at Holkham in 1817 (forty-one mares and geldings, and three mules) contained three *Brags*, four *Smarts*, four *Toppers* and a couple of *Diamants*, as well as such other tried favourites as *Smiler*, *Fanny*, *Dapper*, and *Beauty*, and *Prancer*, *Bonger*, *Dodman* and *Smug*.

Our own Shire Coke, the Hon. Edward Keppel Coke, younger son of the great man, was partial to blacks for colour and faithful to one letter for names. Every mare he had was a C – scores of them, from *Charcoal*, *Cinder* and *Clarice*, and *Cocoa*, *Crusty* and *Catch*, *Chatterbox*, *Cylinder* and *Chintz*, to the celebrated *Czarina* and *Chance* themselves. He fell into the same unchanging habit with his stallions, too – *Candidate* and *Carlist*, *Conjurer*, *Cross-Bow* and many others. Each Coke, like every cart-horse owner, had his favourite names, but they were never elaborate or fancy.

(a) STALLIONS

Three types of name were commonest in the eighteenth century. One sort was descriptive – either literally, such as *Blaze*, *Bald Horse*, *Brown*, *Lame Horse*, *Clubfoot* and *Black Legs*, or else hopefully, like *Samson*, *Farmer's Glory*, *Topper*, or *Waggonshaker*. A second sort consisted really of place names, like *Marston* or *Swebstone*, *Packington Blind Horse* being a typical combination of the two types. The third kind of name was really synonymous with the breeder or owner himself, just like *Morel Lestrange* in 1313 – *Hawksworth's Horse*, *Sims' Horse*, *Codling's Horse*, *Slingsby Horse*, *Smith Colt*, or just *Bulstrode* or *Chadwick*, much as even today a man will buy a colt from Jones or Brown and refer to him at home, whatever name he may use officially, as *Jones* or *Brown*. This kind of name was frequently linked with the second sort. For example, the black Merryman 1553, bred in 1810 by one of the Derbyshire Mellors at Calow had a pedigree (and a long one in the female line, for those days) which went thus: by *Whitehead's Horse of Flentham*, his dam by *Gibson's Horse of Whissendine*, g-dam by *Hurd's Horse*, g.g-dam by *Shuttleworth's Horse of Scalford*. Suffolk men tended, more often than Shire men, to combine all three sorts of name – for example, *Spink's Old High-necked Horse of Eyke*. The high neck helped considerably to identify the animal. In the Shires, if Whitehead, Gibson, Hurd or Shuttleworth happened to possess more than one stallion (and they did) the naming was not very helpful.

Even when "Christian" names became more common, the confusion about identities persisted because most owners were remarkably conservative in their ideas. A man with a successful stallion called *Comet* or *Waxwork* would baptise a promising colt as *Young Comet* or *Young Waxwork*. The inevitable promotion of *Young Waxwork* to the status in due course of *Old Waxwork* in order to make way for a new *Young Waxwork* is enough to defy any attempt at identification today.

There are thirty-four Thumpers in Volume I of the Stud-book, the earliest foaled in 1810. Some are the sons of others, and altogether twenty-one are clearly very closely related. For example, Thumper 2122 (bred near Ely in 1855) was by Stainforth's Thumper (that is 2116, foaled 1845), out of a mare by Cork's Thumper (2113, f Tydd St. Giles in 1831), g-dam by *Porter's Horse*. Thumper 2127 was bred in 1859 by Granger at Stretham, Cambs. and was by *Granger's Thumper* – who never became Granger's *Old Thumper* because the young one was sold to his neighbour and was therefore *Wright's Thumper* until in 1880 the new Society posthumously listed him as Thumper 2127.

Of twenty-eight horses called Merryman in Volume I, six were the sons of others in the book, but Merryman 1562 (foaled 1839) was by Sibthorpe's *Merryman*, too unidentifiable to register. The dam's sire, incidentally, was *Kingham's Old Jenkins* – a sort of name that frequently led to error on stud-cards, which often leave the reader in doubt whether a horse named in a pedigree was really *Kingham's Old Jenkins* or Jenkᵛns' Old Kingham.

There are nineteen registered Nelsons, of which ten are related, including two pairs of full brothers. There are sixteen Napoleons. Seven of them are sons of Napoleon 1592, bred in 1851, and three more have 1592 as their dam's sire. Marshall of Parson Drove near Wisbech had at least two stallions called Magnum Bonum. One of them, together with three sons and a grandson are all registered in the book as Magnum Bonum. Altogether seven horses with this name, all foaled between 1824 and 1836, and all stationed throughout their lives within fifteen miles of each other, are registered with this name: how many more there were, of whom the first Editing Committee lost track, is a matter of guesswork.

Two sons, two g-sons, three g.g-sons and one g.g.g-son of *Henry's Golden Ball* all foaled between 1832 and 1861, were registered in Volume I as Golden Ball, but how many other *Golden Balls* sprang from him one cannot tell. (The other two Golden Balls in the book stemmed from *Young Golden Ball*, also owned by Henry.)

There are twenty-seven horses called Major in Volume I. They consist of the famous Seward's Major 1447, twenty-five of his direct descendants and one doubtfully descended, spanning the years 1838 and 1844–1874, and all operating in Cambs. and Lincs. But if one is in search of a real puzzle one cannot do better than attempt to unravel the breeding of horses used by various members of the Hibbard family, and of their *Farmer's Delights* and *Farmer's Glories* in particular. Or perhaps a study of the Samsons of Volume I is even more confusing. Forty-nine of them are sons, grand-sons, etc., of four earlier Samsons: eighteen are too poorly documented to be certain about: six appear to be three pairs of otherwise unconnected sires and sons; and just three seem to have no connection at all with any other Samson, either registered or otherwise.

However, if the Stud-book brought this chaos to an end, it also ended the sheer poetry of some of the old "address" names – *Locket's Old Brown Redcliffe Horse*, *Elstone's Horse of Thorney Fen*, *Parsons' Horse of Walton Grounds*, *Biddle's Black Horse of Caxton Pastures*, or *Watton's Horse of Matfen Moorhouses*. In addition it brought an end to the more picturesque descriptive names like Orpeth's *Grey Tail*, *Small Tail* and *Old Ruff Knees*. The Committee also frowned upon names which it considered objectionable such as Bang-Up and Hot 'Un (from Hoton in Leicestershire), but did not discourage the many Daniel Lamberts, all named after the celebrated Leicestershire man who weighed over 52 stones and whose girth, at 112 inches, scarcely any stallions could truly rival.

Stallions had of course long been named after famous men or events, and one can guess when the various Wellingtons, Alberts, Raglans, Sebastopols and Inkermans were bred, or Disraeli (and Lord Beaconsfield). The ordinary Toms, Boys, Lads and Bens frequently bore county names. Lancashire Tom and Lincolnshire Tom were thus nicely differentiated, but confusion was never far round the corner, for the best-known Staffordshire Hero always went under the name of Derbyshire Hero when travelling the eastern side.

In comparison with the Thoroughbred, purely whimsical names are, and always have been, very rare among cart-stallions, because frivolity ill becomes size, reliability and weight. But there are names to please the connoisseur – among nineteenth-century horses, Adonis, and the little joke Brigham Young, as well as the more earthy Bangalong, Bargee and Bounce Carty. Clodhopper, Crasher, Crusher and Crackwaggon are resoundingly ponderous names for work or breeding, while Com'd at Last and Cupid are more imaginative. Dewdrop is surprising, whereas Dumpling is not. Earthquake, Elephant, Extra Stout and Explosion speak for themselves, but Essex Chap and Easy Walter are more intriguing. Flanders' Major makes one think of foreign blood (which is misleading, because he was bred and owned by Mr. Shrewsbury Flanders). In Gee Whoa Hoy, Good as Gold, and Good Enough we can read the character of the owner more easily than that of the horse. Ha! Ha!, Half and Half and Half-a-crown reveal the brain of that considerable stallion-owner, George Harrison of Everton, Notts. I'm the Sort, and I'll Try, Just In, Juggernaut – one can go through the alphabet, and always there is more wisdom than wit, right down to Yelling Sweep (another misleading one – his prefix shows he was born in a Huntingdonshire village), Yorkshire Stingo and Zulu Chief.

Amid all the Thumpers, Plumpers, Bumpers, Lumpers and Stumpers, Nimble is refreshing, as is Tea Pot and Newdick's Old Rabbits. But truly choice names are few. One might select from Old Beans, Ready Rhino, Rump Steak, The Old Sort Again, Lord Go Bang, Half Ripe, Birling Bulbous (bred by Mr. Utterby Bowles), Pants, Weighty Will, Brass Bottle, and Passive Resister. The horse of old times that most prompts one's curiosity is perhaps the dam's sire of Brown Stout III 6843. Foaled about 1855, his name was *Bryan's Old Taters and Rubbish*.

It is a pity that the social eminence of the Shire Horse Society caused these homely old names to die out. Perhaps that is why, although he joined the Society in 1880, Mr. Groom, living at Docking, never ventured, in twelve years of membership, to add to the joke by actually registering a single one of his horses and mares himself.

(b) MARES

On the whole, mares' names have been, from time immemorial, more homely still and even less varied than those of stallions. Naturally, they are all stable-names, for the mares stayed at home. If we compile an alphabet of the less sterotyped appellations in the early Stud-books, we shall find affection predominating over eccentricity, even in such names as Harvest Beer, or Taffy.

A is for Artful, for All Fours and Auntie.
B stands for Briony, Bandy and Bangle,
      Busybody, Bang, Buxon and Blunt.

C is old Comfy, Cloddy and Crafty,
     Chucklehock, Crumpet, and Cash.
D is a Dimple, a Dumpling, a Dunce;
     Daffodil, Dainty, Diddle and Dep.
E is for rare ones, like Enigma and Eye-glass.
F is a Frolic, a Fury (or Folliful, Fussy, or Flounce).
G stands for Giddy Girl, Grizzel and Grouse.
H is so plain, such as Homespun or Honest.
I is old Ida, with Idol and Ivy.
J is a Jilt, a Joker, a Jolly Girl – or Jumbo, or Just.
K stands for Kate and Kitty and Keepsake.
L is young Lusty, Landlady, or Lark.
M's just a Muffin or Maggot;
     or Mistletoe, Music and Movement.
N is for Natty and Naughty and Noisy;
     Nimble and Nipper (and Necklace and Nugget and Nut).
O's but a few, such as One Eye, Old Times and Ops.
P compensates with Pickle, Pepper, and Prune;
     Prude and Prim, or Peepshow and Pippin.
Q's represented by Quarrelsome, Queen and old Quits.
R is for Rival and Rustic and Radish,
     and Randy, and Risk It and Rogue.
S has so many, with Salty and Sauce, Slap-bang and Sap,
     Substance, Sturdy and Stout;
     Sensible, Surely and Sober, but Sprightly;
     and Sooty, and Smut, Sultana and Smug.
T's but a Tit or a Tart;
     a Tortoise, Turtle, Tattycoram, or Trim.
U is just Useful, or Uncommon Blossom.
V is for Varnish, Virago or Vic.
W's a Walnut, a Warbler, a Whitenose, a Waif.
X is for X Rays and Xantha (of Hothfield).
But Y is more common – Yatton Romper and Yet,
     and Yokin and Yum Yum.
And Z is a Zomba, a Zany, a Zuler,
     or Zillah, or Zuzn (of Hothfield again).

(c) THE COMMONEST NAMES

From Volume 7 onwards, a stallion could not be given a name that had been used before, unless a prefix or suffix or a number were added. There could not be another plain Champion, but only a Champion II or Champion of Geddington or Moulton Champion (all of which appear in Volume 6).

After 1970, simple names also ceased to be acceptable for mares. Every animal had to be named with a prefix, as most already were. 139963 Jane, foaled in 1970, was the last of the plain ones. The old names had universally become Barnburgh Bonny, Cowerslane Melody, Dunderdales Blossom, Tremoelgoch Beauty, Wheelton Rose, and the like.

(The last simple "Bonny" was 138383, foaled in 1953. She was the 1,704th registered mare to bear the name, alone and unadorned, either as Bonny or Bonnie. The peak

Bonny years, curiously, were 1919–1921, when three volumes contained 210 of them.)

The most-used names in Volumes 1–25 of the Stud-book, spanning the years 1770 (183 Blaze) to 1902, are listed below. The added figures show the number of (e.g.) Bonny II, III, etc.

Mares in Vol. 1–25 (43,931)

Bonny/Bonnie	770 + 31	Rose	242 + 6
Flower	689 + 29	Daisy	235 + 5
Blossom	664 + 34	Gipsy	229 + 8
Diamond	623 + 16	Darby	180 + 11
Beauty/Bute	614 + 20	Whitefoot	169 + 8
Smiler	395 + 26	Depper	149 + 7
Star	350 + 10	Lively	147 + 9
Mettle	334 + 5	Brown	133 + 7
Bounce	294 + 5	Jolly	131 + 7
Jewel	292 + 10	Damsel	115 + 3
Violet	289 + 6	Blackbird	112 + 3
Darling	277 + 7	Trimmer	112 + 3
Smart	273 + 9	Madam	107 + 3
Brisk	263 + 12	Jet	95 + 2

Stallions (22,055)

Champion	95 + 29	Honest Tom	75 + 30
Samson	89 + 40	Farmer's Glory	74 + 11
Drayman	88 + 22	Waxwork	60 + 5

The Obituary Column

SHEER numbers discouraged the Society from attempting to keep an official check on the death or transfer to new owners of pedigree Shires. An Editing Committee recommendation that change of ownership should be compulsorily notified (though not printed in the book) was unfortunately rejected by the Council in 1919 (see A.X.9). It was only in 1974 that this object was achieved in a different way – not by requiring transfer certificates but by a rule that the animal concerned should be re-entered in the Stud-book. One cannot legislate for non-members of course, and so the penalty for non-compliance was that the horse would be ineligible to compete at the Society's show or for any Society prize elsewhere.

The "Obituary of Stallions" section of the Stud-book, begun in 1893, was therefore entirely voluntary. Of course, as a record, it is a failure, though it did not fizzle out until after the volume of 1945, which contained the single item of more or less unimportant information that the Cornish-bred Treswithian Royal 44047 was castrated in July 1945, at the age of three. By this time, 44,240 stallions had been registered in the Stud-book (30,431 of them since the obituary-section had been operating), but only 2,799 deaths or castrations – that is 6% (or 9%) – were recorded.

Of the 2,799 "obituaries", 1,452 were in fact castrations, the most apt being that of New Cut Swell (10055) in the 'nineties. Seven of these were true obituaries as well, since the patients died as a result of the operation, like Moors Mentor and Histon Kingmaker each of whom suffered both fates in succession at the age of seven. Of the other 1,347 animals, the owners of 369 forebore to say whether the horse was dead or gelded. Thirty went so far as to say that their stallion had died, and 160 that he had been destroyed, but did not say why.

The more informative entries include nearly every equine ailment (except of course, such town-and-dirt diseases as glanders), and especially those to which the entire horse is susceptible. Those suffering from quittor should presumably include the two who were listed as "quitter". Some troubles were expressed in veterinary terms: others, like "bursted gut", were not. Senility has many laconic though pleasant euphemisms, such as "decline" or "mature age", as well as the more blunt "worn out".

Mere Duke 15235 was fifteen in 1908 and performed his far too many duties so enthusiastically that he died of exhaustion in the middle of the season. Blyth Echo 2991, on the other hand, had suddenly lost interest in his work at exactly the same age and abruptly departed this life on 25th June 1895. He appears in the obituary as "Shot – useless". It is a little hard on his memory that he is the only Shire stallion listed in official records as being of no service whatever. After all, he had served a thousand mares on behalf of the Forshaws before so suddenly exasperating his new owner. If an ageing horse was relegated in old age from a top-class stable to a less considerate proprietor, a queue of mares wherever he went, with none barred, was bound to result in either disgust, collapse or perhaps paralysis. Nine cases of this last ailment are recorded, including Cheadle

Jumbo 3024, who was permanently affected at the age of eighteen in 1898, Magnus 14162 (a son of Harold, but not among the best 101) who began the 1904 season, when he was thirteen, with much vigour but became paralysed in the middle of April, and the great rough and ever-ready Babingley Nulli Secundus himself, that wide-fronted and single-minded old stager, who at the age of sixteen suffered this distressing malady before the season ever began.

Among the accidental deaths, most of the imaginable acts of God and follies of man or horse are here recorded. Four stallions were killed by lightning, and one by sunstroke. Four were drowned, two ate yew and one tried consuming haws. Five broke their backs and one his neck. Two were strangled and two choked. One perished of a "smashed head".

A stallion's life, if a merry one, was always liable to be cut suddenly short. And the bigger the horse, the briefer the natural life. The Shire, the greatest of all horses, inevitably lasted less long than others, even if disease or calamity did not strike or the gelder's knife transfer him to a lower plane. Few could expect to emulate Bounding Willow 15502 who was destroyed in 1918, but only after successfully completing his season. He had bounded for twenty-six years.

Horse Numbers 1870–1873
and the Census 1917–1934

(*a*) HORSE NUMBERS 1870–1873

It was not until 1917 that the horses of Britain were counted for the first time. Prior to that, it was only in the brief period 1870–1873 that an accurate tally of their numbers was possible.

The Agricultural Returns to the Board of Trade were started in 1866, but did not include horses until 1869, when all horses "in the possession of Occupier of Land" had to be entered on the form. But it was realised that, if the Returns were confined, instead, to "horses used solely for agriculture, unbroken horses, and mares kept solely for breeding", then it would be possible to discover how many there were in the land, for these categories were the only ones exempt from the horse tax. It would simply be necessary to add the Agricultural Returns to the number of taxed animals. (The tax lists were pretty accurate. The Agricultural Returns were less complete, because some old-fashioned farmers refused point-blank to fill in any forms, and the Board of Trade preferred in these cases to make guesses, rather than poke its head into too many hornets nests.) However, after 1873, the tax was abolished, and so, after four years, it again became impossible to count the total number of British horses.

	1870		1871	
	E & W	*G.B.*	*E & W*	*G.B.*
Agricultural Returns	1,093,338	1,266,209	1,080,016	1,254,450
Taxed horses	770,306	841,208	791,006†	864,115
TOTAL*	1,863,644	2,107,417	1,871,022†	2,118,565
	1972		1973	
	E & W	*G.B.*	*E & W*	*G.B.*
Agricultural Returns	1,080,814	1,258,020	1,099,285	1,276,444
Taxed horses	790,306†	857,048	791,906†	865,000†
TOTAL*	1,871,120†	2,115,068	1,891,191†	2,141,444†

* Some horses may have been counted twice. Those only partly involved in agriculture were subject to tax. A few of the taxed animals which changed hands may have incurred two licences in one year.

The correct figure was probably about 2,050,000 in Great Britain in 1870.

† Approximate figures.

N.B. The Army, in addition, owned about 50,000 horses in G.B.

(*b*) THE CENSUS, 1917–1934.

In 1907–1908, supposedly well-informed but quite unofficial estimates had all suggested that there were nearly six million horses in Great Britain and Ireland. They were unanimous, but wholly wrong, and it is difficult to understand why they so grossly overestimated the number. In 1912, the Board of Trade had made its own estimate – about three million. It was later proved to be entirely accurate.

Since horses were as essential to the Army as men, and vitally necessary to get the work of the nation done on the land, in the towns and under the ground, it may seem inconceivable that the Government could be so amateurish as to allow the war to continue for over two and a half years before discovering how many of them there were, especially in view of the fact that horses also consumed vast quantities of increasingly scarce food. But it was so. However, eventually, on 17th April 1917, an Order was made by the Quartermaster-General to the Forces, under Regulation 15 of the Defence of the Realm Regulations, requiring "every person residing in or owning or occupying any land, houses, or other premises in Gtreat Britain who owned any horse or mule within Great Britain on 21st April 1917" to make a return of prescribed particulars. (The following month, a similar Order was made for Ireland.) The police delivered the forms in duplicate and later collected them again, filing one copy and forwarding the other to the Board of Trade, which had undertaken to make the count and tabulate the findings. In point of fact, its staff was too hard-pressed to do the work, and so part-time clerks were obtained through the National Service Department, together with a small number of competen clerical workers from the Railway Clearing House. In London, the Metropolitan Police were under-staffed and over-worked and could not deal with the forms: this resulted in belated returns there in many cases, but on the whole they were reasonably complete.

Later in the year a full report marked 'Confidential', was issued by the Board of Trade Inter-departmental Committee on the Utilisation and Feeding of Horses, which recommended an annual census. A Second Census was in fact conducted eight days defore the war ended, in the same way as the first. Its value is vitiated by the fact that the London returns were so inadequate (the Metropolitan Police again were unable to help) that Greater London was excluded from the Report altogether.

A Third Census was held on 4th June 1920, all police forces this time fully co-operating, and a Fourth on 4th June 1924. Ten years later, on 12th May 1934, a Fifth Census was conducted. Soon afterwards the decision was made that horses were to play no vital part, either militarily or on the civil front, in the next great war, and so no more census were planned. If it is a pity that we have no accurate knowledge of horse-numbers in 1939, it is even more to be regretted that a census was never held in, say, 1900 or 1911 between which dates the peak was reached.

However, the 1917 Returns will give us a pretty accurate indication of this maximum, provided that we add to the figures the number of horses bought up by the Army during the war; had there been no war, they would have been mostly still alive in November 1917 and going about their normal civilian occupations.

(The 1917 census reveals a rather surprising ratio between the human and equine inhabitants of some towns. Of major towns, Preston, that famous centre from which many of the best Shires were sold, had 112 people to only one horse. Gateshead, Salford and Oldham were the next most horseless. Greater London had seventy-two people per horse, and the County of London seventy to one. Merthyr Tydfil and Hereford were at the top, or bottom. of the scale with only thirty-three persons per horse. It was estimated that there were 600,000 urban horses and 2,000,000 rural ones. This means that the ratio over the country as a whole was twenty persons per horse in England and Wales, nineteen per horse in Scotland, and less than eight per horse in Ireland.)

The more one studies the five census, the more unreliable they manifestly appear as a record of the numerical strength of various types of horse. The general practice of each census was to group all horses, other than Thoroughbreds, which were treated separately, into seven classes:

a. Ponies of 14-hands and under.
b. Ponies and cobs over 14-hands, but not more than 15-hands.
    (These two classes were lumped together in the First Census.)
c. Riding horses and hunters over 15-hands.
d. Carriage and trap horses over 15-hands.
e. Horses used wholly or mainly in agriculture.
f. Trade horses of light type.
g. Trade horses of heavy type.

The first four of these classes were clear and sensible, but we are not involved with these. The other three, with which we are here concerned, are absurd in themselves, and, in addition, they were inconsistently described. To make matters worse, many horse owners made the most foolish mistakes in filling up their forms.

As a record useful to the historian, the census therefore have the following flaws:

1. In every one of the five census, all horses under the age of three (other than Thoroughbreds) were classified merely as "light" or "heavy". This vagueness led to widely different interpretations of the meaning of these words.

2. Category (e) is meaningless, since it confuses type with usage. Horses engaged in agriculture were no different from those used in trade: they just happened, at the time of census, to be on a farm and not in town. Furthermore, the category is not subdivided (except in 1934) into "light" and "heavy" types, like categories (f) and (g). Therefore, any sort of little horse used, say, for taking a couple of milk churns down the lane to the road is not differentiated from the weightiest of Shires. (In the Fifth Census there was a subdivision: too late.) In addition, the definition of class (e) posed a problem for the owner who was using any horse of less than 15-hands for jobs on the farm.

3. Classes (f) and (g) were themselves inconsistently defined in the various census.

In 1917, the instructions were admirably clear. Class (f) consisted of "light trade horses and trotting vanners" and category (g) of "heavy draught or dray-horses". That is, all trotting vanners were to be included in (f).

In 1918, "heavy trotting vanners" were classed with heavy draught-horses.

In 1920, this grouping was maintained, (f) being clearly defined as "light trade or draught-horses and light trotting vanners over 15-hands" and (g) as "heavy draught-horses and heavy trotting vanners".

In 1924 and 1934, the word "medium" was introduced, owners being instructed to include in category (f) all draught-horses which normally worked at a trot, "except heavy trotting vanners".

The census figures for 1924 clearly show a large-scale transfer from class (g) to class (f). But it is not possible by simple arithmetic to adjust the numbers in each category in census 1–3 so as to conform to census 4 and 5, or vice versa; the rate at which heavy-horses declined in numbers between 1924 and 1934 was slower than the rate at which light draught-horses declined, but the comparative rate of decline in 1917–1924 is impossible to guess.

4. The 1918 census was made more or less valueless by the omission of Greater London as already mentioned.

5. The 1934 census did not include horses belonging to the four major railway companies and to the London Passenger Transport Board. These actually totalled 14,834. An attempt has been made in the tables A and B which follow to apportion these both for age and type: it is only a guess, but probably a fair one.

6. Horses owned by the Army were not included. This, of course, is to be expected: the purpose of the census was to discover what extra ones would be available in an emergency from civilian sources. Army horses numbered 25,000 before the First World War, over half a million at the end of it, and 12,605 on 1st October 1934. See Appendix 14 for details.

7. Confusion was caused at every census by a multitude of owners who seemed to be quite incapable of realising, in spite of clear instructions on the form, that, "foals, year-lings and two-year-olds" meant what the words are commonly accepted as meaning – that is, animals born in the current or two preceding calendar years. This did not matter at all in 1918 when the census was taken in November: but it has certainly muddled the age-tables for the other census, particularly the 1st and 5th, taken in April and May.

8. An equally large number of owners, every time, failed to appreciate the meaning of "Thoroughbred", even though it was always explained that it referred to "horses whose sires and dams are registered in the General Stud-book". The 3rd Report commented that "so large an increase as that shown in the tables in the number of Thoroughbreds is very improbable. The number shown in 1918 was then remarked upon as probably too low, and the present number seems probably too high. There is a tendency for some owners to count pedigree horses of whatever breed as Thoroughbreds . . . It is to be feared that in some cases owners have shown the same horse twice on their form" – once in its type-class, and once as a Thoroughbred. "Some obvious cases of error in this respect have been corrected, but there are likely to have been others which could not be detected." This was still happening in 1934. (Perhaps it is unfair to ridicule horse-owners on this point. The Second Census demanded a return of stallions also, according to breed. Only one Percheron was returned, in itself an error of several hundred per cent. The Board of Trade, unwilling to make a special column in its Table for this lone creature, added it to the "Suffolk" column!

9. For all these reasons, and no doubt many more besides, the census figures bear little relation to the Agricultural Statistics (See Appendix 15).

(i) *Number of horses (classified according to age): Number of owners: Number of mules and asses*

	1917	1920	1924	1934
1. *Great Britain*				
All horses under 3 y.o.	303,654	354,838	219,392	137,776
Thoroughbreds 3 y.o. and upwards	8,226	9,231	9,725	11,284
Others: 3 and 4 y.o.		259,090	306,863	128,569
5–11 y.o.	1,767,242	963,205	954,875	548,021
12 y.o. and upwards		495,093	401,350	452,691
TOTAL	2,079,122	2,081,457	1,892,205	1,278,341
(Presumed, if no war)	2,379,122			

	1917	1920	1924	1934
1. *Great Britain*				
Number of returns	523,482	501,738	495,549	366,415
Estimated number of owners	507,000	485,000	480,000	354,000
Average no. of horses per owner	4.10	4.29	3.94	3.61
Number of mules	2,455	5,584	3,108	No census
Number of asses: more than	No census	13,615	12,179	No census
2. *England and Wales*				
All horses under 3 y.o.	265,098	308,309	193,600	120,259
Thoroughbreds 3 y.o. and upwards	7,851	8,461	9,225	10,706
Others: 3 and 4 y.o.	228,548	224,705	267,228	112,696
5–11 y.o.	761,457	843,040	831,060	477,564
12 y.o. and upwards	564,850	437,849	354,514	392,354
TOTAL	1,827,804	1,822,364	1,655,627	1,113,579
(Presumed, if no war)	2,090,304			
Number of returns	460,599	441,898	434,601	319,768
Estimated no. of owners	446.000	428,000	421,000	310,000
Average no. of horses per owner	4.10	4.26	3.93	3.59
Number of mules	2,362	5,351	2,983	No census
Number of asses: more than	No census	13,086	11,717	No census

Notes

1917.   Between the outbreak of war and the First Census, about 400,000 horses were purchased in the United Kingdom by the military authorities – about 300,000 in Great Britain (roughly 262,500 in England and Wales and 37,500 in Scotland) and 100,000 in Ireland. Had there been no war and these horses had remained in civilian work, it may be presumed that a census total in 1917 would have been increased by this number.

1918.   This census, spoiled by the omission of Greater London horses, is omitted from this table. By the date of the Census, 366,070 horses had been purchased by the Army in Great Britain, and 100,493 in Ireland – a total of 466,563. On the other hand, at this date. 26,835 had been sold back to civilian owners in Great Britain.

1920.   Between the 1918 and 1920 census, 177,269 horses had been sold back to civilian owners in Great Britain – something under half the number that had been purchased here. (Of course, many of those that were sold were in fact American horses.) Although this table does not reveal it, there were, as a result, a little over 100,000 more horses in Great Britain aged 5–11 years in 1920 than in 1918. This influx of available horses of reasonable working age caused a sharp drop in the number of old horses kept alive in 1920, compared with 1918.

1934.   The figures for 5–11 and 12 and upward have been adjusted so as to include the 14,834 horses owned by railway companies and the L.P.T.B. (see Par. 5 of introduction) omitted from the census. In Great Britain 13,834 horses have been allotted to the 5–11 age group and 1,000 to the twelve and over, and in England and Wales 11,459 and 750 respectively.

MULES. The phenomenal rise in the mule population in 1920 was due to the sale of ex-army animals and was temporary, since the British civilian was never keen on this most useful hybrid. Both in 1920 and 1924, the leading county for these animals was Norfolk (777 and 510) with Yorkshire (369 and 216) second. There were three mules in Radnor in 1920, and one in Rutland. Among towns, Greater London had 499 in 1920 and Birmingham was second with 85. Of the 86 largest towns in England and Wales, ten (including Oxford and Cambridge) had no mules at all. By 1924, when the London mule population had shrunk to 176, over 44% of the country's mules had died. The remainder had carried out considerable migrations. For example, Worcester, which had only 3 in 1920, now claimed 32 and was the leading provincial mule city: equally surprising, the muleless towns were fewer in number. Only Smethwick, Stockport, Swansea and Swindon, which mustered 13 between them in 1920, now had none. Perhaps one day someone will write a thesis on these strange statistics.

ASSES. In all three census (including 1918) in which a return of asses was made, it is certain that the recorded number is less than the real total, because, since the operation was publicised as a "Census of Horses", many persons who owned asses only, and no horses, did not realise they had to take part, and the police did not track them all to their lairs. In 1919, Yorkshire claimed 919 asses, Norfolk 883, Lancashire 854, and Cornwall 829. Greater London had 702 and Blackpool 125. Nine towns had none at all. By 1924, only Leicester and Northampton were officially assless (as they had been in 1920), while London's number had decreased to 596 and Blackpool's had increased to 165.

Bristol and Oxford had the distinction of possessing neither mule nor donkey in 1920 (or of concealing their animals from the police, the Board of Trade and the Army Council). There were four asses in Cambridge.

(ii) Number of horses classified according to type

	1917	1920	1924	1934
1. *Great Britain*				
THOROUGHBREDS	?	19,743	16,990	17,423
LIGHT HORSES				
All under 3 y.o.	?	86,619	62,216	38,870
a. Ponies 14-hands and under		261,931	260,698	165,454
b. Ponies and cobs over 14 to 15-hands	374,634	159,060	170,894	92,433
c. Riding horses and hunters over 15-hands	38,853	42,019	51,575	54,581
d. Carriage and trap horses over 15-hands	76,357	68,137	52,121	17,268
TOTAL	?	620,766	597,504	368,606
DRAUGHT-HORSES				
All under 3 y.o.	?	254,707	149,911	92,767
e. Agricultural	787,175	774,934	753,762	652,920

	1917	1920	1924	1934
1. Great Britain				
f. Light/medium	242,919	163,326	197,514	69,357
g. Heavy	247,304	247,981	176,524	77,268
TOTAL	?	1,440,948	1,277,711	892,312
Aggregate	2,079,122	2,081,457	1,892,205	1,278,341
2. England and Wales				
THOROUGHBREDS	?	18,061	16,205	16,665
LIGHT HORSES				
All under 3 y.o.	?	83,171	57,977	35,812
a. Ponies 14-hands and under		240,095	238,496	153,525
b. Ponies and cobs over 14 to 15-hands	347,822	147,782	158,035	85,694
c. Riding horses and hunters over 15-hands	37,123	40,000	49,040	51,944
d. Carriage and trap horses over 15-hands	69,346	61,786	47,370	16,031
TOTAL	?	572,834	550,918	343,006
DRAUGHT HORSES				
All under 3 y.o.	?	215,538	128,643	78,488
e. Agricultural	662,966	651,289	626,541	548,542
f. Light/medium	218,074	146,972	179,373	61,229
g. Heavy	219,524	217,670	153,947	65,649
TOTAL	?	1,231,469	1,088,504	753,908
Aggregate	1,827,804	1,822,364	1,655,627	1,113,579

CATEGORIES (f) and (g). For reasons explained in Par. 3 above, the relative proportion of these categories from census to census is quite unreliable. In 1917, it seems incredible that there really were more "heavy draught and dray-horses" than "light trade horses and trotting vanners". However, if one accepts that, then the sudden drop in category (f) in 1920 in contrast with category (g) of which the total slightly increased, is accounted for by the transference of "heavy trotting vanners" from (f) to (g). The introduction of the word "medium" to category (f) in 1924 and 1934 caused a sudden swing in the opposite direction.

The only clear and fair comparison is between 1924 and 1934: this decade shows a much faster displacement of the van horse than of the cart horse.

In 1934, the census figures for these categories have been adjusted in the Table so as to include the 14,834 Railway and L.P.T.B. horses (see Par. 5).

(i-ii) Ireland: U.K. (1917)

The first census included Ireland also. Since it was therefore both the first and the last to tally the horses of Great Britain and the whole of Ireland, it is perhaps worth examining how the census justified the pre-war estimate that, in the United Kingdom as it then was, there were three million or more horses:

	1917			1917	
i	*Ireland*	*U.K.*	ii	*Ireland*	*U.K.*
All horses under 3 y.o.*	110,520	414,174	THOROUGHBREDS	?	?
T.B. 3 y.o. & upwards†	6,940	15,166			
Others: 3 & 4 y.o.††		402,010	LIGHT HORSES		
5–11 y.o.	454,191	1,056,988	All under 3 y.o.	?	?
12 y.o. & upward		762,435	a. Ponies 14-hands & under††		
			b. Ponies/cobs 14 to 15-hands††	57,648	432,282
TOTAL	571,651	2,650,773	c. Riding/Hunters ov. 15-hands††	12,773	51,626
(Presumed, if no war)	671,651	3,050,773	d. Carriage/trap ov. 15-hands††	7,643	84,000
			TOTAL	?	?
Number of returns	249,228	772,710	DRAUGHT HORSES		
Est. no. of owners	?	?	All under 3 y.o.	?	?
Av. no. per owner	?	?	e. Agricultural††	328,745	1,115,920
Number of mules	10,320	12,775	f. Light/medium††	12,816	255,735
No. of asses	No census	No census	g. Heavy††	34,566	281,870
			TOTAL	?	?
			Aggregate	571,651	2,650,773

* Inaccurate. For Ireland, figures exclude 2 y.o.
† Inaccurate. For Ireland, figures include Thoroughbreds of all ages.
†† Inaccurate. For Ireland, figures include 2 y.o.
Note that over 80% of the U.K. mules were in Ireland.

(iii) *Horses grouped according to trades*
expressed as percentage of total horses in civilian ownership.

	England and Wales				Scotland	
	Ju '20	Ju '24	Ju '24 Towns* only	Nov '18	Ju '20	Ju '24
1 FARMERS AND MARKET GARDENERS	67.9	69.1	13.2	73.7	76.5	77.5
2 FOOD AND DRINK TRADES	6.6	7.2	1.3	5.1	4.1	4.5
3 OTHER DISTRIBUTIVE TRADES	4.6	4.9	15.7	4.3	4.0	4.3
4 CARTAGE CONTRACTORS	5.2	5.4	23.1	6.7	5.9	5.6
5 MANUFACTURING TRADES (excl. food and drink)	1.7	1.5	3.9	0.8	0.9	1.4
6 LOCAL AUTHORITIES	0.6	0.7	3.5	0.3	0.5	0.6
7 RAILWAY COMPANIES	1.4	1.1	6.5	0.8	0.8	0.7
8 MISCELLANEOUS TRADES	5.7	6.6	7.2	3.8	3.3	3.3
9 CARRIAGE OF PASSENGERS	1.6	0.9	3.9	2.0	1.8	1.1
10 PLEASURE (direct use by owners)	4.7	2.6	1.7	2.5	2.2	1.0
	100.0	100.0	100.0	100.0	100.0	100.0

* By "towns" is meant only those with a human population of over 50,000.

This table is restricted, because

(*a*) the 1917 census did not analyse usage of all horses.

(*b*) the 1918 analysis is vitiated by omission of Greater London from the census.

(*c*) the 1934 census did not analyse the usage of horses, or include any railway horses (14,834).

(*d*) Further, in the analysis of the greater towns, railway horses were not counted in 1917, 1918 and 1920, which destroys the value of the percentages. For example, in 1917 there were 27,405 horses owned by railway companies and most were employed in the larger towns

OTHER DISTRIBUTIVE TRADES (No. 3). In the towns, just over half the horses under this heading were owned by coal merchants – that is about 8% of the total number of horses used in towns. A further number of horses which generally hauled coal are probably included in "general cartage". Perhaps about 10% of all horses in the towns in 1924 were engaged in the coal trade.

MISCELLANEOUS TRADES (No. 8). It is a pity these were not sub-divided. For example, in 1924 the total number of horses and ponies employed by owners of mines and quarries was about 70,000. These represent about 3/5 of those horses and ponies in Great Britain which were grouped in this miscellaneous category, and represented 6.2% of the whole (6.6% in England and Wales, 3.3% in Scotland): that is, over 3.7% of the horses and ponies in Great Britain were employed in mines and quarries.

MANUFACTURING TRADES (5) and LOCAL AUTHORITIES (6). These percentages do not accurately indicate the number of horses on this work, because these categories of employer were also dependent, in some cases heavily dependent, on the services of cartage contractors (4). The railway companies, however, which prior to about 1880 had done much of their work with horses supplied by contractors now for the most part performed it with horses from their own stables.

(iv) *Trade horse numbers in towns: 1920–1934*

All the Census Reports devoted several pages to analyses of the numbers and types of horses in the larger towns – those with a population of over 50,000, or over 30,000 in Scotland. The more one scrutinises them, the more unreliable the figures appear. This is especially so for 1917 and 1918, when in some cases the horses in extensive areas of surrounding countryside were included with those in the neighbouring town, while in other cases the officials had a better idea of where the town ended and the country began. For example, the Bristol figures are very accurate for each year because the city had its own police force and the papers could not be muddled up with returns made by owners in adjacent districts. In contrast, it was the Gloucestershire police who were responsible for collecting the Cheltenham forms, and the temporary clerks at the Board of Trade were incapable of deciding which forms related to Cheltenham town and which to rural places with a Cheltenham address. Not even the influence of Francis Webb-Peploe (whose daughter looms so large in A.XII and XIII), just nominated as the new Vicar of Christ Church, could have caused 2,111 agricultural horses to have gone to work within the boundary of the stately spa. The figures for Wakefield are weird, and those for Swindon preposterous.

The 1920, 1924 and 1934 census are much more reliable in this respect, though even in these some of the major cities have some apparently crazy figures.

The following list is therefore confined to the last three census which are more reliable. Twenty towns have been selected, of which seventeen reach a standard of more than 1,000 returns and/or 3,000 horses and/or 1,000 heavy-horses in either or both of the 1920 and 1924 census, and/or more than 650 returns and/or 1,500 horses and/or 500 heavy-horses in the 1934 census. The other three towns are each included for a special reason – Cardiff to represent Wales: Derby because it showed an exceptional decline in horse numbers between 1924 and 1934 (rather sadly, in view of the vast number of pedigree Shire geldings auctioned there); and Oldham as the centre which had a longer run of continuous town cart horse parades than anywhere else (the series happening to come to an end in the very year 1934).

Bristol is a good example of a considerable drop in heavy-horses by 1934 – a city whose hills gave every incentive to turn to motor haulage. The three Scottish towns showed the least decline at 1934.

One must particularly mistrust the "agricultural horses", not only because (as already mentioned) there were discrepancies in the statisticians' notion of where the town ended and the country began, but because farming land in suburban districts was being sold to building developers at very differing speeds from town to town.

N.B. The 1934 figures have been adjusted as fairly as possible to admit the railway horses which were not included in the census.

		No. of Returns	Total Horses	Draught-horses (3 y.o. & upward)				All Others
				Heavy	Medium & Light	Agri-cultural	Total	
1 ABERDEEN	1920	441	1,924	992	452	117	1,561	363
	1924	504	1,991	755	549	152	1,456	535
	1934	304	1,284	605	283	113	1,001	283
2 BIRMINGHAM	1920	2,821	8,501	3,024	2,124	511	5,659	2,842
	1924	2,422	8,811	3,721	2,081	426	6,228	2,583
	1934	1,243	5,071	1,476	1,523	432	3,431	1,640
3 BRADFORD	1920	1,543	3,647	1,376	886	494	2,756	891
	1924	1,475	3,384	1,250	830	414	2,494	890
	1934	1,240	2,464	483	541	710	1,734	730
4 BRISTOL	1920	1,658	4,491	1,588	938	232	2,758	1,733
	1924	1,466	4,150	1,730	707	194	2,631	1,519
	1934	667	1,607	470	303	147	920	687
5 CARDIFF & BARRY	1920	981	2,179	457	483	139	1,079	1,100
	1924	972	2,327	508	395	227	1,130	1,197
	1934	655	1,317	178	214	203	595	722
6 DERBY	1920	401	1,294	366	313	96	775	519
	1924	434	1,215	438	315	46	799	416
	1934	98	307	52	141	29	222	85
7 EDINBURGH	1920	837	2,980	1,215	991	161	2,367	613
	1924	1,049	4,162	1,525	889	651	3,065	1,097
	1934	774	3,192	1,129	723	644	2,496	696
8 GLASGOW (inc. Govan, Rutherglen, and Partick)	1920	1,749	9,116	5,745	1,659	352	7,756	1,360
	1924	2,146	9,929	5,641	2,148	346	8,135	1,794
	1934	1,325	6,876	3,540	1,756	728	5,024	1,852

		No. of Returns	Total Horses	Draught-horses (3 y.o. & upward)				All Others
				Heavy	Medium & Light	Agricultural	Total	
9 HULL	1920	1,126	3,067	1,123	901	132	2,156	911
	1924	1,135	2,999	1,163	744	131	2,038	961
	1934	688	1,704	656	442	157	1,255	449
10 LEEDS	1920	1,930	4,828	1,652	1,122	402	3,176	1,652
	1924	2,003	4,805	1,640	1,073	483	3,196	1,609
	1934	1,244	3,144	841	583	663	2,087	1,057
11 LIVERPOOL	1920	2,847	13,035	7,498	1,930	480	9,908	3,127
(inc. Bootle,	1924	2,688	10,147	5,098	1,696	511	7,305	2,842
Waterloo &	1934	1,709	5,339	2,505	828	514	3,847	1,492
Seaforth)								
12 LONDON	1920	18,029	91,073	36,839	24,769	6,281	67,889	23,184
(i.e. GREATER	1924	16,510	77,254	27,359	23,540	5,116	56,015	21,239
LONDON)	1934	8,978	41,171	11,915	9,596	3,683	25,194	15,977
13 MANCHESTER	1920	2,168	8,171	3,800	2,091	204	6,095	2,076
	1924	1,949	7,911	4,239	1,640	231	6,110	1,801
	1934	1,648	5,444	1,885	1,360	748	3,993	1,451
14 NEWCASTLE-	1920	868	2,929	1,045	732	107	1,884	1,045
ON-TYNE	1924	935	3,001	877	713	91	1,681	1,320
	1934	621	1,688	328	348	141	817	871
15 NOTTINGHAM	1920	960	2,744	765	709	105	1,579	1,165
	1924	1,016	3,063	1,022	672	134	1,828	1,235
	1934	507	1,573	402	391	129	922	651
16 OLDHAM	1920	432	1,398	770	253	59	1,082	316
	1924	445	1,287	619	241	97	957	330
	1934	270	698	289	118	55	462	236
17 RHONDDA*	1920	421	3,358	796	832	39	1,667	2,691
	1924	634	4,723	755	1,247	60	2,062	2,661
	1934	367	2,887	938	461	108	1,507	1,380
18 SALFORD	1920	673	2,191	1,039	500	121	1,660	531
	1924	592	1,806	831	345	48	1,224	582
	1934	340	1,043	412	222	48	682	361
19 SHEFFIELD	1920	1,613	5,064	2,033	904	557	3,494	1,570
	1924	1,722	4,957	1,806	1,083	541	3,430	1,527
	1934	1,040	2,651	549	381	590	1,520	1,131
20 STOKE-ON-	1920	1,146	3,265	1,507	591	105	2,203	1,062
TRENT (inc.	1924	1,253	3,796	1,264	687	387	2,338	1,458
Burslem,	1934	710	1,795	501	295	259	1,055	740
Hanley,								
Longton &								
Longport)								

* In 1934, Rhondda had more ponies 14-hands and under than any town except Greater London and Sheffield. Its 682 "ponies and cobs over 14-hands to 15-hands" were more numerous than in any town except Greater London. Many of these latter were the exceptional short-legged Shire-types used in the South Wales mines.

It will be seen that the figures do not bear out the sweeping generalisations which have sometimes been made. Miss Edith H. Whetham, for example, dismissed the town horse of the inter-war years in a single sentence: "The urban market for horses came to an end with the first war, when industrial transport shifted from horses to lorries and vans."[1] Heavy town horses in 1934 were 42.6% of what they had been in 1924, and 30.2% of 1920. Vanners and light trade horses were a smaller proportion of what they had been in 1924, though the drop from 1920 was less. The general forecast in 1934 by most observers, not only the horse-users themselves, was that the following ten years would show a much slower rate of decrease in heavy town geldings, or even a slight increase, simply because the congestion of the streets slowed traffic to such an extent that trades in which speed of delivery was not all-important, and in which there were plenty of short-distance rounds, were tending to revert to the horse. However, there were only five years left, not ten, before the next war altered everything. In this half-decade, for which no figures are available, the urban gelding market was so strong that the profitable importation of large numbers of Belgians infuriated the English breeders and dealers, without much harming them.

The linking of (e.g.) Bootle to Liverpool and, particularly, of Barry with Cardiff was somewhat illogical in view of the fact that (e.g.) Gateshead and Tynemouth were listed under their own status, separately, from Newcastle. Tynemouth (26) and Gateshead (27) of all the 91 towns in England and Wales with a population of over 50,000 had the smallest number of heavy town horses in 1934. (In 1920 they had had 95 and 223 respectively.) Hastings had 29 heavy-horses – all but seven of which were twelve years old or over! In fact there were only 165 horses altogether in Hastings in 1934, compared with 742 (219 heavy ones) in 1920. The two towns with the least heavy-horses in 1920 had been Barrow and Stockton, each with 85. But in 1934 they still had 65 and 73 respectively.

(v) *Town horses (3 y.o. and upward) Proportion of types (omitting T.B.)*

	Number per 1,000 horses									
	England and Wales					Scotland				Ireland
	Greater London	Sel- ected towns	Towns with population of 50,000 or more			Towns with population of 30,000 or more				Selected towns
	1917	1917	1920	1924	1934	1918	1920	1924	1934	1917
HEAVY draught-horses and heavy trotting vanners	284	385	377	344	245	518	473	435	390	394
LIGHT/MEDIUM draught-horses & medium trotting vanners over 15-hands	429	302	237	247	204	179	203	211	229	257
AGRICULTURAL	64	62	82	75	144[a]	83	89	92	165[b]	91
Carriage & trap horses over 15-hands	48	43	47	44	33	50	55	52	21	71
Riding horses & hunters over 15-hands	13	10	13	20	36	5	12	25	34	21
Ponies & cobs over 14-hands to 15-hands	162	198	116	132	146	53	54	69	65	166
Ponies 14-hands & under			128	138	192	112	114	116	96	
	1,000	1,000	1,000	1,000	1,000	1,000	1,000	1,000	1,000	1,000

[a] sub-divided on this census as 45 light and medium, 99 heavy.
[b] sub-divided on this census as 28 light and medium, 137 heavy.

British Army Horses, 1914–1934

As a complement or subscript to the tally of horses owned by the civilian population of Great Britain, as shown by the census, the following tables[1] show the numbers of British Army horses.

(*a*) STRENGTH OF ANIMALS 1914–1934

The figures given below are of British Army horses only. They do not include the many thousands brought over (especially in the early months) by the Canadians, the thousands that came to Egypt with Australian and New Zealand troops, or those accompanying Indian divisions landing in France in late 1914 and early 1915: nor of course do they include any in the hands at the date specified of the U.S. Army or of other allies.

1. *Horse and mule strength at various dates*

		No. of horses and mules
1914	July	25,000
	August, on completion of mobilisation	165,000
1915	August	534,951
	31st December	660,000
1916	August	789,135
	31st December	797,174
1917	August	869,931
	31st December	809,248
1918	August	828,360
	30th November	735,409
1919	August	210,090
1920	31st March	110,708
1934	1st October	12,605

2. *Animals in all theatres, 30th November 1918*

	U.K.	France	Italy	Egypt	Salonica	Meso-potamia	East Africa	Aden	Total
HORSES:									
Riding	25,060	93,830	3,932	31,991	9,137	21,784	—	779	187,513
Pack	558	5,084	466	1,795	239	1,692	—	55	9,889
Light Draught	29,717	141,770	5,703	11,501	7,842	13,548	—	219	210,300
HEAVY DRAUGHT	16,200	64,980	3,136	1,442	1,799	—	—	—	87,557
Unclassified	6,752	—	—	7,905	—	355	827	—	15,839
Total	78,287	305,664	13,237	54,634	19,017	37,379	827	1,053	510,098

	U.K.	France	Italy	Egypt	Salonica	Meso-potamia	East Africa	Aden	Total
MULES:									
Riding	—	—	—	835	350	—	—	—	1,185
Pack	211	2,233	1,312	9,506	35,114	16,380	—	1,238	65,994
Draught	10,040	74,369	4,048	31,767	4,702	28,252	—	337	153,515
Unclassified	585	—	—	2,630	—	—	1,402	—	4,617
Total	10,836	76,602	5,360	44,738	40,166	44,632	1,402	1,575	225,311
Total horses and mules	89,123	382,266	18,597	99,372	59,183	82,011	2,229	2,628	735,409
DONKEYS	—	—	—	10,120	—	11	897	—	11,028
CAMELS	—	—	—	32,644	—	2,540	—	1,650	37,034
BULLOCKS	—	—	—	—	—	4,778	3,647	—	8,425
Total animals	89,123	382,266	18,597	142,136	59,183	89,340	6,773	5,278	792,696

(*b*) PURCHASE, 1914–1920

On mobilisation, the establishment of Army horses was raised from 25,000 to 165,000. The extra 140,000 were purchased by impressment in twelve days. After this, compulsory purchase practically came to an end and buying was done in the open market. In Canada and North America purchasing commissions operated which, to save officers from being withdrawn from military duties, consisted very largely of "country gentlemen, large landowners and competent masters of hounds".

The estimated expenditure on the purchase of horses up to 31st March 1920 was £67,505,000.

	Horses	Mules	Total
By purchase in U.K., to 31st March 1920	468,323	0	468,323
By purchase in North America, to 11th November 1918 (when shipping ceased)	428,608	275,097	703,705
By purchase in South America. (The mules for South Africa)	6,819	1,630	8,449
By purchase in Spain (3,000) and Portugal (700)	0	3,700	3,700
Brought to France and England from Australia and New Zealand	28,000	0	28,000
Total	931,750	280,427	1,212,177

(*c*) WASTAGE, 1914–1918

The number of British Army horses and mules which were killed, destroyed, died, missing or cast and sold in all theatres during the war was 529,564.

Up to 1st October 1917 only, the comparable figures for the French and British armies were as follows:

	Dead or missing	Cast	Total Loss
British Army in France and G.B.	225,856	30,348	256,204
French Army in France	376,201	165,513	541,714

The ratio of castings to deaths (again, to 1st October 1917 only) was 1 : 7.4 in the British Army: in the French Army it was 1 : 2.3.

As mentioned in A.X.5, the average annual mortality of animals of the British Forces at home and with the Expeditionary Force was less than 14% for the whole period of the war: and losses on freight ship transports on ocean routes was under 1%. Not the least amazing aspect of this astounding achievement is the fact that, in spite of the increasing strain upon manpower and horsepower and the need to accept lower standards in both, "the health of all animals at home and in all theatres was maintained throughout at a higher standard than in any former war. This standard showed a steady improvement in the later stages of the war."[2] The number of patients under treatment at one time in veterinary hospitals and convalescent depots at home and overseas once reached 90,000. By 11th November 1918 it had fallen to under 60,000, including 3,000 camels.

(d) DISPOSAL AFTER 1918

Before the Armistice, 26,835 horses were sold to civilian users in Great Britain. These were animals no longer fit for service: but they had been sufficiently "reconditioned" to make them of value on farms.

11th November 1918 to 15th March 1919. The sale of surplus horses began soon after the Armistice, commencing with those for destruction and those over twelve years of age. Repatriation from France began on 9th January 1919. By 15th March, the number of animals disposed of, in all theatres, was 225,812 for a total sum of £7,639,560.

11th November 1918 to 31st March 1920. The total of animals sold in this period was as follows:

	For work	For meat
United Kingdom	132,649	6,247
France and Flanders	197,181	40,638
All other theatres	169,371	14,347

From 1st April to 4th June 1920, a further 44,620 animals were sold in Great Britain. From 4th June 1920 to 4th June 1924, 9,151 were sold.

Horse Numbers on Farms, 1869–1975

In comparison with the census (Appendix 13), the Agricultural Statistics throw little light on the heavy-horse picture in general or on the Shire in particular, because they include horses of every type which worked on farms. Nor do they give any real clue to the total number of horses in England and Wales, or in Great Britain, except in the years 1870–1873 when agricultural horses were the only ones not subject to tax (see Appendix 13). The limitations of the following table should be borne in mind.

Although the Agricultural Returns began in 1866, horses were not included until 1869, when, as Mr. Fonblanque of the Board of Trade Statistical Department commented, "the interest so generally taken in the available supply of horses, and their importance as farming Stock, rendered it unadvisable any longer to exclude them".

A number of countries oversea had anticipated the United Kingdom in counting their agricultural horses – in Europe, Belgium, France, the Netherlands, Austria, Prussia, Saxony, Greece, Denmark, Norway and Sweden; and ten British colonies. But many others had not yet done so, including the United States and the Russias.

The following table comprises a summary of the statistics at roughly ten-year intervals from 1869, with some five-year intervals.

(a) The 1869 figures are not comparable with those from 1870–1910, because they included all horses on farms.

(b) The figures in this group comprise only "horses used solely for agriculture, un-broken horses, and mares kept solely for breeding".

(c) As can be seen from the table, these later figures for the first time include stallions and horses other than agricultural ones.

Nineteen fifty-eight was the last year in which complete returns (in June) were made, but no separate figures were published for stallions or unbroken horses which were included among the "others".

(d) From 1959 onwards, horse numbers have not been published in the Agricultural Statistics, though returns have continued to be made quinquennially.

Year	Used for agriculture including mares for breeding	Stallions for service	Unbroken horses One year and above	Unbroken horses Under one year	Other horses on agricultural holdings	Total
(a) 1869						1,274,161
(b) 1870						1,093,338
1879						1,237,098
1889						1,232,184
1899						1,317,786
1909						1,348,503
(c) 1914	791,297	7,500	213,068	102,106	285,576	1,399,549
1919	814,198	7,204	223,623	104,005	237,794	1,386,824
1929	706,765	2,845	89,274	37,583	162,806	999,273
1934	596,326	5,254	82,475	43,780	157,729	885,564
1939	548,921	4,605	110,381	*50,097	131,850	845,854
1944	485,181	2,870	73,602	*31,054	115,206	707,913
1949	335,008	1,940	35,491	*12,182	85,714	470,335
1954	154,899	†416	†6,315	†2,764	92,919	255,313
1958	72,388				94,634	167,022
(d) 1960	45,527				92,923	138,450
1965	19,089				115,444	134,533
1970	12,000				114,000	126,000
1975	5,000				159,000	164,000

* In these years, foals were sub-divided

	Heavy	Light
1939	35,409	14,688
1944	23,062	7,992
1949	5,480	6,702

† Heavy horses only

The Heavy-Horse Breeding Scheme

THE Board of Agriculture's project for assisting the breeders of heavy horses was launched in 1913 as part of the Improvement of Livestock Scheme. Even if the members of the Board had been clairvoyant, they could not have timed it better. The collapse of the existing social order was imminent and, within a very few years, the scheme filled the gap left by the disappearance of that patronage whereby so many old-fashioned landlords allowed their tenants the cheap use of a good stallion or even kept an entire horse mainly for their tenants' benefit.

A Government subsidy had to be hedged about by rules and provisos. The private landlord could do what he liked. The old way of doing things was in most cases much more generous to the struggling small farmer, even though the landlord, when all the accounts were reckoned up, could be shown not to be dispensing charity at all but to be making a profit. It was a truism that cart-horse foals paid the rent. And if it was the landlord himself who expected to get the first pick of the best foals, he did very well out of his generosity in the end. His tenants' mares were virtually an extension of his own stud, and an inexpensive one at that. The breeding of cart horses was different from the breeding of all other species of farm stock in that no man's stud, however big, was numerous enough fully to engage the energy of a stallion. A man of means would not lose by keeping an entire horse for the service of, say, thirty mares: the service of another seventy would not cost any more.

Nevertheless, the old way of patronage depended on whim. The new way was actually more in accordance with the egalitarian spirit of the Shire Horse Society, even though its members at first tended to regard Government assistance with some mistrust. A hiring society gave to the small breeder freedom and independence, which were unimpaired by the new grants and the new assisted nominations. Charity had been personal and laid him under an obligation, however vague and undefined.

Even so, E. B. Shine in Whitehall took a very personal pride in the scheme and specially in the good it achieved in the 'twenties. He rejoiced in the formation of a new society in 1929 – "enquiries for the use of the stallion are reported to have been received from farmers who have not bred a foal for years". Another new society the following year "has ousted three inferior animals which had travelled privately. In both instances, he had Derbyshire in mind. But names were never mentioned. After his retirement in 1933, his successor boasted more and more about the increasing success each year of "a stallion that travelled under the Ministry's scheme" for eight successive seasons. This was Kirkland Mimic himself. The subsidy brought him within the means of even the poorest members of the societies which hired him (see B.VI.11): some of the best mares that he covered would never have felt his weight if it had not been for the scheme. Enoch Bostock's fee was eight guineas for each private nomination, but when the Derbyshire A.S. hired him they could afford to charge only four, and a member entitled to an assisted nomination had to pay a mere two and a half. Fifty-two shillings and sixpence for the best Shire stallion in the land!

(a) NUMBER OF STALLIONS AND MARES 1914–1937

This table shows the number of entire horses in the scheme, the number of mares they covered for members of the societies which hired them, and the number of assisted nominations. Unfortunately, no reliable statistics are extant beyond 1937. And, except in the 'thirties, dependable records do not survive of the relative numbers of stallions of the different breeds taking part in the scheme.

	1				2	3		4
					Mares	Assisted Nominations		
	Stallions in Scheme				served	(a)	(b)	
	(all pure-bred)				by	To	Cumbèrland	Hiring
	(a)	(b)	(c)	(d)	stallions	stallions	and	fee (av)
Year	Shire	Clyde	Suffolk	Total	in Col. 1	in Col. 1	Westmorland	£
1914				72	6,365	1,503	0	231
1915				97	9,122	2,430	385	241
1916				108	9,995	2,181	394	244
1917				110	10,556	2,151	328	258
1918				122	12,281	2,165	321	285
1919				118	10,920	1,996	264	317
1920				105	9,133	1,839	254	345
1921				101	7,888	1,943	255	333
1922				—	—	—	—	—
1923				—	—	—	—	—
1924				87	6,098	0	121	178
1925				96	7,413	1,723	197	194
1926				98	8,165	2,171	220	208
1927				105	8,950	2,599	247	211
1928				114	9,792	2,805	281	217
1929				120	10,196	3,052	283	221
1930	119	17	4	140	12,248	3,604	269	239
1931	126	20	13	159	14,226	4,266	210	235
1932	128	20	14	162	14,624	3,945	198	226
1933	128	22	15	165	15,655	4,280	217	220
1934	132	22	16	170	16,071	4,353	209	221
1935	144	22	19	185	17,548	4,710	208	231
1936	150	22	21	193	18,778	5,078	210	229
1937	154	24	22	200	19,323*	5,668*	*	?

Notes

Subsidy took the form of

(i) direct grants to hiring societies of £40 each (except 1922–1923 when there was no scheme, and 1930, when it was £60); and

(ii) grants of up to £40 (except 1922/3/4 when there were none, and 1931, £30) to assist the nomination of mares of bona fide farmers whose holdings did not exceed

100 acres or were of an annual value for income tax purposes of not more than £100. (Only one assisted nomination per owner.)

Col. 1(b) Clydesdales were hired only by societies in Northumberland, Durham and the North Riding – and, in later years, Hampshire. Clydesdales were also involved in Cumberland and Westmorland (col. 3(b)).

Col. 1(c). In 1930, one Norfolk society hired two of these: in 1931, the same society hired seven. Generally, societies hiring Suffolks were in Suffolk itself, Norfolk and N.E. Essex.

Col. 1(d). There were always between 15 and 30 more stallions in the scheme than there were societies.

Col. 2. These figures include only those mares belonging to members of the hiring society. In addition, owners of stallions often reserved a number of nominations either for their own mares or for open booking. * N.B. 1937 figures include about 200 belonging to col. 3(b).

Col. 3(a). * 1937 figures include about 200 belonging to col. 3 (b).

Col. 3(b). The Cumberland and Westmorland Heavy Horse Society, formed in 1915 did not hire stallions, but was permitted to issue assisted nominations to selected horses travelled by their owners – even in 1924 (because it did not receive a direct grant). * Figures for 1937 are unknown, but are incorporated in the total of mares in Columns 2 and 3(a).

(b) FOALING PERCENTAGES

No precise figures are extant before 1930. In the 1925–1928 service seasons, it appears that just over 60% of the mares were left in foal – more in Wales (rather over 65%) than in England (a little under 60%). The 1929 season resulted in about 59% of the mares served by the subsidised stallions in England and Wales being left in foal. Subsequent percentages, of which details are precisely known, are:

Services in 1930: 58.2%
1931: 59.0%
1932: 58.5%
1933: 58.3%
1934: 58.5% Shire 58.6%, Clydesdale 52.4%, Suffolk 68.1%
1935: 57.4%   59.1%   53.0%   67.2%
1936: 59.3%   60.0%   51.6%   66.0%

(c) SOCIETIES HIRING SHIRE STALLIONS, 1939

This is a list of the 125 societies which were participating in the Government scheme, so far as Shires were concerned, in 1939. Three comments should perhaps be made:

(i) If the number of societies seems small, one should take into consideration the large area which a single travelling stallion could embrace. To indulge in a little mathematical fantasy by way of illustration, let there be a horse starting from his headquarters on a Monday morning and walking in a straight line for just over seven miles. He then turns to describe a perfect circle, of which his headquarters is the centre, and travels almost exactly 45 miles before completing it, finally returning home on Saturday noon. He has walked altogether about 59 miles, tolerable in a week. Even if no mare goes more than five miles to meet him, he could cover mares living within a circle whose radius is, say, 12 miles. (Those within two miles of his headquarters could visit him there on Saturday afternoon.) This is an area of nearly 453 square miles, or 289,900 acres. Two such areas are a little greater than Nottinghamshire (540,016) or Herefordshire (538,924) or Leicester-shire (532,387). It is pointless to pursue the sum further, but if we did we should find 125 stallions theoretically coping with about 56,625 square miles – only 1,398 less than the land area of England and Wales. And if we leave out places where a stallion's services would clearly be unnecessary such as Piccadilly Circus, York Minster, the Severn Tunnel or Snowdonia, there is not much in it.

Of course, in practice there were many large areas where no stallion "club" operated. But they were not so many and so great as one might assume, from the existence of a mere 125 societies in the scheme.

(ii) Societies have been listed on the whole, according to the county in which the main place of their title is situated, but of course several operated largely across the border of another. This partially accounts for the fact that some counties appear to have been poorly organised. For example, Wiltshire. The north and western fringes of this county are within reach of Lechdale (Glos.) and Bath (Som.). In addition, of course, William Cumber's great stallion headquarters was ideally situated in the middle of that part of the county, lying to the north of Salisbury Plain, where most cart horse breeding was done. The private travelling of stallions accounts entirely for the absence of any society at all in that historic centre of Black Horse breeding, Leicestershire, where the mare-owner had an embarrassment of choice. Furthermore, even in the late 'thirties, there were a few old-fashioned landlords who were great Shire supporters – notably A. T. Loyd in Berkshire, Sir Bernard Greenwell in Surrey and, of course, the Dook himself in Derbyshire. So a dearth of hiring associations in any particular county is not necessarily an indication that heavy horse breeding there was not much attended to, though in some cases (e.g. Kent) it is so.

(iii) This list comprises those societies which in 1939 participated in the Government scheme. It is not a complete tally of English and Welsh "clubs". For example, the Montgomeryshire District Entire Horse Association, that first pioneer of the whole movement south of the Scottish border, was pursuing an independent course of its own this year.

Anglesey, 2. Beaumaris & District H.H.S., North West Anglesey S.H.S.
Bedfordshire, 1. Bedfordshire S.H.S.
Berkshire, 2. Reading & District S.H.S., Stanford in the Vale S.H.S.
Brecknock, 4. Breconshire Farmers' S.H.S., Builth & Radnor District S.H.S., Devynock & District S.H.S., Glasbury & District S.H.S.
Buckinghamshire. 2. Newport Pagnell S.H.S. ,Winslow Stud S.H.S.
Caernarvonshire, 2. Caernarvon H.H.S., Lleyn S.H.S.
Cambridgeshire, 2. Cambridge & Isle of Ely S.H.S., Wisbech Stallion Society.
Cardiganshire, 4. Cardigan & District H.H.S., Llandyssul S.H.S., Mid-Cardigan S.H.S., North Cardiganshire S.H.S.
Carmarthenshire, 2. Carmarthenshire United S.H.S., Llanstephan & District S.H.S.
Cheshire, 2. Crewe & District S.H.S., Mobberley & District S.H.S.
Cornwall, 4. East Cornwall H.H.S., Launceston & District H.H.S., St. Columb & District S.H.S., West Cornwall H.H.S.
Cumberland, 1. Cumberland & Westmorland H.H. Breeding S.
Denbighshire, 3. Llangollen & District H.H.S., Ruthin & District S.H.S., Vale of Conway H.H.S.

Derbyshire, 3. Derbyshire A. & H.S., High Peak S.H.S., Pentrich, Shottle & District H.H.S.

Devon, 8. Axminster & District S.H.S., Bampton & District S.H.S., Bideford District H.H.S., Coleridge & District H.H.S., East Devon S.H.S., Newton Abbot & District S.H.S., Tiverton & District S.H.S., Withleigh & Cadeleigh H.H.S.

Dorset. 2. Melplash Agricultural S.H.S., Wimborne, Verwood & District H.H.S.

Durham, 1. Castle Eden & District Cart H.S.

Essex, 1. Saffron Walden S.H.S.

Flintshire, 1. Vale of Clwyd & District Live Stock S.

Glamorgan, 3. East Glamorgan H.H.S., Gower & District S.H.S., Wenvoe S.H.S.

Gloucestershire, 3. Berkeley H.H.S.. United Hunts (Lechlade) A.S., Winchcombe & District H.H.S

Hampshire, 2. Fareham and South Hants. H.H.S., Isle of Wight S.H. Syndicate.

Herefordshire, 3. Kington S.H.S., Ledbury Hunt S.H.S., North Herefordshire S.H.S.

Hertfordshire, 0.

Huntingdonshire, 1. Hunts. Chamber of Agriculture S.H.S. (For Peterborough, see *Northamptonshire*).

Kent, 0.

Lancashire, 2. Furness & Cartmel District S.H.S., Great Eccleston S.H.S.

Leicestershire, 0.

Lincolnshire, 5. Brigg & District S.H.S., Grantham & District A.A., Horncastle & District S.H.S., Saxilby & District S.H.S., Stapleford S.H.S.

Merioneth, 3. Celynin & District S.H.S., Corwen & District H.H.S., Harlech & District H.H.S.

Middlesex, 0.

Monmouthshire, 3. Chepstow & District H.H.S., Monmouth & District H.H.S., St. Mellons & District H.H.S.

Montgomeryshire, 4. Llanfair & District H.H.S., Llanfyllin & District H.H.S., Machynlleth & Llanbrynmair H.H.S., Plasdinam S.H.S.

Norfolk, 3. Framingham, Loddon & District S.H.S., North Norfolk S.H.S., North Walsham & District S.H.S.

Northamptonshire, 1. Peterborough A.S.

Northumberland, 0.

Nottinghamshire, 1. Newark & District S.H.S.

Oxfordshire, 0.

Pembrokeshire, 3. Castlemartin H.H.S., Fishguard, Letterstone & District H.H.S., Haverfordwest & District S.H.S.

Radnor, 2. Knighton & Temeside District S.H.S., Penybont & District S.H.S.

Rutland, 0.

Shropshire, 6. Bishops Castle H.H.S., Bridgnorth & District S.H.S., Chirbury & Montgomery S.H.S., Craven Arms S.H.S., Rea Valley S.H.A., Wen & District S.H.S.

Somerset, 6. Bath H.H.S., Bridgwater S.H.S., Clatworthy & District H.H.S., Evercreech Junction and Frome District S.H.S., Keynsham & District S.H.S., Yeovil Agricultural S.H.S.

Staffordshire, 5. Lichfield S.H.S., Newcastle & District S.H.S., Stone & District S.H.S., Uttoxeter & District S.H.S., West Staffordshire S.H.S.

Suffolk, 1. Stowmarket & District H.H.S.

Surrey, 0.

Sussex, 0.

Warwickshire, 5. Alderminster & District S.H.S., Atherstone Hunt & District S.H.S., Corley & Walsgrave S.H.S., Shipston-on-Stour & District S.H.S., Warwick & District S.H.S.

Westmorland, 0.

Wiltshire, 0.

Worcestershire, 1. Tenbury S.H.S.

Yorkshire, 15. Boroughbridge S.H.S., Brandesburton & District S.H.S., Bridlington S.H.S., Holderness S.H.S., Penistone & District S.H.S., Rotherham S.H.S., Ryedale S.H.S., Scarborough & District Agricultural Club, Selby & District S.H.S., Settle, Ingleton & Bentham District Farmers' Association, Thirsk H.H.S., Thorne & District H.H.S., Vale of Derwent S.H.S., Wetherby & District S.H.S., Whitby & District S.H.S.

Vetting for Soundness at London Shows

THOMAS DYKES used to tell a story about Bob Hutchinson, of Craiksland in Ayrshire, one of the most able Clydesdale men in nineteenth-century Scotland. He was always very strong against horses suffering from hereditary defects, particularly sidebones. Unfortunately an accident with a chaff-cutter (this was in the 1860s) severed both his hands. Nevertheless he continued to keep his stallion business going, though he had to rely upon trusted friends to feel the feet of animals he had in mind to offer for at a sale. On one occasion at Glasgow, Dykes himself and a colleague reported that one horse he was interested in seemed all right.

"Jist try again, man", he said to Tom. "Dan Crawford and I had a share in his father, and if this one's clean he'll be a wee bit exception to the maist of them."

They tried again, and had to confess that he was not after all a wee bit exception.

The severity of Professor Pritchard and others at the early London Shows has been referred to in Part A, and every successive veterinary inspector maintained the tradition of ruthlessness. It is almost impossible to exaggerate the contribution made by these professors and fellows of the Royal College, and their assistants, to the gradual perfection of the Shire as a draught-horse. A glance at the table which follows will indicate the progress that had been made by about 1930 among animals shown in London. If the reader will also consult the table in Appendix 18b, he will see that this vast improvement had extended also to the generality of pedigree stallions. And from them it spread to the ordinary working gelding.

The benefits produced by the rigorous London "vetting" have lasted to the present day. Perhaps no one in England has a wider or more impartial knowledge, either of the Shire or of many other breeds of horse, than the veteran and popular *Horse and Hound* journalist, A. Wyndham-Brown. He began his working life in 1911 as a professional "runner" of horses at the veterinary inspections at several London shows, including the Shire. His vast store of experience extends over so many types of animal and so many tens of thousands of specimens during a period (at the time of writing) of sixty-three years that it is unlikely ever to be rivalled in the future. Indeed, no period of history surely can ever match 1911–1974 for variety and change. He has firmly stated his belief that Shire breeders owe the quality of stallions that they now possess in the 'seventies to the rigorous weeding-out and testing to which these modern horses' progenitors were subjected in the London Show days. If Lord Ellesmere, Street and Coke were architects of the Society, it was Professor Pritchard who laid the foundation stone of soundness. In 1880, he inspected 114 horses with the zeal of a reformer for a fee of 5 guineas. There were twenty-one London Cart Horse parades prior to his death in 1906, with a total of 13,949 horses to be checked and judged. He had either judged or acted as veterinary inspector at nearly all of these shows, without ever charging a fee.

No reliably complete figures have come down to us of the result of the early inspections. Proper statistics begin in 1892, and the following table covers the period from then until

1939. The number of horses rejected may seem, at first consideration, appallingly large, in view of the fact that the standard aimed at had been demonstrated for twelve years and that this was, after all, not just a random assembly of animals, but an exhibition of supposedly the best of the breed.

The various reasons for rejecting a horse were not very systematically listed until after 1900, and this accounts for the high percentage of rejections labelled "other reasons" in the table. Unsoundnesses have been arranged here so as to correspond with the list (in Appendix 18c ii) of rejections under the Horse Breeding Act 1918, though two of those do not occur. The London inspectors did not enquire in the case of stallions, into fertility, as the Ministry's officers were expected to do. Nor, of course, did they need to reject for "poor conformation" – the judges would already have performed this office and, indeed, in the days of large classes, dismissed plenty having perfectly good conformation simply because there were so many which were better.

	1892–1899 (8 years)	1900–1909	1910–1919	1920–1929	1930–1939
No. of horses examined	3,191*	2,863	2,354	2,028	1,226
No. passed sound	2,796	2,663	2,175	1,922	1,200
Rejected:					
Whistling } Roaring }	61	68	58	20	11
Side-bone	170	55	41	41	5
Ring-bone	29	7	12	8	0
Bone spavin	34	14	8	2	1
Cataract	15	19	22	14	2
Shivering	1	12	14	7	1
Stringhalt ·	3	9	19	13	4
Defective genital organs	0	0	0	1	1
Other reasons	82	16	5	0	1
Total rejected	395	200	179	106	26
% rejected	12.3	7.0	7.6	5.2	2.1

* The large number vetted in these years is due to the fact that in the first six of them, 1892–1897, every single horse at the hall was sent to the inspectors before "weeding out" and final judging. From 1898 only the thirty (or less) not "chucked" from each class were vetted.

The Chief Veterinary Inspectors at the Shows 1880–1939 were as follows:

Professor Pritchard	8	1880–1899
R. S. Reynolds	1	1882
Professor Robertson	2	1883, 1885
Professor J. Wortley Axe	9	1886–1905
Professor Duguid	2	1887–1891
Professor Penberthy	15	1885–1926
F. W. Wragg	1	1907
J. Malcolm	3	1909–1913
Professor MacQueen	5	1915–1923
T. Eaton Jones	14	1925–1939

The following also served as Veterinary Inspectors at the London Shows (a few of them additionally to their appearance as Chief Inspector):

R. S. Reynolds, nine times.

Frank Aulton and T. Eaton Jones, seven times.

G. H. Locke, H. Moore, Harry Olver and Ralph Rimmer, six times.

W. S. Carless, G. P. Male, J. G. Runciman and E. A. West, five times.

T. Aubrey, F. L. Gooch, Henry G. Lepper, W. K. Townson and F. W. Wragg, four times.

Joseph Abson, E. H. Curbishley, T. H. L. Duckworth, W. J. Hatton, H. B. Hiles, Thomas Ludlow, Professor MacQueen, Trevor Spencer, W. Trigger and W. Woods, three times.

W. J. T. Bower, J. R. Carless, T. G. Chesterman, Charles Hartley, T. Hicks, George Howe, W. S. King, R. S. Rutherford, M. T. Sadler, William Shipley, Rowland Tayler, George Wartnaby and Professor Williams, twice.

J. S. Barber, G. E. Bowman, W. Crawford, William Dale, Frederick Danby, W. G. B. Dickinson, Professor Duguid, H. H. Ferguson, Percy Gregory, J. B. Gresswell, J. W. Gresswell, W. S. Harrison, J. R. Hewer, G. A. Lepper, T. W. Lepper, S. Locke, Professor McCall, J. W. McIntosh, J. Malcolm, James Martin, A. W. Mason, George Parr, H. Perrins, J. H. Poles, F. H. Potts, F. T. Prince, Professor Pritchard, Captain Russell, S. E. Sampson, W. G. Schofield, F. C. Scott, C. F. Shawcross, Charles Sheather, George Simons, H. P. Standley, Clement Stephenson, Henry Sumner, Henry Sumner, jun., Mark Tailby, H. H. Truman, Albert Wheatley and P. C. Woolston.

'Dolph' Boniface should be mentioned. His task was to assist the Chief Inspector, who always did the testing for wind. He was an employee for nearly fifty years of Sexton, Grimwade and Beck, and trained Bob Broughton eventually to succeed him at London and to help ensure that the strictness of the wind-testing was maintained.

Licensing of Stallions (England and Wales)

(a) THE VOLUNTARY SCHEME, 1911–1919

The number of stallions licensed under the voluntary scheme, which was restricted to animals registered in a stud-book, was as follows:

Year	Shire	Clydesdale	Suffolk	Percheron
1911	96	?	?	
1912	247	57	36	
1913	388	27	40	
1914	636	59	44	
1915	768	114	48	
1916	902	?	?	
1917	1,034	131	87	2
1918	1,183	151	79	16
1919	1,398	188	113	26

(b) THE 1918 CENSUS

The Second Census of Horses (see Appendix 13), and that census only, required owners separately to list stallions which were intended for service in 1919, stating also their breed and whether they were registered in a stud-book. This was no doubt intended to be useful information in respect of the operation of the Horse Breeding Act 1918, which would be effective from 1st January 1920. Here is a summary of the returns, with Scotland added:

	England & Wales	Scotland	G.B.
HEAVY-HORSES			
Registered Shire	2,741	2	2,743
Registered Clydesdale	345	637	982
Registered Suffolk	158	0	158
All non-registered	674	36	710
Total heavy stallions	3,918	675	4,593
Thoroughbreds	297	22	319
Hackney and other light breeds	428	42	470
Ponies	233	145	378
Unregistered light horses	311	14	325
Unregistered ponies	230	18	248
Total stallions	5,417	916	6,333

The total number of stallions was considerably less than that given in the Agricultural Statistics for England and Wales, both in 1918 (7,707) and 1919 (7,204). There is no real accounting for this. Greater London was omitted from the census, but it certainly did not house 1,787 stallions.

The number of Shires and Clydesdales has been slightly adjusted in the above table. The report on the census showed twenty-seven Clydesdales in Somerset and no Shires: it should have been the other way round.

The census forms did not provide a space for registered Percherons. This successfully confused the owners of 20 or more entire horses of this "new" breed. One such stallion was allocated to the Suffolk register and the rest to the Shire, Clydesdale or non-registered category, according to the whim of Board of Trade staff.

Compared with the stallions licensed in the first year of the new Act in 1920 (see next table) there is another oddity. That the number licensed should be less than the actual number of each breed is to be expected – horses not travelling did not require a licence. But why should the number of licensed Suffolks, alone of all breeds, be greater in 1920 by 22% than the *total* number in 1919?

(c) COMPULSORY LICENSING, 1920–1974.

(i) *Licences granted 1920–1938*. The Horse Breeding Act 1918 and the Horse Breeding (England and Wales) Regulations 1919 made it illegal after 1st January 1920 to travel an entire horse of two years old or over for service, or to exhibit it on premises not in the occupation of its owner with a view to its use for service, unless the stallion were currently licensed under the Act. The following table shows the number of licences issued in respect of heavy stallions to the year 1938. Unfortunately figures for 1939 are unreliable, because in the autumn of that year officials at the Ministry had other matters to attend to, more pressing than the enumeration of licensed stallions in days of peace. (Some generalised figures for 1939 appear in the next table.)

LICENCES GRANTED

	Pedigree				Non-pedigree					
	Shire	Clyde	Suffolk	Percheron	Shire	Clyde	Suffolk	Percheron	Others	Total
1920	2,258	286	193	33	172	10	4	9	54	3,019
1921	2,316	266	235	38	147	14	2	1	80	3,099
1922	2,052	237	216	47	122	7	2	2	80	2,765
1923	1,554*	186*	185*	45*	80*	5*	2*	2*	61	2,120
1924	1,151	148	173	53	44	2	2	1	45	1,619
1925	918	125	146	47	35	4	1	0	27	1,303
1926	797	117	139	41	32	5	0	0	22	1,153
1927	732	110	139	41	40	11	0	1	26	1,100
1928	682	112	132	38	38	8	0	0	23	1,033
1929	716	127	127	41	44	6	2	0	26	1,089
1930	706	122	137	42	46	6	2	0	26	1,087
1931	704	118	131	47	57	10	3	1	32	1,103
1932	781	114	134	54	72	16	2	3	35	1,211
1933	789	121	147	56	99	17	7	1	38	1,275
1934	837	138	176	67	125	25	6	4	55	1,433
1935	922	153	202	76	152	31	8	4	68	1,616
1936	1,018	165	221	94	170	26	5	5	71	1,775
1937	1,075	174	240	105	158	30	4	6	64	1,856
1938	1,050	194	260	102	160	30	2	6	64	1,868

* Approximate figures. Totals of each breed (i.e. pedigree and non-pedigree) are exact figures.

The number of persons breaking the law gradually diminished, but unlicensed stallions continued to be discovered on the roads all through the 'thirties. Two or three prosecutions resulted every year, and there was a varying number each season of grooms who had left the licence at home and had an uncomfortable interview with the police.

(ii) *Licences refused 1920–1937.* The following table shows the number of applications for licences which were refused, after veterinary inspection, in sample quinquennial years. It also shows the total number of rejections in the period 1920–1937, omitting 1923 and 1936 (for which years, and also 1938, it is now impossible to compile trustworthy statistics).

LICENCES REFUSED – all heavy stallions

		1920	1925	1930	1935	(16 years) 1920–1937
SHIRES – numbers examined		2,520	950	730	944	18,304
(pedigree)	number refused	262	32	24	22	868
	% refused	10.4	3.4	3.3	2.3	4.7
CLYDESDALES – number examined		332	127	123	156	2,394
(pedigree)	number refused	46	2	1	3	104
	% refused	13.8	1.6	0.8	1.9	4.3
SUFFOLKS – number examined		205	149	143	208	2,519
(pedigree)	number refused	12	3	6	6	98
	% refused	5.9	2.0	4.2	2.9	3.9
PEDIGREE – number examined		34	49	44	77	744
PERCHERONS	number refused	1	2	2	1	28
	% refused	3.0	4.1	4.5	1.3	3.8
ALL OTHERS – number examined		284	69	84	278	2,247
	number refused	35	2	4	16	144
	% refused	12.3	2.9	4.8	5.7	6.4

For the same years, there follows a table showing the grounds on which licences were refused to *pedigree Shires only.*

UNSOUNDNESS – pedigree Shires only

	1920	1925	1930	1935	(16 years) 1930–1937
Whistling	73	12	6	3	266
Roaring	74	9	6	6	233
Side-bone	57	5	5	5	163
Ring-bone	14	1	2	2	45
Bone spavin	4	0	0	0	11
Cataract	19	4	3	3	72
Shivering	6	1	2	0	36
Stringhalt	2	0	0	1	11
Defective genital organs	10	0	0	1	14
Other defects –					
Proved inadequately prolific	0	0	0	0	5
Poor conformation, etc.	3	0	0	1	12
TOTAL	262	32	24	22	868

There were usually one or two animals that had more than one unsoundness. For example, in 1930, one of the roarers was also a shiverer and one of those with sidebone also had a ringbone. Three years earlier one of the rejected Suffolks had bone spavin and stringhalt, and whistled as well.

(iii) *Licences granted 1939–1954.* From 1939, figures are not available to distinguish between stallions registered in a stud-book and other stallions which while recognisable as specimens of one of the four breeds, were un-registered. With this limitation, the statistics are as follow:

Year	Shire	Clydesdale	Suffolk	Percheron	Others	Total
1939	1,092	215	255	92	45	1,699
1940	936	206	220	82	35	1,479
1941	742	188	171	82	14	1,197
1942	696	208	187	86	23	1,200
1943	709	218	203	111	20	1,261
1944	691	211	259	135	22	1,318
1945	629	221	254	164	25	1,293
1946	461	193	231	160	18	1,063
1947	303	141	148	131	11	734
1948	207	112	95	93	19	526
1949	182	85	88	80	16	451
1950	160	62	72	68	16	378
1951	126	46	55	47	12	286
1952	113	38	43	36	24	254
1953	113	32	48	32	16	241
1954	108	30	37	37	15	227

(iv) *New licences 1955–1974.* From 1955, overall totals of licences in force at any one time are not available. The Ministry of Agriculture, Fisheries and Food has kindly supplied a list of the number of *new* licences issued each year but no record is kept of how many seasons a stallion continues his career. Therefore, the number of stallions active in any one year is not officially known.

The following figures show the number of "new stallions" in each of the two decades:

Years	Shire	Clydesdale	Suffolk	Percheron	Others	Total
1955–1964	115	21	66	53	9	264
1965–1974	103	3	19	30	5	160

The figures for 1965–1974 do not appear to reflect the revival. But, in addition to "delayed reaction", there are three points to bear in mind. Firstly, it is certain that, whereas many stallions for whom licences were obtained in the 'fifties were castrated early because there proved to be little demand for their services, in more recent years good entire horses have been kept on at their proper duties for as long as they could successfully perform them: and that, in less hectic days than the Victorian or Edwardian stallion experienced, can be many seasons. Secondly, the number of stallions at stud gives no indication of the amount of breeding that is being done, for it is equally certain that the average number of services per heavy stallion each year is far higher in the 'seventies than twenty years earlier. Thirdly, and in spite of the first two considerations, there were 59 new licences in the last two years of the period recorded above (1973–1974) – more than at any time since the middle 'fifties.

(Incidentally, during the four years 1971–1974, applications were made for eighty-eight heavy stallions. Four were refused licences and had to be castrated. This is 4.5%. In the four sample years 1920, 1925, 1930 and 1935 licences were refused to 1,242 horses out of 26,208 – 4.7%.)

Pedigree Registrations of Shire Mares, 1880–1974

IT has always been the boast of the Shire Society that it published a volume of its Stud-book every year. So well has it kept this going, through good times and bad, that (in spite of delays caused by the two world wars) it has actually issued ninety-seven volumes in only ninety-four years (Volume 1 dated 1880: Volume 97 dated 1973)!

Whence the discrepancy of three volumes? To the extent of one volume only, the error is not real. It is due simply to the fact that Volumes 1–68 were dated according to the year when they were *published* – i.e. the year after the registrations were made which they contained. For example, Volume 48 was dated 1927, and Volume 68 (containing entries accepted in 1946) was dated 1947. But Volume 69, containing entries made in 1947, was also dated 1947. This practice was continued until Volume 81, dated 1959. (Under the former procedure it would have been dated 1960.)

The rest of the discrepancy, that is the other two "extra" volumes, is the result of the fact that the five volumes 82–86, all undated, cover only the three years 1960–1962. After that, one volume a year was issued in the normal way, Volumes 87–97 covering the eleven years 1963–1973.

This confusion having been resolved, it is possible to show the number of horses registered each year (except 1960–1962), and to see the fluctuation caused by boom and and depression. Such a purely numerical guide to the extent of pedigree Shire breeding at various times in the Society's history is of value only if one looks at the mares. The number of stallion-registrations is no guide at all. There are two reasons in particular for this.

In the first place, it can be assumed that the owner of every pedigree mare either breeds from her, or, with few exceptions, attempts to do so. But the number of colts registered in any one year does not necessarily bear any relation to the number of them which, when adult, will be found to be available for service. The number of stallions appearing in the early volumes of the Stud-book was grossly inflated because vast numbers of them (and hardly any mares at all) were due for export. (In Volume 11, there are 2,194, compared with only 1,836 mares). The proportion of horses castrated is even more indeterminable. Early volumes, largely recording horses foaled some years before publication date, naturally contain few which did not do at least some seasons' service. In the early 'twenties, some were gelded virtually as soon as their particulars were published, owing to the Depression. In recent years, the same fate has befallen an increasing number for a different reason – the stringent rules about early registration. Colts have had to be registered which, in earlier times, would not have entered the book, because owners could then adopt a "wait and see" attitude, in some cases registering their horse only when it turned out that there was a good foal needing his father to be accredited. (If the Shire Society had been small enough to have collected, and published, an annual list of living and practising stallions, it would have been a different matter.)

Secondly, a pedigree mare is the actual or potential dam only of pedigree foals: that is,

her owner would not have her covered by any but a pedigree stallion. But pedigree
stallions, including those of the highest class, covered a wide assortment of mares –
pedigree and non-pedigree Shires, "common" mares of every description, and mares
of light type. Many a registered Shire stallion travelled a district where only five mares
in a hundred that he encountered were pure-bred. Of the 2,471 such entire horses recorded in the 1918 census as being available for service in 1919, there is absolutely no way
of enumerating their efforts in furthering the pedigree movement, except to say that, on
average, each of them got only about two foals that year which were put in the Stud-
book. But if one averages out the idleness of the "casual" non-professional stallion at home
with the business of the popular travelling horse, it can be assumed that between them
they covered well over 100,000 mares in their thirteen weeks, and got perhaps 60,000 foals.
This was, indeed, good work in the cause of improving the substance and quality of the
ordinary working horse, but does not tell us much about the pedigree movement.

The following table, therefore, attempts to provide an index to the health and popularity
of pedigree Shire breeding at various times by giving the average number of mares
registered in five-year periods. A seven-year period is adopted for the 1915–1921 boom,
and two four-year periods for the two stages of the slump that followed.

Period of registration*	No. of years	Volume No.	Number of New Mares registered	
			Average per year	Actual for each year
1878–1879	–	1		
1880–1884	5	2–6	585	Uneven and misleading, owing to
1885–1889	5	7–11	1,260	many posthumous registrations
1890–1894	5	12–16	1,987	
1895–1899	5	17–21	2,285	2,085, 1,564, 2,435, 2,123, 3,258
1900–1904	5	22–26	3,243	3,894, 3,250, 2,844, 3,259, 2,879
1905–1909	5	27–31	3,139	3,188, 2,735, 3,123, 3,046, 3,604
1910–1914	5	32–36	3,534	3,024, 3,819, 3,814, 3,418, 3,595
1915–1921	7	37–43	4,369	3,409, 3,528, 3,989, 5,483, 4,376, 5,656, 4,140
1922–1926	5	44–48	1,943	2,660, 2,453, 1,860, 1,494, 1,248
1927–1930	4	49–52	963	1,099, 1,168, 783, 800
1931–1934	4	53–56	758	768, 745, 743, 775
1935–1939	5	57–61	1,019	904, 1,095, 1,038, 1,102, 956
1940–1944	5	62–66	659	553, 581, 761, 815, 584
1945–1949	5	67–71	321	490, 261, 394, 186, 276
1950–1954	5	72–76	255	210, 341, 245, 207, 273
1955–1959	5	77–81	122	170, 140, 134, 96, 68
1960–1964	5	82–88	70	† ?, ?, ?, 49, 55
		(7 vols. in 5 years)		
1965–1969	5	89–93	69	59, 68, 49, 83, 88
1970–1974	5	94–98	99	68, 68, 101, 133, 123

* The dates given in this column are the years in which the registrations were submitted
and approved for publication.

† The five volumes covering the three years 1960–1962 contain 11, 54, 62, 67 and 50
mares – an average of eighty-one mares in each year.

The Shire Horse Society

(a) PATRONS

1879–1910: H.R.H. The Prince of Wales, K.G. (H.M. King Edward VII)
1910–1936: H.M. King George V
1936: H.M. King Edward VIII
1937–1952: H.M. King George VI
From 1952: H.M. Queen Elizabeth II

(b) PRESIDENTS

1879: 3rd Earl of Ellesmere
1880: 5th Earl Spencer, K.G.
1881: The Hon. E. K. W. Coke
1882: 3rd Earl of Powis
1883: Walter Gilbey (Sir Walter Gilbey, Bart)
1884: 1st Duke of Westminster, K.G.
1885: William Wells
1886: H.R.H. The Prince of Wales, K.G. (H.M. King Edward VII)
1887: Lord Egerton of Tatton (1st Earl Egerton, of Tatton)
1888: Anthony Hamond
1889: 1st Lord Wantage, K.C.B., V.C.
1890: H. Chandos-Pole-Gell
1891: 1st Lord Hothfield
1892: R. N. Sutton-Nelthorpe
1893: 2nd Lord Belper
1894: A. C. Duncombe
1895: 1st Lord Tredegar
1896: A. B. Freeman-Mitford, C.B. (1st Lord Redesdale)
1897: Sir Walter Gilbey, Bart   Second term
1898: P. Albert Muntz, M.P. (Sir P. Albert Muntz, Bart)
1899: H.R.H. The Prince of Wales (H.M. King Edward VII)   Second term
1900: 9th Lord Middleton
1901: The Hon. Victor Cavendish, M.P. (9th Duke of Devonshire, K.G.)
1902: 1st Lord Llangattock
1903: Sir Alexander Henderson, Bart, M.P. (1st Lord Faringdon)
1904: Capt. W. H. O. Duncombe (Col. W. H. O. Duncombe)
1905: 1st Lord Rothschild
1906: (J. P. Cross, d. 4th February)
       R. W. Hudson
1907: 4th Lord Bolton
1908: H. H. Smith Carington

1909: 7th Earl Beauchamp, K.C.M.G.

1910: F. E. Muntz

1911: (The Prince of Wales elected in 1910, but became King George V)
9th Earl of Coventry

1912: Sir Walpole Greenwell, Bart

1913: Earl Bathurst, C.M.G.

1914: Sir Berkeley Sheffield, Bart (M.P.)

1915: 1st Lord Northbourne

1916: Robert Whitehead

1917: H.R.H. The Prince of Wales, K.G. (H.M. King Edward VIII: The Duke of Windsor)

1918: 9th Lord Middleton. Second Term

1919: Sir Arthur Nicholson

1920: A. C. Duncombe. Second Term

1921: Sir Walter Gilbey, Bart (II)

1922: (John Rowell, d. 15th March)
A. H. Clark

1923: 9th Duke of Devonshire, K.G.   Second term

1924: Sir Bernard Greenwell, Bart

1925: 3rd Lord Harlech

1926: F. W. Griffin

1927: Mrs. Stanton

1928: Sir Walter Gilbey, Bart (II)   Second term

1929: A. Thomas Loyd

1930: David Davies (1st Lord Davies)

1931: N. W. Smith Carington

1932: Thomas Forshaw

1933: (Sir Edward D. Stern, Bart, d. 17th April)
A. Thomas Loyd   Second term

1934: 9th Duke of Devonshire, K.G.   Third term

1935: Sir Edward Mann, Bart

1936: Christopher Barker

1937: 17th Earl of Derby, K.G.

1938: J. Morris Belcher

1939/1945: William J. Cumber (C.B.E.)

1946: Col. A. Falkner Nicholson, C.B.E.

1947: H. T. L. Young

1948: 10th Duke of Devonshire, K.G.

1949: Col. Stanley Bell, O.B.E. (Sir Stanley Bell)

1950: H. T. L. Young   Second term

1951: W. S. Smith, O.B.E.

1952: Lt.-Col. F. R. P. Barker

1953: A. H. Clark (II)

1954: H. T. L. Young   Third term

1955: Sir Richard Proby, Bart, M.C.

1956: H. T. L. Young   Fourth term

1957: Lord Cornwallis, K.B.E., M.C.

1958: D. Peter Crossman, T.D., D.L.

1959: T. Baker Marsh
1960: Lord Cornwallis, K.B.E., M.C.   Second term
1961: Major Simon Whitbread
1962: Lord Cornwallis, K.B.E., M.C.   Third term
1963/1964: John A. Young
1965/1966: Capt. Peter E. Courage
1967/1968: J. David Kay
1969/1970: Anthony D. Crossman
1971/1972: W. H. Whitbread, T.D., M.A.
1973/1974: R. H. Courage
1975/   : R. N. Gilbey

(c) CHAIRMEN OF THE EDITING COMMITTEE

1879–1880; 1882; 1889–1893	Thomas Brown	8 years
1879; 1883–1888	The Hon. Edward Coke	7 years
1881	Frederic Street	1 year
1894–1909; 1911–1913; 1915–1917; 1919–1923	A. C. Duncombe	27 years
1910; 1914	J. W. Kenworthy	2 years
1918; 1924–1932	A. H. Clark (I)	10 years
1933–1936	Thomas Forshaw	4 years
1937; 1958–1959	J. Morris Belcher	3 years
1938–1954	Col. A. Falkner Nicholson	16 years
1955–1957	H. T. L. Young	3 years
1958–1973	T. Baker Marsh	16 years
1974–	Capt. Peter E. Courage	

(d) CHAIRMEN OF THE FINANCE COMMITTEE

(1878–1880); 1881–1914	Sir Walter Gilbey, Bart (I) (elected at each meeting until 1881)	36 years
1915–1916	H. H. Smith Carington (acting chairman 1914)	2 years
1917–1943	Sir Walter Gilbey, Bart (II)	27 years
1944–1962	William J. Cumber, C.B.E.	19 years
1963–1973	John A. Young	11 years
1974–	J. David Kay	

(e) CHAIRMEN OF THE HORSE-SHOW COMMITTEE

1879	(Thomas Brown)	
1880	(Thomas Brown, Walter Gilbey, Major Dashwood – no chairman)	
1881–1909	Sir Walter Gilbey (I)	29 years
1910; 1912; 1914; 1916–1918	Lord Hothfield	6 years
1911; 1913	Lord Middleton	2 years
1915	Lord Northbourne	1 year
1919–1921	John Rowell	3 years
1922–1932	Sir Walter Gilbey (II)	11 years
1933	Christopher Barker	1 year

1934	A. Thomas Loyd	1 year
1935–1936; 1938–1939	W. J. Cumber	4 years
1937	Col. A. Falkner Nicholson	1 year
1945; 1950–1952	H. T. L. Young	4 years
1946–1949	J. Morris Belcher	4 years

The Horse-Show committee ceased after 1952.

(*f*) SECRETARIES

June 1878	G. M. Sexton
August 1883	John Sloughgrove
November 1916	A. B. Charlton
April 1929	A. G. Holland
June 1963	Roy W. Bird

Spring Show Supporters 1961–1975

THOSE who supported the Spring Show during the darkest years of the early 'sixties are worthy to be recorded, as are those who similarly led the revival which followed. Here, therefore, are listed all who entered animals during the fifteen years to 1975, together with the names of judges.

One or two great names which were prominent in the old time are still to be found here though naturally retirement or death has caused most of these to be poorly represented. But one of the ever-presents is E. J. Holland, who went to Edingale House in 1909, joined the Shire Society in 1918 and won his first Spring Show prize in 1927. In contrast to this doyen of Shire breeders is a large number of men who are not only "new" but in many cases young enough to be his grandsons. Amongst these, in spite of an ever widening geographical spread, there is still a high proportion of classical Shire addresses which would be familiar to eighteenth-century breeders.

For space reasons, addresses have been abbreviated, generally to parish and county (i.e. the actual county, which is not necessarily that to which the Post Office finds it convenient to allocate the inhabitants of many parishes). Old county boundaries and names have been retained, for the sake of uniformity with earlier pages. For example, Crumlin is still regarded as being in "Monmouthshire" rather than in Gwent, its successor; Llanelly as in Carmarthenshire, not Dyfed; and Bewdley in Worcestershire, not "Herefs. and Worcs."

"G" after the address shows that the exhibitor, at least during this period, showed geldings (in hand, or in classes for single horses, pairs or teams in harness with vehicle), but not stallions or mares.

Column 1 indicates the first year of this period that each exhibitor entered horses at the show. (This is not necessarily, of course, the first year he ever exhibited.)

Column 2 gives the number of shows during this period at which he exhibited.

Column 3 shows the total number of his entries during this time, pairs or teams of geldings counting as one entry.

Special praise is due to the five stalwart owners who exhibited at every one of these fifteen shows and to the seven who were represented on each occasion they were eligible. The names of these latter will be found repeated in the list of judges. (Two may appear to have competed at one *more* show than they should. This is because at one show, though judging, they were permitted to exhibit stallions, not in competition, but as candidates for premiums.)

	First Year	No. of Shows	No. of Entries
ANDREW BROS., Barton-on-Humber, Lincs.	63	2	2
W. N. ARBLASTER, Shareshill, Staffs.	74	2	3
B. BAKER, Ilford, Essex (G)	70	4	5

	First Year	No. of Shows	No. of Entries
G. G. BALL, Holmes Chapel, Ches.	61	1	1
G. C. & D. M. BEDFORD, Littleport, Cambs. 71, Ely, Cambs.	62	3	5
W. BEDFORD, & G. H. HANCOCK, Cleckheaton, Yorks. 69–70 Paul & Walter Bedford (sons) 75 W. Bedford snr.	67	4	5
J. F. BELCHER, Hurst, Berks.	74	1	1
P. BENNETT, West Ashling, Sussex (G)	74	1	1
DENYS F. BENSON, East Hanningfield, Essex	66	9	16
C. T. BILLINGS, Crumlin, Mon.	71	1	1
A. BIRTWHISTLE, Heywood, Lancs.	70	1	1
G. E. BOURNES, Brenchley, Kent	69	4	6
R. J. BRICKELL, Witney, Oxon. (Now Enstone, Oxon.)	67	1	1
B. F. BRIGHTMORE, Brampton-en-le-Morthen, Thurcroft, Yorks.	73	1	1
GEORGE BROWNLOW, Gorefield, Cambs.	62	12	26
H. BURKINSHAW, Glapwell, Derbys.	75	1	1
C. BURTON, Haddenham, Cambs.	66	3	3
CALDER BROS., Kidderminster, Worcs. (G)	75	1	2
CAMMIDGE & ROBSON, North Newbald, Yorks.	73	3	6
G. R. CAVE, Chesterton, Cambs.	73	2	2
W. H. CHAMBERS, Swanland Dale, N. Ferriby, Yorks.	63	12	24
HARRY CLAPPISON, Ottringham, Yorks.	63	1	1
CHARLES CLARK, Maidenwell, Lincs.	61	7	10
A. R. & D. CLIXBY, Blyton, Lincs.	61	2	3
J. COLLINS, Hartshead Moor, Yorks.	75	1	1
GEO. E. COLSON, Long Melford, Suffolk	61	2	2
A. CONNER & SONS, Thwing, Yorks. (G)	61	1	1
J. B. COOKE, Deeping High Bank, Spalding, Lincs. From 74 as J. B. Cooke Ltd.	62	14	19
BRIAN COOPER, Ramsdell, Hants.	70	4	4
F. COSGROVE & SON, Hainton, Lincs.	61	13	54
COURAGE, BARCLAY & SIMONDS LTD., Alton, Hants. (G) From 71, Courage Ltd. From 75, at Courage Shire Horse Centre, Maidenhead, Berks.	61	15	59
E. COWARD, Holbeach, Lincs. From 72, E. Coward Ltd., Thorney, Peterborough	66	9	25
T.W. CRITCHLOW, Cubley, Derbys.	66	6	10
J. E. CROSLAND, Aberford, Yorks.	64	2	3
W. CUMBER & SON (THEALE) LTD., Theale, Berks.	61	2	5
D. O. DAVID, Ton Kenfig, Glam.	74	1	1
H. DAVIES, Cy Mau, Wrexham, Denbighs.	74	1	1

	First Year	No. of Shows	No. of Entries
T. L. DAVIES, Ryton, Salop.	72	4	4
WILLIAM DAVIES & SON, Newtown, Mont.	61	2	3
ELTON ESTATES CO. Elton, Peterborough (H. M. T. Jones)	61	14	31
C. C. ETCHES, Mickleover, Derbys. 75, Fenny Bentley, Derby.	68	8	14
BRINLEY EVANS, Llanelly, Carms.	74	1	1
J. DOWNES EVANS, Berriew, Mont.	63	1	1
CHAS. FARNHAM LTD., East Horndon, Essex (G)	65	1	2
MRS. A. M. FINNEY & SONS, Wingerworth, Derbys. 75 G. E. Finney	65	5	7
J. K. FINNEY, Calton Lees, Beeley, Derbys.	67	7	9
F. FLAY, Tongwynlais, Glam.	74	2	2
S. FLETCHER, Stow Bridge, King's Lynn, Norfolk	67	1	1
F. W. FORD, Kirk Ireton, Derbys.	61	1	1
LEONARD FORD, Withington, Ches.	61	2	3
LEONARD FOUNTAIN, Marston Montgomery, Derbys.	61	12	29
JOHN H. FRANK, Horton, Northants.	61	2	2
A. FRANKLIN, Bosley, Ches.	74	2	4
ARTHUR GARDNER, Out Rawcliffe, Lancs. From 66 with son as A. & A. Gardner	61	13	31
S. G. GARRETT, Carr, Maltby, Yorks. From 71, Chapeltown, Yorks.	61	11	18
G. GAYDON, Farnborough, Warks.	61	5	7
C. H. GOODWIN, Walton-on-Trent, Derbys.	65	1	1
T. H. GOSNEY, Stannington, Yorks.	73	1	2
H. E. GRASSBY & SON, Balne, Yorks.	61	1	1
W. H. GRIFFITH, Brynrefail, Caernarvon.	75	1	2
G. GUEST, Darfield, Yorks.	75	1	1
HARRY HALL, March, Cambs.	63	2	2
HAMILTON REMOVALS (W. P. Hamilton), Leeds, Yorks. (G)	68	3	10
HART & BEAVIS, Stapleford, Cambs.	73	1	1
F. HARTLEY, Harthill, Yorks.	74	1	2
P. HARTLEY, Braceby, Lincs.	72	1	3
J. H. HARVEY, Sale, Ches.	70	2	2
R. HAWKSWORTH, Thurvaston, Dalbury Lees, Derbys.	69	2	2
MRS. M. HEYWOOD, Farington, Lancs.	75	1	1
K. P. HICKS, Pulborough, Sussex.	75	1	1
J. B. HILTON, Baston Fen, Lincs. 72, J. B. Hilton & Son	70	2	2
E. J. HOLLAND, Edingale, Staffs.	61	14	36
C. J. HOTCHKISS, Bishop's Castle, Salop	73	3	3
J. HOUSE, Wilton (Salisbury), Wilts.	73	1	1
ROBERT HULL, St. Michaels-on-Wyre, Lancs.	61	13	33
HULL BREWERY CO. LTD., Hull, Yorks. (G)	68	7	18

	First Year	No. of Shows	No. of Entries
A. C. HUMAN, Soham, Cambs.	70	3	4
W. S. INNES, Pentraeth, Anglesey	62	11	19
G. E. IVATT & SONS, Whaplode Drove, Lincs.	64	4	11
A. IVES & SONS, Alverthorpe, Yorks. (G)	63	3	4
G. D. JAMES, Moylgrove, Pemb.	75	1	1
E. G. JARRETT & SON, Stoney Stretton, Yockleton, Salop	74	1	1
JAY TRANSPORT LTD., Dartford, Kent (G)	74	1	3
H. M. T. JONES, see Elton Estates			
HUGH JONES, Llanfechell, Anglesey	62	9	12
J. E. JONES, Berriew, Mont.	62	1	1
R. W. JONES, Llanerch-y-mor, Holywell, Flints.	65	3	6
JOHN JOSEPH, South Cornelly, Pyle, Glam. (son of Ll. J. below)	75	1	1
LLEWELYN JOSEPH & SONS, Nottage, Glam. From 74, South Cornelly, Pyle, Glam.	68	7	12
A. W. KEELING, Alton, Staffs.	61	10	14
E. A. KING, Hillesden, Bucks.	61	1	2
M. & B. KITCHEN & G. TURNER, Crawley Down, Sussex	75	1	1
G. W. KITCHING, Moore, Ches.	75	1	1
C. & K. LEVERETT BROS. Gronant, Prestatyn, Flints.	65	1	1
ARTHUR W. LEWIS, Tanworth-in-Arden, Warks.	61	14	31
MRS. S. A. LEWIS, Ellen's Green, Rudgwick, Sussex.	72	1	1
W. A. LIDSTONE LTD., Slough, Bucks. (G-5m) From 72, Taplow, Bucks. (Gilbert Lidstone, George Green, Slough 1s)	61	15	37
G. P. LINDLEY, Thornhill Lees, Yorks.	69	1	1
R. LIVESEY & SONS, Inskip, Lancs.	73	2	2
P. R. L. LLOYD, Moreton, Ches.	73	1	1
T. LODGE, Denby Dale, Yorks.	74	1	1
C. LUMB, Barkisland, Yorks.	67	3	3
MANN, CROSSMAN & PAULIN LTD., see WATNEY MANN			
G. A. MAPPLETHORPE, North Owersby, Lincs.	74	1	2
T. BAKER MARSH, Knowsley, Lancs.	61	4	4
JOHN MARTINSON, Howden, Yorks.	62	12	35
P. MASON, Barnet, Herts.	66	1	1
L. A. MAY, Colnbrook, Bucks. (G) From 74, Ashford, Middlesex	72	3	3
W. J. MILLS & SON, Truro, Cornwall	63	1	1
A. F. MILLWARD, Whixall, Salop	64	2	2
J. HAROLD MORLEY LTD., Walsall, Staffs. (G-1s) From 73, Streetly, Staffs.	69	6	12
R. T. MORTIMER, Leyland, Lancs. (Son of T. W. below)	75	1	1
T. W. MORTIMER, Leyland, Lancs.	64	5	7

	First Year	No. of Shows	No. of Entries
T. E. MOSS, Eaton (Congleton), Ches.	62	12	33
T. W. O. MOTT & SONS, Little Downham, Cambs.	61	7	7
D. MUGFORD, St. Michael Penkevil, Cornwall	73	1	1
W. W. NAYLOR, Mackworth, Derbys.	63	2	3
MRS. M. NELSON, Camberley, Surrey	73	1	2
G. LLOYD OWEN, Llanfachraeth, Anglesey	66	8	21
A. J. OXBY, Woodhall Spa, Lincs.	62	4	4
ANTHONY PASCOE, Fraddam, Hayle, Cornwall	63	5	7
From 72, as A. Pascoe & Son			
R. PAYZE, Toftwood, East Dereham, Norfolk	75	1	1
B. J. PHILLIPS, Southfleet, Kent (G)	73	1	5
R. A. S. PLEAVIN, Hope, Flints.	61	7	8
HENRY POLLARD, Penryn, Cornwall	64	3	3
73, Mabe, (Penryn)			
A. J. POSNETT, Norley, Ches.	74	1	1
ARTHUR RICHARDSON, Wharles, Lancs.	63	10	14
E. J. RICHARDSON, Woodville, Derbys.-Leics.	61	10	23
F. W. O. RICHARDSON, Bewholme, Yorks.	69	4	5
A. E. ROBINSON, Lissington, Lincs.	70	2	4
G. ROBINSON, Metheringham, Lincs.	74	2	2
H. EADY ROBINSON, Higham Ferrers, Northants.	62	6	9
MRS. G. V. ROOTS, Horam, Sussex	73	1	1
A. S. RUDGE, Hanwell, W.7 (G)	67	3	4
J. RUSSELL, Barnsley, Glos.	61	12	19
G. W. SADLER, Whittlesford, Cambs.	64	3	5
W. SALT & SONS, Denstone, Staffs.	63	12	30
From 71, W. & J. Salt Bros.			
From 73, J. Salt			
From 75, J. & E. Salt			
A. SCRIVENS, Leyland, Lancs.	67	1	1
E. A. SESSIONS, Dalbury Lees, Derbys.	61	5	5
W. H. SIMPSON, West Melton, Yorks.	62	5	7
SEYMOUR SMITH & SONS, Coleshill, Warks.	61	2	2
SOLID FUEL ADVISORY SERVICE (Grosvenor Place, London, S.W.) (G)	75	1	4
JOHN T. D. SPENCE, Bewdley, Worcs. (G)	64	3	3
SOUTHERN LEISURE CENTRE. West Moors, Dorset (G)	75	1	1
FRANK STARLING, Littleport, Cambs. (G)	62	2	2
H. C. STEVENS, Cambridge	62	4	8
J. R. SUCKLEY, Oswestry, Salop	61	14	54
W. SUDELL, Woodplumpton, Lancs.	74	2	2
W. A. SULLY, Wrotham, Kent	66	5	8
H. SUTTON, Lymm, Ches.	61	12	22
RICHARD SUTTON, Longton, Lancs. (G)	64	1	1
G. SWANN (Leggetts Transport) Stalybridge, Ches. (G)	70	4	6

	First Year	No. of Shows	No. of Entries
From 73, G. Swann & Son			
75, Devlin & Swann, Hyde, Ches.			
W. T. TATE, Stainton Dale (Scarborough), Yorks.	73	3	5
MRS. S. TATTON, Cousley Wood, Wadhurst, Sussex.	73	1	1
W. A. TAYLOR, Morton Fen, (Bourne), Lincs.	75	1	1
JOSHUA TETLEY & SON LTD., The Brewery, Leeds, Yorks. (G)	69	2	7
B. THOMAS, Tettenhall Wood, Staffs. (G)	71	3	4
T. TREVOR THOMAS, Three Crosses, Swansea, Glam.	61	4	4
75, T. Trevor Thomas & Sons.			
G. W. THORP, Twycross, Leics.	61	15	20
DANIEL THWAITES & CO. LTD., Star Brewery, Blackburn, Lancs. (G)	62	14	41
C. VINCENT, Chertsey, Surrey	75	1	1
MISS ANN VOS, Lindfield, Sussex	75	1	1
F. W. WALKER, Scarborough, Yorks.	65	3	3
G. T. WARD & SON, Gorefield, Cambs.	61	13	34
From 68 G. T. Ward & Son Ltd.			
J. R. WARD, Weeton, Lancs.	69	3	6
WATNEY MANN LTD. (G)	61	15	48
To 69, Mann, Crossman & Paulin Ltd., Mile End, E.1.			
70 Watney Mann (London & Home Counties) Ltd.			
71 Watney Mann, Albion Brewery, Whitechapel, E.1.			
72 Watney Mann Ltd.			
75 Watney Mann & Truman Brewers Ltd., West Bergholt, Essex.			
K. WELDON, Chapeltown, Yorks.	66	1	1
G. M. WELLINGS & SON, Horderley, Craven Arms, Salop.	75	1	1
J. &. W. WHEWELL LTD., Radcliffe, Lancs. (G-1m, 2s)	61	13	33
WHITBREAD & CO. LTD., Chiswell St., E.C.1 (G)	63	1	4
T. G. WHITE, Yeaveley, Derbys.	65	1	2
J. W. WIDDOWSON, Nether Handley, Yorks.	62	5	8
A. WILKINSON, Green Haworth, Accrington, Lancs.	75	1	1
C. R. WILLIAMS, Sherrards Green, Malvern, Worcs.	74	1	3
D. J. WILLIAMSON, Clenchwarton, Norfolk	74	2	2
F. WILLIAMSON, Chelford, Ches.	65	11	39
HARRY WINSTANLEY, Higher Whitley, Ches.	64	3	3
ARTHUR WRIGHT, Daresbury, Ches.	68	6	16
From 72, Arthur Wright Farms Ltd.			
THOMAS YATES, Windley, Derbys.	61	12	25
J. M. YOUNG, Bosley, Ches.	62	2	3
YOUNG & CO.'S BREWERY LTD., The Ram Brewery, Wandsworth, S.W. 18 (G)	61	15	71

JUDGES

The years shown in parenthesis are those previous to 1961 when the same member had officiated as a judge.

Year	Name
61	John M. Belcher, Edgmond, Salop (47, 55)
69	George Brownlow
72	J. Burton (Haddenham)
64/71	R. O. Cambidge, Kinnerley, Salop
72	W. H. Chambers
67	Charles Clark
66	F. Cosgrove
72	A. E. Cosgrove (son)
63/74	C. C. Etches
64	J. Downes Evans (32, 56)
62/75	Leonard Ford (latterly Holmes Chapel, Ches.)
71	Richard Forshaw, Sutton-on-Trent, Notts (51)
65	G. Gaydon
69	C. H. Goodwin
61/71	J. W. Hiles, Winterton, Lincs. (54)
68	E. J. Holland (52)
66	J. E. Holloway, Ford, Salop
63	Robert Hull
75	W. S. Innes
75	H. M. T. Jones (60)
63/74	J. E. Jones
73	Llewelyn Joseph
65	Arthur W. Lewis
62	T. Baker Marsh (52)
70	T. E. Moss
68	R. A. S. Pleavin
68	R. W. Richards, Bozeat, Northants.
61/70	H. Eady Robinson (36, 43, 53)
62	William Simpson, Chenies, Bucks.
67/73	J. R. Suckley
69	H. Sutton
74	Graham T. Ward (grandson of G.T.)
67	S. T. Ward (son of G.T.) (56)
70	T. G. White
64	E. Lloyd Williams, Llanrwst, Denbighs.
65/73	Thomas Yates
75	T. J. Yates (son)
66	J. M. Young

London and Spring Show Officials, 1880–1975

(*a*) JUDGES, 1880–1960

The following list of Spring Show judges excludes those listed already in Appendix 21 (i.e. those who judged at the Shows in 1961–1975);

A. H. Clark (sen.) judged nine Shows (1890–1918).

Henry Smith of Cropwell Butler, Notts, judged eight Shows (1881–1904).

Thomas Fowler, James Gould (sen.) and F. W. Griffin (6).

John Blundell, Thomas B. Freshney, Edward Green, R. H. Keene, John Rowell and J. W. Rowland (5).

J. Morris Belcher, A. H. Clark (jun.), John T. C. Eadie, Thomas Forshaw, James Gould (jun.), W. T. Lamb, John Morton, John Vaughan and Edmund Whinnerah (4).

W. J. Cumber, Albert Farnsworth, T. H. B. Freshney, Captain Henry Heaton, James Holm, John Nix and Robert Stuart (3).

T. H. Balderston, H. W. Bishop, Peter Blundell, James Bulford, C. R. Chamberlain, Col. T. W. Daniel, A. J. Flowers, John H. Frank, George Gotheridge, Thomas Green, F. W. Ibbotson, J. R. Jones, E. A. Kirk, William Little, Norman R. Lloyd, J. W. Measures, Joseph Paisley, W. H. Potter, William Richardson, W. S. Smith, William Thompson (jun.), T. M. Watson, James Whinnerah and John Wills (2).

Edgar I. Appleby, J. H. Appleby, J. T. Appleby, W. H. Appleby, E. W. Betts, William Brock, A. W. Byron, Chris Catterall, Henry Chandos-Pole-Gell, George Chapman, Harry Clappison, George Cowing, James F. Crowther, John Cumber, Edward Davies, C. I. Douglas, Thomas Ewart, J. R. Faulkner, James Forshaw, James Forshaw (jun.), Joseph Grimes, S. G. Grimes, Milton Harris, W. T. Hayr, E. W. Headington, J. B. Hill, J. B. Hilton, Allan Holm, William Howkins, Thomas Jackson, William Jackson, Robert Jemson, William Jonas, David Jones, George Kendrew, Henry Leggate, A. L. Lester, John Lewis, Arthur Lindley, William McCulloch, Henry Mackereth, Joseph Morton, W. H. Neale, Col. A. F. Nicholson, Henry Overman, Thomas Plowright, R. S. Reynolds, John Rimmer, W. R. Rowland, James G. Runciman, F. G. Starling, Frederic Street, T. P. Stuart, Richard Sutton, C. W. Tindall, A. E. E. Vaughan, Samuel Wade, Joseph Wainwright, Joseph Waltham, William Welch and William Whewell.

(*b*) STEWARDS, 1880–1975

This complete list includes those who were Inspectors under the "Soap and Resin" Rule 25, from 1909–1930.

17 times – Heber G. Martin (1903–1925).

12 – Denys F. Benson (1954–1971) and John Parr (1891–1906).

9 – J. Sturley Nunn and W. S. Smith.

8 – James Heys and William Little.

7 – Thomas Brown, A. H. Clark (sen.), T. Eaton Jones and R. H. Keene.

6 – Denby Collins, Col. T. W. Daniel, E. Hurn, William Jonas, H. M. T. Jones, F. J.

Peacock, Benjamin Rowland, R. G. Thompson and Thomas Wareing.

5 – A. J. Baker, R. S. Brydon, J. Downes Evans, Joseph Martin, F. J. Merson, T. H. Merson and J. D. Ward.

4 – Ben Alderson, John M. Belcher, Cecil Burton, John Cumber, D. E. Davies, Edward Mucklow, Walter R. Odam, William Rowe and Alfred Rowell.

3 – William Barford, J. Morris Belcher, G. Brownlow, T. Brownlow, D. Clixby, A. D. Crossman, J. H. Faulkner, Robert Fish, Percy Heaton, R. G. Heaton, Harry Jackson, W. S. King, J. L. McGowan, T. S. Minton, T. S. Pidduck, R. A. S. Pleavin, Henry Smith, William Thompson (jun.), John Treadwell, Graham T. Ward and S. T. Ward.

2 – Major A. C. Burnaby-Atkins, M.C., C. H. Coxon, Walter Farthing, J. W. Hiles (jun.), Robert Hull, Walter Martin, M. R. Riddington and Frederic Street.

1 – Arthur J. Bird, John Blundell, Henry Brown, R. O. Cambidge, Major Dashwood, J. B. Ellis and Peter Gould.

(c) HONORARY VETERINARY OFFICERS, 1945–1975

(Complete lists of Veterinary Inspectors, 1880–1939, are given in Appendix 17).

1945–1949: Professor Harold Burrow, M.R.C.V.S., D.V.S.M.

1950–1968: James Martin, M.R.C.V.S.

1969–   : S. G. Poles, M.R.C.V.S.

References and Notes

PREFACE

1 *On the Domesticated Animals of the British Islands*, etc. London 1845, p. 608.

PART A

CHAPTER I

1 *The Shire Horse in Peace and War*, Vinton & Co. Ltd., London p. 53.

2 Giraldus Cambrensis, *Itin. Cambriae* op. vi. 143 (see further, V.6, for Robert de Bellême).

3 Anthony Dent and Daphne Machin Goodall, *The Foals of Epona* (Galley Press Ltd. London 1962), pp. 97 f.

4 The first use of the term "charger" to denote a cavalry horse was, according to OED, in 1712, which implies the modern sense of "charge". Nevertheless, there must be some vestige of the older signification behind the word, similar to that applying to "charger" in its meaning of a flat dish which can be loaded with a heavy joint of meat.

5 I am indebted to the Salop County Archivist, Mary C. Hill, for this information, which is drawn from an unpublished and incomplete work on the agriculture of Shropshire, by the late J. W. Slack, and to Mrs. L. C. Lloyd for permission to use it. Sources are Shrewsbury Borough Library 7322-7340, 7263-72, 5922, 9777: Salop Record Office 212/.

6 11 Henry VII c. 13 (1495).

7 23 Henry VIII c. 16 (1531-2).

8 27 Henry VIII c. 6 (1535-6).

9 In this and subsequent Acts, care is taken to define the "hand" or "handful" as containing "four inches of the standard". That is, Henry VIII meant exactly what we mean by a "hand". Otherwise, some bright law-evader might claim local customary measurement, by which a hand was more like three inches. I am indebted to the Standards, Weights and Measures Division of the Department of Trade and Industry for explaining that the four recognised "feet" in general use in this country (9.9 in. in Wales, 11.65 in. and approximately 12.45 in., both used in building, and the northern or Saxon foot of 13.2 in.) were reconciled by a statute of 1305, which settled on a foot of 12 in.: but it did not disturb the older relationships such as "3 barleycorns = 1 thumb, 3 thumbs = 1 palm", which were based on the 9.9 inch foot. The OED quotes a reference as late as 1561 (Eden, *Arte Navig.* 1 xviii 19) which shows how confusion still remained to make definition necessary: "Foure graines of barlye make a fynger: foure fingers a hande: foure handes a foote." On this basis, a mare of 9.3 modern hands, covered by a stallion of 10.2, would have been within the law!

10 32 Henry VIII c. 13 (1540).

11 33 Henry VIII c. 5 (1541–2). This was partially repealed by 4 & 5 Philip & Mary c. 2 (1557) and fully by 21 James I c. 28 (1623).

12 *An Historical Description of the Iland of Britaine* etc, Third Booke chap. 1 in Holinshed's *Chronicles* (1577), for which see the end of section 5.

13 1 Edward VI c. 12 (1547).

14 1 Edward VI c. 12 (1547).

15 2 and 3 Edward VI c. 33 (1548).

16 2 and 3 Philip and Mary c. 7 (1555).

17 1 Elizabeth I c. 7 (1558).

18 5 Elizabeth I c. 19 (1562).

19 Paul L. Hughes and James F. Larkin (ed), *Tudor Royal Proclamations*, Vol. II, Yale Univ. Press 1969. No. 494.

20 id. No. 495.

21 8 Elizabeth I c. 8 (1565).

22 *Tudor Royal Proclamations*. No. 647. (The third Proclamation had been issued from Hampton Court on 3rd Feb. 1567: No. 559.)

23 Holinshed's *Chronicles*, Book III, 8 (first edition 1577).

24 OED says the origin of this word is obscure. It originally tended to mean "an inferior horse", then "a draught horse". It was also used of a "clumsy or stoutly-built female", and OED quotes such expressions as "a jolly great royle", "a great ramping wench, a roile". To call a lady a "gurt roile" was a non-regal way of saying she was a Flemish mare.

25 Quotations are from chapters ii–vi of *The Foure Chiefest Offices belonging to Horsemanship*, London 1580.

26 That is "large bellied" or "long bellied". Blundeville also used the word in the sense "reaching far down" (as coats, sleeves or hair was *side*) when he wrote that one testicle should not be "hanging sider than another, but trussed up round together".

27 Lib. 16.

28 4 James I c. 1 (1606). The position concerning overseas later became confused. Under various Acts from 1682–1809 an export duty was payable on horses, and it was held that these Acts virtually repealed the previous prohibition. But their repeal in 1819 caused a nice point. Did this bring Henry VII's original provisions once again into force? However, there appears to be no record of anyone's being prosecuted for sending a horse out of the country, and so the lawyers had no chance to argue the matter. Even in 1809 John Lawrence wrote that "no impediment to getting any number of horses out of the kingdom has ever come to my knowledge; yet, some few years since, I was informed by a gentleman in the customs, that they could not legally go out of the port of London, but that the export was carried on by sufferance, and against law, from the other parts". (*History and delineation of the horse*, p. 111). The laws about the size of horses for breeding, as amended by Elizabeth, were also still on the statute book, but these were not invoked either.

29 Quoted by Lady Frances Parthenope Verney in *Memoirs of the Verney Family during the Civil War*, Longmans Green & Co. 1892, Vol. 1, pp. 128 f.

30 Sir Charles Firth, *The Regimental History of Cromwell's Army*, Oxford 1940.

31 Thomas Carlyle, *Oliver Cromwell's Letters & Speeches: with Elucidations*, 1857, ed., p. 380. Squire had served with Cromwell as Cornet in the Stilton troop of the Ironsides. Letters to him from Cromwell are variously addressed to "Lieutenant Squire" and "Auditor Squire".

32 Sir Walter Gilbey, *The Great Horse*, 2nd edn. 1899, p. 44.

33 S. R. Gardiner, *History of the Commonwealth and Protectorate*, London 1897, ii, 349.

CHAPTER II

1 *Tour thro' the whole Island of Great Britain*, Letter II (Everyman edn. Vol. 1, p. 129).

2 William Cavendish, 1592–1676. The wonderfully illustrated *Méthode et Invention Nouvelle de dresser les Chevaux* was published in Antwerp in 1657 during his exile. *The New Method and Extraordinary Invention to Dress Horses, and Work them, according to Nature etc.*, published in England in 1667, was – in spite of the similarity of title – a new work.

3 The old verb "wood" means to "go mad, rage, rave". In "Cavelarice" (an earlier hotch-potch, published in 1607 and 1617, which copiously plagiarised Blundeville) it appears as "*wooe* one another". Markham added his belief that if mares "may not have the Horse in the extremitie of their desire, they will runne madde".

4 John Lawrence, *History and Delineation of the Horse*, 1809, p. 105.

5 He left three sons – Sir Thomas (1638–1704), Matthew (1639–1711, rector of Aynho in Northants, doctor of divinity, celebrated antiquary and accomplished violinist) and Richard of Pudsey (near where the great cricketing Hutton, Sir Leonard, was born in 1916). None of these bred horses to any extent, but other members of this remarkable and numerous family have done so. Sir Richard's grandfather was Matthew Hutton, Archbishop of York for almost ten years until his death in 1606. Matthew had three brothers and, from his second and third marriages, twelve children. Among the descendants of one of these were two brothers – John (1691–1768) and Matthew (1692–1758). John bred the stallion Marske (named from the place where he lived), the reputed sire of Eclipse: Matthew was Archbishop successively of York and Canterbury. The last Hutton to own Sir Richard's Markham book was that remarkable character and horse enthusiast the late Ernest Hutton of Eye, after whose death it was unfortunately sold. His brother Horace will long be remembered as a Hackney expert. Among other connexions of the family in modern times is Arthur W. Lewis, Little Ladbrook, Tanworth-in-Arden, one of the best-known Shire men since 1945 and owner of the 1966 champion stallion, Ladbrook What's Wanted.

6 Letter VII.

7 Letter V.

8 Letter VI.

9 Letters I and VII.

10 Letter VII.

11 Letter I.

12 Letter VII.

13 Charles Chenevix Trench says that "the time-honoured legend" that Defoe took part in the Monmouth Rebellion seems to have been confirmed by the discovery of the name "Daniel Foe" in a list of those engaged and later pardoned. (*The Western Rising*, Longmans, 1969, p. 157.)

14 Letter IV.

15 *Kalm's Account of His Visit to England on his Way to America in 1748*. Trans Joseph Lucas, London; Macmillan & Co. Ltd., 1892.

16 "The Clydesdale Horse" in *The Standard Cyclopedia of Modern Agriculture*; later reproduced almost verbatim in *Live Stock of the Farm*, Vol. III (Horses), c. 1913.

17 *Transactions of the Highland and Agricultural Society of Scotland*, 5th series, Vol. XIX, 1907, pp. 24 ff.

18 Op. cit.
19 *Rural Economy of the Midland Counties*, 1790, Vol.1, p. 306.
20 Quoted by L. G. Pine, *The New Extinct Peerage 1884–1971*, 1972, p. 68.
21 *Observations on Livestock*, p. 32.
22 *The Foals of Epona*, pp. 56–8, 220–2.
23 *Lincolnshire Life*, October 1969.
24 *The Black Horsemen: English Inns and King Arthur*, John Baker Ltd., 1971.
25 M. J. Barones van Heemstra and F. C. D. Popken, *Het Friese Paard*, Amsterdam, 1961.
26 *Kings of the Highway*, Hutchinson, 1957, p. 74.

CHAPTER III
 1 Suffolk Stud-book, Vol. 1, p. 43.
 2 Twin-conceptions in cart-mares are in fact more common than is generally realised.
   Usually, one of the twins is aborted at six or seven months and the other is born
   alive at full term. (This is possible because horse-twins, unlike (e.g.) cattle-twins, are
   developed within separate membranes.) Therefore no one but the owner and his
   veterinary surgeon is likely to know what has occurred. In the Thoroughbred, it
   appears that double conceptions comprise between 1.7% and 2.0% of the total.
   Examples of twin live births, however, are rare. Professor Harold Burrow states
   that in the 1930's the Shire stallion Lymm Secundus, travelling in the Wirral, sired in
   the same season three sets of twins on farms within a mile of each other: all these
   foals were born alive at full term and thrived normally. This is a tribute to the mares,
   not to Lymm Secundus. But in the wild, however perfectly they were developed,
   twins would be less fitted than single foals to survive any hazards from exterior
   sources that might threaten them in the first few weeks.
 3 *English Farming Past & Present*, 6th edn., 1961, Heinemann Educ. Books Ltd., and
   Frank Cass & Co. Ltd., p. 181.
 4 *History and Delineation of the Horse*, p. 115.
 5 G. E. Evans, *The Horse in the Furrow*, Faber & Faber Ltd, 1960, p. 150, quoting
   Robert Reyce *The Breviary of Suffolk*, 1816 (1902 ed., John Murray, p. 42).
 6 Quoted by Evans, op. cit., p. 152.
 7 *Tour through the East of England*, 1771, Vol. II, Letter XV.
 8 *Annals of Agriculture*, 1784, Vol. 2, pp. 130–2.
 9 *General View of Suffolk*, 1794, p. 42 f.
10 *Rural Economy of Norfolk*, 1787, Vol. 1, p. 42.
11 *Observations on Livestock*, 2nd ed. 1794, p. 227.
12 *General View*, p. 42.
13 *Tour through the East of England*, II, p. 173 ff.
14 *Observations on Live Stock*, pp. 27 f.
15 *Annals of Agriculture*, Vol. 2, pp. 130–2.
16 *Tour through the East of England*, Letter II, p. 113.
17 W. Pitt, *General View of Leicestershire*, 1809, p. 283.
18 *Observations on Live Stock*, p. 32 f.
19 In *Robert Bakewell, Pioneer Livestock Breeder*, Crosby Lockwood & Son Ltd., 1957.
20 *Rural Economy of the Midland Counties*, Vol.1 pp. 297–302.
21 *Rural Economy of the Midland Counties*,Vol.1, pp. 303 ff.
22 *Tour through the East of England*, Letter II, pp. 108 and 119.
23 *Tour through the East of England*, Letter II, p. 119.

24 Letter dated 26th February 1783 (Pawson, Robert Bakewell, p. 171).
25 *Annals of Agriculture*, Vol. 6, p. 489.
26 Pawson, p. 104.
27 *Rural Economy of Norfolk*, Vol. 1, p. 42 f.
28 Cf. Charles Dickens, *David Copperfield*: " 'I'm a reg'lar Dodman', said Mr. Peggotty, by which he meant snail." Peggotty was a Yarmouth man.
29 Letter dated 20th November 1788 (Pawson, p. 173).
30 Letter dated 8th May 1789 (Pawson, p. 138 f.).
31 *Rural Economy of the Midland Counties*, Vol. 1, pp. 306 ff.
32 *General View of Suffolk*, 1794, p. 42 f.
33 *General View of Leicestershire*, (Monk) 1794, p. 27.
34 *General View of Suffolk*, p. 43.
35 *General View of Leicestershire*, (Pitt) 1808, p. 287.
36 *On the Domesticated Animals of the British Islands* etc., London 1845, p. 609.
37 Numbers after a stallion's name, or preceding a mare's name, indicate their registration in the Shire Stud-book, Volume 1 of which was published in 1880.
38 O.E.D. gives *ball* as an obsolete noun, as in "The ii propertyes of a bauson" (badger): "The fyrste is, to have a white rase or a ball on the forehead" (FitzHerbert *Husb.* 73). Tusser (*Husb.* 185) also referred to a "fine ambling ball". *Bald* comes from Middle English *balled*, of uncertain origin but, like the equivalent words in many other languages from classical Greek to Middle High German, equally applicable either to one who is hairless or to one who has a white patch on the forehead.
39 *General View of Leicestershire*, 1794, p. 36.
40 *Rural Economy of the Midland Counties*, Vol. 1, pp. 470 ff.
41 *Annals of Agriculture*, Vol. 22, pp. 375–83.
42 *Midland Counties*, Vol. 1, pp. 306 ff. and Vol. 2, p. 83.
43 *General View of Leicestershire*, 1809, p. 287.
44 *History and Delineation of the Horse*, p. 119.
45 *Annals of Agriculture*, Vol. 6, p. 463.
46 *Observations on Livestock*, p. 31.
47 *Midland Counties*, Vol. 1, pp. 133 f.
48 *General View of Leicestershire*, 1809, p. 288 f.
49 Both advertisements quoted by Dykes, *Clydesdale Memories*, in Trans. H.A.S.S., 1907.
50 M'Neilage, "The Clydesdale Horse".
51 Trans. H.A.S.S., 1907.
52 *Observations on Livestock*, p. 29 f.
53 *General View of Clydesdale*, 1794, p. 53.
54 *General View of Ayr*, 1793, p. 53.
55 *Heavy Horses: Breeds & Management*, Winston & Co. Ltd., 4th Ed. 1905, p. 80.
56 "The Clydesdale Horse".
57 See Part B, IV–VI.
58 See Part B, VII.
59 See Part B, II.

CHAPTER IV
1 *Rural Rides* (Everyman edn., Vol. 1), p. 93. "From Kensington to Uphusband". Wednesday, 25th September 1822.
2 *The Horse*, Library of Useful Knowledge, London, 1831, pp. 38 ff.

3 *Journal of the R.A.S.E.*, 1st series, Vol. 5, No. 2.

4 "Management of Heavy Horses", in *Livestock of the Farm* (Vol. III, *Horses*), ed. C. Bryner Jones, N.D.

5 Low, *On the Domesticated Animals of the British Islands*, etc., pp. 610 f.

6 *The English Cart Horse Stud-book* (i.e. Shire Stud-book), Vol. 1, p. lxvi

7 "The Clydesdale as a Draught-horse", *Live-stock Journal Almanac*, 1880.

8 Trans. H.A.S.S., 1907, p. 246.

9 *Heavy Horses*, p. 123.

10 *Standard Cyclopedia of Modern Agriculture*.

11 *Select Clydesdale Stud Book*, Vol. 1, 1884, p. xvi.

12 Recounted by W. R. Trotter (of Stocksfield-on-Tyne, a south-of-the-border believer in Lawrence Drew's principles) in *Heavy Horses*, p. 124.

13 *S.C.S.B.*, p. xviii.

14 *S.C.S.B.*, Introduction.

15 *Heavy Horses*, pp. 124 f.

15 *English Cart-Horse Stud-book*, Vol. 2, pp. lxxxv f.

16 J.R.A.S.E. New (2nd) Series, Vol. 7, Part II, 1871.

17 J.R.A.S.E. New (2nd) Series, Vol. 1, Part 1, 1865.

18 Low, op. cit., p. 611.

19 J. M. Wilson (ed.), *Rural Cyclopedia*, Edinburgh and London, 1849, Vol. 2, p. 719.

20 *History and Delineation of the Horse*, p. 123.

21 *The Complete Farrier, and British Sportsman etc.*, 183–, p. 33.

22 William J. Miles, *Modern Practical Farriery; etc.*, 1868, p. 58 f.

23 *Notes sur l'Angleterre*, (1860–70), tr. Edward Hymans as *"Taine's Notes on England"*, Thames & Hudson, 1957, p. 28.

24 Pages 47 and 131.

25 However, Major M. C. Cox assures us of worse things even today. "In France, the large Poitu donkey in that district is used for breeding mules and in that area these stallions are never groomed, nor are the stables in which they live mucked out, consequently they are covered in manure and dirt; it is the belief that the dirtier they are when breeding the better the fertility and the offspring." (*The Shetland Pony Stud-book Society Magazine*, Autumn 1969, p. 20.)

26 J. W. Axe, *The Horse, its treatment in health and disease etc.*, London, 1906, Vol. VIII, p. 235.

27 *Suffolk Stud-book*, Vol. 1.

28 Private service book of his owner, John Jones, Cefn Barrach, Trefeglwys. Mont.

29 *Suffolk Stud-book*, Vol. 1.

30 R. D. Stewart, *Handling Horses*, Hurst and Blackett, N.D. (*c.* 1941).

31 J. W. Axe, op. cit., Vol. VIII, p. 236.

32 Professor Harold Burrow frequently had his attention drawn, in modern times, to the fertility of the sensibly managed travelling stallion which actually *walked* its sixty or so miles a week, compared with those horses which did part of their round by train. The latter was necessary when the route was geographically awkward (or, in the rapid decline of the business after the 1939–45 war, when brood mares were few and scattered). Owners of mares living at the end of the train ride always complained about the ineffectiveness of the horse. Such unanimity, independently voiced in many districts, is impressive.

33 *The Shire Horse*, London, N.D. (*c.* 1885), p. 9.

34 *English Cart-Horse Stud-book*, Vol. II, p. lxxvi.

35 *Three Men in a Boat*, Chapter 1.

36 *Annual Report of the Veterinary Department for 1872*, quoted in J.R.A.S.E. Second series, Vol. 10, No. 1, p. 243.

37 Anna Sewell, *Black Beauty*, 1877, Chapter XXXVIII.

38 38 Geo. III, c. 41.

39 1 & 2 Geo. IV, c. 110.

40 *Liverpool Mercury*, 2nd May, 1863.

CHAPTER V

1 J.R.A.S.E., 2nd series, Vol. 12, Part 1.

2 *The Canal Age*, David & Charles, 1968.

3 *Live-Stock Journal Almanac*, 1879.

4 *Suffolk Stud-book*, Vol. 1.

5 Quoted by Aileen Smiles in *Samuel Smiles and his Surroundings*, Robert Hale Ltd., 1956, p. 65.

6 *The Field*, 16th February, 1878.

7 From a statement made by Dr. J. A. Couture, secretary of the French Canadian Horse Society before the House of Commons, 17th March, 1909. Quoted by W. H. Willson, Secretary of the Canadian Percheron Horse Breeders' Association B.P.S.B., Vol. 1.

8 Trans. H.A.S.S., 1907.

9 For Riddell, see IV.4.

10 *Heavy Horses* (1894), p. 125.

11 *Select Clydesdale Stud-book*, Volume 1, 1884 Introduction.

12 *Heavy Horses*, p. 124.

13 *The Shire Horse in Peace and War*, p. 58.

14 *The Horse in the Furrow*, 1960, p. 163.

15 *Suffolk Stud-book*, Vol. 1, p. 10.

16 *Suffolk Stud-book*, Vol. 1, p. 651.

17 *Among Men and Horses*, London, 1894, p. 343. (The Islington show folded up after 1895.)

18 *Tour through the East of England*, Letter IV, pp. 173 ff.

19 Kevin FitzGerald, *Ahead of their time*, Heinemann, 1968, p. 121.

CHAPTER VI

1 Stud-book, Vol. 1, lxxiii.

2 Thomas F. Plowman, *Fifty Years of a Showman's Life*, John Lane, The Bodley Head, 1919, pp. 23 f.

3 *Tour through the East of England*, Letter IV., p. 172.

4 Aged one year two months, under the name Agronomer. The stud-book version of the name is an error, as are the address of its owner (who was really R. H. Howard of Nocton, Lincs.) and his foaling date, which is given as 1852.

5 The R.A.S.E. catalogue of 1854 listed Sultan as a "Pure cart stallion" and Agronomer as a "Black Lincolnshire stallion".

CHAPTER VII

1 Dykes, Trans. H.A.S.S., 1907, pp. 246 ff.

2 Orwin & Whetham, *History of British Agriculture*, 1846–1914, Longmans, 1964, p. 382.

3 With Prince William (already mentioned several times) he made the William the Conqueror line the second most influential in the breed. See B.VII.
4 James Galbraith and his brother had been staunch Drew men (see VI.11).
5 *Heavy Horses*, p. 132.

CHAPTER VIII

1 *History and Delineation of the Horse*, p. 122.
2 The Veterinary Department of the Privy Council (see Chapter IV.9) was re-named the Agricultural Department in 1883, when it took over responsibility for agricultural statistics from the Board of Trade. The new Board of Agriculture superseded it in 1889.
3 "The London Work Horse in Street and Stable", in *Heavy Horses: breeds and management*, 1894 edition. It has long been out of print, but the only other really good contemporary account of London horses in the 'nineties has been re-issued. This is W. J. Gordon's *The Horse World of London* (The Religious Tract Society, 1893: reprinted 1974 by J. A. Allen & Co. Ltd.), in which the chapters on the carrier's horse, the vestry horse, the brewer's horse and the coal horse are specially relevant.
4 *Heavy Horses*, p. 19.
5 *Heavy Horses*, pp. 116 and 121.
6 *Heavy Horses*, p. 72.
7 Pamphlet *The Shire Horse*, Derby, N. D. (c. 1885).
8 *Heavy Horses*, p. 72.

CHAPTER IX

1 *The Story of the International 1907–1957*, R. S. Summerhays, British Horse Society, 1957.
2 This is the version of the story which is generally accepted by the oldest inhabitants of Etwall parish, except that in true legendary style the offers are given as £1,000 and £2,000 respectively. Mr. Gerald A. Welch, Robert's son, who was born in 1900 and who farmed The Hepnalls from his father's death in 1929 until 1967, gives the figures as stated above, and adds that he has always understood that the second offer came from an American buyer. So it is just possible that Captain Heaton "rescued" him. Local legend, incidentally, elaborates the transatlantic suggestion into an assurance that the colt "went to the U.S.A. where it didn't get a single foal". It is a normal ingredient of this type of Shire legend that the hero goes either to America or, more occasionally to Australia, and that on arrival he either gets several thousand mares in foal, or none at all, or else meets a violent death. Blaisdon Conqueror, for example, according to one legend in the Forest of Dean, was the biggest horse in the world and toured America with enormous success. He was just about to set foot (his feet were 14 inches across!) on ship-board for a second visit when he dropped dramatically dead. In actual fact he travelled for the Montgomeryshire Society in 1904 and died on 27th October, at home, of enteritis.
3 Robert West Howard, *The Horse in America*, Follett, Chicago, 1965, p. 180.
4 I am indebted to *The Draft Horse Journal*, (Febuary 1972.) edited by Maurice and Jeannine Telleen of Iowa, for most of this information about John G. Truman.
5 *Farmer & Stockbreeder*, 7th April 1913.
6 See *Draft Horse Journal*, February 1973 for an account of Iams.
7 Kevin FitzGerald, *Ahead of their Time*.

CHAPTER X

1 *Statistics of the Military Effort of British Empire during the Great War 1914-1920*, War Office, March 1922, Part XXXII.
2 Charles VIII of France (1470–1498) had a favourite one-eyed black horse, called Savoy after the Duke who gave it to him. The horse that caught its foot in a mole-heap and hastened William II's death was called Sorrel, and was also one-eyed. Sir Arthur's horse was brown and differed from them both in that it was not of mean stature.
3 John, Duke of Bedford, *A Silver-plated Spoon*, Cassell, 1959.
4 *Journal of the Ministry of Agriculture*, XLI, No. 1.

CHAPTER XI

1 C. L. Mowat, *Britain Between the Wars 1918–1940*, (1968 edn), p. 203.
2 Idem, p. 252.
3 John Moore, *Portrait of Elmbury*, Collins, 1945, Chapter III.
4 Youatt, *The Horse* etc., 1831 ed., p. 38.

CHAPTER XII

1 For the points which follow, I am indebted to Miss Edith M. Whetham's admirably succinct presidential address to the Agricultural Economics Society in 1970. ("The Mechanisation of British Farming 1910–1945", *J.A.E.*, Vol. XXI, No. 3, pp. 317 ff., September 1970.)
2 Op. cit., p. 319.
3 I am indebted to Mr. Vincent H. Phillips and Mr. R. G. Jones of Adran Traddo-diadau Llafar a Thafodieithoedd, Amgueddfa Werin Cymru, at Castell Sain Ffagan, Caerdydd for the following rendering:

> Thou grey, raven grey horse, of famous stock,
> Remember now where thou wast bred,
> Thy skin was stretched till thou grew strong
> With fodder from Hafod y Beudy.

4 James A. S. Watson and James A. More, *Agriculture, The Science & Practice of British Farming*, 3rd edition revised and enlarged, Oliver & Boyd, 1933, p. 561 f.

CHAPTER XIII

1 William Cobbett, *Rural Rides* (Everyman edn., Vol. 1, p. 73).
2 Op. cit., p. 72.
3 Op. cit., p. 73.
4 This was a long span of two generations. John Edward Cornwallis Rous, 2nd Earl of Stradbroke, 1794–1886, was President of the (East) Suffolk Agricultural Association from its formation in 1831 and the first Suffolk Horse Society Patron in 1877. His son, George Edward John Mowbray Rous, the 3rd Earl, lived 1862–1947. He had been Parliamentary Secretary to the Ministry of Agriculture and Fisheries 1928–1929.
5 *History of the Royal Agricultural Society of England*, 1839–1939, p. 189.
6 Regrettably, all the writer knows about her is that she was not related to Jos Holland or to the Society's Secretary. He believes she came from Cheshire.

CHAPTER XIV

1 Keith A. H. Murray, *History of the Second World War:* U.K. series, "Agriculture", H.M.S.O. and Longmans, Green and Co., 1955.
2 Op. cit., p. 275.
3 As in many other things, more generally acknowledged elsewhere, I am indebted to John M. Porter of Grantham for the report of the conversation with Bill Rastall.
4 I am indebted to Bob Wyatt for this story.
5 Op. cit., p. 339.
6 *The Saturday Book*, 7th Year, Hutchinsons, November 1947.

CHAPTER XV

1 *The Horse in the Furrow*, p. 187.

PART B

CHAPTER II

1 *General View of Leicestershire* (Pitt), 1809, p. 282.
2 *General View of Rutland* (Parkinson), 1808, p. 135.
3 *General View of Derbyshire*, 1794, pp. 25, 32, 59.
4 *General View of Staffordshire*, 1794, p. 63.
5 *General View of Nottinghamshire*, 1794, pp. 23, 24, 49.
6 *General View of Berkshire*, 1794, p. 45.
7 William James and Jacob Malcolm, *General View of Buckingham*, 1794.
8 *General View of Lincolnshire*, 1794, pp. 17, 62 ff., 19.
9 *Tour thro' the East of England*, Vol. 1, p. 469.
10 *General View of Huntingdon* (Maxwell), 1793, pp. 9, 18.
11 *General View of Huntingdon* (Stone), 1793, p. 15.
12 *General View of Cambridge*, pp. 214 ff.
13 Some commentators on Marshall have perversely read the word as "muck" and unfortunately their misquotation has found more readers in modern times than Marshall's original observation.
14 *Rural Economy of Yorkshire*, 1788, Vol. 2, pp. 160 ff.

CHAPTER III

1 *General View of Leicestershire*, 1809, p. 283 f. (It is surprising that Pitt should be so mistaken as to think Bakewell might have put elegance before utility.)

CHAPTER V

1 *Heavy Horses* (1894), p. 24.

CHAPTER VI

1 To John Porter (see *A*cknowledgements).

APPENDIX 9

1 *Observations on Livestock*, 1794 ed., p. 21 f.

APPENDIX 10
 1 *Heavy Horses*, p. 51.
 2 Stud-book, Vol. VII, p. xx.
 3 Federico Tesio, *Breeding the Race Horse*, English edition, tr. Edward Spinola, 1958, J. A. Allen & Company.

APPENDIX 13
 1 *Journal of Agricultural Economics*, Vol. XXI, No. 3, p. 320, September 1970.

APPENDIX 14
 1 Compiled from *Statistics of the Military Effort of the British Empire during the Great War 1914-1920*.
 2 *Statistics*, Part XXXII.

Indices

No apology is offered for the absence of an index of topics, for these so overlap that it would bring more confusion than assistance. How can "action" be divorced from "conformation"? And, when either attribute is applied to a breed, is that not a different matter entirely from the assessment of an individual animal? How is conformation to be separated, in cart-horse history, from soundness? Or unsoundness from hereditary disease, disease from sickness, sickness from management, or management from economy and bad management from cruelty? Imagine, too, an index containing the Black Horse, the Leicestershire, Derbyshire, the Fen Horse and many more. When are these words synonyms, and when are they marks of distinction? Let auction sales be a last example. To mark the fine gradations of these in any helpful way (and to lump them all together would be singularly unhelpful) is to try to disband the rainbow. The Elephant and Castle sales would represent the red, and the Rothschild ones no doubt the violet. But what about all those in between?

The detailed table of Contents is a simpler and more reliable guide to topics than an index could possibly be. Part A of this book is annalistic as to chapters: but each chapter is divided into topics. I have strictly adhered to this principle, except only when a topic is nearly, but not quite, concluded with the close of the period under review in any particular chapter. Then, it has seemed sensible to finish the story by relating "what happened to them all in the end" rather than, in obstinate observance of a self-imposed rule, to include another section about it (perhaps comprising four or five lines) in the next chapter. The eradication of glanders from towns provides an example. Chapter VIII (1889–1900), section 8 ("The Urban Gelding"), recounts the struggle against this scourge. The battle was not won by 1900, but victory only awaited official recognition of the mallein test. This was belatedly given in 1907, and so I have concluded the story of glanders in Chapter VIII – cloaking the extra bit in parentheses.

For Part B, a topical index is, in any case, quite superfluous. There is only one topic, and the theme is better followed in the table of Contents than anywhere else. Its detail consists of individual horses and men, and these have their own indices.

Index to Horses

STALLIONS and mares which are registered in any stud-book are listed in roman type. Their stud-book numbers are not given, except where necessary to differentiate between two animals having the same name.

All other animals are listed in *italic*. These include mares in the modern Grading-up Registers and, to identify them, their number in Register A or B has been given before their names. The names of geldings, however purely bred, are obviously in italic – except those few mentioned which were first registered as stallions, and castrated later: they appear in roman type, with a note. Unregistered animals having identical names are differentiated by the addition of their owners' names in parentheses, or by some other comment. Early horses, not retrospectively registered, often appear to have no real individual names. In those cases, the owner's name has to come first – e.g. *Hean's Horse* and *Ivens' Grey Horse*. (Occasionally Shires were actually registered thus – e.g. Law's Horse 1303.)

Where there are several animals of different breeds having the same name, all Shire horses are listed first (registered animals before unregistered ones), followed by horses of other breeds in alphabetical order of breed.

Horses in Volume I of the Suffolk Stud-book are usually listed there with the owner's name coming first. This has not been done here, in order to maintain uniformity of practice but, as a compromise, the owner's name has been added after – e.g. Winter's Stormer 1329 is indexed as Stormer (Winter's, Suff). Horses whose names begin with the word "The" are indexed under the next word of their name – e.g. *Sinfin Old Horse, The*.

Names beginning with the word "Old" or "Young" – as they commonly used to do, at least for the first or last part of a horse's life – have been either double-indexed or provided with a cross-reference. (But where the word "Old" is part of a prefix – "Old House", "Old Warden" – or is an essential part of the name – as of the horse Old Times – the name is listed only under "O".)

Names are not included at all if they occur only as examples of nomenclature, and not as "real horses". Therefore, few of the names quoted in Appendix 11 are indexed, nor are those which merely show the working of an owner's mind rather than the individuality of a horse – for example, Mr. Elwis' Ebbing Tide and Elastic on page 203 or, on page 272, the resounding and memorable appellations of Mr. Sutton-Nelthorpe's horses.

ABBREVIATIONS

f   *one* following page. E.g. 200f – the horse is mentioned on pages 200 and 201, possibly in a different context the second time.

ff   *two* (but not more) following pages. E.g. 200ff – the horse figures in a narrative extending over pages 200–202, or is mentioned in separate and different contexts, on those three pages.

Bel	Belgian	m	mare
Cl	Clydesdale	Per	Percheron
d	dam	s	stallion, sire
Fl	Flemish	Sh	Shire
gldg	gelding	Suff	Suffolk
g-d	granddam	T.B.	Thoroughbred

Index to Breeders, Owners, People

THIS index comprises the people and companies embraced by its title, and almost no others. Therefore, stallion-hiring societies are not included – except those few mentioned as being actual owners at some time of a horse. Agricultural societies are not here. Nor are repositories, though persons connected with them or owning them will be found among those present.

There are negative and positive reasons for these omissions. Negatively, since the activities of such bodies were often diversified (for example, the Peterborough Agricultural Society was also a hiring society and, additionally to its summer show, promoted a spring stallion show and an autumn mare and foal show), there is no way by which a wider limit can be fixed without crossing the border into an index of topics. To avoid that, choice would become a matter of whim. Not only would the list become cumbersome but unpredictable, and occasionally, where county or regional groups are involved, somewhat vague.

More positively, the use of the table of Contents will be found to provide a more satisfactory way of discovering what has been said about such matters as the activities of various repositories, of the increase and diminution of hiring societies or of Shire classes at various shows. (Furthermore, the reader wishing to see a list – for example – of the hiring societies operating in 1939, or the shows having classes for Shires, will find it simple to turn to the relevant Appendices, 5 and 16. But to flood the Index with their names would make it unwieldy.)

A few points of detail remain to be explained. Owners are not indexed if their names occur only as part of their horses' names and nothing whatsoever is said about them as persons. Mr. Buck does not appear here, because he occurs in the text only by implication – in the stallion always known as *Buck's Horse*. Mr. Ivens does appear, because he is mentioned, not only in *Ivens' Grey Horse*, but as a person (admittedly, somewhat shadowy) existing in his own right.

All authors who have been quoted are indexed, with reference to the text if their name is given there, or to the Notes and References if it is not.

Family relationships have been indicated where such information has been thought to be of help to the enquirer, or is of special significance. This has been done in one of two ways, and sometimes both:

persons marked ★ and bearing the same surname are related: precise relationships are stated in parentheses.

But it is important to bear in mind that this information does not pretend, or attempt, to be complete. Sovereigns, other members of the Royal family, and peers of the realm are exempted. So are all others whose relationships are only of minor interest to the reader of this particular book, though of course of equal importance in every other way.

This practice cannot, in any case, be exhaustive. An index cannot inform the reader that Will Smith was the son-in-law of Fred Griffin or Robert Honeyborn the nephew of Robert Bakewell. (Actually the text does so.) We must be content to observe the male line and forget tail female – for which Shire pedigrees give us some precedent. Secondly, beyond first cousins it would be impossible to go. Given another century of endeavour, I might discover that John Doe, mentioned on page 950, was the son of Mary, nee Hoe, whose mother, a Toe before marriage, was a second cousin of Richard Roe on page 900. But do you really want to know that? And where would be the end of it? Are we not all related to each other anyway?